# DICTIONARY OF INTERNATIONAL TRADE LAW

## Second Edition

D1604964

# DICTIONARY OF INTERNATIONAL TRADE LAW

## Second Edition

**Raj Bhala**
*Associate Dean for International and Comparative Law
& Rice Distinguished Professor
The University of Kansas School of Law*

*Member, Royal Society for Asian Affairs, Council on Foreign Relations,
American Law Institute, and Fellowship of Catholic Scholars*

*Admitted to Practice in New York and the District of Columbia*

*Foreign Legal Consultant, Heenan Blaikie (Canada), LL.P*

**Library of Congress Cataloging-in-Publication Data**

Bhala, Raj.
  Dictionary of international trade law / Raj Bhala. — 2nd ed.
    p. cm.
  ISBN 978-0-7698-5608-7
  1. Foreign trade regulation—Dictionaries. 2. International trade—Dictionaries. I. Title.
K3943.B488 2012
343.08'703—dc23

2012023093

This publication is designed to provide accurate and authoritative information in regard to the subject matter covered. It is sold with the understanding that the publisher is not engaged in rendering legal, accounting, or other professional services. If legal advice or other expert assistance is required, the services of a competent professional should be sought.

NOTE TO USERS
To ensure that you are using the latest materials available in this area, please be sure to periodically check the LexisNexis Law School web site for downloadable updates and supplements at www.lexisnexis.com/lawschool.

Editorial Offices
121 Chanlon Rd, New Providence, NJ 07974 (908) 464-6800
201 Mission St., San Francisco, CA 94105-1831 (415) 908-3200
www.lexisnexis.com

MATTHEW◆BENDER                                                    (2012–Pub.3070)

# DEDICATION

*To my wife and best friend, Kara, whose support defines the word "love."*

# PREFACE

Why write a dictionary? Surely it is a most pedestrian of pursuits? Surely it allows the mind to escape hard research towards a cogent book or article? On the one hand, surely the mental faculties will atrophy? The mind will descend into the complacency of writing a few paragraphs about an idiosyncratic medley of terms. On the other hand, surely the task is an impossible one? Even when a dictionary is confined to a specific subject, as is the present volume, the boundaries of the subject enlarge, the vocabulary expands, the contexts in which words are used change, and the theoretical concepts associated with terminology evolve.

One self-indulgent answer is love for words, the concepts they embody, and the environments in which they are deployed. That is my case. Along with maps, dictionaries always have been a source of fascination and enjoyment. Writing a dictionary is a chance to indulge these intellectual delights. It is a chance to learn more about terms with which I may have passing familiarity, and an opportunity to widen terms in my vocabulary. In so doing, it invites me to study books and articles I have long sought to approach. Yet, that is not the answer — or, at least, not the principal one.

Love for students, is a second, less self-indulgent, and more obvious, answer than the first response. International Trade Law is a highly technical field, with a vocabulary of its own. That is increasingly so. To make matters more difficult, and exciting, International Trade Law is inter-disciplinary, thus so, too, is its terminology. Other subject areas, not the least of which is economics, influence the vocabulary of trade. Economics has its own lingo. Thus, a dictionary can serve the needs and interests of students, as well as scholars and practitioners, to de-mystify the terminology of International Trade Law, and allied fields. Put simply, the jargon is a non-tariff barrier to entry into the discipline. Why not try to reduce that barrier a bit, especially to encourage newcomers to consider entering this fascinating area?

A third, and the most theoretical, answer veers more towards a sense of the importance of words. Understanding the meaning of words advances our vocabulary and knowledge base. Precision in meaning also helps us identify points of agreement, and narrow points of disagreement. That benefit is critical for lawyers, who, after all, are specially trained to be peacemakers. The more we lawyers know about terms, the more accurate we can be in the way we use them, the more command we will have as professionals, and the better service we can be to others.

In the field of International Trade Law, if there is anything to the theory that trade may enhance peace, then perhaps understanding better the words that constitute the field could support that salubrious outcome. Trade is, after all, an increasingly technical field, but one in which many voices speak with sharper and more rhetoric, in louder volumes. Possibly, some of the talking that goes past different sides, and the dialogue of the deaf, might be mitigated if speakers in the trade debate gave great (or greater) care to defining and even economizing on their words — and lowering the volume. In brief, maybe a dictionary can be a reference in service of a desirable global goal.

That answer, of course, depends on the quality of the dictionary. The enterprise of preparing the First Edition of the *Dictionary of International Trade Law* was partly a re-confirmation of how little I know of this marvelous field, and of how much space there is yet into which to grow. It became apparent, and quickly so, that the title *Encyclopedia of International Trade Law* would be too grandiose, and over-sell the volume in a way redolent of how some politicians exaggerate the benefits (or costs) of free trade. But, a journey must start somewhere, with a few steps. The adjective "encyclopedic" was a lodestar for those steps.

Like its predecessor, this Second Edition tries to be comprehensive in defining terms in the field regularly encountered by practitioners, scholars, and students everyday around the world. It seeks, further, to cover as many terms in the related disciplines of Development Economics and International Economics, as they are relevant to International Trade Law, as possible. In so doing, like an encyclopedia, the *Dictionary of International Trade Law* provides references to additional reading for many entries. Note, then, the three audiences: students (again, especially in law and allied graduate programs); scholars (in law schools and allied graduate programs); and practicing attorneys (whether in government, the private sector, non-governmental organizations (NGOs), or international organizations). These audiences are global, because trade tautologically is.

Supplementing the definitions of terms, elaborations of the contexts in which they are used, and exposition of the theories underlying terms, are a number of Maps, Research Tools, and Free Trade Agreements Data. They are set forth in Annexes A, B, and C, respectively. International Trade Law is a field in which careful research is indispensable, but — alas — time is precious. The Annexes, along with the definitions themselves, might assist in this asymmetric milieu.

Also supplementing many of the definitions of terms are *Suggestions for Further Research*. The *Suggestions* are publications in various formats (books, law review articles, book chapters, and other sources), generally from the years 2000 to 2012. As scholarship in the field of International Trade Law has burgeoned, it is impossible to list all potentially relevant publications, lest this *Dictionary* become nothing more than a source index. Where provided, the *Suggestions* are designed to be adequate at least to commence further research, *i.e.*, they are at least a starting point. I eschew listing any of my own publications in the *Suggestions*. Indeed, I recommend strongly that the work of others be consulted. Should the reader be interested in my publications, the reader may find them listed on the University of Kansas School of Law website (www.law.ku.edu). Virtually all of the law review articles are freely downloadable from the Social Science Research Network (SSRN) and KU ScholarWorks.

No dictionary is a static reference. To maintain, and better yet enhance, its quality, new editions are necessary. Each Edition is a commitment to that upward trajectory. That commitment could not be made without the marvelous support of Research Assistants (RAs) at the University of Kansas School of Law — past, present, and assuredly future. With their contributions, the importance of which I cannot overstate, and the comments of readers who consult this *Dictionary* — even if for little purpose other than to check a narrow point — the volume might gain the reputation of "encyclopedic."

With all good wishes,

Raj Bhala
Rice Distinguished Professor
The University of Kansas
School of Law
Green Hall, 1535 West 15th Street
Lawrence, Kansas
U.S.A. 66045

Tel: 785-864-9224
Fax: 785-864-5054

Website: www.law.ku.edu
E-Mail: bhala@ku.edu

# ACKNOWLEDGEMENTS

Simply put, this *Dictionary* is not possible without the contributions of my world-class Research Assistants (RAs) at the University of Kansas School of Law (KU Law). They are:

Owen Andrew Grieb (Overland Park, Kansas), J.D., Class of 2007
Beau Jackson (Wichita, Kansas), J.D., Class of 2009
David Roy Jackson (Virginia), J.D., Class of 2007
Shannon B. Keating (Apple Valley, Minnesota), J.D., Class of 2013
Elizabeth M. Landau (Shawnee, Kansas), J.D. Class of 2012
Sarah Schmidt (Marysville, Kansas), J.D., MA (Economics),
Class of 2013
Devin S. Sikes (Wichita, Kansas), J.D., Class of 2008

Each worked diligently and with enthusiasm, even under considerable time pressure, on many entries in this *Dictionary*. Each added at least one distinct signature to the *Dictionary*. Owen Grieb meticulously checked a large number of entries, and filled in many missing pieces. Beau Jackson added considerable substance to the many entries concerning Africa. David Jackson's work on the Free Trade Agreement (FTA) Tables, his extraordinary efforts on the Tables concerning the EU and China, plus his help with agricultural terms, was at the level of a seasoned trade lawyer. Shannon Keating and Elizabeth Landau completely re-vamped several entries of key terms. Sarah Schmidt contributed roughly 30 new entries from scratch, and updated scores more. She also single-handedly produced the table on Japan's Economic Partnership Agreements (EPAs). Devin Sikes provided much fine research on entries concerning Latin America, was dogged in his pursuit of *Statements of Administrative Action*, and provided first-class information, on short notice, for some critical entries. I am deeply thankful to all of them.

My RAs have, or soon will, graduate. Of course, they are moving onward and upward:

- Owen Grieb practices international business law, making good use of his fluency in Japanese, in Tokyo. He managed to place second in a major New York-based customs and international trade law writing competition while working on the *Dictionary*.

- Beau Jackson held internships at the United States Trade Representative (USTR) and House Ways and Means Committee (Trade Subcommittee), and puts his fluency in Portuguese — gained while in the Peace Corps in Cape Verde — to good use. He practices international trade law with a firm in Washington, D.C.

- David Jackson, who passed the Customs Broker examination while helping with this *Dictionary*, and interned at the United States Department of Agriculture (USDA), practiced customs and international trade law in Kansas City with a renowned firm, employing to good ends his fluency in Chinese. Thereafter, he earned a Masters (LL.M.) degree in Food and Agriculture Law from the University of Arkansas, and joined a law firm specializing in international trade and food and drug law in Washington, D.C.

- Shannon Keating came to KU Law after working on trade and development issues with a non-governmental organization (NGO) in Washington, D.C. Her record at KU Law in her International Trade Law classes was brilliant, evidenced by a CALI Award for her performance on a final examination. Shannon expects to practice in international law, particularly on development issues.

- Elizabeth Landau practices international business law in the New York area. She came to KU Law after getting credentialed and gaining experience as a minister. While interning in Kansas City and Washington, D.C., and completing her final year of legal studies, Elizabeth worked on intricate topics such as the *Harbor Maintenance Tax* case, and she briefed a number of WTO Appellate Body reports. Evidencing her hard work at KU Law, she earned a CALI Award for a top performance on a final International Trade Law examination.

- Sarah Schmidt joined KU Law after working at a large law firm in Washington, D.C. While working on this *Dictionary*, she completed not only her law degree, but also a Master's degree in Economics, plus an internship at the European Union (EU) in Washington, D.C. She plans on specializing in international business law and living overseas. Evidencing the breadth of her knowledge and interests, Sarah earned a top performance on a final examination in Islamic Law (*Sharī'a*) at KU Law.

- Devin Sikes clerked on the United States Court of International Trade (CIT), and thereafter joined the Department of Commerce (Import Administration) as an attorney working on trade remedy cases. He continues to his fluency in Spanish to good use.

I miss the great fun we had amidst our productive endeavors. It is a great consolation to know they are professionally — and, more importantly, personally — happy.

Of course, I take full responsibility for any and all errors in the *Dictionary*, and am most grateful if the reader kindly brings them to my attention at the above coordinates.

# NOTE ON SOURCES

This *Dictionary* is drawn from a prodigious number of sources. Space does not permit a full list of the hundreds of law books, book chapters, and articles I have examined, in varying degrees of intensity, over the years, and to which I remain indebted. That list grows daily. I am indebted to each source for teaching me something new about International Trade Law. The convention I follow is to cite a source, by way of a footnote, in instances of a direct quote from, or direct dependence on, that source. Any other approach would turn this *Dictionary* into little else than a long list of sources.

Yet, it is only proper to acknowledge certain exceptionally high-quality sources explicitly. They cover, in particular, international economics and development economics. They are standard references, core texts, and assorted materials. I consult them extensively and joyfully:[1]

- AUSTRALIAN BUREAU OF AGRICULTURAL AND RESOURCE ECONOMICS, REFORMING WORLD AGRICULTURAL TRADE POLICIES (1999)
- P.T. BAUER, DISSENT ON DEVELOPMENT (1976)
- JOHN BLACK, A DICTIONARY OF ECONOMICS (1997)
- ROBERT J. CARBAUGH, INTERNATIONAL ECONOMICS (7th ed. 1999)
- RICHARD E. CAVES, JEFFREY A. FRANKEL & RONALD W. JONES, WORLD TRADE AND PAYMENTS: AN INTRODUCTION (6th ed. 1993)
- DEPENDENCY THEORY — A CRITICAL REASSESSMENT (Dudley Seers ed., 1981)
- ROBERT M. DUNN, JR. & JOHN H. MUTTI, INTERNATIONAL ECONOMICS (5th ed. 2000)
- THE ECONOMICS OF PREFERENTIAL TRADE AGREEMENTS (Jagdish Bhagwati & Arvind Panagariya eds., 1996)
- MALCOLM GILLIS ET AL., ECONOMICS OF DEVELOPMENT (4th ed. 1996)
- ROBERT GILPIN, THE POLITICAL ECONOMY OF INTERNATIONAL RELATIONS (1987)
- STEVEN HUSTED & MICHAEL MELVIN, INTERNATIONAL ECONOMICS (4th ed. 1998)
- MELVYN KRAUSS, THE NEW PROTECTIONISM (1978)
- MELVYN KRAUSS, HOW NATIONS GROW RICH (1997)
- PAUL KRUGMAN, THE AGE OF DIMINISHED EXPECTATIONS (1990)

---

[1] The *Teacher's Manual* and accompanying textbook, *International Trade Law: Interdisciplinary Theory and Practice* (LexisNexis, 3d edition 2008, and subsequent editions) set out a longer list of consulted works, particularly in the fields of international and development economics. I trust instructors will share the list with interested students as need be.

- PAUL R. KRUGMAN & MAURICE OBSTFELD, INTERNATIONAL ECONOMICS: THEORY AND POLICY (4th ed. 1997)

- V.I. LENIN, IMPERIALISM: THE HIGHEST STATE OF CAPITALISM (1916, Junius Publications Ltd. ed. 1996)

- STUART R. LYNN, ECONOMIC DEVELOPMENT: THEORY AND PRACTICE FOR A DIVIDED WORLD (2003)

- THE MARX-ENGELS READER (Robert C. Tucker ed., 2d ed. 1978)

- THE MIT DICTIONARY OF MODERN ECONOMICS (David W. Pearce ed., 4th ed. 1992)

- JERRY M. ROSENBERG, DICTIONARY OF INTERNATIONAL TRADE (1994)

- W. CHARLES SAWYER & RICHARD L. SPRINKLE, INTERNATIONAL ECONOMICS (2003)

- AMARTYA SEN, DEVELOPMENT AS FREEDOM (1999)

- T.N. SRINIVASAN, EIGHT LECTURES ON INDIA'S ECONOMIC REFORMS (2000)

- IMMANUEL WALLERSTEIN, THE ESSENTIAL WALLERSTEIN (2000)

- CHARLES J. WOELFEL, ENCYCLOPEDIA OF BANKING & FINANCE (10th ed. 1994)

To prepare this *Dictionary*, I also rely on a monstrously large number of news stories from the *Financial Times*, *Economist*, and *International Trade Reporter* (BNA), beginning as far back as 1993. In my humble estimation, these publications include the finest journalists on international trade in the English language. Their stories, which fill three stuffed file cabinets in my garage in Kansas, stories help keep my students and me current. It is quite literally impossible to cite every story I have used. In any event, I suspect the reader would find little value added by a nearly endless list of media stories.

However, special mention deservedly should be made for the many pieces by Alan Beattie, Guy de Jonquières, Frances Williams, and Martin Wolf of the *Financial Times*, and Toshio Aritake, Len Bracken, Rossella Brevetti, Joe Kirwin, Daniel Pruzin, Madhur Singh, Amy Tsui, and Gary G. Yerkey of the *International Trade Reporter*. (*The Economist* does not identify author bylines.) With apologies to them and their colleagues, this *Dictionary* would be nothing but a multi-volume citation list, were I not to adopt a simple policy: a footnote appears only to accompany a direct quote, or extensive use of key data. In brief, then, may I express my deepest thanks and professional respect for these three publications and their staff? May I also express gratitude to the *Khaleej Times*, *Gulf News*, and *The Gulf Today*, for their superb coverage, to which I look, of developments concerning trade and the Middle East?

Finally, in respect of the Maps that appear in this *Dictionary*, they bear no copyright, but do have the handiwork of modest formatting on my part, as tutored by Mr. David Jackson (acknowledged above). The original source of most of them, from which they are freely available and in the public domain, is the University of Texas Map Collection, specifically:

Perry-Castañeda Library Map Collection, UT Library Online,
www.lib.utexas.edu/maps/.

Thanks are due to both this source and Mr. Jackson for the maps, and to Ms. Schmidt for tracking down with alacrity new maps showing South Sudan, which gained independence on 9 July 2011.

Finally, it is readily apparent none of my own publications are mentioned above. That omission is purposeful. It is essential the reader know the *Dictionary* is not intended to be a recycling bin for my prior work. Efficiency dictates some degree of overlap. Adding value mandates examining new and different sources from around the globe. The result ought to be new, insightful, and synthetic. Should it be relevant to pursue any of my other works, they may be found through a variety of search tools, and are listed on the University of Kansas School of Law website (www.law.ku.edu).

# TABLE OF CONTENTS

# INTERNATIONAL TRADE LAW TERMS

## A TO Z

# A

## AACC

Afghan-American Chamber of Commerce.

Formed in 2002, the AACC facilitates business development and investment in Afghanistan between American and Afghan enterprises. The organization is based in McLean, Virginia, in the elite Northern Virginia suburbs of Washington, D.C.

The AACC facilitates financial, investment, and trade links between Afghanistan and the United States. It seeks to promote a free, open, market economy in Afghanistan. Its members include businesses, individuals, and organizations interested in economic opportunities in Afghanistan and the long-term success of that country. One specific project on which the AACC works is establishing and populating with commercially meaningful endeavors in the Reconstruction Opportunity Zones (ROZs).

## ABSOLUTE ADVANTAGE

*See* comparative advantage.

## ABSOLUTE POVERTY

Following the poverty-as-income deprivation approach, economists measure poverty using three principal methodologies. The first methodology, dubbed the "Poverty Line," is to set a minimum income threshold. Then, a "poverty head-count" is taken, *i.e.*, the number of people below the Poverty Line are counted and defined as "impoverished." The most commonly cited threshold is "a dollar a day," meaning a person earning less than U.S. $1.00 per day lives in "absolute" poverty, and thereby is counted among the poorest of the poor. The second method is to calculate a Top/Bottom ratio. The third methodology is a Gini Coefficient, which is derived from a Lorenz Curve.

As for the first measure, the World Bank defines "absolute" poverty as U.S. $1.08 per day, at 1993 Purchasing Power Parity (PPP) terms, or one third of the average consumption level of a country, if that consumption level is above $1.08. (It defines "poverty" as living on less than U.S. $2.00 per day.) The World Bank first published the absolute poverty threshold of $1.08 per day in its 1990 *World Development Report*. The threshold is based on the work of Bank economists, specifically, Martin Ravallion and his two co-authors, who observed the national poverty levels — lines established by six governments in developing countries for their particular societies — tended to cluster around $1.08. By using PPP terms instead of market exchange rates, the poverty line threshold accurately takes into account the fact that lower prices prevail in poor countries.

This Poverty Line reflects minimum levels of basic human needs, namely, staple foods, clothing, shelter, health and sanitation facilities (including access to safe drinking water), and primary education needed to earn an adequate income. The number of people living below the Line can be expressed as a percentage of a total population, or as an absolute figure. Thus, for instance, of the roughly 6.5 billion people on earth, about 20 percent, or 1.2 billion, live below the dollar-a-day threshold. Of the people below the threshold, about 641 million live in Asia.

The latter fact bespeaks a weakness in Asia's generally strong economic record in the post-Second World War era.[1] Most Asian countries have experienced rapid growth in Gross Domestic Product (GDP), and *per capita* GDP, over the last several decades, and the rates of growth have exceeded the rates in Africa, Latin America and the Caribbean, and the Middle East. The relatively faster growth in Asia has helped to eliminate extreme poverty in the region. Further, Asia is projected, between 2008–2015, to cut poverty by half, achieve universal primary education, and reach gender parity in education. Yet, Asia still has an absolute poverty rate of approximately 17 percent — higher than in, for example, Latin America and the Caribbean. Consequently, in Asia, hunger remains widespread, and infant mortality unacceptably high.

Measuring income poverty with an Absolute Poverty threshold like U.S. $1 per day, while simple, also is simplistic. First, because of inflation in the United States, the original 1993 figure of $1.08 is (as of 2005) $1.45.

Second, governments tend to focus more on their own poverty lines — the national poverty lines developed for their own societies. Within a society, relative deprivation matters. Thus, notably, the original developer of the $1.08 threshold, Martin Ravallion of the World Bank, along with co-researchers, suggested in a 2008 World Bank Working Paper that a new line of $1.25 be established:[2]

> They gather 75 national poverty lines, ranging from Senegal's severe $0.63 a day to Uruguay's more generous measure of just over $9. From this collection, they pick the 15 lowest (Nepal, Tajikistan, and 13 Sub-Saharan countries) and split the difference between them. The result is a new international poverty line of $1.25 a day.
>
> Why those 15? The answer is philosophical, as well as practical. In setting their poverty lines, most developing countries aim to count people who are poor in an absolute sense. The line is supposed to mark the minimum a person needs to feed, clothe, and shelter himself. In Zambia, say, a poor person is defined as someone who cannot afford to buy at least two to three plates of *nshima* (a kind of porridge), a sweet potato,

---

[1] *See* Roel Landingin, *Asia Better Off But Still Hungry*, FINANCIAL TIMES, 8 October 2007, at 7.

[2] *See* Martin Ravallion, Shaohua Chen & Prem Sangraula, *Dollar A Day Revisited*, WORLD BANK WORKING PAPER 4620 (2008).

a few spoonfuls of oil, a handful of groundnuts and a couple of teaspoons of sugar each day, plus a banana and a chicken twice a week.

But even in quite poor countries, a different concept of poverty also seems to creep in. . . . It begins to matter whether a person is poor relative to his countrymen; whether he can appear in public without shame, as Adam Smith put it.

This notion of relative deprivation seems to carry weight in countries once they grow past a consumption of $1.95 per person a day. Beyond this threshold, a country that is $1 richer will tend to have a poverty line that is $0.33 higher. . . . The authors thus base their absolute poverty line on the 15 countries in their sample below this threshold.[3]

Interestingly, changing the absolute poverty line from U.S. $1.08 to $1.25 affects the estimate of the number of people who have been lifted out of poverty in recent decades, particularly in China.[4]

Subsequently, the World Bank adopted the $1.25 threshold as the global standard for absolute poverty in August 2008.[5] Again, that standard is based not on market exchange rates, but rather on PPP rates.

Globally, the number of people falling below the old yardstick dropped by over 270 million between 1990 and 2004, to 969 million in 2004. The majority of that decrease — about 250 of the 270 million — occurred in China. With the new yardstick, in 2005 there were 204 million Chinese people subsisting in absolute poverty. Though the number fell between 1990 and 2004 (by 407 million instead of 250 million), the actual number of absolutely poor people in 2005 was roughly 130 million more than estimated earlier.

China is a key case. As *The Economist* reported in December 2011:

Since 1978, China has liberated more people from poverty than any other country in history, partly because China before 1978 consigned more people to poverty than anywhere in history.[6]

In December 2011, the Chinese Communist Party (CCP) adopted a new absolute poverty line near to that of the World Bank threshold of $1.25 per day. The result was that 128 million Chinese in rural areas were deemed poor, as they earned less than 2,300 *yuan* (about $361) annually.[7] Until the revision,

---

[3] *On the Poverty Line*, THE ECONOMIST, 24 May 2008, at 100.

[4] *See* Martin Ravallion, Shaohua Chen & Prem Sangraula, *China is Poorer than We Thought, but No Less Successful in the Fight Against Poverty*, WORLD BANK WORKING PAPER 4621 (2008); *On the Poverty Line*, THE ECONOMIST, 24 May 2008, at 100.

[5] *New Data Show 1.4 Billion Live On Less Than US$1.25 A Day, But Progress Against Poverty Remains Strong, posted at* web.worldbank.org/WBSITE/EXTERNAL/NEWS/0,, contentMDK:21881954~menuPK:34465~pagePK:34370~piPK:34424~theSite PK:4607,00.html.

[6] *Poor by Definition*, THE ECONOMIST, 3 December 2011, at 56.

[7] *See Poor by Definition*, THE ECONOMIST, 3 December 2011, at 56.

the CCP classified 26.9 million rural Chinese as poor, under the previous threshold of 1,196 *yuan* annually.

Third, even if a person has is at or above the line, it does not mean he or she has access to the infrastructure and institutions to lead a full life. There may be no schools for that person to attend, or the quality of the instruction may be dreadful. Health care may not be readily accessible, and when provided, may be sub-standard. Food, while available, may not have the right balance of proteins and carbohydrates to support normal physical and cognitive growth. The environment may be stressed, as in urban slums, drought-stricken rural areas, or famine-prone regions. In brief, an Absolute Poverty threshold says nothing about capability or empowerment.

Given these concerns about an absolute poverty threshold, *The Economist* wisely observed in May 2008:

> Give or take a dime or two, it matters little where a poverty line is drawn. Like a line in the sand, an absolute poverty standard shows whether the economic tide is moving in or out. It does not matter too much where on the beach it is drawn.[8]

*Suggestions for Further Research*:

Books:

1. Collier, Paul, The Bottom Billion — Why the Poorest Countries Are Failing and What Can Be Done About It (2007).

2. Pomfret, Richard, The Age of Equality: The Twentieth Century in Economic Perspective (Cambridge, Massachusetts: Belknap Press, 2011). See also the review of this book, Richard N. Cooper, *Economic, Social, and Environmental*, 90 Foreign Affairs 179 (November/December 2011).

Articles:

1. Lee, Nancy, *More Growth with Income Equality in the Americas: Can Regional Cooperation Help?*, 14 Law & Business Review of the Americas 665–675 (2008).

2. Ocran, Matthew Kofi & Charles K.D. Adjasi, *Trade Liberalisation and Poverty: Empirical Evidence from Household Surveys in Ghana*, 8 Journal of International Trade Law & Policy number 1, 40–59 (2009).

## ABUNDANT SUPPLY

The *Africa Investment Incentive Act of 2006* ("*AGOA IV*") provides for special rules for fabrics or yarns produced in commercial quantities (or "abundant supply") in any designated Sub-Saharan African Country (SSAC) for use in qualifying apparel articles.

Upon receiving a petition from any interested party, the United States International Trade Commission (ITC) determines the quantity of such fabrics

---

[8] *On the Poverty Line*, THE ECONOMIST, 24 May 2008, at 100.

or yarns that must be sourced from the region before applying the third country fabric provision. *AGOA IV* also provides that 30 million square meter equivalents (SMEs) of denim are determined to be in abundant supply beginning 1 October 2006. Various parties have contested this figure, however. The ITC has held hearings to determine if it is an accurate assessment.

## ACCESSION

*See* WTO Member.

## ACCOUNTING RATE

An international telecommunications term referring to the charge imposed by the telephone network operator in one country for calls originating in another country. For example, AT&T charges Philippines Long Distance Telephone (PLDT) a fee (say 19 cents) for calls originating from the Philippines to the United States.

Accounting rates are controversial because they are, in effect, the tariff charged by a monopoly or near-monopoly service provider in the "importing" country (the country into which a call is coming). Lower accounting rates are good for consumers, as they translate into lower phone bills for overseas calls. However, in many countries, the telephone service provider is a state-owned monopoly, or a partially privatized company, and the government is dependent on high accounting rates for revenue. Typically, the government also uses the service provider as a place to employ a large number of workers who, if the company were a competitive private sector one, would be laid off. The United States Federal Communications Commission (FCC) has pushed other countries to lower their accounting rates.

The International Telecommunications Union (ITU) (as of March 2007) is evaluating proposals for accounting rate reform.

## ACE

Automated Commercial Environment.

ACE is an automated system for commercial trade processing intended to streamline business processes, facilitate trade, ensure cargo security, and foster participation in global commerce.[9] ACE replaces the older Automated Commercial System (ACS). It is the only electronic data interchange (EDI) system approved by United States Customs and Border Protection (CBP) for required advance submission of ocean and rail data. The deployment of ocean and rail manifest data will be followed by cargo release and air transportation, laying the foundation for a complete multimodal database.[10]

---

[9] *See* Rossella Brevetti, *CBP Announces Test for ACE Transmission of Ocean, Rail Data*, 27 International Trade Reporter (BNA) 1629 (28 October 2010).

[10] *See generally,* Rossella Brevetti, *CBP Commissioner Bersin Strongly Backs Development of ACE for Trade Processing*, 27 International Trade Reporter (BNA) 1674 (4 November 2010).

## *ACFTA*

*ASEAN — China Free Trade Agreement.*

The free trade agreement (FTA) between China and the *Association of South East Asian Nations (ASEAN)*. In November 2002, China and *ASEAN* signed the Framework Agreement on Comprehensive Economic Cooperation. This Framework Agreement calls for an FTA by 2010 among China and the six elder *ASEAN* countries (the "*ASEAN*-6") — Brunei Darussalam, Indonesia, Malaysia, Philippines, Singapore, and Thailand. It also envisions extension of the FTA to the new, poorer *ASEAN* countries by 2015 — Cambodia, Laos, Myanmar (Burma), and Vietnam (CMLV). On 6 October 2003, at the annual *ASEAN* summit, the Framework Agreement was amended by a Protocol. The *ACFTA* is expected to cover goods, services, and investment.

*Suggestions for Further Research:*

Book Chapters:

1. Wang, Jiangyu, *ASEAN–China Free Trade Agreements: Legal and Institutional Aspects*, *in* ASEAN–China Economic Relations 112–145 (Saw Swee-Hook ed., 2006) (Institute of South East Asian Studies, Singapore).

## ACP

Africa, Caribbean, and Pacific.

African, Caribbean, and Pacific countries that have enjoyed preferential trading arrangements (PTAs) with the European Union (EU) pursuant to the *Lomé* or *Cotonou Conventions*, and the successor Economic Partnership Arrangements (EPAs) to the *Cotonou Convention*.

There are about 78 ACP countries, which tend to be former colonies of EU states. The EU has long had PTAs with ACP countries. In 2005, the EU commenced negotiations with the ACP on a set of regional trade agreements (RTAs) that would replace the single EU–ACP PTA. The EU proposed to call these PTAs "Economic Partnership Agreements," or "EPAs." The EU offered this proposal because of legal difficulties associated with preferences it granted to ACP countries alone. For instance, the WTO found them discriminatory, as the EU did not offer them to other developing countries, in disputes like the 1997 *Bananas* case.

Following the 2004 WTO decision in *European Communities — Conditions for the Granting of Tariff Preferences to Developing Countries*, WT/DS246/AB/R (adopted 20 April 2004), in which the Appellate Body held illegal the discrimination between India and Pakistan created by the European Generalized System of Preferences (GSP) scheme, there was consternation as to the nature and terms of renewal of the *Cotonou Convention*. Moreover, the waiver for the *Cotonou Convention* from the MFN obligation of GATT Article I:1, which the EU obtained on 23 June 2000, expired on 31 December 2007. Thus, the

EU and ACP countries had no choice but to forge a new legal basis for their intended preferences.

The EU approach in four years of negotiations was to persuade the ACP countries to sign EPAs relevant for their particular region, rather than a single, grand agreement to replace the *Cotonou Convention*. After four years of difficult negotiations, in October 2008, 13 Caribbean countries — all the members of the Caribbean Community (CARICOM), plus the Dominican Republic — agreed to sign an EPA. Haiti did not sign, saying it was distracted by hurricanes. Guyana also did not sign, saying it opposed certain terms. Under the EPA, the Caribbean countries will enjoy duty-free access to the EU market.

*Suggestions for Further Research*:

Article:

1. Amao, Olufemi, *Trade Sanctions, Human Rights, and Multinational Corporations: The EU–ACP Context*, 32 Hastings International & Comparative Law Review 379–421 (2009).

## *ACQUIS COMMUNAUTAIRE*

The entire body of European laws is known as the *acquis communautaire*. This term encompasses all treaties, regulations, and directives passed by the European institutions, as well as judgments handed down by the European Court of Justice (ECJ).

## ACR

Average Crop Revenue Plan.

A proposal in the five year 2007 Farm Bill — the *Food and Energy Security Act*, as made in the Senate and approved by the Senate Agriculture Committee in October 2007 — to give American farmers an option as to how they receive subsidies. The Bill allowed farmers to continue obtaining support through the traditional tri-partite programs of direct payments, counter-cyclical payments, and marketing loans. However, the Bill also gave them an option, namely, to abjure the traditional modes of support, and opt instead for subsidies through ACR.[11]

Under the ACR, payments to farmers would be linked to prices in the state in which a farmer is located, not to national prices. Thus, if the state price for a crop fell, then larger payments would be made, as distinct from receiving standard payments based on national prices. The 2007 Bill gave farmers at least one incentive for choosing the ACR scheme — buying less expensive crop insurance than otherwise would be available to them — and allowed for them to opt into the scheme in 2010, 2011, or 2012.

---

[11] *See* Derrick Cain, *Senate Agriculture Committee Approves $280 Billion, Five-Year Farm Policy Bill*, 24 International Trade Reporter (BNA) 1538–1539 (1 November 2007).

## ACTA

*Anti-Counterfeiting Trade Agreement*, a plurilateral accord among countries concerned about intellectual property (IP) infringement that is designed to strengthen the existing domestic and cross-border IP protection regimes.

Accordingly:

> *ACTA* negotiations aim to establish a state-of-the-art international framework that provides a model for effectively combating global proliferation of commercial-scale counterfeiting and piracy in the 21st century. The agreement will also include innovative provisions to deepen international cooperation and to promote strong enforcement practices.[12]

States participating in *ACTA* negotiations include: Australia, Canada, the European Union (EU), Japan, Jordan, Korea, Mexico, Morocco, New Zealand, Singapore, Switzerland, the United Arab Emirates (UAE), and the United States. Plans to draft *ACTA* were first announced in October 2007.

Specifically, in October 2007, the United States Trade Representative (USTR) announced it would seek an *ACTA* with key trading partners. The goal of the accord would be to fight counterfeiting and piracy of intellectual property rights (IPRs). The accord would enhance international cooperation, identify best practices for and strengthen enforcement, develop common standards for enforcement, and improve legal protection, in the area of IPR. During the fall 2007, the USTR negotiating terms of an *ACTA* with Canada, the EU, Japan, Korea, Mexico, Switzerland, and New Zealand, in the hopes that other countries — including developing nations — eventually would join. No timetable was set for the negotiations, nor for subsequent expansion of the member countries.

The *ACTA* is independent of the World Trade Organization *Agreement on Trade-Related Aspects of Intellectual Property Rights (TRIPs)*. It also is independent of any international organization. It is designed to complement *TRIPs* and other existing intellectual property agreements. Countries join *ACTA* on a voluntary basis.[13] Thus, the USTR — Ambassador Susan Schwab — declared *ACTA* "will *not* involve any changes" to the WTO *Agreement on Trade Related Aspects of Intellectual Property Rights (TRIPs)*.[14] While that declaration technically was correct (because the *ACTA* neither would nor could amend *TRIPs*), the USTR hastened to add a point that revealed the true aim of an *ACTA*: create *TRIPs*-Plus standards. The USTR explained that "[r]ather, the goal [of *ACTA*] is to set a new, *higher* benchmark for enforcement that countries can join on a voluntary basis."[15]

---

[12] *Anti-Counterfeiting Trade Agreement (ACTA), posted at* www.ustr.gov/acta.

[13] *See* Christine Mumford, *ACTA Treaty Lauded by Some, Criticized by Others as Secretive*, 25 International Trade Reporter (BNA) 980 (3 July 2008).

[14] *Quoted in U.S., Trading Partners Will Seek Anti-Counterfeiting Trade Agreement*, 24 International Trade Reporter (BNA) 1489 (25 October 2007) (emphasis added).

[15] *Quoted in U.S., Trading Partners Will Seek Anti-Counterfeiting Trade Agreement*, 24 International Trade Reporter (BNA) 1489 (25 October 2007) (emphasis added).

Senator Max Baucus (Democrat-Montana), a supporter of the *ACTA* along with (*inter alia*) the Copyright Alliance (an advocacy group of IP and IP-related organizations), added another motivation for *ACTA*. It might expand protection of American IPRs "eventually through a *new plurilateral WTO agreement*."[16] In other words, *ACTA* might create *TRIPs*-Plus standards, which one day may be multilateralized into the GATT–WTO regime. Why expand that protection in the first place? As the Senator put it: "Intellectual property thieves aren't just stealing American ideas, they're stealing dollars from U.S. businesses and stealing jobs out from under U.S. workers."[17]

Negotiations began in June 2008 and, the 11th and final Round of negotiations took place in Tokyo, Japan between 23 September — 1 October, 2010.[18] On 15 November 2010 parties to the *ACTA* negotiations finalized the text, and it has since been submitted for approval by each party through their individual domestic process.[19]

When negotiations commenced in June 2008, the United States, EU, and 11 other nations were engaged. Over the next four years, these countries met periodically, and discuss matters such as:

- Border measures
- Large-scale infringements of IP laws
- Criminal investigations and prosecutions
- Health and safety risks posed by infringement.

In 2008, the Executive Director of Copyright Alliance, Patrick Ross, stated: "Global piracy annually costs the United States economy $58 billion, nearly 375,000 jobs, $16.3 billion in earnings, and $2.6 billion in tax revenue."[20]

This concern about piracy motivated and underlies the *ACTA*. Note the *ACTA* is not motivated by a sense of failure of the *TRIPs Agreement*, but rather that the world of IP has changed considerably since the Uruguay Round (1986–1993) in which the *TRIPs* accord was negotiated. The idea, then, is not to compete or over-ride *TRIPs*, but to supplement and upgrade its provisions to account for new IP developments. That said, an underlying concern of *ACTA* is that some countries are unable or unwilling to take seriously grave violations of IP rights — possibly, for example, at the scale and severity as

---

[16] *Quoted in U.S., Trading Partners Will Seek Anti-Counterfeiting Trade Agreement*, 24 International Trade Reporter (BNA) 1489 (25 October 2007) (emphasis added).

[17] *Quoted in U.S., Trading Partners Will Seek Anti-Counterfeiting Trade Agreement*, 24 International Trade Reporter (BNA) 1489 (25 October 2007)

[18] *See Anti-Counterfeiting Trade Agreement (ACTA), posted at* www.ustr.gov/acta; Amy Tsui, *U.S. Meets with Other Nations in Geneva on Anti-Counterfeiting Trade Agreement*, 25 International Trade Reporter (BNA) 872–873 (12 June 2008).

[19] *See Anti-Counterfeiting Trade Agreement, 3 December 2010, posted at* www.ustr.gov/webfm_send/2417.

[20] *Quoted in* Christine Mumford, *ACTA Treaty Lauded by Some, Criticized by Others as Secretive*, 25 International Trade Reporter (BNA) 980, 981 (3 July 2008).

occur in China and India, both of which is noticeably absent from the *ACTA* negotiations.

One of the most prevalent criticisms of *ACTA* was the manner in which negotiations were handled. The negotiations, initiated by the Administration of President George W. Bush, were later classified as exempt from the *Freedom of Information Act* (*FOIA*) for security and foreign policy reasons by the Administration of President Barack H. Obama.[21] The lack of transparency created a backlash in the public sector. A lawsuit was filed against the Office of the United States Trade Representative (USTR) in September 2008 under *FOIA*, demanding disclosure of draft texts regarding the *ACTA* negotiations.[22] In response to the call for increased transparency, after the fifth round of talks, draft agendas for subsequent rounds became available to the public. Furthermore, after the eighth round of negotiations, a draft text of the negotiations thus far also was made available to the public. This announcement was met with much applause.

In the United States, the USTR released the draft text on 21 April 2010.[23] In the EU, prior to the release of the draft text, the European Parliament threatened to go to the European Court of Justice (ECJ) if the European Commission (EC) had not made the text public.[24] Finally, the EC also held a stakeholder conference in advance of the eighth round of negotiations to address overall concerns and the issue of transparency.[25]

Despite efforts to increase transparency and quell criticism, on 28 October 2010, weeks after the release of the final *ACTA* draft was made public on 6 October, a group of American law professors circulated a sign-on letter addressed to President Obama requesting the USTR halt its endorsement of *ACTA*. The letter expressed concern

> . . .that the [Obama] Administration is negotiating a far-reaching international intellectual property agreement behind a shroud of secrecy, with little opportunity for public input, and with active participation by special interests who stand to gain from restrictive new international rules that may harm the public interest.[26]

Notwithstanding continued criticism regarding transparency issues that ran the duration of the negotiations, the final *ACTA* draft received public

---

[21] *See* Amy Tsui, *USTR says Sixth Round of ACTA Talks to Include Digital Environment Enforcement,* 26 International Trade Reporter (BNA) 1383 (15 October 2009).

[22] *See* USTR *Official Cites Confidentiality 'Understandings' in ACTA Negotiations,* 25 International Trade Reporter (BNA) 1368 (25 September 2008).

[23] *See* Draft text of the Anti-Counterfeiting Trade Agreement, *posted at* www.ustr.gov/webfm_send/1883.

[24] *See EC Works to Dispel ACTA Controversy; Study Cites Piracy Toll on Jobs, Revenue,* 27 International Trade Reporter (BNA) 422 (25 March 2010).

[25] *See* Joe Kirwin, *EC to Hold Stakeholder Conference to Ease ACTA Transparency Concerns,* 27 International Trade Reporter (BNA) 260 (25 February 2010).

[26] *See* Nathan Pollard, *Law Professors' Letter to Obama Asks for Meaningful ACTA Participation Process,* 27 International Trade Reporter (BNA) 1673 (4 November 2010).

support from groups such as the International Trademark Association, the International Chamber of Commerce's Business Action to Stop Counterfeiting (ICC BASCAP), and the Business Response Group (BRG), an organization consisting of 18 associations around the world.[27] On 23 November 2010 the European Parliament approved a resolution supporting the terms of the accord and called the final draft text "a step in the right direction."[28]

The final draft text addresses copyright, trademark, and intellectual property infringement. Specifically, the definition of intellectual property follows Part II, Sections 1 through 7 of *TRIPs*, which includes: copyright and related rights; trademarks; geographical indicators (GIs); industrial designs; patents; layout designs; protection of undisclosed information; and control of anti-competitive practices in contractual licenses.[29] Exceptions in the draft text limit the scope of coverage, such as provisions setting standards on criminal enforcement that apply only to copyright and trademark violations, and exclude patents from the scope of coverage on border enforcement.[30]

*Suggestions for Further Research*:

Articles:

1. *Focus Issue: Intellectual Property Law Enforcement and the Anti-Counterfeiting Trade Agreement (ACTA)*, 26 American University International Law Review 543–926 (2011).

2. McManis, Charles R., *The Proposed Anti-Counterfeiting Trade Agreement (ACTA): Two Tales of a Treaty*, 46 Houston Law Review 1235–1256 (2009).

3. Port, Kenneth L., *A Case against the ACTA*, 33 Cardozo Law Review 1131–1183 (2012).

4. Sell, Susan K., *TRIPs Was Never Enough: Vertical Forum Shifting, FTAs, ACTA, and TPP*, 18 Journal of Intellectual Property 447–478 (2011).

## ACTPN

Advisory Committee for Trade Policy and Negotiations.

The ACTPN is the senior-most committee counseling the President of the United States on trade law and policy. It is comprised of 750 practitioners, appointed by the President. The ACTPN is organized into 27 committees dedicated to specific fields, such as the Agricultural Policy Advisory Committee (APAC), Labor Advisory Committee (LAC) and the Trade and Environmental Policy Advisory Committee (TEPAC).

---

[27] *See Trademark, Business Groups Hail Final ACTA Text, Urge Implementation*, 27 International Trade Reporter (BNA) 1836 (2 December 2010).

[28] Joe Kirwin, *European Parliament OKs Resolution Backing Terms of Latest ACTA Text*, 27 International Trade Reporter (BNA) 1842 (2 December 2010).

[29] *See* Daniel Pruzin, *Parties to ACTA Issue Final Draft Text; U.S., EU Need to Iron Out Reservations*, 27 International Trade Reporter (BNA) 1540 (14 October 2010).

[30] *See* Daniel Pruzin, *Parties to ACTA Issue Final Draft Text; U.S., EU Need to Iron Out Reservations*, 27 International Trade Reporter (BNA) 1540 (14 October 2010).

The President appoints up to 45 ACPTN members for terms of two years each. Under the *Trade Act of 1974*, as amended, membership must represent broadly key sectors of the American economy affected by trade. The ACPTN considers trade policy issues in the context of overall national interest. The United States Trade Representative (USTR) administers the ACPTN.

*Suggestions for Further Research*:

Article:

1.   Trujillo, Elizabeth, *From Here to Beijing: Public / Private Overlaps in Trade and their Effects on U.S. Law*, 40 Loyola University Chicago Law Journal 691–744 (2009).

## ACTUAL RATE

*See* Applied Rate.

## ACU

Asian Currency Unit.

Following the 1997–99 Asian Economic Crisis, Japan proposed an ACU Index as a device to promote regional stability.[31] The Asian Development Bank added its support to the idea. The roots of the proposal, however, lie in the weakening of the U.S. dollar since the 1960s. Asian countries rely on the dollar as a reserve currency, but the long-term depreciation has caused them difficulties. Moreover, there is resentment created by the fact the dollar, as a global currency standard, liberates the United States from normal constraints on excessive fiscal and trade deficits, and excessively loose monetary policy. During the Vietnam War era, French President Charles De Gaulle dubbed this situation an "arrogant privilege."

An ACU — which has not yet been created — would not be a precursor to a currency like the euro, nor to Asian monetary union. Rather, it would be a measuring device, *i.e.*, a benchmark, for Asian countries to denominate the value of their exports, and price financial instruments like cross-border bonds. The value of the ACU would be derived from a hypothetical Asian currency, which in turn would be a weighted average of actual currencies in the region. Initially, China reacted coolly to the Japanese proposal, fearing the yen would dominate the ACU Index. Subsequently, China's prominent economic growth allayed these concerns, and both countries agree they must reduce their reliance on the U.S. dollar.

## ACWL

Advisory Center on WTO Law, based in Geneva, Switzerland, essentially, a legal aid clinic for poor countries that are WTO Members.

---

[31] *See* Richard McGregor, *Beijing and Tokyo Agree Need for Asian Currency Unit*, FINANCIAL TIMES, 30 August 2006, at 4.

The ACWL was founded in 2001 by several developed country Members of the WTO to help developing and least developing countries in WTO litigation.[32] The ACWL advises poor countries in bringing and defending dispute settlement actions under the WTO *Understanding on Rules and Procedures Governing the Settlement of Disputes (DSU)*. The ACWL plays an important role in helping poor countries build legal capacity, and for which hiring expensive private law firms is not economically viable. Thus, for example, the ACWL helps developing countries challenge trade barriers in developed countries.

Developing and least developed countries account for roughly 80 percent of the WTO Membership, but traditionally did not figure prominently as complainants. In the vast majority of cases from 1995–2000, developed countries were the complainants. Few *DSU* cases were initiated by developing countries. But, since 2005, developing countries have launched the majority of *DSU* cases. By 2010, they were the complainant in the majority of cases. The same trend reversal is true with respect to respondents. Developed countries accounted for the majority of respondents between 1995 and 2009, but developing countries took that position after 2009. Notably, in recent years, the ACWL has advised developing countries in cases challenging trade barriers brought against other developing countries.

Additionally, during the three-year period of 2009–2011, China alone initiated six WTO cases, four against American trade measures, whereas it had brought only two cases during the first seven years of its membership (2001–2008).

Legal advice from the ACWL is free, as is the legal training it provides. In 2010 alone, the ACWL provided 206 legal opinions to developing countries to help them in four DSU cases generated that year. The Center offers legal support in *DSU* proceeding at a discounted rate. The fees the Center charges cover just 8 percent of the cost it incurs. Thus, funding from its developed country benefactors is critical to the survival of the Center. Those benefactors are Australia, Canada, Denmark, Finland, Italy, Netherlands, Norway, Sweden, Switzerland, and United Kingdom, each of which has given U.S. $1 million or more. The United States eschews funding the AWCL, as it does not want to fund litigation that would be brought against itself.

Legal advice from the ACWL includes a range of non-*DSU* matters. For instance, the Center provides legal opinions on matters pertaining to WTO decision-making, including advice on accession negotiations, drafting requests for waivers from GATT–WTO rules, and the Doha Round (*e.g.*, preparing negotiating proposals and responses). It also gives developing and least developed countries opinions on whether draft trade measures they are considering comport with their GATT–WTO obligations.

---

[32] *See* Daniel Pruzin, *Growing Importance of Developing Nations in WTO Dispute Settlement Cited by Officials*, 28 International Trade Reporter (BNA) 1648 (13 October 2011). The statistics cited above are from this source.

# AD

Antidumping, sometimes written as anti-dumping.

Antidumping duties are one of three principal remedies against unfair trade practices, the other two being countervailing duties (CVDs) and measures against imported merchandise infringing on an intellectual property right (IPR). In contrast, safeguard remedies, such as the Escape Clause in Section 201 of the United States *Trade Act of 1974*, as amended, are available to deal with fairly traded foreign products. The AD remedy, like the other remedies, is countenanced by GATT and various WTO agreements. Article VI of GATT allows for AD duties and CVDs, and Article XIX creates the safeguard remedy. Supplementing these Articles are WTO accords on the specific topics of AD, subsidies, and safeguards. The WTO *Agreement on Trade Related Aspects of Intellectual Property Rights (TRIPs)* permits — indeed, encourages — strong enforcement measures against IPR infringement.

The Figure below outlines the principal steps in an AD case brought in the United States. These steps also apply to a CVD case.

Three points are noteworthy at the outset. First, there is no clear line between "unfair" and "fair" trade. That is, there is no general legal theory as to "unfairness" in international trade. Rather, there is simply a list of trade practices deemed "unfair" — dumping, illegal subsidization, and IPR infringement. Second, the AD and CVD remedies long pre-date GATT. The first AD statute in the United States, for instance, dates to 1916. (Interestingly, the *Antidumping Act of 1916* was the subject of a major WTO action, resulting in an adopted Appellate Body ruling against the *Act*, and — ultimately — compliance by the United States.) Third, as tariff rates and non-tariff barriers (NTBs) have been reduced progressively through successive rounds of multilateral trade negotiations, trade remedies remain a (if not the) key tool to impede foreign commerce. Not surprisingly, at every opportunity to weaken trade remedy defenses over several decades, GATT contracting parties and WTO Members instead have either left them alone, or strengthened them.

"Dumping," in the simplest sense, refers to the sale or likely sale of imported merchandise at less than fair value (LTFV). More technically, "dumping" is the sale of subject merchandise (an imported product) in an importing country at a price (after any applicable adjustments to that price) below the price at which the foreign like product (*i.e.*, a product that is like the subject merchandise) is sold in the home market of the exporter (or, in some instances, a third country). The price of subject merchandise in the importing country is called "Export Price" (or "EP" for short).

In cases in which the foreign exporter is affiliated with the importer of subject merchandise, that price is "Constructed Export Price." The word "Constructed" intimates the need to use an arm's length price, namely, between the importer and the first independent buyer of subject merchandise in the importing country. The price at which the foreign like product is sold is called

"Normal Value." In cases in which data for Normal Value are insignificant, incomplete or unavailable, or in which the exporting country is a non-market economy (NME), data on foreign sales are taken from a third country, and the result is "Third Country Price." In some cases, it is necessary to determine Normal Value based on data from the home country of the exporter concerning cost of production, selling, general, and administrative (SG&A) expenses, and profits. Then, the price is called "Constructed Value."

**FIGURE:**

**STEPS IN AN AD OR CVD CASE IN THE UNITED STATES**

*Step 1:*    ***Filing a Petition.***

"Interested party" files petition simultaneously with Department of Commerce (DOC) and International Trade Commission (ITC) (or DOC self-initiates the petition).

*Step 2:*    ***Standing and Sufficiency Determination.***

The DOC checks legal sufficiency of petition, and checks standing by applying the 25 and 50 Percent Tests.

*Step 3:*    ***ITC Preliminary Injury Determination.***

ITC renders a preliminary determination as to "reasonable indication" of material injury or threat thereof.

*Step 4:*    ***DOC Preliminary Dumping Margin or Subsidization Determination.***

If ITC's preliminary determination is affirmative, then DOC renders a preliminary determination as to whether there is a "reasonable basis to believe or suspect" there are LTFV sales (AD case) or illegal subsidization (CVD case). Possibility of alleged critical circumstances.

If ITC's preliminary determination is negative, then petition is dismissed. Case ends.

**FIGURE (continued)**

***Step 5:***     ***DOC Final Dumping Margin or Subsidization Determination.***

If DOC's preliminary determination is affirmative, then DOC (1) estimates magnitude of dumping margin or illegal subsidization, (2) orders suspension of liquidation of entries of subject merchandise, and (3) further orders deposit of estimated AD duties or CVDs, or posting bond to cover estimated duties. Estimated duties must be deposited, or bond posted. ITC commences final injury determination. DOC makes final determination.

Even if DOC's preliminary determination is negative, DOC proceeds to make a final determination as to whether LTFV sales are made, or whether illegal subsidization exists. ITC does not (yet) commence final injury determination.

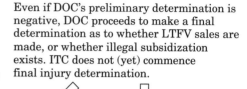

If DOC's final determination is affirmative, then DOC confirms the estimated duty rate (though it is not finalized until the first first Administrative Review).

If DOC's determination is negative, then petition is dismissed. Any suspension of liquidation of entries is lifted, and any estimated duty deposits (or bonds posted) are refunded with interest. Case ends.

***Step 6:***     ***ITC Final Injury Determination.***

If DOC's final determination is affirmative, then ITC renders a final injury determination as to whether there is material injury or threat thereof.

**FIGURE (continued)**

**Step 7:**      *AD or CVD Order.*

If ITC's final injury determination is affirmative, then DOC issues an AD or CVD order to Customs and Borde Protection (CBP). CBP collects estimated AD duties or CVDs. (Suspension of liquidation of entries continues until first Administrative Review, when final duty rate is determined.)

If ITC's final injury determination is negative, then petition is dismissed. Any suspension of liquidation of entries is lifted. Any estimated duty deposits (or bond posted) are refunded with interest. Case ends.

**Step 8:**      *Reviews of AD or CVD Orders.*

ITC conducts Sunset Reviews within 5 years of issuance of AD or CVD order. Administrative Review may occur annually. Changed Circumstances Review may occur if warranted.

**Step 9:**      *Appeals?*

Losing party (petitioner or respondent) may appeal to CIT, and losing party in CIT litigation may appeal to Federal Circuit. In rare instances, appeal from Federal Circuit is made to Supreme Court. In a case where petitioner and respondent are from *NAFTA* Parties, appeal may be to Chapter 19 Panel (rather than U.S. courts). Other Free Trade Agreement (FTA) dispute settlement mechanisms may be available.

**Step 10:**      *WTO Adjudication?*

In some cases, private litigation may generate dispute between sovereign WTO Members, leading to a *DSU* action.

> **Note:**    Settlement through a "price undertaking" can occur at any point. In that instance, a "suspension agreement" results in cessation of the case.

An AD duty may be imposed on imports of subject merchandise up to, or equal to, the "Dumping Margin." The basic formula for this Margin is:

Dumping Margin = Normal Value − Export Price

Expressed as a percentage, the Dumping Margin formula is:

$$\text{Dumping Margin} = \frac{\text{Normal Value} - \text{Export Price}}{\text{Export Price}} \times 100$$

The basic formula can be expanded to capture instances in which Third Country Price or Constructed Value is used as a proxy for Normal Value, or cases in which Constructed Export Price must be employed instead of Export Price. The expanded formula is:

Dumping Margin = Normal Value          –          Export Price

                    (or Third Country,          (or Constructed
                    Price, or                   Export Price)
                    Constructed Value)

Similarly, the equation to express the Margin as a percentage is:

$$\text{Dumping Margin} = \frac{\begin{array}{l}\text{Normal Value} \\ \text{(or Third Country Price,} \\ \text{or Constructed Value)}\end{array} - \begin{array}{l}\text{Export Price} \\ \text{(or Constructed} \\ \text{Export Price)}\end{array}}{\begin{array}{l}\text{Export Price} \\ \text{(or Constructed Export Price)}\end{array}} \times 100$$

Each of the price variables in the formulae are subject to adjustment, so that the calculation of the Dumping Margin—and any AD duty imposed on the basis of this calculation—is made on a fair and equitable basis.

Adjustments are designed to ensure cross-border price data are, in fact, comparable—or, as is commonly said, "apples-to-apples" are being compared. A number of adjustments are permissible. For example, Constructed Export Price may be adjusted—namely, reduced—by the profit allocated to the "total United States expenses."[33] *See* 19 U.S.C. § 1677a(d)(3). This adjustment, known as the "Constructed Export Price profit," or "CEP profit" deduction, entered into United States AD law with the *Uruguay Round Agreements Act of 1994*. Constructed Export Price profit is computed by multiplying "total actual profit" by an "applicable percentage." In turn, an "applicable percentage" is derived by dividing total United States expenses by total expenses. *See* 19 U.S.C. § 1677a(f). Manifestly, some adjustments—like for CEP profit—are highly technical. Not surprisingly, the technical aspects of an adjustment, as well as the question of whether a particular adjustment is appropriate in the first instance, are potential sources of major controversy in an AD case.

In sum, the "dumping margin" refers to the amount by which the Normal Value exceeds Export Price or Constructed Export Price. *See* 19 U.S.C. § 1677b(a)(1). A Dumping Margin is calculated for each entry of subject merchandise. Moreover, Dumping Margins are calculated in both an original investigation and any

---

[33] This example arises in *SNR Roulements v. United States*, 402 F.3d 1358–63 (Fed. Cir. 2005). In that case, the United States Court of Appeals for the Federal Circuit (CAFC) that the Department of Commerce (DOC) may account for credit costs, and inventory carrying costs, by using imputed expenses in one instance, but using actual expenses in the other. The DOC could do so, said the CAFC, as long as the DOC affords a respondent the opportunity to make a showing the amount of imputed expenses is not accurately reflected or embedded in its actual expenses. The CAFC based its ruling on 19 U.S.C. § 1677a, which it said does not address the issue in an unambiguous way.

reviews of outstanding AD orders (*e.g.*, Administrative Reviews, Changed Circumstances Reviews, or Sunset Reviews). *See* 19 U.S.C. § 1675.

Importantly, no AD duty may be imposed on subject merchandise without proof that imports thereof cause, or threaten to cause, material injury to a domestic producer of a like product. In an AD case, therefore, there are two like product determinations—as between the product sold in the exporter's home market and the subject merchandise sold in the importing country, and as between that subject merchandise and a domestically produced good. Some WTO Members, notably the European Union (EU), rely on the "Lesser Duty Rule," imposing an AD duty only in the amount necessary to counter-act dumping. The United States imposes AD duties on the full amount of the Dumping Margin.

Equally importantly, every AD case involves a choice of period of investigation (POI). That is true both for the dumping margin and injury determination phases. While the POI in each phase should—indeed, must—overlap, typically the POI for a dumping margin calculation is shorter than that for an injury determination.

In the United States, appeals of AD determinations from the underlying administrative agencies that render preliminary and final determinations (the Department of Commerce (DOC) for the dumping margin, and the International Trade Commission (DOC) for injury) typically go to the United States Court of International Trade (CIT) in New York, New York. Thereafter, appeal may be take to the United States Court of Appeals for the Federal Circuit, and ultimately, the United States Supreme Court. In some cases involving the *North American Free Trade Agreement* (*NAFTA*), appeal may be made to a Chapter 19 Panel (but, then, not back to domestic courts, unless a constitutional question is presented).

In the EU, appeals go to the European Commission. Generally, Scandinavia and the United Kingdom are against imposing AD duties. Southern Europe, especially Italy and Spain, tend to favor use of the AD remedy. New EU states, from Central and Eastern Europe, are in the middle between these two poles. Thus, a considerable amount of lobbying of individual EU governments occurs in most AD cases.

Finally, as a practical matter, AD cases are expensive propositions. In the EU, the cost to launch an average AD case (as of May 2009) is between €60,000 and €100,000. The United States is the most expensive AD jurisdiction in the world, with the cost to initiate a case far higher than in the EU.

*Suggestions for Further Research*:

Books:

1.  Barrington, Louise, ed., Dumping—A Comparative Approach (1995).

2.  Bovard, James, The Fair Trade Fraud—How Congress Pillages the Consumer and Decimates American Competitiveness (1992).

3.  Czako, Judith, Johann Human & Jorge Miranda, A Handbook on Anti-Dumping Investigations (2003).

4.  Mastel, Greg, Antidumping Laws and the U.S. Economy (1998).

5.  Mastel, Greg & Andrew Szamosszegi, Leveling the Playing Field: Antidumping and the U.S. Steel Industry (February 1999).

6.  Mueller, Wolfgang, Nicholas Khan & Tibor Scharf, EC and WTO Anti-Dumping Law—A Handbook (2nd ed. 2009).

7.  Stewart, Terence P. & Amy S. Dwyer, WTO Antidumping and Subsidy Agreements (1998).

8.  Vakerics, Thomas V., David I. Wilson & Kenneth G. Weigel, Antidumping, Countervailing Duty, and Other Trade Actions (December 1987).

Book Chapters:

1.  Davey, William J., *Antidumping Laws in the GATT and the EC*, in Antidumping Law and Practice: A Comparative Study 295–301 at 296 (John H. Jackson & Edwin A. Vermulst eds., 1989).

2.  Horlick, Gary N., *The United States Antidumping System in* Antidumping Law and Practice 160 (John H. Jackson & Edwin A. Vermulst, eds., 1989).

Articles:

1.  Barnett, Mark A., Sara Khan, Kathy B. Reif & Elizabeth Shryock, *28 U.S.C. § 1581(c)—Review by the Court of International Trade of Antidumping & Countervailing Duty Determinations Issued by the Department of Commerce*, 40 Georgetown Journal of International Law 153–181 (2008).

2.  Bentes, Pablo M., *et al.*, *International Trade*, 44 The International Lawyer 93–111 (2010).

3.  Bolton, Reid M., *Anti-Dumping and Distrust: Reducing Anti-Dumping Duties under the WTO Through Heightened Scrutiny*, 29 Berkeley Journal of International Law 66–93 (2011).

4.  Cho, Sungjoon, *Anticompetitive Trade Remedies: How Antidumping Measures Obstruct Market Competition*, 87 North Carolina Law Review 357–424 (2009).

5.  Dorn, Joseph W., *U.S. Court of International Trade Decisions During 2007 in Appeals of Determinations of the U.S. International Trade Commission*, 40 Georgetown Journal of International Law 219–241 (2008).

6.  Horlick, Gary N. & Eleanor C. Shea, *The World Trade Organization Antidumping Agreement*, 29 Journal of World Trade 5, 26 (1995).

7.  Laroski, Joseph A. Jr. & Valentin A. Povarchuk eds., *International Trade*, 45 The International Lawyer 79–94 (spring 2011).

8.  Long, Qinglan, *Conflicting Positions but Common Interests: An Analysis of the United States Antidumping Policy Toward China*, 7 Richmond Journal of Global Law & Business 133–148 (2008).

9.  Nedzel, Nadia E., *Antidumping and Cotton Subsidies: A Market-Based Defense of Unfair Trade Remedies*, 28 Northwestern Journal of International Law & Business 215–272 (2008).

10. Planert, R. Will, *Enjoining Liquidation in Antidumping and Countervailing Duty Cases: Issues and Pitfalls*, 19 Tulane Journal of International & Comparative Law 505–541 (2011).

11. Von Schriltz, Karl, *U.S. Court of International Trade Decisions in 2008 in Appeals of Determinations of the U.S. International Trade Commission*, 41 Georgetown Journal of International Law 1–51 (2009).

12. Trossevin, Marguerite & Reza Karmaloo, *Judicial Review of Antidumping and Countervailing Duty Determinations by the Department of Commerce: Noteworthy Cases in 2009*, 42 Georgetown Journal of International Law 35–63 (2010).

13. Wood, J. Christopher & Zia C. Oatley, *28 U.S.C. § 1581(c): Judicial Review of Antidumping Duty Determinations Issued by the Department of Commerce*, 41 Georgetown Journal of International Law 117–135 (2009).

## ADA

An acronym occasionally used for the WTO *Antidumping Agreement*, the formal title of which is *Agreement on the Implementation of Article VI of the General Agreement on Tariffs and Trade 1994*.

## ADJUSTMENTS

Arithmetic corrections to terms in the dumping margin formula made to ensure the comparison between sales of a foreign like product and subject merchandise are fair. Adjustments take the form of an addition to, or subtraction from, a term in the formula. Those terms are Normal Value (NV), Export Price (EP), and Constructed Export Price (CEP). The WTO *Antidumping Agreement*, and implementing laws in WTO Members, set out a number of permissible adjustments. Adjustments engage petitioners and respondents in a zero sum game, with each side trying to maximize or minimize the dumping margin, respectively, by arguing for or against a particular adjustment.

## ADJUSTMENT ASSISTANCE

*See* TAA.

## ADMINISTRATIVE GUIDANCE

A term concerning Japanese administrative law.

Administrative guidance (*gyōsei shidō*) refers to suggestions or "unwritten orders" given by Japanese bureaucrats to firms in order to implement official policies. When dealing with businesses, the government officials often issue (typically orally) recommendations or advice. In theory, compliance with the advice is voluntary. But, the implication associated with the advice is non-compliant parties will be obstructed by the relevant government agency in the future in some manner, such as receiving poorer quotas or less government aid. Administrative guidance gives bureaucrats much flexibility in implementing policies, enabling them to steer the private sector in lieu of government regulations.

The former Ministry of International Trade and Industry (MITI) (now known as METI—the Ministry of Economy, Trade and Industry) and the Ministry of Finance were especially well known for using administrative guidance. Because MITI (METI) and MOF have such wide jurisdiction, their use of it was especially significant.

The practice has been criticized on two broad grounds. First, it has left the public uninformed, while fostering an environment of collusion between the ministries and big business. Second, it has caused businesses to give top priority to cultivating smooth relations with authorities.

In response to these criticisms, the Administrative Procedure Law was enacted and went into effect in October 1994. It aims at curbing bureaucratic power by replacing administrative guidance with clear written directives. However, there is some doubt as to whether it has been entirely effective.

*Suggestions for Further Research*:

Book:

1.   Hsu, Robert C., The MIT Encyclopedia of the Japanese Economy 1–2 (MIT Press, 2nd ed. 1999).

## ADMINISTRATIVE REVIEW

Also referred to as a "Periodic Review," an Administrative Review is a review of an outstanding antidumping (AD) or countervailing duty (CVD) order to recalculate the amount of remedial duties owed. Administrative Reviews play a critical role in the American retrospective assessment system. *See* Retrospective assessment.

An Administrative Review may occur once a year during the anniversary month of an outstanding AD or CVD order, and is triggered by a request of an interested party for recalculation of the duties owed. Under United States AD and CVD law, the Department of Commerce (DOC), if requested by an interested party, is required to review and determine the amount of an AD duty or CVD at least once during each 12 month period, beginning on the anniversary date of publication of an AD or CVD order. However, this period may be extended to 18 months following issuance of the order in a case of the first assessment of AD duties or CVDs. The purpose of the extension is to ensure the first Administrative Review covers all entries of subject merchandise that may have been subject to provisional measures. *See* 19 U.S.C. § 1675.

Accordingly, during an Administrative Review of an AD order, the DOC calculates the amount of AD duties owed by each individual importer—the Assessment Rate, or Duty Assessment Rate (or, sometimes, the Final Liquidation Rate)—based on comparisons of the (1) Export Price (or Constructed Export Price) of each individual import transaction to (2) a contemporaneous average Normal Value. That is, the Commerce Department calculates the Assessment Rate using a weighted average Normal Value-to-individual Export Price comparison. Then, the Commerce Department aggregates the total amount of dumping by each importer, and expresses this sum of all the dumping margins as a percentage of that importer's United States imports. The Commerce Department applies to an individual importer the Assessment Rate to imports of subject merchandise for the period examined in the Administrative Review.

Further, the Commerce Department uses the amount of dumping on all imports (*i.e.*, the sum of all the dumping margins) from a particular exporter (regardless of the specific importer) to calculate the Cash Deposit Rate, also called the "Estimated AD Duty Rate." The Cash Deposit Rate applies on future entries from that exporter. If no interested party requests an Administrative Review, then cash deposits assessed on entries in the previous year are automatically determined to be the final duties owed.

Thus, an Administrative Review results in the calculation of two key figures: the (1) Assessment Rate (Duty Assessment Rate), which is the final liability on AD or CVDs owed by an importer for entries of subject merchandise in the previous year, and (2) Going-Forward Cash Deposit Rate, which applies to entries of subject merchandise in the future, at least until the time of the next Review.

## AD VALOREM

From the Latin, on the value of.

*Ad valorem* is a term arising in Customs Law. There are four broad categories of tariffs (duties):

- *ad valorem*
- specific, and
- hybrid (compound)
- mixed (variable per entry or per entry price range).

An *ad valorem* tariff is a tax imposed on the value of imported merchandise. It is expressed as a percentage, such as 10 percent on the value as assessed by customs authorities. If that value is $1,000, then a 10 percent levy would mean a tariff of $100.

A specific duty is a tax imposed on the quantity of imported merchandise. It is expressed as a fixed sum per unit of that merchandise, *e.g.*, $10 per kilogram. A hybrid, or compound, tariff, is a combination of both an *ad valorem* and specific duty. For example, a tariff of 10 percent plus $100 per kilo would be a compound duty. A mixed duty is one in which the rate charges varies with the entry or entry price range of merchandise. For example, a tariff rate quota (TRQ) is a mixed rate, with a lower tariff (or duty-free treatment) applying up to a certain value or volume of imports (in-quota shipments), and then a higher tariff applying after that threshold (above- or out-of-quota shipments).

Economists view *ad valorem* tariffs as more transparent and easier to administer than specific or compound duties. Moreover, tariff revenue adjusts upward (downward) with an increase (decrease) in the price of imported merchandise if the methodology is *ad valorem*. Tariff revenue is fixed, however, under a specific duty, meaning that price inflation does not lead to greater tariff revenue—precisely because a specific duty is set independently of price. Consequently, economists counsel countries to convert specific or compound duties to *ad valorem* tariffs. The difficulty in this conversion is agreeing on the *ad valorem* equivalent, or AVE, to the specific or compound duty being replaced.

*Suggestions for Further Research*:

Book:

1. Dam, Kenneth W., The GATT—Law and International Economic Organization (1970).

## AEC

African Economic Community.

On 3 June 1991, at the Abuja, Nigeria summit, the Organization of African Unity (OAU) agreed to establish the AEC by 2028. The legal instrument for this establishment is the *Treaty Establishing the African Economic Community*, which has been in effect since 12 May 1994.[34] That *Treaty* is commonly known as the *"Abuja Treaty."*

The ultimate goal set out in the *Abuja Treaty* is regional economic integration, a sort of "United States of Africa" or "Common Market of Africa." That goal is being realized incrementally, in six stages over 34 years. It is supposed to be reached through progressively greater coordination, trade barrier elimination, and harmonization. The stages are:

- Stage 1:    5 Years (Years 1–5)

  Strengthening of regional economic communities (RECs), and creating new RECs if needed. The existing RECs are —

  (1) The Arab Maghreb Union (AMU)

  (2) Economic Community of Central African States (ECCAS)

  (3) Common Market of Eastern and Southern Africa (COMESA)

  (4) Southern African Development Community (SADC)

  (5) Economic Community of West African States (ECOWAS)

  (6) Community of Sahel-Saharan States (CEN-SAD)

  (7) Intergovernmental Authority on Development (IGAD)

- Stage 2:    8 Years (Years 6–8)

  Stabilizing tariff and non-tariff barriers to regional trade, and enhancing sectoral integration, especially in the areas of agriculture,

---

[34] *See Treaty Establishing the African Economic Community*, available at www.uneca.org.

communications, energy, finance, industry, transport and, of course, trade, and improving coordination—with a view to harmonization—of activities of the RECs.

- Stage 3:        10 Years (Years 9–10)

  Creation of a free trade area (FTA) and a customs union (CU), but at the level of the RECs.

- Stage 4:        2 Years (Years 11–12)

  Coordination and harmonization of tariff and non-tariff barriers among the RECs, and movement towards a Continental Customs Union.

- Stage 5:        4 Years (Years 12–16)

  Establishment of an African Common Market and adoption of common economic policies.

- Stage 6:        5 Years (Years 17–21)

  Integration of all sectors, establishment of an African Central Bank and single African currency, and creation of African economic and Monetary Union through the election of the first Pan-African Parliament.

*Suggestions for Further Research*:

Book:

1. Asante, Sam, Regionalism and Africa's Development: Expectations, Reality, and Challenges (1997).

Other Source:

1. Asante, Sam, *et al.*, *Towards an African Economic Community* Africa Institute Paper (2001).


## *AFTA* (FIRST MEANING)

*Arab Free Trade Area*.

This free trade agreement (FTA) covers the Arab League countries. On 27 February 1981, the Arab League Members signed the *Agreement on Facilitation and Development of Trade Among Arab States*. To enhance implementation of this *Agreement*, the Arab League members agreed, on 19 February 1997, on arrangements to set up a *Pan Arab Free Trade Area*, or *AFTA*. The idea of *AFTA* originated in part from discussions in the Economic and Social Council of the Arab League. The idea was to enhance trade and economic activity among the Arab states, and establish a regional FTA.

Originally, the Arab League sought to establish *AFTA* within 10 years. However, at the March 2002 Arab Summit in Beirut, and the September 2002 meeting of the League's Economic and Social Council, the member states decided to cut the transitional period for *AFTA* to seven years, ending in January 2005.

Currently (as of December 2007), there are 18 Arab League member states participating in *AFTA*. They are:

- Algeria
- Bahrain
- Egypt
- Jordan
- Iraq
- Kingdom of Saudi Arabia
- Kuwait
- Lebanon
- Libya

- Morocco
- Oman
- Qatar
- Palestine
- Sudan
- Syria
- Tunisia
- United Arab Emirates
- Yemen

There are approximately 320 million consumers in the Arab world. Hence, *AFTA* could constitute one of the larger trading blocs in the world. Under *AFTA*, tariffs are falling by 10 percent per year.

*Suggestions for Further Research*:

Articles:

1.   Fakhri, Michael, *Images of the Arab World and Middle East—Debates about Development and Regional Integration*, 28 Wisconsin International Law Journal 391–429 (2010).

2.   Mohammedi, Omar T., *International Trade and Investment in Algeria: An Overview*, 18 Michigan State Journal of International Law 375–409 (2010).

3.   Sakmar, Susan L., *Globalization and Trade Initiatives in the Arab World: Historical Context, Progress to Date, and Prospects for the Future*, 42 University of South Florida Law Review 919–939 (2008).

## *AFTA* (SECOND MEANING)

*ASEAN* Free Trade Area.

*AFTA* is comprised of Brunei, Burma (Myanmar), Cambodia, Indonesia, Laos, Malaysia, Philippines, Singapore, Thailand, and Vietnam (*i.e.*, the same membership as in *ASEAN*). *AFTA* is a Preferential Trading Arrangement (PTA). *ASEAN* endorsed the creation of *AFTA* in 1992, and implementation began in 1993. The ultimate objective is to achieve total free trade—that is, duty-free trade in both industrial and agricultural products. In February 2000, *ASEAN* began talks with Australia and New Zealand with a view to expanding *AFTA* to include these two countries by 2010.

Initially, the target date for achieving total free trade was 2015 among the original six *ASEAN* members (Brunei, Indonesia, Malaysia, the Philippines, Singapore, and Thailand), which also happen to be the most developed members. For the new—and poorer—members (Burma, Cambodia, Laos, and Vietnam), the target date for zero duties was set as 2018. All members committed themselves to reducing tariffs on most products to between zero and five percent by 2002.

Significantly, *ASEAN* members agreed upon the details of how to achieve the goal of free trade at the 1998 *ASEAN* summit in Hanoi. They devised a plan, known as the "Hanoi Plan," or "Hanoi Action Plan." This Plan embodied the Bogor Goals set out in 1994 by APEC. The thrust of the Goals was free, open trade and investment by 2010 for industrialized countries in the Asia-Pacific region, and by 2020 for developing countries.

Under the Hanoi Plan, *ASEAN* members must reduce their tariffs to five percent or less on over 40,000 manufactured goods, as well as some agricultural products, traded among the members. The centerpiece of the Plan is the "Common Effective Preferential Tariff," or CEPT. There are two tracks to the CEPT.

The "fast track" called for the reduction of tariffs set as of 1999 at above 20 percent to one-half percent by 2003. It mandated the reduction of tariffs set as of 1999 at or below 20 percent to zero-to-five percent by 1 January 2000. Articles on the fast track include chemicals, pulp and paper, and electronics. Roughly 80 percent of the articles subject to *AFTA* tariff cuts (*i.e.*, about 38,000 products) are on the "fast track" list. In the "normal track," tariff reductions for all other products are staged. Tariffs currently above 20 percent had to be reduced to 20 percent by 2001, and must be further reduced to zero-to-five percent by 2003.

The goods on both tracks satisfy a rule of origin. A good must be at least 40 percent manufactured (*i.e.*, at least 40 percent of its value is added) in an *ASEAN* member to qualify for preferential treatment. There is a "General Exception" (GE) list containing items exempt from, or given special treatment as regards, tariff liberalization. Motor vehicle parts (discussed below) are an example of a GE list item. In addition, *ASEAN* members are free to exempt products based on national security or public morality concerns, and because of temporary economic need. Moreover, tariffs on "sensitive" agricultural products will not be phased into the *AFTA* framework until 2010 at the latest, and the integration of some commodities like cloves, rice, sugar, and wheat flour may be delayed beyond this date.

All of the target dates mentioned above are subject to variation. The variations take the form of rather impressive acceleration commitments that underscore the adherence of *ASEAN* to free trade, in spite of protectionist sentiments resulting from the Asian economic crisis. An excellent example occurred in November 1999, when the *ASEAN* leaders agreed to accelerate their overall free trade plan by five years. The six original members (*i.e.*, the developed ones) pledged to eliminate import tariffs on most goods traded in *AFTA* by 2010 instead of 2015. The less developed members would have until 2015 to eliminate tariffs.

Another example of variation involves the CEPT targets. In 1998, the original six members agreed to advance the compliance date for the fast track of 2003 forward to 2002. They also agreed to ensure that tariffs on at least 85 percent of the CEPT articles were cut to between zero to five percent by 1 January 2000, 90 percent by 2001, and 100 percent by 2002. In 1999, they agreed agricultural tariffs would be lowered by 2006. In contrast, the new, less developed *ASEAN* members have longer phase-in periods: Vietnam had until 2006 to comply with the CEPT, though it agreed to cut some tariffs to five percent by 2003. Burma, Cambodia, and Laos had until 2008 to slash all of their tariffs, though they were to reduce tariffs on some articles by 2005. The generous time periods reflect the reliance poor members typically place on tariff revenues. For example, tariffs account for about 60 percent of Cambodia's government revenues.

In May 2000, *ASEAN* members established what might yet prove to be a dangerous precedent: for the first time, they granted to one member a concession—in the form of an extension—on a trade liberalization commitment. The members agreed that Malaysia could have two extra years to reduce its tariffs on autos and auto parts. Like the other *ASEAN* members, Malaysia had committed itself to cutting auto and auto parts tariffs to 20 percent by no later than 1 January 2003. However, the other members agreed Malaysia could keep its tariffs on autos and auto parts at 80 percent until 2005. Thus, the concession granted meant the *ASEAN* playing field in the car industry could not be level until 2005.

Malaysia argued that slashing these tariffs by 2003 would damage, or threaten to damage, its domestic auto industry. In other words, Malaysia sought to protect its controversial national car, the Proton, from foreign competition, as well as its other local manufacturer, Perodua. It has been successful in doing so, given that 90 percent of cars driven in Malaysia are from those two manufacturers (as of March 2006), and over 60 percent of all cars sold in Malaysia are Protons. Thailand—led by former Deputy Prime Minister and WTO Director-General Supachai Panichpakdi—strenuously opposed the extension. Thailand is *ASEAN's* biggest car producer, as it is home to auto and auto parts factories owned by several American, European, and Japanese companies. Thailand argued, unsuccessfully, that Malaysia should have to provide compensation for the concession, possibly in the form of accelerated tariff cuts on other products.

To its credit, by August 2006, *ASEAN* had made considerable strides toward implementing the 1998 Hanoi Plan and building a commercially meaningful *AFTA*. Members had dropped tariffs on nearly all products traded among them to the target band of zero to five percent. The Philippines said it would reinstate the zero to five percent tariff range for plastic and petrochemical products. *ASEAN* members also agreed to implement substantial transformation rules of origin for iron and steel as an alternative to the 40 percent value added test normally required. And, *ASEAN* members began working toward a unified mark for goods to indicate compliance with quality guidelines for the *ASEAN* region. Significantly, in March 2006, Malaysia cut its duty rate from 20 to five percent on automobile imports from *ASEAN* members. The decision was welcomed by Ford and Toyota, which have large production facilities in Thailand. Observe Malaysia refused to abandon high duty rates on non-*ASEAN* cars. It stuck to a general rate of 30 percent (on top of a 10 percent sales tax on all vehicle sales). Depending on the engine size of a non-*ASEAN* car, Malaysia dropped its tariff from 80 to 200 percent to a still high 75 to 125 percent.

By August 2006, considerable challenges remained, of which *ASEAN* members and the *AFTA* Council were aware. Most notably, with respect to goods, *ASEAN* countries exempted about 2,000 products from *AFTA* liberalization. Moreover, many goods faced non-tariff barriers. For example, Malaysia announced in May 2006 it would not phase out its "Approved Permit," or "AP," system for vehicle importation until 2010. This system allows ethnic Malay (*Bumiputra*) companies or individuals to import a limited number of foreign vehicles into Malaysia. The goal of the AP, consistent with the National Economic Program (NEP), is to encourage economic development among the Malays (who generally are Muslim), and thereby re-balance to some degree the economic dominance of Chinese and Indians. The NEP grew out of race riots in Malaysia in 1969, the cause of which was widely interpreted as economic disparity. The AP system is a non-tariff barrier—specifically, a combined license and quota. Fortunately, in their August 2006 meeting, the Council agreed to a standstill on new non-tariff impediments, and to study the problem with a view to eliminating them in a phased manner.

Regarding challenges in the services area, *ASEAN* had yet to deliver on pledges to issue a clear list of service sectors that are either sensitive or subject to temporary exclusion, particularly in services attendant to agriculture, fishery, manufacturing, and mining. Foreign investors thus were uncertain as to whether, and to what extent, they might face restrictions in these sectors. Among the service sectors that appear most ready for rapid liberalization are aviation, information technology, and tourism.

In the long term, of course, *ASEAN* aspires for *AFTA* to be a common market for goods, services, and investment. The initial target date for creating a common market was 2020. However, since at least August 2006, Malaysia, Singapore, and Thailand have pushed for an earlier date—2015. That push comes amidst concerns about competition from emerging economic powers, namely, China and India. Whether *ASEAN* can develop by 2015 the strong institutions needed to administer and enforce free trade rules is open to question. In August 2006, the original *ASEAN* six countries—Brunei, Indonesia, Malaysia, Philippines, Singapore, and Thailand—pledged technical assistance and capacity-building assistance to Burma, Cambodia, and Laos so that they might be able to meet the 2015 deadline.

Another challenge—and opportunity—for *AFTA* is expansion. In 2005–06, talks and accords were struck to include in a free trade zone other Asian nations, such as China, India, Japan, and Korea. For example, in September 2006, Korea and *ASEAN* agreed to implement a two-track arrangement on goods by 1 January 2007. Korea pledged to eliminate duties on 70 percent of "normal track" *ASEAN* products. The six founding members of *ASEAN* said they would cut duties to between zero and five percent on 50 percent of Korean products. The new *ASEAN* members will have extra time to cut their tariffs. By 2010, trade in goods between Korea and *ASEAN* will be duty-free, with the exception of a few sensitive sectors—iron, rice, steel, and certain vehicles.

*Suggestions for Further Research*:

Books:

1.   Bergsten, C. Fred & Marcus Noland, eds., Pacific Dynamism and the International Economic System (1993).

2.   Hafez, Zakir, The Dimensions of Regional Trade Integration in Southeast Asia (2004).

3.   Lincoln, Edward J., East Asian Economic Regionalism (2004).

4.   Matsushita, Mitsuo & Dukgeun Ahn, eds., WTO and East Asia: New Perspectives (2004).

5.   Narine, Shaun, Explaining ASEAN—Regionalism in Southeast Asia (2002).

6.   Sandhu, K.S., et al., eds., The ASEAN Reader (1992).

7.   Tan, Gerald, ASEAN Economic Development and Co-operation (1996).

8.   Tan, Joseph, ed., AFTA in the Changing International Economy (1996).

Book Chapters:

1.   Ahn, Dukgeun, *Trade Remedy Systems for East Asian Free Trade Agreements*, *in* The WTO in the Twenty-First Century — Dispute Settlement, Negotiations, and Regionalism in Asia 423–433 (Yasuhei Taniguchi, Alan Yanovich & Jan Bohanes, eds., 2007).

2.   Lim, C.L., *Free Trade Agreements in Asia and Some Common Legal Problems*, *in* The WTO in the Twenty-First Century — Dispute Settlement, Negotiations, and Regionalism in Asia 434–456 (Yasuhei Taniguchi, Alan Yanovich & Jan Bohanes, eds., 2007).

3.   Lo, Chang-fa, *Dispute Settlement Under Free Trade Agreements: Its Interaction and Relationship with WTO Dispute Settlement Procedures*, *in* The WTO in the Twenty-First Century — Dispute Settlement, Negotiations, and Regionalism in Asia 457–471 (Yasuhei Taniguchi, Alan Yanovich & Jan Bohanes, eds., 2007).

4.   Yuqinq, Zhang, *Regionalism Under the WTO and the Prospect of an East Asian Free Trade Area*, *in* The WTO in the Twenty-First Century — Dispute Settlement, Negotiations, and Regionalism in Asia 472–482 (Yasuhei Taniguchi, Alan Yanovich & Jan Bohanes, eds., 2007).

Articles:

1.   Fink, Carsten & Martin Molinuevo, *East Asian Free Trade Agreements in Services: Key Architectural Elements*, 11 Journal of International Economic Law 263–311 (2008).

2.   Honghua, Men, *East Asian Order Formation and Sino–Japanese Relations*, 17 Indiana Journal of Global Legal Studies 47–82 (2010).

3.   Khaw, L.T., *Protection of Automotive Spare Parts in Malaysia — Changes for the Better?*, 42 IIC: International Review of Intellectual Property & Competition Law 181–200 (2011).

4.   Komuro, Norio, *AFTA Rules of Origin*, 11 International Trade Law & Regulation issue 1, 1–13 (January 2005).

5.   Lau, Terence J., *Distinguishing Fiction from Reality: The ASEAN Free Trade Area and Implications for the Global Auto Industry*, 31 University of Dayton Law Review 435–76 (2006).

6.   Nakagawa, Junji, *No More Negotiated Deals?: Settlement of Trade and Investment Disputes in East Asia*, 10 Journal of International Economic Law 837–867 (2007).

7.   Webster, Timothy, *Bilateral Regionalism: Paradoxes of East Asian Integration*, 25 Berkeley Journal of International Law 434–458 (2007).

8.   Yokoi-Arai, Mamiko, *Implications of Financial Liberalization in the Big States of Asia for Regional Integration*, 43 The International Lawyer 1377–1409 (2009).

Other Source:

1.   Lim, C.L., *"A Mega Jumbo-Jet:" Southeast Asia's Experiments with Trade and Investment Liberalization*, Economy Paper: ASEAN (undated).

## AGENDA 2000

A series of reforms to the Common Agriculture Policy (CAP) of the European Union (EU).

The 1992 MacSharry Reform applied only to beef, cereals, oilseeds, and protein crops. To extend coverage, and to prepare for a new round — the Doha Round — of multilateral trade talks, the EU agreed on "Agenda 2000." Agenda 2000 was agreed upon on 26 March 1999 at the Berlin European Council meeting. In addition to preparing for the new multilateral trade round — or, it might be said, essential to that preparation — Agenda 2000 sought to strengthen CAP policies and provide the EU with a new financial framework for the period for 2000–2006. That period, of course, was one of enlargement, with the EU adding ten (10) new members in 2004. The EU could not approach the Doha Round with a financially confused or unsound CAP in an environment of enlargement.

Accordingly, Agenda 2000 applied the MacSharry Reform to the dairy sector, made further cuts in intervention prices, and boosted direct income support. Significantly for farmers, their income payments to farmers are in nominal terms, *i.e.*, they are not indexed to inflation, and thus can be eroded by cost of living increases. Moreover, the Agenda 2000 boost was not directly proportional to the cuts in intervention prices. The EU thought it unnecessary to do so. Because the price of EU farm goods would fall given the CAP reforms, EU farm products would be more competitive on world markets — and EU farmers would make more money the old fashioned way, namely, through free trade at a market price. Also significant for farmers was the express linking of income payments to satisfaction of environmental conditions — a manifestation of multi-functionality.

## AGOA

*African Growth and Opportunity Act*, initially enacted by the United States on 18 May 2000, and subsequently amended in 2002, 2004, 2006, and 2008. These pieces of legislation are known as *"AGOA I," "AGOA II," "AGOA III," "AGOA IV,"* and *"AGOA V,"* respectively. Collectively, they are called simply *"AGOA."*

*AGOA* is a preference program based in part on the model of the Generalized System of Preferences (GSP). *AGOA* is designed to strengthen the trade and investment relationship between the United States and the countries of Sub-Saharan Africa (SSA), and encourage those countries — through the tangible incentive of trade preferences, and the implementation of legal conditions to obtain preferences — to continue efforts to open their economies and build free markets. Accordingly, *AGOA* provides preferential trade treatment for certain products originating in eligible SSACs. The legislation authorizes the President to determine — on an annual basis — which SSACs are eligible for *AGOA, i.e.,* to be a "Beneficiary Sub-Saharan African Country" (BSSAC).

As suggested, technically, the original *AGOA* legislation is *"AGOA I."* Under the Administration of President George W. Bush, through the *Trade Act of 2002*, amendments to *AGOA I* were made, known as *"AGOA II,"* particularly concerning requirements for duty-free treatment of apparel articles. Under the *AGOA Acceleration Act of 2004* — known as *"AGOA III"*—the Bush Administration modified the earlier legislation, most notably extending the overall program through 30 September 2015. The most recent change to the legislation—now known as *"AGOA IV"*—came through the *Africa Investment Incentive Act of 2006*. This legislation extended the Third Country Fabric Provision for five years (until 30 September 2012), added an abundant supply provision, designated certain denim articles as being in abundant supply, and put forth a "Special Rule" allowing lesser-developed beneficiary SSACs to export certain textile articles under *AGOA*. (Under the Third Country Fabric Provision, a least-developed beneficiary Sub-Saharan African country can use fabric or yarn from outside Africa and the United States to assemble T & A merchandise for export to the United States, and still qualify for duty-free, quota-free (DFQF) treatment under *AGOA*. The normal *AGOA* requirement is a restrictive rule of origin: *AGOA* beneficiaries must use either African or American fabric or yarn.)

Under *AGOA V* — technically, the *Extension of Andean Trade Preference Act*, passed by Congress on 16 October 2008, Pubic Law Number 110–436, 122 Stat. 4976 (2008) — Congress renewed certain textile and apparel (T&A) provisions of the *AGOA*. It also refined the definition of "lesser developed beneficiary sub-Saharan African country," and made technical corrections to *AGOA*.

At first glance, there are many notable successes under *AGOA*. In 2006, over 98 percent of products from *AGOA*-eligible countries entered the United States duty-free, and total United States imports from Africa totaled $59.2 billion, a 17 percent increase from 2005. The real success of *AGOA* has been scrutinized, however, particularly with regard to the disproportionate amount of oil being imported from *AGOA* countries in relation to other products. Indeed, while non-oil *AGOA* trade did increase by seven percent in 2006, oil continued to account for over 90 percent of all imports under *AGOA*. Oil trade is generally regarded as less beneficial in development terms, because this industry often has little impact on hunger and poverty alleviation, and instead — in some parts of Africa — has been associated with tension and civil conflict.

The United States Congress, among other bodies, has been alarmed by these trends, and held hearings to determine what needs to be done to increase non-oil trade under *AGOA*. Suggested solutions include more funding for trade capacity building initiatives, more generous rules of origin (to allow for beneficiary countries to use inputs, such as fabric and yarn, from outside Africa or the United States), and inclusion of products currently ineligible for *AGOA* duty-free treatment, particularly certain agricultural products subject to tariff rate quotas (TRQs).

Pursuant to Section 14 of the *AGOA Acceleration Act of 2004*, the USTR renewed the charter of the Trade Advisory Committee on Africa (TACA) on 27 March 2006. The TACA advises the United States Trade Representative (USTR) on trade and economic policy matters with respect to the countries of sub-Saharan Africa, with an emphasis on maximizing the potential of *AGOA*. Its members are representatives of the private sector and civil society who have substantial experience in American — African trade and investment relations.

While *AGOA* has certainly transformed the trade and investment relationship between the United States and Africa, controversial issues remain regarding the true effectiveness of the program. In respect of the Third Country Fabric Provision, for example, on 14 December 2012, the day before the start of the three-day WTO Ministerial Conference in Geneva, the United States offered to seek to extend it through 2015.[35] This proposal was nearly disingenuous. On 11 July 2011 — five months before the American proposal — Representative Jim McDermott (Democrat-Washington) submitted House Resolution 2493 to amend *AGOA* to extend the third-country fabric provision through the end of 2015.[36] In other words, the legislation already was in Congress when the USTR made its proposal in Geneva.

True, the Senate version of legislation (S. 2007) to extend the third-country fabric provision through September 2015 was introduced by Senators Max

---

[35] *See On Eve of WTO Ministerial, U.S. Details Trade Initiatives Aimed at Helping LDCs*, 28 International Trade Reporter (Breaking News, 14 December 2011).

[36] *See On Eve of WTO Ministerial, U.S. Details Trade Initiatives Aimed at Helping LDCs*, 28 International Trade Reporter (Breaking News, 14 December 2011).

Baucus (Democrat-Montana) and Orin Hatch (Republican-Utah), the Chairman and ranking Minority member of the Senate Finance Committee, respectively, on 15 December 2012.[37] The new legislation included South Sudan (which gained independence from Sudan on 9 July 2011) on the list of Sub-Saharan African nations eligible for *AGOA* DFQF treatment, raising the number of such countries to 48.

*Suggestions for Further Research*:

Articles:

1. Lamar, Stephen E., *The Apparel Industry and African Economic Development*, 30 LAW & POLICY IN INTERNATIONAL BUSINESS 601–622 (summer 1999).

2. Ofodile, Uche Ewelukwa, *Trade, Empires, and Subjects — China–Africa Trade: A New Fair Trade Arrangement, or the Third Scramble for Africa?*, 41 VANDERBILT JOURNAL OF TRANSNATIONAL LAW 505–583 (2008).

Other Sources:

1. COUNCIL ON FOREIGN RELATIONS, MORE THAN HUMANITARIANISM: A STRATEGIC U.S. APPROACH TOWARD AFRICA (Independent Task Force Report Number 56, 2006).

2. OFFICE OF THE UNITED STATES TRADE REPRESENTATIVE, 2007 COMPREHENSIVE REPORT ON U.S. TRADE AND INVESTMENT POLICY TOWARD SUB-SAHARAN AFRICA AND IMPLEMENTATION OF THE AFRICAN GROWTH AND OPPORTUNITY ACT (2007).

## AGRICULTURE

The science of cultivating natural products for human use and consumption, synonymously referred to as "farming."

While "agriculture" obviously involves both animals and plants, more broadly the term encompasses the development of processes and business structures to increase the production, distribution, and mitigation of risk associated with the growing and rearing of living things. There are many sub-disciplines within agriculture, including:

- Apiculture —
  The science of bee keeping.

- Aquaculture —
  The science of fish farming and fisheries production.

- Dairy —
  A classification of ranching, specifically in which animals are raised for milk production, for butter, cheese, yogurt, and milk for drinking.

- Forestry —
  The harvesting of trees for timber.

---

[37] *See* Rossella Brevetti, *Sens. Baucus, Hatch Introduce Bill to Extend Key AGOA Provision*, 29 International Trade Reporter (BNA) 2075 (22 December 2011).

- Horticulture —
  The growing of plants, including garden plants, flowers, trees, vegetables, and ornamentals. There are several sub-specialties within horticulture, including: arboriculture (trees); floriculture (flowers); olericulture (vegetables); and pomology (fruits).

- Poultry —
  The raising of birds raised for food, including turkeys, chickens, and other fowl.

- Ranching —
  The rearing of animals for food and natural products, and typically involving grazing animals kept on pastures. Ranch animals include alpaca, bison, cattle, goats, llamas, ostrich, sheep.

- Viniculture —
  The cultivation of grapes for wine making. The science of making wine is called "oenology."

- Viticulture —
  The cultivation of grapes at a vineyard, from vine to grape.

## AGRICULTURE AGREEMENT

Uruguay Round *Agreement on Agriculture*.

The *Agriculture Agreement* is one of the Multilateral Agreements on Trade in Goods contained in Annex 1A to the *WTO Agreement*.

*Suggestions for Further Research*:

Books:

1.  ANDERSON, KYM & TIM JOSLING, EDS., THE WTO AND AGRICULTURE vols. I and II (2005).

2.  CARDWELL, MICHAEL N., MARGARET R. GROSSMAN & CHRISTOPHER P. RODGERS, AGRICULTURE AND INTERNATIONAL TRADE — LAW, POLICY, AND THE WTO 85–164 (2003).

3.  DESTA, MELAKU GEBOYE, THE LAW OF INTERNATIONAL TRADE IN AGRICULTURAL PRODUCTS — FROM GATT 1947 TO THE WTO AGREEMENT ON AGRICULTURE (2002).

4.  MCMAHON, JOSEPH, THE WTO AGREEMENT ON AGRICULTURE — A COMMENTARY (2006).

Articles:

1.  De La Torre Ugarte, Daniel G. & Alejandro Dellachiesa, Advancing the *Agricultural Trade Agenda: Beyond Subsidies*, 19 GEORGETOWN INTERNATIONAL ENVIRONMENTAL LAW REVIEW 729–750 (2007).

2.  Fabiosa, Jacinto F., *Effect of Free Trade in Agriculture on Developing Countries*, 16 MICHIGAN STATE JOURNAL OF INTERNATIONAL LAW 677–690 (2008).

3. Schoenbaum, *Thomas J. Fashioning a New Regime for Agricultural Trade: New Issues and the Global Food Crisis*, 14 JOURNAL OF INTERNATIONAL ECONOMIC LAW 593–611 (2011).

4. Symposium, *Farming and Food: How We Grow What We Eat*, 3 GOLDEN GATE UNIVERSITY ENVIRONMENTAL LAW JOURNAL 1–180 (2009).

5. Symposium, *Food and Agriculture Systems*, 22 FORDHAM ENVIRONMENTAL LAW REVIEW 493–710 (2011).

6. Tlustosch, Candice Moberg, Comment, *Government Subsidies for Small Grains Farmers Along the U.S.–Canadian Border: International Implications*, 23 WISCONSIN INTERNATIONAL LAW JOURNAL 345–365 (2005).

7. Udo, Chandler H., Note, *Japanese Rice Protectionism: A Challenge for the Development of Agricultural Trade Laws*, 31 BOSTON COLLEGE INTERNATIONAL AND COMPARATIVE LAW REVIEW 169–184 (2008).

Other Source:

1. Ingco, Merlinda & L. Alan Winters, eds., *Agriculture Trade Liberalization in a New Trade Round — Perspectives of Developing Countries and Transition Economies* (World Bank Discussion Paper Number 418, 2000).

## AIA

*ASEAN* Investment Area, comprised of Brunei, Burma (Myanmar), Cambodia, Indonesia, Laos, Malaysia, Philippines, Singapore, Thailand, and Vietnam (*i.e.*, the same membership as in *ASEAN*).

In 1996, *ASEAN* approved of the creation of an investment area, and in 1998 it adopted a framework agreement for the AIA. The goal of AIA is to spur intra-*ASEAN* investment projects and foreign direct investment (FDI) from outside *ASEAN. ASEAN* members agreed to a framework plan for the AIA in 1998. The members, expressing their views through the *ASEAN* Investment Council, are particularly concerned about competition for FDI with China. The largest investors in *ASEAN* (as of 2005) were from the United States, United Kingdom, Japan, France, and Finland. Investors from these countries accounted for more than 50 percent of total FDI into *ASEAN*, with funds focusing on financial and manufacturing sectors, and also in mining and general services. However, China attracted almost twice as much FDI (in 2005) as did all *ASEAN* members combined.

Under the 1998 framework plan, which covers direct (but not portfolio) investment, *ASEAN* members agree to open all industries and remove barriers to investment flows with respect to *ASEAN* investors by 2010, and with respect to all other investors by 2020. For example, national treatment is to be accorded to *ASEAN* investors by 2010, and to all other investors by 2020. However, *ASEAN's* newer and less developed countries have more generous phase-in periods: Vietnam has until 2013, and Burma, Cambodia, and Laos have until 2015 to reduce barriers. *ASEAN* members are free to exempt industries because they are sensitive or for temporary economic reasons, though industries on a member's "temporary exclusion list" must be integrated into the AIA by the start dates listed above. The commitment to opening industries to foreign investment is particularly noteworthy, given the equity limitations traditionally found in the laws and policies of many *ASEAN* members.

*Suggestions for Further Research*:

Article:

1. Kahn, Jordan C., *Investment Protection Under the Proposed ASEAN — United States Free Trade Agreement*, 33 SUFFOLK TRANSNATIONAL LAW REVIEW 225–256 (2010).

# AICO

*ASEAN* Industrial Cooperation program, adhered to by Brunei, Burma (Myanmar), Cambodia, Indonesia, Laos, Malaysia, Philippines, Singapore, Thailand, and Vietnam (*i.e.*, the same membership as in the *Association of South East Asian Nations* (*ASEAN*)).

The program, commenced on 4 April 1996 with a signing in Singapore, is designed to ensure companies taking part in a joint venture or other cooperative manufacturing arrangement in two or more *ASEAN* countries enjoy the benefits of tariff reductions under *ASEAN* free trade agreement (*AFTA*). Specifically, output of companies participating in AICO enjoys a preferential tariff rate of one-half of one percent. To form an AICO arrangement, a prospective company must satisfy three basic requirements:

(1) Be incorporated and operating in any *ASEAN* member.

(2) Have a minimum 30 percent national equity (*i.e.*, at least 30 percent of the shareholders are from the *ASEAN* member state in which the company is incorporated).

(3) Undertake resource sharing (pooling), industrial complementation, or other industrial cooperation activities that are accepted by the country in which the arrangement occurs.

Initially, the AICO program applies only to manufacturing companies. However, enabling provisions exist in a draft agreement for subsequent expansion of the scheme to other sectors.

The AICO program applies to finished products, semi-finished goods, and raw materials made by companies operating cooperative production processes in two or more *ASEAN* countries. It is designed to facilitate foreign direct investment (FDI) in the region by, for example, making it cheaper for companies with subsidiaries or affiliates in multiple *ASEAN* countries to exchange products. Through AICO, the *ASEAN* countries committed to open their manufacturing sectors to *ASEAN* investors and extend national treatment to them as early as 2003.

This commitment was not fully realized. Moreover, *ASEAN* countries face increasing competition for FDI from low-cost producers in other countries, such as Bangladesh, China, and India. The *ASEAN* countries face the challenge of moving higher value labor into higher value output. Some of them suffer from the perception — correct or not — that they did not respond well or successfully to the East Asian financial crisis of 1977–79.

## AID FOR TRADE

Aid for Trade, a scheme to help developing countries, especially least developed countries (LDCs), acquire the trade-related skills and infrastructure needed to implement and benefit from World Trade Organization (WTO) agreements and to expand their trade.[38]

Aid for Trade is a WTO-sponsored program, and was launched in December 2005 at the Hong Kong Ministerial Conference.

The Aid for Trade agenda consists of four key elements, all designed to enhance the participation of poor countries in the world trading system:

(1) Technical assistance.

(2) Infrastructure building.

(3) Production capacity investment.

(4) Adjustment assistance.

Put simply, as the WTO expresses, the idea is to boost "the trade-related skills and infrastructure that are needed to implement and benefit from WTO agreements and to expand their [i.e., poor countries'] trade."[39]

With faster customs clearance times, export volumes from poor countries may increase. An increase in export volumes in those countries allows for an increase in employment and wages, spurring economic growth and poverty alleviation. Some empirical evidence bears out this linkage. According to the United States Agency for International Development (USAID), every one dollar invested in Aid for Trade leads to $42 worth of exports.

In 2006, the WTO created a Task force by the WTO to oversee the initiative. Every two years, a Global Review on Aid for Trade evaluates progress made by the initiative since the previous review. The first review was held in November 2007.

The role of the WTO in the Aid for Trade program is to:

- encourage additional flows of Aid for Trade from bilateral, regional, and multilateral donors to support request for trade-related capacity building from beneficiary countries;

- support improved ways of monitoring and evaluating the initiative; and

---

[38] *See WTO Development — Aid for Trade, posted at* www.wto.org/english/tratop_e/devel_e/a4t_e/aid4trade_e.htm.

[39] Amy Tsui, *Doha Impasse Has Not Yet Affected Aid-for-Trade Programs, WTO Official Says,* 28 International Trade Reporter (BNA) 1073 (30 June 2011) (referring to the WTO website).

- encourage mainstreaming of trade into national development strategies by partner countries.[40]

Funding for Aid for Trade comes from WTO Members, who episodically pledge to give varying amounts. No Member is under any legal obligation to contribute. They may be motivated by a realization that providing assistance is in their self-interest, by purely charitable intentions, or some mix thereof. Ideally, a developing or least-developed country prioritizes its development and trade policies, which can then be matched to requests from donor Members.

By enhancing participation of poor countries in the world trading system, Aid for Trade aims to boost economic growth in such countries, and broadly affect important development criteria, like the empowerment of women. Participation in certain features of the initiative may be open to non-governmental organizations (NGOs) and the private sector, though little of note has occurred in these respects.

*Suggestions for Further Research*:

Article:

1. Cai, Phoenix X.F., *Aid for Trade: A Roadmap for Success*, 36 DENVER JOURNAL OF INTERNATIONAL LAW & POLICY 283–324 (2008).

## AKI Agricultural Knowledge Initiative

A joint United States — India agricultural program operated under the United States — India Trade Policy Forum.

The program concerns technology transfer, and agricultural educational opportunities for academia, government and the private sector from the two countries. Funding is provided by the United States Department of Agriculture (USDA) and Agency for International Development (AID). The program allows India to develop its knowledge capacity in areas such as food processing, biotechnology, water management and academic research.

## ALADI

Latin American Integration Association.

The headquarters of ALADI are in Uruguay.

## *ALBA*

*See TCP*.

## ALL OTHERS RATE (AOR)

*See* Retrospective Assessment.

---

[40] *See* Amy Tsui, *Doha Impasse Has Not Yet Affected Aid-for-Trade Programs, WTO Official Says*, 28 International Trade Reporter (BNA) 1073 (30 June 2011).

## AMBER BOX

Domestic agricultural subsidies that distort trade, *i.e.*, affect the pattern of importation and exportation of primary or processed farm goods. Because of their trade-distorting effect, they are subject to discipline under the Uruguay Round *Agreement on Agriculture*. First, WTO Members have bound their level of Amber Box payments. Second, they have made reduction commitments from these bound levels. Special and differential treatment for developing and least development countries is afforded on these commitments.

During the 2002–2005 marketing years (MYs), the average overall trade-distorting domestic support (OTDS) of the United States was $15.9 billion, with a low of $10.2 billion in 2003 and a high of $18.9 billion in 2005.[41] (In five of the previous eight MYs, ending with 2005, OTDS in the United States exceeded $16.4 billion.) Of this OTDS, during the 2002–2005 MYs, America's Amber Box spending rose from $6.95 billion in 2003 to $12.9 billion in 2005, and averaged $10.3 billion.

In MY 2006, the figure was $7.74 billion, in MY 2007, $6.26 billion, and in MY 2008, $6.25 billion. The Uruguay Round bound limit on Amber Box spending for the United States is $19.1 billion. The proposed Doha Round cut (as of December 2011, based on the December 2008 Draft Agriculture Modalities Text) would lower this limit by 60 percent to $7.64 billion. Interestingly, virtually all American Amber Box support went to two categories of products — dairy ($5.01 billion in MY 2007) and sugar ($1.23 billion in MY 2007).

By way of comparison, the EU lists as per its March 2009 and January 2011 WTO notifications, the following Amber Box support: For MY 2003–2004, the EU reported to the WTO in December 2006 it had spent €30.9 billion in Amber Box support (far below its annual spending limit of €67 billion, bound during the Uruguay Round), and €24.78 billion in the Blue Box. In its March 2009 notification, the EU again stated its Amber Box support for MYs 2004–2005 and 2005–2006, respectively, were €31.2 and €28.4. The commodity product categories to which the EU gave the largest Amber Box payments in MY 2005–2006 were sugar (€7 billion), butter (€4.1 billion), apples (€2.8 billion), and olive oil (€2.6 billion). It subsidies for these products took the form of price support. In its January 2011 notification, the EU said Amber Box spending dropped from by 54 percent, from €26.63 billion in MY 2006–2007, to €12.35 billion in MY 2007–2008. As in previous years, sugar and butter were the largest recipients of product-specific Amber Box support, so the large drop in such support was due mainly to cuts in sugar and butter subsidies: in sugar, a cut from €6.8 billion in MY 2006–2007 to €3.5 billion in MY 2006–2007, and in butter from €3.6 billion in MY 2006–2007 to €2.7 billion in MY 2007–2008.

---

[41] *See* Daniel Pruzin, *U.S. Notifies Farm Support for 2002–2005; Official Confirms Support for Falconer Figure*, 24 International Trade Reporter (BNA) 1417–1418 (11 October 2007).

Also by way of comparison, under its 2001 Protocol of Accession, China is exempt from any subsidy reduction commitments as long as its Amber Box (*i.e.*, trade-distorting) support is less than 8.5 percent of the total value of its domestic agricultural production. China argues that it has stayed well below this cap. In particular, in October 2011 China notified the WTO of the Amber Box subsidies it paid in MYs 2005–2008, as follows:[42]

- In the Amber Box, for product-specific support, China's three most heavily subsidized products are rice, pork, and cotton.

- China's Amber Box cotton subsidies were $530 million in MY 2007 and $410 million in MY 2008. The 2007 figure was 3.3 percent of the total value of China's agricultural production, making cotton the most heavily subsidized product of any commodity in the four MYs, 2005 through 2008. However, the International Cotton Advisory Group, based in the United States, argues China under-reports its true cotton support expenditures. It puts the figure at $1.95 billion for the 2008–2009 MYs, and $1.96 billion for the 2009–2010 MYs.

- China's Amber Box rice subsidies were $773 million in MY 2008 and $767 million for pork in 2008. Both figures were far higher than those for MY 2007.

- China provided non-product specific support of $272 million in 2005, and $1.16 billion in 2008. China claimed the 2008 figure was just 1.5 percent of the total value of its agricultural production.

*Suggestions for Further Research*:

Books:

1. ANDERSON, KYM & TIM JOSLING, EDS., THE WTO AND AGRICULTURE vols. I and II (2005).

2. CARDWELL, MICHAEL N., MARGARET R. GROSSMAN & CHRISTOPHER P. RODGERS, AGRICULTURE AND INTERNATIONAL TRADE — LAW, POLICY, AND THE WTO 85–164 (2003).

3. DESTA, MELAKU GEBOYE, THE LAW OF INTERNATIONAL TRADE IN AGRICULTURAL PRODUCTS — From GATT 1947 TO THE WTO AGREEMENT ON AGRICULTURE (2002).

4. MCMAHON, JOSEPH, THE WTO AGREEMENT ON AGRICULTURE — A COMMENTARY (2006).

Other Source:

1. Ingco, Merlinda & L. Alan Winters, eds., *Agriculture Trade Liberalization in a New Trade Round — Perspectives of Developing Countries and Transition Economies* (World Bank Discussion Paper Number 418, 2000).

---

[42] *See* Daniel Pruzin, *China Reports Agriculture Subsidies for 2005–2008 Well Under WTO Limits*, 28 International Trade Reporter (BNA) 1701 (20 October 2011).

## AMENDED CONTINUOUS BOND DIRECTIVE REQUIREMENT (AMENDED CBD)

*See* Customs Bond.

## AMERICAN FARM BUREAU

The largest farm lobbying group in the United States.

The American Farm Bureau was founded in 1919 by a small group of farmers from 30 states, who gathered in Chicago. They called their organization the "American Farm Bureau Federation." The organization formally was ratified in 1920, and soon became the voice of agriculture at the national level. Subsequently, the body became known simply as the "American Farm Bureau." An explicit goal of the Farm Bureau is to open new world markets to American agricultural products.

## *AMICUS BRIEF (AMICUS CURIAE BRIEF)*

A brief filed by a friend of the court, *i.e.*, one that is not a party to the case at bar. (The plural is *amici*, or *amici curiae*.)

Whether WTO panels or the Appellate Body may accept an amicus brief, and if so the status it may accord to arguments in the brief, is a matter of some controversy in adjudication under the *Understanding on Rules and Procedures Governing the Settlement of Disputes* (*Dispute Settlement Understanding*, or *DSU*). Essentially, the Appellate Body — following its decision in the 1998 *Turtle-Shrimp* case — will look to arguments in an amicus brief if it finds them necessary and helpful.

*Suggestions for Further Research*:

Articles:

1.   Bernstein, Steven & Erin Hannah, *Non-State Global Standard Setting and the WTO: Legitimacy and the Need for Regulatory Space*, 11 JOURNAL OF INTERNATIONAL ECONOMIC LAW 575–608 (2008).

2.   De Brabandere, Eric, *NGOs and the "Public Interest:" The Legality and Rationale of Amicus Curiae Interventions in International Economic and Investment Disputes*, 12 CHICAGO JOURNAL OF INTERNATIONAL LAW 85–113 (2011).

3.   Levine, Eugenia, *Amicus Curiae in International Investment Arbitration: The Implications of an Increase in Third-Party Participation*, 29 BERKELEY JOURNAL OF INTERNATIONAL LAW 200–224 (2011).

4.   Lim, C.L., *The Amicus Brief Issue at the WTO*, 4 CHINESE JOURNAL OF INTERNATIONAL LAW number 1, 85–120 (April 2005).

## AMS

Aggregate Measure of Support.

The term is used in the Uruguay Round *Agreement on Agriculture* to capture the level of domestic support provided by a government for a particular agricultural commodity. AMS is defined in terms of a formula, as follows:

[(Support Price – External Market Price) × (Quantity of Production)]

+   [Non-exempt direct payments or subsidies]

–   [Fees and levies paid by producers]

=   AMS

The support price is the price guaranteed by a government to its farmers for a particular crop. The external market price is determined in terms of import parity for importing countries and export parity for exporting countries. Non-exempt direct payments or subsidies are payments and subsidies not exempted from reduction commitments under the *Agriculture Agreement*. Examples of exempt payments are Blue and Green Box measures. Fees and levies paid by producers are any charges borne by farmers.

AMS is a critical concept because it harmonizes the way in which governmental support for a crop is measured. Only if there is agreement on how to quantify support is it possible to agree upon the extent to which that support ought to be reduced. Thus, AMS is the basis on which reductions in agricultural support schemes are negotiated.

*Suggestions for Further Research*:

Books:

1.  ANDERSON, KYM & TIM JOSLING, EDS., THE WTO AND AGRICULTURE vols. I and II (2005).

2.  CARDWELL, MICHAEL N., MARGARET R. GROSSMAN & CHRISTOPHER P. RODGERS, AGRICULTURE AND INTERNATIONAL TRADE — LAW, POLICY, AND THE WTO 85–164 (2003).

3.  DESTA, MELAKU GEBOYE, THE LAW OF INTERNATIONAL TRADE IN AGRICULTURAL PRODUCTS — FROM GATT 1947 TO THE WTO AGREEMENT ON AGRICULTURE (2002).

4.  MCMAHON, JOSEPH, THE WTO AGREEMENT ON AGRICULTURE — A COMMENTARY (2006).

Other Source:

1.  Ingco, Merlinda & L. Alan Winters, eds., *Agriculture Trade Liberalization in a New Trade Round — Perspectives of Developing Countries and Transition Economies* (World Bank Discussion Paper Number 418, 2000).

## AMU

Arab Maghreb Union. *See* UMAU.

## ANDEAN COMMUNITY

A free trade agreement (FTA) established in May 1969 by the *Cartagena Agreement* whose original members were Bolivia, Colombia, Ecuador, and Peru.

The Community, which is the oldest trading bloc in the western hemisphere, formerly was referred to as the "Andean Pact," and that rubric occasionally is used. The Spanish expression for the "Andean Community" is *Comunidad Andina.*"

Notably, the Andean Pact had set 1999 as a deadline by which to create a common market. The future of the accord is in doubt, owing to membership turmoil and failure to reach the common market goal. There is a distinction between full and associate members. The founders are all full members. In 2005, Argentina, Brazil, Paraguay, and Uruguay became associate members, and in 2006, Venezuela became an associate member. Chile, which was an early member of the Pact but which suspended its membership in 1976, re-joined as an associate member, and later considered re-joining as a full member. Panama contemplated joining the Community.

In 1991, Peru suspended its membership in the Community and unilaterally slashed all tariffs to 15 or 25 percent, and abolished all subsidies. Subsequently, Peru was frustrated with the slow pace of trade liberalization in the other Community members, especially of Colombia and Venezuela to reduce significantly their tariffs. Peru also found the 1999 common market deadline too short. In 1997, Peru decided to withdraw and seek membership in *MERCOSUR*. In April 2006, Peru signed an FTA with the United States, which entered into force in February 2009. Colombia did likewise, signing an FTA with the United States in March, respectively. Chile signed an FTA with the United States in June 2003, and thus elected not to seek full membership in the Community.

Ironically, Peru encouraged Chile to re-join the Community. The irony arose not only because of Peru's history with the Community, but also with Chile. In the 19th century, the two countries warred, with Peru losing a chunk of its southern territory to Chile. Bolivia, too, lost a portion of its territory to Chile in the conflict. Peru continues to dispute its maritime border with Chile, and Bolivia remains bitter about its lost access to the Pacific Ocean. However, a corridor from Bolivia to the sea would require agreement from Peru, because the corridor would be on former Peruvian territory. Despite the long-standing territorial disputes, in August 2006, Chile and Peru broadened a bilateral trade agreement into which they had entered in 1998. Chile agreed to rejoin the Community as an associate member as a result of the agreement.

The Andean Community was jolted in 1996, when Bolivia joined *MERCOSUR* as an associate member on its own, and when Venezuela began negotiations toward membership. In 1996, the Community agreed it would negotiate as a bloc to join *MERCOSUR*. As a first step, in 1999 the Community reached a two year bilateral accord with Brazil on streamlining customs systems. Had the negotiations been successful, a combined *MERCOSUR—* Andean Community FTA would encompass virtually all of South America. That result did not materialize.

Bolivia and Venezuela became full *MERCOSUR* members in December 2005, and Venezuelan President Hugo Chavez announced in April 2006 his country was leaving the Andean Pact. Venezuela formally ended its participation in the Andean Pact in April 2011. That departure, along with the December 2005 FTA between Peru and the United States, and the February 2006 FTA between Colombia and the United States, left the Andean Pact in tatters. Venezuelan President Hugo Chavez declared the *United States — Peru* and *United States — Colombia FTAs* had "mortally wounded" the Community.[43] In at least one technical sense, he was correct. Those FTAs complicated the efforts of the Community to adopt a common tariff. Without a common tariff, it would be unlikely the Community could negotiate a trade accord with the European Union (EU). Still, such negotiations were scheduled to commence in January 2007.

Possibly due to concerns about the viability of the Andean Community, and negotiated bilateral FTAs with some Community members, the United States dropped efforts to form an Andean Trade Pact, *i.e.*, an FTA with Colombia, Ecuador, Peru, and Venezuela. It also backed away from a full scale reform of the *ATPA* through legislation with a rubric of the *Andean Trade Promotion and Drug Eradication Act (ATPDEA)*. Instead, Congress renewed the *Andean Trade Preference Act (ATPA)*, which was set to expire on 31 December 2006, with amendments to it under the *Andean Trade Promotion and Drug Eradication Act (ATPDEA)*.[44] Further, under the *Extension of Andean Trade Preference Act*, passed by Congress on 16 October 2008, Pubic Law Number 110–436, 122 Stat. 4976 (2008), *ATPA* preferences, again as amended by the *ATPDEA*, were renewed. The renewal under the *Extension* legislation applied to Colombia and Peru only until 31 December 2009, because of free trade agreements (FTAs) negotiated with those countries. Moreover, the renewal was applied conditionally to Bolivia and Ecuador until at most 31 December 2009. Once again, at year-end 2009, Congress renewed the *ATPA* for one year, until 31 December 2010, pursuant to H.R. 4284. Pursuant to the *Omnibus Trade Act of 2010*, H.R. 6517, Pub. L. No. 111–344, 124 Stat. 3611 (29 December 2010), Congress renewed the *ATPA* for just six weeks. This temporary renewal was only for selected merchandise from Colombia and Ecuador (but not Peru, which gets such treatment under its FTA with the United States).

Notably, however, the bilateral FTA negotiations were not without controversy. In talks with Colombia in January–February 2006, for example, the United States insisted Colombia accept as equivalent to its own American sanitary and phytosanitary standards (SPS) measures, including food safety inspection. This issue was a stumbling block in the 2005–2006 negotiations for an FTA between the United States and Panama. With respect to the *Central American Free Trade Agreement — Dominican Republic (CAFTA)*, the United States delayed implementation from the original date of 1 January 2006 until

---

[43] *Quoted in* Lucien O. Chauvin, *Ecuador Disrupted by Free Trade Talks with United States; Andean Pact Threatened*, 23 International Trade Reporter (BNA) 640 (6 April 2006).

[44] *See* H.R. 6406, providing for a six month extension, which expired on 30 June 2007. As indicated above, a subsequent extension occurred.

El Salvador and other members accepted American standards. Ultimately, in its FTA with the United States, Colombia behaved more like El Salvador than Panama. Colombia signed a side letter on SPS barriers to agricultural trade, agreeing to recognize American food safety inspection, including of meat products such as beef, pork and poultry. Given that (as of March 2006), Colombia was the second largest market in Latin America for American agricultural products, this recognition was vital to American export interests.

Given the proliferation of FTAs involving not only Colombia, Peru, and the United States, but also Colombia, Peru, and the European Union (EU), and Colombia, Peru, and Canada, the purpose of the Andean Community is very much in doubt.

*Suggestions for Further Research*:

Article:

1. Yong, Camilo A. Rodriguez, *Enhancing Legal Certainty in Colombia: The Role of the Andean Community*, 17 MICHIGAN STATE JOURNAL OF INTERNATIONAL LAW 407–463 (2008–2009).

## ANDEAN PACT

*See* Andean Community.

## ANTI-BRIBERY CONVENTION (OECD ANTI-BRIBERY CONVENTION)

*See* OECD.

## *ANTIDUMPING AGREEMENT (AD AGREEMENT)*

The Uruguay Round *Agreement on Implementation of Article VI of the General Agreement on Tariffs and Trade 1994*.

The *Antidumping*, or *AD*, *Agreement* is one of the Multilateral Agreements on Trade in Goods contained in Annex 1A to the *Agreement Establishing the World Trade Organization (WTO Agreement)*.

## APEC

Asia Pacific Economic Cooperation forum.

Established in 1989, APEC is comprised of (as of December 2007) the following countries:

- Brunei Darussalam
- Burma (Myanmar)
- Cambodia
- Indonesia
- Laos
- Chile
- China
- Hong Kong
- Japan
- Korea

- Malaysia
- Philippines
- Singapore
- Thailand, and
- Vietnam, *i.e.*, all the AFTA and *ASEAN* members, plus
- Australia
- Canada

- Mexico
- New Zealand
- Papua New Guinea
- Peru
- Russia
- Taiwan
- United States.

APEC represents over one-third of the population of the world, over 50 percent of the Gross Domestic Product (GDP) of the world, and over 41 percent of world trade.[45] Since roughly 2000, APEC has had a moratorium on the admission of new members.

It was Australia that took the lead in creating the forum. Interestingly, the forum may well have been born out of fears that (1) the United States would become isolationist and unilateralist, and (2) the world was becoming balkanized into regional trade agreements (RTAs).

In 1993, APEC members began the practice of holding annual meetings attended by heads of state. The annual meetings are preceded by meetings of the trade ministers, who negotiate agreements to be finalized at the annual summit of the presidents and prime ministers.

The Bogor Declaration of 15 November 1994 commits APEC to the long-term goal of achieving free trade among the developing countries of APEC by 2020 and among the developed countries of APEC by 2010. Obviously, that deadline was not met. Still, New Zealand and other developed countries within APEC have encouraged the body to move beyond trade liberalization to allied areas, such as competition policy, so as to ensure non-discriminatory treatment of foreign corporations and to combat cartels extant within APEC.

Progress on APEC's ambitious goals has been mixed. On the positive side, in 1996 APEC was the catalyst behind the WTO negotiations that led to the *Information Technology Agreement (ITA)*. Similarly, at the APEC summit in 1997, the leaders agreed to re-invigorate trade liberalization efforts through the Early Voluntary Sectoral Liberalization (EVSL) program. Tariffs would be cut in 15 sectors, from chemicals to jewelry, ahead of the 2020/2010 target dates. However, Japan refused to cut tariffs in two important sectors, fish and forest products, and APEC was forced to enlist the assistance of the WTO for further work on the EVSL scheme. Essentially, in November 1998, APEC referred to the WTO work on reducing tariffs that it had hoped to accomplish under the EVSL.

---

[45] *See* Murray Griffin, *APEC Ministers, Schwab Call for High Level of Ambition in Doha Chairmen's Draft Texts*, 24 International Trade Reporter (BNA) 977–978 (12 July 2007).

Overall, APEC seems to be adrift, and many observers (including the APEC Business Advisory Council in August 1999) have expressed doubt that the 2020/2010 target dates will be met. It is sometimes joked that it is nothing more than four adjectives in search of a noun. An unhealthy mixture of suspicion and apathy bedevils the organization. Some Southeast Asian members focus on protecting their markets against powerful foreign interests, and are not altogether happy about America's presence in the forum. Japan — which opposed the creation of APEC until it was clear the United States would be permitted to join — is concerned about keeping Southeast Asia's markets open for Japanese trade and investment. The United States has not always bothered to lay out a clear vision for APEC. Thus, the product of most of the annual APEC summits is a bland *communiqué*. After the 1999 Auckland summit, the *Financial Times* queried in reference to the trip to New Zealand undertaken by senior government officials: "Was their journey really necessary? . . . APEC's record on trade liberalization, ostensibly its *raison d'être*, scarcely inspires confidence."

At the November 2009 APEC Summit, hosted by Singapore, the heads of state issued a declaration which laid out specific goals to facilitate trade and investment among the members:

- A collective 25 percent reduction in the cost, time, and number of procedures that APEC businesses face when they start a business, seek credit, enforce contracts, obtain permits, and trade across borders.

- A five percent reduction by 2010 of business transactions costs, building on a cost reduction of 3.2 percent between 2006–2008.

- A "pathfinder" initiative, whereby businesses can more easily obtain benefits under a free trade agreement (FTA) by self-certifying their goods (as originating goods under the FTA) at the point-of-origin of the goods.

However, given the generally poor track record of APEC on follow-up, the extent to which these measures are implemented remains to be seen.

*Suggestions for Further Research*:

Book:

1.   FUNABASHI, YOICHI, ASIA PACIFIC FUSION — JAPAN'S ROLE IN APEC (October 1995).

Book Chapters:

1.   Marceau, Gabrielle, *The Adoption of the "Best Practices" for Regional and Free Trade Agreements in APEC: A Road Towards More WTO-Consistent Regional Trade Agreements?, in* THE WTO IN THE TWENTY-FIRST CENTURY — DISPUTE SETTLEMENT, NEGOTIATIONS, AND REGIONALISM IN ASIA 409–422 (Yasuhei Taniguchi, Alan Yanovich & Jan Bohanes, eds. 2007).

Articles:

1.   Lee, Jaemin, *Juggling Counter-Terrorism and Trade, the APEC Way: APEC's Leadership in Devising Counter-Terrorism Measures in Compliance*

*with International Trade Norms*, 12 U.C. DAVIS JOURNAL OF INTERNATIONAL LAW AND POLICY 257–96 (2006).

2.   Terry, Laurel S., *From GATS to APEC: The Impact of Trade Agreements on Legal Services*, 43 Akron Law Review 875–984 (2010).

Other Source:

1.   ASIA PACIFIC ECONOMIC COOPERATION, THE NEW INTERNATIONAL ARCHITECTURE IN TRADE AND INVESTMENT: CURRENT STATUS AND IMPLICATIONS (March 2007) (especially Chapter 1, *Synthesis Report*, prepared by Henry Gao), *posted at*, www.apec.org/apec/publications/all_publications/human_resources_ development.MedialibDownload.v1.html?url=/etc/medialib/apec_media_ library/downloads/workinggroups/hrdwg/pubs/2007.Par.0002.File.v1.1.

## APHIS

Animal and Plant Health Inspection Service, a division of the United States Department of Agriculture (USDA).

Divisions of APHIS include Animal Health, Plant Health, Import and Export, Biotech Regulation and Sanitary and Phytosanitary Standards Setting.

The central role of APHIS is to protect American agricultural health by the application of scientific measures. For example, APHIS regulates genetically modified organism (GMO) products, administers the *Animal Welfare Act*, and engages in wildlife damage management activities. APHIS plays a joint role, with Customs and Border Protection (CBP), to enforce appropriate importation of agricultural products. APHIS has a joint role with Foreign Agriculture Service in enforcing and addressing sanitary and phytosanitary (SPS) measures and technical barriers to trade (TBT), and with the Food and Drug Administration (FDA) in combating bioterrorism.

Examples of APHIS proposals include permits for the importation of fresh guava fruit from Mexico),[46] allowing imports of baby squash and baby courgettes from Zambia, and amending regulations on imports of live horses, ruminants, swine and dogs from Panama because that country has been removed from the list of regions where screwworm exits.[47] These illustrations are only a few of the numerous regulatory amendments made by APHIS each year. Further examples can be found in publications such as the *Federal Register* and *International Trade Reporter*.

*Suggestions for Further Research*:

Articles:

1.   Aginam, Obijiofor, *Food Safety, South–North Asymmetries, and the Clash of Regulatory Regimes*, 40 VANDERBILT JOURNAL OF TRANSNATIONAL LAW 1099–1114 (2007).

---

[46] *See* 73 Federal Register 60,673 (14 October 2006).
[47] *See* 73 Federal Register 28,382 (16 May 2008).

2.  DeWall, Caroline Smith, *Food Safety and Security: What Tragedy Teaches Us About our 100-Year Old Food Laws*, 40 VANDERBILT JOURNAL OF TRANSNATIONAL LAW 921–935 (2007).

3.  George, Asha M., *Response is Local, Relief is Not: The Pervasive Impact of Agro Terrorism*, 40 VANDERBILT JOURNAL OF TRANSNATIONAL LAW 1155–1170 (2007).

4.  Govern, Kevin H., *Agroterrorism and Ecoterrorism: A Survey of Indo-American Approaches under Law and Policy to Prevent and Defend Against these Potential Threats Ahead*, 10 FLORIDA COASTAL LAW JOURNAL 223–261 (2009).

5.  Hoffman, John T. & Shaun Kennedy, *International Cooperation to Defend the Food Supply Chain: Nations are Talking; Next Step — Action*, 40 VANDERBILT JOURNAL OF TRANSNATIONAL LAW 1171–1187 (2007).

6.  Tauxe, Robert V., *Foodbourne Infections and the Global Food Supply: Improving Health at Home and Abroad*, 40 VANDERBILT JOURNAL OF TRANSNATIONAL LAW 899–919 (2007).

## APICULTURE

The science of beekeeping.

Apiculture is a subset of agricultural science. Bees are an important component of agriculture, as both the producer of honey and the chief pollinator of several crops, including:

| | | |
|---|---|---|
| • almonds | • cantaloupes | • soybeans |
| • apples | • cucumbers | • strawberries |
| • blackberries | • peaches | • watermelons |
| • cherries | • pears | |
| • cranberries | • raspberries | |

The Mid Atlantic Apiculture Research and Extension Consortium, based at the Pennsylvania State University, engages in research on, and provides training in, beekeeping activities. It has been tracking a recent phenomenon known as Colony Collapse Disorder (CCD). CCD is a collective term used to describe the dwindling bee population that has been markedly occurring since late 2006. The cause is yet unknown, but the impact on horticulture worldwide is still yet to be fully realized.

## APPELLATE BODY

A group of seven (7) independent international trade law experts from which three (3) persons are drawn for the purpose of reviewing legal issues presented in a WTO panel report appealed by a disputing party.

The Appellate Body, established under Article 17 of the WTO *Understanding on Rules and Procedures Governing the Settlement of Disputes* (*Dispute Settlement Understanding*, or *DSU*) can uphold, modify or reverse the legal findings and conclusions of the panel. The Appellate Body, as well as the panel, is intended to be independent of the WTO Secretariat. Physically symbolic, at least, is the fact the Appellate Body is located in Geneva in separate facilities from the Secretariat, following an initial period in which it was within the Secretariat complex, but segregated off through secure doors.

The Appellate Body has had a member from China since June 2008, and the presence of a member from the Mainland seems likely to continue. There always have been, and likely always will be, members from the United States, European Union (EU), and Japan. That leaves three open seats not "reserved" for the citizen of any one country. These seats are allocated across Africa, Asia, and Latin America. Of course, this scheme exists in a *de facto*, not *de jure*, sense. The Appellate Body is expected to be independent of the countries from which its members come. Thus far, there have been no credible complaints that it has acted otherwise.

Candidates for the Appellate Body are nominated by Members of the WTO, and undergo interviews by a selection committee. The selection committee includes the WTO Director-General and Chair of the Dispute Settlement Body (DSB). After the selection committee determines which candidate is best suited to fill the vacancy, the candidate is approved (or not) by the DSB.[48] Appellate Body members serve four (4) year terms, which are renewable once. One Appellate Body member serves as Chair. The Chair is appointed by the Appellate Body members, and serves for a term of one (1) year. This term is renewable. The Chair is responsible for organizing and directing the work of the Appellate Body.

In April 2001, the WTO Secretariat proposed Appellate Body members be offered a pension and receive compensation based on full-time work, as opposed to part-time service. According to the Secretariat, Appellate Body members worked "more than 100 percent full time" in 2000.[49] The Secretariat claimed the proposal would not require an amendment to the *DSU*, and be "cost-neutral".[50] The Secretariat further asserted the proposal would help save money in the future. It argued the Appellate Body members should be recognized for their full-time work, and full-time status would signal the time commitment the position requires of new members. The Secretariat also noted other international tribunals provide pension plans to their members, hence the Appellate Body should offer similar options.

The Appellate Body maintains a set of "Working Procedures," which are approved by the Dispute Settlement Body (DSB). These Working Procedures set out the logistical details of filing and arguing an appeal, hearings, and

[48] *See* Daniel Pruzin, *U.S., China Put Forward Two Candidates for Vacancies on WTO Appellate Body*, 24 International Trade Reporter (BNA) 1309 (20 September 2007).

[49] Ravi Kanth, *New Pay, Pension Scheme Proposed for WTO Appellate Body Members*, 18 International Trade Reporter (BNA) 572 (12 April 2001).

[50] Ravi Kanth, *New Pay, Pension Scheme Proposed for WTO Appellate Body Members*, 18 International Trade Reporter (BNA) 572 (12 April 2001).

reports. They include deadlines for steps in the process. In January 2010, the Appellate Body proposed to the DSB three innovations in the Working Procedures, all of which were designed to streamline and make more efficient the process of reviewing WTO panel reports.[51]

First, the Appellate Body called for submission of arguments by a WTO Member on the same day as the Member files an appeal. That would eliminate the seven (7) day gap between notice of an appeal and submission of detailed arguments, and thus would give the Appellate Body more time to consider a case — which, in view of the increasingly large and complex appeals, it desperately needs. (Deadlines for other steps, such as filing counter-appeals, submission of arguments from third parties, and oral arguments, would be accelerated, but the time frame for circulation and adoption of reports would remain the same.) Interestingly, the Appellate Body pointed out the average length of time between (1) circulation of a final a panel report and (2) filing a notice of appeal is 93 days. With that amount of time, the Appellate Body argued it should not be difficult for a Member to prepare its arguments and file them with its notice of appeal.

Second, the Appellate Body said that electronic filing of documents with it should be explicitly authorized. Such filing is increasingly the norm among domestic and international tribunals. Indeed, already WTO Members were circulating a variety of documents via e-mail.

Third, the Appellate Body sought permission to consolidate proceedings in separate but similar disputes. As long as there is "substantial overlap" among the content of panel rulings, then consolidation of appeals would ease the task of the Appellate Body, obviously allowing it to hold one instead of multiple hearings, and produce a single report. Consolidation, said the Appellate Body, could occur at its own initiative, or in consultation with the disputing parties.

*Suggestions for Further Research*:

Book:

1.   VAN DAMME, ISABELLE, TREATY INTERPRETATION BY THE WTO APPELLATE BODY (2009).

Articles:

1.   Alvarez-Jiménez, Alberto, *The WTO Appellate Body's Decision-Making Process: A Perfect Model for International Adjudication?*, 12 Journal of International Economic Law 289–331 (2009).

2.   Alvarez-Jiménez, Alberto, *The WTO Appellate Body's Exercise of Judicial Economy*, 12 JOURNAL OF INTERNATIONAL ECONOMIC LAW 393–415 (2009).

3.   Alvarez-Jiménez, Alberto, *Public Hearings at the WTO Appellate Body: The Next Step*, 59 INTERNATIONAL & COMPARATIVE LAW QUARTERLY 1079–1098 (2010).

---

[51] *See* Daniel Pruzin, *WTO's Appellate Body Proposes Reforms to Accelerate Review Process*, 27 International Trade Reporter (BNA) 64 (21 January 2010).

4.   Cho, Sungjoon, *Of the World Trade Court's Burden*, 20 EUROPEAN JOURNAL OF INTERNATIONAL LAW 675–727 (2009).

5.   Gal-Or, Noemi, *The Concept of Appeal in International Dispute Settlement*, 19 EUROPEAN JOURNAL OF INTERNATIONAL LAW 43–65 (2008).

6.   Fischer, Matthew E., Note, *Is the WTO Appellate Body a "Constitutional Court"? The Interaction of the WTO Dispute Settlement System with the Regional and National Actors*, 40 GEORGETOWN JOURNAL OF INTERNATIONAL LAW 291–310 (2008).

7.   Korotana, Dr. Muhammed, *The Standard of Review in WTO Law*, 15 INTERNATIONAL TRADE LAW & REGULATION issue 2, 72–77 (2009).

8.   Ramirez, Ricardo, *Professor Hudec and the Appellate Body*, 20 MINNESOTA JOURNAL OF INTERNATIONAL LAW 265–273 (2011).

9.   *The WTO Appellate Body's Activities in 2008*, 12 JOURNAL OF INTERNATIONAL ECONOMIC LAW 209–225 (2009).

10.  Van Damme, Isabelle, *Treaty Interpretation by the WTO Appellate Body*, 21 EUROPEAN JOURNAL OF INTERNATIONAL LAW 605–648 (2010).

## APPLIED RATE

The actual rate of duty a country imposes on a particular category of merchandise, as distinct from the bound rate (which is the maximum permissible tariff rate a country may impose on a particular category of merchandise).

The terms "applied rate" and "actual rate" are synonymous. The applied rate is set forth in the Harmonized Tariff Schedule (HTS) of each country. Under the tariff binding principle of GATT Article II:1(b), the actual rate may not exceed the bound rate. There are exceptions, for example, in the case of an antidumping (AD) or countervailing duty (CVD).

Significantly, a bound rate may be higher than the applied, or actual, rate of duty. In that scenario, a country has the flexibility to raise (or lower) its applied rate up to the level of the bound rate. Under the WTO *Agreement on Agriculture*, the concept of a binding, and the distinction between bound and actual levels, also applies to the Aggregate Measure of Support (AMS) and Amber Box subsidies.

*Suggestions for Further Research*:

Books:

1.   HODA, ANWARUL, TARIFF NEGOTIATIONS AND RENEGOTIATIONS UNDER THE GATT AND THE WTO (2001).

2.   MATSUSHITA, MITSUO, THOMAS J. SCHOENBAUM & PETROS C. MAVROIDIS, THE WORLD TRADE ORGANIZATION — LAW, PRACTICE, AND POLICY 112–14 (2003).

## AQUACULTURE

The raising of fish and seafood products for sale and human consumption.

Aquaculture activities in the United States are regulated by the National Oceanic and Atmospheric Administration (NOAA) in the Department of Commerce (DOC). *See National Aquaculture Act of 1980*, Pub. L. No. 96–362, 94 Stat. 1198 (26 September 1980), codified at 16 U.S.C. §§ 2801 *et seq*. The mandate of NOAA is broad. For example, NOAA is the same agency that operates the National Hurricane Center and names all storms. According to NOAA, world demand for seafood products will not be met by current fishing methods. Consequently, farm raised fish and seafood will be increasingly important as a food source in the coming years.

## ARAB LEAGUE

*See* League of Arab States.

## ARABLE LAND

Land in a country that can be used for the cultivation of agricultural products.

For example, only 13 percent of China's land is arable. Of that percentage, approximately 10 percent is not usable because of waste run-off from industrial companies. Some estimates put the percent of poisoned land that had been arable much higher than 10 percent.

## ARTICLE 133 MEETINGS

How does the European Union (EU) formulate its trade policy? The answer is through "Article 133 Committee meetings."

Article 133 refers to a provision in the 1992 *Treaty of Maastricht*, and typically is pronounced "Article 1-3-3." These meetings generally are held on Fridays in Brussels. The Article 133 Committee consists of senior civil servants from each Ministry of Trade in each EU member country. The Ministers of Trade themselves meet once a year. Acting on behalf of the Ministers and their countries, the deputies from these Ministries meet regularly in the Article 133 meetings. They meet with the Trade Commissioner of the European Communities (EC). The EC has the authority to negotiate for the entire EU on goods, and on agriculture, but not on services. Decisions of the Committee must be taken by consensus, which means unanimity among the EC countries. However, as the EU continues with enlargement of its membership, a change in voting rules from consensus to majority may be anticipated. Such a change could prove difficult for traditional powers in the EU, such as France and Germany.

## AS APPLIED CHALLENGE

A challenge to a measure brought under the WTO *Understanding on Rules and Procedures Governing the Settlement of Disputes (Dispute Settlement*

*Understanding* or *DSU*) alleging the way in which the measure is implemented or enforced is a violation of an obligation due by the WTO Member. In contrast to an "as such" claim, an "as applied" claim does not allege that the measure itself is illegal under GATT—WTO rules.

## ASSOCIATION AGREEMENT

An agreement between the European Union (EU) and one or more countries to drop all internal trade barriers as among the countries.[52]

An Association Agreement is technically similar to a Free Trade Agreement (FTA) or Regional Trade Agreement (RTA). Trade negotiations are conducted by the European Commission (EC). Once the EC concludes a trade deal with a foreign country, the final agreement must be approved by each of the 27 EU countries (as well as the other country).[53] The formation of Association Agreements is subject to the requirements set forth in GATT Article XXIV.

Most recently, in the spring of 2010, the EU negotiated with a group of Central American countries to conclude an Association Agreement that covers not only trade, but political dialogue and cooperation regarding fighting terrorism, the environment, energy, and transport.[54] The Central American countries involved are Costa Rica, El Salvador, Guatemala, Honduras, Nicaragua, and Panama. Furthermore, on 1 March 2010 the EU reached an FTA with Peru and Colombia liberalizing trade in industrial goods and fisheries, and increasing market access in agriculture, services, and investments.[55]

In a comparison between EU Association Agreements and United States FTAs there is a divergence in the language of the agreements regarding human rights, beyond labor and the environmental rights. The specific mention of human rights is contained in wide-ranging provisions within multiple Association Agreements. For example, in the EU—Jordan Association Agreement, language calls for discussion of human rights as a mutual point of interest. However, this language is not included in all EU Association Agreements. In comparison, specific language mentioning human rights is entirely absent in any American FTA to date.[56]

---

[52] *See generally* http://ec.europa.eu/trade/creating-opportunities/bilateral-relations/.

[53] *See* Bengt Ljung, *European Union, Peru, Colombia Conclude Comprehensive Free Trade Agreement Talks*, 27 International Trade Reporter (BNA) 298 (4 March 2010).

[54] *See* Bengy Ljung, *EU, Central American Nations on Track to Reach Association Agreement by May*, 27 International Trade Reporter (BNA) 298 (4 March 2010).

[55] *See* Bengt Ljung, *European Union, Peru, Colombia Conclude Comprehensive Free Trade Agreement Talks*, 27 International Trade Reporter (BNA) 298 (4 March 2010).

[56] *See* Raj Bhala, *Four Points about Trade and Human Rights, in* INTERNATIONAL TRADE LAW AND THE WTO (Azizur Rahman Chowdhury ed., Federation Press, Australia, forthcoming 2012).

## AS SUCH CHALLENGE

A challenge to a measure brought under the WTO *Understanding on Rules and Procedures Governing the Settlement of Disputes* (*Dispute Settlement Understanding* or *DSU*) alleging the measure itself is illegal under GATT—WTO rules. If the measure is a statute, then an "as such" challenge is properly called a "statutory challenge." The Appellate Body defines an "as such" challenge, and distinguishes it from an "as applied" challenge, as follows:

> "[A]s such" challenges against a Member's measures in WTO dispute settlement proceedings are serious challenges. By definition, an "as such" claim challenges laws, regulations, or other instruments of a Member that have general and prospective application, asserting that a Member's conduct — not only in a particular instance that has occurred, but in future situations as well — will necessarily be inconsistent with that Member's WTO obligations. In essence, complaining parties bringing "as such" challenges seek to prevent Members *ex ante* from engaging in certain conduct. The implications of such challenges are obviously more far-reaching than "as applied" claims.[57]

## ASA

American Sugar Alliance.

A powerful lobbying group in the United States representing sugar producers and processors.

## ASEAN

*Association of South East Asian Nations*, which is comprised of the 10 South East Asian nations:

- Brunei Darussalam
- Burma (Myanmar)
- Cambodia
- Indonesia
- Laos (Lao PDR)

- Malaysia
- Philippines
- Singapore
- Thailand
- Vietnam

*ASEAN* was founded in 1967 by Indonesia, Malaysia, the Philippines, Singapore, and Thailand.

The primary motive behind establishing *ASEAN* was political security within the boundaries of the founding members, most notably, threats of communist insurgency and ethnic unrest. Ironically, insecurity posed by ethnic and religious tensions continues in parts of Indonesia, the Philippines, and Thailand.

---

[57] Appellate Body Report, *United States — Sunset Reviews of Anti-Dumping Measures on Oil Country Tubular Goods from Argentina*, WT/DS268/AB/R, at ¶ 172 (adopted 17 December 2004).

It took 32 years to unite all 10 nations under its umbrella. The newest members are Vietnam, which was admitted in 1995, Burma and Laos, which were admitted in 1997, and Cambodia, which was admitted in 1999. There are two uninvited Pacific powers, China and the United States, which are not members of *ASEAN*. *ASEAN's* founding purpose was not only to increase economic interchange in South East Asia, but also to keep these two powers out of regional affairs. However, China signed a free trade agreement (FTA) deal of sorts with *ASEAN*. This arrangement is to be negotiated and concluded over 10 years. As for services, China hoped to complete negotiations with *ASEAN* on liberalizing them in 2006. Further, in August 2006, at the annual meeting of *ASEAN* economic ministers, the United States signed a *Trade and Investment Framework Agreement (TIFA)* with *ASEAN*, which is a possible pre-cursor to an FTA.

Not to be left out, India and Korea have sought agreements with *ASEAN*. India proceeded to sign a deal with *ASEAN* in 2003, the *Treaty of Amity and Cooperation*, signed on 8 October 2003 in Bali, Indonesia. However, talks between India and *ASEAN* were suspended in 2005 because India refused to slash a list of 1,400 products it insisted must be excluded from any trade liberalization agreement. By August 2006, India had cut by almost two-thirds the list of excluded goods, and the two sides were back at the negotiating table.

In December 2005, Korea signed an agreement with *ASEAN* to phase in an FTA beginning in July 2006. But, only the better-off *ASEAN* countries had to meet this deadline, *i.e.*, tariff cuts by Burma, Cambodia, Laos, and Vietnam for Korean products would come at a later date. But, sensitive sectors created problems: *ASEAN* insisted on market access for certain food products Korea found sensitive, and conversely, Korea sought market access for its automobiles, mobile phones, and steel, which were sensitive for some *ASEAN* members. Nonetheless, at the August 2006 *ASEAN* economics ministers meeting, *ASEAN* and Korea agreed to cut tariffs starting on 1 January 2007 on a range of products. That agreement was significant, because it occurred in spite of a continuing battle between Thailand, and *ASEAN* member, and Korea, over rice tariffs. Thailand argues Korea unjustifiably blocks exports of its rice to the Korean market to protect Korean rice farmers. Thus, Thailand refused to join the *ASEAN*–Korea deal.

Cambodia originally was slated to join along with Burma and Laos. However, *ASEAN* froze its application for two years in the wake of a *coup d'état*, engineered by Premier Hun Sen, that toppled co-Premier Prince Norodom Ranariddh. The *coup* vitiated the results of United Nations-supported and supervised elections held in 1993, which Prince Ranariddh's party had won and thereafter shared power with Mr. Sen in a formula devised by the Prince's father, King Norodom Sihanouk. The decision to defer Cambodia's application marked an extraordinarily rare instance in which *ASEAN* took a strong position on the internal affairs of another country.

Regarding trade, *ASEAN* members have agreed to liberalize their regimes by extending MFN and national treatment to one another, and increasing transparency in their trade laws. They also have created three principal vehicles for liberalization:

- The *ASEAN Free Trade Area (AFTA)*.
- The *ASEAN* Investment Area (AIA).
- The *ASEAN* Framework Agreement on Services.

At the November 1999 summit of *ASEAN* leaders, the summit chairman, Philippine President Joseph Estrada, went further, articulating a vision of an East Asian common market, with one currency. As an alternative to a common market and single currency, *ASEAN* could become a hub for FTAs in the Asia-Pacific region. In turn, the FTA network could be the foundation for a pan-Asian trading zone. Indeed, at the first "East Asian Summit," held in December 2005 in Kuala Lumpur, Malaysia, the idea of a pan-Asian FTA was mooted.

*ASEAN* supports APEC and WTO on trade matters. However, for two reasons, the vision of a common market and single currency will be difficult to achieve. First, *ASEAN's* newest members — Burma, Cambodia, Laos, and Vietnam — are proving hard to absorb. They are far poorer than the "tiger" nations in *ASEAN*, hence their interests sometimes are at variance with the rest of the members. Indeed, these four nations are sometimes referred to as the "CLMV" group, standing for "Cambodia, Laos, Myanmar, and Vietnam." These least developed countries contrast with the four middle-income developing countries, the so-called "*ASEAN* — 4," which consists of Indonesia, Malaysia, Philippines, and Thailand.

Not surprisingly, some of the *ASEAN* — 4 members pursue an FTA policy independent of *ASEAN*. For example, in 2003, Thailand expressed an interest in an FTA with the United States and EU, and began negotiations with the United States on an FTA in June 2004 (which broke down in January 2006). Thailand has shown a willingness to be a hub for FTAs. For example, on 3 April 2007, Japan signed an EPA with Thailand, called the "JTEPA," for "Japan — Thailand Economic Partnership Agreement." Similarly, Singapore has struck FTAs with the United States and Australia. The *United States — Singapore FTA*, signed by President George W. Bush on 6 May 2003, entered into force on 1 January 2004. The *Australia — Singapore FTA*, signed on 17 February 2003, entered into force on 28 July 2003. This picture is complicated by the FTA deals signed by *ASEAN* with China and India (mentioned above.)

Second, *ASEAN's* traditional policy of non-interference in the internal affairs of members inhibits cooperation on a wide range of trade-related issues. The policy gives comfort to authoritarian leaders in, for example, Burma and Vietnam. But, formation of an integrated economic zone would require agreement on topics such as environmental protection, exchange rate policy, and labor rights — taboo subjects in a non-intervention paradigm. The policy was tested severely in September-October 2007, when Burma's monstrous military leaders shot and killed, beat mercilessly, and detained and mistreated, non-violent Buddhist monks (as well as civilians) in the capital city, Rangoon, and roughly 25 other cities in the country. Triggering the protests of the monks and their civilian supporters was an inhumane doubling of the price of fuel by the military, and more generally 45 years of dreadful mismanagement and abuse by the junta.

With respect to political, diplomatic, and cultural matters, the highest decision-making body of *ASEAN* is the Annual Meeting of Foreign Ministers, also known as the Annual Ministerial Meeting (AMM). Attended by the foreign ministers of the member countries, it is held in the capital city of each *ASEAN* country on a rotating basis. At this Meeting policies are formulated, coordinated, and reviewed. Regarding economic affairs, the highest decision-making body is the Annual Economic Ministers Meeting (AEMM). Regional economic policies are proposed, coordinated, and assessed at the AEMM. There are a number of committees under the AMM and AEMM charged with specific responsibilities that meet periodically. Each *ASEAN* country has a National Secretariat, headed by a Director-General, to conduct the work of *ASEAN* in that country. The permanent Secretariat of *ASEAN*, led by the Secretary-General and staffed with experts in a variety of fields, is located in Jakarta, Indonesia.

*Suggestions for Further Research*:

Books:

1.   BERGSTEN, C. FRED & MARCUS NOLAND, EDS., PACIFIC DYNAMISM AND THE INTERNATIONAL ECONOMIC SYSTEM (1993).

2.   HAFEZ, ZAKIR, THE DIMENSIONS OF REGIONAL TRADE INTEGRATION IN SOUTHEAST ASIA (2004).

3.   LINCOLN, EDWARD J., EAST ASIAN ECONOMIC REGIONALISM (2004).

4.   MATSUSHITA, MITSUO & DUKGEUN AHN, EDS., WTO AND EAST ASIA: NEW PERSPECTIVES (2004).

5.   NARINE, SHAUN, EXPLAINING ASEAN — REGIONALISM IN SOUTHEAST ASIA (2002).

6.   SANDHU, K.S., ET AL., EDS., THE ASEAN READER (1992).

7.   TAN, GERALD, ASEAN ECONOMIC DEVELOPMENT AND CO-OPERATION (1996).

8.   TAN, JOSEPH, ED., AFTA IN THE CHANGING INTERNATIONAL ECONOMY (1996).

Book Chapters:

1.   Ahn, Dukgeun, *Trade Remedy Systems for East Asian Free Trade Agreements*, *in* THE WTO IN THE TWENTY-FIRST CENTURY — DISPUTE SETTLEMENT, NEGOTIATIONS, AND REGIONALISM IN ASIA 423–433 (Yasuhei Taniguchi, Alan Yanovich & Jan Bohanes eds. 2007).

2.   Lim, C.L., *Free Trade Agreements in Asia and Some Common Legal Problems*, *in* THE WTO IN THE TWENTY-FIRST CENTURY — DISPUTE SETTLEMENT, NEGOTIATIONS, AND REGIONALISM IN ASIA 434–456 (Yasuhei Taniguchi, Alan Yanovich & Jan Bohanes eds. 2007).

3.   Lo, Chang-fa, *Dispute Settlement Under Free Trade Agreements: Its Interaction and Relationship with WTO Dispute Settlement Procedures*, *in* THE WTO IN THE TWENTY-FIRST CENTURY — DISPUTE SETTLEMENT, NEGOTIATIONS, AND

REGIONALISM IN ASIA 457–471 (Yasuhei Taniguchi, Alan Yanovich & Jan Bohanes eds. 2007).

    4.  Yuqinq, Zhang, *Regionalism Under the WTO and the Prospect of an East Asian Free Trade Area, in* THE WTO IN THE TWENTY-FIRST CENTURY — DISPUTE SETTLEMENT, NEGOTIATIONS, AND REGIONALISM IN ASIA 472–482 (Yasuhei Taniguchi, Alan Yanovich & Jan Bohanes eds., 2007).

    Articles:

    1.  Lau, Terence J., *Distinguishing Fiction from Reality: The ASEAN Free Trade Area and Implications for the Global Auto Industry*, 31 UNIVERSITY OF DAYTON LAW REVIEW 435–76 (2006).

    2.  Liu, Han-Wei, *A Missing Part in International Investment Law: The Effectiveness of Investment Protection of Taiwan's BIT vis-à-vis ASEAN States*, 16 UNIVERSITY OF CALIFORNIA DAVIS JOURNAL OF INTERNATIONAL LAW & Policy 131–169 (2009).

    3.  Seah, Daniel, *The ASEAN Charter*, 58 INTERNATIONAL & COMPARATIVE LAW QUARTERLY 197–212 (2009).

    Other Source:

    1.  Lim, C.L., *"A Mega Jumbo-Jet:" Southeast Asia's Experiments with Trade and Investment Liberalization, in* THE NEW INTERNATIONAL ARCHITECTURE ON TRADE AND INVESTMENT — CURRENT STATUS AND IMPLICATIONS (APEC Secretariat ed., 2007) (APEC #207-HR-01.2, ECONOMY PAPER).

### *ASEAN* + 3

The 10 members of *ASEAN*, plus Japan, Korea, and China.

In effect, *ASEAN* + 3 is the realization of the vision of former Malaysian Prime Minister Mahathir Mohammed to create an East Asian Economic Group that would exclude the United States. While the *ASEAN* + 3 countries started meeting as early as 2003, the practical effects of their meetings is unclear.

### *ASEAN* 6

The six elder *ASEAN* countries — Brunei Darussalam, Indonesia, Malaysia, Philippines, Singapore, and Thailand.

### ASEM

Asia-Europe Meeting.

An annual summit among senior officials from Asian countries and the European Union (EU), specifically, the *Association of South East Asian Nations* (*ASEAN*) + 3 group and the EU members.

The first such summit was held in March 1996 in Bangkok, Thailand, with subsequent summits held periodically. ASEM activities amount to a dialogue and cooperation in three areas, or pillar topics:

    (1)  Political, specifically, anti-terrorism, migration flows, and human rights.

(2) Economic, namely, reducing trade barriers and discussing WTO matters.

(3) Cultural/Intellectual, especially the protection of cultural heritage.

The activities are intended to complement, in an informal manner, the formal discourse that occurs in the WTO and United Nations (U.N.)

## *ASIA — PACIFIC TRADE AGREEMENT*

The new name, effective November 2005, for the *Bangkok Agreement*.

## ASSESSMENT RATE

Also called the "Duty Assessment Rate" or "Final Liquidation Rate," the final antidumping duty (AD) duty rate, or countervailing duty (CVD) rate, for an individual importer of subject merchandise. *See* Administrative Review, Retrospective assessment.

## ASTP

Australian System of Tariff Preferences.

The ASTP is Australia's Generalized System of Preferences (GSP) scheme. It applies to all products. Initially, it applied to a large number of developing and least developed countries. It was revised by restricting preferential treatment to specified least developed countries and South Pacific Island territories. Significantly, the ASTP does not have a direct shipment requirement.

## *ATC*

The Uruguay Round *Agreement on Textiles and Clothing*.

The *ATC* phased out *Multi-Fiber Agreement* (*MFA*) restrictions over a 10 year period, 1 January 1995-1 January 2005, thus integrating the textile and apparel (T&A) sector into the GATT–WTO regime. Accordingly, *MFA* quotas were eliminated midnight 31 December 2004.

*Suggestions for Further Research*:

Books:

1.   BAGCHI, SANJOY, INTERNATIONAL TRADE POLICY IN TEXTILES — FIFTY YEARS OF PROTECTIONISM (June 2001).

2.   KRISHNA, KALA & LING HUI TAN, RAGS AND RICHES: IMPLEMENTING APPAREL QUOTAS UNDER THE MULTI-FIBRE ARRANGEMENT (1998).

3.   RIVOLI, PIETRA, THE TRAVELS OF A T-SHIRT IN THE GLOBAL ECONOMY: AN ECONOMIST EXAMINES THE MARKETS, POWER, AND POLITICS OF WORLD TRADE (2005).

4.   UNDERHILL, GEOFFREY R. D., INDUSTRIAL CRISIS AND THE OPEN ECONOMY: POLITICS, GLOBAL TRADE, AND THE TEXTILE INDUSTRY IN THE ADVANCED ECONOMIES (1998).

Article:

1. Hall, John A., *"China Casts a Giant Shadow:"* The Developing World Confronts Trade Liberalization and the End of Quotas in the Garment Industry, 5 JOURNAL OF INTERNATIONAL BUSINESS AND LAW 1–46 (2006).

## *ATPA*

*Andean Trade Preference Act.*[58]

A Preferential Trading Agreement (PTA) sponsored by the United States, originally involving Bolivia, Colombia, Ecuador, and Peru, dating from 4 December 1991, the date of enactment of the *ATPA*. The preference is indicated in the Harmonized Tariff Schedule of the United States (HTSUS) as "J," in Column 1 (special duty rates). A key policy goal of the *ATPA* is to reduce the cultivation of illegal crops, such as coca, in the Andean region by giving duty free access to a broad range of licit products from Andean countries entering the American market. In 2009 the top five products benefiting exclusively from *ATPA* were: heavy crude oil; light crude oil; fresh-cut roses; heavy fuel oil; and fresh-cut chrysanthemums.[59]

In 2006, Venezuela pulled out of the Andean Community, making its merchandise (which, after the 1991 inception, qualified for preferences) no longer eligible for duty-free treatment under *ATPA*. In 2008, Bolivia was suspended from the program. That was because, at the time, Bolivia failed to satisfy the eligibility criteria regarding counter-narcotics and, therefore, also was ineligible for duty-free treatment.[60]

*ATPA* preferences were amended in 2002 by the *Andean Trade Promotion and Drug Eradication Act (ATPDEA)*, which was set to expire on 31 December 2006, but renewed by Congress through 31 December 2009. Just prior to expiry, benefits under the *ATPA* and *ATPDEA* extended to over 6,000 products from Bolivia, Colombia, Ecuador, and Peru. *ATPDEA* added approximately 700 additional products to the list of eligible goods under ATPA, including apparel, footwear, oil and its derivatives, and tuna. (*See* Andean Community.)

At the end of 2009, Congress again renewed *ATPA*, until 31 December 2010, but mandated that the United States Trade Representative (USTR) report to Congress by 30 June 2010 on compliance by *ATPA* beneficiaries with eligibility criteria. Eligibility criteria that must be satisfied by member countries includes: expropriation, tax issues, settlement of disputes, following acceptable international rules of trade, worker and human rights, cooperation on narcotics interdiction, and nationalization concerns.[61] The *ATPA* ended up

---

[58] *See* Pub. L. No. 102–182, 105 Stat. 1236 (4 December 1991).

[59] *See* Rossella Brevetti, *ATPA Impact on U.S. Economy was Negligible in 2009, ITC Finds*, 27 International Trade Reporter (BNA) 1569 (14 October 2009).

[60] *See* Len Bracken, *USTR Announces Annual Review of Andean Trade Preference Act*, 27 International Trade Reporter (BNA) 1228 (12 August 2010).

[61] *See* Len Bracken, *USTR Announces Annual Review of Andean Trade Preference Act*, 27 International Trade Reporter (BNA) 1228 (12 August 2010).

lapsing on 12 February 2011. Congress renewed again the *ATPA* in October 2011, retroactively from 12 February 2011, through 31 July 2013. Congress did so via the implementing legislation (H.R. 3078 and S. 1641) for the *United States — Colombia Free Trade Agreement*, and thereby ensured Ecuador receives *ATPA* benefits.

In the 30 June 2010 report, USTR cited several issues of concern including investment, intellectual property rights, and excessive trade barriers to contest Ecuador's eligibility. Based on the USTR report, Congress has the ability to suspend Ecuador, partially or completely, from access to preferences, and to impose additional conditions on Ecuador in order for it to maintain eligibility under *ATPA*.[62]

As an addition to *ATPA*, the United States had goals for a free trade agreement (FTA) with all of the Andean countries, yielding an Andean FTA. But, the United States was successful in reaching bilateral deals with only Peru and Colombia. The *Peru Preferential Trade Agreement (PTPA)* entered into force on 1 February 2009. However, the negotiated *United States–Colombia FTA* has not entered into force as of September 2011. Talks with Ecuador collapsed in early 2006. That same year, in March, Bolivia, under President Evo Morales, rejected the idea of a conventional FTA with the United States.

*Suggestions for Further Research*:

Article:

1.   Grubbs, Kevin, Comment, *The Andean Trade Preference Act: Historical Effectiveness, Modern Trends, and Outlook for the Future*, 16 LAW & BUSINESS REVIEW OF THE AMERICAS 95–118 (2010).

## *ATPDEA*

*Andean Trade Promotion and Drug Eradication Act.*[63]

Andean preferences were originally enacted on 4 December 1991 under the *Andean Trade Preferences Act (ATPA)*. They were renewed, with substantive changes and conditions, through the *ATPDEA*. The *ATPDEA* was enacted on 6 August 2002, as a part of the *Trade Act of 2002*. On 20 December 2006, the *ATPDEA* as part of the Comprehensive Trade Legislation, with *ATPA* preferences was set to expire on 28 February 2008.[64]

But, on 17 October 2008, President George W. Bush signed the *Extension of Andean Trade Preference Act*, Pubic Law Number 110–436, 122 Stat. 4976 (2008), which Congress passed on 16 October 2008,. This *Extension* legislation ensured continued duty-free access to the American market for

---

[62] *See* Len Bracken, *USTR Announces Annual Review of Andean Trade Preference Act*, 27 International Trade Reporter (BNA) 1228 (12 August 2010).

[63] *See* Pub. L. No. 107–210, 116 Stat. 1023 (6 August 2002).

[64] *See Andean Trade Preferences Extension Act*, Pub. L. No. 109–432, 120 Stat. 3194 (20 December 2006).

beneficiary countries in South America through at most 31 December 2009. This *Extension* legislation meant that *ATPA* benefits were extended for —

- Colombia and Peru for one year through 31 December 2009,
- possibly for six months for Bolivia, and
- possibly for one year for Ecuador through 31 December 2009, but with a review after six months.

When the *United States—Peru Free Trade Agreement* was implemented on 1 February 2009, the duty-free market access Peru enjoyed under the *ATPA* became permanent under this FTA. Assuming Congressional passage of the *United States–Colombia FTA*, a similar scenario likely would ensue. Thus, assuming the *ATPA* scheme is renewed beyond 31 December 2009, in practice the key prospective beneficiaries will be Bolivia and Ecuador.

The benefits are contingent, of course, on countries satisfying four criteria. That is, the *ATPDEA* lists four requirements for eligibility as a beneficiary country:

- Investment Policies.
- Trade Policies.
- Counter-narcotics cooperation.
- Workers' rights.

Under the *ATPDEA*, the potentially eligible Andean countries are Colombia, Bolivia, Ecuador, and Peru. But, again, in practice, in the long term, Bolivia and Ecuador are the key ones. The *ATPDEA* requires the President to make findings about country eligibility according to these criteria. For example, President Barack H. Obama had to make findings by 30 June 2009.

In 2008 the United States Department of State found that Bolivia had not met the third criteria. In the view of the State Department, Bolivia failed to demonstrate that it was adhering to its obligations under international counter-narcotics agreements. Accordingly, in 2008, President George W. Bush decided to suspend status as an eligible country under the *ATPA*. Similarly, on 30 June 2009, President Obama extended the determination of his predecessor, agreeing that Bolivia failed to meet the counter-narcotics cooperation eligibility criteria. President Obama certified Ecuador as eligible.

Ecuador's certification by President Obama has caused mild controversy. The United States leases an air force facility, the Eloy Alfaro Air Base, in Ecuador, which it uses for drug interdiction operations. The Foreign Ministry of Ecuador formally notified the United States that it will not renew the lease, when expires in late 2009. The concern is whether Ecuador will ensure there is no slackening of its counter-narcotics cooperation with the United States after the lease expires.

Receiving designation from the United States as a country eligible for *ATPA* benefits is only the first step in receiving duty-free treatment. The next step is to determine whether the specific category of imported merchandise qualifies for this treatment. The *ATPA* and *ATPDEA* extended the benefit to over 6,000 products from eligible countries. The *ATPDEA* itself added about 700 additional products to the list of eligible products under the *ATPA*, including apparel, footwear, oil and its derivatives, and tuna.

## AU

African Union.

The *Constitutive Act of the African Union* was adopted on 11 July 2000 in Lomé, Togo. The *Act* sets out the goals for the AU, including:

> [T]he accelerated socio-economic integration of the African continent, in order to strengthen solidarity and cohesion amongst the peoples of Africa.

Notably, Morocco is not a member of the AU, and the membership of Mauritania was suspended following a coup d'état in that country. The AU has sent peace-keeping forces to a number of conflict zones on the African continent.

*Suggestions for Further Research*:

Articles:

1.   Martorana, Carolyn Scanlon, Note, *The New African Union: Will it Promote Enforcement of the Decisions of the African Court of Human and Peoples' Rights?*, 40 GEORGE WASHINGTON INTERNATIONAL LAW REVIEW 583–610 (2009).

2.   Jalloh, Charles Chernor, *Universal Jurisdiction, Universal Prescription? A Preliminary Assessment of the African Union Perspective on Universal Jurisdiction*, 21 CRIMINAL LAW FORUM 1–65 (2010).

## AUGUST 2003 *MEDICINES AGREEMENT*

*See* Compulsory Licensing.

## AUTOMATICITY

The automatic chronological progression in the WTO dispute resolution process, as set forth in the WTO *Understanding on Rules and Procedures Governing the Settlement of Disputes* (*Dispute Settlement Understanding*, or *DSU*).

The key events in the process for which progression is automatic are the establishment of a panel and its terms of reference, the composition of the panel, the appellate procedure, and the adoption of panel and Appellate Body reports.

## AVE

*Ad valorem* equivalent, that is, an *ad valorem* tariff that provides the equivalent level of protection as a specific duty, hybrid duty, or some other barrier that is not calculated as a percentage of the value of an article of imported merchandise.

The central challenge associated with AVEs is developing a methodology by which to convert a diverse array of bound non-*ad valorem* tariffs into their AVEs. If the conversion to an *ad valorem* duty produces less protection than did the previous specific or hybrid duty it replaces, then the importing country will be unsatisfied. If the conversion boosts the level of protection, then countries with an export interest in the product in question will be upset. In the latter case, there may also be a violation of GATT rules on tariff bindings and modification of tariff schedules.

After several months of negotiations during the Doha Round, in May 2005, WTO Members agreed to a common approach, the "Paris Methodology," to convert bound non-*ad valorem* most favored nation (MFN) duties into their AVEs. The rubric stems from the fact the Methodology was developed in Paris, on the sidelines of a meeting of the Organization for Economic Cooperation and Development (OECD). This Methodology was incorporated into the July 2006 draft modalities text, and subsequently retained as a basis for negotiations.

By way of summary, the Paris Methodology is expressed in the following arithmetic formula:[65]

$$AVE = \frac{(SP \times 100)}{(UV \times XR)}$$

where

$$UV = \frac{V}{(Q \times C_Q)}$$

and where

AVE = *ad valorem* equivalent, expressed as a percentage

SP  = monetary value of a duty per unit of imports
      (*e.g.*, the specific duty)

UV  = unit value of an import
      (*i.e.*, the price per unit of an import)

V  = value of imports (*i.e.*, the total value
     of import flows during a defined period)

Q  = quantity of imports (*i.e.*, the total quantity
     of import flows during the same defined period).

$C_Q$  = conversion factor for quantity units, if relevant

XR  = currency exchange rate, if relevant

---

[65] *See* World Trade Organization, *The Draft Modalities, Version 2006 — Annexes, Annex A: Draft Guidelines for the Conversion of Final Bound Non-Ad Valorem Duties into Ad Valorem Equivalents*, TN/AG/W/3, 12 July 2006.

The Methodology has the advantages of practicality, simplicity, transparency, verifiability, and comparability. Once each WTO Member has applied the Methodology to its bound MFN non-*ad valorem* tariffs to compute the AVEs, using figures for total import flows and data from the period 1999–2001, then it is supposed to submit its AVEs to the WTO. In instances where seasonal tariffs are used (as occurs in some countries on farm products), a separate AVE is calculated for each season.

To posit a highly simplified example of the Paris Methodology, suppose the good in question is wheat, and the country at issue is India. Assume India has imposed a specific duty on wheat equal to U.S. $5.00 per bushel (SP). During the years 1999–2001, India imported a total of 10,000 bushels of wheat (V), the total value of which was U.S. $1 million (V). There is no need to convert prices to U.S. dollars, hence XR is irrelevant, and it is assumed $C_Q$ is 1 (or not needed). Then, the calculation is

$$AVE = \frac{(SP \times 100)}{(UV \times XR)} = \frac{(5 \times 100)}{100} = 5 \text{ percent}$$

where

$$UV = \frac{V}{(Q \times C_Q)} = \frac{1,000,000}{10,000} = 100$$

In brief, the AVE of a specific duty of U.S. $5 per bushel would be 5 percent.

In practice, WTO Members would derive the data necessary to use the Paris Methodology from two sources. First, they may obtain import unit values (UV) at the six-digit level of the Harmonized System (HS) from the United Nations Commodity Trade Statistics Database (Comtrade). Such values are technically called "Comtrade unit values." Second, Members can obtain statistics on import values (V) and quantities (Q) from the WTO Integrated Database (IDB). The IDB provides statistics on international trade at a disaggregated tariff line level.

Sometimes, data may be missing for a particular tariff line, or there may be errors in IDB data. In these circumstances (and where IDB import values for a tariff line is less than U.S. $2,500, on a weighted average for 1999–2001), the Paris Methodology includes alternative approaches.

## AVIAN INFLUENZA (AI)

A disease found in birds, more commonly known as "bird flu."

AI has brought worldwide alarm for its potential to contaminate the poultry food supply and possibly mutate into a human infectious strain. The World Organization for Animal Health (OIE) classifies avian influenza into two categories based on its potential for fatality in birds:

(1) Low pathogenic (also called "low path" or "LPAI").

(2) High pathogenic (also called "high path" or "HPAI").

The latter category is the infamous H5N1 viral strain.

The OIE has designated standards in its Terrestrial Animal Health Code (Chapter 2.7.12) to assist countries in determining risk associated with importing of poultry from affected areas. The OIE considers only high pathogenic AI in commercial flocks as a cause of concern in international trade. It does not consider being of concern the presence of low pathogenic AI in wild birds or commercial flocks, nor the presence of high pathogenic AI in wild birds.

Nevertheless, some countries — such as Sri Lanka — use the presence of LPAI in wild birds to justify imposition of sanitary and phytosanitary standards (SPS) against cross-border trade. That kind of measure, of course, is more rigorous than suggested by the OIE. The result is to protect the poultry industry in the country imposing the measure.

## AWB

Australian Wheat Board.

From 1939 until December 2006, the AWB operated as a "single desk" for wheat exports from Australia. That is, it was a monopoly, controlling all exports of Australian wheat. Australia (as of December 2006) accounts for roughly 14 percent of wheat traded in the world.

In late December 2006, the government of Prime Minister John Howard formally ended the AWB's export monopoly. It did so by authorizing individual grain producers in the country to export their own wheat. That authorization did not take the form of immediate deregulation of the wheat export market, as free traders would have preferred. Rather, Prime Minister Howard's government chose a compromise between the extremes of a single desk and a free market by issuing export permits. For example, the government granted Wheat Australia a permit to ship 300,000 metric tons of wheat to Iraq, and CBH a permit to export 500,000 metric tons to Indonesia. (The grantees are domestic grain producers.) The government also turned down the application of GrainCorp (another domestic producer, to export 230,000 tons).

The AWB had been criticized, both in Australia and overseas (including by American farmers), as an institutional incongruity measured against Australia's generally pro-free trade policies, adduced by its membership in the Cairns Group. Defenders of the AWB, such as Australia's National Party, saw the single desk as a means of increasing the clout of Australia in world wheat markets, for example, with respect to bargaining power over price. Arguably, the decision to end the single desk was eased by a severe drought in Australia. Because of it, Australia's wheat crop output was forecast to fall by 62 percent (for the year 2006). The forecast boosted world prices, and correspondingly — if temporarily — diminished the need for an export monopoly to achieve that end.

Interestingly, the beginning of the end of the AWB's export monopoly was not trade policy but shady dealings with Iraq. Following months of investigation into corruption in the United Nations oil-for-food program, the AWB was found guilty of paying U.S. $227 million in bribes (in the form of kickbacks) to the regime of Saddam Hussein. The leader of the inquiry, Australian judge Terence Cole, recommended criminal charges against 11 former executives of the AWB. With these findings and recommendations, the Australia — in early December 2006 — suspended the AWB's export monopoly for six months. Prime Minister Howard's government made the decision to end it for good on 22 December 2006.[66] As small consolation for the AWB, Australia's Taxation Office said the AWB would not have to pay tax retroactively on the money it paid as kickbacks to officials in Saddam Hussein's Iraq.

---

[66] *See* Raphael Minder, *Canberra Grants Permits to Grain Exporters*, FINANCIAL TIMES, 23–24 December 2006, at 3.

# B

## BALANCE OF TRADE

*See* BOP.

## BALTIC DRY INDEX (BALTIC DRY INDEX OF BULK SHIPPING RATES)

A widely-tracked index of rates for shipping cargo internationally.

If the Baltic Dry Index increases, it means that rates for shipping bulk cargo are increasing, and — therefore — international trade in goods must be increasing (otherwise the rates would not be rising). Conversely, if international trade is falling, then shipping rates decline, and this decline is reflected in a fall in the Baltic Dry Index.

Between May and November 2008, the Baltic Dry Index fell by an astounding 89 percent. That fall occurred because banks were not issuing letters of credit, and because there were rumors in financial markets that some banks that had issued letters of credit previously were not able to honor them. With the collapse of the letter of credit market, commodity shipments became paralyzed, and trade plummeted. In other words, the plummet in the Index was a clear indicator of the fall in world trade associated with the global economic crisis.

### BANGKOK AGREEMENT

An accord signed in 1975 to create the first preferential trade arrangement in Asia among developing countries.

In November 2005, the accord was re-named the *"Asia-Pacific Trade Agreement."* The *Agreement* entered into force on 1 July 2006. The member states are:

- Bangladesh
- China
- India
- Korea
- Sri Lanka
- Lao People's Democratic Republic (Laos)

The United Nations Economic and Social Commission for Asia and the Pacific (UNESCAP), located in Bangkok, Thailand, functions as the Secretariat for the group.

## BARRO STUDY

*See* New Growth Theory, Solow Model.

## BASE PERIOD

The agreed time period that serves as the basis for making measurements and/or reducing trade barriers.

For example, in the Uruguay Round *Agreement on Agriculture*, 1986–88 is selected as the base period for commitments to increase market access and reduce domestic support schemes, and 1986–90 is the base period from which decreases in export subsidies are measured.

## BASIC BOND AMOUNT (BBA) (BASIC BOND REQUIREMENT)

*See* Customs Bond.

## *BASIC TELECOMMUNICATIONS AGREEMENT (1998 BASIC TELECOMMUNICATIONS AGREEMENT)*

*See Telecommunications Agreement.*

## BASKET APPROACH

*See* Product Basket Approach.

## BDC

Beneficiary Developing Country.

A BDC is a country some of the exports of which are eligible for preferential treatment under the United States Generalized System of Preferences Program (GSP) program.

## BECC

The *North American Free Trade Agreement* (*NAFTA*) Border Environment Cooperation Commission.

The BECC is responsible for monitoring the environment in the "high impact" area immediately adjacent to the border between the United States and Mexico.

## BEGGAR-THY-NEIGHBOR (BEGGAR-THY-NEIGHBOR POLICY)

A generic term referring to any government policy designed to improve domestic economic conditions at the expense of other countries.

Typically, the focus of the government's policy is unemployment, and the government seeks to reduce unemployment by increasing exports or reducing imports. In turn, the government tries to achieve this improvement in the trade balance by officially devaluing its currency (or encouraging a market-driven depreciation). Other policy measures the government might try to improve the trade balance, and thereby reduce unemployment, are tariffs, quotas, and export subsidies. The thrust of all of these measures is to shift domestic consumption demand away from imported goods and services, and toward domestically produced goods and services. That way, employment in domestic industries will rise.

The problem with all of these measures is that other countries are hurt by them. Their exports fall, their imports rise, and thus their unemployment rate rises. Consequently, these other countries might retaliate, with their own protectionist measures. In the end, the volume of world trade drops precipitously, and global unemployment rises. This chain reaction occurred during the Great Depression, as one country after another tried to cure its domestic economic woes through competitive devaluations and retaliatory protection that exacerbated problems in other countries.

A contemporary version of beggar-thy-neighbor policies is the reduction of inflation through currency appreciation. As a result of currency appreciation, domestic consumers can buy imports more cheaply, hence import-driven inflationary pressures subside. But, the appreciation of one country's currency means a depreciation of another country's currency (because a foreign exchange rate is the price of one country's currency in terms of another country's currency, like yen/dollar or dollar/euro). Thus, in the second country, the cost of imports rises: that country's currency is weaker, therefore it takes more units of that country's currency to exchange for the relevant foreign currency and pay for imports. In turn, because the cost of imports rises in the second country, import-driven inflation increases in the second country.

## BEHIND THE BORDER

A term typically used to connote measures that serve to protect a domestic producer in an importing country other than tariffs (or other duties and charges (ODC)), and certain sanitary and phytosanitary (SPS) rules, which are applied at the border. At the border measures are applied during the process of customs inspection and clearance. "Behind the border" measures affect trade after that point.

Behind the border measures can be fiscal (*e.g.*, discriminatory indirect taxation) or non-fiscal (*e.g.*, special marketing or display requirements) that impinge market access for foreign merchandise.

## BEIJING CONSENSUS

A generally accepted philosophy of political economy among policymakers and scholars in China that economic reform should be prudent. That is, the excesses of free market capitalism should be avoided, and economic liberalization need not necessarily be accompanied by dramatic political reform.

## BENEFICIARY SSAC

A country in Sub-Saharan Africa (SSA) that is a beneficiary of the United States *African Growth and Opportunity Act (AGOA)*.

Being designated an *AGOA* beneficiary means a country can export most products to the United States duty-free. The Act authorizes the President to designate countries as eligible to receive the benefits of AGOA. To be designated eligible, a Sub-Saharan African Country (SSAC) must satisfy the eight requirements set out in Section 104(a) of *AGOA*, or at least must be making continuous progress toward meeting them. These requirements are:

- Market Economic Reforms.

  Three criteria for market orientation are set out: (1) protection of private property; (2) incorporation of an open, rules-based system; and (3) minimal interference by the government in the economy.

- Liberal Political Reforms.

  Four criteria are mentioned: (1) rule of law; (2) political pluralism; (3) the right to due process; and (4) equal protection under the law.

- Elimination of Barriers to American Trade.

  There are three criteria, all focused on market access for American businesses into SSACs: (1) the provision of national treatment and measures to create an environment favorable to investment; (2) the protection of intellectual property; and (3) the resolution of bilateral trade and investment disputes.

- Development Programs.

  Broad-based economic policies must be put in place. There are six criteria: (1) the reduction of poverty; (2) improved health care; (3) increased educational opportunities; (4) expanded physical infrastructure; (5) the promotion of private enterprise; and (6) the formation of capital markets through micro-credit and other programs.

- Combating Corruption.

  Only one criterion is specified: signing the *Convention on Combating Bribery of Foreign Public Officials in International Business Transactions (Anti-Bribery Convention)*.

- Protecting Worker Rights.

  Internationally recognized worker rights must be protected. Five criteria define these rights: (1) the right of association; (2) the right to organize and bargain collectively; (3) a prohibition on forced or compulsory labor; (4) a minimum age for the employment of children; and (5) acceptable working conditions with respect to minimum wages, hours of work, and occupational safety and health.

- American National Security and Foreign Policy.

  A country must not engage in activities that undermine the national security or foreign policy interests of the United States. No criteria are associated with this requirement.

- Human Rights and Terrorism.

  A country must not engage in gross violations of internationally recognized human rights, must not provide support for acts of international terrorism, and must cooperate in international efforts to eliminate terrorist activities.

The President not only may add countries to the eligibility list, but can also revoke the eligibility of a country.

For example, on 1 January 2004, President George W. Bush removed the Central African Republic and Eritrea from the list of eligible countries, and removed Côte d'Ivoire on 1 January 2005. Mauritania has perhaps had the most interesting experience with *AGOA*, having been removed on 1 January 2006 and then re-designated as eligible on 28 June 2007.

While countries may be generally designated an *AGOA* beneficiary, they must take extra steps to be granted textile and apparel benefits. Thus, their textile and apparel (T&A) exports do not receive duty free access until they are granted an "AGOA Textile and Apparel Visa" by the United States Trade Representative (USTR). To achieve this, a country must demonstrate that it has in place an effective system to prevent illegal transshipment and use of counterfeit documentation, as well as effective enforcement and verification procedures. Twenty-eight of the thirty-eight *AGOA* eligible countries are also declared eligible for *AGOA* T&A benefits (as of December 2007).

*AGOA IV* (which Congress passed in 2005) contains a "Special Rule" for T&A that applies to lesser developed beneficiary countries. Until 30 September 2012, these countries may use non-domestic and non-United States fabric and yarn (so-called "Third Country Fabric") in apparel wholly assembled inside their countries, yet still qualify for duty- and quota-free treatment. Exports under the Special Rule are, however, subject to a cap. Specifically, *AGOA IV* limits imports of apparel made with regional fabric or Third Country Fabric to a fixed percentage of the aggregate square meter equivalents (SMEs) of all apparel articles imported into the United States. Apparel imported into the United States under the Special Rule for lesser developed *AGOA* beneficiary countries is limited to an amount not to exceed 3.5 percent of apparel imported into the United States in the preceding 12-month period.

# BHN

Basic Human Needs, which is a strategy toward poverty alleviation.

BHN, which arose in the late 1970s, emphasizes the provision of public services to the poor, as well as entitlements, including subsidies, to ensure they have effective access to such services. Through access to such services, the human capital of poor people may be enhanced. Such investments in human capital contribute to income, because income comes from assets like human capital (as well as ownership of land and physical capital). In turn, higher human capital promotes overall economic growth.

## BIA

Best information available.

In antidumping (AD) and countervailing duty (CVD) investigations, the United States Department of Commerce (DOC) seeks to use the most reliable data possible for its preliminary and final dumping margin and subsidy determinations. The International Trade Commission (ITC) has the same goal as regards injury determinations. When data submitted by the petitioner or respondent are not reliable, or one of the parties is not cooperative, after an attempt at verifying those data, the DOC or ITC is forced to use the BIA. In some cases, the BIA may be the data submitted by the opposing party.

In this respect, the possibility the DOC or ITC might use BIA is an incentive for both parties — particularly a respondent foreign company — to respond as completely and accurately as possible to the DOC's or ITC's questionnaires. (To be sure, the ITC — but not the DOC — has subpoena power. But, enforcing subpoena's overseas often is impractical or impossible.) "BIA" actually is pre-Uruguay Round terminology. The Uruguay Round *Antidumping Agreement* (at Article 6:8 and Annex II) and 1994 *Uruguay Round Agreements Act* (at 19 U.S.C. § 1677e) speak of "facts available" and "facts otherwise available," respectively.

## BIG PUSH

A development economics strategy for focusing the resources of a country on industrialization. The idea, dating from the 1940s, is advocated by economists like Jeffrey Sachs. He characterizes Sub-Saharan Africa (SSA) as afflicted by a poverty trap, meaning the region is too poor to grow. Only a Big Push will help it industrialize.

More specifically, just as Labor Surplus Models do not expressly address the importance of openness to trade, they do not chart a particular course for industrialization. Should a country make what Paul Rosenstein-Rodan dubbed in 1943 a "Big Push" toward industrialization? He answered "yes," because of five problems endemic to most poor countries:

- *Complementarity*: To industrialize, it is necessary to have complementing suppliers (for inputs into production) and customers (to purchase merchandise). Yet, many poor countries lack a large enough pool of suppliers, and a sizeable internal market, to encourage investment in manufacturing.

- *Indivisibilities*: Industrialization involves high fixed costs and long payback periods. It may be necessary for the government to engage directly in certain projects, or at least provide finance for them.

- *Market imperfections*: Many poor countries lack well-functioning markets. Their markets suffer from the vices of inefficiency and corruption, as well as imperfections like monopoly or oligopoly. It may be necessary for the government to build market institutions, most notably, the rule of law.

- *Infrastructure*: As mentioned earlier, physical infrastructure must support investment in the industrial, and even agricultural, sector. India provides a good example of constraints on growth in some sectors because of poor infrastructure. It is not surprising that much growth has occurred in the high technology sector, or in providing certain services. For example, writing software code, or setting up a call center, do not require port facilities, as the export is done via e-mail or over the phone. Of course, they do require reliable power supply.

- *Savings*: As the Harrod—Domar Model spotlights, savings play an important role in financing capital investment. Yet, poor countries by definition lack a large pool of savings, not to mention a safe and sound banking system to channel savings into investment.

Accordingly, Rosenstein-Rodan called for a major effort toward industrialization. Put simply, the process will not just happen because of a pool of labor surplus — it requires a Big Push.

The Big Push approach engenders two major policy debates: First, what ought the role of the state to be? Second, how balanced ought the growth process be? Typically, a Big Push requires a large degree of state intervention. In contrast, the so-called "Washington Consensus," or neo-liberal theory, which emerged in the 1980s among the American government, International Monetary Fund, and World Bank agreed on a light-handed role for the state in an economy. What matters is the establishment of sound markets, and a state ought to focus on minimizing barriers to entry into markets, ensuring the markets operate in a transparent manner, and intervene only in cases of clear market failure. According to the Washington Consensus, trade liberalization is an important stimulus, for the familiar reason that competition encourages growth and innovation.

As for balance, a Big Push can lead to tremendous industrial growth, but neglect of the agricultural sector. The extreme example, with monstrous results, was the Great Leap Forward in China from 1958–60. Roughly 30 million people starved as Chairman Mao Zedong favored industry over agriculture — a fact discovered decades later when demographers scrutinized Chinese population data and observed serious gaps. Some economists advocate unbalanced growth, like Albert O. Hirschman in his 1958 book *The Strategy of Economic Development*. The advantage of unbalanced growth, argued Hirschman, is linkage. If one or more leading sectors grow, then these sectors will create both backward and forward linkages in the economy. The leading sectors can be export-oriented, as has occurred in Brazil and India in recent decades.

A backward linkage exists when an industry buys inputs from other industries. A forward linkage exists when the output of an industry is purchased by other industries, aside from the final consumer. Both linkages may be measured by the percentage of inputs purchased. For example, in the manufacture of flat screens for computers, a backward linkage would be the purchase of the display panel, and a forward linkage would be the sale of the finished screen to a company assembling laptops (which ultimately sells the laptops to retail customers). A percentage of 38 would mean one industry buys 38 percent of the inputs from another industry (backward linkage), or sells that percentage of its output to other industries (forward linkage). Why are linkages important? Because of the multiplier effect they have on income. In the example, producing flat screens has a positive effect on the revenues of the display panel industry and the laptop industry.

Unbalanced growth can lead to linkages in both directions. Initial investments in a leading sector may result in excess production capacity. Entrepreneurs seeking to produce a different product that uses as an input the output from the leading sector may be able to make use of the spare capacity. If they do, and invest in production and purchase that output, then the result is a forward linkage. The mirror image scenario is where an initial investment creates a shortage. Entrepreneurs fill the supply void by investing in operations to make the input. The result is a backward linkage.

In contrast to the unbalanced growth strategy favored by Hirshman, other economists, notably Ragnar Nurkse, call for balanced growth. His seminal work took the form of lectures at Istanbul and Ankara Universities, which were published in 1958. He argues in favor of a pattern of investments in a range of industries that are mutually supportive. Seeking to avoid isolated advances in one or a few sectors, the Nurkse approach imparts a role to agriculture as well as industry, and to production for domestic consumption as well as exportation. India, in its early stages of growth, pursued a balanced strategy.

*Suggestions for Further Research:*

Books:

1.  HIRSCHMAN, ALFRED O., THE STRATEGY OF ECONOMIC DEVELOPMENT (1958).

2.  LYNN, STUART R., ECONOMIC DEVELOPMENT: THEORY AND PRACTICE FOR A DIVIDED WORLD 43, 56–59 (2003) (including Figures 3-1, 3-3A and 3-3B).

3.  SACHS, JEFFREY, THE END OF POVERTY: ECONOMIC POSSIBILITIES FOR OUR TIME (2005).

Articles:

1.  Rosenstein-Rodan, Paul N., *Problems of Industrialization of Eastern and South-Eastern Europe*, 53 ECONOMIC JOURNAL 202–11 (June-September 1943).

2.  Streeten, Paul, *Balanced versus Unbalanced Growth*, THE ECONOMIC WEEKLY (20 April 1963).

## BILATERAL REQUEST-OFFER

A method for negotiating trade liberalization, be it for goods or services.

Conceptually, there are three steps. First, one country advances a request for enhanced market access to another country, or other countries, with respect to goods or services in which the requesting country has an export interest. The country or countries to which it makes the request obviously are export markets about which it cares. Second, the country or countries receiving the request make an offer on market access. That is, the country or countries respond to a request with a market access offer. Third, the requesting and offering countries negotiate in an effort to narrow the gap between the request and offer.

The request-offer approach was used during the Uruguay Round for agricultural tariffs. The Uruguay Round negotiators established an overall average cut to be imposed on farm tariffs. They used the request-offer approach, on a bilateral basis, to negotiate reductions on individual farm tariff lines.

But, the request-offer approach suffers from three shortcomings. First, it can be time-consuming. Second, it does not automatically reduce tariff peaks, that is, very high tariff rates. Third, it does not necessarily resolve the problem of tariff escalation, which occurs when the tariff on a processed good is higher than the duty rates on the raw materials used as inputs into that good. Accordingly, formulaic approaches often are used, such as the Swiss Formula (which does deal with the latter two problems, by imposing larger percentage cuts on higher tariff rates), or even a simple, across-the-board linear tariff cut (which, however, does not deal with the latter two problems). But, when no agreement can be reached on a formula, there are calls — as they were in April 2011 in the Doha Round — to resort to the request-offer approach.[67]

## BINDING

*See* Bound Rate.

## BINDING OVERHANG

Also referred to as "water" or "the water," binding overhang is the difference between the bound rate of duty and the actually applied rate.

For example, if the bound rate of duty on a product is 10 percent, and the actually applied rate is three percent, then the binding overhang, or water, is seven percent. The binding overhang is important, because it reveals how much room a country has to increase tariffs, before hitting the ceiling (*i.e.*, the bound rate). Moreover, if reductions are applied to bound rates — as is typically the case, and as was expected in the Doha Round, then the greater the binding overhang, the steeper the cuts must be in order to affect applied rates. In the

---

[67] *See* Daniel Pruzin, *As Doha Talks Falter, Efforts Get Under Way on Alternative Approaches to Salvage Gains*, 28 International Trade Reporter (BNA) 644 (21 April 2011).

above example, a 50 percent tariff cut to the bound rate of 10 percent would bring the bound rate down to five percent. But, the applied rate could remain where it is, at three percent, resulting in no new, commercially meaningful market access for exporters of the product in question.

## *BIO DIVERSITY TREATY*

The *Convention on Biological Diversity*, done at Rio de Janeiro, 5 June 1992.[68] In contrast to the *Rio Declaration*, the *Bio Diversity Treaty* is a treaty.

A crucial supplementary agreement to the *Convention on Biological Diversity* was adopted on 29 January 2000, called the *Cartagena Protocol on Biosafety*, named after the city in Colombia in which the first meeting took place on the 22 February 1999. The *Protocol* is a sub-agreement to the *Bio Diversity Treaty*. The *Protocol* entered into force on 11 September 2003, addresses concerns genetically modified organisms (GMOs), which the Protocol dubs "Living Modified Organisms," or "LMOs," and the international trade in such organisms. The *Protocol* enforces the precautionary principle in trade, and requires countries to provide information about the LMOs to be traded in an Advance Information Agreement. (AIA). The *Protocol* also requires the establishment of an international Biosafety Clearinghouse to track trade related information about LMOs, and to assist countries in formulating policies for trade, such as labeling requirements for products containing or made from LMOs.

142 countries have ratified the *Cartagena Protocol*. Notably, the United States has not done so. Further, many of America's free trade agreement (FTA) partners have not signed on as well. They include Australia, Canada, Singapore, Morocco, and Israel. Jordan, Mexico, and Oman are among the United States FTA partners that have ratified the Protocol.

All European Union (EU) members have ratified the *Protocol*. On balance, the *Protocol* adopts a European-style approach to GMO issues. In contrast, the United States views labeling requirements, and the allowance of bans on GMOs, as a trade barrier. Undoubtedly, that stance is due to the estimate that perhaps 90 percent of American agricultural exports do or could contain GMOs (depending on the definition of "genetically modified"). Further, in the United States, GM and non-GM products often are stored in the same grain elevators.

The *Cartagena Protocol* is written in Arabic as well as the other five United Nations (U.N.) languages, Chinese, French, English, Russian, and Spanish. Ironically, Russia is not a party to the *Protocol*.

## BIS (FIRST MEANING)

Bank for International Settlements.

---

[68] *See* (UNEP/Bio.Div./N7-INC5/4, *reprinted in* 31 INTERNATIONAL LEGAL MATERIALS 818) and *Agenda 21* (adopted by the United Nations Conference on Environment and Development, 14 June 1992, U.N. Doc. A/CONF.151/26/Rev.1.)

Founded in 1930 as an international organization (in part to deal with war reparations and payments), this body has taken on considerable importance as a forum for leading central banks to debate international financial matters. The BIS is located in Basle, Switzerland.

## BIS (SECOND MEANING)

Bureau of Industry and Security.

Pursuant to the *Export Administration Act*, as amended, the BIS, which is part of the Department of Commerce (DOC), is responsible for licensing commercial goods and technical data that are susceptible to civilian or military use. Dual use goods are set out on the Commerce Control List (CCL), which the BIS maintains. Exportation is illegal unless authorized by a BIS-granted license. Via internal order, on 18 April 2002, the DOC changed the name of its "Bureau of Export Administration" (BXA) to the BIS.

On 17 March 2008, Assistant Secretary for Export Enforcement, Darryl W. Jackson, delivered a Keynote Address at the BIS Export Control Forum 2008 in Newport Beach, California. In that address, Secretary Jackson listed nine principles to which businesses can adhere if they wish to mitigate fines and penalties:[69]

- Performance by the company of a meaningful risk analysis
- Existence of a formal, written compliance program
- Responsibility of senior officials for overseeing the compliance program
- Provision of adequate employee training
- Adequate screening by the company of customers and transactions
- Compliance by the company to recordkeeping requirements
- Existence of an internal system to report violations
- Existence of internal and external reviews and audits, and reporting of results
- Taking of remedial measures in response to violations

*Suggestions for Further Research:*

Article:

1.   Bartlett III, James E., *et al.*, *U.S. Export Controls and Economic Sanctions*, 41 THE INTERNATIONAL LAWYER 215–227 (2007).

## B.I.S.D. (BISD)

Basic Instruments and Selected Documents.

Published by GATT—WTO in annual supplements, BISD contains all GATT panel reports. The first supplement was published in March 1953, and the last one — number 41, vol. 2 — was published in December 1997.

---

[69] The speech is posted at www.bis.doc.gov/complianceandenforcement.

WTO materials are not contained in the BISD series. Rather, they are available on the WTO's website (www.wto.org). WTO panel and Appellate Body reports are also published in Bernan's Annotated Reporter, *World Trade Organization — Dispute Settlement Decisions*. This Reporter is a multi-volume series, with new volumes issued every few months.

## BIT

Bilateral Investment Treaty.

A BIT is an agreement between two countries specifying all of the terms and conditions under which foreign direct investment (FDI) can be undertaken. Often, a BIT includes clauses on choice of law, choice of forum, and dispute resolution, the latter to be conducted through binding international arbitration. Indeed, largely because of the proliferation of BITs in the last decade, an increasing number of investment-related disputes have been resolved through international arbitration, rather than through diplomatic intervention or domestic lawsuits.

BITs almost always include provisions requiring national treatment and most-favored-nation (MFN) treatment of investors and their covered investments, limits on the use of trade-distorting performance requirements (such as requirements that investments achieve a given level of domestic content), adherence to pubic international law principles on expropriation, transparency obligations of prompt publication of investment-related laws and regulations, and the free transfer of capital and other transfers into and out of the host state. The Department of Commerce (DOC) maintains a "model" BIT, the previous version of which was from 2004. The 2004 DOC model text provided for annexes of non-conforming measures that permit flexibility in the application of some of the treaty's core obligations to specific sectors. The United States does not depart from the core obligations of the model text, however.

The United States (as of December 2007) has BITs with 40 countries, ranging from Albania to Uruguay. The United States sometimes requires a BIT as a precursor to a *Trade and Investment Framework Agreement (TIFA)*, and in turn a *TIFA* as a prelude to a free trade agreement (FTA). For example, Jordan signed a BIT with the United States in 1997, a TIFA in 1999, and an FTA on 24 October 2000.

In April 2012, the United States Trade Representative (USTR) and Department of State released a new Model BIT. The 2012 Model BIT, which runs 42 pages, followed a multi-year review of the 2004 text. That review commenced in 2009, and was undertaken by the Subcommittee on Investment of the Advisory Committee on International Economic Policy.

Like its predecessor, the key aim of the 2012 Model BIT was to serve as a foundation for negotiations on FDI, particularly with respect to providing investors with protection from discriminatory treatment and a binding international arbitration mechanism to settle disputes over alleged breaches of the BIT.

For the most part, the 2012 and 2004 Models BITs are similar. Both contain the core elements of guarantees for foreign investors (*e.g.*, most favored nation (MFN) and national treatment), and an investor-state dispute settlement provisions. However, the 2012 Model includes the following innovations:[70]

- Enhanced transparency obligations (*e.g.*, notice and comment and multilateral appellate procedures).

- Enhanced public participation obligations, including with respect to setting standards (*e.g.*, allowing foreign investors to participate in establishing technical regulations).

- Tougher disciplines on preferential treatment of state-owned enterprises (SOEs), including against indigenous innovation policies (which is a form of forced technology transfer whereby a host nation requires purchase, use, or otherwise accords preference to domestically-created technology), and (in a footnote in the BIT) a clarification of the standard for deciding whether a government has delegated governmental authority to an SOE (and thus for deciding whether that SOE is acting under governmental authority and covered by the BIT).

- Stronger protections for labor and the environment, namely, submission of disputes concerning these topics to non-binding government-to-government consultations, an obligation not to "waive or derogate" from domestic laws and to "effectively enforce" those laws, and a reaffirmation and recognition of international commitments on labor and the environment.

Critics such as labor organizations charged that the labor and environmental provisions were meaningless paper commitments, because no binding dispute settlement mechanism applied to them.

The 2012 Model BIT is a basis for American negotiations in the Trans-Pacific Partnership (TPP) negotiations.

*Suggestions for Further Research:*

Books:

1. DOLZER, RUDOLPH & MARGARET STEVENS, BILATERAL INVESTMENT TREATIES (1995).

2. VANDEVELDE, KENNETH J., BILATERAL INVESTMENT TREATIES – HISTORY, POLICY, AND INTERPRETATION (2010).

---

[70] *See* Len Bracken, *USTR, State Department Release 2012 Model for Bilateral Investment Treaties After Review*, 29 International Trade Reporter (BNA) 649 (26 April 2012).

Book Chapters:

1.   Ziegler, Andreas R., *The Nascent International Law on Most-Favoured-Nation (MFN) Clauses in Bilateral Investment Treaties (BITs)*, in European Yearbook of International Economic Law 2010 (C. Hermann & J.P. Terhechte, eds., 2010).

Articles:

1.   Adlung, Rudolf & Martin Molinuevo, *Bilateralism in Services Trade: Is There Fire Behind the (BIT-)smoke?*, 11 Journal of International Economic Law 365-409 (2008).

2.   Alvarez, José, *A BIT on Custom*, 42 New York University Journal of International Law & Politics 17-80 (2009).

3.   Anderer, Carrie E., Note, *Bilateral Investment Treaties and the EU Legal Order: Implications of the Lisbon Treaty*, 35 Brooklyn Journal of International Law 851-882 (2010).

4.   Anderson, Alan M. & Bobak Razavi, *The Globalization of Intellectual Property Rights: TRIPs, BITs, and the Search for Uniform Protection*, 38 Georgia Journal of International & Comparative Law 265-292 (2010)

5.   Chalamish, Efraim, *The Future of Bilateral Investment Treaties: A De Facto Multilateral Agreement?*, 34 Brooklyn Journal of International Law 303-354 (2009).

6.   Chandler, Aaron M., *BITs, MFN Treatment, and the PRC: The Impact of China's Ever-Evolving Bilateral Investment Treaty Practice*, 43 The International Lawyer 1301-1310 (2009).

7.   Chigara, Ben, *European/Southern African Development Community (SADC) States' Bilateral Investment Agreements (BITs) for the Promotion and Protection of Foreign Investments vs. Post-Apartheid SADC Economic and Social Reconstruction Policy*, 10 Journal of International Trade Law and Policy number 3, 213-242 (2011).

8.   Congyan, Cai, *China–U.S. BIT Negotiations and the Future of Investment Treaty Regime: A Grand Bilateral Bargain with Multilateral Implications*, 12 Journal of International Economic Law 457-506 (2009).

9.   Desierto, Diane A., *Necessity and "Supplementary Means of Interpretation" for Non-Precluded Measures in Bilateral Investment Treaties*, 31 University of Pennsylvania Journal of International Economic Law 827-934 (2010).

10.   Deutsch, Richard, *An ICSID Tribunal Denies Jurisdiction for Failure to Satisfy BIT's "Cooling-Off" Period: Further Evidence of a Sea Change in Investor-State Arbitration or a Meaningless Ripple?*, 33 Houston Journal of International Law 589-604 (2011).

11.   Dolzer, Rudolf, *Fair and Equitable Treatment: A Key Standard in Investment Treaties*, 39 The International Lawyer 87-106 (spring 2005).

12. Dumberry, Patrick, *Are BITs' Representing the "New" Customary International Law in International Investment Law?*, 28 PENN STATE INTERNATIONAL LAW REVIEW 675-701 (2010).

13. Elkins, Zachary, Andrew T. Guzman & Beth Simmons, *Competing for Capital: The Diffusion of Bilateral Investment Treaties 1960-2000* (Response by Christoph Engle), 2008 UNIVERSITY OF ILLINOIS LAW REVIEW 265-317 (2008).

14. Footer, Mary E., *Bits and Pieces: Social and Environmental Protection in the Regulation of Foreign Investment*, 18 MICHIGAN STATE JOURNAL OF INTERNATIONAL LAW 33-64 (2009).

15. Henry, Laura, *Investment Agreement Claims Under the 2004 Model U.S. BIT: A Challenge for State Police Powers?*, 31 UNIVERSITY OF PENNSYLVANIA JOURNAL OF INTERNATIONAL ECONOMIC LAW 935-1011 (2010).

16. Johnson, Alec R., Comment, *Rethinking Bilateral Investment Treaties in Sub-Saharan Africa*, 59 EMORY LAW JOURNAL 919-967 (2010).

17. Lehavi, Amnon & Amir N. Licht, *BITs and Pieces of Property*, 36 YALE JOURNAL OF INTERNATIONAL LAW 115-166 (2011).

18. Liu, Han-Wei, *A Missing Part in International Investment Law: The Effectiveness of Investment Protection of Taiwan's BIT vis-à-vis ASEAN States*, 16 UNIVERSITY OF CALIFORNIA DAVIS JOURNAL OF INTERNATIONAL LAW & POLICY 131-169 (2009).

19. Liu, Qiao & Xiang Ren, Transfer of Funds in China – U.S. BIT Negotiations: Comparing the Articles of Agreement of the IMF, 11 JOURNAL OF INTERNATIONAL TRADE LAW AND POLICY 6-27 (2012).

20. Potts, Jonathan B., Note, *Stabilizing the Role of Umbrella Clauses in Bilateral Investment Treaties: Intent, reliance, and Internationalization*, 51 VIRGINIA JOURNAL OF INTERNATIONAL LAW 1005-1045 (2011).

21. Poulsen, Lauge Skovgaard, *The Significance of South – South BITs for the International Investment Regime: A Quantitative Analysis*, 30 NORTHWESTERN JOURNAL OF INTERNATIONAL LAW & BUSINESS 101-130 (2010).

22. Radi, Yannick, *The Application of the Most-Favoured-Nation Clause to the Dispute Settlement Provisions of Bilateral Investment Treaties: Domesticating the "Trojan Horse,"* 18 EUROPEAN JOURNAL OF INTERNATIONAL LAW 757-774 (2007).

23. Salacuse, Jeswald & Nicholas P. Sullivan, *Do BITs Really Work?: An Evaluation of Bilateral Investment Treaties and Their Grand Bargain*, 46 HARVARD INTERNATIONAL LAW JOURNAL 67-130 (2005).

24. Schill, Stephan W., The Robert E. Hudec Article on Global Trade, *Enabling Private Ordering: Function, Scope and Effect of Umbrella Clauses in International Investment Treaties*, 18 MINNESOTA JOURNAL OF INTERNATIONAL LAW 1-97 (2009).

25. Schill, Stephan W., *Multilateralizing Investment Treaties Through Most-Favored-Nation Clauses*, 27 BERKELEY JOURNAL OF INTERNATIONAL LAW 496-569 (2009).

26. Schreiber, William, *Realizing the Right to Water in International Investment Law: An Interdisciplinary Approach to BIT Obligations*, 48 NATURAL RESOURCES JOURNAL 431-478 (2008).

27. Sheffer, Megan Wells, 2009-2010 V.B. Sutton Award: First Place, Note, *Bilateral Investment Treaties: A Friend or Foe to Human Rights?*, 39 DENVER JOURNAL OF INTERNATIONAL LAW & POLICY 483-521 (2011).

28. Steinberg, Andrew B. & Charles T. Kotuby, Jr., *Bilateral Investment Treaties and International Air Transportation: A New Tool for Global Airlines to Redress Market Barriers*, 76 JOURNAL OF AIR LAW & COMMERCE 457-497 (2011).

29. Wong, Jarrod, *Umbrella Clauses in Bilateral Investment Treaties: of Breaches of Contract, Treaty Violations, and the Divide Between Developing and Developed Countries in Foreign Investment Disputes*, 14 GEORGE MASON LAW REVIEW 135-177 (2007).

30. Yackee, Jason Webb, *Pacta Sunt Servanda and State Promises to Foreign Investors before Bilateral Investment Treaties: Myth and Reality*, 32 FORDHAM INTERNATIONAL LAW JOURNAL 1550-1613 (2009).

31. Yackee, Jason Webb, *Do Bilateral Investment Treaties Promote Foreign Direct Investment: Some Hints from Alternative Evidence*, 51 VIRGINIA JOURNAL OF INTERNATIONAL LAW 397-441 (2011).

## BLUE BOX (BLUE BOX EXEMPTION)

Agricultural support that takes the form of production-limiting subsidies is considered "Blue Box" support.

In brief, Blue Box exemptions are permitted support programs linked to production, but are subject to production limits. Such programs, while not as minimal in their effect on trade as Green Box support, are less trade-distorting than Amber Box payments. Put differently, Blue Box support essentially is Amber Box support, but with a limit on production designed to curb over production.

In the Uruguay Round *Agreement on Agriculture*, a government support scheme that is a production-limiting program is exempted from the Aggregate Measure of Support (AMS), so long as certain requirements are fulfilled. As regards crop support, these requirements (as set forth in Article 6:5 of the *Agriculture Agreement*) are that the government calculates payments to farmers on the basis of (1) a fixed area or yield, or (2) 85 percent or less of the base level of production. As regards livestock support, the requirement (also in Article 6:5) for exemption is that the government calculates payments based on a fixed number of head. These exemptions for payments designed to encourage farmers to limit production are called "Blue Box exemptions."

As of the completion of the Uruguay Round (1986–94), no limits on spending exist for the Blue Box. However, during the Doha Round (2001–present), some WTO Members (especially developing and least developed countries) sought caps on Blue Box support. Certain other Members (such as the United States) proposed limits, but also sought a change in the definition of what qualifies for the Blue Box. Under the change, counter-cyclical payments (which compensate a farmer in inverse relation to the extent to which the market price for a commodity falls below a government-set target price) would be included, effectively enlarging the Box.

According to its March 2009 notification, EU Blue Box support totaled €27.2 billion for Marketing Year (MY) 2004–2005, and €13.4 billion for MY 2005–2006. In its January 2011 notification, the EU said Blue Box support declined by nine percent, from €5.7 billion in 2006–2007 to €5.2 billion in 2007–2008.

As for the United States, in MY 2006, $1.49 billion, and in MY 2007, $893 billion. The United States classified countercyclical payments in the Amber Box, yet explained they were *de minimis* and thus exempt from Amber Box reduction commitments.

*Suggestions for Further Research:*

Books:

1.   ANDERSON, KYM & TIM JOSLING, EDS., THE WTO AND AGRICULTURE vols. I and II (2005).

2.   CARDWELL, MICHAEL N., MARGARET R. GROSSMAN & CHRISTOPHER P. RODGERS, AGRICULTURE AND INTERNATIONAL TRADE — LAW, POLICY, AND THE WTO 85-164 (2003).

3.   DESTA, MELAKU GEBOYE, THE LAW OF INTERNATIONAL TRADE IN AGRICULTURAL PRODUCTS — FROM GATT 1947 TO THE WTO AGREEMENT ON AGRICULTURE (2002).

4.   MCMAHON, JOSEPH, THE WTO AGREEMENT ON AGRICULTURE — A COMMENTARY (2006).

Other Source:

1.   Ingco, Merlinda & L. Alan Winters, eds., *Agriculture Trade Liberalization in a New Trade Round — Perspectives of Developing Countries and Transition Economies* (World Bank Discussion Paper Number 418, 2000).

## BOJ

Bank of Japan, the central bank of Japan.

*Suggestions for Further Research:*

Book:

1.   MURPHY, R. TAGGART, THE WEIGHT OF THE YEN — HOW DENIAL IMPERILS AMERICA'S FUTURE AND RUINS AND ALLIANCE (1996).

Other Source:

1.   INSTITUTE FOR MONETARY AND ECONOMIC STUDIES ED., BANK OF JAPAN, FUNCTIONS AND OPERATIONS OF THE BANK OF JAPAN (2004).

## BONN AGREEMENT

A document formalizing the roadmap for a new Afghanistan signed on 5 December 2001 in Bonn, Germany.

The signatories included much of the leadership of Afghanistan, excluding the Taliban. This *Agreement* establishes the Central Bank of Afghanistan, a Human Rights Commission. It also calls for national elections, which occurred on 9 October 2004 for the Presidency, and on 18 September 2005 for a national assembly.

## BOP

Balance of Payments.

The BOP is a summary statement of a country's economic transactions with the rest of the world during a certain period, such as a quarter or a year. As such, it is an account of the amount of money residents of a country have spent abroad, and the amount of money foreigners have spent in the country. Thus, in the most general sense, the BOP provides a picture of the flows of payments coming into, and going out from, a country.

The BOP is presented as a table that depicts the total amounts the country received from the rest of the world, and the total amounts the country spent overseas. There are three basic parts to this table, the (1) current account, (2) capital account, and (3) foreign exchange reserves. Thus, in simple terms,

$$\text{BOP} = \text{Current Account} +$$
$$\text{Capital Account} +$$
$$\text{Foreign Exchange Reserves}$$

For purposes of international trade law and policy, it is the current account that is the focus of attention. Often when a speaker refers to the "BOP," the reference is imprecise — the speaker really means the current account. Or, to be even more precise, the speaker means the balance of trade.

### The Current Account and Trade in Goods

The current account consists of transactions in which the payment is income to the recipient, or put conversely, an expenditure by the payor. This Account captures the money value of "visible" trade, *i.e.*, trade in goods. This portion of the current account is known as the "balance of trade" — the simple tally of exports and imports of goods alone. In an export transaction, the exporter receives income in the amount of the price of the exported good. The import transaction leads to a payment of income from the importer in the amount of the price of the imported good. The balance of trade is also sometimes called the "merchandise trade balance," or just "merchandise balance," reflecting the fact that it covers trade in physical merchandise.

A balance of trade "surplus" results from an excess of visible exports over visible imports. A "deficit" is the reverse. Often, politicians and commentators call a balance of trade surplus "favorable" and a deficit "unfavorable." These normative labels can be unfortunate, and sometimes bespeak a mercantilist approach to trade. Exports are the price residents of a country must pay in order to buy imports, which they desire to consume. Thus, a deficit suggests the residents are obtaining all of the imports they want, and more, and possibly financing the deficit through sales of overseas assets or loans from foreign lenders.

### The Current Account and Trade in Services

The balance of trade is most certainly the most politically significant component of the current account, indeed, of the entire BOP. However, it is hardly the only portion of this account. This account also captures trade in "invisibles," that is, in services. For example, foreigners spend money in a country on tourism, providing income to the tourist service providers. Conversely, the country's residents spend money overseas on tourism, providing income to foreign tourist service providers. Other examples of services traded that are embraced in the current account are banking, insurance, and shipping. Note, however, that the current account does not include official transfers in military goods or services.

In addition, the current account includes two other important items: factor incomes and gifts. Residents of a country typically hold assets overseas, such as financial instruments (stocks and bonds), real estate, and intellectual property rights. They also may have family or friends who hold jobs overseas, *i.e.*, who are migrant workers. And, they may receive pensions based on jobs they once held overseas. The residents receive income in the form of dividends and interest, remittances from migrant workers, and pensions. The dividends, interest, remittances, and pensions received from abroad are counted as inflows in the current account. Conversely, foreigners hold financial instruments, intellectual property rights, and jobs in the country, and thus earn dividends, interest, royalties, wages, and pensions. These income payments flowing out of the country also are included in the country's current account. Thus, the current account includes incomes of various types paid to and from residents in the country. As for gifts, residents of a country receive gifts from overseas, and send gifts overseas. The current account includes these cross-border payments.

In sum, the current account can be represented formulaically as:

Current Account  =  Balance of Trade (trade in "visibles")  +

Trade in Services (trade in "invisibles")  +

Factor Income Received and Remitted  +

Gifts Received and Remitted

A current account "surplus" means that residents of the country have received more than they have spent, *i.e.*, they have exported more goods and services, and received more property income and gifts, than they have spent on imports of goods and services, property, and gifts. Accordingly, there is a net inflow of money. If they have spent more than they have received, then there is a current account "deficit." However, one must be cautious in drawing too strong an inference from an overall current account surplus or deficit. A surplus position may result from a surplus in services trade that dwarfs a deficit in the merchandise trade balance. A deficit position may arise for converse reasons. Or, a deficit may occur in spite of a strong surplus in services trade and in most categories of merchandise trade. Its sources might be narrow, for example, from the United States' perspective, trade with one or two large partners like Japan and China, or a spike in prices in a key sector, like oil. Thus, in dealing with the current account, just as in dealing with the BOP in general, it is critical to disaggregate data and eschew quick, politically-motivated, consequentialist conclusions.

### The Capital Account

The second major category within the BOP is the capital account. Transactions in the capital account do not generate income to the recipient of a payment, *i.e.*, they do not entail an expenditure of the payor. Rather, the transactions represent a change in the form in which an asset is held. A classic example is an extension of credit. A loan is neither income nor expenditure, but a receipt of funds coupled with a promise to repay the principal balance, plus interest, in the future. The capital account, therefore, covers all changes in a country's official and private assets and liabilities with the rest of the world.

There are two basic parts to the capital account. First, it encompasses inward and outward foreign direct investment. Second, it includes sales and purchases of foreign securities by residents of a country, and sales and purchases of securities in that country by non-residents. When the residents sell financial instruments like stocks and bonds to non-residents, or receive loans from abroad, they obtain funds. When the residents buy securities from non-residents, or loan money to non-residents, they expend funds. The capital account balance is, therefore, the difference between receipts from, and expenditures on, capital transactions with the rest of the world.

A capital account surplus could arise because a country's residents sell securities to foreigners, and receive loans from them. The result is an inflow of funds. A capital account deficit could arise because the residents buy securities from foreigners, and make loans to them. The result is an outflow of funds. Thus, notice that the terms "surplus" and "deficit" should not be thought of automatically in normative terms.

By definition, the overall BOP must balance to zero. Thus, in a general formulaic sense,

| BOP | = | (Exports) | – |
| --- | --- | --- | --- |
| | | (Imports) | – |
| | | (Net Services Flows) | – |
| | | (Income Transfers, Remittances, and Gifts) | – |
| | | (Net Investment Flows) | – |
| | | (Net Official Foreign Currency Reserve flows) | |
| | = | 0 | |

Intuitively, the zero balance makes sense: total money inflows should be offset by total money outflows. (The operative word is "total.") Mechanically, the zero balance should result because the BOP table is constructed on the principle of double-entry book-keeping. Every transaction is recorded in two accounts, as a debit (*i.e.*, a decrease in one account) and as a credit (*i.e.*, an increase in another account).

For example, suppose Boeing sells 10 model 777 civilian aircraft to Air India on credit. The first BOP entry is a credit to the current account, specifically, to exports of physical goods. The offsetting entry is a debit entry in the capital account. The debit is a note payable (that is, an IOU) issued by Air India and held by Boeing, reflecting the loan Boeing has made to its customer. When Air India ultimately pays off the note, the debit entry will be reversed, meaning Air India has extinguished the note payable. There will be a corresponding entry to the capital account to show the inflow of funds from Air India. (Any interest income would be shown in the current account, which, of course, shows income, not mere asset and liability dispositions.)

However, it is not necessarily the case — indeed, not usually the case — that the current and capital accounts will balance individually. It may be that a current account surplus/deficit is offset by a capital account deficit/surplus. However, suppose both the current and capital accounts are in surplus or deficit. Then, foreign exchange reserves, the third major component of the BOP, provides the necessary balancing mechanism. Official foreign exchange reserves constitute the amount of foreign currencies held by the central bank (or treasury) of the country. Changes in these reserves equal the sum of the current and capital account balances.

In practice, even changes in foreign exchange reserves do not always result in a perfect balance in the BOP. Typically, discrepancies arise from two sources: unrecorded transactions (*i.e.*, "leakages" that make BOP accounting less than "total"), and lags between the time the movement of goods is recorded, and the time actual payment for goods is made. Consequently, an errors and omissions entry near the bottom of the BOP table is used to ensure a balance. In some years, and for some countries, this entry, sometimes called the "statistical discrepancy," can be stunningly large.

To understand a BOP table requires an understanding of the sign convention used. In the current account, a plus (+) sign means an outflow of goods and services, and a minus (–) sign means an inflow of goods and services. Thus, a plus sign corresponds to a current account surplus, and a minus sign means a deficit.

The sign convention in the capital account is not quite as intuitive. In the capital account, a minus sign connotes an increase in a country's assets, or a decrease in its liabilities. If the country is acquiring assets, then the residents of that country must be paying funds for the assets to foreigners, hence there is an outflow of funds — which justifies the minus sign. In effect, the country exported capital (money) to import assets. If the country is decreasing its liabilities (*e.g.*, paying off loans), then the residents must be doing so by paying funds to foreigners, and the same logic applies. Conversely, a plus sign in the capital account signifies a decrease in the country's holdings of assets (because the residents are selling assets, and thus receiving an inflow of funds from the foreigners to whom they sell the assets), or an increase in its liabilities (because the residents are receiving funds from foreigners). Thus, a negative capital account balance means a deficit, which is to say the country's accumulation of asset holdings and discharge of liabilities generated a net export of funds from the country to the rest of the world. A positive capital account balance means a surplus, i.e., the country received a net inflow of funds from selling assets and acquiring liabilities.

The sign convention for foreign exchange reserves is the same as that for the capital account. A minus sign means an accumulation of official foreign currency reserves, which are paid for by a net outflow of the country's currency. A plus sign means a net inflow of funds generated by the sale of reserves. Again, caution is required before drawing any inferences. A plus sign in this account is not necessarily a "good" thing. It may result from the central bank selling its holdings of foreign currencies in exchange for the local currency in order to prop up the latter. If this foreign exchange intervention is ineffectual — as such interventions often are — the country will have lost precious currency reserves, and the plus sign in the foreign currency account is hardly a blessing.

There is a common theme to the sign convention in the current, capital, and foreign exchange reserve accounts. A plus sign signifies a net inflow of funds denominated in the country's currency. A negative sign means a net outflow of those funds. The difference among the accounts is what gives rise to the flows: income-generating transactions (the current account); changes in asset and liability positions (the capital account); or changes in official holdings of foreign currencies (the foreign exchange reserve account).

*Suggestions for Further Research:*

Book:

1.   QURESHI, ASIF H. & ANDREAS R. ZIEGLER, INTERNATIONAL ECONOMIC LAW ch. 9 (2nd ed. 2007).

## BOP CRISIS

An immediate BOP problem.

A BOP "problem" is meant to connote that foreign exchange reserves held in the central bank of a country are eroding, or that they are being maintained by borrowing from foreign lenders. The situation is not sustainable in the medium or long term. Foreign lenders eventually will become worried about the credit and sovereign risk they are undertaking, and either charge extraordinarily high interest rates, or simply decline to lend new funds. A BOP "crisis" differs from a BOP "problem" in terms of time. A crisis calls for an immediate response, because the erosion in foreign exchange reserves is not sustainable even in the short run, and the exhaustion of borrowing capacity is fast approaching.

As a general rule, a country ought to maintain three months' worth of imports in its foreign exchange reserves. The logic behind the rule is that if export revenues, property income, gifts, sales of securities, and loans were cut off, so that the country had no source of foreign currency, it could pay for essential imports for three months. Presumably, this time would suffice for it to sort out its difficulties.

To resolve a BOP crisis, a country can pursue either or both of two basic strategies: improve the current account, or improve the capital account. (Either or both strategies may be undertaken in connection with a financial assistance package arranged by the IMF. Of course, such packages usually contain a number of politically difficult and controversial conditions.) The country can improve its current account by boosting exports, thus earning precious new foreign exchange reserves. By devaluing its currency, or encouraging a depreciation of the currency, the country will make its exports more attractive to foreign buyers (subject, of course, to the J-curve effect). It also can enter into a recession in domestic activity, for example, by raising interest rates. The recession will force a decline in imports, and again improve the current account. Of course, raising interest rates tends to make a country's currency more attractive to foreign investors (because they get a higher rate of return on interest-earning assets in the country, and thus demand more of the country's currency to buy these assets). A capital account strategy entails attempts to prevent capital flight, and attract capital into the country. An increase in interest rates can assist toward these ends.

*Suggestions for Further Research:*

Article:

1. Thomas, Chantal, *Balance of Payments Crises in the Developing World: Balancing Trade, Finance, and Development in the New Economic Order*, 15 AMERICAN UNIVERSITY INTERNATIONAL LAW REVIEW 1249–1277 (2000).

## BORDER PROTECTION

Any measure designed to restrain imports implemented at a port of entry in an importing country.

Border protection is to be distinguished from an internal regulation on imports, which applies after the imports have undergone customs clearance at the port of entry.

## BOUND RATE

The maximum permissible tariff rate a country may impose on a particular category of merchandise.

The bound rate is a ceiling agreed upon by a country, typically a WTO Member, during the course of multilateral trade negotiations. This ceiling is bound, in the sense the Member must keep its promise not to increase its tariff above the ceiling. Put differently, the promise is a binding one, and thereby affords certainty and predictability to exporters and importers alike. The tariff binding principle is manifest in GATT Article II:1(b), first sentence. That provision states ordinary customs duties (OCD) are bound at levels set forth in the Schedule of Concessions of a Member. Under GATT Article II:1(b), second sentence, other duties and charges (OCD), also are subject to the discipline of a binding.

Significantly, a bound rate may be higher than the applied, or actual, rate of duty. In that scenario, a country has the flexibility to raise (or lower) its applied rate up to the level of the bound rate. Under the WTO *Agreement on Agriculture*, the concept of a binding, and the distinction between bound and actual levels, also applies to the Aggregate Measure of Support (AMS) and Amber Box subsidies.

*Suggestions for Further Research:*

Books:

1.   HODA, ANWARUL, TARIFF NEGOTIATIONS AND RENEGOTIATIONS UNDER THE GATT AND THE WTO (2001).

2.   MATSUSHITA, MITSUO, THOMAS J. SCHOENBAUM & PETROS C. MAVROIDIS, THE WORLD TRADE ORGANIZATION — LAW, PRACTICE, AND POLICY 112–14 (2003).

Articles:

1.   Hawkins, Slayde, Note, *Skirting Protectionism: A GHG-Based Trade Restriction under the WTO*, 20 GEORGETOWN INTERNATIONAL ENVIRONMENTAL LAW REVIEW 427–450 (2008).

2.   Vranes, Erich, *The WTO and Regulatory Freedom: WTO Disciplines on Market Access, Non-Discrimination and Domestic Regulation Relating to Trade in Goods and Services*, 12 JOURNAL OF INTERNATIONAL ECONOMIC LAW 953–987 (2009).

## BOYCOTT

*See* Secondary Boycott.

## BOX

A generic agricultural term referring to any one of three categories of domestic support: "Green Box," "Blue Box," or "Amber Box." The term arises out of, but is not explicitly used in, the Uruguay Round *Agreement on Agriculture*.

## BOX SHIFTING

A term arising in connection with the WTO *Agreement on Agriculture* and Doha Round negotiations that connotes amending a farm support program so that it qualifies for the Green Box, and thereby is exempt from a reduction commitment, but making no change to the actual level of expenditure.

In other words, the nature or terms of a subsidy are modified just enough to move the program from the Amber Box to the Green Box, and thus get the program out from under an obligation to cut it. During the Doha Round, Brazil, India, and other developing countries urged stricter disciplines on the Green Box to avoid box shifting by developed countries. The United States and European Union (EU) resisted this idea, pointing out Green Box programs — such as support for agricultural research, disease control, environmental protection, regional and restructuring assistance, and rural development and infrastructure — are non- or minimally- trade distorting. They also argued stricter Green Box disciplines would undermine current reforms, which are based on Uruguay Round rules.

## BRAIN DRAIN

An economic, political, and cultural phenomenon created as a result of widespread emigration from less desirable to more desirable places to live.

Safety, career opportunities, educational choices, or political voice options, drive people with high or rising levels of human capital, or aspirations thereof, to move. The country from which they depart is deprived of their brain power, and invested in the new country. Africa has been hard hit with wars, political oppression, and crime. Brain drain has been a secondary but prominent effect of the widespread departure of Africans to the United States and Europe.[71]

## BRAZILIAN TRADE POLICY

*See FTAA.*

## BRETTON WOODS (BRETTON WOODS CONFERENCE, BRETTON WOODS AGREEMENT)

*See IMF.*

## BRIC (BRICS, BRIC COUNTRIES)

A grouping of countries initially consisting of Brazil, Russia, India, and China. In April 2011, South Africa joined the group, thus making the acronym "BRICS" logical.[72]

The "BRIC" acronym was coined by Jim O'Neill of the Wall Street investment firm, Goldman Sachs. Goldman Sachs observes:

> If things go right, in less than 40 years the BRICs economies could together be larger than the G-6 in U.S. dollar terms. By 2025, they

---

[71] *See Home, Sweet home-for Some*, THE ECONOMIST, 13 August 2005, at 37–38.
[72] *See* Kathleen E. McLaughlin, *South Africa Seeks New Markets with BRICS Members at Summit*, 28 International Trade Reporter (BNA) 677 (21 April 2011).

could account for over half the size of the G-6. Of the current G-6, only the United States and Japan may be among the six largest economies in U.S. dollar terms in 2050.[73]

*Suggestions for Further Research:*

Book:

1.   O'NEILL, JIM, THE GROWTH MAP — ECONOMIC OPPORTUNITY IN THE BRICS AND BEYOND (New York, New York: Penguin, 2011). *See also* the review of this book, Stefan Wagstyl, *Ten Years on, Where are the Brics?*, FINANCIAL TIMES, 28 November 2011, at 8.

Article:

1.   Leal-Arcas, Rafael, *The European Union vis-à-vis Brazil and India: Future Avenues in Selected Trade Policy Areas*, 7 JOURNAL OF INTERNATIONAL TRADE LAW AND POLICY number 1 6-26 (2008).

## BRICS

*See* BRIC.

## BTA

Border Tax Adjustment.

A levy imposed on imported merchandise to offset a cost incurred by domestic producers of a like product that is not incurred by producer-exporters of that merchandise.

A BTA may be used to pursue a variety of policy objectives by an importing country, including equalizing costs of complying with environmental rules, such as carbon reduction. For example, a BTA might be designed to penalize an exporting country that does not have an emission reduction regime that the importing country deems equivalent to its own. Thus, a BTA might be an effort to push a foreign country to adopt certain rules on policy matters as diverse as the environment and social welfare. Indeed, the latter topic is the subject of a 1952 GATT case, *Belgian Family Allowances. See* II GATT B.I.S.D. (1ˢᵗ Supp.) 59 (1953) (adopted 7 November 1952).

BTAs are highly controversial under the GATT—WTO legal regime, and are viewed with suspicion by free traders as a form of protectionism. That is for good reason. It is difficult to measure equivalence. That is, how does an importing country decide whether a legal regime in a foreign country is equivalent to the desirable one it has? Protectionist lobbies will mitigate in favor of a finding of no equivalence, and thus a levying of the BTA.

---

[73] Dominic Wilson & Roopa Purushothaman, Goldman Sachs Global Economic Paper Number 99, *Dreaming with BRICs: The Data to 2050* (1 October 2003), available at www2.goldmansachs.com/insight/research/reports/99.pdf.

*Suggestions for Further Research*:

Articles:

1. Brink, Ryan Vanden, *Competitiveness Border Adjustments in U.S. Climate Change Proposals Violate GATT: Suggestions to Utilize GATT's Environmental Exceptions*, 21 COLORADO JOURNAL OF INTERNATIONAL ENVIRONMENTAL LAW & POLICY 85-122 (2010).

2. Eichenberg, M. Benjamin, *Greenhouse Gas Regulation and Border Tax Adjustments: The Carrot and the Stick*, 3 GOLDEN GATE UNIVERSITY ENVIRONMENTAL LAW JOURNAL 283–364 (2010).

# BSE

Bovine spongiform encephalopathy, a type of Transmissible Spongiform Encephalopathy (TSE).

BSE is commonly known as "Mad Cow disease." TSE diseases attack the central nervous system and create sponge-like alterations in the brain. They afflict deer, domestic cats, elk, mink — and humans. The most common TSE in humans is Creutzfeldt-Jackob disease (CJD). BSE is ultimately fatal, killing cows within weeks to months, and humans within an average of four and one-half months. It is believed that exposure of humans to BSE can occur by consuming contaminated food, and that the same agent causing BSE also causes a variant CJD (vCJD), which has an average duration of 14 months. (The average ages of victims of CJD and vCJD are 65 and 29, respectively.)

In 1986, in the United Kingdom, BSE was identified for the first time as a neurological disease in cattle. Cases of the disease have been confirmed (as of May 2007) in over 187,000 animals around the world, yet the majority of them (nearly 180,000 head as of July 2007) have been in the United Kingdom. The United States had no confirmed cases until December 2003, when one infected cow was discovered. The infection was traced to Canada. Canada registered its first case in 1993 — the first one in North America — and linked it to a cow imported from the United Kingdom.

Concern about importation of beef containing BSE spawned SPS restrictions, including quarantines and import bans, by a number of countries. Following the December 2003 confirmation of Mad Cow disease in the United States, Japan, Korea, and Mexico all imposed bans. Together these three countries consumed 90 percent of America's beef exports (with Japan and Korea the first and third largest importers, respectively). Hence, the bans dealt a huge blow to the American cattle industry, costing it billions of dollars. Partial re-openings of the markets occurred in December 2005 in Japan (followed there by another closure in January 2006, because of a problematic veal shipment from one American producer, and subsequent re-opening in July 2006, albeit only for animals 20 months or younger), in December 2005 in Korea (for boneless beef from cattle aged 30 months or less, but with frequent rejections by Korean inspectors of American shipments because of the existence of bone chips), and in March 2004 in Mexico (for boxed beef from cattle less than 30 months old, and for all bone-in beef in 2006). These bans created major legal controversies, and implicated Articles 3.3 and 5 of the WTO *Agreement on the Application of Sanitary and Phytosanitary Measures (SPS Agreement)*, which concern scientific justification for protective measures and risk assessment.

The World Organization for Animal Health (OIE) has enacted provisions in its Terrestrial Animal Health Code (Chapter 2.3.13) to address trade related issues involving countries concerned about BSE in beef products. The OIE provides three tiers of risk classification to denote the level of concern about the BSE contamination in a country:

(1) Negligible Risk.

(2) Controlled Risk.

(3) Undetermined Risk.

The OIE updates its list annually, putting each country in the appropriate risk category. Procedurally, a country applies for a particular risk classification, the OIE makes a recommendation, and the OIE General Assembly then adopts (or, potentially, rejects) that recommendation. The OIE standards require an international veterinary certificate be issued for each shipment of beef products attesting to compliance by an applicant country with the standards for their tier of risk (*e.g.*, for the controlled risk category, ante-mortem and post-mortem inspection of cattle and proof beef is free from contamination).

On 22 May 2007, Mike Johanns, former United States Secretary of Agriculture, announced the OIE classified the United States as a "controlled risk country." That classification meant that the regulatory controls of the United States Department of Agriculture (USDA) met with international approval, such that the United States could once again export beef products as long as they meet the standards. In particular, the United States demonstrated it satisfied the requirements for designation as a "controlled risk" for BSE under Article 2:2:13:4 of the Terrestrial Health Code. Those requirements are (1) conduct of a risk assessment to identify historical and current risk factors, (2) establishment of appropriate measures to manage the identified risks, (3) proof of implementation of appropriate surveillance measures, and (4) proper disposition of any Mad Cow cases.

*Suggestions for Further Research:*

Article:

1. Grossman, Margaret Rosso, *Animal Identification and Traceability Under the U.S. National Animal Identification System*, 2 JOURNAL OF FOOD LAW AND POLICY 231 (2006).

Other Source:

1. World Health Organization, *Bovine Spongiform Encephalopathy Fact Sheet* (November 2002), *posted at* www.who.int.

## BTA

The *Bioterrorism Act (BTA)*.

The formal title is the *Public Health Security and Bioterrorism Preparedness and Response Act of 2002* (Public Law 107-188, 12 June 2002, codified at 42 U.S.C §§ 201 *et seq.*). The *BTA* is a complement to the *Homeland Security Act of 2002*, both of which are post-9/11 responses to concerns about terrorist threats.

*Sources for Further Research*:

Article:

1.  Murray, Sean C., *The Bioterrorism Preparedness and Response Act of 2002 Goes to Geneva, or, Would Bioterror Get the Same Treatment as Biotech Under WTO Rules?*, 7 AVE MARIA LAW REVIEW 499–525 (2009).

## BUSINESSEUROPE

Formerly known as the "Confederation of European Business," or by its French acronym, "UNICE," BusinessEurope lobbies on behalf of major sectors of European business on matters of shared interest, including trade issues.

## BUSINESS ROUNDTABLE

An American association comprised of no less than 160 of the chief executive officers (CEOs) of major corporations and is engaged in lobbying on economic issues of national importance, including international trade matters. Member companies, represented by their CEOs, account for roughly one third of the total value of the United States stock markets and over 40 percent of all corporate income taxes paid.

Significantly, in January 2007 the Business Roundtable said it would end its opposition to inclusion of rigorous labor standards in FTAs. The Roundtable probably had little choice if it hoped for passage of trade agreements by Congress. Congressional opposition to FTAs had been mounting, as Americans became more concerned about the impact of these deals on their jobs and wages and sought some kind of a social contract to mitigate the adjustment costs they felt from free trade. Between 2001 and 2004, income of the bottom 90 percent of Americans fell, and all income growth accrued to the wealthiest 10 percent of Americans. Renewal of Presidential fast-track trade negotiating authority (*Trade Promotion Authority*, or *TPA*, which Congress passed in 2001) became in doubt.[74] The November 2006 elections gave the Democrats

---

[74] *See* Eoin Callan & Caroline Daniel, *"Old-School" Democrats Urge Trade Deal*, FINANCIAL TIMES, 31 January 2007, at 4; Eoin Callan & Caroline Daniel, *Business Backs Bush Trade Talks Drive*, FINANCIAL TIMES, 19 January 2007, at 3; Richard Cowden & Rachel McTague, *Frank Wants "Grand Bargain" With Business To Help Increase Wages, Promote Free Trade*, 24 International Trade Reporter (BNA) 41 (11 January 2007).

control of both the House of Representatives and Senate. TPA was not renewed upon its expiry on 30 June 2007.

## BUY AMERICAN (BUY AMERICAN ACT, BUY AMERICAN LEGISLATION)

Legislation that requires a federal, state, or local governmental entity to purchase goods or services from a vendor in the United States.

In 2003, Representative Duncan Hunter (Republican-California), then-Chairman of the House of Representatives Armed Services Committee, proposed a "Buy American" provision in the 2004 defense authorization bill.[75] The provision required the Pentagon to purchase all essential weapons components from American sources whenever possible. The Administration of President George W. Bush and the then-Chairman of the Senate Armed Services Committee, Senator John Warner (Republican-Virginia), criticized the provision.[76] Senator Warner rejected the measure, because he feared it would lead to increased Pentagon costs, as well as the deterioration of trade relationships with allied countries.

The bill passed, with a significantly watered-down version of the "Buy American" provision.[77] The new, weakened version of Congressman Hunter's provision stipulated the Pentagon evaluate the capacity of American manufacturers to produce weapons parts. It designates funds to build up American manufacturers capabilities in the area of weapons components manufacturing and sets up an incentive program that supports the use of American made machine tools. That is, this version eliminated the original requirement that American manufacturers be favored over foreign manufacturers. A compromise permitted the lease of 20 Boeing 767 air-to-air refueling tankers and 80 Boeing aircraft, as opposed to the 100 stipulated in the original provision. This change in the number of aircraft was estimated to equal more than $4 billion in savings to the Pentagon.

Additionally in 2003, the United States was accused of violating the *WTO Agreement on Government Procurement (GPA)* in awarding post-war reconstruction contracts in Iraq to countries allied with the Americans during the Iraq War. European trade officials claimed this favoritism violated the *GPA*.[78] Then-Undersecretary of Commerce for International Trade, Grant Aldonas, denied the accusations. He claimed the contracts were for humanitarian

---

[75] *See Hunter Stands Firm on Buy American Provisions in Defense Authorization Bill*, 20 INTERNATIONAL TRADE REPORTER (BNA) 1822 (6 November 2003).

[76] *See* Marianne Brun-Rovet, *"Buy America" Dropped From US Arms Bill*, FINANCIAL TIMES, 8 November 2003, at 4.

[77] *See Senate OKs '04 Defense Conference Bill After Buy American Provisions Stripped*, 20 International Trade Reporter (BNA) 1905 (20 November 2003).

[78] *See* Tobias Buck & Edward Alden, *Trade Lawyers Pick Over Small Print in Treaty*, FINANCIAL TIMES, 11 December 2003, at 6.

assistance and, therefore, exempt from *GPA* obligations.[79] Aldonas noted keeping costs low were of great concern, and the contracts would be awarded to the most competitive bidders. That would be the case, he said, regardless of whether that bidder was an ally like Britain, or a country like France, an outspoken critic of the American invasion of Iraq.

In the wake of the global economic recession triggered by the 15 September 2008 collapse of Lehman Brothers, the Obama Administration implemented a fiscal stimulus package of approximately $800 billion. The package was officially entitled the *American Economic Recovery and Reinvestment Act*. A key provision of this *Act* contained a "Buy American" provision, albeit one that called for purchasing entities to conform to international legal obligations of the United States. Those obligations would include the *GPA*, plus government procurement provisions in free trade agreements (*FTAs*).

Despite this proviso, the Buy American provision of the Obama stimulus package proved highly controversial with America's trading partners. The provision catalyzed a general concern that it might lead to protectionist measures in other countries. Undeterred, Congress inserted, a second Buy American provision into the *Foreign Manufacturers Legal Accountability Act of 2009*, which President Obama signed.

The United States is not the only country to enact laws that give preference to domestic producers. For example, China has similar indigenous innovation rules that favor domestic Chinese manufactured goods and technology in government procurement schemes.[80] China maintains these rules do not prohibit foreign businesses from competing for government contracts. International businesses counter that the laws set in motion a dangerous protectionist and anti-foreign business trend. Brazil also favors domestic firms in government procurement programs. The Brazilian law gives preference to domestic companies, even if the domestic products are up to 25 percent more expensive than the competing foreign good.[81] Foreign subsidiaries in Brazil and, in some instances, companies operating in *MERCOSUR* countries would also be eligible for this preference.

In October 2011, a group of over 20 American business associations sent a letter to the United States Congress protesting a "Buy American" provision in President Obama's proposed *American Jobs Act* legislation.[82] The letter accused the 2009 *American Recovery and Reinvestment Act* (*ARRA*) of provoking countries like China and Brazil to erect similar barriers. According to the letter, the

---

[79] *See* Joe Kirwin, *Commerce Official Indicates Countries Opposing Iraq War Could Bid on Contracts*, 20 International Trade Reporter (BNA) 769 (1 May 2003).

[80] *See* Kathleen E. McLaughlin, *Chinese Premier Dismisses Complaints by Foreign Firms on Procurement Rules*, 27 International Trade Reporter (BNA) 1386 (16 September 2010).

[81] *See* Ed Taylor, *Brazil's Congress OKs 'Buy Brazil' Law, Gives Clear Preference to Domestic Firms*, 27 International Trade Reporter (BNA) 1853 (2 December 2010).

[82] *See* Rosella Brevetti, *Business Associations Take Aim at Buy American Provisions in Jobs Bill*, 28 International Trade Reporter (BNA) 1648 (13 October 2011).

"Buy American" provision in the proposed legislation was the reason for the recent consideration of similar government procurement measures by the European Commission (EC) and India.

*Suggestions for Further Research*:

Articles:

1.   Nensala, Sondra Bell, *Homeland Security Presidential Directive 12: How HSPD-12 May Limit Competition Unnecessarily and Suggestions for Reform*, 40 PUBLIC CONTRACTS LAW JOURNAL 619–679 (2011).

2.   Turi, Philip G., Note, *Begging Thy Neighbor: Understanding Canada's Limited Options in Resolving "Buy America,"* 35 CANADA — UNITED STATES LAW JOURNAL 237–256 (2011).

## BYRD AMENDMENT

A provision of United States antidumping (AD) and countervailing duty (CVD) law that permitted allocation of AD duties and CVDs to successful petitioners.

In a celebrated 2003 case, the WTO Appellate Body ruled the *Byrd Amendment* was inconsistent with GATT—WTO rules, essentially because it created a (1) financial incentive to file AD actions, and (2) remedy for dumping that went beyond what those rules contemplated.[83] However, theoretically, to the extent the *Byrd Amendment* remedies could be analogized to a victim's compensation fund, returning collected remedial duties to injured domestic plaintiffs, they held some appeal.

After considerable controversy, the United States repealed the *Byrd Amendment*, effective 1 October 2007.

*Suggestions for Further Research:*

Article:

1.   Rus, Tudor N., *The Short, Unhappy Life of the Byrd Amendment*, 10 NEW YORK UNIVERSITY JOURNAL OF LEGISLATION & PUBLIC POLICY 427–443 (2006–2007).

## BXA

Bureau of Export Administration.

The name of this United States Department of Commerce (DOC) body was changed effective 18 April 2002 to the Bureau of Industry and Security (BIS).

---

[83] *See* WTO Appellate Body Report, *United States — Continued Dumping and Subsidy Offset Act of 2000*, WT/DS217/AB/R, WT/DS234/AB/R (adopted 27 January 2003).

# C

## CACO

Central Asian Cooperation Organization.

*See* Central Asian Economic Community.

## CAEC

*See* Central Asian Economic Community.

## CAEMC

The *Central African Economic and Monetary Community, i.e., CEMAC.*

## CAFC

United States Court of Appeals for the Federal Circuit.

*See* Federal Circuit.

## *CAFTA*

*Central American Free Trade Agreement.*

The members of this free trade agreement (FTA) are the United States, Costa Rica, El Salvador, Guatemala, Honduras, Nicaragua, and the Dominican Republic. The inclusion of the Dominican Republic, at a late stage in *CAFTA* negotiations, sometimes gives rise to the acronym "*CAFTA — DR.*" The United States signed *CAFTA* on 5 August 2004, and implemented it effective 1 March 2006.

*Suggestions for Further Research:*

Articles:

1.   Bravo, Karen E., *Regional Trade Arrangements and Labor Liberalization: (Lost) Opportunities for Experimentation?*, 28 SAINT LOUIS UNIVERSITY PUBLIC LAW REVIEW 71-113 (2008).

2.   Byrnes, Stephen J., *Balancing Investor Rights and Environmental Protection in Investor-State Dispute Settlement under CAFTA: Lessons from the NAFTA Legitimacy Crisis*, 8 UNIVERSITY OF CALIFORNIA DAVIS BUSINESS LAW JOURNAL 102–136 (2007).

3.   Coll, Alberto R., *Wielding Human Rights and Constitutional Procedure to Temper the Harms of Globalization: Costa Rica's Battle Over the Central American Free Trade Agreement*, 33 UNIVERSITY OF PENNSYLVANIA JOURNAL OF INTERNATIONAL LAW 461–561 (2011).

4.   Gantz, David A., *Settlement of Disputes Under the Central American — Dominican Republic — United States Free Trade Agreement*, 30 BOSTON COLLEGE INTERNATIONAL & COMPARATIVE LAW REVIEW 331–410 (2007).

5.  Laun, Christina, Note, *The Central American Free Trade Agreement and the Decline of U.S. Manufacturing*, 17 INDIANA INTERNATIONAL AND COMPARATIVE LAW REVIEW 431–465 (2007).

6.  Morreale, Jessica, Comment, *DR — CAFTA: The Siren Song for Improved Labor Standards for Haitians in the Dominican Republic*, 44 UNIVERSITY OF SOUTH FLORIDA LAW REVIEW 707–727 (2010).

7.  Rajkumar, Rahul, *The Central American Free Trade Agreement: An End Run Around the Doha Declaration on TRIPs and Public Health*, 15 ALBANY LAW JOURNAL OF SCIENCE & TECHNOLOGY 433–475 (2005).

8.  Schmidt, Andrea R., Note, *A New Trade Policy for America: Do Labor and Environmental Provisions in Trade Agreements Serve Social Interests or Special Interests?*, 19 INDIANA INTERNATIONAL & COMPARATIVE LAW REVIEW 167–201 (2009).

9.  Speece, Lyndsay D., Comment, *Beyond Borders: CAFTA's Role in Shaping Labor Standards in Free Trade Agreements*, 37 SETON HALL LAW REVIEW 1101–1126 (2007).

10. Stenzel, Paulette L., *Free Trade and Sustainability Through the Lens of Nicaragua: How CAFTA—DR Should be Amended to Promote the Triple Bottom Line*, 34 WILLIAM & MARY ENVIRONMENTAL LAW & POLICY REVIEW 653–743 (2010).

11. Wang, Vivian H.W., Note, *Investor Protection or Environmental Protection? "Green" Development Under CAFTA*, 32 COLUMBIA JOURNAL OF ENVIRONMENTAL LAW 251–286 (2007).

12. Wold, Chris, *Evaluating NAFTA and the Commission for Environmental Cooperation: Lessons for Integrating Trade and Environment in Free Trade Agreements*, 28 SAINT LOUIS UNIVERSITY PUBLIC LAW REVIEW 201–252 (2008).

## *CAFTA–DR*

*Central American Free Trade Agreement*, which includes the Dominican Republic, a Caribbean country.

*See CAFTA.*

## CAIRNS GROUP

A group of 20 countries particularly interested in trade in agriculture.

The countries are net exporters of farm products. In 2004, the Cairns Group accounted for approximately 25 of world agricultural exports. The Cairns Group consists of:

- Argentina
- Australia
- Bolivia
- Brazil
- Canada

- Indonesia
- Malaysia
- New Zealand
- Pakistan
- Paraguay

- Chile
- Colombia
- Costa Rica
- Fiji
- Guatemala

- Peru
- Philippines
- South Africa
- Thailand
- Uruguay

The newest member, Peru, joined in November 2006. Among the members, the largest agricultural exporters are Argentina, Australia, Brazil, Canada, New Zealand, and Thailand.

The Cairns Group was formed in Cairns, Australia, in August 1986 to promote the liberalization of trade in agriculture. Agricultural exports from the Cairns Group countries exceed that of the United States and European Union (EU) combined. The Cairns Group takes a free-trade stance on agricultural products. Neither the United States nor the EU is a member.

The Cairns Group is not the only body advocating free, or freer, trade in agriculture. In August 2003, the month before the Cancún Ministerial Conference, and during the Doha Round of WTO trade negotiations, the Group of 20 (G-20), emerged as a strong advocate. There is some overlap among the membership, though the membership of the G-20 tends to be larger (despite its name) than the Cairns Group, and tends to fluctuate. Most notably, Brazil is both a Cairns Group and G-20 member. Peru was a founding G-20 member, left that Group shortly after its August 2003 founding, and then re-joined in the summer 2006.

## CAN

Community of Andean Nations.

*See* Andean Pact.

## CAP

The Common Agricultural Policy of the European Union (EU).

Article 38 of the 1957 *Treaty of Rome*, which established the European Economic Community (EEC), states

the common market shall extend to agriculture and trade in agricultural products

and further says

the operation and development of the common market for agricultural products must be accompanied by the establishment of a common agricultural policy.

In other words, the founders of the European project understood integration would be impossible if agriculture were omitted. They also were determined to avoid the food shortages of the Depression and Second World War era, and hence made food security a key aim of the CAP. Interestingly, as of May 2008, according to statistics from the World Trade Organization (WTO), the EU is both the largest importer and exporter of food in the world.

Article 39 of the *Treaty of Rome* lays out the objectives of the CAP. They are:

- To *increase agricultural productivity* by promoting technical progress and by ensuring the rational development of agricultural production and the optimum utilization of the factors of production, in particular, labor. This goal implies what is called "Community preference," meaning the favoring of EU farm products over imports. A combination of subsidies and trade protection is used to implement this goal.

- Thus, to ensure a *fair standard of living for the agricultural community*, in particular by increasing the individual earnings of persons engaged in agriculture. This goal sometimes is called "maintaining regional cohesion," meaning taking steps to ensure the long-term viability of rural communities.

- To *stabilize markets*. The goal of "market stabilization" entails subsidies, which traditionally have been linked to production (or non-production), government purchases of food when prices fall, or both.

- To assure the *availability of supplies*. This goal concerns food security, and as a recent corollary, also entails "food wholesomeness," which pertains to ensuring food meets appropriate sanitary and phytosanitary (SPS) measures.

- To ensure that *supplies reach consumers at reasonable prices*.[83] This goal also concerns food security.

The first common market organization (CMO) under the CAP was established in 1962 for cereals and related goods. In 1964, CMOs for milk and other dairy products were set up. The last CMO, for sugar, was set up in 1968. That year is significant, because continental European leaders, led by France's President, General Charles de Gaulle, sought to have the CAP in place before the United Kingdom joined the European Community (EC) in 1973.

Then, and to the present, the United Kingdom inclines toward a more liberalized view of agricultural trade than many continental states, preferring to keep food prices low and thereby bolster the competitiveness of the industrial sector through low labor costs. Presently, the most aggressive advocates for CAP reform along with the United Kingdom are Denmark, Estonia, Netherlands, and Sweden. Depending on the specific issue, the Czech Republic and Germany also incline toward reform.

The highly complex CAP system, involving a web of subsidies, production targets, and marketing mechanisms, often is criticized as protectionist. The system sets production targets and establishes marketing mechanisms in order to manage agricultural trade within the EU and between the EU and the rest of the world.

---

[83] Gerrit Meester, *European Union, Common Agricultural Policy, and World Trade*, 14 KANSAS JOURNAL OF LAW & PUBLIC POLICY 389, 390 (Winter 2005). (emphasis added).

Enlargement of the EU, in addition to effects on world agricultural trade, is a second source of concern surrounding the CAP. The CAP consumes nearly half of the EU budget, but with a greater number of countries in the EU, particularly from Eastern Europe, CAP benefits cannot continue at the same levels without putting severe pressure on EU finances. Enlargement also means the pattern of beneficiaries is changing. Historically, France has been a sizeable net recipient of CAP subsidies, and EU funding generally. From 2012, France is forecast to be a net contributor to the EU budget.[84]

*Suggestions for Further Research:*

Books:

1.   DAUGBJERG, CARSTEN & ALAN SWINBANK, IDEAS, INSTITUTIONS, AND TRADE — THE WTO AND THE CURIOUS ROLE OF EU FARM POLICY IN TRADE LIBERALIZATION (2009).

2.   KRUGMAN, PAUL R. & MAURICE OBSTFELD, INTERNATIONAL ECONOMICS: THEORY AND POLICY 198–200 (4th ed., 1997).

Articles:

1.   Iannettoni, Tim, Note, *Commission Impossible: The Commission of the European Communities' Attempt to Reform the Common Market Organization for Wine*, 19 INDIANA INTERNATIONAL & COMPARATIVE LAW REVIEW 383–418 (2009).

2.   Leibovitch, Emilie H., *European Union Food Law Update: A Special Look at the Treaty of Lisbon and Its Impact on European Agricultural Policy*, 6 JOURNAL OF FOOD LAW & POLICY 139–149 (2009).

3.   Meester, Gerrit, *European Union, Common Agricultural Policy, and World Trade*, 14 KANSAS JOURNAL OF LAW & PUBLIC POLICY 389–412 (Winter 2005).

## CAP-AND-TRADE (FIRST MEANING)

*See* Carbon Leakage.

## CAP-AND-TRADE (SECOND MEANING)

A radical approach to balancing a trade deficit, advocated by famed billionaire investor of Omaha, Nebraska, Warren Buffet.

The essence of the approach is that an importer of merchandise into a country with a trade deficit, such as the United States, would not be permitted to import that merchandise unless it found an equivalent value of merchandise that is being exported. Key details would include the time period during which the imports and exports would have to coincide.

---

[84] *See* Ben Hall & John Thornhill, *Paris for "Protection, Not Protectionism,"* FINANCIAL TIMES, 25 October 2007, at 2.

*Suggestions for Further Research:*

Article:

1.   Chapman, James, *Linking a United States Greenhouse Cap-and-Trade System and the European Union's Emissions Trading Scheme*, 11 VERMONT JOURNAL OF ENVIRONMENTAL LAW 45–106 (2009).

## CAPABILITY DEPRIVATION

*See* Development as Freedom.

## CAPACITY CONSTRAINT

A limitation on the extent to which a benefit can be realized because of an organizational, structural, or resource impediments.

For example, least developed countries tend to lack sufficient legal resources, in the form of international trade lawyers, to participate effectively in trade negotiations and take advantage of provisions in trade agreements. As another example, some countries lack sufficient teachers for primary, secondary, or tertiary levels. Thus, even if every pupil were funded to go to school, they would not have enough teachers.

*Suggestions for Further Research:*

Article:

1.   Conti, Joseph A., *Learning to Dispute: Repeat Participation, Expertise, and Reputation at the World Trade Organization*, 35 LAW & SOCIAL INQUIRY 625–662 (2010).

## CAPITAL ACCOUNT

*See* BOP.

## CAPTIVE PRODUCTION

A term associated with antidumping (AD) and countervailing duty (CVD) law, specifically, the injury investigation of some AD or CVD cases.

"Captive production" refers to a domestic like product that does not compete directly with imports of merchandise subject to an investigation (subject merchandise). Rather, captive production is consumed by the same producer of the product, or by an affiliate of that producer, as in a vertically-integrated commercial chain. The captively consumed product is an input into a finished or derivative article, or a more advanced version of the product.

At issue is whether captive production should be included in the denominator of the Import Penetration Ratio, or whether an administering authority should focus on the merchant market for the domestic like product. In the merchant market, the like product competes directly with subject merchandise imports.

That is because merchandise typically is sold by respondent producer-exporters to independent buyers in the merchant market.

Neither the WTO *Antidumping Agreement* (Articles 3-4) nor GATT (Article VI) addresses the issue. American trade remedy law, however, does address the matter. Under United States AD and CVD law, the ITC must focus on the merchant market, if certain conditions are met. Specifically, Section 222(b)(2) of the *1994 Uruguay Round Agreements Act* (codified at 19 U.S.C. § 1677(7)(C)(iv)) directs the ITC to focus primarily on the merchant market, if the ITC finds:

(1) a domestic like product that is produced internally and consumed captively in a downstream article does not enter the merchant market for that product, *i.e.*, it does not compete with subject merchandise imports,

(2) the domestic like product is the predominant material input in making the downstream article, and

(3) the domestic like product sold in the merchant market is not generally used to make the downstream article (*i.e.*, the converse of the first condition).

The leading WTO case on captive production is *United States — Anti-Dumping Measures on Certain Hot-Rolled Steel Products from Japan*, WT/DS184/AB/R (adopted 23 August 2001).

In the *Japan Hot-Rolled Steel* case, the Appellate Body agreed with the United States that its statute did not constitute a *prima facie* violation of GATT–WTO obligations. *See*. Essentially, that is because the statute (and the Clinton Administration Statement of Administrative Action for the Antidumping Agreement) directs the International Trade Commission (ITC) to focus "primarily," but not "exclusively," on the merchant market. However, Japan prevailed in showing the ITC — in the case at bar — had focused exclusively on the merchant market, and thereby applied the statute in a manner inconsistent with Articles 3:1 and 3:4 of the WTO *Antidumping Agreement*.

## CARBON LEAKAGE

The problem of a firm that shifts its production facility to a low-regulation jurisdiction in response to new environmental regulations aimed at curbing carbon emissions associated with the product that firm manufactures.

To illustrate, suppose the United States applies tougher regulations to an industry to reduce carbon emissions that occur from the operation of that industry, and use low-carbon technology in their activities. Firms in that industry then shift to China, which (by hypothesis) does not adopt the same stringent regulations. Nothing has been accomplished by the new American regulations, in terms of global carbon emissions. Less carbon is emitted from manufacturing operations in the United States, but more emissions come from China. In other words, the American regulations have shifted the location of emission of carbon, but not the aggregate amount of emissions. The same result occurs even if China applies the same regulations, but does not enforce them.

The problem of carbon leakage is an example of how climate change has become a trade issue. Among the suggested resolutions are (1) a multilateral environmental agreement (MEA) on carbon emissions, (2) taxation of imports based on the carbon emitted to produce those imports, *i.e.*, a carbon tax, or (3) a cap-and-trade regime, whereby countries cap the amount of carbon emissions permitted per industry or firm, but then allow a secondary market for trading permits to emit more than an allocated cap. Note that the second solution raises concerns under GATT Article II, namely, the possible breach of bound tariff levels. It also raises an obvious difficulty under Article I:1, the most-favored nation (MFN) obligation, because imports from countries that did not comply with specified requisites would be targeted for unfavorable tariff treatment. Nonetheless, in March 2009, Steven Chu, the United States Secretary of Energy in the Administration of President Barack H. Obama, declared he personally could support a tariff on products imported from countries that refuse to cut their emissions of greenhouse gases.[85] The carbon tax would help American firms compete internationally against foreign counterparts that are not subject to carbon-reducing environmental regulations, and avoid the need for them to escape the regulations by transferring their operations offshore.

One proposal, made by Gary C. Hufbauer, Steve Charnovitz & Jisun Kim in their 2009 book *Global Warming and the World Trading System*, is for a plurilateral agreement among the 10 largest greenhouse gas emitters, including the United States, European Union (EU), China, Japan, and Russia. They would negotiate a "Code of Good WTO Practice on Greenhouse Gas Emissions Controls." While doing so, they would agree to a "Peace Clause" that would prevent them from applying any trade restrictive measures, either at the border or extraterritorially, against imports. Thus, unilateral actions like border taxes or import bans would be precluded during the period in which the countries bargained over a framework. The goal of the framework — the "Code" — would be to give each country the policy space it needs to establish and implement climate control legislation, and ensure its new rules comport with WTO standards.

*Suggestions for Further Research:*

Book:

1.  HUFBAUER, GARY C., STEVE CHARNOVITZ & JISUN KIM, GLOBAL WARMING AND THE WORLD TRADING SYSTEM (2009).

Articles:

1.  Angelo, Mary Jane, *Corn, Carbon, and Conservation: Rethinking U.S. Agricultural Policy in a Changing Global Environment*, 17 GEORGE MASON LAW REVIEW 593–660 (2010).

---

[85] *See* Lynn Garner, *Carbon Tariff Could Help U.S. Business Compete Globally, Says Secretary Chu*, 26 International Trade Reporter (BNA) 276 (19 March 2009).

2.   Bennett, Lisa, Note, *Are Tradable Carbon Emissions Credits Investments? Characterization and Ramifications Under International Investment Law*, 85 New York University Law Review 1581–1617 (2010).

3.   Brink, Ryan Vanden, *Competitiveness Border Adjustments in U.S. Climate Change Proposals Violate GATT: Suggestions to Utilize GATT's Environmental Exceptions*, 21 Colorado Journal of International Environmental Law & Policy 85–122 (2010).

4.   Charnovitz, Steve, *Reviewing Carbon Charges and Free Allowances Under Environmental Law and Principles*, 16 ILSA Journal of International & Comparative Law 395–412 (2010).

5.   Childs, J. Scott, *Continental Cap-and-Trade: Canada, the United States, and Climate Change Partnership in North America*, 32 Houston Journal of International Law 393–457 (2010).

6.   Condon, Bradly J., *Climate Change and Unresolved Issues in WTO Law*, 12 Journal of International Economic Law 895–926 (2009).

7.   Eichenberg, M. Benjamin, *Greenhouse Gas Regulation and Border Tax Adjustments: The Carrot and the Stick*, 3 Golden Gate University Environmental Law Journal 283–364 (2010).

8.   Ezroj, Aaron, *How Cap and Trade Will Fuel the Global Economy*, 40 Environmental Law Reports, News & Analysis 10696–10705 (2010).

9.   Feng, Lin & Jason Buhi, *Emissions Trading Across China: Incorporating Hong Kong and Macau into an Urgently Needed Air Pollution Control Regime Under "One Country, Two Systems,"* 19 Journal of Transnational Law & Policy 123–177 (2009).

10.   Hornstein, Donald T., *The Environmental Role of Agriculture in An Era of Carbon Caps*, 20 Health Matrix 145–174 (2010).

11.   Hsu, Shi-Ling, *A Prediction Market for Climate Outcomes*, 83 University of Colorado Law Review 179–256 (2011).

12.   Johnson, Lise, *International Investment Agreements and Climate Change: The Potential for Investor-State Conflicts and Possible Strategies for Minimizing It*, 39 Environmental Law Reports, News & Analysis 11147–11160 (2009).

13.   Liang, Mark, Comment, *Green Taxes and the WTO: Creating Certainty for the Future*, 10 Chicago Journal of International Law 359–388 (2009).

14.   McAllister, Lesley K., *The Overallocation Problem in Cap-and-Trade: Moving Toward Stringency*, 34 Columbia Journal of Environmental Law 395–445 (2009).

15.   McKenzie, Michael, *Emissions Reduction Policies of the World Trade Organization*, 13 Asia Pacific Journal of Environmental Law 61–73 1423–1471 (2010).

16.   McLure Jr., Charles E., *The GATT-Legality of Border Adjustments for Carbon Taxesand the Cost of Emissions Permits: A Riddle, Wrapped in a Mystery, Inside an Enigma*, 11 Florida Tax Review 221–294 (2011).

17. Metcalf, Gilbert E. & David Weisbach, *The Design of a Carbon Tax*, 33 HARVARD ENVIRONMENTAL LAW REVIEW 499–556 (2009).

18. Moore, John N. & student Kale Van Bruggen, *Agriculture's Fate Under Climate Change: Economic and Environmental Imperatives for Action*, 86 CHICAGO-KENT LAW REVIEW 87–108 (2011).

19. Nanda, Ved P., *Climate Change and Developing Countries: The International Law Perspective*, 16 ILSA JOURNAL OF INTERNATIONAL & COMPARATIVE LAW 539–556 (2010).

20. Ozbirn, Jasper L., *The Climate Security Act of 2008 and Other Carbon-Based Trade Restrictions: Are They Legal Under International Law?*, 7 LOYOLA UNIVERSITY CHICAGO INTERNATIONAL LAW REVIEW 53–71 (2009).

21. Payne, Cymie, *Local Meets Global: The Low Carbon Fuel Standard and the WTO*, 34 NORTH CAROLINA JOURNAL OF INTERNATIONAL LAW & COMMERCIAL REGULATION 891–917 (2009).

22. Quinn, Elias Leake, Comment, *The Solitary Attempt: International Trade Law and the Insulation of Domestic Greenhouse Gas Trading Schemes from Foreign Emissions Credit Markets*, 80 UNIVERSITY OF COLORADO LAW REVIEW 201–254 (2009).

23. Spence, Samara, Note, *Three Structural Changes for a New System of International Climate Change Mitigation Agreements Based on the WTO Model*, 44 VANDERBILT JOURNAL OF TRANSNATIONAL LAW 1415–1455 (2011).

24. Veel, Paul-Erik, *Carbon Tariffs and the WTO: An Evaluation of Feasible Policies*, 12 JOURNAL OF INTERNATIONAL ECONOMIC LAW 749–800 (2009).

25. Zane, Steven Nathaniel, Note, *Leveling the Playing Field: The International Legality of Carbon Tariffs in the EU*, 34 BOSTON COLLEGE INTERNATIONAL & COMPARATIVE LAW REVIEW 199–225 (2011).

26. Zeller, Bruno, *Systems of Carbon Trading*, 25 TOURO LAW REVIEW 909–942 (2009).

27. Zeller, Bruno, *Uniform Emissions Trading or Tax Schemes: Has the Genie Been (Finally) Let Out of the Bottle?*, 2 ELON LAW REVIEW 57–86 (2011).

## *CARTAGENA PROTOCOL*

*See Bio Diversity Treaty.*

## CARGO MANIFEST

A list of the contents of a shipment of goods (or people, in which case the cargo manifest is called the "passenger list.")

A cargo manifest is used in international air, land, rail, and sea transport. The manifest serves as a security check, for example, to ensure cargo is not dangerous. Different requirements may be imposed by an importing country to the cargo manifests of vessels, based on the originating country of that vessel (*i.e.*, the country in which the vessel is registered). For example, the United States imposes stiffer requirements, in the form of a complete cargo manifest, on vessels registered in Iran, regardless of the origin of the cargo, whereas a French vessel may provide a less-than-complete manifest. This differential could constitute a violation of the MFN obligation, yet possibly be justified on national security grounds. The list of countries to which stiffer requirements are applied is published at 19 C.F.R. Section 4.75. However, as of July 2006, this list had not been updated, and includes countries that no longer exist, like Czechoslovakia, the German Democratic Republic, and Union of Soviet Socialist Republics (U.S.S.R.).

## CARICOM

The Caribbean Community, consisting of 15 Caribbean countries: Antigua and Barbuda, Bahamas, Barbados, Belize, Dominica, Grenada, Guyana, Haiti, Jamaica, Monteserrat, St. Kitts-Nevis, St. Lucia, St. Vincent and the Grenadines, Surinam, and Trinidad and Tobago.

*CARICOM* members vary tremendously in their levels of development: in 1999, *per capita* income in Barbados was $7,500, three times that of Jamaica, and 30 times that of Haiti.

*CARICOM* was established by the *Treaty of Chaguaramas*, signed on 4 July 1973. The 1973 *Treaty* founding *CARICOM* did not provide for the free movement of capital and labor, bilateral investment agreements, intellectual property protection, or liberalization of trade in services. However, while *CARICOM* delayed its planned creation of a single currency, it sought to forge a veritable regional common market by the end of 2000. Toward that end, in 1989, the *CARICOM* heads of government decided to transform their budding common market into a single market and economy, in which factors would move freely to produce goods and provide services. That decision resulted in a report by the West Indian Commission, and creation in 1992 of an Inter-Governmental Task Force (IGTF) to consider how to revise the 1973 *Treaty*.

The IGTF, comprised of representatives of all the CARICOM countries, produced nine protocols between 1993 and 2000, all with a view to amending the *Treaty*. For example, by 1999 *CARICOM* members had re-written sections of the *Treaty* to deal with these matters. In 2000, a Caribbean Court of Justice was created to handle cases on economic matters, including trade disputes. The protocols were combined into a new version of the *Treaty*, which formally is entitled the *Revised Treaty of Chaguaramas Establishing the Caribbean Community, Including the CARICOM Single Market Economy*. The *Revised Treaty* — was signed on 5 July 2001.

Presently, a customs union (CU) is in place, with common tariffs on imports from third countries. *CARICOM* members are concerned that if they do not form a successful common market, they will be unable to deal effectively with blocs like the *North American Free Trade Agreement* (*NAFTA*) and *MERCOSUR*, and they will be ill-positioned in negotiations for a *Free Trade Area of the Americas* (*FTAA*). The *CARICOM* Secretariat is located in Georgetown, Guyana.

*Suggestions for Further Research:*

Article:

1.   Bravo, Karen E., *Regional Trade Arrangements and Labor Liberalization: (Lost) Opportunities for Experimentation?*, 28 SAINT LOUIS UNIVERSITY PUBLIC LAW REVIEW 71–113 (2008).

## CARRY FORWARD

A situation involving a quota system where an exporting country uses in the current year part of its quota allotment assigned to the subsequent year.

## CARRY OVER

A situation involving a quota system where an exporting country uses in the current year its unutilized quota allotment from the past year.

## CARRY TRADE

A carry trade is where an investor converts a low-interest yen into a higher-yielding foreign asset.

Among international financial investors, very low interest rates in Japan, relative to other countries, have led to a controversial practice known as "carry trades." Essentially, an investor borrows money in Japan, denominated in yen, at just 0.5 percent. The investor then takes that money, converts it into another currency — for example, New Zealand (NZ) dollars. Then, with the NZ dollars, the investor purchases a financial asset in New Zealand (*e.g.*, a kiwi bond). The spread (difference) in the returns between the New Zealand asset and a Japanese asset (*e.g.*, a Japanese bond), which the investor could have bought, is great. (For example, as of March 2007, a long-term Japanese government bond pays only 1.7 percent.) The cost of carrying the Japanese debt is small (again, 0.5 percent). Thus, the currency risk (the balance sheet mismatch between having an asset denominated in NZ dollars but a liability in yen) is acceptable.

Carry trades are controversial because (*inter alia*) of the currency risk. If relative rates of interest (on liabilities) or returns (on assets) change, there could be considerable financial market turmoil, even a global crisis.

## CASH DEPOSIT RATE

Also called the "Estimated Antidumping Duty Deposit Rate, or "Estimated AD Duty Deposit Rate," it is the AD duty rate for which an importer of subject merchandise is liable, which applies to all future entries of subject merchandise from an exporter unless and until an Administrative (Periodic) Review occurs. *See* Administrative Review, Retrospective assessment.

## CBERA

The *Caribbean Basin Economic Recovery Act of 1983*, which is the trade component of the *Caribbean Basin Initiative (CBI)*.

Under *CBERA*, the President is authorized to proclaim duty-free treatment for eligible articles from designated beneficiary Caribbean countries and dependent territories. The countries designated as beneficiaries from the CBI program, and thus the ones that potentially may benefit from trade preferences, are:

- Antigua and Barbuda
- Aruba
- Bahamas
- Barbados
- Belize
- British Virgin Islands
- Costa Rica
- Dominica
- Dominican Republic
- El Salvador
- Grenada
- Guatemala
- Guyana
- Haiti
- Honduras
- Jamaica
- Montserrat
- Netherlands Antilles
- Nicaragua
- Panama
- St. Kitts and Nevis
- St. Lucia
- St. Vincent and the Grenadines
- Trinidad and Tobago

The *Act* was expanded in 1990 and amended in May 2000. The 2000 amendment was called the *United States — Caribbean Trade Partnership Act (CBTPA)*, which was a part of the *Trade and Development Act of 2000*. (A different component of the *Trade and Development Act* established preferences for Sub-Saharan Africa, under the *African Growth and Opportunity Act (AGOA)*). The *CBTPA* entered into force on 1 October 2000.

The *CBTPA* remains in effect until 30 September 2008, or an alternative date, if sooner, on which a free trade agreement (FTA) takes effect between the United States and a *CBTPA* country, or a *Free Trade Area of the Americas (FTAA)* is established. The FTA termination criteria affect the countries that are members of the *Central American Free Trade Agreement (CAFTA)*.

*Suggestions for Further Research:*

Article:

1. Wilson, Darryl C., *The Caribbean Intellectual Property Office (CARIPO): New, Useful, and Necessary*, 19 MICHIGAN STATE JOURNAL OF INTERNATIONAL LAW 551–588 (2011).

## CBI (FIRST MEANING)

The *Caribbean Basin Initiative*, an ongoing initiative created under the 1983 *Caribbean Basin Economic Recovery Act* (*CBERA*), and expanded under the *Caribbean Basin Trade Partnership Act* (*CBTPA*).

The purpose of the *CBI* is to facilitate economic development and export diversification among the Caribbean Basin economies. *CBI* preferences, as enlarged by *CBTPA*, were set to expire on 30 September 2008. Via the 2007 Farm Bill, the *CBTPA* was extended through 30 September 2010.

*Suggestions for Further Research:*

Articles:

1.   Anderson, Hon. Justice Winston, *The Caribbean Agricultural Health and Food Safety Agency: Implications for Regional and International Trade*, 12 VERMONT JOURNAL OF ENVIRONMENTAL LAW 253–273 (2011).

2.   Wilson, Darryl C., *The Caribbean Intellectual Property Office (CARIPO): New, Useful, and Necessary*, 19 MICHIGAN STATE JOURNAL OF INTERNATIONAL LAW 551–588 (2011).

## CBI (SECOND MEANING)

Confederation of British Industry.

The largest employer group in the United Kingdom. The CBI, established by Royal Charter in 1965, is a not-for-profit organization and the premiere lobbying organization for businesses in the United Kingdom.

## CBD

*See Bio Diversity Treaty.*

## CBP

The United States Customs and Border Protection, formerly known as the "Customs Service."

Effective 1 March 2003, the United States Customs Service was renamed the United States Bureau of Customs and Border Protection pursuant to the *Homeland Security Act of 2002*, Pub. L. No. 107-296, § 1502, 116 Stat. 2135, 2308-09 (2002). The entity was transferred from the Department of the Treasury to the Department of Homeland Security (DHS).

*Suggestions for Further Research:*

Articles:

1.   Sajdak, Jeffrey, *Protecting and Collecting the Revenue: Pressing Issues United States Customs and Border Protection faces in a Time of Economic Recovery*, 19 TULANE JOURNAL OF INTERNATIONAL & COMPARATIVE LAW 619–625 (2011).

2.   Williams, Kevin & Lexia B. Krown, *United States v. UPS Customhouse Brokerage, Inc.: The Status of Remedies under the CBP Broker Penalty Statute*, 19 TULANE JOURNAL OF INTERNATIONAL & COMPARATIVE LAW 487–504 (2011).

3.   *The Canada — United States Customs Transaction — The Invisible Border?*, 36 CANADA — UNITED STATES LAW JOURNAL 237–259 (2011) (presentations by various speakers).

## CCC (FIRST MEANING)

The Customs Cooperation Council, created by an agreement signed on 15 December 1950, which entered into force on 4 November 1952. Located in Brussels, Belgium, the CCC is responsible for developing the HTS. Following the Uruguay Round, the CCC was renamed the World Customs Organization (WCO).

## CCC (SECOND MEANING)

Commodity Credit Corporation.

The CCC is a division within the United States Department of Agriculture (USDA). The CCC is responsible (*inter alia*) for various domestic agricultural subsidy programs (*e.g.*, direct payments), and export credits and export credit guarantees. Technically, the CCC has no employees. Rather, its operations are conducted by officials employed within other divisions. For instance, the Farm Service Agency (FSA) handles the domestic subsidy operations of the CCC.

More specifically, the CCC is a United States government-owned corporation established to facilitate loans and payments to farmers who may need financial assistance due to the specific economic conditions associated with farming. The CCC was established on 17 October 1933, by President Franklin D. Roosevelt, via Executive Order 6340 (16 October 1933). Responding to the Great Depression, President Roosevelt sought to help stabilize and support farm commodity prices and balance level of commodities produced. The CCC is housed in the USDA.

Ever since 1933, the CCC has operated as a financing institution for American farmers to help them market crops domestically and internationally. Interestingly, the CCC has no staff of its own. Its operations are conducted through the USDA FSA. Foreign Food Aid also flows from the CCC, but through the Foreign Agricultural Service (FAS). Notably, the FSA and FAS report to a single agency of the USDA, namely, the Farm and Foreign Agricultural Service Agency (FFAS). The FFAS is headed by an Under Secretary of Agriculture. Most United States government farm support (subsidy) programs are funded through the CCC.

## CCL

Commerce Control List.

Pursuant to the *Export Administration Act*, the Bureau of Industry and Security (BIS) of the Department of Commerce is responsible for licensing commercial goods and technical data that are susceptible to civilian or military use. Dual use goods are set out on the Commerce Control List (CCL), which the BIS maintains. Exportation is illegal unless authorized by a BIS-granted license.

*See* BIS.

## CEC

The *NAFTA* Commission for Environmental Cooperation.

The CEC was established under Article 10:6(b) of the *North American Agreement on Environmental Cooperation*, which is the Environmental Side Agreement to the *North American Free Trade Agreement* (*NAFTA*). The Article directs the CEC to consider, on an ongoing basis, the environmental effects of *NAFTA*.

*Suggestions for Further Research:*

Articles:

1. Gaines, Sanford E., *Environmental Protection in Regional Trade Agreements: Realizing the Potential*, 28 SAINT LOUIS UNIVERSITY PUBLIC LAW REVIEW 253–271 (2008).

2. Wold, Chris, *Evaluating NAFTA and the Commission for Environmental Cooperation: Lessons for Integrating Trade and Environment in Free Trade Agreements*, 28 SAINT LOUIS UNIVERSITY PUBLIC LAW REVIEW 201–252 (2008).

## *CEFTA*

*Central European Free Trade Agreement*, established in Krakow, Poland, on 21 December 1992 by the former Czechoslovakia (now two countries, the Czech Republic and Slovakia), Hungary, and Poland.

The *CEFTA* entered into force on 1 March 1993. The membership has expanded considerably, to include not only the Czech Republic, Hungary, Poland, Slovakia, but also Slovenia (in 1996), Romania (in 1997), Bulgaria (in 1999), Croatia (in 2003), Macedonia (in 2006). New members added (also in 2006) are Albania, Bosnia & Herzegovina, Moldova, Montenegro, Serbia, and UNMIK/Kosovo.

The original purpose of *CEFTA* was to prepare member countries for accession to the European Union (EU). This purpose remains one of the aims of *CEFTA*. Accordingly, the goal of *CEFTA* was to establish a FTA by 2001. In respect of industrial products, that goal nearly was complete by the fall of 1997. Tariffs on most such goods had been eliminated by then, and remaining tariff barriers fell in January 2000. However, progress on lowering trade barriers on farm products is slow, because the *CEFTA* members seek to protect their fragile agricultural sectors from foreign competition. Moreover, *CEFTA's* trade-creation potential is circumscribed by the tendency of its members to trade more with the EU than with each other.

Indeed, with several *CEFTA* countries now EU members, query whether, and to what extent, *CEFTA* remains commercially or legally meaningful. In 2004, the Czech Republic, Hungary, Poland, and Slovakia joined the EU, and thus ended their participation in *CEFTA*. As of 1 January 2007, with the accession of Bulgaria and Romania to the EU, the remaining members of *CEFTA* are the Western Balkan states plus Moldova. The Table below summarizes accession to and exit from *CEFTA*.

TABLE:
*CEFTA* ENTRY AND EXIT

| Country | Date of Signing of CEFTA Accession Agreement | Date of Application of CEFTA Accession | Date of Leaving CEFTA for EU | CEFTA Member as of 1 January 2007? |
|---|---|---|---|---|
| Czech Republic | 21 December 1992 | 1 March 1993 | 1 May 2004 | No |
| Slovakia | 21 December 1992 | 1 March 1993 | 1May 2004 | No |
| Poland | 21 December 1992 | 1 March 1993 | 1 May 2004 | No |
| Hungary | 21 December 1992 | 1 March 1993 | 1 May 2004 | No |
| Slovenia | 25 November 1995 | 1 January 1996 | Not applicable | Yes |
| Romania | 12 April 1997 | 1 July 1997 | 1 January 2007 | No |
| Bulgaria | 17 July 1998 | 1 January 1999 | 1 January 2007 | No |
| Croatia | 5 December 2002 | 1 March 2003 | Not applicable | Yes |
| Macedonia | 27 February 2006 | 24 August 2006 | Not applicable | Yes |
| Albania | 19 December 2006 | 1 May 2007 | Not applicable | Yes |
| Bosnia & Herzegovina | 19 December 2006 | 1 May 2007 | Not applicable | Yes |

TABLE (continued)

| Country | Date of Signing of CEFTA Accession Agreement | Date of Application of CEFTA Accession | Date of Leaving CEFTA for EU | CEFTA Member as of 1 January 2007? |
|---|---|---|---|---|
| Moldova | 19 December 2006 | 1 May 2007 | Not applicable | Yes |
| Montenegro | 19 December 2006 | 1 May 2007 | Not applicable | Yes |
| Serbia | 19 December 2006 | 1 May 2007 | Not applicable | Yes |
| UNMIK/ Kosovo | 19 December 2006 | 1 May 2007 | Not applicable | Yes |

## CEMAC

The Economic and Monetary Community of Central Africa. *"CEMAC"* stands for the French appellation *Communauté Économique et Monétaire d'Afrique Centrale. CEMAC* was established in March 1994 by a treaty among six members of the Central African Economic and Customs Union (known as "UDEAC," its French acronym). *UDEAC* was founded in December 1964 by the *Brazzaville Treaty*, and became operational on 1 January 1966. The 1964 *Brazzaville Treaty* was revised in 1974.

Under *CEMAC*, the member states have pledged to promote sub-regional integration and form an economic and monetary union. Under *CEMAC*, the member states — which share a common currency, the CFA franc — have pledged to promote sub-regional integration and form an economic and monetary union. In 1994, *CEMAC* successfully introduced quota restrictions and reductions in the range and amount of tariffs. *CEMAC* is not one of the fundamental regional economic communities (RECs) of the African Economic Community (AEC). But, the CEMAC members are associated with the AEC through the Economic Community of Central African States (ECCAS). The 6 *CEMAC* (and *UDEAC*) members are:

- Cameroon
- Central African Republic
- Chad
- Republic of the Congo
- Equatorial Guinea
- Gabon

*Suggestions for Further Research:*

Article:

1.  Bamou, Ernest, *Regional Integration and Economic Performance of the CEMAC Countries: A Multi-Country CGE Analysis*, 7 AFRICAN JOURNAL OF ECONOMIC POLICY issue 2 (2000).

Other Source:

1. Martijn, Jan Kees, & Charalambos G. Tsangarides, *Trade Reform in the CEMAC: Developments and Opportunities*, INTERNATIONAL MONETARY FUND WP/07/137 (June 2007).

## CENTRAL ASIAN COOPERATION ORGANIZATION

*See* Central Asian Economic Community.

## CENTRAL ASIAN ECONOMIC COMMUNITY

Leaders of four former Soviet republics, Kazakhstan, Kyrgyzstan, Tajikistan, and Uzbekistan, discussed for several years the possibility of creating a free trade agreement (FTA), which would be known as the Central Asian Economic Community (CAEC).

These countries seek to stimulate their economies through liberalized intra-regional trade. Their resource-rich economies are heavily dependent on commodities, but commodity prices — particularly for cotton, metals, and oil — have remained depressed. Creation of the FTA has been handicapped by disputes among the countries over tariffs and currency controls.

In January 1998, a "New Silk Road Agreement" was signed by 12 Central Asian nations: Armenia, Azerbaijan, Bulgaria, Georgia, Kazakhstan, the Kyrgyz Republic, Moldova, Romania, Tajikistan, Turkey, Ukraine, and Uzbekistan. Turkmenistan, a self-declared permanently neutral country, remained outside the CAEC. Ambitiously, the Agreement seeks to re-establish the ancient Silk trade route by developing communications and other infrastructure networks linking the countries, and by regulating tariff and customs procedures among the countries. However, the Agreement did not lay out plans for significant economic, much less political, integration.

Beginning in 2000, the CAEC adopted a "Strategy of Integrated Development" for the period 2000–2005. The goal of the Strategy was to establish "common economic space" within the first two years of this period. To implement the goal, the Strategy called for quadripartite interstate consortia in key economic sectors, namely, crop cultivation (with a view to achieving food self sufficiency), gas, hydropower, irrigation, metallic ore extraction, and oil. Investment banking also was identified as a significant sector, and the Central Asian Cooperation and Development Bank was established.

Yet, at a January 2001 summit, CAEC leaders pronounced the project stillborn. The Strategy foundered over three problems. First, each CAEC country pursued its short-term interests, and could not resolve their bilateral squabbles. Second, the CAEC countries lacked sufficient internally generated capital, and in effect were insolvent. Third, each CAEC country was more interested in entering into long-term economic partnerships with developed countries outside the region than in building their own regional community. In 2002, the CAEC countries renamed their group the Central Asian Cooperation Organization (CACO).

*Suggestions for Further Research:*

Article:

1.   Shadikhodjaev, Sherzod, *Trade Integration in the CIS Region: A Thorny Path towards a Customs Union*, 12 JOURNAL OF INTERNATIONAL ECONOMIC LAW 555–578 (2009).

# CEP

Constructed Export Price.

Under United States antidumping (AD) law, the price at which a foreign company sells an allegedly dumped product in an importing country, where the sale to an unrelated American buyer is not made before the product is imported into the United States (*e.g.*, the product is sold to a related party). Under pre-Uruguay Round American antidumping law, CEP was called "Exporters Sales Price" (ESP). As the United States Court of International Trade explained in *Mitsubishi Heavy Industries, Ltd. v. United States*, 15 F.Supp.2d 807–824 (CIT 1998):

> In calculating a dumping margin, Commerce compares United States price to the normal value of the subject merchandise. United States price is calculated using either an export price ("EP") methodology or a constructed export price ("CEP") methodology. Typically, Commerce relies on EP when the foreign exporter sells directly to an unrelated United States purchaser. CEP is used when the foreign exporter makes sales through a related party in the United States. . . .

# *CEPA*

*Closer Economic Partnership Agreement.*

This *Agreement* is among China, Hong Kong, and Macau. The *Agreement*, signed on 29 June 2003, and effective 1 January 2004, followed the 1 July 1997 handover of Hong Kong by the United Kingdom to China. Three Supplements to the *CEPA* have been signed — Supplement I (27 October 2004), Supplement II (18 October 2005), and Supplement III (27 June 2006).

The purpose of the *Agreement* is to unite the three economies, and make operational the "one country, two systems" policy laid out by former Chinese Premiere Deng Xiaoping. From China's standpoint, the *Agreement* provides for Taiwanese entry. The *Agreement* was created under the auspices of a regional trade agreement (RTA) under GATT Article XXIV. In practice, the *Agreement* operates as two bilateral agreements between

- China and Hong Kong, and
- China and Macau.

The *Agreement* allows for the harmonization of tariffs between the three economies. For many products, it allows for duty-free entry of goods among all three economies.

Notably, *CEPA* contemplates, and even permits Taiwanese entry into the *Agreement*. However, political issues surrounding Taiwan's status as an independent country hamper efforts between China and Taiwan to form an express trade agreement across the straits.

*Suggestions for Further Research:*

Articles:

1.  Barfield, Claude, *The Dragon Stirs: China's Trade Policy for Asia — And the World*, 24 ARIZONA JOURNAL OF INTERNATIONAL AND COMPARATIVE LAW 93–119 (2007).

2.  Chuang, Chi, *International Law and the Extraordinary Interaction between the People's Republic of China and the Republic of China on Taiwan*, 19 INDIANA JOURNAL OF INTERNATIONAL & COMPARATIVE LAW 233–323 (2009).

3.  Yu, Peter K., *Sinic Trade Agreements*, 44 U.C. DAVIS LAW REVIEW 953–1028 (2011).

# CEREALS SUBSTITUTES

A generic term for oilseeds, protein crops, and certain other agricultural products.

Generally, the Common Agricultural Policy (CAP) of the European Union (EU) has provided only partial coverage for, or support to, cereals substitutes. Historically, cereals substitutes have been less important to the European agricultural sector than other products. During the early 1960s, when the European Economic Community (EEC) initially implemented the CAP, it emphasized support for relatively more important products. In exchange for subsidies and protection for such products, the EEC agreed with other GATT contracting parties — during the 1960–62 Dillon Round — to low-level tariffs on cereals substitutes. The Dillon Round was the first set of GATT multilateral trade negotiations after the EEC was created in 1957 by the *Treaty of Rome*.

# CET

Common External Tariff.

The tariff applied by all countries that are members of a customs union (CU) to a particular category of merchandise. In entering into a customs union, like the European Union (EU), *MERCOSUR*, or Southern African Customs Union (SACU), individual members give up their sovereign right to set tariff rates, and agree upon a common set of rates with the other members of the union. In this respect, a CU represents one further step of economic integration beyond a free trade agreement (FTA). Both entities eliminate tariff and non-tariff barriers to internal trade among the members. But, FTA members retain their own tariff schedules vis-à-vis merchandise from third countries, whereas CU members have a CET.

Among the CUs of the world, only the EU and SACU are pure, in the sense of having a CET to which all members adhere. MERCOSUR permits deviations from its CET on many products.

## CFIUS

Committee on Foreign Investment in the United States.

CFIUS was established before the *Exon-Florio Amendment*. Its central role is to screen certain proposed acquisitions of American companies by foreign purchasers. In particular, it considers the national security implications of foreign takeovers of United States assets. CFIUS is an inter-agency body whose membership includes senior officials from the Departments of Justice, Homeland Security, and Treasury. CFIUS operates pursuant to Section 721 of the *Defense Production Act of 1950*, as amended by the *Foreign Investment and National Security Act of 2007 (FINSA)* (Section 721) and as implemented by Executive Order 11858, as amended, and regulations at 31 C.F.R. Part 800. CFIUS has the legal authority to block a proposed acquisition, or order divestment of a consummated transaction. *See* 50 U.S.C. Section 2170.

Reviews conducted by CFIUS are *in camera*, and no record is made publicly available. Information about its proceedings and outcomes may come from participants in those reviews, or through other channels. Generally, two categories of proposed takeovers by a foreign entity are likely to raise national security considerations: acquisition of a United States company that (1) makes military, dual-use, or other sensitive products or technologies, and (2) engages in a significant amount of defense contracting that involves such products or technologies.

Prior to *FINSA* there were no statutory or regulatory definitions of "national security," or related terms such as "critical infrastructure." CFIUS had considerable discretion to review deals that — at least ostensibly — would seem unproblematic. In addition, the prospect of a review may be susceptible to abuse by a target company. In particular, raising the specter of a review when no real United States national security concerns are at stake is an appealing takeover defense for an unscrupulous target. Similarly, it is a means for an unscrupulous target to seek a higher price for itself.

In 2005, CFIUS faced immense political pressure from both houses of Congress to scrutinize the possible acquisition of Unocal Corporation, a major United States petroleum exporter and marketer, by a foreign entity, the China National Offshore Oil Corporation (CNOOC). The $18.5 billion proposal by CNOOC for Unocal competing against an offer from Chevron Corporation valued at $17.6 billion.[86] Congress criticized the potential acquisition on grounds of national security, and additionally argued that the CNOOC bid was financed by state loans and subsidies from the Chinese Communist government.[87] On

---

[86] *See China's CNOOC Announces Withdrawal of Bid To Acquire Unocal, Citing Political Opposition*, 22 International Trade Reporter (BNA) 1286 (04 August 2005).

[87] *See Congressional Efforts to Reform CFIUS To Continue Despite CNOOC Withdrawal*, 22 International Trade Reporter (BNA) 1355 (18 August 2005).

24 June 2005, 50 members of the House, in a letter to then Treasury Secretary John Snow, requested CFIUS review the CNOOC bid for Unocal. The request cited concerns regarding "China's ongoing and proposed acquisition of energy assets around the world."[88] Furthermore, proposed legislative amendments by both the House and Senate regarding the possible acquisition were legion. For example, a 25 July amendment to the conference version of an energy bill (H.R. 6) would have required a study of energy investments by China, the findings of which CFIUS would then be required to take into account in its own review of CNOOC. An amendment to the defense authorization bill (S. 1042) called for heightening the security focus of CFIUS, and adding a review process allowing Congress to disapprove transactions.[89] In brief, the support for legislation that would have blocked the acquisition of Unocal by CNOOC was high.

Ultimately, due to the intense public pressure, CNOOC did not undergo a full CFIUS review. CNOOC withdrew its bid on 2 August 2005 and, Unocal accepted the competing offer from Chevron. Even as the bid was withdrawn Congress remained engrossed in the process by which the United States government reviewed foreign acquisitions of American companies.

In 2006, CFIUS reviewed the possible national security implications of an acquisition of Sequoia, a United States company that supplied voting machines used in elections in the United States, by Smartmatic, a privately-owned multinational company. Traditionally, foreign acquirers have applied voluntarily for a CFIUS review before attempting to consummate a transaction. However, pressure from Capitol Hill can influence the work of CFIUS as it clearly did in the CNOOC case.

Following on the heels of such a public event, Congresswoman Carolyn Maloney (Democrat-New York) wrote a letter to the then Treasury Secretary, John Snow, questioning the ties between Smartmatic and the controversial anti-American President of Venezuela, Hugo Chavez. Though the acquisition had been completed months earlier, Smartmatic had little choice but to apply for a review. The then President of Smartmatic, Antonio Mugica, a dual citizen of Venezuela and Spain, vigorously denied any foreign government ownership of Smartmatic shares, saying it was "owned primarily by four young entrepreneurs and their families."[90] However, in the end, Smartmatic decided to sell Sequoia.

A second event in the spring of 2006, once again grabbed the attention of Congress — and the world — when CFIUS did not block the takeover of five port terminals in the United States by Dubai Ports World (DPW) for which DPW paid $6.8 billion.[91] DPW manages port facilities around the world and is

---

[88] *See Fifty House Members Ask Snow To Review Chinese Bid for Unocal*, 22 International Trade Reporter (BNA) 1070 (30 June 2005).

[89]*See Energy Bill to Mandate China Energy Study; Inhofe Seeks to Toughen CFIUS*, 22 International Trade Reporter (BNA) 1242 (28 July 2005).

[90] *Quoted in* Stephanie Kirchgaessner, *CFIUS Probe Blamed for Sale of Voting-Machine Company*, FINANCIAL TIMES, 23–24 December 2006, at 4.

[91] *See* Stephanie Kirchgaessner, *Dubai Ports Takeover Prompt Backlash*, FINANCIAL TIMES, 17 December 2006, at 2.

the world's largest port operator. It was because DPW is owned by Dubai, an Emirate in the United Arab Emirates (UAE), not the business competence of the company, which caused considerable congressional backlash and reignited the debate surrounding the effectiveness of CFIUS.

In a letter to then Treasury Secretary John Snow, New York Senator Chuck Schumer, Oklahoma Senator Tom Coburn, and others argued "US ports are 'the most vulnerable targets for terrorist attack.'" The letter continued: "After the 9/11 attacks, your department complained of a lack of co-operation by the UAE and other Arab countries."[92] The White House continued to back vigorously its decision to allow the acquisition as legislative opposition mounted. Furthermore, on 23 February 2006, the State of New Jersey sued the federal government to block DPW from managing operations at the Port of Newark until the federal government, namely CFIUS, conducted an investigation of national security risks (*Corzine v. Snow*, DC N.J., No. 06-833 (JLL) filed 2/23/06).[93]

Despite cooperation from DPW regarding further investigations DPW was forced to sell. The business was purchased by the American International Group (AIG) for an amount speculated to be above $1 billion. The official sale price was not released by either party.[94]

Following this sale, legislation was introduced to mandate CFIUS reviews in certain circumstances, and tighten the criteria for approval. Many American business leaders opposed such legislation, arguing it would inhibit the entry of foreign capital into the United States, and subject American businesses seeking to acquire foreign companies to retaliatory laws in other countries. The American business owners further argued the United States had created an environment that discouraged foreign investment. In the end, a modest compromise was agreed to.

The combination of these events, which heightened public awareness of the role of CFIUS, prompted Congress to pass and President Bush to sign into law the *Foreign Investment and National Security Act of 2007 (FINSA)* (PL 110-49, July 26, 2007). This *Act* went into effect 22 December 2008.

The *FINSA* affects the CFIUS review process significantly, including changes such as:[95]

- Heightening scrutiny of any transaction where a foreign government or an entity controlled by a foreign government is a party, or whenever a transaction would result in the foreign control of "critical infrastructure."

---

[92] *See* Stephanie Kirchgaessner, *Dubai Ports Takeover Prompts Backlash*, FINANCIAL TIMES, 17 February 2006, at 2

[93] *See* Rossella Brevetti, *Federal District Court Orders Government To Explain UAE Port Deal or Risk Injunction*, 23 International Trade Reporter 324 (2 March 2006).

[94] *See* Robert Wright & Stephanie Kirchgaessner, *DP World Sells USPports for $1bn*, FINANCIAL TIMES, 12 December 2006, at 15.

[95] *See* Edward M. Lebow, *Foreign Direct Investment; The Foreign Investment and National Security Act of 2007*, 37 INTERNATIONAL LAW NEWS 1, 5 (2008).

- Defining "critical infrastructure" to include "systems or assets, whether physical or virtual, so vital to the United States that the incapacity or destruction of such systems or assets would have a debilitating impact on national security." This definition includes energy generation and transportation transactions.

- Codifying the role of CFIUS in the review process.

- Appointing the director of national intelligence as an *ex officio* member of CFIUS. The director must perform a national security threat analysis for all proposed transactions.

- Increasing the role of Congressional oversight by requiring CFIUS to provide an annual report to Congress.

The *FINSA* overhaul of CFIUS focuses primarily on the review process. But, much to the relief of the investment community, this process is, in fact, largely left intact. For example, the definition of "national security" is expanded to include "homeland security" but not expanded so much as to include "economic security." The 30-day review period and 45-day investigation period are not altered, and foreign entities that control 10 percent or less of an American business generally are not subject to CFIUS review, though there are exceptions.

In an example of the new CFIUS procedures at work, on 20 February 2008, Bain Capital Partners LLC, 3Com Corp., and Huawei Technologies withdrew their voluntarily submitted joint CFIUS filling regarding the planned acquisition of 3Com by Bain, with Huawei being a minority owner. The parties were unable to reach a mitigation agreement regarding CFIUS's national security concerns. The withdrawal is regarded as a success of *FINSA*.

*Suggestions for Further Research:*

Book:

1. FOLSOM, RALPH H., MICHAEL W. GORDON & JOHN A. SPANOGLE, JR., PRINCIPLES OF INTERNATIONAL BUSINESS TRANSACTIONS, TRADE & ECONOMIC RELATIONS (2005).

Articles:

1. Clark, Harry L. & Jonathan W. Ware, *Limits on International Business in the Petroleum Sector: CFIUS Investment Screening, Economic Sanctions, Anti-Bribery Rules, and Other Measures*, 6 TEXAS JOURNAL OF OIL, GAS & ENERGY LAW 75–161 (2010–2011).

2. Feng, Yiheng, Note, *"We Wouldn't Transfer Title to the Devil:" Consequences of the Congressional Politicization of Foreign Direct Investment on National Security Grounds*, 42 NEW YORK UNIVERSITY JOURNAL OF INTERNATIONAL LAW AND POLITICS 253–310 (2009).

3. Georgiev, George Stephanov, Comment, *The Reformed CFIUS Regulatory Framework: Mediating Between Continued Openness to Foreign Investment and National Security*, 25 YALE JOURNAL ON REGULATION 125–134 (2008).

4. Sullivan, Matthew C., *CFIUS and Congress Reconsidered: Fire Alarms, Police Patrols, and a New Oversight Regime*, 17 WILLAMETTE JOURNAL OF INTERNATIONAL LAW & DISPUTE RESOLUTION 199–242 (2009).

## C.F.R.

Code of Federal Regulations.

The official regulations of United States government departments and administrative agencies, divided into titles based on subject area. Title 19 of the C.F.R. contains virtually all statutes relating to international trade, including the regulations of the Department of Commerce (DOC). Certain regulations are found in other titles, namely, for criminal matters in Title 18, and for judicial matters, in Title 28.

## CHAPTER 11 (*NAFTA* CHAPTER 11)

*See NAFTA.*

## CHAPTER 19 (*NAFTA* CHAPTER 19)

*See NAFTA.*

## *CHEMICAL TARIFF HARMONIZATION AGREEMENT*

An accord from the Uruguay Round signed by 50 WTO Members.

Under the *Chemical Tariff Harmonization Agreement* (*CTHA*), the signatories agreed to reduce import tariffs on chemical products to 0, 5.5, or 6.5 percent.

## *CHEVRON STANDARD (CHEVRON STANDARD OF REVIEW, CHEVRON TEST)*

The standard of review in the United States used by courts examining decisions made by administrative agencies.

The test comes from the famous United States Supreme Court case of *Chevron, U.S.A., Inc. v. Natural Resources Defense Council, Inc.*, 467 U.S. 837, 81 L. Ed. 2d 694, 104 S. Ct. 2778 (1984). The test is used (*inter alia*) by the United States Court of International Trade (CIT) in reviewing interpretations by the Department of Commerce (DOC) and International Trade Commission (ITC) of statutes with which these agencies are charged to administer.

As the CIT described the test in the case of *NTN Bearing Corporation of America v. United States*, 368 F.3d 1369-78 (Fed. Cir. 2004):

> Our review of Commerce's interpretation of these statutory provisions is governed by the two-part inquiry of *Chevron, U.S.A., Inc. v. Natural Resources Defense Council, Inc.*, 467 U.S. 837, 81 L. Ed. 2d 694, 104 S. Ct. 2778 (1984). First, we must determine "whether Congress has directly spoken to the precise question at issue. If the intent of Congress is clear, that is the end of the matter; for the court, as well as the agency, must give effect to the unambiguously expressed intent of Congress." *Id.* at 842-43. However, "if the statute is silent or ambiguous with respect to the specific issue, the question for the court is whether the

agency's answer is based on a permissible construction of the statute." *Id.* at 843. Where Congress has delegated authority to the agency to promulgate regulations elucidating statutory provisions, the resulting regulations "are given controlling weight unless they are arbitrary, capricious, or manifestly contrary to the statute." *Id.* at 844.

In brief, *Chevron* analysis means a court reviews the interpretation of a statute by an administrative agency; the court applies a two-step analytical paradigm.

First, the court considers whether Congress has directly spoken on the precise question at issue. If so, then the court simply ensures the administrative agency implements the unambiguously expressed intent of Congress. Second, however, if Congress has not directly spoken on the precise question in controversy, then the statute is silent or ambiguous with respect to that question. The court considers whether the interpretation of the agency is a permissible construction of the statute. Critically, the court does not substitute its own interpretation, which it might have preferred, as long as the interpretation of the agency is reasonable.

Note that *Chevron* deference presumes the administrative agency has promulgated its interpretation via a regulation that has undergone notice and comment. Rulings of the United States Customs and Border Protection (CBP), and those of its predecessor, the Customs Service, on classification of articles of merchandise, do not undergo notice and comment. Thus, the United States Supreme Court considered a customs classification decision in the 2002 case of *United States v. Mead*, 533 U.S. 218 (2001). In the *Mead* case, the Court applied so-called "*Skidmore* deference," from *Skidmore v. Swift & Co.*, 323 U.S. 134 (1944), which is a weaker standard of review than the *Chevron* test. (More specifically, on remand from the Supreme Court, the United States Court of Appeals for the Federal Circuit applied the Skidmore test to the classification of day planners and diaries. *See Mead Corp. v. United States*, 283 F.3d 1342 (Fed. Cir. 2002).) The *Skidmore* test is that an agency interpretation, in the form of an opinion letter or other comparable document like an agency manual, enforcement guideline, or policy statement, none of which has the force of law, is entitled to respect, but only to the extent that it has the power to persuade. That is, such interpretations are entitled to deference only if they are persuasive. Thus, under the *Skidmore* test, a court has greater leeway to overturn the decision of an administrative agency, such as a tariff classification determination, than it does under the *Chevron* test. Query whether the Supreme Court decision in *United States v. Eurodif S.A.*, 129 S.Ct. 878 (2008), alters this scheme of review.

Article 17:6(ii) of the WTO *Understanding on Rules and Procedures Governing the Settlement of Disputes (Dispute Settlement Understanding, or DSU)*, contains a *Chevron*-like standard of review. This provision states:

> Where the panel finds that a relevant provision of the Agreement admits of more than one permissible interpretation, the panel shall find the authorities' measure to be in conformity with the Agreement if it rests upon one of those permissible interpretations.

However, the Appellate Body has elaborated on what this provision means in the context of WTO treaty interpretation. In its 2009 Report in *United States — Continued Existence and Application of Zeroing Methodology*, the Appellate Body stated:

270. The Appellate Body has reasoned that the second sentence of Article 17.6(ii) presupposes "that application of the rules of treaty interpretation in Articles 31 and 32 of the *Vienna Convention* could give rise to, at least, two interpretations of some provisions of the *Anti-Dumping Agreement*, which, under that Convention, would both be '*permissible* interpretations.'" [Quoting *Appellate Body Report, United States — Anti-Dumping Measures on Certain Hot-Rolled Steel Products from Japan*, WT/DS184/AB/R ¶ 59 (adopted 23 August 2001).] Where that is the case, a measure is deemed to be in conformity with the *Anti-Dumping Agreement* "if it rests upon one of those permissible interpretations." As the Appellate Body has said, "[i]t follows that, under Article 17.6(ii) of the *Anti-Dumping Agreement*, panels are obliged to determine whether a measure rests upon an interpretation of the relevant provisions of the *Anti-Dumping Agreement* which is *permissible under the rules of treaty interpretation* in Articles 31 and 32 of the *Vienna Convention [on the Law of Treaties]*." [Quoting *Hot-Rolled Steel*, ¶ 60.]

271. The second sentence of Article 17.6(ii) must therefore be read and applied in the light of the first sentence. We wish to make a number of general observations about the second sentence. First, Article 17.6(ii) contemplates a sequential analysis. The first step requires a panel to apply the customary rules of interpretation to the treaty to see what is yielded by a conscientious application of such rules including those codified in the *Vienna Convention*. Only *after* engaging this exercise will a panel be able to determine whether the second sentence of Article 17.6(ii) applies. The structure and logic of Article 17.6(ii) therefore do not permit a panel to determine first whether an interpretation is permissible under the second sentence and then to seek validation of that permissibility by recourse to the first sentence.

272. Secondly, the proper interpretation of the second sentence of Article 17.6(ii) must itself be consistent with the rules and principles set out in the *Vienna Convention*. This means that it cannot be interpreted in a way that would render it redundant, or that derogates from the customary rules of interpretation of public international law. However, the second sentence allows for the possibility that the application of the rules of the *Vienna Convention* may give rise to an interpretative range and, if it does, an interpretation falling within that range is permissible and must be given effect by holding the measure to be in conformity with the covered agreement. The function of the second sentence is thus to give effect to the interpretative range rather than to require the interpreter to pursue further the interpretative exercise to the point where only one interpretation within that range may prevail.

273. We further note that the rules and principles of the *Vienna Convention* cannot contemplate interpretations with mutually contradictory results. Instead, the enterprise of interpretation is intended to ascertain the proper meaning of a provision; one that fits harmoniously with the terms, context, and object and purpose of the treaty. The purpose of such an exercise is therefore to narrow the range of interpretations, not to generate conflicting, competing interpretations. Interpretative tools cannot be applied selectively or in isolation from one another. It would be a subversion of the interpretative disciplines of the *Vienna Convention* if application of those disciplines yielded contradiction instead of coherence and harmony among, and effect to, all relevant treaty provisions. Moreover, a permissible interpretation for purposes of the second sentence of Article 17.6(ii) is not the result of an inquiry that asks whether a provision of domestic law is "necessarily excluded" by the application of the *Vienna Convention*. Such an approach subverts the hierarchy between the treaty and municipal law. It is the proper interpretation of a covered agreement that is the enterprise with which Article 17.6(ii) is engaged, not whether the treaty can be interpreted consistently with a particular Member's municipal law or with municipal laws of Members as they existed at the time of the conclusion of the relevant treaty.[96]

In effect, the Appellate Body says that the *Chevron* test presumes proper application of the *Vienna Convention* Rules. Moreover, when a case comes to it on appeal, its task tends to be examination of whether the legal interpretation rendered by the underlying panel is correct. In other words, the Appellate Body focuses not so much on whether there are multiple possible interpretations that are reasonable, and then defer to one of them as picked by the underlying authority. Rather, once a panel has rendered a legal interpretation, the task of the Appellate Body is to decide whether the panel was legally correct.

*Suggestions for Further Research:*

Articles:

1. Croley, Steven P. & John H. Jackson, *WTO Dispute Procedures, Standard of Review, and Deference to National Governments*, 90 AMERICAN JOURNAL OF INTERNATIONAL LAW 193–213 (1996).

2. Guzman, Andrew T., *Determining the Appropriate Standard of Review in WTO Disputes*, 42 CORNELL INTERNATIONAL LAW JOURNAL 45–76 (2009).

3. Korotana, Dr. Muhammed, *The Standard of Review in WTO Law*, 15 INTERNATIONAL TRADE LAW & REGULATION issue 2, 72–77 (2009).

---

[96] Appellate Body Report, *United States — Continued Existence and Application of Zeroing Methodology* (complaint by European Communities (EC)), WT/DS/350/AB/R ¶¶ 270-273 (adopted 19 February 2009) (emphasis original, footnotes omitted).

4. Magee, Claire, Note, *Using Chevron as a Guide: Allowing for the Precautionary Principle in WTO Practices (Chevron U.S.A., Inc. v. NRDC, Inc., 467 U.S. 837 (1984))*, 21 GEORGETOWN INTERNATIONAL ENVIRONMENTAL LAW REVIEW 6150638 (2009).

5. Tarullo, Daniel K., *The Hidden Costs of International Dispute Settlement: WTO Review of Domestic Anti-Dumping Decisions*, 34 LAW AND POLICY IN INTERNATIONAL BUSINESS 109–181 (2002).

6. Wood, J. Christopher, & Zia C. Oatley, *28 U.S.C. § 1581(c): Judicial Review of Antidumping Duty Determinations Issued by the Department of Commerce*, 41 GEORGETOWN JOURNAL OF INTERNATIONAL LAW 117–135 (2009).

## CHINDIA

A new term (not yet in the *Oxford English Dictionary*) for the combined power of both China's and India's economy, and the recognition of the two most populous countries potential global impact.[97]

"Chindia" was first used by an Indian politician, Shri Jairam Ramesh, looking at the combined effect of the two most populous countries in the world. (He represents the South Indian state of Andhra Pradesh as a member of the *Rajya Sabha* (Upper House) of the Indian Parliament.) Shri Ramesh used the term in his book *Making Sense of Chindia: Reflections on China and India* (Indian Research Press 2005). There have been significant diplomatic efforts between Beijing and New Delhi to improve relations and strengthen trade, finance, and investment ties, and to resolve border disputes in Kashmir from the Sino Indian War of 1962. "Chindia," though, connotes the new environment in which border hostilities are less significant than common economic interests and business synergies.

China, a country with 1.3 billion people, has experienced unprecedented modern economic growth of 9.5 percent per year every year for the past 20 years. India, a country with 1.1 billion people has experienced six percent economic growth per year every year for the past two decades. Economists estimate China may overtake the United States as the largest economy in 40 years, and India may overtake Germany as the third largest economy in 30 years. However impressive these growth rates have been, it is important to remember both countries started with relatively small gross domestic product (GDP) bases, and today only account for six percent of world GDP.

A significant testament to the combined might of both countries is suggested by the reaction of financial markets to creation of a Chindia Index. First Trust created this Index, which is a combination of asset classes from both Chinese

---

[97] *See* Marcus Gee, *Chindia Rising: Not Your Same Old, Golly-gee Asian Superpowers*, THE GLOBE AND MAIL, 30 May 2007, at B-12; Trang Ho, *Chindia ETF Combines 2 of Hottest Economies*, INVESTOR'S BUSINESS DAILY, 22 May 2007, at A11; Jo Johnson, *China and India Pledge to Boost Trade and End Border Dispute*, FINANCIAL TIMES, 12 April 2005, at 5; Martin Wolf, *In This Brave New World Chindia's Uneven Rise Continues*, FINANCIAL TIMES, 21 March 2007, at 13.

and Indian American Depositary Receipts (ADRs). The inception date for the ADRs was 8 May 2007, and the first day of trading was 11 May 2007. Significantly, the Morgan Stanley Capital Index (MSCI) also tracks the performance of Chindian equities, as part of its Emerging Market Stock Indices. For example, in October 2007, the MSCI showed emerging market equities had risen 13 percent (in U.S. dollar terms) in July-September 2007, which was 11 percent better than the rest of the world.[98] Chindia stocks specifically posted gains of nearly 40 percent, handily beating the next best emerging market — Turkey, which had a 20 percent return. More impressively than these three month statistics were MSCI data showing emerging equities have outperformed the rest of the world by more than 100 percent since 2002. Chindia, undoubtedly, had much to do with that superior performance.

## CIRCUMVENTION

A measure taken by exporters to evade an antidumping (AD) or countervailing duty (CVD).

## CIT

The United States Court of International Trade (CIT), located in New York, New York.

Specifically, the CIT is located at the Federal Plaza, next to the Jacob K. Javits Federal Building, and just north of City Hall, on the lower East Side of Manhattan. Most proceedings occur at the Courthouse of the CIT in New York. However, the CIT can hear cases anywhere in the United States. The CIT also is authorized to hold hearings in foreign countries.

The CIT has national jurisdiction over conflicts and disputes arising out of tariff and international trade laws. The jurisdiction of the CIT is set forth in 28 U.S.C. §§ 1581-1585. Basic rules about the Court's procedure are contained in 28 U.S.C. §§ 2631-2646, 2680.

In particular, the CIT has exclusive jurisdiction over

"civil actions that pertain to classification and valuation of imported goods, charges or exactions within the jurisdiction of the Secretary of the Treasury, the exclusion of merchandise from entry under provisions of the customs laws, the liquidation of an entry, the refusal to pay a drawback, and challenges to administrative determinations under antidumping and countervailing duty laws."[99]

Further, the CIT may review administrative determinations certifying and refusing to certify workers, firms or communities eligible for trade adjustment assistance (TAA), as well as administrative decisions to revoke, suspend or

---

[98] See *Chindian Summer*, FINANCIAL TIMES, 5 October 2007, at 16.

[99] Chief Judge Edward D. Re, *Litigation Before the United States Court of International Trade*, *Preface to the First Volume* of Title 19 United States Code Annotated, at XXV-LVIII (2000).

deny a customhouse broker's license. The standard of review applied by the Court in respect of agency determinations requires that final determinations and decisions to suspend investigations must be supported by "substantial evidence on the record." The review is limited to the administrative record compiled by the agency. *See* 19 U.S.C. § 1516a(b)(1)(B). In reviewing interlocutory orders, however, the standard of review is that the order in question must not be arbitrary, capricious, or an abuse of discretion. *See id.* at § 1516a(b)(1)(A). The CIT also has a grant of residual jurisdiction,

> which authorizes it to entertain any civil action arising out of certain laws relating to international trade or the administration or enforcement of those laws.[100]

Notably, the CIT has the authority to conduct jury trials.

As regards procedures and operations, normally, the Chief Judge assigns a single judge to each action before the Court. If the Chief Judge determines that an action involves either

(1) the constitutionality of an Act of Congress, a proclamation of the President, or an executive order, or

(2) has broad or significant implications in the administration or interpretation of the customs laws,

then the Chief Judge may assign the action to a three judge panel.

There are nine judges on the CIT. Each judge is appointed by the President with the advice and consent of the Senate. Judges at the CIT, like all federal judges under Article III of the United States Constitution, are appointed for life. The Table sets out current CIT judges, including those with Senior Status.

**TABLE:**
**JUDGES OF THE UNITED STATES COURT OF INTERNATIONAL TRADE (CIT)**

| *Judge* | *Appointed By President* | *Year of Appointment* | *Home State* |
|---|---|---|---|
| Chief Judge Jane A. Restani | Reagan | 1983 | California |
| Judge Gregory W. Carman | Reagan | 1983 | New York |
| Judge Donald C. Pogue | Clinton | 1995 | Illinois |
| Judge Evan J. Wallach | Clinton | 1995 | Arizona |
| Judge Judith M. Barzilay | Clinton | 1998 | Kansas |
| Judge Delissa A. Ridgway | Clinton | 1998 | |
| Judge Richard K. Eaton | Clinton | 2000 | New York |

---

[100] *Id.*

**TABLE (continued)**

| Judge | Appointed By President | Year of Appointment | Home State |
|---|---|---|---|
| Judge Timothy C. Stanceu | Bush (George W.) | 2003 | Ohio |
| Judge Leo M. Gordon | Bush (George W.) | 2006 | |
| Senior Judge Thomas J. Aquilino, Jr. | Reagan | 1985 | New York |
| Senior Judge Nicholas Tsou- calas | Reagan | 1986 | New York |
| Senior Judge R. Kenton Musgrave | Reagan | 1987 | Florida |
| Senior Judge Richard W. Goldberg | Bush (George H.W.) | 1991 | North Dakota |

There are four Senior Judges at the CIT. Eligible judges may elect to take senior status, which allows them to serve on the Court while handling fewer cases than a judge in active service. Judges of the CIT, again like all Article III judges, may be designated and assigned by the Chief Justice of the United States Supreme Court to perform judicial duties in a United States Court of Appeals or United States District Court.

The CIT has a long and grand history. In its current form, it was established by the *Customs Court Act of 1980*. Before 1980, Congress first empowered the Board of General Appraisers to handle legal matters concerning international trade. Congress did so in 1890. Under the *Customs Administrative Act of 1890*, the Board of General Appraisers was established within the Department of Treasury. The primary function of the Board was to review customs determinations as regards the classification and valuation of imported goods.

Later, in 1926, Congress changed the make-up of this quasi-judicial entity. It created the United States Customs Court, under Article I of the United States Constitution.[101] Although the *Act of May 28, 1926* sought to expand judicial review and promote uniformity in decisions concerning international trade matters, it made no essential changes in the functions, duties, or jurisdiction of the newly created court. In 1956, Congress integrated the Customs Court into the federal judicial system. It did so by declaring the Customs Court was a

---

[101] Article I, Section 8 of the United States Constitution states:

> *Congress* shall have Power to lay and collect Taxes, Duties, Imposts and Excises, to pay the Debts and provide for the common Defence and general Welfare of the United States; but all Duties, Imposts and Excises shall be uniform throughout the United States.

Further, Article I, Section 10, provides:

> no State shall, without the Consent of the Congress, lay any Imposts or Duties on Imports or Exports. . . .

court established under Article III of the Constitution.[102] Finally, with the *Customs Court Act of 1980*, Congress gave the Customs Court its new moniker, the CIT, and explicitly granted it all judicial powers in law and equity.[103]

The United States Court of Appeals for the Federal Circuit has jurisdiction over appeals from the CIT.

*Suggestions for Further Research:*

Book:

1.  REED, PATRICK C., THE ROLE OF FEDERAL COURTS IN U.S. CUSTOMS & INTERNATIONAL TRADE LAW (1997).

Articles:

1.  Alves, Mary Jane, *Reflections on the Current State of Play: Have U.S. Courts Finally Decided to Stop Using International Agreements and Reports of International Trade Panels in Adjudicating International Trade Cases*, 17 TULANE JOURNAL OF INTERNATIONAL & COMPARATIVE LAW 299–352 (2009).

2.  Baisburd, Yohai, John Boscariol, & Cyndee B. Todgham Cherniak, *et al.*, *Customs Law*, 45 THE INTERNATIONAL LAWYER 3–17 (spring 2011).

3.  Barnett, Mark A., *Choices, Choices: Domestic Courts versus International Fora: A Commerce Perspective*, 17 TULANE JOURNAL OF INTERNATIONAL & COMPARATIVE LAW 435–462 (2009).

4.  Barnett, Mark A., *The United States Court of International Trade in the Middle — International Tribunals: An Overview*, 19 TULANE JOURNAL OF INTERNATIONAL & COMPARATIVE LAW 421–432 (2011).

5.  Barnett, Mark A., Sara Khan, Kathy B. Reif & Elizabeth Shryock, *28 U.S.C. § 1581(c) — Review by the Court of International Trade of Antidumping & Countervailing Duty Determinations Issued by the Department of Commerce*, 40 GEORGETOWN JOURNAL OF INTERNATIONAL LAW 153–181 (2008).

6.  Becker, Steven H. & Paul A. Horowitz, *The Court of International Trade's Treatment of the Political Question Doctrine: Placing Totes-Isotoner in the Context of the Court's Recent and Anticipated Jurisprudence*, 17 TULANE JOURNAL OF INTERNATIONAL & COMPARATIVE LAW 533–540 (2009).

7.  Bernstein, Mark A. & Andrea C. Casson, *How Useful is 28 U.S.C. § 1292(d)(1) in Preventing Protracted Litigation and Uncorrectable harm to Litigants in Trade Remedies Cases?*, 19 TULANE JOURNAL OF INTERNATIONAL & COMPARATIVE LAW 455–467 (2011).

---

[102] Article III, Section 1 of the United States Constitution provides:

> The judicial Power of the United States shall be vested in one supreme Court, and in such inferior Courts as the Congress may from time to time ordain and establish. The Judges, both of the supreme and inferior Courts, shall hold their Offices during good Behavior, and shall, at stated Times, receive for their Services, a Compensation, which shall not be diminished during their Continuance in Office.

[103] *See Customs Courts Act of 1980*, Pub. L. No. 96-417, 94 Stat. 1727 (1980).

8. Boscariol, John, *et al.*, *Customs Law*, 44 THE INTERNATIONAL LAWYER 5–23 (2010).

9. Brightbill, Timothy C., Jennifer Kwon & Matthew W. Fogarty, *19 U.S.C. § 1581(c) — Judicial Review of Antidumping and Countervailing Duty Determinations Issued by the Department of Commerce*, 39 GEORGETOWN JOURNAL OF INTERNATIONAL LAW 41–67 (2007).

10. Cameron, Donald B. & Brady W. Mills, *28 U.S.C. § 1581(i) "Residual" Jurisdiction: 2007 Year in Review of Decisions Issued by the U.S. Court of International Trade*, 40 GEORGETOWN JOURNAL OF INTERNATIONAL LAW 123–152 (2008).

11. Cannon, James R., Jr., *2008 Year in Review of Decisions Issued by the U.S. Court of International Trade: Clarifying the Scope of § 1581(i)*, 41 GEORGETOWN JOURNAL OF INTERNATIONAL LAW 83–116 (2009).

12. Cannon, Kathleen W., *Trade Litigation before the WTO, NAFTA, and U.S. Courts: A Petitioner's Perspective*, 17 TULANE JOURNAL OF INTERNATIONAL & COMPARATIVE LAW 389–434 (2009).

13. Carman, Gregory W., *A Critical Analysis of the Standard of Review Applied by the Court of Appeals for the Federal Circuit in Antidumping and Countervailing Duty Cases*, 13. FEDERAL CIRCUIT BAR JOURNAL 203 (2003).

14. Carman, Gregory W., *The Jurisdiction of the United States Court of International Trade: A Dilemma for Potential Litigants,* 22 STETSON LAW REVIEW 157, 160 (1992).

15. Carman, Gregory W., *Forward, Complementing the Court: The Role of Annual Case Review in the Ever-Developing Jurisprudence of the U.S. Court of International Trade*, 40 GEORGETOWN JOURNAL OF INTERNATIONAL LAW 1–2 (2008).

16. Chorev, Nitsan, *The Judicial Transformation of the State: The Case of U.S. Trade Policy, 1974–2004*, 31 LAW & POLICY 31–68 (2009).

17. Coursey, Michael J., *Developments During 2009 Concerning the U.S. Court of International Trade's "Residual" Jurisdiction Under 29 U.S.C. § 1581(i)*, 42 GEORGETOWN JOURNAL OF INTERNATIONAL LAW 169–209 (2010).

18. Davidson, Jeanne E. & Zachary D. Hale, *Developments during 2006 Concerning 28 U.S.C. § 1581(i)*, 39 GEORGETOWN JOURNAL OF INTERNATIONAL LAW 127–164 (2007).

19. Dorn, Joseph W., *U.S. Court of International Trade Decisions During 2007 in Appeals of Determinations of the U.S. International Trade Commission*, 40 GEORGETOWN JOURNAL OF INTERNATIONAL LAW 219–241 (2008).

20. Dorn, Joseph W., *Settlements in the United States Court of International Trade: Practices and Policies*, 19 TULANE JOURNAL OF INTERNATIONAL & COMPARATIVE LAW 433–454 (2011).

21. Franklin, Aaron, *Developments in Cases Arising Under 28 U.S.C. § 1581(a) During 2009*, 42 GEORGETOWN JOURNAL OF INTERNATIONAL LAW 531–554 (2011).

22. Friedman, Lawrence M. & Christine H. Martinez, *What is Persuasive? Pushing World Customs Organizations Materials Through the Skidmore Sieve*, 17 TULANE JOURNAL OF INTERNATIONAL & COMPARATIVE LAW 515–531 (2009).

23. Gerrish, Jeffrey D. & Luke A. Meisner, *Protecting the Right to Judicial Review in Trade Remedy Cases: Preliminary Injunctions and the Impact of Recent Court Decisions*, 19 TULANE JOURNAL OF INTERNATIONAL & COMPARATIVE LAW 469–485 (2011).

24. Greenwald, John D., *After Corus Staal — Is There Any Role, and Should There Be for WTO Jurisprudence in the Review of U.S. Trade Measures by U.S. Courts?*, 39 GEORGETOWN JOURNAL OF INTERNATIONAL TRADE LAW 199–216 (2007).

25. Hadfield, Frances P., *A Question of Evidence, Ethics, and Interpretation: Possible Perils and Pitfalls of the United States Court of International Trade Rules 8 and 11*, 19 TULANE JOURNAL OF INTERNATIONAL & COMPARATIVE LAW 573–586 (2011).

26. Herrmann, John M., *The Global Financial Crisis: Impact on International Trade Matters Potentially Coming before the United States Court of International Trade*, 19 TULANE JOURNAL OF INTERNATIONAL & COMPARATIVE LAW 601–618 (2011).

27. Hughes, Todd M. & Claudia Burke, *Constitutional Litigation and Its Jurisdictional Implications in the Court of International Trade*, 17 TULANE JOURNAL OF INTERNATIONAL & COMPARATIVE LAW 541–553 (2009).

28. Kennedy, Kevin C., *A Proposal to Abolish the U.S. Court of International Trade*, 4 DICKINSON JOURNAL OF INTERNATIONAL LAW 13 (1985).

29. Kipel, Alicia Alexandra, *The Role of the United States Court of International Trade in the Enforcement of Intellectual Property Rights*, 19 TULANE JOURNAL OF INTERNATIONAL & COMPARATIVE LAW 627–649 (2011).

30. Lynch, Michele D., Nasim A. Deylami, Nathaniel J. Halvorson, Skye Mathieson & Kelsey M. Rule, *28 U.S.C. § 1581(c): Judicial Review of Antidumping and Countervailing Duty Determinations by the Department of Commerce*, 42 GEORGETOWN JOURNAL OF INTERNATIONAL LAW 65–95 (2010).

31. McCarthy, Patricia M. & Emily S. Ullman, *Trade Adjustment Assistance Cases: 28 U.S.C. § 158(d) — Department of Labor and Department of Agriculture Decisions Under the Trade Adjustment Assistance Statutes*, 39 GEORGETOWN JOURNAL OF INTERNATIONAL LAW 105–126 (2007).

32. McInerney, John D., *Is It Improper for Commerce to Explain its Disagreement with Remand Orders in Its Remand Redeterminations?*, 17 TULANE JOURNAL OF INTERNATIONAL & COMPARATIVE LAW 491–504 (2009).

33. Mendoza, Julie C. & R. Will Planert, *Agency Remands before the United States Court of International Trade: Objectives and Obstacles*, 17 TULANE JOURNAL OF INTERNATIONAL & COMPARATIVE LAW 463–489 (2009).

34. Pellegrini, John B., *Revocation and Modification of Rulings and Treatments: Does Section 625(c) Work?*, 17 TULANE JOURNAL OF INTERNATIONAL & COMPARATIVE LAW 505–513 (2009).

35. Pickard, Daniel B. & Laura El-Sabaawi, *The Future of Rule 11 Sanctions for Unethical Conduct before the U.S. Court of International Trade*, 19 TULANE JOURNAL OF INTERNATIONAL & COMPARATIVE LAW 587–599 (2011).

36. Pike, Damon V. & Cylinda Parga, *Customs Penalties and Customs Brokers: The Year in Review Under 28 U.S.C. §§ 1581(g) and 1582*, 41 GEORGETOWN JOURNAL OF INTERNATIONAL LAW 53–82 (2009).

37. Pogue, Donald C., *The Emergence of a Tradition in the Discourse on the Court of International Trade*, 39 GEORGETOWN JOURNAL OF INTERNATIONAL LAW 1–2 (2007).

38. Re, Chief Judge Edward D., *Litigation Before the United States Court of International Trade, Preface to the First Volume* of Title 19 United States Code Annotated, at XXV-LVIII (2000).

39. Reed, Patrick C., *Expanding the Jurisdiction of the U.S. Court of International Trade: Proposals by the Customs and International Trade Bar Association*, 26 BROOKLYN JOURNAL OF INTERNATIONAL LAW 819 (2001).

40. Ryan, John M., *Interplay of WTO and U.S. Domestic Judicial Review: When the Same U.S. Administration Determinations Are Appealed Under the WTO Agreements and Under U.S. Law, Do the Respective Decisions and Available Remedies Coexist or Collide?*, 17 TULANE JOURNAL OF INTERNATIONAL & COMPARATIVE LAW 353–387 (2009).

41. Sandler, Gilbert Lee & Morgan L. Frohman, *The Year in Review: 28 U.S.C. § 1581(a) Decisions in 2007 by the CIT and Others*, 40 GEORGETOWN JOURNAL OF INTERNATIONAL LAW 183–217 (2008).

42. Schwinn, Steven D., *Trade Adjustment Assistance at the U.S. Court of International Trade: The Year in Review*, 41 GEORGETOWN JOURNAL OF INTERNATIONAL LAW 137–160 (2009).

43. Sikes, Devin S., *Why Congress Should Expand the Subject Matter Jurisdiction of the United States Court of International Trade*, 6 SOUTH CAROLINA JOURNAL OF INTERNATIONAL LAW AND BUSINESS 253–272 (spring 2010).

44. Simon, Joel K. & Hillel M. Tuchman, *Decisions of the U.S. Court of International Trade Under 28 U.S.C. § 1582: The Year in Review*, 40 GEORGETOWN JOURNAL OF INTERNATIONAL LAW 243–259 (2008).

45. Slater, Valerie A. & Lisa W. Ross, *Judicial Review of the International Trade Commission's Determinations in Antidumping and Countervailing Duty Provisions: An Overview of Decisions in 2006*, 39 GEORGETOWN JOURNAL OF INTERNATIONAL LAW 69–103 (2007).

46. Trossevin, Marguerite & Reza Karmaloo, *Judicial Review of Antidumping and Countervailing Duty Determinations by the Department of Commerce: Noteworthy Cases in 2009*, 42 GEORGETOWN JOURNAL OF INTERNATIONAL LAW 35–63 (2010).

47. Von Schriltz, Karl, *U.S. Court of International Trade Decisions in 2008 in Appeals of Determinations of the U.S. International Trade Commission*, 41 GEORGETOWN JOURNAL OF INTERNATIONAL LAW 1–51 (2009).

48. White Jr., Franklin E., *The Bell Atlantic Corp. v. Twombly Pleading Standard: Has Its Application Been Outcome Determinative in Court of International Trade Cases?*, 19 TULANE JOURNAL OF INTERNATIONAL & COMPARATIVE LAW 543–564 (2011).

49. White Jr., Franklin E. & Justin David Blanset, *Developments During 2009 Concerning 28 U.S.C. § 1581(d) and (g) and 28 U.S.C. § 1582(1)*, 42 GEORGETOWN JOURNAL OF INTERNATIONAL LAW 135–167 (2010).

50. Williams, Barbara S., *Customs Cases: Decisions under 28 U.S.C. § 1581(a) and 28 U.S.C. § 1582*, 39 GEORGETOWN JOURNAL OF INTERNATIONAL LAW 3–39 (2007).

51. Williams, Barbara S., *Critical Decisions by the U.S. Court of Appeals for the Federal Circuit and the U.S. Court of International Trade in Customs 28 U.S.C. § 1581(a) Cases*, 41 GEORGETOWN JOURNAL OF INTERNATIONAL LAW 161–187 (2009).

52. Williams, Barbara S., *Use of Confidential Information in Motion Practice*, 19 TULANE JOURNAL OF INTERNATIONAL & COMPARATIVE LAW 565–571 (2011).

53. Wood, J. Christopher & Zia C. Oatley, *28 U.S.C. § 1581(c): Judicial Review of Antidumping Duty Determinations Issued by the Department of Commerce*, 41 GEORGETOWN JOURNAL OF INTERNATIONAL LAW 117–135 (2009).

54. Young, Kimberly R. & Frederick P. Waite, *Overview of 2009 Decisions by the U.S. Court of International Trade in Appeals Determinations of the U.S. International Trade Commission*, 42 GEORGETOWN JOURNAL OF INTERNATIONAL LAW 5–34 (2010).

## CITA

Committee for Implementation of Textile Agreements.

As its name suggests, CITA is responsible for putting into practice United States trade agreement provisions concerning trade in textiles and apparel (T&A). Its duties include overseeing bilateral safeguard relief in this sector under America's free trade agreements (FTAs), such as the *Central American Free Trade Agreement — Dominican Republic (CAFTA–DR)*, and preferential programs, such as the *Haitian Hemispheric Opportunity through Partnership for Encouragement Act (HOPE Act)*.

## CITT

Canadian International Trade Tribunal.

## CLASS OR KIND OF MERCHANDISE SUBJECT TO INVESTIGATION

The pre-Uruguay Round term in United States antidumping (AD) and countervailing duty (CVD) law for "subject merchandise," *i.e.*, imported articles alleged to be dumped or illegally subsidized, and thus under investigation for violating AD or CVD law.

## CLUSTERING (CLUSTERS, CLUSTER APPROACH)

A strategy for categorizing services sub-sectors and sub-sub-sectors. One way to refine categories is to disaggregate them into functional business lines. Clustering calls for like or similar services to be grouped together.

For instance, consider the Tourism sub-sector, which includes the sub-sub-sectors of Cleaning, Hotel, Transport (land, sea, and air), and Sports and Recreation. The argument in favor of clustering is it leads to a pro-free trade outcome. If WTO Members make commitments in one sub-sector, but not in related sub-sectors, then the full practical benefits of concessions are not realized. To expedite and broaden liberalization, it would be preferable to have commitments on all sub-sectors that are related in practice to one another.

However, there are two arguments against clustering. First, clustering might inhibit a WTO Member from making any commitment whatsoever. Second, a sub-sector may fit well into either one of two clusters. For example, is the "Postal" better put with air transport services or tourist services?

In October 2010, Australia sought to advance service talks in the Doha Round of multilateral trade negotiations through a clusters approach.[104] Proposed concessions could be offered and swapped not in individual sectors, but in related clusters. Australia proposed a transportation cluster embracing logistics/supply chains, which would cover normal and express delivery, inventory, and transit. Backing the clusters approach, the United States called for liberalizing services trade in an information technology cluster that included computer consulting and telecommunications.[105] Yet, by year-end December 2010, the proposal failed to gain traction among the Members.

## CMAA

*See* Customs Mutual Assistance Agreement.

## CMLV

Cambodia, Laos, Myanmar (Burma), and Vietnam.

The term is used in the context of the *Association of South East Asian Nations* (*ASEAN*). CMLV are the new, poorer parties to *ASEAN*. Typically, the *ASEAN*-6 (the older, richer parties to ASEAN) accords CMLV special and differential treatment. For instance, a free trade agreement (FTA) with China, the *ASEAN–China Free Trade Agreement* (*ACFTA*), is expected by 2010 for China and the *ASEAN*-6, but not until 2015 for China and the CMLV.

---

[104] *See* Daniel Pruzin, *Recent Doha Efforts Yield Mixed Results; WTO Members Agree on Need to Continue*, 27 International Trade Reporter (BNA) (21 October 2010).

[105] *See* Daniel Pruzin, *U.S. Envoy Hears Positive Tone on Doha, But Actual Negotiations Are Still Missing*, 27 International Trade Reporter (BNA) 1757 (18 November 2010).

## CMO

Common Market Organization.

Generally speaking, a CMO is a system of subsidies and protection for an agricultural product under the Common Agricultural Policy (CAP) of the European Union (EU). Since the introduction of the CAP, the CMO gradually replaced national market organizations for about 90 percent of final agricultural production in the EU. The goals of a CMO are the same as the aims of the CAP, including a fair standard of living for farmers and increased productivity in agriculture. Under a CMO, single prices for an agricultural product on all European markets is fixed, aid is granted to producers or operators of that product, and mechanisms are established to control production and organize trade of that product with non-EU member countries.

*Suggestions for Further Research:*

Article:

1.  Iannettoni, Tim, Note, *Commission Impossible: The Commission of the European Communities' Attempt to Reform the Common Market Organization for Wine*, 19 INDIANA INTERNATIONAL & COMPARATIVE LAW REVIEW 383–418 (2009).

## CNL

Competitive Need Limitation.

A provision in the United States Generalized System of Preference (GSP) scheme that essentially removes from eligible treatment any article of merchandise if the exporting country has become successful in the American market. Success, or competitiveness, is measured by quantitative benchmarks set forth by statute and regulation. The exporting country itself does not lose Beneficiary Developing Country (BDC) status, unless of course it graduates from the GSP scheme for independent reasons. Rather, the merchandise no longer receives the preferential treatment.

## COAC

The Advisory Committee on Commercial Operations of Customs and Border Protection and Related Homeland Security Functions.

The Advisory Committee makes recommendations to the Commissioner of Customs and Border Protection (CBP), and the Secretaries of Homeland Security and the Treasury.

## COCOM

Coordinating Committee for Multilateral Export Controls.

An informal body based in Paris, COCOM, served as a multilateral forum for cooperation on export control matters. The Cold War focused attention on the need for cooperation and coordination to prevent or restrict sensitive technology shipments to Communist countries. Thus, from 1950-94, Japan, and all North Atlantic Treaty Organization (NATO) countries, save for Iceland, participated voluntarily in COCOM, meeting periodically to set policy, publish lists of controlled items, and develop effective procedures. Their aim was to develop and administer a common set of expert controls to prevent the transfer of sensitive goods and technology to the former Soviet Union and its allies, and certain other countries. Notably, the *Export Administration Act of 1979*, as amended, directed the President to negotiate with COCOM partners on ways to cut the scope of export controls.

COCOM was created in 1949. It ceased functioning on 31 March 1994. On 12 July 1996, COCOM was replaced by the *Wassenaar Arrangement on Export Controls for Conventional Arms and Dual-Use Goods and Technologies*.

*Suggestions for Further Research:*

Articles:

1. Diamond, Andrew F., Note, *Dueling Over Dual-Use Goods: The U.S. Department of Commerce's Misguided Attempt to Promote U.S. Security and Trade with China Through Restrictive Export Controls*, 3 BROOKLYN JOURNAL OF CORPORATE FINANCE & COMMERCIAL LAW 153–183 (2008).

2. Lipson, Michael, *The Reincarnation of COCOM: Explaining Post-Cold War Export Controls*, VI THE NONPROLIFERATION REVIEW number 2, 34 (winter 1999).

## CODEX ALIMENTARIUS COMMISSION ("CODEX")

A commission established in 1963 operating under the aegis of the United Nations (U.N.) Food and Agriculture Organization (FAO) and the World Health Organization (WHO).

The Commission also is known by short names, such as *CAC*, or *Codex*. *Codex* establishes international standards, guidelines, and recommendations on matters relating to human health and food safety. The standards, recommendations, and guidelines which *Codex* provides help to anticipate possible future controversies, and resolve current disputes, concerning sanitary and phytosanitary (SPS) measures and technical barriers to trade (TBT).

These internationally recognized perspectives can specific, such as commodity-by-commodity analysis (for cheddar cheese versus gouda cheese). Or, they can be general, concerning a broad group of people. In the latter category, of particular note, are *Codex* standards for observing Muslim *ḥalal* (permitted) standards or for hygiene of products for infants and mothers. Malaysia led the effort in developing the *ḥalal* standards. Note, however, there remains debate among the four *Sunnite* Schools of Islamic Law (*Sharī'a*) — *Ḥanafī*, *Mālikī*, *Shāfi'ī*, and *Ḥanbalī* — as to *ḥalal* standards.

*Suggestions for Further Research:*

Articles:

1.   Fontanelli, Filippo, *ISO and Codex Standards and International Trade Law: What Gets Said is Not What's Heard*, 60 INTERNATIONAL & COMPARATIVE LAW QUARTERLY 895–932 (2011).

## COEFFICIENT

*See* Swiss Formula Coefficient.

## COLLECTIVE ACTION (COLLECTIVE ACTION PROBLEM, COLLECTIVE ACTION THEORY)

In the WTO context, the problem that no one Member is willing to forego an option that suits its self-interest (such as focusing on its own free trade agreements (FTAs) rather than on multilateral trade negotiations), unless all other Members also forgo this opportunity. But, each Member passes the responsibility to others to take the lead in exerting discipline, and no one ends up going first. The problem of collective action, intuitively, is summarized by the phrase "let George do it." All members in a collective body assume that some other member will take care of the problem, or take the lead in resolving the problem. The end result is that the problem goes unresolved.

Collective action theory was pioneered by an economist, Professor Mancur Olson, in his classic book *The Logic of Collective Action: Public Goods and the Theory of Groups* (1965, rev'd ed. 1971), and also in works such as Albert O. Hirschman, *Exit, Voice, and Loyalty: Reponses to Decline in Firms, Organizations, and States* (1970).

*Suggestions for Further Research:*

Article:

1.   Qasim, Sayera J. Iqbal, Note, *Collective Action in the WTO: A "Developing" Movement Toward Free Trade*, 39 UNIVERSITY OF MEMPHIS LAW REVIEW 153–191 (2008).

## *COLOMBIA FREE TRADE AGREEMENT*

The free trade agreement (FTA) between the United States and Colombia.

*Suggestions for Further Research:*

Article:

1.   Alewelt, Jennifer, Comment, *The Heat is on in Latin America: The Future and Implications of the Colombian Free Trade Agreement*, 39 CALIFORNIA WESTERN INTERNATIONAL LAW JOURNAL 159–195 (2008).

## COMESA

The *Common Market for Eastern and Southern Africa*, established in a 1994 agreement.

The agreement was finalized in 1993 (pursuant to a meeting in Uganda), and fully ratified in December 1994 (at a meeting in Malawi). The agreement creates a free trade agreement (FTA), and calls for formation of a customs union (CU) by 2008. *COMESA* includes 20 African nations, including all three members of the East African Community (EAC).

The *COMESA* members are as follows. (For non-founding members, the date of joining COMESA is set out in parentheses):

- Angola
- Burundi (1 January 2004)
- Comoros
- Congo (Democratic Republic)
- Djibouti (31 October 2000)
- Egypt
- Eritrea
- Ethiopia
- Kenya (31 October 2000)
- Libya

- Madagascar (31 October 2000)
- Malawi (31 October 2000)
- Mauritius (31 October 2000)
- Rwanda (1 January 2004)
- Seychelles
- Sudan (31 October 2000)
- Swaziland
- Uganda
- Zambia (31 October 2000)
- Zimbabwe (31 October 2000)

In 1999, the members agreed to push for the elimination of all internal tariffs in their FTA by October 2000, and called for the avoidance of unilateral measures designed to protect infant industries, raise revenue, or resolve BOP difficulties. These aims are more ambitious than those of SADC. However, not every *COMESA* member is happy with the fast pace. Tanzania — a member of SADC as well as *COMESA* — announced in 1999 its decision to pull out of *COMESA* the following year. Tanzania feared that tariff cuts of 90 percent, which were underway, would hurt its manufacturers.

Squabbles among members have seriously impeded progressive liberalization of trade. For instance, in November 1999, Kenya denied entry to Egyptian rice, flour, and other exports at the preferential tariff rates, because Kenya doubted the origin of these products. Egypt retaliated by delaying the approval of customs documents corresponding to a $20 million shipment of Kenyan tea. The dispute was not resolved until January 2000, after Kenya sent a delegation to verify the origin of Egypt's products, and the trade ministers between the two countries met.

*Suggestions for Further Research:*

Books:

1. HOUNGNIKPO, MATHURIN C. & HENRY KYAMBALESA, ECONOMIC INTEGRATION AND DEVELOPMENT IN AFRICA 99–124 (2006).

2. MSHOMBA, RICHARD E., AFRICA IN THE GLOBAL ECONOMY 175–201 (2000).

Articles:

1.   Ewelukwa, Uché U., *South — South Trade and Investment: The Good, the Bad, and the Ugly — African Perspectives*, 20 MINNESOTA JOURNAL OF INTERNATIONAL LAW 513–587 (2011).

2.   Oduor, Maurice, *Resolving Trade Disputes in Africa: Choosing Between Multilaterlism and Regionalism: The Case of COMESA and the WTO*, 13 TULANE JOURNAL OF INTERNATIONAL & COMPARATIVE LAW 177 (2005).

Other Source:

1.   Khandelwal, Padamja, *COMESA and SADC: Prospects and Challenges for Regional Trade Integration*, INTERNATIONAL MONETARY FUND WP/04/227 (December 2004).

## COMMERCE CLAUSE

Article I, Section 8, Clause 3 of the United States Constitution.

This Clause gives Congress — not the President — the power to regulate commerce with foreign nations, as well as with the Indian tribes. Therefore, all authority of the President in trade matters is delegated by Congress, under the Delegation Doctrine.

*Suggestions for Further Research:*

Article:

1.   Lee, Jennifer M., Comment, *A Match Made in Heaven or a Pair of Star-Crossed Lovers? Assessing Dormant Foreign Commerce Clause Limitations on the Wisconsin — China Relationship*, 2009 WISCONSIN LAW REVIEW 733–762 (2009).

## COMMERCIAL PRESENCE

The existence of a representative office, agency, branch, or subsidiary of a company from one country in the territory of another country.

## COMMODITY CREDIT CORPORATION

*See* CCC (second meaning).

## COMMODITY CROPS

*See* Program Crops.

## COMMON AND DIFFERENTIATED OBLIGATIONS

A term used to connote all parties to an agreement share a common obligation, but the precise requirements each party to which each party must adhere, or duties each party must fulfill, differ.

For example, all parties to an agreement on global warming (such as the *Kyoto Protocol*) may share a commitment to reducing greenhouse gas emissions. But, the extent to which each party must cut emissions, the way in which it cuts the emissions, and the time period for doing so, may differ depending on the party. The differences may relate to the status of a party as a developed, developing, or least developed country, which would suggest a relationship between the concept of "common and differentiated obligations" and "special and differential treatment."

## COMMUNITY INTEREST

An approach to studying whether antidumping (AD) duties and countervailing duties (CVDs) are needed, advocated by (*inter alia*) former European Union (EU) Trade Commissioner Peter Mandelson.

Under the Community interest test, the Directorate-General for Trade of the European Commission (DG-Trade) would analyze whether interests, in addition to those of the domestic industry petitioning for AD or CVD relief, would be served or harmed by imposition of a trade remedy. In particular, the test would take into account the interests of downstream users of the imported merchandise subject to an AD or CVD investigation, such as retail businesses (*e.g.*, firms that use the subject merchandise as an input), and consumers (*i.e.*, end users of the subject merchandise).

During the Doha Round negotiations, the November 2007 draft modalities text on rules, covering AD, CVD, and fishing subsidies issues, proposed a similar approach to the Community interest test. The United States (*inter alia*) opposes any such approach.

## COMPARATIVE ADVANTAGE (COMPARATIVE VERSUS ABSOLUTE ADVANTAGE)

In the 18th century, Adam Smith (1723–1790) focused on absolute advantage. In *The Wealth of Nations* (1776), Smith pointed out that absolute advantage exists when one country is better than a second country at making one commodity, while the second country is better than the first country at making another commodity. Each country is better than the other at making a certain good. As an example, the United States is better at producing software than Ghana, whereas Ghana is better at growing cocoa than the United States. Adam Smith observed that it will be economically beneficial for each country to trade with the other. Smith counseled that each country should specialize in producing the good in which it has an absolute advantage, and export the amount of that good that it does not consume domestically in exchange for imports of a different good in which it lacks an absolute advantage. The result is an increase in the total output of both goods, and an increase in consumption of both goods.

But, Smith was dealing with the "easy" case, where there are two countries and each one has an absolute advantage in a different good. What if one country has an absolute advantage in the production of both products? David Ricardo (1772–1823) provided the answer in *The Principles of Political Economy and Taxation* (1817). In the 19th century, David Ricardo focused on comparative advantage. "Comparative" advantage exists whenever a country has a greater margin of superiority, or a smaller margin of inferiority. Michael Jordan has an absolute advantage over your *Dictionary* author in both basketball and baseball. However, your author has a comparative advantage in baseball, because his margin of inferiority relative to Mr. Jordan — while huge — is smaller than his margin of inferiority relative to Michael in basketball. Someone, or some country, always has a comparative advantage in some activity, even if it has no absolute advantage in any activity. (The only exception to this statement is the nearly impossible case where the margin of inferiority is the same in every single activity.) Thus, it is simply wrong to say that a particular country has no comparative advantage in any good.

Put differently, and in concrete terms, even if Third World countries could produce everything more cheaply than the United States, European Union (EU), and Japan, these three developed countries still would have a comparative advantage in the production of something. Moreover, the cheaper wage rates in Third World countries typically reflect lower productivity. These wage rates mask the need to hire more workers to complete a product, and to overcome problems with infrastructure — both of which suggest higher costs.

Who cares about this difference? Ricardo pointed out that gains from trade follow from comparative, not absolute, advantage. Because a country is sure to have a comparative advantage in the production of some commodity, the scope of Ricardo's argument for free trade is far broader than is often realized. A country that is dreadful at making everything still will have a comparative advantage in making some product, even though in absolute terms it is inefficient at making that product.

A simple arithmetic example illustrates the difference between absolute and comparative advantage, and the gains from free trade.[106] Suppose there are two countries in the world, East and West. Both countries have 1,000 workers, and both countries make two goods — computers and bicycles. West has an absolute advantage in the production of both goods. To make a bicycle, West needs the labor of two workers, whereas East needs four. West uses 10 workers to make a computer, while East uses 100. Clearly, West makes both goods more efficiently than East.

Assume at the outset there is no trade between East and West, and that in each country half of the workers are in each sector. Assume further that, at the outset, West makes 250 bicycles and 50 computers, whereas East makes 125 bikes and five computers. What happens when the two countries begin trading?

---

[106] *See Schools Brief — Trade Winds*, THE ECONOMIST, 8 November 1997, at 85-86.

The starting point of the answer is to observe that even though West has an absolute advantage in both bikes and computers, it has a greater advantage — a bigger edge — in manufacturing computers. Why? Because the ratio of workers used to make bikes in West versus East is 2:4 (*i.e.*, 1:2), but in the computer sector it is 10:100 (*i.e.*, 1:10). And, in terms of output, the ratio of bikes made under autarky in West versus East is 250:125 (*i.e.*, 2:1). In the computer sector, it is 50:5 (*i.e.*, 10:1). Consequently, West has a comparative advantage in computers. Conversely, East has a comparative advantage in making bikes — it has less of an inferiority in this sector than in computers. Thus, with international trade, West will specialize in making computers, and East will concentrate on bikes.

Suppose that West decides to employ 700 workers to make computers, and just 300 workers to make bikes. West's computer output rises to 70, and its bike production falls to 150. Suppose East, on the other hand, focuses on producing just bikes, making 250. World output of both goods has risen (70 computers and 400 bikes after trade, versus 55 computers and 375 bikes before trade), and both countries can consume more if they trade.

At what price will international trade between West and East occur? Neither country will want to import a product that it could make more cheaply itself. Accordingly, West will want at least five bikes per computer. Why? Because in the absence of trade, West makes 250 bikes and 50 computers, thus the price ratio between the two commodities is 250:50 or 5:1. In other words, without trade, 5 bikes = 1 computer. For its part, East will not pay more than 25 bikes per computer. Why? Again, consider the autarky position of East. It makes 125 bikes and five computers, yielding a price ratio of 125:5 or 25:1, *i.e.*,25 bikes = one computer.

With free trade between West and East, the equilibrium world market price of bikes-to-computers will settle somewhere between the 5:1 and 25:1 ratio. Exactly where it settles will depend on demand and supply factors. Suppose that equilibrium is 12:1, *i.e.*, the terms of trade are 12 bikes per computer. Suppose further that 120 bikes are exchanged for 10 computers — West exports 10 computers to East, in return for 120 bikes.

Both countries clearly are better off, said Ricardo, despite the absolute advantage of West in both sectors. West ends up with 270 bikes (150 domestically made bikes, plus 120 imports) and 60 computers (it makes 70, and exports 10). East gets 130 bikes (250 made domestically, less 120 exported) and 10 computers (all imported). In each sector, each country consumes more than it did under autarky. West's consumption of bikes rises from 250 to 270, and its consumption of computers rises from 50 to 60. East's consumption of bikes increases from 125 to 130, and its consumption of computers doubles from five to 10. These gains from trade arise because each country has a comparative advantage in one good — West in computers, East in bikes. The comparative advantage derives from cost differentials: East can produce bikes relatively cheaply compared to West.

*Suggestions for Further Research:*

Books:

1.   BAGWELL, KYLE W., GEORGE A. BERMANN & PETROS C. MAVROIDIS, EDS, LAW AND ECONOMICS OF CONTINGENT PROTECTIONISM IN INTERNATIONAL TRADE (2009). *See also* the review of this book, Jeffrey Kessler, *Book Note*, 46 STANFORD JOURNAL OF INTERNATIONAL LAW 243–245 (2010).

2.   ESTEVADEORDAL, ANTONI & KATI SUOMINEN, THE SOVEREIGN REMEDY? TRADE AGREEMENTS IN A GLOBALIZING WORLD (2009).

3.   RAZEEN, SALLY, NEW FRONTIERS IN FREE TRADE — GLOBALIZATION'S FUTURE AND ASIA'S RISING ROLE (2008).

Articles:

1.   Alessandrini, Donatella, *Transnational Corporations and the Doctrine of Comparative Advantage: A Critique of Free Trade Normative Assumptions*, 11 INTERNATIONAL TRADE LAW & REGULATION issue 1, 14–23 (January 2005).

2.   Ghei, Nita, *Institutional Arrangements, Property Rights, and the Endogenity of Comparative Advantage*, 18 TRANSNATIONAL LAW & CONTEMPORARY PROBLEMS 617–655 (2009).

3.   Gonzalez, Carmen G., *An Environmental Justice Critique of Comparative Advantage: Indigenous Peoples, Trade Policy, and the Mexican Neoliberal Economic Reforms*, 32 UNIVERSITY OF PENNSYLVANIA JOURNAL OF INTERNATIONAL LAW 723–803 (2011).

4.   Gormley, Laurence W., *Free Movement of Goods and Their Use — What's The Use of It?*, 33 FORDHAM INTERNATIONAL LAW JOURNAL 1589–1628 (2010).

5.   Loridas, Kara, Note, *United States — China Trade War; Signs of Protectionism in a Globalized Economy?*, 34 SUFFOLK TRANSNATIONAL LAW REVIEW 403–427 (2011).

6.   Nourse, Victoria & Gregory Shaffer, *Varieties of New Legal Realism: Can A New World Order Prompt A New Legal Theory?*, 95 CORNELL LAW REVIEW 61–137 (November 2009).

## COMPENSATION PRINCIPLE

Virtually any change in economic policy, including trade liberalization, results not only in the improvement of the welfare of some groups in society — the "gainers" or "winners" — but also the diminution of the welfare of other groups in society — the "losers."

One criterion for evaluating whether the policy move is worthwhile is to consider the net welfare effect on society. According to the compensation principle, however, it is possible that the welfare of everyone in the society can be improved from the policy change. This possibility exists if the gainers from the change agree to compensate the losers, by taking some of their gain and sharing it with them.[107] Thus, under the compensation principle, social welfare

---

[107] *See* W. CHARLES SAWYER & RICHARD L. SPRINKLE, INTERNATIONAL ECONOMICS 52 (2003).

potentially improves if gainers compensate losers, so that the policy shift renders all members of society better off.

## COMPETITION POLICY

Essentially, a synonym for antitrust law and regulation.

Trade and competition policy was one of the four Singapore Issues (i.e., issues agreed upon at the December 1996 Singapore Ministerial Conference of the WTO for future multilateral trade negotiations). However, the issue — particularly following the September 2003 Cancún Ministerial Conference — was not pursued in the Doha Round. Many free trade agreements (FTAs), some of which pre-date this Round, have chapters on competition policy. Most (if not all) United States FTAs include such a Chapter, and Australia's FTAs with (for example) Singapore and Thailand have such Chapters.

In the absence of a multilateral agreement on trade and competition policy, there are two basic models for FTA chapters on trade and competition policy. The "American" model emphasizes procedure, and calls for cooperation among domestic antitrust authorities. Such cooperation covers (inter alia) the exchange of confidential information, and cooperation in gathering evidence and the conduct of an investigation, and mutual assistance in enforcement matters. The "European" model focuses on substantive rules about competition, such as monopolization, tying, restrictive business practices, and so forth.

The efficacy of FTA chapters on trade and competition policy is unclear. In part, the strength and resources of antitrust authorities in one country can be a fillip such a chapter, whereas weak antitrust institutions and a lack of legal capacity can mean the chapter has little practical effect.

*Suggestions for Further Research:*

Articles:

1.   Colino, Sandra Marco, *On the Road to Perdition? The Future of the European Car Industry and its Implications for EC Competition Policy*, 28 NORTHWESTERN JOURNAL OF INTERNATIONAL LAW AND BUSINESS 35–88 (2007).

2.   Sokol, Daniel D., *Order without (Enforceable) Law: Why Countries Enter into Non-Enforceable Competition Policy Chapters in Free Trade Agreements*, 83 CHICAGO-KENT LAW REVIEW 231–292 (2008).

## COMPETITIVE ADVANTAGE

A business school explanation relating to the pattern of international trade.

The theory of competitive advantage was developed by Harvard Business School Professor Michael Porter in *The Competitive Advantage of Nations* (1990). Professor Porter attempts to move beyond comparative advantage based on relative cost differentials and consider the extent to which a nation. The process is "highly localized," and "[d]ifferences in national economic structures, values, cultures, institutions, and histories contribute profoundly to competitive success."[108] No single strategy accounted for competitive advantage in a particular industry, and "only strategies tailored to the particular industry and to the skills and assets of a particular firm succeed."[109] Rather, the structure of an industry, and the competitive positions of firms within an industry, determined what strategies would generate a competitive advantage.

Professor Porter's analysis assumes the "basic principles of competitive strategy apply whether a firm is competing domestically or internationally."[110] Accordingly, he engages in four basic inquiries. First, what are the sources of domestic competitive advantage? The answer is the "value chain," which is the way in which a firm creates value for its customers by performing critical discrete activities. "Primary activities" are the production, marketing, delivery, and servicing of a product, whereas "support activities" include the provision of inputs, technology, human resources, and other infrastructural factors such as general management and finance.[111] A firm gains competitive advantage by developing new ways to conduct its primary and support activities through the use of new procedures, technologies, or inputs, and by ensuring that linkages in its value chain are optimal, coordinated, and well managed. Ultimately, the competitive advantage may take the form of a cost advantage, though at what point this gain accrues varies from one firm to another.

Second, how is domestic competitive advantage created? Professor Porter suggests that a firm creates competitive advantage "by perceiving or discovering new and better ways to compete in an industry and bringing them to market."[112] In other words, innovation is the key to creating competitive advantage. A firm must strive to improve its use of technology and find better ways to conduct its activities. In this respect, adaptability is a crucial trait. "Successful firms not only respond to their environment but also attempt to influence it in their favor," and "[o]ne nation's firms supplant another's in international competition when they are in a better position to perceive or respond to such changes."[113]

Third, how is domestic competitive advantage sustained? The answer depends on the (1) source of the advantage, (2) number of sources that generate the advantage, and (3) extent to which a firm seeks to improve and upgrade its advantage. As for the source, a "lower-order" advantage, like low labor costs or cheap raw materials, is easy for other firms to imitate.[114] In contrast, a "higher-order" advantage, like an intellectual property right or brand reputation based on cumulative marketing efforts, is relatively more durable, particularly where a firm engages in sustained and cumulative investment in that advantage.[115]

---

[108] MICHAEL PORTER, THE COMPETITIVE ADVANTAGE OF NATIONS 19 (1990).
[109] MICHAEL PORTER, THE COMPETITIVE ADVANTAGE OF NATIONS 34 (1990).
[110] MICHAEL PORTER, THE COMPETITIVE ADVANTAGE OF NATIONS 53 (1990).
[111] MICHAEL PORTER, THE COMPETITIVE ADVANTAGE OF NATIONS 40 (1990).
[112] MICHAEL PORTER, THE COMPETITIVE ADVANTAGE OF NATIONS 45 (1990).
[113] MICHAEL PORTER, THE COMPETITIVE ADVANTAGE OF NATIONS 34 (1990).
[114] MICHAEL PORTER, THE COMPETITIVE ADVANTAGE OF NATIONS 49–50 (1990).
[115] MICHAEL PORTER, THE COMPETITIVE ADVANTAGE OF NATIONS 50 (1990).

The larger the number of sources of a competitive advantage, the more sustainable that advantage is. Finally, a firm resting on its laurels and failing to improve and upgrade its sources of competitive advantage surely will lose its advantage.

Fourth, how is competitive advantage created through an international strategy, and what role does the nation play in fostering a competitive advantage in the global context? Global configuration and coordination are the answers. Professor Porter focuses on the way in which a firm spreads its "activities among nations to serve the world market," and its ability to coordinate the dispersed activities.[116] A firm gains competitive advantage in the global arena by configuring its value chain activities in an appropriate manner, and ensuring these activities are properly integrated. Further, a firm may enter into a strategic alliance — a long-term agreement with another firm or firms that falls short of a formal merger — to conduct its global strategy. Airlines furnish a good example of this behavior. In turn, a nation succeeds in the global arena if its environment supports the pursuit of proper configuration and coordination strategies.

At bottom, Professor Porter's theory of the competitive advantage of nations is a common-sense argument, laden with business school jargon, in favor of a market economy supported by enlightened government policies. He writes:

> [c]reating competitive advantage in sophisticated industries demands improvement and innovation — finding better ways to compete and exploiting them globally, and relentlessly upgrading the firm's products and processes. Nations succeed in industries if their national circumstances provide an environment that supports this sort of behavior. Creating advantage requires insight into new ways of competing and the willingness to take risks and to invest in implementing them. Nations succeed where the national environment uniquely enables firms to perceive new strategies for competing in an industry. Nations succeed where local circumstances provide an impetus for firms to pursue such strategies early and aggressively. Nations fail where firms do not receive the right signals, are not subject to the right pressures, and do not have the right capabilities.[117]

In other words, the implication for international trade law of Porter's theory is this: a government should ensure entrepreneurs operate in a free trade environment so they are both challenged to adapt and rewarded for their innovations.

## COMPETITIVE LIBERALIZATION

The simultaneous pursuit of trade liberalization negotiations on three levels — multilateral, regional, and bilateral.

---

[116] MICHAEL PORTER, THE COMPETITIVE ADVANTAGE OF NATIONS 54 (1990).

[117] MICHAEL PORTER, THE COMPETITIVE ADVANTAGE OF NATIONS 67-68 (1990).

Allegedly, former Singaporean Prime Minister Lee Kuan Yew developed the strategy in 1993, in the context of the Asia Pacific Economic Cooperation (APEC) forum. In the context of a domestic economy, it means implementing economic reforms to enhance international competitiveness. To help achieve this goal, trade liberalization is necessary at three levels — multilateral, regional, and bilateral. In turn, developing free trade agreements (FTAs) and customs unions (CUs), on a regional or bilateral basis, can lead to liberalization multilaterally through the WTO. Prime Minister Lee argued that if the United States were serious about competitive liberalization of its domestic economy, then it would invite any Asian country to join *North American Free Trade Agreement* (*NAFTA*) that also was committed to deregulation. There would be tension with some Asian countries, in which changing economic structures and policies, is a slow process (*e.g.*, Japan). But, within five years any recalcitrant Asian country would give in, liberalize expeditiously, because it could not afford to stay out of an FTA with the United States.

In brief, competitive liberalization means moving as aggressively as possible toward the goal of global free trade by pursuing trade liberalization on three levels — multilateral, regional, and bilateral — simultaneously. This kind of trade policy is driven by domestic-level economic reforms, *i.e.*, deregulation and the advancement of a free market system. Might it, then, be more accurate to call the strategy "complimentary liberalization," or (as it euphemistically is sometimes dubbed) "parallel liberalization"?

Labels aside, competitive liberalization suffers from a threshold administrative problem. It is a strategy only rich countries can pursue effectively. It requires a considerable number of talented international trade lawyers to pursue three-track negotiations, and the lawyers on each track must coordinate with the lawyers on all other tracks. That is a challenge even for the United States Trade Representative (USTR), and *a fortiori* it is a close-to-insurmountable task for trade ministries in the Philippines, Suriname, or Togo.

Competitive liberalization also suffers from conceptual and practical problems. Consider the following questions:

- How does trade liberalization feed back to domestic-level reforms, particularly in special or sensitive sectors like agriculture and textiles and apparel?

- How do multilateral, regional, and bilateral trade liberalization efforts relate to one another? In particular, is the "Bicycle Theory" of trade negotiations correct, whereby these efforts must continue (as a cyclist must keep pedaling to move forward) or they will come to a halt (as a cyclist would stop, even fall off)?

- Is competitive liberalization a fair concept, particularly when it creates discriminatory treatment through a regional trade agreement (RTA), within the context of non-discriminatory treatment under GATT–WTO rules?

- Does competitive liberalization failure to align properly economic and non-economic benefits from trade liberalization?

The last question requires elaboration.

Consider rents from tariffs in comparison with rents from intellectual property rights (IP). Tariff rents arise from government collection of tariff revenue. IP rents are associated with the ability of a patent, trade or service mark, or copyright owner to exclude all others from manufacturing, distributing, or licensing the good or service embodying the IP, and thus to hold a monopoly position with respect to that good or service. Suppose competitive liberalization were extended to the extreme through RTAs, whereby the United States had an FTA with every country in the world. Rents from tariffs would disappear, because with all trade accorded duty-free treatment, neither the United States nor its FTA partners gain tariff revenue. Would IP rents disappear?

The answer is "no." Holders of patents, trade and service marks, and copyrights — from Adidas to Sony Pictures, from Amazon.com to Roche — assuredly would press the United States and its FTA partners for textual provisions to ensure strict IP protection and enforcement. Thus, exporters and importers of goods would enjoy the disappearance of tariff rents. IP holders would enjoy the maintenance of IP rents. This alignment could create tension. The first group (exporters and importers) would focus on the economic dimensions of the FTAs. The second group (IP rights holders) would be keenly sensitive to IP infringement, and urge rigorous prosecution and penalties. The first group would prefer diplomatic peace to preserve its economic benefits. The diplomatic interests of the second group might call for confrontation to enforce their IP rights, possibly with some disruption in the economic *status quo*. In brief, competitive liberalization in the extreme might not necessarily bring into alignment all economic and non-economic features of FTAs.

That said, the fundamental point to observe is that competitive liberalization itself is not a purely economic strategy. Encouraging trade negotiations on three tracks simultaneously is a hedge against the political risk of failure on one or two of the tracks. In purely American terms, it avoids the United States "putting all its trade eggs in the multilateral basket." More bluntly, it ensures American efforts to obtain market access in other countries are not subject to a veto by any one country, such as France or India, or by any one domestic constituency, such as steel or textile and apparel interests. If blockage occurs on one level, then progress might be made on another level.

*Suggestions for Further Research:*

Articles:

1. Bergsten, C. Fred, *Globalizing Free Trade: The Ascent of Regionalism*, 75 FOREIGN AFFAIRS (May/June 1996).

2. Sutherland, Peter, *The Case for EMU: More than Money*, 76 FOREIGN AFFAIRS (January/February 1997).

3. Zoellick, Robert B., *Campaign 2000: A Republican Foreign Policy*, 79 FOREIGN AFFAIRS (January/February 2000).

## COMPULSORY LICENSE (COMPULSORY LICENSING)

A license granted by a government to permit production of a patented product (or use of a patented process) without the consent of the owner of the patent. That permission is given to a third party, *i.e.*, to someone other than the patent holder.

In effect, a compulsory license suspends the intellectual property right (IPR) — patent protection — of a holder (owner) of that right, but for a specific product and purpose. Typically, the product is a pharmaceutical (*i.e.*, medicine) used to treat a dreaded disease. The purpose usually is to manufacture — by the government or a third party to which the government gives the compulsory license — the product in large, generic quantities and make it available at lower cost than otherwise charged by the patent holder.

Compulsory licensing is permitted under WTO rules, but under strict conditions set out in the *Agreement on Trade Related Aspects of Intellectual Property Rights (TRIPs)*, as amended by the WTO Members. Specifically, Article 31 of the *TRIPs Agreement* allows a WTO Member government, or a third party authorized by a Member government, to make a patented product without permission from the owner (holder) of the patent covering that product. Article 31(h) requires a government issuing a compulsory license to provide the patent holder with "adequate remuneration," which means a modest royalty fee. After all, if a government or third party makes a patented product, or generic version of the product, under a compulsory license, and sells that product at a lower price than the patented item, then the profits of the patent holder are in peril. Consumers may flock to the lower-cost version, if they are able to do so, meaning sales of the patented version will tumble. Unscrupulous traders may arbitrage the product, if there are barriers between markets — buying the cheaper version in one location, and selling it at a higher price against the brand-name patented item in another location. The result might be price suppression or price depression of the patented item.

Notably, Article 31(f) forbids exports of pharmaceuticals (*e.g.*, generic drugs) manufactured under a compulsory license. They must be distributed domestically, *i.e.*, used "predominantly for the supply of the domestic market," which is the territory of the country in which the compulsory license is issued.

Article 31 of the *TRIPs Agreement* says a government cannot issue a compulsory license unless it has tried to obtain authorization from the right holder on "reasonable commercial terms," and those efforts have been unsuccessful within a "reasonable period of time." Yet, this rule is subject to two notable exceptions — for "national emergency or other circumstances of extreme urgency," or (under Article 31(b)) for "cases of public non-commercial use." In these instances, a government need not enter into negotiations with the right holder. As initially drafted in the Uruguay Round, these exceptions were undefined. Would a public health crisis qualify for one of the exceptions? If so, then what kind of disease — only communicable, life-threatening illness, or non-communicable, non-life-threatening ailments — would pass muster?

The ambiguity of the exceptions meant WTO Members were left to their own devices in respect of invoking Article 31. Ironically, and with tragic consequences, in the years following the Uruguay Round (specifically, 1995–2007) developing and least developed countries did not use the flexibility afforded by Article 31 to help poor victims of treat HIV/AIDs and other diseases. They feared retaliation by large, multinational pharmaceutical companies. And, smaller poor countries lacked manufacturing capacity, *i.e.*, even if a government of one of these countries issues a compulsory license, neither it nor any third parties in its territory could make the needed medicine. Yet, Article 31(f) barred exports of pharmaceuticals made under a compulsory license, so a country lacking manufacturing capacity could not lawfully import such products. Put differently, a poor country could not grant a compulsory license to a third party in a country with manufacturing capacity, and then import the generic medicine from that country.

After years of resistance from developed countries, particularly the United States and several EU states, developing and least developed countries succeeded on putting Article 31 revision on the agenda for WTO negotiations. In the Doha Ministerial Conference of November 2001, the topic made its way onto the Doha Development Agenda (DDA), but the *Ministerial Declaration* itself did not fix the problem that compulsory licensing is unhelpful to a country lacking manufacturing capacity. Even the special *Declaration on TRIPs and Public Health*, emanating from the Doha Conference, while referencing specifically the issue Paragraph 6, did not resolve the problem. To be sure, the WTO unleashed a series of public pronouncements asserting the *TRIPs Agreement* ought not to block an appropriate balance between the rights of IPR rights holders, on the one hand, and poor countries — and the vulnerabilities of their people — on the other hand. But, "ought not" and "does not" are legally distinct.

Nearly two years later, in August 2003, the WTO Members agreed to a temporary amendment of the *TRIPs Agreement*. Technically, the 2003 Amendment, sometimes called the *"Medicines Agreement,"* took the form of three waivers from Article 31 of the *TRIPs Agreement* — two waivers from Article 31(f), and one waiver from Article 31(h). The waivers address squarely the legal bar on issuance of a compulsory license by a government in one country lacking manufacturing capacity to a third party in another country, with a view to importing generic drugs made by the third country. To summarize the first waiver from Article 31(f):

- An importing country may issue a compulsory license to a third party, such as a pharmaceutical company, in another country.

- The importing country must notify the WTO of its action, specifically of the patented drug that is the subject of the compulsory license, and the quantity of medicines it seeks a third party to make on its behalf. That country also must attest to its lack of manufacturing capacity.

- The licensed third party may manufacture a pharmaceutical product, on which it is not the patent owner, and make a generic — and typically cheaper — version of the patented drug. The third party must make only the amount of the drug required by the licensing country. It also must package the generic version it makes in a distinctive manner using appropriate colors, shapes, and labels.

- The third party must obtain another license — known as a second compulsory license — to export the drug it makes back to the licensing country. There must be no diversion of the compulsorily licensed drugs to markets, *i.e.*, no shipping of them into markets other than the country issuing the initial license.

- The exporting country in which the third party is situated must give advance notification to the WTO, through a special website, that compulsorily licensed medicines are being exported from its territory.

Under the second waiver from Paragraph 31(f), developing and least developed WTO Members can export or re-export the drugs to countries in a free trade agreement (FTA) or customs union (CU), as long as at least half of those countries are least developed. The third waiver, from Article 31(h), frees a WTO Member importing generic pharmaceuticals under a compulsory license from the obligation of paying compensation to the patent holder of the medicine that is the subject of that license. In brief, the three waivers in the *Medicines Agreement* permits the exportation of generic medicines under a compulsory license issued by a government that lacks the manufacturing capacity to make those medicines, and obviates the need for compensation to the rights holder.

Supplementing the August 2003 *Medicines Agreement* was a Statement read by the Chairman of the WTO General Council on 6 December 2005, in connection with the Hong Kong Ministerial Conference. Significantly, at that Conference, the Members adopted the waivers as a "Decision," thus making the waivers permanent. The Statement was designed to deal with concerns raised by developed countries about unscrupulous and opportunistic behavior in respect of compulsory licensing. The Chairman's Statement embodies an understanding of the Members that compulsory licenses are to be issued in good faith, exportation of generics is to occur only in the event of a public health problem coupled with manufacturing incapacity, and pharmaceutical patents not to be broken to advance national industrial or commercial policy goals.

While the Statement was re-read at the Conference it was not, contrary to the demands of the United States, incorporated expressly by reference into the text of the *TRIPs Agreement*. Whether the Statement forms hard law obligations supplementing that text, as amended by the *Medicines Agreement* (as the United States sought), or whether it creates best endeavor duties (as India and other developing countries argue) is uncertain. What is clear is the three waivers in the *Medicines Agreement*, made permanent in Hong Kong, are the first changes to any Uruguay Round text. Specifically, WTO Members agreed the waivers would become a permanent amendment to the *TRIPs Agreement* as soon as two-thirds of the Membership agreed to the deal, with a deadline for ratification of 1 December 2007. However, by October 2007, only 11 of the then 151 Members had ratified the changes — and no African Member had done so, despite Sub-Saharan African countries being at the forefront of compulsory licensing reform. Thus, the WTO, via a Decision of the TRIPs Council of 23 October 2007, had no choice but to extend the ratification deadline to 1 December 2009. Until ratification, technically the waivers are temporary amendments.

Notably, the EU ratified the changes via the agreement of the European Parliament in October 2007.[118] In doing so, the Parliament also pledged the EU would not include protection of intellectual property rights (IPRs) in bilateral trade agreements with poor countries (albeit without defining the qualifying countries). Further, the Parliament established a U.S. $2.8 million annual fund for technology transfer and research.

Notably, neither the August 2003 *Medicines Agreement* nor December 2005 Chairman's Statement directly addresses pharmaceutical pricing, about which there are least two issues — level and disparity. First, for the poor everywhere — in rich or poor countries — medicine is either unaffordable or foists upon people cruel trade-offs. Second, pharmaceutical prices for the same drug are not uniform globally. Different local market conditions, and cross-border price discrimination, occur. At the same time, the WTO is not responsible for setting drug prices — nor should it be. Market forces of supply and demand are, in an open, capitalistic trading system, the price-setting mechanisms.

The *Agreement* and Statement also do not address the problem of research and development of new medicines for ailments predominant in poor countries. Pharmaceutical companies are wont to invest heavily in drugs to treat diseases prevalent among populations in countries that can pay for those drugs. There is little profit in developing cheap medicines to fight cholera, dengue fever, malaria, or tuberculosis, all of which kill many millions of people in poor countries, yet rare in rich ones. Put simply, a profit making enterprise answerable to shareholders and stock market analysts sees little gain from inventing, making, and distributing drugs to fight diseases if demand is low in wealthy markets, regardless of the demand in impoverished lands. The situation is not so much one of market failure, but of the market operating exactly as predicted, with negative externalities.

These three gaps aside, 33 developed country WTO Members, including the United States, European Union (EU), and Japan forswore using a compulsory license to import drugs. Their action helped ease concerns of major pharmaceutical companies in those countries that inexpensive generic medicines would flow back from third countries and undermine their patents (and, of course, profits). Eleven other Members — notably including China, Israel, Korea,

---

[118] *See* Andrew Bounds, *EU Clears Way for Cheap Drugs*, FINANCIAL TIMES, 25 October 2007, at 3.

Mexico, Qatar, and Turkey — agreed they would invoke the new rules only if they faced a national emergency or extreme urgency. In other words, they abandoned the right to import compulsorily licensed drugs for a mere public non-commercial use.

In November 2006, Thailand — specifically, the Government Pharmaceutical Organization (GPO) — became the first WTO Member to issue a compulsory license to a third party in a foreign country — a generic drug producer in India. The subject of the license was Efavirenz, used to treat HIV/AIDS, the patent on which is held by Merck. For that drug, the GPO authorized domestic production of generic versions until 2011, and importation from India of generic copies until it gains manufacturing capacity. In January 2007, the Thai GPO issued two additional compulsorily licenses for drugs patented by Abbott Laboratories — Kaletra, also an HIV/AIDS medicine, and Plavix, which is a blood-thinning drug used to treat heart disease and strokes. The GPO went even further, issuing another compulsory license, namely, for a tuberculosis (TB) medicine, on which Sanofi-Aventis (a Franco-German drug maker) held the patent. The Thai government also pressed, with success, Sanofi-Aventis to cut the price it charges to patients in the Thai public health system for its malaria treatment.

Accordingly, in the spring of 2007, Thailand formally invoked the compulsory license provisions of the *TRIPs Agreement*, *Doha Declaration on TRIPs*, and *Medicines Agreement* — the first WTO Member to make this legal maneuver. Thailand reminded the world it boasts an ambitious health care program to make life-saving drugs for certain ailments, including HIV/AIDS and tuberculosis (TB), available to any of its needy citizens either free of charge or at a reduced price. Thailand urged that it lacked the capacity to produce these medicines, either at all or in the volumes needed to satisfy domestic demand. The price differential between the patented and generic versions was significant. Thailand imported the Indian-produced version of Efavirenz at one-half the cost of the patented version from Merck. For Kaletra, Thailand argued Abbott had been selling the non-heat stable version to it at U.S. $2,200 per patient, whereas Abbott sold the drug at $500 per patient in Africa. Abbott said Thailand was using compulsory licensing as a tool for price negotiations. It retaliated by withholding seven drugs from the Thai market, including the heat-stable version of Kaletra, which is widely sought after in hot, humid countries for patients for whom the first-line drug therapies has failed.

Unsurprisingly, then, pharmaceutical companies and other critics lambasted Thailand. Why issue a compulsory license for Efavirenz, which (according to Merck) was sold in Thailand at cost of production? Did the compulsory licenses for Efavirenz and Kaletra suggest Thailand was abusing HIV/AIDS as a justification for patent piracy? Why issue a compulsory license for Plavix, which treats non-communicable diseases? Surely there are other countries — least-developed ones where the HIV/AIDS infection rates are higher than in Thailand — which are *bona fide* cases for compulsory licenses? (The adult infection rate in Thailand is 1.5 percent, but 30 percent in Cambodia and parts of Sub-Saharan Africa.) Was Thailand trying to fulfill a promise, made in 2004, to provide HIV/AIDS drugs to 500,000 HIV/AIDS infected citizens, which it had thus far failed to do partly because of rising drug prices? Was the military government, which took power in a September 2006 *coup d'état*, trying to cut drug prices and thus allow for a diversion of funds from health care to defense? (Thailand specifically rejected the latter two charges. The seven percent increase in its health care budget from 1986–2006 simply was outpaced by the prices of name-brand, life-saving drugs.)

Yet, no one — not even the United States Trade Representative (USTR) — accused Thailand of acting unlawfully. True, the Pharmaceutical Research and Manufacturers of America (PhRMA) castigated Thailand for not consulting or negotiating first with (for example) Merck. But, Thailand appropriately justified its decision not to negotiate with the rights holders before breaking the patents under Article 31(b) of the *TRIPs Agreement* — public non-commercial use. And, Thailand provided all requisite notifications. Moreover, major drug companies changed their tact with poor countries. They feared more Thai-like events, and with good reason, as Brazil followed suit, and India, Indonesia, and Kenya announced possible compulsory license issuances. The companies cut prices of certain drugs, even offering to Thailand to do so — if Thailand only would revoke the compulsory licenses. In other words, each company now had to make a cost-benefit calculation on each of its patented drugs as to whether it would lose more money by a voluntary price concession that staved off a compulsory license, or by a compulsory license that opened borders between two countries to generic copies. Whether the possibility that increased availability of generic versions of patented, brand-name drugs might cause a general lowering of prices, however, remains uncertain.

The Brazilian case is particularly intriguing, because it spotlights the issue of drawing distinctions among countries based on the extent of their poverty and infection rates, and ability to pay for brand-name medications. For Efavirenz, Brazil asked Merck to cut the price from $1.57 per patient per day to 65 cents — the amount at which Merck sold it in Thailand. Merck refused. Merck distinguished the two countries: AIDS is more prevalent in Thailand than Brazil, and Brazil is larger and wealthier than Thailand. Therefore, Thailand — but not Brazil — is in Merck's category for pricing at cost. Brazil simply can afford to pay more for drugs than a poorer, harder hit country like Thailand. Not persuaded by a utilitarian calculus, in May 2007, Brazil became the second country to invoke compulsory licenses, overriding Merck's Efavirenz patent. The drug would be available, sourced from India, at 45 cents. Observe that of 180,000 Brazilians who get free anti-retroviral AIDS medicines from the government, 75,000 Brazilians use Efavirenz.

Notably, in March 2012, India granted its first compulsory license since implementing the *TRIPs Agreement* in 2005.[119] The facts for its move were

---

[119] *See* Madhur Singh, *Compulsory License Awarded to Natco to Sell Generic of Bayer's Nexavar in India*, 29 International Trade Reporter (BNA) 414 (15 March 2012).

compelling. In March 2008, India granted a patent to Swiss pharmaceutical giant Bayer to sell Nexavar, to treat kidney and lung cancer, in India. Bayer sold the drug at $5,600 per month, a prohibitive cost for most Indians, who must pay for their medications out of pocket. Natco Pharma, an Indian generic pharmaceutical company, sought from Bayer a license for the patent so that Natco could produce a generic version, called "Sorafenib," of Nexavar. Bayer refused, even though the availability of Sorafenib in India was limited to less than one percent of the patients requiring it. This supply constraint existed because Bayer controlled and imported into India all supplies of the generic version of Nexavar, and Bayer sold them only in a few of India's major cities and certain states.

Natco then applied for a compulsory license to the Indian Controller General of Patents, Designs, and Trademarks. The Controller was impressed Natco could manufacture and sell Sorafenib at 74 rupees ($1.48) per tablet, or 8,800 rupees ($176) per month, and could provide the generic free to patients who could not afford it. Bayer fought the application, saying it could not lower its price because of the research and development it had invested in the medication. Ironically, Bayer also argued pirated (or "at risk") copies were plentiful in the Indian market, so there was no need for an authorized generic version of Nexavar.

The Controller sided with Natco, on the grounds that Bayer not only sold Nexavar at too high a price for Indian patience, but also that it had not worked the patent, *i.e.*, it had not manufactured Nexavar to a reasonable extent. The compulsory license for Natco on the generic version, Sorafenib, mandated that Natco (1) charge no more than 8,880 rupees for a pack for 120 tablets (the amount for one month of therapy), (2) pay to Bayer a quarterly royalty of 6 percent of net sales of Sorafenib, and (3) supply Sorafenib free to at least 600 indigent patients annually. The compulsory license was for the remaining life of the patent Bayer had received on Nexavar, namely until 2020.

In July 2007, Rwanda became the first least developed WTO Member to invoke the new rules on importation of compulsorily licensed pharmaceuticals, *i.e.*, the *TRIPs* Article 31 waivers. Canada subsequently gave notice that it was the country from which the medicines compulsorily licensed by Rwanda would be exported.

In April 2010, a report was submitted to the United Nations Human Rights Council, as part of its first "Universal Periodic Review" of the human rights record of each United Nations member state.[120] This Review process was established in 2006 by the United Nations General Assembly. The process invites public comment, particularly from non-governmental organizations (NGOs), research institutions, and universities. The goal of the process is to assess compliance by each United Nations member with the human rights obligations of the United Nations Charter, Universal Declaration of Human Rights, human rights treaties the member has ratified, voluntary commitments made by the

---

[120] *See Groups' Report to U.N. Says U.S. Policy on Access to Drugs Violates Human Rights*, 27 International Trade Reporter (BNA) 575 (22 April 2010).

member, and international law. The report at issue was provided by Professor Sean Flynn of the American University Washington College of Law, in Washington, D.C. It charged that the United States violated the human rights of poor people around the world. The violation stemmed from the American insistence on promoting intellectual property and pharmaceutical regulations that limit the access of poor people to affordable medicines.

In specific, the report argued the United States uses international trade agreements, as well as diplomatic pressure, foreign aid, and technical assistance, to exalt the protection of intellectual property rights (IPRs) over human rights. That is, the United States champions monopoly rights associated with brand-name patented medicines over the needs of the poor. In consequence, affordable generic medicines have been taken off the market in many developing countries, which in turn has led to price increases for medicines of over 800 percent.

An interesting controversy concerning compulsory licensing and the *TRIPs Agreement* concerns local working requirements. The issue is whether a provision in the domestic law of a WTO Member country that allows for the grant of a compulsory license, even though the patent is not "worked" in that country, is lawful under the *Agreement*. Arguably, a local working requirement violates Article 27 of the *Agreement*, because this Article forbids discrimination between a product that is imported or locally produced. However, as Professor Bryan Mercurio points out in an article co-authored with Mitali Tyagi, Article 2:2 of the *TRIPs Agreement* incorporates most of the *Paris Convention*, including Article 5(A)(2). This provision of the *Paris Convention* — again, arguably — allows working requirements.[121] There is, then, a conflict between Articles 27 of the *TRIPs Agreement* (prohibiting discrimination regardless of whether a product is imported or locally made) and Article 2:2 of that *Agreement* (which, by incorporating Article 5(A)(2) of the *Paris Convention*, permits working requirements).

Applying the principles of treaty interpretation used in WTO adjudication, Professor Mercurio concludes the rule of Article 5(a)(2) must be respected. That is, working requirements are consistent with the *TRIPs Agreement*. As his analysis is technical, he accepts the proposition that as a policy matter, working requirements are controversial. Obviously, a working requirement circumscribes the ability to grant a compulsory license.

*Suggestions for Further Research:*

Articles:

1. Anderson, Horace E., Jr., *We Can Work It Out: Co-Op Compulsory Licensing As the Way Forward in Improving Access to Anti-Retroviral Drugs*, 16 BOSTON UNIVERSITY JOURNAL OF SCIENCE & TECHNOLOGY LAW 167–193 (2010).

---

[121] *See* Bryan Christopher Mercurio & Mitali Tyagi, *Treaty Interpretation in WTO Dispute Settlement: The Outstanding Question of the Legality of Local Working Requirements*, 19 MINNESOTA JOURNAL OF INTERNATIONAL LAW number 2, 275-326 (2010).

2.   Cahoy, Daniel R., *Breaking Patents*, 32 MICHIGAN JOURNAL OF INTERNATIONAL LAW 461–509 (2011).

3.   Chaves, Amanda, Note, *A Growing Headache: The Prevalence of International Counterfeit Pharmaceutical Trade in Developing African Nations*, 32 SUFFOLK TRANSNATIONAL LAW REVIEW 631–654 (2009).

4.   Cotter, Christina, Student article, *The Implications of Rwanda's Paragraph 6 Agreement with Canada for Other Developing Countries*, 5 LOYOLA UNIVERSITY CHICAGO INTERNATIONAL LAW REVIEW 177–189 (2008).

5.   DeRoo, Pier, Note, *"Public Non-Commercial Use" Compulsory Licensing for Pharmaceutical Drugs in Government Health Care Programs*, 32 MICHIGAN JOURNAL OF INTERNATIONAL LAW 347–394 (2011).

6.   Dziuba, Dawn, *TRIPs Article 31bis and H1N1 Swine Flu: Any Emergency or Urgency Exception to Patent Protection?*, 20 INDIANA INTERNATIONAL & COMPARATIVE LAW REVIEW 195–212 (2010).

7.   Epstein, Richard A. & F. Scott Kieff, *Questioning the Frequency and Wisdom of Compulsory Licensing of Pharmaceutical Patents*, 78 UNIVERSITY OF CHICAGO LAW REVIEW 71–93 (2011).

8.   Feldman, James, Note, *Compulsory Licenses: The Dangers Behind the Current Practice*, 8 JOURNAL OF INTERNATIONAL BUSINESS & LAW 137–167 (2009).

9.   Germano, Sara, Note, *Compulsory Licensing of Pharmaceuticals in Southeast Asia: Paving the Way for Greater Use of the TRIPs Flexibility in Low- and Middle-Income Countries*, 76 UNIVERSITY OF MISSOURI-KANSAS CITY LAW REVIEW 273–294 (2007).

10.   Gibson, Christopher, *A Look at the Compulsory License in Investment Arbitration: The Case of Indirect Expropriation*, 25 AMERICAN UNIVERSITY LAW REVIEW 357–422 (2010).

11.   Gumbel, Mike, Comment, *Is Article 31bis Enough? The Need to Promote Economies of Scale in the International Compulsory Licensing System*, 22 TEMPLE INTERNATIONAL & COMPARATIVE LAW JOURNAL 161–190 (2009).

12.   Harris, Donald, *TRIPs After Fifteen Years: Success or Failure, as Measured by Compulsory Licensing*, 18 JOURNAL OF INTELLECTUAL PROPERTY LAW 367–400 (2011).

13.   Lim, Daryl, *Copyright Under Seige: An Economic Analysis of the Essential Facilities Doctrine and the Compulsory Licensing of Copyrighted Works*, 17 ALBANY LAW JOURNAL OF SCIENCE AND TECHNOLOGY 481–558 (2007).

14.   Lin, Tsai-Yu, *Compulsory Licenses for Access to Medicines, Expropriation, and Investor-State Arbitration Under Bilateral Investment Agreements — Are There Issues Beyond the TRIPs Agreement?*, 40 IIC: INTERNATIONAL REVIEW OF INTELLECTUAL PROPERTY & COMPETITION LAW 152–173 (2009).

15.   Manne, Caroline, Note, *Pharmaceutical Patent Protection and TRIPs: The Countries That Cried Wolf and Why Defining "National Emergency" Will Save Them From Themselves*, 42 GEORGE WASHINGTON INTERNATIONAL LAW REVIEW 349–379 (2010).

16. Mellino, Marla L., Note, *The TRIPS Agreement: Helping or Hurting Least Developed Countries Access to Essential Pharmaceuticals?*, 20 FORDHAM INTELLECTUAL PROPERTY, MEDIA & ENTERTAINMENT LAW JOURNAL 1349–1388 (2010).

17. Quadir, Riadh, Note, *Patent Stalemate? The WTO's Essential Medicines Impasse between Pharmas and Least Developed Countries*, 61 RUTGERS LAW REVIEW 437–469 (2009).

18. Ruse-Khan, Henning Große & Thomas Jaeger, *Policing Patents Worldwide? — EC Border Measures Against Transiting Generic Drugs under EC and WTO Intellectual Property Regimes*, 40 IIC: INTERNATIONAL REVIEW OF INTELLECTUAL PROPERTY AND COMPETITION LAW 502–538 (2009).

19. Taubman, Antony, *Rethinking TRIPs: "Adequate Remuneration" for Non-Voluntary Patent Licensing*, 11 JOURNAL OF INTERNATIONAL ECONOMIC LAW 927–970 (2008).

20. Tsai, George, Note, *Canada's Access to Medicines Regime: Lessons for Compulsory Licensing Schemes under the WTO Doha Declaration*, 49 VIRGINIA JOURNAL OF INTERNATIONAL LAW 1063–1097 (2009).

Other Source:

1. New York Law School, Center for International Law, *Is the WTO Providing More Access to Essential Medicines?*, 10 THE INTERNATIONAL REVIEW issue 1, 20–23 (Fall 2007).

## CONFEDERATION OF EUROPEAN BUSINESS

*See* BusinessEurope.

## CONFESSIONAL

A meeting in which trade officials offer their bottom line negotiating positions.

Typically, the meeting is between trade officials from one or more countries, on the one hand, and the Director-General of the WTO, on the other hand.[122] Sometimes, the confessional is held between a trade official of one WTO Member, on the one hand, and the chairperson of a negotiating committee — such as the head of the negotiating group for agriculture talks, or for non-agricultural market access (NAMA) talks during the Doha Round. Having obtained the bottom line figures on a particular disputed issue from individual WTO Members, the Director-General can then use them to effect a compromise among the Members.

The analogy, then, to the Roman Catholic sacrament of reconciliation (confession) is that the officials (penitent disciples) will reveal their true sentiments

---

[122] *See* Daniel Pruzin, *WTO Awaits Results of Lamy "Confessionals" As Doubts Grow About G-8 Meeting on Doha*, 23 International Trade Reporter (BNA) 1052 (13 July 2006).

to the priest (the Director-General or Chairperson of a negotiating group). Confessionals were held in July 2006 and September 2007 in an effort to save the Doha Round — alas (unlike a true sacrament), without success.

## CONNUM

Control Number. CONNUM is a United States antidumping (AD) acronym.

It refers to the control number assigned by the Department of Commerce to a product sub-category, that is, to an averaging group. The Commerce Department assigns CONNUMs when calculating a dumping margin by comparing weighted average Normal Value to weighted average Export Price (or Constructed Export Price). A controversial context in which this occurs is zeroing, specifically, Model Zeroing.

## CONSENSUS (CONSENSUS DECISION-MAKING, CONSENSUS RULE)

*See* WTO.

### CONSOLIDATING AND REFORMING GOVERNMENT ACT OF 2012

A proposal sent by the Administration of President Barack H. Obama to Congress in February 2012 to obtain authority from Congress for the President to reorganize and consolidate federal departments and agencies.

In the two-page proposed *Act* from President Obama, there were four key points:[123]

(1) Any changes proposed by the President must save money.

(2) A reorganization plan would be subject to a fast-track vote by Congress.

(3) The President could make amendments to a plan pending in a Congressional Committee to incorporate Congressional feedback.

(4) The authority of the President to submit reorganization plans would terminate after a set deadline.

That is, first, creation, abolition, consolidation, transfer, or re-naming of any Executive Branch department or agency would be permitted it the change either reduced the overall number of such entities, or yielded cost savings. Second, Congress would be obliged to vote on any plan on an expedited, up-or-down, and no amendment basis. The third point would ensure Congress has an opportunity to comment and suggest modifications to any plan, and also precludes Congress from considering more than three plans simultaneously. The fourth point was manifest in a two-year sunset rule.

Most Presidents in the 20th century have had Congressional authority to rearrange the Executive Branch. However, the last such authority lapsed in

---

[123] *See* Cheryl Bolen, *White House Sends Proposal to Congress Requesting Authority to Reorganize Agencies*, 29 International trade Reporter (BNA) 270 (23 February 2012).

1984, during the tenure of President Ronald Reagan. All of the above-four points were features of previous reorganization authority legislation.

Of course, the bill sent by President Obama to Congress did not specify a specific reorganization plan. But, in a February 2012 memorandum accompanying the proposed *Act*, President Obama indicated he sought to combine six Executive Branch agencies related to international trade:[124]

(1)  The core business and trade functions of the Department of Commerce.

(2)  Office of the United States Trade Representative (USTR).

(3)  Export-Import Bank.

(4)  Overseas Private Investment Corporation (OPIC).

(5)  Trade and Development Agency (TDA).

(6)  Small Business Administration (SBA).

The underlying theory for this kind of reorganization was to unify in a single, one-stop shop, all the key functions directly related in international trade and investment. The proposed integrated entity, therefore, would include activities to help businesses seeking to grow and export, and matters concerning technology, innovation, and statistics. In turn, the new entity would help meet the goal of the Obama Administration in its September 2010 *National Export Initiative* (*NEI*), namely, to double American exports in five years.[125]

## CONSUMER PRODUCT SAFETY COMMISSION

The Consumer Product Safety Commission was established in 1972, and for several years thereafter had a large budget and staff. Its basic mission is to protect American consumers from unsafe products, whether the origin of those products is the United States or a foreign country.

In 1972, only 16 percent of children's toys were imported into the United States. As that number rose, the budget and staff of the Commission declined. Thus, the vulnerability of American consumers to unsafe foreign products, like toys, tended to increase through the 1990s and early part of the new millennium. The years 2007 and 2008 are sometimes called the "Years of Recall." That is because 45 million toys produced in China were recalled, with dangerous defects like lead paint and magnets in the toys. Further recalls, for example, on food made in China, specifically milk products, which contained melamine, were issued. In China, 294,000 children fell ill from those milk products, and at least six kids died.

---

[124] *See* Rossella Brevetti, *President Instructs Agencies on Maximizing Trade Functions Using Administrative Means*, 29 International Trade Reporter (BNA) 276 (23 February 2012).

[125] *See* REPORT TO THE PRESIDENT ON THE NATIONAL EXPORT INITIATIVE: THE EXPORT PROMOTION CABINET'S PLAN FOR DOUBLING U.S. EXPORTS IN FIVE YEARS (Washington, D.C., September 2010), *posted at* www.whitehouse.gov/sites/default/files/nei_report_9-16-10_full.pdf; and National Export Initiative (NEI), www.nei.gov.

It is impracticable, if not impossible, for the Chinese government to police effectively all of its manufacturers to ensure their products meet American safety standards. China has roughly 8,000 toy companies, of which 3,400 export toys to the United States and other countries. Each Chinese producer-exporter sources inputs (such as the rubber tires on "Hot Wheels" cars) from many suppliers and sub-contractors. Many, if not most, of the producer-exporters cannot effectively secure their supply chains, ensuring them for input quality and safety. Moreover, with ferocious competition and thin profit margins, there is a temptation to behave unscrupulously in the short-term, and disregard the long-term reputational, economic, and legal consequences.

Thus, in 2008, amidst considerable concern in the general American public, the United States Congress took action. It passed the *Consumer Product Safety Improvement Act (CPSIA)*, which President George W. Bush signed on 14 August 2008. The House of Representatives passed the bill on a 424-1 vote, and the Senate passed it by 89-3. Also, an inter-agency working group on import safety was created, which includes officials from the Department of Commerce. Among the highlights of the *CPSIA* are the following:

- All manufacturers of merchandise sold into the United States must certify their product has been tested by an accredited third-party tester.[126] Manufacturers must issue certificates with their children's products certifying the products comply with applicable children's safety laws based upon Third Party Conformity Assessment Body tests. The Commission must accredit these Third Party Conformity Assessment Bodies. Accreditation standards are periodically reviewed and revised to ensure the consumer is given the highest level of protection possible. Third party testers undergo audits, and may lose accreditation if they have been subjected to undue influence, or have failed to comply with Commission standards. Resulting injuries or deaths, patterns of failure, and any remedial actions taken by a tester are relevant in considering whether to revoke the accreditation of a tester. Certificates include the date and place of manufacture and testing, and contact information for the test results record holder. The certificates must accompany shipments of products, and must be provided to retailers and distributors. They must be provided in English, but may also be rendered in any other language. In addition to certification requirements, children's products must be affixed with a permanent mark that allows purchasers to identify effectively the product, manufacturer, and other relevant information. All upstream suppliers and sub-contractors must be checked and certified by testers. If a manufacturer is proven wrong, for example, if a toy it exports from China is unsafe, then the manufacturer is liable. Thus, if a toy is found unsafe after being sold by an American retailer like Target, then the manufacturer can be held liable for its erroneous certification. In that sense, the

---

[126] *See The Consumer Product Safety Improvement Act of 2008* Pub. L. No. 110-314 § 102.

liability flows downstream, and does not end after the merchandise clears customs.

- The budget and staff of the Commission are increased.[127] The *CPSIA* authorizes appropriations for the years 2010 through 2014. The appropriations range from a low of $115,640,000 in 2011 to a high of $136,409,000 in 2014. If appropriations allow, then the full time staff of the Commission is to be increased to at least 500 employees with some employees being posted at United States ports of entry or as overseas inspectors.[128] Employees also may work temporarily for foreign governments to receive or provide training, and the agents of foreign governments may work for the Commission.[129]

- The civil money penalties and criminal penalties of the *Consumer Product Safety Act (CPSA*, 15 U.S.C. § 2069 *et seq.*), *Federal Hazardous Substances Act* (15 U.S.C. § 1264 *et seq.*), and *Flammable Fabrics Act* (15 U.S.C. 1194 *et seq.*), are increased. The civil money penalties for single violations of these acts are increased from $5,000 to $100,000. The civil money penalties for a series of violations have been increased to $15 million from $1.25 million. The criminal penalties have been increased to allow up to 5 years imprisonment for violations and may also include forfeiture of assets associated with the violation.[130]

- State Attorney Generals are deputized to enforce the *CPSIA* in federal court. There is no need for a State Attorney General to seek federal permission to take a *CPSIA* case to federal court — they can do so automatically but must provide notice to the Commission. When certain violations of the *CPSA* affect a state or its residents, then the Attorney General of that State may bring an action in any district court for injunctive relief. However, the State Attorney General must notify the Commission before initiating an action. Unless the Commission has consented to an earlier initiation, or immediate protective action is necessary to protect the state's residents, the Attorney General must wait at least 30 days after notifying the Commission before initiating an action.[131]

- The threshold levels for safety are strengthened. The *CPSIA* mandates a progressive reduction of the permissible amount of lead in toys. Lead levels will first be reduced to 600 parts per million, followed by a reduction to 300 parts per million. The following reduction is to

---

[127] *See The Consumer Product Safety Improvement Act of 2008* Pub. L. No. 110-314 § 201.

[128] *See The Consumer Product Safety Improvement Act of 2008* Pub. L. No. 110-314 § 202.

[129] *See The Consumer Product Safety Improvement Act of 2008* Pub. L. No. 110-314 § 208.

[130] *See The Consumer Product Safety Improvement Act of 2008* Pub. L. No. 110-314 § 217.

[131] *See The Consumer Product Safety Improvement Act of 2008,* Pub. L. No. 110-314 § 218.

100 parts per million. However, if this reduction is not technologically feasible, then the permissible amount of lead in toys will be lowered to the lowest amount less than 300 parts per million that is feasible. Lead limitations are reviewed at least every five years with corresponding reductions to lead limitations when possible. Certain items may be excluded from these limitations so long as it can be scientifically proven that no lead absorption into the human body or any other adverse effects can occur because of the exclusion. This exclusion takes into account normal childhood use and abuse of products including swallowing and breaking of the product.[132]

- There are also new standards for products containing certain phthalates. No toy or childcare article may contain more than a 0.1 percent concentration of di-(2-ethylhexyl) phthalate (DEHP), dibutyl phthalate (DBP), benzyl butyl phthalate (BBP), diisononyl phthalate (DINP), diisodecyl phthalate (DIDP), or di-n-octyl phthalate (DnOP). Relatedly, the *CPSIA* establishes the Chronic Hazard Advisory Panel to study all phthalates and phthalate alternatives and their affects on children, pregnant women and other susceptible individuals. The Panel must submit a report to the Commission, which will promulgate rules on permanent bans from toys and childcare products of substances deemed to be hazardous.[133]

- Re-export of recalled items may now be prohibited by the Commission. Before the *CPSIA*, some importers of merchandise that subsequently was recalled would re-export that recalled product, particularly to Kenya. Now, non-conforming products that are refused entry will be destroyed unless the owner of the products requests and is granted permission by the Secretary of the Treasury to re-export non-conforming products in lieu of destruction. Following the grant of permission if the products are not re-exported within 90 days they will be destroyed.[134] The Commission may prohibit the re-export of recalled items to third countries. However, third countries may choose to accept particular shipments of recalled products, and may so inform the Commission of their decision to do so. If the Commission receives third country permission to re-export the items within 30 days of notifying that country of the non-conforming product re-exportation, then the Commission must allow the shipment to take place.[135] The Commission also recommends higher bond amounts (if necessary) to the United States Customs and Border Protection (CBP) to cover the cost of a product's destruction in case it is found to be non-conforming.[136]

---

[132] *See The Consumer Product Safety Improvement Act of 2008,* Pub. L. No. 110-314 § 101.

[133] *See The Consumer Product Safety Improvement Act of 2008,* Pub. L. No. 110-314 § 108.

[134] *See The Consumer Product Safety Improvement Act of 2008,* Pub. L. No. 110-314 § 223.

[135] *See The Consumer Product Safety Improvement Act of 2008,* Pub. L. No. 110-314 § 221.

[136] *See The Consumer Product Safety Act of 2008*, Pub. L. No. 110-314 § 224.

- The *CPSIA* mandates the Commission to expand its website. A new database is to include reports of harm submitted by consumers, government agencies, health care professionals, child services providers, and public safety entities. Reports may be submitted to the Commission on paper, by phone, or electronically. The reports must include the contact information of the person submitting the report, product and manufacturer information, a description of the harm, and a statement that the information is true and accurate to the best of the reporter's knowledge. The Commission must include a disclaimer stating that the accuracy of the reports cannot be guaranteed. If the Commission determines that a submitted report is inaccurate, then it may decline to add the report to the database, add information to the report, or correct any inaccurate information. In the event a publicly available report is determined to be inaccurate, the Commission may take any of those actions, or remove the report. When practical, reports will be transmitted to the manufacturer of the concerned item within five days. The manufacturer may comment on the report, and request that its comments be included in the database.[137] In addition to this database the CPSC also must create an accessible list of accredited third party conformity assessment bodies, along with a link on the web page of the Inspector General that individuals may report anonymously instances of Commission fraud, abuse, and waste.[138] A searchable list of recalled items is available at www.recalls.gov.

- It is illegal for non-conforming baby cribs to enter, or re-enter the stream of commerce, or otherwise be utilized by persons who use cribs in their business. New registration standards affecting all manufacturers of durable infant and toddler products are to promulgated (by August 2009). Products of these types must include a postage pre-paid registration card when sold to consumers. Manufacturers must maintain lists of registered customers for not less than six years to facilitate the dissemination of safety and recall notices.[139]

- Cautionary statement standards are applied to all suppliers of goods subject to such statements. Entities that provide products to retailers must inform the retailer of any applicable cautionary statements. Retailers must inquire of their suppliers whether the products of those suppliers are subject to cautionary statements. Retailers are not found to have violated their responsibilities so long as they make the required inquiries. If a retailer requests information, but is given no information in response, or is given false information, then the retailer is not in violation of its responsibilities. Products offered directly for sale

---

[137] *See The Consumer Product Safety Improvement Act of 2008,* Pub. L. No. 110-314 § 212.

[138] *See The Consumer Product Safety Improvement Act of 2008,* Pub. L. No. 110-314 §§ 102, 205.

[139] *See The Consumer Product Safety Improvement Act of 2008,* Pub. L. No. 110-314 § 104.

through advertisements must not be advertised without applicable cautionary statements. The cautionary statements must be included with, or adjacent to, the advertisement and must be legible.[140]

- Standards found in F-963-07 of the American Society for Testing and Materials International (ASTM International) shall become the standard of Section 9 of the *CPSA* (15 U.S.C. § 2058). When ASTM International proposes revisions to these standards, it must notify the Commission. The Commission must adopt the revision as the new standard within six months, unless the Commission finds the proposed revision does not improve safety standards.[141] The ASTM International standard F-963 was updated as of 2008.

The *CPSIA* does not fix all of the problems that emerged from the Years of Recall. For example, the Commission still has no authority to do overseas inspections. Moreover, the United States has 326 ports that need policing for import safety. Whether the Commission will continue to have the budget and staff, in the long run, to fulfill this major responsibility is uncertain.

Shortly after its passage, the stringent provisions of the *CPSIA* generated considerable industry concern. The National Association of Manufacturers (NAM) and other allies asked for relief from impending, but as of yet unknown, labeling requirements, exemptions from lead limits. They also have queried whether phthalate restrictions will apply to sporting goods and sleepwear. The NAM is particularly worried that unknown new regulations will result in mandatory changes to production processes. The NAM argues changes in production methods may take up to a year to complete, yet specific standards were not (as of April 2009) been announced. As the entry into force date of August 2009 approached, the NAM urged that manufacturers would not have time to adjust to new standards. Given the lack of official guidance, the NAM called for a deferral of the application of labeling requirements until August of 2010.[142]

Apparently to stiffen the resolve of the Commission, 28 United States Senators, led by Jay Rockefeller (Democrat–West Virginia) and Mark Pryor (Democrat–Arkansas), signed a letter to the Acting Chair of the Commission (Nancy A. Nord).[143] In their 9 April 2009 letter, they clarified Congressional intent behind the *CPSIA*. That intent was the Commission is empowered to exercise its authority and enforcement discretion to ensure the legislation is implemented and complied with in a comprehensive manner. In exercising this authority and discretion, the Commission should provide appropriate, commonsense relief and guidance to businesses.

---

[140] *See The Consumer Product Safety Improvement Act of 2008*, Pub. L. 110-314, § 105.

[141] *See The Consumer Product Safety Improvement Act of 2008*, Pub. L. 110-314 § 106.

[142] *See NAM Coalition Says Not Enough Time To Prepare for Label Rules, Asks for Stay*, 26 International Trade Reporter (BNA) 448-449 (2 April 2009).

[143] *See Senators Explain "Congressional Intent," Claim CPSC Has Authority, Discretion*, 26 International Trade Reporter (BNA) 509 (16 April 2009).

*Suggestions for Further Research:*

Articles:

1. Knutson, Katrina, Student Article, *Lead in Their Shoes? The Impact of the Consumer Product Safety Improvement Act on Chinese/American Trade Negotiations*, 31 HAMLINE JOURNAL OF PUBLIC LAW & POLICY 705–734 (2010).

2. Liu, Chenglin, *Profits Above the Law: China's Melamine Tainted Milk Incident*, 79 MISSISSIPPI LAW JOURNAL 371–417 (2009).

3. Weaver, Russell L., Udo Fink & François Lichere, *Protecting Consumers in an Era of World Trade*, 61 ADMINISTRATIVE LAW REVIEW 105–114 (2009).

## *CONSUMER PRODUCT SAFETY IMPROVEMENT ACT*

*See* Consumer Product Safety Commission

## CONSTRUCTED VALUE

Constructed Value.

The value used in lieu of Normal Value when Normal Value is unavailable or inappropriate as a basis for comparison with the Export Price (or Constructed Export Price). That is, Notably, Constructed Value is used when there are no sales of a foreign like product in the comparison market suitable for matching to the subject merchandise.

"Constructed Value" is used in both pre- and post-Uruguay Round American antidumping (AD) law. When making a dumping margin determination, an administering authority such as the United States Department of Commerce (DOC) must compare the Export Price (or Constructed Export Price) of subject merchandise to the Normal Value of a foreign like product.[144] If Normal Value cannot be determined based on the home market of the respondent (the exporter or producer under investigation), then a proxy for that Value must be found. The first alternative is Third Country Price. The second alternative is Constructed Value.[145]

Constructed Value, then, is the market value of a product determined from assumed manufacturing costs and other expenses when no valid basis for comparison exists. Arithmetically, Constructed Value is calculated as follows:

Constructed Value = Cost of materials and fabrication +

Selling, General, and Administrative (SG&A) Expenses +

Profit of the foreign like product in the comparison market +

Cost of packing for export to the United States.

---

[144] *See, e.g.*, 19 U.S.C.§ 1677b(a) (1994).
[145] *See, e.g.*, 19 U.S.C. § 1677b(a)(4).

## CONTINGENCY MEASURE

*See* TDI.

## CONTINUOUS BOND

*See* Customs Bond.

## CONTRACTING PARTY

A country that was a party to GATT. (Observe that, unlike WTO Members, the first letters for GATT contracting parties are not capitalized.)

## CONTRACTING PARTIES (OR CONTRACTING PARTIES)

All of the countries that were members of GATT acting jointly.

## CONVENTION ON BIOLOGICAL DIVERSITY

*See* Bio Diversity Treaty.

## COOL

Country of Origin Labeling.

*Suggestions for Further Research:*

Articles:

1.   Mullins, Matt, Comment, *Not COOL: The Consequences of Mandatory Country of Origin Labeling*, 6 JOURNAL OF FOOD LAW & POLICY 89–102 (2009).

2.   Ross, Carrie, Note, *In the Hot House: Will Canada's WTO Challenge Slaughter U.S. COOL Regulations?*, 36 BROOKLYN JOURNAL OF INTERNATIONAL LAW 299–336 (2010).

## COPYRIGHT

A copyright is a form of intellectual property (IP).

Copyright protects original works of authorship against unauthorized copying. It is, therefore, a property right of the author who created the work to restrict others from (1) reproducing the copyrighted work, (2) preparing derivative works (*e.g.*, an abridgement, adaptation, compilation, dramatization, or translation) based on the copyrighted work, and (3) selling, leasing, or displaying copies of the copyrighted work. As regards works created after 1 January 1978, the protection lasts for the life of the author, plus 50 years after the death of the author. United States copyright law is contained in the *Copyright Act*. The claim of copyright protection is denoted by the famous © symbol.

Works protected by copyright include literature, drama (including pantomimes and choreographic music, plus music accompanying the dramatic production), music, motion pictures and other audiovisual works, sound recordings, and art (*e.g.*, pictorial, graphic, and sculptural works). Increasingly, computer software and databases also are protected. In some instances, the protection also confers performing and recording rights. In brief, a copyright protects the expression of an idea in a fixed (tangible) form — but not the idea itself. The works may be published or unpublished, and the nationality or domicile of the author is irrelevant.

Aside from works that have not been fixed in a tangible form of expression, names, short phrases, slogans, and titles cannot be copyrighted. A work that consists entirely of information that is common property, with no original authorship, cannot be copyrighted. Examples include a calendar or a height/weight chart. The functional part of a useful object cannot be copyrighted (rather, it is eligible for a design patent). Finally, works of the United States government, and works that fall into the public domain, cannot receive copyright protection.

To obtain a copyright, the key criterion is the author creates something new. While it does not need to be terribly new (*i.e.*, it need not be apt, bright, or a breakthrough), it must be more than a trivial change or modification. Put succinctly, the author must create something recognizably original. There must be a new manner of expression, some distinguishable variation. In the United States, applications to register copyrights are made to the Copyright Office of the Library of Congress. Interestingly, in contrast to patents, who created a work first is irrelevant to determining entitlement to copyright protection. If two or more people independently came up with an identical work, then both works could be copyrighted.

In some instances copying is said to be socially desirable, and in these cases, obtaining the permission of the copyright owner is not necessary. The purpose of the use (specifically, whether it is for non-profit or educational uses), the amount and significance of the portion used, the effect of the use on the potential market or value of the copyrighted work, are all factors considered in determining whether use is "fair."

As with a patent or trademark, it is up to the owner of a copyright to enforce the property right. Remedies available to a copyright owner successful in making out an infringement case before a court include an injunction, impounding or destruction of all unauthorized copies, and damages. However, in some cases, infringement may be deemed criminal, in which fines and a jail sentence may be imposed.

*Suggestions for Further Research:*

Articles:

1. Alnajafi, Nada, *Protecting the Past in the Future: How Copyright is Wrong for Egypt and Why Other Sui Generis Laws May Help Protect the Pyramids and Other Cultural Antiquities*, 56 JOURNAL OF THE COPYRIGHT SOCIETY OF THE U.S.A. 243–263 (2009).

2. Burrell, Robert & Kimberlee Weatherall, *Exporting Controversy? Reactions to the Copyright Provisions of the U.S.–Australia Free Trade Agreement: Lessons for U.S. Trade Policy*, 2008 UNIVERSITY OF ILLINOIS JOURNAL OF LAW, TECHNOLOGY & POLICY 259–319 (2008).

3. de Beer, Jeremy & Christopher D. Clemmer, *Global Trends in Online Copyright Enforcement: A Non-Neutral Role for Network Intermediaries?*, 49 JURIMETRICS JOURNAL 375–409 (2009).

4. Griffin, James G.H., *300 Years of Copyright Law? A Not So Modest Proposal for Reform*, 28 JOHN MARSHALL JOURNAL OF COMPUTER & INFORMATION LAW 1–48 (2010).

5. Hariani, Krishna & Anirudh Hariani, *Analyzing "Originality" in Copyright Law: Transcending Jurisdictional Disparity*, 51 IDEA 491–510 (2011).

6. Makeen, Makeen F., *The Protection of Musical Works Under UAE Copyright Law*, 57 JOURNAL OF THE COPYRIGHT SOCIETY OF THE U.S.A. 743–797 (2011).

7. Makeen, Makeen F., The Reception in Public Dilemma Under U.S. Copyright Law, 58 JOURNAL OF THE COPYRIGHT SOCIETY OF THE U.S.A. 355–429 (2011).

8. Mehra, Salil K., *Keep America Exceptional! Against Adopting Japanese and European-Style Criminalization of Contributory Copyright Infringement*, 13 VANDERBILT JOURNAL OF ENTERTAINMENT & TECHNOLOGY LAW 811–824 (2011).

9. Ohly, Ansgar, *The Freedom of Imitation and Its Limits — A European Perspective*, 41 IIC: INTERNATIONAL REVIEW OF INTELLECTUAL PROPERTY & COMPETITION LAW 506–524 (2010).

10. Platt, Robert, *A Comparative Survey of Moral Rights*, 57 JOURNAL OF THE COPYRIGHT SOCIETY OF THE U.S.A. 951–985 (2010) (Nathan Burkan Memorial Competition Winning Paper).

11. Qian, Wang, *Is Downloading of Pirated Content for Private Purposes a Copyright Infringement in China?*, 57 JOURNAL OF THE COPYRIGHT SOCIETY OF THE U.S.A. 667–682 (2010).

12. Wan, Yong, *A Modest Proposal to Amend the Chinese Copyright Law: Introducing A Concept of Right of Communication to the Public*, 55 JOURNAL OF THE COPYRIGHT SOCIETY U.S.A. 603–622 (2008).

13. Wan, Yong, *Moral Rights of Authors in China*, 58 JOURNAL OF THE COPYRIGHT SOCIETY OF THE U.S.A. 455–481 (2011).

14. White, Aaron D., *The Copyright Tree: Using German Moral Rights as the Roots for Enhanced Authorship Protection in the United States*, 9 LOYOLA LAW & TECHNOLOGY ANNUAL 30–90 (2009–2010).

15. Xiao, Emma Yao, Note, *The New Trend: Protecting American Fashion Designs through National Copyright Measures*, 28 CARDOZO ARTS & ENTERTAINMENT LAW JOURNAL 417–443 (2010).

16. Zemer, Lior, *Copyright Departures: The Fall of the Last Imperial Copyright Dominion and the Case of Fair Use*, 60 DEPAUL LAW REVIEW 1051–1114 (2011).

## COPYRIGHT ALLIANCE

A United States advocacy group that lobbies on behalf of American copyright, and copyright-related, firms.

The members of the Copyright Alliance include:

- American Federation of Television & Radio Artists
- American Intellectual Property Law Association
- American Society of Composers, Authors and Publishers
- Broadcast Music Inc.
- Business Software Alliance
- CBS
- Discovery Communications
- Magazine Publishers of America
- Major League Baseball (MLB)
- Microsoft
- Motion Picture Association of America
- National Association of Broadcasters
- National Collegiate Athletic Association (NCAA)
- National Football League (NFL)
- NBC
- Newspaper Association of America
- News Corp.
- Recording Industry Association of America
- Sony Pictures Entertainment
- Time Warner
- Walt Disney

## CORAM PUBLICO

Openly, in front of everyone.

The term is used, for example, as a call for transparency in trade negotiations.

## CORE LABOR RIGHTS

A term aimed to distinguish fundamental labor rights from broad, aspiration-type standards.

The term "core labor rights" sometimes is used interchangeably with "internationally recognized worker rights." That is because core labor rights are widely agreed to be the following, as set out in Conventions of the International Labor Organization (ILO):

- Effective abolition of child labor.

- Elimination of discrimination in employment and occupation.

- Elimination of all forms of forced or compulsory labor.

- Freedom of association and the effective recognition of the right to collective bargaining.

- Acceptable working conditions in respect of minimum wages, hours of work, and occupational safety and health.

Such core labor rights, sometimes called the "ILO Top 5 List," are rights are different from, for example, standards set out in the Social Charter of the European Union (EU). Those standards, which are broader than the core rights, encompass housing, health, education, employment, legal and social protection, movement of persons, and apply non-discrimination obligations in many contexts.

In the United States, from time to time, particularly after May 2007, when Congress and the White House reached an accord in the wake of the expiry of Presidential fast track (trade promotion) negotiating authority, there have been attempts to pass legislation linking core labor rights to possible new trade agreements. For example, in June 2008, Senators Sherrod Brown (Democrat-Ohio) and Byron Dorgan (Democrat-North Dakota) introduced the *Trade Reform, Accountability, Development, and Employment (TRADE) Act*.[146] That legislation would require any country that partners with the United States in a trade agreement to have in force the ILO core labor rights. That is, the country would have to adopt, maintain, and enforce in its domestic laws and regulations those rights, otherwise the United States would not partner with it in a trade deal.

Manifestly, the legislation reflects a direct approach to upgrading labor rights through trade agreements. Rather than await uncertain improvement in those rights through free trade *per se*, the theory underlying the legislation is that trade liberalization ought to be contingent on the existence and application of such rights. Otherwise, trade liberalization may undermine them, or may take an unacceptably long time to achieve them.

*Suggestions for Further Research:*

Article:

1. McGinnis, Megan, Student Article, *Child Farm Labor Under the Fair Labor Standards Act*, 20 KANSAS JOURNAL OF LAW & PUBLIC POLICY 155–180 (2010).

---

[146] *See* Derrick Cain, *Legislation to Require Labor Protections in Trade Agreements Introduced in Senate*, 25 International Trade Reporter (BNA) 871-872 (12 June 2008).

## *COTONOU CONVENTION*

The preferential trading arrangement between the European Union (EU) and a large number of countries, many of which are former European colonies, in the African, Caribbean, and Pacific (ACP) region.

The Fourth *Lomé Convention* ran from 1975–2000, and expired in February 2000. The European Union (EU) favored replacing it with free trade agreements (FTAs) — technically called "Economic Partnership Agreements" (EPAs) — between the EU and each African, Caribbean and Pacific (ACP) region. The ACP seventy-seven (77) countries felt threatened by granting duty-free treatment to EU goods, and were unwilling to accept the loss in tariff revenues. They sought a simple renewal of the *Convention*.

Negotiations commenced in September 1998, compromise was reached in October 1999, and a deal was finalized in February 2000. The compromise had taken 17 months of difficult negotiations to achieve. But, the new *Convention* — called the *Cotonou Convention*, after the capital of Benin, where the *Convention* was signed on 23 June 2000 — is set to last for 20 years, until February 2020.

The essence of the compromise embodied in the *Cotonou Convention* is the continuation of non-reciprocal trade preferences for a limited period of time, in exchange for negotiations toward FTAs with the EU. The EU agreed to renew for an eight year period (*i.e.*, until 2008) the trade preferences on 92 percent of the products it imports from ACP countries. Further, the EU said it would provide duty-free access to substantially all of the products from the 38 poorest ACP countries (along with exports from all other LDCs) by 2005. Of course, the EU and the ACP countries would seek a waiver from the WTO for the renewal. The EU also said it would provide the ACP countries with roughly $13 billion in aid.

In return, the ACP countries pledged to liberalize their economies and, in 2002, initiate talks toward FTAs with the EU. In other words, the FTAs would be negotiated during the extended preferences period. Only the most advanced ACP countries would be obligated to enter into these negotiations. Thus, the 38 poorest ACP countries need not do so. Moreover, the FTAs could be phased in over 12–15 years.

Significantly, an assessment was scheduled for 2004 to determine those ACP countries, other than the least developed ones, that would be capable of entering into an FTA. Also significantly, the *Cotonou Convention* — unlike the *Lomé Convention* — contains no attached protocol on bananas. Revisions to the *Cotonou Convention* are contemplated every five years.

Interestingly, during later phases of the negotiations, the EU persuaded the ACP countries to accept conditions on the promotion of democracy, human rights, and the rule of law. Initially, they refused to agree on a condition concerning good governance (to ensure that EU aid money is not wasted because of corruption), saying that would be difficult to judge. However, by February 2000, the ACP countries agreed to accept "good governance" as a "fundamental element" of the *Cotonou Convention*.

Also, in February 2000, a potential stumbling block arose to reaching a final agreement. The EU insisted that ACP countries take back all illegal immigrants. The ACP countries agreed to take back their own nationals, but the EU wanted the right to deport illegal immigrants back to the country from which they entered the EU, even if that was not their country of origin. Thus, for example, if a Tanzanian illegally entered the EU from Rwanda, Rwanda would have to take the immigrant back. The ACP countries balked at the idea, saying it would impose on them an unfair burden. Accordingly, the EC had to accept that ACP countries would take back only their own citizens, and instead commence negotiations on a bilateral basis with each ACP country on dealing with illegal immigrants who are citizens of another ACP country.

In March 2000, Cuba formally applied for membership in the *Cotonou Convention*. However, the EU objected that Cuba did not yet meet the "political clauses" in the *Convention*, namely, respect for democracy, good governance, and human rights. In April, Cuba withdrew its application, saying that it was protesting a United Nations (U.N.) resolution sponsored by the Czech Republic and backed by a majority of the EU member states that accused Cuba of human rights violations.

In April 2000, the EU requested from the WTO a waiver for the *Cotonou Convention* that would cover the MFN obligation. The United States and the other complainants in the 1997 *EC — Bananas* case (Colombia, Ecuador, Guatemala, Honduras, and Panama) reacted leerily. They sought assurances the waiver would not derail efforts by the EU to bring its banana import regime into compliance with the recommendations of the Appellate Body in that case. Nevertheless, the waiver was granted on 23 June 2000. The waiver, which lasted until 31 December 2007, enabled the EU to continue providing ACP countries with non-reciprocal preferential access to its market. Following the expiry of the waiver — indeed, in negotiations during the four years before the expiry — the EU sought to replace the *Cotonou Convention* with separate EPAs covering groups of ACP countries based on their regional location and interests. In October 2008, the first such EPA was agreed, involving the EU and Caribbean countries.

*Suggestions for Further Research:*

Article:

1. Hilpold, Peter, *EU Development Cooperation at a Crossroads: The Cotonou Agreement of 23 June 2000 and the Principle of Good Governance*, 7 EUROPEAN FOREIGN AFFAIRS REVIEW issue 1, 53–72 (2002).

## COTTON 4 (COTTON FOUR)

Four major cotton producers and exporters in West Africa, namely, Benin, Burkina Faso, Chad, and Mali.

The Cotton 4 has been at the center of the controversy concerning American cotton subsidies, with non-governmental organizations (NGOs) producing studies about the deleterious effect of those subsidies. For example, Oxfam points out that from 2001-03 inclusive, the "Cotton 4" countries — Benin, Burkina Faso, Chad, and Mali — had lost about U.S. 400 million because of America selling subsidized cotton on the world market.

The Cotton 4 has played a key role in the controversy surrounding the inability of the WTO membership to reach consensus on general agricultural trade reform. In 2003, the Cotton 4 presented as its negotiating position for the Cancún Ministerial Conference a "sectoral initiative on cotton," often referred to as the "Cotton Initiative." The Initiative claimed the elimination of cotton subsidies worldwide is essential to ensure the "survival of the cotton sector of West and Central Africa." Other developing countries — those in the Group of 20 (G-20) — supported the Initiative. The refusal by developed countries to agree to its terms was part of the reason for the collapse of the Cancún Conference..

*Suggestions for Further Research:*

Article:

1.  Nedzel, Nadia E., *Antidumping and Cotton Subsidies: A Market-Based Defense of Unfair Trade Remedies*, 28 NORTHWESTERN JOURNAL OF INTERNATIONAL LAW & BUSINESS 215–272 (2008).

     Other Sources:

1.  Anderson, Kym & Ernesto Valenzuela, *WTO's Doha Cotton Initiative: A Tale of Two Issues*, CENTER FOR ECONOMIC POLICY RESEARCH, Discussion Paper Number 5567 (March 2006).

2.  Oxfam (U.K.), *Rigged Rules and Double Standards* (2003).

## COTTON STEP PAYMENTS

The United States Department of Agriculture (USDA) provides so-called "Step payment" programs for upland cotton. As a farm commodity, cotton is entitled to all three of the principal United States agricultural subsidy programs, namely, marketing assistance loans, countercyclical payments, and direct payments. In addition, Step payments are available to cotton — and exclusively to cotton.

Among the Step programs, the second, Step 2 payments, is most famous. That is because of a WTO case in which the Appellate Body ruled the payments inconsistent with various WTO obligations. (Step 1 and Step 3 payments were not at issue in the case.) The Step payments are as follows:

•   Step 1

These payments are associated with marketing assistance loans. Further reductions on the loan repayment rate (also known as the loan rate price) on a marketing assistance loan are authorized. Those further reductions are permitted if a two-pronged price condition is satisfied.

(1) First, the price condition is the adjusted world price (AWP, which is the term used in the 2002 *Farm Bill*, but which in the 2007 *Farm Bill* is called the "Prevailing World Market Price") falls below 115 percent of the loan repayment rate.

(2) Second, the weekly average United States-Northern Europe Price for upland cotton exceeds the average price Northern Europe Price. (The United States-Northern Europe Price is the weekly average price quote for the lowest priced United States upland cotton delivered on c.i.f. terms (cost, insurance, and freight) to Northern Europe. The "Northern Europe Price" is the weekly average of world price quotes for the five lowest prices of upland cotton delivered on c.i.f. terms to Northern Europe.)

When both prongs are met, Step 1 payments are triggered. These payments take the form of a reduction on the loan repayment rate. That reduction allows a farmer to readjust his or her loan rates down. Therefore, the farmer secures a marketing loan gain, or a loan deficiency payment, when market prices actually are still above the loan rate price. The farmer effectively gains a subsidy for higher than loan rate price.

For example, the 2007 *Farm Bill* target loan rate price for upland cotton is 50 cents per pound. In respect of the first prong of the price condition, suppose the Prevailing World Market Price falls below 115 percent of this price, *i.e.*, it falls below 57.5 cents per pound. Assume the second prong of the price condition is satisfied. An upland cotton farmer would be allowed to reduce his or her loan rate price to a price determined by the Secretary of Agriculture.

- Step 2

This kind of subsidy provided cash payments for domestic cotton mills and exporters when the price of cotton fell below 134 percent of the United States loan rate. In effect, Step 2 was an export subsidy, and an import substitution subsidy. However, Step 2 payments were a key target of Brazil's action in the 2005 *Upland Cotton* case. Following Brazil's victory in the case, but not without controversy, the United States repealed Step 2 payments on 1 August 2006, thereby complying with the Appellate Body ruling on this scheme.

- Step 3

The 2002 *Farm Bill* allows the President to establish special import quotas for cotton. These quotas are permitted if supplies of American cotton are low, and market prices are rising. Note the use of the word "quota," which normally connotes a restriction. However, Step 3 actually entails a relaxation of cotton quotas. It does so because of the short supply of domestic cotton, and the rising market prices.

Separately, United States cotton subsidy rules contain a provision for Extra Long Staple Cotton (ELS cotton). As its name suggests, ELS cotton differs from upland cotton by fiber length. The separate rules for ELS cotton operate similarly to the Step 2 program for upland cotton, where prices are below 134 percent of the United States ELS cotton loan rate price. Thus, ELS cotton subsidies — which were not the subject of the 2005 *Upland Cotton* case — could be a target for a subsequent WTO case.

Cotton, along with corn, rice, soybeans, and wheat, is a "program crop" (as distinct from a "specialty crop") under United States agricultural legislation, essentially meaning that it is covered by subsidy programs. It is estimated there are about 20,000 American cotton farmers, as against several million cotton farmers in the Cotton 4 countries.[147]

## COUNCIL OF THE EUROPEAN UNION

*See* European Council.

## COUNTERCYCLICAL PAYMENTS (COUNTER-CYCLICAL PAYMENTS)

Countercyclical payments are one of three cornerstones of American agricultural subsidies that have existed since the first federal farm bill in 1933, during the Depression and Dust Bowl Era, under the Administration of President Franklin D. Roosevelt. Those cornerstones are:

- Marketing assistance loans.

- Direct payments.

- Counter-cyclical payments.

To be sure, the modern-day incarnation of these programs is not identical to the schemes as originally enacted. For example, production flexibility contracts (PFCs) existed before direct payments, and were replaced by them in the 2002 *Farm Bill*. However, the idea of income support — which both incarnations represent — is not new. Likewise, counter-cyclical payments have not been a consistent feature throughout the post-1933 history. However, the idea of shielding farmers from vicissitudes of the market place by offering them support inversely proportional to market prices is not new.

Accordingly, a "countercyclical" payment is a subsidy, generally in the context of agriculture, to a producer the amount of which varies inversely with the difference between

(1) a benchmark, called the "Target Price," which is set by statute (7 U.S.C. Section 7914(c))

and

(2) an actual Market Price (or, if higher, the Loan Rate, under the marketing assistance loan scheme).

Typically, the Target Price is based on historical data concerning market prices for an agricultural commodity. The theory of a countercyclical payment is to provide a farmer with a guarantee of a certain degree of income support in the event the market price for that farmer's output falls below the Target Price. In other words, the countercyclical payment partly shields the farmer from

---

[147] *See* Alan Beattie, *Pile-it-High Advocates Set to Reap Gains*, FINANCIAL TIMES, 9 October 2007, at 4.

fluctuations and vicissitudes in the market, assuring the farmer of a specified minimum price — the Target Price — and, therefore, a certain minimum income level.

Specifically, under the *Farm Security and Rural Investment Act of 2002* — the *2002 Farm Bill*, Public Law 107-171 (13 May 2002), codified in Title 7 of the U.S.C.[148] — to establish the countercyclical payment, the following calculation (in rough terms) is performed.

- First, a direct payment amount is calculated by multiplying base acreage (that is, historic acres planted during a prescribed period, such as the 1998 through 2001 crop years, as statutorily mandated) and program yield (that is, the yield from the base acreage in a statutorily prescribed period, such as 1995, which is statutorily mandated). The direct payment — base acreage times program yield — is decoupled. That is, the direct payment is not linked to the type or amount of production, or to the price of the subsidized commodity.

- Second, the sum of the Market Price (or, if higher, the Loan Rate) and the direct payment is computed.

- Third, this sum is subtracted from the Target Price. The result is called the counter-cyclical rate (CCR).

- Fourth, the CCR (along with base acreage and program yield) is multiplied by 0.85. The result is the amount of the countercyclical payment.

The countercyclical payment is not tied to production, but it does depend on current market values for the commodity in question. If the actual Market Price exceeds the Target Price, then the CCR will be less than zero. Consequently, there will be no payment. Conversely, if the Market Price is less than the Target Price, then the CCR will be positive. In turn, the payment will be positive.

Under the WTO *Agreement on Agriculture*, countercyclical payments are treated as Amber Box subsidies. That is because they are linked to market prices, and thus are trade-distorting. Consequently, countercyclical payments are subject to reduction commitments. The Blue Box was reserved for payments de-coupled from production. However, during the Doha Round, the United States proposed an expanded definition of the Blue Box to accommodate counter-cyclical payments. That proposal was consistent with the significantly greater emphasis the United States placed on counter-cyclical support in the 2007 Farm Bill.

Among the program crops (also called commodity crops), the 2007 *Farm Bill* set as Target Prices for countercyclical support — *i.e.*, the intervention points at which the United Stated Department of Agriculture would begin paying farmers, the following:

- Corn, $2.63 per bushel.
- Wheat, $4.15 per bushel.

---

[148] Conservation provisions of the *2002 Farm Bill* were codified in Title 16 of the U.S.C.

- Soybeans, $6.10 per bushel.

- Oilseeds, which are separately identified as sunflower seed, rapeseed, canola, sesame, safflower, flaxseed, mustard seed, crambe, all of which are at 11.5 cents per pound.

- Rice, $10.50 per hundredweight. (Hundredweight is an old English measure roughly equivalent to 100 pounds.)

- Cotton, 70 cents per pound.

- Sugar (from beet or cane), no counter-cyclical support, but covered by its own separate provision in the 2007 *Farm Bill*, and also protected by tariff rate quotas (TRQs).

- Peanuts, $495 per ton.

- Sorghum, $2.57 per bushel.

- Barley, $2.73 per bushel.

- Oats, $1.50 per bushel.

- Wool (sheep hair, which is a fiber used to make woolen fabric), no counter-cyclical support, but covered by separate provisions in the 2007 *Farm Bill*, including non-recourse marketing assistance loans.

- Mohair (goat hair, which is a fiber used to make woolen fabric), no counter-cyclical support, but covered by separate provisions in the 2007 *Farm Bill*, including non-recourse marketing assistance loans.

- Honey, no counter-cyclical support, but covered by separate provisions in the 2007 *Farm Bill*, including non-recourse marketing assistance loans.

- Dry peas (not English peas, snow peas, sugar snap peas, or other pea types), no counter-cyclical support, but covered by separate provisions in the 2007 *Farm Bill*, including non-recourse marketing assistance loans.

- Lentils, no counter-cyclical support, but covered by separate provisions in the 2007 *Farm Bill*, including non-recourse marketing assistance loans.

- Small chickpeas, no counter-cyclical support, but covered by separate provisions in the 2007 *Farm Bill*, including non-recourse marketing assistance loans.

- Dairy products (including butter, cheese, milk, and non-fat dry milk, but not eggs), no counter-cyclical support, but covered by their own separate provision in the 2007 *Farm Bill*, including a dairy product price support program.

The 2007 *Farm Bill* calls the price against which the Target is gauged the "Effective Price." The Effective Price is the national average market price, or the national average loan rate for a marketing assistance loan, during a specified 12 month Marketing Year (MY), also known as a Crop Year. As American Farm Bills apply for five years, query whether a statutorily-defined benchmark that does not change for such a period actually reflects a market price.

Thus, for example, if the Effective Price of corn hit or fell below $2.63 per bushel, then the USDA would pay a corn farmer the difference between the Effective Price and the $2.63 Target Price. Manifestly, the larger the gap between the two Prices, the greater the payment, hence the rubric "counter-cyclical."

An obvious controversy associated with countercyclical payments concerns cotton. During the Doha Round, the Cotton Four countries, and their sovereign and non-governmental organization (NGO) supporters, urged elimination of cotton subsidies by the United States. That argument was reinforced by a significant legal defeat the United States suffered in the 2005 *Upland Cotton* case. *See United States — Subsidies on Upland Cotton*, WT/DS267/AB/R (adopted 21 March 2005) (complaint by Brazil). However, the 2007 *Farm Bill* lowered the Target Price for cotton from 72 cents per pound to 70 cents per pound.

In the United States, countercyclical payments are made based on a contract from Commodity Credit Corporation (CCC) Form CCC509. These payments are made in one, two or three installments, starting in October of the harvest year, the following February, and the last payment at the end of the marketing year. If a farmer elects to receive fewer installments, then the payments begin in February for two installments, or at the end of the marketing year, should the farmer wait for a single installment payment.

## COURT OF INTERNATIONAL TRADE

*See* CIT.

## CPSC

*See* Consumer Product Safety Commission.

## *CPSIA*

*Consumer Product Safety Improvement Act*.

*See* Consumer Product Safety Commission.

## CREATIVITY

Taking known facts, and known concepts, and putting them together in a novel way.

## CRITICAL CIRCUMSTANCES

Exceptional conditions, typically in an antidumping (AD), countervailing duty (CVD), or safeguard action, which allegedly merit special remedial consideration.

That consideration may take the form of imposing a remedial duty (e.g., an AD duty) further back in time than normally would be the case. For example, the duty may be imposed on subject merchandise entered 90 days prior to the filing of the petition for a trade remedy, rather than as of the filing date. Alternatively, or in addition, special consideration could mean expedited consideration of a petition by administering authorities. For instance, the time frame for a dumping margin or injury determination may be reduced by several weeks.

Critical circumstances often arise — or can arise — where subject merchandise is a perishable good. If a trade remedy petition drags on under a normal time frame, then fruits, vegetables, or other short-life cycle goods may rot awaiting disposition of the petition. United States trade remedy law establishes the grounds for, and remedies in case of, critical circumstances.

## CROSS COMPLIANCE

A term associated with reforms to the Common Agricultural Policy (CAP) of the European Union (EU), especially Agenda 2000 and the 2003 Mid-Term Review of 2000.

The term connotes the requirement for a farmer to adhere to criteria on the environment, food safety, human, animal and plant health and welfare, and maintenance of agricultural land in good condition, in order to receive direct income support under the CAP. That is, cross compliance links direct payments (associated with the Single Payment Scheme of the CAP) to farmers to the extent to which they respect environmental and other requirements. Such requirements are set at the EU, and at national levels.

Essentially, cross compliance is a tool for implementing the concept of multifunctionality into agricultural policy, specifically, promoting environmentally-sustainable agriculture, and certain social values. Further, cross-compliance underscores the nature of single payments as non-trade distorting support to farmers.

Until June 2003, cross-compliance was voluntary and applied only to environmental standards. At that point, it became mandatory and conditionality for receipt of payments broadened beyond environmental matters. Conditions pertaining to the environmental maintenance of agricultural land in good condition are set by EU states. To do so, the EU states take into account the specific characteristics of the agricultural land at issue, including soil and climatic conditions, crop rotation, land use, and existing farming practices, structures, and systems. To be transparent, the states must inform farmers about the requirements, and the way in which they are enforces. Through its Directives and Regulations, the EU establishes management requirements for the environment, and human, animal, and plant health and welfare.

Failure by a farmer to adhere to any of the conditions can result in deductions from direct payments, or cancellation of the entire single payment, to the farmer. To ensure coordinated enforcement, the EU requires that each member state perform spot checks on at least one percent of the farms in its territory annually. The penalty rate depends on the degree of severity of non-compliance. For a case of negligence, the range is 1-15 percent. For intentional non-compliance, the rate is at least 15 percent. Penalties are cumulative, so failure to satisfy multiple conditions, or failure to satisfy a single condition on multiple tracts of land, can result in multiple penalties. Penalties revert to the EU, with member states entitled to retain up to 25 percent of the amount of the penalties. The penalties are used to help fund CAP measures.

The conditions for receiving direct support are considered legally obligatory minimums. Farmers are free, and indeed encouraged, to adopt voluntarily higher standards — good agricultural practices. In some instances, they may receive greater support for doing so.

Note that cross-compliance is distinct from the June 2003 CAP reform that obligates EU states to ensure their area of permanent pasture does not decline as a result of that reform. The "area of permanent pasture" is the ratio of land used for farming in comparison with total agricultural land. The reform mandates that the ratio does not decrease by more than 10 percent relative to the 2003 reference ratio. If a decrease occurs, then member states may impose restrictions to stem the decline. For example, they may require prior authorization for plowing, or obligate the return of arable land to pasture. In sum, maintenance of permanent pasture and cross-compliance are distinct mandates.

## CSI

*Container Security Initiative.*

A post-9/11 program announced by the United States government in January 2002, and sponsored by the United States Customs and Border Protection (CBP). The purpose of CSI is to enhance the security of containers containing merchandise shipped to the United States, and ports from which that merchandise is shipped. Accordingly, there are four core elements to the CSI:

(1) Identifying high-risk containers.

(2) Pre-screening and evaluating containers before they are shipped to the United States.

(3) Using technology to pre-screen high-risk containers to ensure screening can be done rapidly, without decelerating trade flows.

(4) Using so-called "smarter," or more secure, containers.

*Suggestions for Further Research:*

Articles:

1. Bowman, Gregory W., *Thinking Outside the Border: Homeland Security and the Forward Deployment of the U.S. Border*, 44 HOUSTON LAW REVIEW number 2 (2007).

2. Cunningham, Larry, *The Border Search Exception as Applied to Exit and Export Searches: A Global Conceptualization*, 26 QLR 1–55 (2007).

3. Florestal, Marjorie, *Terror On the High Seas*, 72 BROOKLYN LAW REVIEW 385 (2007).

4.   Lobsinger, Eric J., *Post-9/11 Security in a Post-WWII World: The Question of Compatibility of Maritime Security Efforts with Trade Rules and International Trade Law*, 32 TULANE MARITIME LAW JOURNAL 61–129 (2007).

5.   Maney, Kevin P., Comment, *"Said to Contain:" Fear of Incurring Liability Creates a Disincentive for Cargo Carriers to Improve Shipping Container Security by Examining Cargo*, 35 TULANE MARITIME LAW JOURNAL 317–343 (2010).

6.   North, Jennifer L., *The Ins and Outs of Modern Ports: Rethinking Container Security*, 5 SOUTH CAROLINA JOURNAL OF INTERNATIONAL LAW & BUSINESS 191–208 (2009).

7.   Walker, George K., *Self-Defense, the Law of Armed Conflict, and Port Security*, 5 SOUTH CAROLINA JOURNAL OF INTERNATIONAL LAW & BUSINESS 347–410 (2009).

## CSME

Caribbean Single Market and Economy.

The revised *Treaty of Chaguaramas*, signed on 5 July 2001, by the heads of government of the Caribbean community, provides the legal basis for the operation of the CSME. The CSME aims to create a "single economic space where people, goods, services, and capital can move freely."

There are 12 CSME members:

- Antigua & Barbuda
- Barbados
- Belize
- Dominica
- Grenada
- Guyana
- Jamaica
- St. Kitts & Nevis
- Saint Lucia
- St. Vincent & the Grenadines
- Suriname
- Trinidad and Tobago

An additional three countries have not yet signed or otherwise completed the process of joining the CSME:

- Bahamas (which decided against signing as of 5 July 2001)
- Haiti (which has yet to complete the process)
- Montserrat (which is awaiting entrustment from the United Kingdom)

  All 15 of the above countries are CARICOM members.

## CTHA

*See Chemical Tariff Harmonization Agreement.*

## C-TPAT

*Customs–Trade Partnership Against Terrorism.*

A post-9/11 program, launched in November 2001, sponsored by the United States CBP to enhance the security and efficiency of global supply chains through which merchandise is imported into the United States. The program is a partnership between the public and private sectors, that is, between CBP and stakeholders in supply chains (*e.g.*, carriers, customs brokers, freight forwarders, and importers). Participation is voluntary on the part of private sector businesses, but certification as a *C-TPAT* partner entitles a business to the possibility of fewer, faster screenings of its merchandise at the United States border.

*Suggestions for Further Research:*

Articles:

1.   Bowman, Gregory W., *Thinking Outside the Border: Homeland Security and the Forward Deployment of the U.S. Border*, 44 HOUSTON LAW REVIEW number 2 (2007).

2.   Cunningham, Larry, *The Border Search Exception as Applied to Exit and Export Searches: A Global Conceptualization*, 26 QLR 1-55 (2007).

3.   Cunningham, Marjorie x, *Terror On the High Seas*, 72 BROOKLYN LAW REVIEW 385 (2007).

4.   Lobsinger, Eric J., *Post-9/11 Security in a Post-WWII World: The Question of Compatibility of Maritime Security Efforts with Trade Rules and International Trade Law*, 32 TULANE MARITIME LAW JOURNAL 61–129 (2007).

5.   North, Jennifer L., *The Ins and Outs of Modern Ports: Rethinking Container Security*, 5 SOUTH CAROLINA JOURNAL OF INTERNATIONAL LAW & BUSINESS 191–208 (2009).

6.   Walker, George K., *Self-Defense, the Law of Armed Conflict, and Port Security*, 5 SOUTH CAROLINA JOURNAL OF INTERNATIONAL LAW & BUSINESS 347–410 (2009).

## CTE

Committee on Trade and Environment.

A WTO entity established in the Uruguay Round under the *Decision on Trade and Environment*. The *Decision* not only creates the CTE, but also set out its terms of reference. The *Decision* expressly refers to both the *Rio Declaration on Environment and Development* and the *Convention on Biological Diversity*.

## CTH

Change in Tariff Heading.

CTI is a rule of origin to determine whether a substantial transformation has been made to a good in a country, thereby entitling the good to preferential treatment under applicable free trade agreement (FTA) or customs union (CU). A CTH rule is used when non-originating materials, *i.e.*, inputs from one or more countries that are not parties to the FTA or CU, are used in the production of a finished good, where the production occurs in a country that is a member of the FTA or CU, and where the finished good is exported to another FTA or CU member. CTH rules also may be used in the non-preferential context, *i.e.*, for purposes of country of origin labeling, when no FTA or CU is at issue.

As its name suggests, a CTH rule defines a transformation as substantial if the work done on the product in a particular country is enough to cause its tariff classification to change at the sub-heading, *i.e.*, four digit Harmonized System (HS) level. For example, a CTH rule might be appropriate for a case in which crankshaft parts are imported from Brazil into Mexico, and then work is done on the materials in Mexico, before the resulting product — crankshafts — are exported from Mexico to the United States. The Brazilian materials are non-originating, and Mexico and the United States are Parties to the *North American Free Trade Agreement (NAFTA)*. *See Cummins, Inc. v. United States*, United States Court of Appeals for the Federal Circuit, No. 05-1482 (17 July 2006).

Also as with a Change in Tariff Sub-Heading (CTSH) rule, in applying a CTH rule, a comparison is between the (1) tariff classification used when a good enters a FTA or CU member country upon importation from a third country that is not an FTA or CU member, and (2) tariff classification when the good is exported from the country, to a country that is a member of the FTA or CU. If the CTH rule is satisfied, it means the non-originating material imported was substantially transformed before exportation.

## CTSH

Change in Tariff Sub-Heading.

CTSH is a rule of origin to determine whether a substantial transformation has been made to a good in a country, thereby entitling the good to qualify for preferential treatment under applicable free trade agreement (FTA) or customs union (CU) rules. As its name suggests, a CTSH rule defines a transformation as substantial if the work done on the product in a particular country is enough to cause its tariff classification to change at the sub-heading, *i.e.*, six digit Harmonized System (HS) level. CTSH rules also may be used in the non-preferential context, *i.e.*, for purposes of country of origin labeling, when no FTA or CU is at issue.

For example, as with a Change in Tariff Heading (CTH) rule, a CTSH rule might be appropriate for a case in which crankshaft parts are imported from Brazil into Mexico, and then work is done on the materials in Mexico, before the resulting product — crankshafts — are exported from Mexico to the United States. The Brazilian materials are non-originating, and Mexico and the United States are Parties to *North American Free Trade Agreement (NAFTA)*. *See Cummins, Inc. v. United States*, United States Court of Appeals for the Federal Circuit, No. 05-1482 (17 July 2006).

Also as with a CTH rule, in applying a CTSH rule, a comparison is between the (1) tariff classification used when a good enters a FTA or CU member country upon importation from a third country that is not an FTA or CU member, and (2) tariff classification when the good is exported from the country, to a country that is a member of the FTA or CU. If the CTSH rule is satisfied, it means the non-originating material imported was substantially transformed before exportation.

## CU

*See* Customs Union.

An agreement that not only eliminates all internal barriers to trade among the parties, but also establishes a common external tariff (CET) among them. The European Union (EU) and *MERCOSUR* are leading examples of CUs. Like free trade agreements (FTAs), CUs are condoned; subject to lose disciplines, by GATT Article XXIV.

### *CUFTA*

*Canada-United States Free Trade Agreement* of 2 January 1988.

## CULTURE (TRADE AND CULTURE)

*See* Cultural Products.

## CULTURAL INDUSTRIES

*See* Cultural Products.

## CULTURAL PRODUCTS

As yet, there is no broad cultural exemption in the GATT–WTO legal system, though GATT does contain two limited exceptions, in Article IV and Article XX(f). Article IV covers cinematographic films, particularly screen quotas. Article XX(f) contains an exception from GATT obligations for "national treasures of artistic, historic, or archaeological value." With respect to services, the *General Agreement on Trade in Services* (*GATS*) does not contain an exemption for culture. However, the MFN obligation in *GATS* Article II is conditional, and allowed WTO Members to opt out. Similarly, the national treatment obligation in *GATS* Article XVI permits Members to opt into that obligation. Canada took an MFN exemption for film and television co-productions, and it did not make any national treatment commitments in the cultural sector. Thus, "Canada effectively withheld its cultural policies from the *GATS* disciplines and maintained its right to promote Canadian cultural services and suppliers."[149]

Likewise, there is no international instrument that binds countries to a particular relationship between cultural protection and international trade law. Accordingly, there is no standard definition of what qualifies as a "cultural product" for purposes of international trade law. Obvious candidates include film, music, books, and periodicals. The United Nations Educational, Social, and Cultural Organization (UNESCO) offers a broad definition. UNESCO says

---

[149] The Canadian Cultural Industries Sectoral Advisory Group on International Trade, New Strategies for Culture and Trade — Canadian Culture in a Global World i-ii, 1-6, 8-20, 23-24, 26, 30-31 (February 1999).

"culture *includes cultural* heritage, printed matter and literature, music, the performing and visual arts, cinema and photography, radio and television, and socio-*cultural* activities."[150]

*Suggestions for Further Research:*

Book Chapters:

1.  Bruner, Christopher M., *UNESCO, the WTO, and Trade in Cultural Products, in* ESSAYS ON THE FUTURE OF THE WORLD TRADE ORGANIZATION 385–424 (Julien Chaisse & Tiziano Balmelli eds., Editions Interuniversitaires Suisses, 2008).

Articles:

1.  Baskin, Bernard Issac Weinstein, Note, *Historical Heist: An Economic Argument Against Embargoing Chinese Cultural Property*, 8 WASHINGTON UNIVERSITY GLOBAL STUDIES LAW REVIEW 107–138 (2009).

2.  Beppu, Daisuke, Note, *When Cultural Value Justifies Protectionism: Interpreting the Language of the GATT to Find a Limited Cultural Exception to the National Treatment Principle*, 29 CARDOZO LAW REVIEW 1765–1794 (2008).

3.  Bruner, Christopher M., *Culture, Sovereignty, and Hollywood: UNESCO and the Future of Trade in Cultural Products*, 40 NEW YORK UNIVERSITY JOURNAL OF INTERNATIONAL LAW AND POLITICS 351–436 (2008).

4.  Burri-Nenova, Mira, *Trade versus Culture in the Digital Environment: An Old Conflict in Need of a New Definition*, 12 JOURNAL OF INTERNATIONAL ECONOMIC LAW 17–62 (2009).

5.  Delimatsis, Panagiotis, *Protecting Public Morals in a Digital Age: Revisiting the WTO Rulings on US — Gambling and China — Publications and Audiovisual Products*, 14 JOURNAL OF INTERNATIONAL ECONOMIC LAW 257–293 (2011).

6.  Doyle, Christopher, Note, *Gimme Shelter: The "Necessary" Element of GATT Article XX in the Context of the China — Audiovisual Products Case*, 29 BOSTON UNIVERSITY INTERNATIONAL LAW JOURNAL 143–167 (2011).

7.  Gates, Mari-Elise, Note, *Problems in Applying Traditional Cultural Expression Laws to the Unique Medium of Modern Dance*, 48 UNIVERSITY OF LOUISVILLE LAW REVIEW 665–691 (2010).

8.  Kelly, Derek R., Note, *Illegal Tender: Antiquities Protection and U.S. Import Restrictions on Cypriot Coinage*, 34 BROOKLYN JOURNAL OF INTERNATIONAL LAW 491–530 (2009).

---

[150] *Quoted in* THE CANADIAN CULTURAL INDUSTRIES SECTORAL ADVISORY GROUP ON INTERNATIONAL TRADE, NEW STRATEGIES FOR CULTURE AND TRADE — CANADIAN CULTURE IN A GLOBAL WORLD i-ii (February 1999) (emphasis added).

9.  Lee, Kevin, Comment, *"The Little State Department:" Hollywood and the MPAA's Influence on U.S. Trade Relations*, 28 NORTHWESTERN JOURNAL OF INTERNATIONAL LAW & BUSINESS 371–397 (2008).

10.  Nam, Hyung Doo, *The Emergence of Hollywood Ghosts on Korean TVs: The Right of Publicity from the Global Market Perspective*, 19 PACIFIC RIM LAW & POLICY JOURNAL 487–518 (2010).

11.  Patron, Raisa E., Note, *The Looting of Iraqi Archaeological Sites: Global Implications and Support for an International Approach to Regulating the Antiquities Market*, 40 GEORGE WASHINGTON INTERNATIONAL LAW REVIEW 465–496 (2009).

12.  Scully, Kevin, Note, *The Most Dangerous Game: U.S. Opposition to the Cultural Exception*, 36 BROOKLYN JOURNAL OF INTERNATIONAL LAW 1183–1208 (2011).

13.  Turco, Jonathan M., Note, *Leaving Los Angeles: Runaway Productions and the FTAC's 301(A) Petition Under International Law*, 15 SOUTHWESTERN JOURNAL OF LAW & TRADE IN THE AMERICAS 141–166 (2008).

14.  Ya Qin, Julia, *Pushing the Limits of Global Governance: Trading Rights, Censorship and WTO Jurisprudence — A Commentary on the China — Publications Case*, 10 CHINESE JOURNAL OF INTERNATIONAL LAW 271–322 (2011).

## CUMULATION

A rule allowing a good or transaction from one country or region to be added to a good or transaction from another country or region. Generally speaking, the rule allows an imported product to be regarded as originating when it is used in a production process in the importing country. Cumulation may be "bilateral," "full," or "diagonal." *See* rules of origin.

In the context of a free trade agreement (FTA), customs union (CU), or other preferential trade agreement (PTA), cumulation allows FTA members to include inputs from each member — or, sometimes, non-members — when deciding whether a particular product originates within that FTA. For example, suppose American cotton, Costa Rican buttons, Dominican Republic pockets, and Chinese dye go into the manufacture of a shirt, with final assembly of the shirt in Mexico, from which the shirts are shipped to the United States. A cumulation rule under the *United States — Dominican Republic — Central American Free Trade Agreement (CAFTA–DR)* will decide which inputs qualify for purposes of determining *CAFTA–DR* origination. This rule — a preferential rule of origin — may be a product specific rule of origin (PSRO), a value added test, a specified process rule, or some combination thereof.

As intimated, typically cumulation questions arise in the context of a preferential rule of origin. FTAs are one example in which such rules occur. Special schemes for poor countries are another illustration, such as the Pan-European Cumulation System (PECS), or under the United States *Generalized System of Preferences* (GSP) and *African Growth and Opportunity Act* (AGOA) programs. Cumulation also occurs in the context of trade remedies, when imports subject to an investigation (subject merchandise) is aggregated from two or more countries.

## CURRENT ACCOUNT

*See* BOP.

## CURRENCY BOARD

A system whereby a government manages the value of its currency against foreign currencies.

Essentially, a currency board covers excess demand of one currency by stepping in and selling the currency in demand. More specifically, a currency board is legally obligated to buy (sell) foreign currency in exchange for the sale (purchase) of local currency. Further, it is committed to exchanging currencies at a fixed rate, and to ensuring that each unit of local currency is backed by a specified proportion of foreign currency. Consequently, there is no central banking function of issuing local currency in pursuit of a chosen monetary policy to achieve a certain level of interest rates or prices. Rather, local currency is sold (bought) against purchases (sales) of foreign currency.

The Hong Kong Special Administrative Region (SAR) operates a currency board. For instance, suppose people seek to convert more foreign currency (*e.g.*, United States dollars) into local currency (*e.g.*, Hong Kong dollars). The Hong Kong currency board buys the foreign currency, puts it into the SAR reserve account, and sells the local currency. The result, of course, is an increase in the supply of local currency. That increase can lead to inflation, if people spend the local currency on consumption items and the increase in their money outstrips the supply of those items — a classic "too much money chasing too few goods" scenario." That scenario occurred in Hong Kong in the mid-1990s. (Conversely, if they save and invest the local currency, then no inflation results from the money supply increase. In effect, that increase fulfills their demand for money.)

A currency board maintaining a pegged exchange rate, and free foreign capital inflows and outflows, means a loss of control over monetary policy. With free capital flows, the currency board is legally obligated to buy or sell foreign or local currency, in order to maintain a pegged exchange rate. (In the case of Hong Kong, that rate has long been approximately 7.8 Hong Kong dollars to 1 U.S. dollar.) Thus, the supply of local currency depends on foreign capital flows, not on government-set monetary policy *per se*. In turn, insofar as the money supply determines interest rates and price levels, control over those variables is lost. This fact is dubbed by Nobel Prize-winning economist Robert Mundell as the "impossible trinity." He means that no economy can simultaneously and at all times maintain (1) free capital flows, (2) a fixed exchange rate, and (3) control over monetary policy. With a currency board, (1) and (2) are possible, but not (3).

*Suggestions for Further Research:*

Articles:

1.   Beckington, Jeffrey S. and Matthew R. Amon (Student), *Competitive Currency Depreciation: The Need for a More Effective International Legal Regime*, 10 JOURNAL OF INTERNATIONAL BUSINESS & LAW 209–268 (2011).

2.   Bergsten, C. Fred, *The Need for a Robust Response to Chinese Currency Manipulation — Policy Options for the Obama Administration Including Countervailing Currency Intervention*, 10 JOURNAL OF INTERNATIONAL BUSINESS & LAW 269–280 (2011).

3.   Mercurio, Bryan & Celine Sze Ning Leung, *Is China a "Currency Manipulator"?: The Legitimacy of China's Exchange Regime Under the Current International Legal Framework*, 43 THE INTERNATIONAL LAWYER 1257–1300 (2009).

4.   Pettis, Elizabeth L., *Is China's Manipulation of its Currency An Actionable Violation of the IMF and/or WTO Agreements?*, 10 JOURNAL OF INTERNATIONAL BUSINESS & LAW 281–296 (2011).

5.   Restall, Hugo, *Satisfy China's Demand for Money*, 170 FAR EASTERN ECONOMIC REVIEW number 5, 16, 17 (June 2007).

6.   Zimmerman, Claus D., 105 *Exchange Rate Misalignment and International Law*, AMERICAN JOURNAL OF INTERNATIONAL LAW 423–476 (2011).

## CUSTOMARY INTERNATIONAL LAW

Customary International Law (CIL) is a primary source of international law, alongside treaties. There are two traditional elements used to determine (*i.e.*, two criteria for the establishment of) CIL, state practice and *opinio juris*.[151] State practice consists of the repetition of similar conduct by States over time. *Opinio juris* requires these acts to be performed out of a sense of obligation. A third element is often sited, which is that the acts are performed by a large number of states and are not rejected by a large number of states. It is from these elements that rules of law, that is, CIL, are derived.

The existence of CIL is acknowledged in Article 38(1)(b) of the statute of the International Court of Justice (ICJ). This article states that the Court will use international custom while deciding disputes as evidence of general practice accepted as law.[152] This principle was also incorporated into the United Nations Charter in Article 92.

There are many different opinions over what constitutes a rule under CIL. Scholars often turn to records of a State's foreign relations, international obligation legislation, and intergovernmental organizations' resolutions to

---

[151] The ICJ defined "customary law" in *USA v. Nicaragua*, confirming the elements to consist of *opinio juris* as proven by existing state practices. *See* Military and Paramiliary Activities (Nicar. v. U.S.), 1986 I.C.J. 14 (27 June).

[152] The Court also relies on treaty, the general principles of law recognized by civilized nations, and judicial decisions and teachings of the most highly qualified publicists. I.C.J. Art. 38.

determine State practice. Some examples of recognized customary international laws are the prohibition of slavery, torture, or crimes against humanity. Customary laws such as these are often codified in treaty.

While sometimes the substantive content of CIL is difficult to ascertain, there are certain fundamental principles of international law that allow no derogations. These super-customary laws are referred to as "peremptory norms" or "*jus cogens*."[153] A commonly cited example of a peremptory norm is the prohibition against torture.

Some treaties generate rules that become CIL. Professor D'Amato expresses two qualifications to this principle: the treaty provision must be generalizable; and the provision must not be subject to reservation.[154]

There is some debate over the necessity of *opinio juris* and the real origin of CIL. Professor D'Amato argues CIL derives from the results of international controversy.[155] Other scholars disagree, pointing out conflicts are only one type of social interaction, citing negotiations as an example of a peaceful means of creating CIL.[156] Some scholars compare the evolution of CIL to precedents set through common law.[157]

Issues of customary law — its existence and potential relevance or application to a dispute — sometimes arise in WTO litigation. The debate about the precautionary principle in the 1998 *Beef Hormones* case is one example. However, the general approach of the Appellate Body is to focus on the trade agreements in front of it, and focus on treaty interpretation using Articles 31 and 32 of the 1969 *Vienna Convention on the Law of Treaties*. In other words, it tends to eschew references to sources of law other than the GATT–WTO agreements.

## CUSTOMS BOND

Like any bond, a customs bond is a legal instrument designed to secure payment of a possible liability that arises from failure by an importer to adhere to United States trade laws and regulations affecting imported merchandise.[158] There are three parties to a customs bond transaction:

(1) the bond principal, which typically is the importer,

(2) the surety, which is a guarantor that agrees to pay any liability that might arise if the bond principal fails to perform its obligations under American trade laws and regulations; and

---

[153] *See* David Kennedy, International Legal Structures 26–27 (Nomos ed., 1987).

[154] *See* Anthony D'Amato, *Customary International Law: A Reformulation*, 4 International Legal Theory 5 (1998).

[155] *See* Anthony D'Amato, *Customary International Law: A Reformulation*, 4 International Legal Theory 3 (1998).

[156] *See* Andy Feslor, *Reformulating Customary International Law*, 4 International Legal Theory 11 (1998).

[157] *See* Maxwell Chibundu, *Time for Institutional International Law: A Reformulation*, 4 International Legal Theory 7 (1998).

[158] *See* 19 C.F.R. § 113.62.

(3) the beneficiary, which is the United States Customs and Border Protection (CBP).

The bond itself, therefore, is accessory or ancillary to the principal obligation that is supposed to guarantee.

Under United States customs rules, there are three major kinds of deposit requirements incumbent on an importer of merchandise:

(1) Basic Bond Amount (BBA) — Post a bond, which is required of all importers of any merchandise into the United States, whether or not that merchandise is subject to a trade remedy order. The CBP will not permit release from its custody of merchandise unless this bond is posted.[159] The formula for the amount of a continuous BBA is: the greater of U.S. $50,000 or 10 percent of the duties, taxes, and fees paid by the importer during the preceding calendar year. The resulting figure is then rounded to a figure set out in the formula. The BBA also is known as the Basic Bond Requirement (BBR).

(2) Cash Deposit — Post a cash deposit equal to the margin of dumping or subsidization rate calculated in the original investigation, or most recent Administrative (Periodic) Review in which a duty assessment rate is computed, which is standard practice under the retrospective duty assessment system in American antidumping (AD) and countervailing duty (CVD) proceedings.

(3) Enhanced Continuous Bond Requirement (EBR) — Post an enhanced continuous bond equal to 100 percent of the AD or CVD rate established in the original investigation or most recent Review for an exporter of subject merchandise, multiplied by the value of imports entered by the importer of that merchandise during the previous 12 months. When an importer tenders payment of its final liability for AD duties — specifically, when CBP assesses that liability and liquidates entries of subject merchandise to which the liability relates — then the CBP releases the EBR posted by the importer.

Note the different specific types of bonds, namely, a single transaction bond (also called a "single entry bond") versus a continuous bond. A single transaction bond, as its name suggests, covers a single entry of merchandise, *i.e.*, one import transaction. A continuous bond secures payments that arise out of all import transactions by a particular importer during the period for which the bond is effective. The amount of the bond depends in part on the kind of bond the importer seeks to post.

The authority of the CBP to require bonds is set out in Section 1623 of the *Tariff Act of 1930*, as amended. That provision authorizes the Secretary of the Treasury to require or allow a customs official to require the posting of a bond to protect revenue and ensure compliance with any law or regulation for which the Secretary is responsible for enforcement. Under this authority, the Treasury Secretary may prescribe conditions and amounts for bonds. In turn, CBP officials are empowered to determine the sufficiency of a bond in relation to the

---

[159] *See* 19 C.F.R. § 142.4(a).

liability of an importer it secures, review bonds periodically to ensure whether a bond is sufficient, and to require additional security if necessary to protect revenue or ensure enforcement of a law or regulation.[160]

The EBR (including the Amended Continuous Bond Directive Requirement, or Amended CBD) was the subject of WTO litigation, when Thailand and India mounted a successful challenge against it in the 2008 case, *United States — Measures Relating to Shrimp from Thailand* (complaint by Thailand) and *United States — Customs Bond Directive for Merchandise Subject to Anti-dumping/Countervailing Duties* (complaint by India), WT/DS343/AB/R and WT/DS345/AB/R (adopted 1 August 2008).

## CUSTOMS FACILITATION

*See* Trade Facilitation.

## CUSTOMS LAW

A generic term that covers all aspects of the clearance of merchandise across an international boundary, including product classification under the Harmonized System (HS), product valuation, determination of country of origin (*i.e.*, application of rules of origin), assessment of duty liability, administration of technical requirements and of sanitary and phytosanitary standards (SPS), regulation of foreign trade zones (FTZs) and other special entry facilities (such as warehouses and importation under bond), and (especially in the post-9/11 context), adherence to national security and border protection measures.

*Suggestions for Further Research:*

Articles:

1.   Baisburd, Yohai, *et al.*, *Customs Law*, 45 THE INTERNATIONAL LAWYER 3–17 (2011).

2.   Chen, Kelly, *et al.*, *Customs Law*, 43 THE INTERNATIONAL LAWYER 289–309 (2009).

3.   Heath, Christopher, *Customs Seizures, Transit and Trade — In Honour of Dieter Stauder's 70ᵗʰ Birthday*, 41 IIC: INTERNATIONAL REVIEW OF INTELLECTUAL PROPERTY & COMPETITION LAW 881–905 (2010).

## CUSTOMS MUTUAL ASSISTANCE AGREEMENT

An agreement, sometimes abbreviated as "CMAA," between the United States and a foreign country that allows for the exchange of documents, intelligence, and other information to help the two sides prevent and investigate customs law violations.

The United States uses the June 1967 World Customs Organization (WCO, formerly the Customs Cooperation Council (CCC)) model bilateral convention

---

[160] *See* 19 C.F.R. § 113.13.

on mutual administrative assistance for its Customs Mutual Assistance Agreement program. The United States has such programs with a large number of countries. As of November 2006, the United States had entered into CMAAs with the customs authorities of 58 countries, including Canada, China, India, Hong Kong, Mexico, and Russia, plus one with the American Institute in Taiwan (AIT) — Taipei Economic and Cultural Representative Office (TECRO).

## CUSTOMS SERVICE

The United States Customs Service.

The second act of Congress, dated 4 July 1789, authorized the collection of duties on imported goods. The fifth act of Congress, dated 31 July 1789, established customs districts and authorized customs officers to collect import duties. The Bureau of Customs was created in 1927, and re-designated the Customs Service in 1973. In addition to collecting import duties, the Customs Service is responsible for administering trade remedy laws, for example, the collection of AD and CVD duties, and the implementation of IPR laws that apply to imports (such as Section 337). It is also responsible for administering quotas, interdicting and seizing illegally entered merchandise. A Commissioner heads the Customs Service. The President appoints the Commissioner, who is subject to confirmation by the Senate.

In March 2003, the Customs Service was renamed "Customs and Border Protection," or "CBP." The name change and transfer occurred as a part of *the 2002 Homeland Security Act*, Pub. L. 107-296, 60 days after the bill became effective, i.e., 60 days after 24 January 2003, which was 25 March 2003. For the most part, at both ends, it was transferred from the Department of the Treasury to the Department of Homeland Security (DHS). The transition was not entirely smooth, with some Customs officers said to continue displaying their "Treasury Department patches" on their uniforms. The name "Customs Service" remains common among international trade practitioners.

## CUSTOMS UNION

An agreement among two or more countries (more specifically, customs territories) to liberalize trade between or among them, and to harmonize (to a limited extent) their foreign economic policy.

There are two hallmarks to any customs union (CU). First, there is an agreement to drop all internal trade barriers between or among the countries. Second, there is an agreement to harmonize their tariff schedules with respect to imports from third countries. In practice, few customs unions liberalize trade completely on all products immediately upon entry into force. Likewise, few of them develop a comprehensive common external tariff (CET) rapidly.

Thus, a CU is a more economically integrated entity than a free trade agreement (FTA). Not only do goods and services flow freely across the internal geo-political boundaries that delineate the members, but also the members have a common external tariff policy. A customs union, however, need not have a single currency, or even harmonized fiscal and monetary policies. Thus, for many years, the European Union (EU) was a CU, but not a full economic union. The formation of a CU is subject to the skeletal requirements of GATT Article XXIV.

Notably, every common market and monetary union also has a CU. Examples of CUs or CU-like arrangements include the Andean Community, East African Community (EAC), Economic and Monetary Community of Central Africa, EU — Andorra customs zone, EU — San Marino customs zone, EU — Turkey customs zone, Gulf Cooperation Council (GCC), Israel — Palestinian Territories accord (dating from 1994), *MERCOSUR*, South African Customs Union (SACU), Switzerland — Lichtenstein accord, and West African Economic and Monetary Union. Of course, some of these illustrations are more planned than real. And, the economic significance of these illustrations varies depending on its details.

*Suggestions for Further Research:*

Book:

1.   GORMLEY, LAURENCE W., EU LAW OF FREE MOVEMENT OF GOODS AND CUSTOMS UNION (2009).

## CV

*See* Constructed Value.

## CVD

Countervailing duty.

A CVD is an imposition on imports of subject merchandise that have been ruled to be illegally subsidized. In the United States, the Department of Commerce (DOC) is responsible for subsidy investigations, and the International Trade Commission (ITC) for injury investigations. Both are engaged in five year Sunset Reviews of outstanding CVD orders.

GATT Article VI and the WTO *Agreement on Subsidies and Countervailing Measures* (*SCM Agreement*) countenance imposition of CVDs, so long as legal prerequisites set forth in these accords are satisfied. The CVD is designed to counter-act the illegal subsidy. The United States and some countries impose CVDs equal to the full amount of the net countervailable subsidy, as calculated in the subsidy determination phase of a CVD case. The European Union (EU), and certain other countries, follow the "Lesser Duty Rule," whereby they set the CVD at just enough to offset the injurious effects of an illegal subsidy.

*Suggestions for Further Research:*

Books:

1.   ADAMANTOPOULOS, KONSTANTINOS & MARÍA J. PEREYRA, EU ANTI-SUBSIDY LAW AND PRACTICE (London: Sweet & Maxwell 2007).

2. RUBINI, LUCA, THE DEFINITION OF SUBSIDY AND STATE AID — WTO AND EC LAW IN COMPARATIVE PERSPECTIVE (2009).

3. STEWART, TERRENCE P. & AMY S. DWYER, WTO ANTIDUMPING AND SUBSIDY AGREEMENTS (1998).

4. VAKERICS, THOMAS V., DAVID I. WILSON & KENNETH G. WEIGEL, ANTIDUMPING, COUNTERVAILING DUTY, AND OTHER TRADE ACTIONS (December 1987).

Articles:

1. Ahn, Dukgeun & Jieun Lee, *Countervailing Duty Against China: Opening a Pandora's Box in the WTO System?*, 14 JOURNAL OF INTERNATIONAL ECONOMIC LAW 329–368 (2011).

2. Barnett, Mark A., Sara Khan, Kathy B. Reif & Elizabeth Shryock, *28 U.S.C. § 1581(c) — Review by the Court of International Trade of Antidumping & Countervailing Duty Determinations Issued by the Department of Commerce*, 40 GEORGETOWN JOURNAL OF INTERNATIONAL LAW 153–181 (2008).

3. Beckington, Jeffrey S. and Matthew R. Amon (Student), *Competitive Currency Depreciation: The Need for a More Effective International Legal Regime*, 10 JOURNAL OF INTERNATIONAL BUSINESS & LAW 209–268 (2011).

4. Bentes, Pablo M., *et al.*, *International Trade*, 44 THE INTERNATIONAL LAWYER 93–111 (2010).

5. Bergsten, C. Fred, *The Need for a Robust Response to Chinese Currency Manipulation — Policy Options for the Obama Administration Including Countervailing Currency Intervention*, 10 JOURNAL OF INTERNATIONAL BUSINESS & LAW 269–280 (2011).

6. Diamond, Richard, *Privatization and the Definition of Subsidy: A Critical Study of Appellate Body Texturalism*, 11 JOURNAL OF INTERNATIONAL ECONOMIC LAW 649–678 (2008).

7. Dorn, Joseph W., *U.S. Court of International Trade Decisions During 2007 in Appeals of Determinations of the U.S. International Trade Commission*, 40 GEORGETOWN JOURNAL OF INTERNATIONAL LAW 219–241 (2008).

8. Goldburn, Tricia D., Comment, *Dollars & Renminbis: Curbing the United States' Raging Trade Deficit with China by Dismantling the Dollar — RMB Peg*, 25 PENN STATE INTERNATIONAL LAW REVIEW 737–757 (2007).

9. Horlick, Gary N. & Peggy A. Clarke, *WTO Subsidies Discipline During and After the Crisis*, 13 JOURNAL INTERNATIONAL ECONOMIC LAW 859–874 (2010).

10. Jensen, Niels & Joan Fitzhenry, *Countervailing Duties and the Pass-Through of Subsidies: Canadian Lumber and the Australian Position*, 10 INTERNATIONAL TRADE LAW & REGULATION 129–132 (November 2004).

11. Laroski, Joseph A., Jr. & Valentin A. Povarchuk eds., *International Trade*, 45 THE INTERNATIONAL LAWYER 79–94 (spring 2011).

12. de Lima Mantilla, Yuri, *The Survival of the United States Ethanol Subsidies and Tariff: Are There Further Reasons to Keep Them on the Books?*, 15 ILSA JOURNAL OF INTERNATIONAL & COMPARATIVE LAW 203–225 (2008).

13. Lynam, Garrett E., *Using WTO Countervailing Duty Law to Combat Illegally Subsidized Chinese Enterprises Operating in a Non-Market Economy: Deciphering the Writing on the Wall*, 42 Case Western Reserve Journal of International Law 739–773 (2010).

14. Lynch, Michele D., Nasim A. Deylami, Nathaniel J. Halvorson, Skye Mathieson & Kelsey M. Rule, *28 U.S.C. § 1581(c): Judicial Review of Antidumping and Countervailing Duty Determinations by the Department of Commerce*, 42 GEORGETOWN JOURNAL OF INTERNATIONAL LAW 65–95 (2010).

15. Lysons, Sarah E., *Comment, Resolving the Softwood Lumber Dispute*, 32 Seattle University Law Review 407–441 (2009).

16. Mercurio Bryan & Celine Sze Ning Leung, *Is China a "Currency Manipulator"?: The Legitimacy of China's Exchange Regime Under the Current International Legal Framework*, 43 THE INTERNATIONAL LAWYER 1257–1300 (2009).

17. Pettis, Elizabeth L., *Is China's Manipulation of its Currency An Actionable Violation of the IMF and/or WTO Agreements?*, 10 JOURNAL OF INTERNATIONAL BUSINESS & LAW 281–296 (2011).

18. Planert, R. Will, *Enjoining Liquidation in Antidumping and Countervailing Duty Cases: Issues and Pitfalls*, 19 TULANE JOURNAL OF INTERNATIONAL & COMPARATIVE LAW 505–541 (2011).

19. Potter, Simon, *The Softwood Lumber Agreement of 2006: Worth Saving?*, 12 INTERNATIONAL TRADE LAW & REGULATION 98–103 (September 2007).

20. Sykes, Alan O., *Countervailing Duty Law: An Economic Perspective*, 89 COLUMBIA LAW REVIEW 199, 214–18 (1989).

21. Trossevin, Marguerite & Reza Karmaloo, *Judicial Review of Antidumping and Countervailing Duty Determinations by the Department of Commerce: Noteworthy Cases in 2009*, 42 GEORGETOWN JOURNAL OF INTERNATIONAL LAW 35–63 (2010).

22. Windon, James, Note, *The Allocation of Free Emissions Units and the WTO Subsidies Agreement*, 41 GEORGETOWN JOURNAL OF INTERNATIONAL LAW 189–221 (2009).

23. Zheng, Wentong & Robert E. Hudec, Article on Global Trade, *The Pitfalls of the (Perfect) Market Benchmark: The Case of Countervailing Duty Law*, 19 MINNESOTA JOURNAL OF INTERNATIONAL LAW 1–54 (2010).

24. Zimmerman, Claus D., 105 *Exchange Rate Misalignment and International Law*, AMERICAN JOURNAL OF INTERNATIONAL LAW 423–476 (2011).

Other Source:

1. Balassa, Bela, ed., *Subsidies and Countervailing Measures — Critical Issues for the Uruguay Round*, WORLD BANK DISCUSSION PAPERS Number 55 (1989).

# D

## DATA EXCLUSIVITY

An intellectual property (IP) rule on use of original data about a patented product by a would-be generic manufacturer.

Typically, the product context is a pharmaceutical. The rule states that drug regulatory authorities must forbid use of the registration files of an originator of a patented medicine by a party seeking to register a generic version of that product for therapeutic application. The party seeking to register the generic, and manufacture it, as quickly as possible, potentially can benefit from knowledge culled from the original files.

A data exclusivity rule is time bound. For example, the rule might say that for five years after expiry of a patent on a particular medicine, any party seeking to manufacture a generic version of that medicine cannot make use of the registration files of the originator of that medicine. Data exclusivity can delay the entry into a market of generic products.

Data exclusivity rules — both their substance and duration — sometimes are major points of controversy in negotiations over free trade agreements (FTAs), as in the talks between the United States and Thailand in 2006.

## DAVOS MAN

A term coined by Harvard political scientist, Professor Samuel P. Huntington, famed author of *The Clash of Civilizations* (1996). A "Davos Man" is a leader from the world of government, business, non-governmental organizations (NGOs), or the academy attending the annual Davos Summit (formally called the "World Economic Forum") who readily accepts the need for open markets, trade, and investment, and supports globalization. Typically, the entity that leader represents, and even the leader personally, has benefited considerably from economic liberalization since the fall of the Berlin Wall in 1989, though fortunes have changed in the global economic recession of late.

Although some participants at the Summit — held in the Swiss ski resort town of Davos — are women, African, Chinese, or Indian, the "culture" of Davos Man is still sometimes characterized as white, male, and European or Anglo-Saxon. According to *The Economist*, "Davos Man" includes businessmen, bankers, officials, and intellectuals who

> hold university degrees, work with words and numbers, speak some English and share beliefs in individualism, market economics and democracy. They control many of the world's governments, and the bulk of its economic and military capabilities. . . . [The Davos Man does

not] butter up the politicians; it is the other way around . . . finding it boring to shake the hand of an obscure prime minister.[161]

Davos Man, or Woman, prefers to meet the Bill Gates of the world.

*Suggestions for Further Research:*

Other Source:

1.  Beneria, Lourdes, *Global Markets, Gender, and the Davos Man*, First Global Forum on Human Development, 29–31 July 1999, United Nations Headquarters, New York.

## DAVOS SUMMIT

A short-hand expression for the World Economic Forum, which was incorporated in 1971, and which occurs each year in January in the ski resort town of Davos, Switzerland (180 miles from Geneva). The inaugural meeting in 1971 was organized by Klaus Schwab. The Forum is not-for-profit, and not tied to any political or national interests. The Swiss Federal Government supervises the Forum.

Attending the Davos Summit are many of the world's most powerful and influential corporate officials, some intellectuals, and even prominent entertainers. Notable past attendees include Kofi Annan, Tony Blair, Bono, Gordon Brown, Bill Clinton, Bill Gates, and Angela Merkel. Senior governmental officials, who are not heads of state, from many countries also attend. Some academic leaders have participated, including (now former) University of Kansas Chancellor Robert Hemenway.

At the Summit, participants discuss major global problems, including environmental pollution, poverty, and trade. The Summit sometimes is derided, and has been the subject of protests and riots. At the 2005, 2006, and 2007 Summits, participants called for vigorous efforts to conclude the Doha Round — all to no avail. As an "anti-Davos Summit," a "World Social Forum is held at roughly the same time in a developing country.

## DDA

Doha Development Agenda.

*See* Doha Round.

## DE MINIMIS

Insignificant, negligible, or trivial in nature, value, or volume, with the legal consequence that no action is taken.

Several WTO agreements contain *de minimis* rules. For example, Article 5:8 of the *Agreement on Implementation of Article VI of the General Agreement on Tariffs and Trade 1994* (*Antidumping*, or *AD, Agreement*) contains two basic

---

[161] *In Praise of the Davos Man*, THE ECONOMIST, 1 February 1997. *See also* Timothy Ash Garton, *Davos Man's Death Wish*, THE GUARDIAN, 3 February 2005, Comments Section.

*de minimis* thresholds. If either threshold is met, then no antidumping (AD) duty is permitted, and the investigation must be terminated.

- *De minimis* value threshold —
  No AD duty may be imposed if the dumping margin is less than two percent of the Export Price of subject merchandise.

- *De minimis* volume threshold —
  No AD duty may be imposed if the volume of dumped imports is less than three percent of imports of the like product in the importing WTO Member contemplating action.

The *Agreement on Agriculture*, in Article 4, permits WTO Members to provide a *de minimis* level of domestic support, exempting those subsidy payments from the calculation of their Current Total Aggregate Measure of Support (AMS), and from otherwise obligatory reductions.

The establishment of a *de minimis* threshold can be a highly charged affair, pitting the interests of importing countries interested in protecting certain industries against the demand of exporting countries for enhanced market access. The schism may — or may not, depending on the topic and product in question — fall along lines of rich versus poor countries.

Generally speaking, a higher *de minimis* threshold that exempts otherwise actionable conduct from a trade remedy or a trade liberalizing commitment favors protectionist interests. Conversely, a lower *de minimis* threshold bespeaks an inclination to free, or freer, trade.

## DEAUVILLE PARTNERSHIP

*See* MENA (Second Meaning).

## DECOUPLING

The removal of all or part of the link between payment of a subsidy, on the one hand, and performance, on the other hand.

Such coupled subsidies are considered trade distorting, and under the WTO *Agreement on Agriculture*, classified in the Amber Box, and thereby subject to reduction commitments. Agricultural subsidy reform is a familiar context in which this term is used. In that context, decoupling means the amount of payments received by an agricultural producer does not depend on the output of a primary or processed product, or livestock, of that producer. Such payments may qualify for the Green Box under the *Agreement on Agriculture*. Decoupling has been a key aspect of reform by the EU of its CAP.

In June 2008, the Organization for Economic Cooperation and Development (OECD) reported that approximately 60 percent of all agricultural subsidies in OECD countries were based on production, *i.e.*, coupled with output.[162] However,

---

[162] *See OECD Report Says High Commodity Prices Create Opportunity to Slash Farm Subsidies*, 25 International Trade Reporter (BNA) 979 (3 July 2008).

the OECD said increasing efforts are being made to de-link support payments with yield, by employing criteria such as land area under cultivation or livestock number raised. The OECD also reported that roughly 30 percent of all farm subsidies in OECD countries are granted conditionally, with the conditions being environmental and social criteria, restrictions on use of certain inputs, and designation of specific production practices. Overall, then, the OECD analysis suggested a gradual shift toward Green Box programs, and away from trade-distorting Amber Box programs.

*Suggestions for Further Research:*

Articles:

1. Meester, Gerrit, *European Union, Common Agricultural Policy, and World Trade*, 14 Kansas Journal of Law & Public Policy 389–412 (Winter 2005).

2. Phelps, Jess, Note, *Much Ado About Decoupling: Evaluating the Environmental Impact of Recent European Union Agricultural Reform*, 31 Harvard Environmental Law Review 279–320 (2007).

## DEEP FTA (DEEP PTA, DEEP RTA)

*See* Second Generation FTA.

## DEFICIENCY PAYMENT

A payment by a government to a producer of a certain commodity.

Also known as "loan deficiency payment," the amount of the payment is based on the difference between a (1) target price and (2) the domestic market price (or a loan rate, whichever is less). For example, a subsidy payment made to English farmers when prices fall below a level set by government policy would be a deficiency payment.

The United States enters into loan deficiency payment agreements with producers of agricultural products through the Farm Service Agency (FSA) of the Department of Agriculture. Loan deficiency payments for corn, wheat, grain sorghum, soybeans, and wheat are announced each day. Deficiency payments for cotton and rice are announced each week. To maximize revenue, farmers do, or should, monitor market prices, and select deficiency payments at or around their highest levels.

Loan deficiency payments are provided in lieu of Marketing Assistance Loans. The two schemes function in the same way, namely, a counter-cyclical manner. However, loan deficiency payments avoid certain paperwork and administrative burdens associated with Marketing Assistance Loans. In effect, a loan deficiency payment is like applying for, obtaining, and closing out a Marketing Assistance Loan on the same day.

## DEGRESSIVITY

A provision in a trade agreement that calls for, or demands, the progressive liberalization of trade. Typically, degressivity is a requirement associated with a trade remedy. For example, the WTO *Agreement on Safeguards*, and Section 201 of the United States *Trade Act of 1974* (the *Escape Clause*), require progressive liberalization of safeguards restrictions after they have been imposed.

## DEPRECIATION

A decline in the value of a country's currency as a result of market forces, that is, of a relative increase in the supply of the country's currency and/or relative decrease in demand for the country's currency. The term is often mistakenly used synonymously with "devaluation." However, in the event of a devaluation that is viewed as insufficient by the foreign exchange market, traders will be sure to bring about depreciation.

## DET

Differential export taxes.

Differential export taxes exist when a country imposes a duty on one category of exported products that is higher than the levy it puts on a second category of exported products. Typically, the export tax on a basic commodity, such as a primary agricultural product like oilseeds, is higher than the charge on an advanced product, such as a processed food item. A DET is designed to discourage exports of critical inputs and ensure processors and manufacturers have a low-cost domestic source of those inputs. However, a DET also may be an indirect subsidy that arouses the ire of producers in other countries of a good that is like or directly competitive with the low-tariff advanced product.

By discouraging exports of the high-taxed input, the supply of that input is robust in the local economy. In effect, the DET shifts out the supply curve for the input, pushing down its domestic equilibrium price. In turn, producers of an advanced product using that input benefit from its low cost. That benefit redounds in global markets. If those producers export the advanced product, and this product competes with foreign goods that do not have low-cost inputs, the producers enjoy a competitive advantage. Thus, for example, for many years oilseed processors in Canada, the EU, and the United States have opposed DETs put on oilseeds by Argentina. The DETs help Argentine companies that make a good embodying the oilseeds vis-à-vis their Canadian, European, and American competitors.

During the Doha Round, DETs were not the subject of any significant negotiations. In the August 2004 *Framework Agreement*, they were mentioned as part of a group of miscellaneous items.[163] However, draft modalities texts issued in July 2007 and February 2008 by the Chairman of the Agriculture Negotiations, Ambassador Crawford Falconer of New Zealand, made scant reference to the topic. Essentially, the Members felt no strong mandate to negotiate about DETs.

## DEVELOPING COUNTRY

A self-selected country among WTO Members that while not developed, does not meet specific criteria to be a least developed country and, therefore, gets the benefit of certain, but not all, special and differential treatment provisions in GATT — WTO legal regime.

Roughly 80 percent of the WTO Membership qualifies as a "developing" or "least developed" country.

*Suggestions for Further Research:*

Articles:

1.   Busch, Marc L., Eric Reinhardt & Gregory Shaffer, *Does Legal Capacity Matter? A Survey of WTO Members*, 8 WORLD TRADE REVIEW issue 4, 559–577 (2009).

2.   Norris, Laura L., Comment, *The Revolving Door of Emigration: The Economic Influences of Remittances in Developing Countries*, 31 NORTHWESTERN JOURNAL OF INTERNATIONAL LAW & BUSINESS 479–497 (2011).

## DEVALUATION

A decline in the value of a country's currency brought about through an official act of the country's government. A devaluation suggests the country's currency was officially fixed or pegged, to more or less of a degree, to the value of another currency or value of currencies. The term is often mistakenly used synonymously with "depreciation."

For example, for years the United States has pressured China to devalue the *yuan* (*renminbi*, or *Rmb.*) relative to the dollar, which China finally did — albeit modestly — in 2005. As a result of the Plaza Accord of 1985, the value of the United States dollar was allowed to fall versus the Japanese yen and the Deutsche mark. During the two years following that Accord, the dollar depreciated 54 percent against the yen.

## DEVELOPMENT

A broad, amorphous term that often is confused with "growth," but is far broader than growth in the economic sense. "Development" embraces not only economic measures of performance beyond income, but also has cultural,

---

[163] *See* Daniel Pruzin, *WTO Members in Ag Talks Fail to Tackle Growing Problem of Food Export Restrictions*, 25 International Trade Reporter (BNA) 479–480 (3 April 2008).

political, and social dimensions. Pope John Paul II, in a January 2005 address to the members of the diplomatic corps at the Vatican, identified four "development" challenges:

- *Life*: The protection of life from conception to natural death, the sanctity of the family, and the protection of human dignity are under assault from a variety of pressures.

- *Food*: Hundreds of millions of people suffer from serious malnutrition, and millions of children die each year from hunger.

- *Peace*: While peace is the dream of every generation, war and armed conflicts among states, ethnic groups, and peoples within the same territory exist around the world.

- *Freedom*: Each person is born with inalienable human dignity, and each person has a right to life, liberty and security — points agreed to in Articles 1 and 3, respectively, of the *Universal Declaration of Human Rights*, yet not practiced in many parts of the world.

The mere articulation of these challenges bespeaks the breadth of "development." It also intimates "development" may be as much about individual as extrinsic reform, that is, about overcoming evil (be it the arrogance of power, selfishness, hatred, or some other manifestation) with good. That intimation means trade relations are an opportunity for development, but not a panacea to meet the challenges.

Neither development nor growth is an end in itself, and neither has a fixed end point. Both may be called processes. Generating ever-higher levels of income, and thereby achieving "growth," is a long-term process, just as is "developing" along cultural, political, or social lines. However, two broad questions arise when attempting to gauge development.

First, as a normative matter, is it appropriate to allow values about "development" from one country (*e.g.*, the United States) to influence the process of "development" in other (*e.g.*, Islamic) countries? If "development" means a fast-food franchise on every street corner, rap music blaring out of cars, teenagers staying out past midnight wearing risqué garments, movies depicting graphic sex and violence, and divorce rates approaching one-half of all marriages, then a lot of Saudis — and, for that matter — a lot of non-Americans — would rather pursue a different lifestyle. Indeed, many Americans sympathize.

Second, as a theoretical matter, what are the boundaries of "development"? Many would agree they ought to include educational indicia, such as literacy rates and enrollments at primary, secondary, and tertiary levels. Many also would agree they should include statistics on the progress of women, such as male versus female literacy and enrollment rates, and male versus female participation in the labor force. One of the United Nations Millennium Development goals is to achieve universal primary education by 2015. Happily, projections from the United Nations Children's Fund (UNICEF) indicate global school attendance rose from 82 percent in 2001 to 86 percent in 2005, meaning the number of kids not in school fell from 115 million to 100 million.

However, projections also indicate most countries in South Asia and Sub-Saharan Africa will not come close to the goal. The leading obstacles to getting and keeping children in the classroom plague these countries — health crises (especially AIDS), poorly educated mothers (an indicator correlated with low educational levels among children, as 75 percent of children in developing countries not in primary school have mothers with no education), poverty (particularly in rural areas, as 80 percent of children in developing countries not in primary school live in rural areas), and violent conflicts (war and other forms of civil unrest). Moreover, there is considerable empirical evidence that educating girls plays an important role in growth, and is itself an indicator of development. The Millennium Development goal was gender parity in education by the end of 2005, and 125 of 180 countries were on target to reach it. But, much of the Middle East, North Africa, South Asia, and parts of West and Central Africa, failed to come close, with the worst performers being Yemen (61 girls in school for every 100 boys), Niger (67), and Chad (69).

But, to return to the second matter, should the boundaries of "development" also include political rights, and the legal protections that come with them? If so, then what would those rights be? Free elections with universal suffrage? A free press? An independent judiciary? How would each such right be measured? Many countries might not be "developed," despite their high and growing levels of income, if rule of law protections for western-style civil liberties are essential to qualify.

Likewise, should the boundaries include religious freedom, and other such rights many would argue as inalienable and essential to the protection of human dignity? In the address to the diplomatic corps, John Paul II argued the right to religious freedom is at the heart of human freedom, because it deals with the most fundamental relationship of a person, namely, with God, and thus is guaranteed by Article 18 of the *Universal Declaration of Human Rights*. Consider, then, the United States *International Religious Freedom Act of 1998* (22 U.S.C. Section 6401). The United States identified the Kingdom of Saudi Arabia as one among many countries not permitting freedom of worship (*e.g.*, neither Catholic Mass, nor services of any other faith, are lawfully permitted on Saudi territory), and suggested the WTO accession of the Kingdom ought to be delayed until it mends its ways. Should trade be linked to religious freedom? To do so may be noble and morally justified, but is it risky to condition trade on an expansive concept of "development"? Indeed, does an expansive definition undermine progress on basic human rights (say, for instance, freedom from torture), and thus lead to a situation where the best becomes the enemy of the good?

*Suggestions for Further Research:*

Book:

1. COLLIER, PAUL, THE BOTTOM BILLION — WHY THE POOREST COUNTRIES ARE FAILING AND WHAT CAN BE DONE ABOUT IT (2007).

Articles:

1. Bielefeldt, Heiner, *Autonomy and Republicanism: Immanuel Kant's Philosophy of Freedom*, 25 POLITICAL THEORY 524 (1997).

2. Garcia, Frank J., *Book Review — A Philosophy of International Law* (Fernando R. Teson), 93 AMERICAN JOURNAL OF INTERNATIONAL LAW 746 (1999).

3. Kant, Immanuel, *Toward Perpetual Peace: A Philosophical Sketch, in* KANT'S POLITICAL WRITINGS (H. Reiss ed. 1970).

4. La Chimia, Annamaria & Sue Arrowsmith, *Addressing Tied Aid: Towards a More Development-Oriented WTO?*, 12 JOURNAL OF INTERNATIONAL ECONOMIC LAW 707–747 (2009).

5. Moon, Gillian, *Trade and Equality: A Relationship to Discover*, 12 JOURNAL OF INTERNATIONAL ECONOMIC LAW 617–642 (2009).

6. Rawls, John, *The Law of Peoples*, 20 CRITICAL INQUIRY 36 (1993).

7. Sanders, Anselm Kamperman, *Intellectual Property, Free Trade and Economic Development*, 23 GEORGIA STATE UNIVERSITY LAW REVIEW 893–911 (2007).

8. Upham, Frank K., *From Demsetz to Deng: Speculations on the Implications of Chinese Growth for Law and Development Theory*, 41 NEW YORK UNIVERSITY JOURNAL OF INTERNATIONAL LAW & POLITICS 551–602 (2009).

## DEVELOPMENT AS FREEDOM

A theory of development set out by Amartya Sen in a book bearing the rubric "development as freedom." The risk of an expansive definition of "development," and possible dilution of progress on basic human rights, is accepted by Amartya Sen, winner of the 1998 Nobel Prize in Economics. Indeed, in *Development as Freedom* (1999), Sen eagerly embraces the risk — or, perhaps put better, he rejects entirely that such a risk exists. As his title suggests, he defines "development" as the expansion of freedom.

Sen argues the expansion of freedom is not only the pre-eminent end of development, but also the principal means by which development occurs. That is, freedom is both constitutive of development and the instrument of development. As a goal, to develop is to remove different kinds of "unfreedoms" from the lives of people. The main unfreedoms are:

- Poverty, and more generally poor economic opportunities, which robs a person of the freedom to satisfy hunger (sometimes because of famine) or achieve sufficient nutrition, remedy a treatable illness, obtain adequate clothing and shelter, have access to clean water and sanitation, and enter into gainful employment.

- Tyrannical or authoritarian regimes, or overly active repressive states, which rob a person of political and civil liberties (such as participation and uncensored speech), and thereby of the freedom to participate in the economic, political, and social life of a community.

- Systematic social deprivation, including the neglect of public facilities, which robs a person of the freedom to enjoy organized arrangements for functional education (leading to literacy and numeracy), health care (including epidemiological programs), and law and order, and forces a person to spend life fighting unnecessary morbidity.

- Intolerance, which may be based on ethnic, gender, linguistic, racial, or religious grounds, and which robs a person of the ability to enjoy many kinds of freedom.

Why is the removal of unfreedoms the primary goal of development? The answer is the lack of substantive freedoms means the lack of choice and opportunity to exercise the reasoned agency inherent in each person.

Sen uses the term "agency" not in the economic or legal sense of one person employed to act on behalf of another (whether a disclosed or undisclosed principal). Rather, he harkens to the traditional sense of an "agent" as an individual who acts and brings about economic, political, or social change, and whose behavior in the spheres of economics, politics, and society may be judged either by the values and goals of that individual, or by an external set of criteria. As for the term "freedom," Sen focuses on five specific types of freedom:

- *Economic facilities, i.e.*, the opportunity to use economic resources for exchange, production, and consumption, including the freedom to make and exchange goods and services (*i.e.*, to participate in economic production and interchange), made possible through opportunities created by the market mechanism, the freeing of labor from explicit or implicit bondage, made possible through an open labor market, the freedom of access to product markets to obtain inputs into production, and the availability and access to finance, whether the agent is a large enterprise or small establishment.

- *Political freedom*, in the sense of the civil liberty to participate in public discussions and scrutinize policy decisions, to exercise free speech and dissent, and enjoy an uncensored press, to engage in elections among competing candidates and parties to select legislative and executive leaders, to critique leaders, and to choose principles of governance.

- *Social opportunities*, in the sense of facilities like education and health care, which enhance the ability to make use of the other freedoms and thus allow for a better quality of life.

- *Transparency guarantees*, namely, the need for openness so that individuals can deal with each other, and their government, in a lucid manner in confidence all relevant material is disclosed, and so that irresponsible or corrupt behavior is prevented.

- *Protective securities*, which create a safety net to ensure an individual is not vulnerable to abject misery, such as starvation, and which typically consist of income supplements to indigent persons, unemployment benefits, emergency public works projects (to generate income and employment for indigents), and episodic relief programs.

These "real" freedoms, as Sen calls them, are crucial as ends in themselves.

Each real freedom advances human freedom in general, and the overall capability of an individual. He is not naïve about the need for appropriate public regulation, particularly of markets, to ensure some degree of equity in the enjoyment of economic freedom. He emphasizes "development" is the process of expanding each type of real freedom enjoyed by people. This definition contrasts with orthodox approaches to development, which focus on growth, define growth in terms of increases in GNP or *per capita* GNP, and model the process of industrialization and technological change, is obvious.

To illustrate, Sen recounts the example of African-Americans, who enjoy a higher *per capita* income than people in many Third World countries. Yet, they suffer from a lower likelihood of reaching a mature age than people in many such countries, including China, Sri Lanka, and parts of India, such as the southern state of Kerala. Likewise, a rich person who is prevented from participating in public debates and decisions, and from speaking freely, is deprived of something she has reason to value. The process of development ought to include removal of that deprivation. Some illustrations are both shameful and stunning — for example, the fact that a black male in Harlem has less of a chance of living beyond 40 years of age than a man in Bangladesh.

The real freedoms, Sen asserts, also are crucial as instruments of development. Hence, Sen also dubs them "instrumental" freedoms. The expansion of one kind of freedom promotes freedom of other types. That is because different freedoms are linked in a causal way that is empirically demonstrable. For example, social freedoms, such as the opportunity for education and health care, complement individual economic and political freedoms. These opportunities help an individual to overcome economic and political deprivations. The point is simply that instrumental freedoms are interactive.

As another instance of interaction among instrumental freedoms, Sen urges economic and political freedoms are complementary, not competing — contrary to the so-called "Lee Thesis" (named after former Singaporean Prime Minister Lee Kuan Yew), which alleges harsher political conditions, meaning the denial of certain civil liberties, will stimulate rapid economic growth. Political freedom helps promote economic security. Sen — an expert on famines — observes that in world history, no famine has occurred in a functioning democracy. Famines plague colonial territories governed by distant rulers (*e.g.*, in India and Ireland, when they were ruled by the British), in one-party states (like the Ukraine in the 1930s, China during the 1958–61 "Great Leap Forward," and Cambodia under the Khmer Rouge led by Pol Pot), or in military dictatorships (*e.g.*, in Ethiopia, North Korea, and Somalia in recent decades). Rarely if ever are the political leaders in famine-stricken countries the victim of hunger. Political freedom means rulers are held accountable through elections and public criticisms, and thus have a strong incentive to take measures to avert potential economic catastrophes before they occur. In effect, political freedoms offer security for economic facilities.

Still another illustration is economic facilities can generate personal and public wealth to help fund social facilities, such as better schools and health care delivery. Interestingly, life expectancy increases with *per capita* GNP, but the causal chain is not direct. Rather, additional income, if spent on health care and poverty alleviation, helps boost life expectancy. This nexus — from greater income to higher life expectancy through spending on health care and poverty alleviation — explains why Korea and Taiwan, but not Brazil experienced increased life expectancy as *per capita* income grew. What matters is not the fruits of economic growth *per se*, but how those fruits are used. Brazil — in contrast to the East Asian Tigers — largely neglected its public health care system, and tolerated severe social inequalities and high levels of unemployment. In this area, the record of India (especially outside the Southern state of Kerala, which embarked on support-led strategies for education and health care, rather than on growth-mediated processes, *i.e.*, waiting for the effects of fast growth to redound to social programs) and Pakistan resembles that of Brazil.

A final example of the interactive effects of promoting instrumental freedoms concerns social opportunities and economic facilities. Adequate health care reduces mortality rates, which in turn can help reduce birth rates (as there is less necessity to have more children in the hope that some of them reach maturity). In turn, with lower birth rates women can take more full advantage of educational opportunities, enhancing their literacy and numeracy skills. With a stronger skill base, their fertility rate may drop, and they can enter and stay longer in the labor force, thereby earning income and improving their material well-being.

Is income important to development? Indeed, Sen acknowledges, but not as a narrow end in itself. Rather, income matters as a means to expanding substantive freedoms and the ability to enjoy them. The idea is not new. At the start of *Nicomachean Ethics*, which Sen quotes, Aristotle writes "wealth is evidently not the good we are seeking; for it is merely useful and for the sake of something else." That "something else" is to exercise individual volitions, become fuller social persons, and influence the world.

Moreover, as the connections among instrumental freedoms indicate, these freedoms are not a hierarchy with economic facilities at the top. It is commonly believed, but flat wrong, Sen says, that social opportunities can wait until income has grown significantly. Japan raised social standards before it got rich. During the Meiji Era (1868–1911), Japan had a higher literacy rate than Europe, even though industrialization was more advanced in Europe than Japan at the time. Japan developed economically at a rapid pace, and reduced poverty, in part because it had skilled human resources — related to positive social opportunities. He adds a rebuttal to the oft-made argument poor countries cannot afford to spend on education and health care because of their low income: relative cost. In such countries, education and health care are low-cost and labor-intensive. Thus, a poor country — while it has less money — also needs less money to provide these services than a rich country.

Similarly, China in 1979, when economic reform began under Premier Deng Xiaoping, was better prepared, in a social sense, than India, when economic liberalization began there in 1991. After the Communist Revolution of 1949, China — while denying political as well as economic freedoms — improved basic education and health care. By 1979, its people were literate and in respectable health, and good educational and health care facilities existed in most parts of the country. In contrast, following Independence in August 1947, India failed to raise the educational or health care standards of its masses. By 1991, only half of the adult population was literate, and dreaded diseases plagued parts of the country. With elites well-educated and in good health, India in 1991 — in contrast to China in 1979 — was poorly positioned for broadly-based economic growth.

To be fair, denial of political freedoms in pre-reform China was a handicap both to avoidance and response to economic crises. The largest recorded famine in history occurred in China, when at least 30 million died in the Great Leap Forward. In contrast, following Independence, democratic India has not had a famine. Nonetheless, Sen's encapsulation of the point — "The lesson of opening of the economy and the importance of trade has been more easily learned in India than the rest of the message from the same direction of the rising sun" — is a powerful reminder of the importance of non-economic variables like education and health care in readying a population to take advantage of economic liberalization.[164]

Why is the expansion of freedom an instrument of development? Sen offers two justifications — the "evaluative" reason and the "effectiveness" reason. First, the extent to which freedom is advanced is a gauge by which to measure development progress. In a normative sense, the extent to which individuals in a society enjoy substantive freedoms determines the success of that society. Traditional economists give primacy to income, not to the characteristics of human life. Utilitarian philosophers focus on mental satisfaction, on discontent that is creative or dissatisfaction that is constructive. Libertarians are preoccupied with procedures, but forget about the consequences of procedures. Sen, however, urges the enhancement of freedom is (or the) an evaluative criterion for development. In effect, the process of development resembles the history of overcoming unfreedom.

Second, the enhancement of freedom translates directly into the enhancement of the ability of an individual to help herself and influence her society and the world. The fewer the arbitrary governmental hindrances on the exercise of substantive freedoms, the more able a person is to gain not only in income, but also in the complementary spheres of education and health. In a sense, the effectiveness justification emphasizes the favorable consequences of enhanced substantive freedoms. For instance, the exercise of economic freedom, though individual transactions, can lead to higher income and greater efficiency. As another example, the exercise of political freedom can lead to better public

---

[164] AMARTYA SEN, DEVELOPMENT AS FREEDOM 91 (1999).

policy choices through robust debate. In this respect, Sen singles out for criticism ayatollahs and other religious authorities (acting in the name of Islam or another faith), governmental dictators (acting in the name of so-called Asian or other values), and cultural experts (acting as elitist guardians of culture). They insist on adhering to established traditions and obedience to their decisions about these traditions, thus choking off the participatory freedom to which individuals have a right.

The concept of "poverty, as set forth by Amartya Sen in *Development as Freedom* (1999), follows logically from his definition of "development." If "development" is about the expansion of freedom, then "poverty" is about "unfreedom." In turn, "unfreedom" arises for either of two reasons: inadequate processes, or inadequate opportunities. To violate a political freedom, such as voting rights, is to create an inadequate process. To violate an economic freedom, like the right to be free from hunger, is to foster an inadequate opportunity. When these violations occur, it is not possible for an individual to achieve all, or any, of her capabilities.

Accordingly, Sen eschews a focus only on the adequacy of procedures, saying that libertarians (who focus only on appropriate procedures) forget about whether a disadvantaged person is systematically deprived of substantive opportunities). She also eschews a focus only on the adequacy of opportunities, saying that consequentialists (who focus only on outcomes) neglect whether an individual has adequate opportunities or freedom of choice. "Poverty," to Sen, has both a process and opportunity aspect. Inadequate processes and opportunities afflict the poor.

Accordingly, Sen defines "poverty" not as income deprivation, but as capability deprivation. To be "poor" is to lack more than just a high income, though lowness of income is both a handicap for the poor, as it is a leading cause of capability deprivation. To be poor is to lack basic capabilities, such as employment skills (leading to undernourishment), functional education (resulting in illiteracy), or health care (resulting in premature mortality). To inquire into "capability" is to inquire into whether a person can lead the kind of life she values, and has reason to value. Aggregating persons in a society, it is for each society to determine the capability most important to that society.

Sen's definition of "poverty" as capability deprivation, like his definition of "development" as "freedom," runs counter to modern orthodoxies in development economics (though, as he points out, classical economists like Adam Smith took the more expansive view he does). Much of the development economics literature focuses on, or assumes, low income is intrinsically important. Yet, capabilities matter more than income, as Adam Smith suggested in *The Wealth of Nations* (1776). To have a relatively low income in a rich country can be a serious impediment to participation in the life of that country, and immediate community, even though the income level is high in comparison with poor countries. The lack of means makes it impossible to buy consumer electronics and other consumption items, join clubs, go to schools, and pursue ends common in the rich country. Thus, low income is only instrumentally important, whereas deprivations in certain basic capabilities have intrinsic importance.

Moreover, a number of factors call for attention to capability, not income. First, the relationship between low income and capability deprivation differs across individuals, communities, and countries. For instance, parametric variations (*e.g.*, age, gender, proneness to natural disaster, proximity to civil unrest, and disease environment) can affect the relationship between income and capability (*e.g.*, the relationship may be weaker for older people, women, individuals near flood, war-torn, or disease areas, because these parameters themselves affect capability). Some parameters (like age, gender, or illness) may be coupled, and thereby affect the relationship between income and capability. Second, there may be intra-family biases that affect this link. Such biases tend to afflict young girls in various poor countries, who may suffer from smaller food allocation, limited education, extra labor, and bodily degradations (*e.g.*, sexual abuse and female genital mutilation). Third, factors other than low income cause capability deprivation. Instrumental freedoms — political freedoms, social opportunities, transparency guarantees, and protective security — are examples. Fourth, the causal link between income and capability goes in both directions. Enhanced capabilities can lead to higher income, as well as *vice versa*.

European countries, for instance, tend to select a social safety net over high unemployment. In contrast, the United States prefers low unemployment over social security and, more generally, a welfare system. Development "as freedom," therefore, means each country is or ought to be free to order its priorities as to the capabilities. It does not mean freedom in the sense of individuals having maximum ability to pursue liberties in an American-style sense. Rather, the provision of basic capabilities provides for individual freedom. For instance, education helps a person find a job, prosper in it, and build a career. Health care helps a person live well, and recover should illness strike. Significantly, Sen also argues only through a well functioning democracy is it possible to make such choices properly and wisely. That is because only democracy allows for a discourse among different members of society as to what the choices are, the criteria for selection, and the ultimate outcomes.

*Suggestions for Further Research:*

Book:

1.  POMFRET, RICHARD, THE AGE OF EQUALITY: THE TWENTIETH CENTURY IN ECONOMIC PERSPECTIVE (Cambridge, Massachusetts: Belknap Press, 2011). See also the review of this book, Richard N. Cooper, *Economic, Social, and Environmental*, 90 FOREIGN AFFAIRS 179 (November/December 2011).

Article:

1.  Yu, Peter K., *A Tale of two Development Agendas*, 35 OHIO NORTHERN UNIVERSITY LAW REVIEW 465–573 (2009).

## DFQF (DF/QF)

Duty Free/Quota Free.

The acronym indicates preferential treatment of the best sort, in the sense of no tariff or quota barrier being applied to preferred products. DFQF treatment is offered by some developed countries (such as New Zealand) to all products originating in least developed countries.

## DHS

United States Department of Homeland Security.

The DHS is a cabinet-level executive branch agency, and home to the Customs and Border Protection (CBP) and Transportation Security Administration (TSA). Along with the White House Homeland Security Council, the DHS was created by the *Homeland Security Act of 2002*, Pub. L. No. 107–296, 116 Stat. 2135, 25 November 2002.

Creating the DHS represented the largest reorganization of the American government in 50 years — the prior one being establishment of the modern Department of Defense. Stable leadership of the DHS in its formative years has been problematical. President George W. Bush named the former Governor of Pennsylvania, Tom Ridge, as the first DHS Secretary on 24 January 2003, the date the DHS officially began operations. Secretary Ridge resigned on 30 November 2004. President Bush initially nominated New York City Police Commissioner Bernard Kerik to succeed Ridge. Citing personal reasons, Kerik withdrew his nomination. On 11 January 2005, the President nominated Federal Judge Michael Chertoff to succeed Ridge. The Senate confirmed Chertoff on 15 February 2005. By some accounts, morale among many workers at the DHS is poor.

The DHS is an "umbrella" agency under which, in addition to CBP, a number of federal agencies are located. The first Figure below summarizes the general structure of the DHS, as originally created. The second Figure below lays out the detailed organizational structure of the DHS, along with senior posts, at present (as of December 2007).

**Figure:**

**General Structure of the**

**United States Department of Homeland Security**

**(as originally established by the *Homeland Security Act of 2002*)**

Secretary of Homeland Security

Deputy Secretary of Homeland Security

5 divisions within DHS, and an Under Secretary of Homeland Security for each division —

(1) Information analysis and infrastructure protection.
(2) Chemical, Biological, Radiological, Nuclear Countermeasures
(3) Border and Transportation Security
(4) Emergency Preparedness and Response
(5) Management

These Undersecretary positions, and the associated DHS divisions, mirror the 5 primary responsibilities of DHS.

CBP is the 3rd division, along with Immigration and Customs Enforcement (ICE) and Transportation Security Administration (TSA).

Assistant Secretaries for Homeland Security —

No more than 6 such positions, associated with the 5 broad divisions.

No more than 10 Deputy Assistant Secretaries.

Additional Senior Posts —
(1) Inspector General
(2) Commandant of the Coast Guard
(3) General Counsel
(4) Director of the Secret Service
(5) Chief Financial Officer (CFO)
(6) Chief Information Officer (CIO), subsequently renamed the Chief Privacy Officer (CPO)

**FIGURE:**

**ORGANIZATIONAL STRUCTURE OF THE DEPARTMENT OF HOMELAND SECURITY (DHS)**

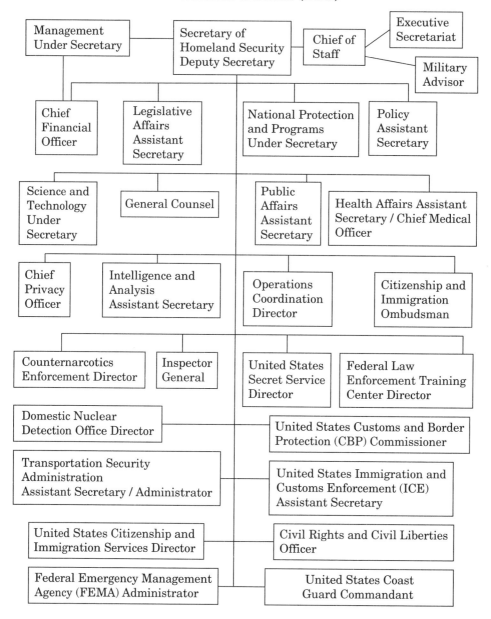

## DIRECTLY COMPETITIVE PRODUCT

*See* Like Product.

## DIRECTLY COMPETITIVE OR SUBSTITUTABLE PRODUCT

*See* Like Product.

## DIRECT PAYMENTS

Direct payments are one of three cornerstones of American agricultural subsidies that have existed since the first federal farm bill in 1933, during the Depression and Dust Bowl Era, under the Administration of President Franklin D. Roosevelt. Those cornerstones are:

- Marketing assistance loans.
- Direct payments.
- Counter-cyclical payments.

To be sure, the modern-day incarnation of these programs is not identical to the schemes as originally enacted. For example, production flexibility contracts (PFCs) existed before direct payments, and were replaced by them in the *Farm Security and Rural Investment Act of 2002* — the *2002 Farm Bill*, Public Law 107–171 (13 May 2002), codified in Title 7 of the U.S.C.[165] However, the idea of income support — which both incarnations represent — is not new. Likewise, counter-cyclical payments have not been a consistent feature throughout the post-1933 history. However, the idea of shielding farmers from vicissitudes of the market place by offering them support inversely proportional to market prices is not new.

The term "direct payment," then, typically arises in the context of agricultural subsidies. This term connotes a transfer of funds from a government to a farmer. Direct payments can be linked to, or coupled with, crop output. However, the touchstone of a direct payment is that it is not based on current production, *i.e.*, it is effectively de-coupled from output. In the United States, direct payments are calculated on the basis of historical acres planted and yield. In turn, the United States bases estimates of historical acres on either:

(1) reported acreage under the former Production Flexibility Contract (PFC) scheme (which did appear to link current production to payments),

or

(2) historical averages of planting between 1998 and 2001.

Because they are not structured on the basis of current yield, the United States does not include them in its calculation of Aggregate Measure of Support (AMS) for the Amber Box, under the WTO *Agreement on Agriculture*.

Specifically, under the *2002 Farm Bill*, to establish a direct payment, the following calculation (in rough terms) is performed.

- First, base acreage is determined. It is historic acres planted during a prescribed period, such as the 1998 through 2001 crop years, as statutorily mandated
- Second, program yield is determined. It is the yield from the base acreage in a statutorily prescribed period, such as 1995, which is statutorily mandated).
- The direct payment is computed. It is equal to the product of base acreage and program yield. That is, the direct payment is base acreage times program yield.

---

[165] Conservation provisions of the *2002 Farm Bill* were codified in Title 16 of the U.S.C.

The direct payment is decoupled. That is because its amount is not linked to the type or amount of production, nor to the price of the subsidized commodity.

In the United States, a direct payment arrangement is established through a contract between the United States Department of Agriculture (USDA), specifically, the Commodity Credit Corporation (CCC), and a farmer. The contractual arrangement typically is started by submitting Form CCC-509 between October and June. The direct payment is made either in one installment, in October, or in two installments, in December and the following October.

Direct payments also can be made to farmers in a manner entirely divorced from output or historic acreage, but in connection with an environmental or social goal. They might then qualify as Green Box payments, under the *Agreement on Agriculture*.

## DIRECTOR-GENERAL

*See* WTO.

## DISTORTION

A broad economic term suggesting that prices or production are higher, or lower, than their equilibrium levels in a competitive market. Causes of distortions include tariffs, taxes, subsidies, non-tariff barriers (NTBs), externalities, imperfect competition, and incomplete information.

## DOC

United States Department of Commerce, located at 14ᵗʰ Street and Constitution Avenue, N.W., in Washington, D.C.

Initially established in 1903 as the Department of Commerce and Labor, the DOC was split off as a separate entity in 1913 by an act of Congress, namely, the *Act of February 14*, 32 Stat. 826, 5. U.S.C. § 591. The DOC's mandate extends far beyond the promotion of the foreign and domestic commerce of the United States.

Most notably, it has major antidumping (AD) and countervailing duty (CVD) responsibilities, conducted by its International Trade Administration (ITA) unit. In addition, the Bureau of Industry and Security (BIS) is responsible for administering export control laws and regulations designed to limit or ban exports of commodities or technology for reasons of national security, foreign policy, or short supply. Until 18 April 2002, the previous name for the BIS was used — the Bureau of Export Affairs (BXA).

The DOC also has responsibility for a large number of areas not directly related to trade. For example, the National Oceanic and Atmospheric Administration (NOAA) tracks national weather forecasts via the National Weather Service (NWS) and the National Hurricane Center. NOAA itself is charged with responsibility for regulating aquaculture (fish farming and fishery activities). The Bureau of the Census, housed in the DOC, not only is responsible for counting people in the United States every 10 years, but also for gathering statistical data on imports and exports, based on their number in the Harmonized Tariff Schedule (HTS). The Census Bureau obtains some of these data from the Customs and Border Protection (CBP), which in turn gathers collects the statistics from entry paperwork for imports. Also associated with the DOC is the United States Patent and Trademark Office (PTO).

*Suggestions for Further Research:*

Articles:

1.  Lynch, Michele D., Nasim A. Deylami, Nathaniel J. Halvorson, Skye Mathieson & Kelsey M. Rule, *28 U.S.C. § 1581(c): Judicial Review of Antidumping and Countervailing Duty Determinations by the Department of Commerce*, 42 Georgetown Journal of International Law 65–95 (2010).

2.  Trossevin, Marguerite & Reza Karmaloo, *Judicial Review of Antidumping and Countervailing Duty Determinations by the Department of Commerce: Noteworthy Cases in 2009*, 42 Georgetown Journal of International Law 35–63 (2010).

3.  Wood, J. Christopher & Zia C. Oatley, *28 U.S.C. § 1581(c): Judicial Review of Antidumping Duty Determinations Issued by the Department of Commerce*, 41 Georgetown Journal of International Law 117–135 (2009).

## DOHA ROUND

The first trade negotiating effort under the auspices of the World Trade Organization, which was born on 1 January 2005, the Doha Round was launched in November 2001 in the Qatari capital, Doha. Formally entitled the "Doha Development Agenda," or "DDA," the Doha Round talks have dragged on without a successful final outcome. In the modern history of the world trading system, dating from GATT on 30 October 1947, the Doha Round is the ninth round of multilateral trade talks.

*Suggestions for Further Research:*

Books:

1.  Buckley, Ross P., The WTO and the Doha Round — The Changing Face of World Trade (2003).

2.  Das, Dilip K., The Doha Round of Multilateral Trade Negotiations: Arduous Issues and Strategic Responses (2006).

3.  Hohmann, Harald, ed., Agreeing and Implementing the Doha Round of the WTO (2008).

4.  Moore, Mike, A World Without Walls — Freedom, Development, Free Trade, and Global Governance (2003).

5.  Moore, Mike, ed., Doha and Beyond — The Future of the Multilateral Trading System (2004).

Book Chapters:

1.  Durling, James P., *Beyond Doha: Reflections on the Future of Trade Remedies, in* The WTO in the Twenty-First Century: Dispute Settlement,

NEGOTIATIONS, AND REGIONALISM IN ASIA 341–366 (Yasuhei Taniguchi, Alan Yanovich & Jan Bohanes eds. 2007).

2. Honma, Masayoshi, *Agricultural Issues in the Doha Development Agenda Negotiations, in* THE WTO IN THE TWENTY-FIRST CENTURY: DISPUTE SETTLEMENT, NEGOTIATIONS, AND REGIONALISM IN ASIA 328–340 (Yasuhei Taniguchi, Alan Yanovich & Jan Bohanes eds. 2007).

3. Stoler, Andrew L., *The Central Place of Market Access for the WTO's Development Round, in* THE WTO IN THE TWENTY-FIRST CENTURY: DISPUTE SETTLEMENT, NEGOTIATIONS, AND REGIONALISM IN ASIA 319–327 (Yasuhei Taniguchi, Alan Yanovich & Jan Bohanes eds. 2007).

Articles:

1. Chang, Seung Wha, *WTO for Trade and Development Post-Doha*, 10 JOURNAL OF INTERNATIONAL ECONOMIC LAW 553–570 (2007).

2. Cho, Sungjoon *Doha's Development*, 25 BERKLEY JOURNAL OF INTERNATIONAL LAW 165–202 (2007).

3. Cho, Sungjoon, *Beyond Doha's Promises: Administrative Barriers as an Obstruction to Development*, 25 BERKELEY JOURNAL OF INTERNATIONAL LAW 395–424 (2007).

4. Cho, Sungjoon, *The Demise of Development in the Doha Round Negotiations*, 45 TEXAS INTERNATIONAL LAW JOURNAL 573–601 (2010).

5. Deb, Uttam & Muhammad Al Amin, *Impact of the Doha Round Negotiation on Bangladesh Agriculture — An Analysis of the Revised Draft Modalities*, 10 JOURNAL OF INTERNATIONAL TRADE LAW POLICY number 2 104–123 (2011).

6. Emerson, Petra L., *An Economic Integration Agreement on Services: A Possible Solution to the Doha Development Round Impasses*, 2 TRADE, LAW AND DEVELOPMENT no. 2, 224–291 (fall 2010).

7. Florestal, Marjorie, *Technical Assistance Post-Doha: Is There Any Hope of Integrating Developing Countries into the Global Trading System?*, 24 ARIZONA JOURNAL OF INTERNATIONAL AND COMPARATIVE LAW 121–132 (2007).

8. Jara, Alejandro, *The WTO and International Trade Law After Doha: Where Do We Go From Here?*, 25 BERKELEY JOURNAL OF INTERNATIONAL LAW 384–394 (2007).

9. Kennedy, Kevin C., *The Doha Round Negotiations on Agricultural Subsidies*, 36 DENVER JOURNAL OF INTERNATIONAL LAW & POLICY 335–348 (2008).

10. Kennedy, Kevin C., *The Status of the Trade-Environment-Sustainable Development Triad in the Doha Round Negotiations and in Recent U.S. Trade Policy*, 19 INDIANA INTERNATIONAL & COMPARATIVE LAW REVIEW 529–552 (2009).

11. Leal-Arcas, Rafael, *The Resumption of the Doha Round and the Future of Services Trade*, 29 LOYOLA LOS ANGELES INTERNATIONAL & COMPARATIVE LAW REVIEW 339–461 (2007).

12. Lewis, Meredith Kolsky, *WTO Winners and Losers: The Trade and Development Disconnect*, 39 GEORGETOWN JOURNAL OF INTERNATIONAL LAW 165–198 (2007).

13. Lovett, William A., *Beyond Doha: Multipolar Challenges for a Globalized World*, 17 TULANE JOURNAL OF INTERNATIONAL & COMPARATIVE LAW 3–37 (winter 2008).

14. Nanda, Ved P., *Selected Aspects of International Trade and the World Trade Organization's Doha Round: Overview and Introduction*, 36 DENVER JOURNAL OF INTERNATIONAL LAW & POLICY 255–273 (2008).

15. *Symposium: The United States, The Doha Round and the WTO — Where Do We Go From Here?*, 37 THE INTERNATIONAL LAWYER number 3 651–833 (fall 2003).

16. Senona, Joseph M., *EPAs and the Doha Round: Development or Discontent*, 8 JOURNAL OF INTERNATIONAL TRADE LAW & POLICY number 1, 60–83 (2009).

17. Sevilla, Christina R., *The WTO Doha Development Agenda: What is at Stake*, 25 BERKELEY JOURNAL OF INTERNATIONAL LAW 423–433 (2007).

18. Udo, Chandler H., Note, *Japanese Rice Protectionism: A Challenge for the Development of Agricultural Trade Laws*, 31 BOSTON COLLEGE INTERNATIONAL AND COMPARATIVE LAW REVIEW 169–184 (2008).

Other Source:

1. McCalla, Alex F. & John Nash, eds., *Reforming Agricultural Trade for Developing Countries: Key Issues for a Pro-Development Outcome of the Doha Round Negotiations* (World Bank Trade and Development Series) (November 2006).

## ĐỔI MỚI

The term given to economic reforms Vietnam initiated in 1986. These reforms included trade and investment liberalization, and de-regulation and privatization of certain sectors. In Vietnamese, "*Đổi*" means life, and "*mới*" means "new." Thus, "*Đổi Mới*" connotes new life, in the sense of new attitude and hope.

*Suggestions for Further Research:*

Article:

1. Gantz, David A., *Đổi Mới, the VBTA and WTO Accession: The Role of Lawyers in Vietnam's No Longer Cautious Embrace of Globalization*, 41 THE INTERNATIONAL LAWYER 873–890 (fall 2007).

## DOMESTIC SUPPORT

A generic term covering agricultural subsidies of many different forms, but excluding export subsidies.

More precisely, "domestic support" includes what in WTO parlance is known as Amber Box, Blue Box, and Green Box subsidies, plus so-called "*De Minimis* Support.*"

The Organization for Economic Cooperation and Development (OECD) produces reviews of agricultural policies in the 30 OECD member countries. In its July 2009 analysis, *Agricultural Policies in OECD Countries, Monitoring and Evaluation*, the OECD observed that these countries spend $265 billion in support (as of 2008).[166] That figure represents 21 percent of total farm receipts. The percentage was 22 in 2007, and 26 in 2006. But, the decline was due not to a change in policy among OECD governments (*i.e.*, an affirmative decision by them to cut subsidies). Rather, it was due to higher world commodity prices, which diminish the need for domestic support.

## DOUBLE COUNTING

*See* NME.

## DOUBLE IMPORT DUTIES

A problem that can afflict a land-locked country whereby tariffs on an imported product destined for that country is paid upon importation at the seaport of another country, and then paid again upon importation at the border of the land-locked country.

For example, despite membership in *MERCOSUR*, Paraguay long complained that duties were collected on shipments coming into ports in Argentina, Brazil, or Uruguay, and then again when those shipments entered Paraguay. Paraguay requested its fellow *MERCOSUR* countries, on whose ports it relies, to forward any duties collected to it, so that it would not have to collect the duties again. Obviously, double duty collection raises the cost of imports. The problem *MERCOSUR* had in honoring Paraguay's request, which it did in 2004, was it lacked a common set of rules for customs agents in the Argentine, Brazilian, and Uruguayan ports to use. Thus, in June 2006, *MERCOSUR* agreed on a customs codex to standardize and harmonize the process of valuation for tariff liability determinations. The common codex entered into force in January 2008.

## DOUBLE SUBSTANTIAL TRANSFORMATION (DOUBLE SUBSTANTIAL TRANSFORMATION TEST)

A rule of origin under the United States Generalized System of Preferences (GSP) scheme that requires inputs that do not originate in a beneficiary developing country (BDC), and which the BDC incorporates into a product eligible for BDC treatment, themselves be substantially transformed into a new and different article — an intermediate product. If the inputs are not substantially transformed in the BDC into an intermediate good, then they cannot be counted in the computation of value added, for purposes of satisfying the 35 percent value added test (which is the general American GSP rule of origin). Thus, two substantial transformations are necessary — (1) the inputs, imported into the BDC from a non-BDC, are transformed in the BDC into an intermediate good, and then (2) the intermediate good in the BDC is transformed into a finished product (or other good) that is eligible for GSP treatment.

An example with contemporary policy implications can be drawn from the textile and apparel (T&A) sector of Bangladesh. This country benefits from the

---

[166] *See* Rick Mitchell, *OECD Suggests U.S. Should Do More on Ag Reform, Criticizes Biofuel Support*, 26 International Trade Reporter (BNA) 913 (9 July 2009).

Everything But Arms (EBA) initiative of the European Union (EU), which grants duty-free and quota-free access to all imports to the EU from least developed countries, with the exception of armaments. The EBA initiative operates on a "double transformation" system largely similar to the rules of origin applied under the United States GSP scheme. Thus, Bangladesh may import cotton from India, a non-BDC, and spin the cotton into yarn that is then woven to create fabric. Fabric, having its own tariff heading, qualifies as an "intermediate good" (thus, a substantial transformation has occurred). The fabric is subsequently cut and sewn into a shirt, which is a finished product eligible for GSP treatment (thus, double substantial transformation has occurred).

As American policy makers consider enacting a Duty-Free Quota-Free (DFQF) initiative for all least developed countries, the performance of countries like Bangladesh under the EBA initiative is helpful in predicting the results of a possible similar program sponsored by the United States. That is particularly so with regard to how such a program might impact — positively or negatively — countries already benefiting from a regional trade preference program with the United States.

The double substantial transformation test was judicially created in *Torrington Co. v. United States*,[167] where the Court of International Trade (CIT) explained that such an analysis furthers the goal of the GSP of facilitating "industrialization, diversification, and economic progression" in developing countries.[168] Congress later codified the test in the Revised Harmonized Tariff Schedule.[169]

# DSB

The Dispute Settlement Body, established by Article 2 of the WTO *Understanding on Rules and Procedures Governing the Settlement of Disputes* (*Dispute Settlement Understanding*, or *DSU*).

All WTO Members are represented on the DSB, because the DSB is the WTO General Council meeting to deal with trade disputes. The DSB is empowered to establish dispute resolution panels, adopt reports issued by a WTO panel or Appellate Body, oversee implementation of panel recommendations that have been adopted by the DSB, and authorize retaliation. The DSB reaches its decisions by consensus. To block adoption of a panel report, all Members must object formally to the report.

# DSU

The *Dispute Settlement Understanding, i.e.*, the 1994 Uruguay Round *Understanding on Rules and Procedures Governing the Settlement of Disputes*.

The *DSU* is one of the Multilateral Trade Agreements, and constitutes Annex 2 to the *Agreement Establishing the World Trade Organization* (*WTO Agreement*). The Figure below summarizes *DSU* procedures.

---

[167] 8 Ct. Int'l Trade 150; 596 F. Supp. 1083 (1984).
[168] 8 Ct. Int'l Trade150, 153; 596 F. Supp. 1083, 1086.
[169] *See* 19 U.S.C. § 1202.

FIGURE:

THE WTO DISPUTE RESOLUTION PROCESS

(including *DSU* references and time deadlines)

---

**Step 1:  Consultations**
*DSU*  Article 4
Time:  60 days

- At all subsequent stages, complainant and respondent are encouraged to consult with each other to settle dispute.

- Director-General may offer good offices for consultations, conciliation, or mediation (*DSU*  Article 5).

↓

**Step 2:  Decision to Establish Panel Is Taken**
*DSU* Article 6
Time:  By 2nd meeting of DSB

- Decision is taken made by DSB.
- Blockage of decision (typically by respondent) is possible only at 1st DSB meeting.

↓

**Step 3:  Panel's Terms of Reference Are Established**
*DSU* Article 7
Time:  0-20 days

- Terms of reference are critical because they are the Panel's subject matter jurisdiction.

↓

**Step 4: Composition of Panel Is Set**
*DSU* Article 8
Time:  20 days (plus an addition 10 days if Director-General is asked to pick panelist)

- Can take up to 50 days after DSB decides to establish a Panel to agree on panel composition.
- Panelists can be chosen up to 50 days after DSB makes decision to create a Panel.

↓

**FIGURE: (Continued)**

---

**Step 5: Examination by Panel**
Time: *See* Step 7

- Panel normally meets twice with complainant and respondent (*DSU* Article 12), and once with third parties (*DSU* Article 10).
  - Upon request, an Expert Review Group may be formed (*DSU* Article 13 and Appendix 4).

---

**Step 6: Interim Review by Panel**
Time: *See* Step 7

- Panel sends descriptive part of its Report to the parties for their comment (*DSU* Art. 15:1), and sends its interim Report to them for their comment (*DSU* Article 15:2).
- Upon request, the parties may hold a review meeting with the Panel (*DSU* Article 15:2).

---

**Step 7: Panel Report Is Issued to the Parties**
*DSU* Article 12:8 and Appendix 3 ¶ 12(j)
Time: Within 6 months of the composition of the Panel (or within 3 months if urgent)

- Panel Report is not yet public

---

**Step 8: Panel Report Is Circulated to DSB**
*DSU* Article 12:9 and Appendix 3 ¶ 12(k)
Time: Within 9 months of establishment of the Panel

- Panel Report becomes public.

**FIGURE: (Continued)**

---

***Step 9 (Possible): Appellate Body Review***
*DSU* Articles 16:4, 17:14
Time: Within 90 days.

- Complainant and/or respondent may appeal legal interpretations, but not findings of fact, in Panel Report.

---

***Step 10: Panel/Appellate Body Reports Are Adopted***
*DSU* Articles 16:1, 16:4, and 17:14
Time: 60 days from Panel Report, unless appealed
Additional 30 days for Appellate Body Report.

- The Reports are adopted by the DSB.
- Total amount of time elapsed from establishment of Panel to the adoption of Report(s) is 9 months, if no appeal, or 12 months, if there is an appeal (*DSU* Article 20).

---

***Step 11: Implementation***
*DSU* Article 21:3
Time: "Reasonable period of time" (RPT)

- Losing Member implements the recommendations contained in Panel/Appellate Body Report.
  - Query the legal nature of the obligation to implement the recommendations.
    - Losing Member proposes, and DSB agrees, upon the meaning of "RPT."
      - If no agreement is reached, then arbitrator defines "RPT."
        - Usually, RPT is set at 15 months.
- Possibility of additional proceedings, in cluding referral to the original Panel (*DSU* Article 21:5), on question of the implementation proposed by the losing Member.
  - Additional proceeding could take up to 90 days.

FIGURE: (Continued)

> **Step 12 (Possible): If No Implementation ...**
> *DSU* Articles 22:2 and 22:6
>
> • Complaining and responding Members negotiate compensation, pending full implementation.

> **Step 13 (Possible): Retaliation**
> *DSU* Article 22:6
> Time: 30 days after expiration of RPT for implementation
>
> • If losing Member does not implement the recommendations contained in Panel/Appellate Body Reports within RPT, and if complainant and respondent do not agree on compensation, then DSB must authorize retaliation pending full compensation.
>
> • The retaliation may be in the same sector, cross-sectoral (*i.e.*, sector other than that at issue), or involve goods/services covered by GATT-WTO agreements other than the agreement(s) at issue. (*DSU* Article 22:3)

> **Step 14 (Possible): Arbitration Concerning Level of Retaliation**
> *DSU* Articles 22:6 and 22:7
>
> • Losing Member that faces retaliation may call for arbitration concerning level of retaliation (specifically, the suspension of procedures and principles of retaliation).

*Suggestions for Further Research:*

Books:

1.   APPELLATE BODY SECRETARIAT, WTO APPELLATE BODY REPERTORY OF REPORTS AND AWARDS 1995–2000 (2006).

2.   CAMERON, JAMES & KAREN CAMPBELL EDS., DISPUTE RESOLUTION IN THE WORLD TRADE ORGANIZATION (1998).

3.   GALLAGHER, PETER, GUIDE TO DISPUTE SETTLEMENT (2002).

4.   GEORGIEV, DENCHO & KIM VAN DER BORGHT, EDS., REFORM AND DEVELOPMENT OF THE WTO DISPUTE SETTLEMENT SYSTEM (2006).

5.  HUDEC, ROBERT E., ENFORCING INTERNATIONAL TRADE LAW — THE EVOLUTION OF THE MODERN GATT LEGAL SYSTEM (1993).

6.  JACKSON, JOHN H., THE JURISPRUDENCE OF GATT & THE WTO — INSIGHTS ON TREATY LAW AND ECONOMIC RELATIONS (2000).

7.  MAVROIDIS, PETROS C. & ALAN O. SYKES, THE WTO AND INTERNATIONAL TRADE LAW/DISPUTE SETTLEMENT (2005).

8.  MITCHELL, ANDREW D., LEGAL PRINCIPLES IN WTO DISPUTES (2008). *See also* Lisa Hemingway, *Book Review*, 13 JOURNAL OF INTERNATIONAL ECONOMIC LAW 515–517 (2010).

9.  OESCH, MATTHIAS, STANDARDS OF REVIEW IN WTO DISPUTE RESOLUTION (2003).

10.  SHAFFER, GREGORY C., DEFENDING INTERESTS — PUBLIC-PRIVATE PARTNERSHIPS IN WTO LITIGATION (2003).

11.  SHAFFER, GREGORY C. & RICARDO MELÉNDEZ-ORTIZ EDS., DISPUTE SETTLEMENT AT THE WTO — THE DEVELOPING COUNTRY EXPERIENCE (2010).

12.  SWACKER, FRANK W., KENNETH R. REDDEN & LARRY B. WENGER, WORLD TRADE WITHOUT BARRIERS vols. 1 and 2 (1995).

13.  TANIGUCHI, YASUHEI, ALAN YANOVICH & JAN BOHANES EDS., THE WTO IN THE TWENTY-FIRST CENTURY — DISPUTE SETTLEMENT, NEGOTIATIONS, AND REGIONALISM IN ASIA (2007) (especially Chapters 1–15).

14.  THOMAS, JEFFREY S. & MICHAEL A. MEYER, THE NEW RULES OF GLOBAL TRADE (1997) (especially Chapter 7).

Book Chapters:

1.  Shaffer, Gregory, *Developing Country Use of the WTO Dispute Settlement System: Why it Matters, The Barriers Posed, in* TRADE DISPUTES AND THE DISPUTE SETTLEMENT UNDERSTANDING OF THE WTO: AN INTERDISCIPLINARY ASSESSMENT 168–190 (James C. Hartigan ed., 2009).

2.  Steger, Debra P., *WTO Dispute Settlement, in* THE WTO AND INTERNATIONAL TRADE REGULATION 53–61 (Philip Ruttley et al. eds. 1998).

3.  Steger, Debra P. & Susan M. Hainsworth, *New Directions in International Trade Law: WTO Dispute Settlement, in* DISPUTE RESOLUTION IN THE WORLD TRADE ORGANIZATION 28–58 (James Cameron & Karen Campbell eds. 1998).

4.  Weiss, Wolfgang, *Reforming the Dispute Settlement Understanding, in* AGREEING AND IMPLEMENTING THE DOHA ROUND OF THE WTO 269–293 (Harald Hohmann, ed., 2008).

Articles:

1.  Antell, Geoffrey & James W. Coleman, *An Empirical Analysis of Wealth and Disparities in WTO Disputes: Do Poorer Countries Suffer from Strategic Delay During Dispute Litigation?*, 29 BOSTON UNIVERSITY INTERNATIONAL LAW JOURNAL 267–286 (2011).

2.  Barceló, John J., *Burden of Proof, Prima Facie Case, and Presumption in WTO Dispute Settlement*, 42 CORNELL INTERNATIONAL LAW JOURNAL 23–43 (2009).

3.  Bentes, Pablo, et al., *International Trade*, 43 THE INTERNATIONAL LAWYER 335–365 (2009).

4.  Bergstrom, Amanda, Comment, *Imbalance of Power: Procedural Inequities within the WTO Dispute Settlement System*, 22 PACIFIC MCGEORGE GLOBAL BUSINESS & DEVELOPMENT LAW JOURNAL 93–109 (2009).

5.  Bodien, Clint, Comment, *Cross-retaliation in the WTO: Antigua and Barbuda's Proposed Remedy Against the United States in an Online Gambling Dispute*, 14 LAW AND BUSINESS REVIEW OF THE AMERICAS 847–856 (2008).

6.  Born, Gary, *A New Generation of International Adjudication*, 61 DUKE LAW JOURNAL 775–879 (2012).

7.  Brewster, Rachel, *Shadow Unilateralism: Enforcing International Trade Law at the WTO*, 30 UNIVERSITY OF PENNSYLVANIA JOURNAL OF INTERNATIONAL LAW 1133–1146 (summer 2009).

8.  Brewster, Rachel, *The Remedy Gap: Institutional Design, Retaliation, and Trade Law Enforcement*, 80 GEORGE WASHINGTON LAW REVIEW 102–158 (2011).

9.  Busch, Marc L. & Krzysztof J. Pelc, *Does the WTO Need a Permanent Body of Panelists?*, 12 JOURNAL OF INTERNATIONAL ECONOMIC LAW 579–594 (2009).

10.  Busch, Marc L., Eric Reinhardt & Gregory Shaffer, *Does Legal Capacity Matter? A Survey of WTO Members*, 8 World Trade Review issue 4, 559–577 (2009).

11.  Cai, Phoenix X.F., *Making WTO Remedies Work for Developing Nations: The Need for Class Actions*, 25 EMORY INTERNATIONAL LAW REVIEW 151–196 (2011).

12.  Carey, Tim, Comment, *Cartel Price Controls vs. Free Trade: A Study of Proposals to Challenge OPEC's Influence in the Oil Market Through WTO Dispute Settlement*, 24 AMERICAN UNIVERSITY INTERNATIONAL LAW REVIEW 783–810 (2009).

13.  Catabagan, Aaron, *Rights of Action for Private Non-State Actors in the WTO Dispute Settlement System*, 37 DENVER JOURNAL OF INTERNATIONAL LAW & POLICY 279–302 (2009).

14.  Charnovitz, Steve, *The Enforcement of WTO Judgments*, 34 YALE JOURNAL OF INTERNATIONAL LAW 558–566 (2009).

15.  Cheng, Tai-Heng, *Precedent and Control in Investment Treaty Arbitration*, 30 FORDHAM INTERNATIONAL LAW JOURNAL 1014–1049 (2007).

16.  Cho, Sungjoon, *Of the World Trade Court's Burden*, 20 EUROPEAN JOURNAL OF INTERNATIONAL LAW 675–727 (2009).

17.  Colares, Juscelino F., *A Theory of WTO Adjudication: From Empirical Analysis to Biased Rule Development*, 42 VANDERBILT JOURNAL OF TRANSNATIONAL LAW 383–439 (2009).

18.  Colares, Juscelino F., *The Limits of WTO Adjudication: Is Compliance the Problem?*, 14 JOURNAL OF INTERNATIONAL ECONOMIC LAW 403–436 (2011).

19.  Conti, Joseph A., *The Good Case: Decisions to Litigate at the World Trade Organization*, 42 LAW & SOCIETY REVIEW 145–181 (2008).

20. Conti, Joseph A., *Learning to Dispute: Repeat Participation, Expertise, and Reputation at the World Trade Organization*, 35 LAW & SOCIAL INQUIRY 625–662 (2010).

21. Cross, Frank B., *Identifying the Virtues of the Common Law*, 15 SUPREME COURT ECONOMIC REVIEW 21–59 (2007).

22. Darling, Jeremy B., Note, *Gambling with Our Future: A Call for Needed WTO Dispute Resolution Reform as Illustrated by the U.S.—Antigua Conflict Over Online Gambling*, 42 GEORGE WASHINGTON INTERNATIONAL LAW REVIEW 381–405 (2010).

23. Davey, William J., Comment, *Compliance Problems in WTO Dispute Settlement*, 42 CORNELL INTERNATIONAL LAW JOURNAL 119–128 (2009).

24. Dillon, Thomas J., Jr., *The World Trade Organization: A New Legal Order for World Trade?*, 16 MICHIGAN JOURNAL OF INTERNATIONAL LAW 349 (1995).

25. Ezeani, Elimma C., *Can the WTO Judges Assist the Development Agenda?*, 10 JOURNAL OF INTERNATIONAL TRADE LAW POLICY number 2 124–150 (2011).

26. Feldman, Alexander M., Note, *Evolving Treaty Obligations: A Proposal for Analyzing Subsequent Practice Derived from WTO Dispute Settlement*, 41 NEW YORK UNIVERSITY JOURNAL OF INTERNATIONAL LAW & POLITICS 655–706 (2009).

27. Flett, James, *Collective Intelligence and the Possibility of Dissent: Anonymous Individual Opinions in WTO Jurisprudence*, 13 JOURNAL OF INTERNATIONAL ECONOMIC LAW 287–320 (2010).

28. Fukunaga, Yuka, *Civil Society and the Legitimacy of the WTO Dispute Settlement System*, 34 BROOKLYN JOURNAL OF INTERNATIONAL LAW 85–117 (2008).

29. Gal-Or, Noemi, *The Concept of Appeal in International Dispute Settlement*, 19 EUROPEAN JOURNAL OF INTERNATIONAL LAW 43–65 (2008).

30. Gantz, David A., *Dispute Settlement Under the NAFTA and the WTO: Choice of Forum Opportunities and Risks for the NAFTA Parties*, 14 AMERICAN UNIVERSITY INTERNATIONAL LAW REVIEW 1025 (1999).

31. Gao, Henry & C.L. Lim, *Saving the WTO from the Risk of Irrelevance: The WTO Dispute Mechanism as a "Common Good" for RTA Disputes*, 11 JOURNAL OF INTERNATIONAL ECONOMIC LAW 899–925 (2008).

32. Gazzini, Tarcisio, *Can Authoritative Interpretation Under Article IX:2 of the Agreement Establishing the WTO Modify the Rights and Obligations of Members?*, 57 INTERNATIONAL & COMPARATIVE LAW QUARTERLY 169–181 (2008).

33. Goldstein, Judith L. & Richard H. Steinberg, *Negotiate or Litigate? Effects of WTO Judicial Delegation on U.S. Trade Politics*, 71 LAW & CONTEMPORARY PROBLEMS 257–282 (2008).

34. Gordon, Robert, *Can the WTO Judges Assist the Development Agenda?*, 10 JOURNAL OF INTERNATIONAL TRADE LAW POLICY number 2 104–123 (2011).

35. Green, Andrew & Michael Trebilcock, *Enforcing WTO Obligations: What Can We Learn from Export Subsidies?*, 10 JOURNAL OF INTERNATIONAL ECONOMIC LAW 653–683 (2007).

36. Greenwald, John D. & Lynn Fisher Fox, *The WTO's Emphasis on Adjudicated Dispute Settlement May be More Drag than Lift*, 24 ARIZONA JOURNAL OF INTERNATIONAL AND COMPARATIVE LAW 134–140 (2007).

37. Harrington, Alexandra R., *They Fought for Trade But Did They Win? An Analysis of the Trends Among Trade Disputes Brought by WTO Member States Before the WTO Dispute Settlement Body*, 16 MICHIGAN STATE JOURNAL OF INTERNATIONAL LAW 315–341 (2007).

38. Harrington, Alexandra R., *Peer Pressure: Correlations between Membership in Regional and Regional Economic Organizations in the Context of WTO Dispute Resolution Claims*, 5 SOUTH CAROLINA JOURNAL OF INTERNATIONAL LAW & BUSINESS 35–73 (2008).

39. Hillman, Jennifer, *Conflicts between Dispute Settlement Mechanisms in Regional Trade Agreements and the WTO — What Should the WTO Do?*, 42 CORNELL INTERNATIONAL LAW JOURNAL 193–208 (2009).

40. Horlick, Gary & Judith Coleman, *The Compliance Problems of the WTO*, 24 ARIZONA JOURNAL OF INTERNATIONAL AND COMPARATIVE LAW 141–147 (2007).

41. Howse, Robert, *Moving the WTO Forward — One Case at a Time*, 42 CORNELL INTERNATIONAL LAW JOURNAL 223–231 (2009).

42. Jackson, John H., *Process and Procedure in WTO Dispute Settlement*, 42 CORNELL INTERNATIONAL LAW JOURNAL 233–240 (2009).

43. Jobodwana, Z. Ntozintle, *Participation of African Member States in the World Trade Organization Dispute Settlement Mechanism*, 7 JOURNAL OF INTERNATIONAL TRADE LAW AND POLICY number 1 61–78 (2008).

44. Karky, Ramesh, *An Issue of Invocability of Provisions of the WTO Covered Agreements Before Domestic Courts*, 17 ANNUAL SURVEY OF INTERNATIONAL & COMPARATIVE LAW 209–224 (2011).

45. Knapp, Kristen A., *Internet Filtering: the Ineffectiveness of WTO Remedies and the Availability of Alternative Tort Remedies*, 28 JOHN MARSHALL JOURNAL OF COMPUTER & INFORMATION LAW 273–312 (2010).

46. Kohona, Palitha T.B., *Dispute Resolution under the World Trade Organization: An Overview*, 28 JOURNAL OF WORLD TRADE 23 (April 1994).

47. Komuro, Norio, *The WTO Dispute Settlement Mechanism: Coverage and Procedures of the WTO Understanding*, 12 JOURNAL OF INTERNATIONAL ARBITRATION 81 (1995).

48. Lagomarsino, Jeffrey, *WTO Dispute Settlement and Sustainable Development: Legitimacy through Holistic Treaty Interpretation*, 28 PACE ENVIRONMENTAL LAW REVIEW 545–567 (2011).

49. Lamy, Pascal, *The Place of the WTO and its Law in the International Legal Order*, 17 EUROPEAN JOURNAL OF INTERNATIONAL LAW 969–84 (2007).

50. Leitner, Kara & Simon Lester, *WTO Dispute Settlement 1995–2008 — A Statistical Analysis*, 12 JOURNAL OF INTERNATIONAL ECONOMIC LAW 195–208 (2009).

51. Lester, Simon, *A Framework for Thinking About the "Discretion" in the Mandatory/Discretionary Distinction*, 14 JOURNAL OF INTERNATIONAL ECONOMIC LAW 369–402 (2011).

52. Lichtenbaum, Peter, *Procedural Issues in WTO Dispute Resolution*, 19 MICHIGAN JOURNAL OF INTERNATIONAL LAW 1195 (1998).

53. Lin, Tsai-Yu, *Compliance Proceedings under Article 21:5 of DSU and Doha Proposed Reform*, 39 THE INTERNATIONAL LAWYER 915–936 (winter 2005).

54. MacLean, Robert G., *The Valuation of Damages in International Investment Disputes*, 14 LAW & BUSINESS REVIEW OF THE AMERICAS 3–18 (2008).

55. Manning, Brian & Srividhya Ragavan, *The Dispute Settlement Process of the WTO: A Normative Structure to Achieve Utilitarian Objectives*, 79 UMKC LAW REVIEW 1–29 (2010).

56. Marchetti, Barbara, *The WTO Dispute Settlement System:Administration, Court, or Tertium Genus?*, 32 SUFFOLK TRANSNATIONAL LAW REVIEW 567–598 (2009).

57. Martin, Mervyn & Maryam Shademan Pajouh, *Rebalancing the Balance: How the WTO's HR Policy Impacts on Its Very Objectives for Welfare Enhancement and Development*, 10 JOURNAL OF INTERNATIONAL TRADE LAW AND POLICY number 3, 243–254 (2011).

58. Menezes de Carvalho, Evandro, *The Decisional Juridical Discourse of the Appellate Body of the WTO: Among Treaties and Dictionaries as Referents*, 20 INTERNATIONAL JOURNAL FOR SEMIOTICS LAW 327–352 (2007).

59. Mercurio, Bryan & Mitali Tyagi, *Treaty Interpretation in WTO Dispute Settlement: The Outstanding Question of the Legality of Local Working Requirements*, 19 MINNESOTA JOURNAL OF INTERNATIONAL LAW 275–326 (2010).

60. Mitchell, Andrew D., *The Legal Basis for Using Principles in WTO Disputes*, 10 JOURNAL OF INTERNATIONAL ECONOMIC LAW 795–835 (2007).

61. Mitchell, Andrew D. & David Heaton, *The Inherent Jurisdiction of WTO Tribunals: The Select Application of Public International Law Required By The Judicial Function*, 31 MICHIGAN JOURNAL INTERNATIONAL LAW 559–619 (2010).

62. Moremen, Philip M., *Costs and Benefits of Adding a Private Right of Action to the World Trade Organization and the Montreal Protocol Dispute Resolution Systems*, 11 UCLA JOURNAL OF INTERNATIONAL LAW AND FOREING AFFAIRS 189–225 ((2006).

63. Nordström, Håkan & Gregory Shaffer, *Access to Justice in the World Trade Organization: A Case for a Small Claims Procedure?*, 7 WORLD TRADE REVIEW issue 4, 587–640 (2008).

64. Nzelibe, Jide, *The Case Against Reforming the WTO Enforcement Mechanism* (Responses by Ernst-Ulrich Petersmann and Christian Tietje), 2008 UNIVERSITY OF ILLINOIS LAW REVIEW 319–387 (2008).

65. Organek, Robin, *Congressional Response to WTO Sanctions: Turning Lemons into Lemonade in the American Jobs Creation Act of 2004*, 16 INTERNATIONAL & COMPARATIVE LAW REVIEW 129–150 (2008).

66. Pauwelyn, Joost & Luiz Eduardo Salles, *Forum Shopping before International Tribunals: (Real) Concerns, (Im)possible Solutions*, 42 CORNELL INTERNATIONAL LAW JOURNAL 77–118 (2009).

67. Petelin, Brandon, Comment, *The United States and International Trade: The Implications of Noncompliance with Dispute Settlement Panel Rulings*, 23 THOMAS M. COOLEY LAW REVIEW 545–595 (2006).

68. Petersmann, Ernst-Ulrich, *Justice as Conflict Resolution: Proliferation, Fragmentation, and Decentralization of Dispute Settlement in International Trade*, 27 UNIVERSITY OF PENNSYLVANIA JOURNAL OF INTERNATIONAL ECONOMIC LAW number 2, 273–366 (summer 2006).

69. Petersmann, Ernst-Ulrich, *Judging the Judges: From "Principal-Agent Theory" to "Constitutional Justice" in Multilevel "Judicial Governance" of Economic Cooperation Among Citizens*, 11 JOURNAL OF INTERNATIONAL ECONOMIC LAW 827–884 (2008).

70. Pfumorodze, J., *Viewpoint — WTO Remedies and Developing Countries*, 10 JOURNAL OF INTERNATIONAL TRADE LAW AND POLICY 83–98 (2011).

71. Rothchild, John A., *Exhausting Extraterritoriality*, 51 SANTA CLARA LAW REVIEW 1187–1239 (2011).

72. Rothstein, Paul, Note, *Moving All-In with the World Trade Organization: Ignoring Adverse Rulings and Gambling with the Future of the WTO*, 37 GEORGIA JOURNAL OF INTERNATIONAL & COMPARATIVE LAW 151–180 (2008).

73. Shaffer, Gregory, *A Structural Theory of WTO Dispute Settlement: Why Institutional Choice Lies at the Center of the GMO Case*, 41 NEW YORK UNIVERSITY JOURNAL OF INTERNATIONAL LAW & POLITICS 1–101 (fall 2008).

74. Shaffer, Gregory, Michelle Ratton Sanchez & Barbara Rosenberg, *The Trials of Winning at the WTO: What Lies Behind Brazil's Success*, 41 CORNELL INTERNATIONAL LAW JOURNAL 383–501 (summer 2008).

75. Shaffer, Gregory C., *How Business Shapes Law: A Socio-Legal Framework*, 42 CONNECTICUT LAW REVIEW 147–183 (November 2009).

76. Shell, G. Richard, *Trade Legalism and International Relations Theory: An Analysis of the World Trade Organization*, 44 DUKE LAW JOURNAL 829 (1995).

77. Slater, Gabriel L., Note, *The Suspension of Intellectual Property Obligations under TRIPs: A Proposal for Retaliating Against Technology-Exporting Countries in the World Trade Organization*, 97 GEORGETOWN LAW JOURNAL 1365–1408 (2009).

78. Steger, Debra P., *WTO Dispute Settlement: Revitalization of Multilateralism After the Uruguay Round*, 9 LEIDEN JOURNAL OF INTERNATIONAL LAW 319 (1996).

79. Steinbach, Armin, *The DSU Interim Review — Need for its Elimination or Extension to the Appellate Body Stage?*, 12 JOURNAL OF INTERNATIONAL ECONOMIC LAW 417–434 (2009).

80. Stiles, Kendall, *The New WTO Regime: The Victory of Pragmatism*, 4 JOURNAL OF INTERNATIONAL LAW & PRACTICE 3 (1995).

81. Taniguchi, Yasuhei, *The WTO Dispute Settlement System as Seen by a Proceduralist*, 42 CORNELL INTERNATIONAL LAW JOURNAL 1–21 (2009).

82. Toohey, Lisa, *China and the World Trade Organization: The First Decade*, 60 INTERNATIONAL & COMPARATIVE LAW QUARTERLY 788–795 (2011).

83. Townsend, David J. & Steve Charnovitz, *Preventing Opportunistic Uncompliance by WTO Members*, 14 JOURNAL OF INTERNATIONAL ECONOMIC LAW 437–468 (2011).

84. Turk, Matthew C., *Why Does the Complainant Always Win at the WTO? A Reputation-Based Theory of Litigation at the World Trade Organization*, 31 NORTHWESTERN JOURNAL OF INTERNATIONAL LAW & BUSINESS 385–437 (2011).

85. Unterhalter, David, *Allocating the Burden of Proof in WTO Dispute Settlement Proceedings*, 42 CORNELL INTERNATIONAL LAW JOURNAL 209–221 (2009).

86. Wang, Angela, *Note, Will China Prevail Over the Current WTO?*, 5 HASTINGS BUSINESS LAW JOURNAL 207–228 (2009).

87. Weiss, Wolfgang, *Security and Predictability Under WTO Law*, 2 WORLD TRADE REVIEW issue 2, 183–219 (2003).

88. Williams, Michael R., Note, *Pirates of the Caribbean (and Beyond): Developing a New Remedy for WTO Noncompliance*, 41 GEORGE WASHINGTON INTERNATIONAL LAW REVIEW 503–540 (2009).

89. Young, Michael, *Dispute Resolution in the Uruguay Round: Lawyers Triumph Over Diplomats*, 29 THE INTERNATIONAL LAWYER 389 (1995).

Other Sources:

1. International Centre for Trade and Sustainable Development (ICTSD), *Towards A Development Supportive Dispute Settlement System in the WTO* (ICTSD Resource Paper Number 5) (March 2003).

2. Lawrence, Robert Z., *The United States and the WTO Dispute Settlement System* (Council on Foreign Relations Special Report, CSR Number 25) (March 2007).

3. United States Government Accounting Office, *World Trade Organization — Issues in Dispute Settlement*, GAO/NSIAD-00-210 (August 2000).

4. United States Government Accounting Office, *World Trade Organization — U.S. Experience to Date in Dispute Settlement System*, GAO/NSIAD/OGC-00-196BR (June 2000).

5. *WTO at 10: Governance, Dispute Settlement, and Developing Countries*, World Trade Organization Tenth Anniversary Conference at Columbia University, New York City, 5–7 April 2006 (available at www.sipa.columbia.edu/wto).

# DUAL SUBSTANTIAL TRANSFORMATION

*See* Double Substantial Transformation.

# DUMPING

"Dumping," in the simplest sense, refers to the sale or likely sale of imported merchandise at less than fair value (LTFV).

*See* AD.

# DUMPING MARGIN

The dumping margin is the amount by which the Normal Value of a foreign like product sold in the home market of an exporter or producer exceeds the Export Price, or Constructed Export Price, of subject merchandise sold in the importing country. Expressed as a percentage, it is this difference divided by Export Price or Constructed Export Price. *See* 19 U.S.C. § 1677b(a)(1).

In some WTO cases, particularly involving zeroing, it has been argued that the term "margin of dumping" and "dumping margin" are not synonymous. That argument has not been successful.

# DUMPING MARGIN DETERMINATION

The phase of an antidumping (AD) investigation in which a dumping margin is calculated.

The essential issue in a dumping margin determination is whether a dumping margin exists, and if so, the quantitative value of that margin. The dumping margin determination is one of two indispensable features of every antidumping (AD) case, the other being the injury determination. In some countries, such as the United States, the dumping margin phase is comprised of two parts — a preliminary determination (which may be affirmative or negative), and a final determination (which may be affirmative or negative). In other countries, each phase consists of just one part, which amounts to a final (affirmative or negative) determination.

Also in some countries, such as the United States, the administering authority responsible for the dumping margin determination is different from the agency responsible for the injury determination. In the United States, the Department of Commerce (DOC) — specifically, the Import Administration (IA) section, handles the dumping margin calculation. The International Trade Commission (ITC) deals with injury determinations. In other countries, the process is unified under one authority.

*Suggestions for Further Research:*

Articles:

1.   Willems, Arnoud R. & Yohan Benizri, *Can EU Injury Margin Calculations Withstand Legal Scrutiny?*, 15 INTERNATIONAL TRADE LAW & REGULATION issue 2, 51–56 (2009).

2.   Wood, J. Christopher & Zia C. Oatley, *28 U.S.C. § 1581(c): Judicial Review of Antidumping Duty Determinations Issued by the Department of Commerce*, 41 GEORGETOWN JOURNAL OF INTERNATIONAL LAW 117–135 (2009).

# DUNKEL DRAFT

The text of draft agreements produced in December 1991, under the direction of former GATT Director-General Arthur Dunkel, following a mini-Ministerial Conference, held in Montreal in 1990, during the Uruguay Round. Many of the final Uruguay Round outcomes, including the *General Agreement on Trade in Services (GATS)*, closely resemble the Dunkel Draft.

The Dunkel Draft was a compromise text designed to jump start stalled Uruguay Round negotiations. The Draft was the only instance in GATT history in which the Director-General used his good offices to produce the outline and details of a possible multilateral trade deal. Many GATT contracting parties opposed the idea of the Director-General acting in this manner. The text itself was widely criticized at the time. But, it worked — that is, the Dunkel Draft became the basis for the final Uruguay Round agreements, which were accepted on 15 December 1993 (when formal negotiations ended), and signed on 15 April 1994 (in Marrakesh, Morocco). The Draft, of course, is the eponym of the former Director-General who produced it.

In December 2006, amidst moribund Doha Round talks, WTO Director-General Pascal Lamy said he would not sponsor a compromise text.[170] Later in the Doha Round, in September 2007, some observers pressed Lamy to produce a "Lamy Text."[171] They argued only the Director-General could guide WTO Members to a compromise, and doing so would guard against any one Member taking the blame for sabotaging the Round and the WTO itself.

*Suggestions for Further Research:*

Book:

1.   STEWART, TERRENCE P., ED., THE GATT URUGUAY ROUND: A NEGOTIATING HISTORY (1986–1982) (1993).

# DUTCH DISEASE

An affliction that befalls a country when it receives a sudden increase in foreign exchange.

---

[170] *See* Daniel Pruzin, *WTO Chief Lamy Plays Down Prospect for Compromise Text to Salvage Doha*, 23 International Trade Reporter (BNA) 1789–90 (21 December 2006).

[171] *See* Gary G. Yerkey, *WTO's Lamy Called on to Come Up with Compromise Text in Doha Trade Talks*, 24 International Trade Reporter (BNA) 1347–1348 (27 September 2007) (noting former Carter and Clinton Administration senior official Stuart E. Eizenstat, and former European Trade Commissioner Hugo Paemen, urged Lamy to produce an eponymous Draft).

The result is a bidding up of the currency of that country, which makes exports from that country more expensive. To fight the ailment, economists recommend (*inter alia*) spending funds (including foreign assistance) in ways that lower costs incurred by exporters, so that they, in turn, can cut prices of their merchandise.[172] Examples include infrastructure projects, such as more and better roads to borders and port facilities.

*Suggestions for Further Research:*

Other Source:

1.   RAJAN, RAGHURAN & ARVIND SUBRAMANIAN, WHAT UNDERMINES AID'S IMPACT ON GROWTH? 6 (IMF Working Paper 05/126, June 2005).

## DUTY ABSORPTION

Duty absorption is a problem arising when an antidumping (AD) order is issued and the importer of subject merchandise is related to the exporter. Essentially, a foreign producer of this merchandise, or the exporter of the merchandise, absorbs the cost of the duties, where the order covers the producer or exporter. Absorption occurs by the producer or exporter reimbursing the importer for the cost of the AD duty.

Between two to four years after issuance of an order, the United States Department of Commerce (DOC) is authorized to consider whether there is a reasonable basis to believe or suspect a foreign producer or exporter is absorbing an AD duty. If so, the DOC examines the matter in any reviews of the order. Moreover, in a Sunset Review, the United States International Trade Commission (ITC) must take into account the findings of the DOC.

According to the Clinton Administration *Statement of Administrative Action* on the WTO *Antidumping Agreement* (at p. 885 of that *Statement*), if duty absorption is occurring, it is not to be treated as a duty as cost. Treating an AD duty as a cost means the duty may be deducted from Export Price if an importer of subject merchandise related to the manufacture of the merchandise is being reimbursed for duties by the manufacturer. That deduction, which lowers Export Price, can effectively double an AD duty or countervailing duty (CVD).

## DUTY ASSESSMENT RATE (DAR)

See Administrative Review, Retrospective Assessment.

---

[172] *See Between Hype and Hope*, THE ECONOMIST, 16 July 2005, at 74.

# E

## E-COMMERCE MORATORIUM

A ban on the imposition and collection of duties on goods that are transmitted digitally over the internet.

At the Second WTO Ministerial Meeting in Geneva in May 1998, Members agreed to this Moratorium. The bank prohibits a Member from imposing a customs duty on an electronic transmission. They understand "electronic transmission" to mean data transmitted via the internet or other mode of telecommunications.[173] The term would include electronically delivered software. The Moratorium does not apply to sales taxes or other internal charges. It also is inapplicable to a good ordered on the internet and shipped physically across an international boundary, such as a purchase by a consumer in the United States of a book on the United Kingdom website of Amazon, amazon.uk.

The WTO Members did not renew this Moratorium at their failed Third Ministerial Conference in Seattle in November–December 1999. But, they adhered to it nevertheless, and subsequently renewed it at their Conferences in Doha in November 2001, Cancún in September 2003, Hong Kong in December 2005, and Geneva in November–December 2009. The Geneva extension carried through until the Eighth Ministerial Conference in December 2011 in Geneva.

The Moratorium is based on compromise wording drawn from texts proposed by Cuba, India, and Pakistan. Interestingly, Cuba insisted on language concerning non-discrimination. Cuba argues that the American trade embargo of Cuban products makes it impossible for Cuba to integration into the global electronic trading system. The Moratorium also contains a work program, which must include non-discrimination, transparency, development issues, and the trade-treatment of software that is sent electronically.

The Moratorium has been successful, in that no WTO Member has imposed a tariff on e-commerce. Indeed, none has explicitly indicated an intention to do so. As a technological matter, it may be difficult to impose and collect such a duty.

## EAC

East African Community, re-established by a treaty signed in Arusha on 30 November 1999 by Kenya, Tanzania, and Uganda. Subsequently, Burundi and Rwanda joined.

The *Arusha Treaty* was ratified by the three EAC member states during the subsequent six months, and enacted by the end of November 2000. The *Treaty* breathed new life into the EAC, which had been long defunct. On 18 June 2007, Burundi and Rwanda formally joined the EAC, bringing the combined population of the Community to 115 million.

---

[173] *See* Daniel Pruzin, *WTO Members on Course for Ministerial Deals on E-Commerce, TRIPs Disputes*, 26 International Trade Reporter (BNA) 1528 (12 November 2009).

The long-term goals of the *Arusha Treaty* are

(1)  the formation of a customs union (CU) with a maximum common external tariff of 25 percent,

(2)  the creation of a common market,

(3)  monetary union, and

(4)  political federation.

In addition, the *Treaty* calls for freedom of movement across their borders for the citizens of the three EAC member states, harmonized investment incentives, a regional tourism strategy, a regional stock exchange, and the eventual creation of an East African court and 32 member legislative assembly.

Little progress has been made toward these ambitious goals. Initially, tariffs among the three EAC member states were scheduled to be eliminated in July 1999, but that timetable was postponed to July 2000. Subsequently, the July 2000 date was abandoned, and no clear timetable for trade liberalization is set forth in the *Arusha Treaty*. The *Treaty* called only for conclusion of a protocol to establish a customs union (CU) within four years, *i.e.*, by 2004. The East African Community Customs Union (comprised of Kenya, Tanzania and Uganda) commenced operation on 1 January 2005, following the official launching ceremonies that were held simultaneously in Kampala, Nairobi and Dar es Salaam on 31 January 2004.

That commencement is more a paper victory than an operational reality. A key reason for the slow pace of trade liberalization is Tanzanian business leaders fear Kenya will dominate any free trade agreement (FTA) or CU. Thus, the Tanzanians seek short-term protective remedies and compensation measures. Their fear is not ungrounded.[174] Kenya is more industrialized than Tanzania. Relative to Kenya, Tanzania faces higher energy costs, higher duties on spare parts, more payroll taxes, more expensive skilled labor, and fewer economies of scale. Burundi and Rwanda, of course, are relatively poorer than the other EAC parties, and have economic worries of their own. At the EAC meetings in August 2007, leaders of the member countries agreed to relegate the establishment of a political federation to economic affairs. They decided to focus on establishing a framework to ensure a functioning CU by 2012.

In November 2012, the United States announced it was launching negotiations with the EAC to form a trade and investment partnership.

*Suggestions for Further Research:*

Articles:

1.  Ewelukwa, Uché U., *South — South Trade and Investment: The Good, the Bad, and the Ugly—African Perspectives*, 20 MINNESOTA JOURNAL OF INTERNATIONAL LAW 513–587 (2011).

2.  Jaconiah, Jacob, *The Parallel Importation of Trademarked Goods in the Framework of the Economic Partnership Agreement between the East African*

---

[174] *See* Tony Zaccharia, *EAC Federation Fears Justified?*, DAILY NEWS (Tanzania), 5 May 2007.

*Community and the European Union*, 42 IIC: INTERNATIONAL REVIEW OF INTELLECTUAL PROPERTY & COMPETITION LAW 673–697 (2011).

## *EAFTA*

*East Asian Free Trade Area.*

In the late 1990s, Japan showed a keen interest in a free trade agreement (FTA) with the *Association of Southeast Asian Nations* (*ASEAN*), and also in building an *EAFTA*. If implemented, *EAFTA* would link Japan with China, (including Hong Kong), Korea, and Taiwan. Motivating Japan was the lack of progress toward an FTA with the United States, coupled with the United States' pursuit of accords with countries other than Japan. Hence, Japan reversed its historic policy of pursuing trade liberalization only through multilateral mechanisms.

## EAI

Enterprise for *ASEAN* Initiative.

The United States announced the EAI in 2002. The Initiative lays out conditions for the United States to enter into free trade agreement (FTA) talks with the *Association of South East Asian Nations* (*ASEAN*) as a group. These conditions are

- All *ASEAN* countries must be WTO Members. (Presently, Laos is not a Member.)

- All *ASEAN* countries must have signed a *Trade and Investment Framework Agreement* (*TIFA*) with the United States. Some individual countries, such as Malaysia, do not have a *TIFA*. However, on 25 August 2006, United States Trade Representative (USTR) Susan C. Schwab met with the 10 economic ministers of *ASEAN* and signed a *TIFA* with the bloc. From the American perspective, at least, the *United States—ASEAN TIFA* will provide a platform for strengthening already deep commercial ties among the United States and *ASEAN* countries.

President George W. Bush first proposed the EAI in the 1980s. At that time, however, it was seen as too visionary. Little progress has been made.

## EARLY HARVEST

A term used in connection with trade negotiations whereby one or more accords are agreed to and implemented, regardless of whether any further deals are negotiated and finalized. Therefore, early harvest is the settling of issues between participants before formal talks begin.

By resolving some issues early, both momentum and goodwill are generated for the formal talks, creating optimistic expectations that remaining — and possibly more difficult — issues will be decided.

The early harvest approach is different from the single undertaking approach, whereby nothing is agreed to until everything is agreed to. The early harvest, as its name suggests, permits negotiations, drafting, finalization, and implementation of one or more texts, regardless of whether progress is made on any other text. The first text or texts agreed to are the first fruits — the early harvest — of the negotiations, which — it is hoped — encourage a positive spirit of cooperation to reach further deals on other topics. Moreover, in contrast to the single undertaking approach, the first or early deals that are reached are not held hostage to the fate of negotiations on other topics. Rather, those deals are decoupled from the outcome of subsequent bargaining.

For example, in the months before the December 2005 WTO Ministerial Conference in Hong Kong, there was hope for an "early harvest" on issues such as

(1) removal by the United States of cotton subsidies,

(2) granting by developed countries of unrestricted access to products, including textile and apparel merchandise, from least developed countries, and

(3) amendment of the *Agreement on Trade Related Aspects of Intellectual Property Rights (TRIPs Agreement)* to incorporate an August 2003 arrangement on importation of generic drugs.

Issues one and two were not resolved before the Ministerial Conference, meaning no early harvest occurred in regard to those issues. However, in December 2005, on the eve of the Hong Kong Ministerial Conference, the third issue was resolved.

## EBA

Everything But Arms, a permanent grant of preferential trade treatment by the European Union (EU) to merchandise from least developed countries.

The EU has a basic, broad Generalized System of Preferences (GSP) program, which originated in 1971. This scheme gives tariff preferences — zero or reduced duties — on 7,000 dutiable tariff lines, which is a larger number than that for the American scheme. The EBA provides duty-free treatment to all imports from least developed countries, except for arms and munitions. Sugar and rice also are an exception until 2009; only thereafter will the EU accord them duty-free treatment. Notably, the broader GSP scheme is reviewed periodically by the EU, but the EBA is a permanent grant of preferential treatment.

## EBR

Enhanced Continuous Bond Requirement.

*See* Customs Bond.

## EC

The European Community, or European Communities.

The name used between 1968–92, under the 1967 *Merger Treaty*, for what has been called the EU since 1992 pursuant to the *Treaty of Maastricht*. From 1957–68, under the 1957 *Treaty of Rome*, the term "EEC" was used.

*Suggestions for Further Research:*

Article:

1. Leal-Arcas, Rafael, *Polycephalous Anatomy of the EC in the WTO: An Analysis of Law and Practice*, 19 FLORIDA JOURNAL OF INTERNATIONAL LAW 569–670 (2007).

## ECCAS

Economic Community of Central African States.

At a summit meeting in December 1981, the leaders of the Central African Customs and Economic Union (UDEAC) agreed in principle to form a wider economic community of Central African states. The ECCAS was established on 18 October 1983 by the UDEAC members (Cameroon, Central African Republic, Chad, Congo (Republic of), Equatorial Guinea, and Gabon), plus São Tomé & Príncipé, Burundi, Rwanda, and the former Zaire (now Democratic Republic of the Congo). Angola held Observer status until 1999, when it became a full member.

The members of ECCAS are:

- Angola
- Burundi
- Cameroon
- Central African Republic
- Chad
- Congo (Democratic Republic of) the Congo
- Congo (Republic of)
- Equatorial Guinea
- Gabon
- Rwanda
- São Tomé and Príncipé

As intimated, Angola has been a member since 1999. All other countries have been members since 1985.

ECCAS began functioning in 1985. It was inactive for several years, because of financial difficulties (non-payment of membership fees) and conflict in the Great Lakes area. The war in the Democratic Republic of the Congo (DRC) was particularly divisive. Rwanda and Angola, for example, fought on opposing sides.

The African Economic Community (AEC) has designated ECCAS a pillar of the AEC. Yet, due to the inactivity of ECCAS between 1992–99, formal contact between the AEC and ECCAS was established only in October 1999. In October 1999, ECCAS signed the *Protocol on Relations between the AEC and the Regional Economic Communities*. In June 1999, The AEC again confirmed the importance of ECCAS as the major economic community in Central Africa at the third preparatory meeting of its Economic and Social Council (ECOSOC).

ECCAS aims to achieve collective autonomy, raise the standard of living of its populations, and maintain economic stability through cooperation. Its ultimate goal is to establish a Central African Common Market. At the Malabo

Heads of State and Government Conference in 1999, leaders identified four priority objectives:

(1) Develop capacities to maintain peace and security.

(2) Work towards physical, economic, and monetary integration.

(3) Establish a culture for human integration.

(4) Build an autonomous financing mechanism for ECCAS.

## ECLAC

The United Nations Economic Commission for Latin America and the Caribbean.

The Economic Commission for Latin America (ECLA) — the Spanish acronym is CEPAL — was established by United Nations (U.N.) Economic and Social Council resolution 106(VI) of 25 February 1948 and began to function that same year. The scope of the Commission's work was later broadened to include the countries of the Caribbean. By Resolution 1984/67 of 27 July 1984, the Economic Council decided to change its name to the Economic Commission for Latin America and the Caribbean (ECLAC). The Spanish acronym — CEPAL — remains unchanged.

ECLAC, which is headquartered in Santiago, Chile, is one of the five regional commissions of the United Nations. It was founded for the purposes of contributing to the economic development of Latin America, coordinating actions directed towards this end, and reinforcing economic relationships among the countries and with the other nations of the world. Later included among its primary objectives was promotion of social development of the region.

In June 1951 the Commission established the ECLAC sub-regional headquarters in Mexico City, which serves the needs of the Central American sub-region. In December 1966, the ECLAC sub-regional headquarters for the Caribbean was founded in Port-of-Spain, Trinidad and Tobago. In addition, ECLAC maintains country offices in Buenos Aires, Brasilia, Montevideo and Bogotá. It has a liaison office in Washington, D.C.

In 1948, the United Nations invited Raúl Prebisch what was then the new ECLA:

> ... Prebisch turned its secretariat in Santiago, Chile, into a launch pad for "structuralism," and its related ideas of "inward development," import substitution and regional integration. Sadly, these were often abused by Latin American governments (and some economists at ECLA itself) to justify exaggerated protectionism and inflationary financing of government.[175]

---

[175] *Misunderstood Moderate*, THE ECONOMIST, 7 March 2009, at 90 (reviewing Edgar J. Dorfman, *The Life and Times of Raúl Prebisch, 1901–1986* (2009)).

Thereafter, in 1964, Prebisch became the first Director-General of the United Nations Conference on Trade and Development (UNCTAD).

*Suggestions for Further Research:*

Book:

1.  DOSMAN, EDGAR J., THE LIFE AND TIMES OF RAÚL PREBISCH, 1901–1986 (2009).

## ECOWAS

Economic Community of West African States.

ECOWAS is a regional group of 15 West African countries. West Africa is one of the poorest regions of the world. ECOWAS was founded on 28 May 1975 with the signing of the *Treaty of Lagos*. When ECOWAS was registered in Nigeria in May 1975, it had 15 members. In 1976, Cape Verde joined ECOWAS as the 16th member. In 2002, Mauritania left the organization.

Currently, there are 15 member countries in the organization:

*   Benin
*   Burkina Faso
*   Cape Verde
*   Côte d'Ivoire
*   Gambia
*   Ghana
*   Guinea
*   Guinea-Bissa

*   Liberia
*   Mali
*   Niger
*   Nigeria
*   Senegal
*   Sierra Leone
*   Tongolese Republic

The mission of ECOWAS is to promote economic integration in all fields of economic activity, particularly industry, transport, telecommunications, energy, agriculture, natural resources, commerce, monetary and financial questions, social and cultural matters. For certain purposes, such as Economic Partnership Agreements (EPAs) with the European Union (EU), ECOWAS negotiates as a bloc, and on behalf of a non-member, Mauritania.

In August 2006, trade, foreign affairs, and cooperation ministers from the ECOWAS members finalized plans for a major restructuring of the organization. Key aspects of the reforms include transformation of the Secretariat to a Commission headed by a President and seven Commissioners, a clearly defined, focused role for each Commissioner, and a predictable rotation system for senior leaders of the organization. The transformation of the Secretariat into a Commission is to be accompanied by the adoption of a new legal regime. The principle of supra-nationality is to be a hallmark of that regime.

Accordingly, four institutions make up ECOWAS:

(1) The Commission.

(2) The Community Parliament.

(3)  The Community Court of Justice.

(4)  The ECOWAS Bank for Investment and Development (EBID).

Of these bodies, the Commission and Bank are pre-eminent.

*Suggestions for Further Research:*

Article:

1.  Gbetnkom, Daniel, *On the Empirics of Market Integration in ECOWAS*, 9 JOURNAL OF ECONOMIC POLICY REFORM 289–303 (2006).

# ECAT

Emergency Committee for American Trade, a lobbying group dealing with matters of trade and foreign direct investment (FDI).

# ECB

European Central Bank. Located in Frankfurt, Germany, the ECB is the central bank for Europe's single currency, the euro. The ECB's main responsibility is to maintain the purchasing power of the euro, and thus price stability in the euro area. The euro area (as of October 2007) comprises the 13 European Union members, each of which has introduced the euro since 1999, replacing its former currency. Participating countries are:

- Austria
- Belgium
- Finland
- France
- Germany
- Greece
- Ireland
- Italy
- Luxembourg
- Netherlands
- Portugal
- Slovenia
- Spain

# ECONOMÍA

The former name for Mexico's *Secretaría de Economía, i.e.*, the *Ministry of the Economy*, or *"Economía."* Formerly called "SECOFI."

*See* SECOFI.

# ECONOMIES OF SCALE

A reduction in the average cost of the product of a firm in the long run as a result of an expansion in the level of output.

There are two types of economies of scale, "internal" and "external." An "internal" economy of scale results from the expansion of output of the individual firm. The firm might achieve this expansion as a result of greater specialization of labor tasks, the use of technology, improved management, or some combination thereof. An "external" economy of scale results from the expansion of output in the industry. Costs fall for all firms in the industry because the expansion of the industry results in greater specialization and training. Government policies may help create external economies of scale.

In brief, an economy of scale suggests that a bigger firm or industry can produce more cheaply than a smaller firm or industry. However, just how much bigger a firm or industry can get before the problems of "big-ness" overwhelm any economies of scale is an important consideration. After all, managing large organizations and the people who work in them is not easy.

## EEC (FIRST MEANING)

The European Economic Community, created in 1957 pursuant to the 1957 *Treaty of Rome*. The name "EEC," based on the 1957 *Treaty*, which founded the EEC, was used from 1957 until 1968.

From 1968–92, the name "European Community" or "European Communities," both abbreviated by "EC," was used. That name was based on the 1967 Merger Treaty. The third and most recent name, used since 1992, is the "European Union," or "EU." This name is taken from the 1992 *Treaty of Maastricht*.

The Table below summarizes the names and legal instruments from which the names are derived. The Table also shows how the membership has expanded from the six founding nations of the EEC, all of which are in Western Europe, to include Central and Eastern European nations:

TABLE:

SUMMARY OF EUROPEAN INTEGRATION

| *Year* | *Treaty or Enlargement* | *Name, Abbreviation, and Period Used* | *Member States* | *Number of Member States* |
|---|---|---|---|---|
| 1957 | *Treaty of Rome* | European Economic Community EEC Used from 1957–68 | Belgium France Germany Italy Luxembourg Netherlands | 6 |
| 1967 | *Merger Treaty* | European Community or European Communities EC Used from 1968–92 | | 6 |

TABLE **(Continued)**

| Year | Treaty or Enlargement | Name, Abbreviation, and Period Used | Member States | Number of Member States |
|------|----------------------|-------------------------------------|---------------|-------------------------|
| 1973 | First Enlargement | EC | Founding 6 plus Denmark Ireland United Kingdom | 9 |
| 1981 | Second Enlargement | EC | All of the above, plus Greece | 10 |
| 1986 | Second Enlargement, continued | EC | All of the above, plus Portugal Spain | 12 |
| 1990 | | EC | All of the above, plus Former East Germany (German Democratic Republic) is reunified with West Germany and thereby gains membership | 12 |
| 1992 | *Treaty of Maastricht* | European Union EU Used since 1992 | | 12 |
| 1995 | Third Enlargement | | All of the above, plus Austria Finland Sweden | 15 |

TABLE (Continued)

| Year | Treaty or Enlargement | Name, Abbreviation, and Period Used | Member States | Number of Member States |
|------|----------------------|-------------------------------------|---------------|-------------------------|
| 2004 | Fourth Enlargement | | All of the above, plus Cyprus Czech Republic Estonia Hungary Latvia Lithuania Malta Poland Slovak Republic Slovenia | 25 |
| 2007 | Fifth Enlargement | | Bulgaria Romania | 27 |

The origins of the EEC date to 1952, when the European Coal and Steel Community (ECSC) was established by treaty.[176] The *ECSC Treaty* expired in 2001, and coal and steel products will thereafter be governed under the EU arrangement.

## EEC (SECOND MEANING)

Eurasian Economic Commission.

The EEC is the governing institution of the Customs Union formed by Belarus, Kazakhstan, and Russia. They created the EEC effective 1 February 2012, and it replaced the "Customs Union Commission." The EEC holds over 100 supra-national powers.[177]

## EECC

Export Enforcement Coordination Center.

---

[176] *See Treaty Establishing the European Coal and Steel Community*, 18 April 1951, 261 U.N.T.S. 140.

[177] *See* Sergei Blagov, *Belarus, Kazakhstan, Russia Customs Union to Form New EEC Governing Body in February*, 29 International Trade Reporter (BNA) 175 (2 February 2012).

The EECC was established on 9 November 2011, by Executive Order 13558, issued by President Barack H. Obama.[178] The EECC is the primary point of contact in coordinating efforts between various United States government departments and agencies concerned with violations of United States export control laws.[179]

The EECC also acts as a contact between federal law enforcement agencies and the intelligence community, and between enforcement authorities and export licensing authorities. The Department of Homeland Security operates the Center, but other departments and agencies cited in the Executive Order include Departments of Commerce, Defense, Energy, Justice, State, and Treasury, and the Office of the Directory of National Intelligence.

## EFFICIENT MARKETS HYPOTHESIS

A theory developed in the 1950s and 1960s that, subject to certain conditions, all of the information available publicly about a financial market instrument relevant to the value of that instrument is reflected in the price of that instrument.[180] Consequently, when new information is revealed, the price of the instrument changes to embody that new information. In 1988, the United States Supreme Court, in *Basic Inc. v. Levinson*, 485 U.S. 224 (1988), accepted a theory of insider trading known as "fraud on the market."

Fraud on the market theory is premised on the efficient markets hypothesis. The Supreme Court agreed that if the market price of a company's stock reflects all publicly available information, then any false or misleading statement by the company will affect adversely the share price of that stock. Investors, who are not insiders in the company, and thus not privy to the truth about the company, rely on the integrity of the share price as an (or the) indicator of the fundamental value of the company. A false or misleading statement defrauds these investors — the market — who purchase the shares of the company. That is true, said the Supreme Court, even if an investor does not rely directly on the false or misleading statement, or even if the investor has no knowledge of the statement — again, because the investor relies on the price, which incorporates the statement.

Securities regulation and jurisprudence in the field is highly developed in the United States and other major markets, including the European Union (EU) and Japan. That is not the case in emerging markets. An issue that arises in the context of services sector liberalization, in both *General Agreement on Trade in Services (GATS)* and free trade agreement (FTA) negotiations, is market access for financial firms providing broker-dealer, underwriter, and fund management services. Developed countries are chary of opening these activities to foreign

---

[178] See Export Enforcement Coordination Center November 9, 2010 Exec. Order No. 13558, 75 FR 69573.

[179] *See* Len Bracken, *Administration Establishes Center for Export Enforcement Coordination*, 27 International Trade Reporter (BNA) 1764 (18 November 2010).

[180] *See Dismal Science, Dismal Sentence*, THE ECONOMIST, 9 September 2006, at 74.

providers from countries with inferior regulations and jurisprudence to protect investors. Conversely, firms from developed countries that gain access to certain emerging markets are (or should be) careful about the integrity of these financial markets.

## *EFTA*

*European Free Trade Association*, established in 1960 by the Stockholm Convention, whose members are Iceland, Liechtenstein, Norway, and Switzerland. Denmark and the United Kingdom joined the European Community (EC) in 1973, thus leaving the *EFTA*. In 1995, Austria, Finland, and Sweden left *EFTA* to join the European Union (EU). These departures spurred *EFTA* to pursue aggressively free trade agreements (FTAs) with as many countries as possible.

*EFTA* countries boast only 12.5 million people. Yet, counting the European Union (EU) as a single trading bloc, *EFTA* (as of 2006) is the 10$^{th}$ largest trader in the world. It is the fifth largest services trader in the world. *EFTA* also is known for having some of the most protected agricultural markets, and highest per farmer subsidy levels, in the world.

*EFTA* has free trade accords with many Eastern European countries (*e.g.*, Bulgaria (agreed to in 1993), Croatia (2001), the Czech and Slovak Republics (1992), Hungary (1993), Poland (1993), Romania (1993), and Slovenia (1995)), as well as with Finland (1961), Israel (1993), Spain (1980), and Turkey (1992). *EFTA* has FTAs in the Middle East, with Jordan (2001), Lebanon (2004), Morocco (1999), the Palestinian Authority (1999), and Tunisia (2004).

Far outside of its region, *EFTA* has concluded FTAs with Chile (2003), Mexico (1999), Singapore (2002), and Hong Kong (2011), plus Korea and the *Southern African Customs Union (SACU)*. Interestingly, the *EFTA — Singapore* accord bans the use of antidumping (AD) measures. The *EFTA — Hong Kong* deal (which entered into force in mid-2012) is the first free trade agreement (FTA) of Hong Kong with a European economy. It covers trade in goods and services, intellectual property, and investment. In these — and possibly other — respects, *EFTA* is racing with the EU to ensure comparable market access terms for its exporters.

Among the highly significant *EFTA* negotiations is the free trade accord with Canada, which *EFTA* had hoped to conclude by December 1999. Had that target date been met, the accord with Canada would have represented the first-ever free trade bridge across the Atlantic. (The *EU — Mexico FTA* snatched that accolade.) The *EFTA — Canada* deal was concluded in 2007, and covered market access generally, plus key specific sectors such as agriculture, government procurement, investment, and services. In particular, the *EFTA — Canada FTA* provides for:

- Immediate (*i.e.*, upon entry into force) elimination of duties on all non-agricultural goods exported by Canada to *EFTA*.

- Immediate (*i.e.*, upon entry into force) elimination, or phased reductions, of tariffs on selected agricultural exports from Canada to *EFTA*, including crude canola oil, beer, durum wheat, and frozen French fries.

- Reduced cost for Canadian firms to obtain machinery, scientific and precision instruments, innovative technologies, and other inputs from *EFTA*.

In addition, the deal covered competition policy and intellectual property rights (IPRs). In April 2009, the Canadian Parliament gave its final approval to the *EFTA* deal, and it entered into force on 1 July 2009. The accord was Canada's first FTA with Europe, and (as of 2008, before implementation of the deal), *EFTA* was the seventh largest export market for Canada in the world.

Along with the FTAs *EFTA* has with Chile, Korea, Mexico, and *SACU*, its FTA with Canada is considered a "second generation" agreement.[181] The second-generation *EFTA* agreements cover a broad range of issues, namely —

- Trade in industrial goods
- Trade in agricultural products
- Trade in services
- Rules on foreign direct investment (FDI)
- Rules on competition policy
- IPR protection
- Government procurement

In these respects, the *EFTA* deals resemble United States FTAs. Interestingly, because *EFTA* does not have a common agricultural policy, individual *EFTA* members negotiate FTA provisions on agricultural market access and subsidies.

However, the *EFTA* FTAs are distinguished from American FTAs in two important ways: *EFTA* intentionally eschews coverage of (1) labor and (2) environmental issues. The *EFTA* policy is that labor and environmental issues are best handled in multilateral venues, such as the International Labor Organization (ILO).

In 1998, Switzerland entered into a bilateral accord with the EU, thereby granting the EU many trade concessions. In 1999, Switzerland agreed to extend these concessions to its fellow *EFTA* members.

As of December 2011, *EFTA* had ambitious plans for new FTA deals. Among the countries with which it is negotiating are Algeria, Colombia, Cyprus, India, Peru, Russia, and Thailand, plus the Gulf Cooperation Council (GCC). *EFTA* expected to conclude a pact with India in early 2012. Additional possible FTA partners are Malaysia and the Philippines, and in November 2011, EFTA announced it was launching negotiations with Costa Rica, Honduras, and

---

[181] Daniel Pruzin, *EFTA Chief Says Group Will Push for Free Trade Deals with Asia, Russia*, 25 International Trade Reporter (BNA) 569 (17 April 2008).

Panama. While *EFTA* would like an agreement with China, China prefers bilateral FTAs, and (in 2008), started negotiations with Iceland.

*Suggestions for Further Research:*

Articles:

1. Fredriksen, Halvard Haukeland, *The EFTA Court 15 Years On*, 59 INTERNATIONAL & COMPARATIVE LAW QUARTERLY 731–760 (2010).

2. Ørebech, Peter, *The Art of Subsidizing Fuel-Free Electricity under the European Economic Area Agreement as Illustrated by Norway's Reversion Instrument*, 86 CHICAGO-KENT LAW REVIEW 109–137 (2011).

# EGSA

Environmental Goods and Services Agreement, a proposed accord under the auspices of the World Trade Organization (WTO).

The purpose of an EGSA would be to eliminate tariffs on environmental goods, and eliminate barriers to trade in environmental services. The United States and European Union (EU) proposed an EGSA in 2007. However, little progress was made toward finalizing an EGSA as part of an overall Doha Round package, particularly with the July 2008 collapse of Doha Round negotiations.

# *ENABLING CLAUSE*

Special and differential treatment under Part IV of GATT poses an obvious legal issue: Under what legal authority is favoring the trade interests of poor over rich countries permissible? In particular, what excuses the blatant departure from the MFN obligation in Article I:1? Until 1979, periodic waivers granted by the CONTRACTING PARTIES answered the question. The permanent answer is language agreed to on 28 November 1979, at the end of the Tokyo Round. The title of the language is the *"Enabling Clause,"* or more formally, the *Decision on Differential and More Favourable Treatment, Reciprocity and Fuller Participation of Developing Countries. See* B.I.S.D. (26th Supp.) 203–05 (1980).

The first Paragraph of the *Enabling Clause* indicates any contracting party (WTO Member) may accord better treatment to a less developed country than to a developed country. Therein lies the permanent waiver from the MFN obligation. Paragraph 2 of the *Enabling Clause* explains the scope of that waiver, containing an itemized list bespeaks a broad scope indeed — from tariff preferences, to non-tariff measures, and from regional to multilateral arrangements.

Notably, Paragraph 5 of the *Enabling Clause* is all about non-reciprocity. It is a reincarnation of GATT Article XXXVI:8 and *Ad Article XXXVI, Paragraph 8.* Paragraph 6 amplifies the non-reciprocity expectation, offering more details. Two of the final three Paragraphs of the *Enabling Clause* embody familiar themes. Paragraph 7 contains broad language about supporting the objectives of GATT vis-à-vis poor countries, and Paragraph 9 (like GATT Article XXXVIII) is about collaboration on trade and development issues.

Paragraph 8 of the *Enabling Clause* makes an important distinction among Third World, or less developed, countries, namely, between developing and least developed countries. Without putting countries into one or the other category, Paragraph 8 calls special attention to the least developed countries. They are, in effect, the poorest countries in the Third World, and generally have a *per capita* Gross National Product (GNP) of less than one United States dollar per day. The distinction between developing and least developed contracting parties does not exist in GATT. But, following Paragraph 8, it was used widely in the Uruguay and Doha Rounds, and is common now in WTO texts.

Suggestions for Further Research:

Article:

1.   Yusuf, Abdulqawi A., *"Differential and More Favorable Treatment"*: The *GATT Enabling Clause*, 14 JOURNAL OF WORLD TRADE LAW 488 (1980).

## ENTRY SUMMARY

The document importers use to clear a shipment of goods through customs, *i.e.*, for Harmonized Tariff System (HTS) classification, tariff imposition, and merchandise processing fee purposes. It is distinct from a cargo manifest.

## ENVIRONMENTAL DUMPING

The phenomenon of companies located in a country with lax environmental standards and enforcement benefiting from this context through low production costs, and making environmentally unfriendly goods that are sold in another country. The exports are dumped not in the technical conventional sense of cross-border price discrimination, but in the environmental sense they embody the lax standards and enforcement of the home country — hence, are unfriendly to the environment relative to the like or directly competitive products in the importing country. *See* social dumping.

## ENVIRONMENTAL SIDE AGREEMENT

The 1993 *North American Agreement on Environmental Cooperation* (associated with *NAFTA*), also sometimes abbreviated as the *"NAAEC."* The *North American Agreement on Environmental Cooperation*, one of two side agreements to the *North American Free Trade Agreement* (*NAFTA*) — the other being the *Labor Side Agreement* — was signed by Canada, Mexico, and the United States in August 1993. It entered into force on 1 January 1994, like the rest of *NAFTA*. The Figure below sets out the institutions of the *Environmental Side Agreement*.

The NAAEC was developed to support the environmental provisions of *NAFTA* by establishing a level playing field with a view to avoiding trade distortions and promoting environmental cooperation. The key objectives of the *NAAEC* are to promote sustainable development, encourage pollution prevention policies and practices, and enhance compliance with environmental laws and regulations. The *NAAEC* also promotes transparency and public participation in the development and improvement of environmental laws and policies.

The *NAAEC* requires that each Party ensure its laws provide for high levels of environmental protection without lowering standards to attract investment. Each Party agrees to enforce effectively its environmental laws through the use of inspectors, monitoring compliance and pursuing the necessary legal means to seek appropriate remedies for violations. Each Party must also provide a report on the state of its environment, develop environmental emergency preparedness measures, promote environmental education, assess environmental impacts, and promote the use of economic instruments. Parties may also appoint National Advisory Committees composed of private sector representatives to assist in implementing the Agreement domestically.

Neither the *Environmental* nor the *Labor Side Agreement* mandates that each Party upgrade its environmental laws to reflect internationally-recognized rules or standards. However, in the summer 2007, the United States Congress reached with the White House an agreement that certain free trade agreements (FTAs) would move beyond the "effective enforcement of existing laws" approach to a requirement that FTA parties implement internationally agreed-upon levels of protection.

FIGURE:

## *NAFTA Environmental Side Agreement Institutions*

---

**COMMISSION FOR ENVIRONMENTAL COOPERATION (CEC)**

- Comprised of the Ministerial Council, Secretariat, and Advisory Committee.
- In Montreal.

---

**Council**

- Consists of the United States Administrator for the Environmental Protection Agency, the Canadian Minister of the Environment, and the Mexican Secretary for Social Development.

- As the governing body of the CEC, the Council is responsible for:
— overseeing all CEC operations
— selecting the Executive Director of the Secretariat
— creating committees or working groups, as necessary.

- Supposed to meet at least once a year.

---

**Joint Public Advisory Committee**

- Comprised of 15 members, 5 appointed from each *NAFTA* Party.

- Responsible for:
— advising the Council
— providing technical information to the Secretariat.

- Supposed to meet at least once a year, at the time of the Council's regular session.

---

**Secretariat**

- Led by an Executive Director.
- Responsible for providing technical, administrative, and operational support to the Council and any committees or groups established by the Council.

---

*In addition to the above Tri-National Organizations:*

A November 1993 agreement between the United States and Mexico establishes 2 bilateral organizations:

- **Border Environment Cooperation Commission (BECC)**, in Ciudad Juarez (Mexico), responsible for assisting border states in both countries to design and finance environmental infrastructure projects in the border region.

- **North American Development Bank (NADBank)**, in San Antonio, responsible for financing environmental projects certified by the BECC, and for providing support for community adjustment and investment projects.

Suggestions for Further Research:

Book:

1. VRANES, ERICH, TRADE AND THE ENVIRONMENT — FUNDAMENTAL ISSUES IN INTERNATIONAL LAW, WTO LAW, AND LEGAL THEORY (2009).

Articles:

1. Chakraborty, Pavel, *Effect of Environmental Standards on India's Market Access Concerns: A Case Study of Marine and Agricultural Products*, 12 ASIA PACIFIC JOURNAL OF ENVIRONMENTAL LAW 85–116 (2009).

2. Diaz, Leticia M. & Barry Hart Dubner, *Environmental Damage and the Destruction of Life — Problems that Add a New Balancing Dimension to International Port Access vs. Efficient Trade Under International Law*, 10 BARRY LAW REVIEW 1–23 (2008).

3. Fuller, Gregory H., Comment, *Economic Warlords: How De Facto Federalism Inhibits China's Compliance with International Trade Law and Jeopardizes Global Environmental Initiatives*, 75 TENNESSEE LAW REVIEW 545–576 (2008).

4. Gaines, Sanford E., *Environmental Protection in Regional Trade Agreements: Realizing the Potential*, 28 SAINT LOUIS UNIVERSITY PUBLIC LAW REVIEW 253–271 (2008).

5. Gentile, Dominic A., Note, *International Trade and the Environment: What is the Role of the WTO?*, 20 FORDHAM ENVIRONMENTAL LAW REVIEW 197–232 (2009).

6. Gresser, Edward, *Labor and Environment in Trade Since NAFTA: Activists Have Achieved Less, and More, Than They Realize*, 45 WAKE FOREST LAW REVIEW 491–525 (2010).

7. Hall, Noah D., *Protecting Freshwater Resources in the Era of Global Water Markets: Lessons Learned from Bottled Water*, 13 UNIVERSITY OF DENVER WATER LAW REVIEW 1–54 (2009).

8. Hassanien, Mohamed R., *Greening the Middle East: The Regulatory Model of Environmental Protection in the United States — Oman Free Trade Agreement, A Legal Analysis of Chapter 17*, 23 GEORGETOWN INTERNATIONAL ENVIRONMENTAL LAW REVIEW 465–511 (2011).

9. Ingelson, Allan & Lincoln Mitchell, *NAFTA, the Mining Law of 1872, and Environmental Protection*, 51 NATURAL RESOURCES JOURNAL 261–285 (2011).

10. Kapterian, Gisele, *A Critique of WTO Jurisprudence on "Necessity,"* 59 INTERNATIONAL & COMPARATIVE LAW QUARTERLY 89–127 (2010).

11. Knox, John H., *The Neglected Lessons of the NAFTA Environmental Regime*, 45 WAKE FOREST LAW REVIEW 391–424 (2010).

12. Lopez, Matthew L., Student Article, *The Effects of Free Trade on the Environment: Conserving the Environment While Maintaining Increased Levels of Economic Prosperity for Developing Countries*, 3 PHOENIX LAW REVIEW 701–728 (2010).

13. Markell, David, *The Role of Spotlighting Procedures in Promoting Citizen Participation, Transparency, and Accountability*, 45 WAKE FOREST LAW REVIEW 425–467 (2010).

14. Schmidt, Andrea R., Note, *A New Trade Policy for America: Do Labor and Environmental Provisions in Trade Agreements Serve Social Interests or Special Interests?*, 19 INDIANA INTERNATIONAL & COMPARATIVE LAW REVIEW 167–201 (2009).

15. Shih, Wen-chen, *Conflicting Jurisdictions Over Disputes Arising from the Application of Trade-Related Environmental Measures*, 8 RICHMOND JOURNAL OF GLOBAL LAW & BUSINESS 351–396 (2009).

16. Studer, Isabel, *The NAFTA Side Agreements: Toward A More Cooperative Approach?*, 45 WAKE FOREST LAW REVIEW 469–490 (2010).

17. Wold, Chris, *Evaluating NAFTA and the Commission for Environmental Cooperation: Lessons for Integrating Trade and Environment in Free Trade Agreements*, 28 SAINT LOUIS UNIVERSITY PUBLIC LAW REVIEW 201–252 (2008).

18. Wold, Chris, *Taking Stock: Trade's Environmental Scorecard After Twenty Years of "Trade and Environment,"* 45 WAKE FOREST LAW REVIEW 319–354 (2010).

## EP

Export Price. A term associated with calculation of a dumping margin in antidumping (AD) cases.

Export Price is the price at which a foreign company sells an allegedly dumped product in an importing country where the sale to an unrelated American buyer is made before the product is imported into the United States. Under pre-Uruguay Round American AD law, Export Price was called "Purchase Price."

## EPA (FIRST MEANING)

United States Environmental Protection Agency.

The EPA is an agency of the federal government charged with protecting the environment: air, water, and land. It began operation on 2 December 1970, created by President Richard M. Nixon through Executive Order.

## EPA (SECOND MEANING)

Economic Partnership Agreement.

The term "EPA" is used by a number of countries, including Japan, to connote its special trade agreements, which loosely also are called "Free Trade Agreements" (FTAs) or "Regional Trade Agreements" (RTAs).

A Table in Annex C presents detailed data on Japan's EPAs.

The United States faults many EPAs for not being true FTAs in that they omit substantial economic sectors (*e.g.*, agriculture), or portions thereof (*e.g.*, exempt autos and auto parts from duty-free treatment on industrial products), or have protracted periods in which trade is liberalized. In other words, the United States tends to eschew the "EPA" label, on the ground that EPAs are less ambitious, from a free trade perspective, than FTAs. Of course, that critique masks the provisions of FTAs that actually manage rather than liberate trade.

The American critique suggests some EPAs may not comport with the requirements of GATT Article XXIV, namely, the requirement in Article XXIV:8 that "substantially all trade" be covered, and perhaps also the requirement in Article XXIV:5 that the accord not impose "higher or more restrictive" measures against trade. These points are noted in the Table.

Prior to October 2002, five of the top 30 economies in the world were not parties to an FTA. Those five economies were China, Hong Kong, Japan, Korea, and Taiwan. The lack of involvement of Japan in FTAs centered around the country's argument that FTAs went against the spirit of the General Agreement on Tariffs and Trade (GATT), in that attention dedicated to FTAs undermined any focus on the multilateral trading system (even though, of course, FTAs are contemplated by GATT Article XXIV).[182] Traditionally, since its accession to GATT, the trade policy of Japan has been steadfastly multilateral.

However, without participating in FTAs, Japan found itself falling behind and unable to compete with other Asian countries, especially China. Furthermore, in other parts of the world significant trade agreements came into force, including the *North American Free Trade Area (NAFTA)*, the *Southern Common Market (MERCOSUR)*, the *Central European Free Trade Area (CETRA)*, and the *ASEAN Free Trade Area (AFTA)*. Japan needed to change its strategy or risk being unable to secure access to markets throughout the world on the same preferential terms that other Asian countries had obtained through their FTAs.

The problem Japan faced became all the clearer as the Doha Round, launched in November 2001, ground on to a halt, *i.e.*, repeated collapses in the Round made it clear Japan could not rely on a new multilateral trade round to secure access to important export markets. So, for Japan, entry into EPAs has marked a watershed in its foreign trade policy.

Pursuant to GATT Article XXIV, World Trade Organization (WTO) rules do allow countries to enter into FTAs. But, that Article requires an FTA to include "substantially all products."[183] The understanding of "substantially all" is interpreted as more than 90 percent of total imports should be covered in the agreements.[184]

---

[182] Hatakeyama Noboru, *Short History of Japan's Movement to FTAs*, JOURNAL OF JAPANESE TRADE & INDUSTRY (November/December 2002), at 24.

[183] GATT Article XXIV.8(b).

[184] Hatakeyama Noboru, *A Short History of Japan's Movement to FTAs (Part 4)*, JOURNAL OF JAPANESE TRADE & INDUSTRY (May/June 2003), at 36.

As early as 1998, Japan began exploring the idea of bilateral trade. As a result of a meeting between then Chairman and CEO of the Japan External Trade Organization (JETRO), Hatakeyama Noboru, and then Mexican Commerce and Industry Minister, Herminio Blanco, the Japanese Ministry of International Trade and Industry (MITI, now Ministry of Economy, Trade and Industry (METI)), Japan established a study team on FTAs. The team produced a report that favored a dual track trade policy, whereby Japan would purse FTAs, while remaining active in the WTO.[185]

However, it was not until 2002 that Japan officially implemented its new approach to FTAs. In that year, the *Japan — Singapore Economic Partnership Agreement (JSEPA)* entered into force. It was the first of many FTAs for Japan. (The JSEPA also evinced a change in Singaporean trade policy, akin to that of Japan, in putting greater emphasis on FTAs given concerns about competition from China and stagnation in the Doha Round.)

Japan continued expanding its new trade policy with the *Association of South East Asian Nations (ASEAN) FTA*. The 2008 *ASEAN FTA* is not only a comprehensive trade agreement with multiple states, but also follows a "double track" approach in which Japan negotiated bilaterally with the individual countries and the region as a whole.

Some additional features of Japan's *EPA* policy are noteworthy:

- Agriculture —

  Japan is the world's largest agricultural importer. Often, it is adamant about protecting its farming sector in FTAs, mostly through excluding rice and other sensitive agricultural sectors from tariff reduction or elimination. Farm lobbies in Japan routinely and strongly oppose FTAs and, therefore, oppose deregulation or opening of the farm market. They argue such moves would lead to a reduction in farm produce output and a loss of billions of dollars for the Japanese farming industry.[186]

  However, such reluctance in opening the agricultural sector seriously restricts Japan FTA negotiations. For example, during negotiations with Mexico, talks were stalled completely in October 2003, because of Japanese reluctance to open its farm markets. It was not until Japan made concessions on certain sensitive farm products, namely, agreeing to open its market to key Mexican products such as pork and orange juice, that a trade agreement was reached.[187]

---

[185] Hatakeyama Noboru, *Short History of Japan's Movement to FTAs*, JOURNAL OF JAPANESE TRADE & INDUSTRY (November/December 2002), at 25.

[186] Toshio Aritake, *Japan to Lose $107 Billion in Exports Unless It Signs More FTAs, METI Says*, 27 International Trade Reporter (BNA) 1641 (28 October 2010).

[187] Martin Fackler, *Mexico First, How a free-trade agreement with Mexico could help Japan compete for Asian partners*, FAR EASTERN ECONOMIC REVIEW (1 April 2004) at 20.

- Competitive Imperialism and China —

  Once again, it was the pressure of China as a rising market that pushed Japan to build trade relationships, even when that included overruling objections from powerful farmers' groups. As Japan continues to negotiate FTAs, it seems inevitable those FTAs will include concessions on sensitive agricultural products, without which FTA talks cannot move forward. Here, then, may be an instance of competitive imperialism.

- Taiwan —

  While the number of Japan's FTAs is increasing, the country also is looking towards other international legal accords to boost growth, which of course has been sluggish in Japan for decades. For example, on 22 September 2011, Japan and Taiwan signed the "Arrangement between the Association of East Asian Relations and the Interchange Association for the Mutual Cooperation on the Liberalization, Promotion and Protection of Investment."[188] This Arrangement, the first between Japan and Taiwan, is an investment pact that applies to investors and their investments.

  Under the pact, a Taiwanese company has the same benefits as a domestic Japanese counterpart when investing in Japan, and *vice versa*. The pact also broadens investment protection to include technology, intellectual property rights (IP), and security. Officials consider the Arrangement a first step towards a more comprehensive FTA.

  Furthermore, the pact offers Japan the opportunity to enter the Chinese market. That is because duties on Taiwanese goods exported to China have been lowered under the *Economic Cooperation Framework Agreement* (*ECFA*), to which China and Taiwan are parties. Japan's need to compete with China thereby can be met, while steering through the thicket of political concerns held by China about dealing directly with Taiwan, and economic concerns held by many Japanese constituencies about opening domestic markets to China.[189]

*Suggestions for Further Research:*

Articles:

1. Lat, Tanya Karina A., Note, *Testing the Limits of GATT Article XX(b): Toxic Waste Trade, Japan's Economic Partnership Agreements, and the WTO*, 21 GEORGETOWN INTERNATIONAL ENVIRONMENTAL LAW REVIEW 367–393 (2009).

2. Ocran, Matthew Kofi, & Charles K.D., Adjasi, *Trade Liberalisation and Poverty: Empirical Evidence from Household Surveys in Ghana*, 8 JOURNAL OF INTERNATIONAL TRADE LAW & POLICY number 1, 40–59 (2009).

---

[188] The English version of the *Arrangement* was signed by Taiwan and Japan, 22 September 2011, *posted at* www.moea.gov.tw/TJI/main/content/wHandMenuFile. ashx?menu_id=3615.

[189] Yu-Tzu Chiu, *Taiwan Legislature Expected to Approve Investment Pact with Japan by Year's-End*, 28 International Trade Reporter (BNA) 1624 (6 October 2011).

3.   Turniov, Anna, *Free Trade Agreements in the World Trade Organization: The Experience of East Asia and the Japan–Mexico Economic Partnership Agreement*, 25 UCLA Pacific Basin Law Journal 336–364 (2008).

## EPA (THIRD MEANING)

Economic Partnership Agreement with the European Union (EU).

The *Lomé Convention*, and its successor, the *Cotonou Convention*, are examples of EPAs the EU maintains with poor countries — in the case of those Conventions, with the African, Caribbean, and Pacific (ACP) countries.

Through EPAs, the EU grants preferential treatment to certain products, under certain conditions, originating in poor countries and exported into the EU. In 2003, the EU commenced negotiations with the ACP on a successor agreement to the *Cotonou Convention*. The negotiations were to have finished by year-end 2007, with the new accord to enter into force in 2008.

However, even as negotiations came to a close, there were criticisms of the new EPA. The National Workers Union (NWU) in Jamaica claims the agreement will place Jamaica at a disadvantage, negatively affecting the lives of workers while benefitting only Europe and not Jamaica. Even so, the Jamaican government stated they intended to sign the final draft of the EPA.[190] Guyana sided with the NWU of Jamaica in their criticism of the EPA. Guyana felt the EU negotiated in "bad faith," and that the country was "bullied" into the agreement.

While criticism is high, there are those who support the EPA, such as the Dominican Republic. Supporters do not want to forgo new market opportunities, and denounce resistance as a product of protectionist measures that have existed for "too long."[191]

## ESCAPE CLAUSE

A term that can refer specifically to Section 201 of the United States *Trade Act of 1974*, as amended, or to GATT Article XIX. The Escape Clause permits remedial action against fairly traded foreign products. The criteria for invoking Article XIX are listed therein, and in the WTO *Agreement on Safeguards*. They are largely tracked — but not verbatim — in Section 201. The more generic term for Escape Clause relief, as the name of the WTO accord suggests, is a "safeguard."

The general safeguard remedy — that is, the Escape Clause, and its multilateral analog condoned by GATT Article XIX and the WTO *Agreement on Safeguards* — is not the only kind of trade remedy against fairly traded

---

[190] Radio Jamaica, *EPA, worst thing since slavery — NWU, posted at*, www.bilaterals. org/article.php3?id_article=13063.

[191] *See* Canute James, *Guyana accuses Europe of bullying in trade deal talks*, FINANCIAL TIMES, 23 July 2008, at 7.

imports. The Table below distinguishes the general safeguard remedy under GATT Article XIX and the *Safeguards Agreement* from two other noteworthy safeguards: (1) the Special Safeguard (SSG) in Article 5 of the WTO *Agreement on Agriculture*, and (2) the Special Safeguard Mechanism (SSM) proposed during the Doha Round.[192]

TABLE:

## COMPARISONS AND CONTRASTS AMONG DIFFERENT KINDS OF SAFEGUARDS

| *Issue* | *General Safeguard under GATT Article XIX, WTO Agreement on Safeguards, and United States Escape Clause* | *SSG under WTO Agreement on Agriculture Article 5* | *SSM discussed in Doha Round* |
|---|---|---|---|
| *Scope:* <br><br> What products are covered? | All products, both agricultural and industrial. | Only agricultural products that have been tarified in the Uruguay Round, *i.e.*, farm goods on which non-tariff barriers have been converted to tariffs under Article 4 of the *Agreement on Agriculture*. No other agricultural products, and no industrial products, are covered. | All agricultural products, but not industrial products. |
| *Usage:* <br><br> Which WTO Members are entitled to invoke the safeguard? | All Members. | All Members, if they have made the appropriate designation in their tariff schedules. | Only developing and least developed countries. Developed countries are ineligible. |

---

[192] *See* World Trade Organization, *An Unofficial Guide to Agricultural Safeguards — GATT, Old Agricultural (SSG) and New Mechanism (SSM)*, 5 August 2008, posted on the WTO website, www.wto.org.

**TABLE (Continued)**

| Issue | General Safeguard under GATT Article XIX, WTO Agreement on Safeguards, and United States Escape Clause | SSG under WTO Agreement on Agriculture Article 5 | SSM discussed in Doha Round |
|---|---|---|---|
| **Legal Criteria:** What triggers the safeguard? | Verbal formula: Increased imports (surge), causation, and injury or threat of injury. | Arithmetic formula: Increased imports (surge), or price decline, *i.e.*, a volume trigger or a price trigger. | Arithmetic formula: Increased imports (surge), or price decline, *i.e.*, a volume trigger or a price trigger. Use volume or price data from previous 3 years. |
| **Relief:** What is the remedy? | Tariff increase or quantitative restriction. | Tariff increase or quantitative restriction. | Tariff increase or quantitative restriction. |
| **Constraints:** What limits are there on using the safeguard? | 4 year time limit, renewable for up to one 4 year period (8 year total). Must negotiate compensation with affected exporting countries. | Tarification and designation in tariff schedule. | For both volume-based (import surge) and price-based trigger, SSM cannot be used on a product that also is subject to a different type of safeguard. For volume-based price trigger (import surge), there would be: (1) a limit on the percentage of products that could be subject to an SSM in a given year; |

**TABLE (Continued)**

| Issue | General Safeguard under GATT Article XIX, WTO Agreement on Safeguards, and United States Escape Clause | SSG under WTO Agreement on Agriculture Article 5 | SSM discussed in Doha Round |
|---|---|---|---|
| | | | (2) a ceiling on the tariff that could be imposed at or above the pre-Doha Round bound duty rate, and (3) a minimum surge required if the tariff imposed exceeded the pre-Doha Round bound duty rate. |
| **Sunset:** Does the safeguard expire? | No, permanent. | Possible expiry or reduction via a Doha Round agreement. | Undecided. |

*Suggestions for Further Research:*

Book Chapters:

1.   Tumlir, Jan, *Emergency Protection against Sharp Increases in Imports, in* IN SEARCH OF A NEW WORLD ECONOMIC ORDER 260, 262 (H. Corbet & R. Jackson eds., 1974).

Articles:

1.   Derrick, Christopher W., Note, *The Evolution of the Escape Clause: The United States' Quest for Effective Relief from Fairly Traded Imports*, 13 NORTH CAROLINA JOURNAL OF INTERNATIONAL LAW AND COMMERCIAL REGULATION 347 (1988).

2.   Kennedy, Kevin C., *Presidential Authority Under Section 337, Section 301, and the Escape Clause: The Case for Less Discretion*, 20 CORNELL INTERNATIONAL LAW JOURNAL 127, 129–30, 158–60 (1987).

3.   Liebman, Benjamin H. & Kasaundra M. Tomlin, *Safeguards and Retaliatory Threats*, 51 JOURNAL OF LAW & ECONOMICS 351–376 (2008).

4.   Maltese, Thomas P., *Congress's Causation Conundrum: Rethinking the United States's Approach to Escape Clause Actions*, 17 KANSAS JOURNAL OF LAW & PUBLIC POLICY 520–541 (2008).

5.   Nicely, Matthew R. & David T. Hardin, *Article 8 of the WTO Safeguards Agreement: Reforming the Right to Rebalance*, 23 ST. JOHN'S JOURNAL OF LEGAL COMMENTARY 699–763 (2008).

6.   Rosenthal, Paul C. & Robin H. Gilbert, *The 1988 Amendments to Section 201: It Isn't Just for Import Relief Anymore*, 20 LAW & POLICY IN INTERNATIONAL BUSINESS 403, 415 (1989).

7.   Sykes, Alan O., *Protectionism as a "Safeguard": A Positive Analysis of the GATT "Escape Clause" with Normative Speculations*, 58 UNIVERSITY OF CHICAGO LAW REVIEW 255, 264 (1991).

## ESP

Exporter's Sales Price, now called "Constructed Export Price," or "CEP" for short.

"Exporter's Sales Price," or "ESP" was the term used in pre-Uruguay Round American antidumping law to refer to a situation in which allegedly dumped merchandise has not yet been sold by a foreign company to an unrelated American buyer at the time the merchandise is imported into the United States (*e.g.*, it is sold to a related party). "Exporter's Sales Price was replaced by "Constructed Export Price" as of 1 January 1995.

## ESTIMATED ANTIDUMPING DUTY DEPOSIT RATE

Also called the Cash Deposit Rate.

*See* Administrative Review, Retrospective assessment.

## EU

The European Union (formerly EC), created pursuant to the *Treaty of Maastricht* of 1992.

Under the 2007 *Treaty of Lisbon Amending the Treaty on European Union and the Treaty Establishing the European Community* (done at Lisbon, 13 December 2007), which entered into force on 1 December 2009, the EU replaced and succeeded the EC as of that date of entry into force. The Council of the European Union and the Commission of the European Communities informed the WTO of this fact on 29 November 2009 through a Verbal Note (WT/L/779).

In the WTO, EU member states each retain their individual seats. At most WTO meetings, the member states are represented by one voice — the EU Trade Commissioner, based in Brussels. For some meetings — most notably, the WTO Budget Committee — each member state represents itself. On matters related to voting, the EU votes as a bloc, with a single vote, and cannot have more votes than the total number of member states.

There are 27 EU member states (as of December 2007). They include Austria, Belgium, Finland, France, Denmark, Germany, Greece, Ireland, Italy, Luxembourg, Netherlands, Portugal, Spain, Sweden, and United Kingdom. With the introduction of monetary union on 1 January 1999, when the euro (?) was launched, and 1 January 2002, when the euro entered into everyday circulation, the EU became even more integrated economically than a "textbook" customs union (CU).

Effective 1 May 2004, pursuant to the Fourth Enlargement, the EU assumed 10 new member states:

- Czech Republic
- Cyprus
- Estonia
- Hungary
- Latvia

- Lithuania
- Malta
- Poland
- Slovak Republic
- Slovenia

As of 1 January 2007, two additional states became EU members — Bulgaria and Romania.

Possibly the most important issue facing the EU is further enlargement. That is because enlargement is inextricably linked to the question of European identity. What is "Europe," and what is the "European project"? The question is most poignant with respect to the application of Turkey for EU membership, but it also arises in respect of potential candidates in Eastern Europe and the Southern Mediterranean. Of course, expansion is also about money, entailing complicated questions of extension of Common Agricultural Policy (CAP) benefits, and in some instances human rights.

The EU is undertaking enlargement not only in the strict sense of expanded membership, but also in the more flexible — but nonetheless ambitious — sense of entry into free trade agreements (FTAs). It is seeking a free trade zone around the Mediterranean, and has negotiated preferential trading arrangements with Morocco, the Palestinian Authority, and Tunisia.

The EU also has an arrangement with Israel, but it has been a victim of Middle East politics. The EU grants preferential tariffs to goods "made in Israel," which the EU interprets to mean Israel's internationally recognized borders. In other words, excluded are Jewish settlements in the West Bank, Gaza strip, and Golan Heights. In March 2000, deputies in the European Parliament produced documentary evidence that exports of carpets, cosmetics, fruit, and wine originated in the settlements. But, Jewish settlers are not the only groups the EU says are flouting the rule of origin. Israel does not recognize the EU's separate trade agreement with the Palestinian Authority. Palestinian exporters often find it easier to ensure their products get preferential treatment by stamping them "Made in Israel" and shipping them through Israeli exporters. The issue presents the EU with a dilemma. On the one hand, the EU does not want European taxpayers to finance the settlements through preferred tariff treatment. On the other hand, the EU wants to play a larger political role in the Middle East peace process, somewhat more on par with the United States, and hence is reluctant to raise the issue too forcefully with either the Israelis or Palestinians. Perhaps the most significant FTA the EU has negotiated is with Mexico.

Regarding monetary union, the following EU members have adopted the common currency, the euro:

- Austria
- Belgium
- Cyprus
- Finland
- Portugal

- France
- Germany
- Greece
- Ireland
- Spain

- Italy
- Luxembourg
- Malta
- Netherlands
- Slovenia

Two countries — ironically, both part of the First Enlargement in January 1973 — opted out of the monetary union. They are the United Kingdom and Denmark. Conversely, Cyprus and Malta were the latest to adopt the euro, each as of 1 January 2008.

The Table below summarizes the structure of the institutions of the EU. The most important decision-making institutions in the EU, which have legislative power, are the Council of the European Union, called the "EU Council," or just "Council," and the European Commission, known simply as the "Commission." These bodies make three kinds of rules — "Regulations," "Directives," and "Decisions." There are critical differences among these categories, as a subsequent Table below summarizes.

**TABLE:**

**STRUCTURE OF EU INSTITUTIONS**

***(Institutions specified in Treaty of Rome, Part Five, Articles 137–198)*[193]**

| Organization (website address) | |
| --- | --- |
| *Membership* | *Function* |
| **EU Parliament** (http://www.europarl.europa.eu) | |
| Members of European Parliament (MEPs) 732 total (later expanded to 736) (Membership as of December 2006) <br> Belgium 24 <br> Czech Republic 24 <br> Denmark 14 <br> Germany 99 <br> Estonia 6 <br> Greece 24 | Acts as a elected body of member representatives from various political parties, and provides guidance on legislation through opinions that are issued, cooperative amendments to council or commission proposed legislation, and a "co-decision" procedure which allows the Parliament to veto Council legislation that it opposes. |

---

[193] Adapted from European Union website, http://europa.eu.

TABLE (Continued)

| EU Parliament (http://www.europarl.europa.eu) | | |
|---|---|---|
| Spain | 54 | Important additions were made to the trade powers of the Parliament through the Lisbon Treaty, which took effect on 1 December 2009. The *Lisbon Treaty* took almost 10 years for each of the 27 EU members to approve, and replaces the *Nice Treaty*, which had been a legal foundation for the EU. Negotiations on the *Lisbon Treaty* began in 2002 with a constitutional convention. But, approval was delayed after Dutch and French voters rejected it in referenda. Negotiators then bundled and packaged various elements into the *Lisbon Treaty*. |
| France | 78 | |
| Ireland | 13 | |
| Italy | 78 | |
| Cyprus | 6 | |
| Latvia | 9 | |
| Lithuania | 13 | |
| Luxembourg | 6 | |
| Hungary | 24 | |
| Malta | 5 | |
| Netherlands | 27 | |
| Austria | 18 | |
| Poland | 54 | |
| Portugal | 24 | |
| Slovenia | 7 | |
| Slovakia | 14 | |
| Finland | 14 | |
| Sweden | 19 | |
| United Kingdom | 78 | |
| | | Under the *Lisbon Treaty*, the Parliament has the power to approve or veto a trade agreement on a "take it or leave it" basis. That basis is redolent of fast-track legislative procedure in the U.S. Congress. The power applies to any multilateral agreement (*e.g.*, negotiated under the auspices of the WTO), regional or bilateral free trade agreement (FTA) or association agreement, or preferential trade arrangement (PTA) (such as the Generalized System of Preferences (GSP)). |
| | | Further, the *Lisbon Treaty* gives the Parliament veto power over the review of antidumping (AD) regulations. Thus, the Parliament shares decision-making authority on AD with the Council of Ministers. That also is true in respect of changes to the Common Agricultural Policy (CAP) — Parliament has veto power over any plans to reform the CAP. |

**TABLE (Continued)**

| EU Parliament (http://www.euparl.europa.eu) | |
|---|---|
| | Finally, the *Lisbon Treaty* allows the Parliament to make amendments to trade legislation proposed by the European Commission. |
| | Arguably, the *Lisbon Treaty* changes enhance the democratic legitimacy of EU trade policy. But, the enhanced powers of the Parliament come at the cost of authority of national governments. The *Lisbon Treaty* eliminates the ability of a national parliament to veto a trade agreement the EU signs with any other country. |
| **European Commission** (http://ec.europa.eu) Trade specific information (http://ec.europa.eu/trade/) | |
| College of Commissioners made up of one representative from each member state. There are also 26 Directorates-General and nine services which are subdivided into directorates and units. Each Directorate General is represents an industry or activity of the EU and work together to implement the College's decisions. | The European Commission is responsible for implementing common policies, administering the EU budget, and managing programs of the EU. The Commission holds a right of initiative to create legislation. A key function of the commission is the coordination of the EU Common Trade Policy, sanctioned under Article 133 of the TEU. The committee involved is called the "Article 133" Committee and works together with the GAERC Council (see below). |
| | The *Lisbon Treaty* expanded the powers of the Commission to a number of trade-related areas: foreign direct investment (FDI), intellectual property (IP), and services. But, exceptions are culture and language diversity, education, health care, and social policies. |

**TABLE (Continued)**

| Council of the European Union (Council of Ministers) — EU Council (http://www.consilium.europa.eu) | |
|---|---|
| Ministers from member states gather and vote on EU issues- the council meets in 9 configurations — General Affairs and External Relations (GAERC), Economic and Financial Affairs (Ecofin), Cooperation in the fields of Justice and Home Affairs (JHA), Employment, Social Policy, Health and Consumer Affairs (EPSCO), Competitiveness (made up of Internal Market, Industry, Research), Transport, Telecom and Energy (TTE), Agriculture and Fisheries (Common Agricultural Policy & Common Fisheries Policy), Environment, Education Youth and Culture (EYC). | The EU Council is the main decision making body of the EU. Ministers from a specific area of responsibility (agriculture, foreign affairs, finance, transportation, etc) will meet and vote on an issue. The council acts in conjunction with the European Parliament or in conjunction with the European Commission to create laws, manage the budget, and formalize any international agreements.<br><br>Under the *Lisbon Treaty*, the Council of Ministers has co-decision making authority with the Parliament on AD regulations and the CAP. |
| **European Council** (http://consilium.europa.eu/) | |
| Heads of State from Member states. | As another form of the EU Council, the heads of state meet to discuss and coordinate political issues within the EU and direct the EU Common Foreign and Security Policy. |
| **Court of Justice of the European Communities** (http://curia.europa.eu/) | |
| **Court of Justice**<br>27 Judges (as of 2007), 8 Advocates General appointed by the governments of the member states for a six-year renewable term. Judges elect a President of the Court for a three-year renewable term. Advocates General provide opinions to cases assigned to them by the Court. The registrar acts as the secretary general of the Court under the President's direction. | **Court of Justice** Jurisdiction covers matters such as: References for preliminary rulings (preliminary review of EU or national legislation), Actions for failure to fulfill obligations (member state obligations under EU law), Actions for annulment (of a law), Actions for failure to act (by EU institutions), Appeals from the Court of the First Instance and Reviews of appeals from the Civil Service Tribunal to the Court of First Instance. |

**TABLE (Continued)**

| Court of Justice of the European Communities (http://curia.europa.eu/) | |
|---|---|
| **Court of First Instance** The Court of the First Instance is made up of judges one from each member state. The Judges appoint a President and a registrar. There are no Advocates General. | **Court of First Instance** Jurisdiction includes EU Institution acts against legal or natural persons, Member state complaints against the EU Commission, member states against the EU Council regarding State aid, Dumping Measures, Compensation actions for damage caused by EU Institutions or staff, Contract actions where the contract specifies the Court of First Instance, trademark issues and appeals from the Civil Service Tribunal. |
| **European Union Civil Service Tribunal** 1 President (elected amongst the Judges to a renewable three-year term), 7 Judges appointed by the EU Council for a renewable 6-year term. | **European Union Civil Service Tribunal** Jurisdiction over disputes between government employees and their employers (communities and their servants). |
| **European Court of Auditors** (http://eca.europa.eu/) | |
| Members of the Court are appointed to a 6-year term by the EU Council and one is selected from each member state. Members elect a President of the Court for a renewable three-year term. | European Court of Auditors reviews, manages, and publishes reports on how the European Union spends funds allocated in its budget. |
| **European Economic and Social Committee** (http://www.eesc.europa.eu/) | |
| 343 members- members are nominated from economic and social interest groups by member state governments and appointed by the EU Council for a renewable four year term. The members fall into one of three categories: employers, employees, and various interests (farmers, artisans, non-profit or-ganizations, scientific and academic community, small business, family associations, and persons with disabilities are included) | A "socio-occupational" advisory panel to the EU Council, Parliament, and Commission on issues affecting the workers of Europe. The EESC was founded in the Treaty of Rome 1957, and affirmed and reinforced in the Single European Act, The Maastricht Treaty, The Amsterdam Treaty and the Treaty of Nice. |

**TABLE (Continued)**

| Committee of the Regions (http://www.cor.europa.eu) | |
|---|---|
| 317 Members and 317 alternates appointed by the EU Council to four-year terms.<br>10 areas of obligatory consultation:<br>• economic and social cohesion<br>• trans-European networks in the field of transport, energy and telecommunications<br>• public health<br>• education and youth<br>• culture<br>• employment<br>• social policy<br>• environment<br>• vocational training<br>• transport. | A political assembly providing local and regional authorities with a voice within the EU. Formed in 1994 (by the Maastricht Treaty), in response to a large amount of EU legislation focused at the local level (3/4 of all EU legislation is implemented at the local and regional level) and to give the public a voice by involving the governments closest to the citizenry. |
| **European Investment Bank** (http://www.bei.org/) | |
| Long term financial institution, publicly owned by the member states of the European Union. | Created by the Treaty of Rome, the European Investment Bank provides long term financing for projects within the member states of the EU. Funding includes support for small and medium enterprises, trans-European networks, investments in economic infrastructure, and environmental protection and improvement initiatives. |
| **European Investment Fund** (http://www.eif.org/) | |
| A tripartite group of investors including the European Investment Bank, The European Union through the European Commission, and a number of European based banks and financial institutions. | The EIF provides venture capital financing in venture capital funds and business incubators supporting small and medium sized enterprises (SMEs) (particularly ones in their early stage or technology oriented) and guarantee instruments to financial institutions that provide loans to SMEs. |

Table **(Continued)**

| European Central Bank (http://www.ecb.int/) | |
|---|---|
| The European Central Bank is part of the European System of Central Banks (ESCB) along with the national central banks of the member states. Eurosystem is the provisional name of the ESCB until all EU countries adopt the Euro. | The central bank for the Euro, Europe's single currency. The bank's main task is to maintain price stability of the Euro. The bank maintains monetary policy, foreign exchange operations, portfolio management and operation of payment systems, as well as the production of banknotes and coinage, statistical analysis and international cooperation. |
| **European Ombudsman** (http://www.ombudsman.europa.eu) | |
| European Parliament appoints an ombudsman to investigate reports of maladministration in the European Union bodies and institutions. | Complaints under the purview of the European Ombudsman include: <br> • administrative irregularities <br> • unfairness <br> • discrimination <br> • abuse of power <br> • failure to reply <br> • refusal of information <br> • unnecessary delay |
| **European Data Protection Supervisor** (http://www.edps.eu.int/) | |
| European Parliament and Council appoint a Data Protection Supervisor and Deputy Supervisor for five-year terms each. | The European Data Protection Supervisor (and Deputy Supervisor assisting) ensure protection of EU citizen personal data processed by Community institutions. Each institution has a Data Protection officer which is appointed by the body the officer represents. |
| **Agencies and other bodies** (http://europa.eu/whoiswho/) | |
| European Network and Information Security Agency (ENISA) <br> European Aviation Safety Agency (EASA) <br> European Medicines Agency (EMA) <br> European Agency for the Management of Operational Coordination at the External Borders (Frontex) | Other key agencies are mentioned as they incorporate the EU institutions and bodies not created by the Treaty of Rome but are nonetheless key to the function of the EU. |

TABLE **(Continued)**

| Agencies and other bodies (http://europa.eu/whoiswho/) | |
|---|---|
| European Agency for Reconstruction (EAR) European Agency for Safety and Health at Work (OSHA) European Maritime Safety Agency (EMSA) European Railway Agency (ERA) European Environment Agency (EEA) European Food Safety Authority (EFSA) Translation Centre for bodies of the European Union (CdT) European Centre for Disease Prevention and Control (ECDC) European Centre for the Development of Vocational Training (Cedefop) European Training Foundation (ETF) European Foundation for the Improvement of Living and Working Conditions (Eurofound) European Monitoring Centre for Drugs and Drug Addiction (EMCDDA) European Monitoring Centre on Racism and Xenophobia (EUMC) Community Plant Variety Office (CPVO) Office for Harmonisation in the Internal Market (trade marks and designs) (OHIM) Eurojust European Police Office (Europol) | |

TABLE:

SUMMARY OF DIFFERENCES IN EU LEGISLATIVE INSTRUMENTS

| EU Legislative Instrument | Regulation | Directive | Decision |
|---|---|---|---|
| Generally Applicable? (*i.e.*, binding on all EU member states?) | Yes | No. Binding only on addressee. | No. Binding only on addressee. |
| Binding in its Entirety? | Yes | No Only results to be achieved are binding. Implementation is left to addressee. | Yes. |
| Directly Applicable? (*i.e.*, member states have no choice as to method of implementation?) | Yes | No. | Yes. |

A "Regulation" is generally applicable to all EU member states. It is binding on them in its entircty. The applicability of a Regulation is direct, meaning that authorities at the national level have no discretion as to how the Regulation is to be implemented. A "Directive" is binding on an EU member state to which it is directed. National authorities in the member state to which the Directive is addressed have the discretion to choose the form and method of implementation of the Directive. A "Decision" is binding in its entirety, and directly so, but only on a member state to which the Decision is addressed. Significantly, most EU legislation concerning the CAP is through Regulation.

*Suggestions for Further Research:*

Articles:

1.   Anderer, Carrie E., Note, *Bilateral Investment Treaties and the EU Legal Order: Implications of the Lisbon Treaty*, 35 BROOKLYN JOURNAL OF INTERNATIONAL LAW 851–882 (2010).

2.   Ashiagbor, Diamond, *Embedded Trade Liberalization in Social Policy: Lessons from the European Union?*, 32 COMPARATIVE LABOR LAW & POLICY JOURNAL 373–404 (2011).

3. Cheng, Priscilla T., Note, *Call a Spade a Spade: Barriers to Harmonization and Conflicting Messages in European Union Internet Gambling Policy*, 36 BROOKLYN JOURNAL OF INTERNATIONAL LAW 693–716 (2011).

4. Dounis, Catherine, Note, *Enforcing Intellectual Property Rights via EU Border Regulations: Inhibiting Access to Medicine or Preventing Counterfeit Medicine?*, 36 BROOKLYN JOURNAL OF INTERNATIONAL LAW 717–750 (2011).

5. Eeckhout, Piet, *The Growing Influence of European Union Law*, 33 FORDHAM INTERNATIONAL LAW JOURNAL 1490–1521 (2010).

6. Errico, John, Note, *The WTO in the EU: Unwinding the Knot*, 44 CORNELL INTERNATIONAL LAW JOURNAL 179–208 (2011).

7. Grosse, Ruse-Khan, Thomas Jaeger Henning & Robert Kordic, *The Role of Atypical Acts in EU External Trade and Intellectual Property Policy*, 21 EUROPEAN JOURNAL OF INTERNATIONAL LAW 901–939 (2010).

8. Howse, Robert L. & Jared M. Genser, *Are EU Trade Sanctions on Burma Compatible with WTO Law?*, 29 MICHIGAN JOURNAL OF INTERNATIONAL LAW 165–196 (2008).

9. Jaconiah, Jacob, *The Parallel Importation of Trademarked Goods in the Framework of the Economic Partnership Agreement between the East African Community and the European Union*, 42 IIC: INTERNATIONAL REVIEW OF INTELLECTUAL PROPERTY & COMPETITION LAW 673–697 (2011).

10. Leal-Arcas, Rafael, *The European Union and New Leading Powers: Towards Partnership in Strategic Trade Policy Areas*, 32 FORDHAM INTERNATIONAL LAW JOURNAL 345–416 (2009).

11. Leal-Arcas, Rafael, *European Union — China Trade Relations*, 2 TRADE, LAW AND DEVELOPMENT no. 2, 224–251 (fall 2010).

12. Shan, Wenhua & Sheng Zhang, *The Treaty of Lisbon: Half Way Toward a Common Investment Policy*, 21 EUROPEAN JOURNAL OF INTERNATIONAL LAW 1049–1073 (2010).

## EU — MEXICO FTA

This free trade agreement (FTA) is the first such agreement the European Union (EU) reached with a Latin American country, and the largest FTA ever negotiated by the EU.

On 24 November 1999, the EU and Mexico agreed in principle to an FTA in which tariffs would be phased out on 95 percent of all products traded between them. The deal was signed at an EU summit in Lisbon on 23 March 2000. Negotiations on the FTA began in November 1998 and took nine rounds, and the FTA entered into force on 1 July 2000. (Technically, the provisions on industrial trade entered into force on that day. The remainder of the FTA took effect when the EU member states completed ratification of a 1997 bilateral agreement — the "Economic Partnership, Political Coordination, and Cooperation Agreement," also known as the "Global Agreement" (EPA). The logic is that the FTA builds on the Global Agreement, which was aimed at liberalizing EU — Mexican trade, hence ratification of that Agreement was necessary.)

Many of the trade-liberalizing commitments in the EU — Mexico FTA are dramatic. They tend to take the form of tariff reduction schedules, which typically are asymmetric. For example, the EU agreed to drop all tariffs on industrial goods from Mexico by 2003. The 2003 date was no accident. The EU wanted to achieve parity with the *North American Free Trade Agreement* (*NAFTA*) by then, as that was when the last *NAFTA* tariffs were phased out.

Specifically, 82 percent of Mexico's industrial exports received duty free treatment when the FTA took effect, and the remaining 18 percent will receive duty-free treatment by 1 January 2003. Mexico agreed to phase out duties on industrial goods from the EU by 1 January 2007, with a four stage phase-out schedule: 47 percent when the FTA entered into force; 4.5 percent over a three year period ending 1 January 2003; 5.5 percent by 1 January 2005; and the remaining 43 percent by 1 January 2007. Mexico also agreed to reduce tariffs on the EU's industrial products in the last two stages to no more than five percent *ad valorem* by 2003. This commitment nearly satisfied the EU's goal of *NAFTA* parity — a level playing field for European firms vis-à-vis American and Canadian firms — by 2003.

For one highly significant industry, cars, the agreed-upon phase-out periods were different, but still ambitious. Mexico could export cars to the EU with a 6.9 percent duty in 2000, a 4.6 percent duty in 2001, a 2.3 percent duty in 2002, and duty free as of 1 January 2003. After a transition period ending in 2005, the EU will mandate 60 percent local content in Mexican cars. Mexico agreed to reduce its tariff on EU cars from 20 percent, also in stages. The EU could export cars to Mexico with a 3.3 percent duty on 1 July 2000, a 2.2 percent duty in 2001, a 1.1 percent duty in 2002, and duty free as of 1 January 2003.

The majority of agricultural trade also comes within the ambit of the EU — Mexico FTA. The FTA liberalizes 62 percent of trade in agricultural products. There are four stages for phasing out tariffs: when the FTA entered into force, by 2003, by 2008, and by 2010. Different products are put in different stages, with the sensitive ones being in the last two stages. The two sides pledged to re-examine in 2003 the possible phase out of tariffs on the 38 percent of agricultural products not covered by the FTA. Those products tend to be ones receiving subsidies from the EU, namely, dairy products, grains, meat, sugar, and some fruits and vegetables. Significantly for the EU, the FTA does cover wines, sprits, and olive oil. Mexico agreed to eliminate tariffs on quality wines in 2003, and on table wines in 2008, subject to negotiation of a deal with the EU on the protection of geographic denominations and traditional expressions. In return, the EU agreed to reduce trade on key Mexican agricultural exports — avocados, concentrated orange juice, and cut flowers.

The FTA agreement is not limited to tariff elimination on industrial and agricultural goods. It covers issues of intellectual property (IP), sanitary and phytosanitary (SPS) measures, technical standards, foreign direct investment

(FDI), government procurement, competition policy, dispute resolution, and rules of origin. The latter topic was the most difficult to work out, as the EU did not want Mexican products with significant American or Canadian content to qualify for preferential treatment.

Finally, the accord provides for the progressive liberalization of trade in services — defined to include energy, the environment, telecoms, and tourism — within 10 years. As for financial services, banks and insurances companies from the EU are authorized to operate directly in Mexico, just like their American and Canadian competitors. Only air transport services, audio-visual services, and maritime cabotage are excluded from coverage. A key provision is a standstill commitment to prevent the adoption of new or more discriminatory measures on services trade.

The EU was clever in choosing Mexico as a FTA partner. It is not simply that Mexico has a burgeoning consumer market to which EU companies can market their wares. Nor is it simply that the EU was seeking to reverse export losses during the 1990s that resulted from trade diversion caused by *NAFTA*. (In 1991, the EU's share of total Mexican trade was 10.6 percent. By 1999, it had tumbled to 6.5 percent. Conversely, American exports to Mexico doubled in the late 1990s, and at the turn of the Millennium, about 80 percent of Mexico's trade was with its *NAFTA* partners.) Rather, in addition, Mexico is the only country other than Israel with preferential access to both the American and Canadian markets. In addition, Mexico has free trade accords with several Latin American countries. As a result, Mexico has access to roughly 60 percent of world trade under preferential conditions. Through FDI in Mexico, European businesses gain the same access. Conversely, Mexico stood to gain much from the FTA with the EU, namely, significantly increased trade and investment.

Interestingly, not everyone was happy with the FTA. The Mexican Citizens' Consultation Forum protested the deal. The Forum represents over 180 social groups and trade unions. It decried the fact that the FTA lacked the labor and environmental protections contained in the *NAFTA* side agreements. Some EU groups voiced concerns about Mexico's human rights record.

*Suggestions for Further Research:*

Article:

1. Bronckers, Marco, *From "Direct Effect" to "Muted Dialogue": Recent Developments in the European Courts' Case Law on the WTO and Beyond*, 11 JOURNAL OF INTERNATIONAL ECONOMIC LAW 885–898 (2008).

## EU REACH

*See* REACH.

## EURASIAN ECONOMIC COMMISSION

*See* EEC (Second Meaning).

## EUROPEAN COMMISSION

The body within the European Union (EU) with the exclusive right to submit legislative proposals. Such proposals may be submitted to the European Parliament. Unless the Commission puts forth a legislative proposal, or if it withdraws a proposal it previously advanced, neither the Parliament nor the European Council can take action. The Commission also is responsible for enforcing EU treaties, and implementing decisions by the Council and Parliament.

Each member state has one representative on the Commission. (Before November 2004, the larger EU member states were represented by two Commissioners.) There terms (since 1995) last for five years, and are parallel to the terms of members of the European Parliament. While the member states choose their Commissioners, the Parliament has final say as to their appointment. That is, the Commission cannot be seated without agreement of the Parliament.

## EUROPEAN COUNCIL

Also known as the Council of the European Union (EU).

A critical body within the EU, consisting of a representative from each EU member state at a ministerial level. The Council meets regularly. There are actually several Councils, for different subject areas. They include the General Affairs Council, which is comprised of the Ministers of Foreign Affairs, the Council of the Ministers of Agriculture, and the EcoFin Council, which consists of the Ministers of Economic Affairs and Ministers of Finance. The General Affairs, Agriculture, and EcoFin Councils meet monthly.

Biannually, the European Council meets in which the composition is the President of the European Commission and the heads of governments of the EU member states. Present for a portion of such meetings is the President of the European Parliament. These meetings are designed to address major policy issues and resolve highly contentious disputes.

Meetings of the Council — regardless of their composition — are chaired by a single member state. That member state holds the chair for six months, after which it moves by rotation to another state. Voting in the Council depends on the subject matter. For instance, on Common Agricultural Policy (CAP) issues, most issues are decided by qualified majority.

## EUROPEAN PARLIAMENT

Sitting in Brussels and Strasbourg, the Parliament is empowered to consult and give advice on legislation submitted to it by the European Commission. The Parliament does not have the power to initiate legislation. If it chooses to do so, the Commission, as well as the Council of the European Union, may ignore the Parliament. Yet, that choice on one particular matter might cause the Parliament to refuse to give advice on another matter.

Under the 1997 *Amsterdam Treaty*, the Parliament exercises co-decisional authority with the Council of the European Union on any agricultural policy relating to food law, or on phytosanitary or veterinary measures aimed directly at protecting public health. Representatives to the Parliament are elected by citizens of European Union (EU) states.

# EVOLUTIONARY APPROACH

A term coined by the WTO Appellate Body in the famous 1998 *Turtle–Shrimp* case to describe its approach to dealing with non-trade issues. *See* Appellate Body Report, *United States — Import Prohibition of Certain Shrimp and Shrimp Products*, WT/DS58/AB/R, ¶ 185 (adopted 6 November 1998).

The Appellate Body explained that the concept of sustainable development is manifest in the Preamble to the *Agreement Establishing the World Trade Organization* (*WTO Agreement*). It further explained it uses a balancing test under GATT Article XX to decide whether a trade restriction on allegedly harmful imports is proportionate to the non-trade objective of protecting the environment.

Thus, there is no one, dramatic, final answer to all trade-and-environment cases. Rather, under the evolutionary approach, the Appellate Body deal with the protection of the environment through the application of trade measures on a case-by-case basis, and over time an accretion of precedents develops.

# EXCLUSION CLAUSE

*See NAFTA Exclusion Clause.*

# EXON–FLORIO AMENDMENT

The shorthand expression for Section 721 of the *Defense Production Act of 1950*, as amended. This 1988 law potentially restricts certain proposed foreign direct investment (FDI) transactions into the United States.

As explained by the House Ways and Means Committee:

> The proposed purchase in 1988 of an 80 percent share of Fairchild Semiconductor Corporation by Fujitsu, Ltd. sparked Congressional interest concerning takeovers of American firms by foreign companies which raise national security considerations. Section 5021 of the *Omnibus Trade and Competitiveness Act of 1988* amended title VII of the *Defense Production Act of 1950* [50 U.S.C. App. § 2170] to add provisions (commonly known as "Exon/Florio," the chief Congressional sponsors) because of concerns that the Federal Government lacked specific authority to prevent such acquisitions.

> The provisions authorize the President, after he makes certain findings, to take actions for such time as he considers appropriate to suspend or prohibit any acquisition, merger, or takeover of a person engaged

in interstate commerce in the United States by or with foreign persons so that such control will not threaten to impair the national security. To activate this authority, the President has to find that there is credible evidence that leads him to believe the foreign interest exercising control might take action that threatens to impair the national security and that other laws do not provide adequate and appropriate authority to protect the national security in the matter. The President has to report the findings to the Congress with a detailed explanation.

In making any decision to exercise the authority under this provision, the President may consider such factors as: (1) domestic production needed for projected national defense requirements; (2) the capability and capacity of domestic industries to meet national defense requirements; and (3) the control of domestic industries and commercial activities by foreign citizens as it affects the capability and capacity of the United States to meet the requirements of national security. The standard of review is "national security"; the provision affects only overseas investment flowing into the United States and is not intended to authorize investigations of investments that could not result in foreign control of persons engaged in interstate commerce nor to have any effects on transactions which are outside the realm of national security.

Among the actions available to the President is the ability to suspend a transaction. The President may also seek appropriate relief in the district courts of the United States in order to implement and enforce the provisions, including broad injunctive and equitable relief including, but not limited to divestment relief.[194]

*Suggestions for Further Research:*

Book:

1.   FOLSOM, RALPH H., MICHAEL W. GORDON & JOHN A. SPANOGLE, JR., PRINCIPLES OF INTERNATIONAL BUSINESS TRANSACTIONS, TRADE & ECONOMIC RELATIONS (2005).

Articles:

1.   Carroll, James F.F., Comment, *Back to the Future: Redefining the Foreign Investment and National Security Act's Conception of National Security*, 23 EMORY INTERNATIONAL LAW REVIEW 167–200 (2009).

2.   Cox, Jason, Note, *Regulation of Foreign Direct Investment After the Dubai Ports Controversy: Has the U.S. Government Finally Figured Out How to Balance Foreign Threats to National Security Without Alienating Foreign Companies?*, 34 JOURNAL OF CORPORATION LAW 293–315 (2008).

---

[194] HOUSE COMMITTEE ON WAYS AND MEANS, 109TH CONGRESS, 1ST SESSION, OVERVIEW AND COMPILATION OF U.S. TRADE STATUTES 251 (Committee Print June 2005).

3.  Heath, Jesse, Note, *Strategic Protectionism? National Security and Foreign Investment in the Russian Federation*, 41 GEORGE WASHINGTON INTERNATIONAL LAW REVIEW 465–501 (2009).

4.  Lalonde, Chris, Note, Dubai or Not Dubai?: *A Review of Foreign Investment and Acquisition Laws in the U.S. and Canada*, 41 VANDERBILT JOURNAL OF TRANSNATIONAL LAW 1475–1502 (2008).

5.  Mostaghel, Deborah M., *Dubai Ports World Under Exon-Florio: A Threat to National Security or a Tempest in a Seaport?*, 70 ALBANY LAW REVIEW 583–623 (2007).

6.  Nensala, Sondra Bell, *Homeland Security Presidential Directive 12: How HSPD-12 May Limit Competition Unnecessarily and Suggestions for Reform*, 40 PUBLIC CONTRACTS LAW JOURNAL 619–679 (2011).

7.  Pudner, Stephen K., Comment, *Moving Forward from Dubai Ports World — The Foreign Investment and National Security Act of 2007*, 59 ALABAMA LAW REVIEW 1277–1304 (2008).

8.  Sothmann, Stephen, Note, *Let He Who is Without Sin Cast the First Stone: Foreign Direct Investment and National Security Regulation in China*, 19 INDIANA INTERNATIONAL & COMPARATIVE LAW REVIEW 203–231 (2009).

## EXPORT CLAUSE

*See* Export Tax.

## EXPORT PERFORMANCE REQUIREMENT

A requirement imposed by a host country government on foreign direct investors that, in exchange for permission to invest in the country, a certain quantity of their production must be exported. A related requirement, known as "product mandating," obligates foreign direct investors to export a certain quantity of their production to specified countries or regions. Along with export performance and local content requirements, trade balancing is a tactic used by host country governments to regulate foreign direct investment (FDI).

## EXPORT TAX

Literally, a tax on the exportation of merchandise.

Export taxes are used from time to time in a variety of countries, typically to assure a low-cost source of supply of the taxed merchandise. For example, in 2007 and 2008, in response to surging world food prices and concerns about food security, several developing countries imposed taxes on staple agricultural commodities. Under the Export Clause of the United States Constitution, export taxes are forbidden. The most recent Supreme Court case arising under the Clause concerned a harbor maintenance tax.

Export taxes are one of the topics in the Non-Agricultural Market Access (NAMA) negotiations of the Doha Round that pit the EU and United States against China, and indeed many developing countries led by Argentina. While the United States Constitution bars such levies, many relatively poorer countries apply them, including not only China and Argentina, but also India and Ukraine. Non-WTO Members, principally Russia (which has export taxes on 450 products, many of which are primary inputs to make steel), also impose these measures.[195]

Developed countries complain that taxing exports unfairly constricts the global supply of important raw materials and inputs. That constriction drives up the prices of these raw materials and inputs, and thus ultimately the cost of finished manufactured products made in their countries. As an example, the export price (in September 2008) from China of coking coal, which is an input into steel, is $680-$730 per metric ton. But, because of a 40 percent export tax on coke, the Chinese domestic price of this input is just $395 per metric ton. Conversely, China and the developing countries insist export taxes are not covered by the DDA mandate. Moreover, they aver that such taxes are necessary to assure their industries of a steady, low-cost source of raw materials and inputs. Of course, that low-cost, such as the difference in the Chinese export and domestic coke prices, is precisely what the EU and United States say is an unfair competitive advantage for Chinese producers of finished goods like steel.

Until 2006, the EU position in the Doha Round was that export taxes should be banned. In that year, it softened its approach, saying WTO Members should agree to maximum permissible export tax rates. Since then, and particularly with the global economic crisis, the EU observed that the number and range of export tax measures has proliferated among supplier countries of key raw materials and inputs. On some taxed items, there was even a global shortage, yet a surfeit in the domestic taxing country. The EU suggested in July 2008 that it might drop its proposal, if consensus was reached on NAMA modalities — a condition that was not fulfilled. Thus, the EU was thoroughly displeased by the deletion from the December 2008 NAMA Text of its modified proposal. Predictably, China, India, Argentina, and other Members stayed on the side of the line they had drawn, insisting the EU drop its proposal.

### Suggestions for Further Research:

Articles:

1.  Khachaturian, Alex, *Reforming the United States Export Tax Policy: An Alternative to the American Trade War with the European Union*, 14 UNIVERSITY OF CALIFORNIA — DAVIS JOURNAL OF INTERNATIONAL LAW AND POLICY 185–203 (2008).

2.  Richmond, William, Casenote, *The First Export Clause Challenge to NAFTA's Deferred Tax Provision (Nufarm America's, Inc. v. United States,*

---

[195] The data above are from Daniel Pruzin, *EU, in New Turnaround on NAMA Issue of Export Taxes, Insists Proposal Still in Play*, 26 International Trade Reporter (BNA) 308 (5 March 2009).

*521 F.3d 1366, 2008)*, 14 LAW & BUSINESS REVIEW OF THE AMERICAS 825–834 (2008).

## EXTERNALITY

Any benefit or cost associated with production or consumption that is not directly incorporated into the price or cost of that product. Also known as a "spillover."

In the context of agriculture, externalities associated with production are called "multi-functionality." It is sometimes argued that government support (*e.g.*, subsidies) for crop production is a way of enhancing positive multi-functionality, such as environmental protection, cultural values, and food security.

# F

## FABRIC

"Fabric" is a generic term used for all flexible materials made of fibers or yarns.

Fabric may be made through a variety of processes, including weaving (which typically is mechanized, and involved one of many types of loom), knitting (on machine or by hand), lace minding (involving knitting machines, hand, or both), braiding (*i.e.*, plaiting), felting (involving matting and pressing fibers together to make cloth), bonding, fusing, or inter locking. "Cloth" and "materials" are synonyms for "fabric."

There are many types of fabric. The Table below sets out examples of different kinds of fabric, with a brief description of each type.

TABLE:

EXAMPLES OF FABRIC TYPES

| Name of Fabric Type | Brief Description |
|---|---|
| Burlap | A loosely woven fabric produced from jute, hemp, or flax fibers. |
| Calico | A light weight woven cotton fabric renowned for its distinctive small image prints. |
| Canvas | A heavy weight cotton fabric used for furniture and outdoor purposes, and for some footwear. |
| Corduroy | A cotton fabric known for its distinctive weave, namely, parallel ridges. Corduroy is measured by the size of the ridges, called "wales." |
| Denim | A heavy weight woven cotton fabric, more dense than canvas, which when dyed indigo is used for blue jeans (dungarees). Blue jeans are a noted American fashion produced by global name brand corporations such as Levi Strauss Co. The name "denim" is derived from the mill that originally produced it, which was located in Nimes, France. In French, *de Nimes* means "of Nimes." |
| Flannel | A woven cotton fabric that is brushed to raise the nap of the fabric to increase softness. Flannel is used for baby clothes, sheets, shirts, and sleepwear. It is favored in winter, because of its warmth. |
| Gabardine | A tightly woven fabric that displays a diagonal patterned weave, and which can be made from cotton, or wool, or other fiber. |

**TABLE (continued)**

| Name of Fabric Type | Brief Description |
| --- | --- |
| Gingham | A lightweight woven cotton fabric renowned for its distinctive checker board pattern. Commonly used for casual, summer dresses and picnic table clothes, gingham is formed by a single color plus white threads. |
| Linen | A class of woven fabrics made from the flax plant, linen is one of the oldest fabrics in existence. It was produced in Ancient Egypt. |
| Muslin | A woven cotton fabric that generally is undyed. Muslin is used as basic fabric for making patterns (draping), in the linings of clothing, or in the backings of quilts. |
| Satin | A type of weave whereby one side of the fabric is shiny, but the other side is dull. |
| Silk | A class of fabrics made from the unwrapped filament of the cocoon of a silkworm. Common forms of silk include dupioni, charmeuse, and organza. Like linen, silk is an ancient fabric. |
| Twill | A type of weave that forms a stiff fabric, typically made from cotton, and of relatively heavy weight. |
| Velvet | A layered fabric made from cotton or silk. The top layer of velvet is cut into short piles, akin to the piles of a rug, and is of the same height. Velvet has rich, thick appearance, and a soft, nearly furry, touch. |
| Worsted | The term "worsted" has two meanings. First, it can refer to a type of fine, smooth yarn that is spun from combed, long stapled wool. Second, it can refer to a fabric made from worsted yarn (as defined in the first meaning). In other words, "worsted" can refer to a yarn type, or to fabric made from that yarn. Threads of worsted yarn are dense, but nonetheless can be woven into a fabric. Worsted fabric has a smooth feel and tends to be durable. |

## FABRIC FORWARD

A rule of origin for textile and apparel (T&A) merchandise that requires the production process, from the weaving of fabric (or other ways of creating fabric) to the completion of the finished article, be conducted in a particular country for the article to qualify as originating in that country.

## FACTORS OF PRODUCTION

A generic term for labor, land, physical capital, human capital, and technology, which are considered the traditional neo-classical factors of production and sources of economic growth.

## FAIR TRADE (FAIR TRADE OR FAIRTRADE)

Fair Trade is a movement of socially conscious consumerism based in part by a reaction to the experiences and consequences of free trade policies. These consequences are often listed as low labor standards in developing countries — subsistence wages and poor working environment conditions.

Fair Trade practices focus on providing producers of commodities a living wage, by reconsidering each step in a supply chain, and working only with distributors of a commodity that pay producers equitably. In short, Fair Trade seeks to recognize the overall value realized in a product, like coffee or chocolate along an entire supply chain, and the deservingness of a producer that adds substantive value (e.g., a coffee or cocoa bean farmer) into production to yield a higher-value finished product.[196]

There is a moral or social justice focus to the Fair Trade movement. Consumers in developed (i.e., rich) countries are concerned about the plight of producers in developing and least developed (i.e., poor) countries. These consumers are concerned specifically with the impact of their purchase decisions as a reward to agents at each step in a product supply chain, and to distributors that sell products. They oppose, in a general sense, the mass-market sales of products at low prices, with sellers paying their suppliers still lower prices, when the result is agents up the commercial chain are compelled to live in poverty and work in inhumane conditions. Charities invest money into fair trading enterprises as a way to help reduce poverty through enforcement of higher wages for producers and better working conditions for upstream workers.

The rationale for Fair Trade is controversial for both rich and poor countries. Advocates argue the focus on Fair Trade is to help developing countries overcome lingering effects of centuries of colonialism, which created an export oriented economy and a commercial infrastructure that promotes exports. Why not re-engineering the value chain of production so that more value stays in a poor country, and is distributed across the society of the producers as a whole?[197]

Others argue Fair Trade is a veiled attempt by developed countries to protect their non-competitive or declining industries.[198] Fair Trade forces developing countries to increase their costs of production, and thus reduces or eliminates their competitive advantage. The hidden agenda is to allow industries in developed countries to continue dominating a market, when market-based pricing mechanisms — if allowed to operate freely — would put an end to their position. Developed countries urge they call for nothing more than equal competitive opportunity on a level playing field, as labor, environmental, and

---

[196] *See* Alan Beattie, *Nestlé Becomes First of Coffee's Big Four to Launch 'Fair Trade' Label*, FINANCIAL TIMES, 7 October 2005, at 4.

[197] *See* John Sweeney, *Why Fairer Trade Does Not Mean an End to Free Trade*, FINANCIAL TIMES, 29 November 2006, at 15.

[198] *See* Jagdish Bhagwati, *An Opportunity for Democrats to Denounce Protectionism*, *Financial Times*, 10 August 2005, at 17.

human rights are respected in their countries. Yet, the question remains whether the playing field can, in fact, be level, or should be so in a market economy?

As a practical matter, how does a consumer know with any certainty that a product labeled "Fair Trade" is, indeed, made through fair practices? How can the consumer be sure the label means profits from the sale of the product are reinvested half-way around the world in villages, to improve educational standards for children or empower women? No sovereign state maintains a cadre of examiners with authority to examine global supply chains or trace the distribution of sale proceeds, and thus certify as "Fairly Traded" — or deny such certification. Rather, interest in buying fair traded products has led to the establishment of certifying organizations, and to an international standards setting organization. Fair trading standards are set internationally by the Fairtrade Labeling Organizations International, (FLO), based in Bonn, Germany. FLO works with 21 countries to harmonize fair trading standards.

*Suggestions for Further Research:*

Books:

1.   BATRA, RAVI, THE MYTH OF FREE TRADE — THE POORING OF AMERICA (1993).

2.   BHAGWATI, JAGDISH, IN DEFENSE OF GLOBALIZATION (2004).

3.   BICHLBAUM, ANDY, MIKE BONANNO & BOB SPUNKMEYER, THE YES MEN — THE TRUE STORY OF THE END OF THE WORLD TRADE ORGANIZATION (2004).

4.   BRECHER, JEREMY & TIM COSTELLO, GLOBAL VILLAGE OR GLOBAL PILLAGE — ECONOMIC RECONSTRUCTION FROM THE BOTTOM UP (2nd ed. 1998).

5.   BROWN, SHERROD, MYTHS OF FREE TRADE — WHY AMERICAN TRADE POLICY HAS FAILED (2004).

6.   BURTLESS, GARY, ROBERT Z. LAWRENCE, ROBERT E. LITAN & ROBERT J. SHAPIRO, GLOBAPHOBIA — CONFRONTING FEARS ABOUT OPEN TRADE (1998).

7.   DE LA DEHESA, GUILLERMO, WINNERS AND LOSERS IN GLOBALIZATION (2006).

8.   DUNKLEY, GRAHAM, THE FREE TRADE ADVENTURE: THE URUGUAY ROUND AND GLOBALISM — A CRITIQUE (1997).

9.   GIDDENS, ANTHONY, THE THIRD WAY AND ITS CRITICS (2000).

10. GILPIN, ROBERT, THE CHALLENGE OF GLOBAL CAPITALISM — THE WORLD ECONOMY IN THE 21ST CENTURY (2000).

11. GRAY, JOHN, FALSE DAWN — THE DELUSIONS OF GLOBAL CAPITALISM (1998).

12. GREIDER, WILLIAM, ONE WORLD, READY OR NOT — THE MANIC LOGIC OF GLOBAL CAPITALISM (1997).

13. IRWIN, DOUGLAS A., FREE TRADE UNDER FIRE (2nd ed. 2005).

14. KELSEY, JANE, RECLAIMING THE FUTURE — NEW ZEALAND AND THE GLOBAL ECONOMY (1999).

15. KENNEDY, PAUL, DIRK MESSNER & FRANZ NUSCHELER EDS., GLOBAL TRENDS & GLOBAL GOVERNANCE (2002).

16. KHOR, MARTIN, RETHINKING GLOBALIZATION — CRITICAL ISSUES AND POLICY CHOICES (2001).

17. LEGRAIN, PHILIPPE, OPEN WORLD:/ THE TRUTH ABOUT GLOBALIZATION (2002).

18. MADELEY, JOHN, HUNGRY FOR TRADE — HOW THE POOR PAY FOR FREE TRADE (2000).

19. MARTIN, HANS-PETER & HARALD SCHUMANN, THE GLOBAL TRAP — GLOBALIZATION & THE ASSAULT ON DEMOCRACY & PROSPERITY (1996).

20. NORBERG, JOHAN, IN DEFENSE OF GLOBAL CAPITALISM (2003).

21. PUSEY, MICHAEL, THE EXPERIENCE OF MIDDLE AUSTRALIA — THE DARK SIDE OF ECONOMIC REFORM (2003).

22. RANSOM, DAVID, THE NO-NONSENSE GUIDE TO FAIR TRADE (2001).

23. RODRIK, DANI, HAS GLOBALIZATION GONE TOO FAR? (March 1997).

24. SCHOLTE, JAN AART, GLOBALIZATION — A CRITICAL INTRODUCTION (2000).

25. SINGER, PETER, ONE WORLD — THE ETHICS OF GLOBALIZATION (2002).

26. STIGLITZ, JOSEPH E., GLOBALIZATION AND ITS DISCONTENTS (2003).

27. STIGLITZ, JOSEPH E., MAKING GLOBALIZATION WORK (2007).

28. STIGLITZ, JOSEPH E. & ANDREW CHARLTON, FAIR TRADE FOR ALL: HOW TRADE CAN PROMOTE DEVELOPMENT (2005).

29. WERTHEIMER, ALAN, EXPLOITATION (1996).

30. WOLF, MARTIN, WHY GLOBALIZATION WORKS (2005).

Articles:

1. Baradaran, Shima & Stephanie Barclay, *Fair Trade and Child Labor*, 43 COLUMBIA HUMAN RIGHTS LAW REVIEW issue 1, 1–63 (fall 2011).

2. Carminati, Giugi, *Is International Trade Really Making Developing Countries Dirtier and Developed Countries Richer?*, 8 UNIVERSITY OF CALIFORNIA DAVIS BUSINESS LAW JOURNAL 205–233 (2007).

3. Dine, Janet, *Democratization: The Contribution of Fair Trade and Ethical Trading Movements*, 15 INDIANA JOURNAL OF GLOBAL LEGAL STUDIES 177–212 (2008).

4. Geis, George S., *The Space between Markets and Hierarchies*, 95 VIRGINIA LAW REVIEW 99–153 (2009).

5. Karbowski, Jessica, Note, *Grocery Store Activism: A WTO Compliant Means to Incentivize Social Responsibility*, 49 VIRGINIA JOURNAL OF INTERNATIONAL LAW 727–787 (2009).

6. Mateikis, William J., *The Fair Track to Expanded Fair Trade: Making TAA Benefits More Accessible to American Workers*, 30 HOUSTON JOURNAL OF INTERNATIONAL LAW 1–87 (2007).

7.   Mumford, Todd, Note, *Voluntary International Standards: Incorporating "Fair Trade" Within Multilateral Trade Agreements*, 14 SOUTHWESTERN JOURNAL OF LAW & TRADE IN THE AMERICAS 171–193 (2007).

8.   Stencel, John, *Free Trade versus Fair Trade*, 36 DENVER JOURNAL OF INTERNATIONAL LAW & POLICY 349–367 (2008).

9.   Weese, Scott B., Note, *International Coffee Regulation: A Comparison of the International Coffee Organization and the Fair Trade Coffee Regimes*, 7 CARDOZO PUBLIC LAW POLICY & ETHICS JOURNAL 275–319 (2008).

## FARM BILL

A generic term referring to major legislation in the United States on agriculture.

The "Farm Bill" is renewed approximately every five years. For example, Congress passed, and the President signed, *Farm Bills* in 1996 and 2002, with 2007 the subsequent renewal year. As explained further below, Congress passed the *2008 Farm Bill*, covering 2008–2012, over the veto of President George W. Bush.

As intimated, the five year cycle is not invariable. There have been both longer and shorter periods covered by farm legislation, for instance, 1990 to 1996, 1956 to 1965, and 1977 to 1981. If and when Congress does not pass a new *Farm Bill* (or extend an existing Bill), or the President vetoes legislation and Congress sustains the veto, then many farm programs either lapse, or revert to permanent agriculture law.

The permanent law, for several programs, was the *Agricultural Adjustment Act of 1938*, and for other programs, the *Agriculture Act of 1949*. Thus, for most supported commodity, reversion to the *1938 Act* or *1949 Act* would be a dramatic change.[199] That is a key reason why periodic Farm Bills suspend application of permanent Law. Specifically, first, with a reversion to *1938 Act* or *1949 Act*, the number of beneficiaries of support would drop dramatically. For instance, absent the *2008 Farm Bill*, a wheat farmer would be eligible under permanent law for parity price support for the 2008 wheat crop only if (1) the farmer had an allotment on his farm that was established in 1958, (2) planted wheat in 2005, 2006, and 2007, and (3) did not exceed the 2008 allotment for his farm. Second, the degree of price support for most crops, under permanent law, would vary drastically from what might be reasonable under a new *Farm Bill*. Some farmers would gain a huge windfall, while others would receive no support. Third, the schedules for payments under permanent law were not synchronized. The *1938 Act* uses a Marketing Year (MY), whereas the *1949 Act* sets price support rates using crop years.

Generally, Farm Bills are extraordinarily controversial, pitting legislators from different parts of the country, representing different agricultural, indus-

---

[199] *See* Sarah Barr, *Congress Could Pass Farm Bill Even Without White House Support, Harkin Says*, 25 International Trade Reporter (BNA) 338–339 (6 March 2008).

trial, and services interests, against one another. In recent years, extreme partisanship has made passage of these Bills even more difficult. For example, the five year, *2008 Farm Bill* (H.R. 2419), as debated in Congress during the fall 2007, winter 2007–2008, and spring 2008, called for $289 billion of expenditures. However, the controversies this massive Bill engendered, coupled with extreme partisanship, prevented its timely passage. Accordingly, Congress considered extending the *2002 Farm Bill* by one year, and did extend it into 2008.[200] It had to do so, because no permanent statute provides for farm support programs, particularly counter-cyclical payments and decoupled direct payments. At the same time, permanent law imposes — for cotton and wheat — acreage allotments and marketing quotas. Permanent law also sets 1 January as the beginning of the MY for milk. Without extending the *2002 Bill* for one year, and thereby falling back on otherwise-applicable permanent legal provisions, Federal support to the milk sector could rise dramatically. The support price for milk, which in November 2007 was $9.90, would rise to between 75 and 90 percent of parity, *i.e.*, to $30.52 to $36.63 (based on October 2007 figures).

In the modern era, major farm legislation initiated in 1933 as part of President Franklin D. Roosevelt's New Deal program. Then, programs established by legislation designed to help much of rural America recover from the Great Depression and the Dust Bowl. From 1933 to approximately 1973, price support was the central goal of farm bills. That goal reflected the acute problem farmers faced in the Depression — low prices. During the 40 years following 1933, farm bills created a variety of mechanisms to ensure robust prices for commodities, including constriction of supply. However, during the Nixon era — *i.e.*, the Administration of President Richard M. Nixon, from 1968–1974 — the policy emphasis of American farm bills changed.

A number of studies — for example, by the Club of Rome, which sponsored an infamous book, *The Limits to Growth* — in that era offered Malthusian-like predictions about a worsening mismatch between population and food supply, with the former increasing so rapidly (especially in many parts of the Third World) that farm output could not keep up, and the environment would be compromised. The doomsday predictions later were debunked, notably by Julian L. Simon in *The Ultimate Resource 2* (1996). Even the Club of Rome disavowed the *The Limits to Growth* four years after its publication. Still, fears about food shortages and soaring food prices had an impact on American agricultural policy. President Nixon re-oriented farm bills by emphasizing schemes to

---

[200] *See* Brett Ferguson, *Conferees Work on Finalizing Farm Bill as President Signs Two-Week Extension*, 25 International Trade Reporter (BNA) 684–685 (8 May 2008); Adam Snider, *Baseline Farm Bill Suggested, But Could Also Be Problematic*, 25 International Trade Reporter (BNA) 416–417 (20 March 2008); Derrick Cain, *House Lawmakers Offer Legislation to Extend Farm Programs for One Year*, 24 International Trade Reporter (BNA) 1642 (22 November 2007).

(1) boost production, and (2) protect farmers if and when commodity prices happened to fall.[201]

First, to encourage output, farm legislation began to emphasize fixed, direct payments to farmers calculated on the basis of their acreage under cultivation (or livestock head raised). That is, the size of the direct payment was linked to the size of the farm, and restrictions on the amount a farmer could receive (the payment per farmer) were weak. Hence, farmers were encouraged not only to produce, but also to increase their farm size, and the largest farms obtained the highest direct payment subsidies. Farmland itself became valuable in part based on the subsidies entrenched in it. Farm owners can, and typically do, further supplement their income by renting part of their farmland out to tenant farmers.

Second, to insure farmers against market vicissitudes, farm bills provided for price-sensitive payments that would compensate farmers if prices fell. The two key price-sensitive subsidy programs were, and still are, the marketing loan assistance scheme and counter-cyclical payments. The marketing loan scheme essentially sets a support price for current production levels. Counter-cyclical payments compensate a farmer if prices fall (sometimes regardless of whether the farmer is producing the crop whose price has fallen). Direct and price-sensitive payments cover only "program crops," such as cotton, corn, rice, soybean, and wheat. "Specialty crops," namely, fruit, vegetables, and nuts, are not covered by American farm subsidies.

Like other laws, farm legislation covers multiple topical areas, and thus is organized into "titles." For example, the *2002 Farm Bill* has 10 titles, with Title I concerning commodity subsidies. Additional topical areas in this and other bills are conservation, research, and food safety. However, commodity subsidies by far are the most controversial provisions in agricultural legislation. Crops eligible for subsidies, called "program crops," are restricted. Which crops should be subsidized? In what amounts should the subsidies be given? How should subsidies be provided? For every existing or prospective new subsidy scheme, there are at least two constituencies — for and against — in the United States.

The raucous over subsidies hardly is purely domestic. Rather, the implications of America's agricultural subsidies for trade negotiations (especially at the multilateral level, *e.g.*, the Doha Round, and for America's vulnerability to legal challenge (again, especially at the WTO level), cause considerable controversy. In other words, large policy issues of free trade and protectionism are embedded in the details of subsidy provisions in the bills.

Notably (as explained below), the *2008 Farm Bill* retains many of the subsidy programs of the 2002 Farm Bill. That is so, despite the fact the United States lost the 2005 *Upland Cotton* case in the WTO. The Senate approved the *2008 Farm Bill* on 14 December 2007 on a 79–14 vote, following passage by the House in 27

---

[201] *See* Alan Beattie, *Pile-it-High Advocates Set to Reap Gains*, FINANCIAL TIMES, 9 October 2007, at 4.

July 2007 on a 231–191 vote. President George W. Bush threatened to veto the bill (arguing the limitations on farm income subsidies for the wealthiest Americans were insufficiently stringent, and also opposing $22.4 billion in new taxes that would increase the scope and size of federal government involvement in farm programs).[202] Only the Senate passage was by a margin sufficient to over-ride a veto. However, in the spring 2008, both the House and Senate passed the *2008 Farm Bill* (H.R. 2419) by a veto-proof margin. On 14 May 2008, the House passed the legislation by 318–106, and the Senate did so on 15 May by 81–15. (The two-thirds margin to over-ride a veto in the House is 290 votes, and 67 in the Senate.)

The formal title of the 2008 *Farm Bill* is the *"Food, Conservation and Energy Act (FCEA) of 2008."* It has approximately 15 Titles covering conservation, nutrition programs (e.g., food stamps, school lunches), and subsidies. The key features of the five (5) year *2008 Farm Bill* are as follows.[203]

- Overall Spending —

  For the five year period 2008 through 2012, agricultural spending is $289 billion, or about one percent of the total federal budget. Nearly three-fourths of this spending goes to domestic food assistance programs. Farmers receive 30 percent of the spending. Of that 30 percent, about 15 percent ($8.3 billion) takes the form of outright farm support (*i.e.*, subsidies) to large, traditional commodities (*e.g.*, cotton, corn, soybeans, sugar, and wheat), slightly over seven percent is crop insurance, and nine percent is to promote conservation.[204] Note that non-traditional crops like fruits and vegetables do not receive outright farm support, but rather must rely on crop insurance or disaster assistance.

- Countercyclical Payments —

  The *2008 Farm Bill* contains price-linked subsidies, especially counter-cyclical support. These payments are triggered by a fall in market prices below a pre-determined fixed level. They are considered trade-distorting, and subject to WTO reduction commitments. Critically, the *Bill* sets a limit of $40,000 per producer participant for direct (*i.e.*, decoupled) payments (discussed below) and counter-cyclical payments.

- Retention of Decoupled Subsidies —

  Direct payments that are decoupled (*i.e.*, not linked to the type or volume of production of crops or livestock head) are retained. They amount to about $5 billion per year. Direct payments are provided to a farmer regardless of market prices or whether the land is farmed. They are computed according to agriculture base acreage. About 76 percent of farmers who get direct payments have sales of over $250,000, and in

---

[202] *See* Derrick Cain, *Harkin Working with OMB's Nussle to Avoid Possible Veto of Farm Bill*, 25 International Trade Reporter (BNA) 191 (7 February 2008).

[203] *See* Adam Snider, *Senate Sends $289 Billion Farm Bill to Bush Amid Calls to Override Promised Veto*, 25 International Trade Reporter (BNA) 743–744 (22 May 2008).

[204] *See* Rick Mitchell, *OECD Suggests U.S. Should Do More on Ag Reform, Criticizes Biofuel Support*, 26 International Trade Reporter (BNA) 913 (9 July 2009).

2006 65 percent of farms with over $1 million in profits got direct payments.[205] Recipients like direct payments because they are reliable and predictable, and point out they are the most trade-friendly. For WTO purposes, the United States schedules these programs as Green Box payments, meaning they are exempt from reduction commitments. However, such the cotton subsidies against which the WTO Appellate Body ruled in the 2005 *Upland Cotton* case brought against the United States by Brazil also are retained in the *2008 Farm Bill*. The Appellate Body held this support, in fact, was linked to the type of commodities produced.

- Reintroduction of Controversial Cotton Subsidy Programs —

  The Step 2 Program, against which the Appellate Body also ruled in the 2005 *Upland Cotton* case, is reintroduced. In the case, the Appellate Body held that the Step 2 compensation to American textile mills and exporters for buying United States cotton (which is higher than cotton available on the world market) is an illegal export subsidy. The United States repealed the Step 2 Program effective 1 August 2006. But, the *2008 Farm Bill* re-establishes the Program. Specifically, domestic cotton mills are paid 4 cents per pound between 2008–2011, and 3 cents per pound in 2012, for buying cotton grown in the United States.

- Controversial Sugar Subsidy Program —

  The United States Department of Agriculture (USDA) is required to allocate production quotas to sugar producers in the United States. (However, there is some dispute as to whether the sugar output actually must come from American sugar producers.) This allocation must equal 85 percent of the expected consumption of sugar in the United States. Thus, the *2008 Farm Bill* essentially guarantees American sugar growers 85 percent of the domestic market. In addition, the USDA must purchase sugar if its price falls below a set support level, and sell the output to producers of ethanol.

- Controversial Dairy Subsidy Program —

  The *2008 Farm Bill* retains the Dairy Promotion and Research Program, under which an assessment — or fee — is charged. Under the 2002 Farm Bill, the fee applied to all milk produced and marketed in the United States, other than Alaska, Hawaii, and Puerto Rico. The fee was used to fun advertising and marketing expenses for American dairy products. The 2007 Bill extends the fee not only to milk produced and marketed in Alaska, Hawaii, and Puerto Rico, but — critically — also to imported dairy products. The EU (among other WTO Members) charges this extension violates WTO rules.

- Continuation of Controversial Ethanol Subsidies and Tariff —

  The *2008 Farm Bill* continues support for the production of ethanol. It extends the tariff on imported ethanol (imposed under HTSUS sub-

---

[205] *See* Liz White, *U.S. Farm Bill Outlook Remains Unclear, Will Face Tough Funding Cuts in Congress*, 28 International Trade Reporter (BNA) 262 (17 February 2011).

headings 9901.00.50 and 9901.00.52) for two years, through 31 December 2010. The Bill ends claims for drawback for additional duties, and substitution drawback, in respect of ethanol, after 20 September 2008.

- Income Limits —

    There are new limits on the eligibility for farm subsidies. Any person making over $500,000 in non-farm adjusted gross income (AGI), or over $750,000 in farm-related income, is ineligible for a direct payment farm subsidy. The *2002 Farm Bill* had no eligibility cap on farm income, and the non-farm earnings cap was $2.5 million.

- Increased Spending on Nutritional Programs —

    The *2008 Farm Bill* increases spending on nutritional programs by over $10 billion.

- Increased Spending on Green Box and Related Programs —

    The *2008 Farm Bill* also hikes spending for conservation, energy research, and specialty crop programs. It establishes a disaster relief scheme on a permanent basis.

- New Optional Average Crop Revenue Election (ACRE) scheme —

    Under the *2008 Farm Bill*, farmers may choose to participate in a revenue-based payment program, the ACRE scheme. Under the ACRE scheme, a farmer receives counter-cyclical support — a revenue guarantee — based on state crop prices. But, if a farmer elects to participate, then that farmer must forego 20 percent of his direct payments, and accept a reduction in loan rates of 30 percent. The *Bill* sets a limit of $32,000 per producer participant for the ACRE program.

- Other Changes Concerning Payments —

    The *2008 Farm Bill* alters the ownership by farmers of commodities, once they have collected a payment for those commodities. It also contains provisions ensuring that payments are attributed directly to a living person. The Bill eliminates the so-called 3-Entity Rule, which was a loophole for circumventing limits on farm payments.

- Customs Law —

    The *2008 Farm Bill* puts a two year moratorium on review by the Customs and Border Protection (CBP) of the "First Sale Rule." It extends Customs User Fees and Merchandise Processing Fees until 14 November 2017.

- Caribbean Basin Preferences —

    The Bill extends the *Caribbean Basin Trade Partnership Act (CBTPA)* through 30 September 2010.

- Administrative Organization —

    The *2008 Farm Bill* calls for a review of the organizational restructuring that has occurred in the USDA and Department of Homeland Security (DHS).

Much of attention is given to the subsidy programs noted above, with claims from many quarters — domestically and abroad — that the support levels exceed thresholds that are the subject of negotiations in the Doha Round. However, it is worth recalling that 17 percent of the expenditures under the Bill go to farmers. Moreover, commodity payments account for 0.25 percent of the entire federal budget, a drop from under the *2002 Farm Bill*, when they made up 0.75 percent.

In June 2008, President George W. Bush vetoed the *2008 Farm Bill*. He objected to four main features of the Bill. First, the Bill contained too many budgetary maneuvers that obfuscated the true cost of programs. Second, the Bill was loaded with wasteful, special interest provisions — old-fashioned pork barrel projects — that were designed solely to secure votes. These objections, accurate as they may be, are a seemingly ineluctable part of modern American farm legislation.

Perhaps more seriously, third, President Bush argued the AGI limits were unacceptably high. The President called for an income cap of $200,000, with no distinction between farm and non-farm income. The Bill appeared to allow for a married couple making up to $2.5 million to receive a direct payment. However, this argument had a strong counter to it. The Internal Revenue Service reportedly informed a proponent of the Bill, Senator Kent Conrad (Democrat—North Dakota) that no couple existed in the United States earning $750,000 from farm income and $500,000 from non-farm endeavors (*i.e.*, non-farm AGI).[206]

Fourth, the President objected to the ACRE program, viewing it as a revenue guarantee with no cap. For example, if corn prices dropped from the May 2008 level of $6 per bushel to $3 per bushel, then countercyclical corn subsidies under that program would be $10 billion. However, this objection met with a strong rebuttal. The National Agricultural Statistics Service of the USDA said in March 2008 that corn prices are unlikely to fall in the short term, because farmers are planting eight percent less acres of corn than in the past, and demand for corn is robust, in part because of its use in ethanol. Further, the Congressional Budget Office reported that the ACRE program would save $400 million.

However, the House and — arguably — the Senate over-rode the veto. On 22 May, the Senate over-rode the veto by 82–13. But, complicating matters was the fact the bill on which the Senate voted to over-ride the veto contained a clerical error. Namely, it omitted the trade title that was supposed to be in the *2008 Farm Bill*, which the Senate and House had passed earlier, and President George W. Bush had vetoed. Because of the difference between the legislation on which the Senate voted, and the bill the President vetoed, doubts were raised as to whether the Senate had, as a matter of constitutional law, over-rode the veto. In other words, the White House was sent, and the President

---

[206] *See* Adam Snider, *Senate Sends $289 Billion Farm Bill to Bush Amid Calls to Override Promised Veto*, 25 International Trade Reporter (BNA) 743–744 (22 May 2008).

vetoed, an incomplete Farm Bill, with one of the 15 titles of the bill inadvertently missing. In consequence, upon the over-ride votes by the House and Senate, 14 of the 15 titles of the bill were law — but not the crucial trade title. No one — on Capitol Hill or in the White House — noticed the mistake until after President Bush delivered the veto.[207]

For its part, on 22 May, the House approved a new bill (H.R. 6124) by a vote of 306–110. This new bill was the correct one. That is, the new bill contained all the agriculture provisions of the original bill (H.R. 2419), which the House and Senate passed previously, and the President vetoed. The new bill approved by the House also contained the trade title, which had been erroneously omitted from the Senate version. This trade title extended preferences for the Caribbean Basin Initiative (CBI), and for Haiti, as well as a declaration program for imports of softwood lumber. To clear up the earlier technical error that could have become a constitutional problem, the Senate passed the *2008 Farm Bill* on 5 June 2008 — technically a new bill (H.R. 6124), which contained the entire bill, including the trade title, passed by the House (H.R. 2419). Senate passage was by a veto-proof margin of 77 to 15.[208]

Three aspects of agricultural legislation sometimes are overlooked. First, a substantial percentage of payments do not go to farmers, but rather for the food stamp program. That is a welfare program to help poor Americans obtain food. For instance, in the *2002 Farm Bill*, spending averaged about $80 billion a year, but the bulk of that spending went not on farm subsidies, but into food stamps. Specifically, during the 2002–2005 Marketing Years (MYs), Green Box expenditures by the United States rose steadily from $58.3 billion in 2002 to $71.8 billion in 2005.[209] The key cause of the increase was a boost in spending on nutrition schemes, specifically, child nutrition, and food stamp programs. A relatively small amount of American Green Box expenditures — $5.3 billion on average annually — went to direct payment programs.

Second, many farmers — especially in the Midwest, growers of specialty crops, or on small or medium sized plots — do not agree entirely with the structure of American subsidy programs. Polls suggest they advocate reform, including caps on *per capita* or per farm payments so that the lion's share of subsidies do not continue to flow to a handful of large, wealthy farmers of particular crops.

Third, farming affects everyone. Single-digit statistics about the role of agriculture in a modern economy — such as that farms in the United States employ less than two percent of the American labor force, or the agriculture processing and marketing employs only about another 1.5 percent of the

---

[207] *See* Adam Snider, *Senate Repasses Farm Bill on 77–15 Vote; President Will Veto Measure Second Time*, 25 International Trade Reporter (BNA) 872 (12 June 2008).

[208] *See* Adam Snider, *Senate Repasses Farm Bill on 77–15 Vote; President Will Veto Measure Second Time*, 25 International Trade Reporter (BNA) 872 (12 June 2008).

[209] *See* Daniel Pruzin, *U.S. Notifies Farm Support for 2002–2005; Official Confirms Support for Falconer Figure*, 24 International Trade Reporter (BNA) 1417–1418 (11 October 2007).

workforce[210] — are relevant. But, no other sector of the economy directly affects every single person from birth to death every day.

As for the *2012 Farm Bill*, the Administration of President Barack H. Obama had two key elements it sought to include:[211]

(1) Reducing federal crop insurance, specifically, the subsidies for such insurance, in order to preserve funding for nutrition assistance schemes. Over 46 million Americans use food stamps (as of November 2011), which is an increase of 50 percent (from November 2008). Private insurance companies provide crop insurance, but the federal government subsidizes payments to those companies by farmers of their premiums for the policies. In the 2011 farm year, private companies over 1.1 million in policies. The premiums and projected indemnities on those policies were, respectively, $11.8 and $11.9 billion. In the 2012 Farm Bill, the President proposed cutting by two percentage points the subsidy level for any crop insurance plan that the government subsidizes at more than 50 percent (*i.e.*, pays for over half of the premiums). The President also proposed to cut the target return on investment of the private crop insurers from 14 to 12 percent.

(2) Reducing direct payments to farmers. After all, such payments were controversial Amber Box subsidies under the WTO Agriculture Agreement, and could be shifted to non-trade distorting, and therefore non-actionable, Green Box schemes.

Critics charged it was unwise to cut crop insurance subsidies. Instead, to save funds, they said the permanent disaster assistance program in the *2008 Farm Bill*, called *Supplemental Revenue Assistance Payments (SURE)*, should be eliminated.

*Suggestions for Further Research:*

Articles:

1.   Berson, Julie C., Comment, *Looking Beyond Efficiency: Applying the Consumer-Choice Standard to Agriculture*, 83 TEMPLE LAW REVIEW 491–527 (2011).

2.   Bunbury, Mark A., Jr., Recent Development, *"Forty Acres and a Mule"* ... *Not Quite Yet: Section 14012 of the Food, Conservation, and Energy Act of 2008 Fails Black Farmers*, 87 NORTH CAROLINA LAW REVIEW 1230–1251 (2009).

3.   Cai, Phoenix X.F., *Think Big and Ignore the Law: U.S. Corn and Ethanol Subsidies and WTO Law*, 40 GEORGETOWN JOURNAL OF INTERNATIONAL LAW 865–917 (2009).

4.   El-Hajj, Jeff, *Confined Animal Feeding Operations in California: Current Regulatory Schemes and What Must be Done to Improve Them*, 15 HASTINGS WEST — NORTHWEST JOURNAL OF ENVIRONMENTAL LAW & POLICY 349–368 (2009).

---

[210] *See* Alan Beattie, *Pile-it-High Advocates Set to Reap Gains*, FINANCIAL TIMES, 9 October 2007, at 4.

[211] *See* Heather Caygle, *Agriculture Secretary Tom Vilsack Defends Proposed Cuts During First Farm Bill Hearing*, 29 International Trade Reporter (BNA) 279 (23 February 2012).

5. Eubanks II, William S., *A Rotten System: Subsidizing Environmental Degradation and Poor Public Health with our Nation's Tax Dollars*, 28 STANFORD ENVIRONMENTAL LAW JOURNAL 213–310 (2009).

6. Foster, Julie, Comment, *Subsidizing Fat: How the 2012 Farm Bill Can Address America's Obesity Epidemic*, 160 UNIVERSITY OF PENNSYLVANIA LAW REVIEW 235–276 (2011).

7. Harwood, Sarah, Comment, *United States Farm Bill — An Antiquated Policy?*, 88 UNIVERSITY OF DETROIT MERCY LAW REVIEW 377–405 (2010).

8. Hazen, Tyler E., Comment, *The Effects of Brazilian Agricultural Property Policies and International Pressures on the Soybean Industry: Incentives for Amazon Deforestation and How it May be Reduced*, 2 SAN DIEGO JOURNAL OF CLIMATE & ENERGY LAW 223–247 (2010).

9. Hernández-López, Ernesto, Law, *Food, and Culture: Mexican Corn's National Identity Cooked in "Tortilla Discourses" Post-TLC/NAFTA*, 20 ST. THOMAS LAW REVIEW 670–690 (2008).

10. Hett, William, Student Note, *U.S. Corn and Soybean Subsidies: WTO Litigation and Sustainable Protections*, 17 TRANSNATIONAL LAW & CONTEMPORARY PROBLEMS 775–808 (2008).

11. Kwan, Charlene C., Note, *Fixing the Farm Bill: Using the "Permanent Provisions" in Agricultural Law to Achieve WTO Compliance*, 36 BOSTON COLLEGE ENVIRONMENTAL AFFAIRS LAW REVIEW 571–606 (2009).

12. Kurz, Natalie Jean, Comment, *Corn Ethanol: Setting Straight A Misguided Attempt to Free the United States from Foreign Oil*, 31 Houston Journal of International Law 377–417 (2009).

13. Lappé, Anna, *Food, Fuel, and the Future of Farming: Conference of Sustainable Agriculture*, 10 VERMONT JOURNAL OF ENVIRONMENTAL LAW 367–378 (2009).

14. McCland, Stacy, Student Article, *Immigration Reform and Agriculture: What We Really Want, What We Really Need, and What Will Happen if They Leave?*, 10 BARRY LAW REVIEW 63–79 (2008).

15. Peterson, Lesley, Note, *Talkin' 'Bout a Humane Revolution: New Standards for Farming Practices and How They Could Change International Trade as We Know It*, 36 BROOKLYN JOURNAL OF INTERNATIONAL LAW 265–298 (2010).

16. Powers, Melissa, *King Corn: Will the Renewable Fuel Standard Eventually End Corn Ethanol's Reign?*, 11 VERMONT JOURNAL OF ENVIRONMENTAL LAW 667–708 (2010).

17. Starr, Sean Charles, Comment, *Sweet Rewards: How U.S. Trade Liberalization and Penetration of Brazilian Ethanol into the U.S. Market Can Stimulate America's Domestic Economy and Strengthen America's International Influence*, 8 DEPAUL BUSINESS & COMMERCE LAW JOURNAL 275–303 (2010).

18. Symposium, *Farming and Food: How We Grow What We Eat*, 3 GOLDEN GATE UNIVERSITY ENVIRONMENTAL LAW JOURNAL 1–180 (2009).

19. Webster, Matthew, *"Jobs Americans Won't Do": Our Farming Heritage, Hazardous Harvests, and a Legislative Fix*, 29 Law & Inequality 249–277 (2011).

20. Wender, Melanie J., Comment, *Goodbye Family Farms and Hello Agribusiness: The Story of How Agricultural Policy is Destroying the Family Farm and the Environment*, 22 Villanova Environmental Law Journal 141–167 (2011).

Other Source:

1.   Oxfam America, Fairness in the Fields: A Vision for the 2007 Farm Bill (2006).

## FAS

*See* Foreign Agricultural Service.

## FAST (FAST CARD)

Free and Secure Trade.

A card that Canadian and Mexican drivers are required to carry if they haul hazardous material (hazmat). The applicable rules are promulgated by the Department of Homeland Security (DHS), specifically, the Transportation Security Administration (TSA) and Customs and Border Protection (CBP). The rules implement Section 7105 of the *Safe, Accountable, Flexible, and Efficient Transportation Equity Act: A Legacy for Users*, Pub. L. No. 109–59 — the *"SAFE Act."* A key mandate of the *SAFE Act* is that no Canadian or Mexican driver can haul hazmats into the United States unless the driver has passed a background check that is similar to the security screening required for American drivers. The *SAFE Act* gave the TSA until February 2006 to set up screening procedures for Canadian and Mexican drivers, which it did, albeit with an extension to August 2006.

Essentially, a FAST card allows for expeditious entry of commercial shipments into the United States from Canada and Mexico. Expedited entry is permitted because the FAST card shows background checks of Canadian and Mexican drivers have been done under the *SAFE Act* and implementing TSA rules. Those checks are akin to the checks the TSA undertakes of American drivers carrying hazmats. With respect to each Canadian and Mexican driver applying for a FAST card, the checks, which the CBP performs, involve:

- Fingerprint background check.
- Name-based background check.
- Verification and validation of driver information.
- Examination of driver identification and documentation.
- Personal interview.
- Photograph.

These procedures are akin to the checks made of American drivers seeking to haul hazmats. That point is significant from the perspective of national treatment obligations under Chapter 3 of the *North American Free Trade Agreement* (*NAFTA*) and GATT Article III:4.

Accordingly, effective 13 November 2006, Canadian and Mexican drivers could not enter the United States with placarded loads of hazmat unless they had a FAST card. The rule is enforced by the CBP.

## FAST TRACK

A special type of negotiating authority for trade agreements, coupled with a procedural mechanism for submitting the agreements to Congress for its consideration for approval.

Procedurally, the essence of fast track, as its name suggests, is expedited consideration by Congress of negotiated trade agreements. Congress sets forth, in its authorization to the Executive Branch to negotiate a trade agreement, broad parameters as to the purposes a proposed trade agreement ought to fulfill. It also tends to include negotiating objectives and guidelines, which may be more or less strict or detailed. Congress does so pursuant to its Constitutional power, under the Commerce Clause (Article I, Section 8, Clause 3 of the United States Constitution) to regulate foreign trade. Moreover, under Article I, Section 7, Clause 1 of the Constitution, bills affecting revenue, such as changes in tariff schedules, must originate in the House of Representatives. The authorization to the Executive Branch is a delegation of authority, and the delegation is made through legislation, typically called "fast track" trade negotiating authority. Recent delegations have gone under the rubric of *"Trade Promotion Authority*," or *"TPA."*

Substantively, the essence of fast track is trust. Congress must trust the President to comply with the negotiating parameters it sets by ensuring the text of any trade agreement embodies those parameters. Conversely, the President must trust Congress to hold to those parameters (*i.e.*, not make up new ones), and to the expedited procedures for consideration of a trade bill. During periods when fast track authority has not been renewed (*e.g.*, 1994–2002, summer-fall 2007), or when its renewal has been in doubt (*e.g.*, spring 2007), the mutual trust has been lacking.

From a sheer practical perspective, delegating negotiating authority makes sense. It would be manifestly impracticable for a foreign government to negotiate with 435 House members and 100 Senators, Congress often — but not always — chooses to delegate trade negotiating authority to the president. At the same time, given the purposes, objectives, and guidelines Congress sets in fast track legislation, a foreign government effectively is negotiating with the Congress, albeit through the Executive Branch.

With delegated authority, then, the United States Trade Representative (USTR) negotiates with other countries, keeping in mind the Congressional purposes and parameters in the fast track legislation. Fast track is famously regarded for its "up or down" voting procedure, whereby Congress cannot amend a negotiated deal. Some commentators view that procedure as undemocratic. In fact, Congressional input exists at several points in the negotiating process, and members from the House Ways and Means Committee and Senate Finance Committee can participate on the negotiating team. The various inputs allow Congress to exercise leverage during the negotiations, and thereby help instill democracy — in the sense of representation of the interests of the broad populace — into the process. When the deal is completed, it is submitted to both houses of Congress for approval by a majority vote. As suggested, Congress must vote on the deal as a single package, and cannot amend the deal. The straight up-or-down vote helps ensure the members of Congress are held accountable to the populace for their positions.

Congress first granted the President — then, President Gerald R. Ford — fast track authority in the *Trade Act of 1974* in connection with the Tokyo Round. Congress renewed that authority periodically (for example, in the *Omnibus Trade and Competitiveness Act of 1988*) to cover the *North American Free Trade Agreement* (*NAFTA*) and the Uruguay Round negotiations. The authority expired in December 1993, hence the rush to finish the Uruguay Round by 15 December 1993. President Clinton became the first President since Gerald Ford to fail to win fast track authority when, in 1997, he abandoned his efforts at re-authorization in the face of stiff opposition from a coalition of unusual bed fellows that crossed traditional political party lines: labor, environmental, human rights, consumer activists, and religious conservatives. The lack of such authority severely hampered the efforts of the Clinton Administration to ignite a Millennium Round of multilateral trade negotiations (as it was dubbed at the time), and push forward *NAFTA* expansion and a *Free Trade Area of the Americas* (*FTAA*).

In 2002, under the *Trade Act of 2002*, specifically, Title XXI of this *Act*, President George W. Bush obtained trade negotiating authority — called *TPA*. (Title XXI of the *Act* bore the rubric of the *Trade Promotion Authority Act*, hence the acronym "*TPA*.") At that time, the Republican Party controlled both houses of Congress, and the *TPA* bill passed the House of Representatives with the support of only 25 Democrats. The essence of TPA is that Congress has 90 days to approve or reject with no changes on a trade agreement that was negotiated and concluded under this authority. The House Ways and Means Committee, and the Senate Finance Committee, are permitted to offer nonbinding recommendations on what ought to be included in the implementing legislation for any trade deal. They do so, if at all, during the mock markup process. But, again, no amendment is permitted from any part of the Congress. Therein lies the "fast track" nature of the procedure — an up or down vote within 90 days.

Using *TPA*, the USTR conducted Doha Development Agenda (DDA) negotiations, and negotiated free trade agreements (FTAs) with Australia, Bahrain, Chile, Colombia, Morocco, Oman, Panama, Peru, and Singapore, plus *CAFTA—DR*. However, *TPA* expired on 30 June 2007. Controversy about its renewal raged, and the issues included not only the Doha Round, but also labor and environmental matters had contributed to the lapse of fast track legislation between 1994 and 2002.

In summer 2007, Congress declined to renew *TPA* for President George W. Bush, partly over concerns that

(1) in the ongoing Doha Round of multilateral trade negotiations, the Administration had not shown sufficient progress to suggest the Round would yield benefits to American agricultural or industrial sectors, and

(2) FTAs proposed by the Administration with certain countries — such as Colombia, Panama, and Peru — raised problems of labor, environmental, or human rights.

In respect of the second concern, Congress insisted any new FTAs —

- Contain special provisions on labor and environmental matters, and specifically use internationally agreed-upon rights as the benchmark (not rules existing in FTA partner countries, as extant rules might be sub-standard from an international perspective).

- Embody relatively flexible provisions on intellectual property right protection (IPR) as regards generic medicines, so as to facilitate trade in them.

Also in respect of the second concern, Congress balked in the summer and fall 2007 at passing an FTA with Colombia because of human rights abuses in that country. Congress said Colombia had a dreadful record of protecting journalists and trade unionists, many of whom had been killed by right-wing paramilitary groups linked to the government. Officials suspected of having ties to these groups had not been prosecuted.

Thus, in an unprecedented move, the House of Representatives changed the rules concerning consideration of the *Colombia FTA*. Implementing legislation was introduced in the 110th Congress by the Administration of George W. Bush. But, one rule change was to delay indefinitely any House action. That meant the bill had to be reintroduced in the House in the 111th Congress, during the Administration of Barack H. Obama. A second rule change was that the House would not apply *TPA* fast track procedures to the *Colombia FTA*. Accordingly, the last FTA submitted by the Bush Administration under *TPA* was the *Korea — United States FTA (KORUS)*, which was signed on 30 June 2007 — the date *TPA* expired.

*Suggestions for Further Research:*

Books:

1.   COHEN, STEPHEN D., ROBERT A. BLECKER & PETER D. WHITNEY, FUNDAMENTALS OF U.S. FOREIGN TRADE POLICY — ECONOMICS, POLITICS, LAWS, AND ISSUES (2nd ed. 2003).

2.   DESTLER, I.M., AMERICAN TRADE POLITICS (4th ed. June 2005).

3.   DEVEREAUX, CHARAN, ROBERT Z. LAWRENCE & MICHAEL D. WATKINS, CASE STUDIES IN TRADE NEGOTIATION, VOLUME 1: MAKING THE RULES, AND VOLUME 2: RESOLVING DISPUTES (Washington, D.C.: Peterson Institute for International

Economics, 2008). *See also* the review of these books by Larry Crump & John S. Odell, *Analyzing Complex U.S. Trade Negotiations*, 24 NEGOTIATION JOURNAL 355–369 (2008).

4.    SHAPIRO, HAL S., FAST TRACK: A LEGAL, HISTORICAL, AND POLITICAL ANALYSIS (2006).

Articles:

1.    Chukwumerije, Okezie, *Obama's Trade Policy: Trends, Prospects, and Portends*, 16 UNIVERSITY OF CALIFORNIA — DAVIS JOURNAL OF INTERNATIONAL LAW & POLICY 39–79 (2009).

2.    Cohee, James R., Note, *The WTO and Domestic Political Disquiet: Has Legalization of the Global Trade Regime Gone Too Far?*, 15 INDIANA JOURNAL OF GLOBAL LEGAL STUDIES 351–374 (2008).

3.    Gantz, David A., *The "Bipartisan Trade Deal," Trade Promotion Authority, and the Future of U.S. Free Trade Agreements*, 28 SAINT LOUIS UNIVERSITY PUBLIC LAW REVIEW 115–153 (2008).

4.    Goldstein, Judith L. & Richard H. Steinberg, *Negotiate or Litigate? Effects of WTO Judicial Delegation on U.S. Trade Politics*, 71 LAW & CONTEMPORARY PROBLEMS 257–282 (2008).

5.    Koh, Harold Hongju, *The Fast Track and United States Trade Policy*, 18 BROOKLYN JOURNAL OF INTERNATIONAL LAW 143 (1992).

6.    McGinnis, John O., *Medellín and the Future of International Delegation*, 118 YALE LAW JOURNAL 1712–1760 (2009).

7.    Pauwelyn, Joost, *New Trade Politics for the 21ˢᵗ Century*, 11 JOURNAL OF INTERNATIONAL ECONOMIC LAW 559–573 (2008).

8.    Rangel, Rep. Charles B., *Moving Forward: A New, Bipartisan Trade Policy that Reflects American Values*, 45 HARVARD JOURNAL ON LEGISLATION 377–419 (2008).

9.    Smith, Charles Anthony, *Credible Commitments and the Early American Supreme Court*, 42 LAW & SOCIETY REVIEW 75–110 (2008).

10. Varellas, James J., *The Constitutional Political Economy of Free Trade: Reexamining NAFTA-Style Congressional Executive Agreements*, 49 SANTA CLARA LAW REVIEW 717–792 (2009).

## FCN TREATY

Treaty of Friendship, Commerce, and Navigation.

FCN Treaties historically have been widely used by the United States and many other countries.

*Suggestions for Further Research:*

Article:

1.    Coyle, John F., *Rethinking the Commercial Law Treaty*, 45 GEORGIA LAW REVIEW 343–407 (2011).

## FCPA

*Foreign Corrupt Practices Act.*

The *Foreign Corrupt Practices Act* was passed by unanimous vote in both Houses of Congress and signed by President Jimmy Carter in 1977.[212] The *FCPA* contains civil sanctions enforced by the Securities and Exchange Commission (SEC) and criminal sanctions enforced by the Department of Justice (DOJ). The statute forbids bribery of foreign government officials, that is, any transfer of a thing of value (above a low *de minimis* threshold) for the purpose of obtaining a benefit (*e.g.*, a government procurement contract.) Summarized, the *FCPA* makes unlawful the "use of the mails or any means or instrumentality of interstate commerce:"[213]

- corruptly,

- in furtherance of an offer, payment, promise to pay, or authorization of the payment or of any money, or offer, gift, promise to give, or authorization of the giving of anything of value,

- to any foreign official [, which includes] any foreign political party or official thereof, any candidate for foreign political office, or to any person, while knowing that all or a portion of such money or thing of value will be offered, given or promised, directly or indirectly to any foreign official,

- for purposes of influencing any act or decision of such foreign official in his official capacity; inducing such foreign official to do or omit to do any act in violation of his lawful duty; securing any improper advantage; or inducing such foreign official to use his influence with a foreign government or instrumentality thereof to affect or influence any act or decision of such government or instrumentality,

- in order to obtain or retain business for or with, or direct business to, any person.[214]

Significantly, the *FCPA* contains an affirmative defense, plus an exemption from the bribery prohibitions.

The affirmative defense is narrow and applies if "the payment, gift, offer, or promise of anything of value that was made, was lawful under the written laws and regulations" of the foreign country.[215] In other words, the affirmative defense is a local law exception. However, that local law "must be affirmatively

---

[212] *Foreign Corrupt Practices Act of 1977*, Pub. L. No. 95–213, 91 Stat. 1494 (codified as amended at 15 U.S.C. §§ 78a, 78dd-1, 78dd-2, 78ff, 78m, 78o (2006)), *amended by Foreign Corrupt Practices Act Amendments of 1988*, 15 U.S.C. §§ 78dd-1 to -3, 78ff (2006) and *International Anti-Bribery and Fair Competition Act of 1998*, 15 U.S.C. §§ 78dd-1 to -3, 78ff (2006).

[213] 15 U.S.C. § 78dd-1(a) (2006).

[214] The summary is provided by, Amy Deen Westbrook, *Enthusiastic Enforcement, Informal Legislation: The Unruly Expansion of the Foreign Corrupt Practices Act*, 45 GEORGIA LAW REVIEW 489, 503–504 (2011).

[215] 15 U.S.C. §§ 78dd-1(c)(1), -2(c)(1), -3(c)(1).

stated and written; neither negative implication, custom, nor tacit approval" is allowed under the affirmative defense.[216]

The exemption is for facilitation, or so-called "grease," payments. The "Grease Payment" exception is an express one to the *FCPA* prohibition of bribery. The exception is for:

> facilitating or expediting payments[s] . . . to expedite or to secure the performance of a routine governmental action. . . .[217]

"Routine governmental action" is defined as:

> only an action which is ordinarily and commonly performed by a foreign official . . . [and] . . . does not include any decision by a foreign official whether, or on what terms, to award new business to or to continue business with a particular party. . . .[218]

Examples specifically mentioned in the *FCPA* include processing governmental papers such as visas, providing phone service, giving police protection, and loading and unloading cargo.[219]

As regards the "Grease Payment" exception, the *FCPA* resembles the *Guidelines* published by the International Chamber of Commerce (ICC). That is, the *Guidelines* contain a similar exemption.[220] In contrast, the *Anti-Bribery Convention of the Organization for Economic Cooperation and Development* (OECD) contains no exception for facilitation payments.[221] This variance is the subject of complaints by some German (and other European) companies, which argue they are at a competitive disadvantage vis-à-vis American firms. That is because American firms are governed by the *FCPA*, and can utilize the exemption, but German companies must work under the *OECD Convention*. These complaints are somewhat ironic, because for years until the Convention was adopted, American businesses argued the *FCPA* handicapped them in their dealings with foreign government officials. A further issue that is important in considering the different anti-bribery regimes is the permissibility (or lack thereof) of tax deductions for facilitation payments.

---

[216] Amy Deen Westbrook, *Enthusiastic Enforcement, Informal Legislation: The Unruly Expansion of the Foreign Corrupt Practices Act*, 45 GEORGIA LAW REVIEW 489, 506 (2011).

[217] 15 U.S.C. §§ 78dd-1 (b), -2(b), -3(b).

[218] 15 U.S.C. §§ 78dd-1(f)(3), -2(h)(4), -3(f)(4).

[219] *See id.* §§ 78dd-1(f)(3)(A)(i)-(v), -2(h)(4)(A)(i)-(v), -3(f)(4)(A)(i)-(v).

[220] *See* COMBATING EXTORTION AND BRIBERY: ICC RULES OF CONDUCT AND RECOMMENDATIONS, (2005), *posted at* www.iccwbo.org/uploadedFiles/ICC/policy/anticorruption/Statements/ICC_Rules_of_Conduct_and_Recommendations%20_2005%20Revision.pdf.

[221] *See* Organization for Economic Cooperation and Development, *Convention on Combating Bribery of Foreign Public Officials in International Business Transactions*, 17 December 1997, 112 Stat. 3302, 37 I.L.M. 1, *posted at* www.oecd.org/dataoecd/4/18/38028044.pdf. 9 December 2009 marked the 10th anniversary of the entry into force of the *OECD Anti-Bribery Convention. See also OECD Recommendation for Further Combating Bribery of Foreign Public Officials in International Business Transactions*, 26 November 2009, *posted at* www.oecd.org/dataoecd/11/40/44176910.pdf.)

Since 2002, enforcement under the *FCPA* has increased significantly. It is estimated there are currently (as of early 2011) 140 open *FCPA* investigations.[222] Compare that number to the first 28 years the *FCPA* was in force, when there were two or three cases initiated a year, and fines generally did not exceed $1,000,000.[223] Due to the upsurge in vigorous enforcement, a number of American businesses and individuals have been caught running afoul of *FCPA* regulations, resulting in billions of dollars in fines paid to the DOJ and SEC, and an increase in the number of individual prison sentences.

For example, in 2007 Lucent Technologies Inc. agreed to pay $2.5 million after an FCPA investigation regarding payments of travel and entertainment expenses for Chinese officials.[224] It was alleged Lucent improperly accounted for certain expenditures related to the Chinese officials in company books and records.

In 2008, Daimler AG paid almost $200 million ($93.6 million to the DOJ and $91.4 million to the SEC, which included $4 million for related alleged violations of the United Nations Oil-for-Food Program) to settle alleged *FCPA* violations.[225] The company neither admitted nor denied the SEC allegations, but did agree to an independent compliance monitor for a period of three years to oversee *FCPA* compliance.

Also in 2008, in one of, if not the, largest case to date, Siemens was ordered to pay $800 million in penalties to United States authorities for *FCPA* violations.[226] $350 million was paid to settle SEC charges and $450 million was paid to settle DOJ criminal charges. The SEC's allegations against Siemens included, but were not limited to: bribes paid in connection with construction regarding transit lines in Venezuela and refineries in Mexico, bribes to obtain business in Argentina regarding the development of national identity cards, and kickbacks to Iraqi ministers under the United Nations Oil for Food Program. The SEC further alleged the violations took place between 12 March 2001 and 30 September 2007, and involved employees at all levels within the company.[227] Siemens neither admitted nor denied the SEC allegations.

---

[222] *See* Amy Deen Westbrook, *Enthusiastic Enforcement, Informal Legislation: The Unruly Expansion of the Foreign Corrupt Practices Act*, 45 Georgia Law Review 489, 496 (2011).

[223] *See* Amy Deen Westbrook, *Enthusiastic Enforcement, Informal Legislation: The Unruly Expansion of the Foreign Corrupt Practices Act*, 45 Georgia Law Review 489, 495 (2011).

[224] *See Lucent Paying $2.5 Million in SEC, DOJ Pacts Over Payments of Chinese Officials' Expenses*, 25 International Trade Reporter (BNA) 79 (17 January 2008).

[225] *See* Yin Wilczek, *Daimler to Pay $200 Million to Settle SEC, DOJ's FCPA Charges, Court Filings Say*, 27 International Trade Reporter (BNA) 514 (08 April 2010).

[226] *See, e.g., SEC Charges Siemens AG for Engaging in Worldwide Bribery, posted at* www.sec.gov/news/press/2008/2008-294.htm.

[227] *See, e.g., SEC Charges Siemens AG for Engaging in Worldwide Bribery, posted at* www.sec.gov/news/press/2008/2008-294.htm.

Regarding the criminal charges brought by the DOJ against the company, Siemens AG, Siemens S.A. — Argentina (Siemens Argentina), Siemens Bangladesh Limited (Siemens Bangladesh), and Siemens S.A. — Venezuela (Siemens Venezuela) all pled guilty to at least one count of violations related to the FCPA.[228] As another instance, in February 2012, Albert (Jack) Stanley, the former Chairman and Chief Executive Officer of Kellogg, Brown & Root, Inc. (KBR), was sentenced to 30 months in prison for FCPA violations.[229] *See United States v. Stanley*, United States District Court for the Southern District of Texas, Criminal Number H-08-597 (24 February 2012). Mr. Stanley participated (with two others) in a conspiracy to bribe Nigerian government officials, resulting in construction contracts worth over $6 billion. Mr. Stanley also was ordered to pay $10.8 million in restitution to KBR, which was the victim in the kickback scheme.

Fines are not the only means of punishment for *FCPA* violations. For instance, in 2010, Virginia resident, Charles Paul Edward Jumet, was sentenced to 87 months in prison for bribing former government officials in Panama.[230] At the time of sentencing, 87 months was the longest prison term imposed for violating the FCPA. Jumet also was ordered to serve three years of supervised release at the end of his prison term and pay a fine of $15,000.

Finally, there exists a cooperation program that can be implemented when there are known *FCPA* violations within a company or by an individual. The SEC announced this cooperation initiative in January 2010. In December 2010, the SEC handed down its first non-prosecution agreement (NPA), in a deal with Carter's Inc., regarding alleged violations by a company sales executive. The SEC has since entered into 25 cooperation agreements (*i.e.*, NPAs) with individuals.[231]

In addition to the use of NPAs, on 17 May 2011 the SEC announced its first-ever deferred prosecution agreement (DPA):

> DPAs are written agreements between the SEC and a cooperating individual or company in which the commission foregoes enforcement action if the company or individual agrees to cooperate, undertake certain measures for a set period of time, pay penalties and/disgorgements, and to tolling of the statute of limitations.[232]

---

[228] *See, e.g., Siemens AG and Three Subsidiaries Plead Guilty to Foreign Corrupt Practices Act Violations and Agree to Pay $450 Million in Combined Criminal Fines*, posted at www.justice.gov/opa/pr/2008/December/08-crm-1105.html

[229] *See Former KBR Chief to Serve 30 Months Over Role in Foreign Bribery Conspiracy*, 29 International Trade Reporter (BNA) 340 (1 March 2012).

[230] *See Virginia Resident's 87-Month Jail Sentence Is Longest for Violation of FCPA*, DOJ Says, 27 International Trade Reporter (BNA) 639 (29 April 2010).

[231] *See* Yin Wilczek, *SEC Signs First Deferred Prosecution Pact; Tenaris to Pay Almost $9M Over Breaches*, 28 International Trade Reporter (BNA) 857 (26 May 2011).

[232] Yin Wilczek, *SEC Signs First Deferred Prosecution Pact; Tenaris to Pay Almost $9M Over Breaches*, 28 International Trade Reporter (BNA) 857 (26 May 2011).

The SEC entered into an agreement with Tenaris S.A. regarding allegations that company employees bribed Uzbekistan officials in order to secure oil pipeline contracts.[233]

In the case of Tenaris, the company self reported *FCPA* violations to the SEC. Furthermore, Tenaris fully cooperated with the SEC and DOJ throughout the case. The DPA agreement was effective from 17 May 2011 to 17 May 2013. During that time Tenaris, was required to ". . . strengthen its FCPA compliance procedures and controls, . . . implement due diligence requirements with respect to the retention and payment of agents, and to provide FCPA training for workers."[234] The DOJ resolved its case against Tenaris through an NPA.[235]

While the cooperation program seemed to work successfully for Tenaris, the program is new and requires further clarity from the SEC. For example, there is a lack of detail available concerning the specific cooperation provided by Tenaris. Therefore, practicing attorneys have little to go on when advising clients regarding whether or not they should cooperate with the SEC.[236]

As recently as 2010, legislation — commonly called the *Dodd-Frank Act*[237] — was adopted to create programs within the SEC to encourage individuals to report violations of laws or regulations, including ones pertaining to the *FCPA*, which take place in their jurisdiction. (The precise scope of what constitutes the jurisdiction of an individual may be unclear.) Significantly, the *Dodd-Frank Act* helps such individuals, who are "whistleblowers," by creating a number of protections for whistleblowers, and by expanding on relief for whistleblowers afforded under the *Sarbanes-Oxley Act*. Further, the *Dodd-Frank Act* clarifies the *FCPA*, and anti-bribery enforcement there under, is subject to the jurisdiction of the SEC. Finally, the *Dodd-Frank Act* also requires issuers to disclose publicly to the SEC payments made to the United States or foreign governments regarding commercial development of oil, natural gas, and minerals.[238]

The "radicalization" of *FCPA* enforcement is a recent phenomenon that has changed the *Act* itself, yet has left the business community with little or no

---

[233] *See* Yin Wilczek, *SEC Signs First Deferred Prosecution Pact; Tenaris to Pay Almost $9M Over Breaches*, 28 International Trade Reporter (BNA) 857 (26 May 2011).

[234] *See* Yin Wilczek, *SEC Signs First Deferred Prosecution Pact; Tenaris to Pay Almost $9M Over Breaches*, 28 International Trade Reporter (BNA) 857 (26 May 2011).

[235] *See* Yin Wilczek, *SEC Signs First Deferred Prosecution Pact; Tenaris to Pay Almost $9M Over Breaches*, 28 International Trade Reporter (BNA) 857 (26 May 2011).

[236] *See* Yin Wilczek, *SEC Signs First Deferred Prosecution Pact; Tenaris to Pay Almost $9M Over Breaches*, 28 International Trade Reporter (BNA) 857 (26 May 2011).

[237] *See* Public Law 111–203, 124 Stat. 1376, codified in scattered sections of the United States Code, including Titles 12 and 15.

Note that the full title of the Dodd-Frank legislation is lengthy, but starts out as the Dodd-Frank Wall Street Reform and Consumer Protection Act. This legislation was the response of the Congress to the financial crisis of 2008–2010.

[238] *See*, Stuart H. Deming, *Anti-Bribery Enforcement, Significant Developments in More Settings*, 40 INTERNATIONAL LAW NEWS 1, 4–6 (Spring 2011).

official guidance regarding compliance.[239] The line between acceptable and unacceptable business practices is not clearly defined. Without official, detailed guidance, companies cannot build effective compliance programs, let alone understand the full scope of *how* to comply. Former General Counsel of the SEC, James Doty, argues "[a]ggressive enforcement, based on an expansive interpretation of a vague statue, a little-used DOJ opinion process, and the temptation perhaps to assume that more draconian criminal enforcement is better, have all lead to a lack of predictability in law enforcement and . . . some incorrect application of" the *FCPA*.[240]

The evolution of the *FCPA* into the ever more aggressive and prominent statute that it is today can be seen as a reaction to various events in the not so distant past. The development of international anti-corruption rules, such as the *OECD Convention*, the 2002 Sarbanes-Oxley Act,[241] and the corruption plagued United Nations Oil-for-Food Program,[242] all encouraged the SEC and DOJ to enforce the FCPA vigorously. Likewise, the global economic crisis triggered by the September 2008 collapse of Lehman Brothers, and Wall Street scandals (including the Bernard L. Madoff $50 billion Ponzi scheme and R. Allen Stanford $8 billion investment fraud)[243] elicited a public perception of regulatory failure and a call for authorities to "do something." One such "something" was increased *FCPA* enforcement. To aid companies in their compliance with *FCPA* regulations general guidance and official classification of acceptable conduct must come from the agencies themselves. The *FCPA* is ". . . a law which is substantively well-suited to the challenges of the 2010s." But, the rigorous enforcement cannot, or at least ought not to, continue without authorities providing formal guidelines so that the private sector has a clearer idea of how best to comply with the *FCPA*.[244]

*Suggestions for Further Research:*

Articles:

1. Benton, Leslie, *et al.*, *Anti-Corruption*, 45 THE INTERNATIONAL LAWYER 345–364 (2011).

---

[239] Amy Deen Westbrook, *Enthusiastic Enforcement, Informal Legislation: The Unruly Expansion of the Foreign Corrupt Practices Act*, 45 GEORGIA LAW REVIEW 489 (2011).

[240] Amy Deen Westbrook, *Enthusiastic Enforcement, Informal Legislation: The Unruly Expansion of the Foreign Corrupt Practices Act*, 45 GEORGIA LAW REVIEW 489, 574 (2011) (*quoting* James R. Doty, *Toward a Reg. FCPA: A Modest Proposal for Change in Administering the Foreign Corrupt Practices Act*, 62 BUSINESS LAWYER 1233, 1233–39 (2007)).

[241] *Sarbanes-Oxley Act of 2002*, Public Law Number 107–204, 116 Stat. 745.

[242] *See generally*, The Independent Inquiry Committee into the United Nations Oil- for-Food Programme ("IIC"), *posted at* www.iic-offp.org/index.html.

[243] Amy Deen Westbrook, *Enthusiastic Enforcement, Informal Legislation: The Unruly Expansion of the Foreign Corrupt Practices Act*, 45 GEORGIA LAW REVIEW 489, 520–521 (2011).

[244] Amy Deen Westbrook, *Enthusiastic Enforcement, Informal Legislation: The Unruly Expansion of the Foreign Corrupt Practices Act*, 45 GEORGIA LAW REVIEW 489, 577 (2011).

2. Bhojwani, Rashna, Note, *Deterring Global Bribery: Where Public and Private Enforcement Collide*, 112 COLUMBIA LAW REVIEW 66–111 (2012).

3. Bonneau, Jacqueline L., Note, *Combating Foreign Bribery: Legislative Reform in the United Kingdom and Prospects for Increased Global Enforcement*, 49 COLUMBIA JOURNAL OF TRANSNATIONAL LAW 365–410 (2011).

4. Brooks, Allen R., Comment, *A Corporate Catch-22: How Deferred and Non-Prosecution Agreements Impede the Full Development of the Foreign Corrupt Practices Act*, 7 JOURNAL OF LAW, ECONOMICS & POLICY 137–162 (2010).

5. Cai, Hongbin, Hanming Fang & Lixin Colin Xu, *Eat, Drink, Firms, Government: An Investigation of Corruption from the Entertainment and Travel Costs of Chinese Firms*, 54 JOURNAL OF LAW & ECONOMICS 55–78 (2011).

6. Carr, Indira, *Fighting Corruption Through the United Nations Convention on Corruption 2003: A Global Solution to a Global Problem?*, 11 INTERNATIONAL TRADE LAW & REGULATION issue 1, 24–29 (January 2005).

7. Cohen, Joel M., Michael P. Holland & Adam P. Wolf, *Under the FCPA, Who is a Foreign Official Anyway?*, 63 BUSINESS LAWYER 1243–1274 (2008).

8. Conti-Brown, Peter, Student Article, *Increasing the Capacity for Corruption?: Law and Development in the Burgeoning Petro-State of São Tomé e Principe*, 12 BERKELEY JOURNAL OF AFRICAN-AMERICAN LAW & POLICY 33–65 (2010).

9. Demas, Reagan R., *Moment of Truth: Development in Sub-Saharan Africa and Critical Alterations Needed in Application of the Foreign Corrupt Practices Act and Other Anti-Corruption Initiatives*, 26 AMERICAN UNIVERSITY INTERNATIONAL LAW REVIEW 315–369 (2011).

10. Einhorn, Aaron, *The Evolution and Endpoint of Responsibility: The FCPA, SOX, Socialist-Oriented Governments, Gratuitous Promises, and a Novel CSR Code*, 35 DENVER JOURNAL OF INTERNATIONAL LAW & POLICY 509–545 (2007).

11. Giudice, Lauren, Note, *Regulating Corruption: Analyzing Uncertainty in Current Foreign Corrupt Practices Act Enforcement*, 91 BOSTON UNIVERSITY LAW REVIEW 347–378 (2011).

12. Grimm, Daniel J., *The Foreign Corrupt Practices Act in Merger and Acquisition Transactions: Successor Liability and Its Consequences*, 7 NEW YORK UNIVERSITY JOURNAL OF LAW & BUSINESS 247–331 (2010).

13. Hinchey, Bruce, Punishing the Penitent: *Disproportionate Fines in Recent FCPA Enforcements and Suggested Improvements*, 40 PUBLIC CONTRACT LAW JOURNAL 393–441 (2011).

14. Jordan, Jon, *Recent Developments in the Foreign Corrupt Practices Act and the New U.K. Bribery Act: A Global Trend Towards Greater Accountability in the Prevention of Foreign Bribery*, 7 NEW YORK UNIVERSITY JOURNAL OF LAW & BUSINESS 845–871 (2011).

15. Jordan, Jon, *The OECD's Call for an End to "Corrosive" Facilitation Payments and the International Focus on the Facilitation Payments Exception Under the Foreign Corrupt Practices Act*, 13 UNIVERSITY OF PENNSYLVANIA JOURNAL OF BUSINESS LAW 881–925 (2011).

16. Koehler, Mike, *The Unique FCPA Compliance Challenges of Doing Business in China*, 25 Wisconsin International Law Journal 397–438 (2007).

17. Koehler, Mike, *The FCPA, Foreign Agents, and Lessons from the Halliburton Enforcement Action*, 36 Ohio Northern University Law Review 457–479 (2010).

18. Kovacich, Matthew J., Comment, *Backyard Business Going Global: The Consequences of Increased Enforcement of the Foreign Corrupt Practices Act ("FCPA") on Minnesota and Wisconsin*, 32 Hamline Law Review 529–569 (2009).

19. Okaru-Bisant, Valentina, *Proposals to Combat the Multilateral Investment Guarantee Agency's Deficiencies: Promoting Private Water Investments and Preventing Corruption and Consumer Risks*, 14 Sustainable Development Law Journal 1–34 (2011).

20. Razzano, Frank C. & Travis P. Nelson, *The Expanding Criminalization of Transnational Bribery: Global Prosecution Necessitates Global Compliance*, 42 The International Lawyer 1259–1286 (winter 2008).

21. Ryznar, Margaret & Samer Korkor, *Anti-Bribery Legislation in the United States and United Kingdom: A Comparative Analysis of Scope and Sentencing*, 76 Missouri Law Review 415–453 (2011).

22. Sanyal, Rajib & Subarna Samanta, *Trends in International Bribe-Giving: Do Anti-Bribery Laws Matter?*, 10 Journal of International Trade Law Policy number 2 151–164 (2011).

23. Singer, Sam, Comment, *The Foreign Corrupt Practices Act in the Private Equity Era: Extracting A Hidden Element*, 23 Emory International Law Review 273–308 (2009).

24. Spahn, Elizabeth, *International Bribery: The Moral Imperialism Critiques*, 18 Minnesota Journal of International Law 155–226 (2009).

25. Trautman, Lawrence J. & Kara Altenbaumer-Price, *The Foreign Corrupt Practices Act: Minefield for Directors*, Virginia Law & Business Review 145–182 (2011).

26. Wallenstein, Joshua C., *Bandits at the Well: FCPA Implications of Extortion at Well Sties in Mexico*, 6 Texas Journal of Oil, Gas & Energy Law 1–22 (2010–2011).

27. Warin, F. Joseph, Michael S. Diamant & Jill M. Pfenning, *FCPA Compliance in China and the Gifts and Hospitality Challenge*, 5 Virginia Law & Business Review 33–80 (2010).

28. Yang, Dean, *Integrity for Hire: An Analysis of a Widespread Customs Reform*, 51 Journal of Law & Economics 25–57 (2008).

29. Young, Kristy E., Pritkin Prize Winner, *The Committee on Foreign Investment in the United States and the Foreign Investment and National Securities Act of 2007: A Delicate Balancing Act that Needs Revision*, 15 University of California — Davis Journal of International Law & Policy 43–70 (2008).

## FDA

The United States Food and Drug Administration (FDA), located in Washington, D.C., with its main offices in Montgomery County, Maryland and field offices in over 150 locations in the United States.

The FDA is an agency in the Executive branch of the Federal government responsible for evaluating the safety of a vast array of food and drug products. In addition to other acts of Congress, the *Food, Drug and Cosmetic Act*, and the *Food and Drug Administration Act*, provide the primary authority and jurisdiction for the FDA.[245] *The Food, Drug and Cosmetic Act* has been amended several times since its original enactment in 1938.

The mission statement of the FDA explains the broad authority of the agency:

> The FDA is responsible for protecting the public health by assuring the safety, efficacy, and security of human and veterinary drugs, biological products, medical devices, our nation's food supply, cosmetics, and products that emit radiation. The FDA is also responsible for advancing the public health by helping to speed innovations that make medicines and foods more effective, safer, and more affordable; and helping the public get accurate, science-based information they need to use medicines and foods to improve their health.[246]

In fulfilling its mission, the FDA oversees the importation, transportation, storage, and sale of approximately U.S. $1 trillion worth of products annually. FDA officials perform tasks such as evaluating applications for new human drugs, complex medical devices, and food additives. Chemists, lawyers, microbiologists, pharmacists, physicians, veterinarians, and other professionals comprise the FDA staff. In 2007, the FDA requested a budget of U.S. $ 2.1 billion from Congress, a 5.3 percent increase from the budget for the 2007 fiscal year.

Products under the jurisdiction of the FDA can be grouped into the following categories: biologics, cosmetics, drugs, foods, medical devices, radiation-emitting electronic products, and veterinary products. Specifically, the FDA has the authority to regulate:

*Biologics*

- Product and manufacturing establishment licensing
- Safety of the nation's blood supply
- Research to establish product standards and develop improved testing methods

*Cosmetics*

- Safety
- Labeling

---

[245] *See* 21 U.S.C. §§ 301–399.

[246] United States Food and Drug Administration, FDA's Mission Statement, posted at www.fda.gov/opacom/morechoices/mission.html.

*Drugs*

- Product approvals
- Over the counter and prescription drug labeling
- Drug manufacturing standards

*Foods*

- Labeling
- Safety of all products (except meat and poultry
- Bottled Water

*Medical Devices*

- Pre-market approval of new devices
- Manufacturing and Performance Standards
- Tracking reports of device malfunctioning and serious adverse reactions

*Radiation-Emitting Electronic Products*

- Radiation safety performance standards for microwave ovens, television receivers, diagnostic
- X-ray equipment, cabinet x-ray systems (such as baggage x-rays at airports), laser products
- Ultrasonic therapy equipment, mercury vapor lamps, and sunlamps
- Accrediting and inspecting mammography facilities

*Veterinary Products*

- Livestock feeds
- Pet foods
- Veterinary drugs and devices[247]

To be sure, there are a number of prominent product and product-related categories not within the ambit of FDA jurisdiction. These include:

- Advertising
- Alcohol
- Consumer products
- Drugs of abuse (*i.e.*, illegal drugs)
- Health insurance
- Meat and poultry
- Pesticides
- Restaurants and grocery stores
- Water

---

[247] *See* U.S. Food and Drug Administration, *What FDA Regulates*, www.fda.gov/comments/regs.html.

Other entities within the Federal government are responsible for overseeing these groups. In some instances, certain state governmental laws or regulations may supplement Federal rules.

The organizational structure of the FDA is complex. The agency is led by a Commissioner, who the President appoints, with the advice and consent of the Senate. (For example, Andrew von Eschenbach has served as the Commissioner since 13 December 2006.) The FDA is subdivided into various centers, each of which specializes in a specific subject matter under the agency's jurisdiction. All offices within the FDA must report to the Office of the Commissioner. Thus, the centers reporting to the Commissioner include:

- Center for Biologics Evaluation and Research
- Center for Food Safety and Applied Nutrition
- Center for Drug Evaluation and Research
- Center for Veterinary Medicine
- Center for Devices and Radiological Health
- National Center for Toxicological Research

In addition, there are other offices that are administrative in nature. They, too, report to the Commissioner. These offices include:

- Office of the Chief of Staff
- Office of Equal Employment Opportunity and Diversity Management
- Office of Regulatory Affairs
- Office of Scientific and Medical Programs
- Office of International and Special Programs
- Office of Operations
- Office of Policy, Planning and Preparedness

Not listed is the Office of General Counsel. Interestingly, the Office of General Counsel provides legal advice to the FDA Commissioner, but reports to the General Counsel of the Department of Health and Human Services (HHS).

The odyssey of the FDA to its current status began in the middle of the 19th century. In 1862, President Abraham Lincoln appointed chemist Charles M. Wetherill to serve in the new Department of Agriculture (USDA). Wetherill and his staff comprised the "Division of Chemistry" in the USDA. In 1901, the "Division of Chemistry" was renamed the "Bureau of Chemistry." The 1906 *Food and Drugs Act* added some regulatory functions to the Bureau of Chemistry, which — in 1927 — was renamed the "Food, Drug, and Insecticide Administration." That name change was initiated when the agency was granted the authority to conduct non-regulatory research.

The FDA received its current moniker in 1930. Until 1940, the FDA remained under the auspices of the USDA. Between 1940 and 1980, the FDA was transferred twice more. In 1940, it came under the control of the now defunct Federal Security Agency. In 1953, the FDA was shifted to the Department of Health,

Education, and Welfare (HEW). Finally, in 1980, HEW was renamed the "Department of Health and Human Services," *i.e.*, HHS. Since then, the FDA remains under the control of that Department. That is why the FDA General Counsel reports to the HHS General Counsel.

One of the sharpest criticisms leveled against the FDA is its use of a three phased system for approving new drugs.

- In Phase I, human subjects are used to study the metabolic and pharmacological actions and side effects of an investigational new drug (IND). The number of subjects included in a Phase I analysis ranges from 20 to 80.

- In Phase II, early controlled clinical studies are conducted to obtain data on the effectiveness of the IND for patients with a particular condition. Phase II testing helps determine the potential short-term side effects of the IND, and involve several hundred subjects.

- Finally, additional studies are performed in Phase III to evaluate the overall benefit-risk relationship of the drug. Phase III studies help the FDA transmit the pros and cons of the IND to the general public, and determine appropriate labeling for physicians. These studies usually involve between several hundred and several thousand subjects.

The essence of the criticisms is that the three Phases are unnecessarily time consuming and expensive. Consequently, the Phases pose a significant barrier to entry into the United States market of medicines tested and available in other countries, and they create a disincentive to developing innovative new pharmaceuticals in the United States.

*Suggestions for Further Research:*

Books:

1. HILTS, PHIL, PROTECTING AMERICA'S HEALTH: THE FDA, BUSINESS, AND ONE HUNDRED YEARS OF REGULATION (2003).

2. SCHACTER, BERNICE ZELDIN, NEW MEDICINES: HOW DRUGS ARE CREATED, APPROVED, MARKETED, AND SOLD (2006).

Book Chapters:

1. Swann, John P., *Food and Drug Administration, in* A HISTORICAL GUIDE TO THE U.S. GOVERNMENT 248–54 (George Thomas Kurian ed., 1998).

Articles:

1. Aginam, Obijiofor, *Food Safety, South—North Asymmetries, and the Clash of Regulatory Regimes*, 40 VANDERBILT JOURNAL OF TRANSNATIONAL LAW 1099–1114 (2007).

2. Anderson, Honorable Justice Winston, *The Caribbean Agricultural Health and Food Safety Agency: Implications for Regional and International Trade*, 12 VERMONT JOURNAL OF ENVIRONMENTAL LAW 255–273 (2011).

3. Chen, Kelly & Rosa Dunnegan-Mallat, *H.R. 3610, the Food and Drug Import Safety Act of 2007*, 42 THE INTERNATIONAL LAWYER 1339–1356 (2008).

4.   Cohoon, Lincoln, Note, *New Food Regulations: Safer Products or More Red Tape?*, 6 JOURNAL OF HEALTH & BIOMEDICAL LAW 343–375 (2010).

5.   DeWaal, Caroline Smith, *Food Safety and Security: What Tragedy Teaches Us About our 100-Year Old Food Laws*, 40 VANDERBILT JOURNAL OF TRANSNATIONAL LAW 921–935 (2007).

6.   Endres, A. Bryan & Michael N. Tarr, *United States Food Law Update: Food Allergy Labels, Reaching Organic Equivalence, Misbranding Litigation, and Regulatory Takings*, 5 JOURNAL OF FOOD LAW & POLICY 223–262 (2009).

7.   Endres, A. Bryan & Michael N. Tarr, *United States Food Law Update: Initial Food Safety Restructuring Efforts, Poultry Production Contract Reforms, and Genetically Engineered Rice Litigation*, 6 JOURNAL OF FOOD LAW & POLICY 103–138 (2010).

8.   Farnese, Patricia L., Canadian Food Law Update, 5 JOURNAL OF FOOD LAW & POLICY 273–285 (2009).

9.   George, Asha M., *Response is Local, Relief is Not: The Pervasive Impact of Agro Terrorism*, 40 VANDERBILT JOURNAL OF TRANSNATIONAL LAW 1155–1170 (2007).

10.  Gilman, Daniel, *Oy Canada&excl; Trade's non-solution to "the Problem" of U.S. Drug Prices*, 32 AMERICAN JOURNAL OF LAW AND MEDICINE 247 (2006).

11.  Hoffman, John T. & Shaun Kennedy, *International Cooperation to Defend the Food Supply Chain: Nations are Talking; Next Step — Action*, 40 VANDERBILT JOURNAL OF TRANSNATIONAL LAW 1171–1187 (2007).

12.  Liu, Chenglin, *The Obstacles of Outsourcing Imported Food Safety to China*, 43 CORNELL INTERNATIONAL LAW JOURNAL 249–305 (2010).

13.  Pagnattaro, Marisa Anne & Ellen R. Peirce, *From China to Your Plate: An Analysis of New Regulatory Efforts and Stakeholder Responsibility to Ensure Food Safety*, 42 GEORGE WASHINGTON INTERNATIONAL LAW REVIEW 1–56 (2010).

14.  Roberts, Michael T., *Cheaters Shouldn't Prosper and Consumers Shouldn't Suffer: The Need for Government Enforcement Against Economic Adulteration of 100% Pomegranate Juice and Other Imported Food Products*, 6 JOURNAL OF FOOD LAW & POLICY 189–233 (2010).

15.  Symposium, *Cultivating Our Future: New Landscapes in Food and Agricultural Law and Policy*, 26 JOURNAL OF ENVIRONMENTAL LAW & LITIGATION 1–146 (2011).

16.  Tai, Stephanie, *Comparing Approaches Towards Governing Scientific Advisory Bodies on Food Safety in the United States and the European Union*, 2010 WISCONSIN LAW REVIEW 627–671 (2010).

17.  Tauxe, Robert V., *Food Borne Infections and the Global Food Supply: Improving Health at Home and Abroad*, 40 VANDERBILT JOURNAL OF TRANSNATIONAL LAW 899–919 (2007).

18.  Trachtman, Elizabeth A., Note, *Food-borne Illnesses Strike U.S. Food Supply: A Discussion of Inadequate Safety Procedures and Regulations in the U.S. and Abroad*, 20 INDIANA INTERNATIONAL & COMPARATIVE LAW REVIEW 385–414 (2010).

19. Trexler, Nathan M., Note, *"Market" Regulation: Confronting Industrial Agriculture's Food Safety Failures*, 17 WIDENER LAW REVIEW 311–345 (2011).

## FDI

Foreign direct investment, sometimes referred to as "direct foreign investment," or "DFI."

Generally speaking, FDI occurs for three reasons:

- Cost, *i.e.*, cost-driven FDI, where foreign operations, integrated in a chain, result in economically efficient production.

- Policy, *i.e.*, policy-driven FDI, where domestic policy lures foreign investment).

- Location, *i.e.*, border-driven FDI, because of economic, social, or political environment around a border.

To be sure, the choice of one particular location for a direct investment may involve two or all three of these factors. Moreover, the importance of rule of law, and the stable, predictable business environment it creates, cannot be underestimated — in theory or practice.

FDI is a matter relevant to international trade law in part because it is commonly thought that investment follows trade, and the more trade, the more investment. As a general empirical matter, that proposition appears to hold true. Moreover, trade agreements typically contain provisions affecting FDI. The WTO *Agreement on Trade-Related Investment Measures* (*TRIMs*) deals with non-discriminatory treatment of FDI, and numerous free trade agreements (FTAs) cover this topic, and often standards for expropriation, as well. Notably, in the WTO *General Agreement on Trade in Services* (*GATS*), the third mode of delivery of service supply — Mode III, defined in *GATS* Article I:2(c) — is FDI.

The *GATS*, and negotiations on liberalization of Mode III service delivery under it, as brought considerable attention to the kinds of barriers that exist to FDI. Such barriers may be put into three categories:

- Barriers to the Entry and Establishment of FDI

Examples of barriers include (1) bans on FDI in certain sectors, (2) quantitative restrictions on foreign ownership, (3) screening, approval, and minimum capital requirements, (4) conditions on location or subsequent investment, and (5) admission taxes.

- Barriers to the Ownership and Control of FDI

Examples of barriers include (1) compulsory joint ventures (JVs) with domestic investors, (2) limitation on the number of foreign members of the board of directors of an investment, or government appointment of certain board members, (3) government approval for certain decisions, (4) restrictions on the rights of shareholders, and (5) mandatory transfers of share ownership to domestic investors within a prescribed period.

- Operational Measures that Inhibit FDI

Examples of barriers include (1) local content, or performance requirements, (2) restrictions on the importation of capital, labor, or raw materials, (3) limitations on the repatriation of capital and profits, or on royalty payments, and (4) licensing (or permit) rules.

Intensive, sector-by-sector (and sub-sector-by-sub-sector) negotiations over the defense or removal of such barriers are part of the Doha Round of negotiations, as well as many FTA talks.

*Suggestions for Further Research:*

Books:

1.   CAMPBELL, DENNIS, ED., INTERNATIONAL PROTECTION OF FOREIGN INVESTMENT (2007).

2.   HEAD, JOHN W., GLOBAL BUSINESS LAW: PRINCIPLES AND PRACTICE OF INTERNATIONAL COMMERCE AND INVESTMENT (2nd ed., 2007).

3.   SALACUSE, JESWALD W., THE LAW OF INVESTMENT TREATIES (2010).

4.   SEID, SHERIF H., GLOBAL REGULATION OF FOREIGN DIRECT INVESTMENT (2002).

5.   SORNARAJAH, M., THE INTERNATIONAL LAW ON FOREIGN INVESTMENT (2004).

Articles:

1.   Alvarez-Jiménez, Alberto, *Foreign Investors, Diplomatic Protection, and the International Court of Justice's Decision on Preliminary Objections in the Diallo Case*, 33 NORTH CAROLINA JOURNAL OF INTERNATIONAL LAW AND COMMERCIAL REGULATION 437–454 (2008).

2.   Alvarez-Jiménez, Alberto, *New Approaches to the State of Necessity in Customary International Law: Insights from WTO Law and Foreign Investment Law*, 19 AMERICAN REVIEW OF INTERNATIONAL ARBITRATION 463–488 (2008).

3.   Brewer, Thomas & Stephen Young, *Investment Issues at the WTO: The Architecture of Rules and the Settlement of Disputes*, 13 JOURNAL OF INTERNATIONAL ECONOMIC LAW 457 (1998).

4.   Bridgeman, Natalie L. & David B. Hunter, *Narrowing the Accountability Gap: Toward a New Foreign Investor Accountability Mechanism*, 20 GEORGETOWN INTERNATIONAL ENVIRONMENTAL LAW REVIEW 187–236 (2008).

5.   Brown, Katherine L., Student Article, *A Comparative Analysis of the Chinese and Czech Legal Systems: Which System is More Favorable to and Provides More Stability for Foreign Direct Investment?*, 8 LOYOLA UNIVERSITY CHICAGO INTERNATIONAL LAW REVIEW 205–227 (2011).

6.   Chacon de Albuquerque, Roberto, *The Disappropriation of Foreign Companies Involved in the Exploration, Exploitation and Commercialization of Hydrocarbons in Bolivia*, 14 LAW & BUSINESS REVIEW OF THE AMERICAS 21–52 (2008).

7.   Claussen, Kathleen, Comment, *The Casualty of Investor Protection in Times of Economic Crisis*, 118 YALE LAW JOURNAL 1545–1555 (2009).

8. Collins, David, *A New Role for the WTO in International Investment Law: Public Interest in the Post-Neoliberal Period*, 25 CONNECTICUT JOURNAL OF INTERNATIONAL LAW 1–35 (2009).

9. Dolzer, Rudolf, *Fair and Equitable Treatment: A Key Standard in Investment Treaties*, 39 THE INTERNATIONAL LAWYER 87–106 (spring 2005).

10. Duong, Wendy, *Effect of Artificial Intelligence on the Pattern of Foreign Direct Investment in the Third World: A Possible Reversal of Trend*, 36 DENVER JOURNAL OF INTERNATIONAL LAW & POLICY 325–334 (2008).

11. Ellig, Jerry & Houman B. Shadab, *Talking the Talk, or Walking the Walk? Outcome-based Regulation of Transnational Investment*, 41 NEW YORK JOURNAL OF INTERNATIONAL LAW & POLITICS 265–340 (2009).

12. Feng, Yiheng, Note, *"We Wouldn't Transfer Title to the Devil:" Consequences of the Congressional Politicization of Foreign Direct Investment on National Security Grounds*, 42 NEW YORK UNIVERSITY JOURNAL OF INTERNATIONAL LAW AND POLITICS 253–310 (2009).

13. Footer, Mary E., *Bits and Pieces: Social and Environmental Protection in the Regulation of Foreign Investment*, 18 MICHIGAN STATE JOURNAL OF INTERNATIONAL LAW 33–64 (2009).

14. Foster, George K., *Striking a Balance between Investor Protections and National Sovereignty: The Relevance of Local Remedies in Investment Treaty Arbitration*, 49 COLUMBIA JOURNAL OF TRANSNATIONAL LAW 201–267 (2011).

15. Francioni, Francesco, *Access to Justice, Denial of Justice, and International Investment Law*, 20 EUROPEAN JOURNAL OF INTERNATIONAL LAW 729–747 (2009).

16. Garnett, Richard, *National Courts, Arbitration and Investment Treaties*, 60 INTERNATIONAL & COMPARATIVE LAW QUARTERLY 485–498 (2011).

17. Gillman, Eric, *Note, Legal Transplants in Trade and Investment Agreements: Understanding the Exportation of U.S. Law to Latin America*, 41 GEORGETOWN JOURNAL OF INTERNATIONAL LAW 263–301 (2009).

18. Glen, Patrick J., *Law as Asymmetric Information: Theory, Application, and Results in the Context of Foreign Investment in Real Estate*, 8 Berkeley BUSINESS LAW JOURNAL 116–151 (2011).

19. Goldstein, Andrea, *Foreign Direct Investment and Mexican Development — A Look at Recent Trends*, 16 LAW & BUSINESS REVIEW OF THE AMERICAS 673–696 (2010).

20. Hallisy, Conaire Michael, Comment, *Riches to Rubles: Problems Russia Must Address to Increase Direct Investment from U.S. Private Equity*, 16 TULSA JOURNAL OF COMPARATIVE & INTERNATIONAL LAW 137–171 (2008).

21. Hiscock, Mary E., *The Emerging Legal Concept of Investment*, 27 PENN STATE INTERNATIONAL LAW REVIEW 765–782 (2009).

22. Huang, Hui, *The Regulation of Foreign Investment in Post-WTO China: A Political Economy Analysis*, 23 COLUMBIA JOURNAL OF ASIAN LAW 185–215 (2009).

23. *Investor—State Arbitration Symposium: Perspectives on Legitimacy and Practice*, 22 SUFFOLK TRANSNATIONAL LAW REVIEW 247–524 (2009).

24. Johnson, Lise, *International Investment Agreements and Climate Change: The Potential for Investor-State Conflicts and Possible Strategies for Minimizing It*, 39 ENVIRONMENTAL LAW REPORTS, NEWS & ANALYSIS 11147–11160 (2009).

25. Kurtz, Jürgen, *The Use and Abuse of WTO Law in Investor—State Arbitration: Competition and Its Discontents*, 20 EUROPEAN JOURNAL OF INTERNATIONAL LAW 749–771 (2009).

26. MacLean, Robert G., *The Valuation of Damages in International Investment Disputes*, 14 LAW & BUSINESS REVIEW OF THE AMERICAS 3–18 (2008).

27. Maniruzzaman, A.F.M., *The Pursuit of Stability in International Energy Investment Contracts: A Critical Appraisal of the Emerging Trends*, 1 THE JOURNAL OF WORLD ENERGY LAW & BUSINESS, no. 2, 119–155 (2008).

28. Moloo, Rahim & Alex Khachaturian, *The Compliance with the Law Requirement in International Investment Law*, 34 FORDHAM INTERNATIONAL LAW JOURNAL 1473–1501 (2011).

29. Morrison, Fred L., *The Protection of Foreign Investment in the United States of America*, 58 AMERICAN JOURNAL OF COMPARATIVE LAW 437–453 (2010).

30. O'Brien, Justin, *Barriers to Entry: Foreign Direct Investment and the Regulation of Sovereign Wealth Funds*, 42 THE INTERNATIONAL LAWYER 1231–1257 (2008).

31. Odumosu, Ibironke T., *The Law and Politics of Engaging Resistance in Investment Dispute Settlement*, 26 PENN STATE INTERNATIONAL LAW REVIEW 251–287 (2007).

32. Okaru-Bisant, Valentina, *Proposals to Combat the Multilateral Investment Guarantee Agency's Deficiencies: Promoting Private Water Investments and Preventing Corruption and Consumer Risks*, 14 SUSTAINABLE DEVELOPMENT LAW JOURNAL 1–34 (2011).

33. Petersman, Ernst-Ulrich, *International Rule of Law and Constitutional Justice in International Investment Law and Arbitration*, 16 INDIANA JOURNAL OF GLOBAL LEGAL STUDIES 513–533 (2009).

34. Rosenberg, Arnold S., *et al.*, *International Commercial Transactions, Franchising, and Distribution*, 45 THE INTERNATIONAL LAWYER 191–204 (2011).

35. Salacuse, Jeswald W., *The Emerging Global Regime for Investment*, 51 HARVARD INTERNATIONAL LAW JOURNAL 427–473 (summer 2010).

36. Salazar, Alberto R. V., *NAFTA Chapter 11, Regulatory Expropriation, and Domestic Counter-Advertising Law*, 27 ARIZONA JOURNAL OF INTERNATIONAL & COMPARATIVE LAW 31–82 (2010).

37. Sarkar, Rumu, *Critical Essay—A "Re-Visioned" Foreign Direct Investment Approach from an Emerging Country Perspective: Moving from a Vicious Circle to a Virtuous Cycle*, 17 ILSA JOURNAL OF INTERNATIONAL & COMPARATIVE LAW 379–392 (2011).

38. Schill, Stephan W., *W(h)ither Fragmentation? On the Literature and Sociology of International Investment Law*, 22 European Journal of International Law 875–908 (2011).

39. Shepston, Megan Overly, Note, *When Private Stakeholders Fail:Adapting Expropriation Challenges in Transnational Tribunals to New Governance Theories (Methanex Corp. v. United States, 44 I.L.M. 1345, 2005; Martina Polasek, Biwater Gauff (Tanzania) Ltd. v. United Republic of Tanzania, 22 ICSID Rev. — Foreign Investment L.J. 149, 2007)*, 71 OHIO STATE LAW JOURNAL 341–380 (2010).

40. Sweeney, Matthew, Note, *Foreign Direct Investment in India and China: The Creation of a Balanced Regime in a Globalized Economy*, 43 CORNELL INTERNATIONAL LAW JOURNAL 207–248 (2010).

41. Sykes, Alan O., *Transnational Forum Shopping as a Trade and Investment Issue*, 37 JOURNAL OF LEGAL STUDIES 339–378 (2008).

42. Trakman, Leon E., *Foreign Direct Investment: Hazard or Opportunity?*, 41 THE GEORGE WASHINGTON INTERNATIONAL LAW REVIEW 1–66 (2009).

43. Trujillo, Elizabeth, *Mission Possible: Reciprocal Deference Between Domestic Regulatory Structures and the WTO*, 40 Cornell International Law Journal 201–263 (winter 2007).

44. Tuck, Andrew P., *The "Fair and Equitable Treatment" Standard Pursuant to the Investment Provisions of the U.S. Free Trade Agreements with Peru, Colombia, and Panama*, 16 Law & Business Review of the Americas 385–408 (2010).

45. Tuck, Andrew P., *United States—Chile FTA Chapter 10: Lessons from NAFTA Chapter 11 Jurisprudence*, 15 LAW & BUSINESS REVIEW OF THE AMERICAS 575–600 (2009).

46. Van Aaken, Anne, *International Investment Law between Commitment and Flexibility: A Contract Theory Analysis*, 12 JOURNAL OF INTERNATIONAL ECONOMIC LAW 507–538 (2009).

47. Vila, Adris Maria, *The Role of States in Attracting Foreign Direct Investment:A Case Study of Florida, South Carolina, Indiana, and Pennsylvania*, 16 LAW & BUSINESS REVIEW OF THE AMERICAS 259–281 (2010).

48. Viñuales, Jorge E., *State of Necessity and Peremptory Norms in International Investment Law*, 14 LAW & BUSINESS REVIEW OF THE AMERICAS 79–103 (2008).

49. Wang, Guiguo, *China's Practice in International Investment Law: From Participation to Leadership in the World Economy*, 34 YALE JOURNAL OF INTERNATIONAL LAW 575–587 (2009)

50. Weimer, Christopher M., Note, *Foreign Direct Investment and National Security Post-FINSA 2007*, 87 TEXAS LAW REVIEW 663–684 (2009).

51. Yalpaala, Kojo, *Rethinking the Foreign Direct Investment Process and Incentives in Post-Conflict Transition Countries*, 30 NORTHWESTERN JOURNAL OF INTERNATIONAL BUSINESS LAW 23–99 (2010).

## FEALAC

Forum for East Asia — Latin America Cooperation.

FEALAC has 34 member states, including Australia, China, Japan, New Zealand, many other East Asian states, and almost all Latin American countries. In August 2011, FEALAC issued a 66-point declaration committing itself to refraining from any protectionist or trade-distorting measures affecting trade in goods or services, or foreign direct investment (FDI).[248] Trade among FEALAC countries (as of 2011) accounts for 13 percent of total world trade. Whether all such countries were faithful to the concepts underlying the declaration, however, is another matter. The *MERCOSUR* countries of Argentina, Brazil, Paraguay, and Uruguay all enacted import-substitution measures in the wake of the global economic slump triggered in 2008. Those measures are designed to purchase goods and services from within the customs union rather than overseas.

## FEDERAL CIRCUIT

The United States Court of Appeals for the Federal Circuit (CAFC), located in Washington, D.C.

Specifically, the court is located in the Howard T. Markey National Courts Building on Lafayette Square. The CAFC was created on 1 October 1982 under Article III of the United States Constitution. The CAFC was born of the decision by Congress to merge the United States Court of Customs and Patent Appeals with the appellate division of the United States Court of Claims. The CAFC is the only court among the 13 circuit courts of appeal in the United States that has national jurisdiction. Further, it is the only circuit court of appeals that is based on subject matter, rather than geographic location. The CAFC mostly hears cases in Washington, D.C. But, it can and periodically does sit in other locations.

The subject matter jurisdiction of the CAFC spans a reasonably focused range of topics, namely:

- International trade
- Government contracts
- Patents
- Trademarks
- Certain money claims against the United States government
- Federal personnel
- Veterans benefits.

The jurisdiction of the CAFC is set forth in 28 U.S.C. §§ 1295–1296. In addition to local rules and internal operating procedures of the CAFC, the basic rules about the procedure of the Court are controlled by Title 28 of the United States Code (U.S.C.) and Federal Rules of Appellate Procedure.

---

[248] *See* David Haskel, *East Asia — Latin America Forum Vows to Boost Bilateral Trade, Fight Protectionism*, 28 International Trade Reporter (BNA) 1448 (8 September 2011).

The CAFC has jurisdiction over appeals from any federal district court, and certain federal courts of limited jurisdiction, namely, the United States Court of International Trade (CIT), United States Court of Federal Claims, and the United States Court of Appeals for Veteran Claims. Further, the CAFC has the authority to hear appeals from decisions made by the following United States government administrative agencies:

- United States International Trade Commission (ITC), for final determinations relating to unfair practices in import trade under Section 337 of the *Tariff Act of 1930*, as amended
- United States Merit Systems Board Protection
- Board of Contract Appeals
- Board of Patent Appeals and Interferences
- Trademark Trial and Appeals Board
- Office of Compliance of the United States Congress
- Government Accountability Office (GAO) Personnel Appeals Board.

Interestingly, the United States Supreme Court recently narrowed the jurisdiction of the CAFC over patent cases to only those actions in which the patent issue arises in the complaint. *See Holmes Group, Inc. v. Vornado Air Circulation Sys., Inc.*, 535 U.S. 826 (2002).

Approximately 55 percent of the docket of the CAFC is filled by administrative law cases, which consist mainly of personnel and veterans claims. Another 31 percent of the docket is comprised of intellectual property (IP) cases, nearly all of which involve patents. A further 11 percent of cases involve money damages against the United States government, including government contracts, tax refund appeals, unlawful takings, and civilian and military pay disputes. Appeals from the CIT make up only a small portion of the remaining docket.

Twelve judges sit on the CAFC, all of whom are appointed by the President with the advice and consent of the Senate. Judges at the CAFC, like all judges under Article III of the United States Constitution, are appointed for life. The Table sets out the current judges of the CAFC.[249]

---

[249] In 2010, President Barack H. Obama appointed Edward Carroll DuMont, a Washington, D.C.-based attorney originally from California, to fill a vacancy on the Court of Appeals for the Federal Circuit. The Senate Judiciary Committee failed to act on his nomination. He would have been the first openly gay federal appellate court judge. In November 2011, he asked the President that his nomination be withdrawn. *See* Tony Dutra, *Edward DuMont Asks Obama to Withdraw His Nomination for Seat on Federal Circuit*, 28 International Trade Reporter 1872 (BNA) (17 November 2011).

## TABLE:

## JUDGES ON THE UNITED STATES COURT OF APPEALS FOR THE FEDERAL CIRCUIT

| Judge | Appointed By President | Year of Appointment | Home State (or Country) |
|---|---|---|---|
| Chief Judge | | | |
| Chief Circuit Judge Randall R. Rader | Bush (George H.W.) | 1989 | Nebraska |
| Judges | | | |
| Judge Evan Jonathan Wallach | Obama | 2011 | Arizona |
| Judge Kathleen ("Kate") M. O'Malley | Obama | 2010 | Ohio |
| Judge Jimmie V. Reyna | Obama | 2010 | New Mexico |
| Judge Sharon Prost | Bush (George W.) | 2001 | Massachusetts |
| Judge Kimberly A. Moore | Bush (George W.) | 2006 | Maryland |
| Judge William C. Bryson | Clinton | 1994 | Texas |
| Judge Richard Linn | Clinton | 1999 | New York |
| Judge Timothy B. Dyk | Clinton | 2000 | Massachusetts |
| Judge Pauline Newman | Reagan | 1984 | New York |
| Senior Status | | | |
| Senior Circuit Judge S. Jay Plager | Bush (George H.W.) | 1989 | New Jersey |
| Senior Circuit Judge Alan D. Lourie | Bush (George H.W.) | 1990 | Massachusetts |
| Senior Circuit Judge Raymond C. Clevenger, III | Bush (George H.W.) | 1990 | Kansas |
| Senior Circuit Judge Alvin A. Schall | Bush (George H.W.) | 1992 | New York |
| Senior Circuit Judge Haldane Robert Mayer | Reagan | 1987 | New York |
| Senior Circuit Judge Arthur J. Gajarsa | Clinton | 1997 | Italy |

A number of senior judges also sit on the CAFC. Eligible judges may elect to take senior status, which allows them to serve on the Court while handling fewer cases than a judge in active service, without retiring completely from the Court. Like all Article III judges, a judge of the CAFC may be designated and assigned by the Chief Justice of the United States Supreme Court to perform judicial duties in a United States Court of Appeals or United States District Court.

Cases at the CAFC are heard by three judge panels. Judges are assigned to the panels randomly. One judge on the panel is designated as the presiding judge. The presiding judge assigns a member of the panel to prepare the opinion of the Court. The United States Supreme Court has jurisdiction over appeals from the CAFC.

When reviewing a judgment of the CIT concerning a final determination of the United States Department of Commerce (DOC) or ITC, the CAFC reapplies that CIT's standard of review. Thus, for example, in an AD case, the CAFC will accords substantial deference to a statutory interpretation by the DOC or ITC. That deference is based on the *Chevron* standard of review. In turn, the Federal Circuit will uphold a CIT determination unless it is unsupported by substantial evidence or otherwise not in accordance with law.

*Suggestions for Further Research:*

Articles:

1.  Baisburd, Yohai, John Boscariol, & Cyndee B. Todgham Cherniak, *et al.*, *Customs Law*, 45 THE INTERNATIONAL LAWYER 3–17 (spring 2011).

2.  Carman, Gregory W., *A Critical Analysis of the Standard of Review Applied by the Court of Appeals for the Federal Circuit in Antidumping and Countervailing Duty Cases*, 13. FEDERAL CIRCUIT BAR JOURNAL 203 (2003).

3.  Chorev, Nitsan, *The Judicial Transformation of the State: The Case of U.S. Trade Policy, 1974–2004*, 31 LAW & POLICY 31–68 (2009).

4.  Dreyfuss, Rochelle Cooper, *The Federal Circuit: A Continuing Experiment in Specialization*, 54 CASE WESTERN RESERVE LAW REVIEW 769 (2004).

5.  Fandl, Kevin J., *2010 International Trade Law Decisions of the Federal Circuit*, 60 AMERICAN UNIVERSITY LAW REVIEW 1121–1157 (2011).

6.  Fitch, Patrick A., *2009 International Trade Law: Decisions of the Federal Circuit*, 59 AMERICAN UNIVERSITY LAW REVIEW 1077–1113 (2010).

7.  Goldfeder, Jarrod M., *2008 International Trade Decisions of the Federal Circuit*, 58 AMERICAN UNIVERSITY INTERNATIONAL LAW REVIEW 975–1049 (2009).

8.  Hall, Munford Page, II & Michael S. Lee, *2007 International Trade Decisions of the Federal Circuit*, 57 AMERICAN UNIVERSITY LAW REVIEW 1145–1196 (2008).

9.  Janicke, Paul M., *Two Unsettled Aspects of the Federal Circuit's Patent Jurisdiction*, 11 VIRGINIA JOURNAL OF LAW & TECHNOLOGY 3 (2006).

10. Linn, Richard, *The Future Role of the United States Court of Appeals for the Federal Circuit Now That It Has Turned 21*, 53 AMERICAN UNIVERSITY LAW REVIEW 731 (2004).

11. Mayer, Haldane Robert, *Reflections on the Twentieth Anniversary of the Court of Appeals for the Federal Circuit*, 52 AMERICAN UNIVERSITY LAW REVIEW 761 (2003).

12. Newman, Pauline, *The Federal Circuit in Perspective*, 54 AMERICAN UNIVERSITY LAW REVIEW 821 (2005).

13. Plager, S. Jay, *A Review of Recent Decisions of the United States Court of Appeals for the Federal Circuit: Foreword: The Price of Popularity: The Court of Appeals for the Federal Circuit 2007*, 56 AMERICAN UNIVERSITY LAW REVIEW 751 (2007).

14. Shuttleworth, Lauren, Note, Is 35 U.S.C. § 271(f) Keeping Pace with the Times? The Law After the Federal Circuit's Cardiac Pacemakers Decision (Cardiac Pacemakers, Inc. v. St. Jude Medical, Inc., 576 F.3d 1348, 2009), 29 JOURNAL OF LAW & COMMERCE 117–139 (2010).

15. Williams, Barbara S., *Critical Decisions by the U.S. Court of Appeals for the Federal Circuit and the U.S. Court of International Trade in Customs 28 U.S.C. § 1581(a) Cases*, 41 GEORGETOWN JOURNAL OF INTERNATIONAL LAW 161–187 (2009).

## FEI—RANIS MODEL

### *The Concept of Labor Surplus and Labor Surplus Models*

Labor Surplus Models represent a conceptual shift from the Harrod—Domar and Solow Models, and from New Growth Theory. To be sure, none of them highlights the role of international trade, but the Labor Surplus Models differentiate between a traditional and modern sector of an economy. That is, they incorporate the realistic observation that many developing or least developed countries have dual economies.

In the traditional, or agricultural, sector, little capital or technology is used — and whatever capital or technology is employed in planting, growing, and harvesting, it is simple. Farming techniques are labor intensive, *i.e.*, a large amount of labor is used per unit of land. Life in this sector is lived at a subsistence level. Farmers consume what they plant, grow, and harvest. By contrast, in the modern sector, also called the industrial or manufacturing sector, production may be capital intensive, *i.e.*, in some countries merchandise may be produced using a large amount of capital per unit of labor. In this dualistic environment, agricultural output is a large percentage of overall output. It may account for one quarter, or even one third, of Gross Domestic Product (GDP), whereas in a developed country agricultural production tends to be less than 10 percent of GDP.

To be sure, identifying just two sectors remains a simplistic way of looking at an economy. Within agriculture, there are many sectors, from the growing of primary commodities to the processing of foods. Likewise, within manufacturing, there are many sectors, from low-value added merchandise like textiles and apparel to high-value added products like transportation equipment. Still, as explored below, Labor Surplus Models have the virtue of highlighting the process of growth through industrialization, and explaining how this process depends on the rural sector.

In particular, as its rubric intimates, the premise of any Labor Surplus Model is the existence of a large amount of labor in the agricultural sector that is unproductive. Specifically, they add nothing to total output, or even may cause it to fall — in economic terms, explained below, they have zero or negative marginal productivity, respectively. This pool of workers is "labor surplus," and it is the base for industrialization. With respect to surplus laborers, the law of diminishing returns, which the classical economist, David Ricardo, articulated, has set in. The Graph shows the law of diminishing returns.

As the Graph suggests, the first few units of labor added to land bring about increased output. But, as more and more units are added, the increases in output level off, and at some point the marginal amount of output falls. ("Marginal" in an economic sense means "additional" or "incremental," but has no normative or pejorative connotation.) At that point, adding more workers to a unit of farmland leads to less and less additional output, because the land cannot accommodate so many workers. (Imagine workers crowded together on a small rice paddy.) No marginal product, or even a negative marginal product, results from the marginal farmer. Eventually, the marginal product of an additional worker may be negative, meaning the addition of a worker actually causes a decline in total output.

It may be rational, from an economic standpoint, for surplus agricultural laborers to migrate to the industrial sector. However, custom and family ties may keep them on the land. Thus, a casual observer of a farm with labor surplus may witness one or more extended families working the land. The wage they earn is at subsistence level, $W_S$. Yet, if the marginal product of a particular worker is less than the value of $W_S$, then that worker represents disguised unemployment. The worker may be engaged in some activity, but in fact he is unemployed, as the value of what he produces does not amount to the wage paid to the worker, even a subsistence wage. Not surprisingly, at $W_S$, it is not possible to generate savings.

## GRAPH:

## LAW OF DIMINISHING RETURNS

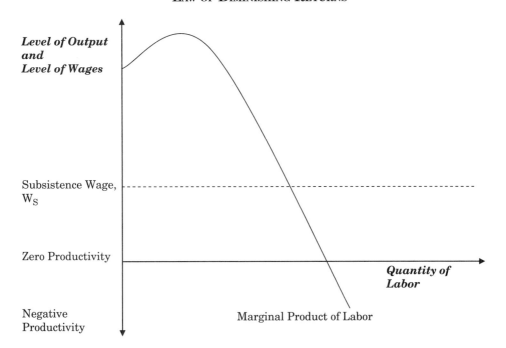

*Level of Output and Level of Wages*

Subsistence Wage, W$_S$

Zero Productivity

*Quantity of Labor*

Negative Productivity

Marginal Product of Labor

The picture in the industrial sector is rather different. There is no surplus labor, and enterprises operate in the rational economic sense of maximizing profits. The wage rate in manufacturing, W$_M$, is low, because of the availability of labor surplus from the agricultural sector. As long as that pool exists, there is no need for capitalists to pay a wage much above subsistence, W$_S$, to attract workers from that pool. That is, W$_M$ is just enough above W$_S$ to coax surplus laborers off the farms and into the factories. For their part, capitalists make use of a different kind of surplus — the difference between the

(1) price at which the merchandise made in their factories is sold to consumers, and

(2) cost of manufacturing — as profit.

The profit is available for re-investment in their enterprises.

The essential teaching of the Labor Surplus Models is industrialization is a process in which labor surplus is transferred from the agricultural sector to the industrial sector. Put simply, industrialization requires getting workers who are not contributing much to agricultural output off the farm and into factories, where they can make a positive impact on merchandise output. In this respect, the dualistic economy is an integrated one — they do not grow independently of one another.

Indeed, agricultural output rises when labor surplus is removed to the industrial sector. Not crowded together on a unit of land (such as a rice paddy), the remaining smaller number of farmers can work more easily and effectively, so their marginal output rises, and total output increases as well. Consequently, both sectors can grow in tandem. Similarly, the government could make use of some of the labor surplus without adversely affecting agriculture, and indeed in support of both agricultural and industrial growth, by employing it to build and improve infrastructure. Depending on the particular country and context, developing roads, power plants, ports, irrigation, and communications facilities may be especially growth-enhancing projects.

In a 1954 article, *Economic Development with Unlimited Supplies of Labor*, and a 1955 book, *The Theory of Economic Growth*, Sir William Arthur Lewis pioneered Labor Surplus modeling. In their book, *Development of the Labor Surplus Economy* (1964), economists John Fei and Gustav Ranis built on the work of Lewis. The first Graph below depicts the basic Lewis Labor Surplus Model. The second Graph below depicts the Fei—Ranis Labor Surplus Model. In the Lewis Model, there are two Panels. Panel I depicts the labor market in the agricultural sector. Panel II shows the labor market in the industrial sector.

### The Lewis Labor Surplus Model

In the Graph of the Lewis Model, the agricultural sector, Panel I, the supply of agricultural labor curve, $S_{AL}$, is perfectly elastic at $W_s$. The perfect elasticity means labor exists in this sector in abundance, and no change in wage is needed to increase the number of laborers in the sector. The Marginal Product curve, which bespeaks the law of diminishing returns, also reflects the demand for labor in the agricultural sector. (In neoclassical economic theory, a worker is paid according to the marginal revenue product made by the worker, *i.e.*, the value of the marginal product. Stated differently, the demand for labor depends on, and varies inversely with, the marginal product of labor, which makes intuitive sense.) In the Lewis Model, the normal equilibrium level of employment would be $L_e$, the intersection of labor supply and demand (marginal product). However, because of labor surplus conditions, and the lack of rational, profit-maximizing behavior, employment is at a higher level. As intimated earlier, it may be at such a high level that marginal productivity goes beyond zero, and is negative. If and when these workers are transferred to the industrial sector, agricultural output would rise.

In the industrial sector, Panel II, a labor market akin to one in which rational profit-maximizing behavior occurs is evident. The supply curve for industrial labor, $S_{IL}$, is flat at $W_M$, which is just above $W_S$. As long as labor surplus exists in the agricultural sector for owners of capital to extract, $S_{IL}$ stays flat at $W_M$. As soon as capitalists exhaust the pool, they have to pay a higher wage rate to attract workers off the farm, who, at this point, are earning more than $W_S$ because labor surplus no longer hamstrings their operations. They can produce and sell more output than before. The demand curve for labor reflects the marginal productivity of workers in industry, $MP_I$, and multiple such curves may be drawn to represent expanding demand. Assuming capitalists reinvest their profits and add new capital equipment, they can rely on the pool of labor surplus from agriculture to keep wages low and profits for investment high. With additional capital equipment, the marginal productivity of industrial workers rises, as is evident from the outward (right-hand) shifts in $MP_I$ curves. Total output also rises, as does the production possibility frontier for the economy.

GRAPH:

THE LEWIS LABOR SURPLUS MODEL

**Panel I:**     **Labor Market in the Agricultural Sector**

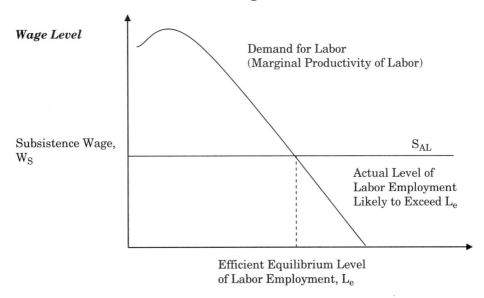

**PANEL II:**     LABOR MARKET IN THE INDUSTRIAL SECTOR

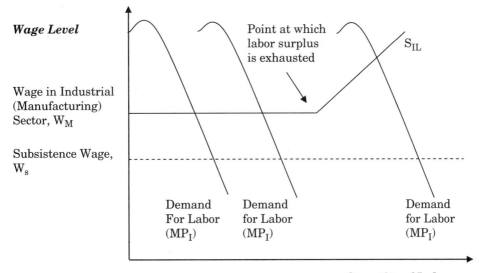

During this phase of industrialization, no harm is done to the agricultural sector. To the contrary, as indicated earlier, the removal of labor surplus from it boosts both marginal productivity of remaining farmers and total agricultural output. However, growth does not continue so easily forever. When the demand for industrial labor exhausts the pool of labor surplus from agriculture, shown by the right-hand most curve, wages rise to the point the demand curve intersects with $S_{IL}$, well above $W_M$. Now, costs to capitalists go up, and they have an incentive to employ capital-intensive processes in order to minimize labor costs. Heretofore, capitalists deployed labor-using, not labor-substituting, methods in order to take advantage of surplus labor. Industrialization and growth enters a new phase.

Notably, withdrawal of any more workers from the agricultural sector will cause a decline in total output from that sector, because such workers have a positive marginal productivity. To prevent this outcome, that is, to allow for a diminution in the number of agricultural laborers without a negative impact on output, it will be necessary to introduce other factors of production, such as capital and technology, into the agricultural sector.

### The Fei—Ranis Labor Surplus Model

In the Fei—Ranis Labor Surplus Model, Panel I is new. However, two of the three Panels are familiar. Panels II and III depict the agricultural and industrial labor markets, respectively. The concepts and processes in Panels II and III are as described for the Lewis Model.

Briefly, in Panel II, the horizontal axis measures the quantity of labor in the agricultural sector, and the vertical axis measures the marginal productivity of labor in that sector. As the quantity of labor increases, *i.e.*, as there are more workers on the farm, marginal productivity falls. At the transition point, it is zero.

In Panel III, the horizontal axis depicts the quantity of labor in the industrial sector. A rightward shift in this axis indicates more workers employed in factories. It corresponds to fewer workers on the farm, because in a labor surplus economy, workers move from the agricultural to the industrial sector. Thus, the transition point, where surplus labor is exhausted, is the same in both sectors.

At the transition point, when labor surplus no longer exists in the agricultural sector, all workers whose marginal productivity is zero have shifted to the industrial sector. If capitalists seek to lure still more workers off the farm, then they must raise wages. That is because the workers remaining on the farm have a positive marginal productivity and, consequently, command wages above subsistence level. They have no incentive to move to factory jobs unless those jobs pay above (possibly well above) subsistence level. The labor supply curve illustrates this fact, as it is flat up to the transition point, but rises thereafter. As usual, the demand curves for labor, which illustrate alternative levels of demand by capitalists for workers, and which reflect the marginal revenue product of those workers, slope downward, reflecting the inverse relationship between wage levels and the willingness and ability of capitalist to employ labor (*i.e.*, the higher the wage rate they must pay, the less the quantity of labor they demand, and in turn the more keen they are to find labor-substitutes).

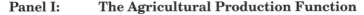

GRAPH:

THE FEI—RANIS LABOR SURPLUS MODEL

**Panel I:     The Agricultural Production Function**

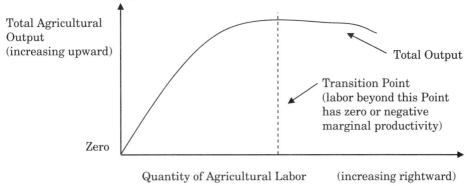

Total Agricultural
Output
(increasing upward)

Total Output

Transition Point
(labor beyond this Point
has zero or negative
marginal productivity)

Zero

Quantity of Agricultural Labor     (increasing rightward)

**Panel II:     The Agricultural Labor Market**

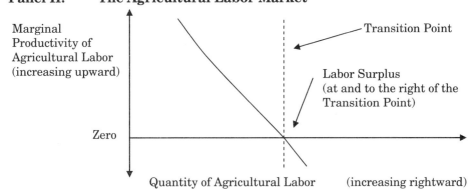

Marginal
Productivity of
Agricultural Labor
(increasing upward)

Transition Point

Labor Surplus
(at and to the right of the
Transition Point)

Zero

Quantity of Agricultural Labor     (increasing rightward)

**Panel III:     The Industrial Labor Market**

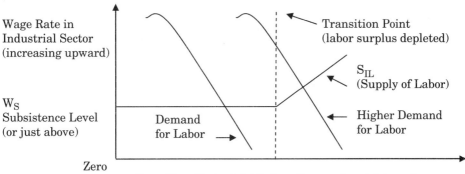

Wage Rate in
Industrial Sector
(increasing upward)

Transition Point
(labor surplus depleted)

$S_{IL}$
(Supply of Labor)

$W_S$
Subsistence Level
(or just above)

Demand
for Labor →

Higher Demand
for Labor

Zero

Quantity of Industrial Labor   (increasing rightward)

With respect to Panel I, the agricultural production function indicates the total output in the agricultural sector. The vertical axis measures total output. An upward movement indicates increased output. The horizontal axis depicts the quantity of workers in the agricultural sector, *i.e.*, in effect, the number of workers on farms. A rightward movement on this axis is an increase in the quantity of those workers. The production function indicates total output falls as the quantity of labor in that sector rises. The reason, of course, is the declining marginal productivity of labor. The transition point indicates the point at which the marginal productivity of agricultural workers is zero. Observe, therefore, the increase in output as labor is withdrawn from the agricultural sector, *i.e.*, a leftward movement on the horizontal axis.

In sum, the three-Panel Fei—Ranis Labor Surplus Model tells a visual story of growth through industrialization, which in turn is fueled by movement of labor surplus from the agricultural to industrial sector. Panel I shows the effect of industrialization on agricultural output, illustrating a rise in total agricultural output as this surplus leaves agrarian lands for factory shop floors. Panel II depicts the rise in marginal productivity of agricultural workers as labor surplus shifts to the industry. Panel III highlights the ability of capitalists to pay a subsistence wage (or just above that level) to attract labor surplus off the farm, but the necessity to increase wages once that pool of workers is depleted. What role exists for international trade in this story?

The short answer is there is no explicit role. Industrialization through labor surplus takes the lead role. However, trade can play a supporting role. First, as industrial output expands, where do capitalists sell the output? They look to their domestic market. However, if and when this market becomes saturated, and profit margins thereby shrink, they look overseas. In other words, export markets may absorb increased industrial production. Second, exports of that production generate revenue that capitalists may use to import capital equipment. Indeed, as their labor costs rise after the transition point, they have an incentive to shift away from labor-intensive, and toward labor-saving, production processes.

In addition to exporting industrial products and importing capital equipment, trade may enter into the labor surplus growth story in two other ways. In the agricultural sector, as Panel I exhibits, output rises after the transition point, *i.e.*, once surplus labor is withdrawn from farms. Who consumes the additional primary and processed farm goods? One answer, of course, is factory workers. Typically, this group expands in size and is based in and around urban areas, such as Bombay, Mexico City, Sao Paolo, and Shanghai. To the extent surplus agricultural output exists, *i.e.*, to the extent a country produces enough food for its own people, it may become a net exporter of agricultural products. That is, the increased agricultural output, made possible by increased marginal productivity, enables the country to generate and export excess production. Naturally, it earns revenues from these exports. It might save these revenues, and channel them into capital investments in the industrial sector. It also might spend some of the revenues on agricultural commodities, in which it does not specialize, *i.e.*, in which it lacks a comparative advantage. For example, China might export rice to Kansas in exchange for beef. In sum, in the process of industrialization in a labor surplus economy, exports and imports are not the principal catalyst. But, they can support that process.

### Critique of Labor Surplus Models and the Role of Trade

China and India are obvious candidates for the label "labor surplus economy." Each has several hundred million people living in rural areas. However, by no means do Labor Surplus Models capture reality in every developing and least developed country. Not all such countries evidence labor surplus. Some countries are under-populated, albeit with fast-growing populations, and rely heavily on foreign workers. While not necessarily developing countries, the six members of the Gulf Cooperation Council (GCC) — Bahrain, Oman, Qatar, Kingdom of Saudi Arabia, Kuwait, United Arab Emirates, and Yemen — illustrate the point. Even if a country has a large supply of labor, it does not mean the country has labor surplus at all times. Some farm workers may be needed, and have a positive marginal productivity, on a seasonal basis — *e.g.*, when crops are planted or harvested. In the off-season, their productivity may be zero. Still, as a generalization, several poor countries in Africa, Asia, and Latin America demonstrate labor surplus characteristics, to one degree or another.

Another less-than-realistic aspect of Labor Surplus Models concerns international trade. These Models do not ascribe any explicit role to exports or imports in the industrialization process. Most developing and least developed countries engage in some trade, however small. In fact, the need to do so can be seen even within a Labor Surplus framework. These Models ascribe the most important role in the story of growth to industrialization, not trade.

As workers are pulled out of the agricultural sector, their consumption level may rise, because they are paid slightly higher wages in industry than the subsistence wage they got as farmers. Domestic production might not satisfy entirely their consumption demand. Some consumer goods may need to be imported to meet the wants of the burgeoning urban population. Were agricultural output to fall because industrialization proceeds beyond the point of extracting surplus labor, then it may be necessary to import food items. As for exports, they may result from higher industrial output. If not all output of a particular kind of merchandise can be consumed directly, then the excess may be exported abroad in exchange for needed imports. In brief, while trade is not the protagonist in a Labor Surplus Model, it could well be an important supporting actor.

*Suggestions for Further Research:*

Books:

1.   FEI, JOHN C. & GUSTAV RANIS, DEVELOPMENT OF THE LABOR SURPLUS ECONOMY: THEORY AND POLICY (1964).

2.   HIRSCHMAN, ALFRED O., THE STRATEGY OF ECONOMIC DEVELOPMENT (1958).

3.   LEWIS, W. ARTHUR, ECONOMIC DEVELOPMENT WITH UNLIMITED SUPPLIES OF LABOR (1954).

4.   LYNN, STUART R., ECONOMIC DEVELOPMENT: THEORY AND PRACTICE FOR A DIVIDED WORLD 43, 56–59 (2003) (including Figures 3–1, 3–3A and 3–3B).

Articles:

1. Grabowski, Richard, *Commercialization, Nonagriculture Production, Agricultural Innovation, and Economic Development*, 29 JOURNAL OF DEVELOPING AREAS 41–62 (October 1995).

2. Rosenstein-Rodan, Paul N., *Problems of Industrialization of Eastern and South-Eastern Europe*, 53 ECONOMIC JOURNAL 202–11 (June-September 1943).

3. Streeten, Paul, *Balanced versus Unbalanced Growth*, THE ECONOMIC WEEKLY (20 April 1963).

## FIBER(S)

"Fiber" (or "fibers") are materials that are continuous or discrete elongated pieces, similar to thread.

Fiber is used in the production of other materials, and can be spun into thread, as well as rope or filaments. Fiber may be natural, such as vegetable fibers like cotton, hemp, jute, and linen, or animal fibers like hair, silk, or wool, or they may be man-made (*e.g.*, acrylic, nylon, polyester, rayon, or spandex). Synthetic fibers, which are a subset of man-made fibers, are made from a chemical process, and sometimes are called "filaments."

## FIBER FORWARD

A rule of origin for textile and apparel merchandise that requires the production process, from the creation of fiber to the completion of the finished article, be conducted in a particular country for the article to qualify as originating in that country.

## FICCI

Federation of Indian Chambers of Commerce and Industry.

## FILL RATE

A term used in the context of quotas or tariff rate quotas (TRQs). The term refers to the amount of actual in-quota imports compared to the quota threshold. The rate is expressed as a percentage. Thus, for example, in 2002 the average fill rate of European Union (EU) TRQs on farm products was 62 percent.[250]

## FINAL LIQUIDATION RATE

*See* Administrative Review, Retrospective assessment.

---

[250] *See* Daniel Pruzin, *WTO Report Criticizes EU Barriers to Farm Imports Despite CAP Reforms*, 24 International Trade Reporter (BNA) 260 (22 February 2007).

## FITTINGS AND TRIMMINGS

A textile and apparel (T&A) term referring to items frequently added to apparel articles, such as bow buds, buttons, decorative lace trim, elastic strips (that are less than one inch width and used in the production of bras), eyes, hooks, labels, sewing thread, snaps, zippers, and zipper tapes.

Under the United States *African Growth and Opportunity Act* (*AGOA*), the origin and value of fittings and trimmings is limited to 25 percent. That is, up to 25 percent of the costs of the components of the assembled article is allowed to secure eligibility — if the value of findings and trimmings exceeds that percentage, then the article is ineligible for an *AGOA* preference. However, for purposes of one *AGOA* preference category, thread is not considered a finding or trimming. In practice, that means the thread must be from the United States.

## FIVE YEAR REVIEW (5 YEAR REVIEW)

*See* Sunset Review.

## FLEXIBILITY (FLEXIBILITIES)

A generic term used to connote an exception to an obligation in an international trade agreement.

The term "flexibility" is not a technical one, but rather encompasses one or more options a WTO Member might have to derogate from an obligation. There are many different kinds of flexibilities. For example, in the context of agriculture negotiations, flexibilities for developing countries might include (1) a maximum (rather than minimum) average tariff cut, (2) a lesser tariff cut than under an agreed-upon formula, (3) smaller cuts on Sensitive Products, along with tariff-rate quota (TRQ) expansions for those Products to ensure some minimum amount of increased market access, (4) smaller, or no, cuts on Special Products, and (5) extended implementation periods during which to take on obligations. The same, or similar, flexibilities may be relevant for agriculture subsidy reductions. Indeed, these derogations were precisely the kinds of flexibilities contemplated during the later stages (2007–2008) of the Doha Round.

From these illustrations, it is apparent that flexibilities fall into two broad categories. Some of them are an unconditional derogation for a category of countries. Special and differential treatment for developing or least developed countries, as in an extended period in which to phase in obligations, are in this category. Others take the form of conditional partial deviation, as is the case with a minimum TRQ expansion (the condition) for a less-than-full tariff cut to a Sensitive Product (the partial deviation).

## FLO

Fairtrade Labeling Organizations International, (FLO).

*See* Fair Trade.

## FMCSA

Federal Motor Carrier Safety Administration.

The FMCSA is a division of the United States Department of Transportation. This division is in charge of regulating commercial transport vehicles on America's highways.

The FMCSA has been at the center of a debate and protracted issue about the entry of Mexican trucks on those highways. It walks a tightrope between guaranteeing the safety of all motorists and traffic on the interstate highway system, and abiding by the provisions of the *North American Free Trade Agreement (NAFTA)* to allowing for cross border trucking services.

## FMV

Foreign Market Value, now called "Normal Value." Foreign Market Value, or "FMV" for short, was the term used in pre-Uruguay Round American anti-dumping (AD) law to refer to the price at which a foreign company sells in its home market merchandise that is the same as or similar to merchandise it allegedly dumps in an importing country. "FMV" was replaced by "Normal Value" as of 1 January 1995.

## FOOD AID (FOOD ASSISTANCE)

The provision of food freely, *i.e.*, donations, at a drastically reduced price, or through extraordinary credit terms.

The United States donates food as international aid to needy countries. It does so through the United States Agency for International Development (USAID) and the Foreign Agricultural Service (FAS). The United States has four basic food assistance programs:

(1) Food For Peace (Public Law 480 programs)

This program offers food assistance to countries under one or more schemes. A country may obtain food aid under more than one of the schemes. Commonly called "P.L. 480," the eponym refers to the statutory origins of the scheme — the 1954 *Agricultural Trade and Development and Assistance Act*, which was Public Law 83–480, passed during the administration of President Dwight D. Eisenhower.

Title I of the *Act*, called *Trade and Development Assistance*, provides food donations in the form of grants or long term loans for governments with little foreign exchange reserves and no other way to meet their food security needs.

Title II of the *Act* is dubbed *Emergency and Private Assistance*. This Title allows for food donations to governments and private organizations in countries in which emergencies may affect adversely food security.

Title III is *Food For Development*. It establishes government-to-government grants of food for least developed countries. The food that is the subject of the grant, in turn, is sold domestically within the country obtaining the grant to support economic development. In other words, the United States gives a poor country a grant of food. That country then sells the food domestically, thereby raising proceeds that it can use for development purposes. Currently, this Title is not active (*i.e.*, the United States is not offering grants under this Title).

(2) Food For Progress

The *Food for Progress Act of 1985* created this second category of food assistance. This Reagan-era *Act* allows for donation or credit sale of American commodities to developing countries and emerging democracies, and for the proceeds of sales of these commodities to be used to fund economic or agricultural programs.

(3) Food For Education

Food For Education is commonly called the McGovern Dole program, after its chief sponsors former Senators George McGovern (Democrat-South Dakota) and Robert Dole (Republican-Kansas). It provides donations of American agricultural products to benefit schools and child nutrition projects in poor countries that are committed to universal education.

(4) Section 416(b)

This program originally was authorized during the administration of President Harry S. Truman under the *1949 Farm Bill* (the *Agriculture Act of 1949*). It allows stocks of commodities of the Commodity Credit Corporation (CCC) to be donated to foreign countries. However, over the years the United States has reduced its stockpile of farm goods. With fewer goods in storage, the Section 416(b) became progressively obsolete. It is currently inactive.

*Suggestions for Further Research:*

Article:

1. Fisher, David, *Fast Food: Regulatory Emergency Food Aid in Sudden-Impact Disasters*, 40 VANDERBILT JOURNAL OF TRANSNATIONAL LAW 1127–1153 (2007).

## FOOD SAFETY

See FDA.

## FOOD SECURITY

Narrowly and conventionally defined, "food security" means a country must be as self-sufficient as possible with respect to the basic dietary needs of its people. Naturally, translated into policy, food security means discouraging imports of agricultural products, and promoting domestic production of substitute items.

However, the idea that food security can be achieved by shutting down international trade and emphasizing self-reliance is sheer folly. As *The Economist* rightly explained:

The argument for self-sufficiency is easiest to counter. Anyone who believes autarky is the route to food security should look at starving North Korea. In world markets trade barriers, not the lack of them, have exacerbated the mess. The commodities that have seen the biggest price spikes are those which tend to be traded least. Only 6% of global rice production, for instance, flows across borders. Unilateral export restrictions, such as those imposed by Vietnam and India, have made matters worse. Global supply is disrupted and domestic farmers discouraged from producing more. The route to deeper, less volatile markets lies through freer trade and fewer distortions. The notion that free trade precludes food security is plainly wrong-headed.[251]

Accordingly, a broader approach to the concept is that "food security" extends beyond self-reliance on food production. Such security is said to exist when all people at all times have access to sufficient, safe, and nutritious food to meet preferences for an active, healthy life. The access may well be provided by the international trading system.

The narrow approach has been influential in China, particularly under Chairman Mao Zedong, India, especially under Prime Ministers Jawaharlal Nehru and Indira Gandhi, and Pakistan for most of its history. In the 1970s, for example, these countries boasted of independence in food, and of being net food exporters. Underlying this definition is that such independence enhances national security. However, in recent years, most countries have moved away from the self-sufficiency approach to embracing (with various degrees of enthusiasm) the idea that food security can be achieved through open trade, market access, and non-trade distorting subsidies.

In 2011, the United Nations Human Rights Council and World Trade Organization (WTO) got in a spat about whether international trade rules harm food security.[252] In November 2011, the Human Rights Council Special Rapporteur on the Right to Food, Olivier de Schutter, argued that countries should limit their reliance on international trade to enhance their food security. He did so in a report published in November 2011 entitled *The World Trade Organization and the Post-Global Food Crisis Agenda: Putting Food Security First in the International Food System*. The Special Rapporteur argued in favor of policy interventions that insulate domestic from international markets, including tariff rate quotas (TRQs), marketing boards, export restrictions, safeguards, and public stockholding of food.

The Special Rapporteur also said that many WTO rules on agriculture are ambiguous, and thus inject uncertainty into international commodity markets, and that the Doha Round negotiations have done nothing to help poor countries increase public investment in agriculture and food security. He also said

---

[251] *The Doha Dilemma*, THE ECONOMIST, 31 May 2008, at 82.

[252] *See* World Trade Organization, *Lamy Rebuts UN Food Rapporteur's Claim that WTO Talks Hold Food Rights "Hostage,"* 14 December 2011, *posted at* ww.wto.org/english/news_e/news11_e/agcom_14dec11_e.htm.

that existing rules do not give poor countries the policy space (*i.e.*, flexibility) they need to increase such investment. Finally, the Special Rapporteur urged that food security be a primary goal of WTO rules and the Doha Round, not a mere byproduct.

The WTO rebutted that international trade is part of the solution to achieve food security. It did so in December 2011 via a letter from its Director-General, Pascal Lamy. The WTO said policy interventions of the kind advocated by the Special Rapporteur distort price signals, which then discourage the efficient allocation of resources within an economy, and diminish domestic purchasing power. In the end, such policies dampen growth in *per capita* Gross Domestic Product (GDP), which is essential to long-run food security. The WTO noted 60 percent of agriculture exports from developing countries go to other developing countries. Hence, any policy measures that dampen this pattern of exports would hurt poor countries. Conversely, the WTO pointed out that under WTO rules, state trading enterprises (STEs) must act in a non-discriminatory manner in accordance with commercial considerations.

As a more enlightened approach, the WTO counseled for the use of Green Box support, under Annex II, Paragraph 2, of the *Agreement on Agriculture*. It also encouraged use of development programs under Article 6:2 of the *Agreement on Agriculture*. That Article allows developing countries to use generally available investment subsidies, and agricultural input subsidies generally available to low-income and resource-poor producers, even if such subsidies distort trade. Developing countries may do so without limitation. The WTO noted that Article 6 also allows for *De Minimis* subsidies, including product-specific support, with special and differential treatment of up to 10 percent of the total value of agricultural production as the *De Minimis* threshold, plus 10 percent of the value of production of each agricultural product as the per-product cap.

The WTO also pointed to development-friendly provisions in the December 2008 Doha Round Draft Modalities Text on Agriculture, particularly concerning:

- Public stockholding for food security, namely, exempting such stocks, if their goal is to support low-income, resource-poor producers, from the Aggregate Measure of Support (AMS) computation, and thus from cuts.

- Domestic food aid, which would be classified in the Green Box).

- Subsidies for relief from natural disasters, which developing countries could provide, in the form of direct payments related to disasters, crop or production insurance, or pest and disease-prevention assistance, without regard to the standard requirement that there must be a loss of more than 30 percent of production value to trigger such support.

Of course, there was no consensus these Doha Round provisions ultimately would be adopted. Moreover, the WTO ignored the mid-to-late 20th century experiences of China and India, albeit controversial, both of which achieved a considerable degree of food security through restrictions on international trade.

Certainly, like poverty, food security is not just an absolute concept. Food security is relative to global trends in agricultural production and population. By 2050 (based on projections as of February 2012), world agricultural output needs to increase by 70 percent to feed and expected 9 billion people.[253]

There are three United Nations agencies dedicated to enhancing food security.[254] Their combined annual budget (as of February 2012) is $4.5 billion. These agencies, each of which is in Rome, are:

(1) Food and Agriculture Organization (FAO), founded in 1945.

(2) World Food Program (WFP), founded in 1961.

(3) International Fund for Agricultural Development (IFAD), founded in 1977.

The very fact they are in Rome is one basis for criticism of them. They might be more effective if they were in the field, particularly in developing and least developed countries. To make matters worse, despite their common headquarter location, they hardly interact. Functioning as independent entities means they overlap and behave inefficiently. Still another criticism is of their leadership, particularly Jacques Diouf of Senegal, who headed the FAO for almost 20 years (from January 1994 through December 2011).[255] Such criticism come from (*inter alia*), Bill Gates, founder of Microsoft, who has donated about $2 billion to food security causes.

*Suggestions for Further Research:*

Articles:

1.   Aoki, Keith, *Food Forethought: Intergenerational Equity and Global Food Supply – Past, Present, and Future*, 2011 WISCONSIN LAW REVIEW 399–478 (2011).

2.   Birchfield, Lauren & Jessica Corsi, *Between Starvation and Globalization: Realizing the Right to Food in India*, 31 MICHIGAN JOURNAL OF INTERNATIONAL LAW 691–764 (2010).

3.   Bobo, Jack A., *The Role of International Agreements in Achieving Food Security: How Many Lawyers does it take to Feed a Village?*, 40 VANDERBILT JOURNAL OF TRANSNATIONAL LAW 1937–947 (2007).

4.   Czarneski, Jason J., *Food, Law & the Environment: Informational and Structural Changes for a Sustainable Food System*, 31 UTAH ENVIRONMENTAL LAW REVIEW 263–290 (2011).

---

[253] *See* Mark Wolski, *Agriculture Secretary Vilsack Calls on China to Work with U.S. to Address Global Hunger*, 29 International trader Reporter (BNA) 290 (23 February 2012).

[254] *See* Javier Blas, *Gates Attacks "Outdated" UN Food Agencies*, FINANCIAL TIMES, 24 February 2012, at 5.

[255] *See* Javier Blas, *Gates Attacks "Outdated" UN Food Agencies*, FINANCIAL TIMES, 24 February 2012, at 5; *Jacques Diouf*, WIKIPEDIA, *posted at* http://en.wikipedia.org/wiki/Jacques_Diouf.

5. Echols, Marsha A., *Paths to Local Food Security: A Right to Food, A Commitment to Trade*, 40 VANDERBILT JOURNAL OF TRANSNATIONAL LAW 1115–1126 (2007).

6. Gonzalez, Carmen G., *Climate Change, Food Security, and Agrobiodiversity: Toward a Just, Resilient, and Sustainable Food System*, 22 FORDHAM ENVIRONMENTAL LAW REVIEW 493–522 (2011).

7. Kaufmann, Christine & Simone Heri, *Liberalizing Trade in Agriculture and Food Security — Mission Impossible?*, 40 VANDERBILT JOURNAL OF TRANSNATIONAL LAW 1039–1070 (2007).

8. Lambert, David P., *The Quest to End Hunger in Our Time: Can Political Will Catch Up with Our Core Values?*, 6 JOURNAL OF FOOD LAW & POLICY 167–188 (2010).

9. Linnekin, Baylen J., *The "California Effect" & the Future of American Food: How California's Growing Crackdown on Food & Agriculture Harms the State & the Nation*, 13 CHAPMAN LAW REVIEW 357–389 (2010).

10. Nierenberg, Lily Endean, Note, *Reconciling the Right to Food and Trade Liberalization: Developing Country Opportunities*, 20 MINNESOTA JOURNAL OF INTERNATIONAL LAW 619–647 (2011).

11. Schoenbaum, *Thomas J. Fashioning a New Regime for Agricultural Trade: New Issues and the Global Food Crisis*, 14 JOURNAL OF INTERNATIONAL ECONOMIC LAW 593–611 (2011).

12. Sealing, Keith E., *Attack of the Balloon People: How America's Food Culture and Agriculture Policies Threaten the Food Security of the Poor, Farmers, and Indigenous Peoples of the World*, 40 VANDERBILT JOURNAL OF TRANSNATIONAL LAW 1015–1037 (2007).

13. Symposium, *Farming and Food: How We Grow What We Eat*, 3 GOLDEN GATE UNIVERSITY ENVIRONMENTAL LAW JOURNAL 1–180 (2009).

14. Symposium, *Food and Agriculture Systems*, 22 FORDHAM ENVIRONMENTAL LAW REVIEW 493–710 (2011).

15. Winter, Lauren, Note, *Cultivating Farmers' Rights: Reconciling Food Security, Indigenous Agriculture, and TRIPs*, 43 VANDERBILT JOURNAL OF TRANSNATIONAL LAW 223–254 (2010).

## FOOD SOVEREIGNTY

The right of people to define their own goals with respect to food, including on matters of food security (namely, the degree of self-reliance), environmental impacts of how food is produced and processed.

*Suggestions for Further Research:*

Articles:

1. Hauter, Wenonah, *The Limits of International Human Rights Law and the Role of Food Sovereignty in Protecting People from Further Trade Liberalization Under the Doha Round Negotiations*, 40 VANDERBILT JOURNAL OF TRANSNATIONAL LAW 1071–1098 (2007).

2.  Linnekin, Baylen J., *The "California Effect" & the Future of American Food: How California's Growing Crackdown on Food & Agriculture Harms the State & the Nation*, 13 CHAPMAN LAW REVIEW 357–389 (2010).

3.  Symposium, *Farming and Food: How We Grow What We Eat*, 3 GOLDEN GATE UNIVERSITY ENVIRONMENTAL LAW JOURNAL 1–180 (2009).

## FOREIGN AGRICULTURAL SERVICE

The agency within the United States Department of Agriculture (USDA) responsible for promoting international agricultural trade, exports of American farm products, and agricultural development.

Specific functions of the Foreign Agriculture Service (FAS) include research on trade trends and scientific issues as they relate to agriculture, resolving agricultural trade barrier controversies, preparing materials for key briefings and meetings, and sponsoring international agricultural training programs. Notably, all agricultural trade negotiations associated with the WTO, and on food aid, are coordinated through the FAS.

The FAS is one of only a few entities in the United States government that operates a Foreign Service unit placing Attachés at key embassies. The FAS is divided into several functional units, called "Offices," as follows:

*   OCRA —

    The Office of Country and Regional Affairs, which analyzes country and region specific trade matters.

*   ONA —

    The Office of Negotiations and Agreements, which is responsible for negotiating and enforcing multilateral and bilateral trade accords.

*   OCBD —

    The Office of Capacity Building and Development, which distributes food aid, funds capacity-building projects, and coordinates educational exchanges.

*   OTP —

    The Office of Trade Policy, which assists in formulating and advancing United States international agricultural trade policy.

*   OFSO —

    The Office of Foreign Service Operations, which coordinates Foreign Service matters.

*   OA —

    The Office of the Administrator, which provides administrative support for the FAS.

*   OSTA —

    The Office of Scientific and Technical Affairs, which tracks the evolution of scientific standards affecting international agricultural trade, monitors the impact on trade of international regulations, and works with APHIS.

- OGA —

  The Office of Global Analysis, which provides commodity-by-commodity analyses.

## FOREIGN EXCHANGE RESERVES

*See* BOP.

## FOREIGN TRADE ZONE

*See* FTZ.

## FOREX

A shorthand expression for foreign exchange.

## FREE RIDER

An economic term that in the international trade law context means a country is not making any trade concessions, yet is profiting from concessions made by other countries, typically by operation of the most-favored nation (MFN) principle.

WTO agreements exhibit both allowance and prohibition of free ridership, depending on the agreement. For example, the *Information Technology Agreement (ITA)* allows for free riding. The benefits of zero- or low-duty treatment on high-technology products are available to all WTO Members, regardless of whether they have made concessions on those products and joined the *ITA*. In contrast, the *Agreement on Government Procurement (GPA)* does not countenance free ridership. The benefits of the market liberalization and transparency in government procurement provided by one Member that is a party to the *GPA* extend only to other Members that also have joined the *GPA*.

## FREE TRADE FUNDAMENTALIST

A person or organization with an adamantine ideological commitment to free trade, regardless of the economic or non-economic consequences that will or are likely to occur, whether domestically or in one or more foreign countries. The free trade fundamentalist is convinced in the righteousness of free trade, notwithstanding evidence to the contrary, holding fast to a narrow interpretation of Adam Smith's absolute advantage and David Ricardo's comparative advantage.

## FSF

Financial Stability Forum.

Based in Basle, Switzerland, the mission of the FSF is to develop and refine standards for banking supervision and regulation. Such standards cover accounting (e.g., mark-to-market rules), capital adequacy, derivatives trading, and pay and bonuses for bankers. The FSF was particularly active in the wake of the global financial crisis that began with the collapse of Lehman Brothers in September 2008.

# FTA

Free Trade Agreement (or, sometimes equivalently, Free Trade Area).

An FTA is an agreement among two or more countries (more specifically, customs territories) to drop all internal trade barriers as among the countries. Each party to and FTA, however, retains its own separate schedule of tariffs for imports from third countries, thus making the FTA a less economically integrated entity than a customs union. The formation of FTAs is subject to the requirements — which are quite slender — set forth in GATT Article XXIV.

FTAs between two countries, of course, are called "bilateral" FTAs. FTAs among more than two countries are dubbed simply "FTAs," or sometimes regional trade agreements (RTAs), even when the countries are not all in the same geographic region.

The *North American Free Trade Agreement (NAFTA)* is the quintessential example of a FTA. By no means is it the only illustration. Indeed, in September 2007, when there were 151 Members of the WTO, only one Member was not a party to an FTA— Mongolia. With several countries involved in multiple FTAs, there are more FTAs than countries. The United States is a party to a large number of FTAs (chronicled in Annex C to this *Dictionary*).

Under the American Constitution, legislation to implement any trade agreement, multilateral or bilateral, must originate in the House of Representatives. That is because such agreements affect revenue, for example, by altering rates of duty, and the Constitution mandates that revenue bills originate in the House. Thus, all FTA bills start off in the House, and then move to the Senate, for consideration.

Interestingly, except for the FTA agreement with the *Association of Southeast Asian Nations (ASEAN)*, China's first FTA came in 2005 with Chile. That FTA was a dramatic illustration of how China is projecting its influence globally, into what the United States traditionally had regarded as its back yard. The *China—Chile FTA* followed the *United States—Chile FTA*, which entered into force on 1 January 2004. China and Chile completed a Services Annex in 2008. Also in 2008, China completed its second FTA with a Latin American country, Peru. In June 2007, Costa Rica changed its diplomatic recognition policy, from Taiwan to China, and is pursuing an FTA with China. That deal would be China's first FTA in Central America.

The *China—Chile FTA* has benefited (*inter alia*), Chilean wine producers. China's burgeoning middle class has a thirst for red wine, which Chilean vineyards can meet with a good quality Malbec varietal. One clever Chilean vineyard markets its brand in China with the label "1421," with considerable success. That is the year China first made contact with Latin America — long before the rest of the west made contact with China. The "1421" label reminds Chinese consumers about this historical fact and the long tradition of Sino—Chilean ties, and might be dubbed an "historical indication" that is loosely tied to a geographical indication (Chilean-origin wine). Of course, "historical indication" is not a recognized concept under intellectual property (IP) law.

Among the many intellectually fascinating and practically consequential questions surrounding FTAs is whether they increase or decrease the propensity of their members to take trade remedy actions against one another. The conventional wisdom is that FTA partners are more inclined to use trade remedies — antidumping (AD), countervailing duty (CVD), and safeguard actions — against each other. That is because the FTA eliminates, or at least lowers, tariff and non-tariff barriers among the members. Accordingly, the members have little other tool than a trade remedy to which to resort if they seek to protect a domestic industry.

However, the experience of India with FTA does not appear to follow the conventional wisdom. Likewise, the experience of the United States with its partners in the *North American Free Trade Agreement (NAFTA)* does not seem to follow the conventional wisdom. If these experiences indeed are accurate and found in other FTAs, then FTAs may be more trade liberalizing than their critics suggest.

*Suggestions for Further Research:*

Articles:

1. Ahn, Dukgeun, *Foe or Friend of GATT Article XXIV: Diversity in Trade Remedy Rules*, 11 JOURNAL OF INTERNATIONAL ECONOMIC LAW 107–133 (2008).

2. Burrell, Robert & Kimberlee Weatherall, *Exporting Controversy? Reactions to the Copyright Provisions of the U.S.—Australia Free Trade Agreement: Lessons for U.S. Trade Policy*, 2008 UNIVERSITY OF ILLINOIS JOURNAL OF LAW, TECHNOLOGY & POLICY 259–319 (2008).

3. Hassanien, Mohamed R., *Greening the Middle East: The Regulatory Model of Environmental Protection in the United States — Oman Free Trade Agreement, A Legal Analysis of Chapter 17*, 23 GEORGETOWN INTERNATIONAL ENVIRONMENTAL LAW REVIEW 465–511 (2011).

4. He, Huaiwen, *The Development of Free Trade Agreements and International Protection of Intellectual Property Rights in the WTO Era — New Bilateralism and Its Future*, 41 IIC: INTERNATIONAL REVIEW OF INTELLECTUAL PROPERTY & COMPETITION LAW 253–283 (2010).

5. Lewis, Meredith Kolsky, *The Prisoners' Dilemma Posed by Free Trade Agreements: Can Open Access Provisions Provide an Escape?*, 11 CHICAGO JOURNAL OF INTERNATIONAL LAW 631–661 (2011).

6. Note, *Keeping Our Balance in the Face of Piracy and Counterfeiting: Limiting the Scope of Intellectual Property Rights Enforcement Provisions in Free Trade Agreements*, 42 GEORGE WASHINGTON INTERNATIONAL LAW REVIEW 159–190 (2010).

7. Powell, Stephen J. & Paola A. Chavarro, *Toward a Vibrant Peruvian Middle Class: Effects of the Peru—United States Free Trade Agreement on Labor Rights, Biodiversity, and Indigenous Populations*, 20 FLORIDA JOURNAL OF INTERNATIONAL LAW 93–146 (2008).

8. Rennie, Dr. Jane, *Competition Provisions in Free Trade Agreements: Unique Responses to Bilateral Needs or Derivative Developments in International Competition Policy?*, 15 INTERNATIONAL TRADE LAW & REGULATION issue 2, 57–71 (2009).

9. Sanders, Anselm Kamperman, *Intellectual Property, Free Trade and Economic Development*, 23 GEORGIA STATE UNIVERSITY LAW REVIEW 893–911 (2007).

10. Sell, Susan K., *TRIPs Was Never Enough: Vertical Forum Shifting, FTAs, ACTA, and TPP*, 18 JOURNAL OF INTELLECTUAL PROPERTY 447–478 (2011).

11. Taylor, C. O'Neal, *Of Free Trade Agreements and Models*, 19 INDIANA INTERNATIONAL & COMPARATIVE LAW REVIEW 569–609 (2009).

12. Tuck, Andrew P., *The "Fair and Equitable Treatment" Standard Pursuant to the Investment Provisions of the U.S. Free Trade Agreements with Peru, Colombia, and Panama*, 16 LAW & BUSINESS REVIEW OF THE AMERICAS 385–408 (2010).

13. Warner, Mildred E., *Regulatory Takings and Free Trade Agreements: Implications for Planners*, 41 URBAN LAWYER 427–443 (2009).

14. Yu, Peter K., *Sinic Trade Agreements*, 44 U.C. DAVIS LAW REVIEW 953–1028 (2011).

## FTAA

*Free Trade Area of the Americas.*

### Vision and Launch

In 1990, President George W. Bush in 1990 proposed a western hemispheric trade agreement, called the "FTAA," which he envisioned would include 34 democracies in North, Central, and South America.[256] Pointedly, it would exclude Cuba, as Cuba had been governed by the Communist regime of Fidel Castro since 1959, and against which the United States had a trade embargo since the Presidency of John F. Kennedy. An FTAA is not a process unto itself, but rather part of a two-pronged strategy — to promote democracy, and to open markets. The two strategies are related. Trade is a means of creating economic opportunities and empowerment, leading to political opportunities and empowerment.

At the 1994 Summit of the Americas, heads of state from the prospective *FTAA* countries announced commencement of negotiations toward their regional trade agreement (RTA).[257] They set an end goal for 2005. That deadline, and every subsequent one, was not reached. Today, little remains of the *FTAA* vision.

---

[256] *See The Road From Santiago*, THE ECONOMIST, 11 April 1998, at 25.

[257] *See* Rossella Brevetti, *FTAA Group Urges That WTO Rules on Standards be Basis of Talks*, 14 International Trade Reporter (BNA) 29 (1 January 1994).

### Initial Proposal

Initially as proposed, the *FTAA* covered a population of 800 million people, more than U.S. $11 trillion in production, and $3.4 trillion in world trade.[258] Prospective *FTAA* countries agreed the *FTAA* would be a single undertaking, completed and implemented as a whole unit.[259] The proposals they submitted envisioned the *FTAA* as an independent agreement co-existing with other existing regional and bilateral agreements.[260]

Trade ministers launched seven *FTAA* Working Groups at the first *FTAA* trade ministerial meeting in Denver, Colorado, and an additional four such Groups at the second *FTAA* trade ministerial meeting in Cartageña, Colombia.[261] Thus, eleven Working Groups were formed covering the following topic areas:

- Market access
- Customs procedure and rules of origin, investments
- Standards and Technical Barriers to Trade (TBT)
- Sanitary and Phytosanitary (SPS) measures
- government procurement
- Intellectual Property Rights (IPRs)
- Services
- Subsidies
- Antidumping (AD) and countervailing duties (CVDs)
- Competition policy.[262]

These topical areas roughly anticipated the chapters in a possible *FTAA* text. A key task of each of the eleven Working Groups was to gather data in advance of formal negotiations.

The 34 countries also agreed negotiations would require some form of independent secretariat support. Once negotiations began, these working groups developed into general and special negotiation committees to address these same topics and develop proposals. The Figure below outlines the FTAA committees.

---

[258] *See* Loren Yager, *Free Trade Area of the Americas: April 2001 Meeting Set for Hard Bargaining to Begin*, United States General Accounting Office, Statement of the Director of International Affairs and Trade, GAO-01-706T (8 May 2001).

[259] *See* Loren Yager, *Free Trade Area of the Americas: April 2001 Meeting Set for Hard Bargaining to Begin*, United States General Accounting Office, Statement of the Director of International Affairs and Trade, GAO-01-706T (8 May 2001).

[260] *See* Rosella Brevetti, *Agreement on How to Launch FTAA Talks Next Year Not Expected at Belo Horizonte*, 14 International Trade Reporter (BNA) 859 (14 May 1997).

[261] *See* Rossella Brevetti, *FTAA Group Urges That WTO Rules on Standards be Basis of Talks*, 14 International Trade Reporter (BNA) 29 (1 January 1994).

[262] *See* Rosella Brevetti, *Agreement on How to Launch FTAA Talks Next Year Not Expected at Belo Horizonte*, 14 International Trade Reporter (BNA) 859 (14 May 1997).

**FIGURE:**

**FTAA NEGOTIATING COMMITTEES**[263]

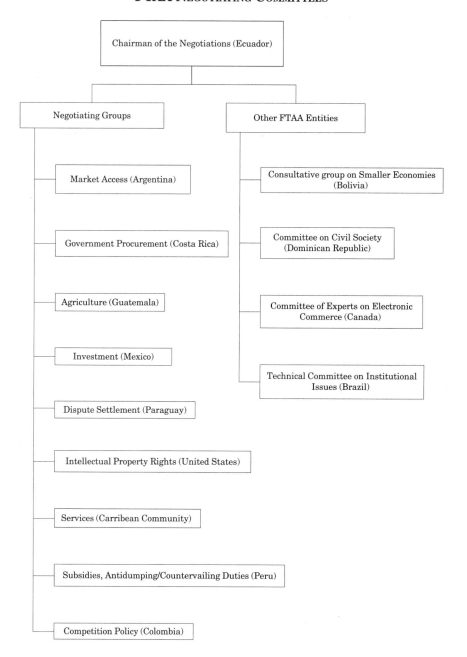

---

[263] A similar Figure appears in, which is unsurprising as the Committee structure is uniformly logical. *See* Loren Yager, *Free Trade Area of the Americas: April 2001 Meeting Set for Hard Bargaining to Begin*, United States General Accounting Office, Statement of the Director of International Affairs and Trade, GAO-01-706T figure 2 at 6 (8 May 2001).

Out of the five proposed approaches to reaching an FTAA, the smaller economies preferred hemispheric negotiations similar to those held under WTO negotiations, in which all countries negotiated.[264] Other possibilities included *North American Free Trade Agreement (NAFTA)* expansion, Southern Common Market *(MERCOSUR)* expansion, negotiations between *MERCOSUR* and *NAFTA*, and regional bloc-to-bloc negotiations.[265]

### American Involvement and Criticism

The United States planned to negotiate country-by-country and not as a member of *NAFTA*.[266] President Clinton advocated for fast-track negotiating authority because it would give the president power to negotiate trade agreements and submit them to Congress for an expedited up-or-down vote only.[267] Without this authority, many countries would not enter trade deals for fear American lawmakers would change them. Following his Presidency, Bill Clinton urged South American business leaders to support moves to reduce trade barriers in the Americas as a means of creating greater economic efficiency and higher growth.[268] He also urged South American representatives of American companies to pressure the United States Congress to pass legislation giving the president fast-track negotiating authority in trade talks.[269,270]

When the White House withdrew its request to Congress for fast track negotiating authority, the Foreign Minister of Colombia predicted negotiations for a free trade accord for the western hemisphere would not be complete by the 2005 deadline.[271] The Canadian representative, Marc Lortie, also felt the speed of negotiations relied partially on political processes.[272] The United States attempted to demonstrate its commitment to the project by approving, as an agreed upon by trade ministers, a timetable of negotiations with the signing of the agreement by 2005.[273] The United States Trade Representative (USTR) at

---

[264] *See Small Countries Face Constraints on FTAA Participation*, 14 International Trade Reporter (BNA) 184 (29 January 1997).

[265] *See Small Countries Face Constraints on FTAA Participation*, 14 International Trade Reporter (BNA) 184 (29 January 1997).

[266] *See Three Framework Proposals to Guide Talks at this Week's FTAA Vice-Ministers' Meeting*, 14 International Trade Reporter (BNA) 357 (26 February 1997).

[267] *See* Jackie Calmes, *Clinton's Trip to South America Seeks to Boost U.S. Support for Trade Plan*, Wall Street Journal A2 (13 October 1997).

[268] *See* Geoff Dyer, *Lower Trade Barriers in Americas, Says Clinton*, FINANCIAL TIMES 5 (16 October 1997).

[269] *See* Geoff Dyer, *Lower Trade Barriers in Americas, Says Clinton*, FINANCIAL TIMES 5 (16 October 1997).

[270] *See* Jackie Calmes, *Clinton's Trip to South America Seeks to Boost U.S. Support for Trade Plan*, WALL STREET JOURNAL, 13 October 1997, at A2.

[271] *See* Stephen Fidler, *Colombia Sees Delay on FTAA*, Financial Times 7 (3 February 1998).

[272] *See* Rosella Brevetti, *Proposal to Accelerate FTAA Talks to be Discussed at Ministers' Meeting*, 17 International Trade Reporter (BNA) 48 (7 December 2000).

[273] *See* Gerard Baker, *Strong Support for Americas Free Trade Area*, FINANCIAL TIMES 1 (20 April 1998).

the time, Charlene Barshefsky, continued to confirm the intent of the United States to approve fast-track authority in Congress.[274]

The *FTAA* faced criticism that regional preferences diverted more trade than they created. Some Latin Americans feared the cost of adjusting to free trade with the most powerful economy in the world would outweigh the benefits especially in smaller and less developed countries.[275] These criticisms conflicted with some Latin American governments, who concluded an *FTAA* would be beneficial based on studies suggesting that American market access would add to growth by boosting exports, and attracting extra foreign direct investment (FDI).[276] However, the general consensus between both groups remained that lack of fast-track would doom the *FTAA* project.[277]

Without fast-track negotiating authority, little progress was made on *FTAA* discussions.[278] The United States could not adequately negotiate, and countries continued to distrust the American political process.

The failure of the Clinton Administration to win Congressional approval for fast-track negotiating authority during the mid and late 1990s prevented serious progress toward creating this zone. Even with the renewal of this authority under the 2002 *Trade Promotion Authority* bill, little progress was made toward an *FTAA* during the Administration of George W. Bush. The initial deadline to complete the *FTAA*, set at the 1994 Miami Summit, was 1 January 2005. This date passed without fanfare. The *FTAA* has yet to be created, and the prospects for its establishment are remote.

Politics are partly to blame. In July 2005, Bolivian President Evo Morales, Cuban President Fidel Castro, and Venezuelan President Hugo Chavez joined other Latin American leaders at a summit. They joined Brazilian President Luis Inácio Lula da Silva in a call to keep the United States out of any free trade accords. President Lula declared "[o]ur nations ceased to be colonies two centuries ago and we have no wish to become colonies again."[279] Similarly, President Chavez has called Mexican President Vincente Fox "the empire's puppy," because of President Fox's support for the United States free trade agenda in Latin America.[280]

The Brazilian Ambassador to the United States, Rubens Barbosa, pointed out not all countries have the same priorities, emphasizing that first priority of his country was to "shore up the World Trade Organization" and its second was

---

[274] *See* Gerard Baker, *Strong Support for Americas Free Trade Area*, FINANCIAL TIMES 1 (20 April 1998).

[275] *See The Road From Santiago*, THE ECONOMIST, 11 April 1998, at 25.

[276] *See The Road From Santiago*, THE ECONOMIST, 11 April 1998, at 25.

[277] *See The Road From Santiago*, THE ECONOMIST, 11 April 1998, at 25.

[278] *See* Geoff Dyer, *Lower Trade Barriers in Americas, Says Clinton*, FINANCIAL TIMES 5 (16 October 1997).

[279] *Quoted in* David Haskel, *Brazil's President Urges Latin Leaders to Leave U.S. Out of Free Trade Plans*, 23 International Trade Reporter (BNA) 1138–39 (27 July 2006).

[280] David Haskel, *EU, Central America Agree to Start Talks on Free Trade; Mercosur, Andean Talks Stall*, 23 International Trade Reporter (BNA) 766–67 (18 May 2008).

to strengthen *MERCOSUR*.[281] These different priorities led to many conflicts. An example can be found in the conflicts as to how the United States and Brazil should proceed in the negotiations.[282] The United States wanted to address first tariff reduction, while Brazil wanted a more general approach based on its growing trade deficit.[283]

In brief, countries were integrating with each other around the United States, but not with the US.[284] USTR Charlene Barshefsky expressed concern about the acceleration of sub-regional integration in the Western Hemisphere not involving the United States.[285] Her goal was to keep the United States at the center of trading relationships.[286] C. Fred Bergsten, Director of the Institute for International Economics, pointed out sub-regional trade blocs can have the effect of creating a barrier to the *FTAA*.[287] Examples he gave were: the belief by members of Congress the *FTAA* failed; the unwillingness of Mexico to share the preferential treatment it receives from *NAFTA*; and unwillingness of Brazil to share the preferential treatment it receives through *MERCOSUR*.[288]

### Reasons for Ultimate Collapse

Why did the *FTAA* ultimately fail? In addition to the negotiating difficulties noted above, there were five key obstacles. First, the support for the *FTAA* among the American business community was countered, and overwhelmed, by a rising tide of opposition in Latin America. Second, the President of the United States failed to persuade Congress to renew fast track trade negotiating authority.

- *Smaller Economies*

    The Working Group for Smaller Economies recommended the *FTAA* have a mechanism built into it to address the needs of smaller economies, and that smaller economies be given differentiated treatment/

---

[281] *See* Rosella Brevetti, *Proposal to Accelerate FTAA Talks to be Discussed at Ministers' Meeting,* 17 International Trade Reporter (BNA) 48 (07 December 2000).

[282] *See* Geoff Dyer, *Lower Trade Barriers in Americas, Says Clinton*, FINANCIAL TIMES 5 (16 October 1997).

[283] *See* Geoff Dyer, *Lower Trade Barriers in Americas, Says Clinton*, FINANCIAL TIMES 5 (16 October 1997).

[284] *See* Rossella Brevetti, *Barshefsky Says She's Concerned About Subregional Integration That Excludes U.S.*, 15 International Trade Reporter (BNA) 644 (15 April 1998).

[285] *See* Rossella Brevetti, *Barshefsky Says She's Concerned About Subregional Integration That Excludes U.S.*, 15 International Trade Reporter (BNA) 644 (15 April 1998).

[286] *See* Rossella Brevetti, *Barshefsky Says She's Concerned About Subregional Integration That Excludes U.S.*, 15 International Trade Reporter (BNA) 644 (15 April 1998).

[287] *See Subregional Integration May Impede FTAA, Expert Says*, 15 International Trade Reporter (BNA) 833 (13 May 1998).

[288] *See Subregional Integration May Impede FTAA, Expert Says*, 15 International Trade Reporter (BNA) 833 (13 May 1998).

longer adjustment periods.[289] Smaller economies account for around 25 out of the 34 countries involved, making them the majority, suggesting those interests are the ones to address.[290] Within the *FTAA* process, countries could negotiate individually or as a group (based on membership in a sub-regional trading block or on commonalities such as size).[291] Small economies were likely to negotiate as a group, because they lacked leverage individually and could pool resources.[292]

- *Intellectual Property*

  The Working Group on Intellectual Property had the task of creating an inventory of all intellectual property treaties and arrangements in the western hemisphere.[293] It also had the task of identifying areas of commonality and divergence in intellectual property laws, regulations, and enforcement measures in the western hemisphere.[294] And, it was asked to identify possible areas for technical assistance that countries may request.[295]

  The United States suggested a draft text focusing on reducing piracy, counterfeiting, and other unauthorized trade in works protected by intellectual property rights.[296] It also called for a text that reduced barriers to obtaining intellectual property rights in the hemisphere. *MERCOSUR* agreed to submit proposals on business facilitation matters.[297]

- *Services*

  While not the dominant approach used, the United States wanted a negative list in the *FTAA* Services Chapter.[298] Similar to the approach taken in *NAFTA*, all service sectors would be covered except those a member country put on its negative list in its services schedule.[299] *MERCOSUR*

---

[289] *See* Rosella Brevetti, *Jamaican Envoy Says FTAA Lacks Consensus for Regional Integration Fund*, 15 International Trade Reporter (BNA) 20 (7 January 1998).

[290] *See* Rosella Brevetti, *Jamaican Envoy Says FTAA Lacks Consensus for Regional Integration Fund*, 15 International Trade Reporter (BNA) 20 (7 January 1998).

[291] *See* Rosella Brevetti, *Jamaican Envoy Says FTAA Lacks Consensus for Regional Integration Fund*, 15 International Trade Reporter (BNA) 20 (7 January 1998).

[292] *See* Rosella Brevetti, *Jamaican Envoy Says FTAA Lacks Consensus for Regional Integration Fund*, 15 International Trade Reporter (BNA) 20 (7 January 1998).

[293] *See* Rossella Brevetti, *FTAA Intellectual Property Group Agrees on Work Plan, Deadlines*, 13 International Trade Reporter (BNA) 1095 (3 July 1997).

[294] *See* Rossella Brevetti, *FTAA Intellectual Property Group Agrees on Work Plan, Deadlines*, 13 International Trade Reporter (BNA) 1095 (3 July 1997).

[295] *See* Rossella Brevetti, *FTAA Intellectual Property Group Agrees on Work Plan, Deadlines*, 13 International Trade Reporter (BNA) 1095 (3 July 1997).

[296] *See* Rossella Brevetti, *U.S. Suggests Draft FTAA Language on Intellectual Property for Declaration*, 13 International Trade Reporter (BNA) 1786 (20 November 1996).

[297] *See* Rossella Brevetti, *U.S. Suggests Draft FTAA Language on Intellectual Property for Declaration*, 13 International Trade Reporter (BNA) 1786 (20 November 1996).

[298] *See U.S. Wants "Negative List" Approach in FTAA Services Chapter*, 15 International Trade Reporter (BNA) 1602 (23 September 1998).

[299] *See U.S. Wants "Negative List" Approach in FTAA Services Chapter*, 15 International Trade Reporter (BNA) 1602 (23 September 1998).

countries preferred a positive list approach, such as what is used in the *General Agreement on Trade in Services (GATS)*, making countries bound only to the extent that they schedule a sector.[300]

- *FDI*

  The Working Group on Investment discussed topics such as investor protection in the pre-establishment phase, national treatment, application of treaties at a subnational level, expropriation and compensation, top managerial personnel, transfers, performance requirements, general exceptions, and dispute settlement.[301]

  There were protests over the prospect of including an investor-state provision similar to *NAFTA* Chapter 11.[302] The American negotiators were adamant the *FTAA* include an investor-state provision.[303] Critics said the inclusion of that Chapter would make public health care, education and other services vulnerable to the threat of foreign lawsuits.[304]

- *Labor and the Environment*

  There was significant conflict over the role and extent of labor and environmental provisions in the *FTAA*. Many domestic market supporters believed the *FTAA* would benefit multinational corporations at the cost of job opportunities and their home markets.[305] There was also concern that high standards would decrease competitive levels.[306]

  For all practical purposes, FTAA negotiations collapsed in the early 2000s, not with a bang, but with a whimper. There was no formal declaration they were dead. Rather, they just tapered off.

### Potential Renewed Interest

With the death (again, undeclared) of the Doha Round of multilateral trade negotiations, there could be renewed interest in *FTAA* negotiations. Industrialists in Brazil, in particular, appear interested in reducing trade barriers across the western hemisphere for their merchandise, all the more so because of the disappointing performance of *MERCOSUR*.

---

[300] *See U.S. Wants "Negative List" Approach in FTAA Services Chapter*, 15 International Trade Reporter (BNA) 1602 (23 September 1998).

[301] *See Countries Exchange Views on FTAA Investment Chapter*, 13 International Trade Reporter (BNA) 1869 (4 December 1996).

[302] *See Proposed Investor-State Provision in FTAA Opposed*, 18 International Trade Reporter (BNA) 479 (22 March 2001).

[303] *See Proposed Investor-State Provision in FTAA Opposed*, 18 International Trade Reporter (BNA) 479 (22 March 2001).

[304] *See Proposed Investor-State Provision in FTAA Opposed*, 18 International Trade Reporter (BNA) 479 (22 March 2001).

[305] *See* Sara Catherine Smith, *The Free Trade Area of the Americas: Is There Still A Place for the World Trade Organization?*, 13 TULSA JOURNAL OF COMPARATIVE & INTERNATIONAL LAW 321 (2006).

[306] *See* Sara Catherine Smith, *The Free Trade Area of the Americas: Is There Still A Place for the World Trade Organization?*, 13 TULSA JOURNAL OF COMPARATIVE & INTERNATIONAL LAW 321 (2006).

The United States and Brazil have co-chaired several rounds of *FTAA* negotiations. Typically, they have been at loggerheads, with most other countries watching sometimes-heated negotiations from the sidelines. Until these two largest players agree on both substantive and procedural points, little progress is or can be made. Complicating matters following the launch of the Doha Round of WTO trade negotiations in November 2001, the United States and Brazil became have been engaged actively in multilateral discussions and debates.

Accordingly, Brazil's trade policy is a critical factor in success or failure of an *FTAA*. Brazil is one of the rare countries of the world with a small ratio of trade to Gross Domestic Product (GDP). One aspect of Brazil's trade policy is to expand trade, and thus increase its share in national income. Historically, Brazil has a clear, long-standing Brazilian preference to liberalize trade through the multilateral regime. That is because Brazil has done well in its performance in the GATT—WTO system.

For example, at the November 2001 Doha Ministerial Conference, Brazil won important concessions on setting the agenda for the Doha Round. First, Brazil secured agreement that agricultural issues would be considered explicitly as an agenda item.

Second, it persuaded other Members that antidumping (AD) issues also would be an explicit item. Third, Brazil played a major role in negotiations over patent protection and compulsory licensing for pharmaceuticals used to treat HIV/AIDS. In addition to these triumphs, Brazil also has won important WTO cases, including a subsidy dispute with Canada over Embraer jets (the *Aircraft* case, Appellate Body Report, *Canada — Export Credits and Loan Guarantees for Regional Aircraft*, WT/DS222/AB/R (adopted 19 February 2002) (complaint by Brazil)), a dispute with the United States over cotton subsidies (Appellate Body Report, *United States — Subsidies on Upland Cotton*, WT/DS267/AB/R (adopted 21 March 2005) (complaint by Brazil)), and a dispute with the EU over sugar subsidies (Appellate Body Report, *European Communities — Export Subsidies on Sugar*, WT/DS266/AB/R (adopted 19 May 2005) (complaint by Brazil)).

These successes in the multilateral trade arena lead to a second aspect of Brazilian trade policy. It is, in effect, a subset of Brazil's broad foreign policy calculus. Brazil sees itself as a potential member of the United Nations Security Council. Trade policy ties in — or should link to — the objective of the country to play a highly prominent role on the world stage. In turn, *MERCOSUR* and an *FTAA* may be incommensurate — in terms of ambition — with Brazil's global self-image and vision.

As for an *FTAA*, the likelihood of such an accord appears small. Brazil developed the policy that it would begin with a "*SAFTA*," *i.e.*, a *South American Free Trade Agreement*. Then, as the leader of *SAFTA*, Brazil would negotiate a link between *SAFTA* and *NAFTA*. The *SAFTA—NAFTA* accord would approximate an *FTAA*. Unfortunately for Brazil, and other trade liberalization reformers in North and South America, this strategy failed. Four reasons account for the failure, inability, and even hesitancy of Brazil to play a leading role in western hemispheric integration.

First, the United States made it clear concessions offered in the Doha Round on issues of critical interest to Brazil — agriculture, antidumping (AD), and intellectual property (IP) — do not carry over to an *FTAA*. If the United States made an offer in the Round to cut agriculture trade barriers or subsidies, or deal with AD or IP controversies, then it would not automatically bring that offer into *FTAA* discussions. The effective segregation of WTO and *FTAA* talks meant the matters in which Brazil had the greatest interest were not open in the regional context. To be sure, this segregation was not necessarily wrong-headed. To deal effectively with agriculture, from a free trade perspective, the best approach is to have all the "sinners" at the negotiating table — especially the United States, European Union (EU), Japan, and Korea. It is unrealistic to expect *ad hoc*, piecemeal reforms through FTAs to contribute to significant agricultural trade liberalization. Not surprisingly, Brazil — joined by Canada, Mexico, and others — favor the multilateral approach.

Second, *MERCOSUR* — the practical manifestation of a *SAFTA*, albeit with fewer than all South American countries as members — has been an economic disappointment. To be sure, from 1994–97, trade between Brazil and Argentina expanded greatly. Yet, the history of *MERCOSUR* makes the general lackluster performance of this customs union unsurprising. Brazil and Argentina brought to an end their military governments at about the same time. Each country saw *MERCOSUR* as a vehicle to advance its own democratic processes. In other words, *MERCOSUR* was conceived in the 1980s by the Brazilian President José Sarne and Argentine President Raúl Alfonsín for political, not economic, motives.

Third, Brazil has been unable to lead the expansion of *MERCOSUR* to include a few key countries. For example, Chile made a strategic decision to attempt to join *NAFTA* instead of *MERCOSUR*. Chile has a unified MFN tariff rate of six percent. In preliminary discussions with Chile, the *MERCOSUR* countries (Argentina, Brazil, Paraguay, and Uruguay) spoke of a CET of 18 percent. The gap between six and 18 percent simply was not bridgeable, leading Chile to focus more on *NAFTA* membership. In the end, Chile signed an FTA with the United States in June 2003, which entered into force on 1 January 2004. As another example, *MERCOSUR* has not expanded into the Andean region. Special problems posed by Venezuela have blocked such expansion. Here, too, the effect has been to weaken the possible significance of *MERCOSUR*. The absence of Chile and Venezuela from *MERCOSUR* diminishes the potential political and economic force of the bloc.

Fourth, macroeconomic factors in Brazil sometimes have conspired against the success of *MERCOSUR*. The "PT" (*i.e., Partido dos Trabalhadores*, or Workers' Party) government of President Luiz Lula de Silva has championed *MERCOSUR*. (President Lula was elected in 2002, and re-elected in 2006, to four year terms in office.) But, it has done so at a time when the IMF is playing a new role in Latin America. Guidance from the IMF on macroeconomic policies factor into *MERCOSUR* and *FTAA* policy. (Obviously, it also affects IMF financing operations. In August 2002, Brazil reached agreement with the IMF for a loan, which the IMF disbursed in 2003.) Generally, President Lula followed the macroeconomic policies of his predecessor, President Fernando Cardoso, on macroeconomic policies. These policies bear four hallmarks:

- *Government Expenditure Targets*:

  President Lula not only accepted a surplus target for internal government expenditures, but (at 4.25 percent) one larger than his predecessor.

- *Current Account Targets*:

- President Lula targeted a current account surplus of $15 billion. If this target were reached, then Brazil's current account deficit as a percentage of GDP would change from over four percent to less than one percent.

- *Emphasis on Agriculture*:

  President Lula emphasized the importance of increasing the size of the agricultural sector, especially through improvements in productivity, and the dominance of this sector in shaping Brazil's trade policy. Growing the agriculture sector is connected directly to improving Brazil's current account picture. In the past, and potentially in the future, the real expansion that can create a trade surplus is agricultural expansion. This emphasis also contrasts with Brazilian macroeconomic policies of the 1970s, which stressed industrialization. While industry and services are important to Brazil, in its trade policy the country speaks of both free and fair trade, especially in agriculture.

- *Emphasis on Foreign Direct Investment (FDI)*:

  President Lula continued to stress the importance of attracting FDI.

Significantly, these macroeconomic policies have not inclined Brazil to strengthen *MERCOSUR*. To the contrary, they have inclined Brazil toward a Chilean-style trade policy, as distinct from a Mexican-style one.

The Mexican economy is about 85 percent integrated into the United States, in the sense of trade and FDI relationships. Before *NAFTA*, Mexican exports accounted for about 15 percent of GDP. After *NAFTA* (as of May 2003), they are about 30 to 35 percent of the country's GDP. The reason for the growth is burgeoning trade under *NAFTA* with the United States. In contrast, Brazil seeks a far more diversified economy than Mexico, in terms of trade and investment links with a variety of nations. In this respect, the economy of Chile, which is not excessively dependent on any one country, is a model for Brazil.

If an *FTAA* is unlikely, in part because of the aforementioned factors associated with the trade policy of Brazil, then might a bilateral FTA between Brazil and the United States be a realistic possibility? The answer is "no," or at least "not likely." In the FTAs with Chile and Singapore, the United States emphasized the need for "WTO Plus" commitments. Such commitments can help make the FTA commercially meaningful, as they liberalize trade in a broader, deeper way than under multilateral rules. But, a *United States — Brazil FTA* almost certainly would have to be "WTO Minus."

What would a "WTO Minus" FTA amount to, in terms of legal details? Presumably, the scope of product coverage would be limited. Agriculture would not play a central role in the accord. This fact may be inferred from the difficult negotiations Brazil has led, on behalf of *MERCOSUR*, to create a FTA with the EU. Brazil insists on broader market access for farm products than the EU is willing to concede, especially in view of the interest of some EU members in preserving Common Agricultural Policy (CAP) subsidies. Thus, the target date for finishing EU — *MERCOSUR* negotiations — the end of 2003 — came and went without a deal. Presumably, then, a WTO-Minus *United States — Brazil FTA* would be on lowering industrial tariffs and liberalizing service market access. The results would not be a basis to create obligations for an *FTAA*, or a multilateral accord under WTO auspices. Given these limitations, the United States appears quite unwilling to enter into such an FTA.

*Suggestions for Further Research:*

Articles:

1.  González, Anabel, *Revitalizing the U.S. Trade Agenda in Latin America: Building on the FTA Platform*, 12 Journal of International Economic Law 539–546 (2009).

2.  Powell, Stephen J., *Expanding the NAFTA Chapter 19 Dispute Settlement System: A Way To Declare Trade Remedy Laws in A Free Trade Area of the Americas?*, 16 Law & Business Review of the Americas 217–240 (2010).

3.  Symposium, *Trade Integration in the Americas: Revisiting the Washington Consensus*, 16 Law & Business Review of the Americas 3–269 (2009).

## FTAAP

*Free Trade Area of the Asia-Pacific.*

An idea proposed at the Asia Pacific Economic Cooperation (APEC) summit meeting in Santiago, Chile, in 2004. The idea did not materialize, even as a possible second best solution to a collapsed Doha Round, because of the heterogeneity in the trade regimes of the Asia-Pacific countries. Harmonizing rules in controversial sectors like agriculture, and melding the many free trade agreements (FTAs) into a unified accord, would be difficult. The level of detail cannot be overestimated. For example, just in the context of a bilateral FTA, Japan and Korea have haggled for many years over market access for gim seaweed, a specific type of seaweed. Thus far, the idea has gained little traction.

*Suggestions for Further Research:*

Article:

1.  Rushford, Greg, *Asia Drags Down the Free Trade Cause*, 170 Far Eastern Economic Review number 8, 29–33 (October 2007).

## FTZ

Foreign Trade Zone.

A special manufacturing area physically set in the United States, usually near a major air, sea, rail, or land port, but legally treated as outside the United States for purposes of customs. That is, an FTZ, while situated in the United States on specially designated land, is outside the customs territory of the United States for the purposes of Customs Law, specifically, payment of customs duties.

FTZs were created under the *Foreign Trade Zones Act of 1934*, and are regulated by the United States Foreign Trade Zones Board (FTZB). The regulations of the FTZB are published at 15 C.F.R. Part 400. Companies must apply to the FTZB on certain matters. The Board is managed by the Import Administration (IA) section of the International Trade Administration (ITA), within the Department of Commerce (DOC).

In an FTZ, companies (both foreign and domestic) set up manufacturing operations. An FTZ provides manufacturers with the opportunity to process goods in the United States, and employ American workers, and United States customs after completing the processing. Indeed, the key American policy goal FTZs serve is to increase output and create jobs. Companies are induced to operate in FTZs by a reduction in tariff liability. When merchandise enters the customs territory of the United States from an FTZ, typically it does so at a reduced (or even zero) tariff, in comparison with tariffs on individual components entered into the FTZ that would have been applicable, had these components entered the United States customs territory directly from overseas. The special customs rules that apply to FTZs are set out in statute and regulation. *See* 19 C.F.R. Part 146.

Essentially, a company operating in an FTZ calculates *a priori* the tariff liability that would be owed on individual components, were they imported directly into the United States, versus the tariff on a processed product, where it entered directly into the customs territory. The company then chooses to enter the components into an FTZ, and designates them either as "privileged" or non-privileged status." That designation provides the company with certainty and predictability as to the tariff it will pay on a product it processes in the FTZ, once it withdraws it from the FTZ into the customs territory of the United States. By making the correct status designation, the company reduces its tariff liability in comparison with straight importation into the United States.

Notably, since 1991 FTZ users have been entitled to enter goods into an FTA that are subject to an antidumping (AD) or countervailing duty (CVD) order, engage in further manufacturing of those goods, and then export the finished products, without having to pay the AD duty or CVD that otherwise would be applicable if they entered those goods into the customs territory of the United States. Only if the user enters the finished good into the United States, as opposed to exporting it, does the user pay the AD duty or CVD. The American business community, as represented by the United States Council for International Business (U.S. CIB), supports this rule as striking a balance between (1) enforcing AD and CVD orders on subject merchandise that enters the United States and (2) encouraging companies to use FTZs, in which Americans are employed, as a manufacturing and export platform.[307]

However, in December 2010, the FTZB proposed eliminating the exemption from AD duties and CVDs on subject merchandise imported into an FTZ, manufactured into a finished good, and subsequently exported. The proposed change in the law would mean that AD duties and CVDs on this subject merchandise must be paid, even though that merchandise technically never is entered for consumption into the customs territory of the United States. The U.S. CIB vigorously opposed the proposed change. It and other critics charged that levying such duties would constitute a *de facto* trade remedy without either (1) a full, fair legal proceeding or (2) ascertaining whether denial of duty-free status to the inputs was in the public interest.

In February 2012, the International Trade Administration (ITA) of the Department of Commerce (DOC) issued the first revision of its FTZ regulations in over 20 years.[308] The new regulations cut by over 50 percent the regulatory burden on applicants for and users of an FTZ. That is, the revision simplified the process for (1) designating a new FTZ location for an individual company, and (2) manufacturers to follow to enjoy FTZ benefits.

# FX

A short-hand, globally used expression for foreign exchange. An equivalent expression is "Forex."

---

[307] *See* Rossella Brevetti, *Businesses Warn Administration FTZ Proposal Would Hurt Competitiveness*, 28 International Trade Reporter (BNA) 1718 (20 October 2011).

[308] *See Commerce to Announce Final Rule That Will Overhaul Foreign-Trade Zones*, 29 International Trade Reporter (BNA) 275 (23 February 2012).

# G

## G-4

The Group of Four countries.

The G-4 consists of four key players in multilateral trade negotiations, namely, the United States, European Union (EU), Brazil, and India. The G-4 was a core negotiating entity in the Doha Round.

Brazil and India have both been championed as, and championed themselves as, the leading advocates for poor countries — both developing and least developed ones. That role is one they played in the Uruguay Round, and continuing through the Doha Round has at times generated considerable personal animosity with negotiators from the United States and EU. For instance, with respect to several agricultural commodities, Brazil is an efficient producer. During the Doha Round, the United States and EU have charged Brazil with thinly-veiled self-interest. Brazil might have more to gain from subsidy reductions in developed countries than would poor countries Brazil claims to represent. The United States and EU have noted hypocrisy in some of India's negotiating positions, being rather more interested in protecting their inefficient producers unjustifiably than with strengthening them through exposure to international competition.

The G-4 took the lead in 2006-2007 to spur the Doha Round to a successful conclusion. Its effort to reach a deal on agriculture and industrial tariffs, as a spring board to an agreement on other topics, failed in July 2007 with a split between developed and developing countries at a meeting in Potsdam, Germany.

## G-5

The Group of Five countries.

The G-5 consists of Brazil, China, India, Mexico, and South Africa. They are important players in multilateral trade negotiations individually. However, they occasionally band together to exert a stronger collective influence than they could do acting alone. For example, in July 2009, they urged the G-8 at its summit in L'Aquila, Italy, to commit to reaching an ambitious, balanced conclusion to the Doha Round in 2010 on the basis of extant modalities texts. That is, they sought a specific time frame, not ambiguous "as soon as possible" language. In the end, the G-5 issued a statement with a specific commitment, but in its communiqué, the G-8 left the time frame open.

## G-6

The Group of Six countries.

The G-6 grouping was established before the December 2005 WTO Ministerial Conference in Hong Kong. The G-6 consists of the Australia, Brazil, European

Union (EU), India, Japan, and United States. The shared interest of these WTO Members was to push forward in the Doha Round, and break stalemates on critical issues such as agricultural market access, domestic agricultural support, and agricultural export subsidies.

## G-7

The Group of Seven countries.

The G-7 consists of the leading industrial countries, namely, Canada, France, Germany, Italy, Japan, the United Kingdom, and the United States.

## G-8

The Group of Seven (G-7), plus Russia.

## G-10

The Group of Ten countries, which includes Iceland, Israel, Japan, Korea, Liechtenstein, Mauritius, Norway, Switzerland, and Taiwan.

The G-10 members are all developed countries. They are known in part for maintaining some of the highest agricultural tariffs and subsidies in the world. In the Doha Round, the G-10 generally resisted ambitious cuts to these tariffs and subsidies, and resisted even capping duty rates on agricultural products.

*Suggestions for Further Research:*

Article:

1.   Alexander, Kern, *Global Financial Standard Setting, the G10 Committees, and International Economic Law*, 34 BROOKLYN JOURNAL OF INTERNATIONAL LAW 861-881 (2009).

## G-11

The Group of Eleven countries, which is a discussion forum in the Doha Round of multilateral trade negotiations.

The G-11 consists of Argentina, Australia, Brazil, Canada, China, EU, India, Japan, Mauritius, South Africa, and the United States. Thus, it has both developed and developing countries, all of which have played significant roles in the Doha Round.

## G-15

The Group of 15 countries.

The G-15 is a group of 15 developing countries that act as the main political organ for the non-aligned movement and advocate for developing country interests.

## G-20 (FIRST MEANING)

The Group of Twenty countries that negotiates as a bloc in the World Trade Organization (WTO), such as during the Doha Round.

The G-20 is a group of developing countries with the self-appointed mission of lobbying for free, or freer, trade in agriculture. The G-20 is comprised of agricultural exporting nations, such as:

| | |
|---|---|
| • Argentina | • Mexico |
| • Bolivia | • Nigeria |
| • Brazil | • Pakistan |
| • Chile | • Paraguay |
| • China | • Philippines |
| • Cuba | • South Africa |
| • Egypt | • Thailand |
| • India | • Venezuela |
| • Indonesia | • Zimbabwe |

Formed in August 2003, the G-20 coalesced in the September 2003 Ministerial Conference in Cancún, and the membership has varied to some degree. Peru was a founding member, withdrew shortly after the founding, and then re-joined in the summer of 2006.

The G-20 successfully called attention to trade issues of importance to poor countries. Thereafter, the G-20 put forward proposals in the Doha Round, and effectively blocked any multilateral trade accord that failed to take account of poor country interests.

*Suggestions for Further Research:*

Article:

1.    Rolland, Sonia E., *Developing Country Coalitions at the WTO: In Search of Legal Support*, 48 HARVARD INTERNATIONAL LAW JOURNAL 484-551 (summer 2007).

## G-20 (SECOND MEANING)

A group of 20 leading industrial and major emerging developing countries that meets occasionally to discuss issues of international economic importance.

The G-20 was created in response to the 1997-99 Asian financial crisis, and first met in December 1999 in Berlin. It is a forum for discussing global economic governance and stability, and resolving cross-border problems. The G-20 consists of the following 19 countries:

| | |
|---|---|
| • Argentina | • Canada |
| • Australia | • China |
| • Brazil | • France |

- Germany
- India
- Indonesia
- Italy
- Japan
- Kingdom of Saudi Arabia
- Korea

- Mexico
- Russia
- South Africa
- Turkey
- United Kingdom
- United States

The 20th member of the G-20 is the EU, which is represented by the President of the European Commission and the European Central Bank. However, the EU has been urged to slim down its representation at the G-20. In March 2010, WTO Director-General stated:

> The frank reality is that it does not make sense, not for political reasons, not for institutional reasons . . . if one European takes the floor on one topic and then another European takes the floor on the same topic. . . . Nobody listens because either it's the same thing and it gets boring, or it's not the same thing and it will not influence the result at the end of the day. So the right solution is at least to make sure that they speak with one mouth.[309]

Thus far, not only has the EU rejected any effort to cut its representation at the G-20, but also it has expanded this representation following the approval of the Treaty of Lisbon.

The G-20 members collectively account for 90 percent of world Gross National Product (GNP), 80 percent of world trade, and two-thirds of world population.[310]

At its 2004 meeting in Berlin, the G-20 agreed to an "Accord for Sustained Growth," and a "Reform Agenda." The G-20 met in November 2008 at the "Summit on Financial Markets and the World Economy" to address the world financial crisis. At that Summit, in addition to the G-20, so-called "extraordinary presence" was allowed to the Netherlands, Spain, International Monetary Fund (IMF), World Bank, and Financial Stability Forum. It met again in April 2009 in London to deal with the global economic slump, and included the Director-General of the World Trade Organization (WTO).

G-20 meetings routinely result in grandiloquent and resolute language, manifest in a final communiqué that affirms the commitment of countries to avoid trade protectionism, deal with financial instability, and negotiate important new agreements. Yet, the efficacy of the G-20 is questioned not only by

---

[309] *Quoted in* Joe Kirwin, *WTO Chief Calls on European Union to Streamline its Representation at G-20*, 27 International Trade Reporter (BNA) 496 (8 April 2010).

[310] *See FACTBOX — What is the G20?*, REUTERS, 30 March 2009, posted at www.reuters.com; *Summit Pledge to "Restore Growth,"* BBC NEWS, 15 November 2008, posted at http://bbc.co.uk.

scholars such as Dr. Razeen Sally,[311] but also by empirical evidence produced by none other than the World Bank. In March 2009, the World Bank published a study identifying 47 trade-restrictive measures that countries, including 17 of the G-20 nations, had implemented since the onset of the global economic crisis in fall 2008.[312] Prime illustrations were:

- *Tariff increases*, which made up one-third of the trade-restrictive measures:

  For example, Ecuador raised tariffs on over 600 products, and Russia boosted tariffs on used cars.

- *Non-tariff barriers*:

  For instance, Argentina imposed non-automatic import licensing requirements for auto parts, leather goods, televisions, textiles, and toys. Indonesia announced all imports of five categories of merchandise — electronics, food and beverages, garments, shoes, and toys — could be admitted only at five of its air or sea ports.

- *Tightened Product or Sanitary Standards*:

  For example, China banned imports of some kinds of Belgian chocolates, British sauce, Dutch eggs, Irish pork, and Spanish dairy products. India banned imports of Chinese toys.

- *Export Subsidies*:

  The EU temporarily implemented new subsidies for exports of butter, cheese, and milk powder.

- *Sector-Specific Subsidies*:

  Several governments had subsidized their domestic auto industry, with the amount summing to $48 billion. The United States had provided direct subsidies of $17.4 billion, and Argentina, Brazil, Canada, China, France, Germany, Italy, Sweden, and the United Kingdom had given either direct or indirect subsidies to their national producers.

In June 2011, for the first time in its history, agriculture ministers from the G-20 countries met. They did so amidst record-high commodity prices, and worked out a five-point mechanism to deal with price volatility in agricultural commodities, especially food.

The mechanism, dubbed the *Action Plan on Food Price Volatility and Agriculture*, is comprised of five points that were based on a proposal from

---

[311] *See, e.g.,* Razeen Sally, *The Quest for a Global Solution is Misguided*, FINANCIAL TIMES, 19 March 2009, at 9.

[312] *See* Diana I. Gregg, *World Bank Takes 17 Nations in G-20 to Task for Implementing Trade-Restricting Measures*, 26 International Trade Reporter (BNA) 406 (26 March 2009).

France. Highlights of the *Action Plan* include a commitment among G-20 countries to:

(1) Increase innovation in agricultural production, especially wheat crops.

(2) Increase information about and transparency of agricultural markets.

(3) Improve agricultural policy coordination among countries, including a prohibition on export restraints on shipments of food for humanitarian purposes.

(4) Enhance the way in which financial markets for agricultural commodity derivatives function.

(5) Develop appropriate risk management tools, including to establish an international system for emergency humanitarian food reserves.

Yet, the *Action Plan* does not deal with several topics that contribute to price volatility, namely, the regulation of financial markets and instruments dealing with agricultural commodities (in particular, to curb speculation), biofuel subsidies (*e.g.*, to plant corn for ethanol, which may displace production of food crops), and export restrictions not associated with humanitarian food shipments.

*Suggestions for Further Research:*

Book:

1. SALLY, RAZEEN, NEW FRONTIERS IN FREE TRADE — GLOBALIZATION'S FUTURE AND ASIA'S RISING ROLE (2008).

# G-33

The Group of 33 countries.

A group of newly industrialized countries (NICs), and developing countries, which formed during the Doha Round of multilateral trade negotiations. Consisting of 46 countries, the G-33 includes several G-20 countries, such as China and India, along with Argentina, Brazil, Indonesia, Korea, Nigeria, Pakistan, Peru, Philippines, Thailand, and roughly 20 African and Caribbean nations. Specifically, the G-33 members are:

- Antigua and Barbuda
- Barbados
- Belize
- Benin
- Botswana
- Bolivia
- China
- Congo
- Côte d'Ivoire
- Cuba

- Dominica
- Dominican Republic
- El Salvador
- Grenada
- Guatemala
- Guyana
- Haiti
- Honduras
- India
- Indonesia

- Jamaica
- Kenya
- Korea
- Madagascar
- Mongolia
- Mauritius
- Mozambique
- Nicaragua
- Nigeria
- Pakistan
- Panama
- Peru
- Philippines
- Saint Kitts and Nevis
- Saint Lucia
- Saint Vincent and the Grenadines
- Senegal
- Sri Lanka
- Suriname
- Tanzania
- Trinidad and Tobago
- Turkey
- Uganda
- Venezuela
- Zambia
- Zimbabwe

The G-33 offered proposals in the Doha Round, particularly on the criteria used to designate agricultural commodities as "special," and thereby exempt such products from any agreed-upon tariff cuts. The G-33 also advocated special safeguard rules for sensitive and special products, that is, the Special Safeguard Mechanism (SSM).

## G-77

The Group of Seventy-Seven countries.

The G-77 is a group of developing countries set up in 1964 at the end of the first United Nations Conference on Trade and Development (UNCTAD). Originally, the G-77 numbered 77, but now it exceeds 130 countries.

## GAA

Globalization Adjustment Assistance.

The idea, endorsed by Senator Max Baucus (Democrat-Montana), that Trade Adjustment Assistance (TAA) should be expanded into GAA.[313] The expansion would mean government benefits would be offered to workers displaced by any aspect of globalization, not just trade or a free trade agreement (FTA).

## GAO

United States Government Accountability Office, formerly known as the "General Accounting Office."

The GAO often publishes useful studies on trade and trade-related issues.

---

[313] *See* Rossella Brevetti, *Sen. Baucus Urges TPA Renewal With Labor, Enforcement Provisions*, 24 International Trade Reporter (BNA) 37 (11 January 2007).

## *GATB*

*General Agreement on Trade in Bananas*, one of two key documents that settled the Bananas War.

The Bananas War had plagued the world trading system since before the creation of the WTO (specifically, 1993) and had become the longest-running dispute in WTO history. The EU, which is the largest importer of bananas in the world and imports (as of 2008) over 70 percent of the fruit from Latin America, battled several Latin American countries over bananas, many of which market their fruit through prominent American companies like Chiquita Brands and Dole.[314] Following losses in 11 GATT and WTO cases, including a November 2008 Appellate Body ruling in favor of the United States and Ecuador that discriminatory EU tariffs giving preference to ACP bananas (which are far more expensive than Latin bananas) continued to violate WTO rules, the EU promised to change its offending regime.

The EU pledged to implement a single-tariff (*i.e.*, tariff-only) regime by 1 January 2006, and grant at least the same level of market access to third country exporters as to its preferred ACP trading partners.[315] Indeed, without such a pledge, third country producers (located mainly in Latin America) had threatened in November 2001 to block the launch of the Doha Round. While the EU did drop its quota and licensing system, and shift to a tariff-only system in 2006, it also maintained a duty-free quota of 775,000 tons for ACP producers. Thus, the regime generated one of the legal cases against the EU, yielding another WTO judgment that it discriminatory.

Initially in the regime it commenced in 2006, the EU set the tariff at 230 per metric ton. Latin American countries challenged that rate successfully in two WTO arbitration proceedings, as the 230/ton level failed to maintain equivalent market access for their banana exports to the EU. The EU responded by dropping the tariff to 176/ton, but also set up an annual duty-free quota of 775,000 metric tons for ACP exporters. Ecuador (the world's largest banana exporter) and the United States (headquarters of two major banana distributors, Chiquita and Dole) prevailed against the EU in WTO proceedings, obtaining rulings that the EU quota was illegal because it unfairly discriminated among WTO Members.[316]

---

[314] *See* Joshua Chaffin, *End of Banana Wars Brings Hope for Doha*, FINANCIAL TIMES, 16 December 2009, at 8. As of June 2010, the EU imported $4 billion worth of bananas. *See* Len Bracken, *U.S., EU Agree to Settle Dispute Over Latin American Bananas, USTR Says*, 27 International Trade Reporter (BNA) 856 (10 June 2010).

[315] *See* Raj Bhala, *The Bananas War*, 31 McGEORGE LAW REVIEW 839-971 (Summer 2000); Alan Beattie, Expectations Low as Doha talks Begin — EU Regime in Dispute, Financial Times, 22 July 2008, at 4; Daniel Pruzin, *WTO's Lamy Delivers Compromise Text Aimed at Resolving Banana Dispute*, 25 International Trade Reporter (BNA) 1048-1049 (17 July 2008) (*quoting* an unnamed Latin American official).

[316] Those rulings also included a WTO Appellate Body compliance report, issued 26 November 2008, which upheld two Panel decisions that the EU had failed to comply with previous adjudicatory rulings, as its banana import regime continued to discriminate in favor of ACP bananas and against Latin and other non-ACP

To avoid further adjudicatory proceedings, WTO Director-General Pascal Lamy agreed to mediate a solution. His report, delivered on 12 July 2008, suggested a compromise whereby the EU would make an immediate down payment to Latin American exporters of a large cut to its 176/ton tariff, and make further cuts across a defined transition period. Specifically, the final tariff would be 114/ton, which the EU would reach over an eight-year period starting on 1 January 2009, with an immediate cut on that date of 28/ton.[317] (The July 2008 Text called for the EU to reach the final rate of 114/ton by the end of 2016.) Thus, there would be a tariff cut of just over 35 percent (from 176/ton to 114/ton). In exchange, the Latin banana exporting countries would drop all WTO litigation and rights of retaliation against the EU, and acquiesce to the EU giving ACP exporters duty-free access.[318]

The Lamy compromise pleased no one — even though, ironically, a single tariff-only regime of 176/ton was the deal struck years earlier to end the Bananas War.[319] The ACP countries — most of which were former British, French, or Portuguese colonies — feared for their historical preferences. If a banana tariff cut through the Lamy compromise were too steep, then their access to the EU market would be jeopardized. Likewise, if bananas were not designated as "Sensitive" and subject to the July 2008 Text proposal of an 85 percent tariff reduction, the new tariff would be 26.4/ ton — effectively eroding the ACP margin of preference.

The ACP position was influential in the EU. It accorded with the commercial interests of the two major banana producers in the EU, France, and Spain, which have considerable operations in the ACP. The EU insisted that if it cuts its banana tariff via the compromise, then the compromise must unambiguously permit it to exclude bananas (along with melons, rum, and sugar) from the list of tropical products slated for Doha Round tariff reductions. That is, the EU should be allowed to declare bananas as a "Sensitive Product," so that it does not have two legal obligations to slash banana tariffs. Further, the EU was adamant that any deal on bananas would have to be contingent on an overall Doha Round agreement in agriculture.

---

supplying countries. *See* Daniel Pruzin, *Latin Countries Slam EU Inaction on Banana Tariffs, Push 2008 Side Deal*, 26 International Trade Reporter (BNA) 155 (29 January 2009).

[317] *See* Daniel Pruzin, *Latin Countries Slam EU Inaction on Banana Tariffs, Push 2008 Side Deal*, 26 International Trade Reporter (BNA) 155 (29 January 2009).

[318] *See* Daniel Pruzin, *EU Official Optimistic on Banana Deal, But Latin Exporters See Key Differences*, 26 International Trade Reporter (BNA) 484 (9 April 2009).

[319] *See* Raj Bhala, *The Bananas War*, 31 McGeorge Law Review 839-971 (Summer 2000); *EU, Latin America Look to WTO Talks for Banana Deal*, Reuters, 5 December 2008, posted at www.reuters.com.

Note that a few Latin banana exporting countries, namely, Colombia, Costa Rica, Ecuador, Guatemala, and Panama, were reported to have agreed with the EU to the deal. *See* Daniel Pruzin, *EU Official Optimistic on Banana Deal, But Latin Exporters See Key Differences*, 26 International Trade Reporter (BNA) 484 (9 April 2009). Of course, Colombia and Costa Rica were Banana Framework Agreement (BFA) countries, and thus had cut a deal with the EU in the past.

The EU position, shaped by the ACP, was the diametric opposite of the Latin American stance. For Latin banana exporting countries, resolving the Bananas War was a separate matter. There should be no deal in the Round without its settlement. Latin American countries attacked the Lamy compromise as "very much biased" in favor of the EU, which they said already had agreed in negotiations to an immediate 20 percent cut in the 176/ton figure.[320] The implementation period, too, was a battlefront, with the EU arguing for a transition period of 15 years, and the Latin American exporting countries demanding four or five years. In brief, the Bananas War heated up, and Ecuador — the largest banana exporter in the world — said that without a settlement it found agreeable, it would not join a consensus to conclude the Doha Round agriculture modalities.[321]

Seeking some middle ground, the EU proposed in February 2009 that the 114/ton end-tariff for non-ACP bananas apply even if there were no, or a delayed, Doha Round deal.[322] Negotiations proceeded through 2009, particularly with the EU on one side, and five key Latin banana exporters on the other side — Colombia, Costa Rica, Ecuador, Guatemala, and Panama. Once all countries agreed on a bananas deal, then the EU would commence cuts for three years. The EU would freeze any further reductions for three years, if the Round were not concluded, and then resume the cuts, regardless of the status of the Round.

Accordingly, the new EU proposal meant a cut from the initial MFN tariff of 176/ton to 114/ton by 2019 (approximately an eight-year period, and three years later than the July 2008 Text specified), with a reduction to 136/ton in the interim. As a down payment, the EU would make an immediate cut of 28/ton (to 148/ton) from 176/ton (with "immediate" meaning in October 2010).[323] The 136/ton rate would apply from 2011 to 2014, followed by gradual cuts. The final result of a 114/ton tariff would be reached by the end of 2019 (instead of 2016, under the Lamy compromise), if the Round were not concluded.[324]

---

[320] Daniel Pruzin, *WTO's Lamy Delivers Compromise Text Aimed at Resolving Banana Dispute*, 25 International Trade Reporter (BNA) 1048-1049 (17 July 2008) (*quoting* an unnamed Latin American official).

[321] *See UPDATE 1 — Ecuador Threatens Doha Deal Over Banana Dispute*, REUTERS, 26 November 2008, posted at www.reuters.com.

[322] *See* Joshua Chaffin, *"Banana Wars" Pact Between EU and Latin America Nears Fruition*, FINANCIAL TIMES, 18 November 2009, at 4; Daniel Pruzin, *EU Official Optimistic on Banana Deal, But Latin Exporters See Key Differences*, 26 International Trade Reporter (BNA) 484 (9 April 2009).

[323] *See* Daniel Pruzin, *EU, Latin Americans Conclude Banana Deal, But Haggling Remains Over Tropical Products*, 26 International Trade Reporter (BNA) 1662 (3 December 2009).

[324] Note that following the Seventh WTO Ministerial Conference in Geneva in November-December 2009, the precise details of the transition period were not entirely clear. By one account, following the cut in October 2010 to 148/ton, the EU would reduce the tariff in annual installments to 132/ton in 2013. If no Doha Round agreement were reached by the end of 2013, then the 132/ton rate would remain in effect until the Round was completed. *See* Daniel Pruzin, *EU, Latin Americans Conclude Banana Deal, But Haggling Remains Over Tropical Products*, 26 International Trade Reporter (BNA) 1662 (3 December 2009).

Likewise, the EU would cut tariffs on other tropical products, such as pineapples and sugar, at least until the outcome of the Doha Round was clear.

As part of its proposal, the EU insisted on three conditions.[325] First, any settlement would obligate Latin American countries drop their outstanding legal challenges at the WTO, and waive any rights of retaliation they had based on their previous adjudicatory victories. (After their major victory at the Appellate Body level in 1997, the United States and Ecuador won the right to retaliate against the EU.[326] The United States was authorized to impose $191 million of sanctions, which it did on goods from coffee makers to handbags, though it lifted the sanctions in 2001. Ecuador was authorized to impose $202 million in trade sanctions on EU imports, including — for the first time in the annals of GATT–WTO dispute resolution — the right to suspend intellectual property protection and wholesale distribution rights for EU goods and services. Ecuador never imposed the sanctions.) The EU did not want to come to a settlement in the Bananas War, only to have that War reignited by another legal fight, or suffer retaliation based on a previous one. The EU wanted the "Peace Clause" to take effect as soon as the settlement deal was signed by all relevant parties.[327] However, some of those parties — potential complainants — argued the Clause should not enter into force until the EU registered the deal with the WTO. Until such registration — technically known as "certification," whereby the WTO approves in the tariff schedule of the EU and the new rates become legally binding[328] — the EU could renege on the deal.

Second, the EU would be permitted to continue to grant duty-free access to ACP bananas. The EU had no interest in entirely abandoning its former colonies. Moreover, indubitably, these cuts would greatly erode the margin of preference historically enjoyed by the ACP countries. To help the ACP countries face adjustment costs and restructure, the EU would grant them 190 million in development aid. That figure was too low to mollify some ACP producers, such as Cameroon, and Caribbean countries queried how the EU would divide the funds among ACP countries with divergent interests.[329] After all, as the Trade Minister of Trinidad poignantly noted, banana exports are critical to Caribbean economies, and not exporting them would be "like not exporting watches from Geneva."[330]

---

[325] *See* Jonathan Lynn, *EXCLUSIVE — Banana Deal Emerging — Trade Sources*, REUTERS, 2 November 2009, posted at www.reuters.com.

[326] *See* Daniel Pruzin, *EU, Latin, U.S. Officials Welcome Beginning of End to WTO Dispute on Banana Imports*, 26 International Trade Reporter (BNA) 1733 (17 December 2009).

[327] *See UPDATE 1 — EU Says Banana Deal Near, Some Producers Unhappy*, REUTERS, 2 December 2009, posted at www.wto.org.

[328] *See* Daniel Pruzin, *EU, Latin Americans Conclude Banana Deal, But Haggling Remains Over Tropical Products*, 26 International Trade Reporter (BNA) 1662 (3 December 2009).

[329] *See UPDATE 1 — EU Says Banana Deal Near, Some Producers Unhappy*, REUTERS, 2 December 2009, posted at www.wto.org.

[330] *UPDATE 1 — EU Says Banana Deal Near, Some Producers Unhappy*, REUTERS, 2 December 2009, posted at www.wto.org (*quoting* Mariano Browne).

Third, bananas would be treated as a normal agricultural good, not as a tropical product. Consequently, bananas would not be subject to the faster, deeper tariff cuts imposed on tropical products under the proposed July 2008 Doha Round agricultural text. If they were, then the problem of preference erosion would be exacerbated, against the interests of the ACP, because those cuts would be applied on top of the special transitional rules for bananas.

This purported middle ground appeared to the ACP to be tilted in favor of the EU and Latin America. In May 2009, the ACP asked the EU for compensation of 500 million, along with any agreed-upon tariff-cutting deal.[331] No less than that level of compensation would be needed to cover the drastic economic losses, and the attendant social dislocations and political instability, which assuredly would occur immediately after the EU implemented any deal. The ACP averred they would occur because, in a liberalized trading regime for bananas, its fruit would lose yet more share of the EU market to competition from Latin suppliers, *i.e.*, Latin bananas would flood the EU market, drowning out the ACP bananas. Initially, the EU balked at the compensation figure, offering what the ACP regarded as a paltry sum — 100 million — before boosting it to 190 million.

Happily, on 15 December 2009, the Bananas War finally ended with a settlement along the above-delineated lines of the EU's middle-ground proposal of February 2009. The settlement consists of two key documents.

First, there is the *GATB*, formally signed on 31 May 2010. The signatories to *GATB* were the EU and 11 Latin American countries — Brazil, Colombia, Costa Rica, Ecuador (which is the largest banana exporter in the world), Guatemala, Honduras, Mexico, Nicaragua, Panama, Peru, and Venezuela.[332] Second, on 8 June 2010, the EU and United States signed a separate, linked deal, called the "*Agreement on Trade in Bananas Between the United States of America and the European Union.*" The only material changes rendered by this *Agreement* and *GATB* from the above-described parameters in the February 2009 EU proposal concerned the exact transition dates and compensation figure:[333]

- The EU will cut its MFN tariff on bananas from Latin America and any other non-ACP origin from 176 per ton to 114 per ton by 1 January 2017 (or, possibly, 2019). The overall cut in the tariff, from 176 per ton to 114 per ton, is 35 percent.

---

[331] *See* Darren Ennis & Bate Felix, *African States Seek 500 Mln Euros in EU Banana Deal*, REUTERS, 29 May 2009, posted at www.reuters.com.

[332] *See* Len Bracken, *U.S., EU Agree to Settle Dispute Over Latin American Bananas, USTR Says*, 27 International Trade Reporter (BNA) 856 (10 June 2010).; Daniel Pruzin, *EU, Latin, U.S. Officials Welcome Beginning of End to WTO Dispute on Banana Imports*, 26 International Trade Reporter (BNA) 1733 (17 December 2009).

[333] *See* Daniel Pruzin, *EU, Latin Nations Formally Sign Agreement on Bananas; First Tariff Cuts Take Effect*, 27 International Trade Reporter (BNA) 828 (3 June 2010); Daniel Pruzin, *EU, Latin, U.S. Officials Welcome Beginning of End to WTO Dispute on Banana Imports*, 26 International Trade Reporter (BNA) 1733 (17 December 2009); Joshua Chaffin, *End of Banana Wars Brings Hope for Doha*, FINANCIAL TIMES, 16 December 2009, at 8; Darren Ennis & Jonathan Lynn, *UPDATE 1 — EU, U.S., Latin America to Initial Banana Deal*, REUTERS, 15 December 2009, posted at www.reuters.com.

- The EU will make an immediate, initial cut (*i.e.*, a down payment) to 148 per ton (as of 1 June 2010, retroactive to 15 December 2009, when the *Agreement* and *GATB* were initialed).

- After the first cut, the EU will drop its tariff to 143 per ton on 1 January 2011, 136 per ton on 1 January 2012, and 132 on 1 January 2013.

- As of 1 January 2013, if there is a Doha Round agreement on agriculture, then the EU will continue to cut the tariff to 127 in 2014, 122 in 2015, and 117 in 2016. Thus, the final rate of 114 will apply on 1 January 2017.

- However, if there is no final Doha Round deal on farm trade, then the EU will freeze its tariff at 132 for two years — 2014 and 2015 — before re-commencing cuts in January 2016. Then, it will reach the final rate of 114 per ton in January 2019. In other words, the final duty level will be achieved two years faster under the scenario of a successful outcome to the Doha Round, which itself is an incentive for some Members to achieve that success.

- The EU agreed to boost the compensation figure to ACP countries to roughly 200 million.

Accordingly, the Latin countries agreed to all three of the EU's aforementioned conditions. First, there will be no more law suits, and an end to all legal proceedings, as soon as the EU inscribes its new tariff commitment into its legally-binding Schedule of Concessions. Second, the EU can continue its tariff-only preference for ACP bananas under the new Economic Partnership Agreements the EU reached with ACP countries, which entered into force in January 2008, and which are WTO compliant. Third, bananas will be treated as a good subject to normal tariff reductions under any Doha Round deal (not accelerated duty elimination as a tropical good).

## *GATS*

*General Agreement on Trade in Services*, one of the Uruguay Round multilateral trade agreements (MTAs).

The *GATS* is set forth in Annex 1B to the Uruguay Round *Agreement Establishing the World Trade Organization* (*WTO Agreement*). The MTAs on Goods (including GATT) are found in Annex 1A, and *Agreement on Trade-related Aspects of Intellectual Property Rights* (*TRIPs Agreement*) is contained in Annex 1C.

*Suggestions for Further Research:*

Books:

1. ARUP, CHRISTOPHER, THE NEW WORLD TRADE ORGANIZATION AGREEMENTS — GLOBALIZING LAW THROUGH SERVICES AND INTELLECTUAL PROPERTY (2000).

2. CLAESSENS, STIJIN & MARION JANSEN EDS., THE INTERNATIONALIZATION OF FINANCIAL SERVICES — ISSUES AND LESSONS FOR DEVELOPING COUNTRIES (2000).

3.  KELSEY, JANE, RECLAIMING THE FUTURE — NEW ZEALAND AND THE GLOBAL ECONOMY (1999).

4.  KELSEY, JANE, SERVING WHOSE INTERESTS? THE POLITICAL ECONOMY OF TRADE IN SERVICES AGREEMENTS (2008).

5.  KELSEY, JANE, ED., NO ORDINARY DEAL — UNMASKING THE TRANS-PACIFIC PARTNERSHIP FREE TRADE AGREEMENT (2010).

6.  LITAN, ROBERT E., PAUL MASSON & MICHAEL POMERLEANO EDS., OPEN DOORS — FOREIGN PARTICIPATION IN FINANCIAL SYSTEMS IN DEVELOPING COUNTRIES (2001).

7.  ORGANIZATION FOR ECONOMIC COOPERATION AND DEVELOPMENT (OECD), TRADE IN SERVICES — NEGOTIATING ISSUES AND APPROACHES (2001).

8.  RAGHAVAN, CHAKRAVARTHI, DEVELOPING COUNTRIES AND SERVICES TRADE — CHASING A BLACK CAT IN A DARK ROOM, BLIND FOLDED (2002).

9.  SAUVÉ, PIERRE, *TRADE RULES BEHIND BORDERS: ESSAYS ON SERVICES, INVESTMENT AND THE NEW TRADE AGENDA* 41 (2003).

10. SAUVÉ, PIERRE & ROBERT M. STERN, GATS 2000 — NEW DIRECTIONS IN SERVICES TRADE LIBERALIZATION (2000).

11. STEPHENSON, SHERRY M ED., SERVICES TRADE IN THE WESTERN HEMISPHERE — LIBERALIZATION, INTEGRATION, AND REFORM (2000).

12. WTO SECRETARIAT, GUIDE TO THE GATS — AN OVERVIEW OF ISSUES FOR FURTHER LIBERALIZATION OF TRADE IN SERVICES (2001).

13. WTO SECRETARIAT, TRADE IN SERVICES DIVISION, A HANDBOOK ON THE GATS AGREEMENT (2005).

Book Chapters:

1.  Gao, Henry S., *Reflections on the Relationship between WTO Negotiations and Dispute Settlement: Lessons from the GATS, in* THE WTO IN THE TWENTY-FIRST CENTURY — DISPUTE SETTLEMENT, NEGOTIATIONS, AND REGIONALISM IN ASIA 367-380 (Yasuhei Taniguchi, Alan Yanovich & Jan Bohanes eds. 2007).

Articles:

1.  Abu-Akeel, Aly K., *Definition of Trade in Services Under the GATS: Legal Implications*, 32 THE GEORGE WASHINGTON UNIVERSITY JOURNAL OF INTERNATIONAL LAW AND ECONOMICS 189-210 (1999).

2.  Adlung, Rudolf & Antonio Carzaniga, *MFN Exemptions Under the General Agreement on Trade in Services: Grandfathers Striving for Immortality?*, 12 JOURNAL OF INTERNATIONAL ECONOMIC LAW 357-392 (2009).

3.  Adlung, Rudolf & Martin Molinuevo, *Bilateralism in Services Trade: Is There Fire Behind the (BIT-)smoke?*, 11 JOURNAL OF INTERNATIONAL ECONOMIC LAW 365-409 (2008).

4.  Bloom, Heather A., *Upping the Ante: The Unlawful Internet Gambling Enforcement Act's Noncompliance with World Trade Organization Law*, 5 SOUTH CAROLINA JOURNAL OF INTERNATIONAL LAW & BUSINESS 75-106 (2008).

5.  Bodien, Clint, Comment, *Cross-retaliation in the WTO: Antigua and Barbuda's Proposed Remedy Against the United States in an Online Gambling Dispute*, 14 LAW AND BUSINESS REVIEW OF THE AMERICAS 847-856 (2008).

6.  Carlson, Eric J., Note, *Drawing Dead: Recognizing Problems with Congress' Attempt to Regulating the Online Gambling Industry and the Negative Repercussions to International Trade*, 32 SUFFOLK TRANSNATIONAL LAW REVIEW 135-160 (2008).

7.  Chander, Anupam, *Trade 2.0*, 34 YALE JOURNAL OF INTERNATIONAL LAW 281-330 (2009).

8.  Cheng, Priscilla T., Note, *Call a Spade a Spade: Barriers to Harmonization and Conflicting Messages in European Union Internet Gambling Policy*, 36 BROOKLYN JOURNAL OF INTERNATIONAL LAW 693-716 (2011).

9.  Codd, Kathryn, Note, *Betting on the Wrong Horse: The Detrimental Effect of Non-Compliance in the Internet Gambling Dispute on the General Agreement on Trade in Services (GATS)*, 49 WILLIAM & MARY LAW REVIEW 941-971 (2007).

10. Cottier, Thomas & Markus Krajewski, *What Role for Non-Discrimination and Prudential Standards in International Financial Law?*, 13 JOURNAL OF INTERNATIONAL ECONOMIC LAW 817-835 (2010).

11. Crosby, Daniel C., *Banking on China's WTO Commitments: "Same Bed, Different Dreams" in China's Financial Services Sector*, 11 JOURNAL OF INTERNATIONAL ECONOMIC LAW 75-105 (2008).

12. D'Angelo, Carlo, *Overseas Legal Outsourcing and the American Legal Profession: Friend or "Flattener"?*, 14 TEXAS WESLEYAN LAW REVIEW 167-195 (2008).

13. Darling, Jeremy B., Note, *Gambling with Our Future: A Call for Needed WTO Dispute Resolution Reform as Illustrated by the U.S.–Antigua Conflict Over Online Gambling*, 42 GEORGE WASHINGTON INTERNATIONAL LAW REVIEW 381-405 (2010).

14. De Meester, Bart, *Testing European Prudential Conditions for Banking Mergers in the Light of Most Favored Nation in the GATS*, 11 JOURNAL OF INTERNATIONAL ECONOMIC LAW 609-647 (2008).

15. Delimatsis, Panagiotis & Pierre Sauvé, *Financial Services Trade After the Crisis: Policy and Legal Conjectures*, 13 JOURNAL OF INTERNATIONAL ECONOMIC LAW 837-857 (2010).

16. Delimatsis, Panagiotis, *Determining the Necessity of Domestic Regulations in Services: The Best is Yet to Come*, 19 EUROPEAN JOURNAL OF INTERNATIONAL LAW 365-408 (2008).

17. Dogan, Irem, Note, *Taking a Gamble on Public Morals: Invoking the Article XIV Exception to GATS*, 32 BROOKLYN JOURNAL OF INTERNATIONAL LAW 1131-1156 (2007).

18. Emerson, Petra L., *An Economic Integration Agreement on Services: A Possible Solution to the Doha Development Round Impasses*, 2 TRADE, LAW AND DEVELOPMENT no. 2, 224-291 (fall 2010).

19. Enriques, Luca, *Regulators' Response to the Current Crisis and the Upcoming Reregulation of Financial Markets: One Reluctant Regulator's View*, 30 University of Pennsylvania Journal of International Law 1147-1155 (summer 2009).

20. Footer, Mary E., *The International Regulation of Trade in Services Following Completion of the Uruguay Round*, 29 The International Lawyer 453, 465 (1995).

21. Gadbaw, R. Michael, *Systemic Regulation of Global Trade and Finance: A Tale of Two Systems*, 13 Journal of International Economic Law 551-574 (2010).

22. Ganesh, Selvi, *Educational Service and International Law*, 50 Indian Journal of International Law number 4 617-635 (October — December 2010).

23. Gkoutzinis, Apostolos, *International Trade in Banking Services and the Role of the WTO: Discussing the Legal Framework and Policy Objectives of the General Agreement on Trade in Services and the Current State of Play in the Doha Round of Trade Negotiations*, 39 The International Lawyer 877-914 (winter 2005).

24. Gordon, Jennifer, *People Are Not Bananas: How Immigration Differs from Trade*, 104 Northwestern University Law Review 1109-1145 (2010).

25. Gupta, Amar & Deth Sao, *Harmonization of International Legal Structure for Fostering Professional Services: Lessons from Early U.S. Federal — State Relations*, 18 Cardozo Journal of International & Comparative Law 239-294 (2010).

26. Hamann, Georgia, Note, *Replacing Slingshots with Swords: Implications of the Antigua — Gambling 22:6 Panel Report for Developing Countries and the World Trading System*, 42 Vanderbilt Journal Transnational Law 993-1028 (2009)

27. Harrington, Lorraine L., *Note. Loaded Dice: Do National Internet Gaming Statutes Violate WTO Fair Trade Access Standards?*, 24 Arizona Journal of International and Comparative Law 769-802 (2007).

28. Hill, Louise L., *Services as Objects of International Trade: Bartering the Legal Profession*, 39 Vanderbilt Journal of Transnational Law 347-78 (2006).

29. Hufbauer, Gary & Sherry Stephenson: *Services Trade: Past Liberalization and Future Challenges*, 10 Journal of International Economic Law 605-630 (2007).

30. Kilby, Mitchell E., Comment, *The Mouse that Roared: Implications of the WTO Ruling in U.S. — Gambling*, 44 Texas International Law Journal numbers 1 &2, 233-268 (fall/winter 2008).

31. King, Nancy J. & Kishani Kalupahana, *Choosing Between Liberalization and Regulatory Autonomy under GATS: Implications of U.S.–Gambling for Trade in Cross Border E-Services*, 40 Vanderbilt Journal of Transnational Law 1189-1299 (2007).

32. Leal-Arcas, Rafael, *The Resumption of the Doha Round and the Future of Services Trade*, 29 Loyola Los Angeles International & Comparative Law Review 339-461 (2007).

33. Leroux, Eric H., *Eleven Years of GATS Case Law: What Have We Learned?*, 10 JOURNAL OF INTERNATIONAL ECONOMIC LAW 749-793 (2007).

34. Li, Chao Feng & Andrew McGee, *The View on Chinese License Regulation for Insurance Companies*, 8 JOURNAL OF INTERNATIONAL TRADE LAW & POLICY number 1, 25-39 (2009).

35. Liu, Cynthia, Note, *Internet Censorship as a Trade Barrier: A Look at the WTO Consistency of the Great Firewall in the Wake of the China-Google Dispute*, 42 Georgetown Journal of International Law 1199-1240 (2011).

36. Mangin, Elanor A., Note, *Market Access in China — Publications and Audiovisual Materials: A Moral Victory with a Silver Lining*, 25 BERKELEY TECHNOLOGY LAW JOURNAL 279-310 (2010).

37. Marchetti, Juan A & Petros C. Mavroidis, *The Genesis of the GATS (General Agreement on Trade in Services)*, 22 European Journal of International Law 689-721 (2011).

38. Martin, Mervyn, *Sole Distribution Agreements in the Context of the General Principles of Free Trade and Competition*, 35 SYRACUSE JOURNAL OF INTERNATIONAL LAW AND COMMERCE 77-94 (2007).

39. Mattoo, Aaditya & Deepak Mishra, *Foreign Professionals in the United States: Regulatory Impediments to Trade*, 12 JOURNAL OF INTERNATIONAL ECONOMIC LAW 435-456 (2009).

40. Nesson, Charles R. & Andrew Woods, Commentary on the Law of Poker, 8 RICHMOND JOURNAL OF GLOBAL LAW AND BUSINESS 11-18 (2008) (transcription).

41. Owens, Tracy M., Comment, *It's A Numbers Game: Financial Data Restrictions in China Don't Add Up to WTO Compliance*, 20 PACIFIC MCGEORGE GLOBAL BUSINESS & DEVELOPMENT LAW JOURNAL 383-406 (2007).

42. Perry, Kristina L., *The Current State of the Unlawful Internet Gambling Enforcement Act and Recently Adopted Prohibition on Funding of Unlawful Internet Gambling*, 8 RICHMOND JOURNAL OF GLOBAL LAW AND BUSINESS 29-36 (2008).

43. Rose, J. Nelson, *Internet Gaming and the Law*, 8 RICHMOND JOURNAL OF GLOBAL LAW AND BUSINESS 3-10 (2008) (transcription).

44. Sakmar, Susan L., *Bringing Energy Trade into the WTO: The Historical Context, Current Status, and Potential Implications for the Middle East Region*, 18 INDIANA INTERNATIONAL & COMPARATIVE LAW REVIEW 89-111 (2008).

45. Sherman, Laura B., Comment, *A Fundamental Misunderstanding: FCC Implementation of U.S. WTO Commitments*, 61 FEDERAL COMMUNICATIONS LAW JOURNAL 395-406 (2009).

46. Silver, Carole, *The Variable Value of U.S. Legal Education in the Global Legal Services Market*, 24 GEORGETOWN JOURNAL OF LEGAL ETHICS 1-57 (2011).

47. Symposium, *Medical Tourism Meets Health Law: U.S.–EU Dialogue*, 26 WISCONSIN INTERNATIONAL LAW JOURNAL 591-964 (2008).

48. Terry, Andrew & Heather Forrest, *Where's the Beef? Why Burger King is Hungry Jack's in Australia and Other Complications in Building A Global Franchise Brand*, 28 NORTHWESTERN JOURNAL OF INTERNATIONAL LAW & BUSINESS 171-213 (2008).

49. Terry, Laurel S., *From GATS to APEC: The Impact of Trade Agreements on Legal Services*, 43 AKRON LAW REVIEW 875-984 (2010).

50. Thornberg, Christopher F. & Frances L. Edwards, *Failure of Trade Liberalization: A Study of the GATS Negotiation*, 10 JOURNAL OF INTERNATIONAL BUSINESS & LAW 325-348 (2011).

51. Vena, Chris, Comment, *More than Best Friends: Expansion of Global Law Firms into the Indian Legal Market*, 31 NORTHWESTERN JOURNAL OF INTERNATIONAL LAW & BUSINESS 195-223 (2011).

52. Voon, Tania & Andrew Mitchell, *Open for Business? China's Telecommunications Service Market and the WTO*, 13 JOURNAL OF INTERNATIONAL ECONOMIC LAW 321-378 (2010).

53. Vranes, Erich, *The WTO and Regulatory Freedom: WTO Disciplines on Market Access, Non-Discrimination and Domestic Regulation Relating to Trade in Goods and Services*, 12 JOURNAL OF INTERNATIONAL ECONOMIC LAW 953-987 (2009).

54. Wang, Jiangyu, *Financial Liberalization and Regulation in East Asia: Lessons from Financial Crises and the Chinese Experience of Controlled Liberalization*, 41 JOURNAL OF WORLD TRADE issue 1 211-241 (2007).

55. White, Robin C.A., *Revisiting Free Movement of Workers*, 33 FORDHAM INTERNATIONAL LAW JOURNAL 1564-1587 (2010).

56. White, Timothy B., Comment, *Internet Gaming Trade Commitments: The Exaggerated Fears of U.S. Vulnerability under Multiple Trade Agreements*, 33 SOUTHERN ILLINOIS UNIVERSITY LAW JOURNAL 321-342 (2009).

57. Yokoi-Arai, Mamiko, *GATS' Prudential Carve Out in Financial Services and its Relation with Prudential Regulation*, 57 INTERNATIONAL & COMPARATIVE LAW QUARTERLY 613-648 (2008).

58. Zaidi, Kamaal R., *Harmonizing Trade Liberalization and Migration Policy Through Shared Responsibility: A Comparison of the Impact of Bilateral Trade Agreements and the GATS in Germany and Canada*, 37 SYRACUSE JOURNAL OF INTERNATIONAL LAW & COMMERCE 267-297 (2010).

Other Sources:

1. *Decision on Financial Services*, ¶ 1, *in* URUGUAY ROUND TRADE AGREEMENT, HOUSE OF REPRESENTATIVES DOCUMENT 316, 103D CONGRESS, 1ST SESSION 1703 (27 September 1994).

2. Kindt, John W., *Testimony before the Subcommittee on Crime, Terrorism, and Homeland Security, United States House of representatives, Legislative Hearing on H.R. 4777: The "Internet Gambling Prohibition Act,"* 5 April 2008, 8 RICHMOND JOURNAL OF GLOBAL LAW AND BUSINESS 19-27 (2008).

3. World Trade Organization Press Release, *The WTO's Financial Services Commitments Will Enter into Force as Scheduled*, PRESS/120 (15 February 1999).

4. World Trade Organization Press Release, *Successful Conclusion of the WTO's Financial Services Negotiations*, PRESS/86 (15 December 1997).

# GATT

A generic and somewhat imprecise term, typically used to cover GATT 1947, GATT 1994, and the institutional apparatus — particularly the pre-WTO GATT Secretariat — associated with GATT.

As to the institution, the GATT originally was housed in Villa Bocage, in Geneva Switzerland. It remained in that location from 1947 until 1977. In 1975, the International Labor Organization (ILO), created under the 1919 *Treaty of Versailles*, moved from its facility in Geneva — Centre William Rappard — which it had occupied since 1926. The new home of the ILO, also in Geneva was in the neighboring district of Grand Saconnex, to which it moved in 1975. The shift in the ILO's location opened up Centre William Rappard, which the GATT occupied in 1977, following two years of renovation and remodeling (1975-1977).

In 1977, the building vacated by the ILO changed names from the "ILO Building" to Centre William Rappard. The Centre is named after William Emmanuel Rappard, a Swiss diplomat, University Professor, and leading internationalist. From 1945-1956, he served on the Swiss Delegation to the ILO, before which he played a significant role in bringing the League of Nations to Geneva.

Centre William Rappard originally was constructed between 1923-1926, following the design of the Swiss architect, Georges Épitaux (1873-1957). His design was based on a classical Florentine villa, with an interior courtyard, august entrance, and sweeping staircase ascending from that entrance. The land on which the Centre sits was donated in 1923 by the Swiss Confederation to the League of Nations. (Switzerland had purchased the site, an estate forming the property of two families, in 1921.)

The Centre contains many fine works of art, some of which were hidden and re-discovered in 2007. One notable work is a six by three meter mural entitled *The Dignity of Labour*, painted by the French artist Maurice Denis (1870-1943). Commissioned by the International Federation of Christian trade unions, the mural depicts Jesus Christ in a workshop in Nazareth. He has put down his carpentry tools, and is speaking with a group of workers, some of whom sport 20th century work garments. The workers include several Christian trade unionists. Denis painted the mural at his home. In May 1931, the mural was brought to Geneva and placed on the left side of the main staircase.

In 1995, when the new World Trade Organization (WTO) succeeded the GATT, it remained in the same home, Centre William Rappard, the address of which is Rue de Lausanne 154, Ch-1211, Geneva 21, Switzerland. In 1998, a major new conference center was built next to Centre William Rappard. It accommodates large meetings, such as of the General Council.

*Suggestions for Further Research:*

Other Source:

1.   WORLD TRADE ORGANIZATION, THE WTO BUILDING — THE SYMBOLIC ARTWORK OF THE CENTRE WILLIAM RAPPARD, HEADQUARTERS OF THE WORLD TRADE ORGANIZATION (March 2008) (available at www.wto.org).

## GATT 1947

General Agreement on Tariffs and Trade, dated 30 October 1947 and entered into force on 1 January 1948. *See* 19 U.S.C. § 3501(1)(A).

According to GATT 1994, GATT 1947 remains in force after the entry into force, on 1 January 1995, of *WTO Agreement* and related MTAs.

The text of GATT was drafted in two sets of pivotal meetings of delegates from many countries. These meetings occurred in 1946 and 1947, as follows:

- First Session of the Preparatory Committee of the United Nations Conference on Trade and Employment, held in London from 15 October to 20 November 1946, and known as the "London Preparatory Conference." The key summary of this Session is the *London Report*, First Session of the Preparatory Committee (1946).

- Second Session of the Preparatory Committee of the United Nations Conference on Trade and Employment, held in Geneva from 10 April to 30 October 1947, and known as the "Geneva Preparatory Conference." The key summary of this Session is *Report of the Second Session of the Preparatory Committee of the United Nations Conference on Trade and Employment*, United Nations Document EPCT/186 (1947), *i.e.*, the *Geneva Report*.

*Suggestions for Further Research:*

Books:

1.   BAGWELL, KYLE & ROBERT W. STAIGER, THE ECONOMICS OF THE WORLD TRADING SYSTEM (2002).

2.   BARTON, JOHN H., JUDITH L. GOLDSTEIN, TIMOTHY E. JOSLING & RICHARD H. STEINBERG, THE EVOLUTION OF THE TRADE REGIME — POLITICS, LAW, AND ECONOMICS OF THE GATT AND THE WTO (2006).

3.   BEANE, DONALD G., THE UNITED STATES AND GATT — A RELATIONAL STUDY (2000).

4.   BUTLER, MICHAEL A., CAUTIOUS VISIONARY — CORDELL HULL AND TRADE REFORM, 1933-1937 (1998).

5.   CAPLING, ANN, AUSTRALIA AND THE GLOBAL TRADE SYSTEM — FROM HAVANA TO SEATTLE (2001).

6. DAM, KENNETH W., THE GATT — LAW AND INTERNATIONAL ECONOMIC ORGANIZATION (1970).

7. ECKES, ALFRED E., JR. ED., REVISITING U.S. TRADE POLICY — DECISIONS IN PERSPECTIVE (2000).

8. GARDNER, RICHARD N., STERLING–DOLLAR DIPLOMACY — THE ORIGINS AND THE PROSPECTS OF OUR INTERNATIONAL ECONOMIC ORDER (1969).

9. GEHRING, MARKUS W., JARROD HEPBURN & MARIE-CLAIRE CORDONIER SEGGER, WORLD TRADE LAW IN PRACTICE (2006).

10. HELLER, FRANCIS H. & JOHN R. GILLINGHAM, THE UNITED STATES AND THE INTEGRATION OF EUROPE — LEGACIES OF THE POSTWAR ERA (1996) (especially Chapter 10).

11. IRWIN, DOUGLAS A., PETROS C. MAVROIDIS, AND ALAN O. SYKES, THE GENESIS OF THE GATT (2008).

12. JACKSON, JOHN H., WORLD TRADE AND THE LAW OF GATT (1969).

13. JACKSON, JOHN H., THE WORLD TRADING SYSTEM (2nd ed. 1997)

14. KENWOOD, A.G. & A.L. LOUGHEED, THE GROWTH OF THE INTERNATIONAL ECONOMY 1820-2000 (4th ed. 1999).

15. KIRSHNER, ORIN, ED., THE BRETTON WOODS–GATT SYSTEM — RETROSPECT AND PROSPECT AFTER FIFTY YEARS (1996).

16. LOW, PATRICK, TRADING FREE — THE GATT AND U.S. TRADE POLICY (1993).

17. O'ROURKE, KEVIN H., ED., THE INTERNATIONAL TRADING SYSTEM, GLOBALIZATION AND HISTORY vols. I and II (2005).

18. OSTRY, SYLVIA, THE POST-COLD WAR TRADING SYSTEM — WHO'S ON FIRST? (1997).

19. RUGGIE, JOHN GERARD, ED., MULTILATERALISM MATTERS — THE THEORY AND PRAXIS OF AN INSTITUTIONAL FORM (1993).

20. TREBILCOCK, MICHAEL J. & ROBERT HOWSE, THE REGULATION OF INTERNATIONAL TRADE (3rd ed. 2005).

21. WILCOX, CLAIR, A CHARTER FOR WORLD TRADE (1949).

22. ZEILER, THOMAS W., FREE TRADE FREE WORLD — THE ADVENT OF GATT (1999).

Articles:

1. Alessandrini, Donatella, *WTO and Current Trade Debate: An Enquiry into the Intellectual Origins of Free Trade Thought*, 11 INTERNATIONAL TRADE LAW & REGULATION 53-60 (March 2005).

2. Archie, Charles V., Comment, *China Cannot Have Its Cake and Eat It, Too: Coercing the PRC to Reform its Currency Exchange Policy to Conform to Its WTO Obligations*, 37 NORTH CAROLINA JOURNAL OF INTERNATIONAL LAW & COMMERCIAL REGULATION 247-305 (2011).

3. Dam, Kenneth W., *Cordell Hull, The Reciprocal Trade Agreements Act, and the WTO — An Essay on the Concept of Rights in International Trade*, 1 NEW YORK UNIVERSITY JOURNAL OF LAW AND BUSINESS 709-730 (2005).

4. Du, Michael Ming, *The Rise of National Regulatory Autonomy in the GATT/WTO Regime*, 14 JOURNAL OF INTERNATIONAL ECONOMIC LAW 639-675 (2011).

5. Emmerson, Andrew, *Conceptualizing Security Exceptions: Legal Doctrine or Political Excuse?*, 11 JOURNAL OF INTERNATIONAL ECONOMIC LAW 135-154 (2008).

6. Feichtner, Isabel, *The Waiver Power of the WTO: Opening the WTO for Political Debate on the Reconciliation of Competing Interests*, EUROPEAN JOURNAL OF INTERNATIONAL LAW 615-645 (2009).

7. Galantucci, Robert, *Compassionate Consumerism within the GATT Regime: Can Belgium's Ban on Seal Product Imports be Justified Under Article XX?*, 39 CALIFORNIA WESTERN INTERNATIONAL LAW JOURNAL 281-312 (2009).

8. Garner, Richard N., *The Bretton Woods–GATT System After Sixty-Five Years: A Balance Sheet of Success and Failure*, 47 COLUMBIA JOURNAL OF TRANSNATIONAL LAW 31-71 (2008).

9. Gormley, Laurence W., *Silver Threads Among the Gold ... 50 Years of the Free Movement of Goods*, 31 FORDHAM INTERNATIONAL LAW JOURNAL 1637-1691 (2008).

10. Kapterian, Gisele, *A Critique of WTO Jurisprudence on "Necessity,"* 59 INTERNATIONAL & COMPARATIVE LAW QUARTERLY 89-127 (2010).

11. Luan, Xinjie & Julien Chaisse, *Preliminary Comments on the WTO Seals Products Dispute: Traditional Hunting, Public Morals, and Technical Barriers to Trade*, 22 COLORADO JOURNAL OF INTERNATIONAL ENVIRONMENTAL LAW & POLICY 79-121 (2011).

12. Mangin, Elanor A., Note, *Market Access in China — Publications and Audiovisual Materials: A Moral Victory with a Silver Lining*, 25 BERKELEY TECHNOLOGY LAW JOURNAL 279-310 (2010).

13. Miller, Gary, Note, *Exporting Morality with Trade Restrictions: The Wrong Path to Animal Rights*, 34 BROOKLYN JOURNAL OF INTERNATIONAL LAW 999-1044 (2009).

14. Note, *(In)efficient Breach of International Trade Law: The State of the "Free Pass" After China's Rare Earths Export Embargo*, 125 HARVARD LAW REVIEW 602-625 (2011).

15. Ozbirn, Jasper L., Comment, *An Analysis and Synthesis of the Decisional Law Applying Article XX(g) of the General Agreement on Tariffs and Trade*, 21 PACIFIC MCGEORGE GLOBAL BUSINESS & DEVELOPMENT LAW JOURNAL 371-413 (2008).

16. Rehm, John B., *Developments in the Law and Institutions of International Economic Relations: The Kennedy Round of Trade Negotiations*, 62 AMERICAN JOURNAL OF INTERNATIONAL LAW 2, 403 (1968).

17. Scott, James, *Developing Countries in the ITO and GATT Negotiations*, 9 JOURNAL OF INTERNATIONAL TRADE LAW AND POLICY number 1, 5-24 (2010).

18. Smith, Bryant Walker, *Water as a Public Good: The Status of Water Under the General Agreement on Tariffs and Trade*, 17 CARDOZO JOURNAL OF INTERNATIONAL & COMPARATIVE LAW 291-314 (2009).

19. Smith, Tyler, Note, *Much Needed Reform in the Realm of Public Morals: A Proposed Addition to the GATT Article XX(a) "Public Morals" Framework Resulting from China — Audiovisual (China — Measures Affecting Trading Rights and Distribution Services for Certain Publications and Audiovisual Entertainment Products, WT/DS363/R (2009)*, 19 CARDOZO JOURNAL OF INTERNATIONAL & COMPARATIVE LAW 733-773 (2011).

Other Source:

1. *A Brief History of the GATT, in* TRADE POLICIES FOR A BETTER FUTURE — THE "LEUTWILER REPORT," THE GATT AND THE URUGUAY ROUND 160-64 (1987).

## GATT 1994

The General Agreement on Tariffs and Trade 1994, as annexed to the *Agreement Establishing the World Trade Organization (WTO Agreement). See* 19 U.S.C. § 3501(1)(B).

By virtue of Article II:2 of *WTO Agreement* and Annex 1A to that *Agreement*, GATT 1994 is one of the Multilateral Trade Agreements (MTAs). Article 1 of GATT 1994 explains that GATT 1994 consists of GATT 1947; legal instruments that entered into force under GATT 1947 before the entry into force of the *WTO Agreement* (namely, protocols and provisions relating to tariff concessions, protocols of accession, decisions on waivers under Article XXV of GATT 1947, and other decisions of the Contracting Parties); Understandings reached during the Uruguay Round (namely, Understandings on the Interpretation of Article II:1(b), XVII, the Balance of Payments (BOP) provisions, Article XXIV, waivers of obligations, and Article XXVIII of GATT 1994); and the Marrakesh Protocol to GATT 1994.

*Suggestions for Further Research:*

Other Source:

1. GATT SECRETARIAT, THE RESULTS OF THE URUGUAY ROUND OF MULTILATERAL TRADE NEGOTIATIONS (November 1994).

## GATT COUNCIL

A pre-Uruguay Round body that consisted of representatives from the contracting parties.

The GATT Council was established in 1959 under the authority of GATT Article XXV:1 to consider urgent matters, supervise the work of committees, prepare negotiating sessions, and engage in other functions delegated to it by the contracting parties. Technically, it was the organ of GATT that adopted, or declined to adopt, panel reports. The General Council of the WTO now stands in its stead.

## GATT-WTO REGIME

A generic term encompassing all pre- and post-Uruguay Round legal instruments and institutions, namely, GATT 1947, Agreement Establishing the World

Trade Organization (*WTO Agreement*), Multilateral Trade Agreements (MTAs), and GATT and WTO as institutions. A synonym is the "GATT-WTO system." International relations scholars, however, sometimes impute special meaning to the noun "regime."

## GCC

The Gulf Cooperation Council.

The GCC was created in 1981 in Riyadh, Kingdom of Saudi Arabia. Six Arab countries in the Gulf (that is, the Persian or Arabian Gulf) region — Bahrain, Saudi Arabia, Kuwait, Oman, Qatar, Saudi Arabia, and the United Arab Emirates (UAE) — agreed to form the "Cooperation Council for the Arab States of the Gulf." The group commonly is known as the "Gulf Cooperation Council" (GCC). As a Persian country, Iran is not a member. The other two Gulf Arab nations, Iraq and Yemen, also did not join, though Yemen (as of 2006) is seeking full membership.

The purpose of the GCC is to promote stability and economic cooperation in the Gulf region. In 1991, during the first Gulf War, the GCC formed a regional military force with Egypt and Syria, which was used to liberate Kuwait and is available for peacekeeping purposes. The GCC also has a fund for Arab development. Most notably from a trade perspective, in January 2003, the GCC eliminated tariff and many non-tariff barriers on trade among member states, and established a customs union (CU).

In December 2001 at a GCC Heads of State Summit, GCC leaders agreed to an across-the-board common external tariff (CET) of five percent on imports originating from non-GCC countries, with implementation beginning January 2003. Considerable challenges face the GCC, including agreement on distribution of revenues, setting common technical standards, and deciding the products to which a tariff higher than the five percent CET will apply. Some GCC countries have tariffs of 15 to 20 percent or more on certain products.

Bahrain, for instance, has a 20 percent duty on 12 millimeter steel bars. Some of the GCC countries impose a duty of 100 percent or more on goods the consumption of which Islamic Law (*Shari'a*) forbids, namely, alcohol, pork, and pork products. For example, Bahrain puts a 125 percent duty on alcohol, Oman and Qatar a 100 percent duty on alcohol, and the Kingdom of Saudi Arabia bans the importation of it under GATT Article XX(a) (the public morality exception) of alcohol altogether. Additionally, most GCC countries impose a 100 percent tariff on tobacco products.

Notably, like the European Union (EU), the GCC aspires to create a common currency, and thus achieve monetary union.[334] Along with the elimination of trade barriers, the GCC declared in 2001 that it would establish a single

---

[334] *See* Will McSheehy, *Economists Fear Plan for Monetary Union Among Gulf States is Losing Momentum*, FINANCIAL TIMES, 23 September 2005.

currency as a means of boosting intra-regional trade. The original target date for a GCC monetary union was 1 January 2010, with the new currency to float freely by 2015. To meet this deadline, Kuwait agreed in January 2003 to end its 27 year-long link to a basket of currencies (the exact identities and weighting of which Kuwait does not disclose). Kuwait was the only GCC country to peg its currency to a unit other than the U.S. dollar, *i.e.*, the other GCC countries had not yet made the switch from dollar pegging to a basket link, which was necessary to support monetary union.

However, in 2005 the GCC did not meet its interim deadline for agreement on specific convergence criteria. Disagreements persisted, despite technical assistance from the European Central Bank (ECB), over the formation and name of a common currency, and the location of a central bank.[335] In September 2006, the GCC agreed to put its Central Bank in Abu Dhabi at the objection of the UAE. The UAE had requested to be the headquarters for the bank since 2004. Because of the decision to base the bank in Abu Dhabi the UAE withdrew from plans to join the monetary union in May 2009. The withdrawal of the UAE followed Oman, which already had withdrawn from the project.

As for the currency name, it might be *"karam"* — the Arabic word for "generosity." However, several GCC countries implemented unilateral measures to support growth and help their own banking systems, particularly in the global economic recession that struck following the September 2008 collapse of Lehman Brothers on Wall Street.

Thus, in March 2009, the GCC announced it was postponing the date for the launch of a single currency.[336] The GCC had little choice. It had no common regulatory or monetary policy framework in place to cover critical issues like reserve management. Indeed, as of March 2009, none of the six GCC governments had endorsed formally a single currency agreement — even though the accord they reached in 2001 laid out basic economic criteria to support a single currency, namely:

- Each GCC country would maintain an inflation rate of two percent or less.

- Each GCC would limit its annual fiscal deficit to no more than three percent of Gross Domestic Product (GDP).

Implementing the first criterion was not possible, because the GCC had not harmonized statistical and data collection and evaluation, and thus had no common measure for inflation. In an effort to maintain some momentum toward a monetary union, the GCC planned to launch a Monetary Council, as a precursor to a Central Bank, sometime in 2009.

On a positive note, effective 1 January 2008, the GCC declared it had formed a common market. The rules of the common market not only broadened and

---

[335] *See* Ralph Atkins & Mark Schieritz, *ECB to Advise Gulf States on Monetary Union Plan*, FINANCIAL TIMES, 18 April 2006.

[336] *See* Robin Wigglesworth, *Gulf Countries Extend Currency Union Deadline*, FINANCIAL TIMES, 25 March 2009, at 6.

deepened trade liberalization; they also drew the GCC countries closer together in other economic aspects. GCC citizens are treated equally for economic purposes, and can move freely among the countries for both education and employment. Additionally, GCC citizens can purchase homes or companies, obtain health services, and work in any of the member countries. However, the GCC nations tend to extreme niggardliness in granting citizenship. Thus, the customs union does not enhance the legal rights of the millions of migrant workers in the GCC, who are as a practical matter indispensable to the Gulf economies.

In spring 2010, the GCC signed a free trade agreement (FTA) with Pakistan.[337] This FTA was catalyzed by political and military events in Pakistan, and occurred at the urging of the United States. The United States called on the GCC to help Pakistan economically, as it fought Taliban militants in the volatile northwest region of Waziristan. Pakistan engaged in numerous bloody battles in the fall of 2009 to evict the Taliban from the Swat and Buner areas. Pakistan needed assistance to offset drops in foreign direct investment (FDI), as investors became increasingly skittish about the long-term stability of the country, particularly in the poor areas vulnerable to militancy. From a business standpoint, the FTA was not too difficult to arrange. There are long-standing, close ties between Pakistan and the GCC, given the large number of expatriate Pakistani workers in the GCC. Moreover, the nature of the Pakistani and GCC economies is complimentary. Pakistan exports leather, rice, textiles, and sporting goods, and imports petroleum — the mirror image of the GCC.

The GCC also has an FTA with Singapore, signed in December 2008, which grants tariff-free access to 99 per cent of Singapore's domestic exports, while all GCC goods entering Singapore have tariff-free access. As of April 2009, the GCC was negotiating an FTA with Indonesia, and considering reviving FTA negotiations with the EC, which were suspended in December 2008. On 22 June 2009 the GCC signed an FTA with the Ministers of the *European Free Trade Association (EFTA)* — Switzerland, Norway, Iceland, and Liechtenstein — covering trade in goods, services, competition policy, and government procurement among other sectors. Finally, as recently as June 2010, China made securing an FTA with the GCC a top priority.

*Suggestions for Further Research:*

Article:

1. Azmat, Gani, *The Effect of Business Environment on Trade in Gulf Cooperation Council Countries*, 10 JOURNAL OF INTERNATIONAL TRADE LAW AND POLICY number, 3 200-212 (2011).

---

[337] *See* Toula Vlahou, *Pakistan, Gulf Cooperation Countries to Sign Free Trade Agreement this Spring*, 27 International Trade Reporter (BNA) 82 (21 January 2010).

## GDP

Gross Domestic Product.

GDP is a slightly narrower measure of income earned than Gross National Product (GNP). GDP is the total value of all finished output of goods and services produced in an economy. *Per capita* GDP is the final value of finished goods and services produced in the territory of a country in one year, divided by the number of persons (whether or not nationals) in that country.

It does not matter whether or where the output is consumed, invested, or used by a government. The value of the output is income to its producer. Therefore, GDP is defined equivalently as all income earned within the territory of a country, whether or not produced by nationals (*i.e.,* citizens) or non-nationals of that country. Like GNP, GDP may be measured at current price levels in a country, or at constant prices.

The letter "D" in GDP serves to emphasize the income measured is earned within the territorial jurisdiction of the country. That is, GDP measures economic activity within the domestic territory of a country. For example, income earned by a Filipino receptionist working at the Sheraton Hotel in Bahrain would be included in the GDP of Bahrain, but not in the GDP of the Philippines. That is true even if the receptionist repatriates all or some of the income. Likewise, income earned by Sheraton Hotel in Bahrain would be included in the GDP of Bahrain, not the United States, even though Sheraton is an American-based multinational corporation. That is because the facility in question is located in Bahrain. In brief, for GDP, the owner of the asset producing income is irrelevant. Rather, the location of the income-generating activities matters.

As with GDP, the letter "G" in GNP indicates the calculation is an aggregate one. No subtraction is made for consumption of capital. Also, as with GNP, the letter "P" in GDP suggests the value of output absorbed in the manufacturing process — namely, intermediate or semi-finished goods — is excluded.

## GEARY KHAMIS EQUATION SYSTEM

A method to estimate a synthetic world market price for a commodity.

The estimation is based on aggregation of data on (1) international prices and (2) various country purchase power parity (PPP). One hallmark of the system is it allows an economist to assign one price to a quantity of a commodity, regardless of where that commodity was grown.

The United Nations (U.N.) uses the Geary Khamis system in its economic analyses. In particular, the U.N. Food and Agricultural Organization (FAO) uses the system to compare agricultural commodity trade volumes by value, on a country-by-country basis.

## GENERAL EXCLUSION ORDER

Under Section 337 of the United States *Tariff Act of 1930*, as amended, a general exclusion order affects all shipments of merchandise under investigation infringing on a valid intellectual property right (IPR). In contrast, a specific, or limited, order focuses on merchandise only from persons violating Section 337.

*Suggestions for Further Research:*

Articles:

1.　de Blank, Bas & Bing Cheng, *Where is the ITC Going After Kyocera?*, 25 SANTA CLARA COMPUTER & HIGH TECHNOLOGY LAW JOURNAL 701-721 (2009).

2.　Lim, Lily & Sarah E. Craven, *Injunctions Enjoined; Remedies Restructured*, 25 SANTA CLARA COMPUTER & HIGH TECHNOLOGY LAW JOURNAL 787-819 (2009).

3.　Lyons, Michael J., Andrew J. Wu, & Harry F. Doscher, *Exclusion of Downstream Products After Kyocera: A Revised Framework for General Exclusion Orders*, 25 SANTA CLARA COMPUTER & HIGH TECHNOLOGY LAW JOURNAL 821-838 (2009).

## GENERIC (GENERICS)

A product, typically a drug, which is a copy of a patented product where the patent has expired, that has no trademark, or both.

If the copy is of a product on which the patent has expired, then the copy is generic from a patent point of view. If the copy is of a product on which there is no trademark, then it is generic from a trademark point of view. The distinction between the two viewpoints is not necessarily significant. A patented drug almost always is sold under a brand name that is trademarked. Conversely, copies of a patented drug typically are made by a distinct manufacturer (not the original patent holder). Often, they are sold under the name of the chemical ingredient (*e.g.*, "paracetamol," which is a key ingredient in many pain killers). If the generic copy is sold under a brand name that is trademarked, it still is generic from a patent point of view.

Whether a product is "generic" is a factually and legally different question from whether a product infringes on an intellectual property right (IPR). A generic copy is legal if made after expiration of a patent or trademark, or pursuant to a voluntary or compulsory license. Otherwise, the copy is considered counterfeit, or pirated, and, therefore, illegal.

*Suggestions for Further Research:*

Articles:

1.　Galantucci, Robert, Note, *Data Protection in a U.S. — Malaysia Free Trade Agreement: New Barriers to Market Access for Generic Drug Manufacturers*, 17 FORDHAM INTELLECTUAL PROPERTY, MEDIA & ENTERTAINMENT LAW JOURNAL 1083-1123 (2007).

2.　Young, Adam R., Note, *Generic Pharmaceutical Regulation in the United States with Comparison to Europe: Innovation and Competition*, 8 WASHINGTON UNIVERSITY GLOBAL LEGAL STUDIES REVIEW 165-185 (2009).

## GENEROSITY

Hardly a traditional international trade term, but indubitably a term — and concept — of increasing importance, especially during and after the Uruguay Round (1986-94) when evaluating existing or proposed trade rules. The underlying issue is how effective are preferential trade programs for developing and least developed countries?

A lawyer-like answer is "it depends," namely, on the program in question, the beneficiary country and products at issue, time period examined, and — most of all — on the criteria for effectiveness. For instance, in 1992 the Organization for Economic Cooperation and Development (OECD) published a study examining data on Generalized System of Preferences (GSP) programs from 1976-88. Two conclusions stood out.

First, exports from poor countries rose by one to two percent as a result of these programs. Obviously, that suggests GSP programs hardly give much of a boost. Second, a small number of large, relatively better-off developed countries capture the lion's share of benefits. In 1987, six countries accounted for two-thirds of all exports of GSP merchandise. Despite these conclusions, a generalization that such programs enhance macroeconomic performance (*e.g., per capita* Gross Domestic Product (GDP), employment, and the like), help diversify exports, or alleviate poverty — or, conversely, that they do not, is risky. That said, two broad arguments leveled against preferences for developing countries should be weighed.

One line of argument faults developing and least developed countries for focusing too heavily on obtaining preferential treatment. Such treatment is an asset the value of which is diminishing over time. The value of preferential trade treatment, in the form of a zero or low applied rate, depends on the rate that otherwise would be imposed on a product, *i.e.*, on the Most Favored Nation (MFN) rate. If GSP, *African Growth and Opportunity Act (AGOA)*, or *Caribbean Basin Initiative (CBI)* treatment means a product enters duty free, and the MFN rate on that product is 20 percent, then the margin of preference is 20 percent (*i.e.*, the difference between normal and preferential trade treatment). If the MFN rate is two percent, then the margin of preference is just two percent. However, these simple calculations are misleading. They exclude the cost of compliance with GSP eligibility criteria. Suppose the requirements demand significant time and investment by lawyers and business officials at the exporter and importer, which amount to about one percent of the value of the imported merchandise. Then, the margin of preference in the examples drops to 24 percent and one percent, respectively.

Notwithstanding compliance costs, margins of preference from GSP, *AGOA*, or *CBI*-style treatment erode as MFN rates among developed countries decline. Because of successive rounds of multilateral trade negotiations under GATT–WTO auspices, those rates indeed have declined, and done so dramatically. While tariff peaks in the Schedules of Concessions of developed countries remain on some products of export importance to developing and least developed countries, as a general observation tariffs on industrial products imposed by major countries like the United States and European Union (EU) average in the range of two to six percent. Duty-free treatment on industrial products is foreseeable, and already exists under the *Information Technology Agreement* (*ITA*), negotiated in the wake of the Uruguay Round. If and when that happens, preferences will be of even more dubious value.

Aside from diminishing margins of preferences, poor countries are faulted for subjecting themselves to conditionality. A developed country imposing requirements for GSP treatment, or preferences for Africa, can change the rules anytime, and even withdraw the preferential treatment itself. In contrast, tariff reductions negotiated and bound as part of an MTN, or through a free trade agreement (FTA) or customs union (CU), are permanent (albeit subject to modifications, for which compensation must be paid). Why not, then, focus on the real prize? In sum, then, the first line of argument against preferential trading programs criticizes poor countries for "begging" for "ever-smaller scraps from the table." It might be added that not only is the process demeaning, but also it pits some poor countries against others (particularly where two or more of them export a like product and seek duty-free treatment for it), thereby playing into a modern "divide-and-conquer" strategy, which some critics allege certain developed countries pursue. To be sure, a poignant rebuttal is "they divide, we conquer," indicating clearly that the Third World hardly is monolithic.

A second line of argument is addressed to developed countries, the sponsors of GSP-program. The eligibility criteria are so onerous that developing and least developed countries cannot take full advantage of duty-free or low-tariff treatment:

- *Conditions for Beneficiary Designation*:

  Some poor countries do not satisfy all of the requirements to be designated as a Beneficiary Developing Country (BDC) under the GSP program, a textile and apparel (T&A) Beneficiary Sub-Saharan African Country (SSAC) under *AGOA*, or qualify for the *CBI*. The self-interested nature of some criteria tends to serve the interests of the sponsoring country, and bespeaks a giving that is more self-referential than charitable.

- *Graduation of BDCs*:

  Graduation requirements in the GSP program ensure a country loses its status as a beneficiary once it reaches a certain income level. For example, in 1988, during the Uruguay Round and in connection with the *Omnibus Trade and Competitiveness Act*, the United States struck the East Asian Tigers — Hong Kong, Korea, Singapore, and Taiwan — from the list of GSP BDCs. The point of the GSP program is not to benefit other rich countries, and graduation potentially opens up opportunities for truly needy countries. Still, whether the income graduation criteria are appropriate, or whether they lead to premature ineligibility, may be debated.

- *Conditions for Product Eligibility*:

  Several products cannot receive preferential treatment. Indeed, some products are excluded by statute, and some of these items are ones in which several beneficiaries would have a keen export interest (*e.g.*, leather goods and textile and apparel).

- *Competitive Need Limits on Products*:

  Competitive need limitations ensure merchandise from a GSP BDC is stricken from the list of eligible products if imports of it pose a significant competitive threat to a domestic industry in the sponsoring country.

In sum, the extent to which rich countries may be faulted for a lack of generosity, as manifest in the intense conditionality on which they insist, is increasingly an issue in international trade.

## GENEVA PREPARATORY CONFERENCE

*See* GATT 1947.

## GEOGRAPHICAL INDICATION (GEOGRAPHIC INDICATION)

A place name, or words associated with a place, used to identify a product that has a particular reputation for quality, or other feature, and that is associated with the place.

A geographic indication tells the place of origin of a good that has characteristic qualities resulting from that origin. In other words, it is the place name, or the words associated with a place, used to identify a product.

The product so identified has a particular quality, reputation, or other characteristic based on its origin from the place. Quintessential product sectors in which geographical indications are used or sought are beer, cheese, ham, and wines and spirits. Famous examples would be "Beaujolais," "Bordeaux," "Burgundy," "Champagne," "Pilsen," "Roquefort," of "Tequila." Other well known examples include "Parma ham" and "Toscano olive oil." A synonymous term is "appellation of origin." The European Union (EU) is particularly interested in seeing tighter regulation on the use of place names, especially on wine. At least as to wine, Australia, Canada, New Zealand, and the United States support the *laissez-faire status quo* in which a winery can use a place name for its product even regardless of where it makes the wine.

One example of the disputes that can arise is a long-running battle about the use of the name "Budweiser" between the owners of Budejovicky Budvar, a Czech brewery in Budweis, in the Czech region of Budvar, and Anheuser-Busch of St. Louis, Missouri. Following a takeover in 2008, the latter company was renamed "Anheuser-Busch InBev." The acquirer was the Belgian brewing company, InBev.

In 1996, the EU Office for the Harmonization of the Internal Market (OHIM) — *i.e.*, the EU's Trademark Office — rejected an application from Anheuser-Busch to use the "Budweiser" and "Bud" names throughout the EU in connection with beer, malted alcoholic beverages, and non-alcoholic beverages. Budvar unsuccessfully opposed the application by arguing it (Budvar) already had registered the identical name for a trademark in Austria and Germany, and thus owned the commercial right to the name. Budvar also pointed out it was using the names in parts of the EU, such as France, Italy, and Portugal, and cited in its favor certain international agreements and bilateral treaties.

Disagreeing with Budvar, the OHIM awarded trademark rights to the name "Bud" to Anheuser-Busch and its new Belgian Parent, Inbev. The OHIM reasoned the trademark sought by Anheuser-Busch was identical to that of Budvar, and the products in question were identical, too. Subsequently, Budvar took the matter to court. In March 2009, the second highest court in the EU, the European Court of First Instance (CFI) — also called by its new name, the "General Court" — upheld the decision of OHIM. The CFI stated OHIM, which functions (*inter alia*) as the trademark agency for the EU, was right to accept the Anheuser-Busch application for EU-wide rights. The CFI said Budvar adduced insufficient evidence to support its position.

Budvar appealed the Court of Justice of the European Union, that is, the European Court of Justice (ECJ), which is the highest court in the EU. Anheuser-Busch argued the trademark held by Budvar expired, and that in the CFI proceedings, the CFI found Budvar did not actually produce evidence it had owned that trademark. The failure to adduce such evidence in the prior proceedings, urged Anheuser-Busch, was contrary to new EU rules implemented in 2005 that require an opponent of a trademark to produce evidence it holds the trademark. In July 2010, the ECJ rejected the Anheuser-Busch argument, and ruled in Budvar's favor.[338] The ECJ said the 2005 evidentiary requirements should not be applied retroactively. Thus, the ECJ held Anheuser-Busch could not register a trademark for the name "Budweiser" throughout the EU. This ruling gave Budvar the exclusive right to the name in some EU states. Further, in July 2010, the General Court held the OHIM was wrong to award trademark rights to the name "Bud" to Anheuser-Busch and its new Belgian parent, AB Inbev.[339] That is, the General Court overruled the OHIM trademark award to Anheuser-Busch, thereby preventing Anheuser-Busch from registering the mark.

The case took another twist in March 2011, when the ECJ issued another ruling (C-96/09) in which it struck down certain parts of the July 2010 CFI ruling. The ECJ found that the General Court committed three errors in that

---

[338] See Bengt Ljung, *Siding with Czech Brewery, ECJ Rules "Budweiser" Mark Not for Anheuser-Busch*, 27 International Trade Reporter (BNA) 1195 (5 August 2010).

[339] *See* Joe Kirwin, *Anheuser-Busch Wins Round in EU in Dispute Over "Bud" Trademark Rights*, 28 International Trade Reporter (BNA) 595 (7 April 2011).

ruling. The ECJ also said registration of a trademark throughout the EU (*e.g.*, of "Bud" and "Budweiser") may be prevented (*i.e.*, denied to Anheuser-Busch) only when the mark actually is used (*e.g.*, by Budvar) in a sufficiently significant manner, in the course of trade, in a substantial part of the territory of the EU in which it is protected. The ECJ said use in the course of trade must be assessed separately in each of the territories in which the mark is protected.

Under a provisional 2007 deal, Anheuser-Busch uses the name "Budweiser" in North America and the United Kingdom, but uses "Bud" in continental Europe so as to differentiate it clearly from the Czech "Budweiser" product.

The only multilateral accord in place on the use of geographic indications for wine is the 1957 *Lisbon Agreement*, which is administered by World Intellectual Property Organization (WIPO). The *Agreement* obligates countries simply to register with WIPO their use of place names for wine. Among WTO agreements, the *Agreement on Trade-Related Aspects of Intellectual Property Rights* (*TRIPs*) contains three provisions that provide protection to GIs.

First, *TRIPs* Article 22 offers basic GI protection for all products against unfair competition. Thus, Article 22:2(a) forbids communications about a product that mislead consumers as to its true origin, and Article 22(3) contains a similar position concerning trademarks. Article 22:2(b) requires every WTO Member to provide a legal means for redress against acts of unfair competition.

*TRIPs* Article 23 provides special (that is, enhanced or higher) protection for wine and spirits, which account for the majority of GIs in the world (as of May 2008). Article 23:1 forbids use of a geographic name in respect of a wine or spirit that is not the same as the place of production of that product. The obvious intent is to prevent consumer confusion or deception. Article 23:2 forbids a WTO Member from registering a trademark that is misleading as to the true origin of a wine or spirit product. Thus, subject to a few exceptions, GI protection must be afforded to wines and spirits, even if misuse of the GI would not cause the public to be misled.

Third, *TRIPs* Article 24 sets out exceptions to the rules of Articles 22 and 23. There is an exception that grandfathers trademarks established before the *TRIPs Agreement* entered into force (or, if later, before the true country of origin of the product established a system of GIs to protect its product). Another exception exists for common, customarily used, names.

As its name suggests, the essence of a GI is the link between a product and the location in which it is produced. In other words, the status of the product, in terms of its locus of production, is what matters. Hence, GIs reflect a so-called "status" approach to intellectual property (IP), as distinct from a focus on the inventor of a product. The emphasis on a nexus between a product and its characteristics, on the one hand, and the place in which it is produced, on the other hand, is called "*terroir*" (a French term), or the "*terroir* theory." The word "*terroir*" loosely translated as "terrain." The EU adheres to this theory, whereas the United States generally does not.

Wine connoisseurs appreciate *"terroir"* refers to the environment of a vine from which grapes are harvested and used to make wine. More generally, *terroir* is a collaborative effort among land, climate, and other environmental inputs in a particular place, plus labor of local expertise. There are two key results from this collaboration. First, the product bears a distinct, identifiable taste that conjures up signature qualities of that place. Second, that taste can be produced only in that location.

These two results, however, are disputed. First, inputs can be transported and combined from their original location to another one, far away from that original location. That is manifestly the case with grape varietals in the world wine industry. Second, the quality of a product in its original location is not as even and predictable as touted, and products in a new location may actually have a higher quality. Again, various wine varietals make the point.

Given the dearth of legal protection at the international level for GIs, and the strong sentiments about them and the *terroir* theory, it is not surprising that the EU — led by France and Italy — have championed stronger protections in the Doha Round.[340] The topic is referred to in Paragraphs 18 of the Doha Development Agenda (DDA), and reiterated in December 2005 in Paragraph 39 of the Hong Kong Ministerial Declaration. Specifically, three broad issues are at play in the Doha Round:

- International Registration:

    The purpose of the registry would be to facilitate protection for wines and spirits, not to increase the level of protection. It would need to be useful, in the sense of not be burdensome administratively or financially, and developing countries likely would require special treatment that is precise, effective, and operational. However, a number of key questions are unresolved.[341]

    Should a multilateral system for registering GIs for wines and spirits, which benefit from enhanced protection under Article 23 of the *TRIPs Agreement (i.e.*, protection beyond the standard level of protection in Article 22), be created? If so, then how and what kind of system? How would registration be effected and notified, and how would much would it cost? Would participation be mandatory or voluntary? What would be the legal effects of registration and participation in the system? When making a decision about registration of a geographical indication, what significance should a national authority give to international registration at the WTO? Note that discussions on a multilateral GI registry for wines and spirits pre-date the Doha Round by four years, having started in 1997 pursuant to *TRIPs* Article 23:4, and were folded into the DDA.

---

[340] *See* Guy Dinmore, *Italy-France Form "Trade Axis to Counter Emerging Nations,* FINANCIAL TIMES, 12 June 2008, at 2.

[341] *See* World Trade Organization, *Members Accept New Chair's Approach in Intellectual Property Talks,* 4 March 2010, posted at www.wto.org.

- Extension of Protection:

  Should enhanced protection for GIs, of the type offered in Article 23 of the *TRIPs Agreement* to wines and spirits, be extended beyond wines and spirits, to other products? If so, then how, and to which other products?

- Patents, Biodiversity, and Disclosure:

  Should GI protection exist for patents and biodiversity, and if so, what would the relationship be between the WTO *TRIPs Agreement* and the United Nations *Convention on Biological Diversity (CBD)*? Further, what disclosure requirements ought to exist for patents so as to avoid bio-piracy of genetic resources?

On 9 June 2008, the Chairman of the Doha Round Negotiations on GIs, Manzoor Ahmad, the Ambassador of Pakistan to the WTO, issued a report on the state-of-play of those talks on the first issue. Simultaneously, the Director-General of the WTO, Pascal Lamy, circulated a report on the second and third issue.[342]

In respect of the first issue, in December 2010, the new Chairman of the GI negotiations, Ambassador Darlington Mwape of Zambia, identified six elements that would be necessary for any registration system of a GI term: Notification; Registration, Legal Effects (Consequences of Registration); Fees and Costs; Special and Differential Treatment; and Participation.[343] Of the six elements, two posed the greatest challenges in terms of reaching a consensus among WTO Members: Legal Effects and Participation.

In January-February 2011, the Members produced a composite text of about one and one-half pages that encompassed these elements and the proposals on them. The text contained square brackets, indicating Members had reached no consensus on the options. Finally, after 13 years of discussions, in March 2011, WTO Members crafted a complete nine-page text. But, it contained 208 square brackets around portions of rival language, or 30 pairs of square brackets per side in the seven central pages of the text. Thus, the text bespoke a wide divergence on many key issues.[344] Each set of brackets was followed by an abbreviation for the country or countries championing the language inside that set. Moreover, the overall text was not compiled by all the Members, but rather a

---

[342] Both reports are available on the WTO website, www.wto.org. *See also* Daniel Pruzin, *Lamy Says Compromise Possible on Some, but Not All, TRIPs Issues*, 25 International Trade Reporter (BNA) 1135 (31 July 2008) (summarizing the state of play on the eve of the July 2008 collapse in Doha Round negotiations).

[343] *See* April 2011 Geographical Indications Document, Part I ¶ 11; World Trade Organization, *Geographic Indications Talks Gear Up for 2011 Endgame*, 10 December 2010, *posted at* www.wto.org.

[344] *See* World Trade Organization, Intellectual Property: Geographical Indications Negotiations — Formal Meeting, *Geographic Indications Draft Completed Swiftly But with 208 Differences*, 3 March 2011, *posted at* www.wto.org.

sub-set of them, that is, key representatives from certain Members that represented coalitions of Members.

In April 2011, as part of the issuance of reports and draft texts across all areas of the Doha Round negotiations, the WTO published the composite text, along with a report from the Chairman of the GI negotiations.[345] Hacked up by so many square brackets, the April 2011 Draft Composite Text was anything but a final deal.[346] Apparently, it was the same text the Members had worked out in March, and with the same 208 square brackets. The best that could be said, in the words of the Chairman Mwape, was:

> 18.  ... *The devil being in the details,* I do believe that working on treaty-language formulations regarding the structure, operation and implications of the Register has — for the first time — helped all delegations to have a clearer view of each other's positions, proposals and wordings.
>
> 19.  While I am aware that *there still is a long way to go,* I do believe that the Draft Composite Text . . . provides a good basis on which to continue negotiations towards a multilateral system of notification and registration for geographical indications for wines and spirits.[347]

---

[345] The WTO issued three documents on 21 April dealing with IP and GI matters. *See:*
(1)  World Trade Organization, Council for Trade-Related Aspects of Intellectual Property Rights, Special Session, *Multilateral System of Notification and Registration of Geographical Indications for Wines and Spirits — Report by the Chairman, Ambassador Darlington Mwape (Zambia) to the Trade Negotiations Committee,* TN/IP/21 (21 April 2011), *posted at* www.wto.org. Hereinafter, April 2011 Geographical Indications Document.
(2)  Council for Trade-Related Aspects of Intellectual Property Rights, Special Session, Attachment, *Multilateral System of Notification and Registration of Geographical Indications for Wines and Spirits — Draft Composite Text, Revision,* JOB/IP/&num;/Rev.1 (20 April 2011), *posted at* www.wto.org. Hereinafter, April 2011 Geographical Indications Draft Composite Text.
(3)  World Trade Organization, General Council, Trade Negotiations Committee, *Issues Related to the Extension of the Protection of Geographical Indications Provided for in Article 23 of the TRIPs Agreement to Products Other than Wines and Spirits and those Related to the Relationship between the TRIPs Agreement and the Convention on Biological Diversity — Report by the Director-General,* WT/GC/W/633, TN/C/W/61 (21 April 2011), posted at www.wto.org. Hereinafter, April 2011 TRIPs Article 23 — CBD Document.
*See also* World Trade Organization, *Intellectual Property: Geographical Indications Negotiations — Formal Meeting, Geographical Indications Draft Completed Swiftly But with 208 Differences* (3 March 2011), *posted at* www.wto.org (reporting on the status of the negotiations and production of the nine-page draft composite text).

[346] The adjective "composite" arises, as the Chairman explained in his April 2011 Report, because:

> The various textual proposals submitted before a certain deadline were collated into a "composite text" before meetings, and further supplemented, complemented or amended by textual comments during the drafting sessions.

April 2011 Geographical Indications Document, Part I ¶ 12.

[347] April 2011 Geographical Indications Document, Part I ¶18-19.

That is, with a synthesis of competing proposals in front of them, the WTO Members could see the many details on which they disagreed, and thereby appreciate how far apart they were on basic concepts that those details reflected.

The April 2011 Draft Composite Text dealt with each of the six elements Ambassador Mwape had identified four months earlier as crucial:

(1) Notification (which is related to "participation," discussed below) —

What procedure should be used to explain how a term would be notified, and which WTO Member would be responsible for providing notification?

The April 2011 Draft Composite Text suggested notification was up to each WTO Member. If a Member opted to give notice, then its notification would have to identify the pertinent GI, and do so in the relevant language.[348] The notification also (*inter alia*) would have to "identify the quality, reputation, or other characteristic which is essentially attributable to the geographical origin of the wine or spirit" in question, name the relevant "territory, region or locality," and refer to the relevant domestic laws under which the wine or spirit was geographically protected.[349]

(2) Registration —

Registration of a GI product would be valid for 10 years, and the registration could be renewed for further periods of a decade with no limit on the number of renewals.[350] But, the duration of registration begged a key question: what could be registered?

That is, what should be the scope of products eligible for registration, namely, all products, or only wines and spirits as under *TRIPs* Article 23?[351] There was strong disagreement on this point, and it implicated the fundamental purpose for which the Doha Round was launched, namely, fighting poverty and thereby Islamist extremism.

The Joint Proposal Group — Argentina, Australia, Canada, Chile, Costa Rica, Dominican Republic, Ecuador, El Salvador, Guatemala, Honduras, Japan, Korea, Mexico, New Zealand, Nicaragua, Paraguay, South Africa, Taiwan, and the United States — argued there was no mandate to extend a registry system beyond wines and spirits, nor to provide other products with the high level of protection given to wines and spirits (so-called "GI extension"). Other WTO Members believed that not to incorporate products other than wines and spirits would be

---

[348] *See* April 2011 Geographical Indications Draft Composite Text ¶ B.2(a), B.6.

[349] April 2011 Geographical Indications Draft Composite Text ¶ B.2(b), (d), (h)-(i).

[350] *See* April 2011 Geographical Indications Draft Composite Text ¶ D.4(a). Interestingly, a Member could notify the WTO Secretariat that its courts or administrative bodies have refused registration of a product, on grounds set forth in *TRIPs* Articles 22-24, and thus multilateral registration would be denied. *See id.* at ¶ D.4(f).

[351] *See* April 2011 Geographical Indications Document, Part I ¶ 13.

to solidify comparative advantages held by rich countries. In turn, poor, Muslim countries that do not specialize in such products would be disadvantaged. After all, under Islamic Law (*Sharī ʿa*), the consumption of alcohol is forbidden (*harām*), so how could they lawfully benefit from a multilateral registry for wine and spirit GIs?[352]

Certainly, as a policy matter, it was in keeping with the fundamental purpose of the Round to interpret the scope of the negotiating mandate broadly. But, the opponents of GI extension had the ear of the Chairman. Ambassador Mwape indicated that establishing a multilateral registry for products other than wines and spirits was a matter "to be resolved at a different and higher level."[353] Thus, the April 2011 Draft Composite Text limited the registry to wines and spirits within Chapter 22.04 and 22.08, respectively, of the Harmonized System.[354]

Clarification also was needed as to what happens after notification of a GI, that is, how a registration system would be run, what role the WTO would play in the system, how a GI product would be registered (*e.g.*, what would be recorded, or appear on the register), and how registrations would be updated to account for changes in notifications or GIs that no longer are used. The Composite Text suggested a rather top-down approach, with the WTO Secretariat managing the registry, being responsible for compiling, maintaining, and updating it, and spreading information to all Members about the registration of a particular wine or spirit.[355]

(3) Legal Effects —

What should the legal consequences of registration be, *i.e.*, what commitments or obligations are associated with registration of a term? Such effects included extra-territoriality, with the issue being whether registration of a geographical indication in the system by one member would create legal obligations in another Member. If so, then a follow-on matter is whether the burden of proof on whether a term is eligible for protection shifts to that other Member.

Indubitably, the April 2011 Draft Composite Text was messiest in the area of Legal Effects. Consider the opening paragraph on the topic:

> [**E.1** Each [participating][JP,IND,SG,BRA,CUB] WTO Member [commits to ensure][JP,BRA] [shall provide][EU] that [its procedures include the provision to][JP,BRA] [domestic authorities shall][EU] consult the [Database][JP] [Register and take its information into account][EU] when making decisions regarding registration and/ or protection of trademarks and geographical indications [for

[352] *See* RAJ BHALA, UNDERSTANDING ISLAMIC LAW (*Sharīʿa*) ch. 45 (2011).
[353] *See* April 2011 Geographical Indications Document, Part I ¶ 13.
[354] *See* April 2011 Geographical Indications Draft Composite Text ¶ X:1-2.
[355] *See* April 2011 Geographical Indications Draft Composite Text ¶ D.1-3.

wines and spirits][JP,SG,BRA] in accordance with its [laws and regulations][JP,BRA,COL] [and][COL] [domestic procedures][EU,COL].][JP,EU,COL]

[[In the framework of these domestic procedures and in the absence of proof to the contrary in the course of these procedures,][EU] [Registration of an indication on][HKC] the Register shall be considered as a *prima facie* evidence][HKC,EU]

[(a)  of interested parties who may enforce the protection of the geographical indication;][HKC]

[[(b)]  [HKC]that in the [notifying][IND] Member [that consults the Register][EU] the registered geographical indication satisfies the definition of "geographical indication" laid down in Article 22.1 of the *TRIPS Agreement*; [and][HKC]][HKC,EU]

[(c)  that the indication is protected in the country of origin (*i.e.*, Article 24.9 of the *TRIPS Agreement* does not apply)

in any domestic courts, tribunals or administrative bodies of the participating Members in any judicial, quasi-judicial or administrative proceedings related to the geographical indication. The issues will be deemed to have been proved unless evidence to the contrary is produced by the other party to the proceedings. In effect, a rebuttable presumption is created in relation to the above three issues.[92]][HKC]

[In the framework of these domestic procedures, domestic authorities shall consider assertions of genericness as laid down in Article 24.6 of the *TRIPS Agreement* only if these are substantiated.][EU356]

[92] For jurisdictions where there is a distinction between legal burden and evidential burden of proof, the proposed legal tool will shift the evidential burden of proof on issues (a)-(c) mentioned in this paragraph.

What did this all-but-impenetrable language amount to? (The superscripts, of course, referred to countries that championed the language contained in the brackets with those references.)

The answer is it embodied three different paradigms for GI registration. That is, embedded in the Text were three alternative multilateral registry proposals, none of which had been reconciled with any other.[357]

---

[356] April 2011 Geographical Indications Draft Composite Text ¶ E.1.

[357] *See* World Trade Organization, *Geographic Indications Draft Completed Swiftly But with 208 Differences*, 3 March 2011, *posted at* www.wto.org; World Trade Organization, *Geographic Indications Talks Gear Up for 2011 Endgame*, 10 December 2010, *posted at* www.wto.org.

First, there was a Joint Proposal sponsored by the Joint Proposal Group. This Proposal stated that the registry of GI terms would be a voluntary database. WTO Members could choose whether or not to participate in it. An intellectual property authority in a Member that participates in the registry would consult the database when deciding whether to give GI or trademark protection in its country.

Second, there was a proposal, dating from July 2008, from over 100 WTO Members — the W/52 Group — for a multilateral registry. It was derived from, but was a modified, stripped-down version of, an EU proposal. It was a negotiated compromise among those 100 Members that envisaged a system applying to all Members. A Member could choose whether or not it wanted to register its own GI terms in the system. But, at a minimum, all Members would have to take into account the fact that a particular term is registered in the multilateral registry system as *prima facie* evidence, in the absence of proof to the contrary, that (1) an interested party exists to enforce the GI, (2) the term satisfies the definition of a GI under the *TRIPs Agreement*, and (3) the GI is protected in its country of origin.

Thus, in contrast to the original EU proposal, registration would not create an irrefutable presumption that a registered term should be protected in every Member (save for any Member that challenges the term). But, this *prima facie* evidence would have to be accepted in an adjudicatory or administrative hearing about the GI in any WTO Member participating in the registry system. Here, then, was an extraterritorial effect: among consenting Members, registration created a rebuttable presumption on these three matters.

As regards this modified EU proposal, WTO Members were not in agreement about certain other follow-on legal effects of the existence of *prima facie* evidence. In particularly, they could not decide whether:

- Additional legal procedures and effects for that term (*e.g.*, concerning eligibility as a "GI," challenges, and exceptions) would depend on the domestic law of the Member in question? In other words, how significant would the extraterritorial effect of the existence of *prima facie* evidence be? Would it create obligations in the legal systems of other countries beyond the three aforementioned matters?

- The burden of proof would shift from the owner of the geographically-indicated product as to whether a term qualifies as a "geographical indication?"

- Large costs would result, imposed on the legal systems of other countries?

On these issues, WTO Members supporting the Joint Proposal answered in the affirmative. In contrast, the EU and Switzerland said the new registry system they proposed would not have any further extraterritorial effects, because a Member still could use its own legal rules and procedures to determine whether to protect a term.[358]

The third proposal embedded in the Composite Text came from Hong Kong. Hong Kong proposed that if a term is registered, that fact would be *prima facie* evidence that could be rebutted about who owns the term, and that it is protected in the country of origin. But, this presumption would operate only among Members that opted to participate in the registration system.

(4)  Fees and Costs —

What fees and costs are associated with registering a term, and what parties ought to bear them? Some Members thought costs should be covered by the budget of the WTO. Hence, all Members would contribute to funding the registry. Other members called for user fees, *i.e.*, Members would be charged only if they registered a geographical indication term.

The April 2011 Draft Composite Text suggested that any multilateral registry system would recover fully its operating costs under a user pays principle.[359] That principle could discriminate against developing and least developed countries, not all of which might be able to afford to pay for registering their GI products. But, there was no consensus as to whether either or both categories of poor countries ought to receive special and differential treatment in respect of fees and costs in the form of exemptions.[360]

(5)  Special and Differential Treatment —

What preferential rules, if any, should be establishment for poor countries?

Some developing countries in the so-called "W/52 Group" (which includes not only Brazil, China, and India, but also the EU and Switzerland) sought a transition period for themselves of 10 years. That is, developing countries would have 10 years after a registry comes into being before they have to consult the terms of the register.[361] They sought 20 years for least developed countries.[362]

The Joint Proposal Group disagreed. This Group championed a voluntary registry system. Therefore, delays as to when a developing our least developed country would have to consult the registry would be

---

[358] *See* April 2011 Geographical Indications Draft Composite Text ¶ E.2(a)-(c).
[359] April 2011 Geographical Indications Draft Composite Text ¶¶ B.2(j) and fn. 2, F.1.
[360] *See* April 2011 Geographical Indications Draft Composite Text ¶ G.3.
[361] *See* April 2011 Geographical Indications Draft Composite Text ¶ G.1.
[362] *See* April 2011 Geographical Indications Draft Composite Text ¶ G.2.

measured in terms of an unspecified number of years from the date such a country voluntarily agreed to participate in the registry.

Also in dispute was the nature and range of technical assistance that should be provided to poor countries. Ought it to consist of translating a GI notice from the vernacul ar language of a developing or least developed country into one of the three WTO languages (English, French, and Spanish)?[363] Should it also include financial assistance, with a view to building institutional and legal capacity to participate in the GI protection system?[364]

(6)  Participation —

Should participation in the registry be voluntary or mandatory? The April 2011 Draft Composite Text contained bracketed language stating participation would be voluntary.[365] Or, as a third alternative, should a Member be able to choose whether to register a geographically indicated term, but always be obligated to consult the registry? The Text contained bracketed language with this option, too.

Questions of participation linked closely to that of extraterritoriality (discussed earlier). Should registration of a term have implications for some or all WTO Members? The April 2011 Draft Composite Text suggested not, *i.e.*, the legal effects of registration would operate only on Members participating in the registry.[366] But if that were the case, then what good would the registry be?

On the one hand, it would bolster protection among Members already inclined to protect each other's GIs. On the other hand, it would do nothing for GI protection among non-participating Members, which is precisely where a party interested in a particular GI would want security from counterfeit wines and spirits. Put differently, the multilateral registry really was a plurilateral one, and reached no further than the countries opting to be in the plurality. Two provisions, at the end of the Draft Composite Text, compounded this problem. One provision called for review of the scope of participation after four years from establishment of a registry.[367] The second provision permitted any Member to terminate participation in the system anytime.[368] Both provisions intimated how tentative — that is, how little certainty and predictability — the registry would afford.

---

[363] *See* April 2011 Geographical Indications Draft Composite Text ¶ G.4.

[364] *See* April 2011 Geographical Indications Draft Composite Text ¶ G.5-6

[365] *See* April 2011 Geographical Indications Draft Consolidated Text ¶ A.1.

[366] *See* April 2011 Geographical Indications Draft Consolidated Text ¶ A.1(b).

[367] *See* April 2011 Geographical Indications Draft Consolidated Text ¶ H.1.

[368] *See* April 2011 Geographical Indications Draft Consolidated Text ¶ I.1.

In sum, the Composite Text indeed was "made up of various parts."[369] But, unlike a true "composite" material, they had not been "blended" together well, so the Text hardly was a good "synthetic building material," much less one that had concerns of poor, Islamic countries at its core.[370]

On the second issue, GI extension, the June 2008 report of the Director-General made clear some Members oppose completely any extension of GI products beyond wines and spirits, while others essentially insist on it. As indicated earlier, that schism remained right through to the spring 2011, when the April 2011 appeared.

Specifically, the EU and Old World countries strongly favored expanding coverage of GIs beyond wines and spirits, in effect, to all products. China and Kenya insist that a multilateral register must not discriminate in favor of wines and spirits. Conversely, as intimated earlier, the United States, along with certain New World countries such as Argentina, Australia, Canada, and New Zealand, were reluctant to bring the question of extended GI protection into the WTO, or within the scope of the Doha Round. They believed the existing trademark protection regimes are adequate to accommodate protections beyond wines and spirits, and they are chary of imposing large GI protection costs on their food industries.

Amidst this disagreement, the relationship of GI extension to the needs and interests of developing and least developed Muslim countries was lost. In his April 2011 TRIPs Article 23 — CBD Document, the WTO Director-General, Pascal Lamy paid scant attention to this relationship:

> On extension of GI protection, the first issue mentioned in my mandate, the structured discussions covered:
>
> - Factors for and against expanding the protection of Article 23 of the *TRIPS Agreement* to goods other than wines and spirits, including the comparative merits of the "misleading-the-consumer" and unfair competition tests under Article 22, and the Article 23 "correctness" test.
>
> - How the costs and burdens of GI protection and its enforcement should be managed, so as to balance legal certainty and predictability (which proponents claim for Article 23 protection), and case-by-case application of the consumer deception and unfair competition rule under Article 22.
>
> - The rationale for the current higher level protection for wines and spirits — contrasting a claim for a non-discriminatory, level playing field for all products and sectors, against the view that the current arrangement represents a balanced package in the Uruguay Round and that wine and spirits were subject to specific forms of labelling regulation in some national systems.

---

[369] THE OXFORD AMERICAN DICTIONARY AND THESAURUS 286 (2003) (entry for "composite").
[370] THE OXFORD AMERICAN DICTIONARY AND THESAURUS 286 (2003) (entry for "composite").

-   Broader trade issues, such as the impact of higher protection on continuing market access for food exports to third country markets and the relevance of GI protection to agricultural trade.

-   The *development dimension of GI protection, some arguing that higher protection for wine and spirit GIs principally benefited industrialized countries, not those developing countries whose GI interests concerned textiles, handicrafts, agricultural products or foodstuffs; others argued that higher GI protection may impede certain valuable exports of developing countries.*[371]

Of the five points, only the fifth one raised the linkage between GI protection and development. But, it did not specifically mention poverty alleviation, or the follow-on implications for the appeal of Islamist extremism. Moreover, the Director-General's summary of the discussions was remarkable for its silence: the Members had not agreed to anything relating to the "development dimension of GI protection."[372]

Rather, their talks produced five "clusters" of themes:

12. Cluster 1, on differences between protection under [*TRIPs*] Articles 22 and 23: whether and how a GI could be prevented from becoming generic in third markets without Article 23 protection; *the scope of the proposal to extend GI protection, in terms of products covered, their link with their geographical origin, and the role of a GI identifying a product*; whether Article 22 protection is costly and burdensome because of the need for evidence to prove that use of a GI is misleading or confusing to the consumer; and whether Article 22 or 23 protection was preferable for policy reasons. [Article 22 requires Members to provide the legal means for GI protection for all products, using accepted trademark laws, to prevent misleading the public as to the geographic origin of a good, if that origin is the essential attribute conveying quality, reputation, or other characteristics to the product. Article 23 mandates additional GI protection for wines and spirits, without these strictures.]

13. Cluster 2, on the effects of extending higher protection to additional products: *effects of higher protection being extended to GIs for different products, including in third country markets; whether increased market access had resulted from higher protection*; and the impact of higher protection on market access for products with generic descriptions.

14. Cluster 3, on Members' experiences with GI protection under the existing standards: *implications of Article 23 protection in third country markets for trade in wines and spirits*; the nature of problems

---

[371] April 2011 *TRIPs* Article 23 — CBD Document, Part A.1 ¶ 9 (emphasis added).
[372] April 2011 *TRIPs* Article 23 — CBD Document, Part A.1 ¶ 9. *See id.*, Part A.1 ¶¶ 10-11, Part A.2 ¶ 17.

claimed to arise from current levels of protection; and *whether a useful analogy could be drawn between wines and spirits and other products.*

15.  Cluster 4, on the contrasts between GI protection and other forms of IP: whether and if so how GIs differed from other forms of IP, *whether any possible trade benefits from GI extension could be equally available through alternative branding and marketing strategies*, and the relative costs involved; and the complementary character of marketing and GI protection; implications of extension of the scope of GI protection for continuing market access for products legitimately presented with generic terms or other *TRIPS* exceptions to GI protection.

15.  Cluster 5, on how exceptions under Article 24 would apply under an extension system: for instance, whether the existing sector-specific exception for the names of grape varieties could be adapted and applied for other products, such as cheese and other processed foods.[373]

On none of these clusters of themes, most notably whether to extend GI protection and if so, what heightened protection would result, was there consensus:

*Delegations continued to voice the divergent views that have characterized this debate, with no convergence evident on the specific question of extension of Article 23 coverage: some Members continued to argue for extension of Article 23 protection to all products; others maintained that this was undesirable and created unreasonable burdens.* It was clarified that trademark systems were legitimate forms of protecting GIs, in line with the general principle that Members are entitled to choose their own means of implementing their *TRIPS* obligations. *Extension proponents sought guarantees that the trademark system could and would protect their GIs at the higher level for all goods.* Discussions clarified that GI extension did not mean that existing exceptions under the *TRIPS Agreement*, such as for generic terms and prior trademark rights, would cease to apply. . . .[374]

Worse yet for poor countries, there seemed to be a sub-text in some of these themes, namely, opposition among at least some Members to helping poor countries.

For example, on Cluster 1, Members obviously could not agree on what additional products, if any, to give GI protection under Article 23 like that of wines and spirits. On Cluster 2, Members fretted that extending GI protection would damage market access to non-alcoholic products, when in fact it such protection bolsters the reputational advantage, and desirability, of wines and spirits. On Cluster 3, Members patronizingly suggesting that GI protection might not

---

[373] April 2011 *TRIPs* Article 23 — CBD Document, Part A.1 ¶¶ 12-16 (emphasis added).

[374] April 2011 *TRIPs* Article 23 — CBD Document, Part A.1 ¶ 17 (emphasis added).

help products other than wines and spirits. On Cluster 4, Members callously suggested countries exporting non-alcoholic goods forget about GI protection and focus on branding those goods.

And yet, the needs and interests of poor countries in respect of GI protection should be obvious. Muslim countries are the origin of many world-renowned non-alcoholic products. Bangladesh produces fine silk in Rajshahi. Jordan has personal beautification from the Dead Sea area. Pakistan, along with northern India and Nepal, produces pashmina goat wool, and in the Pakistani and Indian Kashmir, elegant pashmina shawls are created from this wool.[375] Saudi Arabia is home to several species of the world's finest dates. Iran (though not yet a WTO Member) boasts the best pistachios, and carpet designs named after some of its cities — Qom, for example — are stunningly gorgeous. None of these products — Rajshahi silk, Dead Sea soap, Pashmina shawls, Saudi dates, Iranian pistachios, or Qom carpets — benefits from GI protection. Providing it through a WTO-sponsored GI registry might well boost jobs and incomes in these countries, simply by giving the relevant products the legal protection from counterfeiting and the market cache to command elevated prices.

On the third topic, patents, biodiversity, and disclosure, the Director-General reported in December 2008 there were four major different positions among WTO Members. The differences, however, are partly over the appropriate forum and vehicle to use to achieve substantive outcomes. The April 2011 *TRIPs* Article 23 — CBD Document evinced no bridging of these differences. During their talks between December 2008 and April 2011, Members broadly agreed on obvious general principles like the importance of prior informed consent and equitable sharing of benefits — both of which are enshrined in the *CBD*. They also accepted the need for avoiding erroneous patents through, for example, a database system for traditional knowledge and genetic resources, the use of contracts, and disclosure requirements.[376] But, much of their discussions seemed non-substantive.[377]

Their substantive discussions covered the legal character of misappropriation, measures to address misappropriation and benefit-sharing, national-based approaches, and costs and benefits of mandatory disclosure requirements.[378] Yet, on these topics, they reached no consensus. Nothing in the Director-General's December 2008 Report nor in the April 2011 *TRIPs* Article 23 — CBD Document indicated Members were concerned primarily with identifying and addressing the needs and interests of poor Muslim countries in respect of traditional knowledge, genetic material, and an equitable sharing with them of benefits derived from these kinds of IP.

---

[375] *See* http://en.wikipedia.org/wiki/Pashmina.
[376] See April 2011 *TRIPs* Article 23 — CBD Document, Part B.1 ¶¶ 18-21, Part B.2 ¶ 27.
[377] *See* April 2011 *TRIPs* Article 23 — CBD Document, Part B.1 ¶¶ 18-21.
[378] *See* April 2011 *TRIPs* Article 23 — CBD Document, Part B.1 ¶¶ 22-26, Part B.2 ¶ 27.

Thus, WTO Members remained entrenched in one of four positions.[379] The first one was championed by a group led by Brazil and India. This group included Bolivia, Colombia, Cuba, Dominican Republic, Ecuador, Peru, and Thailand, and was supported by several African and other developing countries. This group was concerned about bio-piracy of genetic resources. Thus, it sought to amend the *TRIPs Agreement* to require a patent applicant disclose the country of origin of generic resources and associated traditional knowledge used in the invention in question. Further, the applicant would have to prove it received "prior informed consent" (a term and concept from the *CBD*), plus show it will provide for "fair and equitable sharing" of benefits. No patent application would be processed unless it satisfied these requirements.

Switzerland articulated the second position. Here, there would be changes to the regulations of the *Patent Cooperation Treaty* (*PCT*) of the World Intellectual Property Organization (WIPO). The changes would be implemented in domestic law, and essentially require an inventor, upon applying for a patent, to disclose the source of genetic resources and traditional knowledge. Failing to make that disclosure would trigger a delay in the patent, or even invalidation of a patent already granted (if fraud were involved).

The EU advocated the third position. It said all patent application should disclose the source or origin of genetic material. There should be legal consequences for failure to make this disclosure. The penalties would go beyond the usual patent law remedies.

Finally, the United States firmly opposed any mandatory disclosure concerning genetic resources in a patent application. It argued for national legislation and contractual commitments to ensure the goals of the *CBD* — access to genetic resources and sharing of benefits — are achieved. (As of August 2008, the United States had not ratified the *CBD*.) The commitments could include certain disclosure obligations, including one to announce the commercial application of genetic resources or traditional knowledge.

*Suggestions for Further Research:*

Book:

1. ECHOLS, MARSHA A., GEOGRAPHICAL INDICATIONS FOR FOOD PRODUCTS: INTERNATIONAL LEGAL AND REGULATORY PERSPECTIVES (2008).

Articles:

1. Bashaw, Bradley M., Comment, *Geographical Indications in China: Why Protect GIs with Both Trademark Law and AOC-Type Legislation?*, 17 PACIFIC RIM LAW & POLICY JOURNAL 73-102 (2008).

---

[379] *See* World Trade Organization, *TRIPS: Issues — Article 27:3(b), Traditional Knowledge, Biodiversity, posted at* www.wto.org (listing and summarizing proposals and countries associated with them).

2. Blakeney, Michael, *Book Review*, 15 INTERNATIONAL TRADE LAW & REGULATION issue 2, 78 (2009) (reviewing Marsha A. Echols, *Geographical Indications for Food Products: International Legal and Regulatory Perspectives* (2008)).

3. Chen, Jim, *A Sober Second Look at Appellations of Origin: How the Untied States will Crash France's Wine and Cheese Party*, 5 MINNESOTA JOURNAL OF GLOBAL TRADE 29 (1996).

4. Evans, G.E., *The Comparative Advantages of Geographical Indications and Community Trade Marks for the Marketing of Agricultural Products in the European Union*, 41 IIC: INTERNATIONAL REVIEW OF INTELLECTUAL PROPERTY & COMPETITION LAW 645-674 (2010).

5. Gervais, Daniel J., *Reinventing Lisbon: The Case for a Protocol to the Lisbon Agreement (Geographical Indications)*, 11 CHICAGO JOURNAL OF INTERNATIONAL LAW 67-126 (2010).

6. Hansen, David R., *Protection of Traditional Knowledge: Trade Barriers and the Public Domain*, 58 JOURNAL OF THE COPYRIGHT SOCIETY U.S.A. 757-794 (2011).

7. Hughes, Justin, *Champagne, Feta, and Bourbon: The Spirited Debate About Geographical Indications*, 58 HASTINGS LAW JOURNAL 299 (2006).

8. Jiang, Gee, *Dual Protection of Geographical Indications in China — An Enhanced Protection Standard or a Labyrinth for Right Holders?*, 432 IIC: INTERNATIONAL REVIEW OF INTELLECTUAL PROPERTY & COMPETITION LAW 926-952 (2011).

9. Munzer, Stephen R. & Kal Raustiala, *The Global Struggle Over Geographical Indications*, 18 EUROPEAN JOURNAL OF INTERNATIONAL LAW 337 (2007).

10. Nation, Emily, Comment, *Geographical Indications: The International Debate Over Intellectual Property Rights for Local Producers*, 82 UNIVERSITY OF COLORADO LAW REVIEW 959-1008 (2011).

11. Nieuwveld, Lisa Bench, *Is This Really About What We Call Our Food or Something Else? The WTO Food Name Case over the Protection of Geographical Indications*, 41 THE INTERNATIONAL LAWYER 891-922 (fall 2007).

12. Raustiala, Kal & Stephen R. Munzer, *The Global Struggle Over Geographic Indications*, 18 EUROPEAN JOURNAL OF INTERNATIONAL LAW 337-365 (2007).

13. Reeves, Andrew M., Note, *Protecting our Barefoots: Policy Problems in the International Wine Market*, 27 ARIZONA JOURNAL OF INTERNATIONAL & COMPARATIVE LAW 835-871 (2010).

14. Russell, Alexandra Basak, Note, *Using Geographical Indications to Protect Artisanal Works in Developing Countries: Lessons From A Banana Republic's Misnomered Hat*, 19 TRANSNATIONAL LAW & CONTEMPORARY PROBLEMS 705-728 (2010).

15. Shayesteh, Shokat, *Protection of Geographical Indications in Iran and its Comparison with the TRIPS Agreement*, 39 IIC — INTERNATIONAL REVIEW OF INTELLECTUAL PROPERTY AND COMPETITION LAW 963-973 (2008).

16. Shimura, Kaiko, Note, *How to Cut the Cheese: Homonymous Names of Registered Geographic Indicators of Foodstuffs in Regulation 510/2006*, 33 Boston College International & Comparative Law Review Review 129-151 (2010).

17. Staten, Tunisia L., *Geographical Indications Protection Under the TRIPs Agreement: Uniformity Not Extension*, 87 Journal of Patent & Trademark Office Society 221 (2005).

18. Waggoner, Justin M., *Acquiring A European Taste for Geographical Indications*, 33 Brooklyn Journal of International Law 569-595 (2008).

19. Wells, Jennifer, Student Article, *In Vino Veritas: Grapes, Greed, and Lawsuits in the Napa Valley*, 16 Hastings West — Northwest Journal of Environmental Law & Policy 515-540 (2010).

## GHG

Greenhouse gas.

*Suggestions for Further Research:*

Article:

1. Hawkins, Slayde, Note, *Skirting Protectionism: A GHG-Based Trade Restriction under the WTO*, 20 Georgetown International Environmental Law Review 427-450 (2008).

## GINI COEFFICIENT

The third of three major methods of measuring poverty, along with Absolute Poverty (*i.e.*, a Poverty Line) and a Top/Bottom Ratio, the Gini coefficient is named after the early 20th century Italian statistician, Corrado Gini.

A Gini coefficient (also called a "Gini Concentration Ratio") is the most sophisticated tool for measuring income-based poverty. The coefficient

> ranges between 0 (signifying "perfect" or maximum equality), and 1 (signifying maximum inequality).
>
> The coefficient indicates the gap between two percentages: the percentage of the population, and the percentage of income received by each percentage of the population. If, say, 1% of the population receives one percent of total income, and all subsequent percentages of the population receive the corresponding percentages of total income, the Gini coefficient is 0 — there is no gap between the income and the population percentages. If, at the other extreme, all of the economy's income were acquired by a single recipient, the gap would be maximized, and the coefficient would be 1.[380]

---

[380] Arthur C. Brooks & Charles Wolf, Jr., *All Inequality is Not Equal*, 171 Far Eastern Economic Review 23-24 (June 2008).

The amount (and changes) in a Gini coefficient can have major social and political, as well as economic, consequences for a society.

> If the coefficient approximates 0, income received by each individual (or family, or household) would be exactly the same — each percentage of the population would receive the corresponding percentage of income; the system's survival would be jeopardized by an absence of pecuniary incentives for entrepreneurship, innovation and productivity. If . . . the coefficient approximates 1, all of the economy's income would be acquired by a single recipient. The system's survival would depend precariously on the altruism of that single recipient, with the risk of revolution if altruism is insufficient![381]

(The multifarious implications of a Gini coefficient are considered below.)

Mathematically, a Gini coefficient is derived from a Lorenz Curve. A Lorenz Curve, shown in the Graph below, is plotted in a square box where the left-hand vertical side measures the cumulative percentage of income in a country, and the lower-horizontal side gauges the cumulative percentage of recipients of income (*i.e.*, population percentiles). In the lower left-hand corner of the square, the zero point, there is no income and there are no recipients of income. At the upper right-hand corner of the square, 100 percent of the income, and 100 percent of the people, in a country are accounted for.

**GRAPH:**

**THE LORENZ CURVE**

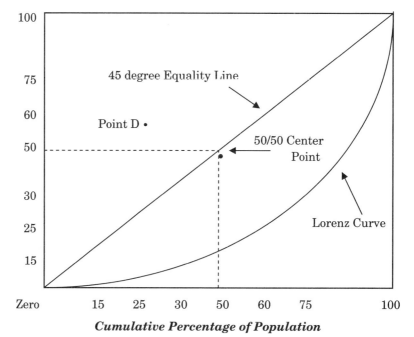

*Cumulative Percentage of Population*

[381] Arthur C. Brooks & Charles Wolf, Jr., *All Inequality is Not Equal*, 171 FAR EASTERN ECONOMIC REVIEW 23-24 (June 2008).

The 45-degree "Equality Line" connecting the lower-left hand and upper-right hand corner shows perfect equality.

On the Equality Line, at each cumulative percentage of income, the same percentage of the population receives that income. For example, in the center of the square, on the 45-degree line, 50 percent of the income generated in the country is received by 50 percent of the people. Below that "50/50 Center Point," 25 percent of the income is received by 25 percent of the people. Above that Center Point, 75 percent of the people get 75 percent of the income. Not surprisingly, therefore, the 45-degree line is the benchmark against which to measure inequality of income distribution. In brief, plotting data on a country, the larger a curve is away (to the right) from this line, the greater the income inequality in that country. (What about points above, *i.e.*, to the left, of the 45-degree line? They are not observed in reality. For instance, Point D would mean the bottom 25 percent of the population gets 50 percent of the income, suggesting an extreme redistribution that renders them no longer at the bottom.)

An example, with hypothetical data from Bangladesh (where income is stratified) and Sweden (where it is not) is shown below. The curve $LC_B$ is the Lorenz Curve for Bangladesh, and $LC_S$ is the Lorenz Curve for Sweden.

**GRAPH:**

**HYPOTHETICAL LORENZ CURVES FOR SWEDEN AND BANGLADESH**

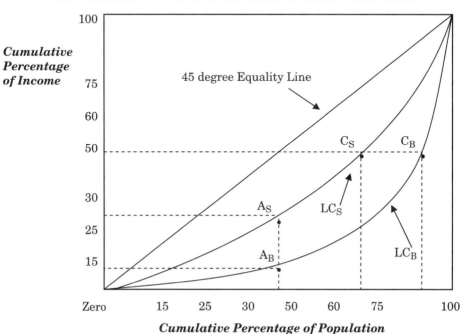

Using this example, $LC_B$ represents greater income inequality than $LC_S$, because $LC_B$ deviates further from the 45-degree equality benchmark than $LC_S$.

To read these curves, consider and contrast specific points on them, such as $A_B$ and $A_S$. At $A_B$, 50 percent of the population in Bangladesh receives less than 15 percent of the income. But, at $A_S$, 50 percent of the Swedish population receives over 25 percent of the income. Or, contrast points $C_B$ and $C_S$. At point $C_B$, 50 percent of the income in Bangladesh goes to well over 75 percent of the population, implying the other 50 percent of income is shared by far less than 25 percent of the population. At point $C_S$, however, 50 percent of the income in Sweden goes to about 70 percent of the population, indicating the remaining 50 percent of income accrues to about 30 percent of the people. Neither society is perfectly egalitarian, but poverty — in terms of the unequal distribution of income — is worse in Bangladesh than Sweden.

Gini coefficients are derived from a Lorenz Curve. Essentially, they are the area between the Lorenz Curve for a country and the 45-degree equality line, divided by the total area underneath (to the right and bottom of) that line.

Arithmetically, the formula is:

$$\text{Gini Coefficient} = \frac{\text{Extend of Deviation from Perfect Equality (Area between Lorenz Curve and 45-degree line)}}{\text{Total Income (Area underneath 45 degree line)}}$$

$$= \frac{A}{A + B}$$

where the areas "A" and "B" are shown in the Graph of the Lorenz Curve below.

**GRAPH:**

**CALCULATION OF GINI COEFFICIENT FROM THE LORENZ CURVE**

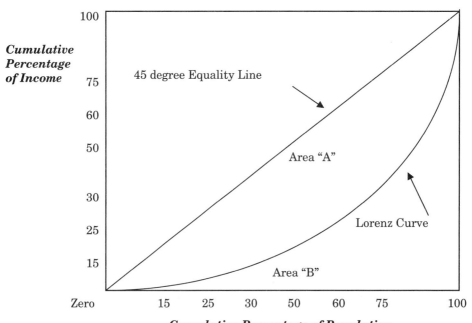

*Cumulative Percentage of Population*

A Gini coefficient of zero represents perfect equality. Every person (or family) earns the same amount of income. There is no gap between the Lorenz Curve and the 45-degree line, hence the numerator in the ratio is zero. A Gini coefficient of one bespeaks complete inequality — in effect, all income is controlled by one person (or family). Thus, the lower the Gini coefficient, which is associated with a less "bloated" Lorenz Curve, the more equal the distribution of income in a country.

Depending on the country, Gini coefficients range from roughly 0.25 (in Japan and Scandinavia) to 0.60 (in some Latin American and Sub-Saharan African countries). Generally speaking, higher income countries have lower Gini coefficients — an observation consistent with the Kuznets Curve. But, among middle- and low-income countries, it is hard to render a general statement, as some have more, and some less, income inequality. Also as a general matter, there is a high degree of correlation between the Gini coefficient for a country and the Top/Bottom ratio for that country.

When studying Lorenz Curves and Gini coefficients, four caveats should be observed. First, equality and equity are not synonymous, at least not to economists. Equality suggests every person earns the same income, but equity is a normative concept that distinguishes right from wrong using some philosophical or theological paradigm. Income equality may be — indeed, is — regarded in some paradigms as inequitable.

Second, Gini coefficients of zero or one are extreme referential standards. Neither perfect equality (zero) nor inequality (one) is observed in reality. However, seemingly modest changes — from, say, 0.42 to 0.36 — can indicate fairly important changes in a country in terms of increased income equality. Conversely, a modest redistribution of income, say one percent, from the top to the bottom 20 percent of the population might not change the Gini Coefficient by a large amount. However, the redistribution could mean a lot to poor people, in terms of the marginal difference it makes to their income. In other words, it is important not to focus on the extremes and thereby become insensitive to actual changes in distribution.

Third, the Lorenz Curves from which Gini coefficients are derived can intersect, *i.e.*, cross over one another. In turn, the different income distributions evinced by the Curves can generate the same Gini Coefficient. A hypothetical example is shown in the Graph below, involving India and Canada. $LC^{India}$, for India, exhibits a steep slope at the top (upper right hand), but a gentle slope at the bottom (lower left hand). The steep portion indicates more extreme income inequality at the higher income range, but more equality at the lower income end. Put bluntly, poor people in India are poor, with few gradations among them. But, among the rich in India, there is considerable stratification. $LC^{Canada}$, for Canada, shows the opposite pattern. There is considerable inequality at the lower range, but at the upper end, there is less inequality among rich people. Thus, the caveat is two different Lorenz Curves can generate the same value for a Gini coefficient when each has different degrees of inequality along the Curve.

GRAPH:

DIFFERENT HYPOTHETICAL LORENZ CURVES GENERATING SAME GINI COEFFICIENT

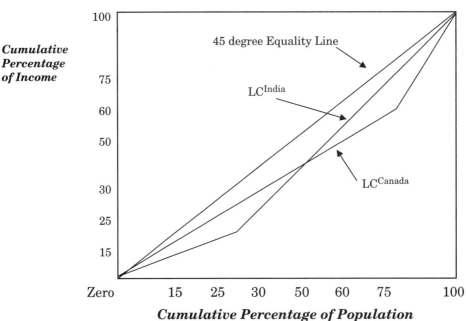

**Cumulative Percentage of Population**

Fourth, an increase in the value of the Gini coefficient indicates worsening income inequality, but making a judgment as to whether that movement is "good" or "bad" requires some caution.

> . . . [The] judgment [as to whether a shift in a Gini Coefficient closer to, or further from, equality is "good" or "bad"] depends on whether the strengthened incentives toward higher productivity that might be associated with a movement toward higher inequality are offset by the aggravation of social tensions that might be associated with the same movement.
>
> In turn, such a judgment is likely to depend critically on how and why the change in inequality has occurred, rather than on the magnitude of the change. For example, whether the coefficient's change is (or is perceived to be) due to favoritism, nepotism, and corruption, or instead to innovation, productivity and entrepreneurship; whether the change is viewed as earned, fair and legitimate, or instead as connived, unfair and illegitimate.[382]

To be sure, the general presumption is that an upward movement in the value of a Gini coefficient is likely to have adverse economic, social, and political ramifications. But, more than just the math must be checked. The degree of the change, and especially the reasons for it, must be examined.

---

[382] Arthur C. Brooks & Charles Wolf, Jr., *All Inequality is Not Equal*, 171 FAR EASTERN ECONOMIC REVIEW 23-24 (June 2008).

*Suggestions for Further Research:*

Books:

1. COLLIER, PAUL, THE BOTTOM BILLION — WHY THE POOREST COUNTRIES ARE FAILING AND WHAT CAN BE DONE ABOUT IT (2007).

2. POMFRET, RICHARD, THE AGE OF EQUALITY: THE TWENTIETH CENTURY IN ECONOMIC PERSPECTIVE (Cambridge, Massachusetts: Belknap Press, 2011). See also the review of this book, Richard N. Cooper, *Economic, Social, and Environmental*, 90 FOREIGN AFFAIRS 179 (November/December 2011).

Articles:

1. Lee, Nancy, *More Growth with Income Equality in the Americas: Can Regional Cooperation Help?*, 14 LAW & BUSINESS REVIEW OF THE AMERICAS 665-675 (2008).

2. Ocran, Matthew Kofi & Charles K.D. Adjasi, *Trade Liberalisation and Poverty: Empirical Evidence from Household Surveys in Ghana*, 8 JOURNAL OF INTERNATIONAL TRADE LAW & POLICY number 1, 40-59 (2009).

## GLOBAL SYSTEM OF TRADE PREFERENCES (GLOBAL SYSTEM OF TRADE PREFERENCES AMONG DEVELOPING NATIONS)

*See* GSTP.

## GLOBALIZATION

An umbrella term that covers the cross-border movement of goods, services, intellectual property, finance, people, and ideas.

Globalization is not new to human history. There have been several eras in which trade, investment, and finance has been robust, and in which people have traveled and relocated in large numbers. However, what is distinct about globalization in the late 20$^{th}$ and early 21$^{st}$ century is its pervasiveness, intensity, and technology. In particular, contemporary technological conduits (such as the internet) make movement nearly instantaneous, widely accessible, and highly visible.

One of many examples of globalization is that over 50 percent of world trade in goods, and 75 percent of services trade, is in intermediate products or services used to make or offer other goods or services.[383] The Boeing 787 Dreamliner is a case in point: its engines are made in the United Kingdom and United States, its doors are made in Sweden and France, its flaps and ailerons are made in Canada and Australia, the fuselage is made in Japan, Italy, and the United States, its horizontal stabilizers are made in Italy, its landing gear is

---

[383] *See* Rick Mitchell, *Protectionist Measures Had Small Role in 12.5% Trade Plunge of 2009, OECD Says*, 27 International Trade Reporter (BNA) 854 (10 June 2010).

made in France; and its wings are made in Japan. Overall, there are 43 suppliers in over 135 production sites around the world.[384]

# GMA

Grocery Manufacturers' Association.

The GMA is the leading American lobby organization on behalf of grocery stores. The GMA looks critically at American farm subsidy programs. It points out (*inter alia*) that such subsidies complicate international trade negotiations, as during the Doha Round. In so doing, foreign countries are less inclined to liberalize market access for American grocery stores, to the disadvantage of GMA members.

# GMO

Genetically Modified Organism.

As its name suggests, a GMO is produced as a result of genetic engineering. "Genetic engineering" is a form of bio-technology, and the term is a broad one, embracing an array of processes such as cross-breeding, plant hybridization, and fermentation. The common feature of all genetic engineering is manipulation of genetic material (namely, DNA) inside the cells of a living organization to block an undesirable trait, or to add a desired trait.

To block a gene that controls an undesirable trait, "anti-sense technology" is used. For example, a tomato is bred with delayed ripening in order to get a fresher flavor. To add a desirable trait, "recombinant DNA technology" is used. This process involves transferring genetic material from one species (such as a miro-organism, *e.g.*, bacteria, or an animal) to another species (such as a plant). Recombinant DNA is used to transfer genetic material from a bacterium into the cells of corn to produce insect-resistant corn plants, and into soybeans to yield pesticide-resistant soybeans. It is also used to insert fish genes into plants to increase tolerance to cold.

An enormous number of foods — far more than the average consumer realizes — contain have been genetically engineered. Examples include:

- milk and other dairy products from cows that receive growth hormones;
- canola plants, corn, soybeans, and tomatoes, which are altered to withstand herbicide application;
- corn, tomatoes, and potatoes, into which pesticides are built;
- canola plants, cantaloupe, corn, cucumbers, grapes, potatoes, soybeans, squash, and tomatoes, which are manipulated to resist plant viruses;

---

[384] Rick Mitchell, *Protectionist Measures Had Small Role in 12.5% Trade Plunge of 2009, OECD Says*, 27 International Trade Reporter (BNA) 854 (10 June 2010) (reporting on a May 2010 report from the Organization for Economic Cooperation and Development, *Trade and the Economic Recovery: Why Open Markets Matter*).

- peppers and tomatoes, which are altered to resist plant fungi;

- peas, peppers, tomatoes, and tropical fruits, which are engineered for a longer shelf life and better processing quality;

- corn, soybeans, and sunflowers, which contain altered levels of nutrients;

- fruits with skins, and tomatoes, which are manipulated to endure freezing;

- coffee beans, which are altered for caffeine content;

- potatoes, which are engineered to absorb less oil when fried.

In addition, various enzymes (*i.e.*, proteins for speeding up biological processes) are used to make beer, baked goods, fruit juice, oil, sugar, and wine. Rennet (chymosin) is genetically engineered to make cheese.

Proponents of GMOs point out that genetically-engineered food production results in reduced use of pesticides, herbicides, and fertilizers, enhanced nutrition, resistance to drought, temperature, and disease, better appearance and flavor, and longer shelf-life. Perhaps most importantly, they argue GMOs result in an increase in world food supply and, therefore, a decrease in world hunger.

Opponents counter that GMOs may be unsafe to human, animal, or plant life or health. As yet, there are few long-term studies on the safety of GMOs used in food, or of the effect of GMOs on the environment. Will the use of GMOs result in unsustainable agricultural development (perhaps by disturbing the eco-system)? For example, *bacillus thuringiensis*, or $B_t$, is a natural biological pesticide. It may be rendered useless due to widespread use of $B_t$-engineered crops. Further, genetically-engineered crops that contain the $B_t$ toxin, such as corn, generate pollen that pollute organic fields and may be killing Monarch butterflies. Will the use of GMOs create pesticide-resistant and herbicide-resistant plants? Will this use alter the toxicity levels of naturally occurring food toxins? Will GMOs endanger individuals who have food allergies or sensitivities if these persons unknowingly ingest altered food? Will the alteration of the genetic structure of food lead to new allergens?

Opponents also question the ethics of creating novel organisms. Why should humans create forms of life, via crossing plants and animals or other species, which would not occur through traditional means of reproduction? The question is all the more poignant if the process inflicts cruelty on animals.

The United States is the world's largest producer and exporter of products containing GMOs. For example, in 1999, 35 percent of the corn, 55 percent of the soybeans, and about half of the cotton grown in the United States were genetically modified. About 60 percent of processed foods contained these or other GMO ingredients. Thus, not surprisingly, the United States is quite opposed to efforts to restrict trade in such products. It maintains that no credible scientific evidence has emerged to prove GM products are harmful to health, and that most attempts to restrict trade in them are disguised protections against successful (if not dominant) American companies.

The United States Food and Drug Administration (FDA) does not require labeling of genetically-engineered foods unless (1) the new genetically engineered food is nutritionally different from the non-genetically engineered version, or (2) the characteristics of the genetically engineered food differ significantly from what is normally expected (*e.g.*, the introduction of an allergen or toxin). However, there have been various efforts to legislate a GMO labeling system in the United States.

Many advocates of stricter labeling requirements intone that consumers have the right to choose between genetically and non-genetically engineered foods. Labeling would make this right a reality, enabling consumers to avoid products because of their beliefs about health and science, or on ethical, religious, or spiritual grounds. Moreover, these advocates urge that public health officials could trace the cause and course of unforeseen public health problems, and minimize its adverse consequences, through appropriate labeling. Finally, labeling would force agri-businesses to make a more compelling case that GMOs are safe.

Similarly, many Europeans advocate an approach based on the precautionary principle, arguing they should not have to wait until damaging effects are manifest before taking action. In 1998, the European Union (EU) passed mandatory labeling legislation. The rules require that all foods containing ingredients with a GM content level of one percent or more bear a label to inform consumers of that fact. European companies had a choice: continue to use GM ingredients, and place labels on their products; or, buy non-GMO inputs and avoid labeling. The vast majority of the companies chose the latter course, thus rendering labeling nearly as effective as a ban. This effect worries GMO advocates.

In January 2000, the United States acquiesced to the EU's new GMO labeling rules. The United States preferred not to challenge the rules at the WTO. Ironically, the United States feared it might win such a case. After prevailing in the *Beef Hormone* dispute, public perception in the EU was that the United States was forcing GM products on reluctant European consumers. Another victory would reinforce anti-American sentiment.

That said, a WTO challenge did ensue, yielding the longest Panel Report to date. Following the Report, which was not appealed, in October 2007 the EU Commission finally decided to approve for importation four genetically engineered crops — three types of maize, and one type of sugar beet.[385] However, the approval was subject to the stipulation the crops be used only as animal feed, not consumed directly by humans. Moreover, the approval brought the total of GM crops the EU approved to just 15. The October 2007 EU decision came after rulings in 2005 and 2006 by the European Food Safety Authority that the GM maize and GM sugar beet varieties were safe. Notwithstanding those rulings, several EU states tried to veto importation of the varieties. Under EU law, the Commission has final decision-making authority on GM issues whenever member states are in disagreement.

---

[385] *See GM Approval*, FINANCIAL TIMES, 25 October 2007, at 3.

The EU is hardly the only sponsor of labeling requirements. In January 2000, 130 countries — including the United States and the EU member states — agreed to an international protocol on trade in GM seeds and crops. The accord, called the "Cartagena Protocol" was the first accord under the 1992 United Nations *Convention on Biological Diversity*. (The Bio-safety Protocol was completed in Montreal, but named after the Colombian city where talks in 1999 had failed.) Under the Protocol, a country must notify other countries when it approves a new bio-engineered seed or crop for domestic use. An international shipment of GMOs must be identified as such, so that an importing country can reject the shipment. These features of the Protocol suggest a modest acknowledgment of the legitimacy of the precautionary principle.

However, significantly, labels need not state clearly that a shipment actually does contain GMOs. The United States, Canada, and other agricultural exporting countries objected that precise labeling would be impossible for bulk commodities, *i.e.*, shipments that mix grain from multiple sources. Accordingly the Protocol requires only that a label state a shipment "may contain" GMOs, without any reference to their type or nature. Moreover, the Protocol does not create any new regulatory authorities, and countries remain able to take disputes to the WTO.

In February 2000, Japan's Ministry of Health and Welfare (MHW) announced it would require labeling of foods made from GMOs, and of allergy-inducing foods (effective 1 April 2001). (The Ministry designates over two dozen foods that are "allergy-inducing." Examples include barley, buckwheat noodles (soba), chestnuts, crabs, eggs, fish, milk, rice, shrimp, soybeans, squid, tangerine oranges, and wheat.) The purpose of the MHW labeling requirements is to secure food safety. In addition, the Ministry of Agriculture, Forestry, and Fisheries (MAFF) has a labeling program aimed at enhancing freedom of choice for consumers (without necessarily addressing food safety). The Japanese requirements apply to all foods, whether of domestic or foreign origin. In May 2000, the MHW took an important further step in regulating the use of GMOs in food products. It said it would require safety examinations and inspections of all imported foods to ascertain whether they are or contain GMOs. Third parties make the safety examinations before the covered products are exported. The inspections occur after they arrive in Japan.

Likewise, in May 2000, Korea's Ministry of Agriculture and Fisheries decided to implement labeling requirements (effective March 2001). Korea maintains that its requirements are consistent with the U.N. Bio-safety Protocol. The labeling formula follows the "may contain" rule with respect to possible GMO content. If a good is a GMO, or definitely contains a GMO, then the label must state this fact. Violations of Korea's requirements carry fines of up to 30 million won (about $27,000) or three years in prison.

There is an important First World — Third World dimension to the labeling debate. A number of Third World countries fear that GM products lead to dependency on the supplying companies. For example, certain agricultural seeds that are resistant to pests cannot necessarily be stored for long periods, or produce only one crop, thus requiring farmers to purchase new seed each year from the American company (which, of course, controls the patent to that seed). Conversely, First World agri-businesses are eager to shore up their image in developing countries, and seek strategies to do so.

One example, announced in May 2000, is to give "golden rice" free to the Third World. Golden rice is genetically engineered to contain the anti-oxidant and pigment beta-carotene, which gives the rice a distinctive yellow color. That ingredient is essential in fighting blindness caused by vitamin A deficiency, a problem afflicting half a million people in the Third World every year. The two German professors who invented the rice (Ingo Potrykus and Peter Beyer) agreed to sell the commercial rights to it (through a small German intermediary company, Greenovation) to AstraZeneca, an Anglo-Swedish company that, along with the Rockefeller Foundation, funded the development of the rice. In turn, AstraZeneca licensed the non-commercial rights back to the inventors so that they can distribute the golden rice for free to government-run agricultural institutes and breeding centers in China, India, and other Asian countries. Farmers in these countries are allowed to earn up to $10,000 each year without paying a royalty. AstraZeneca covers the cost of the "give away" by commercializing golden rice in developed countries, essentially marketing it to health-conscious consumers as a "functional food."

*Suggestions for Further Research:*

Books:

1.    BODIGUEL, LUC & MICHAEL CARDWELL, THE REGULATION OF GENETICALLY MODIFIED ORGANISMS — COMPARATIVE APPROACHES (2010).

2.    POLLACK, MARK A. & GREGORY C. SHAFFER, WHEN COOPERATION FAILS — THE INTERNATIONAL LAW AND POLITICS OF GENETICALLY MODIFIED FOODS (2009).

Articles:

1.    Ansari, Abdul Haseeb & Nik Ahmad Kamal Nik Mahmod, *Biosafety Protocol, SPS Agreement, and Export and Import Control of LMOs/GMOs*, 7 JOURNAL OF INTERNATIONAL TRADE LAW AND POLICY number 2, 139-170 (2008).

2.    Blas, Emily A., Case Note, *Monsanto v. Geertson Seed Farms: Why the National Environmental Policy Act of 1969 Fails to Protect the Environment from Current Biotechnology (Monsanto Company v. Geertson Seed Farms, 130 S. Ct. 2743, 2010)*, 14 SUSTAINABLE DEVELOPMENT LAW JOURNAL 35-47 (2011).

3.    Blaustein, Samuel, *Splitting Genes: The Future of Genetically Modified Organisms in the Wake of the WTO/Cartagena Standoff*, 16 PENN STATE ENVIRONMENTAL LAW REVIEW 367-401 (2008).

4.    Bussell, Charles J., Note, *As Montville, Maine Goes, So Goes Wolcott, Vermont? A Primer on the Local Regulation of Genetically Modified Crops*, 43 SUFFOLK UNIVERSITY LAW REVIEW 727-748 (2010).

5.    Cannon, Joshua B., Note, *Statutory Stones and Regulatory Mortar: Using Negligence Per Se to Mend the Wall Between Farmers Growing*

*Genetically Engineered Crops and Their Neighbors*, 67 WASHINGTON & LEE LAW REVIEW 653-691 (2010).

6. DeBona, Michael, Comment, *Letting a Hundred Transgenic Flowers Blossom: The Future of Genetically Modified Agriculture in the People's Republic of China*, 22 VILLANOVA ENVIRONMENTAL LAW JOURNAL 89-115 (2011).

7. Eliason, Antonia, *Science versus Law in WTO Jurisprudence: The (Mis) interpretation of the Scientific Process and the (In)sufficiency of Scientific Evidence in EC–Biotech*, 41 NEW YORK UNIVERSITY JOURNAL OF INTERNATIONAL LAW & POLITICS 341-406 (2009).

8. Federici, Valery, Note, *Genetically Modified Food and Informed Consumer Choice: Comparing U.S. and EU Labeling Laws*, 35 BROOKLYN JOURNAL OF INTERNATIONAL LAW 515-561 (2010).

9. Glass-O'Shea, Brooke, *The History and Future of Genetically Modified Crops: Frankenfoods, Superweeds, and the Developing World*, 7 JOURNAL OF FOOD LAW & POLICY 1-33 (2011).

10. Hishaw, Jillian S., *"Show-Me" No Rice Pharming: An Overview of the Introduction of and Opposition to Genetically Engineered Pharmaceutical Crops in the United States*, 3 JOURNAL OF FOOD LAW & POLICY 209-227 (2007).

11. Hutchinson, Marguerite A., Comment, *Moving Beyond the WTO: A Proposal to Adjudicate GMO Disputes in an International Environmental Court*, 10 SAN DIEGO INTERNATIONAL LAW JOURNAL 229-263 (2008).

12. Kariyawasam, Kanchana *Legal Liability, Intellectual Property, and Genetically Modified Crops: Their Impact on World Agriculture*, 19 PACIFIC RIM LAW & POLICY JOURNAL 459-485 (2010).

13. Laxman, Lekha & Abdul Haseeb Ansari, GMOs, Safety Concerns, and International Trade: Developing Countries' Perspective, 1.    Gani,    Azmat, *The Effect of Business Environment on Trade in Gulf Cooperation Council Countries*, 10 JOURNAL OF INTERNATIONAL TRADE LAW AND POLICY number 3 281-307 (2011).

14. Lesicko, Christine K., Note, *Attempting to (De)regulate Genetically Modified Crops: The Supreme Court Overrules the Injunction Denying Deregulation of Roundup Ready Alfalfa (Monsanto v. Geertson Seed Farms, 130 S.Ct. 2743 (2010))*, 18 MISSOURI ENVIRONMENTAL LAW & POLICY REVIEW 351-377 (2011).

15. Partlet, Aubrey, Note, *Organic Foods Production: What Consumers Might Note Know About the Use of Synthetic Substances*, 21 LOYOLA CONSUMER LAW REVIEW 392-406 (2009).

16. Peck, Alison, *The New Imperialism: Toward an Advocacy Strategy for GMO Accountability*, 21 GEORGETOWN INTERNATIONAL ENVIRONMENTAL LAW REVIEW 37-72 (2008).

17. Peck, Alison, *Leveling the Playing Field in GMO Risk Assessment: Importers, Exporters, and the Limits of Science*, 28 BOSTON UNIVERSITY INTERNATIONAL LAW JOURNAL 241-280 (2010).

18. Peel, Jacqueline, *A GMO by Any Other Name . . . Might be an SPS Risk!: Implications of Expanding the Scope of the WTO Sanitary and Phytosanitary Measures Agreement*, 17 EUROPEAN INTERNATIONAL LAW JOURNAL 1009-1031 (2006).

19. Rowe, Elizabeth A., *Patents, Genetically Modified Foods, and IP Overreaching*, 64 SMU LAW REVIEW 859-893 (2011).

20. Schlosser, Adam, Comment, *A Meating of the Minds: Possible Pitfalls and Benefits of Certified Organic Livestock Production and the Prodigious Potential of Brazil*, 4 JOURNAL OF FOOD LAW & POLICY 209-242 (2008).

21. Schramm, Daniel, Note, *The Race to Geneva: Resisting the Gravitational Pull of the WTO in the GMO Labeling Controversy*, 9 VERMONT JOURNAL OF ENVIRONMENTAL LAW 93-129 (2007).

22. Sella-Villa, David E., Note, *Gently Modified Operations: How Environmental Concerns Addressed Through Customs Procedures Can Successfully Resolve the U.S.–EU GMO Dispute*, 33 WILLIAM & MARY ENVIRONMENTAL LAW & POLICY REVIEW 971-1016 (2009).

23. Shaffer, Gregory, *A Structural Theory of WTO Dispute Settlement: Why Institutional Choice Lies at the Center of the GMO Case*, 41 NEW YORK UNIVERSITY JOURNAL OF INTERNATIONAL LAW & POLITICS 1-101 (2008).

24. Smith, Tempe, Note, *Going to Seed?: Using Monsanto as a Case Study to Examine the Patent Antitrust Implications of the Sale and Use of Genetically Modified Organisms*, 61 ALABAMA LAW REVIEW 629-648 (2010).

25. Stephenson, Andrea L., *Germany's Ban on Monsanto's Modified Maize (MON 810): A Violation of International Law*, 2 TRADE, LAW AND DEVELOPMENT no. 2, 292-328 (fall 2010).

26. Stockhorst, Lee, Note, *Super Crops or a Super Problem? The Battle over BT Corn (Monsanto Company v. Bayer Bioscience N.V., 514 F.3d 1229, 2008)*, 15 MISSOURI ENVIRONMENTAL LAW & POLICY REVIEW 531-553 (2008).

27. Strauss, Debra M., *The Application of TRIPs to GMOs: International Intellectual Property Rights and Biotechnology*, 45 STANFORD JOURNAL OF INTERNATIONAL LAW 287-320 (2009).

28. Tai, Stephanie, *Comparing Approaches Towards Governing Scientific Advisory Bodies on Food Safety in the United States and the European Union*, 2010 WISCONSIN LAW REVIEW 627-671 (2010).

29. Young, Margaret A., *The WTO's Use of Relevant Rules of International Law: An Analysis of the Biotech Case*, 56 INTERNATIONAL & COMPARATIVE LAW QUARTERLY 907-930 (2007).

## GNP

Gross National Product.

GNP is the broadest measure of income earned by nationals of a country. GNP is the total value of all finished output of goods and services produced by nationals of a country. *Per capita* GNP is the final value of all finished goods and services produced by nationals of a country in one year, divided by the number of nationals (*i.e.*, citizens) of that country.

It does not matter whether or where the output is consumed, invested, or if it used by a government. The value of the output is income to its producer. Therefore, GNP is defined equivalently as all income earned by nationals — but only nationals, *i.e.*, citizens, of a country — regardless of where the nationals earn the income. The letter "N" in "GNP" serves to emphasize nationals of the country earned the income being measured. GNP may be computed in terms of current (also called "nominal") price levels in the country.

However, the prices of income-generating output (*e.g.*, agricultural commodities, manufactured goods, services) change over time. Consequently, a more reliable measurement than current GNP is "constant" GNP. Essentially, "constant" GNP is current GNP, corrected for price inflation (or deflation) using a numerical factor that sets a specific year as the base year from which to define a price index (*e.g.*, prices in 2005 equal 100).

For example, the income of a Filipino receptionist working at the Sheraton Hotel in Bahrain would be included in the GNP of the Philippines, but not of Bahrain, because the receptionist is a national of the Philippines. Indeed, to the extent the receptionist repatriates the earnings, the economy of the Philippines directly benefits. In addition to the Philippines, Bangladesh, India, Sri Lanka, and various other poor countries send workers to Persian Gulf countries to earn income, which then is repatriated to the home countries.

As another example, the income earned by the Sheraton Hotel in Bahrain would be included in the GNP of the United States, but not of Bahrain. That is because, as an American-based multinational corporation, Sheraton Hotels are a national of the United States. Many such corporations rely for a large percentage of their revenues on foreign-generated income. Yet, for purposes of computing GNP, the location in which income is produced is irrelevant. What matters is the nationality of the owner of the asset producing the activities.

As for the letter "G," standing for "Gross," it indicates the calculation is an aggregate one, with no subtraction for items like consumption of capital. ("Capital consumption" refers to the decline in value of equipment, which occurs because as equipment ages, becomes obsolete, or is used, and because of technological enhancements.) The letter "P," standing for "Product," suggests only the value of real output produced is included in GNP. The value of output absorbed in the manufacturing process — namely, intermediate or semi-finished goods — is excluded.

As a practical matter, there are three ways to compute national income — the GNP or GDP — of a country: the income approach, the expenditure approach, and the output approach. Under the income approach, the incomes derived from each type of economic activity, that is, the income accruing to all owners of factors of production, is summed. Thus, income from self-employment, trading profits, rent, and property income from abroad are added together. Only the incomes and profits of residents of the country are included in the calculation. Transfer payments (*e.g.*, welfare), that is, payments that are not made to factors of production for current services, also are excluded.

Under the expenditure approach, spending on final goods and services is aggregated. The principal categories of spending are consumption (C), investment (I) (*i.e.*, expenditures that add to the capital stock, as distinct from consumption), government purchases (G), and net exports (*i.e.*, exports less imports, or X–M). These categories give rise to the familiar macroeconomic equation

$$GNP \quad = \quad C + I + G + (X - M),$$

or, using "Y" to symbolize GNP,

$$Y \quad = \quad C + I + G + (X - M)$$

Under the output approach, the values of products of each of the various sectors in the economy are summed. Thus, the value added by agricultural and extractive industries, manufacturing industries, construction, and services, along with net property income from abroad, are aggregated. GDP is reported both in "nominal" or "current" terms (*i.e.*, uncorrected for inflation), and in "real" or "constant" terms (*i.e.*, corrected for inflation).

## GOING-FORWARD CASH DEPOSIT RATE

*See* Administrative Review, Retrospective assessment.

## *GPA*

*Government Procurement Agreement, i.e.*, the World Trade Organization (WTO) *Agreement on Government Procurement*, typically referred to as the "*Government Procurement Agreement*" or "*GPA*."

Government procurement is a significant economic sector. In most countries, government procurement accounts for 15-20 percent of Gross Domestic Product (GDP). The *GPA* was concluded as part of the Tokyo Round (1973-7199), but revised in the Uruguay Round (1986-1994). In brief, the *GPA* requires:

- Most Favored Nation (MFN) treatment for suppliers from different countries of goods and services to governments.

- National treatment for foreign suppliers, vis-à-vis domestic contractors.

- Procedural fairness, including transparency, in international competition for government procurement.

The *GPA* applies to government procurement contracts at both the central and sub-central levels above a certain value threshold. The thresholds are defined in terms of International Monetary Fund (IMF) Special Drawing Rights (SDRs):

- Central government purchases of goods and services above SDR 130,000 (approximately U.S. $200,000).

- Sub-Central government purchases of goods and services above SDR 200,000 (approximately U.S. $305,000).

- Purchases of goods and services by Public Utilities above SDR 400,000 (approximately U.S. $610,000).

- Public sector procurement of construction contracts above SDR 5 million (approximately U.S. $7.7 million).

The *GPA* relies on a "Positive List" approach whereby WTO Members designate the central and sub-central governmental and quasi-governmental entities subject to *GPA* terms. They list the covered entities in Annexes to the *GPA*.

Also in those Annexes, Members state the minimum value threshold to which it will apply the *GPA* for a covered entity. Obviously, the higher the minimum threshold, the less the number of opportunities for foreign procurement providers to bid on a project. Further, countries can — and do — restrict bidding by foreigners for various policy reasons. For example, the United States does so under the *Small Business Act of 1953*. Malaysia does so as part of its affirmative action program for Malays.

The *GPA* contains a number of legal obligations applicable to signatory countries and their covered entities. For example, there are rules about transparency and fair bidding procedures, non-discriminatory treatment, and the use of local content requirements. *GPA* signatories must conduct their procurement operations in a fair, predictable, and transparent manner and not discriminate against foreign suppliers, in favor of domestic ones. These obligations, of course, affect only procurement operations covered by the *GPA*.

The *GPA* is not part of the Uruguay Round single undertaking. Rather, it is a plurilateral accord. Just 42 of the 153 WTO Members are signatories (as of December 2011). The value of the government procurement market in these 42 signatories is $1.6 trillion annually.[386] These signatories include:

| | |
|---|---|
| - Armenia | - Korea |
| - Aruba | - Liechtenstein |
| - Canada | - Norway |
| - European Union (and its 27 member states) | - Singapore |
| - Hong Kong | - Switzerland |
| - Iceland | - Taiwan |
| - Israel | - United States |
| - Japan | |

---

[386] *See* Daniel Pruzin, *Key WTO Members Vow to Conclude Procurement Talks by December Ministerial*, 28 International Trade Reporter (BNA) 1647 (13 October 2011).

WTO Members negotiating accession to the *GPA* include:

- Albania
- China
- Georgia
- Jordan
- Kyrgyzstan

- Moldova
- Oman
- Panama
- Ukraine

Furthermore, while stating that the country did not have plans at the time for negotiating accession, on 10 February 2010 the government procurement committee did accepted India as an observer.[387] Members seeking to join the *GPA* must negotiate concessions — that is, specific commitments as to public entities subject to *GPA* disciplines, and value thresholds above which those disciplines apply — with existing signatories.

Note that unlike the 1996 WTO *Information Technology Agreement* (*ITA*), which also is a plurilateral accord, the *GPA* does not allow for free riding. That is, as a closed plurilateral deal, the benefits from the *GPA* are not available to all WTO Members, ones that are parties to the *GPA* and ones that are not. The *GPA* benefits only redound to Members that are party to the *GPA*. In contrast, as an open plurilateral deal, *ITA* benefits are enjoyed by all WTO Members, whether or not they participate in the *ITA* by making a commitment to eliminate duties on information technology products. Stated differently, in an open plurilateral bargain, immediate, unconditional most favored nation (MFN) treatment applies to all Members, regardless of whether they are signatories to the bargain. With a closed deal, the MFN principle operates immediately and unconditionally only among the signatories.

China presents an interesting case concerning *GPA* membership. China's first offer for accession, submitted in December 2007 was highly criticized by several WTO Member countries for extensive exclusion of regional, provincial, and municipal governments. The offer also excluded procurement of services and public utilities from coverage under the *GPA*. The United States commented to the WTO that the offer was "substantially below the standards" of other WTO members.[388] China was further criticized for seeking an implementation period of 15 years.[389] China's accession to the *GPA* would mean access to a $35 billion per year market for United States companies, according to the United States Department of Commerce.[390] Hence, an explanation for the sharp criticism of China's first offer.

---

[387] Daniel Pruzin, *U.S., EU Other Criticize Draft China Procurement Rules as Discriminatory*, 27 International Trade Reporter 210 (BNA) (18 February 2010).

[388] *See* Daniel Pruzin, *U.S. Slams China's Offer to Open Procurement Market as Inadequate*, 25 International Trade Reporter (BNA) 306 (28 February 2008).

[389] Daniel Pruzin, *Chinese Official Indicates Procurement Offer Likely to Fall Short of U.S., Partners' Wishes*, 27 International Trade Reporter (BNA) 858 (10 June 2010).

[390] *See* Daniel Pruzin, *China Submits 'Modest' Offer to Open Government Procurement Market*, 25 International Trade Reporter (BNA) 116 (24 January 2008).

In June 2010 China agreed to submit a second, revised offer that Beijing deems will be "ambitious." However, the proposal will not subject state-owned enterprises (SOEs) to *GPA* requirements.

Taiwan also presents an interesting case concerning *GPA* membership.[391] Taiwan agreed to join the *GPA* as part of its WTO entry terms, and completed terms of accession to the *GPA* in December 2002. Its accession, effective 15 July 2009, was as a separate customs territory. However, China — which had not signed the *GPA* as part of its WTO accession terms — held Observer status on the WTO *GPA* Committee. Hong Kong is also a member of the *GPA* Committee. Operating through Hong Kong, China blocked the Committee from accepting Taiwan into the *GPA*, because China objected to the official names Taiwan used to designate some of its central government bodies. The Taiwanese bodies at issue included the Presidential Office, the Executive Yuan (*i.e.*, the national parliament), and the Ministry of Defense. Believing the names suggested Taiwan was a sovereign nation independent from China, and not merely a separate customs territory, China asked Taiwan to change the names.

In June 2006, the United States and EU proposed a compromise, which the Committee accepted, stating that nomenclature is provided "only for the purpose of providing clarity in defining commitments in the framework of the accession to the *Agreement* . . . [and] none of the nomenclature and other terminology used have implications for sovereignty." Ultimately, in December 2008, the parties to the *GPA* gave final approval for the accession of Taiwan.

The United States is a champion of the *GPA*, even calling in WTO accession negotiations (such as with China and the Kingdom of Saudi Arabia) for an applicant to join the *GPA* despite its status as a plurilateral accord. However, the EU has criticized the United States for not sufficiently opening up its own government procurement markets. For example, the EU's *U.S. Barriers to Trade and Investment Report for 2006* observed:

- Lack of transparency in federal government procurement, because notices are published on just one electronic website (*www.fedbizoppos.gov*).
- Lack of transparency in sub-federal government procurement.
- "Buy America" restrictions that demand or prefer procurement from a United States supplier.
- Set aside schemes for small businesses, mandated by the *Small Business Act of 1953*.
- Limitations on bidding opportunities for foreign suppliers in state government procurement, because of the extra-territorial effect of state sanctions (*e.g.*, a state rule prohibiting state government procurement from a foreign supplier if that supplier does business with Burma or Sudan). [392]

---

[391] *See* Daniel Pruzin, *WTO Members Reach Agreement to Facilitate Taiwan Joining Government Procurement Pact*, 23 International Trade Reporter (BNA) 872 (8 June 2006).

[392] *See* Gary G. Yerkey, *EU Presses U.S. to Improve Offer in WTO Public Procurement Talks*, 24 International Trade Reporter (BNA) 336 (8 March 2007).

This Report is emblematic of a broader trend in international trade law interests of developed nations in the post-Uruguay Round era. They are finding among the biggest obstacles to their exporters are not necessarily conventional trade barriers like tariffs, but difficult-to-find-and-root-out barriers. The latter category includes not only barriers to government procurement, but also hidden subsidies, sanitary and phytosanitary (SPS) measures, and technical barriers to trade (TBT).

In any event, scrambling to preserve some measure of credibility in the wake given the moribund state of the Doha Round, in May 2011 Director-General Lamy said negotiations on expanding the WTO *Agreement on Government Procurement (GPA)* might be part of a package of deliverable items at the December 2011 Ministerial Conference.[393] Of course, GATT contracting parties adopted the *GPA*, originally a Tokyo Round (1973-1979) text, on a plurilateral basis in 1979.[394] They revised that text in the Uruguay Round (1986-1994), again adopting it on a plurilateral basis. Yet, never before had *GPA* negotiations, which launched in 1999 before the Doha Round, been linked to or part of the Doha Round. The Director-General was stretching outside the Round for a victory to tout, and for good reason. A revised *GPA* could add $100 billion to world GDP, which would be only 0.2 percent of global output, but would be over half the gains estimated from the entire Round package covering goods and services.[395] Yet, with four major hurdles to cross, *GPA* negotiations were far from complete.

First, the United States and EU awaited a credible offer, with significant central and sub-central government coverage, from China, so that China would be a party to the *GPA*. As part of its 11 December 2001 terms of accession to the WTO, China promised to join the *GPA*.[396] But, it has been slow in working toward keeping its promise. China submitted its initial offer — the government

---

[393] *See* Daniel Pruzin, *WTO's Lamy Says Public Procurement Deal Could be in December Deliverables Package*, 28 International Trade Reporter (BNA) 846 (26 May 2011).

[394] *See* Daniel Pruzin, *GPA Chairman Warns of Setback in Government Procurement Talks*, 28 International Trade Reporter (BNA) 1923 (1 December 2011).

[395] *See* Alan Beattie, *Rich Economies Look to Deal on Services Outside Doha Meeting*, Financial Times, 13 December 2011, *posted at* www.ft.com/intl/cms/s/0/1bc018d4-24df-11e1-8bf9-00144feabdc0.html&num;axzz1gXpXx3yj.

That said, the estimates of economists about the Doha Round are dubious. On the eve of the December 2011 Geneva Ministerial Conference, the World Bank confessed its initial estimates of the extent to which the Round, if completed, would stimulate growth and reduce poverty around the world were far too ambitious. *See* Beattie, Alan, *Miserly Progress Made*, Financial Times, 13 December 2011, at 9 (*quoting* Bernard Hoekman, Director, International Trade Department, World Bank).

[396] *See* Daniel Pruzin, *WTO's Lamy Says Public Procurement Deal Could be in December Deliverables Package*, 28 International Trade Reporter (BNA) 846 (26 May 2011).

WTO Members sought through accession negotiations with Russia the same commitment, *i.e.*, that it would join the *GPA*. The other two "BRIC" countries — Brazil and India — showed no interest (as of October 2011) in joining the *GPA*, though India held observe status effective February 2010. *See* Daniel Pruzin, *WTO Report Cites Potential in New Market Access Opportunities from GPA Accessions*, 28 International Trade Reporter (BNA) 1738 (27 October 2011).

entities that it scheduled under the *GPA* positive-list approach — in December 2007. That offer was grossly inadequate, in terms of entities covered, and China revised it in July 2010.

To the chagrin of the United States and EU, the revised offer was insufficient. They called on China to expand the central government entities covered.[397] They also asked China to include procurement by all sub-central governments in all of China's 22 provinces and 5 autonomous regions, and in the four municipalities (Beijing, Chongqing, Shanghai, and Tianjin) under central government authority. The United States and EU also said China needed to include the 23 municipalities at the prefecture level. In respect of all these requests, the United States and EU noted that China should include subordinate agencies operating under the relevant entities.

Second, the EU demanded more ambitious offers of coverage from Canada, Japan, and Korea. With Japan, for example, the EU insisted it lower its thresholds for government construction contracts that would be subject to *GPA* disciplines.[398] The EU also demanded Japan allow foreign suppliers to bid on procurement contracts issued by private Japanese railway operators. Japan affirmatively scheduled the Japan Railways (JR) Group as a covered state entity in its *GPA* commitments.[399] But, in the 1990s, and finishing in 2006, Japan privatized fully three of the six regional networks in the JR Group. An independent governmental agency, the Japan Railway Construction, Transportation and Technology Agency, owns the other three networks. Yet, because of the earlier privatizations, Japan sought to remove the JR Group, hence the conflict with the EU.

Third, the United States had to open further its government procurement market. The United States, said the EU, needed to schedule more central government entities, and subject more state governments to *GPA* disciplines. (Thirteen of the 50 states had not scheduled any of their official entities in the *GPA*: Alabama, Alaska, Georgia, Indiana, Nevada, New Jersey, New Mexico, North Carolina, North Dakota, Ohio, South Carolina, Virginia, and West Virginia. Georgia refused to see its entities covered by the *GPA*.)[400] The United States also needed to reduce the competitive distortions created by its set-aside programs. That is, the Europeans wanted the Americans to eliminate the exemption the Americans inserted in the *GPA* from *GPA* disciplines for procurement schemes that require certain federal procurement contracts be

---

[397] *See* Pruzin, Daniel, *WTO's Lamy Says Public Procurement Deal Could be in December Deliverables Package*, 28 International Trade Reporter (BNA) 846 (26 May 2011).

[398] *See* Daniel Pruzin, *Deal on Revised WTO Procurement Accord Will Depend on U.S., EU, Japan Trade-Offs*, 28 International Trade Reporter (BNA) 892 (2 June 2011).

[399] *See* Daniel Pruzin, *GPA Chairman Warns of Setback in Government Procurement Talks*, 28 International Trade Reporter (BNA) 1923 (1 December 2011).

[400] *See* Daniel Pruzin, *GPA Parties' Negotiations Go Down to Wire in Attempt to Reach WTO Procurement Deal*, 28 International Trade Reporter (BNA) 1960 (8 December 2011); Daniel Pruzin, *GPA Chairman Warns of Setback in Government Procurement Talks*, 28 International Trade Reporter (BNA) 1923 (1 December 2011).

awarded to small and medium-sized enterprises (SMEs).[401] Ironically given its much-ballyhooed interest in the environment, the EU also sought an end to American procurement rules that prefer "green" firms that endeavor to protect the environment.

Until the United States and other countries enhanced their offers, the EU would adhere to strict reciprocity vis-à-vis such countries when fashioning its offers and awarding government procurement contracts. Thus, it would open up the EU procurement market to Iceland, Lichtenstein, Norway, and Switzerland, but not to Canada, Japan, Korea, or the United States.[402] That is, in December 2010, the EU tabled a revised offer expanding the list of its entities covered by the *GPA*, and thus open to foreign procurement bids, but expressly excluding these four countries from any benefits associated with the expanded list.

Fourth, expanded *GPA* coverage pursuant to the first three points would have to be accompanied by special and differential treatment for developing countries.[403] Most poor countries could not (or would not) assume the same degree of liberalization obligations in their markets for government procurement of goods and services as would most rich countries. Consensus would be needed on reduced commitments and extended phase-in periods for poor countries.

In sum, these four hurdles meant the likelihood of completing an accord to expand the *GPA* was low, at least in the short or medium-term.[404] To their credit, during the December 2011 WTO Ministerial Conference in Geneva, the EU and Japan resolved some of their differences, largely because Japan agreed to modest enhanced market access for foreign procurement bidding on contracts in the Japanese rail sector.[405] Japan insisted on excluding from *GPA* coverage the three JR Group entities that had been privatized. But, Japan agreed to apply in a non-discriminatory, transparent manner its strict rail operational safety regulations. (The EU had accused Japan of shutting out foreign bidders by claiming only Japanese firms could meet these regulations, particularly in respect of seismic resistance.[406])

---

[401] *See* Daniel Pruzin, *Deal on Revised WTO Procurement Accord Will Depend on U.S., EU, Japan Trade-Offs*, 28 International Trade Reporter (BNA) 892 (2 June 2011).

[402] *See* Daniel Pruzin, *Deal on Revised WTO Procurement Accord Will Depend on U.S., EU, Japan Trade-Offs*, 28 International Trade Reporter (BNA) 892 (2 June 2011).

[403] *See* Daniel Pruzin, *GPA Talks Chair Cites Growing Confidence in WTO Procurement Deal in December*, 28 International Trade Reporter (BNA) 1689 (20 October 2011).

[404] The EU and United States could not even agree on what form a *GPA* deal, if reached, should take. The Europeans favored an entirely new accord, because of EU rules under the Treaty of Lisbon. The United States insisted on a revision to the existing *GPA*, because with its lack of fast-track trade negotiating authority, Congress might not pass a new accord. *See* Daniel Pruzin, *Deal on Revised WTO Procurement Accord Will Depend on U.S., EU, Japan Trade-Offs*, 28 International Trade Reporter (BNA) 892 (2 June 2011).

[405] *See* Daniel Pruzin, *Negotiators Clinch WTO Procurement Deal*, 28 International Trade Reporter (BNA) (Breaking News, 15 December 2011).

[406] *See* Daniel Pruzin, *French Minister Cites Last-Minute Japanese Concessions in Salvaging Procurement Deal*, 28 International Trade Reporter (BNA) 2046 (22 December 2011).

As a result, trade ministers from over 40 WTO Members proudly proclaimed agreement on a revised *GPA*. They claimed it would expand market access for government procurement by $80-$100 billion annually through the addition of covered central governmental entities in Aruba, EU, Hong Kong, Israel, Korea, Lichtenstein, and Switzerland, and the addition of covered sub-central entities in Canada, Israel, Japan, and Korea.[407] Many of the newly-included entities procured services, such as telecommunications, in which the United States had a keen export interest. Indeed, in their concessions, Aruba, Hong Kong, Israel, Japan, Korea, Singapore, and Switzerland added over 50 categories of services.

The trade ministers stuck by their rosy estimate of trade gains from the revised *GPA*, even though their deal left unchanged most of the value thresholds at which a procurement contract becomes subject to *GPA* rules (though some thresholds for covered entities in Aruba, Japan, and Israel fell).[408] Moreover, despite a top up of the American offer to offset the exclusion of Georgia from *GPA* coverage, the EU continued to treat the United States on the basis of reciprocity. (The United States topped up its offer by including the Social Security and Transportation Security Administration, though excluding textile and apparel (T&A) merchandise by these two entities, and by including the Department of Agriculture, and telecommunications projects funded by the Rural Utilities Service.[409]) The EU also chafed at the American refusal to remove special preferences in procurement by small and medium sized enterprises (SMEs) and minority-owned businesses.

Likewise, the EU continued to treat Japan on the basis of reciprocity. The EU still quarreled with Japan over foreign procurement by the JR Group, saying access for European bidders remained insufficient. And, though Japan lowered its procurement threshold from 130,000 to 100,000 Special Drawing Rights (SDRs) for goods, it refused to drop the threshold from 15 million SDRs for construction contracts.[410] Japan did agree, however, to open its procurement market to foreign bidding on large infrastructure projects in its earthquake-destroyed regions.[411]

---

[407] *See* Daniel Pruzin, *Negotiators Clinch WTO Procurement Deal; Expanded Access Valued at $80-100 Billion*, 28 International Trade Reporter (BNA) 2043 (22 December 2011).

[408] *See* Daniel Pruzin, *Negotiators Clinch WTO Procurement Deal; Expanded Access Valued at $80-100 Billion*, 28 International Trade Reporter (BNA) 2043 (22 December 2011).

[409] The United States added 14 central government entities to coverage under the *GPA*. In addition to the four mentioned above, it added the following ten: Advisory Council on Historic Preservation; Court Service and Offender Supervision Agency for the District of Colombia; Federal Energy Regulatory Commission; Federal Labor Relations Authority; Millennium Challenge Corporation; National Assessment Governing Board; National Endowment for the Arts; National Endowment for the Humanities; United States Marine Mammal Commission; and United States Access Board. *See* Daniel Pruzin, *U.S. Paper Details Additional Federal Entities Subject to Disciplines Under Revised GPA*, 28 International Trade Reporter (BNA) 2045 (22 December 2011).

[410] 130,000 SDR is equivalent to roughly U.S. $200,000 (as of December 2011).

[411] *See* Daniel Pruzin, *French Minister Cites Last-Minute Japanese Concessions in Salvaging Procurement Deal*, 28 International Trade Reporter (BNA) 2046 (22 December 2011).

In brief, the December 2011 *GPA* deal was a quick and partial fix, leaving the fundamental disagreements involving the United States, EU, and Japan unresolved. If that was the best WTO Members could manage, small wonder why it failed to inspire the Members to agree on more important, core Doha Round issues. Aside from the *GPA* deal, and the accession of Russia to the WTO, the Conference produced no other systemically important innovations. Nevertheless, the difficulties manifest in the April 2011 Documents, on matters that properly were in the Round, could not be offset or covered up easily by a *GPA* deal.

In 2009, Canada grew alarmed by the "Buy American" provisions favoring American companies under the *American Recovery and Reinvestment Act (AARA)*. This provision stated all *AARA* funded projects must be carried out using only domestically produced steel, iron and manufactured goods.[412] (These projects were publicly funded, and designed to stimulate the American economy. Some, but not all, of them were government procurement contracts.) Canada was acutely affected by this measure, given the significant importance (indeed, dependence) of the Canadian economy on the United States, including on government procurement contracts handed out by Washington, D.C. close relationship between the American and Canadian economies. The "Buy American" provision in the *AARA* included a requirement that the Buy American procurement rule be carried out "in a manner consistent with international trade commitments." But, the Canadians complained state and municipal governments misinterpreted or even ignored this requirement.

Responding to Canadian concerns, the United States and Canada entered negotiations. In 2010, they signed a bilateral agreement on sub-national government procurement.[413] This accord allowed American companies to compete for Canadian provincial and municipal government contracts not covered by the *GPA* until September 2011. American companies also received a permanent right to compete for Canadian provincial and territorial procurement contracts, in accordance with the *GPA*. Canadian companies have the ability to compete for sub-national procurement contracts in the 37 American states covered by the *GPA*, as well as selected projects of the *AARA*.

*Suggestions for Further Research:*

Books:

1.   ARROWSMITH, SUE, ED., GOVERNMENT PROCUREMENT IN THE WTO (2003).

2.   ARROWSMITH, SUE, & MARTIN TRYBUS EDS., PUBLIC PROCUREMENT — THE CONTINUING REVOLUTION (2003).

---

[412] Rosella Brevetti, *U.S., Canadian Officials at Preliminary Stage of Exploring Expansion of Procurement Pact*, 28 International Trade Reporter (BNA) 404 (10 March 2010).

[413] Rosella Brevetti, *USTR Kirk, Van Loan Sign Agreement on U.S.-Canadian Government Procurement*, 27 International Trade Reporter (BNA) 233 (18 February 2010).

Articles:

1.  Gao, Henry, *The Bid Challenge Procedures Under the WTO Government Procurement Agreement: A Critical Study of the Hong Kong Experience*, 16 PUBLIC PROCUREMENT LAW REVIEW issue 4 211-254 (2007).

2.  Goodwin, David P. *et al.*, *Government Procurement*, 44 THE INTERNATIONAL LAWYER 261-272 (2010).

3.  Kessler, David A., *Protection and Protectionism: The Practicalities of Offshore Software Development in Government Procurement*, 38 PUBLIC CONTRACTS LAW JOURNAL 1-46 (2008).

4.  Mathieson, Skye, Note, *Assessing China's Public Procurement Market: Which State-Influenced Enterprises Should the WTO's Government Procurement Agreement Cover?*, 40 PUBLIC CONTRACT LAW JOURNAL 233-266 (2010).

5.  Miller, Drew B., Note, *Is It Time to Reform Reciprocal Defense Procurement Agreements?*, 39 PUBLIC CONTRACT LAW JOURNAL 93-111 (2009).

6.  Nackman, Mark J., *A Critical Examination of Offsets in International Defense Procurements: Policy Options for the United States*, 40 PUBLIC CONTRACT LAW JOURNAL 511-529 (2011).

7.  Nensala, Sondra Bell, *Homeland Security Presidential Directive 12: How HSPD-12 May Limit Competition Unnecessarily and Suggestions for Reform*, 40 PUBLIC CONTRACTS LAW JOURNAL 619-679 (2011).

8.  Wang, Ping, *Coverage of the WTO's Agreement on Government Procurement: Challenges of Integrating China and Other Countries with a Large State Sector into the Global Trading System*, 10 JOURNAL OF INTERNATIONAL ECONOMIC LAW 887-920 (2007).

9.  Wang, Ping, *China's Accession to the WTO Government Procurement Agreement — Challenges and the Way Forward*, 12 JOURNAL OF INTERNATIONAL ECONOMIC LAW 663-706 (2009).

10.  Reich, Arie, *The New GATT Agreement on Government Procurement — the Pitfalls of Plurilateralism and Strict Reciprocity*, 31 JOURNAL OF WORLD TRADE 2 (April 1997).

11.  *Efforts to Open Foreign Procurement Markets: Hearing Before the H.R. Subcomm. on Legis. & Nat'l Sec., Comm. on Gov't Operations*, 103rd Cong. (1994) (statement of Allan I. Mendelowitz, Managing Director International Trade, Finance, and Competitiveness General Government Division).

12.  Corr, Christopher F. & Zissis, Kristina, *Convergence and Opportunity: The WTO Government Procurement Agreement and U.S. Procurement Reform*, 18 NEW YORK LAW SCHOOL INTERNATIONAL & COMPARATIVE LAW JOURNAL 306 (1999).

13.  Jones, Glower W. et al., *Leveling the Playing Field: Public Procurement in Europe*, 24 INTERNATIONAL BUSINESS LAWYER 298-326 (July/August 1996).

14.  Arrowsmith, Sue, *Towards a Multilateral Agreement on Transparency in Government Procurement*, 47 INTERNATIONAL AND COMPARATIVE LAW QUARTERLY 793 (October 1998).

15. Arrowsmith, Sue, *Towards an Agreement on Transparency in Government Procurement*, 9 PROGRAM FOR THE STUDY OF INTERNATIONAL ORGANIZATION(S) WTO SERIES 7 (1998).

16. Lees, Frederick J., *Transnational Norms of Government Procurement* (26 October, 2001) (unpublished manuscript).

17. Rege, Vinod, *Transparency in Government Procurement — Issues of Concern and Interest to Developing Countries*, 35 JOURNAL OF WORLD TRADE 489 (August 2001).

## GPT

General Preferential Tariff, which is the Canadian Generalized System of Preferences (GSP) scheme, and which Canada initiated on 1 July 1974. In 2004, Canada renewed the GPT for 10 years.

The GPT covers 185 countries and customs territories, whereas the United States GSP scheme covers 143 countries (as of January 2008). Unlike the American GSP, the Canadian GPT has no graduation requirement. Of the 185 countries to which the GPT is available, 49 are least developed countries. Burma is not eligible, nor is a country when it joins the European Union (EU).

The GPT offers duty-free or reduced tariffs on eligible merchandise. Except for one narrow category of items, the GPT accords duty-free treatment to all merchandise from least developed countries. The exception is known as "Supply Management Items," which are dairy, eggs, and poultry. Notably, textiles, clothing, and footwear (TCF) from least developed countries enter Canada duty-free.

Among the notable features of the GPT is a generous *de minimis* threshold (tolerance level) for non-originating imports. In addition, the GPT relaxes rules of origin for least developed countries. For them, up to 60 percent of the content of a product may consist of such imports. For developing countries, the figure is 40 percent.

## GRAY MARKET GOODS (GREY MARKET GOODS)

A gray market good is a foreign-manufactured good, bearing a valid United States trademark that is imported without the consent of the United States trademark holder. Section 526 of the *Tariff Act of 1930*, as amended, 19 U.S.C. § 1526, bars importation of certain (but not all) gray market goods.

In *K Mart Corporation v. Cartier, Inc.*, 486 U.S. 281 (1988), the United States Supreme Court considered federal regulations permitting the importation of gray market goods based on "common control" (*i.e.*, where a foreign and United States trademark are owned by the same person, or are under common control), or "authorized use" (*i.e.*, where the articles made overseas bear a recorded trademark under authorization from the American owner). The majority decision identified three general contexts in which gray market goods arise.

In Case 1, a domestic firm purchases from an independent foreign firm the rights to register and use the foreign firm's trademark as a United States trademark and to sell its foreign-manufactured products here. These rights are very valuable if the foreign firm already has registered the trademark in the United States, or if the product has already earned a reputation for quality, the right to use that trademark can be very valuable. Suppose the foreign manufacturer could import the trademarked goods and distribute them here, despite having sold the trademark to a domestic firm. Then, the domestic firm would be forced into sharp intra-brand competition involving the very trademark it purchased. Likewise, intra-brand competition could arise if the foreign manufacturer markets its good outside the United States, and a third party that purchases the good abroad could legally import it. The parallel importation, if permitted, would create a gray market that would jeopardize the trademark holder's investment.

In Case 2, a domestic firm registers the United States trademark for goods that are manufactured abroad by an affiliated manufacturer. For example, a foreign firm might seek to control distribution of its good in the United States by incorporating a subsidiary here. Thus, the subsidiary would register under its own name a United States trademark that is identical to its parent's foreign trademark. Any parallel importation by a third party that buys the good abroad (or even by the affiliated foreign manufacturer itself) would create a gray market. As another example, an American-based firm might establish abroad a manufacturing subsidiary corporation. Or, it might own an unincorporated manufacturing division. In either instance, the overseas facility would produce the goods bearing a United States trademark, and then import them for domestic distribution. If the trademark holder or its foreign subsidiary sells the trademarked goods abroad, the parallel importation of the goods competes on the gray market with the holder's domestic sales.

In Case 3, the domestic holder of a United States trademark authorizes an independent foreign manufacturer to use it. Typically, the holder sells to the foreign manufacturer an exclusive right to use the trademark in a particular foreign location, but conditions the right on the foreign manufacturer's promise not to import its trademarked goods into the United States. Here too, if the foreign manufacturer or a third party imports into the United States, the foreign-manufactured goods will compete on the gray market with the holder's domestic goods.

*Suggestions for Further Research:*

Articles:

1.  Bird, Robert C. & Peggy E. Chaudhry, *Pharmaceuticals and the European Union: Managing Gray Markets in an Uncertain Legal Environment*, 50 VIRGINIA JOURNAL OF INTERNATIONAL LAW 719-756 (2010).

2.  Buckley, Marianne, Comment, *Looking Inward: Regional Parallel Trade as a Means of Bringing Affordable Drugs to Africa*, 412 SETON HALL LAW REVIEW 625-669 (2011).

3.  Chow, Daniel, *Exhaustion of Trademarks and Parallel Imports in China*, 51 SANTA CLARA LAW REVIEW 1283-1309 (2011).

4.   Conley, Christopher B., Comment, *Parallel Imports: The Tiered Debate of the Exhaustion of Intellectual Property Rights and Why the WTO Should Harmonize the Haphazard Laws of the International Community*, 16 TULSA JOURNAL OF INTERNATIONAL & COMPARATIVE LAW 189-211 (2007).

5.   Conroy, Amy E., Note, *The Gray (Goods) Elephant in the Room: China's Troubling Attitude Toward IP Protection of Gray Market Goods*, 36 BROOKLYN JOURNAL OF INTERNATIONAL LAW 1075-1109 (2011).

6.   Grant, Joseph Karl, *The Graying of the American Manufacturing Economy: Gray Markets, Parallel Importation, and a Tort Law Approach*, 88 OREGON LAW REVIEW 1139-1187 (2009).

7.   Jaconiah, Jacob, *The Parallel Importation of Trademarked Goods in the Framework of the Economic Partnership Agreement between the East African Community and the European Union*, 42 IIC: INTERNATIONAL REVIEW OF INTELLECTUAL PROPERTY & COMPETITION LAW 673-697 (2011).

## GREEN BOX (GREEN BOX EXEMPTIONS)

Agricultural support that has little trade-distorting effect, *i.e.*, that does not affect the pattern of imports and exports, or does so only minimally, and that does not have the effect of providing price support to producers, is classified as "Green Box" subsidies.

Under the Uruguay Round *Agreement on Agriculture*, government support measures that satisfy criteria designed to ensure support is no worse than minimally trade-distorting are exempt from domestic reduction commitments, because of their non- or minimally-distorting effect on trade. That is, payments that qualify for the Green Box are exempt from reduction commitments. Such measures are known as "Green Box exemptions," and are set forth in Annex 2 of the *Agreement*. These measures not linked to market variables such as prices, production, factors used in production, or exports.

Specific Green Box program examples include agricultural research (*e.g.*, into conservation and ethanol fuels), certain types of direct payments to farmers (namely, support de-coupled from the amount or type of crop grown), disease control, domestic food aid (*e.g.*, the United States Food Stamp program, child nutrition programs, and purchases of fruits and vegetables for school lunches), environmental protection, income insurance, infrastructure support, natural disaster relief, regional assistance, restructuring aid, and certain other safety-net programs. All such subsidies are considered to have no effect on trade, or at worst a minimally distorting effect on the value, volume, and pattern of imports and exports.

During the 2002-2005 Marketing Years (MYs), Green Box expenditures by the United States rose steadily from $58.3 billion in 2002 to $71.8 billion in 2005.[414]

---

[414] *See* Daniel Pruzin, *U.S. Notifies Farm Support for 2002-2005; Official Confirms Support for Falconer Figure*, 24 International Trade Reporter (BNA) 1417-1418 (11 October 2007).

The key cause of the increase was a boost in spending on nutrition schemes, specifically, child nutrition, and food stamp programs. A relatively small amount of American Green Box expenditures –$5.3 billion on average annually — went to direct payment programs.

*Suggestions for Further Research:*

Books:

1.   ANDERSON, KYM & TIM JOSLING EDS., THE WTO AND AGRICULTURE vols. I and II (2005).

2.   CARDWELL, MICHAEL N., MARGARET R. GROSSMAN & CHRISTOPHER P. RODGERS, AGRICULTURE AND INTERNATIONAL TRADE — LAW, POLICY, AND THE WTO 85-164 (2003).

3.   DESTA, MELAKU GEBOYE, THE LAW OF INTERNATIONAL TRADE IN AGRICULTURAL PRODUCTS — FROM GATT 1947 TO THE WTO AGREEMENT ON AGRICULTURE (2002).

4.   MCMAHON, JOSEPH, THE WTO AGREEMENT ON AGRICULTURE — A COMMENTARY (2006).

Other Source:

1.   Ingco, Merlinda & L. Alan Winters eds., *Agriculture Trade Liberaliztion in a New Trade Round — Perspectives of Developing Countries and Transition Economies* (World Bank Discussion Paper Number 418, 2000).

## GREEN PROTECTIONISM

The use of tariff and non-tariff barriers to support environmental objectives.

One such objective is to offset the costs of compliance with domestic carbon reduction rules applicable to industries in an importing country by imposing a border tax adjustment (BTA) on merchandise from foreign countries that do not have the same or similar rules.

## GREEN REVOLUTION

An agricultural movement in the 1950s, 1960s, and 1970s focusing on the development and implementation of agricultural technology to boost productivity in the farm sector. The Ford and Rockefeller Foundations funded the research for the movement, and Dr. Norman Earnest Borlaug conducted the critical research.

The term "Green Revolution" was first used in 1968 by the Director of the United States Agency for International Development (U.S. AID), to connote changes brought about by the increased agricultural productivity and consequent declines in hunger. Dr. Borlaug, who was born in Iowa on 25 March 1914, is the figure most closely associated with the Green Revolution. Indeed, his unofficial moniker is "Father of the Green Revolution." In 1970, he won the Nobel Peace Prize for his work on corn and wheat varieties.

Simply put, Dr. Borlaug's research catalyzed the Green Revolution. Applying Green Revolution technologies, agricultural productivity in India and Mexico increased markedly in the 1950s and 1960s. The Indian Punjab, for instance, became an efficient, high-volume producer of wheat, in part through planting, fertilizing, and harvesting appropriate wheat varieties, and using tractors. Consequently, India, Mexico, and many other poor countries were able to feed better their populations, and rescue large numbers of their people from chronic hunger.

## GREEN ROOM

Physically, the term refers to a large room across from the Office of the Director-General of the WTO in the WTO Secretariat in Geneva. Traditionally, the room bore that color.

The "Green Room," as a process connotes informal consultations and negotiations, under the auspices of the Director-General, held in that Room, among a small subset of WTO Members. The Green Room process is designed to seek consensus among the subset on an issue, and then present the outcome to the broader Membership. The process originating under GATT, and was criticized for favoring major developed countries such as the United States and European Union (EU), and excluding developing and least developed countries. However, the process became legitimized under WTO Director-Generals Supachai Panitchpakdi and Pascal Lamy, who enlarged participation by inviting more countries into the Room.

## GRI

The General Rules of Interpretation for the Harmonized Tariff System (HTS).

## GROSS NATIONAL HAPPINESS

A concept developed by the King of Bhutan, Jigme Wangchuck. The concept is a compliment, if not alternative, to traditional economic indicators such as Gross National Product (GNP). Gross National Happiness is a way to evaluate the desire of the Bhutanese people to eke out a place for their tiny country in a globalized world, but also maintain their heritage and tradition as a Buddhist Kingdom.

Following the forcible annexation of Tibet by China on 28 March 1959, and the assimilation of Sikkim into India, formally concluded on 16 May 1975, Bhutan is the last Buddhist Kingdom in the world. (Both dates concluded processes that began in the 1950s.) There are 635,000 people in Bhutan, 80,000 of whom live in the capital, Thimphu, which boasts it is the only capital city with no traffic lights.

## GROUP OF THREE TRADE PACT

A trade agreement between Mexico, Colombia, and Venezuela.

In May 2006, President Hugo Chavez of Venezuela announced his country was pulling out of the Pact.

## GSP

The Generalized System of Preferences.

A scheme by which one country (namely, developed one) accords duty-free, reduced-tariff, and/or quota-free treatment to merchandise imported from and originating in another country (usually, a developing or least developed one). The grant of preferential treatment is unilateral, and the preferences take the form of eliminating, or significantly reducing, import duties below the otherwise applicable rates — typically, the MFN rates.

Such a scheme plainly violates the MFN obligation in GATT Article I:1. However, in Paragraph 1 of the 1979 *Enabling Clause*, the GATT CONTRACTING PARTIES agreed to a permanent waiver for such schemes. Most developed countries — Australia, Canada, European Union (EU), Japan, and the United States — operate GSP schemes.[415]

GSP schemes tend to be criticized on seven grounds:

- The criteria to qualify as a beneficiary country for GSP treatment are too onerous, and sometimes politically-driven

- The criteria for a specific class of merchandise to qualify for eligibility for preferential treatment are too onerous.

- Restrictions on designating beneficiary countries (such as graduation requirements), and eligible merchandise (such as exemptions from preferential treatment, or competitive need limitations) are imposed to protect domestic industries in the importing developing country that produce a like or directly competitive product.

- Preferences are an asset the value of which is diminishing, because the margin of preference is reduced with multilateral reductions in tariff barriers, and/or with reductions in those barriers through free trade agreements (FTAs). That is, as MFN rates fall, the difference between duty-free (or reduced duty) treatment and the MFN rate also falls. To be sure, the extent to which this phenomenon occurs, and affects products of keen export interest to poor countries, depends on the product and country at issue.

- Rules of origin can be complicated, in both theory and administration, and the cost of compliance swallows all or most of the benefit from any preference realized.

- Preferential schemes typically are subject to legislative renewal, and the timing and outcome of this renewal is uncertain.

---

[415] The Canadian scheme, the Generalized Preferential Tariff, is discussed in the GPT entry

- Preferential schemes are insufficiently nuanced, giving benefits on the basis of large categories of poor countries, when in fact the levels of economic development of the countries in the beneficiary category is heterogeneous. What is more helpful to poor countries is a targeted preferential arrangement, *i.e.*, one focused on key products that are of interest to those countries, including textiles, clothing, and footwear (TCF).

- The beneficiaries of preferential schemes are, or include, multinational corporations (MNCs) that use GSP beneficiary countries as platforms in which to manufacture eligible articles, and from which they export this merchandise. These companies may have little long-term interest in the development of the beneficiary country, instead focusing on the contribution to profit margins made by GSP treatment. If that treatment is altered or lost, the companies may shift their platforms to other countries.

- Preferential schemes complicate multilateral trade negotiations, such as the Doha Round, because GSP beneficiary countries resist efforts to make deep cuts on tariffs on manufactured items, in the context of non-agricultural market access (NAMA) discussions. Those countries are concerned about the erosion of tariff preferences, if NAMA rates fall, and about competition from China.

The United States GSP program originated in 1974 with *Trade Act* of that year. It is still sponsors the scheme, though it is vulnerable to all of the above criticisms. The Table below summarizes renewals and amendments by the United States of its GSP scheme.

Of consternation to American importers of GSP-eligible products, and to their producer-exporters in poor countries, is episodic uncertainty about renewal. For example, in the *Omnibus Trade Act of 2010* (H.R. 6517), which is distinct from a *Miscellaneous Tariff Bill* (*MTB*), Congress deliberately excluded GSP renewal, while extending for six weeks the *Andean Trade Preference Act* (*ATPA*), which grants duty-free treatment to certain merchandise from Colombia and Ecuador, and also for six weeks, *Trade Adjustment Assistance* (*TAA*), which offers workers dislocated by trade compensation, training, and health care benefits. The reasons for this failure include local political interests and posturing dwarfing broader national interests. Senator Jeff Sessions (Republican–Alabama) complained that GSP treatment should not be given to sleeping bags from Bangladesh.

The Alabama Republican triggered a raging debate over whether to designate non-down sleeping bags as an import-sensitive article and, therefore, ineligible for GSP treatment.[416] Following the 1989 fall of the Berlin Wall, in 1992, to help the textile industry of the former Czechoslovakia, sleeping bags, the U.S. designated sleeping bags as not being import sensitive. So, they

---

[416] *See* Len Bracken, *Sleeping Bags No Longer GSP Eligible; No Change to AGOA in Preference Reviews*, 29 International Trade Reporter (BNA) 9 (5 January 2012).

became eligible for duty free treatment, though ironically, Czechoslovakia never manufactured them. Subsequently, one of the world's poorest countries, Bangladesh, began exporting this product to the U.S. Because of GSP treatment, Bangladeshi sleeping bags were not subject to the U.S. MFN duty rate of 9 percent.

In 2010, when the GSP program required yet another Congressional renewal, Senator Jeff Sessions (Republican-Alabama) vigorously opposed such action unless President Barack H. Obama agreed to designate non-down sleeping bags as import sensitive, and thereby remove them from GSP eligibility. Why? Because in Alabama was a sleeping bag manufacturer that purportedly prospered once the GSP scheme lapsed and its Bangladeshi competitors had to pay a nine percent tariff. The Senator responded that those competitors were not Bangladeshi, but Chinese. That is, a Chinese company established manufacturing and export operations in Bangladesh to avoid the 9 percent rate.

To secure renewal of not only the GSP program, but also of *Trade Adjustment Assistance (TAA)*, and to obtain passage of implementing legislation for free trade agreements (FTAs) with Colombia, Korea, and Panama, President Obama did as Senator Sessions asked. To critics, the President appeased the Senator, setting an adverse precedent that could prompt other legislators to hold hostage trade bills unless their protectionist demands were met. The legal reality is GSP eligibility depends on the country of origin of merchandise, based on rules of origin. It does not depend on the country of origin of the owners of the production and export facilities located overseas in a BDC. Hence, the fact the owners of the sleeping bag facility in Bangladesh are Chinese (or American, or of any other nationality) is irrelevant; what matters is the value added to the product in Bangladesh.

In cases such as sleeping bags, the concerns of American importers are disfavored relative to domestic producer constituencies. Those importers include many small and medium-sized enterprises (SMEs), which rely on tariff-free treatment for GSP-eligible merchandise, which they use as inputs into finished goods. Failure to renew GSP, or postponement in such renewal, raises the cost of GSP-eligible merchandise to consumers of that merchandise. Those consumers are not only individual retails customers, but also businesses. Perhaps worse yet, the relative deprivation suffered by producer-exporters in monstrously poor countries like Bangladesh is ignored. In turn, the efforts of poor countries to grow economically and alleviate poverty are undermined.[417]

As of November 2011, under the American GSP program, there are 129 beneficiary developing countries (BDCs). Overall, up to 4,800 products are eligible for duty-free treatment under the program. Specifically, BDCs may export roughly 3,400 types of products to the United States and obtain duty-free treatment. Additionally, the United States designates 44 BDCs

---

[417] *See* Len Bracken & Rossella Brevetti, *House, Senate Pass Trade Agreements with South Korea, Colombia, Panama*, 28 International Trade Reporter (BNA) 1653 (13 October 2011).

as "least developed." These countries can export a further 1,400 products that are eligible for duty-free treatment.

Similarly, the EU program, which originated in 1971, suffers from some of these faults, notwithstanding the EU Everything But Arms (EBA) scheme. The basic, broad EU GSP scheme gives tariff preferences — zero or reduced duties — on 7,000 dutiable tariff lines, which is a larger number than that for the American scheme. The EBA provides duty-free treatment to all imports from least developed countries, except for arms and munitions, and also except for sugar and rice. However, in 2009, sugar and rice will be accorded duty-free treatment.

Notably, the broader GSP scheme is reviewed periodically by the EU, but the EBA is a permanent grant of preferential treatment. The EU GSP scheme has an escape clause. The EU can invoke it in the interests of a domestic industry to suspend temporarily a preference.

Interestingly, under the EU GSP scheme, a beneficiary developing country may obtain additional preferences — beyond those ordinarily available under the scheme — if they adhere to core labor standards of the International Labor Organization (ILO). That is also true in respect of a narrow category of environmental practices, namely, adherence to the International Tropical Timber Convention. The benefits cover tropical timber products.

Japan, too, commenced its GSP scheme in 1971. Its current iteration of the scheme (as of January 2008) lasts through March 2011. Japan gives preferences to 141 developing countries and 14 customs territories. The preferences cover 3,500 tariff lines. They take one of two forms: duty-free treatment, or tariff reductions down to a "ceiling." In the latter instance, Japan grants eligible imports preferential treatment on a first-come, first-serve basis, with a limit that it adjusts annually. Like the EU, Japan also has an escape clause in its scheme. Japan offers duty-free treatment to least developed countries. The list of eligible merchandise is wider than that for regular GSP treatment.

Like the American GSP scheme, Japan's program has product and country graduation provisions. Depending on the competitiveness of a product, and the developmental stage of a country, preferential treatment can be lost — graduated from, as it were. The product competitiveness criteria are imports exceeding 50 percent of total imports and 1 billion yen for two straight years. The developmental stage variables are the high-income criteria set by the World Bank. Also like the American scheme, Japan allows for cumulative treatment under its GSP rules of origin, albeit only for an approved multi-country trade arrangement. Japan has approved the arrangement involving Indonesia, Malaysia, Philippines, Thailand, and Vietnam.

It may be New Zealand offers the best illustration of generosity through a GSP-type scheme. New Zealand's scheme started in 1972, and it has revised the scheme on several occasions since that year. For all developing countries, all merchandise except textiles, clothing, and footwear (TCF), and glass and ceramics, get an 80 percent tariff preference (or, on some articles, more), or duty-free treatment. With rare exceptions (involving the aforementioned articles), all merchandise from all least developed countries get duty-free treatment in New Zealand. There are no product-specific graduation requirements, though New Zealand graduates a beneficiary country once its Gross National Product (GNP) exceeds 70 percent of the New Zealand GNP.

GSP schemes in many countries have undergone recent, or are undergoing presently, significant overhauls, partly to address the above criticisms of them. Notably, under the *Enabling Clause*, any country — rich or poor — can create preferential schemes under the Enabling Clause. Poor countries have been faulted for not doing so. Often, poor countries themselves impose the highest tariff barriers to products originating in poor countries.

TABLE:

GSP RENEWALS AND AMENDMENTS

| *Statute* | *Effective or Approval Date* | *Sunset (Expiry) Date for GSP Program* | *Period (ending on Sunset Date)* | *Amendments?* |
|---|---|---|---|---|
| *Trade Act of 1974* (Title V) | Effective and approved 3 January 1975, with implementation occurred on 1 January 1976 | 3 January 1985 | 10 years | Not applicable. Minor amendments in *Tax Reform Act of 1976* (Section 1802) (approved 4 October 1976) and *Trade Agreements Act of 1979* (Section 1111) (approved 26 July 1979). |
| *Trade and Tariff Act of 1984* (Title V) | Approved 30 October 1984 | 4 July 1993 | 8 ½ years | Significant amendments (effective 4 January 1985) to criteria for designating beneficiary developing countries and limiting duty-free treatment. |
| *Omnibus Budget Reconciliation Act of 1993* (Section 13802) | Approved 10 August 1993 | 30 September 1994 | 15 months | None. |
| *Uruguay Round Agreements Act of 1994* (Section 601) | Approved 8 December 1994 | 31 July 1995 | 10 months | None. |

TABLE (continued)

| Statute | Effective or Approval Date | Sunset (Expiry) Date for GSP Program | Period (ending on Sunset Date) | Amendments? |
|---|---|---|---|---|
| *Small Business Jobs Protection Act of 1996* (Title I, Subtitle J) | Approved 20 August 1996 | 31 May 1997 | 1 year and 10 months | Amendments (effective 1 October 1996) plus revisions and reorganizations to the GSP statute, and a technical correction under the *Miscellaneous Trade and Technical Corrections Act of 1996* (approved 11 October 1996). |
| *Omnibus Appropriations Bill for Fiscal Year 1999* (Section 1011) | 21 October 1998 Public Law 105-277 | 30 June 1999 | Approximately 8 months | None. |
| *Ticket to Work and Work Incentives Improvement Act of 1999* (Section 508) | 17 December 1999 Public Law 106-170 | 30 September 2001 | Approximately 1 year, 9 months | None. |
| *African Growth and Opportunity Act (AGOA I)* | 18 May 2000 | 30 September 2008 (for eligible Sub-Saharan African countries) | Approximately 8 years, 4 months | Extension of regular and enhanced GSP benefits for eligible Sub-Saharan African countries. |
| *Trade Act of 2002* (Section 4101(a)) | 6 August 2002 Public Law Number 107-210 | 31 December 2006 (*See* 19 U.S.C. Section 2465, on date of termination.) | Approximately 4 years, 4 months | Amendments to (1) eligibility criteria to prohibit beneficiary designation to a country that does not support the United States to combat and (2) definition of worker rights to include worst forms of child labor. |

**TABLE (continued)**

| Statute | Effective or Approval Date | Sunset (Expiry) Date for GSP Program | Period (ending on Sunset Date) | Amendments? |
|---|---|---|---|---|
| *Tax Relief and Health Care Act of 2006* | 20 December 2006<br><br>Public Law Number 109-432 | 31 December 2008 (except for countries included in *AGOA*) | 2 years | Also provides Permanent Normal Trade Relations (PNTR) for Vietnam, extends the *African Growth and Opportunity Act* (*AGOA*) through 30 September 2015 and continues the *AGOA* third country fabric provision through 30 September 2012, modifies the Harmonized Tariff Schedule (HTS) (especially Chapter 99), creates a special program for Haiti under the Caribbean Basin Initiative (CBI), called the *Haitian Hemispheric Opportunity through Partnership Encouragement Act* (*HOPE Act*), and extends the *Andean Trade Preference Agreement* (*ATPA*) through 30 June 2007 (or 31 December 2007 if an *ATPA* country signs an FTA with the United States). |
| *Extension of Andean Trade Preference Act*<br><br>(Section 4, codified at 19 U.S.C. § 2465) | 16 October 2008<br>H.R. 7222,<br><br>Public Law Number 110-436, 122 Stat. 4976 (2008) | 31 December 2009 | 1 year | Also renews *Andean Trade Preference Act* (*ATPA*) and *Andean Trade Promotion and Drug Eradication Act* (*ATPDEA*), through December 31, 2009 for Colombia and Peru (given the free trade agreements (FTAs) |

TABLE (continued)

| Statute | Effective or Approval Date | Sunset (Expiry) Date for GSP Program | Period (ending on Sunset Date) | Amendments? |
|---------|---------|---------|---------|---------|
| | | | | negotiated with those countries), and through June 30, 2009 for Bolivia and Ecuador. Also renews certain textile and apparel (T&A) provisions of the *African Growth and Opportunity Act* (*AGOA*), refines the definition of "lesser developed beneficiary sub-Saharan African country," and makes technical corrections to *AGOA*, and amends the *Central American Free Trade Agreement* (*CAFTA — DR*) by establishing an earned import allowance program for T&A articles. |
| *To Extend the Generalized System of Preferences and the Andean Trade Preferences Act, and For Other Purposes* | H.R. 4284, Public Law Number 111-124, 123 Stat. 3484 (2009), codified at 19 U.S.C. §§ 58c, 2465, 3203, 3206, 6655. Signed by President Barack H. Obama on 28 December 2009. | 31 December 2010 | 1 year | Also extends the *Andean Trade Preferences Act* (*ATPA*) for same period. Eschews broad reform of GSP or *ATPA* schemes. Requires the USTR to report to Congress by 30 June 2010 on compliance by *ATPA* beneficiaries with eligibility criteria, including with respect to Ecuador and its respect for the rule of law. |

TABLE (continued)

| Statute | Effective or Approval Date | Sunset (Expiry) Date for GSP Program | Period (ending on Sunset Date) | Amendments? |
|---|---|---|---|---|
| The Trade Adjustment Assistance Extension Act of 2011 | H.R. 2832, Public Law Number 112-40. Enacted by Congress 12 October 2011, signed by President Barack H. Obama on 21 October 2011. | 31 July 2013 | 2 ½ years | The Omnibus Trade Act of 2010 failed to renew the GSP. Hence, the GSP expired on 31 December 2010. The 2011 legislation, which also renewed the Trade Adjustment Assistance (TAA) scheme, renewed the GSP program retroactively to 1 January 2011. |

*Suggestions for Further Research:*

Book:

1.   COTTIER, THOMAS, ET AL., HUMAN RIGHTS AND INTERNATIONAL TRADE (Oxford University Press, 2005) (containing several chapters on the GSP and conditionality).

Articles:

1.   Bartels, Lorand, *The Trade and Development Policy of the European Union*, 18 EUROPEAN JOURNAL OF INTERNATIONAL LAW 715-756 (2007).

2.   Bartels, Lorand, *The WTO Legality of the EU's GSP+ Arrangement*, 10 JOURNAL OF INTERNATIONAL ECONOMIC LAW number 4 869-886 (October 2007).

3.   Chaisse, Julien, Debashis Chakraborty & Biswajit Nag, *The Three-Pronged Strategy of India's Preferential Trade Policy: A Contribution to the Study of Modern Economic Treaties*, 26 CONNECTICUT JOURNAL OF INTERNATIONAL LAW 415-455 (2011).

4.   Franklin, Aaron, Note, *Targeted Tariff Preferences to Reduce Corruption in Developing States*, 41 GEORGETOWN JOURNAL OF INTERNATIONAL LAW 1011-1041 (2010).

5.   Grossman, Gene & Alan Sykes, *A Preference for Development: The Law and Economics of GSP*, 4 WORLD TRADE REVIEW 41 (2005).

6.   Huhs, John, *Trade Preferences for Developing Countries: Options for Ordering International Economic and Political Relations*, 20 STANFORD LAW REVIEW 1150-75 (1968).

7. Kishore, Dr. Pallavi, *Conditionalities in the Generalized System of Preferences as Instruments of Global Economic Governance*, 45 THE INTERNATIONAL LAWYER 895-902 (fall 2011).

8. Lawrence, Veronica M., Note, *An Entrepreneur's Best Friend: The U.S. GSP Program and Its Positive Impact on Small Business*, 2 ENTREPRENEURIAL BUSINESS LAW JOURNAL 593-614 (2007).

9. Patel, Monica, Note, *Expanding the Role of Trade Preference Programs*, 95 MINNESOTA LAW REVIEW 1490-1523 (2011).

10. Switzer, Stephanie, *Environmental Protection and the Generalized System of PSuggestions for Further Research: A Legal and Appropriate Linkage?*, 57 INTERNATIONAL & COMPARATIVE LAW QUARTERLY 113-147 (2008).

11. Tuzin, Alexander H., *Vietnam's Eligibility to Receive Trade Benefits Under the U.S. Generalized System of Preferences*, 7 LOYOLA UNIVERSITY CHICAGO INTERNATIONAL LAW REVIEW 193-212 (2010).

Other Source:

1. Huenemann, Jon E., *Tariff Preferences for Developing Countries: The Industrialized Country Debate and the Implications*, Miller & Chevalier, 2 FOCUS ON TRADE POLICY issue 1 (16 January 2008).

# GSTP

Global System of Trade Preferences, or Global System of Trade Preferences Among Developing Nations.

An agreement under the auspices of United Nations Conference on Trade and Development (UNCTAD) to stimulate South-South trade, *i.e.*, trade among developing and least developed countries.[418] Over 40 countries are signatories to the GSTP accord, including:

| | |
|---|---|
| • Bangladesh | • Mexico |
| • Chile | • Nigeria |
| • China | • North Korea |
| • Egypt | • Pakistan |
| • India | • South Africa |
| • Indonesia | • South Korea |
| • Iran | • Thailand |
| • Malaysia | • Vietnam |

• *MERCOSUR* bloc

(Argentina, Brazil, Paraguay, Uruguay, and Venezuela)

---

[418] *See* Daniel Pruzin, *Developing Countries Reach Framework for Future "South-South" Tariff Cutting Deal*, 23 International Trade Reporter (BNA) 1793-94 (21 December 2006).

The GSTP signatories account for 17.5 percent of total world exports ($1.8 trillion in exports as of 2005).

Starting in June 2004 in Sao Paulo, Brazil, the GSTP launched a round of tariff reduction negotiations. In recognition of the location of the launch, the negotiations are known as the "Sao Paulo Round." However, notable non-participants in the round included China and South Africa. Negotiations were scheduled to conclude by the end of 2007. South-South tariff cuts could boost trade among poor countries significantly, if the reductions are large, with few exemptions, and phased in rapidly.

For example, exports among GSTP countries (in 2005) were worth $200 billion in 2000, and $405 billion in 2005. An UNCTAD study estimates a 30 percent across-the-board tariff reduction would boost exports by $11.7 billion, and a 20 percent cut would add $7.7 billion in exports. Most importantly, over half of the export increases would result from trade diversion. That is, meaning GSTP countries would import more from each other, and less from non-GSTP competitors.

Impressively, on the sidelines of the Seventh WTO Ministerial Conference in Geneva from 30 November–2 December 2009, developing countries announced a South–South trade pact.[419] They began negotiating this pact in 2004. Twenty-two, or by some accounts 23 if North Korea is included, countries committed themselves to negotiations on this pact:

- Algeria
- Chile
- Cuba
- Egypt
- India
- Indonesia
- Iran
- Korea (North)
- Korea (South)
- Malaysia

- *MERCOSUR* bloc
- Mexico
- Morocco
- Nigeria
- Pakistan
- Sri Lanka
- Thailand
- Vietnam
- Zimbabwe

(Argentina, Brazil, Paraguay, Uruguay, and Venezuela)

The 22 countries (excluding North Korea) account for 2.6 billion people, 15-18 percent of global trade, nearly 50 percent of all trade among developing countries, 43 percent of global agricultural production, and 16 percent of

---

[419] *See* Daniel Pruzin, *South-South Pact Hits Resistance, Core Group to Proceed with Interim Deal*, 26 International Trade Reporter (BNA) 1602 (26 November 2009); Daniel Pruzin, *Developing Country Trade Initiatives Set to Take Center Stage at WTO Ministerial*, 26 International Trade Reporter (BNA) 1567 (19 November 2009).

global industrial production.[420] They are diverse in their tariff profiles. The simple average tariffs of these countries ranges from six percent (in Chile) to 26.2 percent (Iran). The highest average agricultural tariff is 66.4 percent (in Egypt), and the highest average industrial tariff is 25.8 percent (Iran).

However, not all of these countries participated with equal vigor. North Korea never attended a negotiation meeting, and Algeria and Iran surely were limited in their ability to negotiate by virtue of the fact neither is a WTO Member. Some major developing countries — namely, China and South Africa — declined even to commit to the talks.

Under the pact, countries agreed to make linear (*i.e.*, across-the-board), line-by-line cuts of between 20 and 30 percent on applied tariffs for all agricultural and industrial goods. Moreover, they agreed at least 70 percent of their tariff lines must be subject to these linear cuts. The countries submitted draft schedules by 31 May 2010, and then took four months to review and verify them. Negotiations — that is, consultations and requests-and-offers — continued through 30 September 2010 to achieve steeper tariff cuts on merchandise of keen export interest. Final schedules were due on that date, and they became an integral part of the Final Agreement of the Sao Paolo Round. To account for their lack of Membership in the WTO, special terms were arranged for Algeria and Iran.

By November 2009, just before the WTO Ministerial Conference, it became clear not all of the 22-23 participating countries were prepared to join the pact. Accordingly, the pact was joined by only a core group of countries, namely India, the members of *MERCOSUR*, several of the members of the *Association of South East Asian Nations (ASEAN)*, and a few African countries. Yet, 20 countries did sign onto the modalities agreement:[421]

- Algeria
- Chile
- Egypt
- India
- Indonesia
- Iran
- Korea (North)
- Korea (South)
- Malaysi

- *MERCOSUR* bloc Cuba
  (Argentina, Brazil, Paraguay, and Uruguay)
- Nigeria
- Pakistan
- Sri Lanka
- Thailand
- Vietnam
- Zimbabwe

---

[420] *See* Frances Williams, *Poorer Nations Sign Deal on Trade Tariff Cuts*, FINANCIAL TIMES, 3 December 2009, at 6; Daniel Pruzin, *Developing Country Ministers Hail "South–South" Trade Breakthrough*, 26 International Trade Reporter (BNA) 1642 (3 December 2009). The figures are as of year-end 2008.

[421] *See* Daniel Pruzin, *Morocco Joins Mexico in Shying Away from "South–South" Trade Agreement*, 26 International Trade Reporter (BNA) 1694 (10 December 2009).

The modalities agreement was supposed to lead to a final deal, so the fact that 20 of the 22 negotiating countries signed on to it suggested they were optimistic about a final outcome.

To be sure, critics pointed out that exceptions to the agreed-upon tariff cuts, *i.e.*, up to 30 percent of tariff lines, meant some countries could exempt entire product headings, such as automobiles or textiles and apparel (T&A).[422] Critics also pointed out the pact lacked a dispute settlement mechanism, and thus was unenforceable, and failed to deal with non-tariff barriers such as customs clearance hassles and technical standards. Thus, Mexico (which as of December 2009 was reducing unilaterally its average industrial tariff from 10.6 to 4.2 percent by 2012) said it would not join, as the cuts called for by the pact were too small. Morocco, too, declined to join. Likewise, Chile found the cuts unambitious, and indicated it might not join. Thailand was unclear as to whether it would join.

In December 2010, 11 nations confirmed their participation in the pact, and solidified the arrangements for cutting tariffs under it. These countries were:

- Argentina
- Brazil
- Cuba
- Egypt
- India
- Indonesia
- Korea (South)
- Malaysia
- Morocco
- Paraguay
- Uruguay

Under the deal, these signatory countries agreed to cut their tariffs by 20 percent on 70 percent of the goods traded among them.[423] In consequence, 47,000 different products would be covered by the tariff cuts.

Nevertheless, UNCTAD, under whose auspices — not those of the WTO — the South–South pact was negotiated, contends that a linear cut of 20 percent would stimulate export revenues by $7.7 billion, and a 30 percent would yield increased export revenues of $11.7 billion. Over 50 percent of the export benefits would accrue because of trade diversion, meaning more trade among GSTP countries, and less between GSTP and non-GSTP countries. Asian GSTP countries would capture about 75 percent of the total export gains under either the 20 or 30 percent tariff cut scenario.

Without question, the fact the pact occurred through UNCTAD, not the WTO, indicates the frustration many developing countries have with the WTO and the Doha Round. The pact took only four pages and five years to complete, and thus was a stark contrast to the several hundred pages of Doha Round texts produced between 2001 and 2009. The pact may even be a harbinger of an increasingly prominent role for UNCTAD, and a marginalization of the WTO,

---

[422] *See* Daniel Pruzin, *Developing Country Ministers Hail "South–South" Trade Breakthrough*, 26 International Trade Reporter (BNA) 1642 (3 December 2009).

[423] *See* Ed Taylor, *Brazil, India and Nine Emerging Nations Sign Trade Accord Lowering Tariffs by 20 Percent*, 27 International Trade Reporter (BNA) 1951 (23 December 2010).

in respect of developing country trade interests — precisely the opposite of the conventional wisdom about the two international organizations.

*Suggestions for Further Research:*

Article:

1.   Ewelukwa, Uché U., *South — South Trade and Investment: The Good, the Bad, and the Ugly — African Perspectives*, 20 MINNESOTA JOURNAL OF INTERNATIONAL LAW 513-587 (2011).

# GTLP

Global Trade Liquidity Program.

The GTLP is a mechanism to make trade finance more available, and was established by the Group of 20 (G-20) at its April 2009 London Summit. The G-20 injected $250 billion into the GTLP in an effort to combat the effects of global economic recession, one of which was to render banks highly reluctant to extend trade finance, and thus drive up the cost of such finance. Their reluctance was due in part to the sorry state of their own balance sheets, suggesting that cleaning off toxic assets from their accounts also was critical to getting trade finance "unstuck."

The GTLP is an umbrella for export credit and investment agencies, and multilateral development banks such as the World Bank. The G-20 designated the $250 billion to be used in the two years following the establishment of the GTLP, *i.e.*, 2010 and 2011.

# H

## HAGUE CONFERENCE

The Hague Conference on Private International Law.

The purpose of this organization is to work toward the progressive unification of the rules of private international law. The Hague Conference actively develops conventions in areas of private law on a diverse array of subjects, including traditional fields like conflicts of law, evidence, and judicial assistance, and contemporary issues like inter-country adoption and child abduction.

## HARMONIZED SYSTEM (HARMONIZED COMMODITY DESCRIPTION AND CODING SYSTEM)

*See* HS.

## HARROD–DOMAR MODEL

A model of economic growth that stresses the importance of capital as a determinant of growth.

### *The Basic Model*

What are the determinants of economic growth? Put in economic terms, if growth is the dependent variable, what are the independent variables, that is, the factors that cause, or are associated with, the dependent variable? Whole courses in Departments of Economics are offered to explore these issues. As an international trade lawyer, it is easy to concentrate on the roles played by boosting exports and obtaining imports needed to make merchandise for exportation. Yet, increasing growth from a low level, which typifies underdevelopment, and increasing the rate of growth from a low percentage, requires more than just stimulating trade. Other independent variables are involved, as a simple economic production function suggests:

$$Y = f(K, L, N, T, (X - M))$$

where

| | |
|---|---|
| Y | = Income or Output |
| f | = a function of, *i.e.*, depends on |
| K | = capital |
| L | = labor |
| N | = land |
| T | = technology |
| X | = exports |
| M | = imports |
| X – M | = net exports |

This production function conveys in arithmetic terms the following concept: the level of output depends on the stock of capital, labor supply, amount of land, state of technology, and net exports. It is simple, in that it excludes other possible determinants of growth, and in that it fails to differentiate within each factor of production (*e.g.*, skilled versus unskilled labor, or arable versus non-arable land).

The production function can be converted into a dynamic one, illustrating growth in output, simply by changing each term from a static level to a change in that level. Arithmetically, "change in" is symbolized by a small triangle, $\Delta$, so a production function focusing on growth would be:

$$\frac{DY}{Y} = f\left[\frac{DK}{K}, \frac{DL}{L}, \frac{DN}{N}, \frac{DT}{T}, \frac{D(X-M)}{(X-M)}\right]$$

This production function says, in arithmetic terms, that the rate of growth of output depends on the rates of growth of capital, labor, land, technology, and net exports.

Is one independent variable particularly important in the story of growth? In a series of papers spanning from 1939 to 1948, two economists working independently of one another, Sir Roy Harrod and Evsey Domar, answered the question with essentially two words: capital accumulation. The Harrod–Domar Model posits that the most important factors in stimulating economic growth, and thus in moving a country from underdeveloped to developed status, is to invest in capital, by which they meant factories, machines, assembly lines, and so forth. In turn, capital investment depends on savings. Thus, a high savings rate creates a pool of funds available for investment. If these funds are used wisely for investment — and not pocketed by elites for purely consumptive or corrupt purposes — then growth as measured by Gross National Product (GNP) or Gross Domestic Product (GDP) will rise.

To be sure, capital may be obtained locally or from abroad, and in the latter event imports play a role in capital accumulation. Export markets may be important for output generated by accumulated capital. However, trade is not the main determinant of growth in the Harrod–Domar Model. Rather, the process of capital accumulation, through the use of unconsumed surplus for investment, is the simple focus of the Model. The higher the savings rates, the greater the potential capital investment and, therefore, the greater the possible rate of growth.

Arithmetically, the Harrod–Domar Model may be expressed on the basis of two critical concepts. The first concept, "MPS," stands for "Marginal Propensity to Save." The second concept, "ICOR," stands for "Incremental Capital—Output Ratio." As its name suggests, MPS is the proportion of any change in the income of an individual or household that is saved. For example, if income rises from $100 to $150, and of the $50 increase, $10 is saved, then MPS is 20 percent.

MPS is calculated by dividing the increased saving into the increased income. Thus, the arithmetic definition of MPS is:

$$MPS = \frac{\Delta S}{\Delta Y}$$

where "S" stands for "Saving," "Y" stands for "Output" or "Income," and the small triangle $\Delta$ is the arithmetic symbol for "change."

Thus, the variable $\Delta Y$ refers to a change in output (again, measured in terms of GNP or GDP).

Similarly, "ICOR" is the addition to the stock of capital in a country that is needed to produce an extra unit (valued, for example, in U.S. dollars) of output. The letter "K" is used to stand for "capital," and $\Delta K$ stands for increase in capital. An increase in K occurs through Net Investment, which is abbreviated with "I." That is, by definition:

$$\Delta K = I$$

because a change in the capital stock, by definition, occurs because of net investment in capital.

Therefore, the arithmetic definition of ICOR is:

$$ICOR = \frac{\Delta K}{\Delta Y} = \frac{I}{\Delta Y}$$

While the letter "Y" stands for national income, measured as GNP or GDP, there are two components of this variable. That is, to be more precise, it is useful to differentiate the demand and supply sides of a macroeconomy.

To maintain an equilibrium rate of growth in an economy, the level of total demand for goods and services, known as "Aggregate Demand," must equal the level of total supply of goods and services, known as "Aggregate Supply." Accordingly, Aggregate Demand is abbreviated Yd, and Aggregate Supply is abbreviated Ys. If Yd exceeds Ys, then inflation could result, as demand for goods and services exceed supply. Conversely, if Ys exceeds Yd, then recession (or worse, depression) could occur, as goods and services are being produced but not consumed. The preferable state is where Yd and Ys are balanced. With this greater precision, ICOR may be defined as follows:

$$ICOR = \frac{\Delta K}{\Delta Ys} = \frac{I}{\Delta Ys}$$

This definition highlights the fact ICOR is a measurement of output, relating to the supply side of a macroeconomy. Of course, if the economy is in balance, or if that issue is assumed or abstracted from, then the general $\Delta Y$ symbol may be used.

Harrod and Domar explained an equilibrium growth rate of national income, *i.e.*, growth in GNP (or GDP) from one equilibrium level to a higher level, required growth in Ys and Yd at the same pace. They theorized this balanced pace would result from Net Investment, I (or $\Delta K$, as explained below). The increased income, $\Delta Y$, resulting from one equilibrium growth rate would generate increased savings, $\Delta S$, which then could be used for investment in the capital stock. The additional capital stock, or Net Investment, I (or $\Delta K$), then would generate more income, Y, some of which could be saved and then invested — and so on. The result was an upward spiral of net investment generating increased income, saving a portion of the new income for additional capital, and the additional capital producing yet more income.

Expressed arithmetically, this positive cycle is as follows:

*Equation #1, Aggregate Demand —*

$$Yd = \frac{I}{MPS}$$

*Equation #2, Aggregate Supply —*

$$Ys = (K) \times \frac{(\Delta Y)}{(\Delta K)} = \frac{K}{ICOR}$$

(because ICOR as defined above is $\Delta K$ divided by $\Delta Y$).

The first equation explains the components of Aggregate Demand. This equation makes two points. First, higher levels of capital stock, *i.e.*, greater net investment, represented by "I," generate more income, and therefore higher Aggregate Demand (as people consume some of their additional income), Yd. Second, there is an inverse relationship between MPS and Aggregate Demand, *i.e.*, the lower the percentage of additional income that people save, the more they must be consuming that income, hence the higher the level of Aggregate Demand.

The second equation sets out the components of Aggregate Supply. It makes two points. First, there is a direct relationship between the capital stock, K, and Aggregate Supply. With a higher stock, more output can be produced. Second, there is an inverse relationship between ICOR and Aggregate Supply. A low ICOR suggests efficient use of capital. That is because a low ICOR means a small addition to capital stock generates a large increase in output. Stated equivalently, the lower the ICOR, the higher the effect on Aggregate Supply.

Perhaps the most important equation in the Harrod–Domar Model is the third equation, below. *Equation #3* is nothing more than an arithmetic re-arrangement of *Equation #2*:

*Equation #3, Rates of Growth of Output and the Capital Stock —*

It is possible to re-state Equation #2, which is

$$Ys = (K) \times \frac{(\Delta Y)}{(\Delta K)} = \frac{K}{ICOR}$$

as

$$\frac{Ys}{(\Delta Y)} = \frac{(K)}{(\Delta K)}$$

or inverting both sides of the expression,

$$\frac{\Delta Y}{Ys} = \frac{\Delta K}{K}$$

Some economists use the symbol "I," meaning "Net Investment," interchangeably with "$\Delta K$." That is because a change in the capital stock, by definition, occurs because of net investment in capital. Thus, *Equation #3* may be expressed as:

$$\frac{\Delta Y}{Ys} = \frac{I}{K}$$

The left-hand side of the expression is the rate of growth of Aggregate Supply, or in layman's terms, productive capacity. The right-hand side of the expression is the rate of growth of Net Investment. The equation expresses the powerful idea that the rate of growth of productive capacity depends on the rate of growth of additions to capital stock. Put simply, growth is a story of capital accumulation — the thesis argued by Harrod and Domar.

The Model they built also sets out conditions for macroeconomic equilibrium. As indicated earlier, for this equilibrium, Aggregate Demand and Aggregate Supply should equal one another. Hence, a fourth equation represents the condition for a static macroeconomic equilibrium:

*Equation #4, Static Macroeconomic Equilibrium* —

$$Yd = Ys$$

therefore,

$$\frac{I}{MPS} = \frac{K}{ICOR}$$

and this equivalence can be rearranged to state

$$\frac{I}{K} = \frac{MPS}{ICOR}$$

This statement is insightful. Net Investment, I, in the capital stock, K, occurs in direct proportion to the MPS, and in inverse proportion to ICOR.

In other words, here again, there are two relationships. First, there is a direct relationship between Net Investment and savings. A high the savings rate (measured by a high MPS), provides for a large pool of funds available to invest, and thereby possibly a high Net Investment level. Second, there is an inverse relationship between Net Investment and the productivity of new capital. If new capital equipment is productive (measured by a low ICOR), then a large amount of new output may be generated by that capital. With more output, it is possible to engage in more New Investment — indeed, some of that output itself may be capital equipment. In brief, *Equation #4* says that at any particular equilibrium level, the amount of Net Investment depends directly on savings (measured by a high MPS) and inversely on the productivity of capital (measured by a low ICOR).

Finally, it is possible to turn the static equilibrium into an equilibrium growth rate, *i.e.*, to convert the *Equation #4* from a static condition to a stable growth path. That conversion occurs simply by changing the static variables in *Equation #4* to growth rates, using the small triangle symbol, $\Delta$. (Observe there is no need to change MPS or ICOR to growth rates, as by definition these variables already are based on changes in underlying variables.) Thus:

*Equation #5, Stable Macroeconomic Growth Rate —*

$$\Delta Yd = \Delta Ys$$

or

$$\frac{\Delta I}{\Delta K} = \frac{MPS}{ICOR}$$

In effect, *Equation #5* defines a rate of growth in Net Investment, *i.e.*, a change in Net Investment, $\Delta I$, in terms of a change in the overall capital stock, I (or $\Delta K$). Thus, *Equation #4* may be expressed as:

$$\frac{\Delta I}{I} = \frac{MPS}{ICOR}$$

What does this equation mean? It says the rate of growth of Net Investment depends directly on the propensity to save (gauged by MPS) and inversely on the productivity of capital (gauged by ICOR).

Two final equations round out the Harrod–Domar Model. *Equation #6* expresses the rate of growth of Aggregate Supply, where $\Delta Ys$ means "change in" Aggregate Supply. *Equation #7* expresses the rate of growth of Aggregate Demand, where $\Delta Yd$ means "change in" Aggregate Supply." These equations result from converting the first two equations to growth rates. That conversion is done simply by dividing the change in Aggregate Supply or Aggregate Demand by, respectively, the level of Aggregate Supply or Aggregate Demand:

*Equation #6, Rate of Growth of Aggregate Supply —*

$$\frac{\Delta Ys}{Ys} = \frac{\dfrac{I}{ICOR}}{Ys}$$

Using the definition of Ys in *Equation #2*, this expression may be manipulated arithmetically as follows:

$$\frac{\Delta Ys}{Ys} = \frac{\dfrac{I}{ICOR}}{\dfrac{K}{ICOR}} = \frac{I}{ICOR} \times \frac{ICOR}{K}$$

$$= \frac{I}{K} = \frac{\Delta K}{K}$$

$$\frac{\Delta Ys}{Ys} = \frac{I}{K}$$

But, in a static equilibrium (*Equation #4*),

$$\frac{I}{K} = \frac{MPS}{ICOR}$$

Thus

$$\frac{\Delta Ys}{Ys} = \frac{I}{K} = \frac{MPS}{ICOR}$$

In brief, *Equation #6* expresses the rate of growth of productive capacity (the left-hand side), saying this rate depends on the rate of growth in Net Investment (the right-hand side). Net Investment, in turn, depends on savings and the productivity of capital.

It is worth pausing to reflect on *Equation #6*. It is the most famous mathematical aspect of the Harrod–Domar Model, and sometimes is expressed as

$$g = \frac{\Delta s}{\Delta k} = \frac{MPS}{ICOR}$$

where "g" stands for the growth rate of total output, $\Delta s$ is the savings rate, *i.e.*, the MPS, and $\Delta k$ is the change in the capital stock, *i.e.*, ICOR. This expression embodies the powerful idea at the heart of the Harrod–Domar Model: the rate of growth of output depends directly on the savings rate and inversely on ICOR. The higher the savings rate, the greater the output, because more funds are available for investment in productive capital. The lower ICOR, the more efficient capital is, *i.e.*, the greater the contribution an incremental unit of capital makes to output.

The final equations in the Harrod–Domar Model concern growth in aggregate demand (*Equation #7*) and equilibrium growth rates (*Equation #8*):

*Equation #7, Rate of Growth of Aggregate Demand —*

$$\frac{\Delta Yd}{Yd} = \frac{\dfrac{\Delta I}{MPS}}{Yd}$$

*Equation #7* captures the rate of growth of demand for output (the left-hand side). Using the definition of Yd in *Equation #1*, this expression may be manipulated arithmetically as follows:

$$\frac{\Delta Yd}{Yd} = \frac{\dfrac{\Delta I}{MPS}}{\dfrac{I}{MPS}} = \frac{\Delta I}{MPS} \times \frac{MPS}{I}$$

$$= \frac{\Delta I}{I}$$

Assuming there is equilibrium in the growth rates between Aggregate Demand (*Equation #6*) and Aggregate Supply (*Equation #7*), then the following a relationship would exist:

*Equation #8, Macroeconomic Equilibrium Growth Rates —*

$$\frac{\Delta Ys}{Ys} = \frac{MPS}{ICOR} = \frac{\Delta Yd}{Yd} = \frac{\Delta I}{I}$$

This relationship results from the combination of *Equations #6* and *#7*, and the assumption of equilibrium. In brief, *Equation #8* states the rate of growth of Aggregate Demand would equal the rate of growth of Aggregate Supply, and the rate would depend directly on savings and the productivity of capital.

As a simple example, suppose MPS is 20 percent, and ICOR is three. The resulting equilibrium growth rate would be 6.67 percent (the result of dividing 0.20 into three, converting the result, 0.066, into a percent, and rounding up). However, if the savings rate drops to five percent, and capital becomes less productive as indicated by an ICOR of five, then growth falls to just one percent (the result of dividing 0.05 into five, and converting the result, 0.01, into a percent). Put simply, faster growth requires more savings, higher productivity of capital investments, or both.

It also is possible to use the Model to work backwards from a desired rate of growth. Economic policy officials can select a desired or target rate of growth and then compute the necessary savings and capital — output figures to achieve that target. Once they have agreed on those figures, they can implement appropriate fiscal and monetary policies to promote the necessary savings and capital productivity. "Getting it right" is important, because of the consequences of error. If the rate of growth of output is too fast *i.e.*, in excess of growth in Aggregate Demand, then recession (or depression) will follow. But, if it is too slow, *i.e.*, slower than the growth in Aggregate Demand, then inflation will occur.

## *Critique of the Harrod–Domar Model:*

The Harrod–Domar Model has the virtue of simplicity. In consequence, its policy implications are clear. The two critical points of the Model are:

- The rate of growth of output, or Aggregate Supply, depends directly on capital accumulation and the productivity of capital. As Equations #3 and #4 indicate, growth essentially is a story dominated by capital. Savings, which derive from increased output generated by new capital, are relevant insofar as they are the funds used to finance new capital accumulation. Thus, as *Equation #6* states:

$$\frac{\Delta Y}{Ys} = \frac{I}{K} = \frac{MPS}{ICOR}$$

In brief, growth depends on the productivity of new investment and the proportion of income that is saved.

- An equilibrium rate of growth occurs when the growth rate of Aggregate Supply, $\Delta Ys$, equals the growth rate in Aggregate Demand, $\Delta Yd$. To attain a particular equilibrium rate of growth, it is necessary to establish a rate of growth of investment that depends on the savings rate and the productivity of capital. Once again, the critical relationship, Equation # 4, is:

$$\frac{\Delta I}{I} = \frac{MPS}{ICOR}$$

Here again, the effect of new capital on output and the percent of new income saved are the critical variables.

However, the virtue of the Harrod–Domar Model — simplicity — also is a vice. The Model equates growth with capital accumulation, and capital accumulation means industrialization. The policy implications are to encourage centralized planning in pursuit of target goals using a small number of variables. In reality, growth occurs in a more diffuse, decentralized manner, and there are multiple sources of growth.

In the Harrod–Domar Model, labor is not an explicit source of growth. Yet, labor obviously exists as a factor of production. In most developing and least developed countries, the size of the labor force grows over time. How can a poor country ensure full employment for its expanding workforce? The answer from the Harrod–Domar Model is to achieve a rate of growth of output and investment, based on MPS and ICOR that equals the rate of growth of the labor face.

Even with respect to capital accumulation, the Harrod–Domar Model does not differentiate among types of capital. The Model does not address whether capital investments should be dedicated to the production of more capital goods, consumer goods, or some of both. The choice can be made by a central planning commission, as India did for much of its post-August 1947 Independence Period. Or, it can be made by private sector businesses, possibly directed with incentives from the government. A related, and highly limiting, assumption of the Model is ICOR does not change with increases in capital stock, nor with different rates of growth of investment.

That is, the Harrod–Domar Model presumes ICOR is invariant over time, as all investments are the same. Or, put it in economic terms, is determined exogenously (*i.e.*, explained by factors outside of the Model). In reality, this assumption is unlikely to be true. It is surely the case investment in a powerful computer will boost output more than investment in a typewriter. In other words, in terms of their impact on output, not all capital improvements are equal. Further, as a country acquires more capital, it concomitantly may become more efficient in the use of its capital stock, hence ICOR may fall. Not surprisingly, the economists C. Rangarajan and R. Kannan demonstrated that the ICOR for India changed from 3.37 in the early 1950s to 6.56 in the late 1970s, meaning over three decades, capital became less productive. These economists also showed ICOR differs depending on the sector of the Indian economy for which it is measured — from a low of 0.48 in banking and insurance to a high of 10.33 in electricity, gas, and water utilities.

As for trade, the Harrod–Domar Model provides no explicit role. Rather, the Model implicitly assumes the economy is closed. In fact, however, even viewed from the "capital paradigm" of this Model, trade may be relevant. As regards imports, a country — especially a developing or least developed country with no manufacturing base to speak of — may have no choice but to import new capital equipment, to encourage foreign direct investment (FDI), or both. Such a country does not have the productive capacity to make machine tools. It must either buy the tools from overseas, or rely on foreign-based multinational corporations to set up production facilities in its territory. Similarly, the country may have to import raw materials, intermediate goods, or spare parts in order to manufacture capital equipment, rely on FDI, or both. With respect to exports, a country that generates more output from its additional capital may not be able to consume all it produces. Market access overseas may be the outlet for surplus production, which the country exports.

Interestingly, the need to import capital equipment (or the inputs necessary to make this equipment) creates an incentive for the country to maintain an over-valued exchange rate. That way, the value of its currency is strong against other currencies, particularly hard currencies like the U.S. dollar, Japanese yen, and euro. As the country will have to exchange its currency into hard currency to pay for capital imports, an over-valued rate will result in a larger amount of hard currency, and thus support importation. Conversely, if a country is concerned about exporting surplus production, then an under-valued exchange rate allows foreign buyers to translate their currency at a cheap rate. The result is to stimulate exports. A number of countries in Asia, including

China, Korea, Malaysia, and Taiwan, pursued this exchange-rate policy at one stage or another in their development. They did so by pegging their currency to the U.S. dollar (or a basket of currencies including the dollar), or by permitting their currency to trade within a band.

A final shortcoming of the Harrod–Domar Model is the implicit assumption of a well-functioning banking system. How are additional savings channeled into investment in capital equipment? The answer is a credit market, specifically, a banking system, into which savers deposit their funds, and from which capitalists obtain finance to build new factories and buy new equipment. However, there may be no well-developed credit market. What if savers do not trust the safety and soundness of banks, or simply are not satisfied with the returns the banks offer on their savings. They might send their funds — legally or not — outside of the country (a problem known as "capital flight," where "capital" in that context refers to financial, not physical, capital). What if capitalists find the cost of borrowing from banks too high? Not surprisingly, then, the existence of an efficient means for allocating credit, as well as the cost of credit, are important determinants of capital investment.

Given the aforementioned limitations of the Harrod–Domar Model, it should not come as a surprise there are several other notable theories of the determinants of economic growth. Economist Robert Solow won the 1987 Nobel Prize for his "Solow," or "Neo-Classical Model." That Model highlights the importance of labor as well as capital. Economist Robert Barro, among other scholars, has explored determinants well beyond capital and labor. Not to be left out, political scientists — such as Seymour Martin Lipset — have offered explanations, including the so-called "Lipset Hypothesis."

*Suggestions for Further Research:*

Book:

1. LYNN, STUART R., ECONOMIC DEVELOPMENT: THEORY AND PRACTICE FOR A DIVIDED WORLD 50-52 (2003) (including Development Spotlight 3-1).

Articles:

1. Domar, Evsey, *Expansion and Employment*, 37 AMERICAN ECONOMIC REVIEW 34-35 (March 1947).

2. Domar, Evsey, *The Problem of Capital Formation*, 38 AMERICAN ECONOMIC REVIEW 777-94 (December 1948).

3. Harrod, Roy, *An Essay in Dynamic Theory*, 49 ECONOMIC JOURNAL 14-33 (March 1939).

4. Rangarajan, C. & R. Kannan, *Capital — Output Ratios and the Indian Economy (1950-51 to 1989-90)*, 42 INDIAN ECONOMIC JOURNAL 1-16 (July–September 1994).

5. Stern, Nicholas, *The Determinants of Economic Growth*, 101 ECONOMIC JOURNAL 122-33 (January 1991).

## HAVANA CHARTER

The legal instrument negotiated in 1947, and finished in 1948 in Havana, Cuba, which would have established an International Trade Organization (ITO). Also known as the *"ITO Charter."*

The drafting history of the *Havana Charter* is largely parallel to that of the GATT. For the *Charter*, the key drafting conferences, which occurred between 1946-48, were:

- First Session of the Preparatory Committee of the United Nations Conference on Trade and Employment, held in London from 15 October to 20 November 1946, and known as the "London Preparatory Conference." The key summary of this Session is the *London Report*, First Session of the Preparatory Committee (1946).

- The 1947 New York Preparatory Conference, held from 20 January to 25 February 1947. The key summary of this Conference is The *New York Report*, United Nations Document EPCT/34 (29 May 1947), concerning the *"New York Draft."*

- Second Session of the Preparatory Committee of the United Nations Conference on Trade and Employment, held in Geneva from 10 April to 30 October 1947, and known as the "Geneva Preparatory Conference." The key summary of this Session is *Report of the Second Session of the Preparatory Committee of the United Nations Conference on Trade and Employment*, United Nations Document EPCT/186 (1947), *i.e.*, the *Geneva Report*.

- The Havana Conference, held from 21 November 1947 to 24 March 1948. The key summary of this Conference is United Nations Conference on Trade and Employment, *Havana Reports*, United Nations Document ICITO/1/8 (1948).

*Suggestions for Further Research:*

Books:

1.   BAGWELL, KYLE & ROBERT W. STAIGER, THE ECONOMICS OF THE WORLD TRADING SYSTEM (2002).

2.   BARTON, JOHN H., JUDITH L. GOLDSTEIN, TIMOTHY E. JOSLING & RICHARD H. STEINBERG, THE EVOLUTION OF THE TRADE REGIME — POLITICS, LAW, AND ECONOMICS OF THE GATT AND THE WTO (2006).

3.   BEANE, DONALD G., THE UNITED STATES AND GATT — A RELATIONAL STUDY (2000).

4.   BUTLER, MICHAEL A., CAUTIOUS VISIONARY — CORDELL HULL AND TRADE REFORM, 1933-1937 (1998).

5.   CAPLING, ANN, AUSTRALIA AND THE GLOBAL TRADE SYSTEM — FROM HAVANA TO SEATTLE (2001).

6.   DAM, KENNETH W., THE GATT — LAW AND INTERNATIONAL ECONOMIC ORGANIZATION (1970).

7. Eckes, Alfred E., Jr. ed., Revisiting U.S. Trade Policy — Decisions in Perspective (2000).

8. Gardner, Richard N., Sterling–Dollar Diplomacy — The Origins and the Prospects of Our International Economic Order (1969).

9. Heller, Francis H. & John R. Gillingham, The United States and the Integration of Europe — Legacies of the Postwar Era (1996) (especially Chapter 10).

10. Jackson, John H., World Trade and the Law of GATT (1969).

11. Jackson, John H., The World Trading System (2nd ed. 1997)

12. Kenwood, A.G. & A.L. Lougheed, The Growth of the International Economy 1820-2000 (4th ed. 1999).

13. Kirshner, Orin, ed., The Bretton Woods–GATT System — Retrospect and Prospect After Fifty Years (1996).

14. Low, Patrick, Trading Free — The GATT and U.S. Trade Policy (1993).

15. O'Rourke, Kevin H., ed., The International Trading System, Globalization and History vols. I and II (2005).

16. Ostry, Sylvia, The Post-Cold War Trading System — Who's on First? (1997).

17. Ruggie, John Gerard, ed., Multilateralism Matters — The Theory and Praxis of an Institutional Form (1993).

18. Trebilcock, Michael J. & Robert Howse, The Regulation of International Trade (3rd ed. 2005).

19. Wilcox, Clair, A Charter for World Trade (1949).

20. Zeiler, Thomas W., Free Trade Free World — The Advent of GATT (1999).

Articles:

1. Alessandrini, Donatella, *WTO and Current Trade Debate: An Enquiry into the Intellectual Origins of Free Trade Thought*, 11 International Trade Law & Regulation 53-60 (March 2005).

2. Dam, Kenneth W., *Cordell Hull, The Reciprocal Trade Agreements Act, and the WTO — An Essay on the Concept of Rights in International Trade*, 1 New York University Journal of Law and Business 709-730 (2005).

3. Rehm, John B., *Developments in the Law and Institutions of International Economic Relations: The Kennedy Round of Trade Negotiations*, 62 American Journal of International Law 2, 403 (1968).

Other Source:

1. *A Brief History of the GATT, in* Trade Policies for a Better Future — The "Leutwiler Report," the GATT and the Uruguay Round 160-64 (1987).

## HAVANA CONFERENCE

*See Havana Charter.*

# HDI

Human Development Index.

If development is a far broader concept than growth, then it is appropriate to construct an index of development that takes into account more than just the hallmark of growth, which is income. In 1990, the United Nations Development Program (UNDP) began publishing just such an index — the HDI. In 1994, it revised the way it constructs the index to allow for comparison of countries over time, instead of static relative rankings, in part by defining a possible range of minimum and maximum values for each variable in the index.

The essential theory of the HDI is a country with a higher income is not necessarily more developed than one with a lower income. For example, in 1998 the United States sat atop the world in terms of *per capita* Gross Domestic Product (GDP) ($29,605), but scored second to Canada on the HDI (0.929 for the United States, and 0.935 for Canada). Comparing the relative levels of development of countries depends on a mix of factors.

There are three variables on which the HDI focuses, as follows. Observe the HDI is not a complete break from orthodox measures of growth, as the third variable is income.

- *Health*: To measure the level of health of people in a country, the HDI examines average life expectancy at birth. A longer life expectancy indicates better health. The possible range is from 25 to 85 years.

- *Knowledge*: To gauge the level of education of people in a country, the HDI covers two factors: literacy rates and average number of years of schooling. The higher the literacy rate and average number of years of schooling, the higher level of education. Literacy rates may range from zero to 100 percent. Average years of schooling may range from zero to 15 years. They are measured using the combined primary, secondary, and tertiary enrollment ratios (in effect, the percentage of children in school at these levels). As between these two factors, literacy is given a two-thirds weight, and enrollment a one-third weight.

- *Income*: Income matters, of course, and the HDI incorporates *per capita* GDP using the Purchasing Power Parity (PPP) method, with a deflator to account for price inflation (putting the income figure in real, as opposed to nominal, terms). The range is from U.S. $100 to $40,000. However, as explained below, an adjustment is made to take account of the law of diminishing marginal utility to income. The average world real *per capita* income, in PPP terms, establishes a threshold level. The actual income level of a country is not adjusted if it is below that threshold. If the actual income level is above the threshold, then it is discounted according to a formula (known among economists as "Atkinson's formula for the utility of income"). The maximum figure of $40,000 requires discounting, and the discounted amount is $6,154.

Arithmetically, the UNDP calculates the value for each variable using the formula explained below.

In the formula, $X_A$ is the actual value of the variable for a particular country, $X_{MAX}$ is the maximum value possible, and $X_{MIN}$ is the minimum value possible:

$$\text{Value of Variable} = \frac{X_A - X_{MIN}}{X_{MAX} - X_{MIN}}$$

For example, in 1994, life expectancy in Egypt was 64.3 years, the adult literacy rate was 50.5 percent, the combined enrollment ratio at the first, second, and third levels was 69 percent, and adjusted real *per capita* GDP on PPP terms was U.S. $3,846. (The world average real *per capita* income in PPP terms that year was $5,835. The actual figure for Egypt is below this threshold, so no adjustment is needed.) Using the formula, and the aforementioned minimum and maximum values, the variable scores are:

For Life Expectancy:

$$\text{Egyptian Score} = \frac{64.3}{85 - 25} = 0.66$$

For Adult Literacy:

$$\text{Egyptian Score} = \frac{50.5 - 0}{100 - 0} = 0.51$$

For Enrollment:

$$\text{Egyptian Score} = \frac{69 - 0}{100 - 0} = 0.69$$

For Education (combining Adult literacy and Enrollment):

$$\text{Egyptian Score} = (66.66 \text{ percent weight}) \times (0.51) +$$
$$(33.33 \text{ percent weight}) \times (0.69)$$
$$= 0.57$$

For Income:

$$\text{Egyptian Score} = \frac{3,846 - 0}{6,154 - 0} = 0.62$$

Then, to compute the HDI for a country, the UNDP takes the average of the three variables. In the example of Egypt, the result would be:

$$\text{HDI for Egypt} = \frac{0.66 + 0.57 + 0.62}{3} = 0.62$$

Significantly, especially for the poor living in places like the Cairo slums (known as the "City of the Dead"), this HDI put Egypt at number 109 of 175 countries the UNDP ranked in 1994. Comparing the HDI against Egypt's performance on real *per capita* GDP (PPP terms), the result was –22. The negative sign means Egypt's HDI score was 22 notches worse than its ranking solely on income (which was 87 out of 175). Many countries in the Middle East, especially oil-exporting ones, score well on income charts, but lowly on indexes of social development like the HDI.

However, a significant aspect of how the UNDP constructs the HDI is its weighting of the three factors, particularly income. Put in the jargon of economics, there is diminishing marginal utility of income. Accruing income (like consuming most goods or services) is subject to the law of diminishing returns. A person — or country — derives a great deal of satisfaction — or utility — from the first dollar of income earned. Levels of utility from incremental — or marginal — amounts of income are positive — but not forever. Each additional dollar of income brings a little less satisfaction than the previous one. At some point, a person (or country) has more than enough income needed or desired, and additional amounts do not confer much satisfaction at all. Indeed, after a large amount of income, the increments may cause more trouble than they are worth (*e.g.*, because of time and energy consumed in managing the additional money and protecting it from theft and fraud). Put simply, to a poor person, one dollar brings huge satisfaction, but to a billionaire, it means virtually nothing.

Thus, recognizing the phenomenon of diminishing marginal utility of income, the UNDP incorporates it by adjusting statistics on income. If a country has a high *per capita* income, the UNDP discounts that income. Conversely, it assigns a greater weight to the *per capita* income of poor countries. In other words, the higher the *per capita* income, the less the weight the UNDP gives it, in proportion to health and knowledge, in the HDI.

Despite that adjustment, the HDI has failed to impress many economists. Indeed, that adjustment is a source of criticism. The maximum real *per capita* income figure of $40,000, discounted to $6,154, effectively puts a cap on the contribution income can make to development in the HDI. Suppose a country moves from the income level of Laos to that of Singapore, and the upward trend continues. The HDI disregards increases beyond the maximum. Yet, surely those increases, to Singapore-style levels and beyond, matter, albeit with diminishing returns.

Among other deficiencies they cite are the weighting of the variables and positive correlation among the variables. Assigning coefficients to weigh health, education, and income ultimately depends on subjective preferences. Those preferences differ depending on a range of factors — time, culture, and so forth. For example, perhaps Americans do not experience diminishing returns to income to the same degree that Scandinavians do. Yet, the UNDP essentially imposes its preferences when weighing variables. As for the variables themselves, health, knowledge, and income are not statistically independent of one another. People with higher incomes tend to be healthier and better educated than those with lower incomes, precisely because they can afford to spend on gym memberships and law school tuition. Consequently, the addition of two other variables may say little beyond what income data reveal.

## HEADLINE NUMBER

A number associated with trade negotiations, or a trade agreement, which attracts attention from the media.

Classic examples of a headline number are the overall average tariff cut, and the overall average cut in farm subsidies. Depending on the context, a headline number can be misleading. It may connote more, or less, trade liberalization than actually is proposed, or occurs, in negotiations or an agreement, respectively. It is necessary to look behind the headline number, at exceptions (*e.g.*, for sensitive products), implementation periods, peculiarities of definitions of key terms, and so on.

## HFCS

High Fructose Corn Syrup.

An artificial sweetener and sugar substitute. Mexico's scheme for taxing HFCS, and beverages containing it, was the subject of a major trade dispute with the United States, both under the WTO and the *North American Free Trade Agreement (NAFTA)*.[424]

## HIPC

Highly indebted poor country.

HIPCs are the most indebted countries in the world, with a ratio of debt to foreign exchange earnings of 250 percent or more.

## HISTORICAL INDICATION

*See* FTA.

## HLRCC

High-Level Regulatory Cooperation Council.

The HLRCC was created in May 2010 as a joint initiative between President Barack H. Obama of the United States and President Felipe Calderón of Mexico. The HLRCC identifies areas of mutual interest for increased regulatory

---

[424] *See* WTO Appellate Body Report, *Mexico — Tax Measures on Soft Drinks and Other Beverages*, WT/DS308/AB/R (adopted 24 March 2006) (complaint by United States, with Canada, China, European Communities, Guatemala, and Japan as third party participants).

cooperation between the two countries.[425] The Council is comprised of senior-level regulatory, trade, and foreign affairs officials from both the United States and Mexico.[426]

The six major goals of the council set out in the terms of reference are:

- make regulations more compatible and simple;
- increase regulatory transparency;
- promote public participation;
- improve the analysis of regulations;
- link regulatory cooperation to improved border-crossing and customs procedures; and
- increase technical cooperation.[427]

Such increased regulatory cooperation is a means to promote economic growth, lower costs, increase trade, and better protect the environment, health and safety of the populace of the United States and Mexico.[428]

Thus, for example, in February 2012, the United States and Mexico announced for 2012 and 2013 an HLRCC work plan to cover the following areas of mutual interest to the United States and Mexico: conformity assessment (that is, accreditation of conformity assessment bodies); e-health records (namely, decreasing the time required to implement electronic health record systems); food (in particular, enhancing food safety); nanotechnology (including sharing information about such technology); oil and gas exploration, drilling, and production (specifically, minimizing risks in these activities); and transportation (especially with a view to ensuring all trucks are inspected at a consistently high level, without regard to the country of origin of the truck).[429]

The Council is not part of or called for by the *North American Free Trade Agreement* (*NAFTA*), and Canada plays no role in it. In other words, it is a bilateral, non-*NAFTA* institution. However, there is a United States — Canada Regulatory Cooperation Council (RCC), which is the analog to the United States — Mexico HLRCC. The RCC was created in February 2011 by President Obama and Canadian Prime Minister Stephen Harper.

---

[425] *See,* Len Bracken, *Obama, Calderón Work to Expand Trade, Streamline Regulations; ITA Seeks Comments,* 28 International Trade Reporter (BNA) 403 (10 March 2011).

[426] *See,* Rossella Brevetti, *Obama, Mexico's Calderon Discuss Obstacles to Resolving Truck Dispute,* 27 International Trade Reporter (BNA) 791 (27 May 2010).

[427] *See,* Len Bracken, *Obama, Calderón Work to Expand Trade, Streamline Regulations; ITA Seeks Comments,* 28 International Trade Reporter (BNA) 403 (10 March 2011).

[428] *See,* Rossella Brevetti, *Obama, Mexico's Calderon Discuss Obstacles to Resolving Truck Dispute,* 27 International Trade Reporter (BNA) 791 (27 May 2010).

[429] *See* Rossella Brevetti, *U.S.-Mexico Regulatory Group Launches Work Plan for Cooperation Over Two Years,* 29 International Trade Reporter (BNA) 384 (8 March 2012).

## *HOPE ACT*

The *Haitian Hemispheric Opportunity through Partnership for Encouragement Act* (*HOPE Act*).

The *HOPE Act* legislation was part of the *Tax Relief and Health Care Act of 2006*, Public Law 109–432, 20 December 2006. The *Act* took effect 20 March 2007. Under the *HOPE Act*, imports of qualifying textile and apparel (T&A) from Haiti are entitled to duty-free treatment if it is determined by the President that Haiti meets certain requirements. The *2006 Act* is also known as *HOPE I*. Furthermore, *HOPE Act* benefits go above and beyond those benefits already provided to Haiti by the Caribbean Basin Initiative (CBI).

However, *HOPE I* benefits are not limitless in their generosity. Notably, Section 213(b) of the *HOPE Act* restricts access to the American market of Haitian T&A. For each 12 month period beginning 20 December, a quantitative limit is set on Haitian T&A. The limit is defined in terms of a percentage of the aggregate square meter equivalents (SMEs) of all apparel articles imported into the United States in the most recent 12 month period for which data are available. The limits are computed and published by the Committee for the Implementation of Textile Agreements (CITA).

CITA gathers relevant data for a 12 month period running through 31 October of each year. Based on that data, CITA sets a quantitative limit, measured in SMEs, for Haitian T&A exports eligible for preferential treatment. This limit applies for a one year period beginning 20 December of one year and ending on 19 December of the next year. Thus, for example:

- The limit for 20 December 2007 through 19 December 2008 was 1.25 percent of the aggregate SMEs of all apparel articles imported into the United States, based on data from the 12 month period ending 31 October 2007. This limit translated into 313,000,534 SMEs of Haitian apparel eligible for duty-free treatment.

- Based on data from the 12 month period ending 31 October 2008, the limit for 20 December 2008 through 19 December 2009 was 305,093,845 SMEs of Haitian apparel eligible for duty-free treatment. Any Haitian apparel article exported to the United States in excess of these limits would be subject to the normally applicable tariff.

- Based on data from the 12 month period ending 31 October 2009, the limit on Haitian T&A eligible for duty-free treatment for 20 December 2009 through 19 December 2010 was 284,904,116 SMEs. Again, shipments in excess of this cap faced the normal most-favored nation (MFN) tariff.

Manifestly, the quantitative restriction set by CITA progressively falls. That legal fact intimates the limits of the generosity of the *HOPE Act*. Arguably, if a preferential option is to be accorded to the poor, then Haiti — being the poorest nation in the western hemisphere — should have no cap placed on it, or at least one that is relatively high and passive.

More recently, the *2008 Farm Bill* included provisions that expanded the *2006 HOPE Act*. The provisions in the *2008 Farm Bill* allow for duty-free imports of certain woven and knit apparel made in Haiti. Specifically, the provisions contain six stand-alone rules for T&A to qualify for duty-free treatment. For example, two of the six provisions read as follows:

> A capped benefit for woven apparel meeting a wholly assembled/knit-to-shape rule regardless of the fabric's source-the cap is 70 million square meter equivalents (SMEs);

> An uncapped benefit for certain types of apparel meeting a wholly assembled/knit-to-shape rule, where the apparel is made from non-U.S. fabrics found to be in "short supply."

These additional provisions are known as *HOPE II*. *HOPE II* specifically expanded the *HOPE I* program by addressing the limits of complex rules of origin found in the *2006 Act* and addressing labor rights and labor laws in Haiti. To address such issues, the *2008 Act* conditioned benefits on the establishment of an independent labor ombudsman office and a program operated by the International Labor Organization (ILO). To receive *HOPE II* duty-free treatment, Haitian producers are required to participate in the ILO program. Put simply, *Hope II* adds a layer of conditionality to receive preferential treatment.

In mid-January 2010, a devastating earthquake hit Haiti leaving its T&A industry operating at approximately 50 percent capacity. Reacting to the tragedy, President Obama signed into law on 25 May 2010 the *Haiti Economic Lift Program (HELP) Act of 2010*. The *HELP Act* affected *HOPE I* and *HOPE II* by renewing these *Acts* through 2020. That extension was essential, because certain key provisions in the *HOPE* legislation originally were set to expire at the end of 2010.

## HORIZONTAL

Across product categories or services sectors.

"Horizontal" is used to connote the scope of coverage of trade negotiations or a trade agreement. That scope is across-the-board, or applying to all areas. Thus, for example, horizontal negotiations could involve trade-offs among agricultural, industrial, and service sectors. The opposite adjective, of course, is "vertical," which connotes depth within a particular product category or services sector.

Horizontal negotiations presume the number of open, unresolved issues across different sectors is not excessively large. There is no specific figure as to the maximum number of outstanding issues permissible for horizontal negotiations can occur. In remarks made in Chicago, Illinois in February 2008 about Doha Round progress, United States Trade Representative Susan C. Schwab said the reduction of bracketed text from 750 items in 2007 to 150 items in early 2008 was progress. But, 150 brackets still were too many, from the perspective of Ambassador Schwab, to commence the proverbial horse-trading of one sector (*e.g.*, market access on farm products) against a different one (*e.g.*, cuts to industrial tariff rates) associated with horizontal negotiations.[430]

## HS

Harmonized System, formally known as the Harmonized Commodity Description and Coding System.

The HS is the basis for common classification of goods for customs purposes, as reflected in the Harmonized Tariff Schedules (HTS). The HS is an international nomenclature developed by the World Customs Organization (WCO) for classifying products. Products are grouped according to appropriate categories, and every product is assigned a six digit code. Beyond the six digit level, countries are free to introduce additional digits to make distinctions for tariff or statistical reporting purposes.

As of 2006, 169 countries used the HS, meaning 98 percent of world trade was classified under the HS. In American trade parlance, the acronym "HTS," for "Harmonized Tariff Schedule," often is used interchangeably with "HS." The WCO periodically updates, amends, and corrects the HS. The HS is not to be confused with a separate classification system for services.

## HTCG

High Technology Cooperation Group.

The HTCG is a joint United States — India entity that meets annually. It examines ways to streamline export controls that impede bilateral trade.

## HTS

The Harmonized Tariff Schedule, which each WTO Member maintains for goods.

In the United States, the HTS of the United States — the HTSUS — is referred to at 19 U.S.C. §3501(2). The HTS replaced the Tariff Schedule of the United States (TSUS) on 1 January 1989. The Harmonized System (HS) categorizes products at the six digit level, and affords countries the opportunity to refine classifications to the eight and 10 digit level. The HTSUS uses eight and 10 digit classifications for many products. The HTS is not to be confused with the separate schedule for services.

---

[430] *See* Daniel Pruzin, *WTO NAMA Chair Defends Draft Text Against Charges of Backsliding in Talks*, 25 International Trade Reporter (BNA) 288–289 (28 February 2008).

*Suggestions for Further Research:*

Articles:

1.   Lewis, Jason, *Gender-Classified Imports: Equal Protection Violations in the Harmonized Tariff Schedule of the United States*, 18 CARDOZO JOURNAL OF LAW & GENDER 171–197 (2011).

## HTSUS

The Harmonized Tariff Schedule of the United States.

*See* HTS.

## HUBS AND SPOKES

A term associated with the critique of Regional Trade Agreements (RTAs).

The critique is the proliferation of Free Trade Agreements (FTAs) and Customs Unions (CUs) results in a hub-and-spoke arrangement in the world trading system. The "hubs" are the major trading powers, such as the United States, European Union (EU), and Japan, which are at the center of FTAs or CUs. The "spokes" are small economies, which are linked to the dominant powers, but which are unconnected to each other. The overall pattern is radial.

In such an arrangement, the advantage lies with rich country hubs, because they have secured barrier-free access in their major export markets, and sources of supply for needed imports. Poor country spokes, however, potentially put themselves in a position dependent on the hubs, as they lower trade barriers on rich country imports, and thus divert trade away from otherwise-cheaper producers, namely, in other unconnected spokes.[431] The spokes also lose tariff revenue, simply because of the duty-free treatment they accord goods form the hub.

In reality, the world trading system is messier than the neat, radial pattern of a hub-and-spoke arrangement. That is because of FTAs and CUs that interlock and overlap. For example, Mexico is a Party to the North American Free Trade Agreement (*NAFTA*), but also a member of dozens of other FTAs. The EU is a CU, but has FTA-type accords with many countries. Bahrain is a member of the Gulf Cooperation Council (GCC), but also has an FTA with the United States.

Cumulation rules, such as the Pan-European Cumulation System (PECS), and as in the United States Generalized System of Preferences (GSP) and *African Growth and Opportunity Act* (*AGOA*) programs, can stitch together the spokes into a uniform network, essentially by allowing inputs from one FTA partner to qualify in the origin calculation with respect to a different FTA partner. In theory, at least, a large network of FTAs woven tightly together with cumulation rules could simulate multilateral trade liberalization.

---

[431] *See Least Favored Nation*, THE ECONOMIST, 5 August 2006, at 68.

## HUMAN DEVELOPMENT INDEX

*See* HDI.

## HUMAN RIGHTS

*See* Trade—Human Rights Link

# I

## IA

Import Administration.

*See* ITA.

## IBRD

International Bank for Reconstruction and Development, a part of the World Bank Group. *See* World Bank.

## IBRAHIM INDEX OF AFRICAN GOVERNANCE

A measure of the quality of governance in the 48 Sub-Saharan African countries, published annually, with an associated substantial cash prize for an individual leader.

The Index is the eponym of Mr. Mohammed Ibrahim, a British entrepreneur of Sudanese birth who made a fortune in the mobile-phone industry. In 2005, he sold his company, Celtel, to MTC, a Kuwait based firm, for $3.4 billion. Concerned about the overall condition of governance in Sub-Saharan Africa, Mr. Ibrahim worked with two academics, Robert Rotberg and Rachel Gisselquist, both of Harvard University, to develop a system for evaluating governance. The system — the Ibrahim Index — was publicly proclaimed in 2006, and the first cash prize awarded that year.

Five sets of criteria comprise the Index:

- Safety and Security
- Rule of Law and Corruption
- Participation and Human Rights
- Economic Opportunity
- Human Rights

The Table below sets out the results from the first year, 2007, which were based on 2005 data. One observation from those results made is the positive correlation between being an island country and good governance, with Mauritius, Seychelles, and Cape Verde in the winners list, but no island nations on the loser side.[432]

---

[432] *See It's Better to be Out to Sea*, The Economist, 29 September 2007, at 51.

## TABLE:
### IBRAHIM INDEX OF AFRICAN GOVERNANCE — FIRST YEAR RESULTS

| Country (Among 48 Sub-Saharan African countries) | | Top 10 Winners Best Governed | Bottom 10 Losers Worst Governed |
|---|---|---|---|
| 1 | 39 | Mauritius | Sierra Leone |
| 2 | 40 | Seychelles | Burundi |
| 3 | 41 | Botswana | Central African Republic |
| 4 | 42 | Cape Verde | Angola |
| 5 | 43 | South Africa | Liberia |
| 6 | 44 | Gabon | Guinea-Bissau |
| 7 | 45 | Namibia | Sudan |
| 8 | 46 | Ghana | Chad |
| 9 | 47 | Senegal | Congo (Democratic Republic of) |
| 10 | 48 | São Tomé & Príncipe | Somalia |

Scores on each criterion are summed up and averaged to yield an overall result.

Associated with the Ibrahim Index is a cash prize, awarded annually, for achievement in African leadership. The winner is an African leader who not only best sponsors security, health, education, and economic development, but also transfers power democratically to a successor. The prize is $5 million, plus a $200,000 stipend for life. The individual winner need not be the same as the country that tops the league table on governance. While perhaps an incentive to individual leaders to provide good governance, this prize has been criticized as waste, in that the funds could be put to better and more direct use for the benefit of poor people.

## IBSA

India, Brazil, and South Africa.

In March 2006, these three countries agreed to establish a Free Trade Agreement (FTA). They were motivated, in part, by the lack of progress in the Doha Round of multilateral trade negotiations. Surging volumes of trade among the three countries also motivated them. For example, between

2004–06, Brazil's trade with India increased 170 percent, and Brazil's trade with South Africa increased 86 percent.

## ICANN

Internet Corporation for Assigned Names and Numbers.

This non-profit organization is responsible for (1) assigning domain name registration authority, (2) Internet protocol (IP) space allocation, and (3) protocol port number assignment. In short, ICANN is the organization that structures the naming taxonomy of the Internet.

In practice, ICANN doles out two of these three responsibilities. First, it subcontracts the opportunity to administer Top Level Domains, like .com, .gov, and .net, and Country Domains, like .cn, .de, .nz, .uk, to entities. Those entities are called "registries" or "Network Information Centers" (NICs). Registries or NICs may be companies, non-profits, or government agencies. They create the sub-domain names based on a registration process the registry or NIC establishes. Second, ICANN delegates to various registries or NICs the tasks of assigning IP ranges, and matching an IP address (*i.e.*, the numerical reference to the server that represents the domain) to the domain name they have created within their .com or .net, or other appropriate registry or NIC. Third, the registry or NIC then provides this information via a publicly searchable database, called a "WHOIS" database. A computer user types in "whois" and the domain name, and the registry or NIC provides the administrative and technical contact information for each domain it has assigned.

Due to the popularity and financial potential of the Internet, ICANN has come under attack for its lack of transparency in how it assigns responsibilities to various registries and NICs. There are complaints about American domination of the Internet naming conventions (*e.g.*, United States websites are known by .com, .org, .net, and others, but have no country suffix, whereas British, Canadian, German, and New Zealand websites have to add a two letter country signifier to the end of their addresses, such as ".co.uk" in the British Broadcasting Corporation website bbc.co.uk). In relation to United States involvement in the management of internet systems, another concern is the assignment of registry or NIC functions for two of the largest top-level domains, namely, .com and .net, to a single American company — VeriSign.

Finally, there are privacy concerns based on the broader access of the WHOIS database and the physical address and telephone contact information that is available.

*Suggestions for Further Research:*

Articles:

1. Alramahi, Moe, *The Legal Nature of Domain Names*, 8 JOURNAL OF INTERNATIONAL TRADE LAW & POLICY number 1, 84–94 (2009).

2.  Symposium, *I Think I Can, I Think ICANN: Regulating the Internet ... Or Not*, 21 PACIFIC MCGEORGE GLOBAL BUSINESS & DEVELOPMENT LAW JOURNAL 1–110 (2008).

# ICSID

International Center for the Settlement of Disputes.

Part of the World Bank Group, ICSID is located in Washington, D.C. Through ICSID arbitration, sovereign governments and private foreign investors may resolve disputes.

*Suggestions for Further Research:*

Book:

1.  QURESHI, ASIF H. & ANDREAS R. ZIEGLER, INTERNATIONAL ECONOMIC LAW ch. 14 (2nd ed. 2007).

Articles:

1.  Bermann, George, Jack J. Coe, Jr., Christopher R. Drahozal & Catherine A. Rogers, *Restating the U.S. Law of International Commercial Arbitration*, 113 PENN STATE LAW REVIEW 1333–1342 (2009).

2.  Bjorklund, Andrea K., *The Emerging Civilization of Investment Arbitration*, 113 PENN STATE LAW REVIEW 1269–1299 (2009).

3.  Claussen, Kathleen E., *Engaging Closed Societies through International Arbitration: Lessons from the Cuban Experience*, 17 LAW & BUSINESS REVIEW OF THE AMERICAS 11–25 (2011).

4.  Deutsch, Richard, *An ICSID Tribunal Denies Jurisdiction for Failure to Satisfy BIT's "Cooling-Off" Period: Further Evidence of a Sea Change in Investor-State Arbitration or a Meaningless Ripple?*, 33 Houston Journal of International Law 589–604 (2011).

5.  Franck, Susan D., *The ICSID Effect? Considering Potential Variations in Arbitration Awards*, 51 VIRGINIA JOURNAL OF INTERNATIONAL LAW 825–914 (2011).

6.  Greiman, Virginia A., *The Public / Private Conundrum in International Investment Disputes:Advancing Investor Community Partnerships*, 32 WHITTIER LAW REVIEW 395–454 (2011).

7.  Kasenetz, Eric David, Note, *Desperate Times Call for Desperate Measures: The Aftermath of Argentina's State of Necessity and the Current Fight in the ICSID*, 41 GEORGE WASHINGTON INTERNATIONAL LAW REVIEW 709–747 (2010).

8.  Kim, Dohyun, Note, *The Annulment Committee's Role in Multiplying Inconsistency in ICSID Arbitration:The Need to Move Away from an Annulment-Based System*, 86 NEW YORK UNIVERSITY LAW REVIEW 242–279 (2011).

9.  Krawiec, Daniel A., *Sempra Energy International v. The Argentine Republic: Reaffirming the Rights of Foreign Investors to the Protection of ICSID Arbitration*, 15 LAW & BUSINESS REVIEW OF THE AMERICAS 311–337 (2009).

10. Parish, Matthew T., Annalise K. Nelson & Charles B. Rosenberg, *Awarding Moral Damages to Respondent States in Investment Arbitration*, 29 BERKELEY JOURNAL OF INTERNATIONAL LAW 225–245 (2011).

11. Overly, Megan Shepston, Note, *When Private Stakeholders Fail: Adapting Expropriation Challenges in Transnational Tribunals to New Governance Theories (Methanex Corp. v. United States, 44 I.L.M. 1345, 2005; Martina Polasek, Biwater Gauff (Tanzania) Ltd. v. United Republic of Tanzania, 22 ICSID Rev. — Foreign Investment L.J. 149, 2007)*, 71 OHIO STATE LAW JOURNAL 341–380 (2010).

12. Simma, Honorable Bruno, *Foreign Investment Arbitration: A Place for Human Rights?*, 60 INTERNATIONAL & COMPARATIVE LAW QUARTERLY 573–596 (2011).

13. Supnik, Kate M., Note, *Making Amends: Amending the ICSID Convention to Reconcile Competing Interests in International Investment Law*, 59 DUKE LAW JOURNAL 343–376 (2009).

14. Vincentelli, Ignacio A., *The Uncertain Future of ICSID in Latin America*, 16 LAW & BUSINESS REVIEW OF THE AMERICAS 409–455 (2010).

15. Wang, Guiguo, *China's Practice in International Investment Law: From Participation to Leadership in the World Economy*, 34 YALE JOURNAL OF INTERNATIONAL LAW 575–587 (2009).

## IDA

International Development Association, a part of the World Bank Group. *See* World Bank.

## IFAD

International Fund for Agricultural Development. *See* Food Security.

## IFC

International Finance Corporation, a part of the World Bank Group.

## IFI (IFIS)

International financial institution(s), an umbrella term covering the International Monetary Fund (IMF) and multilateral development banks (*i.e.*, the World Bank and regional development banks).

## IFPRI

International Food Policy Research Institute.

## IIF

Institute for International Finance.

Members of the IIF include the central banks of many countries, plus leading creditors. Certain members of debt restructuring groups, such as the Paris Club or London Club, also belong to the IIF.

# ILO

International Labor Organization, created by the *Treaty of Versailles* in 1919 and based in Geneva, Switzerland. Over 150 countries are ILO members.

*Suggestions for Further Research:*

Book:

1.   QURESHI, ASIF H. & ANDREAS R. ZIEGLER, INTERNATIONAL ECONOMIC LAW ch. 15 (2nd ed. 2007).

Articles:

1.   Arthurs, Harry, *Extraterritoriality by Other Means: How Labor Law Sneaks Across Borders, Conquers Minds, and Controls Workplaces Abroad*, 21 STANFORD LAW & POLICY REVIEW 527–553 (2010).

2.   Banks, Kevin, *Trade, Labor and International Governance: An Inquiry into the Potential Effectiveness of the New International Labor Law*, 32 BERKELEY JOURNAL OF EMPLOYMENT & LABOR LAW 45–142 (2011).

3.   Baradaran, Shima & Stephanie Barclay, *Fair Trade and Child Labor*, 43 COLUMBIA HUMAN RIGHTS LAW REVIEW issue 1, 1–63 (fall 2011).

4.   Bravo, Karen E., *Regional Trade Arrangements and Labor Liberalization: (Lost) Opportunities for Experimentation?*, 28 SAINT LOUIS UNIVERSITY PUBLIC LAW REVIEW 71–113 (2008).

5.   Brown, S. Denay, Note, *Protecting the Children: The Need for a Modern Day Balancing Test to Regulate Child Labor in International Business*, 20 JOURNAL OF TRANSNATIONAL LAW & POLICY 129–156 (2010–2011).

6.   Burkeen, Annette, *Private Ordering and Institutional Choice: Defining the Role of Multinational Corporations in Promoting Global Labor Standards*, 6 WASHINGTON UNIVERSITY GLOBAL STUDIES LAW REVIEW 205–254 (2007).

7.   Charnovitz, Steve, *The Influence of International Labor Standards on the World Trading Regime: A Historical Review*, 126 INTERNATIONAL LABOR REVIEW 565 (1987).

8.   Charnovitz, Steve, *Environmental and Labor Standards in Trade*, 15 WORLD ECONOMICS 335 (1992).

9.   Choudhury, Barnali, *The Façade of Neutrality: Uncovering Gender Silences in International Trade*, 15 WILLIAM & MARY JOURNAL OF WOMEN & LAW 113–159 (2008).

10. Compa, Lance, *Labor Rights and Labor Standards in International Trade*, 25 LAW & POLICY IN INTERNATIONAL BUSINESS 165, 166–67 (1993).

11. Cooney, Sean, *Making Chinese Labor Law Work: The Prospects for Regulatory Innovation in the People's Republic of China*, 30 FORDHAM INTERNATIONAL LAW JOURNAL 1050–1097 (2007).

12. Desierto, Diane A., *Leveraging International Economic Tools to Confront Child Soldiering*, 43 NEW YORK UNIVERSITY JOURNAL OF INTERNATIONAL LAW & POLITICS 337–418 (2011).

13. Dowling Jr., Donald C., *U.S.-Based Multinational Employers and the Social Contract Outside the United States*, 26 AMERICAN BAR ASSOCIATION JOURNAL OF LABOR & EMPLOYMENT LAW 77–100 (2010).

14. Drouin, Renée-Claude, *Promoting Fundamental Labor Rights Through International Framework Agreements: Practical Outcomes and Present Challenges*, 31 COMPARATIVE LABOR LAW & POLICY JOURNAL 591–636 (2010).

15. Estreicher, Samuel, *"Think Global, Act Local:" Employee Representation in a World of Global Labor and Product Market Competition*, 4 VIRGINIA LAW & BUSINESS REVIEW 81–95 (2009).

16. González-Garibay, Montserrat, *The Trade-Labour and Trade-Environment Linkages: Together or Apart?*, 10 JOURNAL OF INTERNATIONAL TRADE LAW POLICY number 2 165–184 (2011).

17. Gould IV, William B., *Labor Law Beyond U.S. Borders: Does What Happens Outside of America Stay Outside of America?*, 21 STANFORD LAW & POLICY REVIEW 401–426 (2010).

18. Hall, John A., *The ILO's Better Factories Cambodia Program: A Viable Blueprint for Promoting International Labor Rights?*, 21 STANFORD LAW & POLICY REVIEW 427–460 (2010).

19. Hecker, Michael, *A Lesson from the East: International Labor Rights and the U.S. — Cambodian Trade Agreement of 1999*, 26 BUFFALO PUBLIC INTEREST LAW JOURNAL 39–71 (2007–2008).

20. Helms, Grant E., Note, *Fair Trade Coffee Practices: Approaches for Future Sustainability of the Movement*, 21 INDIANA INTERNATIONAL & COMPARATIVE LAW REVIEW 79–109 (2011).

21. Jakubowski, Laura, Note, *International Commerce and Undocumented Workers: Using Trade to Secure Labor Rights*, 14 INDIANA JOURNAL OF GLOBAL LEGAL STUDIES 509–525 (2007).

22. Kolben, Kevin, *Integrative Linkage: Combining Public and Private Regulatory Approaches in the Design of Trade and Labor Regimes*, 48 HARVARD INTERNATIONAL LAW JOURNAL 203–256 (2007).

23. Kolben, Kevin, *Wal-Mart is Coming, But It's Not All Bad: Wal-Mart and Labor Rights in Its International Subsidiaries*, 12 UCLA JOURNAL OF INTERNATIONAL LAW AND FOREIGN AFFAIRS 275–332 (2007).

24. Kuehnert, Daniel Richard, Note, *The International Labor Organization and a Possible End to Violence Against Union Members in Colombia*, 7 WASHINGTON UNIVERSITY GLOBAL STUDIES LAW REVIEW 593–617 (2008).

25. Lazar, Wendi S., *Employment Agreements and Cross Border Employment — Confidentiality, Trade Secret, and Other Restrictive Covenants in a Global Economy*, 24 LABOR LAWYER 195–211 (2008).

26. Likosky, Michael B., *Gender Arbitrage: Law, Luxury and Labor*, 23 WISCONSIN JOURNAL OF LAW, GENDER & SOCIETY 293–311 (2008).

27. Lofaso, Anne Marie, *Toward a Foundational Theory of Workers' Rights: The Autonomous Dignified Worker*, 76 UNIVERSITY OF MISSOURI-KANSAS CITY LAW REVIEW 1–65 (2007).

28. Lu, Haina, *New Developments in China's Labor Dispute Resolution System: Better Protection for Worker Rights?*, 29 COMPARATIVE LABOR LAW & POLICY JOURNAL 247–273 (2008).

29. Marzán, César F. Rosado, *Of Labor Inspectors and Judges: Chilean Labor Law Enforcement After Pinochet (and What the United States Can Do To Help)*, 54 ST. LOUIS UNIVERSITY LAW JOURNAL 497–523 (2010).

30. Mustapha, Kemi, Note, *Taste of Child Labor Not So Sweet: A Critique of Regulatory Approaches to Combating Child Labor Abuses by the U.S. Chocolate Industry*, 87 WASHINGTON UNIVERSITY LAW REVIEW 1163–1195 (2010).

31. Nham, Mayoung, Note, *The Right to Strike or the Freedom to Strike: Can Either Interpretation Improve Working Conditions in China?*, 39 GEORGE WASHINGTON INTERNATIONAL LAW REVIEW 919–945 (2007).

32. Nkowani, Zolomphi, *International Trade and Labour: A Quest for Moral Legitimacy*, 8 JOURNAL OF INTERNATIONAL TRADE LAW & POLICY number 1, 4–24 (2009).

33. Perez-Lopez, Jorge F., *Conditioning Trade on Foreign Labor Law: The U.S. Approach*, 9 COMPARATIVE LABOR LAW JOURNAL 253 (1988).

34. Perez-Lopez, Jorge F., *Promoting International Respect for Worker Rights Through Business Codes of Conduct*, 17 FORDHAM INTERNATIONAL LAW JOURNAL 1 (1993).

35. Pritikin, Martin H., *Fine-Labor: The Symbiosis Between Monetary and Work Sanctions*, 81 UNIVERSITY OF COLORADO LAW REVIEW 343–424 (2010).

36. Redd, Julius, Note, *Liberty's Irony: A Path to Liberation Via the Worst Forms of Child Labour Convention?*, 11 RUTGERS RACE & LAW REVIEW 368–409 (2010).

37. Scully, Katherine, Note, *Blocking Exit, Stopping Voice: How Exclusion from Labor Law Protection Puts Domestic Workers at Risk in Saudi Arabia and Around the World*, 41 COLUMBIA HUMAN RIGHTS LAW REVIEW 825–881 (2010).

38. Tapiola, Kari & Lee Swepston, *The ILO and the Impact of Labor Standards: Working on the Ground After an ILO Commission of Inquiry*, 21 STANFORD LAW & POLICY REVIEW 513–526 (2010).

39. Thomas, Chantal, *Convergences and Divergences in International Legal Norms on Migrant Labor*, 32 COMPARATIVE LABOR LAW & POLICY JOURNAL 405–441 (2011).

40. Thornton, Sarah A., Comment, *Importing Prison Labor Products from the People's Republic of China: Re-examining U.S. Enforcement of Section 307 of the Trade and Tariff Act of 1930*, 3 PACIFIC RIM LAW & POLICY JOURNAL 437, 457–58 (1995).

41. Tóth, Mariann Arany, *The Right to Dignity at Work: Reflections on Article 26 of the Revised European Social Charter*, 29 COMPARATIVE LABOR LAW & POLICY JOURNAL 275–316 (2008).

42. Trebilcock, Anne, *Putting the Record Straight About International Labor Standard Setting*, 31 COMPARATIVE LABOR LAW & POLICY JOURNAL 553–570 (2010).

43. Weiss, Marley S., *International Labor and Employment Law: From Periphery to Core*, 25 AMERICAN BAR ASSOCIATION JOURNAL OF LABOR & EMPLOYMENT LAW 487–507 (2010).

44. White, Robin C.A., *Revisiting Free Movement of Workers*, 33 FORDHAM INTERNATIONAL LAW JOURNAL 1564–1587 (2010).

Other Sources:

1. Bravo, Karen E., *Transborder Labour Liberalization: A Path to Enforcement of the Global Social Contract for Labour*, POLICY BRIEF, THE FOUNDATION FOR LAW, JUSTICE AND SOCIETY AND THE CENTRE FOR SOCIO-LEGAL STUDIES, UNIVERSITY OF OXFORD (2009) (www.fljs.org).

2. Lyle, F., *Worker Rights in U.S. Policy in* U.S. DEPARTMENT OF LABOR, FOREIGN LABOR TRENDS 20 (1991).

## IMF

International Monetary Fund, headquartered in Washington, D.C.

The IMF was created at the end of the Second World War — specifically, at the Bretton Woods Conference in July 1944, in which 44 countries participated, and which produced the *Bretton Woods Agreement* — as part of an attempt to build a more stable international economic system that would support peace, security, and prosperity than had existed before the War. The *Charter* governing the IMF also came out of this watershed conference. The IMF *Charter* has been amended three times, in 1969, 1978, and 1992. Notably, at the Conference, the participants viewed developing countries "as objects, not subjects, of history" — a view that no longer is tenable.[433]

Following worldwide economic depression and a horrific global conflict, the founders of the IMF — most notably John Maynard Keynes of Great Britain and Harry Dexter White of the United States — sought to create an institution that would help stimulate post-War economic growth by restoring stability in exchange rates and enforcing currency convertibility. In turn, exchange rate stability and currency convertibility, by giving businesses certainty and

---

[433] Diana I. Gregg, Zoellick *Cautions on Taking Dollar for Granted, Questions More Fed Power*, 26 International Trade Reporter (BNA) 1354 (8 October 2009) (*quoting* Robert Zoellick, President World Bank).

predictability (*i.e.*, eliminating or greatly reducing foreign exchange rate risk), would lead to reconstruction of the multilateral trading system. The IMF was a key institution, along with the World Bank, to advance this cause.

Generally speaking, the history of the IMF can be divided into two phases. During the first phase — the IMF's "first life," as it were, the Fund administered the "par value system" (discussed below). This period lasted from 1946-1971. In its first life, but following the collapse of the par value system in 1971, the IMF was rather adrift. The second phase — or "second life" — of the IMF began in 1982 and continues to the present day, with the debt crisis (also discussed below). The IMF became a, if not the, focal point for managing immediate and long-term implications of the crisis. Also in its second life, but starting in 1997 with the Asian economic crisis, the IMF became involved in regional and international financial crisis management, and rescues of specific countries. Especially in its second life, the mission of the IMF has been criticized from two opposing view points. On the one hand, some critics find the Fund guilty of mission creep, meaning it acts in an *ultra vires* manner by interfering with sovereign affairs of individual members (such as internal governance), providing bail outs, and getting involved in issues such as environmental degradation, poverty alleviation, and women's rights. On the other hand, other critics say the IMF is insufficiently sensitive to social concerns. It is focused too narrowly on economic matters and macro-economic statistical performance (*e.g.*, aggregate Gross Domestic Product (GDP) growth).

The original focus of the IMF was to promote and oversee the operation of the "par value system," commonly referred to as the "fixed exchange rate system." Under this system, the "par value" of the currency of each member state of the IMF was expressed in terms of gold or United States dollars. All exchange transactions were to be on the basis of these par values. The anchor of the system was the convertibility of dollars into gold at the rate (as of August 1971) of U.S. $35.00 per one ounce of gold. Simply put, the par value system was one of fixed exchange rates, tethered with a gold standard. The system prevailed until the early 1970s.

However, in the early 1970s, the par value system collapsed. Effective 15 August 1971, President Richard M. Nixon closed the gold window, *i.e.*, de-linked the dollar from gold, ending convertibility of dollars into gold. Economic changes throughout the world — including the realignment of many the exchange rates of many currencies, and the devaluation of the U.S. dollar — made it apparent certain IMF provisions needed dramatic revision. These circumstances — together with the First Amendment to the *Fund Agreement* in 1969, which created the Special Drawing Rights (SDRs) Department — left the IMF with a more modest role. The amended IMF *Charter* effectively conveyed sovereignty over exchange rates back to individual member states. Consequently, the IMF had a general mission of overseeing compliance by each member with its obligations to collaborate with the IMF and other members.

The emergence of the international debt crisis in the early 1980s, created the opportunity for the IMF to play an active role in international finance, namely, through serving as a source of financing for less developed countries (LDCs). That crisis was triggered in 1982 by announcements by Mexico and Brazil that they could not meet their debt servicing obligations. The Fund provides this financing primarily through "stand-by arrangements," a process in which a member state obtains assurances from the Fund that drawings will be permitted in the future when needed. Stand by arrangements help a member avoid the catastrophic effects that often follow a severe balance of payments (BOP) problem.

To be sure, these arrangements have been widely, though not roundly, criticized for infringing on the sovereignty of LDCs, the economic circumstances of which effectively compels them to borrow from the Fund. The most controversial element in the IMF assistance program is "conditionality." Conditionality typically is manifest in:

- Performance criteria

- Program reviews by the IMF Executive Board

- Prior actions

Essentially, these conditions mandate that financial aid from the IMF — a "bailout," as it is colloquially called — be tied to a program of economic reform by the member-borrower. The ideological underpinnings of the reforms are that of the "Washington Consensus," *i.e.*, they embody structural changes of a capitalist, free-market nature. Supporters of that Consensus argue that strict economic discipline, along with honest efforts to deal with rampant corruption and promote the rule of law, is precisely the medicine many LDCs need.

Another major source of controversy is the weighted voting system of the IMF. The weights are based on "quota allocations," which are subscriptions to capital of the IMF made by member states. The larger the capital contributions a member makes, the higher the quota allocation, and thus the greater its voting power. In other words, in this system, countries with the largest "quotas" — meaning (*inter alia*) they provide the most financial support to the institution — hold a disproportionately large amount of voting power in the institution. The top five shareholders are:

- United States, which holds a 17 percent quota, and thus has a 17 percent voting power.

- Japan, which has about a six percent quota, and thus roughly six percent voting power.

- Germany, which has the same allocation and voting power as Japan.

- France

- United Kingdom.

(Note that there are so-called "basic votes," which are fundamental votes all IMF member countries have, above which proportionality takes hold.) Overall, members of the European Union (EU) hold a 30 percent representation in the IMF, although the EU accounts for about 20 percent of global

Gross Domestic Product (GDP). The EU states have rejected any effort to reduce its quota allotments.

Not surprisingly, the IMF is criticized — again, widely — as being dominated by hegemonic powers, which harbor neo-colonialist intentions. To be sure, under the 1944 *Charter*, the United States had a 25 percent subscription. Yet, its current 17 percent block still gives the United States effective control over major IMF decisions. That is because of the so-called "85 percent rule," which states major decisions about IMF affairs — such as amending the *Charter* or changing quota allocations — require an 85 percent affirmative vote. Any country with 15 percent or more voting power, therefore, has an effective veto power. The only such country is the United States. Moreover, under current quotas, the Group of Seven (G-7) countries combined have about 40 percent of the allocations, and thus roughly 40 percent voting stake. That power among the major powers is essentially insurmountable, unless a major chasm arises within those powers.

To be sure, some efforts have been made at quota allocation reform, including slight upward adjustments for Brazil, China, Korea, and Turkey. These revisions reflect the increasing status in the global economy of those countries. However, the revisions are far from the major overhaul called for by friends and critics alike of the IMF.

The practical import of these criticisms may be less than the elevated rhetorical volume suggests. Private capital flows — by, for example, mutual funds, hedge funds, and other investment vehicles channeled by major private sector players such as Goldman Sachs, Hong Kong Shanghai Bank, Merrill Lynch, Morgan Stanley, and the like — dwarf the entire portfolio of loanable funds of both the IMF and World Bank combined. A country needing an IMF "bailout," as it were, is in bad shape indeed, as it can attract only the most risk-loving of investors. The extent to which the country follows an IMF-style reform package may be a signal to private portfolio investors that it is on a sound economic path, and thereby might have attractive investment opportunities. Yet, the example of Malaysia during the 1997–99 Asian economic crisis — which publicly spurned an IMF package, in sharp contrast to Indonesia and other Southeast Asian countries — showed international financial markets that adopting IMF conditions was neither necessary nor sufficient for restoring economic health. In brief, neither the magnitude nor the nature of IMF assistance is as significant as the enormous attention devoted to it intimates.

The IMF has 184 member countries, seven fewer than the United Nations, but considerably more than the WTO. When it began in 1944, the IMF had 45 members — roughly double the number of original contracting parties to GATT in 1947, which was 23. Notable exceptions to IMF membership include Cuba (which was an original member but withdrew in 1964, yet is a WTO Member and was an original contracting party) and North Korea. To join the IMF, a country must apply, and then be accepted by a majority of the existing members. The chief executive of the IMF is the Managing Director, who is selected by the Executive Board to serve a five year term. This selection, too, generates controversy. Russia, along with many LDCs, publicly has decried the post-War "gentlemen's understanding" that an American citizen heads up the World Bank, and a European runs the IMF. Why not appoint officials from LDCs? To do so might draw on and emerging pool of world-class financial talent from those countries, and help expand that pool to serve those countries.

In any event, the Executive Board of the IMF sets and policies, and is responsible for most decisions. The Board consists of 24 Executive Directors, who are appointed by the five largest contributing countries (as listed above). Political oversight of the IMF is primarily conducted by the International Monetary and Financial Committee (IMFC). The IMFC has 24 members, namely, the finance ministers or central bank governors from the same countries that are represented on the Executive Board. The Development Committee, which also has 24 members of ministerial rank, advises the Boards of Governors of the IMF and World Bank about issues facing developing countries.

Decision-making is the context for yet another controversy surrounding the IMF. Many critics accuse the IMF of not being transparent. Stated in this manner, that criticism is unfocused. In fact, the IMF — like the World Bank and WTO — posts thousands of documents on line. In other words, documentary transparency is not a major problem. Rather, it is transparency in decision-making that is of concern. Operational secrecy, *i.e.*, the practice of making key decisions behind closed doors, and then announcing them *fait accompli*, is the greater issue.

*Suggestions for Further Research:*

Books:

1. BIRD, GRAHAM, THE IMF AND THE FUTURE: ISSUES AND OPTIONS FACING THE FUND (2003).

2. DAM, KENNETH W., THE RULES OF THE GAME — REFORM AND EVOLUTION IN THE INTERNATIONAL MONETARY SYSTEM (1982).

3. GRANVILLE, BRIGITTE, ED., ESSAYS ON THE WORLD ECONOMY AND ITS FINANCIAL SYSTEM (2000).

4. HEAD, JOHN W., LOSING THE GLOBAL DEVELOPMENT WAR: THE FUTURE OF THE GLOBAL ECONOMIC ORGANIZATIONS: A CONTEMPORARY CRITIQUE OF THE IMF, THE WORLD BANK, AND THE WTO (2005).

5. HEAD, JOHN W., GLOBAL BUSINESS LAW: PRINCIPLES AND PRACTICE OF INTERNATIONAL COMMERCE AND INVESTMENT (2nd ed. 2007).

6. JAMES, HAROLD, INTERNATIONAL MONETARY COOPERATION SINCE BRETTON WOODS (1996).

7. LISSAKERS, KARIN, BANKS, BORROWERS, AND THE ESTABLISHMENT — A REVISIONIST ACCOUNT OF THE INTERNATIONAL DEBT CRISIS (1991).

8. QURESHI, ASIF H. & ANDREAS R. ZIEGLER, INTERNATIONAL ECONOMIC LAW chs. 5–10 (2nd ed. 2007).

Articles:

1.  Alexander, Kern, *International Regulatory Reform and Financial Taxes*, 13 JOURNAL OF INTERNATIONAL ECONOMIC LAW 893–910 (2010).

2.  Arner, Douglas W., *The Global Credit Crisis of 2008: Causes and Consequences*, 43 THE INTERNATIONAL LAWYER number 1, 91–136 (spring 2009).

3.  Beckington, Jeffrey S. & Matthew R. Amon (Student), *Competitive Currency Depreciation: The Need for a More Effective International Legal Regime*, 10 JOURNAL OF INTERNATIONAL BUSINESS & LAW 209–268 (2011).

4.  Bergsten, C. Fred, *The Need for a Robust Response to Chinese Currency Manipulation — Policy Options for the Obama Administration Including Countervailing Currency Intervention*, 10 JOURNAL OF INTERNATIONAL BUSINESS & LAW 269–280 (2011).

5.  Buckley, Ross P., *Improve Living Standards in Poor Countries: Reform the International Monetary Fund*, 24 EMORY INTERNATIONAL LAW REVIEW 119–146 (2010).

6.  Caliari, Aldo, *Updating the International Monetary System to Respond to Current Global Challenges: Can it Happen with the Existing Legal Framework?*, 20 MINNESOTA JOURNAL OF INTERNATIONAL LAW 588–618 (2011).

7.  Feldstein, Martin, *Refocusing the IMF* 77, FOREIGN AFFAIRS number 2, 20–33 (March/April 1998).

8.  Garcia, Frank J., *Global Justice and the Bretton Woods Institutions*, 10 JOURNAL OF INTERNATIONAL ECONOMIC LAW 461–481 (2007).

9.  Garicano, Luis & Rosa M. Lastra, *Towards a New Architecture for Financial Stability: Seven Principles*, 13 JOURNAL OF INTERNATIONAL ECONOMIC LAW 597–621 (2010).

10. Garner, Richard N., *The Bretton Woods–GATT System After Sixty-Five Years: A Balance Sheet of Success and Failure*, 47 COLUMBIA JOURNAL OF TRANSNATIONAL LAW 31–71 (2008).

11. Goldburn, Tricia D., Comment, *Dollars & Renminbis: Curbing the United States' Raging Trade Deficit with China by Dismantling the Dollar — RMB Peg*, 25 PENN STATE INTERNATIONAL LAW REVIEW 737–757 (2007).

12. Hagan, Sean, *Enhancing the IMF's Regulatory Authority*, 13 JOURNAL OF INTERNATIONAL ECONOMIC LAW 955–968 (2010).

13. Head, John W., *Supranational Law: How the Move Towards Multilateral Solutions Is Changing the Character of "International Law"* 16 UNIVERSITY OF KANSAS LAW REVIEW 627–28 (1993).

14. Hufbauer, Gary & Daniel Danxia Xie, *Financial Stability and Monetary Policy: The Need for Surveillance*, 13 Journal of International Economic Law 939–953 (2010).

15. Lowenfeld, Andreas F., *The International Monetary System: A Look Back Over Seven Decades*, 13 JOURNAL OF INTERNATIONAL ECONOMIC LAW 575–595 (2010).

16. Manship, Flora, Comment, *Collateral Damage of the IMF's Global Economic Relief: A Case Study of Zimbabwe*, 24 EMORY INTERNATIONAL LAW REVIEW 821–871 (2010).

17. Mercurio, Bryan & Celine Sze Ning Leung, *Is China a "Currency Manipulator"?: The Legitimacy of China's Exchange Regime Under the Current International Legal Framework*, 43 THE INTERNATIONAL LAWYER 1257–1300 (2009).

18. Pettis, Elizabeth L., *Is China's Manipulation of its Currency An Actionable Violation of the IMF and/or WTO Agreements?*, 10 JOURNAL OF INTERNATIONAL BUSINESS & LAW 281–296 (2011).

19. Symposium: *Law-Based Nature of the New International Financial Infrastructure*, 33 THE INTERNATIONAL LAWYER number 4, 847–1014 (winter 1999).

20. Symposium: *Law-Based Nature of the New International Financial Architecture*, Part II: Articles and Selected Essays, 34 THE INTERNATIONAL LAWYER number 1, 85–234 (spring 2000).

21. Symposium — *International Monetary and Financial Law in the New Millennium: Dedication Conference of Sir Joseph Gold Library Collection*, 35 THE INTERNATIONAL LAWYER number 4, 1335–1669 (winter 2001).

22. Symposium — *Developing the IMF, the World Bank, and the Regional Development Banks: The Future of Law and Policy in Global Financial Institutions*, 17 KANSAS JOURNAL OF LAW AND PUBLIC POLICY (fall 2007).

23. Torres, Hector R., *Reforming the International Monetary Fund — Why Its Legitimacy is at Stake*, 10 JOURNAL OF INTERNATIONAL ECONOMIC LAW 443–460 (2007).

24. Zimmerman, Claus D., 105 *Exchange Rate Misalignment and International Law*, AMERICAN JOURNAL OF INTERNATIONAL LAW 423–476 (2011).

Other Sources:

1. Auboin, Marc, *The Trade, Debt and Finance Nexus: At the Cross-Roads of Micro- and Macroeconomics*, WTO Discussion Paper Number 6 (2004).

2. BANDOW, DOUG & IAN VÁSQUEZ, EDS., PERPETUATING POVERTY — THE WORLD BANK, THE IMF, AND THE DEVELOPING WORLD (Cato Institute, 1994).

3. BERGSTEN, C. FRED, ED., INTERNATIONAL ADJUSTMENT AND FINANCING: THE LESSONS OF 1985–1991 (Institute for International Economics 1991).

4. Cartellieri, Ulrich & Alan Greenspan, *Global Risk Management*, Group of Thirty, The William Taylor Memorial Lectures Number 3 (1996).

5. Corrigan, E. Gerald, *The Financial Disruptions of the 1980s: A Central Banker Looks Back*, Group of Thirty, The William Taylor Memorial Lectures Number 1 (1993).

6. Eatwell, John, *International Financial Liberalization: the Impact on World Development*, United Nations Development Program (UNDP) Office of Development Studies, Discussion Paper Number 12 (September 1996).

7.   Hakim, Jonathan R., ed., *Investment Banking and Development Banking*, IFC Occasional Papers, Capital Markets Series (1985).

8.   Wyplosz, Charles, *Exchange Rate Regimes: Some Lessons from Postwar Europe*, Group of Thirty Occasional Paper Number 63 (2000).

## IMPORT PENETRATION RATIO

One of several economic statistics that may be used in an antidumping (AD) or countervailing duty (CVD) investigation, specifically, in assessing whether a petitioner is injured, or threatened with injury, by imports of allegedly dumped or illegally subsidized merchandise.

The arithmetic formula for the Import Penetration Ratio is:

$$\text{Import Penetration Ratio} = \frac{\text{Imports of Subject Merchandise}}{\text{Total United States Market}} \times 100$$

The Ratio is one of the all relevant economic variables the United States International Trade Commission (ITC) may examine in determining material injury or threat thereof. Under certain circumstances, the ITC may exclude from the denominator of the Ratio captive production of the domestic like product. A higher Ratio — which arithmetically happens with a smaller denominator — is evidence subject merchandise is having an injurious or threatening effect on domestic producers of a like product.

## IMPOSSIBLE TRINITY

*See* Currency Board.

## IMPORT SUBSTITUTION

A trade policy pursued by most Latin American and many African countries in the 1950s through 1970s, the countries of the Indian Subcontinent in the 1950s through early 1990s, and some Far East countries (such as Korea) in the 1950s and 1960s, whereby imports were discouraged in preference to domestic products.

As its name implies, the policy is to substitute domestically produced like products for imported goods. Generally, the policy is designed to encourage the development of local manufacturing, but it can be applied to the industrial as well as agricultural sectors. The policy is effected by a combination of high tariff and non-tariff barriers, and restrictions on foreign direct investment (FDI).

The consensus of mainstream economists is that the policy is less successful in stimulating economic growth than a policy of openness to trade and foreign direct investment.

*Suggestions for Further Research:*

Article:

1.   James Scott, *Developing Countries in the ITO and GATT Negotiations*, 9 JOURNAL OF INTERNATIONAL TRADE LAW AND POLICY number 1, 5–24 (2010).

## IMPORTER SECURITY FILING

Effective 26 January 2009, an Importer Security Filing (ISF) is required for all containerized ocean freight shipments to the United States.

The filing is lodged with the United States Customs and Border Protection (CBP). The ISF is part of the "10 + 2" security initiative, designed to secure America's borders from terrorist threats, such as the smuggling of weapons of mass destruction (WMDs) in shipping containers. Through documentation like the ISF, the CBP ascertains the contents of containers, and also the integrity of the supply chain, i.e., the sources of inputs and intermediate goods used to make finished merchandise. Thus, data for products on sellers, manufacturers, buyers, consolidators, and ocean carriers (including, as to the latter, the bill of lading) must be obtained by foreign producer-exporters, or importers of foreign merchandise. Ideally, such data should be obtained, and the process for securing and transmitting the data established, at least 48 hours before cargo lading (*i.e.*, the preparation of a bill of lading for the cargo in question) at a foreign port of discharge. Any inaccurate data should be rectified at least 24 hours before merchandise arrives in a United States port of entry.

Compliance with ISF rules is mandatory. Failure to file a complete, accurate ISF in a timely fashion carries a potential liquidated damage penalty of U.S. $5,000 per filing. In addition, CBP can stop merchandise from entry into the United States (or a foreign trade zone (FTZ)) by issuing a "Do Not Load" order for merchandise with a missing, incomplete, or inaccurate ISF. An importer may arrange for the preparation and filing of ISFs on their behalf by an ISF Service Provider, with which it contracts to perform this function.

## INDIAN ECONOMIC REFORMS

Commencing in 1991 under then-Minister of Finance, and later Prime Minister, Manmohan Singh, India undertook a series of dramatic economic reforms. They include de-regulation, privatization, and rationalization. For example:

- Reduction of tariffs on industrial goods from an average of 15 percent to an average of 12.5 percent.

- Extension of patent protection to pharmaceuticals, agricultural chemicals, and certain food products.

- Relaxation of investment (equity share ownership) caps on foreign direct investment (FDI) in certain sectors, such as telecommunications.

- Creation of Special Economic Zones (SEZs).

However, there are a number of areas in which India's reforms are inchoate, or have run into problems.[434] They include:

- Upgrading and expanding physical infrastructure needed to support economic growth, such as roads, railroads, air and sea ports, energy

---

[434] *See A Himalayan Challenge*, THE ECONOMIST, 13 October 2007, at 84–85; Gary G. Yerkey, *U.S. Expects India to Play Greater Role in Coming Months to Help Revive WTO Talks*, 24 International Trade Reporter (BNA) 10 (4 January 2007).

(especially electricity) generation, sanitation facilities, and telecommunication systems.

- Opening certain sectors to FDI, including retail stores (especially large, multi-brand retailers).

- Continuing privatization of state-owned enterprises (SOEs), which (as of October 2007) still account for 38 percent of total output in the formal non-farm sector, are one-third less productive than private firms, and have grown less rapidly than firms benefiting from privatization (*e.g.*, in the information technology (IT) and privatization sectors).

- Eliminating investment caps on foreign ownership of local financial service providers, especially in banking and insurance.

- Cutting tariffs further, which (as of October 2007) average about 20 percent, among the highest figures in the world.

- Drastically reducing government subsidies, which (as measured as a percentage of Gross Domestic Product (GDP)) are the second highest in the world among countries surveyed by the Organization for Economic Cooperation and Development (OECD).

- Reforming the labor market, specifically to make it more flexible by eliminating (1) restrictive employment protection laws against collective dismissals, and (2) the requirement manufacturing firms obtain government permission to lay off workers at any factory with more than 100 employees.

- Modernizing and strengthening copyright and patent laws.

- Enforcing intellectual property (IP) laws, especially with respect to pharmaceuticals (India is a leading center for counterfeit medicines), software (74 percent of which in India is pirated), and entertainment (notably, movies and music, the pirating of which damages Bollywood).

There are many theoretically intriguing and practically relevant comparisons and contrasts to be drawn between the Indian economic reform experience, on the one hand, and the experiences of India's neighbors — especially China and Pakistan — on the other hand. For example, because of India's labor laws that make hiring and firing so difficult, 87 percent (as of October 2007) of employment in the manufacturing sector is with firms that employ less than 10 workers. In China, only five percent of industrial jobs are at firms with fewer than 10 workers. Consequently, Chinese firms can develop and maximize economies of scale, absorb new technology, and enjoy higher labor productivity, than Indian companies.

The difficulties encountered in India's reform project are a source of ironic contrast with China. Communist parties in India have blocked or impeded reforms, partly out of concerns the changes benefit the rich and widen income disparities. Reform-minded governments, such as the Congress Party-led coalition headed by Prime Minister Manmohan Singh, rely on the Communist parties for support. Conversely, with a monopoly on political power, the Communist Party of China can push through necessary reforms — albeit after internal consultations, negotiations, and debate.

*Suggestions for Further Research:*

Books:

1.  CHAMBERS, MICHAEL R., ED., SOUTH ASIA IN 2020: FUTURE STRATEGIC BALANCES AND ALLIANCES (November 2002).

2.  COHEN, STEPHEN P., INDIA — EMERGING POWER (2001).

3.  DAS, TARUN, COLETTE MATHUR & FRANK-JÜRGEN RICHTER, INDIA RISING — EMERGENCE OF A NEW WORLD POWER (2005).

4.  GANGULY, SUMIT & NEIL DeVOTTA EDS., UNDERSTANDING CONTEMPORARY INDIA (2003).

5.  GULATI, ASHOK & TIM KELLEY, TRADE LIBERALIZATION & INDIAN AGRICULTURE (1999).

6.  HOSSAIN, MOAZZEM, IYANATUL ISLAM & REZA KIBRIA, SOUTH ASIAN ECONOMIC DEVELOPMENT — TRANSFORMATION, OPPORTUNITIES AND CHALLENGES (1999).

7.  HUSAIN, ISHRAT, PAKISTAN — THE ECONOMY OF AN ELITIST STATE (1999).

8.  KHAN, SHAHRUKH RAFI, ED, 50 YEARS OF PAKISTAN'S ECONOMY — TRADITIONAL TOPICS AND CONTEMPORARY CONCERNS (1999).

9.  KRUEGER, ANNE O. & SAJJID Z. CHINOY EDS., REFORMING INDIA'S EXTERNAL, FINANCIAL, AND FISCAL POLICIES (2003).

10. LAL, DEEPAK, UNFINISHED BUSINESS — INDIA IN THE WORLD ECONOMY (1999).

11. MYRDAL, GUNNAR, ASIAN DRAMA — AN INQUIRY INTO THE POVERTY OF NATIONS (abridged ed., 1971).

12. PAL, IZZUD-DIN, PAKISTAN, ISLAM & ECONOMICS — FAILURE OF MODERNITY (1999).

13. SINGH, INDERJIT, THE GREAT ASCENT — THE RURAL POOR IN SOUTH ASIA (1990).

14. SRINIVASAN, T.N., EIGHT LECTURES ON INDIA'S ECONOMIC REFORMS (2000).

15. SRINIVASAN, T.N. & SURESH D. TENDULKAR, REINTEGRATING INDIA WITH THE WORLD ECONOMY (March 2003).

16. ZAIDI, S. AKBAR, ISSUES IN PAKISTAN'S ECONOMY (1999).

Articles:

1.  Buckley, Ross P., *The Economic Policies of China and India, and of the Washington Consensus:An Enlightening Comparison*, 27 WISCONSIN INTERNATIONAL LAW JOURNAL 707–726 (2010).

2.  Ranjan, Prabhash, *Treaties in Trade and Investment and the Indian Legal Regime: Should We Mind the Gap?*, 11 AUSTRALIAN JOURNAL OF ASIAN LAW 56–81 (2009).

3.  Singhania, Monica & Akshay Gupta, *Determinants of foreign Direct Investment in India*, 10 JOURNAL OF INTERNATIONAL TRADE LAW AND POLICY 64–81 (2011).

4.  Viswanathan, K.G., *The Global Financial Crisis and Its Impact on India*, 9 JOURNAL OF INTERNATIONAL BUSINESS & LAW 41–62 (2010).

## INFORMED COMPLIANCE

A customs law concept that refers to the shared responsibility between customs officials, on the one hand, and the import community, on the other hand.

The concept is found in United States customs law. Essentially, United States Customs and Border Protection (CBP) — formerly, the Customs Service — communicates its requirements for importation to the private sector. Those responsible for importing are expected to conduct their transactions in accordance with these requirements. The requirements concern key customs law issues like merchandise description, tariff classification, valuation, country of origin marking, quotas, and intellectual property rights (IPRs), plus special matters pertaining to textiles and apparel (T&A).

The cornerstone of informed compliance is that importers are expected to exercise reasonable care in their importing operations. Whether care is "reasonable" depends on the facts and circumstances surrounding a particular import transaction.

The theory of informed compliance is that it benefits both sides. When importers comply voluntarily — on the "honor system," as it were — then they are less likely to have their shipments examined, or entries reviewed, by customs officials. Conversely, customs officials need not spend resources on redundant examinations or entry reviews for the cargo of importers who are reliable as regards compliance.

The CBP publishes a wealth of information to facilitate informed compliance. The material is available on its web site (www.cbp.gov).

*Suggestions for Further Research:*

Book:

1.  LANE, MICHAEL H., CUSTOMS MODERNIZATION AND THE INTERNATIONAL TRADE SUPERHIGHWAY (1998).

## INJURY DETERMINATION

The phase of an antidumping (AD), countervailing duty (CVD), or safeguard investigation in which injury, or threat thereof, is considered.

The essential issue in an injury determination is whether a domestic producer of a product that is like the merchandise subject to the investigation (subject merchandise) is injured, or threatened with injury, by reason of that merchandise. An injury determination is one of two indispensable features of every AD or CVD case, the other being the dumping margin or subsidization calculation, respectively. In some countries, such as the United States, the injury phase is comprised of two parts — a preliminary determination (which may be affirmative or negative), and a final determination (which may be affirmative or negative). In other countries, each phase consists of just one part, which amounts to a final (affirmative or negative) determination.

Also in some countries, such as the United States, the administering authority responsible for the injury determination is different from the agency responsible for the dumping margin or subsidization determination. That is, the investigation process is bifurcated. In the United States, the Department of Commerce (DOC) — specifically, the Import Administration (IA) section, handles the dumping margin calculation. The International Trade Commission (ITC) deals with injury determinations. In other countries, the process is unified under one authority.

In a safeguard action, proof of injury is one of several criteria that must be fulfilled before imports may be restricted. In the United States, the ITC is responsible for all aspects of a safeguard action.

*Suggestions for Further Research:*

Books:

1.   BARRINGTON, LOUISE, ED., DUMPING — A COMPARATIVE APPROACH (1995).

2.   BOVARD, JAMES, THE FAIR TRADE FRAUD — HOW CONGRESS PILLAGES THE CONSUMER AND DECIMATES AMERICAN COMPETITIVENESS (1992).

3.   CZAKO, JUDITH, JOHANN HUMAN & JORGE MIRANDA, A HANDBOOK ON ANTI-DUMPING INVESTIGATIONS (2003).

4.   MASTEL, GREG & ANDREW SZAMOSSZEGI, LEVELING THE PLAYING FIELD: ANTIDUMPING AND THE U.S. STEEL INDUSTRY (February 1999).

5.   MASTEL, GREG, ANTIDUMPING LAWS AND THE U.S. ECONOMY (1998).

6.   STEWART, TERRENCE P. & AMY S. DWYER, WTO ANTIDUMPING AND SUBSIDY AGREEMENTS (1998).

7.   VAKERICS, THOMAS V., DAVID I. WILSON & KENNETH G. WEIGEL, ANTIDUMPING, COUNTERVAILING DUTY, AND OTHER TRADE ACTIONS (December 1987).

Book Chapters:

1.   Davey, William J., *Antidumping Laws in the GATT and the EC*, IN ANTIDUMPING LAW AND PRACTICE: A COMPARATIVE STUDY 295–301 at 296 (John H. Jackson & Edwin A. Vermulst eds., 1989).

2.   Horlick, Gary N., *The United States Antidumping System in* ANTIDUMPING LAW AND PRACTICE 160 (John H. Jackson & Edwin A. Vermulst, eds., 1989).

Articles:

1.   Dorn, Joseph W., *U.S. Court of International Trade Decisions During 2007 in Appeals of Determinations of the U.S. International Trade Commission*, 40 GEORGETOWN JOURNAL OF INTERNATIONAL LAW 219–241 (2008).

2.   Horlick, Gary N. & Eleanor C. Shea, *The World Trade Organization Antidumping Agreement*, 29 JOURNAL OF WORLD TRADE 5, 26 (1995).

3.   Schriltz, Karl Von, *U.S. Court of International Trade Decisions in 2008 in Appeals of Determinations of the U.S. International Trade Commission*, 41 GEORGETOWN JOURNAL OF INTERNATIONAL LAW 1–51 (2009).

## INSIDE THE BELTWAY (INSIDE THE WASHINGTON, D.C. BELTWAY)

A reference to institutions, officials, and/or conventional wisdom found within the Washington, D.C. Depending on its use, the reference can be factual and non-judgmental, or normative and pejorative.

The beltway itself is Interstate 495, which essentially loops around Washington, D.C. The beltway is infamous for ubiquitously heavy traffic volume, monstrous jams, interminable construction projects, and hideous suburban sprawl.

To many inside the Beltway, the thinking on international economic and legal affairs is of the most sublime quality, worthy of the utmost respect, and of unquestionable sagacity. To many others inside the Beltway — and without doubt to most of mainstream America, and many abroad — many of the pro-mulgators of inside the Beltway thinking are self-absorbed, self-promotional, and self-referential. The conventional thinking, in practice, often lacks com-mon sense, shows little appreciation for abilities and talents outside the belt-way, and — in some instances — has negative consequences. The Washington Consensus — both as an economic ideology, and as it was promoted stylistically by some officials — affords one illustration of both inside-the-Beltway thinking and why that thinking, like the Beltway itself, is sclerotic.

In brief, inside-the Beltway thinking embodies the views and paradigms of "the establishment" (a term which is problematic to the extent it is ill- or un-defined).

## INTERLININGS

A textile and apparel (T&A) term referring to the part of a garment inside the outer portion of that garment.

Examples include chest-type plates; "hymo" pieces; and "sleeve headers." Under the United States *African Growth and Opportunity Act (AGOA)*, the ori-gin and value of interlinings is limited to 25 percent. That is, up to 25 percent of the cost of components of an assembled article may include interlinings that originate in neither the United States nor a Beneficiary.

If the 25 percent threshold is exceeded, then the article is not entitled to duty-free treatment. Additionally, this benefit terminates if the President determines that such interlinings are made in the United States in commercial quantities.

## INTERNAL SUPPORT

A term used with respect to trade in agriculture to encompass any measure established by a government to maintain producer prices at a level above those prevailing in the international marketplace.

Examples of internal support include direct payments to producers, deficiency payments (*i.e.*, a payment based on the difference between a target price and a domestic market price), and input and marketing cost reduction measures.

## INTERNATIONALLY RECOGNIZED WORKER RIGHTS

*See* Core Labor Rights.

## INVERTED TARIFF

A situation where higher import duties are imposed on products further down the production chain.

With an inverted tariff, the highest duty is on raw materials use (*e.g.*, leather), a less-high duty is on the semi-processed product (*e.g.*, leather uppers used for shoes), and the lowest duty is on the finished product (*e.g.*, completed shoes, the leather uppers plus soles). Stated conversely, an inverted tariff exists when the duty rate applied to a finished product is lower than the duty rate applicable to one or more components in that product. In brief, the tariff varies inversely with the degree of processing — it is highest on the least processed good, and lowest on the most processed good.

An inverted tariff structure is designed to encourage domestic manufacturers to source inputs locally, not from overseas.

An inverted tariff is the opposite of "tariff escalation." Tariff escalation is designed to protect domestic processing industries, and discourage the development of manufacturing activities in the countries in which raw materials originate. It is sometimes used by developing countries to protect infant industries, and by some developed countries to protect declining industries facing stiff import competition from less developed countries (LDCs) and newly industrialized countries (NICs).

## INVERTED U CURVE

*See* Kuznets Curve.

## IP

Intellectual property.

The principal forms of IP include patents, trademarks, copyrights, and semiconductor mask works. In addition, trade secrets are protected in the WTO *Agreement on the Trade Related Aspects of Intellectual Property Rights* (*TRIPs*), and in the United States under state law.

*Suggestions for Further Research:*

Articles:

1. Benoliel, Daniel & Bruno Salama, *Towards an Intellectual Property Bargaining Theory: The Post-WTO Era*, 32 University of Pennsylvania Journal of International Law 265–368 (2010).

2. Harris, Daniel P., *The Honeymoon is Over: The U.S.–China WTO Intellectual Property Complaint*, 32 Fordham International Law Journal 96–187 (2008).

3. Moscato-Wolter, Amy, *What is the McLaw in Malaysia?*, 5 AKRON INTELLECTUAL PROPERTY JOURNAL 231–249 (2011).

4. Stone, Charles R., Comment, *What Plagiarism Was Not: Some Preliminary Observations on Classical Chinese Attitudes Toward What the West Calls Intellectual Property*, 92 Marquette Law Review 199–230 (2008).

# IPR

Intellectual property right.

The term is a generic one. It embraces the legal rights associated with a patent, trademark, copyright, semiconductor mask work, or other form of intellectual property (IP).

*Suggestions for Further Research:*

Books:

1. NETANEL, NEIL WEINSTOCK, ED., THE DEVELOPMENT AGENDA — GLOBAL INTELLECTUAL PROPERTY AND DEVELOPING COUNTRIES (2008).

2. ODAGIRI, HIROYUKI, AKIRA GOTO, ATSUSHI SUNAMI & RICHARD R. NELSON EDS., INTELLECTUAL PROPERTY RIGHTS, DEVELOPMENT, AND CATCH UP — AN INTERNATIONAL COMPARATIVE STUDY (2010).

Articles:

1. Dounis, Catherine, Note, *Enforcing Intellectual Property Rights via EU Border Regulations: Inhibiting Access to Medicine or Preventing Counterfeit Medicine?*, 36 BROOKLYN JOURNAL OF INTERNATIONAL LAW 717–750 (2011).

2. He, Huaiwen, *The Development of Free Trade Agreements and International Protection of Intellectual Property Rights in the WTO Era — New Bilateralism and Its Future*, 41 IIC: INTERNATIONAL REVIEW OF INTELLECTUAL PROPERTY & COMPETITION LAW 253–283 (2010).

3. Kipel, Alicia Alexandra, *The Role of the United States Court of International Trade in the Enforcement of Intellectual Property Rights*, 19 TULANE JOURNAL OF INTERNATIONAL & COMPARATIVE LAW 627–649 (2011).

4. Lane, Eric, *Clean Tech Reality Check: Nine International Green Technology Transfer Deals Unhindered by Intellectual Property Rights*, 26 SANTA CLARA COMPUTER & HIGH TECHNOLOGY LAW JOURNAL 533–557 (2010).

5. Note, *Keeping Our Balance in the Face of Piracy and Counterfeiting: Limiting the Scope of Intellectual Property Rights Enforcement Provisions in Free Trade Agreements*, 42 GEORGE WASHINGTON INTERNATIONAL LAW REVIEW 159–190 (2010).

6. Nguyen, Xuan-Thao, *The China We Hardly Know: Revealing the New China's Intellectual Property Regime*, 55 ST. LOUIS UNIVERSITY LAW JOURNAL 773–810 (2011).

7. Peck, Brian & Siyuan An (Student), *China's Indigenous Innovation Policy in the Context of its WTO Obligations and Commitments*, 42 GEORGETOWN JOURNAL OF INTERNATIONAL LAW 375–447 (2011).

8.   Stauber, Demian & Zhonggi Zhou, *Protection of Intellectual Property Rights at Trade Fairs in China — Analysis of the Current Legal Framework and Comparison with Other Approaches*, 10 UNIVERSITY OF CALIFORNIA AT DAVIS BUSINESS LAW JOURNAL 207–236 (2010).

9.   Wilson, Darryl C., *The Caribbean Intellectual Property Office (CARIPO): New, Useful, and Necessary*, 19 MICHIGAN STATE JOURNAL OF INTERNATIONAL LAW 551–588 (2011).

## ISF

*See* Importer Security Filing.

## ISO

International Organization for Standardization, commonly called the International Standards Organization.

The ISO establishes standards for business, government, and society on a wide range of products, thus yielding some degree of harmonization on standards. As the ISO explains, it is:

> is the world's **largest developer** and publisher of **International Standards**.

> [The] ISO is a **network** of the national standards institutes of **161 countries**, one member per country, with a Central Secretariat in Geneva, Switzerland, that coordinates the system.

> [The] ISO is a **non-governmental organization** that forms a bridge between the public and private sectors. On the one hand, many of its member institutes are part of the governmental structure of their countries, or are mandated by their government. On the other hand, other members have their roots uniquely in the private sector, having been set up by national partnerships of industry associations.

> Therefore, ISO enables a **consensus** to be reached on solutions that meet both the requirements of business and **the broader needs of society**.[435]

The work of the ISO is relevant to the WTO *Agreement on Technical Barriers to Trade (TBT Agreement)*, which calls for the use of relevant international standards.

*Suggestions for Further Research:*

Article:

---

[435] International Organization for Standardization, *About ISO, posted at* www.iso.org/iso/about.htm (emphasis original).

1.   Fontanelli, Filippo, *ISO and Codex Standards and International Trade Law: What Gets Said is Not What's Heard*, 60 INTERNATIONAL & COMPARATIVE LAW QUARTERLY 895–932 (2011).

## ISRAEL — UNITED STATES FREE TRADE AGREEMENT

The *Israel — United States Free Trade Agreement*, dated 22 April 1985.

## *ITA* (FIRST MEANING)

The *Information Technology Agreement*, concluded in December 1996 at the first WTO Ministerial Conference in Seattle, and signed in March 1997. The *ITA*, negotiated under WTO auspices, initially covered more than 90 percent of world trade in information and technology products. These products — grouped into about 180 categories — range from computers and semiconductors to monitors and telecommunications equipment. The *Agreement* eliminated all tariffs on these products as of 1 January 2000. On a limited number of products, and for some developing countries, phase-in periods lasti ng up to 2005 applied.

The *ITA* is a plurilateral bargain, hence many WTO Members are not parties to it. The Members that have signed on include most developed countries, major developing countries like India, Indonesia, Malaysia, and the Philippines, small developing countries like El Salvador and Panama, and about a dozen countries in Eastern Europe and the former Soviet Union. As of December 2007, there were 70 WTO Member signatories to the *ITA*. Yet, they account for 97 percent of world trade in IT products. Four years later, in December 2011, there were 73 of 153 WTO Members that had joined the *ITA*. Clearly, the pace of expanding the signatories to the *ITA* is slow. One device essentially to compel joining the *Agreement* is the accession process: countries seeking to join the WTO are likely to be asked to join the *ITA*, too.

In March 2012, Colombia joined the *ITA*, making it the 74th signatory. With this development, the ITA participants accounted for about 97 percent of world trade in IT products.

Note that unlike the WTO *Agreement on Government Procurement (GPA)*, which also is a plurilateral accord, the *ITA* allows for free riding. Benefits from the *ITA* are available to all WTO Members, ones that are parties to the *ITA* and ones that are not. That is, *ITA* benefits are enjoyed by all WTO Members, whether or not they participate in the *ITA* by making a commitment to eliminate duties on information technology products. In contrast, *GPA* benefits extend only to Members that are party to the *GPA*. If they do not join the *GPA* and liberalize their government procurement markets, then they do not benefit from the liberalization of those markets by Members that are parties to the accord. In brief, the *ITA* is an open plurilateral accord, whereas the *GPA* is a closed one.

In March 2000, the United States voiced concerns that many Members that are party to the *ITA* were not living up to their obligations. For example, the

United States cited customs authorities in Thailand as demanding a certificate of origin before allowing high-tech imports to pass duty free, and European Union (EU) customs officials as continuing to impose a 14 percent duty on set top boxes (*i.e.*, communication devices that provide internet access through TVs).

In October 2006, the United States again argued some WTO Members that are parties to the *ITA* were undermining it.[436] They were not giving duty-free treatment to products entitled to it. Such products included certain set-top boxes, computer flat panel displays, computer multifunction units, and digital cameras. For example, most EU member countries classified an LCD monitor as a computer monitor, and gave it zero duty treatment, the Netherlands classified it as a video monitor. Thus, the Netherlands imposed a 14 percent tariff. And, throughout the EU, a 14 percent tariff applied to LCD monitors larger than 19 inches.

In general, the United States said, the *ITA* must not be interpreted narrowly as applying only to older or less sophisticated versions of a product. Rather, it must apply to newer, more sophisticated versions — otherwise, the *ITA* will be less and less useful in liberalizing trade as product innovation occurs.

Efforts at reaching an "*ITA II*," *i.e.*, a second-generation *ITA* that would cover products not embraced by the first generation accord, thus far have failed. The proposed *ITA II* accord would have enlarged the scope of duty free treatment to include an additional 200 products. However, the draft *ITA II* deal was a casualty of the collapse of the 1999 WTO Ministerial Conference in Seattle.

In May 2008, the United States and Japan launched WTO actions against the European Union (EU). The essence of the claim was the EU imposed tariffs on new technology consumer products that ran afoul of the *ITA*. The products at issue were facsimile machines, flat panel displays, input or output unites, and set-top boxes with a communication function.

*Suggestions for Further Research:*

Articles:

1.   Forbes, Reshad & Christos Sakellariou, *The WTO to Settle Dispute over EU Tariffs for IT Products: The ITA Case*, 15 INTERNATIONAL TRADE LAW & REGULATION issue 1, 14–22 (2009).

2.   Peng, Shin-yi, *Taxing Innovation? — The Evolving Coverage of the Information Technology Agreement*, 64 TAX LAWYER 79–96 (2010).

## ITA (SECOND MEANING)

The International Trade Administration unit of the United States Department of Commerce (DOC).

---

[436] *See* Daniel Pruzin, *U.S. Voices Concern to WTO About Tariffs on High-Tech Goods; Criticism Aimed at EU*, 23 International Trade Reporter (BNA) 1528–29 (26 October 2006).

The principal — or, at least the most renowned — responsibility of the ITA is the calculation of dumping margins and subsidization amounts towards the possible imposition or review of antidumping (AD) or countervailing duty (CVD) orders. The ITA does so through its Import Administration, or IA, division. Notably, the IA has assigned special AD/CVD enforcement teams tasked only with China investigations — the China/NME section (where "NME" stands for "non-market economy").

The ITA and IA also are responsible for:

- Approving and managing Foreign Trade Zones (FTZ).

- Supervising statutorily authorized imports of materials for the physically disabled (through the Nairobi Protocol).

- Overseeing the importation of scientific instruments and watches (through the Florence Agreement Protocol).

- Reviewing market access and trade agreement compliance issues, through the Market Access and Compliance (MAC) section.

- Economic research, through the Manufacturing and Services (MAS) section, which is part of the "Industry Analysis" branch.

Related to these ITA functions is the Foreign Service branch of the DOC. This branch is staffed by diplomats stationed in United States embassies to promote American trade overseas.

## ITC

The United States International Trade Commission, located in Washington, D.C.

Initially established in 1916 as the United States Tariff Commission, the ITC received its contemporary name from the Trade Act of 1974, as amended. The ITC is an independent, quasi-judicial agency that not only conducts studies and issues reports on trade matters, but also administers important trade remedy laws. For example, it is responsible for injury determinations in AD and CVD cases, and for adjudicating Section 201 and 337 cases. The ITC also is responsible for providing the President with advice on trade negotiations, and on the Generalized System of Preferences (GSP).

The President appoints Commissioners to the ITC for nine year terms. Of the six Commissioners in total, not more than three may be of the same political party. The President designates the Chair and Vice-Chair for two year terms, and successive Chairs may not be of the same political party.

*Suggestions for Further Research:*

Articles:

1. Bugg, Robert E., Note, *The International Trade Commission and Changes to United States Patent Law*, 76 Brooklyn Law Review 1093–1119 (2011).

2.  Dorn, Joseph W., *U.S. Court of International Trade Decisions During 2007 in Appeals of Determinations of the U.S. International Trade Commission*, 40 GEORGETOWN JOURNAL OF INTERNATIONAL LAW 219–241 (2008).

3.  Von Schriltz, Karl, *U.S. Court of International Trade Decisions in 2008 in Appeals of Determinations of the U.S. International Trade Commission*, 41 GEORGETOWN JOURNAL OF INTERNATIONAL LAW 1–51 (2009).

4.  Young, Kimberly R. & Frederick P. Waite, *Overview of 2009 Decisions by the U.S. Court of International Trade in Appeals Determinations of the U.S. International Trade Commission*, 42 GEORGETOWN JOURNAL OF INTERNATIONAL LAW 5–34 (2010).

## ITO

International Trade Organization.

The entity that would have been created by the *Havana Charter* if that *Charter* had entered into force. Some observers regard the WTO as a reincarnation of the failed ITO, though the ITO *Charter* was broader in scope than the *Agreement Establishing the World Trade Organization (WTO Agreement)* and its Annexes, thus suggesting the WTO is a more narrowly-focused institution than the ITO would have been.

*Suggestions for Further Research:*

Article:

1.  Scott, James, *Developing Countries in the ITO and GATT Negotiations*, 9 JOURNAL OF INTERNATIONAL TRADE LAW AND POLICY number 1, 5–24 (2010).

## ITO CHARTER

A synonym for "Havana Charter."

# J

## J CURVE

An economic proposition about the effect of a depreciation or devaluation of a country's currency on that country's balance of trade, specifically, its current account.

The J-Curve posits that immediately after the decline in the value of the country's currency relative to the value of the currencies of its trading partners, the country may experience a current account deficit. However, this deficit will be eliminated over time, and eventually the country will experience a surplus balance. There is, in other words, a lag in the effect of an exchange rate adjustment on the current account.

The reason is that the volume of a country's imports and exports cannot possibly react immediately to the exchange rate change. Importers already have placed orders weeks, or even months, in advance with foreign sellers. Exporters are filling orders placed by foreign buyers weeks or months earlier. Thus, the volume of imports stays high, and the volume of exports remains low, in the period immediately following the depreciation or devaluation.

In addition, the position of importers and exporters in the country worsens if both groups are quoting prices in their country's currency. For example, suppose the Indian *rupee* depreciates in value relative to the United States dollar. Indian importers must pay more *rupees* to import goods from the United States. American exporters want dollars for their goods, and it takes more *rupees* to buy each dollar to pay for the goods. Therefore, the cost of imports into India, denominated in *rupees*, rises. As for Indian exporters, suppose they want *rupees* for their goods. American buyers do not need to spend so many dollars to buy rupees to pay for the goods, because the *rupee* is cheaper relative to the dollar following the depreciation. Thus, the dollar value of Indian exports falls. In brief, devaluation or depreciation results in an immediate rise in the domestic (*rupee*) price of imports, and an immediate fall in the foreign (dollar) price of exports.

However, in time the change in relative prices — specifically, the increase in the price of imports, and decrease in the price of exports, as denominated in the country's currency — that is caused by the exchange rate shift will take effect. Importers will curtail their purchases, because imports have become more expensive. Exporters will find that demand for their products has increased because those products, in foreign currency terms, are cheaper. The exporters will, therefore, expand output — assuming they are able to do so, given constraints on factors of production. In brief, the expectation is that over time, importers and exporters alike will negotiate new trade contracts. The result will be a decline in the volume of imports, and an increase in the volume of exports, hence an improved current account balance.

Graphically, if time is plotted on the horizontal (X) axis, and the balance of trade on the vertical (Y) axis, then the time path of the current account will approximate the shape of the letter "J." The downward portion of the "J," corresponding to the static or worsening deficit immediately after devaluation, is generally anticipated to last about two to three quarters. Thereafter, movement is expected on the upward portion, as the balance improves.

*Suggestions for Further Research:*

Book:

1.   BREMMER, IAN, THE J CURVE: A NEW WAY TO UNDERSTAND WHY NATIONS RISE AND FALL (2006).

Articles:

1.   Backus, David, Patrick Kehoe & Finn Kydland, *Dynamics of the Trade Balance and the Terms of Trade: The J-Curve?*, 84 AMERICAN ECONOMIC REVIEW 84–103 (1994).

2.   Beckington, Jeffrey S. & Matthew R. Amon (Student), *Competitive Currency Depreciation: The Need for a More Effective International Legal Regime*, 10 JOURNAL OF INTERNATIONAL BUSINESS & LAW 209–268 (2011).

3.   Bergsten, C. Fred, *The Need for a Robust Response to Chinese Currency Manipulation — Policy Options for the Obama Administration Including Countervailing Currency Intervention*, 10 JOURNAL OF INTERNATIONAL BUSINESS & LAW 269–280 (2011).

4.   Goldburn, Tricia D., Comment, *Dollars & Renminbis: Curbing the United States' Raging Trade Deficit with China by Dismantling the Dollar — RMB Peg*, 25 PENN STATE INTERNATIONAL LAW REVIEW 737–757 (2007).

5.   Mercurio, Bryan & Celine Sze Ning Leung, *Is China a "Currency Manipulator"?: The Legitimacy of China's Exchange Regime Under the Current International Legal Framework*, 43 THE INTERNATIONAL LAWYER 1257–1300 (2009).

6.   Pettis, Elizabeth L., *Is China's Manipulation of its Currency An Actionable Violation of the IMF and / or WTO Agreements?*, 10 JOURNAL OF INTERNATIONAL BUSINESS & LAW 281–296 (2011).

## *JACKSON–VANIK AMENDMENT*

Section 402 of Title IV of the *Trade Act of 1974*, as amended. The *Jackson-Vanik Amendment* is codified at 19 U.S.C. Section 2431 *et seq.* The *Amendment* requires the President to deny MFN treatment to a non market economy (NME) country that:

> (1)   was ineligible for such treatment as of the date of enactment, and

> (2)   denies or seriously restricts the right of its citizens to emigrate.

Section 401 of Title IV of the *1974 Trade Act* forbids the President from granting Permanent Normal Trade Relations (PNTR) to a country subject to review under the *Amendment*. Hence, Congressional action is needed to remove a country from the review process.

The political concern underlying the *Amendment* was the intolerable treatment of ethnic and religious minorities, most notably Jews, Catholics, and Evangelical Christians, by Soviet bloc governments. Congress was particularly concerned the Administration of President Richard M. Nixon, in pursuit of a policy of détente with the former Union of Soviet Socialist Republics, would grant MFN treatment to the Soviet Union and its allies, regardless of persecution of religious minorities. Secretary of State Henry Kissinger aggressively pursued this policy, but some in Congress saw it as little else than appeasement, and thus a compromise on universal human rights principles.

How could this legislation — which limits America's adherence to the unconditional MFN principle — be justified under GATT? It did not need to be. None of the targets of Title IV was a GATT contracting party or WTO Member. Some of them did accede to the WTO, but by that time the United States was prepared to, and did, remove the countries from the scope of the application of Title IV.

Significantly, the *Jackson-Vanik Amendment* empowers the President to waive its requirements for full compliance. A country may qualify for a waiver if the President (1) determines that a waiver will substantially promote the objective of freedom of emigration and (2) has received assurances from the country that its emigration practices will lead substantially to the achievement of this objective. The President must submit an annual report to Congress regarding each country that obtains a waiver.

The President's waiver authority is subject to annual renewal by Congress. Renewal occurs automatically upon a recommendation from the President by 3 June of each year that extending the waiver authority for another year will further the purposes of the *Jackson-Vanik Amendment*. By joint resolution, Congress can disapprove of the extension either generally or with respect to a specific country. If it seeks to prevent renewal, then each house of Congress must pass the joint resolution by a simple majority vote within 60 days of the expiration of the previous waiver. The disapproval resolution would take effect 60 days after its enactment. However, the disapproval resolution would be subject to a presidential veto, which Congress would have to override by a two-thirds vote. In every year since 1976, the President's waiver authority has been renewed.

The exercise of waiver authority, however, has been political in two very clear senses. First, does the President really have the facts to justify a waiver in a particular case? Second, does the President enjoy sufficient support in both houses of Congress to survive a joint resolution disapproving of the exercise of the waiver authority?

During the Cold War, no NME country was found to be in full compliance with the *Jackson-Vanik* freedom of emigration requirements. However, that is not to say the United States denied most favored nation (MFN), *i.e.*, PNTR, treatment to every NME. Between 1976 and 1989, the President concluded bilateral commercial agreements with, and waived the *Jackson-Vanik* requirements for, three countries: Romania (effective 3 August 1975), Hungary (effective 7 July 1978), and China (effective 1 February 1980). Each country thereby received MFN treatment from the United States. The bilateral agreements were renewed for additional three year periods, and the waivers were extended annually.

By far the most widely covered and divisive case of the application of the *Jackson-Vanik Amendment* and attendant waiver authority is China. In 1979, following President Jimmy Carter's recognition of the People's Republic of China (PRC), the United States and China signed a bilateral trade agreement that provided mutual MFN benefits. The agreement took effect in 1980. However, because China was a NME, the United States granted it MFN status subject to the requirements of the *Jackson-Vanik Amendment*. Only if the President determined that China permitted free and unrestricted emigration would China receive MFN treatment. And, only if the President determined that excusing the requirements would substantially promote the objectives of the *Amendment* could he recommend waiving them in successive 12 month periods.

The *Jackson-Vanik Amendment* thus opened a new front on the raucous debate about "China policy." In general, on one side falls the business community, which is mesmerized by China's dramatic economic growth and eager to help "tap" the China market. On the other side falls a coalition of strange bedfellows: organized labor, environmentalists, religious conservatives, and human rights activists. Respectively, they condemn substandard labor conditions, heavily pollution by industries, suppression of free expression of religious belief, and suppression of freedom of speech and assembly. Caught in between these two extremes is the United States government. It must avoid promoting a policy that alienates either side, while confronting the problem of how trade policy with China fits in with the broader national security question of how the United States should "engage" China and whether China's ascendancy is (as Chinese leaders claim) a "Peaceful Rise."

The clash among these three forces has produced an annual controversy over waiver of the *Jackson-Vanik* requirements for China. It is not surprising that in every year (at least until the PRC acceded to the WTO, on 11 December 2001) since the Tiananmen Square incident (4 June 1989), members of Congress have introduced bills to terminate China's MFN status or place conditions on it. But, in no year has both houses of Congress passed such a bill. Indeed, in virtually every year, both houses defeated efforts to deny a 12 month extension of the President's *Jackson-Vanik* waiver authority and thereby China's MFN status.

About the only notable change Congress has made, which occurred in 1998, was to change the designation from MFN to "NTR," for Normal Trade Relations, *i.e.*, PNTR. Technically, MFN is the more accurate term — no country gets a more favorable trade arrangement than any other country. But, at least to those not bothered about precision or tradition, the new designation seems to have defused the renewal process: China just gets the "normal" treatment that almost everyone else gets.

Of course, the *Jackson–Vanik Amendment* applied to Russia on the accession of that country to the WTO. As of April 2010, it was generally agreed that Russia complied fully with the freedom of emigration provisions in the *Amendment*. When Russia released the "Schneerson Archive" (which had been seized during the Second World War by the Nazis, but later returned to the Soviet Union), one Congressman — Representative Brad Sherman (Democrat — California), Chairman of the House Subcommittee on Terrorism, Nonproliferation, and Trade — said: "The Jews of the Soviet Union are no longer held hostage, but their sacred papers are."[437] Another Congressman, Representative Dana Rohrabacher (Democrat — California), argued China was a "totalitarian monster," which Russia is not, as Russia has experienced greater human rights, religious freedom, and has opposition political parties and newspapers (albeit with some selective repression of journalists).[438] Moreover, nearly 2.5 million Jews (as of March 2012) had emigrated from Russia to Europe.[439] Thus, he argued, it was a contradiction to have supported China in its WTO accession, but not support Russia in its bid.

As for Russia, its accession was approved by the WTO at the 15–17 December 2011 Geneva Ministerial Conference. At the urging of the Administration of President Barack H. Obama, Congress removed Russia from the *Jackson-Vanik* process, and Congress considered repeal of the *Jackson-Vanik Amendment*. After all, Russia was the last country to which that legislation was relevant. However, the United States had not completed the legislative changes it needed to make to the 1974 *Jackson-Vanik Amendment* in time for the WTO approval of the Russian accession terms in December 2011. That is, the United States failed to grant Russia unconditional MFN treatment by that time. Accordingly, in December 2011, the United States had to submit a notice to the WTO that it was invoking the non-application provisions of GATT and the *WTO Agreement*.[440] Until Congress waived the *Jackson-Vanik* review for Russia, American firms would be ineligible for many preferential terms that the United States negotiated in the accession package, thereby putting them at a competitive disadvantage vis-à-vis other foreign firms operating in Russia. In the meantime, Russia felt (in the words of Sergei Guriev, President,

---

[437] *Quoted in* Len Bracken, *Lawmakers, Witnesses Vary on Graduating Russia from Jackson — Vanik Requirements*, 27 International Trade Reporter (BNA) 668 (6 May 2010).

[438] *Quoted in* Len Bracken, *Lawmakers, Witnesses Vary on Graduating Russia from Jackson — Vanik Requirements*, 27 International Trade Reporter (BNA) 668 (6 May 2010).

[439] *See* Len Bracken, *Kirk, Baucus, Cardin See Russia Trade, Human Rights Concerns Being Addressed*, 29 International Trade Reporter (BNA) 400 (15 March 2012).

[440] *See* Len Bracken, *Russian Economist Sees Continuity on WTO Membership with Putin Victory*, 29 International Trade Reporter (BNA) 365 (8 March 2012).

Center for Economic and Financial Research, New Economic School, Moscow) "humiliated."[441]

In place of the *Jackson-Vanik Amendment*, Congress debated the *Sergei Magnitsky Rule of Law Accountability Act of 2011* (S. 1039), named after the 137-year old lawyer Sergei Magnitsky, a lawyer who was tortured to death in a Russian jail (Matrosskaya Tishina prison) in November 2009.[442] He worked for the Moscow law firm of Firestone Duncan. While working on a tax case affecting a hedge fund based in London, he supposedly committed the "crime" of accusing police of participating in a $230 million tax fraud. The *Act* proposed to put Russian officials implicated in human rights abuses on a black list. American visas would be revoked for any person involved in such crimes. Further, the *Act* would oblige the United States Secretary of the Treasury to freeze and prohibit any transactions in American property by such persons, and order American financial institutions to take certain measures against entities involved in money laundering or conspiracy. Oddly, given its human rights rhetoric, the Obama Administration opposed this *Act*. It argued it already had legal authority to blacklist dubious Russian, and the *Act* would antagonize Russia.

The grant of NTR to Russia, and eventual waiver of the *Jackson-Vanik Amendment*, followed similar action by the United States with respect to Georgia and Kyrgyzstan (both in 2000), Armenia (in 2005), and Ukraine (in 2006). Until its repeal, however, the *Amendment* remained applicable to seven former Soviet republics. The United States waived application to Vietnam in 2006.

*References:*

Books –

1. ASLUND, ANDERS & GARY HUFBAUER, THE UNITED STATES SHOULD ESTABLISH NORMAL TRADE RELATIONS WITH RUSSIA (Washington, D.C., Peterson Institute for International Economics, 2012).

## JIIA

Japan Institute of International Affairs.

Established in 1959 by Japan's great post-Second World War Prime Minister, Shigeru Yoshida, the JIIA is a leading think tank in Japan on international relations. The JIIA is dedicated to research on long- and medium-term issues involving international politics and security, and to promoting communication and understanding between Japan and other countries.

---

[441] *Quoted in* Len Bracken, *Russian Economist Sees Continuity on WTO Membership with Putin Victory*, 29 International Trade Reporter (BNA) 365 (8 March 2012).

[442] *See* Charles Clover & Anna Fifield, *Congress Urges Sanctions on Russian Officials Over Abuses*, FINANCIAL TIMES, 29 November 2011, at 3.

# K

## KIMBERLY PROCESS WAIVER

*See* Trade — Human Rights Link.

## *KORUS*

The *United States — Korea Free Trade Agreement.*

Negotiations, which commenced in June 2006, proceeded slowly on *KORUS*. Negotiations concluded at the end of March 2007, following eight formal rounds of talks over a 10 month period. *KORUS* was signed on 30 June 2007. Both dates are significant. The authority of the President to negotiate trade agreements under *Trade Promotion Authority (TPA)* expired on 30 June 2007, and the deadline for the President to notify Congress of a new agreement that would be submitted to Congress was three months before the expiry, *i.e.*, 1 April 2007. Ratification took years, during which there was no clear timetable for legislative action, amidst a great deal of politicking in the United States, and an economic slump around the world. Finally, *KORUS* was approved by the United States Congress in October 2011, and Korean legislature in November 2011. It entered into force on 1 January 2012.

Without doubt, *KORUS* is the most significant commercial accord h the United States has signed since the *North American Free Trade Agreement* (*NAFTA*, which entered into force on 1 January 1994). Korea boasts the 10th largest economy in the world, and third largest one in Asia (with a 2005 Gross Domestic Product of nearly U.S. $1 trillion). For goods, Korea is the seventh largest trading nation (both exports and imports of goods, with U.S. $278 billion and $248 billion, respectively, as of 2005). For services, Korea is the largest exporter in the world (U.S. $40 billion in 2004), and the sixth largest importer (U.S. $50 billion in 2004). Bilateral trade between Korea and the United States is enormous. Korea is America's seventh largest trading partner (as of 2006), and America is Korea's third largest trading partner. The pattern of trade is diverse. The United States exports aircraft, beef, corn, fruit, manufactured products, plastics, pork, semiconductor chips, vegetables, and wheat to Korea. Korea ships autos and auto parts, apparel, appliances, and electronics, among a broad array of products, to America. Nonetheless, the Korean market is particularly protected in respect of certain sectors — notably, agricultural goods and cars. *KORUS* holds out the promise of boosting significantly American market access in those sectors.

The negotiations were conducted with both sides facing substantial political and economic risks. From the American side, controversial issues included Korean tariff barriers on beef, pork, poultry, and certain horticulture, as well as autos. From the Korean side, American insistence on yarn — forward rules of origin for textiles and apparel (T&A) posed difficulties, as Korea favored less strict rules of origin.

Reactions to *KORUS* in both the United States and Korea have been mixed. On one side, the American business community, in large part — particularly financial services firms — has expressed strong support for the accord. In the middle, major American agricultural groups have delayed a full response until South Korea formally agrees to lift its restrictions on imports of beef shipments from the United States. On the other side, some United States automobile manufacturers and major unions have criticized it. A detailed examination of the terms of *KORUS* (set out in Tables in Annex C of this *Dictionary*) suggests their criticisms are unfounded. Moreover, Korea rightly points out that American cars tend to be too large for congested, narrow roads in Korea, and consumer too much gas in Korea, where gas is heavily taxed and thus far more expensive than in the United States. While American car advocates complain Korean nationalism is a non-tariff barrier to their vehicles, Koreans point out that many wealthy buyers in Korea simply prefer prestigious, high-performance cars made by BMW and Lexus — as is the case among elites in America.

As intimated, beef trade has proven especially controversial, and triggered massive street protests in Korea (*e.g.*, in April-May 2008). In April 2008, the United States Trade Representative (USTR) signed a beef import protocol with Korea, supposedly paving the way for a resumption of American beef exports to Korea. Protests blocked implementation of that protocol until the two countries agreed to an exchange of side letters. Those letters tightened safety restrictions, specifically, permitting Korea to ban importation of certain additional cattle parts, and reaffirming the right of Korea to take measures to protect the health of the Korean people. Further, the United States Department of Agriculture (USDA) agreed it would monitor a pledge by American exporters to ship to Korea beef only from cattle less than 30 months of age.

Notably, *KORUS* contains a dispute settlement mechanism. In the event of a disagreement between the United States and Korea as to how to interpret a provision of the FTA, or of conflict over the application of the agreement (where one party accuses the other of acting inconsistently with an FTA provision), this mechanism is to be used. The Figure below outlines the mechanism.

FIGURE:

### *KORUS* DISPUTE SETTLEMENT MECHANISM

---

### *Consultations*

Request for consultations is made by the complaining party.

The two parties have 60 days to reach a mutually-agreeable solution to their dispute.

### *Referral to Joint Committee*

If consultations fail to achieve a mutually-agreeable solution, then either the complaining or respondent party may refer the dispute to the Joint Committee.

### *Joint Committee Consideration*

Joint Committee endeavors to resolve the dispute.

### *Dispute Settlement Panel — Adjudication and Initial Report*

Upon failure to resolve the dispute by at the Joint Committee level, a dispute settlement Panel is established.

The Panel must adjudicate the case, and produce an initial report of findings and decisions within 180 days of its establishment.

The Panel circulates its initial report to the parties for comment.

Settlement could be induced by issuance of the draft report.

**FIGURE (continued)**

---

### *Dispute Settlement Panel — Final Report*

Following the receipt of comments (if any) on its initial report, the Dispute Settlement Panel may modify its report as needed.

The Panel then issues its final report, which embodies its ruling.

Here, again, the parties may reach a mutually acceptable resolution.

---

---

### *Dispute Settlement Panel — Compliance Review*

The Dispute Settlement Panel may undertake a Compliance Review, the purpose of which is to ascertain whether the losing party has adhered to the ruling of the Panel in its final report.

---

*Suggestions for Further Research:*

Articles:

1.   Choi, Won-Mog, *Aggressive Regionalism in Korea — U.S. FTA: The Present and Future of Korea's FTA Policy*, 12 JOURNAL OF INTERNATIONAL ECONOMIC LAW 595–615 (2009).

2.   Kim, Ho Cheol, *Does Annex 22-B of the Proposed United States–Korea Free Trade Agreement Contemplate and Allow for Trade with respect to North Korea?*, 40 GEORGETOWN JOURNAL OF INTERNATIONAL LAW 67–97 (2008).

3.   Lee, Soonghyun Daniel, Note, *Laissez-Faire International Investor-State Dispute Resolution Settlement Mechanism: The Inadequacy of Adopting U.S. Legal Standards for the KORUS FTA*, 18 TRANSNATIONAL LAW & CONTEMPORARY PROBLEMS 499–523 (2009).

4.   Shin, Hi-Taek, *The Domestic Decision-Making Process and its Implications for International Commitments: American Beef in Korea*, 34 YALE JOURNAL OF INTERNATIONAL LAW 567–574 (2009).

5.   Skibola, Nicole, *The U.S. — Korea Free Trade Agreement: The Evolution of Fair Trade Through the Free Trade System*, 10 UNIVERSITY OF CALIFORNIA DAVIS BUSINESS LAW JOURNAL 183–206 (2010).

6.   Suh, Younghyun & Yoon-Young Angela Choe, *Negotiators as Mediators: The Case of 1987–1995 Korea — United States Bilateral Trade Negotiations*, 26 NEGOTIATION JOURNAL 435–452 (2010).

Other Sources:

1.   Congressional Research Reports for the People: *The Proposed South Korea-U.S. Free Trade Agreement* (KORUS FTA), http://opencrs.cdt.org/document/RL33435 (last visited 31 August 2007).

2.   New York Law School, Center for International Law, *KORUS: A Trade Agreement Binding the United States and Korea?*, 10 THE INTERNATIONAL REVIEW 24–27 (fall 2007).

## KUZNETS CURVE

An inverted "U" curve relating to the age old question "What causes poverty?," or phrased differently, "Why are some people poor?"

In the 1950s and 1960s, the famous economist Simon Kuznets argued that greater income inequality accompanies early stages of growth. However, as growth proceeds, income tends to become more equal. In graphical terms, plotting income inequality (on the vertical axis) against income (on the horizontal axis) is an inverted U pattern, known as the "Kuznets Curve," shown on the Graph below.

The reason for the early-stage inequity is wealthier people earn and save more than poorer people, and reinvest their savings in productive enterprises. As those enterprises grow, they afford employment opportunities for others. Eventually a middle class begins to develop and enlarge, as experienced in Brazil, Mexico, and India. Kuznets also said no one level of income is the transition point for all countries between greater and reduced inequality.

GRAPH:

THE KUZNETS CURVE (INVERTED U)

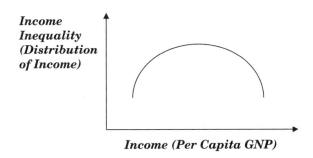

*Income (Per Capita GNP)*

Empirically, the Kuznets Curve has been tested often. It is evident from many of the tests, particularly ones using cross-section (as opposed to time-series) data, and which include data from Latin American countries. That said, of course, whether and the extent to which trade — as distinct from other possible factors affecting income distribution, such as asset ownership, education enrollment, or population growth — plays a role in shaping the inverted U curve remains open to debate.

## KYOTO CONVENTION

The 1974 *International Convention on the Simplification and Harmonization of Customs Procedures*. Annex D.1 of this *Convention* contains rules of origin. The *Convention* originally was signed on 25 September 1974. The World Customs Organization (WCO) Council adopted a revised version on 30 June 1999, which entered into force on 3 February 2006.[443]

The purpose of the *Kyoto Convention* is to establish uniform customs procedures, and thereby providing a predictable and efficient environment for international commerce. Annex D.1 of the *Convention* contains rules of origin.

## KYOTO PROTOCOL

An international environmental treaty, which was adopted on 11 December 1997, and which entered into force 16 February 2005, designed to combat global warming.

The *Kyoto Protocol* is a complement to the 1992 (adopted) United National Framework Convention on Climate Change (UNFCCC). The *Protocol* establishes emissions targets for six greenhouse gases:

(1)  $CO_2$- Carbon Dioxide

(2)  $CH_4$- Methane

(3)  $N_2O$- Nitrous Oxide

(4)  HFCs- Hydrofluorocarbons

(5)  PFCs- Perfluorocarbons

(6)  $SF_6$- Sulfur Hexafluoride

These targets are based on measures of tons of $CO_2$ gases, informally known as "Kyoto units." Each country has to commit to reductions in these gases. Canada and Japan have a six percent reduction commitment, the European Union (EU) an eight percent reduction commitment, and the United States a seven percent reduction commitment. As is widely known, the United States has not ratified the *Kyoto Protocol*.[444]

---

[443] The revised *Convention* is posted at World Customs Organization, *www.gfptt.org/uploadedEditorImages/00000311.pdf.*

[444] *See* Fiona Harvey, *Climate Change Move Leaves World Guessing*, FINANCIAL TIMES, 2 June 2007, at 3.

Notably, under the *Kyoto Protocol*, some countries are entitled to increase production of gases, namely, Norway one percent more, Australia eight percent more, and Iceland 10 percent more. New Zealand has a zero percent change commitment.

Countries can affect an increase in target emission allowances through reforestation and land management activities (creating "sinks"), or through the sponsorship of clean energy development mechanisms (CDMs) in poor countries. Countries can also trade their excess units with other countries which may need them, *i.e.*, the *Kyoto Protocol* establishes a secondary market in emission allowances trading.

Entry into force of the *Kyoto Protocol* occurred when a combination of countries representing 55 percent of the total emitters of greenhouse gases globally individually ratified the treaty. A separate set of accords, called the "Marrakesh Accords," were agreed upon in 2001 to provide guidance on the mechanisms for *Protocol* implementation. The commitment period to reduce these greenhouse gas emissions is from 2008 through 2012, with an unclear projection forward after 2012. The *Protocol* may need to be renegotiated to extend beyond 2012, which would prove highly controversial. That is because, in part, of the list of countries — in addition to the United States — that never ratified it: Australia, China, India, and Russia.

*Suggestions foor Further Research:*

Book:

1.   HUFBAUER, GARY C., STEVE CHARNOVITZ & JISUN KIM, GLOBAL WARMING AND THE WORLD TRADING SYSTEM (2009).

Articles:

1.   Griffin, Ronald C., *A Prairie Perspective on Global Warming and Climate Change: The Use of Law, Technology, and Economics to Establish Private Sector Markets to Compliment Kyoto*, 17 SOUTHEASTERN ENVIRONMENTAL LAW JOURNAL 95–135 (2008).

2.   Halvorssen, Anita M., *UNFCCC, the Kyoto Protocol, and the WTO — Brewing Conflicts or Are They Mutually Supportive?*, 36 DENVER JOURNAL OF INTERNATIONAL LAW & POLICY 369–379 (2008).

3.   Hawkins, Slayde, Note, *Skirting Protectionism: A GHG-Based Trade Restriction under the WTO*, 20 GEORGETOWN INTERNATIONAL ENVIRONMENTAL LAW REVIEW 427–450 (2008).

4.   Ponnamblam, Arjun, Note, *U.S. Climate Change Legislation and the Use of GATT Article XX to Justify a "Competitiveness Provision" in the Wake of Brazil–Tyres*, 40 GEORGETOWN JOURNAL OF INTERNATIONAL LAW 261–289 (2008).

# L

## *LABOR SIDE AGREEMENT*

The 1993 *North American Agreement on Labor Cooperation*, associated with the North American Free Trade Agreement (*NAFTA*). Sometimes abbreviated the "*NAALC*," the accord commonly is called the "*Labor Side Agreement*." It was the first time in which the United States negotiated an agreement concerning labor standards as a supplementary accord to an international trade agreement. The Figure below sets out the institutions of the *Labor Side Agreement*.

The *Labor Side Agreement* calls upon *NAFTA* Parties to enforce effectively their existing labor laws. This requirement ensures the Parties do not compete against each other in a "race to the bottom," with each Party trying to attract trade and investment by relaxing its labor rules more than the others. That is, the requirement sets existing labor rules as a minimum standard, or floor. However, that approach to addressing trade and labor issues is problematical for two reasons.

First, it does not obligate a country to upgrade its labor laws. A country might not meet certain internationally recognized worker rights. The *Side Agreement* requires a "stand still" at the level of existing labor protections, and no lowering of them, but leaves Parties free to enhance worker rights — or not. Second, the approach the Side Agreement takes does not mandate harmonization of worker rights across borders. Theoretically, American, Canadian, and Mexican worker rights could be effectively enforced by each Party, yet remain materially different in substance, in perpetuity.

To deal with challenge of upward harmonization, the United States Congress and the White House agreed, in the summer 2007, to a new approach. This approach would apply both to labor and environmental matters. It would require the United States to negotiate special provisions in free trade agreements (FTAs) mandating each signatory ensure its labor and environmental rules are at the level of internationally accepted standards — and, of course, to enforce effectively those standards. This approach is notable because (*inter alia*) the metrics for acceptable labor and environmental practices is an international one, not a self-interested, unilateral benchmark set by a one country.

Undoubtedly, the new approach would have been impossible without a change in power of Congress from Republicans to Democrats following the November 2006 election. Congress contemplates applying the new approach retroactively, to certain FTAs the United States Trade Representative (USTR) had more or less viewed as completed. It also expects the USTR to execute the new approach in any new FTAs.

## FIGURE:

### *NAFTA LABOR SIDE AGREEMENT* INSTITUTIONS

**Tri-National Institutions:**

**COMMISSION FOR LABOR COOPERATION (CLC)**

- Consists of Ministerial Council and supporting Secretariat.
  - In Dallas.

**Council**

- Consists of United States Secretary of Labor, Canadian Minister of Human Resources Development, and Mexican Secretary of Labor and Social Welfare.
  - Responsible for:
— overseeing the implementation of the Labor Side Agreement
— hiring the Executive Director of the Secretariat
— directing the work of the Secretariat.

**Secretariat**

- Led by an Executive Director.
  - In Dallas.
  - Responsible for:
— assisting the Council in exercising its functions
— preparing reports and studies.

**National Institutions:**

**NATIONAL ADMINISTRATIVE OFFICES (NAOs)**

- One federal office located in each *NAFTA* Party.
- United States NAO is located in the Bureau of International Labor Affairs of the Department of Labor, Washington, D.C.
- Canadian NAO is located in the Ministry of Human Resources Development, Ottawa.
- Mexican NAO is located in the Secretary of Labor and Social Welfare, Mexico City.
- Each NAO is led by a Secretary.
  - NAOs are responsible for:
— receiving public complaints about non-enforcement of labor law
— serving as a domestic focal point for parties interested in Labor Side Agreement issues
— disseminating information on CLC activities
— requesting consultations with other NAOs.

*Suggestions for Further Research:*

Articles:

1. Albertson, Paula Church, *The Evolution of Labor Provisions in U.S. Free Trade Agreements*, 21 STANFORD LAW & POLICY REVIEW 493–511 (2010).

2. Alvarez, José E., *The WTO as Linkage Machine*, 96 AMERICAN JOURNAL OF INTERNATIONAL LAW issue 1, 146–158 (2002).

3.  Arthurs, Harry, *Extraterritoriality by Other Means: How Labor Law Sneaks Across Borders, Conquers Minds, and Controls Workplaces Abroad*, 21 STANFORD LAW & POLICY REVIEW 527–553 (2010).

4.  Banks, Kevin, *Trade, Labor and International Governance: An Inquiry into the Potential Effectiveness of the New International Labor Law*, 32 BERKELEY JOURNAL OF EMPLOYMENT & LABOR LAW 45–142 (2011).

5.  Bravo, Karen E., *Regional Trade Arrangements and Labor Liberalization: (Lost) Opportunities for Experimentation?*, 28 SAINT LOUIS UNIVERSITY PUBLIC LAW REVIEW 71–113 (2008).

6.  Bravo, Karen E., *Free Labor&excl; A Labor Liberalization Solution to Modern Trafficking in Humans*, 18 TRANSNATIONAL LAW & CONTEMPORARY PROBLEMS number 3 545–616 (fall 2009).

7.  Buchanan, Ruth & Rusby Chaparro, *International Institutions and Transnational Advocacy: The Case of the North American Agreement on Labor Cooperation*, 13 UCLA JOURNAL OF INTERNATIONAL LAW & FOREIGN AFFAIRS 129–159 (2008).

8.  Cabin, Michael A., Note, *Labor Rights in the Peru Agreement: Can Vague Principles Yield Concrete Change?*, 109 COLUMBIA LAW REVIEW 1047–1093 (2009).

9.  Enriquez Andres, John, Note, *The Raiding of the Pearl: The Effects of Trade Liberalization on Philippine Labor Migration, and the Filipino Migrant Worker's Experience*, 10 RUTGERS RACE & LAW REVIEW 523–581 (1009).

10.  Estreicher, Samuel, *"Think Global, Act Local": Employee Representation in a World of Global Labor and Product Market Competition*, 24 LABOR LAWYER 253–265 (2009).

11.  Gibbs, Emily, Comment, *Free Movement of Labor in North America: Using the European Union as a Model for the Creation of North American Citizenship*, 45 UNIVERSITY OF SOUTH FLORIDA LAW REVIEW 265–288 (2010).

12.  González-Garibay, Montserrat, *The Trade-Labour and Trade-Environment Linkages: Together or Apart?*, 10 JOURNAL OF INTERNATIONAL TRADE LAW POLICY number 2 165–184 (2011).

13.  Gould IV, William B., *Labor Law Beyond U.S. Borders: Does What Happens Outside of America Stay Outside of America?*, 21 STANFORD LAW & POLICY REVIEW 401–426 (2010).

14.  Gresser, Edward, *Labor and Environment in Trade Since NAFTA: Activists Have Achieved Less, and More, Than They Realize*, 45 WAKE FOREST LAW REVIEW 491–525 (2010).

15.  Marzán, César F. Rosado, *Of Labor Inspectors and Judges: Chilean Labor Law Enforcement After Pinochet (and What the United States Can Do To Help)*, 54 ST. LOUIS UNIVERSITY LAW JOURNAL 497–523 (2010).

16.  Morreale, Jessica, Comment, *DR — CAFTA: The Siren Song for Improved Labor Standards for Haitians in the Dominican Republic*, 44 UNIVERSITY OF SOUTH FLORIDA LAW REVIEW 707–727 (2010).

17. Mustapha, Kemi, Note, *Taste of Child Labor Not So Sweet: A Critique of Regulatory Approaches to Combating Child Labor Abuses by the U.S. Chocolate Industry*, 87 WASHINGTON UNIVERSITY LAW REVIEW 1163–1195 (2010).

18. Pritikin, Martin H., *Fine-Labor: The Symbiosis Between Monetary and Work Sanctions*, 81 UNIVERSITY OF COLORADO LAW REVIEW 343–424 (2010).

19. *Proceedings of the Canada — United States Law Institute Conference on An Example of Cooperation and Common Cause: Enhancing Canada — United States Security and Prosperity Through the Great Lakes and North American Trade*, 24 CANADA — UNITED STATES LAW JOURNAL 1–488 (2010).

20. Ruiz, Cameron & Christopher David, *The Borders of Collective Representation: Comparing the Rights of Undocumented Workers to Organize Under United States and International Labor Standards*, 44 UNIVERSITY OF SOUTH FLORIDA LAW REVIEW 431–452 (2009).

21. Russo, Robert, *A Cooperative Conundrum? The NAALC and Mexican Migrant Workers in the United States*, 17 LAW AND BUSINESS REVIEW OF THE AMERICAS 27–38 (2011).

22. Sack, Jeffrey, *U.S. and Canadian Labour Law: Significant Distinctions*, 25 AMERICAN BAR ASSOCIATION JOURNAL OF LABOR & EMPLOYMENT LAW 241–258 (2010).

23. Schmidt, Andrea R., Note, *A New Trade Policy for America: Do Labor and Environmental Provisions in Trade Agreements Serve Social Interests or Special Interests?*, 19 INDIANA INTERNATIONAL & COMPARATIVE LAW REVIEW 167–201 (2009).

24. Su, Yang & Xin He, *Street as Courtroom: State Accommodation of Labor Protest in South China*, 44 LAW & SOCIETY REVIEW 157–184 (2010).

25. Thomas, Chantal, *Globalization and the Border: Trade, Labor, Migration, and Agricultural Production in Mexico*, 41 McGEORGE LAW REVIEW 867–889 (2010).

26. White, Robin C.A., *Revisiting Free Movement of Workers*, 33 FORDHAM INTERNATIONAL LAW JOURNAL 1564–1587 (2010).

27. Zheng, Yin Lily, Note, *It's Not What is On Paper, But What is in Practice: China's New Labor Contract Law and the Enforcement Problem*, 8 WASHINGTON UNIVERSITY GLOBAL STUDIES LAW REVIEW 595–617 (2009).

## LABOR SURPLUS MODEL

*See* Fei — Ranis Model.

## LAC

The Latin American and Caribbean Region.

## *LACEY ACT*

The 1900 *Lacey Act* is the oldest United States wildlife protection statute, combating trafficking in "illegal" wildlife, fish, or plants. Over the last century, numerous amendments have been made to the *Lacey Act* that ultimately expanded its protections.

The *2008 Farm Bill* expanded the protections of the *Lacey Act* to include a broader range of plants and plant products, making it unlawful to trade wood products or other plants that were amassed in violation of relevant laws of the United States or foreign countries. As amended, the *Act* makes it unlawful to import certain plants and plant products without an import declaration. The purpose of the amendment is to curb illegal logging and illegal harvesting of plants.

Under the *2008 Farm Bill* amendment, the declaration importers are required to submit for a plant or plant product must contain the scientific name of the plant, value of the import, quantity of the plant, and name of the country from which the plant was harvested.[445] Paper and paperboard products that contain recycled content must include the average percent of recycled content, but are not required to account for species or country of harvest.[446] However, exempt from the import declaration requirements are "common cultivar" (except trees) and "common food crop" (which include roots, seeds, parts, or products thereof), definitions of which are determined by the Animal and Plant Health Inspection Service (APHIS) of the Department of Agriculture, and Fish and Wildlife Service (FWS) of the Department of the Interior (DOI). [447]

APHIS enforces the following Harmonized Tariff Schedule of the United States (HTSUS) Chapters that are affected by the amendments to the *Lacey Act*, including: Chapter 6 (live trees, plants, bulbs, cut flowers, and ornamental foliage, etc.); Chapter 44 (word and articles of wood); Chapter 47 (wood pulp); Chapter 48 (paper and articles thereof); Chapter 92 (musical instruments); and Chapter 94 (furniture). These Chapters are part of the proposed phase-in schedule, occurring throughout 2009, for the new *Lacey Act* requirements. Additional Chapters regarding plants and plant products will be phased in after the initial phase-in periods including: Chapter12 (oil seeds, miscellaneous grain, seed, fruit, plant, etc.); Chapter 13 (gums, lacs, resins, vegetable saps, extract, etc.); and Chapter 45 (cork and articles of) among numerous other Chapters. All phase-in schedules are announced in a *Federal Register* notice.[448]

The import declaration requirement, ushered in 2008, may affect approximately 30,000 entries of plants and plant products into the United States per day, according to estimates by officials.[449] This volume of work is the reason

---

[445] *See* Rossella Brevetti, *Key Democrats Support Stretching Out Phase-in of New Lacey Act Requirements*, 25 International Trade Reporter (BNA) 1508 (23 October 2008).

[446] *See* Rossella Brevetti, *CBP Delays Enforcement of Lacey Act's Plant Import Declarations for One Month*, 26 International Trade Reporter (BNA) 447 (2 April 2009).

[447] *See* Rossella Brevetti, *APHIS Proposes Definitions for Lacey Act Exclusion of Common Food Crops, Cultivars*, 27 International Trade Reporter (BNA) 1214 (12 August 2010).

[448] *See* Rossella Brevetti, *AHPIS Proposes Phased-In Enforcement of New Lacey Act Declaration Requirements*, 25 International Trade Reporter (BNA) 1482 (16 October 2008).

[449] Rossella Brevetti, *Lacey Act Amendment Will Affect 30,000 Entries Daily, Official Says*, 25 International Trade Reporter (BNA) 1540 (30 October 2008).

for the phase-in period, and for requests from some Members of Congress and business community to increase the list of exceptions. The Bureau of Customs and Border Protection (CBP) aids APHIS in the collection of data of import declaration requirements.

## LAS

See League of Arab States.

## LAW OF DIMINISHING COOPERATION

An observed pattern in trade negotiations, namely, that the greater the degree of stress, in the sense of regional or global economic hardship, the greater the degree of cooperation on trade matters among countries. Conversely, as economic crisis recedes, cooperation diminishes, as countries feel they are not facing an imminent threat that demands their cooperation. The pattern, then, is a direct relationship between the severity of economic problems and cooperation to resist protectionism and liberalize trade.

## LDBDC

Least Developed Beneficiary Developing Country, *i.e.*, a country some of the exports of which are eligible for preferential treatment under the United States Generalized System of Preferences (GSP) program.

## LDC (FIRST MEANING)

Less Developed Country.

The term can be used generically to encompass both developing countries and least developed countries, a distinction found in many Uruguay Round multilateral trade agreements (MTAs). Generally speaking, least developed countries are those less developed countries with an annual *per capita* Gross National Product (GNP) of less than $1,000.

Synonyms for "less developed country" sometimes used "lesser developed country," "poor country," "Third World country," or "under developed country."

## LDC (SECOND MEANING)

*See* Least Developed Country.

## LEADERSHIP

Taking ownership of an idea and acting upon it.

## LEAGUE OF ARAB STATES

The Arab League, or LAS, founded in Cairo, Egypt on 22 March 1945 via the *Alexandria Protocol*.

The basic goal of the Arab League is to strengthen and coordinate the economic, political, social, and cultural programs of its member countries, and to mediate disputes between them or between them and a third country.[450] Pursuant to a *Joint Defense and Economic Cooperation Agreement*, which LAS countries signed on 13 April 1950, the Arab League committed itself to work together on military defense.

Arab Members of the World Trade Organization (WTO) have sought observer status for the Arab League. However, Israel and the United States oppose grating the LAS this status.[451]

## LEAST DEVELOPED COUNTRY

According to United Nations (U.N.) criteria a least developed country is among the poorest of poor countries. The key criterion is a *per capita* Gross National Product (GNP) of less than U.S. $1 per day.

Under some WTO agreements, least developed countries are entitled to special and differential treatment, and such treatment may be in excess of that accorded to developing countries. The Table below presents least developed countries and their status as GATT contracting parties or WTO Members.

TABLE:
LEAST DEVELOPED COUNTRIES —
STATUS AS WTO MEMBERS AND GATT CONTRACTING PARTIES[29]

| Country | WTO: Date of Accession or Application to WTO GATT: Date of Accession as GATT Contracting Party (if applicable) |
|---|---|
| Afghanistan | WTO: Applied 21 November 2004 |
| Angola | WTO: 1 December 1996 GATT: 8 April 1994 |
| Bangladesh | WTO: 1 January 1995 GATT: 16 December 1972 |
| Benin | WTO: 22 February 1996 GATT: 12 December 1963 |
| Bhutan | WTO: Applied 17 December 1999 |
| Burkina Faso | WTO: 3 June 1995 GATT: 3 May 1963 |

---

[450] *See* WIKIPEDIA, *Arab League*, http://en.wikipedia.org/wiki/Arab_League.

[451] *See Arab Members of WTO Threaten to Block International Organizations from Ministerial*, 28 International Trade Reporter (BNA) 1950 (1 December 2011).

[452] See WORLD TRADE ORGANIZATION, GATT ACTIVITIES 1994–1995, at 201–04 (April 1996).

TABLE (continued)

| Country | WTO: Date of Accession or Application to WTO GATT: Date of Accession as GATT Contracting Party (if applicable) |
|---|---|
| Burundi | WTO: 23 July 1995<br>GATT: 13 Marcy 1965 |
| Cambodia | WTO: 13 October 2004 |
| Cape Verde | WTO: Applied 11 November 1999 |
| Central African Republic | WTO: 31 May 1995<br>GATT: 3 May 1963 |
| Chad | WTO: 19 October 1996<br>GATT: 12 July 1963 |
| Democratic Republic of the Congo | WTO: 1 December 1996<br>GATT: 3 May 1963 (for Congo) |
| Djibouti | WTO: 31 May 1995<br>GATT: 16 December 1994 |
| Ethiopia | WTO: Applied 13 January 2003 |
| Gambia | WTO: 23 October 1996<br>GATT: 22 February 1965 |
| Guinea (Republic of) | WTO: 25 October 1995 |
| Guinea-Bissau | WTO: 31 May 1995 |
| Haiti | WTO: 30 January 1996<br>GATT: 1 January 1950 |
| Laos | WTO: Applied 16 July 1997 |
| Lesotho | WTO: 31 May 1995<br>GATT: 8 January 1988 |
| Madagascar | WTO: 17 November 1995<br>GATT: 30 September 1963 |
| Malawi | WTO: 31 May 1995<br>GATT: 28 August 1964 |
| Maldives | WTO: 31 May 1995<br>GATT: 19 April 1983 |
| Mali | WTO: 31 May 1995<br>GATT: 11 January 1993 |
| Mauritania | WTO: 31 May 1995<br>GATT: 20 September 1963 |
| Mozambique | WTO: 26 August 1995<br>GATT: 27 July 1992 |
| Myanmar | WTO: 1 January 1995<br>GATT: 29 July 1948 (original contracting party) |

**TABLE (continued)**

| Country | WTO:<br>*Date of Accession or Application to WTO*<br>GATT:<br>*Date of Accession as GATT Contracting Party (if applicable)* |
|---|---|
| Myanmar | WTO: 1 January 1995<br>GATT: 29 July 1948 (original contracting party) |
| Nepal | WTO: 23 April 2004 |
| Niger | WTO: 13 December 1996<br>GATT: 31 December 1963 |
| Rwanda | WTO: 22 May 1996<br>GATT: 1 January 1966 |
| Samoa | WTO: Applied 15 April 1998, Accession approved 15–17 December 2011 |
| São Tome and Príncipé | WTO: Applied 14 January 2005 (has Observer status) |
| Senegal | WTO: 1 January 1995<br>GATT: 27 September 1963 |
| Sierra Leone | WTO: 23 July 1995<br>GATT: 19 May 1961 |
| Solomon Islands | WTO: 26 July 1996<br>GATT: 28 December 1994 |
| Sudan | GATT: Applied 11 October 1994 |
| Tanzania | WTO: 1 January 1995<br>GATT: 9 December 1961 |
| Togo | WTO: 31 May 1995<br>GATT: 20 March 1964 |
| Uganda | WTO: 1 January 1995<br>GATT: 23 October 1962 |
| Vanuatu | WTO: Applied 7 July 1995 |
| Yemen | WTO: Applied 14 April 2000 |
| Zambia | WTO: 1 January 1995<br>GATT: 10 February 1982 |

*Suggestions for Further Research:*

Articles:

1.   Busch, Marc L., Eric Reinhardt & Gregory Shaffer, *Does Legal Capacity Matter? A Survey of WTO Members*, 8 WORLD TRADE REVIEW issue 4, 559–577 (2009).

2.  Hsieh, Pasha L., *China's Development of International Economic Law and WTO Legal Capacity Building*, 13 JOURNAL OF INTERNATIONAL ECONOMIC LAW 997–1036 (2010).

## LESSER DUTY RULE

A rule in antidumping (AD) law that calls upon an administering authority to impose an AD duty only in the amount necessary to counter-act dumping.

Some WTO Members, notably the European Union (EU) and Brazil, rely on the Lesser Duty Rule. In contrast, the United States imposes AD duties on the full amount of the Dumping Margin. Whether all Members should be obliged to have the Lesser Duty Rule in their AD law was a major controversy in the trade remedy negotiations of the Doha Round.

The logic of the Lesser Duty Rule is public interest, or more particularly, consumer interest. Why not impose less of an AD duty, if the less-than-full dumping margin duty will rectify dumping? That lesser AD duty will impose less of a cost on consumers of the subject merchandise in the importing country.

The rebuttal to this logic is that AD law has a remedial purpose, namely, to rectify dumping. That is the only purpose of the law, and consumer interests are intentionally not put into the mix, so as not to distort or dilute the purpose. Moreover, imposing an AD duty puts more pressure on a foreign country to lower its trade barriers. Those barriers contribute to dumping. The foreign tariff and non-tariff barriers insulate the foreign market from global competition, and thus allow a foreign producer-exporter to enjoy monopolistic or semi-monopolistic status in its home market. With that status, the producer-exporter garners super-normal profits, and uses them to cross-subsidize losses from dumping on overseas markets. A severe AD duty is more likely to force the foreign country government to dismantle those barriers than a lesser one, or so the argument goes.

## LEWIS MODEL

*See* Fei—Ranis Model.

## LIFDC

Low-income food-deficit country.

The acronym is used (inter alia) by the United Nations Food and Agriculture Organization (FAO). LIFDCs are poor countries that are net food importers. There are 82 LIFDCs in total, of which

- 44 are in Africa
- 25 are in Asia
- Four are in Latin America
- Nine are in Europe and Oceania.

LIFDCs are particularly vulnerable to increases in the cost of food imports. Their food import bills can rise for three basic reasons:

(1) An increase in commodity prices, especially cereals, corn (maize), rice, and wheat.

(2) An increase in oil prices.

(3) An increase in transportation (freight) costs.

In 2006–2008, all three factors conspired against the LIFDCs. [453] For example, in 2006-2007, the LIFDCs faced a 37 percent increase in international cereals prices. In consequence, food riots broke out in Burkina Faso, Cameroon, Côte D'Ivoire, Egypt, Ethiopia, and Haiti, Indonesia, Madagascar, Philippines, and Senegal. The military was called out in Pakistan and Thailand to prevent theft of food.

To reduce food import prices, LIFDCs can cut import tariffs (as well as post-border levies). Thus, in 2006–2008, Côte D'Ivoire, Ethiopia, Liberia, Senegal, and Zimbabwe all took this action for cereals, as did the Kingdom of Saudi Arabia in respect of rice. However, many food exporters took diametrically opposite measures. Cambodia, Egypt, India, and Vietnam banned rice exports, Tanzania banned all agricultural commodity exports, and Zimbabwe banned corn exports. Bangladesh, Malaysia, and Philippines imposed price-stabilization measures. These export restrictions are designed to promote domestic food security, specifically, ensuring a steady supply of reasonably priced food, and prevent farmers from selling their crops at relatively higher world market prices.

## LIKE PRODUCT

Essentially, a good that closely resembles, but need not be identical to, another good.

The term "like product" is commonly used in GATT and WTO accords to delineate the scope of particular obligations. For example, trade remedies such as antidumping (AD) duties and countervailing duties (CVDs) are designed to protect domestic producers in an importing country of a "like product," i.e., one that is "like" merchandise imported from overseas that allegedly is dumped or receiving an unlawful subsidy.

The term — specifically, the test for determining "likeness" — also is the subject of considerable case law. Briefly, based on the landmark 1996 Appellate Body ruling in *Japan — Alcoholic Beverages*, there is no single, immutable test. Each dispute requires a case-by-case analysis accounting for three principal variables: the physical characteristics of a product, consumer tastes and preferences as regards the product, and end uses of the product.

---

[453] *See* Daniel Pruzin, *U.N. Body Warns of Major Spike in Food Import Bill of Poorest Nations*, 25 International Trade Reporter (BNA) 556 (17 April 2008).

Critically, "like product" is not the same as "directly competitive or substitutable product." The distinction arises between the two categories in GATT Article III:2, which is the national treatment obligation for fiscal (internal tax) measures. The first sentence of Article III:2 applies only to "like" products. The second sentence of Article III:2 (supplemented by the Interpretative Note, *Ad Article III, paragraph 2*) applies to "directly competitive or substitutable" products. Briefly, "like" products is the narrower of the two categories. All like products are directly competitive or substitutable with one another, but the reverse is not true.

The term "like product" also should not be confused with "directly competitive product." That distinction arises in Article XIX:1 of GATT and Article 2:1 of the WTO *Agreement on Safeguards*, which indicate that the general safeguards remedy may be deployed to protect domestic producers in an importing country of a product that is "like," or that is "directly competitive" with, foreign merchandise under investigation. Here again, "like" products is the narrower of the two categories. All "like" products are substitutes, but the reverse is not true.

What about the relationship between "directly competitive" and "directly competitive or substitutable products"? Literally, the terms appear to overlap, with the former category being the narrower of the two. However, this question — both theoretically and in terms of practical relevance — appears to be an open one.

*Suggestions for Further Research:*

Article:

1.   Stedeford, Todd & Amanda S. Persad, *The Influence of Carcinogenicity Classification and Mode of Action Characterization on Distinguishing "Like Products" Under Article III:4 of the GATT and Article 2:1 of the TBT Agreement*, 15 NEW YORK UNIVERSITY ENVIRONMENTAL LAW JOURNAL 377–419 (2007).

# LIPSET HYPOTHESIS

A hypothesis about the linkage between economic growth and political development. Simply put, it is that prosperity stimulates democracy. The Hypothesis is named after the political scientist Seymour Martin Lipset, who proposed it in a 1959 article.

This Hypothesis, as Lipset himself acknowledges, is grounded in Aristotle's political philosophy. In Book VI of *Politics*, Aristotle argued that only in a wealthy society, in which a small number of citizens live in real poverty, is it possible for the mass of people to participate in politics in an intelligent manner and eschew irresponsible demagoguery. Empirical evidence strongly supports the Lipset Hypothesis.[454]

---

[454] *See, e.g.,* STEPHAN HAGGARD & ROBERT R. KAUFMAN, THE POLITICAL ECONOMY OF DEMOCRATIC TRANSITIONS, 27–28 (1995); ALEX HADENIUS, DEMOCRACY AND DEVELOPMENT, 77–82 (1992).

Increased standards of living lead to increased democracy, albeit at a gradual pace. A number of countries in East Asia, including South Korea and Taiwan, and some Latin American countries, such as Chile, are examples of increased democratization following closely enhanced economic performance. Conversely, a country that installs political freedoms without substantial economic development tends not to retain those freedoms. Examples include some Sub-Saharan African countries, which developed democracies in the early 1960s, following independence from colonial powers. Many of those democracies proved to be too far ahead of economic growth and, in part consequently, not enduring.

What might be said about the reverse causal direction, the effect of democracy on growth? The theory for a direct relationship — that democracy causes growth — is weak. Among the growth-enhancing features of democracy are, possibly, the checks and balances against dictatorship (a point Alexis de Tocqueville made in *Democracy in America* (1835)), increased education and an expanded middle class, and enhanced power of working and middle classes against landlords.

The data reveal a weak relationship, and overall democracy is not a critical determinant of economic growth. At a low level of "political rights," defined in terms of meaningful participation in the political process, as manifest in the right of all adults to vote and hold office, the ability of elected officials to make decisions about public policies, and influence of minority parties on policy, some expansion of these rights stimulates growth. However, too much democracy can cause economic distortions, and damage growth. This phenomenon may result from the heightened concern for social programs, income redistribution, and land reform, which accompany increased democratization. These rich-to-poor programs result from the increased prominence of interests groups in political systems with representative legislative bodies. In other words, the relationship between democracy and growth is non-linear, like an inverted "U." At a low level of democracy, expanding rights stimulates growth. But, after a moderate amount of democracy is achieved, further democratization cuts into growth. These findings are replicated when democracy is defined in terms of "civil liberties," such as the right to education, travel, and worship. What would be instances of a "moderate" democratization, beyond which liberalization probably would reduce growth? One answer is the level of political freedom achieved by Malaysia and Mexico by 1994, and by Chile, South Korea, and Taiwan in the 1990s.

It is important to add a caveat. In principle, nothing precludes an authoritarian regime from providing growth-enhancing economic freedoms, and conversely nothing forces it to engage in central planning. A number of regimes led by strong central figures, arguably including Chile (under General Augusto Pinochet), Iran (under the Shah), Peru (under President Alberto Fujimori), and Singapore (under Prime Minister Lee Kuan Yew) illustrate the point. A considerable degree of protection of property rights characterized each illustration. Adversity, from the perspective of economic growth, occurs when a dictatorial regime uses its power to loot the country, or makes foolish investments in non-productive investments for corrupt reasons. A number of Sub-Saharan African countries, plus a few Latin American countries and the former Marco regime in the Philippines, exemplify this point.

In brief, harkening to Plato's *Republic*, a dictator may be a benevolent, wise philosopher king whose personal objectives are to promote growth for the populace, or a malicious dictator whose personal objectives are orthogonal to the interests of the people. Consequently, economists dub dictatorship a risky investment. However, lest democracies become self-satisfied, they can become complacent, paralyzed by internal wrangling and self-promotional behavior of leaders, and corruption. A review of the history of the Roman Republic (roughly 501 B.C. to 31–27 B.C.) surely illustrates this point.

What is the "bottom line" on the link between democracy and growth? Perhaps it is the argument made by Milton Friedman in *Capitalism and Freedom* (1962). In that book, the Nobel Prize winning economist famously argued economic and political freedoms are mutually reinforcing.

*Suggestions for Further Research:*

Article:

1.   Lipset, Seymour Martin, *Some Social Requisites of Democracy: Economic Development and Political Legitimacy*, 53 AMERICAN POLITICAL SCIENCE REVIEW 69–105 (1959).

## LIMITED EXCLUSION ORDER

Under Section 337 of the United States *Tariff Act of 1930*, as amended, a general exclusion order affects all shipments of merchandise under investigation infringing on a valid intellectual property right (IPR). In contrast, a specific, or limited, order focuses on merchandise only from persons violating Section 337. *See also* general exclusion order, PEO, and TEO.

## LINKAGE ISSUES

*See* Trade — Energy link, Trade — Environment link, Trade — Human Rights link, and Trade — Labor link.

## LIQUIDATION (LIQUIDATION OF ENTRIES)

A customs law term referring to completion of all documentation associated with an entry of a shipment of merchandise, and requires final computation of the duties and fees due on an entry.

"Suspension of liquidation" means the relevant customs authority — which, in the United States, is Customs and Border Protection (CBP) — defers calculation of the amount and rate of tariff duty applicable to each individual entry until a later date. The merchandise may enter the United States (or be entered into a warehouse, foreign trade zone (FTZ), or put in temporary importation in bond). But, as that entry is not liquidated, liability for final payment of duties (if any) remains. Following an affirmative preliminary dumping margin or subsidy determination by the United States Department of Commerce (DOC) in an antidumping (AD) or countervailing duty (CVD) case, liquidation of entries of subject merchandise is suspended.

*Suggestions for Further Research:*

Article:

1. Planert, R. Will, *Enjoining Liquidation in Antidumping and Countervailing Duty Cases: Issues and Pitfalls*, 19 TULANE JOURNAL OF INTERNATIONAL & COMPARATIVE LAW 505–541 (2011).

## LISBON TREATY

*See* EU.

## LMO

Genetically modified living organism.

*See* GMO.

## LOAN DEFICIENCY PAYMENT

*See* Deficiency Payment.

## LOCAL CONTENT REQUIREMENT

A requirement imposed by a host country government on foreign direct investors that, in exchange for permission to invest in the country, the investors must purchase a certain amount of local raw materials or intermediate goods and incorporate them into the investors' products.

Along with export performance and trade balancing requirements, local content strictures are a tactic used by host country governments to regulate foreign direct investment (FDI). There is considerable debate over the impact of local content requirements, particularly with regard their effects on economic growth in developing countries.

*Suggestions for Further Research:*

Book:

1. MORAN, THEODORE H., PARENTAL SUPERVISION: THE NEW PARADIGM FOR FOREIGN DIRECT INVESTMENT AND DEVELOPMENT (2001).

Articles:

1. Lahiri, Sajal & Yoshiyasu Ono, *Foreign Direct Investment, Local Content Requirement, and Profit Taxation*, 108 THE ECONOMIC JOURNAL 444–57 (1998).

2.   Qiu, Larry D. & Zhigang Tao, *Export, Foreign Direct Investment, and Local Content Requirement*, 66 JOURNAL OF DEVELOPMENT ECONOMICS 101–25 (2001).

# LOMÉ CONVENTION

A system of trade preferences granted by the European Union (EU) to approximately 71 African, Caribbean, and Pacific (ACP) developing countries — the socalled "ACP" or "Lomé" countries. The EU negotiated this Convention in 1975. The First Convention, and each of its subsequent editions, set forth a means for the European Community (EC) to aid the ACP countries, partly through a system of preferences such as lower tariffs or duty-free treatment. Many of the Lomé countries are former European colonies. Thirty-nine of the Lomé countries are among the world's 48 poorest countries.

In June 1998, Cuba was granted observer status, with no guarantee of future membership in the absence of substantial progress on human rights and good governance, and political freedom. Cuba applied for full membership in February 2000, but the EU insisted on greater democracy and respect for human rights before considering the matter. In fact, the EU was split over the matter. France, Italy, and Spain favored membership, saying it was the best way to encourage reform in Cuba. Britain, the Netherlands, and Sweden were hesitant, wanting concrete signs of improvement before granting membership.

The Fourth Lomé Convention was signed on 15 December 1989 by the EU and the ACP countries, many of which are now WTO Members.[455] This edition contained a protocol concerning bananas, implemented fully in 1993, which became the subject of the infamous *Bananas* dispute — the Bananas War — between the United States and EU.

The Fourth Lomé Convention expired in February 2000. The EU favored replacing the trade preference scheme in the Fourth Convention with free trade agreements (FTAs) between the EU and each ACP region. However, the ACP countries felt threatened by granting duty-free treatment to EU goods, and were unwilling to accept the loss in tariff revenues. Hence, they preferred a simple renewal of the Convention.

In October 1999, a compromise solution was reached, and finalized in February 2000. The new *Cotonou Convention* was signed in May 2000.

*Suggestions for Further Research:*

Book:

1.   BABARINDE, OLUFEMI A, THE LOMÉ CONVENTIONS AND DEVELOPMENT: AN EMPIRICAL ASSESSMENT (1994).

---

[455] *See* African, Caribbean and Pacific States — European Economic Community: Final Act, Minutes and Fourth ACP-EEC Convention of Lomé, 15 December 1989, 29 INTERNATIONAL LEGAL MATERIALS 783 (1990).

Articles:

1.  Montana, Ismael Musah, *The Lome Convention from Inception to the Dynamics of the Post-Cold War, 1957–1990s*, 2 AFRICAN AND ASIAN STUDIES issue 1 63–97 (2003).

2.  Nilsson, Lars, *Trading Relations: Is the Roadmap from Lome to Cotonou Correct?*, 34 APPLIED ECONOMICS 439–52 (2002).

## LONDON PREPARATORY CONFERENCE

*See* GATT 1947.

## LOONIE

A nickname for the Canadian currency, *i.e.*, the Canadian dollar.

The amusing name is derived from an aquatic, diving bird — the loon. That bird is depicted on a Canadian one-dollar coin, which Canada introduced in 1987. "Loonie" (or its variant, "loony") means crazy. The allusion in this meaning is to the loon, which when trying to escape from a threatening situation or manifest danger acts crazily and cries wildly. In the foreign exchange context, that allusion presumably depends on the performance of the Canadian dollar.

## LORENZ CURVE

*See* Gini Coefficient.

## *LOUVRE ACCORD*

*See Plaza Accord.*

## LTFV

Less Than Fair Value. In general, dumping occurs when a foreign company sells its product in an importing country at LTFV. This value implies a price in the importing country that is less than the price at which the foreign company sells the same or a similar product in its home country, or a price below its cost of production. To determine whether LTFV sales are made, a dumping margin calculation, in which Normal Value (or a proxy for it, namely, Third Country Price or Constructed Value) and Export Price (or Constructed Export Price) are compared, is necessary. Thus, the dumping margin equals the difference between Normal Value (or its proxy) and Export Price (or Constructed Export Price).

## LTL

Less than truckload.

An environment in which a conventional, full truck carrier does not haul a shipment of merchandise. Rather, the shipment is in a trailer pulled by, or small container atop or on, a vehicle. An LTL shipment raises border security concern that the trailer or container is not sealed properly to avoid tampering, unauthorized access, and the introduction of illicit materials. High security seals and controlled access are remedies, and are required of carriers for participation in the *Customs — Trade Partnership Against Terrorism (C-TPAT)* program.

# M

## MACSHARRY REFORM (MACSHARRY REFORMS)

A major package of reforms undertaken by the European Union (EU) to its Common Agricultural Policy (CAP) in 1992. The former EU Agricultural Commissioner, who served from 1989–92, is the eponym. Proposed by Commissioner MacSharry in 1991, and approved by the Council of the European Union in 1992, the reforms changed the philosophy underlying the EU. As initially conceived, the CAP required farmers to earn income from the market, but the government would intervene as necessary to affect prices. With the Reform, the EU began backing away from intervention, and moving toward direct income support.

Accordingly, the MacSharry Reform involved –

- Cutting support (intervention) prices and mandated production restrictions. For example, the EU eliminated all price support for oil seeds and protein crops, cutting it by 20 and 33 percent for beef and cereals, respectively.

- Assisting producers by providing direct income payments to farmers. The variables to determine income compensation were historical areas under cultivation, yield, and livestock units, *i.e.*, these variables were used in the formula to determine direct income payments. Such payments became conditional on set asides, *i.e.*, farmers setting taking arable land out of cultivation (for crops), or establishing maximum densities per hectare (for livestock).

Following the MacSharry Reform, the EU successfully pushed for creation of a "Blue Box" during Uruguay Round negotiations on the *Agreement on Agriculture*. The 1992 deal creating this Box, known as the "Blair House Accord" (after the Washington, D.C. location where it was reached), meant subsidies whereby farmers are paid based on setting aside parts of their fields, are exempt from AMS reduction commitments. In other words, the EU's direct income support to farmers is put in the Blue Box.

The EU has implemented other major changes to the CAP changes since the MacSharry Reform. They include Agenda 2000 and the 2003 Mid-Term Review of Agenda 2000. None of these changes, however, affected the EU sugar subsidies. Reforms to sugar came only after a successful WTO action in 2005 brought against the EU by Brazil.

*Suggestions for Further Research:*

Books:

1. BALDWIN, RICHARD & CHARLES WYPLOSZ, THE ECONOMICS OF EUROPEAN INTEGRATION (2007).

2. FOLMER, C., ET AL., THE COMMON AGRICULTURAL POLICY BEYOND THE MACSHARRY REFORM (1995).

## MAFF

Ministry of Agriculture, Forestry, and Fisheries of Japan.

## MAILBOX

A term associated with the WTO *Agreement on Trade-Related Aspects of Intellectual Property Rights (TRIPs)*.

The term refers to the requirement in the *TRIPs Agreement* incumbent on WTO Members that do not yet provide product patent protection for pharmaceuticals and agricultural chemicals. The requirement is set forth in Article 70:8. In brief, since 1 January 1996, when the *TRIPs Agreement* entered into force, these Members have been obligated to establish a means by which an application for a patent for pharmaceuticals and agricultural chemicals can be filed. A related requirement, in *TRIPs* Article 70:9, states these Members must put in place a system for granting exclusive marketing rights for the products whose patent applications have been filed.

Mailbox protection is the subject of the first WTO case on the *TRIPs Agreement, India — Patent Protection. See* WTO Appellate Body Report, *India — Patent Protection for Pharmaceutical and Agricultural Chemical Products*, WT/DS50/AB/R (adopted 16 January 1998) (complaint by United States).

## *MAQUILADORA*

A factory operating in Mexico, owned by foreigners (typically Americans), used for the final assembly of goods. *Maquiladora* plants tend to be near the Mexican border with the United States. The term has Arabic origins referring to a portion of grain. The term was used widely in colonial Mexico, when "*maquila*" was the charge millers collected for processing other people's grain.

*Suggestions for Further Research:*

Books:

1.  KAMEL, RACHAEL & ANYA HOFFMAN, THE MAQUILADORA READER: CROSS-BORDER ORGANIZING SINCE NAFTA (1999).

2.  STODDARD, ELLWYN R., MAQUILA: ASSEMBLY PLANTS IN NORTHERN MEXICO (1987).

3.  WILSON, PATRICIA, EXPORTS AND LOCAL DEVELOPMENT: MEXICO'S NEW MAQUILADORAS (1992).

Other Source:

1.  Gruben, William & Sherry Kiser, *The Border Economy: NAFTA and Maquiladoras: Is the Growth Connected?*, FEDERAL RESERVE BANK OF DALLAS (June 2001).

## MARGIN OF DUMPING

*See* Dumping Margin.

## MARK

A generic intellectual property (IP) term encompassing trademarks and service marks.

## MARK UP

*See* Mock Mark Up.

## MARKETING LOAN (MARKETING ASSISTANCE LOAN)

Marketing assistance loans are one of three cornerstones of American agricultural subsidies that have existed since the first federal farm bill in 1933, during the Depression and Dust Bowl Era, under the Administration of President Franklin D. Roosevelt. Those cornerstones are:

- Marketing assistance loans.
- Direct payments.
- Counter-cyclical payments.

To be sure, the modern-day incarnation of these programs is not identical to the schemes as originally enacted. For example, production flexibility contracts (PFCs) existed before direct payments, and were replaced by them in the *Farm Security and Rural Investment Act of 2002* — the *2002 Farm Bill*, Public Law 107–171 (13 May 2002), codified in Title 7 of the U.S.C.[456] However, the idea of income support — which both incarnations represent — is not new. Likewise, counter-cyclical payments have not been a consistent feature throughout the post-1933 history. However, the idea of shielding farmers from vicissitudes of the market place by offering them support inversely proportional to market prices is not new.

Marketing assistance loans, in contrast to direct payments and countercyclical payments, are short-term, non-recourse loans that a farmer can take out during harvest time. The purpose of a marketing assistance loan, as its name intimates, is to cover expenses so that crops just harvested can be sold later in the year when a farmer-borrower expects crop prices to be higher than at harvest time. Prices traditionally are lowest at harvest time, simply because crop supply is at a maximum then, as all farmers of the same crop in a region are harvesting simultaneously. In other words, a marketing assistance loan enables a farmer-borrower to withhold some or all of that producer's crop supply from the market, and await a post-harvest rise in prices.

Simply put, marketing loan assistance is a price support program for current levels of production. Like counter-cyclical support, marketing loan assistance is a price-sensitive subsidy. But, counter-cyclical support provides compensation specifically when prices tumble.

---

[456] Conservation provisions of the *2002 Farm Bill* were codified in Title 16 of the U.S.C.

By "short-term," it is meant that the tenure of loans is less than one year. Specifically, for all commodities other than cotton, the duration is nine months, and for cotton it is 10 months. By "non-recourse," it is meant that the collateral pledged by the farmer-borrower to secure the loan is the just-harvested crops only. No other assets of the farmer-borrower are available to the lender in the event of default. Thus, the non-recourse feature of the loan, discussed in 7 U.S.C. Section 7934, ensures there is no risk to the borrower. In sum, a marketing assistance loan is non-recourse loans to permit a farmer to repay debt obligations, without incurring financial hardship arising from crop price fluctuations.

The lender of a marketing assistance loan is the United States Commodity Credit Corporation (CCC). The loans are managed by the Farm Services Agency (FSA). Both the CCC and FSA are part of the United States Department of Agriculture (USDA). The CCC has no employees; rather all, domestic activities of the CCC are conducted by the FSA. Loans are issued for a commodity based on a price of that commodity. The price of a crop on which a loan is based is called the "loan rate," or put more accurately, the "loan rate price," which is set out by statute in 7 U.S.C. Section 7932. To take a simplified example, suppose a Kansas wheat farmer obtains a loan for 1,000 bushels of wheat, and the loan rate price is $4.00 per bushel. The loan amount would be $4,000.

Marketing assistance loans are repaid in one of three ways, as follows. The USDA, specifically the FSA, monitors the market price of each commodity, and publicizes weekly the national price, a county-by-county price (if available), for each county of each state in the United States. The county-by-county price is called the "Posted County Price" (PCP). (At times, and for certain crops, there may be adjacent counties in which the PCP for the same commodity differs. In such instances, farmers have been known to cross county lines to go to grain elevators offering the higher of the prices.) For cotton and rice, the FSA also publishes a world market price, called the "Prevailing World Market Price."

- First, a farmer can repay the loan plus interest as a standard loan. Generally, a farmer would do so after selling the crops at a higher price, that is, at a market price, which is above the loan rate price.

  In the example above, it the market price were $5.00 per bushel, then the Kansas wheat farmer would sell 1,000 bushels at $5,000, pay off the $4,000 loan, plus interest, and keep the balance.

- Second, if the actual market price available to a farmer (which may or may not be the same as the PCP) is below the loan rate price, then a farmer simply can forfeit the crops to the United States government. The government then takes the crops as collateral, and closes out the loan, thus invoking and fulfilling the non-recourse provision of the loan. The benefit to the farmer is the loan rate price — rather then dealing with the market, the farmer simply hands over the crops to the government and pockets the value of the loan, which is at the loan rate price.

  In the example above, suppose the market price per bushel of wheat is $3.00. Then, the farmer could turn over the 1,000 bushels to the government, which then would use the wheat — or the sale proceeds thereof, which would be $3,000 — to offset the indebtedness. In this instance, the government would lose $1,000, plus interest, or to put it differently, it would have subsidized the farmer in the amount of $1,000 plus interest.

As a different example, suppose a farmer obtains a loan at the loan rate of $2.50 per bushel, and the market price falls to $1.75 per bushel. What is the obligation of the farmer to repay the government? The answer is the market price, $1.75 per bushel, which the farmer can effectively fulfill by forfeiting the crops to the government. The farmer does not lose the difference of 75 cents between the higher loan rate and lower market price. Conversely, of course, if the market price exceeded the loan rate — say the market price were $3 per bushel, and the loan rate still at $2.50 per bushel — then the farmer must repay the government at the loan rate. In that scenario, the farmer benefits from the 50 cent per bushel differential between the higher market price and fixed loan rate.

- Third, suppose the market price of the commodity drops and stays below the loan rate price for the entire period of the loan. Then, a farmer can sell the crop at that lower price, and repay the loan from the proceeds of that lower priced sale. The FSA adjusts the loan to the PCP (or, in the case of cotton or rice, to the Prevailing World Market Price). Then, the farmer would keep the difference between the loan rate and the PCP rate as a "marketing loan gain" (MLG).

In the above example, suppose the market price for wheat is $2.50 per bushel, and stays below the loan rate of $4.00. A farmer could sell the wheat at $2.50 per bushel, thus earning $2,500. The farmer would use these sale proceeds to pay the loan, and the FSA would adjust downward the loan amount to the PCP of $2.50. In effect, the FSA re-sets the loan amount *post hoc*. In this example, the farmer benefits in the amount of the difference between the higher original loan rate price, $4.00, and the PCP, which is the re-set price, $2.50, *i.e.*, by $1.50 per bushel, of a total of $1,500. That MLG is a subsidy from the government to the farmer.

Would a farmer ever prefer to forfeit crops (the second methodology) rather than go through the MLG (the third methodology)? The answer is "yes." For example, suppose the loan rate price is $4.00 per bushel of wheat, the actual market price is $2.00 per bushel, and the PCP is $2.50. A Kansas wheat farmer may be better off forfeiting the crop to the government, rather than selling the crop at $2.00 per bushel. The benefit to the farmer is the $4.00 loan rate price on which the marketing assistance loan was based. In contrast, accrual of any MLG would be based on the differential between the $4.00 loan rate price and the $2.50 PCP, *i.e.*, the MLG is $1.50. The farmer then sells the price at $2.00 per bushel on the market, and reaps a gain of $3.50 total — the actual sale price ($2.00) plus the MLG ($1.50). By forfeiting the crops, the farmer gains 50 cents per bushel more than by going through the MLG methodology.

To avoid some of the unnecessary administrative paperwork involved in a MLG, a farmer-borrower can opt not to take out a marketing assistance loan when the PCP rate is below the loan rate price at harvest time. At that time, the farmer simply could apply for a Loan Deficiency Payment (LDP) instead. The United States government simply would issue a check to the farmer (who, in this instance, is not a borrower) for the difference between the (1) loan rate price and (2) PCP rate price.

Observe the marketing assistance loan program can have an effect similar to a counter-cyclical payment subsidy scheme. That is because the loan rate price effectively functions as a minimum, or floor, price for a crop, which a farmer is guaranteed regardless of the market. The first payment methodology above indicates the farmer never has to pay back more than the loan rate price. That is a desirable situation in which the price of the commodity in question rises, a few months after harvest, above the loan rate price. The farmer sells the crop at the actual market price, pays back the full amount of the marketing assistance loan, with interest, and earns a profit. The entire transaction is based on actual market conditions, and there are no price distortions or subsidies.

The second payment methodology above shows the farmer may end up paying less than the loan rate price, where the market price is below the loan rate price. The farmer essentially repays nothing — no loan principal or interest. The farmer turns over his or her crop, which the government uses to offset the loan balance. But, the offset is only partial, meaning the government loses money on the loan transaction, *i.e.*, it subsidizes the farmer. Effectively, the government buys the crop from the farmer at the established loan rate price, which is above the market price for the crop. In that sense, the loan rate price operates as a minimum price for the farmer. The crop purchase transaction does not accurately reflect market conditions, in that the government purchases crop at an off-market, namely above-market, price — the loan rate price.

The third payment methodology suggests a farmer may end up paying less than the loan rate persists above the PCP rate. This methodology most clearly demonstrates the counter-cyclical effect of the marketing assistance loan program, and is the most obvious instance of price distortion in commodity markets. In the second methodology, the government may hold grain from the farmer in storage, or donate it to foreign countries — not necessarily sell it on the market. But, in the third methodology, the farmer sells grain on the market at a price below the loan rate price. This price is a loss to the government, and would be a loss to the farmer, if the government effectively step in and re-write the terms of the loan. This re-writing of loan terms shields the farmer from price risk and volatility of actual market conditions. That effect of shielding the farmer from vicissitudes is redolent of a counter-cyclical subsidy.

Notably, in the United States, participation by a farmer in the marketing assistance loan program has no bearing or effect on that farmer's participation in either a counter-cyclical payment or direct payment program. That is, an American farmer can participate in all three programs simultaneously. In contrast, small farmers in poor countries do not have these participation options. Not surprisingly, the United States subsidy programs are one reason cited by poor countries to explain why American agricultural exports command strong positions in many overseas markets. Note, too, poor countries contend the effect of the American subsidy programs is price suppression or price depression, as large volumes of United States farm exports — encouraged in part by subsidy programs — find their way onto world markets. Indeed, Brazil made this very argument, with success, in the 2005 *Upland Cotton* case.

Under the WTO *Agreement on Agriculture*, marketing assistance loans are treated as Amber Box subsidies. That is because of their counter cyclical function. Therefore, marketing assistance loans are subject to reduction commitments. Uruguay Round negotiators, of course, reserved the Blue Box for payments de-coupled from production. However, during the Doha Round, the United States proposed an expanded definition of the Blue Box to accommodate counter-cyclical payments. That proposal was consistent with the significantly greater emphasis the United States placed on counter-cyclical support in the 2007 *Farm Bill*.

The program crops (also called commodity crops), the 2007 *Farm Bill* set for marketing loans reflects a broader set of commodities than are available for direct or countercyclical payments. That is, there are more crops for which a farmer can obtain a marketing assistance loan than for which a direct or counter-cyclical payment is available. An example is honey.

Target Prices set as Loan Rates for the marketing assistance loan support — *i.e.*, the stated levels of prices that the United States recognizes as an effective floor for commodity prices are as follows in the 2007 *Farm Bill*. These prices are the loan rate prices referred to above:

- Corn, $1.95 per bushel.
- Wheat, $2.94 per bushel.
- Soybeans, $5.00 per bushel.
- Oilseeds, which are separately identified as sunflower seed, rapeseed, canola, sesame, safflower, flaxseed, mustard seed, crambe (an industrial oilseed added by the Secretary of Agriculture in 1998), all of which are at 10.7 cents per pound.
- Rice, $6.50 per hundredweight. (Hundredweight is an old English measure roughly equivalent to 100 pounds in the U.S. system.) Note that Short, Medium and Long Grain Rice are specified separately in the *Farm Bill*, but the price remains the same.
- Upland Cotton, 52 cents per pound. Extra Long Staple (ELS) Cotton is 79.77 cents per pound. (LDPs on ELS Cotton only are prohibited)

- Sugar (from beet or cane), no marketing loan support, but covered by its own separate provision in the 2007 *Farm Bill*, and also protected by tariff rate quotas (TRQs).

- Peanuts, $355 per ton.

- Sorghum, $1.95 per bushel.

- Malt Barley, $2.50 per bushel, Feed Barley $1.90 per bushel.

- Oats, $1.46 per bushel.

- Wool (sheep hair, which is a fiber used to make woolen fabric) Graded Wool, $1.10 per pound, Non-Graded Wool, 40 cents per pound.

- Mohair (goat hair which is a fiber used to make woolen fabric) $4.20 per pound.

- Honey, 60 cents per pound.

- Dry peas (not English peas, snow peas, sugar snap peas, or other pea types), $5.40 per hundredweight.

- Lentils, $11.28 per hundredweight.

- Small chickpeas, $8.54 per hundredweight.

- Dairy products (including butter, cheese, milk, and non-fat dry milk, but not eggs), no counter-cyclical support, but covered by their own separate provision in the 2007 *Farm Bill*, including a dairy product price support program.

The 2007 *Farm Bill* calls the price against which the Target is gauged the "Effective Price." The Effective Price is the national average market price, or the national average loan rate for a marketing assistance loan, during a specified 12 month Marketing Year (MY), also known as a Crop Year. As American Farm Bills apply for five years, query whether a statutorily-defined benchmark that does not change for such a period actually reflects a market price.

An obvious controversy associated with these types of countercyclical payments concerns cotton. During the Doha Round, the Cotton Four countries, and their sovereign and non-governmental organization (NGO) supporters, urged elimination of cotton subsidies by the United States. That argument was reinforced by a significant legal defeat the United States suffered in the 2005 *Upland Cotton* case. *See United States — Subsidies on Upland Cotton*, WT/DS267/AB/R (adopted 21 March 2005) (complaint by Brazil). However, the 2007 *Farm Bill* maintains marketing loans for cotton, albeit with a calculated world market price. Query if that makes these subsidies a target of future cases in the Dispute Settlement Body (DSB).

The United States has eliminated Step 2 counter cyclical payments based on the resolution of the *Upland Cotton* case, but some economists theorize the impact to of the elimination will be minimal in the face of the other counter cyclical programs including marketing assistance loans. Indeed, an econometric study done in July 2005 conducted at Texas Tech University suggests the elimination of Step 2 payments is unlikely to have much impact on world market prices for cotton.[457] Moreover, Brazil has challenged the United States in the WTO as to whether it has fully complied with the Appellate Body recommendations in the *Upland Cotton* decision in respect of eliminating or reforming the other contentious subsidy schemes.

## MAXIMUM RESIDUE LEVEL

*See* MRL.

## MCC

*See* Millennium Challenge Corporation.

## MCCA

*Mercado Común Centroamericano.* The Spanish acronym for the Central American Common Market.

The MCCA, established in December 1960 by the *General Treaty on Central American Economic Integration*, originally included El Salvador, Guatemala, Honduras, and Nicaragua. Costa Rica joined in July 1962. The MCCA consists of Costa Rica, El Salvador, Guatemala, Honduras, and Nicaragua. Panama is considering joining the bloc. However, Panama's distinctive economy, one dominated by banking and other financial services, and shipping through the Canal Zone, coupled with the economic difficulties in Latin America, has made it difficult for Panama to join a regional trade agreement (RTA).

In May 2000, three of the Central American countries — El Salvador, Guatemala, and Nicaragua — signed a free trade agreement (FTA). The exclusion of the other countries fueled tensions in the region, which already had existed over frontier disputes between Belize and Guatemala, between Costa Rica and Nicaragua, and between Honduras and Nicaragua.

*Suggestions for Further Research:*

Book:

1.   BULMER-THOMAS, VICTOR, THE ECONOMIC HISTORY OF LATIN AMERICA SINCE INDEPENDENCE 268–393 (2nd ed. 2003).

Articles:

1.   Bulmer-Thomas, Victor, *The Central American Common Market: From Closed to Open Regionalism*, 26:2 WORLD DEVELOPMENT 313–22 (1998).

2.   Rodas-Martini, Pablo, *Intra-Industry Trade and Revealed Comparative Advantage in the Central American Common Market*, 26:2 WORLD DEVELOPMENT 337–44 (1998).

---

[457] *See* Samarendu Mohanty, Suwen Pan, Mark Welch & Don Ethridge, *The Impacts of Eliminating the Step 2 Program on the U.S. and World Cotton Market*, Texas Tech University Cotton Economics Research Institute, Briefing Paper, CER-BR05-01, July 2005, available at www.aaec.ttu.edu/ceri/policy/publications.

## MCL

Munitions Control List.

Pursuant to the *Arms Export Control Act*, the Department of State is the responsible licensing agency for exports from the United States of defense articles and services. Defense articles and services requiring a license are indicated on the MCL, which the State Department maintains.

## *MCP AGREEMENT*

The *Agreement on Multi-Chip Integrated Circuits*.

The United States, European Union (EU), Korea, and Taiwan signed this *Agreement* in March 2006.[458] Under the 1996 WTO *Information Technology Agreement* (*ITA*), semiconductor products receive duty-free treatment from the signatory countries. However, an MCP allows several semiconductor chips to be bundled into a single product. Examples of goods containing MCPs are cell phones, personal organizers, and MP3 players. Being a recent innovation, MCPs are not covered by the *ITA*.

## MCTL

Militarily Critical Technologies List.

The *Export Administration Act of 1979*, as amended, established, for the first time, separate and distinct criteria and procedures to impose export controls for two long-standing policy purposes — protecting United States national security and furthering American foreign policy interests. The *Act* not only laid out time deadlines for processing export license applications, but also mandated creation of the MCTL. The purpose of the MCTL is to ensure the CCL (Commerce Control List) of goods and technology maintained by the Department of Commerce (DOC) is both adequate and focused narrowly on items most militarily important, and introduced foreign availability of a good controlled by the United States as a criterion in making a licensing decision.

## MDG

Millennium Development Goal.

In the 2000 Millennium Declaration, the United Nations set forth eight (8) MDGs to be achieved by 2015:[459]

---

[458] *See U.S., EU, Korea, Taiwan Sign Pact Ending All Duties on Multi-Chip Integrated Circuits*, 23 International Trade Reporter (BNA) 492 (30 March 2006).

[459] *Aspirations and Obligations*, THE ECONOMIST, 10 September 2005, at 67–68; *Between Hype and Hope*, THE ECONOMIST, 16 July 2005, at 74; *Helping Africa Help Itself*, THE ECONOMIST, 2 July 2005, at 11; *The $25 Billion Question*, THE ECONOMIST, 2 July 2005, at 24–26.

- *Eradicate extreme poverty and hunger*:

  Specifically, this MDG is to cut poverty and hunger in half. It is, of course, assumed that living in poverty means (*inter alia*) living with hunger. Accordingly, one strategy to reduce hunger is to boost income.

  The World Bank defines the international poverty line at one dollar a day, or more specifically, U.S. $1.08 per day, using 1993 dollars in PPP terms. In 2002, 1,072,000,000 people lived on less than a dollar a day, and on average they fell short by $113. The MDG is to reduce that amount to 446,800,000 people by 2015. Based on present trends, by 2015 there will be 826,700,000 people living below the poverty line; hence the projected shortfall in meeting the target will be 379,900,000 people. China already has met the goal of cutting poverty in half — over a decade early. However, at present trends, Sub-Saharan Africa (SSA) will be decades late in achieving it. In many Sub-Saharan African Countries (SSACs), *per capita* income levels remain below the levels of the 1960s.

  Related to the goal of cutting poverty and hunger in half is to increase access to clean water, so that by 2015 no more than 315.3 million people will lack access to clean water. In 2002, 1,036,600,000 people lacked access to clean water. At current trends, by 2015, 525.2 million will not have clean water, implying a shortfall of 209.9 million people.

- *Universal primary education, i.e., enrolling every child in primary school*:

  A number of countries do not come close to this zero-tolerance goal, particularly when gender differences are considered. For example, only 40 percent of primary-school pupils in Pakistan are girls. Overall, in 2002, 109,900,000 children were not enrolled in primary school. At present trends, by 2015, 46,700,000 children will not be enrolled in primary school.

- *Promote gender equality and empower women*:

  This MDG reflects a concern about the status of women around the world.

- *Reduce child mortality*:

  This MDG concerns death before the fifth birthday, and the aim is to cut the child mortality level by two-thirds, to a level of 4.2. In 2003, the level was 10.5, and the level projected for 2015 on current trends is 8.6, leaving a shortfall of 4.4. As of 2005, only one African country even registered births and deaths in accordance to United Nations standards. A related objective is to spare adults from untimely deaths, *i.e.*, to increase life expectancy. In many SSACs, life expectancy is falling.

- *Improve maternal health*:

  This goal reflects a concern about the status of women as mothers and caretakers of children, and the link between this status and the poverty and hunger of children.

- *Reduce infectious diseases, notably HIV/AIDS and malaria*:

  Shifting priorities in medical research is essential to meeting this MDG. Of the $75 billion spent annually on medical research, 90 percent is devoted to the health issues affecting 10 percent of the world's population. Achieving this goal also requires accurate recordkeeping. As of 2005, no African country regularly measured infection rates for tuberculosis.

- *Protect the environment*:

  This MDG aims to ensure environmental sustainability.

- *Establish a global partnership for development*:

  Specifically, this MDG aims to increase assistance to poor countries from rich countries so that each rich country devotes 0.7 percent of its GDP to foreign aid. Overall, not surprisingly, in its 2005 *Human Development Report*, the United Nations Development Program stated "[t]he currency of pledges from the international community is by now so severely debased by non-delivery that it is widely perceived as worthless.

  In May 2005, the oldest 15 EU members agreed to spend 0.51 percent of their national income by 2010 on foreign aid. Collectively, the EU set a target of 0.56 percent of combined income. At the same time, in 2004, the EU spent $55 billion on its CAP. Yet, as of 2008, the average aid from 22 donor countries was only 0.28 per cent of their national incomes. Only five countries, Denmark, Luxembourg, the Netherlands, Norway, and Sweden met the millennium pledge amount. Because these five countries met the pledge amount, the overall average percent of national income contributed was raised to 0.7 percent.

  Interestingly, the 0.7 percent figure dated from a pledge that wealthy countries made in 1970, to spend this proportion of their income on aid.[460] Few countries, most of which are Nordic, meet this target. Consequently, aid advocates see the MDG as part of a long legacy of broken promises.

  Notably, the United States has not met the MDG of spending 0.51 percent of GDP on aid. America is reluctant to commit over five to 10 years to foreign assistance defined in terms of a fixed share of national income. In comparison to the MDG, the Marshall Plan of the post-Second World War period required an average one percent of America's national income for four years.

  Furthermore, in 2005 at the Gleneagles (Scotland) Summit, the G-8 pledged to increase development aid to Africa to $25 billion annually by 2010. As of 2008 the entire G-8 was set to backtrack on that pledge.

---

[460] *See* Chris Giles, *G8 Accused of Cover-Up on Failure to Meet Aid Targets*, FINANCIAL TIMES, 16 May 2011, at 4.

There is, of course, a debate about the efficacy of aid. Critics charge it makes recipient governments dependent on aid, and that every dollar of aid given to a government leads to a reduction of 28 cents in tax revenue collected by that government. They also point out aid results in an increase in the price of skilled workers, and thereby crowds out export industries.

In general, at present trends, will any of the MDGs be met?

The answer to this question requires a forecast, of course. The outlook is not good. For example, the number of chronically hungry people in the world rose from 848 million in 2003–2005 to nearly 1 billion (specifically, 963 million) in 2008.[461] Thus, the first MDG of halving world hunger between 1990 and 2015 is further off than ever before. As another example, no SSAC will achieve a MDG on target. Indeed, there is little doubt that many, if not all, of the MDGs will be missed.

Thus, in May 2011, a document from the Group of 8 (G-8), leaked to the media, indicated the G-8 countries were trying to cover up their failure to meet the MDGs.[462] The G-8 prepared the document, a draft accountability report, for the May 2011 G-8 Summit in Deauville, France. The draft report claimed the G-8 had increased annual aid by nearly $49 billion, from 2004 through 2010, which was only $1 billion per year short of the target the G-8 set in its 2005 Gleneagles, Scotland Summit. But, the Organization for Economic Cooperation and Development (OECD) pointed out the G-8 figures failed to account for inflation, which had been notable between 2004 and 2010. Thus, in 2010, the G-8 was $19 billion short of the 2005 goal. Moreover, the G-8 had increased aid to Africa in this period by just $11 billion, whereas they promised a $25 billion hike. And, of the 15 EU countries that pledged to boost aid to 0.51 percent of their national income by 2010, seven (including France, Germany, and Italy) had failed to do so.

However, while specific MDGs might not be met, there still is evidence of progress in some areas. Take, for example, the goal of eradicating extreme poverty. In Sub-Saharan Africa, the absolute poverty rate has fallen by almost one percentage point a year since 1990. Another example of progress is in the area of reducing child mortality. In Niger, between 1990 and 2007, the number of children who died before their fifth birthday was reduced from 302 to 176. Despite what would appear to be a huge success, Niger most likely will fall below the goal of reducing child mortality by two-thirds.

This "failure" in meeting goals can be prejudiced by uniform or across the board MDGs, which means some countries must work much harder than others to meet goals. The low starting point for countries such as Niger can hinder seriously their ability to meet goals even when they are making progress.

---

[461] *See* Javier Blas, *Almost 1 bn People Now Going Hungry*, FINANCIAL TIMES, 10 December 2008, at 6.

[462] *See* Chris Giles, *G8 Accused of Cover-Up on Failure to Meet Aid Targets*, FINANCIAL TIMES, 16 May 2011, at 4.

In contrast to Niger's MDG "failure" is a uniform goal that seemingly has lead to an MDG "victory," namely, halving the poverty rate by 2015 from its 1990 level of 46 percent. In 2005 the poverty rate fell to 27 percent, and with 10 years to meet the goal, success seemed likely. However, the drop in poverty was due primarily to a decrease in China's poverty rate from 60 percent in 1990 to 16 percent in 2005. China, along with India, accounts for a majority of the world's poor. The performance of these two countries in eradicating poverty greatly affects the MDG, in contrast to the effect a country such as Niger would have on a uniform MDG goal, notwithstanding the impressive progress the smaller country has made.

*Suggestions for Further Research:*

Book:

1. UNITED NATIONS DEVELOPMENT PROGRAM, HUMAN DEVELOPMENT REPORT (2005).

Other Source:

1. Scarnecchia, D. Brian & Terrence McKeegan, *The Millennium Development Goals — In Light of Catholic Social Teaching*, International Organizations Research Group, White Paper Number 10, 2009, *posted at* www.c-fam.org.

## MEA

Multilateral Environmental Agreement.

The relationship between MEAs, on the one hand, and GATT–WTO rules, on the other hand, is highly contentious.

*Suggestions for Further Research:*

Book:

1. VRANES, ERICH, TRADE AND THE ENVIRONMENT — FUNDAMENTAL ISSUES IN INTERNATIONAL LAW, WTO LAW, AND LEGAL THEORY (2009).

Articles:

1. Alvarez, José E., *The WTO as Linkage Machine*, 96 AMERICAN JOURNAL OF INTERNATIONAL LAW issue 1, 146–158 (2002).

2. Bilsky, Eric A., *Conserving Marine Wildlife Through World Trade Law*, 30 MICHIGAN JOURNAL OF INTERNATIONAL LAW 599–641 (2009).

3. Blodgett, Mark S. & Richard J. Hunter, Jr., *The Environment and Trade Agreements: Should the WTO Become More Actively Involved?*, 33 HASTINGS INTERNATIONAL & COMPARATIVE LAW REVIEW 1–19 (2010).

4. Carranza, Miguel A. Elizalde, *MEAs with Trade Measures and the WTO: Aiming Toward Sustainable Development?*, 15 BUFFALO ENVIRONMENTAL LAW JOURNAL 43–96 (2007–2008).

5. Charnovitz, Steve, *The WTO's Environmental Progress*, 10 JOURNAL OF INTERNATIONAL ECONOMIC LAW 685–706 (2007).

6.  Cheyne, Ilona, *Proportionality, Proximity and Environmental Labeling in WTO Law*, 12 JOURNAL OF INTERNATIONAL ECONOMIC LAW 927–952 (2009).

7.  Czarnezki, Jason J., *The Future of Food Eco-Labeling: Organic, Carbon Footprint, and Environmental Life-Cycle Analysis*, 30 STANFORD ENVIRONMENTAL LAW JOURNAL 3–49 (2011).

8.  Dagne, Teshager Worku, *The Debate on Environmentally Motivated Unilateral Trade Measures in the World Trade Organization: The Way Forward*, 9 WASHINGTON UNIVERSITY GLOBAL STUDIES LAW REVIEW 427–456 (2010).

9.  Emory Jr., Richard W., *Improving National Enforcement for Better Governance Implementing Multilateral Environmental Agreements*, 36 DENVER JOURNAL OF INTERNATIONAL LAW & POLICY 381–388 (2008).

10. Gentile, Dominic, Note, *International Trade and the Environment: What is the Role of the WTO?*, 20 FORDHAM ENVIRONMENTAL LAW JOURNAL 197–232 (2009).

11. González-Garibay, Montserrat, *The Trade-Labour and Trade-Environment Linkages: Together or Apart?*, 10 JOURNAL OF INTERNATIONAL TRADE LAW POLICY number 2 165–184 (2011).

12. Hall, Noah D., *Protecting Freshwater Resources in the Era of Global Water Markets: Lessons Learned from Bottled Water*, 13 UNIVERSITY OF DENVER WATER LAW REVIEW 1–54 (2009).

13. Kapterian, Gisele, *A Critique of WTO Jurisprudence on "Necessity,"* 59 INTERNATIONAL & COMPARATIVE LAW QUARTERLY 89–127 (2010).

14. Kishore, Pallavi Dr., *A Comparative Analysis of Secretariats Created Under Select Treaty Regimes*, 45 THE INTERNATIONAL LAWYER 1051–1082 (winter 2011).

15. Lopez, Matthew L., Student Article, *The Effects of Free Trade on the Environment: Conserving the Environment While Maintaining Increased Levels of Economic Prosperity for Developing Countries*, 3 PHOENIX LAW REVIEW 701–728 (2010).

16. Moloo, Rahim & Justin Jacinto, *Environmental and Health Regulation: Assessing Liability Under Investment Treaties*, 29 BERKELEY JOURNAL OF INTERNATIONAL LAW 1–65 (2011).

17. Nanda, Ved P., *Climate Change and Developing Countries: The International Law Perspective*, 16 ILSA JOURNAL OF INTERNATIONAL & COMPARATIVE LAW 539–556 (2010).

18. Skinner, Jonathan, Note, *A Green Road to Development: Environmental Regulations and Developing Countries in the WTO*, 20 DUKE ENVIRONMENTAL LAW & POLICY FORUM 245–269 (2010).

19. Symposium, *China's Environmental Governance: Global Challenges and Comparative Solutions*, 12 VERMONT JOURNAL OF ENVIRONMENTAL LAW 591–734 (2011).

20. Symposium, *China's Asset Management Platforms and Cleantech Sector*, 19 CARDOZO JOURNAL OF INTERNATIONAL & COMPARATIVE LAW 525–591 (2011).

21. Weber, Katherine, *Can You Eat Your Fish & Save It Too? Improving the Protection of Pirated Marine Species through International Trade Measures*, 25 JOURNAL OF LAND USE & ENVIRONMENTAL LAW 265–304 (2010).

## *MEDICINES AGREEMENT*

Also called the August 2003 *Medicines Agreement*.

*See* Compulsory Licensing.

## **MEEPC**

Middle East Economic Partnership Caucus.

A group of Congresspersons interested in ways to increase trade, and enhance economic relations, between the United States and moderate countries (as identified by the United States) in the Middle East.

## *MEFTA*

*Middle East Free Trade Agreement.*

A policy goal of the United States, articulated in May 2003 by President George W. Bush, to create a free trade agreement (FTA) between the United States and all countries in the Middle East by 2013. The goal is to be reached by building on a network of bilateral FTAs between the United States and individual Middle Eastern countries.

Query the extent to which the United States has progressed toward this goal, which is plainly as much or more about politics and national security as it is about economics. There are FTAs linking the United States with Bahrain, Jordan, Morocco, Oman, but their commercial significance is uneven. The United States has made modest progress toward FTAs with the United Arab Emirates (UAE), but rejects (for the time being) such an accord with the largest Arab Muslim country — Israel. Query, too, whether Israel — which has an FTA with the United States — would be brought into *MEFTA*. Similarly, how might Libya or Palestine fit in? Finally, query why certain major Middle Eastern economies –Iran and Turkey, for instance — are not (as yet, anyway) part of the *MEFTA* vision.

To be sure, the *MEFTA* vision is based largely on a peace-through-trade approach, which has been a hallmark of American trade policy since at least the era of Cordell Hull, Secretary of State to President Franklin D. Roosevelt. Yet, the moves and counter-moves by the United States and European Union (EU) suggest a different basis for the vision — competitive imperialism. Ultimately, the success of the vision may depend on the extent to which Middle Eastern countries themselves put aside differences and focus, rather pragmatically, akin to South East Asian countries, on economic development, and on the extent to which the United States offers specific terms in FTAs to the long-run benefit of those countries.

## MEMBER

A country that is a Member of the World Trade Organization. Under Article XI:1 of the *Agreement Establishing the World Trade Organization* (*WTO Agreement*), a contracting party to GATT that accepts the *WTO Agreement* and related Multilateral Trade Agreements is an original Member. Sources differ as to the capitalization of the first letter, though the better convention — in terms of visual clarity, at least — seems to use the upper case "M."

## MENA (FIRST MEANING)

Middle East North Africa, *i.e.*, the countries of that region.

## MENA (SECOND MEANING)

Middle East North Africa, with a view to a regional trade agreement (RTA) of some kind involving the MENA countries.

Essentially the *Middle East Free Trade Agreement* (*MEFTA*) idea of the Administration of President George W. Bush, but reincarnated after considerable delay in the Administration of President Barack H. Obama. In November 2011, the President's Export Council (PEC) recommended strengthening trade ties with the MENA region, specifically, by:[463]

- Identifying areas to engage MENA with a view to increased trade and foreign direct investment (FDI), including in services and government procurement.

- Promoting development in sectors that are engines of growth for the MENA countries.

- Supporting environmentally sustainable technologies.

- Regarding governments of MENA countries as partners with which to work on reforms necessary to increase trade and FDI, including on tariff reductions and customs facilitation.

- Building regional institutions and mechanisms that would allow for regulatory convergence, common standards, and governance.

However, United States Trade Representative (USTR) Ron Kirk opined in November 2011 that the United States was "probably two or three steps away" from an FTA with the MENA countries as a region.[464]

At the 2011 G-8 Summit, the G-8 established the Deauville Partnership. The purpose of this Partnership is to develop a coordinated response to the Arab Spring for the MENA region, particularly with respect to supporting a

---

[463] *See* Rossella Brevetti, *President's Export Council Recommends Expanding ITA, Strengthening MENA Trade*, 28 International Trade Reporter (BNA) 1884 (24 November 2011).

[464] *Quoted in* Rossella Brevetti, *President's Export Council Recommends Expanding ITA, Strengthening MENA Trade*, 28 International Trade Reporter (BNA) 1884 (24 November 2011).

democratic transition to accountable, transparent government that would yield an economic framework in which sustainable, inclusive growth occurs.[465]

## MERCANTILISM

The theory, popular in 16th and 17th century England, that it is best for a nation to maintain a large trade surplus. Because international trade payments would be made in gold, it was believed a nation would be stronger economically by receiving a net influx of gold as a result of its trade surplus. Insofar as its currency was tied to a gold standard, the increase in gold reserves would justify monetary expansion, and thereby overall economic growth. In brief, given the gold supply as a transmission mechanism of sorts, a balance of payments (BOP) surplus would lead to an increase in the money supply and thus stimulate the economy.

The logical policy conclusion of this view was protectionism. That is, it was thought protectionist devices ought to be used to achieve this effect. In turn, to implement these policies, strong government intervention in international trade markets was required. For example, the British government used a series of Navigation Acts (regulating the carriage of goods at sea), limited the trade of its colonies to England, the mother country, subsidized exports, and set high tariffs on imported manufactured goods. Naturally, that sort of intervention was facilitated by colonialist domination.

It was mercantilism that both Adam Smith in *The Wealth of Nations* (1776) and David Ricardo in *The Principles of Political Economy and Taxation* (1817) attacked. Both pointed out that mercantilism was, on balance, inefficient for society, because it emphasized the interests of producers over consumers. But, in addition to the critique of mercantilism from the perspective of Smith's invisible hand and Ricardo's theory of comparative advantage, it can be said that mercantilism is self-defeating in the long run. An increase in domestic money supply can lead to increases in prices, *i.e.*, inflation. In turn, any trade surplus may disappear as foreigners find goods too expensive, and the end results are real losses.

*Suggestions for Further Research:*

Books:

1. IRWIN, DOUGLAS A., AGAINST THE TIDE — AN INTELLECTUAL HISTORY OF FREE TRADE (1996).

2. SALLY, RAZEEN, NEW FRONTIERS IN FREE TRADE — GLOBALIZATION'S FUTURE AND ASIA'S RISING ROLE (2008).

## MERCHANT MARKET

*See* Captive Production.

---

[465] *See* Len Bracken, *Atlantic Council's Dunne Backs Trade Focus for U.S. Assistance to Egypt, Libya, Tunisia*, 29 International Trade Reporter (BNA) 426 (15 March 2012).

## *MERCOSUR*

The *Mercado Común del Sur*, or Southern Common Market, which is a customs union established in 1991 by the Treaty of Asuncion.

The *MERCOSUR* bloc consists of roughly 250 million people, led by Brazil, the world's seventh largest economy. Arguably, in economic power, the bloc rivals, or even exceeds the *Association of South East Asian Nations (ASEAN)*.[466] After the European Union (EU) and the *North American Free Trade Agreement (NAFTA)*, *MERCOSUR* is the third largest single market and trade bloc in the world.

*MERCOSUR's* founding four members are Argentina, Brazil, Paraguay, and Uruguay. In December 2005, Bolivia and Venezuela joined these four countries with a view to gaining full *MERCOSUR* membership.[467] Venezuela launched membership talks in 2001. As of December 2012, Venezuela's status as a full member depended on approval by the legislature of Paraguay, and by some accounts, Bolivia was listed as an associate member.[468] Thus, Venezuela and Bolivia, along with Chile, Colombia, Ecuador, and Peru, are associate members in *MERCOSUR*. That means they enjoy preferential access to the bloc, but do not adopt the common external tariff (CET) of *MERCOSUR*, and have no voting rights in *MERCOSUR*. Counting the original four members plus Venezuela, *MERCOSUR* accounts for 76 percent of the Gross Domestic Product (GDP) of South America.

Full membership requires consensus among all four members, which means approval by all four members, effectively giving any one of them a veto. Argentina, Brazil, and Uruguay had granted approval for Venezuela. But, conservatives in the Paraguayan Congress opposed the undemocratic, socialist policies pursued by Venezuela under its President, Hugo Chavez. They specifically pointed out that the Chavez regime has failed to satisfy the standards concerning freedom in the so-called "democratic clause" of the *MERCOSUR* agreement.[469] Moreover, they feared that once in, the fact that *MERCOSUR* operates by consensus — which, again grants a member an effective veto — would put too much power in the hands of President Chavez.

During 1991–1994, *MERCOSUR* created a free trade agreement (FTA), though a less ambitious one than *NAFTA*. *MERCOSUR* lacks agreements to achieve free trade in services, or deal with intellectual property (IP) and

---

[466] *See* David Haskel, *Latin Leaders Seek to Boost External Trade but Still Vow to Protect Domestic Markets*, 28 International Trade Reporter (BNA) 1143 (7 July 2011).

[467] *See* David Haskel, *Venezuela's Full Membership in MERCOSUR Seen as Boon to Exporters by Other Members*, 23 International Trade Reporter (BNA) 1262–63 (24 August 2006).

[468] *See* David Haskel, *Venezuela Seen unlikely to Win Mercosur Membership Anytime Soon*, 28 International Trade Reporter (BNA) 1665 (13 October 2011); David Haskel, *Latin Leaders Seek to Boost External Trade but Still Vow to Protect Domestic Markets*, 28 International Trade Reporter (BNA) 1143 (7 July 2011).

[469] *See* David Haskel, *Venezuela's Admission, Free Trade talks with EU, Top MERCOSUR Leaders' Agenda*, 28 International Trade Reporter (BNA) 2027 (15 December 2011).

government procurement issues.[470] Moreover, while most goods now move tariff-free within *MERCOSUR*, there were some notable exceptions: cars, sugar, and so-called "sensitive" products (that range from chicken to shoes). Tariffs on most of these exceptions became zero in 2000, though autos and auto parts remain a sticking point. In May 2000, Argentina and Brazil agreed to phase out by 2006 remaining restrictions on trade between the two countries in autos and auto parts.

Free trade within *MERCOSUR* for the auto industry has proved highly controversial. Argentina is particularly concerned about the ability of its auto firms to withstand competition from Brazil, and refused to start free trade in this sector as scheduled at the start of 2006. For their part, Brazilian auto producers are eager to see trade liberalization in this sector, in part because of worries about losing market share in Mexico. In June 2006, the Argentina and Brazil reached a new 24 month bilateral auto agreement that would create free trade in the automotive sector — eventually.[471] This bilateral agreement is a continuation, with some adjustment, of the "flex" rules to which the two countries agreed in 2002. Under those rules, the amount — measured in terms of value — of cars Argentina (Brazil) is allowed to export duty-free to Brazil (Argentina) depends on the amount Argentina (Brazil) imports from Brazil (Argentina). In other words, the amount of zero tariff exports are linked to the amount of duty-free imports.

The basic bargain was for every U.S. $100 of autos imported by one country, the other country could export $260 duty-free. Under the June 2006 revision to the flex rules, for every U.S. $100 in cars exported from one country to another (*e.g.*, exported from Argentina to Brazil), cars worth $195 worth (and $210 in the first 12 months for every $100 exported) can be imported (*e.g.*, imported by Argentina from Brazil) without paying the standard *MERCOSUR* tariff rate of 35 percent. Significantly, the bilateral deal does not cover auto parts, which face tariffs of 14–18 percent. As of August 2006, Brazil discounted by 40 percent the tariff it imposed on auto parts from any country, while Argentina imposed a duty of two percent on a list of 40 auto parts.

This regime is manifestly one of managed trade, though perhaps a modestly freer one than the 1995–2000 quota system that prevailed between the two countries. Satisfying the interests of Argentine and Brazilian car producers is not the only problem to resolve if *MERCOSUR* is to move away from managed trade in the auto industry. In August 2006, the auto parts manufacturers from all *MERCOSUR* countries held their first "*MERCOPARTS*" conference in Punta del Este, Uruguay. Auto parts makers from Paraguay and Uruguay called for a bigger share of the *MERCOSUR* market, complaining Argentine and Brazilian competitors are pushing them out, partly through bilateral

---

[470] *See* David Haskel, *In EU FTA Talks, Mercosur Offers to Open Services in Exchange for Ag Liberalization*, 23 International Trade Reporter (BNA) 498–99 (30 March 2006).

[471] *See* Ed Taylor, Brazil, *Argentina Extend Auto Accord Until July 1, as Negotiations Continue*, 23 International Trade Reporter (BNA) 372 (9 March 2006).

agreements on cars and car parts.[472] Their calls reflected the positions of their governments, which argue the larger *MERCOSUR* countries impose their own agendas on the smaller countries. Paraguay and Uruguay said they ought to have at least a one percent share each of the *MERCOSUR* auto parts market.

Notably, effective 1 July 2008, Brazil and Argentina agreed to liberalize fully trade in autos between them, and establish joint production of 6 million vehicles annually — 5 million units in Brazil, and 1 million units in Argentina — by 1 July 2013.[473] The pact was signed on 30 May 2008 in Buenos Aires, Argentina. It is designed to last for six years, from 2008 to 2013, and thus replace the need to negotiate deals annually. However, it still smacks of managed trade. Specifically, the deal permits Argentina to export to Brazil $2.50 worth of autos and auto parts for every $1 of autos and auto parts imported from Brazil. Conversely, the deal allows Brazil to export $1.95 of autos and auto parts to Argentina for every $1 of those goods it imports from Argentina. Interestingly, too, are some of the foreign beneficiaries of the deal. Major multinational car companies — Ford, Fiat, General Motors, Renault, Peugeot, and Volkswagen — all have built production facilities in Argentina and Brazil to make cars both for domestic markets and export.

In the auto industry, at least, FTAs between or among third countries sometimes have ramifications for *MERCOSUR*. For example, under the *EU–Mexico FTA*, Mexico lowered its tariffs on EU — but not Brazilian — cars from 20 percent to 3.3 percent in July 2000, and scheduled further reductions. Moreover, in early 2000, Mexico rescinded preferential tariffs on Brazilian cars, raising duties from eight percent to an average of twenty 20. (Brazilian tariffs on Mexican cars were about 35 percent.) Brazil and Mexico patched together an auto deal in April 2000, essentially agreeing to a set of tariff-rate quotas (TRQs).

As for creation of a CU, *MERCOSUR* articulated this goal in 1995, with a five year implementation program for further liberalization of intra-regional trade, standardization of trade-related rules, harmonization of economic policies, and establishment of a common external tariff (CET). The CET is set at 11 different levels, ranging from zero to 20 percent depending on the product, and is being phased in over time. The CET on capital goods is to converge at 14 percent by 2001, and the CET on computers and telecommunications equipment was to converge toward 16 percent by 2006. In June 2006, *MERCOSUR* set 1 January 2014 as a final deadline for full trade liberalization, which presumably would mean establishment of a CET.

In 1999, the heads of state of *MERCOSUR's* founding members approved an ambitious long-term plan to harmonize their economies. The EU's *Treaty of*

---

[472] *See* David Haskel, *Uruguayan, Paraguayan Auto Parts Makers Ask for Bigger Share of MERCOSUR's Market*, 23 International Trade Reporter (BNA) 1261–62 (24 August 2006).

[473] *See* David Haskel, *Argentina, Brazil Agree on Bilateral Pact to Liberalize Automobile Trade by 2013*, 25 International Trade Reporter (BNA) 846–847 (5 June 2008).

*Maastricht* was their model, and they aimed for a "Little Maastricht." *MERCOSUR* committed itself to studying the feasibility of coordinating economic policies, establishing targets for key variables (*e.g.*, fiscal deficits, inflation, and debt), and (ultimately) monetary union. It also committed itself to harmonizing national statistics so as to facilitate comparisons, establishing common standards for fiscal responsibility (*e.g.*, legal limits on public spending), and reporting on efforts to reach economic stability. Among the motivations for macro-economic convergence was the need for external discipline to introduce long-overdue reforms — the very discipline that EU targets had imposed on Italy, and which helped Italy to introduce needed fiscal changes. The possibility Argentina might "dollar-ize" its economy also catalyzed efforts to achieve deeper integration that might spawn a more powerful trading bloc. Since 1999, various high-level meetings have been held to coordinate economic policy.

Expansion of membership is a critical issue facing *MERCOSUR*. Bolivia (land-locked, and South America's poorest country) and Chile (an economic success story, but which felt jilted by the United States in its efforts to join *NAFTA*) became associate members of *MERCOSUR* in 1996. With associate membership, Bolivia and Chile entered into the *MERCOSUR* FTA. They agreed to reduce their tariffs on a wide range of products over a phase-out period. Yet, they were not subject to its CET regime and, therefore, continued to act unilaterally as regards trade barriers to third country products. Chile has the most open economy in South America. Chile boasts a very low, uniform duty rate that is far below *MERCOSUR's* variegated common external tariff regime, an FTA with the United States. Consequently, Chilean membership in the CU is problematical as long as *MERCOSUR* is relatively protectionist, and remains suspicious about bilateral FTAs with the United States.

Notably, the necessity of raising tariffs to meet the *MERCOSUR* CET was not a problem for Venezuela, when it joined in December 2005. The *MERCOSUR* CET for cars, trucks, and pickups is 35 percent, while Venezuela's pre-*MERCOSUR* rate was 15 percent (for trucks and pickups). For medicines, the CET is 14 percent, while Venezuela's rate was five percent. For cargo ships and oil rigs, the CET is 14 percent, whereas Venezuela (which gets over 80 percent of its export earnings from crude oil) accorded these products duty-free treatment. In all instances, Venezuela agreed to raise its tariffs to the CET level, and overall to comply with the CET, no later than four years after *the MERCOSUR* presidents or foreign ministers (including Venezuela) sign a protocol for Venezuela on which the *MERCOSUR* countries agreed in June 2006. The signature occurred among the presidents on 4 July 2006, meaning the deadline for Venezuela to adopt the *MERCOSUR* CET is 4 July 2010. Notably, not all the other *MERCOSUR* countries gave Venezuelan goods the benefit of reduced duties immediately. Paraguay and Uruguay were allowed eight years — until 2013 — to lower their tariffs on most exports originating in Venezuela, and an additional one year for duties on sensitive products.

In 1996, the Andean Community agreed to negotiate as a group to join *MERCOSUR*, and talks began. In 1998, the two blocs signed a framework agreement calling for the gradual reduction of tariffs between *MERCOSUR* and the Community, and expressed the goal of signing a free trade accord by 2000. That goal proved excessively optimistic, as difficult issues of implementation remain, particularly with respect to the streamlining of customs procedures and the list of products to be streamlined. However, Peru became an associate member of *MERCOSUR* in August 2003. Interestingly, also since 1996, Mexico has negotiated with *MERCOSUR* for a formal relationship, possibly associate membership, and in June 2006 reiterated its interest in affiliate membership status. As noted above, in December 2005, two of the Andean Community countries — Bolivia and Venezuela — became full *MERCOSUR* members. Chile remains an associate member, as do Colombia, Ecuador, and Peru.

In 1997, Canada started informal discussions with *MERCOSUR* about a link, culminating in a 1998 accord establishing a framework for negotiating bilateral foreign investment agreements, cooperating on customs matters, and identifying trade and investment barriers. (Interestingly, the signing of the deal was delayed several months because of a dispute between Canada and Brazil over aircraft subsidies. Montreal-based Bombardier Inc., the lead contractor for a North Atlantic Treaty Organization pilot training program, did not award a $56 million contract to Brazil's Embraer SA for the supply of aircraft. Bombardier, saying it was a purely business decision, awarded the contract to an American supplier. However, it was suggested that Bombardier rejected Embraer's bid because the company received heavy subsidies from the Brazilian government. That government had asked the Canadian government to intervene on behalf of Embraer. Ultimately, Canada and Brazil took their dispute to the WTO.) Also in 1997, Peru sought associate membership, and *MERCOSUR* sought an association agreement with Caribbean common market, *CARICOM*.

The EU (which is *MERCOSUR's* largest trading partner) and *MERCOSUR* (which is the EU's largest trading partner in Latin America) began discussions on an EU — *MERCOSUR* FTA area based on a 1995 agreement they signed setting out a model for negotiations. The unachieved goal was to have an *EU — MERCOSUR FTA* in place on 1 January 2005. Spain is especially eager to cement ties with Latin America, and ensure that *MERCOSUR* members boost their trade ties with the EU, not simply the United States.

However, the commencement of negotiations was stalled, because of concerns within the EU about reforming the Common Agricultural Policy (CAP) and thereby opening the EU market to cheaper *MERCOSUR* agricultural exports. The CAP limits sales of agricultural goods from *MERCOSUR*, such as cereals, dairy products, meat, and wine. While EU–*MERCOSUR* trade expanded throughout the 1990s, the principal reason for the growth was trade liberalization in *MERCOSUR*, not increased market access in the EU. In a 1998 report, the European Commission's budget directorate found that if a full free trade deal were signed between the two blocs, and EU farmers thereby were exposed to competition, then the EU would have to pay its farmers

$14.9 billion a year in compensation for the effects of the deal — a staggering sum that the EU could not afford.

Thus, EU members squabbled among themselves as to how to proceed. Spain, as well as the *MERCOSUR* members, sought to begin talks as soon as possible, whereas France, Germany, and Ireland preferred to defer negotiations until 1 July 2002 or even later. In June 1999, the EU members reached a compromise:

(1) talks on removing non-tariff barriers (NTBs) in all areas of trade (including agriculture and services) began in November 1999;

(2) talks on lowering non-agricultural tariffs and liberalizing trade in services would not begin until 1 July 2001, and would parallel multilateral negotiations under the auspices of the WTO; and

(3) talks on lowering agricultural tariffs would not begin until after 2001, *i.e.*, after WTO negotiations are concluded.

Chile, an associate member of *MERCOSUR*, also was included in the talks. At bottom, each side has something the other wants. *MERCOSUR* wants increased access to the European agriculture market. The EU wants increased access to *MERCOSUR's* services market.

However, once they commenced, in 1999, negotiations for an *EU—MERCOSUR* accord snagged over familiar issues. *MERCOSUR* demanded better access to EU agricultural markets, in terms of lower tariff and quota restrictions, and cuts in EU farm support. After all, *MERCOSUR* countries are among the world's largest exporters of beans, beef, and grains.[474] *MERCOSUR* also was interested in the free movement of peoples. *MERCOSUR* argued it had offered major concessions to the EU in terms of cutting tariffs and NTBs on automobiles, and on market access for government procurement.

The EU called for enhanced market access on industrial goods, insurance and other financial services, and maritime services, government procurement, investment protection, and for better protection of copyrights. As of December 2007, the two sides remained far apart.[475] Complicating matters was a dispute in 2005–06 between Argentina and Uruguay over construction of two large pulp mills in Uruguay. Argentina claimed the mills would pollute a river shared by the two countries. The companies building the mills were from Finland and Spain. The mills would entail a $1.6 billion investment in Uruguay, its largest FDI ever.

Interestingly, *MERCOSUR* has FTAs with several countries outside of Latin America. They include FTAs with Egypt and Israel. *MERCOSUR* also is considering an FTA with the Palestinian National Authority.

---

[474] *See* David Haskell, *Venezuela's Admission, Free Trade Talks with EU, Top MERCOSUR Leaders' Agenda*, 28 International Trade Reporter (BNA) 2027 (15 December 2011).

[475] *See* David Haskel, *EU, Central America Agree to Start talks on Free Trade; Mercosur, Andean Talks Stall*, 23 International Trade Reporter (BNA)766–67 (18 May 2006).

In addition to membership expansion, one of the key difficulties facing *MERCOSUR* is that Brazil is the dominant partner (in the way that the United States is the linchpin in *NAFTA*). This fact is a constant source of tension, as the other partners fear the potential of Brazil's industrial might. For example, in 1999 the most severe dispute since the founding of *MERCOSUR* erupted between Brazil and Argentina.

Their dispute was triggered by two related factors: (1) Brazil's January 1999 40 percent devaluation of its currency, and (2) the strength of the Argentine *peso* resulting from the currency peg, maintained by Argentina between the *peso* and United States dollar. These factors caused Brazilian goods to become roughly 40 percent cheaper in 1999 than 1998, leading Argentina to threaten, and on some products actually impose, restrictions. Argentine producers claimed the two factors had given their Brazilian competitors an unfair advantage. The products at issue were steel, textiles and apparel (T&A), and footwear.

In April 1999, Argentina imposed a $410 per ton surcharge on Brazilian steel exports. In June, Argentina took a safeguard action, placing import quotas on five categories of Brazilian textile and apparel (T&A) products (specifically, five types of Brazilian cotton fabrics). In September, Argentina mandated that Brazilian footwear exporters obtain a special import license and quality certificate. Until September, Brazil insisted it would not retaliate, though it did postpone talks on trade liberalization in autos, a key Argentine export to Brazil. Brazilian footwear manufacturers even offered to limit voluntarily their exports to Argentina to 2 million pairs in 1999. However, Argentina insisted on a 1.5 million quota, and talks collapsed. Finally, in September, Brazil struck back — albeit reservedly.

Brazil declared roughly 400 Argentine export products would lose their preferential status as regards licensing and be treated like non-*MERCOSUR* products. In other words, the 400 Argentine products would have to endure administrative procedures that would cause delays of up to 60 days before Brazil would grant an import license. In contrast, the normal rule for *MERCOSUR* goods is that Brazil grants import licenses within 24 hours. In addition, Brazil's Ministry of Agriculture announced that it would inspect the facilities of Argentine manufacturers of milk and milk products (*e.g.*, cheese and yogurt) to determine if they met Brazilian technical and sanitary standards. (Argentina is Brazil's principal supplier of these products.) If the facilities did not measure up, then they would not be certified, and hence prohibited from exporting to Brazil.

The 1999 Brazil–Argentina dispute never really healed, or at least was not patched up in a way favoring free trade. In February 2006, these countries agreed to a "Competitive Adjustment Mechanism."[476] Under this special safeguard, any

---

[476] *See* David Haskel, *Argentina, Brazil Start Safeguard System To Shield Industries From Mutual Imports*, 23 International Trade Reporter (BNA) 247–28 (16 February 2006).

industry in either country affected by cheap imports is protected by a series of quotas. Imports in excess of the quota thresholds would be subject to a tariff of 90 percent of the duty applicable to the same product originating outside of *MERCOSUR*. Argentina cheered the deal. It had a bilateral trade deficit (in 2005) with Brazil of almost U.S. $4 billion, and had watched its exports to Brazil fall by 25 percent and imports from Brazil rise by 40 percent — all despite the Brazilian real appreciating sizably against the Argentine peso. Predictably, Brazilian businesses saw the safeguards deal as lamentable.

In fact, Brazil and Argentina require import permits before merchandise can be imported from the other country.[477] Certain products qualify for automatic licenses, but for goods that do not, the process to obtain a permit can be time consuming — sometimes taking months. In February 2011, Argentina actually increased the number of products that require licensing from 400 to 600. In May, Brazil retaliated by cancelling the eligibility of imported cars for automatic licensing. Argentina was stung by this move, because it is the largest source of imported cars in Brazil, accounting for 43 percent of all car imports to Brazil (as of 2010). In effect, import licensing smacks of import substitution, a policy to which Argentina and Brazil have adhered, but which they ostensibly ended by joining *MERCOSUR*.

*MERCOSUR* contains a dispute resolution mechanism, namely, it creates an arbitration court. There is no right of appeal from decisions of this court. That court has been used, for example, to adjudicate disputes between Brazil and Argentina. In March 2000, the *MERCOSUR* arbitration court ruled against Argentina's textile safeguard action, and gave Argentina 15 days to lift the quotas. The court agreed with Brazil's argument that *MERCOSUR* prohibits the use of safeguards by one member against another, and Argentina accepted the verdict.

Interestingly, *MERCOSUR* has a "democracy clause." This provision has prevented Cuba from joining the bloc, though whether "democracy" could be defined (or re-defined) to encompass a Cuban-style political system has been raised by some *MERCOSUR* officials. This issue bespeaks a fundamental challenge for *MERCOSUR*: not only are its members economically diverse, but they are politically diverse too. In addition to the interpretation and application of the democracy clause, political diversity reveals itself in the approach of the bloc to the United States. For all its trade squabbles with the United States, Brazil tends toward pragmatism in its approach. In contrast, Venezuela under President Hugo Chavez appears to steer *MERCOSUR* towards becoming an anti-imperialist group. One context in which political relations with the United States arises is the role of the dollar in *MERCOSUR* trade. In August 2006, Argentina and Brazil held discussions on ways to "de-dollarize" *MERCOSUR* trade. Arguably for political reasons, they thought increasing the number of commercial transactions paid for in local currency would be wise.

---

[477] *See* Ed Taylor, *Brazil-Argentina Negotiations Produce Agreement to Expedite Import Licensing*, 28 International Trade Reporter (BNA) 950 (9 June 2011).

Businesses were not so sure, especially given the relatively greater fluctuations in the Argentine peso and Brazilian real than the U.S. dollar.

In September 2006, Uruguay presented *MERCOSUR* with yet another challenge: the possibility of a bilateral FTA with the United States. *MERCOSUR* officially bans bilateral deals between one of its members, on the one hand, and a non-member, on the other hand. However, in 2004, the United States overtook *MERCOSUR* as the largest export market for Uruguay. In November 2005, the United States and Uruguay signed a Bilateral Investment Treaty (BIT). Uruguay also has been frustrated by the lack of productive integration and macroeconomic coordination among *MERCOSUR* members, and the dominance of the bloc by Brazil. In May 2006, Uruguay openly floated the idea of detaching from *MERCOSUR* as a full member, *i.e.*, downgrading its status to an associate member, so as to liberate itself from regional dependence. In September 2006, President Tabare Vazquez of Uruguay asked for permission from his fellow *MERCOSUR* leaders to negotiate an FTA with the United States — the leading export market for Uruguay. The response was stiff resistance.[478] Uruguay's President argued bilateral FTAs would stimulate *MERCOSUR* to improve its performance. Article 21 of the 1991 *MERCOSUR* treaty allows associate members to participate in *MERCOSUR* as an FTA, but deviate from the CET, and allows such members to negotiate FTAs with non-*MERCOSUR* countries. Accordingly, Uruguay could invoke Article 21 to pursue its goals. In January 2007, Uruguay took another significant step toward an FTA, when it signed a *Trade and Investment Framework Agreement (TIFA)* with the United States.

In contrast, land-locked Paraguay has shown no interest in an FTA with the United States, despite having complaints similar to Uruguay concerning Brazilian and Argentine domination of *MERCOSUR*. The Foreign Minister of Paraguay, Leila Rachid, declared in June 2006 that it would never sign an FTA with a country that was unwilling to liberalize its farm trade regime. That stance reflects in part the position of Paraguay as an overwhelmingly agrarian society.

Impressively, on the sidelines of the Seventh WTO Ministerial Conference in Geneva from 30 November–2 December 2009, *MERCOSUR* made an important declaration. Along with the *Southern African Customs Union (SACU)*, and India, MERCOSUR announced progress toward a free trade agreement (FTA). This progress built on the June 2004 preferential trade agreement (PTA) between *MERCOSUR* and *SACU*, and on talks between *MERCOSUR* and India.

*Suggestions for Further Research:*

Books:

1.   FILHO, MARCÍLIO TOSCANO FRANCA, LUCAS LIXINSKI & MARÍA BELÉN OLMOS GIUPPONI, THE LAW OF MERCOSUR (2010).

---

[478] *See* David Haskel, *Brazil's President Urges Latin Leaders to Leave U.S. Out of Free Trade Plans*, 23 International Trade Reporter (BNA) 1138–39 (27 July 2006).

2. PORRETTA-DORIA, RAFAEL, MERCOSUR: THE COMMON MARKET OF THE SOUTHERN CONE (Carolina Academic Press 2005).

Book Chapters:

1. Markwald, Ricardo & Joao Bosco Machado, *Establishing an Industrial Policy for MERCOSUR, in* MERCOSUR — REGIONAL INTEGRATION, WORLD MARKETS 63, 64 (Riordan Roett ed. 1999).

Articles:

1. Bravo, Karen E., *Regional Trade Arrangements and Labor Liberalization: (Lost) Opportunities for Experimentation?*, 28 SAINT LOUIS UNIVERSITY PUBLIC LAW REVIEW 71–113 (2008).

2. Brown, Kristin L., Comment, *Venezuela Joins Mercosur: The Impact Felt Around the Americas*, 16 LAW & BUSINESS REVIEW OF THE AMERICAS 85–93 (2010).

3. Gari, Gabriel, *Legal Instruments for the Liberalization of Trade in Services at the Sub-Regional Level: The MERCOSUR Case*, 25 PENN STATE INTERNATIONAL LAW REVIEW 659–705 (2007).

4. Richelson, Sarah, Student Note, *Trafficking and Trade: How Regional Trade Agreements Can Combat the Trafficking of Persons in Brazil*, 25 ARIZONA JOURNAL OF INTERNATIONAL AND COMPARATIVE LAW 857–898 (2008).

# METI

Ministry of Economy, Trade, and Industry of Japan, located in Tokyo.

In the 1960s, Japan emerged as the second largest economy in the world. METI, formerly known as the "Ministry of International Trade and Industry" ("MITI"), played a central role in shaping Japanese economic growth. It issued industrial policy plans, roughly every five years, which at least through the 1990s were considered seriously by Japanese businesses. It was among the most powerful ministries in the Japanese government, and indeed among the most powerful players in the Japanese economy. In 2001, "MITI" was re-named "METI."

In its June 2006 report, *The New Economic Growth Strategy*, METI explained that in 10 years China will become the second largest economy in the world. India, too, might overtake Japan in economic size, shortly after a decade. To avoid a loss of economic status and competitiveness, *The New Economic Growth Strategy* called for closer ties between Japan and other Asian countries, a renewed emphasis on innovation and productivity to become a global innovation center (*e.g.*, by creating an innovation superhighway to research and develop new products and technologies through collaboration by academia, business, and government), modernization of services businesses (*e.g.*, health care), increased inward investment (*e.g.*, by a special foreign direct investment (FDI) zone that would offer tax relief to foreign companies), and the promotion of Japanese commercial brand identity (*e.g.*, for products like fashion, fruit, organically grown rice, sake, and vegetables).[479]

---

[479] *See* Toshio Aritake, *Japan Issues New Trade Policy Calling for Closer Asian Ties, Increase in Innovation*, 23 International Trade Reporter (BNA) 909 (15 June 2006).

## *MFA*

*Multi-Fiber Arrangement.*

Under the 1974 *MFA*, countries whose markets were disrupted by increased imports of textiles and apparel from other countries could negotiate the imposition of quotas. *MFA* quota restrictions were phased out under the Uruguay Round *Agreement on Textiles and Clothing (ATC)* over a 10 year period commencing on 1 January 1995. The last *MFA* quotas were abolished 31 December 2004.

In the *Turkey — Textiles* case, the WTO Panel provided historical background on the *MFA*, as follows:

> 2.25   The gradual removal of QRs [quantitative restrictions] in major developed countries during the 1950s, in the wake of general liberalization efforts pursued in the GATT, brought about substantial increases in textiles and clothing imports into major developed countries originating in low-cost countries. To alleviate the difficulties caused to their producers, some importing countries convinced exporters of cotton textiles to conclude voluntary export restraint agreements. In an attempt to find a multilateral solution to the problem, in 1960 the GATT CONTRACTING PARTIES recognized the phenomenon of market disruption, thus setting the ground for selective safeguard action in the area of textile and clothing products (as a departure from the requirements of Article XIX of GATT 1947).

> 2.26   Thereafter, discriminatory restraints took the form of the 1961 *Short-Term Arrangement Regarding International Trade in Cotton Textiles*, followed in 1962 by the *Long-Term Cotton Textiles Arrangement* (1962–1973). The *Arrangement Regarding International Trade in Textiles or Multifibre Arrangement* ("*MFA*") entered into force in 1974, extending the coverage of the restrictions on textiles and clothing from cotton products, to include wool and man-made fibre products (and, from 1986, certain vegetable fibre products). [As the Panel observes in a footnote, "Operationally, the *MFA* (like the cotton arrangements) provided rules for the imposition of restraints, either through bilateral agreements or, in cases of market disruption or threat thereof, through unilateral action. Importing countries were also required, with certain exceptions, to allow for an annual growth rate in the restraints."]

> 2.27   During its 21 years of existence, from 1974 to 1994, the *MFA* underwent numerous operational changes and adaptations. The restraints under the *MFA* developed into a complex network of restrictions, bilaterally negotiated (or imposed in the case of unilateral actions) at short intervals, often every year or so. In the last year of its existence, the *MFA* had 44 participants, six of which (Canada, Norway, the United States and the European Communities, plus Austria and Finland,) applied restraints. Such restraints were used almost exclusively to protect their markets against imports of textiles and clothing

from developing countries and, to a lesser extent, from former state-trading countries, also *MFA* members.

2.28    After more than three decades of special and increasingly complicated regimes governing international trade in textile and clothing products, seven years of negotiations during the Uruguay Round resulted in the *ATC* [WTO *Agreement on Textiles and Clothing*]. Through the transitional process embodied in the *ATC*, by 1 January 2005 the extensive and complex system of bilateral restraints will come to an end and importing countries will no longer be able to discriminate between exporters in applying safeguard measures.[480]

*Suggestions for Further Research:*

Books:

1.    BAGCHI, SANJOY, INTERNATIONAL TRADE POLICY IN TEXTILES — FIFTY YEARS OF PROTECTIONISM (June 2001).

2.    KRISHNA, KALA & LING HUI TAN, RAGS AND RICHES: IMPLEMENTING APPAREL QUOTAS UNDER THE MULTI-FIBRE ARRANGEMENT (1998).

3.    RIVOLI, PIETRA, THE TRAVELS OF A T-SHIRT IN THE GLOBAL ECONOMY: AN ECONOMIST EXAMINES THE MARKETS, POWER, AND POLITICS OF WORLD TRADE (2005).

4.    UNDERHILL, GEOFFREY R.D., INDUSTRIAL CRISIS AND THE OPEN ECONOMY: POLITICS, GLOBAL TRADE, AND THE TEXTILE INDUSTRY IN THE ADVANCED ECONOMIES (1998).

Article:

1.    Hall, John A., *"China Casts a Giant Shadow:" The Developing World Confronts Trade Liberalization and the End of Quotas in the Garment Industry*, 5 JOURNAL OF INTERNATIONAL BUSINESS AND LAW 1–46 (2006).

## MFN

Most Favored Nation.

The MFN principle is set forth in GATT Article I:1 and calls for WTO Members not to discriminate among like products and the rules relating to the importation or exportation of goods, or payment for them, on the basis of their origin or destination. The principle — a pillar obligation of GATT — is a broad one, encompassing not only customs duties and the way in which they are levied, but also all rules and formalities relating to importation, exportation, and payment for imports or exports. The principle is found in a number of WTO accords.

In developing and least developed countries, both applied and bound MFN rates tend to be far higher than in developed countries. Average applied MFN

---

[480] WTO Panel Report, *Turkey — Restrictions on Imports of Textile and Clothing Products*, WT/DS34/R (adopted as modified by the Appellate Body 19 December 1999) (complaint by India).

rates in most developed countries are quite low, as a result of successive rounds of multilateral trade negotiations since the founding of GATT on 30 October 1947. For example (as of April 2009), the average applied MFN rate of the European Union (EU) is 6.7 percent (a slight drop from 6.9 percent in 2006). Note that the EU has tariff peaks, as do many WTO Members. The highest EU applied MFN rate is 604.3 percent, imposed on isoglucose.

*Suggestions for Further Research:*

Book Chapter:

1.  Ziegler, Andreas R., *The Nascent International Law on Most-Favoured-Nation (MFN) Clauses in Bilateral Investment Treaties (BITs), in* EUROPEAN YEARBOOK OF INTERNATIONAL ECONOMIC LAW 2010 (C. Hermann & J.P. Terhechte, eds., 2010).

Articles:

1.  Adlung, Rudolf & Antonio Carzaniga, *MFN Exemptions Under the General Agreement on Trade in Services: Grandfathers Striving for Immortality?*, 12 JOURNAL OF INTERNATIONAL ECONOMIC LAW 357–392 (2009).

2.  Bamberger, Kenneth A. & Andrew T. Guzman, *Keeping Imports Safe: A Proposal for Discriminatory Regulation of International Trade*, 96 CALIFORNIA LAW REVIEW 1405–1445 (2008).

3.  Benoit, Charles, Note, *Picking Tariff Winners: Non-Product Related PPMs and DSB Interpretations of "Unconditionality" within Article I:1*, 42 GEORGETOWN JOURNAL OF INTERNATIONAL LAW 583–604 (2011).

4.  Boscariol, John W. & Orlando E. Silva, *The Widening Application of the MFN Obligation and Its Impact on Investor Protection*, 11 INTERNATIONAL TRADE LAW & REGULATION 61–67 (March 2005).

5.  Broude, Tomer, *The Most-Favoured Nation Principle, Equal Protection, and Migration Policy*, 24 GEORGETOWN IMMIGRATION LAW JOURNAL 553–563 (2010).

6.  Chandler, Aaron M., *BITs, MFN Treatment, and the PRC: The Impact of China's Ever-Evolving Bilateral Investment Treaty Practice*, 43 THE INTERNATIONAL LAWYER 1301–1310 (2009).

7.  Mansfield, Edward D. & Helen V. Milner, *Regime Type, Veto Points, and Preferential Trading Arrangements*, 46 Stanford Journal of International Law 219–242 (2010).

8.  Maruyama, Warren H., *Preferential Trade Arrangements and the Erosion of the WTO's MFN Principle*, 46 Stanford Journal of International Law 177–197 (2010).

9.  Qin, Julia Ya, *Defining Nondiscrimination under the Law of the World Trade Organization*, 23 BOSTON UNIVERSITY INTERNATIONAL LAW JOURNAL 215–297 (2005).

10. Radi, Yannick, *The Application of the Most-Favoured-Nation Clause to the Dispute Settlement Provisions of Bilateral Investment Treaties: Domesticating the "Trojan Horse,"* 18 EUROPEAN JOURNAL OF INTERNATIONAL LAW 757–774 (2007).

11. Schill, Stephan W., *Multilateralizing Investment Treaties Through Most-Favored-Nation Clauses*, 27 BERKELEY JOURNAL OF INTERNATIONAL LAW 496–569 (2009).

12. Vranes, Erich, *The WTO and Regulatory Freedom: WTO Disciplines on Market Access, Non-Discrimination and Domestic Regulation Relating to Trade in Goods and Services*, 12 JOURNAL OF INTERNATIONAL ECONOMIC LAW 953–987 (2009).

13. Warburton, Christopher E.S., *International Trade Law and Trade Theory*, 9 JOURNAL OF INTERNATIONAL TRADE LAW AND POLICY number 1, 64–82 (2010).

## MID-TERM REVIEW OF AGENDA 2000

In 2003, in connection with the "Mid-Term Review of Agenda 2000," the European Union (EU) approved further Common Agricultural Policy (CAP) changes.

As with prior reforms, the 2003 package aimed to reduce production surpluses by lowering intervention prices and de-coupling subsidies from output. The EU decreased support prices for butter by 25 percent (across four years) and skim milk powder by 15 percent (over three years). As with Agenda 2000, increases in income support only partly compensate for these decreases. Most notably, the EU replaced multiple direct income payments with a single farm payment.

Significantly, the EU entirely de-linked the single farm payment from what a farmer produces. The policy underlying disengaging income subsidies and farm production is to liberate farmers, and thereby increase farm efficiency. Without having to pay attention to support payments, a farmer can make planting, growing, and harvesting decisions based on market signals. Continuing the theme of multi-functionality, in the 2003 reform the EU made the single payment contingent on satisfying not only environmental conditions, but also standards on animal and plant welfare and food safety. These contingencies are known as "cross-compliance."

Details of the 2003 reforms are complicated and crop specific. Notably, full de-coupling does not occur for all products, and for some products occurs only over a lengthy phase in period. Individual EU member states have discretion to retain some links, on certain products, between income support and output.

*Suggestions for Further Research:*

Book:

1. THOMSON, KENNETH J., ET AL., THE CAP AND THE REGIONS: THE TERRITORIAL IMPACT OF THE COMMON AGRICULTURAL POLICY 129–49 (2005).

Articles:

1. Fouilleux, Eve, *CAP Reforms and Multilateral Trade Negotiations: Another View on Discourse Efficiency*, 27:2 WEST EUROPEAN POLITICS 235–55 (2004).

2. Swinbank, Alan & Carsten Daugbjerg, *The 2003 CAP Reform: Accommodating WTO Pressures*, 4:1 COMPARATIVE EUROPEAN POLITICS 47–64 (2006).

Other Source:

1. Conforti, Piero, et al., *The Mid-Term Review of the Common Agricultural Policy: Assessing the Effects of the Commission Proposals*, Working Paper n. 18, NATIONAL INSTITUTE OF AGRICULTURAL ECONOMICS, ITALY (2002).

## MIDDLE INCOME TRAP

The inability of a country to grow beyond the levels associated with a middle income country.

Examples include Argentina, the former Soviet Union, and Venezuela. China, arguably, is in the middle income trap.[481] Hundreds of millions have been lifted out of poverty since the Chinese Communist Party (CCP) took power in 1949, albeit at great human cost. China has reached the status of a borderline middle income country. In the first decade of China's Membership in the WTO (2001–2011), Chinese *per capita* Gross Domestic Product (GDP) grew at an average annual rate of 10 percent, from U.S. $800 to $3,300.[482] During the 2011–2020 decade, its *per capita* GDP is expected to rise threefold, to roughly U.S. $13,000. That will put China squarely among middle income countries. Yet, to be a fully developed nation, *per capita* GDP must rise to significantly higher levels. How to achieve this feat is a subject of debate.

First, to climb out of the middle income trap, an economy needs rebalancing. It must move away from dependence on agriculture and industry, and from an investment-centered growth. It must move toward greater dependence on services and consumption-driven growth. For China, these shifts are difficult because companies and industries that have been favored by the Chinese Communist Party (CCP), such as heavy industry like steel, will lose some of their benefits, as will coastal regions in China and certain CCP provincial and military elites. Benefits, and the power that goes with them, must flow to other sectors and regions, as well as consumers and migrant workers. Yet, China remains investment-centric: over 40 percent of household wealth (as of June 2011) was held as bank deposits, and they earn a real interest rate of -2.3 percent because of inflation.

Second, China suffers from inflation and asset bubbles. Prices of goods and property have risen sharply, and there is easy recourse to credit of dubious quality. To help escape the middle income trap, credit should be allocated through market mechanisms. That way, interest rates would be set in line with money supply and

---

[481] *See* George Magnus, *China Can Yet Avoid a Middle-Income Trap*, FINANCIAL TIMES, 30 June 2011, at 11. Unless otherwise noted, the data and four insights above are drawn from this article.
[482] *See* Daniel Pruzin, *Experts Say China Exerts Growing Influence, Generates Rising Tensions in WTO Matters*, 28 International Trade Reporter (BNA) 1135 (7 July 2011).

demand, and the price of financial capital would be appropriate. But, the CCP is chary of relinquishing power to allow for such mechanisms to flourish.

Third, developed countries have strong institutions and the rule of law. The CCP governs not through neutral legal institutions, but rather exercises direct primacy over all organs of the state and the judiciary. In other words, China lacks the institutional and legal framework necessary to escape the middle income trap. Thus, the Fraser Institute ranks (as of June 2011) China as 82nd among 141 countries studied on institutional quality. But, establishing the necessary framework is a threat to the power of the CCP.

Fourth, the CCP itself suffers from a crisis of legitimacy. Social unrest is considerable, and human rights abuses are common. The Party has different factions, and their rivalries sometimes result in party officials, state owned enterprises (SOEs), or the military intruding into policy decisions. The result is political uncertainty. Some party officials are corrupt. At bottom, many Chinese wonder whether the CCP is a rightful governing entity that can lead China out of the middle income trap.

## MILC

Milk Income Loss Contract program.

A United States Department of Agriculture (USDA) subsidy program to support small and medium-sized dairy farmers. The MILC scheme is part of the National Dairy Market Loss Payment program. Essentially, MILC gives counter-cyclical support.

Under the *2002 Farm Bill*, if dairy prices dropped, producers received 34 percent of the difference between a base price ($16.94 per hundred weight) and market price. Under proposed *2007 Farm Bill*, that percentage falls to 31 percent (in 2009), 28 percent (in 2010), 25 percent (in 2011), and 22 percent (in 2012). The index used to measure dairy prices is the Boston (Massachusetts) Class I price of milk.

The Farm Services Agency (FSA) manages the MILC program, as it does all other programs coordinated through the Commodity Credit Corporation (CCC).

## MILLENNIUM CHALLENGE CORPORATION

A government-owned corporation created in January 2004 to fund international initiatives focused on (1) Anti-Corruption, (2) Environment, (3) Health, and (4) Freedom of the Press.

Countries apply to the Millennium Challenge Corporation (MCC) for aid. Their applications are assessed on the basis of their ability to rule justly, provide economic freedom, and invest in their own people. Successful applicants, *i.e.*, countries the MCC deems worthy of aid, are then able to apply for either

(1) a multi-year grant, called a "Compact," or

(2) a smaller grant, called a "Threshold Agreement."

The two schemes differ not only in duration and size, but also in orientation. The purpose of a Threshold Agreement is to help a country meet the criteria (specific policy indicators) it lacks for a Compact.

15 countries have signed a Compact with the MCC. They are:

- Armenia
- Benin
- Cape Verde
- El Salvador
- Georgia
- Ghana
- Honduras
- Lesotho
- Madagascar
- Mali
- Mongolia
- Morocco
- Mozambique
- Nicaragua
- Vanuatu.

21 countries have signed Threshold Agreements with the MCC. They are:

- Albania
- Burkina Faso
- Guyana
- Indonesia
- Jordan
- Kenya
- Kyrgyz Republic
- Malawi
- Moldova
- Niger
- Paraguay
- Peru
- Philippines
- Rwanda
- São Tomé and Principe
- Tanzania
- Timor-Leste
- Uganda
- Ukraine
- Yemen
- Zambia.

## MINIMUM IMPORT PRICE (MINIMUM IMPORT PRICE SYSTEM)

A scheme whereby a country established a minimum value for the price of imported merchandise, and uses that price as a basis for customs valuation.

The WTO *Agreement on Customs Valuation* mandates use of Transaction Value, or where unavailable, Deductive Value or Computed Value. The central suspicion aroused by minimum import pricing is that values established by the government of an importing country will be the actual price paid or payable by the importer, and thus compel the importer to pay an artificially high duty (assuming the applicable tariff is *ad valorem*).

Accordingly, minimum import pricing generally is illegal under WTO rules. The leading Appellate Body Report on the topic is *Argentina — Measures Affecting Imports of Footwear, Textiles, Apparel and Other Items*, WT/DS56/AB/R (adopted 27 March 1998) (complaint by United States). The Kingdom of

Saudi Arabia, in its WTO accession negotiations, sought unsuccessfully to retain its system of minimum import pricing.

## MINISTERIAL CONFERENCE

The highest decision-making body of the WTO.

Pursuant to Article IV:1 of the *Agreement Establishing the World Trade Organization (WTO Agreement)*, a Ministerial Conference must be held "at least once every two years." Embarrassingly for the WTO, which prides itself on being a rules-based body, this schedule has not always been followed. No Ministerial Conference was held between 2005 and 2009.

The Table below sets out these Conferences and the principal events for which each one is remembered.

TABLE:
**WTO Ministerial Conferences**

| Number | Date | Location | Principal Events |
|---|---|---|---|
| 1st | 9–13 December 1996 | Singapore | Identification of 4 "Singapore Issues" for future negotiations: foreign direct investment (FDI); trade and competition policy; customs facilitation; and transparency in government procurement. |
| 2nd | 18–20 May 1998 | Geneva | Celebration of 50th Anniversary of GATT. |
| | | | Moratorium agreed to on collection of duties on goods transmitted digitally via the internet — the "E-Commerce Moratorium." |
| 3rd | 30 November– 3 December 1999 | Seattle | Failure of attempt to launch a "Millennium Round" amidst violent protests against globalization and the WTO, particularly on issues of labor and environmental rights, and the effects of trade liberalization on poor countries. |
| 4th | 9-14 November 2001 | Doha | Launching the Doha Development Agenda in an Arab country shortly after the terrorist attacks of September 11. |

TABLE (continued)

| Number | Date | Location | Principal Events |
|---|---|---|---|
| 5<sup>th</sup> | 10–14 September 2003 | Cancún | Failure to agree on modalities (*i.e.*, a blue print) for Doha Round negotiations, and collapse of talks over agricultural market access and subsidies, and the Singapore Issues. |
| 6<sup>th</sup> | 13–18 December 2005 | Hong Kong | Limited progress in Doha Round negotiations, despite impending deadline of 30 June 2007, when Trade Promotion Authority for the United States President expired. |
| | | | Agreement on amendments to Article 31 of the *Agreement on Trade-Related Aspects of Intellectual Property Rights* (*TRIPs*) to allow export of generic medicines made under a compulsory license to WTO Members lacking manufacturing capacity. |
| | | | Extension of deadline for compliance with *TRIPs Agreement* for least developed countries through 1 January 2013. |
| 7<sup>th</sup> | 30 November– 2 December 2009 | Geneva | Theme of "The WTO, the Multilateral Trading System, and the Current Global Economic Environment." |
| | | | First Ministerial Conference in four (4) years, despite obligation to hold one every two (2) years under Article IV:1 of the *WTO Agreement*. |
| | | | By design, no discussion of Doha Round, and no *a priori* aim of negotiating a Ministerial Declaration. |
| | | | Effort to achieve a "FIT" Conference, meaning full participation, inclusiveness, and transparency, with a lean, non-extravagant atmosphere. |

**TABLE (continued)**

| Number | Date | Location | Principal Events |
|---|---|---|---|
| | | | Extension of moratorium in Article 64:2 of the *Agreement on Trade Related Aspects of Intellectual Property Rights* (*TRIPs*) on WTO Members bringing non-violation nullification or impairment complaints through the 8th Ministerial Conference. |
| | | | Extension of the E-Commerce Moratorium (initially agreed to at the 2nd Ministerial Conference), that is, on the collection of duties on goods transmitted digitally over the internet, through the 8th Ministerial Conference. |
| | | | Announcement by developing countries of the framework for a South — South trade pact under the Global System of Trade Preferences (GSTP) agreement, which is under the auspices of the United Nations Conference on Trade and Development (UNCTAD). |
| | | | Announcement by *MERCOSUR*, the Southern African Customs Union (*SACU*), and India of progress toward a free trade agreement (FTA), building on the June 2004 preferential trade agreement (PTA) between *MERCOSUR* and *SACU*, and talks between *MERCOSUR* and India. |
| 8th | 11–15 December 2011 | Geneva | Pledge made in November 2010, following Group of 20 (G-20) Summit in Seoul, Korea, to redouble efforts to complete Doha Round in 2011, and produce revised negotiating texts in agriculture and non-agricultural market access (NAMA) by April or mid-2011, in advance of presidential elections in France, India, and United States. |

**TABLE (continued)**

| Number | Date | Location | Principal Events |
|---|---|---|---|
| | | | Approval of terms of accession to the WTO for Montenegro, Russia, and Samoa. (Vanuatu became a Member before the Ministerial Conference, as of 26 October 2011.) |
| | | | Extension of the E-Commerce Moratorium (initially agreed to at the 2nd Ministerial Conference), that is, on the collection of duties on goods transmitted digitally over the internet, through the 9th Ministerial Conference. |
| | | | Extension of deadline indefinitely for compliance with *TRIPs Agreement* for least developed countries. |
| | | | Extension of moratorium in Article 64:2 of the *Agreement on Trade Related Aspects of Intellectual Property Rights* (*TRIPs*) on WTO Members bringing non-violation nullification or impairment complaints through the 9th Ministerial Conference. |
| | | | Continuation of waiver for 15 years to all WTO Members to provide preferential treatment to services and service suppliers from least developed countries. |
| | | | Assistance to facilitate the accession of least developed countries to the WTO. |
| 9th | 2013 | | |

Despite the obligation in Article IV:1 of the *WTO Agreement*, no Conference was held in 2007. There were many meetings in connection with the Doha Round negotiations, none of which produced a successful outcome.

The venue depends on whether a WTO Member offers to host a Conference. If no Member volunteers, then the default venue is Geneva. Many Members are reluctant to host a Conference because of concerns about violent protests, and the expensive and time-consuming security arrangements that need to be made in anticipation of them. Thus, hosting is not seen as a badge of honor, prestige, or standing in the international community the way it once was.

## MISCELLANEOUS TARIFF BILL

See MTB.

## MITI

The Ministry of International Trade and Industry (*Tsūsho-sangyō-shō*).

MITI was one of the most powerful agencies in the Japanese government. During the post-Second-World War period, until 2001, MITI managed Japanese trade and industry, providing industries with administrative guidance and other direction, both formal and informal, on modernization, technology, investments in new plants and equipment, and domestic and foreign competition. In 2001, its role was taken over by the newly created "Ministry of Economy, Trade, and Industry," or "METI."

*Suggestions for Further Research:*

Article:

1.   Kiyota, Kozo & Tetsuji Okazaki, *Industrial Policy Cuts Two Ways: Evidence from Cotton-Spinning Firms in Japan, 1956–1964*, 53 JOURNAL OF LAW & ECONOMICS 587–609 (2010).

## MNC

Multinational Corporation, also known as "TNC" for "Transnational Corporation."

*Suggestions for Further Research:*

Articles:

1.   Dowling Jr., Donald C., *U.S.-Based Multinational Employers and the Social Contract Outside the United States*, 26 AMERICAN BAR ASSOCIATION JOURNAL OF LABOR & EMPLOYMENT LAW 77–100 (2010).

2.   Kita, Matthew H., Comment, *It's Not You, It's Me: An Analysis of the United States' Failure to Uphold Its Commitment to OECD Guidelines for Multinational Enterprises in Spite of No Other Reliable Alternatives*, 29 PENN STATE INTERNATIONAL LAW REVIEW 359–384 (2010).

3.   Stiglitz, Joseph E., *Regulating Multinational Corporations: Towards Principles of Cross-Border Legal Frameworks in a Globalized World Balancing Rights with Responsibilities*, 23 AMERICAN UNIVERSITY INTERNATIONAL LAW REVIEW 451–558 (2008).

## MNC PROVISION

*See* NME.

## MOCK MARK UP

A term referring to the process by which the United States Congress considers trade agreements (as well as other legislation).

During the "mark up" process, a Congressional committee with jurisdiction over a trade agreement makes and considers recommendations to the Executive branch about legislation designed to implement a trade agreement. The recommendations are non-binding, particularly if the agreement is considered by Congress under fast-track or trade promotion authority (TPA), whereby Congress committed not to amend the agreement under the authority it delegated to the President to negotiate the agreement. (After all, the delegation typically contains careful parameters the Congress expects the President to satisfy in any agreement.)

Following the mock mark up, the President then submits formal implementing legislation to Congress, which may or may not include the recommendations made by the committee. Under Trade Promotion Authority (TPA) and other fast track procedures, Congress must vote on the formal legislation without amendment within a prescribed time period (such as 90 days). Thus, the word "mock" connotes that the legislation the committee is "marking up" is in draft form, not the actual bill to be voted on.

## MODALITY (MODALITIES)

A way to proceed, plan of action, or blue print, specifically, the means by which reductions in trade barriers are effected. Once a modality is agreed, then commitments are made (typically calculated on the basis of tables of data, which may be attached to schedules of concessions) trade liberalization occurs by implementing that modality.

That is, general or specific formulas and figures, including coefficients in those formulas, figures, and other devices used to cut tariffs on agricultural and industrial goods, and subsidy programs. In effect, a "modality" is a road-map to get from the status quo to a new and different reality. However, the practical effects of applying a modality are not always entirely clear until full tariff and services schedules have been prepared. That is, the exercise of scheduling concessions pursuant to the modalities by which those concessions are made yields a clear picture of the actual trade-liberalizing effects of the modalities.

That is a point the Administration of President Barack H. Obama made in the spring 2009, when it called for new ideas to re-ignite the Doha Round negotiations. One such idea was an alternative approach, whereby scheduling would start, even before final agreement on modalities, so as to test what new market access American exporters might gain from the modalities. This test — and the transparency it would bring with it — was important to Congress, which was deeply skeptical of the draft modalities texts that had been produced thus far in the Round. However, most of the rest of the WTO Membership firmly rejected any scheduling exercises before a final deal on modalities was reached.

## MODES OF DELIVERY (MODES OF SUPPLY)

The ways in which services may be provided by a firm from one country to customers in another country.

There are four modes, all of which are defined in and covered by the *General Agreement on Trade in Services (GATS)*, and Chapters 11 and 14 of the *North American Free Trade Agreement*:

(1) Cross-border supply (*i.e.*, the service provider transmits the service across an international boundary to a service consumer in the territory of that consumer). An example is an international phone call.

(2) Consumption abroad (*i.e.*, the service consumer travels across an international boundary to the territory of the service provider). An example is tourism.

(3) Establishment of a commercial presence (*i.e.*, foreign direct investment (FDI)), such as a branch, agency, or representative office. An example is a bank operating in a foreign country.

(4) Movement of natural persons (*i.e.*, temporary migration by the service provider to provide the service, which is the mirror image of the second mode). An example is a fashion model displaying a new line in a foreign country.

They are referred, respectively, to as "Modes I, II, III, and IV." These Roman numerals are used in Schedules of Services Concessions.

## MODULATION

A term associated with the Common Agricultural Policy (CAP) of the European Union, specifically, reforms ushered in with the 2003 Mid-Term Review of Agenda 2000.

"Modulation" refers to the reduction in direct income payments to large EU farms. The cost savings are used to fund rural development policy initiatives.

## MOFAT

The Korean Ministry of Foreign Affairs and Trade. The responsibilities of MOFAT include international trade negotiations.

Korea waited until April 2004 before adopting an aggressive free trade agreement (FTA) policy, in contrast to other Asian countries. The policy, which MOFAT itself calls a "shotgun" approach, produced an FTA with Chile (in April 2004), and FTA negotiations with Singapore and *EFTA* in 2005–06. In May 2006, MOFAT announced agreement with nine of the 10 members of the *Association of South East Asian Nations (ASEAN)* states to eliminate tariff barriers by 2010 on 90 percent of merchandise.[483] Owing

---

[483] *See* James Lim, *South Korea's MOFAT Outlines Goals of Draft Free Trade Agreement with U.S.*, 23 International Trade Reporter (BNA) 761 (18 May 2006).

to differences on agricultural product protection, MOFAT could not reach agreement with Thailand.

## MOFCOM

Ministry of Commerce of China, formerly called Ministry of Foreign Trade and Economic Cooperation (MOFTEC).

As the Table below depicts, MOFCOM has broad responsibility for all international trade matters affecting China. As the Table also suggests, while a centralized body in charge of trade matters, MOFCOM itself is somewhat decentralized, with diffuse centers of power.

TABLE:

MINISTRY OF COMMERCE (MOFCOM)

OF THE PEOPLE'S REPUBLIC OF CHINA[484]

| *Official* | *Departments within the Ministry* | *Offices, Commissions, Associations, Bureaus, Agencies within the Ministry* | *Responsibilities of the Official and/or Other Relevant Organizations Affiliated with the Ministry* |
|---|---|---|---|
| Minister of Commerce  *Bo Xilai* | Department of Human Resources | General Office | Responsible for overall affairs |
| Vice Minister of Commerce  *Yu Guangzhou* | Department of General Economic Affairs  Department of European Affairs  Department of Foreign Affairs  Department of Retired Cadres Affairs | China-Europe Association | MOFCOM Party Committee  China Foreign Trade Center |

---

[484] As of 1 October 2007. All information in this Table is taken directly from the official website of MOFCOM, and re-organized for clarity and legibility. The English language version of the website is www.mofcom.gov.cn (visited on several occasions between September 2006 and October 2007). The specific officials are listed (by surname, then given name, in italics) in part because their seniority affects the responsibilities assigned to them. The functional lines of MOFCOM appear to be, therefore, defined to some degree by the individual official.

**TABLE (continued)**

| Official | Departments within the Ministry | Offices, Commissions, Associations, Bureaus, Agencies within the Ministry | Responsibilities of the Official and/or Other Relevant Organizations Affiliated with the Ministry |
|---|---|---|---|
| Vice Minister of Commerce<br><br>Wei Jiangguo | Department of West Asian and African Affairs<br><br>Department of Electromechanical Products and Science and Technology Industry<br><br>Department of Aid to Foreign Countries | The Executive Bureau of International Economic Cooperation | China Chamber of Commerce for Import and Export of Machinery and Electronic Products |
| Vice Minister of Commerce<br><br>Ma Xiuhong | Department of Treaty and Law<br><br>Department of American and Oceanian Affairs<br><br>Department of Foreign Investment Administration | Investment Promotion Agency<br><br>China Association of Enterprises with Foreign Investment | China Council for International Investment Promotion |
| Vice Minister of Commerce<br><br>Liao Xiaoqu | Department of Policy Research<br><br>Department of Taiwan, Hong Kong, and Macau Affairs<br><br>Department of Information Technology | China Association of International Trade<br><br>Association of Economy and Trade across Taiwan Straits | China International Institute of Multinational Corporations<br><br>China International Electronic Communications Center |

TABLE **(continued)**

| *Official* | *Departments within the Ministry* | *Offices, Commissions, Associations, Bureaus, Agencies within the Ministry* | *Responsibilities of the Official and/or Other Relevant Organizations Affiliated with the Ministry* |
|---|---|---|---|
| Vice Minister of Commerce<br><br><br><br>*Gao Hucheng* | Department of Foreign Trade | Bureau of Fair Trade for Imports and Exports<br><br>Bureau of Industry Injury Investigation<br><br>Office of the Representative for Trade Negotiations<br><br>Quota and License Administration Bureau | China Chamber of Commerce for Import and Export of Textiles |
| Vice Minister of Commerce<br><br><br><br>*Jiang Zhengwei* | Department of Commercial Reform and Development | National Office for the Rectification and Regulation of Market Economic Order<br><br>MOFCOM Logistics Bureau | Province, Autonomous Region, and Municipality Contact |
| Vice Minister of Commerce<br><br><br><br><br><br><br>*Yi Xiaozhun* | Department of International Trade and Economic Affairs<br><br><br><br><br>Department of WTO Affairs | China Asia Pacific Association for Promoting Economic and Trade Cooperation | |
| Vice Minister of Commerce | | Bureau of Discipline Supervision and Investigation | Responsible for Discipline Inspection |

## TABLE (continued)

| Official | Departments within the Ministry | Offices, Commissions, Associations, Bureaus, Agencies within the Ministry | Responsibilities of the Official and/or Other Relevant Organizations Affiliated with the Ministry |
|---|---|---|---|
| Wang Hemin | | MOFCOM Discipline Inspection Commission | Discipline Inspection Group |
| Assistant Minister of Commerce | Department of Asian Affairs | China International Contractors Association | Responsible for assisting Ma Xiuhong in the Investment Promotion Agency |
| Chen Jian | Department of Foreign Economic Cooperation | Association of International Engineering Consultants | China International Economic Cooperation Society |
| Assistant Minister of Commerce | Department of Finance | Trade Development Bureau | Chinese Academy of International Trade and Economic Cooperation |
| Fu Ziying | | China Enterprises Association | MOFCOM Training Center |
| | | China International Freight Forwarders Association | Accounting Society for Foreign Economic Relations and Trade in China |
| | | | Statistical Society for Foreign Economic Relations and Trade in China |
| Assistant Minister of Commerce | Department of Market System Development | | Responsible for assisting Liao Xiaoqi in the Department of Policy Research |
| Huang Hai | Department of Market Operation Regulation | | China Chamber of Commerce of Metals, Minerals, and Chemicals Importers and Exporters |

TABLE (continued)

| Official | Departments within the Ministry | Offices, Commissions, Associations, Bureaus, Agencies within the Ministry | Responsibilities of the Official and/or Other Relevant Organizations Affiliated with the Ministry |
|---|---|---|---|
| | | | China Chamber of Commerce for Import and Export of Light Industrial Products and Arts-Crafts |
| | | | China Chamber of Commerce of Import and Export of Foodstuffs, Native Product and Animal By-Products |
| | | | China Chamber of Commerce for Import and Export of Medicines and Health Products |
| | | | Slaughter Technique Identification Center |
| Assistant Minister of Commerce | | MOFCOM General News Agency | Responsible for assisting the Minister of Commerce *Bo Xilai* and the General Office |
| *Chong Quan* | | MOFCOM Special Commissioners Offices (in different localities) | |
| | | Economic and Commercial Counselors Offices of the Chinese Embassies (in foreign countries) | |

TABLE (continued)

| Official | Departments within the Ministry | Offices, Commissions, Associations, Bureaus, Agencies within the Ministry | Responsibilities of the Official and/or Other Relevant Organizations Affiliated with the Ministry |
|---|---|---|---|
| Assistant Minister of Commerce | | China Association for NGO Cooperation | Responsible for assisting *Wei Jiangguo* in the Department of Aid to Foreign Countries |
| *Wang Chao* | | | Also responsible for assisting *Chen Jian* in the Department of Foreign Economic Cooperation |

The following is a list of countries (and, in some instances, capital and/or port cities) in which China maintains a Commercial Counselor Office in its Embassy (as of October 2007). The extent of this list is a testament to the global interests of China.

- Aden
- Albania
- Algeria
- Angola
- Antigua and Barbuda
- Argentina
- Armenia
- Australia
- Austria
- Azerbaijan
- Bahamas
- Bahrain
- Bangladesh
- Barbados
- Belarus
- Benin
- Bolivia

- Bosnia and Herzegovina
- Botswana
- Brazil
- Brunei
- Bulgaria
- Burma
- Burundi
- Capo Verde
- Cambodia
- Cameroon
- Canada
- Central Africa
- Chile
- Colombia
- Comoros
- Congo (Brazzaville)

- Congo (Kinshasa)
- Côte d'Ivoire
- Croatia
- Cuba
- Cyprus
- Czech Republic
- Denmark
- Djibouti
- Douala
- Ecuador
- Egypt
- Eritrea
- Estonia
- Ethiopia
- Fiji
- Finland
- France

- Gabon
- Georgia
- Germany
- Ghana
- Greece
- Guinea
- Guinea-Bissau
- Guyana
- Equatorial Guinea
- Hungary
- Iceland
- India
- Indonesia
- Iran
- Iraq
- Ireland
- Israel
- Istanbul
- Italy
- Jamaica
- Japan
- Jordan
- Kazakhstan
- Kenya
- Kiribati
- Korea (South)
- Korea (People's Republic of)
- Kuwait
- Kyrgyzstan
- Laos
- Latvia
- Lebanon
- Lesotho
- Libya
- Lithuania
- Macedonia

- Madagascar
- Malaysia
- Mali
- Malta
- Morocco
- Mauritania
- Mauritius
- Mexico
- Micronesia
- Mozambique
- Moldova
- Mongolia
- Namibia
- Nepal
- Netherlands
- New Zealand
- Niger
- Nigeria
- Norway
- Oman
- Pakistan
- Papua New Guinea
- Peru
- Philippines
- Poland
- Portugal
- Qatar
- Romania
- Russia
- Rwanda
- Samoa
- Saudi Arabia
- Serbia and Montenegro
- Seychelles
- Sierra Leone
- Singapore

- Slovakia
- Slovenia
- South Africa
- Spain
- Sri Lanka
- St. Lucia
- Sudan
- Suriname
- Sweden
- Switzerland
- Syria
- Tajikistan
- Tanzania
- Thailand
- Togo
- Tonga
- Trinidad and Tobago
- Tunis
- Turkey
- Turkmenistan
- Uganda
- United Arab Emirates
- United Kingdom
- United States
- Ukraine
- Uruguay
- Uzbekistan
- Vanuatu
- Venezuela
- Vietnam
- Yemen
- Zambia
- Zanzibar
- Zimbabwe

## MOFTEC

*See* MOFCOM.

## MOU

Memorandum of Understanding.

## MRA

Mutual Recognition Agreement.

An agreement between two or more countries to recognize the testing and related standards used in each country for products. Thus, for example, if Countries A and B recognize each other's standards for testing whether cosmetics are safe for human health, and Country B exports cosmetics to Country A, then Country A will not perform its own separate testing on the cosmetics from Country B. Because such testing could be a non-tariff barrier (NTB), the MRA is a trade-liberalizing device.

## MRL

Maximum Residue Level.

A scientific standard for the maximum amount of pesticide residue allowed in a traded agricultural product. MRLs are often codified and maintained by the *Codex Alimentarius* Commission. The United States Department of Agriculture (USDA) Foreign Agricultural Service (FAS) maintains an International Database for MRLs. The Database is searchable by crop or pesticide.

## MTAs

The Uruguay Round Multilateral Trade Agreements.

According to Article II:2 of the *Agreement Establishing the World Trade Organization* (*WTO Agreement*), and Annexes 1, 2 and 3 to this *Agreement*, the MTAs are comprised of

- Multilateral Agreements on Trade in Goods, which are contained in Annex 1A
- *General Agreement on Trade in Services* (*GATS*), in Annex 1B
- *Agreement on Trade Related Aspects of Intellectual Property Rights* (*TRIPs*), in Annex 1C
- *Understanding on Rules and Procedures Governing the Settlement of Disputes* (*Dispute Settlement Understanding*, or *DSU*), in Annex 2
- Trade Policy Review Mechanism (TPRM), in Annex 3.

The MTAs do not include the Plurilateral Trade Agreements (PTAs), which Annex 4 contain. United States law, specifically the *Uruguay Round Agreements Act of 1994*, identifies and implements the MTAs. *See* 19 U.S.C. § 3501(4).

The organization structure of the MTAs is logical. Annex 1 contains agreements on three kinds of cross-border transactions, goods, services, and intellectual property (IP), in Annexes 1A, 1B, and 1C, respectively. (The fourth kind of international transaction, concerning financial flows, is not strictly within the purview of the WTO.) Annex 2 has the accord setting out a methodology for resolving disputes about such transactions, or measures that affect them. Annex 3 sets out a mechanism for review trade policies of Members, to ensure consistency with WTO standards. The final Annex deals with accord not accepted by all Members.

*Suggestions for Further Research:*

Books:

1. BUCKLEY, ROSS P., ED., THE WTO AND THE DOHA ROUND: THE CHANGING FACE OF WORLD TRADE (2003).

2. CROOME, JOHN, GUIDE TO THE URUGUAY ROUND AGREEMENTS (1999).

3. JACKSON, JOHN H., THE WORLD TRADING SYSTEM — LAW AND POLICY OF INTERNATIONAL ECONOMIC ORGANIZATIONS (2nd ed. 1997).

4. MATSUSHITA, MITSUO, THOMAS J. SCHOENBAUM & PETROS C. MAVROIDIS, THE WORLD TRADE ORGANIZATION — LAW, PRACTICE, AND POLICY (2nd ed. 2005).

5. STEWART, TERENCE P. ED., THE WORLD TRADE ORGANIZATION — MULTILATERAL TRADE FRAMEWORK FOR THE 21ST CENTURY AND U.S. IMPLEMENTING LEGISLATION (1996).

6. TREBILCOCK, MICHAEL J. & ROBERT HOWSE, THE REGULATION OF INTERNATIONAL TRADE (3rd ed. 2005).

7. VAN DEN BOSSCHE, PETER, THE LAW AND POLICY OF THE WORLD TRADE ORGANIZATION: TEXT, CASES AND MATERIALS (2005).

Other Source:

1. ORGANIZATION FOR ECONOMIC COOPERATION AND DEVELOPMENT (OECD), THE NEW WORLD TRADING SYSTEM — READINGS (1994).

## MTB

Miscellaneous Tariff Bill, which is legislation in the United States for duty suspensions.

In brief, through an MTB, Congress suspends for a prescribed period American tariffs on imports of inputs used in the domestic manufacturing process that are not produced in the United States. An MTB is distinct legislation from bills to renew or extend certain programs, like the Generalized System of Preferences (GSP). In respect of duty suspensions for imported merchandise, a non-partisan process analyzes proposals to make sure no domestic producer of a like product exists.

More specifically, a MTB requests the temporary reduction or suspension of duties on certain United States imports, or requests other technical corrections to the United States Harmonized Tariff System (HTS), that is, to the

Harmonized Tariff Schedule of the United States (HTSUS).[485] The purpose of an MTB is to help manufacturers in the United States compete domestically and internationally by temporarily suspending or reducing duties on intermediate goods and materials that they use in the manufacturing process, but which are not produced in the United States, or (if they are) where there is no domestic opposition to the duty changes.[486]

Most products that receive tariff relief are inputs or components used in American manufactured goods. For example, Church & Dwight Co. Inc., a producer of various consumer products such as baking soda and specialty cleaners, imports a palm oil by-product to manufacture a feed additive for dairy cows. The by-product (an input into the feed additive) is not produced in North America. So, Church & Dwight imports the by-product from Indonesia and Malaysia. As another example, Solutia Inc., a chemical manufacturer, imports an input from a Solutia plant in Belgium to manufacture rubber and tires in the United States.[487] The input, like the palm oil by-product in the first example, is not produced in the United States. In both cases, the companies ask Congress for the imported input in which they are interested to be included in a MTB, through which the normal, applied most favored nation (MFN) duty rate is suspended or reduced. If Congress enacts the MTB, then the President thereby is authorized to make the duty amendments called for in the Bill. Such tariff relief saves companies thousands and sometimes millions a year in production costs.

The MTB passed by Congress in 2006 expired on 31 December 2009. It was not until August 2010 that President Barack H. Obama signed the MTB, extending the 2006 MTB. It was renamed the *U.S. Manufacturing Enhancement Act* (Pub. Law No. 111–227).[488] The bill expired on 31 December 2012, and contains retroactive duty suspension, dating back to 1 January 2010, for certain products. However, that bill failed to include new duty suspension requests. Therefore, a second draft MTB, posted by the House Ways and Means Committee on 24 November 2010, built on the first bill, and contained over 300 total tariff suspensions and reductions, including those that had been new tariff suspensions requests.[489] An explanation for the delay in passing the expired MTB legislation is due to House Republicans,

---

[485] Miscellaneous Tariff Bills, *posted at* www.ustr.gov/trade-topics/industry-manufacturing/industrial-tariffs/miscellaneous-tariff-bills.

[486] *See Congress, Trade Agencies Need to Start Working Soon on Miscellaneous Tariff Bill*, 26 International Trade Reporter (BNA) 955 (16 July 2009).

[487] *See Congress, Trade Agencies Need to Start Working Soon on Miscellaneous Tariff Bill*, 26 International Trade Reporter (BNA) 955 (16 July 2009).

[488] *See* Amy Tsui, *Over 55 Groups Write Congress Asking MTB Not be Banned as Earmarks in Next Session*, 27 International Trade Reporter (BNA) 1760 (18 November 2010).

[489] *See* Amy Tsui, *Ways and Means Posts Draft of Second MTB, Expects House Consideration in Few Weeks*, 27 International Trade Reporter (BNA) 1834 (2 December 2010).

who at the time supported (*inter alia*) a one-year moratorium on earmarks in appropriations legislation and tariff legislation.[490]

## MTN

Multilateral Trade Negotiations.

A generic term referring to a round of multilateral trade negotiations conducted under the auspices of the GATT or WTO.

## MULTILATERAL AGREEMENTS ON TRADE IN GOODS

The set of agreements (and associated legal instruments, which are principally Understandings) reached during the Uruguay Round concerning trade in goods. These agreements entered into force on 1 January 1995, and are binding on all Members. They are contained in Annex 1A to the *Agreement Establishing the World Trade Organization (WTO Agreement)*. There are 13 such agreements:

(1)   GATT 1994

(2)   *Agreement on Agriculture*

(3)   *Agreement on the Application of Sanitary and Phytosanitary Standards* (*SPS Agreement*)

(4)   *Agreement on Textiles and Clothing (ATC)*

(5)   *Agreement on Technical Barriers to Trade (TBT Agreement)*

(6)   *Agreement on Trade-Related Investment Measures (TRIMs Agreement)*

(7)   *Agreement on Implementation of Article VI of the GATT 1994* (*Antidumping*, or *AD, Agreement*)

(8)   *Agreement on Implementation of Article VII of the GATT 1994 (Customs Valuation Agreement)*

(9)   *Agreement on Preshipment Inspection (PSI Agreement)*

(10)  *Agreement on Rules of Origin*

(11)  *Agreement on Import Licensing Procedures*

(12)  *Agreement on Subsidies and Countervailing Measures (SCM Agreement)*

(13)  *Agreement on Safeguards*

## MULTI-FUNCTIONALITY

The concept that agriculture is more than about producing food.

Agriculture plays commodity and non-commodity roles in a society, and not all of them (especially the non-commodity roles) can be fulfilled effectively

---

[490] *See* Rossella Brevetti, *Businesses, Groups Urge House Leaders to Take Action on Miscellaneous Tariff Bill*, 27 International Trade Reporter (BNA) 698 (13 May 2010).

through free market mechanisms. The non-commodity roles the agricultural sector serves include:

- Cultural and national identity
- Environmental protection
- Food and national security
- Landscape preservation
- Rural employment
- Sustainable development

Initially the United States and other nations traditionally inclined toward free trade in agriculture viewed the concept of multi-functionality with suspicion. Was it, they inquired, an argument for protection? However, by the mid-2000s, multi-functionality had gained widespread acceptability as a legitimate concept.

*Suggestions for Further Research:*

Books:

1.   CARDWELL, MICHAEL N., MARGARET R. GROSSMAN & CHRISTOPHER P. RODGERS, AGRICULTURE AND INTERNATIONAL TRADE — LAW, POLICY, AND THE WTO 85–164 (2003).

2.   MARSDEN, TERRY & JONATHAN MURDOCH, BETWEEN THE LOCAL AND THE GLOBAL: CONFRONTING COMPLEXITY IN THE CONTEMPORARY AGRI-FOOD SECTOR (2006).

Articles:

1.   Harvey, David R., *Agri-Environmental Relationships and Multi-Functionality: Further Considerations*, 26 THE WORLD ECONOMY 705–25 (2003).

2.   Potter, Clive & Jonathan Burney, *Agricultural Multifunctionality in the WTO — Non-Trade Concern or Disguised Protectionism?*, 18 JOURNAL OF RURAL STUDIES 35–47 (2002).

3.   Raoult-Wack, Anne-Lucie & Nicolas Bricas, *Food Sector Development: Multifunctionality and Ethics*, 3 CIGR JOURNAL OF SCIENTIFIC RESEARCH AND DEVELOPMENT (2001).

## MULTILATERALISM

Cooperation among a large group of nations, or among all or virtually all nations.

Multilateralism is a principle on which the WTO, like its GATT predecessor, operates. But, Professor Razeen Sally of the London School of Economics (LSE) argues that it always has been a fiction, and it would be better to speak of "minilateralism."[491]

---

[491] *Quoted in* Alan Beattie, *Retread Required*, FINANCIAL TIMES, 1 December 2009, at 7.

## *MUTATIS MUTANDIS*

A public international law term appearing frequently in WTO dispute settlement reports.

The term is used to note the application of an implied, mutually understood set of changes. An example from an appeal before the WTO is this: "Brazil and Canada requested that the Appellate Body apply, *mutatis mutandis*, the Procedures Governing Business Confidential Information adopted by the panel in this case."[492]

Both "*mutatis*" and "*mutandis*" come from the Latin verb "*muto*," meaning "to change."

*Suggestions for Further Research:*

Book:

1.   PAUWELYN, JOOST, CONFLICT OF NORMS IN PUBLIC INTERNATIONAL LAW — HOW WTO LAW RELATES TO OTHER RULES OF INTERNATIONAL LAW (2003).

## MY

Marketing Year.

Also known as Crop Year, the term is used in agricultural legislation — such as United States farm bills — to identify a 12 month period. That period is the basis for calculation of a variety of metrics, including the Effective Price used when determining counter-cyclical payments.

---

[492] WTO Panel Report, *Brazil — Export Financing Program for Aircraft*, WT/DS46/R (adopted 2 August 1999) (complaint by Canada).

# N

## *NAAEC*

The 1993 *North American Agreement on Environmental Cooperation* (associated with *NAFTA*), *i.e.*, the *Environmental Side Agreement*.

## *NAALC*

The 1993 *North American Agreement on Labor Cooperation* (associated with *NAFTA*), *i.e.*, the *Labor Side Agreement*.

## NACC

The North American Competitiveness Council.

The NAAC was launched by the United States, Canada, and Mexico on 15 June 2006. Its aim is to increase the global competitiveness of businesses located in the *North American Free Trade Agreement* (*NAFTA*) region. The NACC consists of senior business officials from the *NAFTA* Parties. Each *NAFTA* Party has a NACC, consisting of 10 individuals.

In turn, the NACCs from each country meet annually with another body, the Security and Prosperity Partnership (SPP) of North America. The SPP is comprised of governmental officials, particularly commerce and security ministers, from the *NAFTA* Parties. The SPP was formed on 23 March 2005, and aims to cut trade barriers and boost economic growth, but at the same time enhance the security of the *NAFTA* Parties. The NACC makes recommendations to the SPP, and is particularly keen on enhancing the competitiveness of sectors such as automotive, manufacturing, steel, transportation, and various service businesses against competition from China and India. The NACC and SPP also are concerned with issues of emergency management, energy security, and SPS protection. However, in March 2010, the NAFTA Parties decided to disband the SPP.[493]

## NADBANK

The North American Development Bank, created by the *North American Free Trade Agreement* (*NAFTA*).

NADBank is devoted to financing environmental infrastructure projects on the border between the United States and Mexico. However, the funding of NADBank is parlous, and the future of NADBank precarious.

## *NAFTA*

The *North American Free Trade Agreement* of 1993, the Parties to which are Canada, Mexico, and the United States.

---

[493] *See* Rossella Brevetti, *SPP Forum for NAFTA Members is Scrapped But Work Continues*, 27 International Trade Reporter (BNA) 395 (18 March 2010).

The Parties signed *NAFTA* on 17 December 1992. On 15 December 1993, the United States Congress approved the accord through the *North American Free Trade Implementation Act*, specifically, Section 101 thereof, 19 U.S.C. Section 3311(a). *NAFTA* entered into force on 1 January 1994. The Figure below sets out the basic institutions of *NAFTA*, and their responsibilities.

*NAFTA* is a comprehensive trade agreement that affects virtually every aspect of doing business between or among the Parties. All trade between the United States and Canada has been duty-free since 1998, except for certain supply-managed agricultural products. Mexico eliminated 50 percent of its industrial tariffs, and many non-tariff barriers, immediately upon the entry into force of *NAFTA*. By 2003, Mexico had phased out virtually all industrial tariffs. Mexico phased out agricultural tariffs across 15 years, with all farm import tariffs eliminated as of 1 January 2008. The last remaining barriers were to certain beans, corn, corn syrup, and milk. In other words, on 1 January 2008, Mexico fully implemented *NAFTA*.

FIGURE:

BASIC *NAFTA* INSTITUTIONS

---

**FREE TRADE COMMISSION (FTC)**

Comprised of the USTR, Trade Minister of Canada, and Secretary for Trade and Industrial Development of Mexico.
Responsible for:

- Overseeing the implementation of *NAFTA*.
- Resolving disputes about the application or interpretation of *NAFTA*.
- Supervising the work of the Secretariat, Committees, and Working Groups.
- Establishing new committees and working groups, as needed.

---

**NAFTA Secretariat**

Comprised of a United States Section (located in the DOC in Washington, D.C.), Canada Section (located in Ottawa), and a Mexico Section (located in Mexico City)
Responsible for:

- Assisting the FTC, and

- Assisting Chapter 19 and 20 dispute resolution panels by
— supervising the appointment and maintenance of panelists,
— insuring the code of conduct and conflicts of interests rules for panelists are followed,
— engaging in overall case management,
— receiving and safeguarding confidential information,
— serving as a liaison to national administrative authorities, and
— administering the budget for the *NAFTA* dispute resolution process.

---

**Various Working Groups and Committees**

*Suggestions for Further Research:*

Books:

1.  APPLETON, BARRY, NAVIGATING NAFTA 146–155 (1994).

2.  BOWMAN, GREGORY W., NICK COVELLI, DAVID A. GANTZ & IHN HO UHM, TRADE REMEDIES IN NORTH AMERICA (2009). *See also* the review of this book, Kevin C. Kennedy, *Book Review*, 19 MICHIGAN STATE JOURNAL OF INTERNATIONAL LAW 145–161.

3.  CANNON JR., JAMES R., RESOLVING DISPUTES UNDER NAFTA CHAPTER 19 (1994).

4.  FOLSOM, RALPH H., MICHAEL WALLACE GORDON & DAVID GANTZ, NAFTA AND FREE TRADE IN THE AMERICAS — A PROBLEM-ORIENTED COURSEBOOK (2nd ed. 2005).

5.  HUFBAUER, GARY CLYDE & JEFFREY J. SCHOTT, NAFTA — AN ASSESSMENT 5 (rev'd ed. October 1993).

6.  HUFBAUER, GARY CLYDE & JEFFREY J. SCHOTT, NORTH AMERICAN FREE TRADE: ISSUES AND RECOMMENDATIONS 5–7, 44, 155, 168 (1992).

7.  KENNEDY, KEVIN C., ED., THE FIRST DECADE OF NAFTA: THE FUTURE OF FREE TRADE IN NORTH AMERICA (2004).

8.  NEFF, RICHARD E. & FRAN SMALLSON, NAFTA — PROTECTING AND ENFORCING INTELLECTUAL PROPERTY RIGHTS IN NORTH AMERICA (1994).

9.  WETHINGTON, OLIN, FINANCIAL MARKET LIBERALIZATION — THE NAFTA FRAMEWORK (1994).

10. WISE, CAROL, ED., THE POST-NAFTA POLITICAL ECONOMY — MEXICO AND THE WESTERN HEMISPHERE (1998).

Book Chapters:

1.  Bello, Judith H. & Alan F. Holmer, *The North American Free Trade Agreement: Its Major Provisions, Economic Benefits, and Overarching Implications, in* THE NORTH AMERICAN FREE TRADE AGREEMENT 1–7 (Judith H. Bello *et al.*, eds. 1994).

Articles:

1.  *Achieving Canada — United States Economic Competitiveness through Regulatory Convergence — A Common Cause Agenda*, 36 CANADA — UNITED STATES LAW JOURNAL 77–120 (2011) (presentations by various speakers).

2.  Adams, Daniel N., Comment, *Back to Basics: the Predestined Failure of NAFTA Chapter 19 and its Lessons for the Design of International Trade Regimes*, 22 EMORY INTERNATIONAL LAW REVIEW 205–245 (2008).

3.  Alexander, Klint W. & Bryan J. Soukup, *Obama's First Trade War: The U.S. — Mexico Cross-Border Trucking Dispute and the Implications of Strategic Cross-Sector Retaliation on U.S. Compliance Under NAFTA*, 28 BERKELEY JOURNAL OF INTERNATIONAL LAW 313–342 (2010).

4.  American Bar Association, Canadian Bar Association, and Barra Mexicana Joint Working Group, *Dispute Settlement under a North American Free Trade Agreement*, 35 CANADA — UNITED STATES LAW JOURNAL 125–147 (2011).

5. Arizona Journal of International and Comparative Law ed., Symposium — *NAFTA and the Expansion of Free Trade: Current Issues and Future Prospects*, 14 ARIZONA JOURNAL OF INTERNATIONAL AND COMPARATIVE LAW number 285–573.

6. Benedict, Bret, Comment, *Transnational Pollution and the Efficacy of International and Domestic Dispute Resolutions Among the NAFTA Countries*, 15 LAW & BUSINESS REVIEW OF THE AMERICAS 863–890 (2009).

7. Brown, Catherine & Christine Manolakas, *Tax Discrimination and Trade in Services: The Search for Balance in Canada–U.S. Relations*, 40 GEORGETOWN JOURNAL OF INTERNATIONAL LAW 3–65 (2008).

8. Canova, Timothy A., *Closing the Border and Opening the Door: Mobility, Adjustment, and the Sequencing of Reform*, 5 THE GEORGETOWN JOURNAL OF LAW AND PUBLIC POLICY 341–414 (summer 2007).

9. Colares, Juscelino F., *Alternative Methods of Appellate Review in Trade Remedy Cases: Examining Results of U.S. Judicial and NAFTA Binational Review of U.S. Agency Decisions from 1989 to 2005*, 5 JOURNAL OF EMPIRICAL LEGAL STUDIES 171–196 (2008).

10. Cone, Sydney M. III, *Canadian Softwood Lumber and "Free Trade" Under NAFTA*, 51 NEW YORK LAW SCHOOL LAW REVIEW 840–852 (2006–2007).

11. Cook, Aaron, Note, *The NAFTA Superhighway: Paving the Way to a Prosperous North America — An In-Depth Analysis of the Impacts of the NAFTA Superhighway and Recommendations for Its Implementation*, 19 INDIANA INTERNATIONAL & COMPARATIVE LAW REVIEW 459–495 (2009).

12. Edson, Andrew G., Note, *Road Block: The U.S.–Mexican Trucking Dispute*, 16 LAW & BUSINESS REVIEW OF THE AMERICAS 323–332 (2010).

13. Gantz, David A., *Dispute Settlement Under the NAFTA and the WTO: Choice of Forum Opportunities and Risks for the NAFTA Parties*, 14 AMERICAN UNIVERSITY INTERNATIONAL LAW REVIEW 1025 (1999).

14. Gantz, David A., *Dispute Resolution Under the North American Free Trade Agreement,* 9 JOURNAL OF AMERICAN-CANADIAN STUDIES 13 [Korea] (2000).

15. Gantz, David A., *Resolution of Trade Disputes Under NAFTA's Chapter 19: The Lessons of Extending the Binational Panel Process to Mexico,* 29 LAW & POLICY IN INTERNATIONAL BUSINESS 297 (1998).

16. Gray, Michelle E., Comment, *Broadening NAFTA Article 1105 Protections: A Small Price for International Investment,* 48 HOUSTON LAW REVIEW 383–420 (2011).

17. Harp, Seth, Note, *Globalization of the U.S. Black Market: Prohibition, the War on Drugs, and the Case of Mexico,* 85 NEW YORK UNIVERSITY LAW REVIEW 1661–1693 (2010).

18. Hernández-López, Ernesto, *Law, Food, and Culture: Mexican Corn's National Identity Cooked in "Tortilla Discourses" Post-TLC/NAFTA,* 20 ST. THOMAS LAW REVIEW 670–690 (2008).

19. Hing, Bill Ong, *NAFTA, Globalization, and Mexican Migrants,* 5 JOURNAL OF LAW, ECONOMICS & POLICY 87–175 (2009).

20. Howe, Olivia D., *Recent Developments in NAFTA*, 16 LAW & BUSINESS REVIEW OF THE AMERICAS 137–141 (2010).

21. Kagalwalla, Adnan, Note, *NAFTA Chapter 11 Tribunals and Their Impact on Signatory States: A Parallel System and its Many Potential Dangers*, 3 ENTREPRENEURIAL BUSINESS LAW JOURNAL 95–112 (2008).

22. Kahn, Jordan C., *Striking NAFTA Gold: Glamis Advances Investor-State Arbitration*, 33 FORDHAM INTERNATIONAL LAW JOURNAL 101–155 (2009).

23. Lee, Nancy, *More Growth with Income Equality in the Americas: Can Regional Cooperation Help?*, 14 LAW & BUSINESS REVIEW OF THE AMERICAS 665–675 (2008).

24. Long, Melissa, *Recent Developments in NAFTA*, 14 LAW & BUSINESS REVIEW OF THE AMERICAS 875–884 (2008).

25. MacDonald, Chad, Note, *NAFTA Cross-Border Trucking: Mexico Retaliates After Congress Stops Mexican Trucks at the Border*, 42 VANDERBILT JOURNAL OF TRANSNATIONAL LAW 1631–1662 (2009).

26. McClintock, Michael C., *NAFTA's 13th Year: Steadily Increasing Trade Between the United States and Mexico, Transportation Infrastructure Crisis, Building a "Dry Canal" Across Southern Mexico, and More*, 14 SOUTHWESTERN JOURNAL OF LAW & TRADE IN THE AMERICAS 171–193 (2007).

27. Murphy, Jr., Ewell E., *NAFTA and the New Mexican Presidency*, 33 CANADA — UNITED STATES LAW JOURNAL 49–58 (2008) (The Annual Henry T. King Jr. Address on Northern American Relations Before the Greater Cleveland International Lawyers Group).

28. Nafziger, James A.R. & Angela M. Wanak, *United Parcel Service, Inc. v. Government of Canada: An Example of a Trend in the Arbitration of NAFTA-Related Investment Disputes*, 17 WILLAMETTE JOURNAL OF INTERNATIONAL LAW & DISPUTE RESOLUTION 49–79 (2009).

29. Pan, Eric J., *Assessing the NAFTA Chapter 19 Binational Panel System: An Experiment in International Adjudication*, 40 HARVARD INTERNATIONAL LAW JOURNAL 382–394, 440–445 (1999).

30. Pauwelyn, Joost and Luiz Eduardo Salles, *Forum Shopping before International Tribunals: (Real) Concerns, (Im)possible Solutions*, 42 CORNELL INTERNATIONAL LAW JOURNAL 77–118 (2009).

31. Powell, Stephen J., *Expanding the NAFTA Chapter 19 Dispute Settlement System: A Way To Declare Trade Remedy Laws in A Free Trade Area of the Americas?*, 16 LAW & BUSINESS REVIEW OF THE AMERICAS 217–240 (2010).

32. *Proceedings of the Canada — United States Law Institute Conference on An Example of Cooperation and Common Cause: Enhancing Canada — United States Security and Prosperity Through the Great Lakes and North American Trade*, 24 CANADA — UNITED STATES LAW JOURNAL 1–488 (2010).

33. Richman, Erica, Comment, *The NAFTA Trucking Provisions and the Teamsters: Why They Need Each Other*, 29 NORTHWESTERN JOURNAL OF INTERNATIONAL LAW & BUSINESS 555–575 (2009).

34. Romero, David Jiménez & Eduardo Ortega Castro, *Mexican Energy Reform*, 14 LAW AND BUSINESS REVIEW OF THE AMERICAS 859–867 (2008).

35. Sands, Christopher, Canada—United States Law Institute Distinguished Lecturer, March 23, 2009 at the University of Western Ontario Faculty of Law, *The Obama Opportunity for Canada*, 35 CANADA — UNITED STATES LAW JOURNAL 149–180 (2011).

36. Spitz, Laura, *The Evolving Architecture of North American Integration*, 80 UNIVERSITY OF COLORADO LAW REVIEW 735–792 (2009).

37. Stanton, Paul Kibel, *Grasp on Water: A Natural Resource that Eludes NAFTA's Notion of Investment*, 34 ECOLOGY LAW QUARTERLY 655–672 (2007).

38. Stanton, Paul Kibel & Jonathan R. Schutz, *Rio Grande Designs: Texans' NAFTA Water Claim Against Mexico*, 25 BERKELEY JOURNAL OF INTERNATIONAL LAW 228–267 (2007).

39. Starr, Pamela K., *The Two "Politics of NAFTA" in Mexico*, 16 LAW & BUSINESS REVIEW OF THE AMERICAS 839–853 (2010).

40. Swan, Alan C., *NAFTA Chapter 11 — "Direct Effect" and Interpretive Method: Lessons from Methanex v. United States*, 64 UNIVERSITY OF MIAMI LAW REVIEW 21–88 (2009).

41. *The Canada — United States Regulatory Regime as the Road to Recovery*, 36 CANADA — UNITED STATES LAW JOURNAL 261–284 (2011) (presentations by various speakers).

42. *The Economic Impact of Canada — United States Regulatory Convergence: From the Canada — United States Auto Pact to the North American Free Trade Agreement and Beyond*, 36 CANADA — UNITED STATES LAW JOURNAL 41–75 (2011) (presentations by various speakers).

43. Trujillo, Elizabeth, *Disaggregating the Regional-Multilateral Overlap: The NAFTA Looking Glass*, 19 INDIANA INTERNATIONAL & COMPARATIVE LAW REVIEW 553–568 (2009).

44. Truskett, Harve A., Comment, *"This Does Not Matter in Mexico:" Mexico–U.S. Competition Law — Conflicts and Resolutions*, 30 HOUSTON JOURNAL OF INTERNATIONAL LAW 779–814 (2008).

45. Tuck, Andrew P., *United States–Chile FTA Chapter 10: Lessons from NAFTA Chapter 11 Jurisprudence*, 15 LAW & BUSINESS REVIEW OF THE AMERICAS 575–600 (2009).

46. Van Landingham, R. Chris, Comment, *Do We Have an Agreement? Examining the Constitutionality and Legality of the Security and Prosperity Partnership of North America, and the Legal Ramifications of Its Informality*, 27 PENN STATE INTERNATIONAL LAW REVIEW 937–957 (2009).

47. Westbook, Jay Lawrence, *Legal Integration of NAFTA Through Supranational Adjudication*, 43 TEXAS INTERNATIONAL LAW JOURNAL 349–358 (2008).

48. Worrell, Erin M., Comment, *Free Trade, Free Migration: A Path to Open Borders and Economic Justice in the North American Free Trade Agreement*

*and the Security and Prosperity Partnership of North America*, 23 TEMPLE INTERNATIONAL & COMPARATIVE LAW JOURNAL 113–142 (2009).

49. Zamora, Stephen, *A Proposed North American Regional Development Fund: The Next Phase of North American Integration Under NAFTA*, 40 LOYOLA UNIVERSITY CHICAGO LAW JOURNAL 93–140 (2008).

50. Zamora, Stephen, *Rethinking North America: Why NAFTA's Laissez Faire Approach to Integration is Flawed, and What To Do About It*, 56 VILLANOVA LAW REVIEW 631–670 (2011).

Other Source:

1. *Building A North American Community*, Council on Foreign Relations Independent Task Force Report Number 52 (2005).

## NAFTA EXCLUSION CLAUSE

Article 2005:6 of *NAFTA* is the *"Exclusion Clause."* It states:

> Once dispute settlement procedures have been initiated under Article 2007 or dispute settlement proceedings have been initiated under the GATT, the forum selected shall be used to the exclusion of the other, unless a Party makes a request pursuant to paragraph 3 or 4.

The WTO Appellate Body quoted the *Clause* in its Report, *Mexico — Tax Measures on Soft Drinks and Other Beverages*, WT/DS308/AB/R (adopted 24 March 2006) (complaint by United States), partly to support its finding that the Panel in the case was correct in exercising jurisdiction.

*Suggestions for Further Research:*

Article:

1. Gantz, David, *Dispute Settlement Under the NAFTA and the WTO: Choice of Forum Opportunities and Risks for the NAFTA Parties,* 14 AMERICAN UNIVERSITY INTERNATIONAL LAW JOURNAL 1025 (1999).

## NAFTA FTC

*NAFTA* Free Trade Commission.

## NAFTA PARTY

A Party to *NAFTA, i.e.*, Canada, Mexico, or the United States.

## NAM

National Association of Manufacturers.

A prominent, Washington, D.C.-based industry association lobbying on behalf of the trade interests of American manufacturing companies.

## NAMA

Non-agricultural market access.

# NAMA 11

A negotiating group during the Doha Round of multilateral trade talks consisting of developing countries. The NAMA 11 includes:

- Argentina
- Brazil
- Egypt
- India
- Indonesia

- Namibia
- Philippines
- South Africa
- Tunisia
- Venezuela

# NATIONAL DAIRY MARKET LOSS PAYMENT PROGRAM

*See* MILC

# NATIONAL TREATMENT

The requirement, set forth most prominently in GATT Article III, that WTO Members treat imported goods no less favorably than domestically-produced like products once the imports have passed customs.

*Suggestions for Further Research:*

Articles:

1.  Archibald, Catherine Jean, *Forbidden by the WTO? Discrimination Against a Product When its Creation Causes Harm to the Environment or Animal Welfare*, 48 NATURAL RESOURCES JOURNAL 15–51 (2008).

2.  Staiger, Robert W. & Alan O. Sykes, *International Trade, National Treatment, and Domestic Regulation*, 40 JOURNAL OF LEGAL STUDIES 149–203 (2011).

3.  Vranes, Erich, *The WTO and Regulatory Freedom: WTO Disciplines on Market Access, Non-Discrimination and Domestic Regulation Relating to Trade in Goods and Services*, 12 JOURNAL OF INTERNATIONAL ECONOMIC LAW 953–987 (2009).

4.  Ya Qin, Julia, *Defining Nondiscrimination under the Law of the World Trade Organization*, 23 BOSTON UNIVERSITY INTERNATIONAL LAW JOURNAL 215–297 (2005).

# NATO

North Atlantic Treaty Organization.

On 24 August 1949, 12 nations founded NATO. The founding document is the *North Atlantic Treaty*, 63 Stat. 2241, TIAS No. 1964, 34 U.N.T.S. 243, signed 4 April 1949. The *Treaty* entered into force on 24 August 1949.

There are 26 NATO members. These members, and dates on which they gained membership, are:

| | |
|---|---|
| • Belgium | 24 August 1949 |
| • Bulgaria | 29 March 2004 |

- Canada                              24 August 1949
- Czech Republic                      12 March 1999
- Denmark                             24 August 1949
- Estonia                             29 March 2004
- France                              24 August 1949
- Germany
  (Federal Republic of)              6 May 1955
  Germany
  (following reunification)          3 October 1990
- Greece                              18 February 1952
- Hungary                             12 March 1999
- Iceland                             24 August 1949
- Italy                               24 August 1949
- Latvia                              29 March 2004
- Lithuania                           29 March 2004
- Luxembourg                          24 August 1949
- Netherlands                         24 August 1949
- Norway                              24 August 1949
- Poland                              12 March 1999
- Portugal                            24 August 1949
- Romania                             29 March 2004
- Slovakia                            29 March 2004
- Slovenia                            29 March 2004
- Spain                               30 May 1982
- Turkey                              18 February 1952
- United Kingdom                      24 August 1949
- United States                       24 August 1949

The fundamental purpose of NATO is to provide collective security for its members. Article 5 of the NATO treaty explains that an attack on one member is considered an attack on all members:

> The Parties agree that an armed attack against one or more of them in Europe or North America shall be considered an attack against them all and consequently they agree that, if such an armed attack occurs, each of them, in exercise of the right of individual or collective self-defense recognized by Article 51 of the Charter of the United Nations, will assist the Party or Parties so attacked by taking forthwith, individually and in concert with the other Parties, such action as it deems necessary, including the use of armed force, to restore and maintain the security of the North Atlantic area.

Any such armed attack and all measures taken as a result thereof shall immediately be reported to the Security Council. Such measures shall be terminated when the Security Council has taken the measures necessary to restore and maintain international peace and security.

Manifestly, Article 5 contemplates Europe and North America as the attack location, and thus expresses concern for the security of North Atlantic area.

The Article 5 Mutual Defense Clause was implicated, for the first time ever, in August 2003, in response to the terrorist attacks of 11 September 2001. The first deployment of NATO forces outside of the Euro-Atlantic area western European theater was in Afghanistan, in August 2003. Accordingly, Article 5 provides an international legal basis for NATO operations against terrorists and sponsors thereof.

## NEGATIVE CONSENSUS (NEGATIVE CONSENSUS DECISION-MAKING, NEGATIVE CONSENSUS RULE)

*See* WTO.

## NEGATIVE LIST (NEGATIVE LIST APPROACH)

A pro-free trade way of liberalizing trade.

Under the Negative List approach, all barriers to trade are eliminated, except for goods or services specifically itemized on a list. That is, trade liberalizing obligations apply across-the-board, unless a good or service is exempted by virtue of its placement on the Negative List. Put colloquially, everything is covered unless indicated to the contrary.

The Negative List approach is used, for example, in the *North American Free Trade Agreement* (*NAFTA*) Chapter 12 on Cross-Border Trade in Services, and in Chapter 14 on Financial Services.

The contrasting methodology, which is less ambitious from a free-trade perspective, is a Positive List approach. The Positive List approach is used, for instance, in the WTO *Agreement on Government Procurement* (*Government Procurement Agreement*, or *GPA*).

## NEO-CLASSICAL GROWTH MODEL

*See* Solow Model.

## NEPAD

New Partnership for Africa's Development.

This significant economic initiative is supported by the Group of Seven (G-7), the United Nations (U.N.) General Assembly, and African leaders. A key feature of NEPAD is self-policing of economic and political matters through inspections and reports of one country by another or others.

NEPAD originated on 23 October 2001 in Abuja, Nigeria, after many discussions about a new vision for development, an African renaissance, the importance of a partnership with mutual obligations, the need for a peer review mechanism to assess performance of a country by other countries (which NEPAD creates — the "African Peer Review Mechanism" (APRM), whereby governments voluntarily submit to scrutiny of their economic management and political standards), and the potential benefits of globalization. The NEPAD Secretariat is located in Johannesburg, South Africa, and depends heavily on the support of the South African government for facilities and staff.

There is a debate as to whether the 53 nation African Union (AU) ought to take over NEPAD, which would entail moving the Secretariat to Addis Ababa, Ethiopia, where the AU is headquartered.[494] The AU has established a peace and security council, and a pan-African parliament. However, the principal argument against such a takeover and move is NEPAD would become bogged down in AU bureaucracy.

*Suggestions for Further Research:*

Books:

1.   ADESINA, JIMI O., ET AL., AFRICA AND DEVELOPMENT CHALLENGES IN THE NEW MILLENNIUM: THE NEPAD DEBATE (2006).

2.   FRANCIS, DAVID J., UNITING AFRICA: BUILDING REGIONAL PEACE AND SECURITY SYSTEMS (2006).

3.   SMITH, MALINDA, BEYOND THE "AFRICAN TRAGEDY": DISCOURSES ON DEVELOPMENT AND THE GLOBAL ECONOMY 49–84 (2006).

4.   TAYLOR, IAN, NEPAD: TOWARD AFRICA'S DEVELOPMENT OR ANOTHER FALSE START? (2005).

Articles:

1.   Aka, Philip C., *Politics and Development in Africa: Incorporating the Influence of the Movement for Popular Participation on Assessment of NEPAD*, 3 HUMAN RIGHTS & GLOBALIZATION LAW REVIEW 79–148 (2009/2011).

2.   Mosoti, Victor, *The New Partnership for Africa's Development: Institutional and Legal Challenges of Investment Promotion*, 5 SAN DIEGO INTERNATIONAL LAW JOURNAL 145–78 (2004).

## NEW GROWTH THEORY

A theory of economic growth that emphasizes the role of technology.

The list of economic, social, demographic, and governmental factors in 1997 study by Robert J. Barro, *Determinants of Economic Growth*, amounts to a criticism of the Solow Model. The Model is simplistic in that it does not account for these forces as independent variables affecting growth. Indeed, while the Model

---

[494] *See* David White, *Leaders Split Over Plan for AU to Take Over NEPAD*, FINANCIAL TIMES, 28 January 2005, at 4.

does not mandate technology is an exogenously determined variable, it does not expressly incorporate this relevant factor either. It implicitly presumes technology is freely available to all economic actors. Yet, not all firms have access to the same technology. Further, some countries provide greater incentives, through the legal availability and enforcement of intellectual property rights (IPRs), for intellectual property (IP), *e.g.*, patent, copyright, and trademark rights.

Thus, in 1986, economist Paul Romer built a variation of the Model to include technological change as an endogenous factor (*i.e.*, as a variable determined by the Model, not a "given" taken on the basis of outside forces). His variation, and subsequent work by other economists, has produced what is known as "New Growth Theory."

New Growth Theory emphasizes the role of technology in growth. To be sure, New Growth Theory is not the first to spotlight this role. In 1962, the Russian economist Alexander Gerschenkron argued poor countries could grow rapidly using sophisticated technology in existence they did not have to invent or manufacture. New Growth Theory emphasizes that innovations in ways to produce merchandise or provide services, and the learning associated with this kind of change, stimulates growth.

Moreover, according to New Growth Theory, new knowledge gained is not subject to diminishing returns. Rather, an individual firm may experience constant returns to capital from advancement in technology. For example, if inputs into production are doubled, then output from the firm doubles. Some industries (*e.g.*, in the high-technology sector) may experience increasing returns to scale (where a doubling of inputs would lead to more than double the volume of output). Possibly, technology may allow an economy, overall, to benefit from increasing returns to scale.

Two obvious policy implications follow from New Growth Theory.[495] First, a country would do well, in the sense of promoting growth, to encourage its individuals and firms to develop technology. The important incentive is the innovator be allowed to seek and harness the rewards from the innovation, *i.e.*, to benefit from the profits of technology. As a corollary, a country ought to ensure a high-quality education system, through which it develops human capital. Second, there is no necessary endpoint, no Steady State, at which an economy must end up or to which it must converge. With technological change, economic progress may continue indefinitely. Countries are likely to diverge, and the gap between wealth and poverty to widen, depending on their environments for technological change and human capital building.

*Suggestions for Further Research:*

Books:

1.   BARRO, ROBERT J., DETERMINANTS OF ECONOMIC GROWTH — A CROSS-COUNTRY EMPIRICAL STUDY (1997).

---

[495] *See Old Before their Time*, THE ECONOMIST, 5 March 2005, at 76.

2. GERSCHENKRON, ALEXANDER, ECONOMIC BACKWARDNESS IN HISTORICAL PERSPECTIVE (1962).

3. LYNN, STUART R., ECONOMIC DEVELOPMENT: THEORY AND PRACTICE FOR A DIVIDED WORLD 52–54 (2003) (including Development Spotlight 3–2).

Articles:

1. Berkowitz, Daniel, Johannes Moenius & Katharina Pistor, *Legal Institutions and International Trade Flows*, 26 MICHIGAN JOURNAL OF INTERNATIONAL LAW 163–98 (2004).

2. Davis, Kenneth E., *What Can the Rule of Law Variable Tell Us About Rule of Law Reforms?*, 26 MICHIGAN JOURNAL OF INTERNATIONAL LAW 141–61 (2004).

3. Kuttner, Robert L., *Development, Globalization, and Law*, 26 MICHIGAN JOURNAL OF INTERNATIONAL LAW 19–38 (2004).

4. Romer, Paul, *Increasing Returns and Long-Run Growth*, 94 JOURNAL OF POLITICAL ECONOMY 1002–37 (October 1986).

5. Romer, Paul, *Endogenous Technical Change*, 98 JOURNAL OF POLITICAL ECONOMY 71–102 (October 1990).

6. Solow, Robert M., *A Contribution to the Theory of Economic Growth*, 70 *Quarterly Journal of Economics* 65–94 (February 1956).

## NEW SHIPPER

A company that did not export a good that is subject to an antidumping (AD) or countervailing duty (CVD) order during the period of investigation (POI) — the subject merchandise — and that is not affiliated with any company that did export or produce the subject merchandise.

## NEW SHIPPER LOOPHOLE

The ability, under United States law, of an importer of a good from a new shipper to choose whether to post a bond or security, rather than a cash deposit, for estimated antidumping (AD) or countervailing duties (CVDs).

The loophole, specifically the choice of the bond, allows importers to evade AD duties or CVDs that otherwise should apply. That is because once the imports in question are processed, the importer may default on the bond — and thereby avoid paying the full amount of AD or CVD duties. The problem occurred especially with respect to merchandise exported from China. Under the *Miscellaneous Trade and Technical Corrections Act of 2006* (H.R. 4944) the United States closed this loophole.[496]

Essentially, from 1 April 2006 through 30 June 2009, the United States suspended the "bonding privilege" importers had, to choose between posting a

---

[496] *See* 19 U.S.C. § 1675(a)(2)(B) (New Shipper Reviews); 19 C.F.R. § 351.214 (conduct of New Shipper Reviews).

bond or security, or a cash deposit of estimated AD duties or CVDs. This suspension means that for each entry of merchandise for consumption, or withdrawn from a warehouse for consumption, on or after 1 April 2006, Customs and Border Protection (CBP) collects a cash deposit of estimated AD duties or CVDs from all new shippers, with the notable exception of goods imported from Canada or Mexico. Similarly, except for goods from Canada or Mexico, CBP collects a cash deposit of estimated duties for each entry of merchandise during a New Shipper Review.

## NEW SHIPPER REVIEW

The review of an antidumping (AD) or countervailing duty (CVD) order to establish an individual weighted average dumping margin, or individual subsidization rate, for an exporter or foreign producer that did not export or produce the subject merchandise during the period of investigation (POI) during the original investigation. Under United States AD and CVD law, a New Shipper Review is required.

## NEW YORK PREPARATORY CONFERENCE

*See Havana Charter.*

## NFIDC

Net Food Importing Developing Country.

NFIDCs gained particular attention during the Doha Round, in view of concerns about food security amidst rising food prices (particularly in 2007–2008), and the emphasis in that Round on liberalizing world agricultural trade. It was widely appreciated that decades of globalization generally, and trade liberalization specifically, had brought great gains in world economic output. Thus, the positive link between an open economy and growth, measured by *per capita* GDP, was unassailable. But, to all but diehard free trade economists, the relationship between openness and poverty alleviation was far less certain.

For example, the link among international trade, food prices, farm subsidies, and poverty reduction is complex. As *The Economist* aptly summarized:

> ... For years reformers have advocated freer trade on the grounds that market distortions, particularly the rich world's subsidies, depress prices and hurt rural areas in poor countries, where three-quarters of the world's indigent live. The Doha Round of trade talks is dubbed the "development round" in large part because of its focus on farms. But now [May 2008], high food prices are being blamed for hurting the poor....

> ... Different types of reform have diverse effects on prices. When countries cut their tariffs on farm goods, their consumers pay lower prices. In contrast, when farm subsidies are slashed, world food prices rise. The

lavishness of farm subsidies means that the net effect of fully freeing trade would be to raise prices, by an average of 5.5% for primary products and 1.3% for processed goods, according to the World Bank.

... In crude terms, food-exporting countries gain in the short term, whereas net importers lose. Farmers are better off; those who buy their food fare worse. Although most of the world's poor live in rural areas, they are not, by and large, net food sellers. [According to a 2008 study of 9 poor countries by two World Bank economists, M. Ataman Aksoy and Aylin Isik-Dikmelik], ... even in very rural countries, such as Bangladesh and Zambia, only one-fifth of households sell more food than they buy. That suggests the losers may outnumber the winners.

But things are not so simple. ... [N]et food buyers tend to be richer than net sellers, so high food prices on average, transfer income from richer to poorer households. And prices are not the only route through which poverty is affected. Higher farm income boosts demand for rural labour, increasing wages for landless peasants and others who buy rather than grow their food. ... [T]his income effect can outweigh the initial price effect. Finally, the farm sector itself can grow. Decades of under investment in agriculture have left many poor countries reliant on imports: over time that can change.

The World Bank has often argued that the balance of all these factors is likely to be positive. Although freer farm trade — and higher prices — may raise poverty rates in some countries, it will reduce them in more.[497]

Evidently, it is difficult to generalize about the effects of freer farm trade on poverty in a global sense. The nature of reforms — how and when trade barriers are dismantled and farm subsidies reduced — along with the distinction between NFIDCs and food-exporting countries, and the milieu in specific countries, matter greatly.

## NFTC

National Foreign Trade Council.

A prominent, Washington, D.C.-based association engaged in lobbying on international trade issues.

## NFU

National Farmers Union.

The NFU is a major agricultural lobby in the United States.

## NGO

Non-Governmental Organization.

---

[497] *The Doha Dilemma*, THE ECONOMIST, 31 May 2008, at 82.

*Suggestions for Further Research:*

Articles:

1.  Alpert, Rachel, *Contained Change: International Non-Governmental Organizations Come to Syria in the Wake of the Iraq Refugee Crisis*, 42 GEORGE WASHINGTON INTERNATIONAL LAW REVIEW 57–122 (2010).

2.  Bernstein, Steven & Erin Hannah, *Non-State Global Standard Setting and the WTO: Legitimacy and the Need for Regulatory Space*, 11 JOURNAL OF INTERNATIONAL ECONOMIC LAW 575–608 (2008).

3.  Catabagan, Aaron, *Rights of Action for Private Non-State Actors in the WTO Dispute Settlement System*, 37 DENVER JOURNAL OF INTERNATIONAL LAW & POLICY 279–302 (2009).

4.  De Brabandere, Eric, *NGOs and the "Public Interest:" The Legality and Rationale of Amicus Curiae Interventions in International Economic and Investment Disputes*, 12 CHICAGO JOURNAL OF INTERNATIONAL LAW 85–113 (2011).

5.  Fukunaga, Yuka, *Civil Society and the Legitimacy of the WTO Dispute Settlement System*, 34 BROOKLYN JOURNAL OF INTERNATIONAL LAW 85–117 (2008).

6.  Helmer, Elena & Stuart Deming, *Non-Governmental Organizations: Anticorruption Compliance Challenges and Risks*, 45 THE INTERNATIONAL LAWYER 597–624 (summer 2011).

7.  Qi, Mei, Note, *Developing a Working Model for Legal NGOs in China*, 10 WASHINGTON UNIVERSITY GLOBAL STUDIES LAW REVIEW 617–639 (2011).

8.  Sapra, Seema, *The WTO System of Trade Governance: The Stale NGO Debate and the Appropriate Role for Non-State Actors*, 11 OREGON REVIEW OF INTERNATIONAL LAW 71–107 (2009).

9.  Van den Bossche, Peter, *NGO Involvement in the WTO: A Comparative Perspective*, 11 JOURNAL OF INTERNATIONAL ECONOMIC LAW 717–749 (2008).

10.  Yin, Deyong, *China's Attitude Toward Foreign NGOs*, 8 WASHINGTON UNIVERSITY GLOBAL STUDIES LAW REVIEW 521–543 (2009).

## NIC

Newly Industrializing Country.

## NIEO

New International Economic Order, a term coined by the great Argentine economist Raúl Prebisch.

In the 1970s, developing countries called for a complete re-alignment of their economic relations with developed countries. They sought, in particular, an improvement in their Terms of Trade (TOT), and better arrangements for borrowing. Specific proposals included

(1)  measures to boost the price of primary product exports relative to the price of manufactured good imports so as to improve the TOT,

(2) improved access to developed country markets, particularly with respect to manufactured products, in order to foster industrialization in developing countries, and

(3) relief from the crushing burden of debt servicing, so as to free up funds for internal investment.

The NIEO was embodied in a 1974 United Nations General Assembly Resolution, *Declaration on the Establishment of a New International Economic Order*, G.A. Res. 3201, U.N. GAOR, 6th Sess., Supp. No. 1, at 3, U.N. Doc. A/9559 (1974), *reprinted in* 13 INTERNATIONAL LEGAL MATERIALS 715. Whether developed countries have responded meaningfully to the NIEO proposals is arguable.

*Suggestions for Further Research:*

Books:

1.   BARAN, PAUL, THE POLITICAL ECONOMY OF GROWTH (1957); MALCOLM GILLIS ET AL., ECONOMICS OF DEVELOPMENT 32–33 (4th ed. 1996).

2.   DOSMAN, EDGAR J., THE LIFE AND TIMES OF RAÚL PREBISCH, 1901–1986 (2009).

3.   LENIN, V.I., IMPERIALISM: THE HIGHEST STATE OF CAPITALISM (1916, Junius Publications Ltd. ed. 1996).

4.   TUCKER, ROBERT C., ED., THE MARX-ENGELS READER (2nd ed. 1978) (especially the excerpts from Karl Marx, *Das Kapital*, at 294–438, and *The British Rule in India* (10 June 1853) at 657–658).

Book Chapters:

1.   Furtado, Celso, *"The Brazilian Model" of Development, in* THE POLITICAL ECONOMY OF DEVELOPMENT AND UNDERDEVELOPMENT 324–33 (Charles K. Wilber ed. 1979).

Article:

1.   Griffin, Keith & John Gurley, *Radical Analyses of Imperialism, the Third World, and the Transition to Socialism*, 23 JOURNAL OF ECONOMIC LITERATURE 1090 (1985).

Other Sources:

1.   *Declaration on the Establishment of a New International Economic Order* (adopted by the U.N. General Assembly 1 May 1974), G.A. Res. 3201 (S-VI), 6 (Special) U.N. GAOR, 6th Spec. Sess. Supp. No. 1, at 3, U.N. Doc. A/9559 (1974), *reprinted in* 3 INTERNATIONAL LEGAL MATERIALS 715 (1974).

2.   Resolution on Permanent Sovereignty Over Natural Resources (adopted by the U.N. General Assembly 14 December 1962), G.A. Res. 1803, U.N. GAOR, 17th Sess., Supp. No. 17, at 15, U.N. Doc. A/5217 (1963), *reprinted in* 2 INTERNATIONAL LEGAL MATERIALS 223 (1963).

3.   Resolution on Permanent Sovereignty Over Natural Resources (adopted by the U.N. General Assembly 17 December 1973), G.A. Res. 3171, U.N. GAOR, 28th Sess., Supp. No. 30, at 52, U.N. Doc. A/9030 (1973), *reprinted in* 13 INTERNATIONAL LEGAL MATERIALS 238 (1974).

## NIPPON KEIDANREN

The Japan Business Federation (or Japanese Economic Federation).

Nippon Keidanren is the largest business lobby in Japan. Among its activities are economic missions to foreign countries in conjunction with the Prime Minister of Japan.

## NME

Non market economy, *i.e.*, a country with a socialist or communist economic system.

NME countries typically have applied to them special rules on dumping margin calculations and subsidy determinations. Such rules include the use of third countries as proxies from which to obtain data to make such calculations and determinations. In turn, depending on which third country is used as a proxy, the dumping margin calculation or subsidy determination can be skewed against the NME.

In the United States, in 1979 the Department of Commerce (DOC) agreed with Congress that in a NME, prices are fictional. The DOC developed a methodology — NME analysis — for dealing with antidumping (AD) investigations of subject merchandise from an NME. Under this methodology, the DOC would ask a respondent producer-exporter about the factors of production, and inputs, it used to manufacture subject merchandise, and the quantity of each factor and input used. Then, the DOC would go to a third-country that is a market economy, such as India, and value the factors and inputs of the subject merchandise according to the prices in a third country. The DOC would use the third-country factor and input prices in its calculation of Constructed Value, and then compare the resulting Constructed Value against Export Price (or Constructed Export Price) to arrive at a dumping margin. In sum, under the NME AD methodology, the DOC values factors of production and inputs into a finished product at third country prices, with India being a typical third country, as a proxy for fictional prices in the NME itself.

For example, suppose the NME is China, subject merchandise is a car, labor is a key factor of production, and one of the inputs used is steel. Assume the DOC finds that 100 hours of labor and 10 kilograms of steel are used by the Chinese respondent producer-exporter. The wage rate in China (in U.S. dollars) is $2 per hour, and the price of that steel in China (in U.S. dollars) is $15 per kilo. Because the DOC treats China as an NME, it regards the wage rate and steel price as unreliable, and looks to the comparable values in India. Assume those values are a wage rate of $3 per hour, and a steel price of $20 per kilo. In computing Constructed Value, the DOC would use the Indian wage rate and steel price. (Observe that the DOC uses Constructed Value as a proxy for Normal Value and Third Country Price.) Manifestly, because they are higher than the Chinese levels, Constructed Value will be higher than it would have been had the DOC used the Chinese wage rate and price levels. In turn, for any given value of Export Price (or Constructed Export Price), the dumping margin will be enlarged.

The DOC continues to use this approach in NME cases. Notably, China agreed as part of its WTO accession negotiations that it would be treated as an NME for AD purposes for 15 years following its accession (which occurred on 11 December 2001). Thus, in 2016, the NME issue with respect to China effectively will be over. Notably, the concession China granted was a major aim of the United States Trade Representative (USTR) in negotiating the accession, and then-Chinese Vice Premier Zhu Rongji knew it.

In an important 2006 AD investigation involving lined paper from China, the Chinese asked for removal of NME status, at least for the subject merchandise and sector in question. The DOC rejected the Chinese request, giving several reasons why China still should be treated as an NME for AD purposes:

(1) The Chinese government exerts significant control over foreign exchange, particularly by limiting capital account flows.

(2) There are no independent trade unions in China, no right to strike, and labor mobility is regulated by the government, all of which affects the determination of wage rates.

(3) The Chinese government remains heavily involved in foreign direct investment (FDI) regulation.

(4) The Chinese government continues to direct bank lending and other resource allocations.

(5) There is still a lack of the rule of law in China.

(6) The Chinese government continues to own all of the land in China.

Thus, the DOC rejected the Chinese argument for removal of its NME status.

In 1984, the question of NME status first arose in the context of countervailing duty (CVD) investigations. The exporting countries at issue were Soviet bloc countries, such as the former Czechoslovakia and East Germany, along with the Union of Soviet Socialist Republics (USSR) itself. Domestic industries in the United States argued that CVD law could not be used in an NME context, because it is impossible in that context to measure the benefit of a subsidy to a firm receiving the subsidy. The firm is a state-owned enterprise, indeed a hallmark of an NME is state-ownership of all productive enterprises. Thus, a subsidy is a financial contribution from one arm of a socialist or communist government to another arm of the same government. There is little, if any, transparency in the arrangement. In the landmark case of *Georgetown Steel Corporation v. The United States*, 801 F.2d 1308–18 (Fed. Cir. 1986), the United States Court of Appeals for the Federal Circuit essentially stated that it could not see why the application of CVD law to an NME would be unreasonable. Nevertheless, the case was widely understood to mean that CVD ought not to be applied in that context.

One month after the 2006 lined paper AD case, an important case emerged concerning the application of CVD law to an NME — China. The American petitioners asked the DOC to remove China's status as an NME, and thereby apply CVD law to Chinese exports. The DOC applied its NME analysis, and agreed that for CVD purposes, China is not an NME, hence CVD law can be applied to China. The DOC relied on the following key findings:

(1) The Chinese government does not set 90 percent of the wages or prices in China.

(2) The Chinese currency, the *yuan* (*renminbi*) is freely convertible.

(3) The private sector in China is flourishing.

(4) The Chinese government allows some flexibility in credit and resource allocation.

(5) Overall, the Chinese economy no longer looks like that of the former Soviet Union, which was the kind of paradigm in which the Georgetown Steel decision was reached.

In turn, the DOC treated China as market economy, and applied CVD law, in five major cases in 2006–2008, involving products such as coated free sheet paper, pipes, and pneumatic off-road tires. Overall, between March 2007, when the DOC announced the reversal of its long-standing policy not to apply the CVD remedy to NMEs, and September 2009, when the CIT issued its landmark GTX decision (discussed below), there were 19 cases filed against China that involved parallel CVD and NME AD investigations.[498]

Obviously, the different outcomes in the AD and CVD context raise theoretical and practical questions. As a theoretical matter, why is it justified to treat China (or any other country) as an NME for one trade remedy (AD), but not in the other trade remedy (CVD)? Are the criteria used different, and if so, should they be? Moreover, is it appropriate to characterize an entire economy that is in transition, such as China, as either "market" or "NME"? Or, does it make more sense to identify on a sector-by-sector or industry-by-industry basis "market" versus "non-market" status, as occurs under Canadian trade remedy law?

As a practical matter, it is difficult — if not impossible — to defend the asymmetric treatment of a factor of production or input in the AD and CVD contexts. That is, the asymmetry between treating China as an NME for AD purposes, and applying CVD law to China, thereby treating it as a market economy, is not logical. The problem of asymmetric treatment in parallel CVD — NME AD investigations is sometimes called "double counting," which reflects what happens because of the treatment.

The "first count" occurs as follows, in an AD investigation: an input price is not useable because the country of the respondent is an NME, such as China. A proxy is used, namely, the price of the input in India, as a basis for calculating Constructed Value in China. The result typically is a higher figure for

---

[498] *See* Rossella Brevetti, *CIT Ruling Rejects Commerce's Interpretation in China AD / CVD Case*, International Trade Reporter (BNA) 1268 (24 September 2009).

Constructed Value, because the price of the input in India is higher than the price of the comparable input in China. In other words, in the NME AD investigation, the DOC cannot base Normal Value on price data from the NME — because the country of the respondent is an NME. The DOC must use a proxy for Normal Value, the alternative being Constructed Value (or, conceivably, Third Country Price). In computing Constructed Value, the DOC identifies the factors of production and inputs used by the respondent producer in the NME. But, the DOC values those factors and inputs using figures from a market economy. In theory, at least, the DOC selects a market economy that is at a comparable level of development to the NME in question, and also is a significant producer of comparable merchandise to that under investigation. In practice, as the hypothetical example suggests, it is debatable whether China and India indeed are comparable.

The "second count" then happens in a CVD investigation of the same subject merchandise as the NME AD case: the in-country (*i.e.*, in China) input price in the CVD investigation is not usable under Article 14(d) of the WTO *Agreement on Subsidies and Countervailing Measures (SCM Agreement)*. The DOC, therefore, uses the price of the input in India. Consequently, the cost of production of the subject merchandise is elevated, because of the Indian input price (again, it is higher than that of the comparable input in China). With a higher cost of production, the subsidization rate ultimately computed by the DOC also is higher. In turn, the CVD is increased. In brief, the double-counting problem is one of cumulatively counting a higher input price in both an AD and CVD investigation, and building that higher price into the AD duty and CVD.

As just suggested, the incongruity is evident in the context of factors of production and inputs used in subject merchandise. To give a fuller illustration, consider the following hypothetical simultaneous investigation of subject merchandise for alleged dumping and illegal subsidization. Assume the DOC treats the exporting country — China — as a NME for AD, but not CVD, purposes. In practice, for the AD investigation, the DOC will value an input into the subject merchandise using the price from the Indian market. That also is true for the values of the factors of production, like wage rates. In other words, the DOC will use Indian prices as a proxy for unreliable Chinese prices. In the CVD investigation, the DOC also uses the value of inputs and factors from India.

Thus, following the illustration outlined above, the DOC would ask the Chinese respondent producer-exporter what factors and inputs it uses in the manufacturing of the subject merchandise. Focusing just on the input, suppose the producer-exporter says it uses input X, which in China is valued (in U.S. dollar terms) at $100. The DOC would explain that because China is a NME for AD purposes, it does not trust the $100 value of input X, and will not take that figure into the computation of Constructed Value. The DOC thus turns to India, and values input X according to Indian pricing, which by assumption is $200. Constructed Value then includes the higher $200 figure for input X, and when compared with Export Price (or Constructed Export Price), the dumping margin is elevated (*ceteris paribus, i.e.*, assuming all other variables are constant).

Turning to the CVD investigation, the DOC would not treat China as an NME, but rather as a market economy. Therefore, in applying CVD law to China, the DOC must figure out the cost of production of the subject merchandise, and the degree to which that cost is subsidized by the government of China. The DOC asks the respondent producer-exporter what factors and inputs it employs to make the subject merchandise. The answer again (focusing on the inputs) is that input X is used, and the value of that input according to Chinese pricing is $100. However, the DOC values input X at $200, the Indian price, not the Chinese price. That is, the DOC uses in the CVD investigation the input value from the parallel NME AD investigation. Worse yet, the DOC essentially treats the $200 price for input X as a subsidized price — subsidized by the Chinese government. That is because the DOC computes a subsidization rate for the subject merchandise based on the third-country (Indian) input price.

Therein lies the asymmetry: for AD purposes, the inputs and factor values are elevated simply because they are Indian instead of Chinese figures. The result is an exacerbated dumping margin. For CVD purposes, the DOC says the subject merchandise is subsidized, but its determination is based on valuations from the Indian — not Chinese — market. The asymmetry is perverse, because the AD methodology used by the DOC is that for NMEs, but the CVD methodology it uses is that for market economies. After all, until March 2007, the DOC had said it could not apply CVDs to NMEs because subsidies are too difficult to calculate in those countries, and treated China as an NME for subsidy purposes — and, there are no special CVD rules for NMEs. Again, the DOC is treating China as an NME for AD purposes, but as a market economy for CVD purposes. In doing so, the DOC is not making any adjustment in its AD or CVD methodologies to avoid double counting.

Moreover, with the asymmetry, the subsidization rate is elevated because the DOC uses Indian prices. It is not logical, consistent, or fair to assert simultaneously that subject merchandise is dumped using Indian prices, and also say it is subsidized, using Indian prices. India has nothing to do with conferring a subsidy to the respondent producer-exporter. The subsidy, if it exists, is paid by an organ of the Chinese government. Using Indian factor and input prices as a justification for finding the input is subsidized by the Chinese government makes little sense.

What is the defense the DOC offered of the above methodology in a case involving a simultaneous CVD/NME AD investigation? Briefly put, it is that American trade remedy law does not instruct the DOC that it cannot engage in these practices. That defense failed spectacularly in September 2009, in a key case before the United States Court of International Trade

(CIT), *GPX Tire Corp. v. United States*, Ct. Int'l Trade, No. 08–00285 (Slip. Op. 09–103, 18 September 2009).[499] In *GPX Tire*, the CIT ordered the DOC to make a choice:

- Either cease imposing the CVD law against China, or

- Change the NME methodology in AD cases to reflect the application of CVD duties to China and thereby correct the problem of double-counting.

To be sure, the CIT decision may not be the last word on the matter. The CIT remanded the case to the DOC. After a final judgment by the CIT that the DOC has complied with its order, an appeal to the United States Court of Appeals for the Federal Circuit is possible. Nevertheless, the CIT ruling is the first on the merits of the March 2007 decision by the DOC to apply the CVD law to China, and of the DOC's defense of double counting.

The petitioners in the underlying parallel CVD and NME AD investigations that gave rise to the *GPX Tire* decision were the Titan Tire Corp. of Des Moines, Iowa, and the United Steel, Paper and Forestry, Rubber, Manufacturing, Energy, Allied Industrial and Union of Pittsburgh, Pennsylvania. In the CIT case, the petitioners were joined by Bridgestone Americas, Inc., and Bridgestone Americas Tire Operations, LLC. The respondents in the underlying investigations, and plaintiffs in the CIT proceedings, were GPX International Tire Corp. and Hebei Starbright Tire Co. Ltd. In the underlying investigations, the DOC rendered final affirmative determinations, resulting in the application of CVDs and NME AD duties to the product at issue — pneumatic off-the-road tires from China.

Before the CIT, the plaintiffs raised two key issues and arguments:

(1) The CVD statute could not be applied to an NME, *i.e.*, the DOC was wrong to apply that statute to China. The DOC misread the statute, and misinterpreted the applicable precedent, namely, the 1986 *Georgetown Steel* case, which precludes application of the statute to NMEs.

(2) Applying to China both the CVD statute, and the AD law using the NME methodology, resulted in double-counting. Chinese respondents were punished twice for the same allegedly unfair trade practice.

Essentially, the CIT ruled in favor of the DOC on the first, but not the second, issue.

On the first issue, the CIT held that the statutory language did not bar the DOC from applying the CVD law to imports from China. The CIT concluded that the *Georgetown Steel* case was ambiguous as to whether the DOC could or could not apply the CVD remedy to NMEs — the *Georgetown Steel* court did not forbid imposition of CVDs on imports from an NME. But, the CIT said there was no need for it to resolve this ambiguity. Rather, the CIT cited

---

[499] *See* Rossella Brevetti, *CIT Ruling Rejects Commerce's Interpretation in China AD / CVD Case*, International Trade Reporter (BNA) 1268 (24 September 2009).

*National Cable & Telecommunications Association v. Brand X Internet Services*, 545 U.S. 967 (2005). In that case, the Supreme Court held that before a court engages in judicial construction of a statute in a manner that may trump the interpretation of that statute by the relevant agency, the court must conclude that the statute unambiguously requires construction by the court.

Thus, the CIT looked to the relevant CVD statute — 19 U.S.C. Sections 1671 and 1677(5) — to see what they said about imposing CVDs against NME imports. Drawing in part on legislative history, the CIT held the statutory language does not deprive the DOC of the authority to impose CVDs on NME imports. In other words, the DOC indeed can apply the CVD law to a NME like China. But, the CIT reminded the DOC it has the discretion not to impose CVDs when it applies the NME AD methodology. The CIT warned it is not clear how — or even whether — the CVD and NME AD statutes work together in the event of a parallel investigation. These statutes give no guidance as to how the DOC is to account for the instances when they overlap in a parallel CVD — NME AD investigation.

On the second issue, the CIT held that the interpretation of the DOC of the NME AD statute, in relation to the CVD statute, was unreasonable. It was both unlawful and unfair for the DOC to impose CVDs on China under the normal market economy methodology, while simultaneously imposing AD duties based on the NME methodology. The CIT said that if the DOC wanted to apply the CVD remedy to China, against which the DOC also uses the NME AD methodology, then the DOC had to take corrective action. Otherwise, this kind of parallel investigation, and imposition of a parallel remedy, was wrong.

Specifically, the DOC had to avoid double-counting of market-economy CVDs and NME AD duties. It simply had failed to explain clearly the extent to which it was, or was not, double-counting. That is, the DOC had to adopt additional policies and procedures in its NME AD and CVD methodologies to account for the imposition of CVDs to products from and NME country. In its NME AD investigation, the DOC did not compare the Export Price of the subject merchandise with the Normal Value of the foreign like product in China. Had it done so, then both sides of the Dumping Margin formula would be equally affected by any subsidy, as both the price of the merchandise sold in the United States and in China potentially would be affected by the subsidy — in all probability, both would be lower on account of the subsidy.

Instead, the DOC used a proxy for Normal Value, namely Constructed Value, for which it relied on data from a third country, such as India. Those data were unaffected by any Chinese subsidy, because the Chinese government obviously did not confer financial contributions to firms and enterprising operating in the third country. Thus, in the NME AD investigation, the DOC compared an Export Price that is potentially affected by the Chinese subsidy against Constructed Value that is not affected by a subsidy. The result likely was a widened dumping margin, because Export Price was reduced by the subsidy, but not Constructed Value. Then, in the parallel CVD investigation, the DOC computed a subsidization rate, and based a CVD on it.

Herein was the double-counting, said the CIT. First, the NME AD methodology incorporated the effect of the subsidy on Export Price, without any adjustment to the proxy for Normal Value, Constructed Value. The result was a dilated dumping margin. Second, the subsidization rate reflected the subsidy, too. The DOC did not make any adjustment to this rate when computing the value of the subsidy. (As the earlier hypothetical illustration suggest, the DOC may even base the rate on unsubsidized input prices from a third country, which are sure to be higher than the subsidized prices in China.) Note the double-counting is even worse to the extent the DOC uses in Constructed Value input prices, as well as factor prices, from India. The end result is a double penalty against China — once in the AD duty, and once in the CVD — for the same breach, namely, a subsidy. The CIT challenged the DOC to consider whether it could impose all the remedy necessary through an NME AD duty, because that duty alone most likely accounts for the measurable competitive advantage respondents get from a subsidy. If the DOC persisted in entertaining parallel investigations, then, again, it needed to take steps to eschew double-counting.

Another way to characterize the CIT holding in *GPX Tire* on the second issue is as follows: the DOC could not change its anti-subsidy policy and apply CVDs to China on the ground that China is now a hybrid economy, without also refining its CVD rules, NME AD rules, or both to account for the fact that China really is a hybrid economy. Failure to fine-tune the rules suggested the DOC was doing nothing more than sticking China with as many trade remedies as could be piled on at once. That result was blatantly protectionist.

A third issue also was at play in *GPX Tire*. The DOC had decided that the date of the accession of China to the WTO — 11 December 2001 — was the cutoff date for the DOC to identify and measure subsidies in China. The plaintiffs challenged this bright-line rule as arbitrary. China was in a continuing state of reform and transition. It was only fair that the DOC evaluate the type of subsidy, and whether it is measurable, at a particular time, based on specific facts. The CIT agreed with the plaintiffs, ordering the DOC to drop its arbitrary line and look at Chinese subsidies after the WTO accession date, in an ongoing manner.

On a final point, the CIT also ruled against the DOC. One of the respondents in the underlying parallel CVD and NME AD investigations — Hebei Starbright Tire — asked the DOC for treatment as a market-oriented enterprise. The DOC blithely responded that it could not address this request. The reason? The DOC had not yet developed procedures to apply market-oriented AD rules to an individual respondent in an NME. The CIT had no patience for the DOC's response. The DOC had behaved in an arbitrary and capricious manner, and the CIT ordered it to address the request and fill in the gaps in its procedures.

One interesting episode in the saga about China's status as an NME is how China treats Russia. In 1997, China investigated silicon metals from Russia for potential dumping. Russia petitioned China for status as a market economy. China agreed to grant the petition. China reasoned that it did not want to be a hypocrite. To deny Russia's request, while contemporaneously seeking market-economy status from the United States in WTO accession negotiations, seemed inconsistent — even if there might be good reasons to treat Russia and China differently. Of course, China was unsuccessful in the accession negotiations. However, it did seek and obtain market economy status in its free trade agreement (FTA) with New Zealand.

Finally, note that the United States NME AD rules contain a "Multinational Corporation" (MNC) provision. *See* 19 U.S.C. § 1677(c). The MNC provision addresses the pricing practice of certain MNCs: they offset lower-priced home market sales with higher-priced third country sales. This practice hides the dumping of merchandise from the home market, which is under investigation. Under the MNC provision, a special rule is applied to calculate Normal Value (*i.e.*, the price of a foreign like product) of goods produced and exported by an MNC. In particular, if a respondent is affiliated with a company in another country, and the respondent has no viable home market to calculate Normal Value, then the Department of Commerce (DOC) uses the Normal Value of the affiliate as the Normal Value for the respondent — but only if the Normal Value for the affiliate is higher than the Normal Value for the respondent. In effect, the MNC provision allows the DOC to use a higher third country price (the price of goods associated with the MNC affiliate in the third country), instead of the lower home market price (the price of the goods associated with the MNC respondent).

In *Ad Hoc Shrimp Trade Action Committee v. United States*, No. 2009–1375, the United States Court of Appeals for the Federal Circuit affirmed a decision by the United States Court of International Trade (31 ITRD 1456), ruling on the MNC provision. The Appeals Court said the DOC reasonably determined that the MNC provision does not apply to a case in which the non-exporting country (*i.e.*, the country of the MNC affiliate) is a NME and Normal Value is based on the factors-of-production (*i.e.*, Constructed Value) methodology. The MNC provision itself is silent as to whether it applies if the non-exporting country is an NME and Normal Value is based on Constructed Value, and the Court applied *Chevron* deference to the determination of the DOC. (However, a dissenting opinion stated that the MNC rule does set forth three conditions for when it applies, and when it does not, and those conditions were met in the case at bar.) The case involved a dumping margin calculation for frozen warmwater shrimp from Thailand. The CIT ruled that the MNC provision did not apply to a Thailand-based company, Thai I-Mei Foods Co., which had affiliates in China and Vietnam. Both China and Vietnam are NMEs.

*Suggestions for Further Research:*

Articles:

1. Alford, William P., *When is China Paraguay? An Examination of the Application of the Antidumping and Countervailing Duty Laws of the United States to Nonmarket Economy Nations*, 61 SOUTHERN CALIFORNIA LAW REVIEW 79–135 (1987).

2. Ansel, Aaron, Note, *Market Orientalism: Reassessing An Outdated Anti-Dumping Policy Towards the People's Republic of China*, 35 BROOKLYN JOURNAL OF INTERNATIONAL LAW 883–934 (2010).

3. Clarke, Lauren W., Note, *The Market-Oriented Enterprise Approach: The Best Response to the Questionable United States Trade Practices Scrutinized in GPX International Tire Corp. v. United States, 715. F.Supp. 25 1337 (2010)*, 60 CATHOLIC UNIVERSITY LAW REVIEW 809–840 (2011).

4. Cong, Do Thanh, *Catfish, Shrimp, and the WTO: Vietnam Loses its Innocence*, 43 VANDERBILT JOURNAL OF TRANSNATIONAL LAW 1235–1264 (2010).

5. Gao, Henry, *China's Participation in the WTO: A Lawyer's Perspective*, 11 SINGAPORE YEAR BOOK OF INTERNATIONAL LAW 1–34 (2007).

6. Laroski, Jr., Joseph A. & Valentin A. Povarchuk eds., *International Trade*, 45 THE INTERNATIONAL LAWYER 79–94 (spring 2011).

7. Lynam, Garrett E., *Using WTO Countervailing Duty Law to Combat Illegally Subsidized Chinese Enterprises Operating in a Non-Market Economy: Deciphering the Writing on the Wall*, 42 Case Western Reserve Journal of International Law 739–773 (2010).

8. McDaniel, Christopher Blake, Note, *Sailing the Seas of Protectionism: The Simultaneous Application of Antidumping and Countervailing Duties to Non-Market Economies — An Affront to Domestic and International Laws*, 38 GEORGIA JOURNAL OF INTERNATIONAL AND COMPARATIVE LAW 741–767 (2010).

9. Trendl, Thomas J., Jamie B. Beaber, Michael T. Gershberg, Laura Ardito & Christopher Falcone, *Commentary on Developments in Section 1581(c) NME Cases*, 42 GEORGETOWN JOURNAL OF INTERNATIONAL LAW 97–134 (2010).

10. Watts, Dana, Note, *Fair's Fair: Why Congress Should Amend U.S. Antidumping and Countervailing Duty Laws to Prevent "Double Remedies,"* 1 TRADE, LAW AND DEVELOPMENT number 1, 145–170 (spring 2009).

## NON-DISCRIMINATION

A generic term that encompasses both most favored nation (MFN) and national treatment obligations under Articles I and III of the General Agreement on Tariffs and Trade (GATT), and under similar rules in other trade agreements.

*Suggestions for Further Research:*

Book Chapters:

1. Weiss, Friedl, *The Principle of Non-Discrimination in International Economic Law: A Conceptual and Historical Sketch, in* INTERNATIONAL LAW BETWEEN UNIVERSALISM AND FRAGMENTATION — FESTSCHRIFT IN HONOUR OF GERHARD HAFNER 269–286 (Isabelle Buffard, James Crawford, Alain Pellet & Stephan Wittich, eds., Leiden, Netherlands: Martinus Nijhoff Publishers, 2008).

Articles:

1.  Diebold, Nicholas, F., *Standards of Non-Discrimination in International Economic Law*, 60 INTERNATIONAL & COMPARATIVE LAW QUARTERLY 831–865 (2011).

2.  Efrat, Asif, *A Theory of Internationally Regulated Goods*, 32 FORDHAM INTERNATIONAL LAW JOURNAL 1466–1523 (2009).

3.  Moon, Gillian, *Fair in Form, but Discriminatory in Operation — WTO Law's Discriminatory Effects on Human Rights in Developing Countries*, 14 JOURNAL OF INTERNATIONAL ECONOMIC LAW 553–592 (2011).

4.  Staiger, Robert W. & Alan O. Sykes, *International Trade, National Treatment, and Domestic Regulation*, 40 JOURNAL OF LEGAL STUDIES 149–203 (2011).

5.  Wylie, Candice A., *A Comparative Analysis of Non-Discrimination in Multilateral Agreements, North American Free Trade Agreement (NAFTA), Energy Charter Treaty (ECT), and General Agreement on Tariffs and Trade (GATT)*, 18 WILLAMETTE JOURNAL OF INTERNATIONAL LAW & DISPUTE RESOLUTION 64–108 (2010).

6.  Ya Qin, Julia, *Defining Nondiscrimination under the Law of the World Trade Organization*, 23 BOSTON UNIVERSITY INTERNATIONAL LAW JOURNAL 215–297 (2005).

## NON-PREFERENTIAL RULE OF ORIGIN

*See* Rule of Origin.

## NORTH AMERICAN FREE TRADE AGREEMENT

*See NAFTA.*

## NORTH AMERICAN SUPER CORRIDOR

A proposal launched during the Administration of President Barack H. Obama with Mexican officials, implemented through a working group to enhance highway, railroad, and seaway infrastructure between the United States and Mexico, and reduce trade-related congestion between the two countries.

The Super Corridor would be a multi-modal transportation system to connect the ports of Colima, Lazaro Cardenas, Manzanillo, and Michoacan to the United States. There already are highway and rail linkages, but enhancing the network would benefit importers and exporters alike. Not surprisingly, a key issue that has held up progress on the Corridor is funding and sharing the financial burden between the two countries.

## NOTIFICATION

An obligation contained in many international trade agreements to promote transparency, and minimize the chances for disagreement.

Notification requirements vary considerably as to how, when, to whom, and by whom notice must be given, and the substantive and stylistic nature of the notice. Their common denominator, however, is that all parties to a trade agreement are entitled to know about a measure contemplated, or enacted, by one of them that may affect their rights or obligations under the agreement.

In the GATT—WTO system, one of the several accords that contains a notification requirement is the *Agreement on Agriculture*. Each WTO Member is obligated to provide the WTO with notice of its agricultural subsidy programs. Such notice is informative in its own right, and also helps ascertain whether a Member is adhering to its bound obligations concerning subsidy limits. Regrettably, major farm subsidy countries lag considerably in providing notification, *i.e.*, this *Agreement* illustrates one of the problems associated with a notification requirement — what can be done if a Member (or, worse yet, several Members) fail to provide timely notice? The Table below depicts the considerable extent to which the European Union (EU), Japan, and the United States are behind in their farm subsidy notifications:[500]

TABLE:

DELAYED NOTIFICATIONS ON AGRICULTURE SUBSIDIES

| WTO Member | Date Notification of Agricultural Subsidy Programs Submitted | Marketing Years (MYs) Covered by Notification | Gap between Notification Date and End of MYs |
|---|---|---|---|
| EU | December 2006 | 2002–2003 2003–2004 | 2 years |
| Japan | March 2008 | 2005 | 2 years, 3 months |
| United States | October 2007 | 2002–2005 | 1 year, 10 months |

Failure to provide timely notice has an important practical consequence, which operates in favor of the tardy notice-giver. Suppose a WTO Member provides notice in Year eight that indicates it exceeded its applicable Amber Box spending level in Years two and three. Presently, there is no serious legal sanction for the tardy notice. Moreover, there is no retroactively applicable remedy for exceeding the spending caps. For an unscrupulous WTO Member, a protracted delay creates the opportunity (or at least temptation) to adjust or tamper with data to show compliance with obligations.

---

[500] *See* Daniel Pruzin, *Spending on Agricultural Subsidies Declines for Third Year in Japan, WTO Data Indicate*, 25 International Trade Reporter (BNA) 443–444 (27 March 2008).

## NRC

Nuclear Regulatory Commission.

Pursuant to the *Atomic Energy Act*, the Nuclear Regulatory Commission (NRC) is the United States governmental body responsible for licensing exports of nuclear materials and technology.

## NTB

Non-tariff barrier, *i.e.*, any barrier to trade other than a tariff.

A synonymous term is non-tariff measure ("NTM"). NTBs include licensing rules, quotas, product testing and certification requirements, and food, health, and safety requirements.

## NTE

National Trade Estimate Report on Foreign Trade Barriers.

The United States Trade Representative (USTR) issues the NTE on an annual basis (on or before March 31). The NTE is submitted to the President, the Senate Finance Committee, and appropriate committees in the House of Representatives, and is publicly available. The NTE covers barriers to market access for exports of American goods and services, and problems in protecting and enforcing American intellectual property rights (IPRs). The NTE is complemented by a separate, annual "Special 301 Report" on the state of IPR protection and enforcement in foreign countries.

## NTR

Normal Trade Relations.

A term preferred by some Congressmen in lieu of most-favored nation (MFN). They point out the United States offers MFN treatment to most countries in the world, so that such treatment actually is "normal." They also urge that the term "NTR" is less politically caustic, particularly with respect to China, because it does not imply China is somehow getting more favorable trade treatment than any other country. "NTR" may well be a euphemism. "MFN," of course, means that no country is favored over another, because each is getting the most-favored treatment. "NTR" is officially used in United States trade law.

## NUISANCE TARIFF

A tariff so low that the cost a government incurs in collecting this tariff exceeds the revenue generated by the tariff.

## NULLIFICATION OR IMPAIRMENT

Damage to the benefits and expectations of a WTO Member that are associated with its membership that result from (1) the failure of another Member to carry out its WTO obligations, or (2) the application of a trade measure by another Member, regardless of whether it conflicts with that Member's WTO obligations.

The first type is called "violation nullification or impairment." It is made actionable by GATT Article XXIII:1(a). It involves a claim of a violation of a GATT—WTO text. It also is what lawyers conventionally think of in terms of a legal claim — namely, a violation of a relevant substantive textual provision.

The second type is known as "non-violation nullification or impairment" and is rendered actionable by GATT Article XXIII:1(b). Non-violation nullification or impairment allows one Member to bring a legal action against another Member by showing that it has been deprived of an expected benefit because of an action taken by the other Member, even though that action does not violate a specific provision of a GATT—WTO text. In principle, the action may concern goods, services, or intellectual property (IP). That is, legal grounds for a claim exist, even though the relevant substantive text has not been violated.

Essentially, nullification or impairment is the basis for a legal claim under the pre-Uruguay Round dispute settlement rules of GATT Article XXIII. It remains one basis (among others) for a claim under the *Understanding on Rules and Procedures Governing the Settlement of Disputes* (*Dispute Settlement Understanding*, or *DSU*). Notably, the concept is reincarnated (including the non-violation species) in the *General Agreement on Trade and Services* (*GATS*) (in Article XXIII) and the *Agreement on Trade Related Aspects of Intellectual Property Rights* (*TRIPs*) (in Article 64:2, setting out a non-violation claim, with effect five years after the *TRIPs Agreement* entered into force).

In respect of the *TRIPs* provision, the WTO has continued the prohibition on bringing non-violation nullification or impairment claims concerning intellectual property benefit through a succession of extensions relating to GATT Article XXIII(b)-(c). WTO Members do not agree on the issue of whether a non-violation claim has a place in the *TRIPs* context. That is, they debate whether non-violation is a feasible concept in the context of intellectual property — can there be a claim in which one Member argues that the action of another Member deprives the first Member of an expected intellectual property benefit, where there is no violation of an intellectual property agreement? Would not any deprivation necessarily entail a violation of an agreement?

Accordingly, WTO Members have agreed to refrain from bringing disputes under the *TRIPS Agreement* under a non-violation nullification or impairment theory. Thus, for instance, an extension was agreed at the Seventh WTO Ministerial Conference of 30 November—2 December 2009. At that Conference, the extension was granted until the Eighth Conference, held in Geneva in 2011.[501] At the Geneva Conference, the Members again renewed the extension, until the Ninth Ministerial Conference, scheduled for 2013.

---

[501] *See* Daniel Pruzin, *WTO Members on Course for Ministerial Deals on E-Commerce, TRIPs Disputes*, 26 International Trade Reporter (BNA) 1528 (12 November 2009); Daniel Pruzin, *WTO Members Endorse Agenda, Organization of Ministerial Conference*, 26 International Reporter (BNA) 1457 (29 October 2009).

*Suggestions for Further Research:*

Book:

1.  PETERSMAN, ERNST-ULRICH, ED., INTERNATIONAL TRADE LAW AND THE GATT/ WTO DISPUTE SETTLEMENT SYSTEM (1997).

Book Chapters:

1.  Roessler, Frieder, *The Concept of Nullification and Impairment in the Legal System of the World Trade Organization, in* INTERNATIONAL TRADE LAW AND THE GATT/WTO DISPUTE SETTLEMENT SYSTEM 125–38 (Ernst-Ulrich Petersmann ed. 1997).

Articles:

1.  Durling, James P. & Simon N. Lester, *Original Meanings and the Film Dispute: The Drafting History, Textual Evolution, and Application of the Non-Violation Nullification or Impairment Remedy*, 32 THE GEORGE WASHINGTON JOURNAL OF INTERNATIONAL LAW AND ECONOMICS 211–269 (1999).

2.  Frankel, Susy, *Challenging TRIPs-Plus Agreements: The Potential Utility of Non-Violation Disputes*, 12 JOURNAL OF INTERNATIONAL ECONOMIC LAW 1023–1065 (2009).

## NUSACC

National United States — Arab Chamber of Commerce.

NUSACC publishes report on trade, investment, and financial relations between the United States and Arab world.

## NV

Normal Value.

The price at which a foreign company sells a product in its home country. This product is the same as or similar to a product the company is alleged to dump in an importing country. Under pre-Uruguay Round American anti-dumping (AD) law, Normal Value was called "Foreign Market Value or "FMV."

# O

## OAS

The Organization of American States.

## OAU

Organization of African Unity.

The OAU was established by the OAU *Charter*, adopted on 23 May 1963. South Africa was admitted to the OAU on 23 May 1994.

## OCD

Ordinary customs duties.

The term is used in GATT Article II:(1)(b), first sentence, which contains the tariff binding principle. Essentially, "OCD" refers to tariffs, as distinct from other duties and charges (ODC).

*Suggestions for Further Research*:

Books:

1.  HODA, ANWARUL, TARIFF NEGOTIATIONS AND RENEGOTIATIONS UNDER THE GATT AND THE WTO (2001).

2.  MATSUSHITA, MITSUO, THOMAS J. SCHOENBAUM & PETROS C. MAVROIDIS, THE WORLD TRADE ORGANIZATION — LAW, PRACTICE, AND POLICY 112–14 (2003).

## OCR

Out of cycle review.

An analysis conducted at a time different from what is prescribed by law. For example, Special 301" is Section 182 of the *Trade Act of 1974*, as amended, 19 U.S.C. Section 2242. (It was added to the *1974 Act* by Section 1303 of the *Omnibus Trade and Competitiveness Act of 1988*.) Special 301 requires the United States Trade Representative (USTR) to provide information on an annual basis to Congress about countries that lack, or fail to enforce, intellectual property rights (IPRs). The USTR must provide the information within 30 days after issuing its annual analysis of foreign trade barriers under Section 301 of the *Trade Act of 1974*. The Section 301 analysis is formally called the *National Trade Estimate Report* (*NTE*). (*See* 19 U.S.C. § 2241(b).) The 30 day rule means the USTR must put out the Special 301 Report on or before 30 April of each year. However, the USTR may, and in fact does, conduct OCRs.

# ODC

Other duties and charges.

The term is used in GATT Article II:(1)(b), second sentence, which contains a discipline on ODC relating to the tariff binding principle in the prior (first) sentence. Essentially, "ODC" refers to non-tariff monetary impositions on foreign merchandise.

*Suggestions for Further Research*:

Books:

1. HODA, ANWARUL, TARIFF NEGOTIATIONS AND RENEGOTIATIONS UNDER THE GATT AND THE WTO (2001).

2. MATSUSHITA, MITSUO, THOMAS J. SCHOENBAUM & PETROS C. MAVROIDIS, THE WORLD TRADE ORGANIZATION — LAW, PRACTICE, AND POLICY 112–14 (2003).

# OECD

The Organization for Economic Cooperation and Development.

The OECD was created on 30 September 1961 pursuant to a *Convention* signed in Paris on 14 December 1960. Headquartered in Paris, its members are:

| | | |
|---|---|---|
| • Australia | • Hungary | • Norway |
| • Austria | • Iceland | • Poland |
| • Belgium | • Ireland | • Portugal |
| • Canada | • Israel | • Slovak Republic |
| • Chile | • Italy | • Slovenia |
| • Czech Republic | • Japan | • Spain |
| • Denmark | • Korea | • Sweden |
| • Estonia | • Luxembourg | • Switzerland |
| • Finland | • Mexico | • Turkey |
| • France | • Netherlands | • United Kingdom |
| • Germany | • New Zealand | • United States |
| • Greece | | |

The Ctommission of the European Communities takes part in the work of the OECD.

As the above list of members indicates, the OECD covers the world's richest economies. There are some key emerging countries that, as of August 2010, are not members: Brazil, China, India, Indonesia, Russia, and South Africa. As of April 2010, there also were some smaller significant countries not in the "club": Estonia (a leader in e-government and e-commerce), Israel (which has considerable scientific and technological expertise), and Slovenia (a leader in public sector communication).

However, in 2007 the OECD invited Estonia, Israel, Russia, and Slovenia to enter into accession negotiations — as well as Chile, which became a member in January 2010. The membership of Estonia, Israel, and Slovenia occurred in May 2010. Similarly, the OECD has expanded its engagement with Brazil, China, India, Indonesia, and South Africa. Note that part of the motivation of the OECD for adding members is to enhance its global influence.

Notably, Palestinian Authority leadership tried to prevent the entry of Israel. To be sure, the Israeli economy has been characterized by an overall stellar performance and remarkable spirit of entrepreneurship in Israel. However, the Palestinians pointed out that the OECD was violating its own rules by including a country with a poor human rights record. Moreover, argued the Palestinians, the Israeli economic data could not be trusted. Israel presented data in the form of statistics, including output, from Jewish farms and businesses operating in the Occupied Territories. Israel, and the OECD, countered that the inclusion of these data did not represent a judgment on the final status of the Territories.

Once invited to begin accession negotiations, a country undergoes scrutiny by existing OECD members as to various benchmarks, instruments, and standards. The criteria cover topics such as anti-corruption, competition laws, consumer protection, corporate governance, economic reform, environmental protection, intellectual property (IP) protection, and removal of restrictions on sharing bank and tax information. The process can be lengthy. For example, it took two years for Chile to complete its accession talks, which began in 2007. Chile signed the OECD accession agreement in January 2010. During the accession process, roughly 20 OECD committees reviewed Chile's laws and policies on which the OECD has criteria.

Article 1 of the *1960 Convention* indicates the OECD is designed to:

(1) "achieve the highest sustainable economic growth and employment and a rising standard of living in Member countries, while maintaining financial stability, and thus to contribute to the development of the world economy;"

(2) "contribute to sound economic expansion" in Member countries and non-Member less developed countries (LDCs), and;

(3) "contribute to the expansion of world trade on a multilateral, non-discriminatory basis in accordance with international obligations."

Accordingly, the OECD produces a number of policy studies and analyses in areas such as bank regulation, employment policy, international trade, pension reform, social affairs, and tax policy.

The OECD expanded its work in 1997 with an *Anti-Bribery Convention* that aims to establish "legally binding standards to criminalize bribery of foreign public officials in international business transactions and provides for a host of related measures that make this effective."[502] The *Convention* entered into force on 15 February 1999, with 39 OECD member state signatories and four non-member state signatories — Argentina, Brazil, Bulgaria, and South Africa. In February 2012, Russia became the 39th party to the *Convention*.[503] Joining the *Convention* is a key requirement for accession to the OECD.

The key requirement of the *Anti-Bribery Convention* is that a party to it must pass domestic legislation that criminalizes bribery of foreign public officials, establishes penalties against corrupt acts, and bans the tax deductibility of bribes.[504] In 2009, the OECD strengthened the Convention provisions banning the tax deductibility of bribes.

In 2008, numerous American business groups, in a 20 May letter to the George W. Bush Administration, called for increased enforcement of the provisions of the *Anti-Bribery Convention*. The business groups saw transnational bribery as a serious threat to investment, economic development, democracy, and national security. The letter specifically targeted Canada, Japan, and the United Kingdom as being lax in following through on their international commitment to crack down on foreign bribery.[505]

*Suggestions for Further Research*:

Article:

1.   Kita, Matthew H., Comment, *It's Not You, It's Me: An Analysis of the United States' Failure to Uphold Its Commitment to OECD Guidelines for Multinational Enterprises in Spite of No Other Reliable Alternatives*, 29 PENN STATE INTERNATIONAL LAW REVIEW 359–384 (2010).

## OFAC

Office of Foreign Assets Control.

A body within the United States Department of the Treasury responsible for administering certain sanctions imposed by the United States against foreign governments, entities, or persons.

## OFFSET (OFFSETS)

A measure used to encourage local development or improve the balance-of-payments accounts by means of domestic content, licensing of technology, investment requirements, counter-trade or similar requirements.

---

[502] *See generally*, OECD, *posted at* www.oecd.org/document/21/0,3746,en_2649_34859_2017813_1_1_1_1,00.html.

[503] *See* Rick Mitchell, *Accession Instrument for Anti-Bribery Pact Brings Russia Closer to OECD Membership*, 29 International Trade Reporter (BNA) 285 (23 February 2012).

[504] *See* Rick Mitchell, *Accession Instrument for Anti-Bribery Pact Brings Russia Closer to OECD Membership*, 29 International Trade Reporter (BNA) 285 (23 February 2012).

[505] Gary G. Yerkey, *U.S. Companies Call on Bush Administration to Press U.K., Japan, Canada Over Bribery*, 25 International Trade Reporter (BNA) 831 (5 June 2008).

Such measures sometimes are conditions for obtaining government approval for a license, or for government procurement. Generally, they are illegal under GATT — WTO texts. For example, Article XVI of the WTO *Agreement on Government Procurement*, while not a prophylactic ban on offsets, looks askance at them.

*Suggestions for Further Research*:

Article:

1.  Nackman, Mark J., *A Critical Examination of Offsets in International Defense Procurements: Policy Options for the United States*, 40 PUBLIC CONTRACT LAW JOURNAL 511–529 (2011).

## OFFSHORING (OFF-SHORING)

*See* Outsourcing.

## OIC

Organization of the Islamic Conference.

The OIC consists of 57 Muslim countries representing 1.5 billion Muslims. The OIC meets annually, alternating in Malaysia and Pakistan. At the 2005 meeting in Kuala Lumpur, Malaysia, the OIC agreed to establish a permanent secretariat in that city.

Collectively, the Gross Domestic Product (GDP) of the OIC countries is less than five percent of total world income. Other than Malaysia and the Kingdom of Saudi Arabia, few OIC members have attracted significant foreign direct investment (FDI). Trade among OIC countries is small, about $800 billion annually, which represents about seven percent of total world trade. At the 2005 meeting, the OIC Chairman, Malaysian Prime Minister Abdullah Ahmad Badawi, called for an "Islamic free trade agreement" among the OIC members.[506] The benefits would include increased trade, development, and economic clout.

## OIE

The acronym for the *World Organization for Animal Health*, or in French *Office International des Epizooties*.

The OIE was established in 1924 in Paris. The official French name of the original founding document is *Arrangement International Pour La Création, à Paris, d'un Office International Des Épizooties*, translated as *International Agreement for the Creation at Paris of an International Office of Epizootics*. *See* 57 LNTS 135, TIAS 8141, 26 UST 1840. The *OIE Treaty* was signed in Paris on 25 January 1924, and entered into force on 17 January 1925. However, the

---

[506] *Muslims Urge Islamic Free Trade*, BBC NEWS, 3 October 2005, posted at *http:///news.bbc.co.uk*.

United States did not ratify it for another half century. For the United States, the *OIE Treaty* took effect on 29 July 1975.

The OIE is an impartial, international organization responsible for setting standards for animal health. Specifically, it establishes internationally recognized health standards for animals, both aquatic and terrestrial, and encodes those standards into a legal code for each. The *Aquatic Animal Health Code* ensures the sanitary conditions for the international trade of aquatic animals, namely fish, mollusks, and crustaceans. The *Terrestrial Animal Health Code* ensures the sanitary conditions for the international trade of terrestrial animals, defined as mammals, birds, and bees. This *Code* may be more famous given its analysis of avian influenza and bovine spongiform encephalopathy (BSE) and standards for maintaining poultry and cattle health regarding these newsworthy conditions. Both the Aquatic and Terrestrial Animal Health Codes are available in their entirety on the official OIE website (www.oie.int).

The global prominence of the OIE has risen in recent years for at least two reasons. First, there have been a number of cross-border animal diseases or disease risk issues. Thus, for example, the role of the OIE has established standards concerning avian influenza and bovine spongiform encephalopathy (BSE, or mad cow disease). Second, WTO accords, notably the *Agreement on the Application of Sanitary and Phytosanitary Measures (SPS Agreement)* has brought to light cross-border animal disease and disease risk issues, and the importance of reaching common ways of dealing with them.

OIE membership has grown to 169 countries. Each country nominates a delegate to participate in organizational functions, such as working groups, regional commissions, and specialist commissions focusing on laboratories and the review and development of both animal health codes.

## OMA

Orderly Market Arrangement, or Orderly Marketing Arrangement.

*See* VER.

## ONE TRANCHE ECONOMY

A pejorative term used to describe a developing or least developed country that draws draw down on the first tranche of a loan from the International Monetary Fund (IMF) — as it is entitled to do automatically once the IMF approved the loan. But, subsequently, the country abandons its economic restructuring program, on which further tranche draws are conditional, simply to avoid politically unpopular decisions and appease preferred interest groups.

President Pervez Musharraf dubs Pakistan — at least as it stood when he took over in a military *coup d'etat* in October 1999 — a "one-tranche country."[507]

---

[507] Pervez Musharraf, In the Line of Fire 184 (2006).

## OPEC

Organization of Petroleum Exporting Countries, a cartel of major oil producing and exporting countries, which endeavors to regulate the supply of oil produced by its members through quotas, and thereby influence the world market price of oil.

*Suggestions for Further Research*:

Articles:

1.  Bartels, Brian P., *Preventing Coffee Cooperation from Grinding to a Halt: An Institutional Analysis of International Coffee Agreements and Recommendations for Achieving Long-Term Cooperation in the International Coffee Trade*, 42 CREIGHTON LAW REVIEW 279–321 (2009).

2.  Carey, Tim, Comment, *Cartel Price Controls vs. Free Trade: A Study of Proposals to Challenge OPEC's Influence in the Oil Market Through WTO Dispute Settlement*, 24 AMERICAN UNIVERSITY INTERNATIONAL LAW REVIEW 783–810 (2009).

## OPEN REGIONALISM

The creation of a free trade and investment area by two or more countries, with the key feature of the area being that its benefits extend to non-members on a reciprocal basis.

The region is "open" in the sense that non-members can benefit from the liberalized trade and investment rules, subject to them providing reciprocal treatment to the members. The concept has been considered by Asia Pacific Economic Cooperation (APEC) forum, but never defined by the group.

## OPEN SKIES

A term arising in the context of international air transport services.

In theory, "open skies" means free trade in civil aviation services, for passenger and cargo traffic. That is, subject to over-riding regulatory concerns, such as for safety and the environment, airlines and air cargo companies will be able to fly between or among countries that are parties to an open skies arrangement. Such freedom covers not only international flights, but also domestic flights. Thus, for example, in a true open skies deal between the United States and United Kingdom, any airline from either country could carry passengers between and within the two countries. Likewise, companies such as DHL and FedEx could carry shipments between and within the countries. In practice, however, open skies deals are rarely about free trade, and much more about managed trade. Ports of entry tend to be limited to one or a few airports, with limited landing spaces. Onward carriage within a country tends to be restricted to domestic companies.

A number of countries, including the United States and United Kingdom, have spent years trying to agree on an open skies deal. There is no multilateral accord under WTO auspices setting forth open skies obligations, though the *General Agreement on Trade in Services (GATS)* covers transport services.

*Suggestions for Further Research*:

Articles:

1. Kelly, Lawrence J., *Is that "Whoosh" You Hear a New Whisper-Jet Whisking Across U.S. Skies, or the Perotvian "Sucking Sound" of Jobs Leaving the Country? A Review of the Impact of U.S. — EU Open Skies Agreement Negotiations on the Leverage, Lifestyle, and Legal Standing of U.S. Aviation Labor*, 14 LAW & BUSINESS REVIEW OF THE AMERICAS 699–736 (2008).

2. Mushkat, Miron & Roda Mushkat, *The Political Economy of Hong Kong's "Open Skies" Legal Regime: An Empirical and Theoretical Exploration*, 10 SAN DIEGO INTERNATIONAL LAW JOURNAL 381–438 (2009).

3. Patel, Bimal, *A Flight Plan Towards Financial Stability — The History and Future of Foreign Ownership Restrictions in the United States Aviation Industry*, 73 JOURNAL OF AIR LAW & COMMERCE 487–525 (2008).

## OPIC

The United States Overseas Private Investment Corporation.

OPIC is located in Washington, D.C. The mission of OPIC is to provide insurance against political risk associated with foreign direct investment (FDI) by American companies.

There are exceptions in the *North American Free Trade Agreement (NAFTA)* and other United States free trade agreements (FTAs) that make clear a foreign business (*e.g.*, in *NAFTA*, a Canadian or Mexican company) are ineligible for OPIC insurance.

*Suggestions for Further Research*:

Book:

1. HEAD, JOHN, GLOBAL BUSINESS LAW (2nd edition 2007).

Article:

1. Inniss, Ashton B., Note, *Rethinking Political Risk Insurance: Incentives for Investor Risk Mitigation*, 16 SOUTHWESTERN JOURNAL OF INTERNATIONAL LAW 477–505 (2010).

## OTDS

Overall trade-distorting domestic support.

A concept associated with agricultural subsidies, referring to the aggregate level of spending by a country on such subsidies that distort trade, as distinct from non-trade distorting (Green Box) subsidies. Essentially, OTDS is the sum of Amber Box, Blue Box, and *De Minimis* support.

The concept was introduced during the Doha Round, essentially to rectify a problem embedded in the WTO *Agreement on Agriculture* from the Uruguay Round. That problem was the exclusion from the calculation of Aggregate

Measure of Support (AMS) of Blue Box and *De Minimis* support, and thus the exemption of Blue Box and *De Minimis* support from reduction commitments. The consequence was far less dramatic cuts to farm subsidies than many, especially in developing and least developed countries, had anticipated developed countries would be obliged to make under the *Agreement*.

In Marketing Year (MY) 2006, $11.34 billion, and in MY 2007, OTDS for the United States was $8.52 billion. The average for MYs 2002–2005 was $15.9 billion. The OTDS limit proposed for the United States in the Doha Round (as of December 2011, based on the December 2008 Draft Agriculture Modalities Text) was $14.46 billion.

*Suggestions for Further Research*:

Books:

1.    ANDERSON, KYM & TIM JOSLING EDS., THE WTO AND AGRICULTURE vols. I and II (2005).

2.    CARDWELL, MICHAEL N., MARGARET R. GROSSMAN & CHRISTOPHER P. RODGERS, AGRICULTURE AND INTERNATIONAL TRADE — LAW, POLICY, AND THE WTO 85–164 (2003).

3.    DESTA, MELAKU GEBOYE, THE LAW OF INTERNATIONAL TRADE IN AGRICULTURAL PRODUCTS — FROM GATT 1947 TO THE WTO AGREEMENT ON AGRICULTURE (2002).

4.    MCMAHON, JOSEPH, THE WTO AGREEMENT ON AGRICULTURE — A COMMENTARY (2006).

Other Source:

1.    Ingco, Merlinda & L. Alan Winters eds., *Agriculture Trade Liberalization in a New Trade Round — Perspectives of Developing Countries and Transition Economies* (World Bank Discussion Paper Number 418, 2000).

## OUTSOURCING (OUT-SOURCING)

Also known as off-shoring, outsourcing refers to a shift from one country to another of the source from which a good or service is obtained.

For example, if an input into a good (such as cotton in a shirt) traditionally is sourced in the United States, but the source shifts to Pakistan, then outsourcing has occurred in respect of the cotton. Another example, which received considerable media attention during the 2004 American Presidential Election, is the movement of relatively simple service sector jobs, such as back-office functions, call centers, consumer (customer) relations, certain publication production operations, software support lines, and even simple legal services from the United States to developing countries such as India.

Free trade theory suggests outsourcing may well be an expression of the Law of Comparative Advantage. However, in the Classical and Neo-Classical demonstration of that Law, decisions about specialization of production (*i.e.*, which country makes what based on relative cost advantage) do not involve intra-firm trade. Outsourcing typically entails a shift in the locus of production or service provision within a firm, from a plant or facility in a high-cost developed country to a low-cost developing country. Not only does the job loss in developed countries cause controversy (as, it would, when multiple unaffiliated firms are involved), but also there can be near-cruelty associated with that job loss. Reportedly, some firms have asked their long-standing mid-level managers to travel frequently, or even move, from the United States to developing countries essentially to train workers in those countries to succeed them in their jobs. In other words, the American workers are given the choice of quitting immediately, or hanging on for a short period by participating in their own outsourcing.

To be sure, outsourcing is not a unidirectional or irreversible phenomenon. There are significant difficulties in operating facilities in developing countries like India, from poor infrastructure to corruption. That is, relatively cheaper labor costs in such countries must be weighted against comparatively higher expenses on other matters. Moreover, the costs of moving an entire plant or service center from, say, Ohio, to Hyderabad can be significant.

*Suggestions for Further Research*:

Articles:

1. Burns, Michael J. & James McConvill, *An Unstoppable Force: The Offshore World in a Modern Global Economy*, 7 HASTINGS BUSINESS LAW JOURNAL 205–221 (2011).

2. Roan, Tyson B., *Anything But Doomed: Why Restrictions on Offshoring Are Permissible under the Constitution and Trade Agreements*, 13 EMPLOYEE RIGHTS & EMPLOYMENT POLICY JOURNAL 209–251 (2009).

3. Symposium Issue — *Global Sourcing and the Global Lawyer*, 38 GEORGETOWN JOURNAL OF INTERNATIONAL LAW 399–753 (2007).

# OUTWARD PROCESSING

The completion of certain parts of a manufacturing process in another country, using inputs in that process from a preference-granting country so as to obtain a trade preference from that country upon importation of the semi-finished or finished article.

For example, in December 2007, Canada proposed to enhance the competitiveness of its textile and apparel (T&A) industry by encouraging developing countries to use Canadian textiles in the manufacture of apparel. Suppose a developing country imported Canadian textiles, and incorporated them into an apparel article. Canada then would grant a trade preference to that article, in the form of a conditional remission of customs duties on the article. The condition, of course, was that the article be made, in whole or part, of Canadian textiles. Manifestly, such programs are designed and stand to benefit, the preference-granting country, as well as help a developing or least developed country. In this instance, the Canadian outward processing initiative could help Canadian textile firms against American or other foreign competitors.

# P

## P&D

Pickup and Delivery.

An environment in which a carrier picks up merchandise and delivers it to a designated destination. Multiple P&D transactions by a single carrier raise border security concern that the cargo hold of the carrier is susceptible to tampering, unauthorized access, and the introduction of illicit materials. High security seals and controlled access are remedies, and are required of carriers for participation in the *Customs — Trade Partnership Against Terrorism* (*C-TPAT*) program.

## PACIFIC ALLIANCE

An effort at regional integration among Chile, Colombia, Mexico, and Peru.

These four countries are the largest Latin American countries with coastlines along the Pacific Ocean. In April 2011, in Lima, Peru, they signed an agreement to develop a framework agreement. That framework agreement would coordinate free trade agreements (FTAs) the countries already have bilaterally with each other.[508] For example, in 2010 an FTA between Chile and Peru entered into force. Mexico and Peru completed an FTA in April 2011. Panama signed the April 2011 document as an observer, with the option of joining as a full member once it finalized bilateral trade deals with the other four countries. For example, as of April 2011, Panama was finalizing an FTA with Mexico.

The Pacific Alliance hopes to cover not only traditional trade issues concerning customs rules, tariff and non-tariff barriers, and remedies, but also topics such as migration, police cooperation, and even stock market integration. Indeed, Chile, Colombia, and Peru began efforts to integrate their stock markets at the end of 2010, at which point their combined market capitalization was almost $720 billion. The largest stock market capitalizations in Latin America are the bourses of Brazil and Mexico.

The Pacific Alliance is the first Latin trading bloc to be established since *MERCOSUR*. Arguably, it is a political counter-weight to *MERCOSUR*. *MERCOSUR* consists of Argentina, Brazil, Paraguay, and Uruguay. But, three of the Alliance countries — Chile, Colombia, and Peru — are associate members (as are Bolivia and Ecuador). Arguably, too, the Alliance undermines the Andean Community. Two of the Alliance countries — Colombia and Peru — are Community members. Thus, how, if at all, the Alliance relates to regional integration through these other vehicles is uncertain.

---

[508] *See* Lucien O. Chauvin, *Pacific Alliance Presidents Sign Pact Linking Chile, Colombia, Mexico, Peru*, 28 International Trade Reporter (BNA) 789 (12 May 2011). The figures noted above are from this source.

## *PAFTA*

*Pan-Arab Free Trade Area.*

*See AFTA* (FRIST MEANING).

## PANEL

A group of independent experts assigned the task of adjudicating an international trade dispute.

A WTO panel consists of three experts, which, like the Appellate Body, is supposed to be independent of the WTO Secretariat. Rules concerning panels are set forth in Articles 6-16 and 18-19 of the *Understanding on Rules and Procedures Governing the Settlement of Disputes (Dispute Settlement Understanding, or DSU)*.

*Suggestions for Further Research:*

Article:

1. Busch, Marc L. & Krzysztof J. Pelc, *Does the WTO Need a Permanent Body of Panelists?*, 12 JOURNAL OF INTERNATIONAL ECONOMIC LAW 579–594 (2009).

## PAR VALUE (PAR VALUE SYSTEM)

*See* IMF.

## PARAGRAPH 6 SYSTEM

A system of notification concerning compulsory licensing under an amendment to the WTO *Agreement on Trade Related Aspects of Intellectual Property Rights (TRIPs Agreement)*.

The origins of the system date to the November 2001 Ministerial Conference in Doha, Qatar. Negotiations produced a "Medicines Agreement" in August 2003, and a final deal amending the *TRIPs Agreement* — the first change to any WTO accord — approved at the December 2005 Hong Kong Ministerial Conference.

Under the Paragraph 6 system, one country is allowed to produce and export a pharmaceutical product under a compulsory license (*i.e.*, make and ship a generic version of a patented product without the approval of the patent holder) to another country that lacks the manufacturing capacity to produce that medicine itself. In the summer 2005, Rwanda became the first WTO Member to invoke Paragraph 6, and in September 2007 Canada became the first Member to give notice it would make and ship a generic medicine — to Rwanda — under this system. In practice, then, Rwanda began to import generic versions of patented HIV/AIDS medicines from Canada, in order to address its public health crisis. Though Rwanda is the first country to take advantage of this *TRIPs Agreement* amendment, other poor countries have indicated an interest in doing so — but cite pressure from developed countries not to invoke Paragraph 6.

That pressure evinces a major battle at the intersection of trade and intellectual property (IP). Simply and simplistically put, on the one hand are defenders of intellectual property rights (IPRs), who focus on the need to protect IP to induce and reward innovation, protect public safety, and guard against fraud. On the other hand are developing and least developed countries, which fact acute public health crises and are too poor to cover the costs of patented medicines.

Following the first 10 years of its operation (2001–2011), the Paragraph 6 system has spawned a debate about its efficacy.[509] Advocates of the system say it does work, and point to the case of generics exported from Canada to Rwanda. They also argue that the system allows poor countries to bargain more aggressively with pharmaceutical companies than otherwise would be the case, because they have the ultimate option of invoking Paragraph 6. Critics of the system say that the fact only Rwanda has invoked Paragraph 6 proves the system is a failure. It is a failure, they argue, because it is too complicated. As for lower pharmaceutical prices, critics urge they have fallen for reasons distinct from Paragraph 6, particularly the fact that poor countries are purchasing pharmaceuticals on large scales.

## PARALLELISM

A term arising in the context of the general safeguard remedy under GATT Article XIX and the WTO *Agreement on Safeguards*.

The scope of application of a safeguard remedy should be consistent with — that is, parallel to — the foreign merchandise examined during a safeguard investigation. After all, if an importing Member includes merchandise from all sources in its injury and causation determination, but excludes merchandise originating in certain countries (namely, partners in a free trade agreement (FTA) or customs union (CU)) from remedial action, then application of the remedy is discriminatory. The problem, however, is some FTAs and CUs call for exactly this kind of exemption from a global safeguard remedy.

In the 2000 *Argentina Footwear Safeguard* case, the Appellate Body held Argentina could not rely on its status as a party to *MERCOSUR*, nor on GATT Article XXIV, as a defense for its safeguard remedy applied to footwear imports only from non-*MERCOSUR* countries.[510] In the 2001 *Wheat Gluten* case (in which the United States exempted its *North American Free Trade Agreement (NAFTA)* partner, Canada, from a safeguard),[511] and 2002 *Line Pipe* case (in

---

[509] *See* World Trade Organization, *10-Year Old WTO Declaration Has Reinforced Health Policy Choices, Lamy Tells Symposium*, 23 November 2011, *posted at* www.wto.org.

[510] *See* WTO Appellate Body Report, *Argentina — Safeguard Measures on Imports of Footwear*, WT/DS121/AB/R (complaint by European Communities) (adopted 12 January 2000).

[511] *See* WTO Appellate Body Report, *United States — Definitive Safeguard Measures on Imports of Wheat Gluten from the European Communities*, WT/DS166/AB/R (complaint by the European Communities) (adopted 19 January 2001).

which the United States excluded both *NAFTA* partners, Canada and Mexico, from a safeguard),[512] the Appellate Body affirmed imports included in an Escape Clause investigation must correspond to imports targeted for remedial action.

## PARALLEL IMPORTS

*See* Gray Market Goods.

## PARALLEL LIBERALIZATION

A euphemism for competitive liberalization.

*See* Competitive Liberalization.

## PARALLEL MARKET

*See* Gray Market Goods.

## PARIS CLUB

A consortium of private lenders from developed countries, including Canada, Japan, European Union (EU) states, and Japan, which help finance (or re-finance) highly indebted countries.

The consortium is informal. Its financing arrangements are collective and *ad hoc* in nature. The focus of the creditors constituting the Paris Club is on debt restructuring, and the Club also assists countries with currency crises. There are rules of engagement with the Paris Club, and in total 84 countries have agreements (as of December 2007) with the Paris Club. The first project of the Paris Club was the 1956 Argentine debt restructuring.

The Paris Club is not the only such consortium. Another one is the London Club of private lenders from wealthy countries The International Institute of Finance (IIF), located in Washington, D.C., acts as a sort of consortium of consortia.

## PARIS METHODOLOGY

*See* AVE (*ad valorem* equivalent).

## PART IV

The final Part of the GATT, entitled "Trade and Development," consisting of Articles XXXVI, XXXVII, and XXXVIII.

---

[512] *See* WTO Appellate Body Report, *United States — Definitive Safeguard Measures on Imports of Circular Welded Carbon Quality Line Pipe from Korea*, WT/DS202/AB/R (adopted 2 March 2002).

Negotiations on Part IV were concluded on 8 February 1965, and it entered into force on 9 June 1966. Rarely amended, the last change to GATT was the addition of Part IV.

## PARTIAL DESIGNATION

The consideration of sub-categories, or parts of large categories, of products as being Sensitive.

This term was widely used in the Doha Round, in connection with expansion of in-quota volume thresholds on tariff rate quotas (TRQs) for sensitive products. Such products potentially benefit from less-than-agreed upon tariff reductions. But, to ensure a minimum amount of enhanced market access for exporters of these products, importing countries designating them "sensitive," and thus shielding them from the full force of otherwise-obligatory tariff cuts, should expand TRQs. Domestic consumption in the importing country is one way to base the expansions. But, for purposes both of designating a product as sensitive, and identifying domestic consumption data on which products is relevant, partial designation is relevant.

Partial designation permits, for example, disaggregation of a broad category like carrots, or cheese, into smaller categories such as baby carrots, or hard cheese. Another illustration is the broad category "wheat" under the Harmonized System (HS). There are 28 different types of wheat sub-products, at the six-digit HS level. Partial designation allows for them to be distinguished and treated distinctively.

## PARTICIPATION

As distinct from transparency, which concerns the accessibility (*e.g.*, publication) of trade measures, "participation" refers to the degree to which individuals, groups (formal or informal), organizations (business, non-governmental, and so forth), and sovereign states are entitled to be involved in the affairs of a body, and the degree to which — as a practical matter — they can do so effectively.

Transparency and participation, at bottom, are concepts that implicate both fairness and efficiency. Sometimes an increase of either or both transparency or participation suggests actual or potential tensions between fairness and efficiency. But, the two concepts are distinct. Transparency is more about observation, with the follow-on concern of applying relevant trade measures. Participation is about action, including in the formulation, implementation, and enforcement of those measures.

*Suggestions for Further Research:*

Book:

1.  GALLAGHER, PETER, PATRICK LOW & ANDREW L. STOLER, MANAGING THE CHALLENGES OF WTO PARTICIPATION — 45 CASE STUDIES (2005).

Article:

1. Bonzon, Yves, *Institutionalizing Public Participation in WTO Decision Making: Some Conceptual Hurdles and Avenues*, 11 JOURNAL OF INTERNATIONAL ECONOMIC LAW 751–777 (2008).

2. Charnovitz, Steve, *Transparency and Participation in the World Trade Organization*, 56 RUTGERS LAW REVIEW 927–959 (2004).

3. Dunoff, Jeffrey L., *Public Participation in the Trade Regime: Of Litigation, Frustration, Agitation and Legitimation*, 56 RUTGERS LAW REVIEW 961–970 (2004).

4. Gathii, James Thuo, *Process and Substance in WTO Reform*, 56 RUTGERS LAW REVIEW 885–925 (2004).

5. Howse, Robert, *For a Citizen's Task Force on the Future of the World Trade Organization*, 56 RUTGERS LAW REVIEW 877–884 (2004).

6. Livshiz, David, *Updating American Administrative Law: WTO, International Standards, Domestic Implementation and Public Participation*, 24 WISCONSIN INTERNATIONAL LAW JOURNAL 961–1016 (2007).

7. Markell, David, *The Role of Spotlighting Procedures in Promoting Citizen Participation, Transparency, and Accountability*, 45 WAKE FOREST LAW REVIEW 425–467 (2010).

8. Sapra, Seema, *The WTO System of Trade Governance: The Stale NGO Debate and the Appropriate Role for Non-State Actors*, 11 OREGON REVIEW OF INTERNATIONAL LAW 71–107 (2009).

9. Trujillo, Elizabeth, *From Here to Beijing: Public/Private Overlaps in Trade and their Effects on U.S. Law*, 40 LOYOLA UNIVERSITY CHICAGO LAW JOURNAL 691–744 (2009).

10. Van den Bossche, Peter, *NGO Involvement in the WTO: A Comparative Perspective*, 11 JOURNAL OF INTERNATIONAL ECONOMIC LAW 717–749 (2008).

## PATENT

A patent is a form of intellectual property (IP).

It is a grant of a property right by government to an inventor (or to the heirs or assigns of the inventor). The property right is a monopoly, specifically, the right to exclude others from making, using, or selling the invention that is the subject of the patent. In other words, what is granted is not the right to make, use, or sell, but rather the right to exclude others from the commercial exploitation of the invention with respect to the particular invention. Interestingly, Article I, Section 8 of the American Constitution empowers Congress to enact patent laws in order to promote progress in science and the arts by giving inventors and artists the exclusive rights to their discoveries and works. Article 33 of the WTO *Agreement on Trade-Related Aspects of Intellectual Property Rights (TRIPs Agreement)*, implemented by Section 532(a) of the *Uruguay Round Agreements Act of 1994* (35 U.S.C. § 154), requires that the monopoly last for 20 years. Because a patent is personal property, it can be sold to others, mortgaged, and bequeathed in a will. However, through certain free trade agreement (FTA) negotiations, including with Thailand in January 2006, the United States has sought a "TRIPs Plus" standard of 25 year protection.

The right conferred by a patent applies only in the geographical territory over which the granting government has control. Thus, an applicant seeking to get protection in more than one country needs to file an application in each country.

In the United States, the Patent and Trademark Office (PTO) is responsible for granting patent applications. The PTO grants one of three basic types of patents. A "utility" patent protects a mechanical, electrical, or chemical invention that concerns a new machine or a new process, or an improvement of an existing machine or process. A "design" patent may be granted for new, original, and ornamental designs. It protects the aesthetic or external appearance of an item. A "plant" patent protects a new variety of plant, such as a new tree, shrub, or flower, which is reproduced in an asexual manner.

There is a broad distinction between "product" and "process" patents. The names of the categories suggest their contents: "product" patents protect final products (e.g., a machine, a particular composition of matter, as in a chemical composition, or any manufactured item), while "process" patents protect the means of producing a product (i.e., the industrial or technical method used to make the product). Thus, for example, a patent on a medicine used to treat human infertility would be a product patent, but a patent on a particular method of synthesizing that drug would be a process patent. The *TRIPs Agreement* focuses on product patents, which some developing countries believe cuts against their interests. They argue that protecting the way in which a pharmaceutical product is made is legitimate, but the monopoly right ought to stop there so that anyone can come up with a different production process to make the same end product. That way, developing countries would not be dependent on American and European pharmaceutical companies for important medicines.

Only the inventor may apply for a patent (though under American law, the citizenship of the inventor is irrelevant). To receive a patent, the applicant must fulfill three general criteria. First, the subject matter of the application must be useful. That is, it must have a useful purpose, some utility, which includes the idea of operativeness. A machine that could not operate to perform its intended purpose would not be useful. Similarly, a mere idea or suggestion cannot be patented. Second, the subject matter must be new. If the invention has been described in a printed publication anywhere in the world, or if it has been in public use or on sale for more than a year, a patent cannot be obtained. Third, the subject matter must be non-obvious. That means an invention must be sufficiently different from what has been used or described before so that it is not obvious to a person having ordinary skill in the area of technology related to the invention. Merely substituting one material for another, or changing size, would not be patentable.

Sometimes, an applicant puts the words "Patent Pending" on the subject matter of the application. The words provide notice to the world that a patent application has been filed. However, the words have no legal effect. Patent protection does not start until the patent actually is granted.

Suppose two or more applications are filed by different inventors claiming the same, or substantially the same, patentable subject matter. A patent can be granted to only one of the applicants. Hence, it is the job of the administering authority, such as the PTO, to determine who is the first inventor and thereby entitled to the patent.

Patent infringement occurs when a person other than the patentee makes, uses, or sells the invention without authorization from the patentee to do so. The patentee can sue for relief, and obtain not only an injunction against further infringement, but also damages for the past infringement. Typical defenses are challenges to the validity of the patent, and arguments that the activities do not constitute infringement.

A patentee is free to license — *i.e.*, give authorization to — others to make, use, or sell the invention. For example, they may require that a patented invention be manufactured in the country within a certain number of years, otherwise the patent right in that country becomes void. In addition, some countries have rules on compulsory licensing, though such rules are circumscribed the by *TRIPs Agreement*.

There are two major patent treaties. The first is the *1967 Paris Convention for the Protection of Industrial Property*. The *Paris Convention* requires member countries to guarantee to the citizens from other countries the same rights in patent and trademark matters that they give to their own citizens — in effect, national treatment. The Convention also contains a right of priority for patent and trademark applications, namely, that priority is based on the first application filed. Once an application is filed in one country, the applicant may file in other countries to get protection therein. The *Convention* makes clear that the latter applications are deemed to have been filed as if they were filed on the same day as the first application. Over 100 countries, including the United States, are *Paris Convention* members.

Second, there is the *Patent Cooperation Treaty*, which was negotiated in Washington, D.C., concluded in June 1970, and entered into force on 24 January 1978. About 44 countries, including the United States, follow the *Patent Cooperation Treaty*. The *Treaty* makes filing a patent application for the same invention in multiple jurisdictions easier by, *inter alia*, establishing a standardized application format and centralized filing procedure.

*Suggestions for Further Research:*

Book:

1.  FOSTER, FRANK H., & ROBERT L. SHOOK, PATENTS, COPYRIGHTS & TRADEMARKS 143–53 (1989).

Articles:

1.   Bugg, Robert E., Note, *The International Trade Commission and Changes to United States Patent Law*, 76 BROOKLYN LAW REVIEW 1093–1119 (2011).

2.   Chien, Colleen V., *Patently Protectionist? An Empirical Analysis of Patent Cases at the International Trade Commission*, 50 WILLIAM & MARY LAW REVIEW 63–114 (2008).

3.   Curtin, Gerald V., Jr., Comment, *The Basics of ASICs: Protection for Semiconductor Mask Works in Japan and the United States*, 15 BOSTON COLLEGE INTERNATIONAL AND COMPARATIVE LAW REVIEW, 113, 114–16, 120–26 (1992).

4.   Ernstmeyer, James, Note, *Does Strict Territoriality Toll the End of Software Patents?*, 89 BOSTON UNIVERSITY LAW REVIEW 1267–1303 (2009).

5.   Erstling, Jay A., & Ryan E. Strom, *Korea's Patent Policy and Its Impact on Economic Development: A Model for Emerging Countries*, 11 SAN DIEGO INTERNATIONAL LAW JOURNAL 441–480 (2010).

6.   Feldman, Catherine Schulte, Case Comment, *Patent Law — No Infringement for Extraterritorial Completion of Method Patents (Cardiac Pacemakers, Inc. v. St. Jude Medical, Inc., 576 F.3d 1348, 2009)*, 33 SUFFOLK TRANSNATIONAL LAW REVIEW 391–407 (2010).

7.   Germinario, Claudio, *Double Patenting in the Practice of the European Patent Office*, 42 IIC: INTERNATIONAL REVIEW OF INTELLECTUAL PROPERTY & COMPETITION LAW 387–395 (2011).

8.   Große Ruse-Khan, Henning & Thomas Jaeger, *Policing Patents Worldwide? — EC Border Measures Against Transiting Generic Drugs under EC and WTO Intellectual Property Regimes*, 40 IIC: INTERNATIONAL REVIEW OF INTELLECTUAL PROPERTY AND COMPETITION LAW 502–538 (2009).

9.   Hahn, Robert W., & Hal. J. Singer, *Assessing Bias in Patent Infringement Cases: A Review of International Trade Commission Decisions*, 21 HARVARD JOURNAL OF LAW & TECHNOLOGY 457–508 (2008).

10.  Hamilton, Maria Raia, *Process Patents and the Limits of the International Trade Commission's Jurisdiction: Finding the Line in the Sand*, 50 IDEA 161–213 (2010).

11.  Ho, Cynthia M., *Unveiling Competing Patent Perspectives*, 46 HOUSTON LAW REIVEW 1047–1114 (2009).

12.  Johnson, Andrea L., *Transborder Licensing: A New Frontier for Job Creation*, 13 TULANE JOURNAL OF TECHNOLOGY & INTELLECTUAL PROPERTY 103–131 (2010).

13.  Keyhani, Dariush, *Patent Law in the Global Economy: A Modest Proposal for U.S. Patent Law and Infringement without Borders*, 54 VILLANOVA LAW REVIEW 291–307 (2009).

14.  Kumar, Sapna, *The Other Patent Agency: Congressional Regulation of the ITC*, 61 FLORIDA LAW REVIEW 529–580 (2009).

15. Lee, Nari, Patent *Term Extension in Japan in Light of the Pacific Capsule Decision*, 42 IIC: INTERNATIONAL REVIEW OF INTELLECTUAL PROPERTY & COMPETITION LAW 442–457 (2011).

16. Liu, Yinliang, *Patenting Business Methods in the United States and Beyond — Globalization of Intellectual Property Protection is Not Always an Easy Game to Play*, 42 IIC: INTERNATIONAL REVIEW OF INTELLECTUAL PROPERTY & COMPETITION LAW 395–416 (2011).

17. Luginbuehl, Stefan & Thomas Pattloch, *The Awakening of the Chinese Patent Dragon — The Revised Chinese Patent Law 2009*, 42 IIC: INTERNATIONAL REVIEW OF INTELLECTUAL PROPERTY AND COMPETITION LAW 130–150 (2011).

18. Ma, Lin & Junjie Zheng, *Patent Criminal Enforcement in the People's Republic of China*, 41 IIC: INTERNATIONAL REVIEW OF INTELLECTUAL PROPERTY & COMPETITION LAW 4–30 (2010).

19. Oddi, A. Samuel, *Plagues, Pandemics, and Patents: Legality and Morality*, 95 IDEA 1–45 (2011).

20. Royker, Edo, Student Article, *Foreign Patents Under U.S. Bankruptcy Code Section 365(n)*, 27 EMORY BANKRUPTCY DEVELOPMENTS JOURNAL 497–522 (2011).

21. Schade, Jürgen, *Is the Community (EU) Patent Behind the Times? — Globalization Urges Multilateral Cooperation*, 41 IIC: INTERNATIONAL REVIEW OF INTELLECTUAL PROPERTY & COMPETITION LAW 806–818 (2010).

22. Schroeder, John R., Note, *Should Foreign Sales Exhaust U.S. Patent Rights Post Quanta?*, 55 ST. LOUIS UNIVERSITY LAW JOURNAL 713–739 (2011).

23. Schwartz, David L., *Courting Specialization: An Empirical Study of Claim Construction Comparing Patent Litigation Before Federal District Courts and the International Trade Commission*, 50 WILLIAM & MARY LAW REVIEW 1699–1737 (2009).

24. Sheehe, Johanna, Comment, *Indian Patent Law: Walking the Line?*, 29 NORTHWESTERN JOURNAL OF INTERNATIONAL LAW & BUSINESS 577–599 (2009).

25. Smolczynski, Vincent M., Note, *"Willful Patent Filing:" A Criminal Procedure Protecting Traditional Knowledge*, 85 CHICAGO-KENT LAW REVIEW 1171–1198 (2010).

26. Volkheimer, Tim, Note, *Patents and the Free Movement of Goods: A Shift Towards European Arbitrariness?*, 15 COLUMBIA JOURNAL OF EUROPEAN LAW 495–509 (2009).

27. Wu, Rachel T., Comment, *Awaking the Sleeping Dragon: The Evolving Chinese Patent Law and Its Implications for Pharmaceutical Patents*, 34 FORDHAM INTERNATIONAL LAW JOURNAL 549–594 (2011).

28. Wuestehube, Linda, *U.S. Patent Applications and Export Control Regulations: Seven Habits for Highly Effective Offshore Outsourcing*, 14 INTELLECTUAL PROPERTY LAW BULLETIN 109–122 (2010) (SFIPLA Writing Competition Winner).

29. Yueh, Linda, *Patent Laws and Innovation in China*, 29 INTERNATIONAL REVIEW OF LAW & ECONOMICS 304–313 (2009).

Other Sources:

1.　PATENT AND TRADEMARK OFFICE, GENERAL INFORMATION CONCERNING PATENTS 1–5, 12–13, 20, 23–29, 31–32 (December 1992).

2.　PATENT AND TRADEMARK OFFICE, BASIC FACTS ABOUT REGISTERING A TRADEMARK 1–5 (September 1993).

## *PEACE CLAUSE*

Article 13 of the Uruguay Round *Agreement on Agriculture*.

Under this *Clause*, agricultural subsidies cannot be challenged under GATT–WTO rules, most notably, the WTO *Agreement on Subsidies and Countervailing Measures (SCM Agreement)*, particularly Articles 3 and 5 thereof. Each Member state enjoyed that immunity provided subsidies did not exceed their 1992 levels in any given year.

The impetus behind the *Peace Clause* was the European Union (EU), which during the Uruguay Round negotiations sought a temporary immunity from lawsuits against its Common Agricultural Policy (CAP). The EU intended to reform the CAP, and in the meantime, the United States agreed — via the *Clause* — not to bring legal challenges against the CAP. The EU agreed upon modestly significant de-coupling changes to the CAP in summer 2003. On 26 June 2003, the EU reformed CAP by decoupling (albeit partially in some instances) farm subsidies from production, and moving to a single farm payment.

The *Peace Clause* expired at the end of 2003. Efforts by some WTO Members to renew it, thereby extending the immunity it embodies, in the Doha Round have not been successful.

The leading dispute on the *Peace Clause* is the 2005 *Brazil Cotton* case.[513]

*Suggestions for Further Research:*

Book:

1.　Moyer, H. Wayne, AGRICULTURAL POLICY REFORM: POLITICS AND PROCESS IN THE EU AND US IN THE 1990S (Wayne Moyer & Tim Josling eds., 2002).

Article:

1.　Gillon, William A., *Agriculture*, 10 DRAKE JOURNAL OF AGRICULTURAL LAW 7, 19–56 (2005).

## PEC

President's Export Council.

PEC is the principal national advisory council to the President of the United States on issues of international trade, specifically, on the promotion and expansion of American exports through government policies.

---

[513] *See* Appellate Body Report, *United States — Subsidies on Upland Cotton*, WT/DS267/AB/R (adopted 21 March 2005) (complaint by Brazil).

# PECS

Pan-European Cumulation System.

A device introduced by the European Union (EU) in 1997, and extended to Turkey in 1999, to allow merchandise manufactured in different countries to qualify as originating in the EU, and thus obtain duty-free treatment. The device addresses the situation in which the EU has a free trade agreement (FTA), or FTA-like accord, with individual countries that contribute inputs to a finished product, but the countries are not all linked together — for example, because they are not all EU members. In effect, as the letter "C" in its name suggests, PECS is a cumulation rule.

For example, suppose a finished article has inputs from Hungary, Poland, and Turkey. Then, under PECS, the inputs from each country may be added together for purposes of determining whether the article qualifies as "European." The United States *Generalized System of Preferences (GSP)* and *African Growth and Opportunity Act (AGOA)* programs contain cumulation rules as well.

*Suggestions for Further Research:*

Other Source:

1.   Baldwin, Richard, *Multilateralizing Regionalism: Spaghetti Bowls as Building Blocks on the Path to Global Free Trade*, Center for Economic Policy Research Discussion Paper Number 5775 (August 2006).

# PEO

Permanent Exclusion Order.

An order to exclude permanently from a territorial jurisdiction specified articles from overseas. The articles may be, for example, foreign merchandise that infringes on an intellectual property right (IPR) in the jurisdiction in which the merchandise, but for the PEO, would enter. A PEO is a remedy that may be obtained under Section 337 of the *United States Tariff Act of 1930*, as amended, 19 U.S.C. Section 1337.

# PERIODIC REVIEW

A synonym for an Administrative Review of an antidumping (AD) or countervailing duty (CVD) order.

A Periodic, or Administrative, Review may occur once a year during the anniversary month of an outstanding AD or CVD order. The Review is triggered by a request of an interested party for recalculation of remedial duties owed.

*See* Administrative Review.

# PHRMA

Pronounced "Farma," the acronym "PhRMA" stands for the "Pharmaceutical Research and Manufacturers of America."

PhRMA is a powerful group lobbying on intellectual property (IP) protection issues on behalf of major American companies.

## *PLAZA ACCORD*

An agreement signed on 22 September 1985 at the Plaza Hotel in New York City by in 1985 among the world's most industrialized nations to cooperate in reducing the United States current account deficit by joint foreign exchange intervention.

The countries included the United States, Canada, France, West Germany, Italy, Japan, and the United Kingdom (*i.e.*, the Group of Seven, or G-7). The essential feature of the *Plaza Accord* was coordinated action by finance ministries and central banks to reduce the value of the U.S. dollar relative to other currencies, *i.e.*, to encourage depreciation of the dollar.

Under the *Plaza Accord*, the parties assumed additional obligations. In particular:

- The United States promised to cut its federal deficit
- Japan pledged a looser monetary policy, as well as financial sector reforms.
- West Germany agreed to make certain tax cuts.

These obligations complemented the fundamental purpose of the accord.

Simply, if simplistically, put, the Plaza Accord essentially worked. By the end of 1987, the U.S. dollar had fallen by 54 percent against the Japanese Yen and West German Deutschemark (DM). The *Accord* was followed by the *Louvre Accord*, in 1987, with the aim of stabilizing the decline of the U.S. dollar.

*Suggestions for Further Research:*

Book:

1. MURPHY, R. TAGGART, THE WEIGHT OF THE YEN — HOW DENIAL IMPERILS AMERICA'S FUTURE AND RUINS AN ALLIANCE (W.W. Norton Co. 1996).

## PNTR

Permanent normal trade relations.

"PNTR" is frequently used in the context of obtaining a removal from the annual MFN waiver process under the *Jackson-Vanik Amendment* to the *Trade Act of 1974*.

## POI

Period of investigation. The time period used in a trade remedy investigation.

For example, in an antidumping (AD) case, there is a POI for examining whether dumping occurs. Typically, the POI for the dumping margin determination by the United States Department of Commerce is one year. In an AD case, there also is a POI to considering whether dumping caused injury. Typically, for an injury determination by the United States International Trade Commission, the POI is approximately three years. The POIs should overlap, and in almost no case should either be less than three months.

Establishing the appropriate POI can be a highly contentious issue in an AD case. Depending on the precise time period from which data are taken, there may or may not be significant dumping margins or injury. Likewise, in a countervailing duty (CVD) or safeguards case, choice of the POI may determine the outcome of the case.

*Suggestions for Further Research:*

Book:

1. CZAKO, JUDITH, JOHANN HUMAN & JORGE MIRANDA, A HANDBOOK ON ANTI-DUMPING INVESTIGATIONS (2003).

## POINT OF STUFFING

The time and place at which cargo is put into a container, and then sealed.

This point is a key vulnerability in the security of international trade shipments, because it is the last opportunity to insert items into a container. This vulnerability is addressed (*inter alia*) by the United States *SAFE Port Act*, specifically the *Container Security Initiative (CSI)*.

## POLICY SPACE

The freedom of a country to implement a trade measure.

In effect, "policy space" concerns the ability of a country to act without violating its international legal obligations under applicable trade agreements. A large policy space indicates a country has considerable autonomy to take action, whereas a small policy space means there are disciplines in a trade accord that constrain its room to maneuver. For example, in coping with high prices and shortages of food in 2007–2008, WTO Members that imported food had three options: reduce food import tariffs; impose taxes on food exports; or subsidize consumption of food. Their policy space was set by GATT–WTO disciplines, such as GATT Articles II, IX, and XX. Fundamentally, the size of policy space is a question about balance between sovereignty and interdependence.

## POLLUTER PAYS PRINCIPLE

A rule in environmental law about allocation of costs associated with cleaning up pollution.

The polluter pays principle seeks to allocate the costs of pollution to the actor that engaged in polluting. The polluter should bear the expenses of implementing measures decided by governmental authorities that are necessary to ensure the environment is in an acceptable state. If these costs are borne by the government or subsequent property owners, then the polluter reaps a production subsidy.

The polluter pays principle forces the polluter to internalize the costs. As a result of such internalization, consumers may pay higher prices for the goods and services provided by the would-be polluter. However, the purpose of polluter pays principle is to deter the would-be polluter from polluting in the first place.

The polluter pays principle is not incorporated into Chapters 7B or 9 of the *North American Free Trade Agreement* (*NAFTA*), nor is it found in the *NAFTA Environmental Side Agreement*.

*Suggestions for Further Research:*

Articles:

1.   Benedict, Bret, Comment, *Transnational Pollution and the Efficacy of International and Domestic Dispute Resolutions Among the NAFTA Countries*, 15 Law & Business Review of the Americas 863–890 (2009).

2.   Crawford, Colin, *Some Thoughts on the North American Free Trade Agreement, Political Stability and Environmental Equity*, 20 Brooklyn Journal of International Law 585 (1995).

3.   Rowbotham, Elizabeth J., *Dumping and Subsidies — Their Potential Effectiveness for Achieving Sustainable Development in North America*, 27 Journal of World Trade 145 (1993).

4.   Stevens, Candice, *Interpreting the Polluter Pays Principle in the Trade and Environment Context*, 27 Cornell International Law Journal 577 (1994).

## POSITIVE LIST (POSITIVE LIST APPROACH)

A way of liberalizing trade that is less ambitious, from a free trade perspective, than the Negative List approach.

Under a Positive List approach, no barriers to trade are eliminated, except for barriers on goods or services specifically itemized on a list. That is, trade liberalizing obligations do not apply across-the-board. Rather, they are presumed not to apply, *i.e.*, they apply only to goods or services identified on the List. Put colloquially, nothing is covered unless listed. In 1993, the Parties to the *North American Free Trade Agreement* (*NAFTA*) initially suggested use of a Positive List approach to services trade liberalization, though they later agreed on a Negative List approach.

## POVERTY

*See* Absolute Poverty, Development as Freedom, Gini Coefficient, MDG, Top/Bottom Ratio.

## POVERTY LINE

*See* Absolute Poverty.

## POVERTY TRAP

A situation in which a country or region is too poor to grow.

Arguably, most African countries south of the Sahara Desert are in a poverty trap.[514] It faces geographic adversity, because less than 25 percent of the population in Sub-Saharan Africa (SSA) lives within 100 kilometers of the coast. SSA also is bedeviled by disease, accounting for 85 percent of annual worldwide deaths due to malaria, and 75 percent of all deaths due to HIV/AIDS each year. Such factors make it difficult for SSA to attract foreign capital, or for people in the region to save themselves. The gross national savings (as of 2003) in SSA averages 16 percent of Gross Domestic Product (GDP), whereas in East Asia it is 42 percent.

Generally, there are diverging viewpoints as to the best, or most appropriate, strategies for economic development. The specific issue of how to escape a poverty trap is no exception. Jeffrey Sachs and William Easterly take rather different approaches to seeing SSA out of the poverty trap.

Sachs focuses on what he terms the "poverty trap" of disease, physical isolation, environmental stress, political instability, and lack of access to capital, technology, medicine, and education. The goal of development, he argues, should be to help the poorest people of the world reach the first rung on the "ladder of economic development" so they can rise above mere a subsistence level, which is their present state in the poverty trap. Getting up to the first rung — slightly above subsistence level — would empower them, namely, give them a modicum of control over their economic futures and lives. To do get to that first rung, Sachs proposes an increase in foreign aid that, while certainly large, is within the bounds of what has been promised in the past. For the United States, for instance, his proposals would raise foreign aid from 0.14 percent of Gross National Product (GNP) to 0.7 percent. In presenting his argument, Sachs argues globalization should be embraced rather than fought, and puts forth a case for why international institutions such as the United Nations (U.N.), International Monetary Fund (IMF), and World Bank need to play a strong role in this effort.

The key to success, Sachs says, lies more in a fortified financial commitment from rich countries, and less in the obsession of the United States and certain other developed countries over misrule in the Third World. True, corruption in poor countries exists and impedes development. But, says Sachs, it ought not to be an excuse by rich countries to avoid helping the poorest people of the world. In sum, Sachs proposes a large-scale, comprehensive international strategy for eradicating extreme poverty.

In contrast, Easterly argues the best chance for on-the-ground development success is piecemeal problem solving — not grandiose, top-down plans. He points out in the last five decades, the United States and a few other developed

---

[514] *See The $25 Billion Question*, THE ECONOMIST, 2 July 2005, at 24–26.

nations have spent over \$2.3 trillion on foreign aid, and yet there is shamefully little to show for it. Easterly criticizes aid agency managers such as those at the U.N., IMF, and World Bank, as well as politicians from rich countries, who propose major "interventions" to end world poverty. Thus, Easterly counsels against the U.N.–World Bank program to achieve "Millennium Development Goals" (MDGs) by 2015. Such plans have no mechanism for judging success or failure. Aid agencies are held accountable neither for modest lapses nor debacles, contends Easterly. Spending decisions in these agencies, and on foreign assistance, are driven by feel-good posturing of politicians and entertainment industry celebrities from rich countries.

Easterly contrasts the traditional "Planner" approach of most aid projects with the "Searcher" approach that has worked well in democracies of the western world. "Searchers" view problem-solving as an incremental discovery process. They rely on competition and feedback to figure out what works. "A Planner thinks he already knows the answers," Easterly writes, while a Searcher "admits he doesn't know the answers in advance; he believes that poverty is a complicated tangle of political, social, historical, institutional and technological factors."[515] In sum, Easterly advocates a small-scale approach, led by "searchers," which stresses homegrown solutions to the challenges of extreme poverty.

*Suggestions for Further Research:*

Books:

1. EASTERLY, WILLIAM, THE WHITE MAN'S BURDEN: WHY THE WEST'S EFFORTS TO AID THE REST HAVE DONE SO MUCH ILL AND SO LITTLE GOOD (2006).

2. SACHS, JEFFREY D., THE END OF POVERTY: ECONOMIC POSSIBILITIES FOR OUR TIME (2005).

Other Sources:

1. Easterly, William, *A Modest Proposal* (reviewing JEFFREY D. SACHS, THE END OF POVERTY: ECONOMIC POSSIBILITIES FOR OUR TIME (2005)) WASHINGTON POST, 13 March 2005.

2. Easterly, William, *Author's Response* (a response to Book Review by Jeffrey D. Sachs on 22 April 2006) 367:9528 THE LANCET 2060 (24 June 2006).

3. Sachs, Jeffrey D., *Up From Poverty* (a response to William Easterly's Book Review on 13 March 2005) WASHINGTON POST, 27 March 27, 2005.

4. Sachs, Jeffrey D., *How to Help the Poor: Piecemeal Progress or Strategic Plans?* (reviewing William Easterly, THE WHITE MAN'S BURDEN: WHY THE WEST'S EFFORTS TO AID THE REST HAVE DONE SO MUCH ILL AND SO LITTLE GOOD (2006)) 367:9519 THE LANCET 1309–1310 (22 April 2006).

---

[515] WILLIAM EASTERLY, THE WHITE MAN'S BURDEN: WHY THE WEST'S EFFORTS TO AID THE REST HAVE DONE SO MUCH ILL AND SO LITTLE GOOD 6 (2006).

## PP

Purchase Price, now called Export Price, or EP for short.

Purchase Price, or PP for short, was the term used in pre-Uruguay Round American antidumping (AD) law in a situation in which a sale of allegedly dumped merchandise from a foreign company to an unrelated American party occurs before that merchandise is imported in the United States. Export Price replaced Purchase Price as of 1 January 1995.

## PPP

Purchasing Power Parity.

A method of comparing national income — either Gross National Product (GNP) or Gross Domestic Product (GDP) — and other economic growth statistics that accounts for different price levels across countries. There is an obvious problem when relying on any one of these measurements of "growth" in a country to make comparisons and contrasts across countries. Price levels differ across countries. The price of identical, like, similar, or substitutable merchandise — whether the good is a baseball, protein bar, or textbook — often differs across countries. The reasons for the variance include market conditions, such as competition among suppliers, demand and income levels among consumers, inflation, protection, and taxation. Such variations also exist for the same or comparable services, be they banking, dental, or legal.

Consequently, comparisons of growth — and, as a closely related matter, income levels — among countries using raw GNP or GDP data are misleading, insofar as cross-country differences may be explained in part by price variations. Typically, the raw data overstates the true extent of growth and income differences. The correction economists make is to put the data on "Purchasing Power Parity" (PPP) terms. That is, economists measure and compare growth and income using

- GNP (PPP terms)
- *Per Capita* GNP (PPP terms)
- GDP (PPP terms)
- *Per Capita* GDP (PPP terms)

Measuring income at market prices means valuing the quantity of goods and services in a country at the price levels for those goods and services prevailing in that country during a particular point or period in time. To make cross-country comparisons, the resulting figures must be converted from local currency (*e.g.*, Chinese *yuan*) into a common currency (*e.g.*, U.S. dollars). In contrast, PPP terms means valuing the quantity of goods and services at price levels prevailing in a chosen country during a particular year — say the United States in the year 2005.

With income statistics put on a PPP basis, no exchange conversion is necessary, because from the outset goods and services from all countries are valued in terms of a common currency. Typically, that currency is the U.S. dollar. Essentially, PPP is a way to correct for differences in prices across countries, and for the possibility exchange rate fluctuations undermine the reliability of cross-country GNP comparisons. The device eliminates the need to convert valuation of goods and services in a foreign currency to valuation in a standard set of prices denominated in a major currency.

There is a second, and subtle, advantage to measuring GNP, GDP, and so on in PPP terms. PPP helps correct for the fact not every type of good or service is traded across borders. For example, childcare services are not traded among countries, and in general, water is not traded across international boundaries either (though countries do share boundary waters pursuant to treaties). Indeed, in many Third World countries, a large portion of national income is comprised of goods and services that are not traded internationally. This fact creates a problem if cross-country comparisons are made using GNP at market prices.

In each country, the ratio of the price of goods and services that are traded internationally to the price of goods and services that are not traded internationally will differ. The differences will depend in part on the importance of non-traded goods and services in each the economy of a country. Yet, at the same time, exchange rates are determined in part by the flow of goods and services that are traded internationally. That is to say, exchange rates do not embody economic activity in non-traded sectors. As a result, when a GNP statistic measured at market prices (such as Chinese *yuan*) is converted to a major currency (such as U.S. dollars), the exchange rate used for the conversion is "incomplete." In turn, the comparison of GNP statistics across countries is misleading. The PPP measure circumvents the problem by valuing goods and services produced in each country on the basis of prices prevailing in one country. Thus, the fact the ratio of prices in traded versus non-traded sectors differs from one country to the next does not matter, because the prices in only one country are used for valuation.

To understand how income-based measures of growth are calculated and compared in PPP terms, consider the following example involving the GDP of China and the United States. To simplify, suppose the output of the United States consists of rice (to represent all agricultural products), navigational equipment for long-haul commercial aircraft (to represent advanced manufactured products), and pediatric dental services for children age five or under (to represent the service sector). Suppose further the output of China consists of rice and dental services, but not navigational equipment. Chinese manufacturing, at a less advanced stage, consists of H-shaped steel beams (used, for example, in building construction).

The Table below presents the volume of output for each category and country in a given year. It also specifies the price of each good or service in the American market, measured in U.S. dollars, in a specified base year (2005). Using the PPP method, the output of each country is valued in dollars.

**TABLE:**

**EXAMPLE OF PPP GDP — CHINA AND THE UNITED STATES**

| Output (Good or Service) ⟹ Country and Measurement | Rice | H-Shaped Steel Beams | Navigational Equipment for Long-Haul Commercial Civil Aircraft | Pediatric Dental Services for Children Age 5 Or Under |
|---|---|---|---|---|
| Volume of Output in China | 100 kilos | 500 tons | China does not make this good. It relies on imports. | 1 million dental visits (*i.e.*, the number of dental visits in China by kids age 5 or under was 10 million) |
| Volume of Output in United States | 200 kilos | The United States does not make this good domestically. It relies on imports. | 100 units | 5 million dental visits (*i.e.*, the number of dental visits in the U.S. by kids age 5 or under was 50 million) |
| Price of Output in United States, in 2005, in U.S. dollars | $10 per kilo | $100 per beam (price of imported H-beams) | $1,000 per unit | $50 per visit |
| PPP Value of Output in China | 100 × $10 = $1,000 | 500 × $100 = $50,000 | Zero, because no domestic (Chinese) production. | 1 million × $50 = $50 million |
| PPP Value of Output in United States | 200 × $10 = $2,000 | Zero, because no domestic (American) production. | 100 × $1,000 = $100,000 | 5 million × $50 = $250 million |

PPP GDP of China (Total PPP Value of Output): $50,051,000

PPP GDP of United States (Total PPP Value of Output): $250,102,000

If the comparison of the value of the output of each country is in U.S. dollars, and if China's output initially is measured in local currency at price levels prevailing in China, then the Chinese currency — the *yuan* — needs to be converted into dollars. No doubt that exchange rate, at any point in time, reflects only the goods and services China and the United States trade internationally. No doubt the exchange rate selected today might be different from the one tomorrow.

What if the *yuan* depreciates relative to the dollar after the conversion is made? Then, China's GNP — in dollar terms — will be overstated. It will have been valued at the exchange rate just before the depreciation. Conversely, if the *yuan* appreciates after the conversion, then China's dollar-denominated GNP will be understated. That output will have been valued at the lower rate, the one prevailing before the appreciation. Thus, when the comparison of China and the United States is done the next time, the results will differ — in part because of the exchange rate fluctuation that occurred since the last comparison.

Using PPP not only avoids the problem of traded versus non-traded sectors in different countries, but also helps ensure GNP comparisons are not adulterated by exchange rate fluctuations. After all, these fluctuations do not necessarily mean the real quality of life in the countries being compared has changed. At market prices, GNP, or *per capita* GNP, figures not measured in PPP terms can present a misleading picture of growth. But, getting the truest possible picture of the quality of life is what we must have if we are to draw reliable inferences about problems in less developed countries, and how (if at all) international trade law and policy can be altered to remedy the problems.

Accordingly, a PPP comparison is premised on a common set of prices in one currency. The common standard typically used by economists is dollar-denominated prices prevailing in the United States during a reference year. In the Table, the reference year is 2005. The Table sets forth the hypothesized prices prevailing in the United States during 2005, in U.S. dollars. The cells in the last row of the Table show the value of the good or service produced in the United States at those prices. The cells in the penultimate row show the value of the good or service produced in China, but the valuation is computed at those same prices. By using the common set of prices in one currency, the near-certainty that the prices of those goods and services in China, denominated in *yuan*, in 2005 were different, is immaterial. Likewise, any *yuan–*dollar exchange rate fluctuations have no effect on the valuation. The PPP GDP of each country, set forth at the bottom of the Table, simply is the sum of the cells in the row pertaining to each country.

To emphasize, because prices change from year to year with inflation or deflation, it is critical to select a particular year, such as 2005, as a basis for measurement. Comparisons of GDP (or GNP) over time would be distorted by inflation or deflation if the prices used to measure goods and services were those prevailing in the year of measurement. Thus, to measure "real" (as distinct from "nominal") GDP (either at market prices or in PPP terms), economists typically select a "base" year and stick with it. That is, they calculate the value of goods and services produced in various countries on the basis of prices from only one year.

It should not come as a surprise that when GDP and *per capita* GDP are measured in PPP terms, the differences between low- and high-income countries are compressed. After all, the output volumes of poor countries measured at price levels prevailing in the United States. Almost certainly, those levels are higher than the prices for the same goods and services in poor countries. In turn, critics of the multilateral trading system should take heed. The lot of poor people anywhere is horrific, and in least developed countries, by definition, they earn less than a dollar a day. Yet, the actual statistical gap between low- and high-income countries should not be exaggerated, and exaggerations ought not to be a basis for criticizing the trading system.

## PPP (ABSOLUTE VERSUS RELATIVE VERSION)

The term "Purchasing Power Parity" as understood by economists to refer to a theory about foreign exchange rates.

The PPP theory holds that the long-run determinant of the exchange rate between two currencies is the amount of goods and services that each currency can purchase. Consider a homogeneous basket of goods that can be traded between two countries. Assume there are no transport costs, trade barriers on those goods, or other transactions costs. What would happen if the price of the goods in one country were cheaper than the price of the same goods in the other country?

The answer is traders would engage in arbitrage, buying the basket of goods in the lower-price country and selling these goods in the higher-priced country. The traders would profit from the difference. To arbitrage, the traders would have to obtain the currency of the lower-price country, so as to pay for the goods. When they sold the goods in the higher-priced country, they would receive the currency of that country.

For example, suppose textile and apparel products sell for less in India than in the United States. Under the above assumptions, traders will obtain Indian rupees, buy those products in India, sell them in the United States, and receive dollars. When they purchase rupees, their demand for that currency bids up its price, measured against other currencies, such as the dollar. The dollars they obtain from selling the products in the American market may be what they use to buy rupees, thus implying a sale of dollars and decline in the value of the dollar against the rupee. At some point, this process should lead to an equilibrium exchange rate between the rupee and dollar.

Thus, price levels of tradable goods (here, textile and apparel products) determine the equilibrium exchange rate. That statement is the "absolute" version of the PPP theory. There also exists a "relative" version of purchasing power parity. It states changes in relative price levels determine changes in the equilibrium exchange rate. That is, starting from a particular, or base, exchange rate, the future of this rate depends on movements in the price levels in the two countries.

Arbitrage limits the extent to which prices of the products in the two countries differ, and accordingly circumscribes the difference between the exchange rates. In theory, arbitrage could wipe out all or almost all of the price difference. Under the *ceteris paribus* assumption, (*i.e.*, all other variables held constant) assumption, buying textile and apparel in India means the price of those products in the Indian market rises with the increased demand, while selling them in the American market means prices drop with the increased supply. Ultimately, a unit of a currency (*e.g.*, one U.S. dollar or the equivalent thereof in Indian rupees) should be able to pay for the same product, or basket of products, in every country in which the product is sold (*e.g.*, the United States and India). This proposition is what "parity" in "purchasing power" means. Yet, how it occurs, even in theory, is not intuitive — and thus is worthy of illustration.

Suppose U.S. $1 equals 2 Mexican pesos, and $1 buys twice as many baseballs (to take one of many tradable goods) in the United States as in Mexico. Assume $1 buys two baseballs in the United States. But, if a trader converts $1 into 2 pesos, then the trader can buy only one baseball in Mexico. That is because the price of baseballs in Mexico is 2 pesos per baseball.

There will be no demand from the United States for Mexican baseballs, because they are more expensive than the equivalent American product. But, for the same reason, there will be a demand for American baseballs. A trader can exchange 2 pesos for $1, and get two baseballs. If engaging in arbitrage, the trader then could sell the two baseballs in Mexico at a price of 2 pesos each, for a total of 4 pesos. At what exchange rate would it cease to be profitable to arbitrage, *i.e.*, to buy the cheaper American baseballs using dollars and sell them in the Mexican market to receive *pesos*? Asked differently, at what exchange rate would the price of baseballs in the United States and Mexico equalize?

The answer is when U.S. $1 equals 4 Mexican pesos. With $1, a trader could buy two baseballs in the United States. Likewise, the trader could exchange the $1 for 4 pesos. With the 4 pesos, the trader could buy two baseballs in Mexico, at a price of 2 pesos per baseball. The same basket of goods — here, two baseballs — has the same value, $1 or 4 pesos, regardless of the country, which is just another way of articulating the PPP theory — the same unit of currency ($1 or 4 pesos) buys the same goods (two baseballs). The rate of $1 to 4 pesos becomes an equilibrium rate, because any movement away from it induces traders to arbitrage.

To be sure, the price of neither baseballs nor any other product equalizes. In reality, a unit of currency cannot buy the same bundle of goods in all countries. For a number of reasons, parity in purchasing power typically is not observed. Not all products are homogeneous or tradable. Equally obvious, both transportation costs and tariffs exist. In recent decades, flows of large sums of financial capital, associated with short-term investments in stocks, bonds, and other financial instruments, not to mention in derivatives and in foreign currencies themselves, have affected exchange rates. Many examples can be found in the 1997–99 Asian financial crisis, including the affect of rapid (some critics would say speculative) shifts in funds into and out of Thailand, leading to a plummet in the *baht*. The result of such movements has been increased volatility in exchange rates. Not surprisingly, parity in purchasing power has not been a significant determinant of those rates.

The poor empirical results as regards PPP establishing equilibrium exchange rates do not affect the use of PPP when comparing economic performance of countries. In other words, the fact a unit of currency fails to buy the same bundle of goods in all countries does not mean comparisons in income measurements like Gross National Product (GNP) should be made without converting the measurements to a common currency (like U.S. dollars). The PPP comparison provides the necessary correction, setting income statistics in terms of a common set of prices and a single currency in a base year, and thus ensures the measurements are not distorted by exchange rates.

## PRECAUTIONARY PRINCIPLE

The principle that a country ought to be able to restrict or ban importation of a certain product as a precaution against the possibility the product might pose a danger to human, animal, or plant life, even though scientific evidence as to whether a danger actually exists is insufficient, inconclusive, or uncertain.

Put succinctly, it is the principle that

> in the presence of uncertainty, it is appropriate for a regulator to act *before* resolving the uncertainty, if delay might result in an irreparable harm to human or animal life or the environment.[516]

The Precautionary Principle is different from a zero-risk approach, whereby no risk whatsoever is tolerated.

Obviously, the danger with the Precautionary Principle is that it may be deployed against imports for reasons that, at bottom, are protectionist. Trade-restrictive measures can be justified by the principle only insofar as they are proportionate to the potential harm, and are implemented in a non-discriminatory and least trade-distorting manner. Because abuse of the principle can undermine free trade, the principle is not expressly recognized in the WTO *Agreement on the Application of Sanitary and Phytosanitary Measures (SPS Agreement)*, which focuses instead on sound scientific evidence.

Despite the lack of express authority in the *SPS Agreement*, Article 5:7 of the *Agreement* essentially embodies the concept of the Precautionary Principle. In the 1998 *Beef Hormones* case, the Appellate Body endorsed the concept. The European Union (EU) used the principle to ban imports of American beef treated with growth hormones, though in the *Beef Hormones* case, the Appellate Body ruled against the ban. The EU also has cited the principle in support of

---

[516] Michael J. Trebilcock & Robert Howse, *The Regulation of International Trade* 209–10 (3rd ed. 2005).

its reluctance to license the sale of genetically modified organisms (GMOs). In *Beef Hormones*, the EU challenged the premise that the *Agreement* does not allow for trade-restrictive measures on precautionary grounds. It pointed to Article 5:7, which authorizes provisional SPS measures "on the basis of available pertinent information" (*e.g.*, from international organizations or other WTO Members) in instances where "relevant scientific evidence is insufficient."

To counter accusations of protectionism, in February 2000 the EU published a definition of the Precautionary Principle. The EU said that when action is deemed necessary, *i.e.*, when it is agreed there is an unacceptably high risk for society to bear, the action must be proportionate and non-discriminatory. Moreover, the action must be based on a cost-benefit analysis of action versus inaction. The EU said the use of a trade-restrictive measure predicated on the precautionary principle should be accompanied by an identification of the burden of proof as to what scientific evidence would be necessary for a comprehensive risk assessment.

*Suggestions for Further Research:*

Book:

1.  ATAPATTU, SUMUDU, EMERGING PRINCIPLES IN INTERNATIONAL ENVIRONMENTAL LAW (2006).

Articles:

1.  Bernetich, John, Note, *Sovereignty and Regulation of Environmental Risk Under the Precautionary Principle in WTO Law*, 35 VERMONT LAW REVIEW 717–739 (2011).

2.  Kogan, Lawrence A., *The Extra-WTO Precautionary Principle: One European "Fashion" Export the United States Can Do Without*, 17 TEMPLE POLITICAL & CIVIL RIGHTS LAW REVIEW 491–604 (2008).

3.  Magee, Claire, Note, *Using Chevron as a Guide: Allowing for the Precautionary Principle in WTO Practices (Chevron U.S.A., Inc. v. NRDC, Inc., 467 U.S. 837 (1984))*, 21 GEORGETOWN INTERNATIONAL ENVIRONMENTAL LAW REVIEW 6150638 (2009).

4.  Mercurio, Bryan & Diana Shao, *A Precautionary Approach to Decision Making: The Evolving Jurisprudence on Article 5:7 of the SPS Agreement*, 2 TRADE, LAW AND DEVELOPMENT no. 2, 195–223 (fall 2010).

## PREFERENTIAL RULE OF ORIGIN

*See* Rule of Origin.

## *PRIMA FACIE* CASE

"*Prima facie*" is Latin for at first sight, thereby connoting something that is preliminary, or a view obtained before further investigation.

A general legal term that, in the context of WTO adjudication through the *Understanding on Rules and Procedures Governing the Settlement of Disputes* (*Dispute Settlement Understanding*, or *DSU*), means a complainant must, at a minimum, offer evidence and arguments that are sufficient to identify the

(1)  challenged measure, and the importance of that measure,

(2)  relevant provisions of the GATT–WTO legal regime, and obligations contained in those provisions, and

(3)  basis for the claim that the measure is inconsistent with those obligations.

The requirement of making out a *prima facie* case, and what such a case consists of, is one part of the procedural common law of the WTO Appellate Body.[517]

## PRIMARY BOYCOTT

*See* Secondary Boycott.

## PRIMARY PRODUCT

Raw crops, or basic agricultural commodities.

That is, agricultural products that are not processed. An example would be cocoa.

## PROCESSED PRODUCTS

Agricultural products that undergo processing.

An example would be chocolate, made from refining cocoa.

## PRODUCT BASKET APPROACH

Also called the "basket" approach, a strategy for negotiating reductions in tariffs on industrial products, used for the Uruguay Round Chemical Tariff Harmonization Agreement, and proposed for non-agricultural market access (NAMA) talks in the Doha Round.

---

[517] *See, e.g.*, Appellate Body Report, *United States — Measure Affecting Imports of Woven Wool Shirts and Blouses from India*, WT/DS33/AB/R at p. 16 (adopted 23 May 1997); Appellate Body Report, *Canada — Measures Affecting the Importation of Milk and the Exportation of Dairy Products — Second Recourse to Article 21:5 of the DSU by New Zealand and the United States*, WT/DS103/AB/RW2, WT/DS113/AB/RW2, at ¶ 66 (adopted 17 January 2003); Appellate Body Report, *United States — Sunset Reviews of Anti-Dumping Measures on Oil Country Tubular Goods from Argentina*, WT/DS268/AB/R, at ¶¶ 263–264 (adopted 17 December 2004); Appellate Body Report, *United States — Measures Affecting the Cross-Border Supply of Gambling and Betting Services*, WT/DS285/AB/R, at ¶ 141 (adopted 20 April 2005); Appellate Body Report, *United States — Laws, Regulations and Methodology for Calculating Dumping Margins ("Zeroing")*, WT/DS294/AB/R (adopted 9 May 2006).

In October 2010, Japan tried to kick-start NAMA negotiations by proposing a product basket approach.[518] Rather than take on large sectors, and mandate a single tariff cut for all tariff lines within a particular sector, why not divide each sector into smaller numbers of tariff lines? That would allow for different tariff reduction commitments on different lines within a single, large product sector.[519] For example, electronics could be divided into consumer goods and business goods. Japan's proposal had the benefit of tradition behind it, namely, the use of this approach for the Uruguay Round *Chemical Tariff Harmonization Agreement*.[520] Nevertheless, the proposal to use a basket approach in the Doha Round was met with confusion. Several WTO Members — including the United States — found it vague.

## PROGRAM CROP (PROGRAM CROPS)

A primary agricultural commodity eligible for a subsidy under an American Farm Bill, also called (in the plural) "commodity groups."

Major subsidies go to corn, cotton, dairy products, rice, sorghum, soybeans, sugar, and wheat. Some support is given to chickpeas, dry beans, honey, mohair, peanuts, and wool. No other crops — including fresh fruit and vegetables — receive subsidies. Over 80 percent of all United States agricultural subsidies go to program crops.

Consequently, only about 25 percent of United States farmers qualify for commodity subsidies, and among the qualifying farmers, 10 percent of them get 72 percent of the subsidies. Ironically, fresh fruits and vegetables have been the fastest growing sector in American agriculture (between 1996–2006). While these commodities are unsubsidized, they account for over 50 percent of the value of farm output (as of 2006).

Under the 2002 *Farm Bill*, which was in effect for five years, there were nine program crops. The 2007 *Farm Bill*, formally entitled the *Farm, Nutrition, and Bioenergy Act of 2007*, H.R. 2419, expands the number of program crops to 25, as follows. The direct payment prices for these crops, as applicable, also are set out below:

- Corn, 28 cents per bushel.
- Wheat, 52 cents per bushel.
- Soybeans, 44 cents per bushel.
- Oilseeds, which are separately identified as sunflower seed, rapeseed, canola, sesame, safflower, flaxseed, mustard seed, crambe, all of which are at 0.8 cents per pound.

---

[518] *See* Daniel Pruzin, *Recent Doha Efforts Yield Mixed Results; WTO Members Agree on Need to Continue*, 27 International Trade Reporter (BNA) (21 October 2010).

[519] *See* Daniel Pruzin, *U.S. Envoy Hears Positive Tone on Doha, But Actual Negotiations Are Still Missing*, 27 International Trade Reporter (BNA) 1757 (18 November 2010).

[520] *See* Daniel Pruzin, *U.S. Envoy Hears Positive Tone on Doha, But Actual Negotiations Are Still Missing*, 27 International Trade Reporter (BNA) 1757 (18 November 2010).

- Rice, $2.35 cents per hundred weight.
- Cotton, 6.67 cents per pound.
- Sugar (from beet or cane), no direct payment price, but covered by its own separate provision in the 2007 *Farm Bill*, and also protected by tariff rate quotas (TRQs).
- Peanuts, $36 per ton.
- Sorghum, 0.35 cents per bushel.
- Barley, 24 cents per bushel.
- Oats, 2.4 cents per bushel.
- Wool (sheep hair, which is a fiber used to make woolen fabric), no direct payment price, but covered by separate provisions in the 2007 *Farm Bill*.
- Mohair (goat hair, which is a fiber used to make woolen fabric), no direct payment price, but covered by separate provisions in the 2007 *Farm Bill*.
- Honey, no direct payment price, but covered by separate provisions in the 2007 *Farm Bill*.
- Dry peas (not English peas, snow peas, sugar snap peas, or other pea types), no direct payment price, but covered by separate provisions in the 2007 *Farm Bill*.
- Lentils, no direct payment price, but covered by separate provisions in the 2007 *Farm Bill*.
- Small chickpeas, no direct payment price, but covered by separate provisions in the 2007 *Farm Bill*.
- Dairy products (including butter, cheese, milk, and non-fat dry milk, but not eggs), no direct payment price, but covered by their own separate provision in the 2007 *Farm Bill*.

The direct payment subsidy is paid by the United States Department of Agriculture (USDA) to a farmer of a program crop based on the farmer's historical acreage. In other words, the direct payment is (or is supposed to be) de-coupled from production. The subsidies are paid regardless of world market prices.

Farmers of these crops are paid subsidies regardless of the downstream use of their output. Thus, for example, corn farmers are subsidized for their corn crop, even when that crop is used for high fructose corn syrup (HFCS) or ethanol. Similarly, soybean farmers receive a subsidy whether their output is used for hydrogenated vegetable or tofu. Still another example is sorghum, which is used for molasses.

Note the 2007 *Farm Bill* keeps countercyclical payments.

*Suggestions for Further Research:*

Book:

1.   POLLAN, MICHAEL, THE OMNIVORE'S DILEMMA: A NATURAL HISTORY OF FOUR MEALS (2006).

Other Source:

1. OXFAM AMERICA, FAIRNESS IN THE FIELDS: A VISION FOR THE 2007 FARM BILL (2006).

## PROSPECTIVE NORMAL VALUE (PROSPECTIVE NORMAL VALUE SYSTEM)

A method for assessing liability for antidumping (AD) duties.

In a prospective normal value system, the relevant governmental authority announces a "Prospective Normal Value" before collecting any AD duties. The Prospective Normal Value applies to future entries of subject merchandise. The authority assesses AD duties on the basis of the difference between Prospective Normal Value and the prices of individual export transactions (*i.e.*, Export Price or Constructed Export Price) for the merchandise. In a prospective normal value system, an exporter or foreign producer may decide to raise its Export Prices to the level of Prospective Normal Value, and thereby avoid liability for payment of an AD duty on each export transaction for which it raised Export Price. While a refund of any excess duties occurs later, following Article 9:3:2 of the *Antidumping Agreement*, in a prospective normal value system, liability for payment of AD duties is final at the time of importation of subject merchandise.

The Appellate Body discussed, albeit briefly, prospective normal value systems in its 2007 *Japan Zeroing* Appellate Body Report. *See United States — Measures Relating to Zeroing and Sunset Reviews*, WT/DS294/AB/R at ¶¶148–154 (adopted 23 January 2007) (complaint by Japan). In this kind of system, does the AD duty collected at the time of importation represent a "margin of dumping?" Can the total amount of AD duties levied in such a system exceed the "margin of dumping" for an exporter or foreign producer? To both questions, the Appellate Body said, the answer is "no."

The Panel reasoned that in a prospective normal value system, liability to pay AD duties is incurred only to the extent that prices of individual export transactions are less than Normal Value. Therefore, thought the Panel, under Article 9:4(ii) of the *Antidumping Agreement*, the concept of "dumping" and a "margin of dumping" can apply on a transaction-specific basis to a price of an individual export transaction that is below Normal Value. Moreover, in a prospective normal value system, liability for an AD duty is triggered whenever the price of an individual export transaction is below the Prospective Normal Value, regardless of other export transactions in which the price exceeds Prospective Normal Value. That was a kind of zeroing — disregarding transactions above the benchmark of Prospective Normal Value. Why, then, asked the Panel, should zeroing be forbidden in a retrospective system, such as that used by the United States?

In over-ruling the Panel, the Appellate Body gave a simple answer: in both prospective and retrospective systems, duty liability may be assessed on a transaction-specific basis, but the margin of dumping must be established in accordance with Article 2 of the *Antidumping Agreement*; that margin is the ceiling for the amount of AD duties that can be collected in respect of sales made by an individual exporter or foreign producer; and duties paid in excess of that ceiling may be claimed by the importer as a refund. In sum, the Agreement is neutral as to whether a WTO Member should adopt a prospective or retrospective system for the collection of AD duties, favoring neither over the other. The critical disciplines are on the establishment of the dumping margin for an exporter or foreign producer, the use of that margin as a ceiling on collection of duties associated with sales made by that exporter or foreign producer, and the entitlement of an importer to a refund of excess duties.

## PROTECTIONIST ABUSE

A term to connote the abuse of a trade remedy for a protectionist purpose.

To be sure, all trade remedies — when imposed — afford protection to a domestic producer of a product that is like the merchandise subject to the remedy. However, "protectionist abuse" suggests some producers have lost their international competitive advantage, *i.e.*, they are no longer cost-competitive in the global marketplace. Accordingly, imposition of a trade remedy is at odds with free trade theory.

What kind of petitioner is the "protectionist abuser"? The profile is a petitioner that has lost its comparative advantage in manufacturing merchandise vis-à-vis a respondent that makes the like product. The petitioner is unwilling or unable to reduce its cost structure to meet global competitive pressures, fails to incorporate technological innovations in its manufacturing process and product design, or is insensitive to changes in consumer tastes. Its strategy for survival is to restore the *status quo ante* by raising the cost of imported merchandise.

Imposition of an antidumping (AD) duty on the imports achieves the goal. To a lesser extent, filing the petition serves this goal. The petition itself harasses the competitive respondent, generates uncertainty about the respondent's future prices and liabilities, and raises the respondent's legal fees. Litigation in domestic courts may drag on for over a decade, thereby enabling a petitioner to delay final liquidation of entries of merchandise. Thus, Judge Richard Richard Posner writes:

> Of course, the concerns that actually animate anti-dumping, countervailing-duty, and other measures directed against allegedly "unfair" trade practices of foreign producers go far beyond a concern with predatory pricing. *The dominant concern is to protect U.S. industry from foreign producers that have genuinely lower costs, whether because they pay lower wages, incur fewer pollution-control and other regulatory costs, are better managed, have better workers, or have more modern plants and equipment.* Policies so motivated are called "protectionist"....[521]

---

[521] RICHARD A. POSNER, ECONOMIC ANALYSIS OF LAW 310–11 (4th ed. 1992) (emphasis added).

The petitioner eagerly manipulates the calculation of a dumping margin to maximize that margin, and exploits permissive injury and causation standards, to support its dubious claim.

In effect, "protectionist abuse" means the petitioner seeks governmental assistance — the AD law — to negate the economic law of comparative advantage with respect to specific merchandise. Whenever the government obliges, it gives greater priority to the interests of the inefficient petitioner than to the importing country (not to mention the global economy) as a whole. Professor Dam explains:

> Local firms suffer "injury" (in the sense that they make less, or lose more, money than they otherwise would) whenever the import price is the same or lower than the price they charge. *That injury is no greater when dumping is present than when the import price merely reflects the comparative advantage of the exporter.* But it is only when consumers in another country are charged a higher price that this injury triggers government action under antidumping laws. And this government action normally occurs, unless the "injury" criterion is unusually stringently construed, *whatever the level of efficiency of local firms. Indeed, the less efficient the local firms, or the greater their local monopoly, the more easily the requisite injury can be shown (even though the local consumer's need for the low-priced goods is comparatively greater.)*[522]

In contrast, a "meritorious" AD action is — or should be — one that involves predatory dumping.

That is, a petitioner should demonstrate that an exporter sells merchandise in the petitioner's market at below the exporter's average variable cost of production. The exporter seeks to drive the petitioner out of business and perhaps ultimately gain a monopoly position in an importing country. The petition has "merit" because absent predatory dumping, the petitioner would be a financially robust and competitive company. Consequently, the petitioner, along with consumers of its product, are at risk.

To differentiate a protectionist abuser from meritorious petitioner, AD law must be clear and unequivocal. A protectionist abuser is sure to exploit ambiguities. Arguably, neither the WTO *Antidumping Agreement*, nor implementing legislation such as the United States *Uruguay Round Agreements Act of 1994*, meets this criterion.

## PSE

Producer Support Estimate.

A measure used by the Organization for Economic Cooperation and Development (OECD) to determine the extent of governmental assistance to

---

[522] KENNETH W. DAM, THE GATT — LAW AND INTERNATIONAL ECONOMIC ORGANIZATION 168–69 (1970) (emphasis added).

the agricultural sector. Essentially, PSE is the amount of government aid to farmers as a percentage of total farm revenue, that is, total support as a percentage of total farm receipts. In effect, PSE measures how much of a farmer's income comes from the government, aggregated across a country. PSE includes not only budgetary payments to farmers, via direct funding and other subsidies, but also market price support, such as guaranteed prices and protection through tariffs.[523]

Between 2003 and 2005, the PSE for the OECD countries averaged 30 percent, meaning that government subsidies and other kinds of support accounted for a third of all farm revenue in the developed world. However, in non-OECD countries — which, of course, are relatively poor — the average PSE tends to be lower. During the same period, it was three percent in Ukraine, five percent in Brazil, and eight percent in Bulgaria, China, and South Africa. In Russia, PSE was 17 percent. Romania (part of the European Union (EU)) had a PSE of 27 percent. In other words, the unsurprising pattern is that PSE tends to be higher in richer countries. However, the OECD has noted that, given concerns about adverse effects of globalization on their farmers, PSEs in some developing countries have trended upward.

In its July 2010 report, *Agricultural Policies in OECD Countries*, the OECD reported the PSE for OECD countries rose to $252.5 billion, or 22 percent, in 2009, an increase from 21 percent in 2008 and the same as in 2007.[524] It was the first increase since 2004, occurring because declines in agricultural commodity prices following record highs in 2008 triggered government support programs that stabilize domestic prices and farm incomes. The PSEs for 2009 for certain OECD members was:

- Canada, 20 percent, an increase from 13 percent in 2008
- EU, 24 percent, an increase from 22 percent in 2008
- Korea, 52 percent, an increase from 46 percent in 2008
- Norway, 66 percent, in increase from 60 percent in 2008
- Switzerland, 63 percent, an increase from 57 percent in 2008
- United States, 10 percent, an increase from eight percent in 2008

Notably, because Australia ended exceptional payments associated with the restructuring of its dairy industry, its PSE fell between 2008 and 2009.

Notably, in its September 2011 report, the OECD said the PSE for China had risen by more than 40 percent in 2010, to a total of over $147 billion.[525] In contrast, in 2010, the total EU farm support budget was $101 billion, and the total American budget was $25.5 billion. China, then, easily is one of the

---

[523] *See* Daniel Pruzin, *China Reports Agriculture Subsidies for 2005–2008 Well Under WTO Limits*, 28 International Trade Reporter (BNA) 1701 (20 October 2011).

[524] Rick Mitchell, *OECD Says Market-Distorting Subsidies to Rich-Nation Farmers Still a Problem in '09*, 27 International Trade Reporter (BNA) 1025 (8 July 2010).

[525] *See* Daniel Pruzin, *China Reports Agriculture Subsidies for 2005–2008 Well Under WTO Limits*, 28 International Trade Reporter (BNA) 1701 (20 October 2011).

largest — if not the largest — agricultural subsidizers in the world. The reasons for the increase in Chinese farm subsidies in 2010 are two-fold: the Chinese Communist Party (CCP) spent more on market price support, and the Chinese currency (the *renminbi* (*RMB*), or *yuan*) appreciated relative to the U.S. dollar (thus making expenditures denominated in RMN translate into more dollars).

*Suggestions for Further Research:*

Other Source:

1.  ORGANIZATION FOR ECONOMIC COOPERATION AND DEVELOPMENT (OECD), AGRICULTURAL POLICIES IN NON-OECD COUNTRIES (March 2007).

# PSI

Pre-shipment inspection.

The practice of checking the details of shipments of imports (*e.g.*, price, quantity, and quality) before exportation. Specifically, PSI is

> an examination, on behalf of a foreign government or other contracting principal, of the quality and quantity of goods exported to that country or principal and an evaluation of whether or not the transaction value of the goods corresponds, within acceptable limits, to the export market price generally prevailing in the country of origin of the goods. The examination is conducted by private inspection companies [known as pre-shipment inspection, or PSI, companies] retained for that purpose by the governments of many developing countries to perform quantity and quality inspections and price comparisons on their imports. These inspections are generally conducted within the country of export [*e.g.*, at a seaport or airport].[526]

*Suggestions for Further Research:*

Books:

1.  CROOME, JOHN, RESHAPING THE WORLD TRADING SYSTEM 16, 51–2, 99, 189–93, 280, 297–99 (1995).

2.  STEWART, TERENCE P., ED., THE GATT URUGUAY ROUND: A NEGOTIATING HISTORY (1986–1992) vol. I 715-38 (1993).

Book Chapters:

1.  Sandstrom, Mark R., Julia M. Cheung & Michele D. Lynch, *Market Access, in* THE WORLD TRADE ORGANIZATION 117, 127–30 (Terence P. Stewart ed. 1996).

---

[526] TERENCE P. STEWART ED., THE GATT URUGUAY ROUND: A NEGOTIATING HISTORY (1986–1992) vol. I 738-39 (1993).

## PSRO

Product-specific rule of origin.

Many of the free trade agreements (FTAs) to which the United States is a party, including the *North American Free Trade Agreement* (*NAFTA*) and recent agreements, rely heavily on PSROs.

## PROSPECTIVE ASSESSMENT (PROSPECTIVE REMEDY)

*See* Retrospective Assessment (Retrospective Remedy).

## PTA (FIRST MEANING)

Preferential Trading Agreement, Preferential Trading Area, or Preferential Trading Arrangement.

These three phraseologies are synonymous. PTA, in effect, is a synonym for a regional trade agreement (RTA), but not to be confused with Plurilateral Trade Agreement.

*Suggestions for Further Research:*

Book:

1.   SALLY, RAZEEN, NEW FRONTIERS IN FREE TRADE — GLOBALIZATION'S FUTURE AND ASIA'S RISING ROLE (2008).

Articles:

1.   Bowman, Gregory W., *The Domestic and International Policy Implications of "Deep" versus "Broad" Preferential Trade Agreements*, 19 INDIANA INTERNATIONAL & COMPARATIVE LAW REVIEW 497–527 (2009).

2.   Chaisse, Julien, Debashis Chakraborty & Biswajit Nag, *The Three-Pronged Strategy of India's Preferential Trade Policy: A Contribution to the Study of Modern Economic Treaties*, 26 CONNECTICUT JOURNAL OF INTERNATIONAL LAW 415–455 (2011).

3.   Mansfield, Edward D., & Helen V. Milner, *Regime Type, Veto Points, and Preferential Trading Arrangements*, 46 STANFORD JOURNAL OF INTERNATIONAL LAW 219–242 (2010).

4.   Maruyama, Warren H., *Preferential Trade Arrangements and the Erosion of the WTO's MFN Principle*, 46 STANFORD JOURNAL OF INTERNATIONAL LAW 177–197 (2010).

5.   Patel, Monica, Note, *Expanding the Role of Trade Preference Programs*, 95 MINNESOTA LAW REVIEW 1490–1523 (2011).

6.   Srinivasan, T.N., *Global Trading System: Decline of Nondiscrimination and Rise of Preferential Trade Arrangements and Agreements*, 46 STANFORD JOURNAL OF INTERNATIONAL LAW 199–217 (2010).

7.   Sykes, Alan O., *The Law, Economics, and Politics of Preferential Trading Arrangements: An Introduction*, 46 STANFORD JOURNAL OF INTERNATIONAL LAW 171–175 (2010).

## PTA (SECOND MEANING)

Plurilateral Trade Agreement.

The agreements and associated legal instruments reached during the Uruguay Round that entered into force on 1 January 1995, but which have been accepted only by some Members. The Plurilateral Trade Agreements are binding only on the Members that accept them. According to Article II:3 of the *Agreement Establishing the World Trade Organization (WTO Agreement)*, and Annex 4 to that *Agreement*, the Plurilateral Trade Agreements are:

- *Agreement on Trade in Civil Aircraft*
- *Agreement on Government Procurement (GPA)*
- *International Dairy Agreement*
- *International Bovine Meat Agreement.*

In September 1997, the WTO decided to dissolve the *Dairy* and *Bovine Meat Agreements*, which initially had come into effect in 1980 after the Tokyo Round. The Uruguay Round made these two PTAs obsolete. In particular, the Uruguay Round *Agreements on Agriculture* and the *Application of Sanitary and Phytosanitary Standards (SPS Agreement)*, and the WTO committees working on SPS and agricultural matters, covered the matters dealt with under these PTAs. Thus, the *Dairy* and *Bovine Meat Agreements* expired at the end of 1997.

The *Dairy Agreement* created an International Dairy Council, which established minimum export prices for trade in milk fat (including butter), milk powders, and some types of cheese. The Council's members were Argentina, Bulgaria, Chad, the European Union (EU), Japan, New Zealand, Norway, Romania, Switzerland, and Uruguay. Its price-setting proved ineffectual, because the United States, a major dairy exporter, was not a party to the agreement. Thus, the Council stopped setting these prices in 1995. Under the Bovine Meat Agreement, an International Meat Council was created, whose members were Argentina, Australia, Brazil, Bulgaria, Canada, Chad, Colombia, the EU, Japan, New Zealand, Norway, Paraguay, Romania, South Africa, Switzerland, and Uruguay. The Council served as a forum for discussing trade in meat. Like the Dairy Council, however, its effectiveness was limited by the absence of the United States.

There are two species of Plurilateral Agreements: open versus closed. With an "open" deal, all of the benefits created by the deal extend immediately and unconditionally to every WTO Member, regardless of whether the Member is a signatory to the deal and assumes its obligations. Such benefits include market access, so with an open arrangement, a non-signatory gets the benefit of the liberalized market access provided by the deal, even though that non-signatory makes no market access concessions of its own. In effect, an open deal applies the obligation of immediate, unconditional MFN treatment to all Members.

With a "closed" deal, only participants (that is, signatories) to the deal are entitled to its benefits. Unless a Member signs the deal and makes market opening concessions of its own, it cannot make use of any market access provisions of the deal. Thus, a closed Plurilateral Agreement forbids free ridership. It adheres to the MFN obligation in an immediate, but conditional way: the condition is that only a Member that is a party to the accord gets its benefits.

Both species are found among WTO texts: the *GPA* is closed, as is the 1979 *Agreement on Trade in Civil Aircraft* (and both are in Annex 4 to the *WTO Agreement*), while the *ITA* is open. As for the 1997 *Agreement on Financial Services* and 1997 *Agreement on Telecommunications*, both of which are post-Uruguay Round deals negotiated under the auspices of the *General Agreement on Trade in Services (GATS)*, they fit the open pattern. Under these 1997 *Agreements*, MFN treatment is extended immediately and unconditionally to all Members, unless a specific exemption is invoked under *GATS* rules. Note that *GATS* Article II:1 calls for immediate, unconditional MFN treatment, though Article II:2 allows a Member to derogate from that obligation by scheduling exemptions (in yet another appendix, the *Annex on Article II (MFN) Exemptions*). The *Annex on Financial Services* (specifically, Paragraph 1 of the *Second Annex*) also respects the general *GATS* MFN rule of Article II, but allows for derogations from MFN treatment, and the *Annex on Telecommunications* (in footnote 15) refers to the general *GATS* MFN rule.

## PTA (THIRD MEANING)

Peoples Trade Agreement.

*See* TCP.

## PTO

The United States Patent and Trademark Office.

The PTO handles applications for patents, trademarks, and service marks. Accepted applications are registered with the PTO. Copyrights are dealt with and registered by the Copyright Office of the Library of Congress.

## *PTPA*

*Peru Trade Promotion Agreement*, which entered into force on 1 February 2009.

The *PTPA* is the *United States — Peru Free Trade Agreement*. The United States Congress passed implementing legislation for the *PTPA*, the *United States — Peru Trade Promotion Agreement Implementation Act*, H.R. 3688, 110th Congress, 1st Session, 13 November 2007, in 2007. (The House of Representatives passed the Act 285–132 in November 2007, and the Senate did so the following month by a 77–18 vote. President George W. Bush signed the *Act* into law on 14 December 2007). The *PTPA* is the second free trade agreement (FTA) between the United States and a country in South America, the 2004 Chile FTA being the first such accord.

## PUBLIC CHOICE THEORY

A theory about the behavior of public officials based on economic insights.

In effect, Public Choice Theory is the application of microeconomic analysis to political behavior. The Theory has application to international trade law and policy.

As Professor Sykes explains, Public Choice Theory

> suggests that policymaking under democratic government depends on the interplay of special interest forces in the political "marketplace." There is generally no reason to expect the democratic process system- atically to yield "efficient," "equitable," or otherwise "correct" outcomes by any idealized criterion for measuring the success of policy. Rather, elected officials will pursue their self interest. They will "supply" policy initiatives to interest groups that "demand" them, with the currency of the political marketplace in the form of votes or campaign contribu- tions, for instance. Ultimately, well-organized groups — those most adept at lobbying and most capable of "paying" for policy initiatives — will have their interests vindicated, while diffuse, poorly organized interest groups may suffer.
>
> ...
>
> Public choice [theory] predicts that elected officials will concern them- selves far more with the impact of trade policy on producer interests than on consumer interests. Individual firms in import-competing or export-oriented industries often have much to gain from specific trade policy measures. And, especially in industries with a relatively small number of large firms, free-rider problems need not seriously impede efforts to influence policy, either because each firm has sufficient incen- tive to act individually or because interested firms can organize them- selves to act collectively through a trade association or lobbying coalition. In contrast, the number of consumers is large and the amount at stake for each consumer on a given trade issue is modest. Consequently, the costs to each consumer of acting individually in an effort to influ- ence the political process will usually exceed the potential gains. Thus, severe free-rider problems will often thwart the task of organizing con- sumers to act collectively to support liberal trade policies.[527]

Thus, the Theory predicts a politician will focus on concerns of producers adversely impacted by trade liberalization as opposed to consumers beneficially affected by such liberalization.

---

[527] Alan O. Sykes, *Protectionism as a "Safeguard": A Positive Analysis of the GATT "Escape Clause" with Normative Speculations*, 58 UNIVERSITY OF CHICAGO LAW REVIEW 255, 275–76 (1991).

# PUDD

Potentially Uncollectible Dumping Duties.

This term is used in United States antidumping (AD) law, specifically in the Department of Commerce (DOC) *Antidumping Manual*. The *Manual* defines PUDD as follows:

> The PUDD is the amount of dumping duties that would have been col-
> lected from the U.S. sales under investigated [*sic*] [*i.e.*, of the subject
> merchandise] had an antidumping duty order been in effect during the
> period [of] investigation (*i.e.*, before the investigation began). The
> PUDD is used to establish a dumping margin which will remain in
> effect until the annual reviews established [*sic*] rates based upon the
> entries for which liquidation was suspended pursuant to the prelimi-
> nary determination and for the year following the Antidumping Duty
> Order. ... The calculation of the PUDD is, in effect, a two-step process.
> First, PUDD is determined for each U.S. sale by multiplying the per
> unit dollar margin for that sale by the total number of items sold.
> Second, the PUDD for each of the U.S. sales are [*sic*] summed to arrive
> at a total PUDD. The total PUDD is then used to calculate a weighted–
> average margin for the investigation. . . .[528]

Essentially, "PUDD" is an acronym for the "dumping margin," and tends to be employed in the context of calculating a weighted average dumping margin.

To appreciate the above definition, it is important to recall that the United States AD duty remedy applies on a retrospective basis. That is, AD duty liability attaches at the time of entry of subject merchandise, even though duties are not actually imposed at that time, because the investigation has not been completed. Following a preliminary affirmative dumping margin determination, the DOC issues an order to Customs and Border Protection (CBP) to collect security, namely, a cash deposit or bond, to cover estimated AD duties, and to suspend liquidation of entries of subject merchandise. The DOC determines the final AD duty due, relating back to the time of entry, later on, at the final dumping margin determination stage and through annual Administrative Reviews upon request of an interested party.

*Suggestions for Further Research:*

Book:

1.   CZAKO, JUDITH, JOHANN HUMAN & JORGE MIRANDA, A HANDBOOK ON ANTI-
DUMPING INVESTIGATIONS (2003).

# PURCHASING POWER PARITY

*See* PPP, PPP (Absolute versus Relative Version).

---

[528] U.S. DEPARTMENT OF COMMERCE, IMPORT ADMINISTRATION, ANTI-DUMPING MANUAL, Chapter 6, at 9 (1997 ed.). The *Manual* is available on the DOC website at http://ia.ita. doc.gov.

# Q

## QIZ

Qualified Industrial Zone.

Products originating in a QIZ are eligible for preferential legal treatment. That treatment may take the form of tax benefits, employment rules, or duty-free treatment.

For example, through H.R. 3074, *West Bank and Gaza Strip Free Trade Benefits*, Pub. L. No. 104-234, approved 2 October 1996, Congress amended the *United States–Israel Free Trade Area Implementation Act of 1985*, Pub. L. No. 99-47, 99 Stat. 82. The amendment provides for duty-free treatment to articles from designated industrial parks between West Bank and Israel, and Gaza Strip and Israel, and from Qualified Industrial Zones (QIZs) between Israel and Jordan and Egypt and Jordan. This amendment followed two significant developments.

First, on 17 October 1995, the United States, Israel, and Palestinian Authority exchanged letters agreeing to the elimination of duties on articles originating in the West Bank and Gaza Strip. The Palestinian Authority made three pledges:

(1) To give American products duty-free access.

(2) To prevent illegal transshipment of non-Israeli and non-Palestinian origin goods, which are ineligible for duty-free treatment.

(3) To support every effort at ending the Arab economic boycott of Israel.

Second, in May 1996, the United States and Israel agreed to an amendment of their free trade agreement (FTA) whereby they established "Qualified Industrial Zones" (QIZs) between Jordan and Israel. QIZs also exist between Israel and Egypt. The QIZs were designed to rectify the discriminatory effects of the *FTA* on Palestinians.

Thus, the United States accords articles originating in designated industrial parks and QIZs receive the same tariff treatment as Israeli products under the *FTA*. Obviously, these benefits are designed to encourage Arab–Israeli economic and social cooperation. Preferential rules of origin are a legal device for this encouragement. The same preferential rules of origin as exist in the *United States–Israel FTA* apply to all products from the industrial parks or QIZs. However, there must be minimum amount of Israeli, Palestinian, Jordanian, or Egyptian content to qualify for duty free treatment.

Between 1996 and June 2005, the United States designated 10 QIZs in Jordan. The first such Zone grew from 1,800 employees and eight firms when it was established in 1998 to 7,000 employees and 50 firms by June 2005.

# QR

Quantitative restriction.

A generic term covering a wide array of non-tariff barrier to trade. The most prominent examples of QRs include quotas, and import or export licenses. Tariff rate quotas (TRQs) have features of both tariffs and quotas, but generally are considered tariff barriers.

*Suggestions for Further Research:*

Article:

1.   Derlén, Mattias & Johan Lindholm, *Article 28 E.C. and Rules on Use: A Step Towards A Workable Doctrine on Measures Having Equivalent Effect to Quantitative Restrictions*, 16 COLUMBIA JOURNAL OF EUROPEAN LAW 191-231 (2010).

# QUALIFIED MAJORITY VOTING

A term frequently arising in the context of decision making in the European Union (EU), to connote that decisions are taken by majority vote, but certain parties have more votes than others.

In the EU context, it means the voting weight given to a member state in the Council of the European Union depends on the population (*i.e.*, number of inhabitants) and size (*i.e.*, economic and political significance) of that member state. Most legislation of the Council on Common Agricultural Policy (CAP) matters is considered under qualified majority voting.

# QUOTA

A quota is a control on the quantity of a specific class of merchandise that can be imported or exported lawfully during a certain period. Usually, that period is one year.

Once the stated limit of a particular good is reached, the import or export of further units is prohibited. Indeed, these restrictions are strictly quantitative in nature and hold no more than a specified amount of a particular good may be permitted entry or exported during the relevant period.

A quota may appear in two forms. First, it may be global, whereby a control is placed on the entire world supply of a particular good. Second, the quota could be country-specific. That is, a quota could limit the export or import of a particular class of goods to or from any country or countries. The forms are not mutually exclusive. An importing country could maintain a global quota, giving country-specific share allocations in the quota to individual exporting countries.

To be sure, quotas are seen as protectionist because they serve as a non-tariff barrier to trade. Accordingly, GATT Articles XI and XIII strictly regulate quotas and other quantitative restrictions.

*Suggestions for Further Research:*

Books:

1. BERGSTEN, FRED, KIMBERLY ELLIOTT, JEFFREY SCHOTT & WENDY TAKACS, AUCTION QUOTAS AND UNITED STATES TRADE POLICY (1987).

2. JACKSON, JOHN H., WORLD TRADE AND THE LAW OF GATT § 13.1 at 305–06 (1969).

3. MATSUSHITA, MITSUO, THOMAS J. SCHOENBAUM & PETROS C. MAVROIDS, THE WORLD TRADE ORGANISATION — LAW, PRACTICE AND POLICY 123–24 (2003).

## QUOTA RENT

The difference between the (1) price of a commodity without the application of a quota (*i.e.*, the unencumbered market equilibrium price), and (2) price of that commodity resulting from quota restrictions.

These restrictions, which may exist on imports or production, almost invariably drive up the internal (*i.e.*, domestic) price of the product in question by restricting the supply of that product. (Only if the quota level is set above market demand would the quota price not rise above the market price.) The price differential is captured by the enterprises and individuals receiving government authorization to import or produce the good.

# R

## R & D

Research and Development.

## RAM

Recently Acceded Member.

The term refers to a new Member of the WTO, though in principle could apply to other international bodies. As of March 2007, the RAMs and their dates of accession to the WTO, are:

| | |
|---|---|
| • Albania | 8 September 2000 |
| • Armenia | 5 February 2003 |
| • China (People's Republic of) | 11 December 2001 |
| • Croatia | 30 November 2000 |
| • Ecuador | 1 January 1996 |
| • Jordan | 11 April 2000 |
| • Kingdom of Saudi Arabia | 11 December 2005 |
| • Kyrgyzstan (Kyrgyz Republic) | 20 December 1998 |
| • Macedonia (Former Yugoslav Republic of Macedonia (FYROM)) | 4 April 2003 |
| • Moldova | 26 July 2001 |
| • Oman | 9 November 2000 |
| • Panama | 6 September 1997 |
| • Taiwan (Chinese Taipei) | 1 January 2002 |
| • Vietnam | 11 January 2007 |

During the Doha Round, RAMs called for special and differential treatment above and beyond what might be provided to developing countries in any final multilateral trade deal.[529]

Note the early date of 1 January 1996, when Ecuador acceded to the WTO. Other countries, such as the United Arab Emirates (UAE), acceded after that date, but are not considered RAMs.

*Suggestions for Further Research:*

Article:

1.   Gao, Henry, *China's Participation in the WTO: A Lawyer's Perspective*, 11 SINGAPORE YEAR BOOK OF INTERNATIONAL LAW 1–34 (2007).

---

[529] *See* Daniel Pruzin, *China, Other New WTO Members Seek Special Terms on Farm Tariff, Subsidy Cuts*, 24 International Trade Reporter (BNA) 369 (15 March 2007).

## RCC

United States — Canada Regulatory Cooperation Council.

*See* HLRCC.

## REACH

Registration, Evaluation, Authorization, and Restriction of Chemicals, known as REACH formed from the shortened name Registration, Evaluation, and Authorization of Chemicals.

REACH is regulatory legislation passed by the European Union (EU) effective 1 June 2007, requiring registration of essentially all chemicals for use in the EU, whether imported or made in the EU.[530] The legislation is Regulation (EC) No. 1907/2006 of the European Parliament and of the Council of 18 December 2006. The legislation established a regulatory agency, the European Chemicals Agency (ECHA), based in Helsinki, Finland, to implement REACH and process registration applications submitted by the chemical manufacturers' industry for the chemicals it uses. Registration applications were required beginning in 2008. Preregistration took place between 1 June 2008 and 1 December 2008. During that period companies were required to pre-register chemical substances in order to benefit from an extended phase-in period for full registration. A failure to preregister meant companies could not continue to manufacture or import substances until submission of a full registration dossier.[531] The EHCA received 2.2 million preregistrations, covering 100,000 substances, during the preregistration period.[532] Full registration deadlines for preregistered chemicals will take place in 2010, 2013 or 2018 depending on the production volume and toxicity of a substance.[533]

The overall goal of REACH is to increase human safety and protect the environment. REACH requires companies to demonstrate they have used the safest chemical in their manufacturing processes. If a safer chemical exists that is equivalent to the chemical being used, REACH obligates companies to commit to substituting the safer chemical for the less safe chemical. Also, REACH distinguishes between existing and new chemicals. The cutoff date for an existing chemical is any chemical commercially available in the EU before and including 1981. New chemicals are those sold after 1981.

---

[530] *See* Arthur Rogers, *European Parliament Passes REACH; Enactment Expected by End of Year*, 23 International Trade Reporter (BNA) 1798–1799 (21 December 2006).

[531] *See* Stephen Gardner, *REACH Preregistration Period Closes with Far More Notifications Than Expected*, 25 International Trade Reporter (BNA) 1750 (11 December 2008).

[532] *See* Stephen Gardner, *REACH Preregistration Period Closes with Far More Notifications Than Expected*, 25 International Trade Reporter (BNA) 1750 (11 December 2008).

[533] *See* Pat Rizzuto, *EU Agency Lists Nearly 40,000 Chemicals as Preregistered Under REACH Regulation*, 25 International Trade Reporter (BNA) 1488 (16 October 2008).

Specifically, REACH targets toxic or dangerous chemicals, existing and new, that cause health hazards, characterized as "substances of very high concern." These include:

- CMRs — carcinogens that are mutagenic (causing genetic mutations) or reprotoxic (causing infertility and affecting future generations).

- PBTs — chemicals that are persistent (linger in the body not expelled), bio-accumulative (collect in human tissue), and are toxic.

- vPvBs — chemicals which are very persistent, and very bio-accumulative.

The "substances of very high concern" are compiled on a "candidate list." The substances on the candidate list totaled 38 as of June 2010. ECHA expects to add 40 substances to the list in 2011.[534] By 2012 the list is expected to total 136 substances and by 2020 could total 500.[535] Substances on the candidate list can be formally prioritized for restriction, and the continued use of the substance will only be allowed if specific authorization is granted. Furthermore, it is required that the restricted substance is eventually replaced with a safer alternative. Also, the substance can be out right banned. Entering substances on the candidate list is a step towards outlawing the most dangerous chemicals.[536]

Once a substance is included on the candidate list, suppliers and retailers of the substance are required to provide safety data for products that contain the substance to their customers. Manufacturers of products that contain the substance are required to provide safe-use information to consumers upon request. Finally, importers or producers of products containing the substance must notify ECHA of their use of the substance.[537] However, the European Environmental Bureau (EEB), a European federation of advocacy groups, found that retailers are failing to comply with requests for safety data as required under REACH. EEB sent 158 safety data requests to 60 retailers and received answers to only half of the requests. Furthermore, answers conformed to REACH requirements in only 22 percent of the responses.[538] Under REACH, a request for information should be answered ". . .within 45 days, should detail any SVHCs *(substances of very high concern)* contained in a product, and should provide information on safe use of the product."[539]

---

[534] *See* Stephen Gardner, *EU Agency Says Listing of Chemicals for Bans Under REACH to Increase in 2011*, 27 International Trade Reporter (BNA) 1554 (14 October 2010).

[535] *See* Stephen Gardner, *EU Commission Says up to 500 Chemicals Could be Restricted Under REACH by 2020*, 27 International Trade Reporter (BNA) 823 (3 June 2010).

[536] *See* Stephen Gardner, *EU Agency Says Listing of Chemicals for Bans Under REACH to Increase in 2011*, 27 International Trade Reporter (BNA) 1554 (14 October 2010).

[537] *See* Stephen Gardner, *EU Agency Says Listing of Chemicals for Bans Under REACH to Increase in 2011*, 27 International Trade Reporter (BNA) 1554 (14 October 2010).

[538] *See* Stephen Gardner, *Retailers Fail REACH Product Information Test, EU Environmental Federation Says*, 27 International Trade Reporter (BNA) 1596 (21 October 2010).

[539] Stephen Gardner, *Retailers Fail REACH Product Information Test, EU Environmental Federation Says*, 27 International Trade Reporter (BNA) 1596 (21 October 2010).

Enforcement of such measures is the responsibility of individual member states. However, penalties for violations of REACH vary widely from member state to member state. Fines are the most common penalty and maximum fines range from less than €5,000 in Latvia and Lithuania to €55 million in Belgium.[540] Countries are also not in agreement on the use of criminal or administrative penalties or both to enforce REACH. Finally, in some countries, the potential fine incurred for a violation is not high enough to match what it costs to comply with REACH.[541]

REACH is highly controversial legislation. It has created concerns for foreign chemical manufacturers and their EU importing counterparts.[542] Among the outstanding issues are who should submit applications to REACH for registration of chemicals, what recourse a foreign company might have against an adverse ECHA decision, and the fees charged by the European Commission to companies that seek to register a chemical (especially in respect of claims of confidentiality as to commercially valuable data). The European Commission is required to review the scope and implementation of REACH by 1 June 2012 and will make proposals to revise REACH if necessary, at that time.[543]

*Suggestions for Further Research:*

Articles:

1.   Brownfield, David, Comment, *Reform of U.S. Chemicals Regulations May Not be Out of REACH*, 21 Pacific McGeorge Global Business & Development Law Journal 223–249 (2008).

2.   Motaal, Doaa Abdel, *Reaching REACH: The Challenge for Chemicals Entering International Trade*, 12 Journal of International Economic Law 643–662 (2009).

3.   Rieger, RA Eric, *Turning Reach into Practice — First Experiences in Setting Up Consortia*, 10 Business Law International number 2, 166–182 (May 2009).

---

[540] *See* Stephen Gardner, *Penalties for REACH Violations Vary Widely Among EU Member Countries, Report Finds*, 27 International Trade Reporter (BNA) 667 (6 May 2010).

[541] *See* Stephen Gardner, *Penalties for REACH Violations Vary Widely Among EU Member Countries, Report Finds*, 27 International Trade Reporter (BNA) 667 (6 May 2010).

[542] *See* Pat Phibbs-Rizzuto, *Chemical Firms Told to Think Through Options to 'Preregister' Chemicals for REACH*, 24 International Trade Reporter (BNA) 238 (15 February 2007); Pat Phibbs-Rizzuto, *U.S. Chemical Makers Said to Face Challenge Proving Legal Standing in European Courts*, 24 International Trade Reporter (BNA) 238–239 (15 February 2007); Pat Phibbs-Rizzuto, *EU Chemicals to Subject Substances of 'Very High Concern' to Intense Scrutiny*, 24 International Trade Reporter (BNA) 239–240 (15 February 2007).

[543] *See* Stephen Gardner, *European Industry Group Highlights Problems Encountered in Complying with REACH Rules*, 26 International Trade Reporter (BNA) 780 (11 June 2009).

## RECIPROCITY

The give-and-take process that characterizes virtually all international trade negotiations, whereby one country balances the concessions it is offers against the concessions it is offered.

## REMEDIES

*See* Trade Remedies.

## REQUEST-OFFER

*See* Bilateral Request-Offer.

## RETROSPECTIVE ASSESSMENT (RETROSPECTIVE ASSESSMENT SYSTEM, RETROSPECTIVE BASIS, RETROSPECTIVE REMEDY)

A term concerning the temporal manner in which trade remedies are applied.

Under United States antidumping (AD) and countervailing duty (CVD) law, liability for an AD duty or CVD attaches at the time of entry of subject merchandise. Duties are not actually assessed until completion of an investigation, of course. But, the liability for such duties is triggered at the moment of entry of the offending merchandise. Consequently, once final duties are calculated through an original investigation or subsequent review, such as an Administrative Review, they are assessed backwards in time, to the moment of importation of the subject merchandise. Through an Administrative Review, the AD duty or CVD rate can change.

The United States is the only nation in the world with a retrospective system of duty assessment. In contrast, for example, under European Union (EU) AD and CVD law, liability applies only prospectively. Thus, in the EU, duties are collected only from and after the date they are finally calculated. That is, under a prospective system, AD duties and CVDs are collected at the time subject merchandise is entered, at an amount calculated before that entry.

More specifically, under United States AD and CVD law, the following procedures occur:

- During the preliminary dumping margin or subsidization determination stage, and assuming a preliminary affirmative injury determination by the International Trade Commission (ITC), the DOC:

    (1) Retrospective assessment of AD duties occurs, meaning that final liability for payment of the duties is determined after the importation of subject merchandise, through an assessment review — the Administrative Review — that covers a discrete period of time (typically, one year) after the subject merchandise is imported.

    (2) Imposes an estimated AD duty or CVD deposit rate (also called the "cash deposit rate") equivalent to the overall weighted average

dumping margin or subsidization rate for each respondent individually investigated. This rate is based on data from transactions during the period covered by the original investigation.

(3)   Calculates an All Others Rate (AOR) applicable to respondents not individually examined (which may not exceed the weighted average dumping margin established with respect to the respondents selected for investigation). This rate is based on data from transactions during the period covered by the original investigation.

(4)   Publishes a Notice of Antidumping Duty Order, or Notice of a Countervailing Duty Order, stating the estimated AD duty or CVD deposit rate and all others rate.

Note that up through 22 February 2007, in AD cases, the DOC used Model Zeroing in original investigations in connection with points (1) and (3).

- Following a final affirmative dumping margin or subsidization determination stage by the DOC, and assuming a final affirmative injury determination by the ITC:

(1)   Retrospective assessment of AD duties and CVDs occurs, meaning that final liability for the duties is determined after the importation of subject merchandise.

(2)   Initial collection of cash deposits occurs upon each entry of subject merchandise.

(3)   The collection of cash deposits in point (2) is at the estimated AD duty or CVD deposit rate for each individually-investigated respondent, and at the all others rate for other respondents.

Note that the ability to require security — the cash deposits — is essential to the operation of a retrospective assessment system. Without these deposits, the administering authority, such as the DOC, has no security that it will be paid when it determines final liability for an AD or CVD duty later on (in the next phase, below). That is, without the obligation to post this security, an importer of subject merchandise would be allowed to enter merchandise despite being suspected of dumping, simply because the authority has not computed a final duty assessment rate for that merchandise, and could do so for about 12 months until the authority makes that calculation.

- Administrative (Periodic) Reviews:

(1)   If no request is made for a Periodic Review, then the cash deposits made on entries of subject merchandise during the previous year (and collected in point (2) above) are automatically assessed as the final AD duties or CVDs for that year. That is, if no Review occurs, then DOC instructs CBP to assess AD duties at the cash deposit rate, and liquidate entries of subject merchandise at that rate. In effect, the estimated AD duty deposit rate becomes the final duty assessment rate.

(2)  Upon request by an interested party (which includes respondents, domestic entities, and importers), the DOC conducts an annual Periodic Review, during the anniversary month of the AD or CVD order.

(3)  The purpose of a Periodic Review is to determine the final amount of AD duties or CVDs owed during the previous year on entries of subject merchandise during that previous year.

(4)  The Review covers all sales of subject merchandise made by the relevant respondent.

(5)  The Review results in calculation of a going-forward cash deposit rate that applies to all future entries of subject merchandise from the relevant respondent (applicable at least until the time of the next annual Review). This rate is based on data from transactions during the period covered by the Review. Liability for posting the cash deposit rests with importers of subject merchandise.

(6)  The Review also results in calculation of a "duty assessment rate," which applies to each importer that imports subject merchandise from the relevant exporter. Sometimes, this rate is called the "final liquidation rate," because it is set at the same time the entries of subject merchandise are finally liquidated.

(7)  Final liability for payment of the AD duties or CVDs lies with the importer of subject merchandise, and is equal to the duty assessment rate. That is, the DOC calculates a duty assessment rate for each importer that imports subject merchandise from an exporter of that merchandise (as per point (6)), and then sets the final liability for payment of AD duties by that importer equal to the duty assessment rate for that importer.

(8)  Depending on the case, the duty assessment rate may equal the previous cash deposit rate, be greater than the cash deposits, or be less than the cash deposits. Where it is equal, no additional money is owed. Where the duty assessment rate is higher than the cash deposited, the importer of subject merchandise is liable for the difference. Where the assessment rate is lower than the cash that has been on deposit, the importer is eligible for a refund of the difference, with interest.

In AD cases, the DOC uses Simple Zeroing to calculate the going-forward cash deposit rate (used for the subsequent year) and the duty assessment rate (the final AD duty liability applied to the previous year).

A retrospective system of duty assessment has the virtue of precision. It penalizes dumped or illegally subsidized goods from the moment they are imported (or nearly so). That is because the penalty — the remedial duty — dates backwards, and is assessed and collected as soon as a preliminary affirmative dumping margin or subsidization determination is obtained. But, this system is complicated, and thus involves considerable resources to operate.

Moreover, respondents in AD and CVD cases complain that it creates unpredictability. They do not know what their final AD or CVD rate (duty assessment rate or final liquidation rate) is (i.e., whether it is higher or lower than the cash deposit rate) until an Administrative Review.

In 2008, the United States General Accounting Office (GAO) issued a report in which it said large amounts of AD duties and CVDs remain uncollected under the retrospective American system. The GAO encouraged Congress to consider changing American trade remedy law to a prospective system. But, the report also said that 84 percent of the uncollected duties arose from just four products, all of which were subject merchandise from China. The report triggered a debate about the merits of the two types of systems, but no changes to the American rules.

## REVENUE ASSURANCE PRINCIPLE

A concept arising in the context of United States agricultural legislation that the income of farmers should be guaranteed, even if the nature of the subsidies they receive to support their income changes.

Thus, if because of WTO obligations, subsidy payments that are trade-distorting (e.g., the United States Marketing Loan Program) are reduced, then they should be replaced by non- or less trade distorting support (e.g., direct income payments). That way, the income of farmers remains whole. In brief, the principle connotes the idea that the form of subsidy payments may change, but not the substantive level of support. This principle is applicable in other countries and contexts, such as the European Union (EU) and Common Agricultural Policy (CAP).

## REVERSE CONSENSUS (REVERSE CONSENSUS DECISION-MAKING, REVERSE CONSENSUS RULE)

See WTO.

## REVERSE ENGINEERING (FIRST MEANING)

The construction of a product by taking apart another, like or similar product, to discover how the latter product was built.

The term often is used in the intellectual property (IP) context, particularly in respect of developing generic medicines based on patented pharmaceutical products.

## REVERSE ENGINEERING (SECOND MEANING)

A negotiating strategy whereby participants focus first on coming to an agreement on detailed, technical issues. Then, they build upward, as it were, on resolution of larger issues that involve so-called "headline" numbers, i.e., figures that attract widespread attention.

In effect, "reverse engineering" is a bottom-up, specific-to-general strategy. Its purpose is to establish confidence-building measures that both engender trust and a positive atmosphere, and produce substantive results that can serve as a foundation for a broad accord. The strategy was used unsuccessfully in the winter 2006 and spring 2007 during the Doha Round.

## *RIO DECLARATION*

The *Rio Declaration on Environment and Development*, which is Annex I to the *Report of the United Nations Conference on Environment and Development*.

That *Report* came out of meetings held on 3-14 June 1992 in Rio de Janeiro, Brazil. The *Rio Declaration* is not a treaty. It contains a list of 27 principles on sustainable development and the importance of balancing sovereignty against the use of resources by countries to alleviate poverty.

## ROLE OF CAPITAL

*See* Harrod–Domar Model.

## ROO

*See* Rule of Origin.

## ROSTOW MODEL

*See* Stages of Growth

## ROUND

*See* GATT, MTN, WTO.

## ROZ

Reconstruction Opportunity Zone.

A ROZ is a public-private venture, in that a governmental authority establishes its boundaries and the incentives for doing business therein, and private enterprises then populate the zone with commercially meaningful endeavors. However, ROZs also serve a national security purpose, namely, countering narcotics trafficking and terrorism by providing salubrious employment opportunities for individuals and businesses in or near unstable or conflict areas.

One key incentive to operating in a ROZ is duty-free access to the American market for merchandise originating in the Zone. The United States has worked with Jordan on ROZs in that country, though they are called "Qualified Industrial Zones" (QIZs).

In August 2006, the United States discussed with Pakistan the possibility of establishing ROZs on the border between Afghanistan and Pakistan. The aim would be to help improve the economic conditions in this border region, and in turn render the climate there less hospitable to extremist sentiments. The United States would give products originating in an ROZ receive duty-free treatment from the United States. Pakistan, of course, prefers a full free trade agreement (FTA), an idea President Pervez Musharraf first raised with President George W. Bush in December 2004, and reiterated in August 2006 by Pakistan's Minister of Commerce, Humayun Akhtar Khan. The Administration of President Barack H. Obama, however, has followed the preference of the previous Administration, namely, for ROZs over an FTA.[544]

*Suggestions for Further Research:*

Book:

1.  HUFBAUER, GARY C., SUSTAINING REFORM WITH A U.S. — PAKISTAN FREE TRADE AGREEMENT (2006).

# RPT

Reasonable Period of Time.

The term frequently is used in the context of the time allowed to a losing WTO Member to compliance with recommendations in a WTO panel or Appellate Body report. The default RPT under the *Understanding on Rules and Procedures Governing the Settlement of Disputes (Dispute Settlement Understanding, or DSU)* is 15 months. However, typically the RPT is subject to negotiation between the winning and losing Members, especially in cases in which implementing a recommendation requires a major or controversial domestic legislative change.

# RTA

Regional Trade Agreement, Regional Trade Arrangement, or Regional Trading Arrangement, *i.e.*, a generic term enveloping both a free trade agreement (FTA) and/or a customs union (CU).

Also called a PTA (not to be confused with a Plurilateral Trade Agreement). It is important to distinguish an RTA from non-preferential free trade, thus "PTA" is a superior term.

As of November 2009, there were over 430 RTAs that had been notified to the WTO.[545] Yet, the WTO Committee on Regional Trade Agreements had not issued a single decision as to whether any of them complied with the requirements of GATT Article XXIV and Article V of the *General Agreement on Trade in Services (GATS)*.

---

[544] *See* Rossella Brevetti, *U.S. Commits to Improved Market Access for Pakistan*, 27 International Trade Reporter (BNA) 466 (1 April 2010).

[545] Daniel Pruzin, *Senior Officials to Address Talks on Rules; Advocates Call for Progress in Light of Crisis*, 26 International Trade Reporter (BNA) 1605 (26 November 2009).

*Suggestions for Further Research:*

Book Chapters:

1.   Bhagwati, Jagdish & Arvind Panagariya, *Preferential Trading Areas and Multilateralism — Strangers, Friends, or Foes?*, in THE ECONOMICS OF PREFERENTIAL TRADE AGREEMENTS 1–55 (Jagdish Bhagwati & Arvind Panagariya eds. 1996

2.   Summers, Lawrence, *Regionalism and the World Trading System*, in POLICY IMPLICATIONS OF TRADE AND CURRENCY ZONES (symposium sponsored by the Federal Reserve Bank of Kansas City 1991)

Articles:

1.   Abbott, Frederick M., *A New Dominant Trade Species Emerges: Is Bilateralism a Threat?*, 10 JOURNAL OF INTERNATIONAL ECONOMIC LAW 571–583 (2007).

2.   Ahn, Dukgeun, *Foe or Friend of GATT Article XXIV: Diversity in Trade Remedy Rules*, 11 JOURNAL OF INTERNATIONAL ECONOMIC LAW 107–133 (2008).

3.   Bhagwati, Jagdish, *Preferential Trade Agreements: The Wrong Road*, 27 LAW AND POLICY IN INTERNATIONAL BUSINESS 865 (1996)).

4.   Bjukovic, Ljiljana, *Dispute Resolution Mechanisms and Regional Trade Agreements: South American and Caribbean Modalities*, 14 UNIVERSITY OF CALIFORNIA — DAVIS JOURNAL OF INTERNATIONAL LAW AND POLICY 255–296 (2008).

5.   Bravo, Karen E., *Regional Trade Arrangements and Labor Liberalization: (Lost) Opportunities for Experimentation?*, 28 SAINT LOUIS UNIVERSITY PUBLIC LAW REVIEW 71–113 (2008).

6.   Brummer, Chris, *The Ties that Bind? Regionalism, Commercial Treaties, and the Future of Global Economic Integration*, 60 VANDERBILT LAW REVIEW 1349–1408 (2007).

7.   Carmody, Chi, *Metrics and the Measurement of International Trade: Some Thoughts on the Early Operation of the WTO RTA Transparency Mechanism*, 28 SAINT LOUIS UNIVERSITY PUBLIC LAW REVIEW 273–294 (2008).

8.   Chaisse, Julien, Debashis Chakraborty & Biswajit Nag, *The Three-Pronged Strategy of India's Preferential Trade Policy: A Contribution to the Study of Modern Economic Treaties*, 26 CONNECTICUT JOURNAL OF INTERNATIONAL LAW 415–455 (2011).

9.   Cimbolic, Brian, *The Impact of Regional Trade Areas on International Intellectual Property Rights*, 48 IDEA — THE INTELLECTUAL PROPERTY LAW REVIEW 53–68 (2007).

10. Devuyst, Youri & Asja Serdarevic, *The World Trade Organization and Regional Trade Agreements: Bridging the Constitutional Credibility Gap*, 18 DUKE JOURNAL OF COMPARATIVE AND INTERNATIONAL LAW 1–75 (2007).

11. Emmerson, Andrew, *Conceptualizing Security Exceptions: Legal Doctrine or Political Excuse?*, 11 JOURNAL OF INTERNATIONAL ECONOMIC LAW 135–154 (2008).

12. Fakhri, Michael, *Images of the Arab World and Middle East — Debates about Development and Regional Integration*, 28 WISCONSIN INTERNATIONAL LAW JOURNAL 391–429 (2010).

13. Gao, Henry & C.L. Lim, *Saving the WTO from the Risk of Irrelevance: The WTO Dispute Mechanism as a "Common Good" for RTA Disputes*, 11 JOURNAL OF INTERNATIONAL ECONOMIC LAW 899–925 (2008).

14. Gathii, James Thuo, *African Regional Trade Agreements as Flexible Legal Regimes*, 35 NORTH CAROLINA JOURNAL OF INTERNATIONAL LAW & COMMERCIAL REGULATION 571–667 (2010).

15. Gathii, James Thuo, *The Under-Appreciated Jurisprudence of Africa's Regional Trade Judiciaries*, 12 OREGON REVIEW OF INTERNATIONAL LAW 245–282 (2010).

16. Gathi, James Thuo, *The Neoliberal Turn in Regional Trade Agreements*, 86 WASHINGTON LAW REVIEW 421–474 (2011).

17. Gounder, Neelesh & Biman Chand Prasad, *Regional Trade Agreements and the New Theory of Trade — Implications for Trade Policy in Pacific Island Countries*, 10 JOURNAL OF INTERNATIONAL TRADE LAW AND POLICY 49–63 (2011).

18. Harrington, Alexandra R., *Peer Pressure: Correlations between Membership in Regional and Regional Economic Organizations in the Context of WTO Dispute Resolution Claims*, 5 SOUTH CAROLINA JOURNAL OF INTERNATIONAL LAW & BUSINESS 35–73 (2008).

19. Hillman, Jennifer, *Conflicts between Dispute Settlement Mechanisms in Regional Trade Agreements and the WTO — What Should the WTO Do?*, 42 CORNELL INTERNATIONAL LAW JOURNAL 193–208 (2009).

20. Kim, Jong Bum & Joongi Kim, *The Role of Rules of Origin to Provide Discipline to the GATT Article XXIV Exception*, 14 JOURNAL OF INTERNATIONAL ECONOMIC LAW 613–638 (2011).

21. Langille, Joanna, Note, *Neither Constitution Nor Contract: Understanding the WTO by Examining the Legal Limits on Contracting Out through Regional Trade Agreements*, 86 NEW YORK UNIVERSITY LAW REVIEW 1482–1518 (2011).

22. Leal-Arcas, Rafael, *Proliferation of Regional Trade Agreements: Complementing or Supplanting Multilateralism?*, 11 CHICAGO JOURNAL OF INTERNATIONAL LAW number 2, 597–629 (winter 2011).

23. Nsour, Mohammad F., *Regional Trade Agreements in the Era of Globalization: A Legal Analysis*, 33 NORTH CAROLINA JOURNAL OF INTERNATIONAL LAW & COMMERCIAL REGULATION 359–435 (2008).

24. Picker, Colin, *Regional Trade Agreements v. The WTO: A Proposal for Reform of Article XXIV to Counter this Institutional Threat*, 26 UNIVERSITY OF PENNSYLVANIA JOURNAL OF INTERNATIONAL ECONOMIC LAW 267 (2005).

25. Richelson, Sarah, Student Note, *Trafficking and Trade: How Regional Trade Agreements Can Combat the Trafficking of Persons in Brazil*, 25 ARIZONA JOURNAL OF INTERNATIONAL AND COMPARATIVE LAW 857–898 (2008).

26. Sanders, Anselm Kamperman, *Intellectual Property, Free Trade and Economic Development*, 23 GEORGIA STATE UNIVERSITY LAW REVIEW 893–911 (2007).

27. Schaefer, Matthew, *Ensuring that Regional Trade Agreements Complement the WTO System: U.S. Unilateralism a Supplement to WTO Initiatives?*, 10 JOURNAL OF INTERNATIONAL ECONOMIC LAW 585–603 (2007).

28. Taylor, C. O'Neal, *Regionalism: The Second-Best Option?*, 28 SAINT LOUIS UNIVERSITY PUBLIC LAW REVIEW 155–199 (2008).

29. Taylor, C. O'Neal, *The U.S. Approach to Regionalism: Recent Past and Future*, 15 ILSA JOURNAL OF INTERNATIONAL & COMPARATIVE LAW 411–447 (2009).

30. *The Human Element: The Impact of Regional Trade Agreements on Human Rights and the Rule of Law*, 42 UNIVERSITY OF MIAMI INTER-AMERICAN LAW REVIEW 197–366 (2011).

31. Voon, Tania, *Eliminating Trade Remedies from the WTO: Lessons from Regional Trade Agreements*, 59 INTERNATIONAL & COMPARATIVE LAW QUARTERLY 625–667 (2010).

32. Yokoi-Arai, Mamiko, *Implications of Financial Liberalization in the Big States of Asia for Regional Integration*, 43 THE INTERNATIONAL LAWYER 1377–1409 (2009).

33. Yu, Peter K., *Sinic Trade Agreements*, 44 U.C. DAVIS LAW REVIEW 953–1028 (2011).

34. Zaidi, Kamaal R., *Harmonizing Trade Liberalization and Migration Policy Through Shared Responsibility: A Comparison of the Impact of Bilateral Trade Agreements and the GATS in Germany and Canada*, 37 SYRACUSE JOURNAL OF INTERNATIONAL LAW & COMMERCE 267–297 (2010).

Other Source:

1. Robinson, Sherman & Karen Thierfelder, *Trade Liberalization and Regional Integration: The Search for Large Numbers*, Trade and Macroeconomics Division (TMD) Discussion Paper Number 34, International Food Policy Research Institute (Washington, D.C., January 1999).

## RULE OF ORIGIN (RULES OF ORIGIN)

A rule that clarifies, ideally with accuracy, precision, certainty, the country of origin of a product.

Rules of origin may be "non-preferential," meaning that no trade preference is at stake. Or, they may be "preferential," meaning that preferences such as duty free treatment may be available. The preferences may arise in connection with a free trade agreement (FTA), customs union (CU), or preferential trading arrangement (PTA) for poor countries. The term rule of origin sometimes is abbreviated "ROO."

Closely related to preferential rules rules of origin is the concept of "cumula-tion." Essentially, cumulation concerns whether inputs into a product, and value added to a product, in one country can count towards conferring origin on that product in another country. At one extreme, if cumulation is "bilateral," then it means that only materials from, and work done in, either of two countries to an FTA or CU qualify for conferring origin on that product. For example, in an FTA between the United States and Ghana, if only inputs originating in either of those two countries, and only work done in those two countries, counted towards conferring origin on a product for purposes of preferential treatment, then the regime would be one of "bilateral" cumulation. In effect, "bilateral" cumulation favors only the use of products originating in, and labor of, the other member (or other members) of an FTA or CU, to qualify for the preferential trade treatment at stake.

At the other extreme, "full" cumulation allows for materials from, and work done in, in a broad array of countries to count towards origin within a particular FTA or CU. For example, if an FTA involving the United States and Ghana were to allow all inputs and other value added from any developing or least developed country to count towards a determination as to whether a finished product originated in Ghana (or the United States), then the regime would be one of "full" cumulation. A more restrictive, but still "full," cumlation regime would allow for any input or work in Africa to qualify. Evidently, "full cumulation" favors the use of products originating in, and labor of, a wide array of countries, whether or not the countries are party to the FTA or CU for which preferential treatment is sought, as long as the countries fit within a category (such as one based on development level or geographical location).

In between these extremes of "bilateral" and "full" cumulation is "diagonal" cumulation. Here, inputs and labor qualifies toward conferring origin, and thus obtaining a preference, under an FTA or CU, as long as the inputs originate in, or labor is performed in, a country that is linked by another FTA or CU to one of the countries that is a member of the first FTA or CU. For example, suppose the United States has separate bilateral FTAs with both Ghana and Gabon. A diagonal rule of origin would allow inputs or value added to a product in Gabon to qualify for origin in Ghana, for purposes of obtaining duty-free treatment under the United States — Ghana FTA.

Trade creation and trade diversion are effects — foreseeable *a priori* and observable *a posteriori* — of different cumulation rules. Manifestly, full cumulation allows businesses the greatest flexibility in sourcing inputs and performing work on a product. Trade is most likely to be created, and least likely to be diverted, because full cumulation preferential rules of origin are the most flexible. Yet, such rules risk giving the benefits of duty-free treatment under an FTA or CU to non-members.

Conversely, bilateral cumulation is the tightest discipline on ensuring only members get the benefit of preferential treatment under an FTA or CU, and thus most likely to create trade between (or among) the members. But, bilateral cumulation creates the greatest artificial incentive — or distortion — to engage in productive activity within the members of an FTA or CU, *i.e.*, to divert trade. The effects of diagonal cumulation are in between these extremes.

Both trade creation and trade diversion, among the countries that qualify diagonally, are likely to occur to some degree. However, preferential rules of origin that allow for diagonal cumulation risk fostering dependency of peripheral countries (e.g., African, Caribbean, and Pacific (ACP) nations) on a major trading power (*e.g.*, the EU) that is the hub of a network of FTAs or CUs. Diagonal cumulation effectively ties them to the center — and to each other — by favoring use of materials and labor only in the network. Notably, the EU tends to rely on diagonal rules in its PTAs, since at least 1997.

*Suggestions for Further Research:*

Books:

1.   AMERICAN BAR ASSOCIATION (SECTION OF INTERNATIONAL LAW AND PRACTICE AND DIVISION FOR PROFESSIONAL EDUCATION), THE NORTH AMERICAN FREE TRADE AGREEMENT: ITS SCOPE AND IMPLICATIONS FOR NORTH AMERICA'S LAWYERS, BUSINESSES AND POLICYMAKERS (1993) (especially Chapter on *Rules of Origin — Autos: A Case Study*, by Jon R. Johnson).

2.   CADOT, OLIVIER, ANTONI ESTEVADEORDAL, AKIKO SUWA-EISENMANN & THIERRY VERDIER EDS., THE ORIGIN OF GOODS — RULES OF ORIGIN IN REGIONAL TRADE AGREEMENTS (2006).

3.   SERKO, DAVID, IMPORT PRACTICE 326 (2nd ed. 1991).

4.   VERMULST, EDWN, PAUL WAER & JACQUES BOURGEOIS EDS., RULES OF ORIGIN IN INTERNATIONAL TRADE — A COMPARATIVE STUDY (1994).

5.   VON MEHREN, PHILIP T., CROSS-BORDER TRADE AND INVESTMENT WITH MEXICO (1997) (especially Chapter 6, *NAFTA's Special Rules for Specific Types of Goods*).

Book Chapters:

1.   Angulo, Carlos, *The NAFTA Rules of Origin and their Consequences for Maquiladoras: A Mexican Perspective, in* MAKING FREE TRADE WORK IN THE AMERICAS 80–91 (Boris Kozolchyk ed. 1993).

2.   Gantz, David A., *Maximizing the Regional Benefits of North American Economic Integration: Rules of Origin Under NAFTA, in* MAKING FREE TRADE WORK IN THE AMERICAS 52–79 (Boris Kozolchyk ed. 1993).

Articles:

1.   Asakura, Hironori, *The Harmonized System and Rules of Origin*, 27 JOURNAL OF WORLD TRADE 5, 6–8, 17, 19–20 (1993).

2.   Hoekman, Bernard, *Rules of Origin for Goods and Services — Conceptual Issues and Economic Considerations*, 27 JOURNAL OF WORLD TRADE 81, 84–85 (1993).

3.   James, William E., *APEC and Preferential Rules of Origin — Stumbling Blocks for Liberalization of Trade?*, 31 JOURNAL OF WORLD TRADE 113–134 (June 1997).

4.   Kim, Jong Bum & Joongi Kim, *The Role of Rules of Origin to Provide Discipline to the GATT Article XXIV Exception*, 14 JOURNAL OF INTERNATIONAL ECONOMIC LAW 613–638 (2011).

5.  Komuro, Norio, *AFTA Rules of Origin*, 11 INTERNATIONAL TRADE LAW & REGULATION issue 1, 1–13 (January 2005).

6.  LaNasa III, Joseph A., *Rules of Origin under the North American Free Trade Agreement: A Substantial Transformation into Objectively Transparent Protectionism*, 34 HARVARD INTERNATIONAL LAW JOURNAL 381, 404–05 (1993).

7.  LaNasa III, Joseph A., *Rules of Origin and the Uruguay Round's Effectiveness in Harmonizing and Regulating Them*, 90 AMERICAN JOURNAL OF INTERNATIONAL LAW 625, 636–40 (1996).

8.  Mabrouk, Hatem, *Rules of Origin as International Trade Hindrances*, 5 ENTREPRENEURIAL BUSINESS LAW JOURNAL 97–176 (2010).

9.  Malkawi, Bashar H., *Rules of Origin Under U.S. Trade Agreements with Arab Countries — Are They Helping and Hindering Free Trade?*, 10 JOURNAL OF INTERNATIONAL TRADE LAW AND POLICY 29–48 (2011).

10. Palmeter, N. David, *Pacific Trade Liberalization and Rules of Origin*, 27 JOURNAL OF WORLD TRADE 49, 53–54, 61 (1993).

11. Simpson, John P., *North American Free Trade Agreement — Rules of Origin*, 28 JOURNAL OF WORLD TRADE 33, 34, 37–38, 40–41 (1994).

12. Vergano, Paolo R. & Margareta Djordjevic, *Understanding Rules of Origin — the Coffee Example*, 10 INTERNATIONAL TRADE LAW & REGULATION issue 5, 96–105 (September 2004).

# RWG

Redistribution With Growth.

A strategy toward poverty alleviation. Advocates of RWG stress the need to increase the productivity and purchasing power of poor people, which can occur through appropriate commodity market interventions, dynamic redistribution of assets (*e.g.*, land reform), and progressive taxation. Better services, through their positive effects on human capital, can increase the productivity and purchasing power of the poor. Arguably the most successful, but also controversial, exemplar of RWG is Malaysia.

*Suggestions for Further Research:*

Books:

1.  CHENERY, HOLLIS, MONTEK S. AHLUWALIA, C.L.G. BELL, JOHN H. DULOY & RICHARD JOLLY, REDISTRIBUTION WITH GROWTH: POLICIES TO IMPROVE INCOME DISTRIBUTION IN DEVELOPING COUNTRIES IN THE CONTEXT OF ECONOMIC GROWTH (Oxford University Press for The World Bank and Institute of Development Studies, University of Sussex, 1974).

2.  EDWARDS, E.O., ED., EMPLOYMENT IN DEVELOPING COUNTRIES (1974).

3.  GREEN, ROY E., ED., ENTERPRISE ZONES: NEW DIRECTIONS IN ECONOMIC DEVELOPMENT (1991).

# S

## S & D TREATMENT

*See* Special and Differential Treatment.

## SAA

*See* Statement of Administrative Action.

## SAARC

South Asian Association for Regional Cooperation, a preferential trade agreement among Afghanistan, Bangladesh, Bhutan, India, Maldives, Nepal, Pakistan, and Sri Lanka. The SAARC was established in 1985 in New Delhi, India.

The SAARC entered into force on 8 December 1995, and essentially took a decade to negotiate after its initial establishment. Afghanistan became the group's eighth member in April 2007. At the 13th SAARC summit in Dhaka, China, the European Union (EU), Japan, South Korea and the United States were granted observer status of the group; however, despite a similar request in March 2007, Iran has not been granted such status.

The original seven SAARC members agreed on five principal areas of cooperation:

- Agriculture and Rural Development
- Telecommunications, Science, Technology and Meteorology
- Health and Population Activities
- Transport; and
- Human Resources Development

The group has since expanded its operations to encourage cooperation in the following sectors:

- Women, Youth and Children; and
- Environment and Forestry

With a billion people, a formidable military, and nuclear weapons capability, India dominates the South Asian region. Thus, India is viewed by the other six SAARC members as hegemonic, though India discounts this view as paranoid. To the other six members, SAARC is a forum for uniting against India in the hopes of a stronger bargaining position. To India, SAARC is a forum for fostering economic and social progress in the region. The arrangement also is hobbled by major political-strategic disputes, most notably that between India and Pakistan over Kashmir.

Thus far, the progress has been unimpressive. The lists of goods on which each SAARC member offers tariff preferences are insufficient. For example, when SAARC was created, India offered up 106 items, Pakistan 35, Sri Lanka 31, and Bangladesh 12. By early 1997, SAARC members had agreed to cut tariffs on about 2,000 items, with India offering 911, Bangladesh 513, Pakistan 375, and Sri Lanka 32.

However, thousands of key products remained immune from tariff reductions. Moreover, trade within the region accounts for only about three percent of the total trade of the SAARC members, and the items covered by the SAARC tariff preferences are a tiny portion of this amount. In truth, large-scale trade in the region is through black markets and smugglers. For instance, gold and heroin are traded from Pakistan in exchange for whisky from India, and jute and hides are traded from Bangladesh in exchange for consumer goods from India. It is estimated that black-market trade between India and Pakistan exceeds $1 billion annually, which is double or quadruple the value of official trade. Finally, non-tariff barriers abound in the region. A case in point, linked to the Kashmir dispute, is Pakistan's bar on imports from India of all but roughly 577 items.

Still, since 1991 Sri Lanka has pushed for a South Asian FTA, and in May 1997, SAARC endorsed the idea. Finally, on 6 January 2004, a SAARC-backed FTA, the *Agreement on South Asian Free Trade Area (SAFTA)*, was signed at the 12th Summit at Islamabad. *SAFTA* came into effect on 1 January 2006. However, many of the cuts excluded "sensitive" goods protected by SAARC member countries.

In late-2005, SAARC called for the creation of the SAARC Development Fund, a financial institution that would serve as an umbrella organization for all SAARC development funding. In 2007, a plan to adopt a single currency for the bloc was made by Sri Lankan President Mahinda Rajapaske at the 14th SAARC summit in New Delhi.

## *SACU*

The Southern African Customs Union, which consists of Botswana, Lesotho, Namibia, South Africa, and Swaziland.

The primary impetus of *SACU* is to facilitate trade amongst the member nations, and to spark economic development and integration in the region. Originally, *SACU* was established through the *Customs Union Agreement of 1910*, making it the oldest customs union (CU) in the world.

That *1910 Agreement* was signed by the then Union of South Africa, and the then High Commission territories of Bechuanaland, Basutoland, and Swaziland. With the independence of Botswana, Lesotho, South Africa, and Swaziland, the *1910 Agreement* was updated in 1969. The *Agreement* has twice since been renegotiated, the last of which occurred in 2002. Namibia joined *SACU* after gaining its independence in 1990.

The institutional framework of *SACU* is headed by the Council of Ministers, which is comprised of one Minister (Trade of Finance) from each Member state. The Council is the supreme decision-making body in *SACU*, and all measures must be passed by consensus. The Customs Union Commission is an administrative body composed of senior trade and finance officials who advise the Council and oversee implementation of the *2002 Agreement*. The Secretariat runs the day-to-day operations of *SACU* and ensures that all protocols and measures of the Council and Commission are followed. *SACU* also has a Tribunal composed of an independent body of experts that reports directly to the Council. The Tribunal settles any dispute arising out of the interpretation or application of the 2002 Agreement.

Lastly, there are two independent bodies that are integral to *SACU*. The Tariff Board is an independent body of trade experts that advises the Council on the levels and changes of tariffs, including antidumping (AD) duties and other trade remedies. In addition, four Technical Liaison Committees (on Agriculture, Customs, Trade and Industry, and Transport) advise the Commission on its work.

Like *MERCOSUR*, *SACU* is a customs union whereby all goods are freely tradable amongst the Member nations. That is, no tariff or quantitative restriction is imposed on goods originating from other Member countries, unless otherwise noted in the 2002 Agreement. However, trade liberalization does not extend to agriculture, services, or government procurement. In effect, *SACU* is a common policy on industrial tariffs. SACU imposes a common external tariff (CET) on all goods originating from non-Member countries, as well as a common excise tariff for all its members. All customs and excise duties collected in the common customs area are paid into a common pool, whereby the revenue is shared by all members under the auspices of a revenue-sharing formula devised in the 2002 Agreement.

*SACU* maintains a common negotiating mechanism. That is, no Member shall negotiate or enter into a preferential agreement with a third party without concurrence and taking into account of the other Member states. In 1999, the EU and *SACU* entered into a free trade agreement (FTA). However, the deal is not a comprehensive one. That is in part because *SACU* provides duty-free treatment only for goods. On 16 December 2003, *SACU* concluded a preferential trading arrangement (PTA) with *MERCOSUR*.

The United States and *SACU* launched FTA negotiations in 2003. Those talks stalled when *SACU* members felt American demands were too high in respect of liberalization of their trade and investment regimes. In early 2006, the United States and *SACU* agreed to create a framework for deepening bilateral commercial ties. However, the parties deemed an FTA between them to be their "long term" objective.[546]

Impressively, on the sidelines of the Seventh WTO Ministerial Conference in Geneva from 30 November–2 December 2009, *SACU* made an important declaration. Along with *MERCOSUR* and India, *SACU* announced progress toward a free trade agreement (FTA). This progress built on the June 2004

---

[546] *See* Gary G. Yerkey, *U.S., SACU Agree to Create 'Framework' But Free Trade Agreement Now Longer Term*, 23 INTERNATIONAL TRADE REPORTER (BNA) 621 (2006).

preferential trade agreement (PTA) between *SACU* and *MERCOSUR*, and on talks between *MERCOSUR* and India.

*Suggestions for Further Research:*

Articles:

1.   Ewelukwa, Uché U., *South — South Trade and Investment: The Good, the Bad, and the Ugly — African Perspectives*, 20 MINNESOTA JOURNAL OF INTERNATIONAL LAW 513–587 (2011).

2.   Gathii, James Thuo, *African Regional Trade Agreements as Flexible Legal Regimes*, 35 NORTH CAROLINA JOURNAL OF INTERNATIONAL LAW & COMMERCIAL REGULATION 571–667 (2010).

## SADC

The Southern African Development Community.

SADC is comprised of SACU plus nine other Southern African countries. Thus, the members of SADC include the SACU countries, namely,

- Botswana
- Lesotho
- Namibia

- South Africa
- Swaziland

plus the non-SADC countries of

- Angola
- Congo (Democratic Republic of)
- Madagascar
- Malawi
- Mauritius

- Mozambique
- Tanzania
- Zambia
- Zimbabwe.

Originally, the SADC was formed on 1 April 1980 as a loose alliance of nine States in Southern Africa known as the Southern African Development Coordinating Conference (SADCC). The *Lusaka Declaration*, the group's founding document, deemed the primary objective of the SADCC to coordinate development projects amongst the Member nations and lessen economic dependence on the then apartheid South Africa. In 1992, the adoption of a *Declaration* and Treaty transformed the SADCC into the SADC.

The Figure below summarizes the institutional framework of SADC. SADC is run by eight principal bodies. The Summit, comprising of Heads of State, is the ultimate decision-making body of the group. It is responsible for the overall policy direction of the SADC. The Council of Ministers consists of Ministers from each Member State and is responsible for ensuring the policies of the SADC are properly implemented. An Integrated Committee of Ministers oversees four core areas of integration, namely,

- Trade, Industry, Finance and Investment
- Infrastructure and Services

- Food, Agriculture and Natural Resources
- Social and Human Development and Special Programs.

Each Committee is comprised of two Ministers from each Member state and reports directly to the Council. The Secretariat is the principal executive institution of the SADC and is responsible for strategic planning, coordination and management of SADC programs. The Organ on Politics, Defense and Security (OPDS) is run by a Troika. The Troika consists of three members: the Chair, the outgoing Chair, and the incoming Chair. Lastly, the SADC's founding treaty calls for a tribunal which has yet to be established.

**FIGURE:**

**SADC ORGANIZATIONAL STRUCTURE**[547]

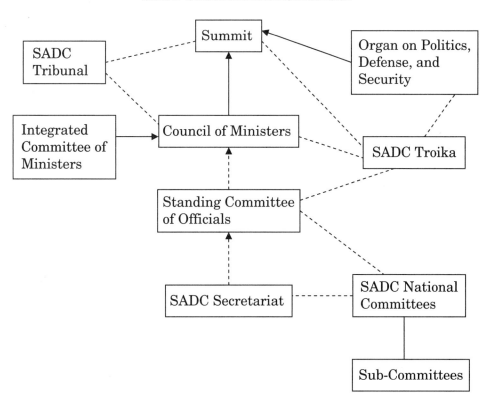

The ultimate objective of SADC is to increase the harmonization and rationalization amongst the Member nations so as to enable the pooling of resources to achieve self-reliance and improve the living standards of the people of the region. Other objectives of the group include:

- Evolving common political values, systems and institutions;
- Promoting and defending peace and security;

---

[547] Adapted from official SADC website Chart on "SADC Institutional Framework."

- Promoting and maximizing productive employment and utilization of the resources of the Region;

- Achieving sustainable utilization of natural resources and effective protection of the environment; and

- Strengthening and consolidating the long standing historical, social and cultural affinities and links among the people of the Region.

To be sure, the aim of SADC is economic integration among Southern African countries through a free trade agreement (FTA). However, the pace of trade liberalization is deliberately slower than that of COMESA.

Negotiations for a free trade pact, which commenced at least as far back as the late 1990s, never came to fruition, though a *Protocol on Trade* was signed in 1996. The *Trade Protocol* calls for an 85 percent reduction of internal trade barriers. The *Protocol* is posted on the Official SADC website (www.sadc.int).

*Suggestions for Further Research:*

Book:

1. EVANS, DAVID, ET AL., SADC: THE COST OF NON-INTEGRATION (1999).

Articles:

1. Chigara, Ben, *European / Southern African Development Community (SADC) States' Bilateral Investment Agreements (BITs) for the Promotion and Protection of Foreign Investments vs. Post-Apartheid SADC Economic and Social Reconstruction Policy*, 10 JOURNAL OF INTERNATIONAL TRADE LAW AND POLICY number 3, 213–242 (2011).

2. Ewelukwa, Uché U., *South — South Trade and Investment: The Good, the Bad, and the Ugly — African Perspectives*, 20 MINNESOTA JOURNAL OF INTERNATIONAL LAW 513–587 (2011).

## *SAFE ACT*

See *SAFETEA — LU Act.*

## SAFEGUARD

*See* Escape Clause, SSG, and SSM.

## *SAFETEA — LU ACT*

The *Safe, Accountable, Flexible and Efficient Transportation Equity Act: A Legacy for Users (SAFETEA–LU). SAFETEA-LU*, signed by President George W. Bush on 10 August 2005, guarantees U.S. $244.1 billion in funding for highways, highway safety and public transportation. In particular, *SAFETEA–LU* contains five primary objectives:

- Improving safety;

- Reducing traffic congestion;

- Improving efficiency in freight movement

- Increasing inter-modal connectivity; and
- Protecting the environment

*SAFETEA-LU* provides funding for projects during the five year period 2005–2009. *SAFETEA–LU* appears mainly in various sections of Title 23 of the United States Code.[548]

The *SAFETEA-LU* also drew heavy criticism for numerous in-state projects that were questionable at best. One of the projects "earmarked" to receive funds that caused the most ire, dubbed the "Bridge to Nowhere," was a bridge nearly as long as the Golden Gate Bridge and higher than the Brooklyn Bridge connecting two towns with a total population of 8,050 in southeast Alaska.

*See* FAST (FAST Card).

## SAFE PORT ACT

The *Security and Accountability for Every Port Act of 2006*, which has the clever acronym the "*SAFE Port Act*", was enacted by Congress on 13 October 2006.[549] The *Act* appropriates nearly U.S. $9 billion in funds to the Department of Homeland Security (DHS) from 2007–11.

There are eight parts to the *Safe Port Act*:

(1) Security of United States Seaports.

(2) Security of International Supply Chain.

(3) Administration.

(4) Agency Resources and Oversight.

(5) Domestic Nuclear Detection Office.

(6) Commercial Mobile Service Alerts.

(7) Other Matters.

(8) Unlawful Internet Gambling Enforcement.

The primary impetus of the *Act* is to improve security of American ports. To help achieve greater security, the Act created a Domestic Nuclear detection office within the DHS and appropriated funds towards an integrated Deep Water Program, a long-term Coast Guard Modernization Program.

The *Act* also contains an important provision on online gambling. Title VIII of the *Act* is known as the *Unlawful Internet Gambling Enforcement Act of 2006 (UIGEA)*.[550] The *UIGEA* prohibits a financial institution from transferring funds to an internet gambling site. However, the *UIGEA* does grant exceptions to the general ban, namely, when funds are transferred to online sites involving fantasy sports and horse racing. In early 2007, Congressman Barney

---

[548] *See Safe, Accountable, Flexible and Efficient Transportation Equity Act of 2005: A Legacy for Users*, Pubic Law Number 109-59, 119 Stat. 1144 (codified as amended in scattered sections of 23 U.S.C.).

[549] *See Security and Accountability for Every Port Act of 2006*, 6 U.S.C. § 901 (2006).

[550] *See Unlawful Internet Gambling Enforcement Act of 2006*, 31 U.S.C. §§ 5361–67 (2006).

Frank (Democrat — Massachusetts) called for the repeal of the *UIGEA* from the *Safe Port Act*. Congress took no final action.[551]

## SAFTA (FIRST MEANING)

*Agreement on South Asian Free Trade Area.*

*See* SAARC.

## SAFTA (SECOND MEANING)

*Singapore — Australia Free Trade Agreement*, which entered into force on 28 July 2003.

*Suggestions for Further Research:*

Article:

1. Rennie, Jane, *The Evolution of Competition Law in Singapore and Thailand and its Implications for Bilateral Competition Policy in SAFTA and TAFTA*, 15 INTERNATIONAL TRADE LAW & REGULATION issue 1, 1–13 (2009).

## SAO PAULO ROUND

*See* GSTP.

## SAR

Special Administrative Region.

China operates SARs, most notably, Hong Kong, in which it retains ultimate sovereign control, but permits decentralization in many economic and legal matters.

Chinese Premier Deng Xiaoping originally proposed the idea of a SAR, whereby China would rule under "one country, two systems." Each SAR has its own Basic Law, or a set of legal rules adopted by the National People's Congress of the People's Republic of China to act as the controlling legal authority for the region. A Chief Executive, who is appointed by an election committee whose members are generally sympathetic to China's views, acts as the head of the government for each SAR. To be sure, control over matters of foreign policy and external affairs are retained by the Chinese central government in Beijing. Notably, the Hong Kong SAR is in the process of moving towards direct election of its Chief Executive. This move has been encouraged by (*inter alia*) Cardinal Joseph Zen of Hong Kong.

On 19 December 1984, the British and Chinese government signed the Sino-British *Joint Declaration*, which guarantees the SAR status of Hong Kong for 50 years. It also ensures no socialist system or policies would be implemented before the expiration of 50 years, and the capitalist system and way of life will remain the same. The *Basic Law of Hong Kong* later incorporated

---

[551] Karen L. Werner, *House Passes Internet Gambling Bill Updating Wire Act, Enhancing Penalties*, 23 INTERNATIONAL TRADE REPORTER (BNA) 1072 (2006).

these guarantees. The Seventh National People's Congress of the People's Republic of China adopted the *Basic Law* on 4 April 1990. It came into effect on 1 July 1997.

The SAR of Macau was established in 1999.

For China, a "bottom line" reality is that successful performance of the Hong Kong and Macau SAR is indispensable to China's articulated theory of "Peaceful Rise." Under that rubric, China posits its ascendancy onto the global economic and political stage is a peaceful one, posing no threat of conflict to other sovereign nations. Were China to flout the Joint Declaration and Basic Law, were People's Liberation Army (PLA) troops to patrol openly on the streets of Hong Kong, and were China to suppress brutally non-violent demonstrations, then it would belie its commitment to being a peaceful, rising power. Worse yet, it would cast doubt on whether, having arrived on the global stage, it would be a "Peaceful Risen" China.

*Suggestions for Further Research:*

Book:

1.   Neves, Miguel Santos & Brian Bridges eds., Europe, China and the two SARS: Towards a New Era (2000).

Articles:

1.   Chan, Johannes, *Judicial Independence: Controversies on the Constitutional Jurisdiction of the Court of Final Appeal of the Hong Kong Special Administrative Region*, 33 The International Lawyer number 4, 1015–1023 (winter 1999).

2.   Chen, Albert, *Constitutional Crisis in Hong Kong: Congressional Supremacy and Judicial Review*, 33 The International Lawyer number 4, 1025–1040 (winter 1999).

3.   Gao, Henry, *China's Participation in the WTO: A Lawyer's Perspective,* 11 Singapore Year Book of International Law 1–34 (2007).

4.   Luke, Frances M., *The Imminent Threat of China's Intervention in Macau's Autonomy: Using Hong Kong's Past to Secure Macau's Future*, 15 American University International Law Review 717 (2000).

5.   Rapoport, Erik Alexander, *Extradition and the Hong Kong Special Administrative Region: Will Hong Kong Remain a Separate and Independent Jurisdiction after 1997?*, 4 Asian Law Journal 135 (1997).

## SCHEDULE (SCHEDULE OF CONCESSIONS)

The document that embodies commitments on market access and national treatment made by a country.

These commitments may be made unilaterally or after negotiation. That is, a Schedule is a detailed list of bound tariff rates (plus certain non-tariff barriers (NTBs)), and exceptions thereto, established by a country. WTO Members lodge their Schedules with the WTO. Every Member's Schedule is constructed on the basis of a harmonized product classification system, the HS, agreed to under the auspices of, and maintained by, the World Customs Organization (WCO).

Separate Schedules are associated with GATT and *General Agreement on Trade in Services (GATS)* commitments. That is, each WTO Member has two Schedules — one for goods, and one for services. The latter records market access and national treatment commitments on services sectors, sub-sectors, and sub-sub-sectors to which a Member has bound itself. It also indicates areas in which the Member has made no, or only partial, commitments. Thus, to be precise, it is best to refer to a "Schedule of Concessions" for Goods vis-à-vis a "Schedule of Concessions for Services," or respectively, the "Goods Schedule" as distinct from the "Services Schedule."

Notably, the Goods Schedule of a Member also includes commitments made by the Member on agricultural subsidies and domestic support for the farm sector.

## SCHEDULE XX

The schedule of tariffs for the United States as annexed to the Uruguay Round Agreements, specifically, to the Marrakesh Protocol to the GATT 1994. The formal name is "Schedule XX — United States of America."

Under authority delegated by Congress, the President from time to time modifies Schedule XX. For instance, President George W. Bush modified Schedule XX on 29 December 2006 by President George W. Bush.[552] That modification adjusted the rule of origin requirements under United States free trade agreements (FTAs) with Australia, Bahrain, Jordan, Morocco and Singapore.

## SCHEDULING

The process of turning a proposal or guideline into a legally binding obligation.

## *SCM AGREEMENT*

Uruguay Round *Agreement on Subsidies and Countervailing Measures.*

The *SCM Agreement* is one of the Multilateral Agreements on Trade in Goods contained in Annex 1A to the *WTO Agreement.*

*Suggestions for Further Research:*

Books:

1.   Kraus, John, The GATT Negotiations: A Business Guide to the Results of the Uruguay Round 33–36 (1994).

---

[552] *See* 19 U.S.C. § 3501(5), Proclamation Number 8097, 72 Federal Register 429 (4 January 2007).

2. STEWART, TERENCE P., ED., THE GATT URUGUAY ROUND: A NEGOTIATING HISTORY (1986–1992) vol. I 809-1007(1993).

3. SWACKER, FRANK W., KENNETH R. REDDEN, & LARRY B. WENGER, I WORLD TRADE WITHOUT BARRIERS § 4-2(d)(1)(vi) at 218–222 (1995).

Book Chapters:

1. Anderson, M. Jean & Gregory Husisian, *The Subsidies Agreement, in* THE WORLD TRADE ORGANIZATION 299 (Terence P. Stewart ed., 1996)

2. Herlach, Mark D. & David A. Codevilla, *Major Changes in U.S. Countervailing Duty Law: A Guide to the Basics, in* THE GATT, THE WTO, AND THE URUGUAY ROUND AGREEMENTS ACT 53–83 (Practising Law Institute, September 1995).

3. Lorentzen, Ronald K., *Overview of Major Changes Contained in the Uruguay Round Antidumping and Subsidies Agreements, in* I THE COMMERCE DEPARTMENT SPEAKS ON INTERNATIONAL TRADE AND INVESTMENT 513–43 (Practising Law Institute, 1994).

4. Lunn, Mark P., *Multilateral Action Under the "Serious Prejudice" Provision, in* I THE COMMERCE DEPARTMENT SPEAKS ON INTERNATIONAL TRADE AND INVESTMENT 661–80 (Practising Law Institute, 1994).

5. McCartin, Terrence J., *Red, Yellow or Green: GATT 1994's Traffic Light Subsidies Categories, in* I THE COMMERCE DEPARTMENT SPEAKS ON INTERNATIONAL TRADE AND INVESTMENT 611–58 (Practising Law Institute, 1994).

6. Stewart, Terence P., *The Countervailing Duty Law and the Subsidies Code: A Domestic Counsel's Perspective, in* THE GATT, THE WTO, AND THE URUGUAY ROUND AGREEMENTS ACT 263–402 (Practising Law Institute, September 1995).

Articles:

1. Archie, Charles V., Comment, *China Cannot Have Its Cake and Eat It, Too: Coercing the PRC to Reform its Currency Exchange Policy to Conform to Its WTO Obligations*, 37 NORTH CAROLINA JOURNAL OF INTERNATIONAL LAW & COMMERCIAL REGULATION 247–305 (2011).

2. Christoff, Ann E., Note, *The Chinese Automobile Industry and the World Trade Organization: China's Non-Compliance with WTO Regulations through its Subsidizing Automobile Manufacturers*, 19 INDIANA INTERNATIONAL & COMPARATIVE LAW REVIEW 137–166 (2009).

3. Coppens, Dominic, *How Much Credit for Export Credit Support under the SCM Agreement*, 12 JOURNAL OF INTERNATIONAL ECONOMIC LAW 63–113 (2009).

4. Diamond, Richard, *Privatization and the Definition of Subsidy: A Critical Study of Appellate Body Texturalism*, 11 JOURNAL OF INTERNATIONAL ECONOMIC LAW 649–678 (2008).

5. Horlick, Gary N., & Peggy A. Clarke, *The 1994 WTO Subsidies Agreement*, 17 WORLD COMPETITION 41, 42–51 (June 1994).

6.  Seminerio, Frank A., Comment, *A Tale of Two Subsidies: How Federal Support Programs for Ethanol and Biodiesel Can be Created in Order to Circumvent Fair Trade Challenges under World Trade Organization Rulings*, 26 PENN STATE INTERNATIONAL LAW REVIEW 963–995 (2008).

7.  Wise, Judith, *Hunger and Thieves: Anticipating the Impact of WTO Subsidies Reform on Land and Survival in Brazil*, 31 AMERICAN INDIAN LAW REVIEW 531–551 (2006–2007).

8.  Zampetti, Americo Beviglia, *The Uruguay Round Agreement on Subsidies: A Forward-Looking Assessment*, 29 J. WORLD TRADE 5, 10–16 (Dec. 1995).

Other Source:

1.  SENATE COMMITTEE ON FINANCE, SENATE COMM. ON AGRIC., NUTRITION, AND FORESTRY, AND SENATE COMMITTEE ON GOVERNMENTAL AFFAIRS, URUGUAY ROUND AGREEMENTS ACT, SENATE REPORT NUMBER 412, 103d Congress, 2d Session 88–90 (1994).

## SDR

Special Drawing Right.

An international reserve asset, created in 1969 via an Amendment to the Articles of Agreement of the International Monetary Fund (IMF). SDRs have attributes of money, in that it is a means of payment, store of value, and unit of account. Yet, they are a credit entered on the books and records of the IMF, and are issued to IMF members without any sacrifice by the members of real resources. Accordingly, Professors Qureshi and Ziegler urge that SDRs are a *sui generis* instrument.

*Suggestions for Further Research:*

Book:

1.  QURESHI, ASIF H. & ANDREAS R. ZIEGLER, INTERNATIONAL ECONOMIC LAW ch. 8 (2nd ed. 2007).

## SDT

*See* Special and Differential Treatment.

## SECONDARY BOYCOTT

A form of economic sanction, as distinct from a primary boycott, in which a country implements a punishment against not only the target country (the primary boycott), but also against all other countries that do business with that target country.

A number of United States sanctions are secondary boycotts, including the 1996 *Helms–Burton Act* (targeted at Cuba) and the 1996 *Iran and Libya Sanctions Act* (targeted initially at Iran and Libya, but later amended to remove Libya). The Arab boycott of Israel is both a primary and secondary boycott. Secondary boycotts are highly controversial, because they are an effort by the sanctioning country to compel third countries to participate in the sanctions regime, even in the absence of a multilateral consensus in favor of the regime.

*Suggestions for Further Research:*

Articles:

1.   Bartlett III, James E., et al., *Export Controls and Economic Sanctions*, 43 INTERNATIONAL LAWYER 311–333 (2009).

2.   Meyer, Jeffrey A., *Second Thoughts on Secondary Sanctions*, 30 UNIVERSITY OF PENNSYLVANIA JOURNAL OF INTERNATIONAL LAW 905–967 (2009).

## *SECOFI*

*Secretaría de Comercio y Fomento Industrial (SECOFI)* is the former name for Mexico's *Secretaría de Economía, i.e.,* the *Ministry of the Economy,* or *"Economía."*

Former Mexican President Vicente Fox changed *SECOFI* to *Economía* after he took office in 2000. The main objectives of *Economía* are to promote Mexican-owned companies' competitiveness and economic growth in both domestic and international markets. The Secretary of *Economía* who took office in December 2006 is Eduardo Sojo Garza Aldape.

*See Economía.*

## SECOND GENERATION FTAS

Second Generation Free Trade Agreements, also called "deep FTAs."

The *Peru — Canada Free Trade Agreement (FTA)* is the first of a new breed of FTAs, branded as "Second Generation FTAs." This "new" FTA is distinguished from previous FTAs as being significantly more comprehensive than the first generation accords. The Second Generation FTAs include provisions addressing government procurement, investment protection, competition policy, enforcement of intellectual property rights, labor, and the environment. In comparison, the *Canada — European Free Trade Association FTA (Canada — EFTA FTA)*, which was signed in January 2008, is considered a first-generation accord. Among other notable omissions, it does not address labor, the environment, or services in any section of the agreement.

The *Peru — Canada FTA* was negotiated in less than one year, and signed on 29 May 2008. Issues are covered in the main text of the agreement and in annexes. The provisions relating to the environment are found in a side agreement.[553] Aside from the earliest of its FTAs (namely, with Israel and Canada), all of America's agreements would fit within the "Second Generation" rubric.

---

[553] Lucien O. Chauvin, *Canada Pushes Second-Generation FTAs Covering Range of Issues, Emerson Says*, 25 International Trade Reporter (BNA) 889 (12 June 2008).

## SECTION 201

*See* Escape Clause, SSG, and SSM.

## SECTION 301

A unilateral trade remedy of the United States.

The term "Section 301" commonly is used to include Sections 301–309 of the *Trade Act of 1974*, as amended, and codified at 19 U.S.C. §§ 2411-2419. The existence and use of Section 301 has proved highly controversial, and been the subject of studies as to the efficacy of this weapon. A few other countries, including WTO Members, have unilateral remedies loosely akin to Section 301.

*Suggestions for Further Research:*

Books:

1. BAYARD, THOMAS O. & KIMBERLY ANN ELLIOTT, RECIPROCITY AND RETALIATION IN U.S. TRADE POLICY (1994).

2. LOW, PATRICK, TRADING FREE 89, 91 (1993).

3. OYE, KENNETH A., ECONOMIC DISCRIMINATION AND POLITICAL EXCHANGE: WORLD POLITICAL ECONOMY IN THE 1930S AND 1980S (1992)

4. VAKERICS, THOMAS V., DAVID I. WILSON & KENNETH G. WEIGEL, ANTIDUMPING, COUNTERVAILING DUTY, AND OTHER TRADE ACTIONS (1987).

Book Chapters:

1. McMillan, John, *Strategic Bargaining and Section 301*, *in* AGGRESSIVE UNILATERALISM: AMERICA'S 301 TRADE POLICY AND THE WORLD TRADING SYSTEM 203 (Jagdish Bhagwati & Hugh T. Patrick, eds., 1990).

Articles:

1. Bayard, Thomas O., Comment On Alan Sykes' *"Mandatory Retaliation for Breach of Trade Agreements: Some Thoughts on the Strategic Design of Section 301,"* 8 BOSTON UNIVERSITY INTERNATIONAL LAW JOURNAL 301, 322 (1987).

2. Bello, Judith Hippler & Alan F. Holmer, *The Heart of the 1988 Trade Act: A Legislative History of the Amendments to Section 301*, 25 STANFORD JOURNAL OF INTERNATIONAL LAW 1, 12–14 (1988).

3. Bello, Judith Hippler & Alan F. Holmer, *Section 301 of the Trade Act of 1974: Requirements, Procedures, and Developments*, 7 NORTHWESTERN JOURNAL OF INTERNATIONAL LAW & BUSINESS 633, 636–37 (1986).

4. Bliss, Julia Christine, *The Amendments to Section 301: An Overview and Suggested Strategies for Foreign Response*, 20 LAW & POLICY IN INTERNATIONAL BUSINESS 501 (1989).

5. Borrus, Michael & Judith Goldstein, *United States Trade Protectionism: Institutions, Norms, and Practices*, 8 NORTHWESTERN JOURNAL OF INTERNATIONAL LAW & BUSINESS 328, 352 (1987).

6. Broiles, David, *When Myths Collide: An Analysis of Conflicting U.S.- Japanese Views on Economics, Law, and Values*, 1 TEXAS WESLEYAN LAW REVIEW 109 (1994).

7. Cline, William R., *"Reciprocity": A New Approach to World Trade Policy?*, POLICY ANALYSES IN INTERNATIONAL ECONOMICS (1982).

8. Diamond, Richard, *Changes in the Game: Understanding the Relationship Between Section 301 and U.S. Trade Strategies*, 8 BOSTON UNIVERSITY INTERNATIONAL LAW JOURNAL 351, 352–53, 357, 360 (1990).

9. Eichmann, Erwin P. & Gary N. Horlick, *Political Questions in International Trade: Judicial Review of Section 301?*, 10 MICHIGAN JOURNAL OF INTERNATIONAL LAW 735, 761–64 (1989).

10. Fisher, Bart S. & Ralph G. Steinhardt, III, *Section 301 of the Trade Act of 1974: Protection for U.S. Exporters of Goods, Services, and Capital*, 14 LAW & POLICY IN INTERNATIONAL 569, 570 (1982).

11. Hansen, Patricia I., Note, *Defining Unreasonableness in International Trade: Section 301 of the Trade Act of 1974*, 96 YALE LAW JOURNAL 1122, 1130–31 (1987).

12. Jones, W. Davis, *The Relationship between Trade and Effective Enforcement*, 36 DENVER JOURNAL OF INTERNATIONAL LAW & POLICY 389–394 (2008).

13. Maruyama, Warren, *Section 301 and the Appearance of Unilateralism*, 11 MICHIGAN JOURNAL OF INTERNATIONAL LAW 394, 400 (1990).

14. Matsushita, Mitsuo, *A Japanese View of United States Trade Laws*, 8 NORTHWESTERN JOURNAL OF INTERNATIONAL BUSINESS LAW 30, 52–56 (1987).

15. Moyer, Marc A., Comment, *Section 301 of the Omnibus Trade and Competitiveness Act of 1988: A Formidable Weapon in the War Against Economic Espionage*, 15 NORTHWESTERN JOURNAL OF INTERNATIONAL LAW & BUSINESS 178, 190–204 (1994).

16. Nara, Fusae, Note, *A Shift Toward Protectionism Under § 301 of the 1974 Trade Act: Problems of Unilateral Trade Retaliation Under International Law*, 19 HOFSTRA LAW REVIEW 229, 256–66 (1990).

17. Phillips, Steven R., *The New Section 301 of the Omnibus Trade and Competitiveness Act of 1988: Trade Wars or Open Markets?*, 22 VANDERBILT JOURNAL OF TRANSNATIONAL LAW 491, 500–01, 551 (1989).

18. Puckett, A. Lynne & William L. Reynolds, *Rules, Sanctions and Enforcement Under Section 301: At Odds with the WTO?*, 90 AMERICAN JOURNAL OF INTERNATIONAL LAW 675 (October 1996).

19. Stern, Paula, *Reaping the Wind and Sowing the Whirlwind: Section 301 as a Metaphor for Congressional Assertiveness in U.S. Trade Policy*, 8 BOSTON UNIVERSITY INTERNATIONAL LAW JOURNAL 1, 8–13 (1990).

20. Sykes, Alan O., *Constructive Unilateral Threats in International Commercial Relations: The Limited Case for Section 301*, 23 LAW & POLICY IN INTERNATIONAL BUSINESS 263–276 (1992).

21. Thatcher, K. Blake, Comment, *Section 301 of the Trade Act of 1974: Its Utility Against Alleged Unfair Trade Practices by the Japanese Government*, 81 NORTHWESTERN UNIVERSITY LAW REVIEW 492, 497–99 511–12 (1987).

22. Turco, Jonathan M., Note, *Leaving Los Angeles: Runaway Productions and the FTAC's 301(A) Petition Under International Law*, 15 SOUTHWESTERN JOURNAL OF LAW & TRADE IN THE AMERICAS 141–166 (2008).

## SECTION 337

Section 337 of the *United States Tariff Act of 1930*, as amended.[554]

This remedy exists against one form of unfair trade practice, namely, infringement by foreign merchandise of an intellectual property right (IPR). That is, it is unlawful under Section 337 to import any article into the United States that infringes on a patent, trademark, or copyright that is valid and enforceable in the United States. Section 337 also prohibits the importation of a semiconductor chip that infringes on a registered mask work that is valid and enforceable in the United States. Recent examples of goods subject to Section 337 review include digital processors; endoscopic probes; foam footwear; insulin delivery devices; lighters; orthodontic aligners; and portable digital media players, amongst others.

Four elements are required for a petitioner to lodge a successful a Section 337 claim. First, the petitioner must own a valid and enforceable IPR. Second, the imported goods in question must infringe on that IPR right. Third, the petitioner must be an industry in the United States that exists or is in the process of being established. Lastly, there must be a relationship between that industry and the articles protected by the IPR.

The petitioner in a Section 337 action is the right holder of the IPR. That is, the complainant is the right holder seeking to enforce its right against the alleged infringed goods. Once a petitioner lodges a complaint, the International Trade Commission (ITC) has the sole authority to investigate alleged violations of Section 337. However, the ITC does have the authority to self-initiate a Section 337 action.

The remedy includes the possibility of a temporary exclusion order (TEO) or permanent exclusion order (PEO). However, any remedy is subject to Presidential approval. The President has 60 days to overturn the decision for policy reasons.

Section 337 has come under fire from other WTO members, namely, the European Communities (EC). In the 1989 *Section 337* case, a GATT Panel determined Section 337 violated Article III:4 of GATT.[555] The United States responded initially by blocking the GATT Panel Report. The United States

---

[554] *See* 19 U.S.C. § 1337.

[555] *See* Statement by United States Trade Representative Ambassador Carla Hills on Section 337 and Enforcement of Intellectual Property Rights (7 November 1989) *quoted in* Jeffrey S. Neeley & Hideto Ishida, *Section 337 and National Treatment under GATT: A Proposal for Legislative Reform*, 13 FORDHAM INTERNATIONAL LAW JOURNAL 276, 277 (1989).

declared it would change Section 337 only if a comprehensive Uruguay Round agreement improved intellectual property (IP) protection. In 1994, after the *Agreement on Trade-Related Aspects of Intellectual Property Rights (TRIPs)* was finalized, amendments were made to Section 337 under the Clinton Administration, though the European Union (EU) subsequently questioned whether the statute was in full compliance with GATT–WTO obligations.

*Suggestions for Further Research:*

Book:

1.  WARSHOFSKY, FRED, THE PATENT WARS 103–108 (1994).

Book Chapters:

1.  Herrington, Wayne W., *Protecting Trademarks and Copyrights by Section 337 Proceedings at the International Trade Commission*, in INTERNATIONAL TRADEMARKS AND COPYRIGHTS: ENFORCEMENT AND MANAGEMENT 71–114 (2004).

Articles:

1.  Abbott, Kenneth W., *GATT Dispute Settlement Panel*, 84 AMERICAN JOURNAL OF INTERNATIONAL LAW 274, 279 (1990).

2.  Allison, Richard G., Note, *Section 337 Proceedings before the International Trade Commission: Antiquated Legislative Compromise or a Model Forum for Patent Dispute Resolution?*, 5 NEW YORK UNIVERSITY JOURNAL OF LAW & BUSINESS 873–904 (2009).

3.  Barons, Lisa, Note, *Amending Section 337 to Obtain GATT Consistency and Retain Border Protection*, 22 LAW & POLICY IN INTERNATIONAL BUSINESS 289 (1991).

4.  de Blank, Bas & Bing Cheng, *Where is the ITC Going After Kyocera?*, 25 SANTA CLARA COMPUTER & HIGH TECHNOLOGY LAW JOURNAL 701–721 (2009).

5.  DuChez, Neil F., Note, *Synopsis of the Extraterritorial Protection Afforded by Section 337 as Compared to the Patent Act*, 14 MICHIGAN TELECOMMUNICATIONS & TECHNOLOGY LAW REVIEW 447–456 (2008).

6.  Krupka, Robert G., *et al.*, *Section 337 and the GATT: The Problem or the Solution?*, 42 AMERICAN UNIVERSITY LAW REVIEW 779, 783, 821 (1993).

7.  Laroski, Joseph A., Jr. & Valentin A. Povarchuk eds., *International Trade*, 45 THE INTERNATIONAL LAWYER 79–94 (spring 2011).

8.  Lim, Lily & Sarah E. Craven, *Injunctions Enjoined; Remedies Restructured*, 25 SANTA CLARA COMPUTER & HIGH TECHNOLOGY LAW JOURNAL 787–819 (2009).

9.  Lyons, Michael J., Andrew J. Wu, and Harry F. Doscher, *Exclusion of Downstream Products After Kyocera: A Revised Framework for General Exclusion Orders*, 25 SANTA CLARA COMPUTER & HIGH TECHNOLOGY LAW JOURNAL 821–838 (2009).

10.  Neeley, Jeffrey S. & Hideto Ishida, *Section 337 and National Treatment under GATT: A Proposal for Legislative Reform*, 13 FORDHAM INTERNATIONAL LAW JOURNAL 276, 277 (1989).

11. Spangler, Anne L., Note, *Intellectual Property Protection and Import Trade: Making Section 337 Consistent with the General Agreement on Tariffs and Trade*, 43 HASTINGS LAW JOURNAL 217, 251–71 (1991).

# SECTION 421

*Section 421 of the Trade Act of 1974*, as amended.

Section 421 is a special safeguard remedy for use by the United States against imports that cause or threaten to cause disruption to the American market. The remedy dates from the Cold War. In the late 1960s and early 1970s, under a policy of détente pursued by President Richard M. Nixon and his Secretary of State, Henry Kissinger, the United States and former Union of Soviet Socialist Republics (U.S.S.R.) sought peaceful competition and co-existence. The United States gradually opened its markets to products from the Soviet Union and its allies in Central and Eastern Europe. But, with the lowering of trade barriers, United States producers of like products were concerned about possible surges of imports from the Soviet bloc. Section 421 was the answer for domestic producers and labor unions alike, not only to an actual import surge, but even the threat of one into the American market. The precise remedies could vary from case to case, but included raising tariff and non-tariff barriers. Section 421 petitions are brought to the International Trade Commission, which makes a recommendation to the President. The President has absolute discretion to accept, reject, or modify the ITC finding.

Section 421, as such, does not violate GATT–WTO legal regime. However, a highly controversial application of this remedy occurred in September 2009, when President Barack H. Obama accepted the recommendation of the ITC to impose it on tires from China. The ITC voted four - two affirmatively on a Section 421 petition, and called for a three-year tariff on Chinese tires of 40 percent, 35 percent, and 30 percent, on top of the normal most-favored nation (MFN) rate of four percent. China immediately called for WTO dispute settlement consultations with the United States.

To be sure, under its terms of accession to the WTO, which occurred on 11 December 2001, China agreed that the United States could apply Section 421 to its exports. Many extant WTO Members sought, and obtained, the same result — a special safeguard for use against China in the event of market disruption. Moreover, China also agreed under its terms of accession that it would be a non-market economy (NME), making application of antidumping (AD) law easier. Note that Section 421 is useable against more than just NMEs, but it is a rarely used remedy overall. Several Section 421 petitions were brought under the Administration of President George W. Bush, but President Bush rejected every affirmative recommendation to take action.

In 2013, the twin conditions concerning China — use of the special safeguard and designation of an NME — lapse. Until then, because of the multilateral nature of China's accession commitments, any WTO Member can follow a

Section 421 action taken by the United States by invoking the product specific remedy as they have implemented it in their own domestic law.

## SED

Strategic Economic Dialogue.

The China — United States Strategic Economic Dialogue (SED) is a framework for discussion between America the People's Republic of China on economic relations and other bilateral, regional, and global issues affecting the countries. President Barack H. Obama of the United States and President Hu Jintao of China initiated the SED in 2009. The SED replaced an earlier initiative, the Senior Dialogue and Strategic Economic Dialogue, initiated by President George W. Bush and President Hu Jintao in 2006.[556]

Meetings take place in either the United States or China, with the parties convening twice a year between 2006 and 2008 and once per year in 2009 and 2010. The SED talks are a valuable tool in addressing concerns regarding foreign exchange rates (particularly the alleged under-valuation of the Chinese *yuan* relative to the dollar) investment policies, product safety, intellectual property (IP), energy, the environment, and trade. Both countries participate actively in the discussions and remain committed to maintaining a market for open investment and growth.[557]

## SEMICONDUCTOR MASK WORK

A semiconductor mask work is a form of intellectual property (IP). The specific circuit layout pattern on a silicon computer chip is called the "mask work."

Computer chips are made of silicon, because of the unique "semi-conducting" properties of silicon. Specifically, silicon can conduct electricity under certain circumstances, and resist it under other circumstances. Silicon also has a unique ability to serve as a transistor, thereby avoiding the need for cumbersome, heat-generating vacuum tubes and switches to regulate the path for the flow of electric current. The pathways can be etched directly on a silicon chip. An integrated circuit on a chip not only performs transistor like on-off functions, but also engages in logic functions (*e.g.*, data storage, process, and manipulation). Accordingly, a "semiconductor mask work" consists of two or more layers of metallic semiconducting material into which is etched a pre-determined pattern. The semiconductor mask work is designed to perform electronic circuitry functions.

---

[556] For general information on the SED, see *U.S.-China Strategic and Economic Dialogue, posted at* csis.org/publication/us-china-strategic-and-economic-dialogue-0; *posted at* www.treasury.gov/initiatives/Pages/china.aspx.

[557] *See* Amy Tsui, *With China's Investor Role Growing, U.S. Welcomes Chinese FDI, Envoy Says*, 25 International Trade Reporter (BNA) 802 (29 May 2008).

In 1984, Congress enacted the *Semiconductor Protection Act* to protect layouts that define the circuits and functions on a chip.[558] Under that *Act*, Congress defines a "mask work" as:

> A series of related images, however fixed or encoded, having or representing the predetermined, three-dimensional pattern of metallic, insulating, or semiconductor material present or removed from the layers of a semiconductor chip product, and in which the relation of the images to one another is such that each image has the pattern of the surface of one form of the semiconductor chip product. 17 U.S.C. § 901(a)(2).

This *sui generis* form of protection was necessary because existing IP law was inadequate. Chip producers had a hard time getting patent protection for semiconductor mask works, because a chip and its layout did not necessarily meet the new and non-obvious tests. Moreover, the two to three year period spent waiting for a decision to be made on a patent application was too long. By the time the decision was made, the chip market had evolved considerably. Copyright law could help protect only a technical drawing of a chip, but not the objects made from the drawing. Thus, it could not bar others from copying a circuit layout and selling the results — *i.e.*, from mass production by a competitor. Moreover, copyright law did not protect articles merely because they were useful. It focused on the aesthetic, not utilitarian, aspect of the subject matter, as a pre-condition for protection.

Thus, the *Semiconductor Act* creates a new form of IP — namely, chips — and protects them from unauthorized copying. The key right is to the exclusive right of reproduction, and to import and distribute works that contain the mask work. Of course, the owner of the mask work may license the rights to make, import, and distribute the chip. Unlike copyrights, protection does not extend to derivative works. But, as with copyrights, the owner's rights are limited by the "fair use" doctrine. Analysis and research is a fair use. So, too, is reverse engineering (*i.e.*, dissolving the successive layers of silicon on a chip to discover the circuit pattern), as long as the purpose of the reverse engineering is not to completely strip down a chip to determine its make-up in order to replicate the mask work. The term of protection is 10 years from the date of registration or from the date of the first commercial exploitation, whichever date is earlier.

Four requirements must be satisfied to obtain protection under the *Semiconductor Act*. First, the mask must be set on a semiconductor chip. Second, the design of the circuit laid out on the chip must be original, which means it must be created independently. Third, the owner must meet certain citizenship or domicile requirements. In general, if the owner is a foreign national, then protection is possible only if the owner's home country affords protection of semiconductor mask works to Americans. Fourth, the owner must register the mask work within two years of it being commercially exploited

---

[558] *See* 17 U.S.C. §§ 901-914.

anywhere in the world. Registration is done at the Copyright Office of the Library of Congress. As with the other forms of IP, an owner of a semiconductor mask work must enforce its rights. Remedies for infringement are damages and the destruction of infringing products.

*Suggestions for Further Research:*

Book:

1. NISHI, YOSHIO & ROBERT DOERING EDS. HANDBOOK OF SEMICONDUCTOR MANUFACTURING TECHNOLOGY (2000).

# SERVICE MARK

A service mark is a form of intellectual property (IP).

Specifically, a service mark is any word, name, phrase, symbol or design (or combination of words, names, symbols, or designs) used in the trade of a service to identify the source or origin of that good, and to distinguish the service from all other services.

A service mark arises from either (1) actual use of the mark, or (2) filing an application to register the mark with the appropriate governmental authority stating that the applicant already has used, or intends to use, the mark in commerce. In the United States, the Patent and Trademark Office (PTO) is responsible for handling applications for, and registering, service marks. Note, therefore, that because use can establish the right to a mark, it is not necessary to register the mark to have that right. Anyone claiming rights in a service mark can use the "SM" designation to alert the public to the claim. However, under American law, federal registration creates a presumption of ownership of a mark, and only as a result of this registration can the ® symbol be used. American trade and service mark law is set forth in the *Trademark Act of 1946*, commonly known as the *"Lanham Act."*[559]

The first party who either uses the mark in commerce or files an application has the ultimate right to register the mark. A service mark can last indefinitely if the owner continues to use the mark to identify its service. The term of federal registration is 10 years, with 10 year renewal terms.

The key criterion in determining whether to grant a registration request is whether there is a conflict between the proposed service mark and an existing service mark. Where there is a likelihood of confusion, *i.e.,* where consumers would be likely to associate the applicant's service with the service of another party that already has a service mark, the application will be denied. To find a conflict, the proposed and extant service marks need not be identical, and the services do not have to be identical.

A second criterion used to determine whether to grant an application request is the nature of the service mark. If it is merely descriptive of the service, or a

---

[559] *See* 15 U.S.C. §§ 1051 *et seq.*

feature of the service, then an application for registration likely will be refused. Moreover, applications to register a geographic term or surname also may be refused. Finally, a service mark cannot consist of (1) immoral, deceptive, or scandalous material, (2) the name, picture, or signature of a living person (without that person's consent), or (3) the official flag of a country or sub-central government.

As with a copyright, patent, or trademark, it is up to the owner of a service mark to enforce the property right in the event of possible infringement.

## SIECA

Secretariat for Central American Economic Integration.

SIECA was established by *Tratado General de Integración Económica Centroamericana* (*General Treaty of Central American Economic Integration*), signed in Managua, Nicaragua, on 13 December 1960. SIECA has legal personality, with headquarters in Guatemala City, Guatemala.

The fundamental purpose of SIECA is to help Central America nations integrate into the global economy, namely, through world trade. The principal function of SIECA is to provide technical and administrative assistance toward this integration. It does so mainly in the form of work studies and field analyses. An important initial step in this process is formation of a Central American customs union (CU).

The Figure below summarizes the organizational structure of SIECA. A *Secretaria General* (Secretary General), who is appointed by the *Consejo de Ministros de Integración Económica* (Council of Ministers of Economic Integration), leads SIECA. The Secretary General is in charge of the *Dirección Ejecutiva* (Executive Direction). In turn, the Executive Direction houses three separate committees: General Direction of Integration and Trade; General Direction of Legal Affairs; and General Direction of Information Technologies.

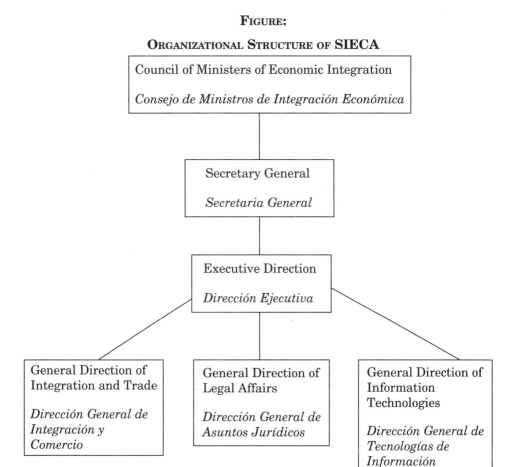

FIGURE:

ORGANIZATIONAL STRUCTURE OF **SIECA**

Council of Ministers of Economic Integration

*Consejo de Ministros de Integración Económica*

Secretary General

*Secretaria General*

Executive Direction

*Dirección Ejecutiva*

General Direction of Integration and Trade

*Dirección General de Integración y Comercio*

General Direction of Legal Affairs

*Dirección General de Asuntos Jurídicos*

General Direction of Information Technologies

*Dirección General de Tecnologías de Información*

Additionally, the Secretariat houses an independent body established by the *Central American Free Trade Agreement–Dominican Republic* (*CAFTA–DR*), the Secretary of Environmental Affairs of *CAFTA-DR* (SEA), which reviews claims from the public that a *CAFTA–DR* Member failed to effectively enforce its environmental law. The Environmental Chapter of *CAFTA–DR*, Chapter 17, allows members of the public to submit allegations of such failure to an independent body. Article 17:7 specifies the filing requirements. The SEA of *CAFTA-DR* has operated since 2 October 2006.[560]

# SINGAPORE ISSUES

Four issues identified at the first WTO Ministerial Conference in 1996, held in Singapore. These issues are —

(1) foreign direct investment (FDI),

(2) trade (or customs) facilitation,

---

[560] Rossella Brevetti, *CAFTA-DR Environmental Affairs Council Establishes Secretariat, Outlines Functions,* 23 INTERNATIONAL TRADE REPORTER (BNA) 914–15 (15 June 2006).

(3)  transparency in government procurement, and

(4)  trade and competition policy.

As a result of these issues, the Ministerial Conference set up three new working groups: on trade and investment, on competition policy, and on transparency in government procurement. In addition, the Ministerial Conference instructed the WTO Goods Council to look at ways to simplifying trade procedures (*i.e.*, trade facilitation).

The European Union (EU), among other WTO Members, favored inclusion of all four issues in the Doha Round. Facing stiff opposition, especially from developing and least-developed countries. Much to the relief of, and following considerable urging by, developing and least-developing countries, these issues were not revisited at the 2003 Cancún Ministerial Conference. On 1 August 2004, the EU was forced to drop the first, third, and fourth issues from the Doha Round talks.

*Suggestions for Further Research:*

Books:

1.  ARROWSMITH, SUE, ED., GOVERNMENT PROCUREMENT IN THE WTO (2003).

2.  ARROWSMITH, SUE & MARTIN TRYBUS EDS., PUBLIC PROCUREMENT — THE CONTINUING REVOLUTION (2003).

3.  GRAHAM, EDWARD M. & J. DAVID RICHARDSON EDS., GLOBAL COMPETITION POLICY (December 1997).

4.  KENNEDY, KEVIN, COMPETITION LAW AND THE WORLD TRADE ORGANIZATION: THE LIMITS OF MULTILATERALISM (2001).

5.  STATE SECRETARIAT OF ECONOMIC AFFAIRS (SWITZERLAND) & SIMON J. EVENETT (WORLD TRADE INSTITUTE, BERNE), THE SINGAPORE ISSUES AND THE WORLD TRADING SYSTEM: THE ROAD TO CANCÚN AND BEYOND (SECO Publication Number 1, June 2003).

Article:

1.  Wisner, Robert & Nick Gallus, *The Emergence of WTO Competition Law: The Mexico — Telecommunications and Canada — Wheat and Grain Decisions*, 10 INTERNATIONAL TRADE LAW & REGULATION issue 5, 91–95 (September 2004).

Other Sources:

1.  *World Trade Organization: Status of Issues to be Considered at Singapore Ministerial Meeting*, HEARING BEFORE THE SUBCOMMITTEE ON TRADE OF THE HOUSE COMMITTEE ON WAYS AND MEANS, 103ᴿᴰ CONGRESS 1–19 (1996) (statement of JayEtta Z. Hecker, Associate Director, International Relations and Trade Issues, National Security and International Affairs Division).

2.  *World Trade Organization: Observations on the Ministerial Meeting in Singapore*, HEARING BEFORE THE SUBCOMMITTEE ON TRADE OF THE HOUSE COMMITTEE ON WAYS AND MEANS, 104ᵀᴴ CONGRESS 1–14 (1997) (statement of JayEtta Z. Hecker, Associate Director, International Relations and Trade Issues, National Security and International Affairs Division).

## SINGLE ENTRY BOND (SINGLE TRANSACTION BOND)

*See* Customs Bond.

## SINGLE PAYMENT SCHEME

A term associated with reforms to the Common Agriculture Policy (CAP) of the European Union (EU), especially Agenda 2000 and the 2003 Mid-Term Review of 2000.

The term connotes the receipt by a farmer of a single annual payment as farm support, instead of several assistance payments during the year. To be eligible for a single payment, a farmer requires payment entitlements. The single payment scheme (SPS) is calculated on the number of payments received by the farmer during a specific reference period, or by the number of eligible hectares during the first year of implementation of the scheme.[561]

The term also connotes a shift to non-trade distorting support, as the SPS contemplates support regardless of exportation, production, or non-production. In effect, the single payment (in theory) is entirely de-coupled from economic activity. Though the EU claims the primary impetus of the SPS is to guarantee farmers more stable income, the intention of the SPS was to de-couple grants payments from production, as many WTO Members (*inter alia*) criticized the EU for unfairly subsidizing its farmers. However, in conjunction with the environmental and social values of the EU, receipt of the single payment is contingent on a farmer satisfying criteria in support of those values. That contingency is known as cross-compliance.

The implementation and grants afforded to farmers vary from country to country. For most EU states, the SPS was implemented between 2005 and 2007. Different rules apply to the 10 new countries that joined the EU in May 2004, which have until 2011 to phase in the scheme, as well as to states joining the EU subsequently, namely, Bulgaria and Romania, which had until 2012. All new states may elect to adopt the SPS or to phase it in over a period from 2005–2013.

## SINGLE UNDERTAKING

An approach to trade negotiations whereby nothing is agreed to until everything is agreed.

That is, every item of the negotiation is part of a whole and indivisible package. Thus, an agreement in one legal area or economic sector is contingent on a deal being reached in all other areas and sectors. A different strategy is called the "early harvest approach," whereby one or a few deals are agreed to and implemented, on the basis of which negotiations on other topics are pursued.

The single undertaking approach was first used in the Uruguay Round. However, its use in the Doha Round has provoked considerable criticism. The

---

[561] *See* Commission Regulation (EC) 1782/2003, 2003 J.O. (L 270) 20–41.

advantage of the single undertaking approach is it provides for a comprehensive set of trade liberalizing obligations, and the obligations are carefully balanced. The disadvantage is that considerable progress made on one issue is not finalized until all other issues are resolved. If resolution does not occur on a particular matter, then that progress is lost.

*Suggestions for Further Research:*

Articles:

1.  Lanoszka, Anna, *The Promises of Multilateralism and the Hazards of "Single Undertaking:" the Breakdown of Decision Making within the WTO*, 16 MICHIGAN STATE JOURNAL OF INTERNATIONAL LAW, 655–675 (2008).

2.  Rolland, Sonia E., *Redesigning the Negotiation Process at the WTO*, 13 JOURNAL OF INTERNATIONAL ECONOMIC LAW 65–110 (2010).

3.  Wolfe, Robert, *The WTO Single Undertaking as Negotiating Technique and Constitutive Metaphor*, 12 JOURNAL OF INTERNATIONAL ECONOMIC LAW 835–858 (2009).

## SME (FIRST MEANING)

Small and Medium Sized Enterprise.

SMEs are those enterprises that employ less than a specified ceiling and whose turnover does not exceed a certain amount. In the European Union (EU), an SME is an enterprise employing less than 250 persons, whose annual turnover does not exceed 50 million, and/or whose annual balance sheet total does not exceed 43 million euros.[562]

In the United States, however, the classification of SMEs is more complex.[563] The government agency established for SMEs, the Small Business Association (SBA), revises the numerical definitions for all for-profit industries. This numerical definition is called a "size standard." The SBA considers a number of economic characteristics of a particular industry when setting size standards. These facts include competition within the industry; average firm size; start-up costs; entry barriers; distribution of firms by size; technological changes; competition from other industries; growth trends, historical activity within an industry; and other unique factors occurring in the industry which may distinguish small firms from other firms.

## SME (SECOND MEANING)

Square Meter Equivalent.

The term is used in the context of international trade textiles and apparel (T&A). SMEs allow for different kinds of textiles and apparel to be compared

---

[562] *See* Commission Regulation 96/280, 2003 O.J. (L 124) 39.
[563] 13 C.F.R. § 121 (2006).

and measured against one another. Typically, a harmonized unit for measuring different T&A articles is necessary in order to administer trade agreements dealing with them, particularly provisions concerning quotas or tariff rate quotas (TRQs). Moreover, the commonality provided by the SME unit facilitates collection of balance of payments (BOP) statistics, as regards imports and exports of T&A.

## SMOOT–HAWLEY TARIFF ACT (SMOOT–HAWLEY TRADE ACT)

A key portion of the *Tariff Act of 1930*, as amended, sponsored by Senator Reed Smoot (Republican-Oregon) and Congressman Willis Hawley (Republican-Ohio), which raised American duty rates on over 20,000 imported articles to historic or near-historic levels in response to the economic depression of the times.

Protectionism in the United States manifest in the *Smoot–Hawley Tariff Act* was met with protectionist responses in other countries, and coupled with competitive currency devaluations, with each country seeking to protect its jobs and incomes, and export unemployment and wage decline to other countries. This beggar-thy-neighbor scenario exacerbated the Great Depression, which was caused by erroneous economic policy responses, namely, a lack of Keynesian fiscal stimulus (and instead adherence to balanced-budget style policies), contractionary monetary policies, and restrictive exchange rate policies (namely, clinging to the gold standard).

Smoot–Hawley duties still exist in the Harmonized Tariff Schedule of the United States (HTSUS) as the Column 2 non-MFN rates. But, they apply to a tiny and diminishing number of countries.

*Suggestions for Further Research:*

Books:

1.  BEAUDREAU, BERNARD C., MAKING SENSE OF SMOOT–HAWLEY: TECHNOLOGY AND TARIFFS (2005).

2.  IRWIN, DOUGLAS A., THE BATTLE OVER PROTECTION: A HISTORY OF U.S. TRADE POLICY (2009).

3.  IRWIN, DOUGLAS A., PEDDLING PROTECTIONISM: SMOOT — HAWLEY AND THE GREAT DEPRESSION (2011). *See also* the review of this book, Niall Meagher, *Book Review*, 14 JOURNAL OF INTERNATIONAL ECONOMIC LAW 507–511 (2011).

Articles:

1.  Berglund, Abraham, *The Tariff Act of 1930*, AMERICAN ECONOMIC REVIEW (1930).

2.  Irwin, Douglas A., *Antebellum Tariff Politics: Regional Coalitions and Shifting Economic Interests*, 51 JOURNAL OF LAW & ECONOMICS 715–741 (2008).

3.  McDonald, Judith, Anthony Patrick O'Brien & Colleen Callahan, *Trade Wars: Canada's Reaction to the Smoot–Hawley Tariff*, JOURNAL OF ECONOMIC HISTORY (December 1007).

## SOCIAL DUMPING

The phenomenon whereby companies located in a country with lax labor standards and enforcement benefit from this state through low production costs, making labor unfriendly goods that are sold in another country.

The exports are dumped not in the technical sense of cross-border price discrimination, but in the sense they embody low working conditions and poor enforcement of labor rights in the home country. Hence, these goods are unfriendly to workers manufacturing like or directly competitive products in the importing country.

*See* Environmental Dumping.

*Suggestions for Further Research:*

Book Chapters:

1.   Corden, W. Max & Neil Vousden, *Paved with Good Intentions: Social Dumping and Raising Labor Standards in Developing Countries*, in GLOBALISATION UNDER THREAT: THE STABILITY OF TRADE POLICY AND MULTILATERAL AGREEMENTS 124–43 (Zdenek Drabek ed., 2001).

2.   Pizzuti, Felice R., *Globalization, Welfare State and Social Dumping*, in GLOBALIZATION, INSTITUTIONS, AND SOCIAL COHESION 127–58 (Maurizio Franzini and Felice R. Pizzuti eds., 2001).

## SOCIAL JUSTICE

Generally speaking, "social justice" is "justice in society in general," which is to say it "is concerned with the common good."[564] More specifically, "social justice" concerns rights and duties at a societal level, that is, the obligations owed by individuals and groups in their design and operation of societal frameworks (such as the legal system, the economy, and the political system) in which these individuals and groups interact.

Social justice should not be confused with the other three types of justice — though it often is. Those types are:

*   Commutative justice —

Commutative justice covers the obligations arising from relationships between and among individuals, and involves respect for the rights of another person, including for the property of that person. Commutative justice "binds individual to individual in the sphere of private transactions."[565] A classic example is a contractual relationship between two parties, whereby rights and obligations are established, whether the subject matter be goods, services (including labor in exchange for a wage), or property. As Saint Thomas Aquinas explains in *Summa Theologica*,

---

[564] RODGER CHARLES, S.J., AN INTRODUCTION TO CATHOLIC SOCIAL TEACHING 27 (1999).
[565] MONSIGNOR DAVID BOHR, CATHOLIC MORAL TRADITION 337 (rev'd ed. 1999).

Commutative justice is concerned with the mutual dealings between two people. . . . In commutations something is paid to an individual chiefly in buying and selling. Hence it is necessary to equalise thing with thing — equality in *arithmetic* proportion.[566]

Essentially, commutative justice demands "economic justice in exchange of goods by barter or selling," which means "there must be exact equivalence between what is agreed and what is paid."[567] Indeed, this type of justice "commands that exchange be of equal value . . . [and because it] operates by the standard of strict equality," it is "violated by theft, fraud, and unjust damage."[568] Thus, for example, commutative justice would entail a right of restitution for payment of funds already made in the event of non-performance of a duty.

• Distributive justice —

Distributive justice concerns the obligations of a community or government to the individual members of the community or citizens of the polity, particularly as regards the allocation of public social goods. In *Summa Theologica*, Saint Thomas Aquinas states:

> [D]istributive justice distributes common goods proportionately. . . . In distributive justice we find equality in *geometric* proportion; a person's station is considered.[569]

The benefits and burdens of membership in a community, or of citizenship in a country, are regulated by the governing authority of that community or country. How that authority distributes these benefits and burdens is a question of distributive justice. In brief, this type of justice pertains to "the distribution of the goods and honors of the State among its citizens according to their contribution to the commonweal."[570] As a general criterion for distributive justice, the allocation ought to be in some relation to the needs and contributions of the members of the community or polity. A classic example is a progressive tax system, implying payment based on ability to pay, coupled with the expenditure of tax revenues on the housing, food, education, and health needs of the poor. In contrast, "[p]erversions" of distributive justice "include all kinds of corruption, favoritism toward individuals or groups, all kinds of oppression, [and] all unrelieved poverty."[571]

---

[566] SAINT THOMAS AQUINAS, SUMMA THEOLOGICA, IIª IIᵃᵉ Q. 61 Art. 1, Art. 2, *quoted in* RODGER CHARLES, S.J., AN INTRODUCTION TO CATHOLIC SOCIAL TEACHING 28 (1999) (emphasis original).

[567] RODGER CHARLES, S.J., AN INTRODUCTION TO CATHOLIC SOCIAL TEACHING 27 (1999).

[568] MONSIGNOR DAVID BOHR, CATHOLIC MORAL TRADITION 337–338 (rev'd ed. 1999).

[569] SAINT THOMAS AQUINAS, SUMMA THEOLOGICA, IIª IIᵃᵉ Q. 61 Art. 1, Art. 2, *quoted in* RODGER CHARLES. S.J., AN INTRODUCTION TO CATHOLIC SOCIAL TEACHING 28 (1999) (emphasis original).

[570] RODGER CHARLES, S.J., AN INTRODUCTION TO CATHOLIC SOCIAL TEACHING 27 (1999).

[571] MONSIGNOR DAVID BOHR, CATHOLIC MORAL TRADITION 338 (rev'd ed. 1999).

- Legal justice —

Legal justice refers to the obligations of a person to a community, or of a citizen to a government. Commutative justice, as well as distributive justice, is a species of "particular" justice. But, "legal" justice also is called "general" justice. This appellation is based on coverage. "Legal" or "general" justice "pertains both to the bearers *and* subjects of authority who practice it by passing and furthering legislation favorable to the common welfare."[572] In other words, legal justice is about what an individual owes to a collective body (whereas distributive justice is the converse). The individual could be an ordinary one, or one who is a leader in political society. A classic example is the duty of an individual to pay his fair share of taxes, where this share is calculated according to a criterion of general justice, such as the ability to pay.

Social justice concerns arise in international trade law in many contexts, from agricultural subsidies and cultural protection to service market liberalization and special and differential treatment.

What distinguishes "social justice" from other types of justice is its use of moral reasoning to take "into account the fact that relationships between persons have an *institutional or structural dimension*."[573] In overtly Catholic Christian terms, social justice is

> the obligation of all parties to apply the Gospel to the structures, systems, and institutions of society which are the framework in which all human relationships take place.[574]

Social justice demands that individuals and groups empowered to create and implement these frameworks "take an active interest in necessary social and economic reform."[575] In doing so, they serve God, as Saint Thomas Aquinas points out in *Summa Theologica*:

> Justice is a habit whereby a man renders to each one his due by constant and perpetual will. *Just as love of God includes love of neighbor, so too the service of God includes rendering to each one his due.*[576]

Interestingly, while the philosophical and theological roots of the concept of "social justice" are ancient, the term itself is relatively new. In *Quadragesimo Anno*, Pope Pius XI uses the term "social justice" eight times.[577] This 1931 Encyclical may be one of the first instances in which the term appears, at least in Roman Catholic social teaching.

---

[572] MONSIGNOR DAVID BOHR, CATHOLIC MORAL TRADITION 338 (rev'd ed. 1999) (emphasis added).

[573] MONSIGNOR DAVID BOHR, CATHOLIC MORAL TRADITION 337 (rev'd ed. 1999) (emphasis added).

[574] RICHARD P. McBRIEN, CATHOLICISM 946 (new ed. 1994).

[575] RICHARD P. McBRIEN, CATHOLICISM 946 (new ed. 1994).

[576] SAINT THOMAS AQUINAS, SUMMA THEOLOGICA, IIa IIae Q. 58 Art. 1 ad 6, *quoted in* RODGER CHARLES, S.J., AN INTRODUCTION TO CATHOLIC SOCIAL TEACHING 26 (1999) (emphasis added).

[577] *See* MONSIGNOR DAVID BOHR, CATHOLIC MORAL TRADITION 337 (rev'd ed. 1999).

*Suggestions for Further Research:*

Books:

1. BARRERA, ALBINO, O.P., MODERN CATHOLIC SOCIAL DOCUMENTS & POLITICAL ECONOMY (2001).

2. BOHR, MONSIGNOR DAVID, CATHOLIC MORAL TRADITION (rev'd ed. 1999).

3. CATECHISM OF THE CATHOLIC CHURCH (2nd ed. 1997) (especially ¶¶ 1928-1942 at 468-472, ¶ 2411 at 899).

4. CHARLES, RODGER, S.J., AN INTRODUCTION TO CATHOLIC SOCIAL TEACHING (1999).

5. EVANS, BERNARD F., LAZARUS AT THE TABLE — CATHOLICS AND SOCIAL JUSTICE (2006).

6. GARCIA, FRANK J., TRADE, INEQUALITY, AND JUSTICE: TOWARD A LIBERAL THEORY OF JUST TRADE (2003).

7. HARDON, JOHN A., S.J., THE CATHOLIC CATECHISM (1981).

8. KAPSTEIN, ETHAN B., ECONOMIC JUSTICE IN AN UNFAIR WORLD — TOWARD A LEVEL PLAYING FIELD (2006).

9. MASSARO, THOMAS, S.J., LIVING JUSTICE — CATHOLIC SOCIAL TEACHING IN ACTION (2000).

10. McBRIEN, RICHARD P., CATHOLICISM (new ed. 1994).

11. O'BRIEN, DAVID J. & THOMAS A. SHANNON EDS., CATHOLIC SOCIAL THOUGHT — THE DOCUMENTARY HERITAGE (1992).

12. PEARCE, JOSEPH, SMALL IS STILL BEAUTIFUL — ECONOMICS AS IF FAMILIES MATTERED (2006).

13. PIEPER, JOSEF, THE FOUR CARDINAL VIRTUES (1965).

14. PONTIFICAL COUNCIL FOR JUSTICE AND PEACE, COMPENDIUM OF THE SOCIAL DOCTRINE OF THE CHURCH (2004).

15. RULAND, VERNON, CONSCIENCE ACROSS BORDERS — AN ETHICS OF GLOBAL RIGHTS AND RELIGIOUS PLURALISM (2002).

16. SCAPERLANDA, MICHAEL A. & TERESA STANTON COLLETT, RECOVERING SELF-EVIDENT TRUTHS — CATHOLIC PERSPECTIVES ON AMERICAN LAW (2007).

17. SCHALL, JAMES V., ROMAN CATHOLIC POLITICAL PHILOSOPHY (2004).

18. THOMPSON, J. MILBURN, JUSTICE & PEACE — A CHRISTIAN PRIMER (1997).

19. ZWICK, MARK & LOUISE, THE CATHOLIC WORKER MOVEMENT — INTELLECTUAL AND SPIRITUAL ORIGINS (2005).

Articles:

1. Berg, Thomas C., *Intellectual Property and the Preferential Option for the Poor*, 5 JOURNAL OF CATHOLIC SOCIAL THOUGHT number 1, 193–233 (2008).

2. Bjorklund, Andrea K., *Causation, Morality, and Quantum*, 32 SUFFOLK TRANSNATIONAL LAW REVIEW 435–450 (2009).

3. de Blanco, Eglé Iturbe, *Women: Power and Development in Latin America*, 5 UNIVERSITY OF ST. THOMAS LAW JOURNAL 675–697 (2008).

4. Diebold, Nicolas F., *The Morals and Order Exceptions in WTO Law: Balancing the Toothless Tiger and the Undermining Mole*, 11 JOURNAL OF INTERNATIONAL ECONOMIC LAW 43–74 (2008).

5. Domínguez, Jorge I., *The Politics of Hope: Free Politics and Free Markets in Latin America*, 5 UNIVERSITY OF ST. THOMAS LAW JOURNAL 625–638 (2008).

6. Elizabeth, V.S., *Distributive Justice — Poverty and Economic Development*, 28 PENN STATE INTERNATIONAL LAW REVIEW 463–475 (2010).

7. Garcia, Frank J., *Book Review — A Philosophy of International Law* (Fernando R. Teson), 93 AMERICAN JOURNAL OF INTERNATIONAL LAW 746 (1999).

8. Garcia, Frank J., *Trade and Inequality: Economic Justice and the Developing World*, 21 MICHIGAN JOURNAL OF INTERNATIONAL LAW 975 (2000).

9. Garcia, Frank J., *Building a Just Trade Order for a New Millennium*, 33 THE GEORGE WASHINGTON INTERNATIONAL LAW REVIEW 1015 (2001).

10. Garcia, Frank J., *Global Justice and the Bretton Woods Institutions*, 10 JOURNAL OF INTERNATIONAL ECONOMIC LAW 461–481 (2007).

11. Lang, Andrew T.F., *Re-thinking Trade and Human Rights*, 15 TULANE JOURNAL OF INTERNATIONAL AND COMPARATIVE LAW 335–413 (2007).

12. Pérez-Perdomo, Rogelio, *Lawyers, Rule of Law, and Social Justice: A Latin American Perspective*, 5 UNIVERSITY OF ST. THOMAS LAW JOURNAL 730–742 (2008).

13. Petersmann, Ernst-Ulrich, *Multilevel Judicial Governance of International Trade Requires a Common Conception of Rule of Law and Justice*, 10 JOURNAL OF INTERNATIONAL ECONOMIC LAW 529–551 (2007).

14. Reitz, John C., *Politics, Executive Dominance, and Transformative Law in the Culture of Judicial Independence*, 5 UNIVERSITY OF ST. THOMAS LAW JOURNAL 743–807 (2008).

15. Symposium Issue: *The South-North Exchange on Theory, Culture, and Law (SNX 2006), Free Market Fundamentalism: A Critical Review of Dogmas and Consequences*, 5 SEATTLE JOURNAL FOR SOCIAL JUSTICE 497–720 (2007).

## SPECIAL 301

A unilateral trade remedy of the United States, which focuses on intellectual property rights (IPRs).

Special 301 is part of the *Trade Act of 1974*, as amended, and codified at 19 U.S.C. § 2242.

## SOE

State-Owned Enterprise.

An entity created and wholly owned by a State that exercises a particular power of the State. SOEs are a mainstay of many developing countries, particularly in such sectors as utilities, infrastructure industries, transportation and telecommunications. SOEs are often criticized for the inefficient management and misuse of government resources through bloated employee salaries and opaque practices.

Moreover, SOEs distort trade by using any one or more of at least six different methods:[578]

(1)  SOEs receive subsidies, such as exemptions or reductions from tax.

(2)  SOEs do not base decisions on maximizing profits or shareholder wealth, but rather on an array of non-market criteria.

(3)  SOEs are exempt from regulations imposed on private sector business associations.

(4)  SOEs operate in a non-transparent manner.

(5)  SOEs are favored by their parent governments for purchases and sales of goods and services.

(6)  Credit is channeled to SOEs from state-owned banks, laborers in SOEs are controlled through state-approved labor unions, and pension and investment funds in which SOEs are involved are distorted by state officials.

Finally, SOEs can raise sensitive questions of national security. China is a case in point.

First, Chinese SOEs are said to be the source of some cyber-warfare attacks against the United States.[579] Some Chinese telecommunications share the same genealogy as the People's Liberation Army (PLA). Second, proposed acquisitions of American companies by certain Chinese SOEs have raised national concerns of the Committee for Foreign Investment Review in the United States. Third, China has shifted sourcing of certain goods away from the United States to its own SOEs, as in the case of polysilicon (the major input into solar cells). China used to source this item from the United States, but now does so from SOEs, which in turn export 95 percent of their solar production. In consequence, American polysilicon suppliers, and the solar industry, has been injured, and global markets for solar products have been distorted.

The International Monetary Fund (IMF) and World Bank, through the use of conditionality, often require borrowers to reduce the budgets of SOEs and/or, in some instances, to divest the state of the SOE altogether. Such divestments have led to 20 - 30 million layoffs in China over the last decade.

*Suggestions for Further Research:*

Books:

1.  FERNANDEZ, JUAN ANTONIO, CHINA'S STATE-OWNED ENTERPRISE REFORMS: AN INDUSTRIAL AND CEO APPROACH (2007).

2.  TONINELLI, PIERANGELO MARIA, THE RISE AND FALL OF STATE-OWNED ENTERPRISES IN THE WESTERN WORLD (2000).

---

[578] *See* Len Bracken, *Attorney Highlights Trade Distortions of Chinese SOEs That Harm U.S. Firms*, 29 International Trade Reporter (BNA) 289 (23 February 2012).

[579] *See* Len Bracken, *Attorney Highlights Trade Distortions of Chinese SOEs That Harm U.S. Firms*, 29 International Trade Reporter (BNA) 289 (23 February 2012).

Articles:

1. Dickinson, Andrew, *State Immunity and State-Owned Enterprises*, 10 BUSINESS LAW INTERNATIONAL 97–127 (May 2009).

2. Luehr, Christopher, Note, *Red Banking: Chinese State-Owned Commercial Bank Reform and the Basel II Accord*, 20 MINNESOTA JOURNAL OF INTERNATIONAL LAW 171–197 (2011).

3. Pomeranz, William E., *Russian Protectionism and Strategic Sectors Law*, 25 AMERICAN UNIVERSITY INTERNATIONAL LAW REVIEW 213–224 (2010).

4. Tan, Lay-Hong & Jiangyu Wang, *Modeling an Effective Corporate Governance System for China's Listed State-Owned Enterprises: Issues and Challenges in a Transitional Economy*, 7 JOURNAL OF CORPORATE LAW STUDIES (part I) 143–183 (April 2007).

## SOFTWOOD LUMBER (SOFTWOOD LUMBER CASE)

A short-hand reference to a long-running series of legal battles between the United States and Canada.

The majority of the litigation involved allegations by the United States that the Canadian government illegally subsidized exports of softwood lumber to the United States. The United States imposed countervailing duties (CVDs), which (inter alia) were estimated to raise the average cost of a newly-constructed American home by $1,200. Some litigation also involved anti-dumping (AD) action, specifically over the zeroing methodology employed by the United States Department of Commerce (DOC) in estimating the dumping margin of softwood lumber that was subject merchandise. The litigation occurred at the levels of domestic administrative agencies and courts (including the Court of International Trade (CIT)), *North American Free Trade Agreement (NAFTA)* panels, and under the WTO *Understanding on Rules and Procedures Governing the Settlement of Disputes (Dispute Settlement Understanding, or DSU)*.

*Suggestions for Further Research:*

Articles:

1. Quayat, David, *The Forest for the Trees: A Roadmap to Canada's Litigation Experience in Lumber IV*, 12 JOURNAL OF INTERNATIONAL ECONOMIC LAW 115–151 (2009).

2. Sillivent, Shane R., Comment, *The New Softwood Lumber Agreement Between the United States and Canada: Finally Seeing the Forest Instead of Merely the Trees?*, 13 LAW AND BUSINESS REVIEW IN THE AMERICAS, 971–982 (2007).

## SOLOW MODEL

A model of economic growth that stresses the role of capital and labor in growth.

The Solow Model yields the conclusion that all economies ultimately trend toward a "Steady State" of investment.

## *The Basic Solow Model*

The "Solow Model", or "Neo-Classical Growth" Model, is the result of work on growth theory by economist Robert Solow, for which he won the 1987 Nobel Prize in Economics. Solow relies on a production function with two factors, capital (K) and labor (L). Total output (Y), or Aggregate Supply, which is the dependent variable, is a function (*f*) of capital and labor. That is, both combine to produce output. In arithmetic terms:

$$Y = f(K, L)$$

The Solow Model identifies two independent variables as affecting Aggregate Demand, namely, Consumption (C) and Investment (I). However, the Model captures the distinction between Net Investment (I) and Depreciation (D). Further, in contrast to the Harrod–Domar Model, the Solow Model posits the ratio of capital to output — *i.e.*, the Incremental Capital/Output Ratio (ICOR) — changes as the capital stock grows.

The Solow Model produces what is known as a "Steady State" level of investment. This level equals the rate of depreciation in the capital stock. In this Steady State, the ratio of capital to labor (K divided by L) and the ratio of output per labor (Y divided by L) is stable, with the latter variable a measure of productivity. Accordingly, the central insight is that a developing or least-developed country grows by increasing its stock of capital. Once the country reaches a Steady State, it will invest enough to replace capital that depreciates. But, net investment and growth no longer occur. In that Steady State, the country will produce a constant level of output per laborer.

What constraints exist on investment, and thus on the Steady State? The key constraint is savings — a higher savings rate can support greater investment, and thus a higher Steady State. A second constraint is the size of the labor force. If that size increases, then more investment will be needed to support the larger population, and thereby stay at the Steady State level of output per person.

Expressed in arithmetic form, the Model is as follows:

*Equation #1: The Production Function —*

The production function in which capital and labor produce output (Aggregate Supply),

$$Y = f(K, L)$$

is expressed in per labor terms, *i.e.*,

$\dfrac{Y}{L} = y$, which means output per unit of labor

$\dfrac{K}{L} = k$, which means capital per unit of labor

$$\frac{L}{L} = 1$$

Small letters are used to express a variable in per labor terms. As regards labor, because the same term (L) is in the numerator and the denominator, labor is no longer an explicit stand-alone independent variable. The resulting production function is:

$$y = f(k)$$

This expression conveys the idea total output per labor depends on the amount of capital per labor.

For macroeconomic equilibrium, total output (Aggregate Supply) must equal Aggregate Demand. Aggregate Demand (Y) depends on two independent variables, Consumption expenditures (C) and Investment (I). Thus:

*Equation #2: Aggregate Demand —*

$$Y = C + I$$

The Aggregate Demand function, like the Production Function, can be put in per labor terms, namely,

$\dfrac{C}{L}$ = c, which refers to consumption per unit of labor, that is, consumption per worker

$\dfrac{I}{L}$ = i, which refers to investment per unit of labor, that is, investment per L worker

Thus, Aggregate Demand is:

$$y = c + i$$

However, this expression can be restated based on the tautology that consumption is income not saved. If the savings rate, S, in per labor terms is expressed as "s," then every dollar of income per labor, y, not consumed must be saved, because a worker has only those two choices — to spend or not to spend the income. Arithmetically:

$$c = y - (s) \cdot (y)$$
$$= (1 - s) \cdot y$$

For example, if income per worker (y) is $100, and the savings rate per worker is 20 percent, then consumption per worker is $80. In turn, the Aggregate Demand function becomes:

$$y = (1 - s) \cdot y + i$$

The above Aggregate Demand function can be manipulated to establish an equation for investment, as follows:

*Equation #3: Investment —*

$$y = (1 - s) \cdot y + i$$
$$i = y - (1 - s) \cdot y$$

i = y — (y — s•y)

i = s•y

This expression states investment depends on the proportion of income that is saved. In this respect, the Solow and Harrod–Domar Models share an important similarity. Both stress the importance of savings to investment in capital equipment, and thereby to growth in output.

Using the expression for total output (Aggregate Supply),

y = $f$ (k)

it is possible to substitute "$f$ (k)" for the variable "y" in the investment equation. In other words:

i = s x y

becomes:

i = s•$f$ (k)

Literally, this expression says investment per unit of labor equals the savings rate multiplied by some function of capital per unit of labor, where the dot (•) is the symbol for multiplication and the function, $f$, is not specified in detail. Conceptually, the insight is simply that investment depends on income saved, and the use of that income for capital investment.

Unlike the Harrod–Domar Model, the Solow Model takes into account the fact capital equipment depreciates through use, wear and tear, and technological obsolescence. Accordingly, what matters for growth is net investment in the capital stock. Depreciation, D, may be expressed as a fixed percentage, "d," occurring each year, and the small triangle Δ (the Greek letter "delta"), is used to mean "change in." Thus:

*Equation #4: Depreciation and Net Investment in Capital —*

Δk = change in the stock of capital per unit of labor

= i — (d•k)

That is, net investment equals gross investment in capital minus depreciation in existing capital equipment.

The last two equations lead to an expression for the Steady State level of investment:

*Equation #5: The Steady State Equilibrium —*

Combining *Equation #4*, which is

i = s•$f$ (k)

with *Equation #5*, which is

Δk = i — (d•k)

yields an expression for the Steady State level of investment:

Δk = s•$f$(k) — (d•k)

By definition, in the Steady State, investment in new capital offsets depreciation exactly — there is neither growth nor diminution in the capital stock. In arithmetic terms:

$\Delta k = s \cdot f(k) - (d \cdot k) = 0$

or, simply:

$s \cdot f(k) - (d \cdot k) = 0$

$s \cdot f(k) = (d \cdot k)$

The Solow Model, while somewhat more refined than the Harrod–Domar Model, is not conceptually complex.

In particular, the five salient features of the Solow Model are:

- Growth depends on net investment in the capital stock, which accounts for depreciation, and labor.
- Net investment requires savings.
- The productivity of capital can grow over time.
- Net investment continues to increase until a Steady State level is increased, at which point it falls to zero, implying depreciated capital equipment is replaced, but the stock of capital is not increased.
- In the Steady State, the capital–output ratio and output per worker stabilizes.

The last two points suggest that as poor countries grow, their rates of growth will converge with the growth rates in rich countries. Why?

The simple answer is diminishing returns to capital. The level of productivity of capital differs from one country to another. By definition, a poor country has less capital equipment per worker than a rich country. Therefore, the productivity of a unit of capital in the poor country should be higher than that in a rich country. The higher rate of return to capital in the poor country than in the rich country should cause faster growth in the poor country than in the rich country. Stated differently, for capital equipment in the poor country, the law of diminishing returns (whereby the additional units of output generated from increments to capital get ever-smaller as the stock of capital accumulates) is a distant prospect.

In the rich country, capital equipment presumably has been deployed everywhere it can make a positive marginal contribution to output. In turn, owners of capital will seek to invest in equipment in poor countries, where returns to those investments are higher than in the capital-saturated rich countries. As this process of capital flow from rich to poor countries continues, investment — and consequently output — growth is rapid. In the long run, however, each poor country reaches a Steady State, *i.e.*, growth slows over time from the rapid rates seen in countries like China (eight - 12 percent *per annum*) to the rates characteristic of rich countries (one - three percent *per annum*).

### Critique of the Solow Model — The Barro Study

The work of economist Robert Barro sheds considerable light on the Solow Model and the Steady State. In particular, it questions whether each country must have the same Steady State. Barro showed it is not necessarily the case each country will have the same Steady State. Convergence in investment and growth rates — if, indeed, it occurs — does not mean identical rates. Rather, the Steady State is unique to each country. A number of factors influence that State, including:

- Economic variables, such as the savings rate of a country, and the imports into and exports from that country.

- Social and demographic variables, such as the level of human capital, population size, and quality of health, among people in a country. (Express reference to human capital indicates the need to broaden the concept of capital in the Solow Model from just capital equipment to include education and experience.)

- Government variables, including an appropriate mix of fiscal and monetary policies, and a low level of corruption.

Indeed, in February 1996 Barro delivered the Lionel Robbins Memorial Lectures at the London School of Economics (LSE). Published as *Determinants of Economic Growth* (1997), the lectures offer a number of insights.

Among the noteworthy aspects of these insights is the methodology Barro used to obtain them. His data were comprehensive, covering roughly 100 countries and the years 1960 to 1990. He employed a variety of econometric tools, particularly sophisticated multivariable regression analysis, as well as simple correlation coefficients:

- *Modified Model*:

Barro modified the Solow Model, essentially by broadening the number of independent variables to account for the same dependent variable, the growth rate in income (ouput). Conceptually, the Barro Model uses the following arithmetic expressions:

Growth in *Per Capita* GDP = $f$ (Steady State Level of Output, Actual Level of Output)

where

Steady State Level of Output = $f$ (Government Variables and Private Sector Variables)

As explained below, the Government Variables include infrastructure support, regulatory and tax policies, rule of law, and terms of trade. Private Sector Variables include fertility and savings rates, and willingness to work. Similarly, as also discussed below, the Actual Level of Output depends on several variables.

- *Steady State*:

The Steady State level of output of a country is a level that occurs in the long run and, in some sense, is a target level. The Steady State depends on the policies of the government of that country, and on the behavior of households in that country. The key household factors are savings, work effort, and fertility. An increase in the Steady State leads to an increase in the growth rate of output, but only for a transitory period. As output rises, diminishing returns eventually set in, and growth is restored to a rate that depends essentially on technological progress.

Generally, the growth rate in output of a country varies inversely with the gap between its existing level of output and its Steady State (both measured in *per capita* Gross Domestic Product (GDP) terms). The larger the gap between actual and Steady State levels, the faster the growth. Conversely, as this gap narrows, implying ever-closer movement to the target, the growth rate slows.

- *Existing Output*:

Differences in growth rates among countries depend on the actual level of output of a country. There is an inverse relationship between current level of output and the growth rate of output, *i.e.*, as the Solow Model predicts, the lower the initial level of output (measured by real *per capita* GDP), the faster the growth rate (in real *per capita* GDP). Conversely, a higher starting level of output is associated with a lower growth rate. This inverse relationship reflects "conditional convergence."

"Absolute convergence" would occur if the characteristics of the economies of all countries were the same, except for the capital intensities (that is, the intensiveness with which capital equipment is used in agricultural and industrial production) in each economy. If this situation existed, then the *per capita* income growth rate of poor countries would outpace that of rich countries, until convergence occurred. In reality, the features of economies in different countries differ. There are variations in access to technology, fertility rates, government policies, savings rates, and work ethic. Consequently, convergence occurs in a conditional sense, meaning convergence of output growth rates across countries depends on these kinds of variables.

- *Catch Up*:

If the growth rate of a country is below its Steady State, then that country needs to catch up, not only to the Steady State level, but also to the levels of income achieved by relatively richer countries. Holding constant the various factors contributing to growth (*i.e.*, *ceteris paribus*), in practice poor countries do grow faster, in terms of *per capita* income, than rich countries. That is, conditional convergence of poor with rich countries tends to occur — but at a slow pace.

That is, the catch up process takes a long time. Overall, the rate of conditional convergence is 2.5 percent per year. This rate (which is the coefficient on the actual level of output as an independent variable) is low. Practically speaking, it means each year, the growth in output eliminates 2.5 percent of the gap between the actual level of output and the Steady State level. Further, the 2.5 percent conditional convergence rate means it takes about 27 years for a country to move half way toward its Steady State level of output. It takes about 89 years to get 90 percent of the way to this level.

- *Technology*:

To catch up, technology (including the transfer of technology from rich to poor countries) is important. Capital accumulation alone cannot sustain growth indefinitely, because diminishing returns occur. However, technological progress helps avoid diminishing returns in the long run, and also overcome population pressures about which Thomas Malthus warned in *An Essay on the Principle of Population* (1798). With such progress, which presumes a country does not run out of ideas, positive rates of *per capita* income growth can occur for long periods. Data from some countries indicate the length of time is over a century, with no tendency to fall.

To be sure, technology is not diffuse and freely available. In the Solow Model, technology is exogenous, *i.e.*, not explained by the Model itself, as the Model does not contain any theory of technical progress. Implicitly, the Model assumes imitation is cheaper than innovation, and technology spreads through imitation. In reality, technology results from costly, purposive research. Accordingly, incentives are needed for the discovery of new ideas. In practical terms, the key incentive is *ex post* monopoly power, that is, legal protection for monopoly profits earned from intellectual property. Without such protection, the costs of research are not recouped, and there is no financial reward to engage in it.

- *Additional Independent Variables*:

In addition to the existing level of output and technology, a number of other factors prove important in having a positive causal effect on the rate of growth of output as measured in terms of *per capita* GDP. Most importantly, these factors are —

(1) *Education*:

There is a direct relationship between education level, particularly secondary and tertiary schooling for males, and the growth rate of *per capita* output. An extra year of upper-level schooling for males boosts the output growth rate by 1.2 percent annually. Primary education of males has an insignificant direct effect on growth, but it obviously is relevant in an indirect sense because it is necessary to proceed to the secondary and tertiary levels.

Surprisingly contrary to expectations, and to the hypothesis that the education of women is a key to economic growth, female education at various levels does not have a direct, significant effect on output growth rates. However, this variable may operate in a less obvious manner. For example, female primary education levels and fertility rates tend to be related inversely, and strongly so, and fertility rates and output growth rates tend to be related directly. Thus, improving female education leads to lower fertility, which in turn boosts output growth. A similar causal chain may work through infant mortality.

(2) *Health Care*:

Good health care, as measured by life expectancy, relates positively to economic growth. The higher the level of life expectancy, the greater the growth rate of real *per capita* GDP.

(3) *Fertility Rate*:

There is an inverse relationship between the total fertility rate and the growth rate of *per capita* output. A growing population means part of the investment made by a country in capital equipment is used to provide capital to new members of the labor force, not to increase the amount of capital per worker, and thus not to increase the productivity of existing workers. Moreover, with population growth, the economy devotes resources to child rearing instead of the production of output. Consequently, a drop in the total fertility rate results in a higher growth rate of *per capita* output.

(4) *Government Consumption*:

There is an inverse relationship between this variable, which is measured in relation to GDP, and the growth rate of *per capita* output. Low levels of government consumption (measured in relation to GDP), particularly expenditures on welfare, appropriate policies concerning financial market regulation, international trade, and taxation, and the provision of infrastructure, lead to higher output growth. Significantly, government expenditures on defense and education are excluded from consideration, because these outlays tend to improve productivity. Put simply, through its behavior, the government has great potential to do good or ill as regards growth, and big government is bad for growth.

(5) *Rule of Law*:

The rule of law may be measured by an index score, where the index includes basic law and order, corruption, enforcement of contracts, protection of property (including intellectual property) rights, quality of the government bureaucracy, and risk of expropriation. A strong rule of law framework makes a country attractive as a host for investment, and a reliable trading partner. Accordingly, there is a direct relationship between the strength of the rule of law and growth rate in *per capita* output. In fact, an increase of one rank in the index score stimulates the growth rate by 0.5 percent.

(6) *Terms of Trade*:

There is a significant positive relationship between the terms of trade and expansion of domestic output (measured in terms of real GDP). That is, an improvement in the ratio of export to import prices stimulates output, as well as employment. However, an improvement in the terms of trade leading to higher income and consumption, but not to increases in the amount of physical goods produced, has no effect on real GDP.

(7) *Regional Position*:

Countries in some regions grow faster than in other regions. This fact is evident from the Table below.

TABLE:

AVERAGE *PER CAPITA* GROWTH RATES

| Period and Region | 1975–1985 | 1985–1990 |
|---|---|---|
| All Countries | 1.0 percent (124 countries) | 1.0 percent (129 countries) |
| East Asia | 3.7 percent (12 countries) | 4.0 percent (15 countries) |
| Latin America | – 0.1 percent (24 countries) | – 0.4 percent (29 countries) |
| Sub-Saharan Africa | – 0.3 percent (43 countries) | 0.1 percent (40 countries) |

(8) *Investment Ratio*:

Generally, there is a direct relationship between the savings rate and the Steady State level of output per worker, which in turn leads to a higher growth rate for a particular initial value of output (measured by GDP). This relationship is based on the Solow-type Model in which the savings rate is exogenous and equals the ratio of investment to output, and in which the economy is closed to trade. However, with an open economy, the reverse causal process may occur. Higher growth opportunities may generate higher investment rates, and thus higher savings rates.

Empirically, there is a positive effect of the investment ratio on growth, but the reverse relationship also exists. Moreover, a number of variables stimulate investment, including long life expectancy (which is a proxy for human capital) and maintenance of the rule of law. Conversely, government consumption (as a percentage of GDP) and the inflation rate relate negatively to the investment ratio.

• *Democracy*:

A democratic political system, as measured by elections, also is helpful to growth, *i.e.*, it is true that prosperity is good for democracy. As a country becomes more prosperous (as measured by increased real *per capita* GDP, longer life expectancy, and a narrower gap between male and female educational levels), the propensity of its people to experience democracy increases. This linkage — that prosperity stimulates democracy — is known as the "Lipset Hypothesis."

• *Inflation*:

Inflation (measured in terms of the growth rate over each period in a consumer price index) up to a rate of 15 to 20 percent *per annum* is not necessarily harmful to growth. The evidence is unclear. However, at rates above 15 to 20 percent, inflation has a negative effect on growth. Empirically, an increase in the inflation rate of 10 percentage points causes a drop in the annual GDP growth rate of a 0.3 to 0.4 percentage point. Small as this drop may sound, it can add up — after 30 years, the level of real GDP would fall by six to nine percent. The rationale is businesses and households cannot perform well, in an economic sense, if inflation is high (and, for that matter, if it is unpredictable). One policy prescription is to encourage central bank independence, both as a matter of law (*e.g.*, legal rules to ensure a central bank can maintain a commitment to price stability) and in practice (*e.g.*, a habit of central bank governors fulfilling their legal term in office).

Given the range of variables on which growth is contingent, it ought not to be surprising that the empirical evidence for convergence of growth rates among rich countries is mixed. In a 2005 study entitled *Economic Policy Reforms in OECD Countries: Going For Growth*, the Organization for Economic Cooperation and Development (OECD) reported that from the end of the Second World War through the 1980s, the richest countries in the world converged toward the same level of per capita income.[580]

However, in the 1990s and early 2000s, convergence ended. Average per capita income growth from 1993–2003 in the United States soared above that of the European Union (EU), with the result that per capita income in EU countries (specifically, the euro area) was 30 percent below that of the United States. For the EU to close the gap, recommended the Organization for Economic Cooperation and Development (OECD), it must not only continue to improve productivity (measured by output per hour of labor) and remove unnecessary labor market regulations, but also encourage work from its increasingly aging labor force by reducing generous pension and early retirement benefits, cutting unemployment programs, and increasing minimum retirement ages.

*Suggestions for Further Research:*

Books:

1. BARRO, ROBERT J., DETERMINANTS OF ECONOMIC GROWTH: A CROSS-COUNTRY EMPIRICAL STUDY (1997).

2. BARRO, ROBERT J. & XAVIER SALA-I-MARTIN, ECONOMIC GROWTH (2nd ed 2003).

3. GERSCHENKRON, ALEXANDER, ECONOMIC BACKWARDNESS IN HISTORICAL PERSPECTIVE (1962).

4. LYNN, STUART R., ECONOMIC DEVELOPMENT: THEORY AND PRACTICE FOR A DIVIDED WORLD 52–54 (2003) (including Development Spotlight 3–2).

5. MALTHUS, THOMAS R., AN ESSAY ON THE PRINCIPLE OF POPULATION (1798).

Articles:

---

[580] *See Old Before their Time*, THE ECONOMIST, 5 March 2005, at 76.

1. Berkowitz, Daniel, Johannes Moenius & Katharina Pistor, *Legal Institutions and International Trade Flows*, 26 MICHIGAN JOURNAL OF INTERNATIONAL LAW 163–98 (2004).

2. Davis, Kenneth E., *What Can the Rule of Law Variable Tell Us About Rule of Law Reforms?*, 26 MICHIGAN JOURNAL OF INTERNATIONAL LAW 141–61 (2004).

3. Kuttner, Robert L., *Development, Globalization, and Law*, 26 MICHIGAN JOURNAL OF INTERNATIONAL LAW 19–38 (2004).

4. Lipset, Seymour Martin, *Some Social Requisites of Democracy: Economic Development and Political Legitimacy*, 53 AMERICAN POLITICAL SCIENCE REVIEW 69–105 (1959).

5. Romer, Paul, *Increasing Returns and Long-Run Growth*, 94 JOURNAL OF POLITICAL ECONOMY 1002-37 (October 1986).

6. Romer, Paul, *Endogenous Technical Change*, 98 JOURNAL OF POLITICAL ECONOMY 71–102 (October 1990).

7. Solow, Robert M., *A Contribution to the Theory of Economic Growth*, 70 QUARTERLY JOURNAL OF ECONOMICS 65–94 (February 1956).

## SOUTH–SOUTH TRADE (SOUTH–SOUTH TRADE DEAL)

*See* GSTP.

## SOVEREIGN WEALTH FUND

A vehicle by which a government invests money, other than foreign exchange reserves, in financial assets on behalf of the country.

*Suggestions for Further Research:*

Articles:

1. Gilson, Ronald J. & Curtis Milhaupt, *Sovereign Wealth Funds and Corporate Governance: A Minimalist Response to the New Mercantilism*, 60 STANFORD LAW REVIEW 1345–1369 (2008).

2. Langland, Eric, Comment, *Misplaced Fears Put to Rest: Financial Crisis Reveals the True Motives of Sovereign Wealth Funds*, 18 TULANE JOURNAL OF INTERNATIONAL & COMPARATIVE LAW 263–286 (2009).

3. Lee, Yvonne C.L., *A Reversal of Neo-Colonialism: The Pitfalls and Prospects of Sovereign Wealth Funds*, 40 GEORGETOWN JOURNAL OF INTERNATIONAL LAW 1103–1149 (2009).

4. Lindberg, Seth Robert, Note, *Sovereign Wealth Fund Regulation in the E.U. and U.S.: A Call for Workable and Uniform Sovereign Wealth Fund Review within the E.U.*, 37 SYRACUSE JOURNAL OF INTERNATIONAL LAW & COMMERCE 95–126 (2009).

5. Keller, Amy, Note, *Sovereign Wealth Funds: Trustworthy Investors or Vehicles of Strategic Ambition? An Assessment of the Benefits, Risks, and Possible Regulation of Sovereign Wealth Funds*, 7 GEORGETOWN JOURNAL OF LAW & PUBLIC POLICY 333–372 (2009).

6. O'Brien, Justin, *Barriers to Entry: Foreign Direct Investment and the Regulation of Sovereign Wealth Funds*, 42 THE INTERNATIONAL LAWYEr 1231–1257 (2008).

7. Sarkar, Rumu, *Sovereign Wealth Funds as a Development Tool for ASEAN Nations: From Social Wealth to Social Responsibility*, 41 GEORGIA JOURNAL OF INTERNATIONAL LAW 621–645 (2010).

## SPAGHETTI BOWL

A metaphor coined and popularized by economist Jagdish Bhagwati, initially in 1993, to represent the myriad of trade rules associated with the ever-growing number of free trade agreements (FTAs).

This spaghetti bowl of regulations — not the least of which are preferential rules of origin — is difficult, if not impossible, to untangle. The metaphor, however, is vulnerable in at least two respects.

First, Professor Bhagwati is implacably opposed to FTAs. Hence, the metaphor is pejorative. But, bad pasta is not what most people think of when they envision a spaghetti bowl, unless their experience with Italian cuisine has been uniformly poor (which is highly unlikely). A metaphor based on a widely held negative item might be more persuasive. Second, whereas an omelet truly cannot be unscrambled, some spaghetti (depending on its nature and how it is cooked) in some bowls (especially smaller ones that are clear or white) can be without too much difficulty. A metaphor more along the lines of a Gordian knot might be more effective.

*Suggestions for Further Research:*

Book Chapters:

1. Bhagwati, Jagdish, *Regionalism and Multilateralism: An Overview*, in New DIMENSIONS IN REGIONAL INTEGRATION (J. de Melo & A. Panagariya eds., 1993).

## SPECIAL 301

A blacklisting provision of United States trade law focusing on alleged infringements of intellectual property rights (IPRs).

Each year, the United States Trade Representative publishes a "Special 301 Report." This Report evaluates the state of IPR protection and enforcement in foreign countries. The Report complements the USTR's annual National Trade Estimate Report on Foreign Trade Barriers (NTE).

The scope and slant of the Special 301 reports has created controversy. In April 2008, 27 Democratic members of the House of Representatives — led by Henry A. Wasman (Democrat-California) — wrote to USTR Ambassador Susan Schwab to urge that the Special 301 go beyond consideration of IPR protection and a narrow focus on innovation enhancement.[581] The Report also should

---

[581] *See House Democrats Urge USTR to Consider Drug Access in Annual Review of IPR Rights*, 25 International Trade Reporter (BNA) 558 (17 April 2008).

cover the commitment of the United States to respecting measures that improve the access of poor people in developing and least-developed countries to life-saving medicines. They were alarmed by a reference in the 2008 NTE Report in which the USTR said compulsory licenses issued by Thailand are for addressing public health emergencies. The House Democrats explained the characterization was too narrow, because the WTO *Agreement on Trade Related Aspects of Intellectual Property Rights (TRIPs)* permits countries to determine when a compulsory license may be needed, and does not restrict the context only to emergency situations.

*Suggestions for Further Research:*

Articles:

1.   Bello, Judith H. & Alan F. Holmer, *"Special 301": Its Requirements, Implementation, and Significance*, 13 FORDHAM INTERNATIONAL LAW JOURNAL 259, 260, 263, 269 (1989).

2.   Bliss, Julia Christine, *The Amendments to Section 301: An Overview and Suggested Strategies for Foreign Response*, 20 LAW & POLICY IN INTERNATIONAL BUSINESS 501, 523–24 (1989).

3.   Chang, Y. Kurt, *Comment, Special 301 and Taiwan: A Case Study of Protecting United States Intellectual Property in Foreign Countries*, 15 NORTHWESTERN JOURNAL OF INTERNATIONAL LAW & BUSINESS 206 (1994).

4.   Shi, Wei & Robert Weatherley, *Harmony or Coercion? China — EU Trade Dispute Involving Intellectual Property Enforcement*, 25 WISCONSIN INTERNATIONAL LAW JOURNAL 439–490 (2007).

Other Source:

1.   U.S. GENERAL ACCOUNTING OFFICE, INTELLECTUAL PROPERTY RIGHTS — U.S. TRADE REPRESENTATIVE INVESTIGATIONS OF FOREIGN COUNTRY PRACTICES, GAO/GGD-94-168FS (July 1994).

## SPECIAL AND DIFFERENTIAL TREATMENT

Special and differential treatment, sometimes abbreviated "S & D treatment" or "SDT."

Special and differential treatment distinguishes poor from rich countries with respect to their legal rights and obligations. In effect, it is legalized discrimination in favor of poor countries, in recognition of their status as poor countries. The discrimination is designed to assist them in their economic growth and broader development objectives.

There are six prominent types of special and differential treatment:

(1) Longer time periods to implement an agreement or a specific obligation under a trade agreement.

(2) Permission to retain tariff or non-tariff barriers to protect infant industries.

(3) Measures to increase trading opportunities, such as preferential market access through duty-free, quota free (DFQF) treatment.

(4) Aid, that is, aid-for-trade.

(5) Technical assistance to help build infrastructure, capacity, and the rule of law.

(6) Requirements that all countries take care of the trade interests of the recipients of special and differential treatment.

Special and differential treatment is afforded to developing and least-developed countries under Part IV of GATT and in several Uruguay Round agreements.

The origins of this treatment are found in concepts prominent in the Marxist-Leninist critique of international trade. Special and differential treatment is based on a normative judgment that Third World Countries ought to receive preferences — a "break" — as regards multilateral trade obligations in order to facilitate their development and ease adjustment costs they might otherwise incur owing to trade liberalization. In the 1950s, decolonization and an explosion in the number of developing and least developed countries increased the call for the treatment.

Under GATT, there are 12 special and differential treatment rules that are both procedural and substantive in nature:

- GATT Preamble (paragraph 1), concerning raising standards of living, ensuring an increase in real income, and developing the full use of the world's resources.

- GATT Article I:2-4, concerning exceptions to general MFN treatment for preferences in force when GATT was negotiated.

- GATT Article XVIII, concerning governmental assistance to economic development and the use of protective measures against imports.

- GATT Article XXIV:11, concerning the establishment of special trade relationships between India and Pakistan

- GATT Article XXVIII:3(b) *bis*, concerning tariff negotiations and the needs of developing countries.

- GATT Article XXXVI:1-7, contained in Part IV of GATT, which deals with Trade and Development, and concerns principles and objectives of the GATT contracting parties (*i.e.*, WTO Members)

- GATT Article XXXVI:8, also in Part IV of GATT on Trade and Development, concerning non-reciprocity in commitments made by developed to less-developed countries.

- GATT Article XXXVI:9, also in Part IV of GATT on Trade and Development, concerning efforts to give effect to principles and objectives relating to trade and development.

- GATT Article XXXVII:1, also in Part IV of GATT on Trade and Development, concerning trade and trade-related measures by developed countries that affect imports from less developed countries.

- GATT Article XXXVII:3(a)-(b), also in Part IV of GATT on Trade and Development, concerning price and market access commitments of developed contracting parties to less developed countries.

- GATT Article XXXVII:3(c), also in Part IV of GATT on Trade and Development, concerning commitments of developed countries to less developed countries on applying trade measures.

- GATT Article XXXVIII, also in Part IV of GATT on Trade in Development, concerning joint action by the contracting parties to GATT (*i.e.*, by WTO Members).

The Generalized System of Preferences (GSP) scheme, offered by the developed to developing countries at the Tokyo Round in 1979, is one example of special and differential treatment afforded under GATT. Under the GSP, certain exports from beneficiary developing countries receive duty-free treatment.

However, special and differential treatment, under the auspices of multilateral trade agreements promulgated at the Uruguay Round, tends to take the form of longer phase-in periods for obligations, longer phase-out periods for offending measures, and a suspension of the requirement to reciprocate for concessions received from developed countries. For example, developing countries were required to implement the Uruguay Round *Agreement on Customs Valuation*, *Agreement on Trade-Related Investment Measures* (*TRIMs*), and *Agreement on Trade-Related Aspects of Intellectual Property Rights* (*TRIPs*) 1 January 2000 (rather than the normal 1 January 1995 date, or in the case of the *TRIPs Agreement*, 1 January 1996).

Yet, despite this delayed implementation date, many developing countries experienced difficulties meeting the deadline and requested further extensions. Thus, in May 2000, the WTO General Council agreed to procedures for reviewing requests for extending the *TRIMs* implementation period. Essentially, the procedures amount to a case-by-case examination in accordance with *TRIMs* Article 5:2. The General Council also agreed to examine difficulties some developing countries were having in complying not only with the *Customs Valuation*, *TRIMs*, and *TRIPs Agreements*, but also with the accords on antidumping (AD), countervailing duty (CVD), sanitary and phytosanitary (SPS), and various other matters.

The grant of a compulsory license by a WTO Member is an example of a controversial type of special and differential treatment afforded under the *TRIPs Agreement*. *TRIPs* allows developing countries to issue compulsory licenses in order to override patent rights and import generic copies of medicines needed to address serious public health problems. In 2007, Brazil issued a compulsory license for the HIV/AIDS drug efavirenx, commonly known as or STOCRIN.[582]

---

[582] Amy Tsui, *Merck Asks Brazil to Reconsider Decision To Issue Compulsory License for AIDS Drug*, 24 INTERNATIONAL TRADE REPORTER (BNA) 660 (2007).

*Suggestions for Further Research:*

Books:

1. ACEMOGLU, DARON & JAMES ROBINSON, WHY NATIONS FAIL: THE ORIGINS OF POWER, PROSPERITY, AND POVERTY (2012). *See also* the review of this book, *The Big Why*, THE ECONOMIST, 10 March 2012, at 95.

2. ADHIKARI, RAMESH & PREMA-CHANDRA ATHUKORALA, DEVELOING COUNTRIES IN THE WORLD TRADING SYSTEM — THE URUGUAY ROUND AND BEYOND (2002).

3. CROOME, JOHN, GUIDE TO THE URUGUAY ROUND AGREEMENTS (1999).

4. GALLAGHER, PETER, GUIDE TO THE WTO AND DEVELOPING COUNTRIES (2000).

5. GARCIA, FRANK J., TRADE, INEQUALITY, AND JUSTICE: TOWARD A LIBERAL THEORY OF JUST TRADE (2003).

6. HOEKMAN, BERNARD, AADITYA MATTOO & PHILIP ENGLISH, DEVELOPMENT, TRADE, AND THE WTO — A HANDBOOK (2002).

7. MICHALOPOULOS, CONSTANTINE, DEVELOPING COUNTRIES IN THE WTO (2001).

8. ROLLAND, SONIA E., DEVELOPMENT AT THE WORLD TRADE ORGANIZATION (2012).

9. TRACHTMAN, JOEL P. & CHANTAL THOMAS, DEVELOPING COUNTRIES IN THE WTO LEGAL SYSTEM (2009).

10. WHALLEY, JOHN (COORDINATOR), THE URUGUAY ROUND AND BEYOND — THE FINAL REPORT FROM THE FORD FOUNDATION PROJECT ON DEVELOPING COUNTRIES AND THE GLOBAL TRADING SYSTEM (1989).

Articles:

1. Antell, Geoffrey & James W. Coleman, *An Empirical Analysis of Wealth and Disparities in WTO Disputes: Do Poorer Countries Suffer from Strategic Delay During Dispute Litigation?*, 29 BOSTON UNIVERSITY INTERNATIONAL LAW JOURNAL 267–286 (2011).

2. Cai, Phoenix X.F., *Aid for Trade: A Roadmap for Success*, 36 DENVER JOURNAL OF INTERNATIONAL LAW & POLICY 283–324 (2008).

3. Cai, Phoenix X.F., *Making WTO Remedies Work for Developing Nations: The Need for Class Actions*, 25 EMORY INTERNATIONAL LAW REVIEW 151–196 (2011).

4. Carminati, Giugi, *Is International Trade Really Making Developing Countries Dirtier and Developed Countries Richer?*, 8 UNIVERSITY OF CALIFORNIA DAVIS BUSINESS LAW JOURNAL 205–233 (2007).

5. Conti, Joseph A., *Learning to Dispute: Repeat Participation, Expertise, and Reputation at the World Trade Organization*, 35 LAW & SOCIAL INQUIRY 625–662 (2010).

6. Dunoff, Jeffrey L., *Hudec's Methods — And Ours*, 20 MINNESOTA JOURNAL OF INTERNATIONAL LAW 437–479 (2011).

7. Ewart, Andrea M., *Small Developing States in the WTO: A Procedural Approach to Special and Differential Treatment Through Reforms to Dispute Settlement*, 35 SYRACUSE JOURNAL OF INTERNATIONAL LAW AND COMMERCE 27–76 (2007).

8.   Ezeani, Elimma C., *Can the WTO Judges Assist the Development Agenda?*, 10 JOURNAL OF INTERNATIONAL TRADE LAW POLICY number 2 124–150 (2011).

9.   Gordon, Robert, *Can the WTO Judges Assist the Development Agenda?*, 10 JOURNAL OF INTERNATIONAL TRADE LAW POLICY number 2 104–123 (2011).

10.  Martin, Mervyn & Maryam Shademan Pajouh, *Rebalancing the Balance: How the WTO's HR Policy Impacts on Its Very Objectives for Welfare Enhancement and Development*, 10 JOURNAL OF INTERNATIONAL TRADE LAW AND POLICY number 3, 243–254 (2011).

11.  Mitchell, Andrew D. & Joanne Wallis, *Pacific Pause: The Rhetoric of Special & Differential Treatment, The Reality of WTO Accession*, 27 WISCONSIN INTERNATIONAL LAW JOURNAL 663–706 (2010).

12.  Osakwe, Chiedu, *Developing Countries and GATT / WTO Rules: Dynamic Transformations in Trade Policy Behavior and Performance*, 20 MINNESOTA JOURNAL OF INTERNATIONAL LAW 365–436 (2011).

13.  Scott, James, *Developing Countries in the ITO and GATT Negotiations*, 9 JOURNAL OF INTERNATIONAL TRADE LAW AND POLICY number 1, 5–24 (2010).

14.  Sutrisno, Nandang, *Substantive Justice Formulated, Implemented, and Enforced as Formal and Procedural Justice: A Lesson from WTO Special and Differential Treatment Provisions for Developing Countries*, 13 JOURNAL OF GENDER, RACE & JUSTICE 671–703 (2010).

15.  Thrasher, Rachel Denae & Kevin Gallagher, *21st Century Trade Agreements: Implications for Development Sovereignty*, 38 DENVER JOURNAL OF INTERNATIONAL LAW & POLICY 313–350 (2010).

Other Sources:

1.   Martin, Will & L. Alan Winters, *The Uruguay Round and the Developing Economies*, World Bank Discussion Paper Number 307 (1995).

2.   UNITED NATIONS CONFERENCE ON TRADE AND DEVELOPMENT, WTO ACCESSIONS AND DEVELOPMENT POLICIES (2001).

3.   Weiss, Wolfgang, *The Role of the WTO in Global Development Policy*, in GLOBAL GOVERNANCE — REPORTS AND DISCUSSIONS OF A SYMPOSIUM HELD IN TRIER ON OCTOBER 9TH AND 10TH, 2003 (Bernd von Hoffman, ed.) 101–129 (2004).

## SPECIAL SAFEGUARD

*See* SSG.

## SPECIAL SAFEGUARD MEASURE

*See* SSM.

## SPECIALTY CROP

A crop that, under American agricultural legislation, is not eligible for subsidies.

Fruit, vegetables, and nuts are specialty crops. In contrast, cotton, corn, rice, soybean, and wheat are "program" (or "commodity") crops, and are eligible for agricultural support payments according to the terms set out in a farm bill. Consequently, growing specialty crops is riskier than growing program crops. Moreover, private insurance to indemnify against crop failure (*e.g.*, caused by drought, heat, or pests) is available only for a few specialty crops — such as cherries and tomatoes used for processing.

Note the term "specialty" crop is a misnomer, in the sense the vast majority of crops are not eligible for American subsidies, *i.e.*, they are the normal case. Note, also, that in the five year 2007 Farm Bill — the *Food and Energy Security Act* — as made in the Senate and approved by the Senate Agriculture Committee in October 2007 — the statutory definition of "specialty crop" was broadened. The Bill stated the term should cover dried fruits, floriculture, horticulture (including herbal farming and turf grass sod), and nursery crops.[583]

## SPECIFICITY TEST

The test established by the WTO *Agreement on Subsidies and Countervailing Measures* (*SCM Agreement*), particularly Article 2, to help differentiate countervailable from non-countervailable subsidies.[584]

If a subsidy exists — that is, if a government provides a financial contribution that confers a benefit on recipients — then it may not be offset by a countervailing duty (CVD) if that subsidy is generally available. The subsidy must be specific to an enterprise or industry, or group of enterprises or industries for it to be countervailable. The Specificity Test operates in tandem with the Traffic Light System, which considers the substantive nature of the subsidy program at issue.

*Suggestions for Further Research:*

Article:

1.   Southwick, James D., Note, *The Lingering Problem with the Specificity Test in United States Countervailing Duty Law*, 72 MINNESOTA LAW REVIEW 1159 (1988).

## SPP

Security and Prosperity Partnership (SPP) of North America.

*See* NACC.

---

[583] *See* Derrick Cain, *Senate Agriculture Committee Approves $280 Billion, Five-Year Farm Policy Bill*, 24 International Trade Reporter (BNA) 1538–1539 (1 November 2007).

[584] *See also* 19 U.S.C. § 1677(5A)(D)(iii).

## SPS MEASURE

Sanitary and Phytosanitary Measure.

A measure affecting international trade that concerns human, animal, or plant life or health, of food safety. "Sanitary" refers to human and animal life or health. "Phytosanitary" refers to plants and plant products.

## *SPS AGREEMENT*

Uruguay Round *Agreement on the Application of Sanitary and Phytosanitary Standards*.

The *SPS Agreement* is one of the Multilateral Agreements on Trade in Goods contained in Annex 1A to the *WTO Agreement*. The essence of the *SPS Agreement* is a balance between (1) protecting the legitimate, sovereign right of each WTO Member to establish sanitary and phytosanitary (SPS) measures according to the risk assessments and tolerance thresholds of its population, and (2) ensuring that SPS measures are not protectionist measures and disguised restrictions on trade in favor of preferred domestic producer constituencies. The *SPS Agreement* strikes this balance by adopting scientific justification for an SPS measure as the key operative legal standard, maintaining a reasonably flexible definition of science, and strongly encouraging the use of international standards for SPS measures.

On 30 May 2008, the WTO Members confirmed a *Decision on SPS Transparency*.[585] The *Decision* is formally entitled *Recommended Procedures for Implementing the Transparency Obligations of the SPS Agreement* (Article 7). It had been approved on 2–3 April 2008, at the meeting of the WTO Sanitary and Phytosanitary Measures Committee (SPS Committee). The SPS Committee adopted the Decision *ad referendum* (*i.e.*, to be considered, subject to the agreement of a superior, meaning that all material points had been agreed, though some minor points — details — had yet to be resolved by the authority with final decision-making power).

The *Decision* contains procedural and substantive recommendations on how governments should provide information on new or proposed SPS measures. Members are to use new forms and formats for supplying information, and sponsor an on-line data base where they post notifications and other relevant information. The *Decision* also urges Members to provide notification when they adopt an international standard as an SPS measure. (Technically, such notice is optional. A Member is legally obligated to provide notification only if it adopts an SPS measure that does not follow an international standards.) Concomitant with the *Decision* is adaptation by the WTO Secretariat of its electronic system so that it can manage and circulate notifications from a Member about SPS measures to all other Members. The *Decision* entered into force in late 2008.

---

[585] *See* (G/SPS/7/Rev.3 and G/SPS/W/215/Rev.2), *posted at* www.wto.org.

*Suggestions for Further Research:*

Books:

1. GRUSZCZYNSKI, LUKASZ, REGULATING HEALTH AND ENVIRONMENTAL RISKS UNDER WTO LAW — A CRITICAL ANALYSIS OF THE SPS AGREEMENT (2010).

2. SCOTT, JOANNE, THE WTO AGREEMENT ON SANITARY AND PHYTOSANITARY MEASURES — A COMMENTARY (2009).

Articles:

1. Aginam, Obijiofor, *Food Safety, South–North Asymmetries, and the Clash of Regulatory Regimes*, 40 VANDERBILT JOURNAL OF TRANSNATIONAL LAW 1099-1114 (2007).

2. Archibald, Catherine Jean, *Forbidden by the WTO? Discrimination Against a Product When its Creation Causes Harm to the Environment or Animal Welfare*, 48 NATURAL RESOURCES JOURNAL 15–51 (2008).

3. Ballet, Lucas, Comment, *Losing Flavor: Indonesia's WTO Complaint Against the U.S. Ban on Clove Cigarettes*, 26 AMERICAN UNIVERSITY INTERNATIONAL LAW REVIEW 515–541 (2011).

4. Bamberger, Kenneth A. & Andrew T. Guzman, *Keeping Imports Safe: A Proposal for Discriminatory Regulation of International Trade*, 96 CALIFORNIA LAW REVIEW 1405-1445 (2008).

5. Bradley, Caroline, *Consultation and Legitimacy in Transnational Standard-Setting*, 20 MINNESOTA JOURNAL OF INTERNATIONAL LAW 480–512 (2011).

6. Büthe, Tim, *The Globalization of Health and Safety Standards: Delegation of Regulatory Authority in the SPS Agreement of the 1994 Agreement Establishing the World Trade Organization*, 71 LAW & CONTEMPORARY PROBLEMS 219–255 (2008).

7. Chen, Kelly & Rosa Dunnegan-Mallat, *H.R. 3610, the Food and Drug Import Safety Act of 2007*, 42 THE INTERNATIONAL LAWYER 1339–1356 (2008).

8. Cho, Sungjoon, *From Control to Communication: Science, Philosophy, and World Trade Law*, 44 CORNELL INTERNATIONAL LAW JOURNAL 249–278 (spring 2011).

9. Cortez, Elvira, Comment, *Total Recall on Chinese Imports: Pursuing an End to Unsafe Health and Safety Standards Through Article XX of GATT*, 23 AMERICAN UNIVERSITY INTERNATIONAL LAW REVIEW 915–942 (2008).

10. Countryman, Philip, *International Trade and World Health Policy: Helping People Reach their Full Potential*, 21 PACE INTERNATIONAL LAW REVIEW 241–279 (2009).

11. Das, Kasturi, *Coping with SPS Challenges in India: WTO and Beyond*, 11 JOURNAL OF INTERNATIONAL ECONOMIC LAW 971-1019 (2008).

12. DeWaal, Caroline Smith, *Food Safety and Security: What Tragedy Teaches Us About our 100-Year Old Food Laws*, 40 VANDERBILT JOURNAL OF TRANSNATIONAL LAW 921–935 (2007).

13. Du, Michael M., *Standard of Review Under the SPS Agreement After EC — Hormones II*, 59 INTERNATIONAL & COMPARATIVE LAW QUARTERLY 441–459 (2010).

14. Foster, Caroline E., *Public Opinion and the Interpretation of the World Trade Organization's Agreement on Sanitary and Phytosanitary Measures*, 11 JOURNAL OF INTERNATIONAL ECONOMIC LAW 427–458 (2008).

15. George, Asha M., *Response is Local, Relief is Not: The Pervasive Impact of Agro Terrorism*, 40 VANDERBILT JOURNAL OF TRANSNATIONAL LAW 1155–1170 (2007).

16. Gillman, Eric, *Making WTO SPS Dispute Settlement Work: Challenges and Practical Solutions*, 31 NORTHWESTERN JOURNAL OF INTERNATIONAL LAW & BUSINESS 439–477 (2011).

17. Haseeb Ansari, Abdul & Nik Ahmad Kamal Nik Mahmod, *Biosafety Protocol, SPS Agreement, and Export and Import Control of LMOs/GMOs*, 7 JOURNAL OF INTERNATIONAL TRADE LAW AND POLICY number 2 139–170 (2008).

18. Hill, Tamara L., *Comment, the Spread of Antibiotic-Resistant Bacteria through Medical Tourism and Transmission Prevention Under International Health Regulations*, 12 CHICAGO JOURNAL OF INTERNATIONAL LAW 273–308 (2011).

19. Hoffman, John T. & Shaun Kennedy, *International Cooperation to Defend the Food Supply Chain: Nations are Talking; Next Step — Action*, 40 VANDERBILT JOURNAL OF TRANSNATIONAL LAW 1171–1187 (2007).

20. Huang, Hao, Note, *Maximizing Chinese Imports' Compliance with United States Safety and Quality Standards: Carrot and Stick from Whom?*, 18 SOUTHERN CALIFORNIA INTERDISCIPLINARY LAW JOURNAL 131–160 (2008).

21. Lat, Tanya Karina A., Note, *Testing the Limits of GATT Article XX(b): Toxic Waste Trade, Japan's Economic Partnership Agreements, and the WTO*, 21 GEORGETOWN INTERNATIONAL ENVIRONMENTAL LAW REVIEW 367–393 (2009).

22. Liberman, Jonathan, & Andrew Mitchell, *In Search of Coherence Between Trade and Health: Inter-Institutional Opportunities*, 25 MARYLAND JOURNAL OF INTERNATIONAL LAW 143–186 (2010).

23. Mitchell, Andrew & Tania Voon, *Regulating Tobacco Flavors: Implications of WTO Law*, 29 BOSTON UNIVERSITY INTERNATIONAL LAW JOURNAL 383–425 (2011).

24. Murray, Craig, Note, *Implementing the New International Health Regulations: The Role of the WTO's Sanitary and Phytosanitary Agreement*, 40 GEORGETOWN JOURNAL OF INTERNATIONAL LAW 625–653 (2009).

25. Orellana, Marcos, *Evolving WTO Law Concerning Health, Safety and Environmental Measures*, 1 TRADE, LAW AND DEVELOPMENT number 1, 103–144 (spring 2009).

26. Shapiro, Hal S., *The Rules That Swallowed the Exceptions: The WTO SPS Agreement and Its Relationship to GATT Articles XX and XXI*, 24 ARIZONA JOURNAL OF INTERNATIONAL AND COMPARATIVE LAW 199–233 (2007).

27. Stathopoulos, Anastasia S., Note, *You Are What Your Food Eats: How Regulation of Factory Farm Conditions Could Improve Human Health and Animal Welfare Alike*, 13 NEW YORK UNIVERSITY JOURNAL OF LEGISLATION AND PUBLIC POLICY 407–444 (2010).

28. Tauxe, Robert V., *Foodbourne Infections and the Global Food Supply: Improving Health at Home and Abroad*, 40 Vanderbilt Journal of Transnational Law 899–919 (2007).

29. Vesilind, Pamela A., *Continental Drift: Agricultural Trade and the Widening Gap between European Union and United States Animal Welfare Laws*, 12 Vermont Journal of Environmental Law 223–254 (2011).

30. Wagner, Markus, *Law Talk v. Science Talk: The Languages of Law and Science in WTO Proceedings*, 35 Fordham International Law Journal 151–200 (2011).

# SRM

A sanitary and phytosanitary standard (SPS) acronym for "specified risk material."

In general, a SRM is that part of a ruminant animal most likely to be infected by Bovine Spongiform Encephalopathy (BSE). However, the exact definition of SRM varies by jurisdiction. In the United States, the United States Department of Agriculture (USDA) identifies which materials are identified as SRM and thus inedible. The USDA expressly forbids the introduction of SRMs into the market. Such materials include the eyes, brain and spinal cord in cattle 30 months and older.

SRMs have become a vital tool for many WTO Members over the last decade, particularly in their efforts to combat the spread of epidemics, such as mad cow disease. In one such instance, Japan placed a ban on American beef in response to finding spine in shipments at Japanese ports in early-2006.[586]

# SSA

Sub-Saharan Africa.

Sub-Saharan Africa is the term that describes the area of the African continent, which lies south of the Sahara Desert. The region houses just over 10 percent of the world's population.

However, SSA has succumbed to many ills over the last half-century. Governments within the region are often wrought with corruption and instability. Many of the poorest countries in the world lie within the region: in 2004, nearly 50 percent of its population lived on less than a dollar a day. Since 1965, nearly all of the countries with declining average *per capita* Gross National Product (GNP) levels, which reflect declining growth rates, have been in Sub-Saharan Africa.

Despite these troubles, the growth performance of SSA from 2004 to 2006 was its highest in the previous three decades. This phenomenon was thanks to high oil revenues and increased debt relief.

---

[586] *See* Toshio Aritake and Derrick Cain, *U.S. Officials Bolster Inspection Efforts After Japan Moves to Ban U.S. Beef Again*, 23 International Trade Reporter (BNA) 138–39 (26 January 2006).

*Suggestions for Further Research:*

Books:

1.  AZAM, JEAN-PAUL, TRADE, EXCHANGE RATE, AND GROWTH IN SUB-SAHARAN AFRICA (2007).

2.  COLE, ROY, SURVEY OF SUB-SAHARAN AFRICA: A REGIONAL GEOGRAPHY (2007).

3.  COLLINS, ROBERT O. & JAMES M. BURNS, A HISTORY OF SUB-SAHARAN AFRICA (2007).

## SSAC

Sub-Saharan African Country.

There are 53 countries in total on the African continent (54, if Western Sahara is counted as an independent entity). Forty-eight of those countries, divided by region below, are considered SSACs:

Central Africa —

- Burundi
- Central African Republic
- Congo (Democratic Republic of)
- Congo (Republic of)
- Rwanda

East Africa —

- Dijibouti
- Eritrea
- Ethiopia
- Kenya
- Somalia
- Sudan
- Tanzania
- Uganda

Southern Africa —

- Angola
- Botswana
- Lesotho
- Malawi
- Mozambique
- Namibia
- South Africa
- Swaziland
- Zambia
- Zimbabwe

West Africa —

- Benin
- Burkina Faso
- Cameroon
- Chad
- Côte d'Ivoire
- Equitorial Guinea
- Gabon
- The Gambia
- Guinea-Bissau
- Liberia
- Mali
- Mauritania
- Niger
- Nigeria
- Senegal
- Sierra Leone

- Ghana
- Guinea

Island Nations —

- Cape Verde
- Comoros
- Madagascar

- Togo

- Mauritius
- São Tomé and Príncipe
- Seychelles

The remaining countries, all in North Africa and Arabic-speaking, are Algeria, Egypt, Libya, Morocco, and Tunisia. Those countries lying on the demarcation line, namely, Chad, Mali, Sudan, Niger, and Mauritania, are technically part of both North and Sub-Saharan Africa.

*Suggestions for Further Research:*

Books:

1. AZAM, JEAN-PAUL, TRADE, EXCHANGE RATE, AND GROWTH IN SUB-SAHARAN AFRICA (2007).

2. COLE, ROY, SURVEY OF SUB-SAHARAN AFRICA: A REGIONAL GEOGRAPHY (2007).

3. COLLINS, ROBERT O. & JAMES M. BURNS, A HISTORY OF SUB-SAHARAN AFRICA (2007).

## SSG

Special safeguard, not to be confused with a special safeguard mechanism (SSM).

A term arising in connection with Article 5 of the WTO *Agreement on Agriculture*. This Article condones use of a special safeguard, subject to a trigger volume or trigger price, if a WTO Member has indicated in its tariff schedule that the product in question could be subject to a SSG. Application of an SSG obviously means diminution in market access. The SSG is simply an additional duty imposed on specific imports. Indeed, even some free trade agreements (FTAs), such as the *North American Free Trade Agreement* (*NAFTA*) and the *United States–Chile FTA*, have a similar provision.

Note that under Article 5 *Agriculture*, an importing WTO Member may impose an SSG on an agricultural product that it has subjected to tariffication. In turn, "tariffication," under Article 4:2 of the *Agreement*, means conversion of the form of protection from a non-tariff barrier (*e.g.*, discretionary import licensing, import ban, quota, or variable duty) to a tariff. However, several developing countries gave up their right to invoke the SSG, because rather than tariffy a product, they set a ceiling bound rate on it.

The SSG is an additional duty imposed on certain goods only upon the satisfaction of four conditions. First, the WTO member must have a reservation in its tariff schedule to apply an SSG. Second, the value of imports must fall below a reference price (which would make the additional duty a price-based SSG) or the volume of imports must surge above a specific threshold (which would make the additional duty a volume-based SSG). Third, minimum access commitments cannot be affected by the SSG, nor can the SSG be applied to imports taking place within tariff quotas. Lastly, under Appendix II of the *Agreement on Agriculture*, the Member must notify the WTO if it plans to use an SSG prior to the implementation of the duty.

Long seen as a protectionist device, the extension of SSGs became a highly contentious topic in the Doha Round negotiations. Many developing countries lobbied for the elimination of SSGs, because they claim goods produced by their domestic farmers are denied market access in developed countries. Instead, developing countries called for the creation of an SSM, whereby only developing countries could invoke this tool to protect their domestic farmers.

Although over 1,477 SSGs were notified to the WTO by the end of May 2005, the number of SSGs actually implemented was much higher due to the fact that most WTO Members ignore the *Agreement on Agriculture's* reporting requirements. From 1995 to 2000, Korea, the European Communities (EC), and the United States accounted for more than 70 percent of all SSGs notified. By mid-August 2007, Switzerland, Norway, Iceland, Morocco, and Mexico were the Members with the most reservations in their schedules.

*Suggestions for Further Research:*

Article:

1. Thacker, Cody A., *Agricultural Trade Liberalization in the Doha Round: The Search for a Modalities Drift*, 33 GEORGIA JOURNAL OF INTERNATIONAL AND COMPARATIVE LAW 721 (2005).

## SSM

Special safeguard measure, not to be confused with a special safeguard (SSG) on agricultural products.

Many WTO Members, particularly developing and least developed countries, criticized Article 5 of the WTO *Agreement on Agriculture* for establishing an SSG that could be used against their farm exports, but not allowing them to apply SSG measures against foreign imports. There is ambiguity in Article 5 as to whether a WTO Member had to designate a product as potentially subject to an SSG by the conclusion of the Uruguay Round. Accordingly, in the Doha Round, many WTO Members called for a new remedy — an SSM — that would allow them to take action against foreign farm products, subject to agreed-upon triggers and disciplines.

During the Doha Round, at least one proposed SSM was based on Article 5 of the *Agreement on Agriculture*. In late 2005, the Group of 33 (G-33) submitted a suggestion to the WTO for the creation of an SSM. The G-33 proposal requires any developing country must meet the requirements of Article 5 of the *Agreement on Agriculture* before it can impose an SSM. In the Doha Round developing countries argued that if they bind more tariffs and cut those tariffs already bound, they will limit their ability to increase duties in the case of emergency, thus leaving their domestic farmers unprotected from foreign imports of like or similar goods.

Notably absent from SSM proposals are justification or compensation requirements. Developing countries argue that any SSM need not satisfy these requirements. That is because, first, developed countries need not satisfy these requirements to impose an SSG. Second, normal safeguards require technical and legal expertise that most developing countries do not have.

## STATEMENT OF ADMINISTRATIVE ACTION

The definitive legislative history that accompanies some United States trade legislation.

That is, a *Statement of Administrative Action*, or *SAA*, is the official United States government's interpretation of a particular trade agreement. An SAA accompanied the *North American Free Trade Implementation Act of 1993*, which implemented the *North American Free Trade Agreement* (*NAFTA*) into United States law, the *Uruguay Round Agreements Act of 1994*, which implemented the Uruguay Round texts into American law, and all trade agreements that have come into effect after 2002. There is no SAA for the *Israel–United States Free Trade Agreement* (FTA), nor does there appear to be one for the *United States–Jordan FTA*. It is possible the Administration of President Ronald Reagan drafted an SAA for the *Israel FTA*, but elected not to submit it to Congress. That is, for trade agreements negotiated prior to 2002, records suggest an SAA accompanied both the Israel FTA (1985) and Jordan FTA, or was supposed to have accompanied these deals. But, an SAA could not be found for either agreement. Accordingly, citations to existing SAAs are listed in the References below.

In 2002, Congress passed the *Bipartisan Trade Promotion Authority Act* (*TPA*). After entering into an FTA, the President is required to submit to Congress the final text of the agreement, as well as an SAA.[587] Of course, the FTA can only take effect if it is approved by the enactment of an implementing bill.[588]

As regards the Uruguay Round *SAA*, the United States Court of Appeals for the Federal Circuit explained in a footnote in the case of *The Timken Company v. United States*, 354 F.3d 1334-47 (Fed. Cir. 2004):

> The *SAA* is "an authoritative expression by the United States concerning the interpretation and application of the Uruguay Round Agreements and this *Act* in any judicial proceeding in which a question arises concerning such interpretation or application." 19 U.S.C. § 3512(d).

---

[587] *See* 19 U.S.C. § 2191.
[588] *See* 19 U.S.C. § 3805(a)(1)(D).

In addition, the Court of International Trade has explained:

> [The *NAFTA SAA*] described and the *NAFTA Implementation Act* authorized the promulgation of regulations "as necessary or appropriate to implement immediately applicable U.S. obligations under the NAFTA," NAFTA SAA, H.R. Doc. No. 103-159, vol. 1, at 463, as well as those regulations that were necessary or appropriate to carry out the actions proposed in the SAA. 19 U.S.C. § 3314(b); *see also* Bestfoods v. United States, 165 F.3d 1371, 1374 (Fed. Cir. 1999).

*Former Employees of Quality Fabricating, Inc. v. U.S. Department of Labor*, 343 F.Supp.2d 1272, 1276 (Ct. Int'l Trade 2004).

Despite the importance of these documents as the authoritative interpretation of the United States government respective trade agreement, locating an SAA is not an easy task. The University of Kansas library system is a depositary for all federal government materials. Accordingly, a search (in 2007) for these documents began in the stacks of the Wheat Law Library at the University of Kansas School of Law. Documents for the House of Representatives, namely, implementation acts and other supplementary material of each agreement, were examined. This led to the discovery of all but four SAAs for the following FTAs: the *Israel FTA* (1985); the *Jordan FTA* (2001); the *Australia FTA* (2005); and the *Morocco FTA* (2005). The search moved to another library at the University of Kansas, Anschutz Library. Investigations at Anschutz proved fruitless. Indeed, after several phone calls to the United States Government Printing Office (GPO), it was determined that the GPO did not have *any* SAA available, either in print or electronic form.

The House of Representatives Subcommittee on International Trade, in the House Ways and Means committee, also was solicited for help in locating these missing documents. No one at the Ways and Means Committee had a copy of the documents, nor knew where to find one. However, links were provided to the Ways and Means website, where the SAAs for the *Australia FTA* and *Morocco FTA* are available in portable document format (.pdf). The Subcommittee on International Trade was asked to confirm the .pdf version of these documents (see below) were the final version of each SAA. No response was given.

Local LexisNexis and Westlaw representatives were contacted to determine if they had these documents on file. Despite the fact each company used several reference attorneys to help locate the documents, the remaining SAAs could not be found.

This search endeavor should cause concern. One of the main goals of an SAA is to promote transparency through the publication of an official, authoritative interpretation of a particular trade agreement. In the Kansas experience, quite the opposite occurred: the SAAs were difficult to find and two separate government entities do not know how to obtain a copy of one of the documents. The fact that these documents were difficult to obtain suggests the documents fail to meet its primary aim of increasing transparency. Query whether the difficulty in obtaining an SAA undercuts the value of each document.

*Suggestions for Further Research:*

Article:

1. Buys, Cindy G. & William Isasi, *An "Authoritative" Statement of Administrative Action: A Useful Political Invention or A Violation of the Separation of Powers Doctrine?*, 7 NEW YORK UNIVERSITY JOURNAL OF LEGISLATION AND PUBLIC POLICY 73–114 (2003).

Other Sources:

1. *NAFTA Implementation Act, Statement of Administrative Action*, HOUSE OF REPRESENTATIVES DOCUMENT NUMBER 103–159, at 450 (4 November 1993).

2. *NAFTA Implementation Act, Statement of Administrative Action*, HOUSE OF REPRESENTATIVES DOCUMENT NUMBER 103–159, at 450 (4 November 1993).

3. *Uruguay Round Agreements Act, Statement of Administrative Action*, HOUSE OF REPRESENTATIVES DOCUMENT NUMBER 103-826I, at 822 (27 September 1994), *reprinted in* 1994 U.S.C.C.A.N. 3773, 4040.

4. *Statement of Administrative Action*, The "United States-Australia Free Trade Agreement Implementation Act," H.R. 4759, 108th Cong. (6 July 2004), *posted at,* waysandmeans.house.gov/Media/pdf/australia/hr4579SAA.pdf.

5. *Statement of Administrative Action*, The "United States-Bahrain Free Trade Agreement Implementation Act," H.R. 4340, 109th Cong. (16 November 2005), *posted at,* waysandmeans.house.gov/Media/pdf/109cong/hr4340StatementofAdminAction.pdf.

6. *Statement of Administrative Action*, The "United States-CAFTA-DR Free Trade Agreement Implementation Act," H.R. 3045, 109th Cong. (23 June 2005), *posted at,* waysandmeans.house.gov/media/pdf/109cong/dr-cafta/hr3045saa.htm.

7. *Statement of Administrative Action*, The "United States-Chile Free Trade Agreement Implementation Act," H.R. 2738, 108th Cong. (8 July 2003), *posted at,* waysandmeans.house.gov/media/pdf/chile/hr2738ChileSAA7-15-03.pdf.

8. *Statement of Administrative Action*, The "United States-Morocco Free Trade Agreement Implementation Act," H.R. 4842, 108th Cong. (15 July 2004), *posted at,* waysandmeans.house.gov/Media/pdf/morocco/hr4842saa.pdf.

9. *Statement of Administrative Action*, The "United States-Oman Free Trade Agreement Implementation Act," H.R. 5684, 109th Cong. (26 August 2006), *posted at,* waysandmeans.house.gov/Media/pdf/109cong/HR5684/AdminAction.pdf.

10. *Statement of Administrative Action*, The "United States-Singapore Free Trade Agreement Implementation Act," H.R. 2739, 108th Cong. (15 July 2003), *posted at,* waysandmeans.house.gov/media/pdf/singapore/hr2739Singapore-SAA7-15-03.pdf.

11. *Statement of Administrative Action*, The "United States-Israel Free Trade Area Implementation Act," H.R. 2268, 99th Cong. (6 March 1985). Unavailable or not readily available.

12. *Statement of Administrative Action*, The "United States-Jordan Free Trade Agreement Implementation Act," H.R. 2603, 107th Cong. (26 July 2001). Unavailable nor not readily available.

## STABILIZATION CLAUSE

A provision of a contract between a private investor engaged in foreign direct investment (FDI) and the host country government that is designed to guarantee the stability of the key conditions of the contract that affect the return on investment (ROI). Simply put, the clause is a legal device to hedge against political and legal risk in a foreign country.

A stabilization clause is supposed to protect the private investor against future changes in law or regulation that the host country government might implement. The clause constrains the legislative and regulatory power of the host country government to amend the legal regime in a way that would adversely affect the contract retroactively, or even to annul the contract. Even though the host country has a sovereign right to implement such changes, and apply them retroactively, for example, on the ground of public interest, the country bargains away this right as regards the particular contract at issue. Stabilization clauses are used, for example, in international petroleum contracts and concession agreements between international oil companies (IOCs) and host governments.

There are two kinds of stabilization clauses. "Traditional" stabilization clauses freeze the *status quo*, meaning that the laws and regulations in effect at the time the contract is signed shall apply for the duration of the contract. The host country government cannot enact subsequent rules that are inconsistent with the contract. "Modern hybrid-stabilization" clauses are flexible, in that they allow the state to make changes, but only if it compensates the private investor in the event a change imposes a financial burden on that investor.

The mere presence of a stabilization clause in a contract does not ensure its efficacy. Other factors, such as other provisions in the contract, the law governing the contract, the availability and place of arbitration, and the availability of protection under an investment treaty, affect the efficacy of a stabilization clause.

*Suggestions for Further Research:*

Article:

1. Emeka, J. Nna, *Anchoring Stabilization Clauses in International Petroleum Contracts*, 42 THE INTERNATIONAL LAWYER 1317-1338 (winter 2008).

## STAGES OF GROWTH (STAGES OF GROWTH THEORY OR STAGES OF GROWTH MODEL)

A model of economic growth that highlights the progressive movement of a country through different levels and kinds of economic activity.

### The Basic Theory

Is there a pattern to the process of economic growth through which most poor countries proceed as they gain in riches? Economist Walt W. Rostow answered "yes" in a famous book initially published in 1960, *The Stages of Economic Growth*. To be sure, he was not the first to do so. Karl Marx and Vladimir Lenin developed and refined, respectively, a deterministic model of economic development in which they categorized stages of production, namely, primitive, feudalism, capitalism, socialism, and communism. Rostow, however, was no communist — indeed, the sub-title of his book is "A Non-Communist Manifesto."

Rostow marshaled a massive amount of historical evidence and found that five stages characterized economic growth. The Graph, below, summarizes these stages.

GRAPH:

ROSTOW'S STAGE THEORY

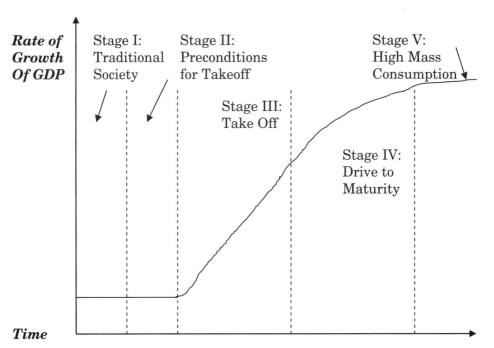

The five stages Rostow identifies are as follows:

• *Traditional Society*:

Poor countries have traditional societies stuck in a vicious cycle of poverty. Earnings are at a subsistence level, so saving is low or non-existent. With no sizeable savings pool, there is no investment. With no investment, there is no growth.

- *Pre-Conditions for Take Off*:

  To break the vicious cycle of poverty, poor countries must create the pre-conditions for a takeoff. These pre-conditions, when in place, will lead to self-sustained growth. There are four key pre-conditions. First, a class of entrepreneurs must develop. By definition, an entrepreneur is willing to take risks in business. Second, people must accumulate savings, and their savings must be channeled into investments. These investments are in productive methods, in both the agricultural and manufacturing sectors. Entrepreneurs play the key role here, as they draw on the savings pool to make investments. Third, people work diligently, whether for themselves or as employees of others. In effect, there is a strong work ethic dedicated to growth. Fourth, there is national unity. The fourth pre-condition allows for enlarged markets for output and specialization of production.

- *Take Off*:

  Given the pre-conditions, at some point there is an increase in investment from less than five percent of total output to more than 10 percent of total output. When this 10 percent threshold is crossed, a country enters the Take Off stage. With higher investment, the growth rate of output accelerates. To be sure, growth may not be even across all sectors. It may be unbalanced (as discussed later), but leading sectors would grow rapidly. Improved technology leads to yet greater productivity and output, and profits are reinvested, as well as allow for new sectors. The financial system improves, in order to mobilize savings and channel them into investments more efficiently than before. The demand for output rises, so as to absorb increased production.

- *Drive to Maturity*:

  In this stage, the ratio of investment to income increases to between 10 and 20 percent, and the savings rate correspondingly grows to that range. Output *per capita* rises, and the leading sectors of the economy change.

- *High Mass Consumption*:

  The final stage results from sustained high investment activity and savings rates. While income growth rates taper off, as the name of this stage connotes, most people enjoy a high degree of material comfort. In comparison with the earlier Stages, especially the first three Stages, it is easy to see the change in the mix of employment and output.

There is a relationship between sources of national income and employment, on the one hand, and the stage at which a country is in, on the other hand. Among low-income countries (which are at earlier stages in the Rostow Model), agriculture accounts for roughly 25 percent of total output, and two-thirds of employment. As these countries grow (*i.e.*, move through the last two stages), agriculture becomes a less significant source of income and employment in relation to manufacturing. Eventually, both agriculture and manufacturing account for a smaller proportionate share of aggregate income and employment than services.

Looking at the historical evidence for major developed countries, Rostow argued they hit the Take Off and Drive to Maturity Stages at slightly different periods. The Table below summarizes these periods.

TABLE:

MAJOR DEVELOPED COUNTRIES, THE TAKE OFF, AND THE DRIVE TO MATURITY

| *Country* | *Take Off Stage* | *Drive to Maturity Stage* |
|---|---|---|
| Great Britain | 1783–1802 | By 1850 |
| Japan | 1878–1900 | By 1940 |
| Russia/Soviet Union | 1890–1914 | By 1950 |
| United States | 1843–60 | By 1900 |

### Critique of Stages of Growth Theory

As conceptually appealing as Rostow's Stages of Growth Model may be, it is important to appreciate the critical questions that have been asked of the Model. First, is the Model too simplistic? Rostow paints with a broad brush. Not every country goes through the five stages in lock step. The more nuanced the review of the economic history of one country in comparison with that of another, the more likely differences will emerge. Another way to put this question is what level of generalization of comparative economic development history is too general?

Second, how does a country get from one stage to another? The Model provides an exposition of the internal dynamics of capitalist economic development. But, it does not explain how the transition is made from one developmental stage to another. Is the story one of channeling increased savings into investment in capital equipment? Or, are other factors important, such as good governance? Might the transition mechanisms be different from one country to another, or one region to the next? Is it possible to skip a stage?

Third, what role does international trade play in each stage, and in the transition from one stage to another? The Model is largely silent as to imports and exports. Yet, in reality, imports are necessary for most countries to industrialize. Exports of surpluses are needed to generate revenues to pay for needed imports. In brief, a closer inspection of the link between trade and stages of income growth than the Model affords is desirable.

An example of a group of countries that provokes all three questions are oil-exporters, particularly in the Arab Middle East. A cursory view of cities like Abu Dhabi and Dubai in the United Arab Emirates (UAE), Doha in Qatar, Manama in Bahrain, and Riyadh in the Kingdom of Saudi Arabia suggests these countries are in the High Mass Consumption stage. They bear all the indicia of that stage, and more (including, for example, health problems like high obesity rates). A closer inspection of these countries reveals features of Traditional Society. There is little in the way of industrialization. Virtually all exports are energy or energy–related, and almost all other items are imported. There are large, poor rural and semi-rural areas where subsistence herding and farming occurs. Dependence on state subsidies, generated from oil and gas exports, means education and health care costs are covered. But, government nannying also creates disincentives to entrepreneurship.

Such countries, members of the Organization of Petroleum Exporting Countries (OPEC) have not passed through Rostow-type stages the way Great Britain, Japan, or the United States did. Might the Arab OPEC countries be able to jump from Traditional Society to High Mass Consumption, *i.e.*, skip industrialization and move straight to reliance on services? That surely is the aspiration of some of them, including Bahrain and the Emirates, which seek to be regional financial hubs and look to Singapore as a model of development.

*Suggestions for Further Research:*

Books:

1.  LENIN, V.I., IMPERIALISM: THE HIGHEST STAGE OF CAPITALISM (1917, 1969 ed.)

2.  LYNN, STUART R., ECONOMIC DEVELOPMENT: THEORY AND PRACTICE FOR A DIVIDED WORLD 33, 47–49 (2003) (including Figure 3-2).

3.  ROSTOW, W.W., THE STAGES OF ECONOMIC GROWTH: A NON-COMMUNIST MANIFESTO (3ᴿᴰ ED. 1990).

Article:

1.  Domar, Evsey, *Expansion and Employment*, 37 AMERICAN ECONOMIC REVIEW 34–35 (March 1947).

# STANDARD OF REVIEW

The legal rule by which an appellate adjudicatory body examines the decision and supporting rationale rendered by a lower adjudicatory body. Article 17:6 of the WTO *Understanding on Rules and Procedures Governing the Settlement of Disputes (Dispute Settlement Understanding*, or *DSU)*, establishes a standard of review applicable in all cases.

Notably, however, a different standard is set for the Appellate Body out in Article 17:6 of the WTO *Antidumping Agreement*. Of course, this standard applies only in antidumping (AD) cases. There has been considerable controversy as to whether the Appellate Body has been faithful to this standard, or has exceeded its authority.

*Suggestions for Further Research:*

Articles:

1.  Cai, Phoenix X.F., *Between Intensive Care and the Crematorium: Using the Standard of Review to Restore Balance to the WTO*, 15 TULANE JOURNAL OF INTERNATIONAL & COMPARATIVE LAW 465–539 (2007).

2.  Guzman, Andrew T., *Determining the Appropriate Standard of Review in WTO Disputes*, 42 CORNELL INTERNATIONAL LAW JOURNAL 45–76 (2009).

## STATUTORY CHALLENGE

*See* As Such Challenge.

## STE

State Trading Enterprise.

STEs are governmental and non-governmental enterprises that deal with goods for import and/or export. STEs can include marketing boards, such as the Kansas City Board of Trade, or the Karnataka State Agricultural Marketing Board (KSAMB) in India. STEs are most common in economies where agriculture is an important sector, particularly in trade, and they often enjoy monopoly control over imports and exports.

STEs should not be confused with state-owned enterprises (SOEs). An STE need not be state owned, and its mission and function is narrowly focused on importation and/or exportation. By contrast, SOEs are government owned (wholly or partly), and may engage in a wide-range of functions, including manufacturing operations. Finally, STEs may be found in non-communist, non-socialist economies, such as Australia and Canada. SOEs are more typically characteristic of non-market economies (NMEs).

Article XVII of GATT 1994 speaks specifically to STEs and their operations.[589] Although a major lacuna of Article XVII is it never defines what a "STE" is, it mandates that STEs — in purchasing or selling either imports or exports — are to act in accordance with general principles of non-discrimination. In addition, STEs are only to be swayed by commercial considerations when making decisions on imports and exports. The WTO has a Working Party dedicated to STEs.

*Suggestions for Further Research:*

Book:

1.  COTTIER, THOMAS & PETROS C. MAVROIDIS EDS., STATE TRADING IN THE TWENTY-FIRST CENTURY (1998).

Book Chapters:

1.  Curtiss, Catherine, *Against the Grain: U.S. — Canada Wheat Trade Dispute, in* THE FIRST DECADE OF NAFTA: THE FUTURE OF FREE TRADE IN NORTH AMERICA 145–65 (Kevin Kennedy ed. 2004).

---

[589] *See also Understanding on the Interpretation of Article XVII of the General Agreement on Tariffs and Trade 1994*, 15 April 1994, Marrakesh Agreement Establishing the World Trade Organization, Annex 1A, 1867 U.N.T.S. 187, 33 International Legal Materials 1153 (1994).

Article:

1. Zhang, Catherine Xiaoying, *Business Negotiation between Westerners and Chinese State-Owned Enterprises*, 42 The International Lawyer 1303–1316 (2008).

Other Source:

1. Organization for Economic Co-Operation and Development, State Trading Enterprises in Agriculture (2001).

## STEADY STATE (STEADY STATE LEVEL OF INVESTMENT)

*See* Solow Model.

## STEP PAYMENTS (STEP 1, STEP 2, STEP 3)

*See* Cotton Step Payments

## STERILIZATION

A term associated with foreign exchange and monetary policy operations conducted by a central bank.

When a central bank intervenes in a foreign exchange market to maintain or reduce the value of its currency against foreign currencies, by definition it purchases foreign currency and sells local currency. The sale of local currency increases the money supply in the local country, which can lead to inflation. In particular, if the supply of local currency outstrips growth in output, and if people spend the extra currency on consumption items, then the scenario is quintessentially "too many dollars chasing too few goods." (Of course, if people save the extra currency, and invest it in assets denominated in local currency, then there is no inflationary effect.) To avoid this outcome, the central bank may follow its foreign exchange intervention with issuances of bonds, particularly medium- and long-term debt obligations. When people buy the bonds, they pay for them with the extra currency, and thus the surplus currency is mopped up — or sterilized.

The converse situation also can occur. If a central bank seeks a higher value of its currency against foreign currencies, then it may intervene in the foreign exchange market by selling foreign currency, paying for it with local currency. The central bank can offset the contraction in the supply of local currency, and reduce the risk of deflation, by purchasing debt obligations. It injects local currency into the domestic economy simply by paying for the debt with that currency. Here, the diminution in the supply of local currency following foreign exchange sales is offset by sterilization in the form of asset purchases.

## STR

United States Special Representative for Trade Negotiations, or Special Trade Representative, now called the "United States Trade Representative" or "USTR" for short.

The *Trade Expansion Act of 1962* established the STR to serve as the chief American trade negotiator, with the rank of Ambassador. The *1962 Act* required the president to appoint an STR and establish an agency to make recommendations to the President on policy issues arising from trade agreements. The *Trade Act of 1974* made the Office of the STR an agency within the executive office of the President, expanded the STR's duties, and elevated it to Cabinet rank. The STR was re-designated as the USTR by a reorganization plan issued pursuant to the Reorganization Plan Number 3 and Executive Order 12188. That *Act* assigned a number of duties to the USTR, including:

- The overall responsibility to develop, coordinate, and implement American trade policy;

- The designation of the USTR as the President's principal advisor and chief spokesperson on trade;

- The duty to protect the rights of the United States under all bilateral and multilateral agreements;

- The position of Vice Chair of the Overseas Private Investment Corporation (OPIC), a non-voting member of the Export-Import Bank Board of Directors, and a member of the National Advisory Committee on International Monetary and Financial Policies;

- The duty to develop and coordinate trade in services matters; and

- The obligation to oversee direct investment matters.

These duties were later codified by the *Omnibus Trade and Competitiveness Act of 1988*. Also in this *Act* was a requirement that the USTR coordinate America's trade policy with other government agencies.

*Suggestions for Further Research:*

Book:

1. DRYDEN, STEVE, TRADE WARRIORS: USTR AND THE AMERICAN CRUSADE FOR FREE TRADE 33–59 (1995).

## STRUCTURAL IMBALANCE

A chronic disequilibrium associated with cross-border trade in goods or services, which may be measured from the perspective of one country (*e.g.*, the United States) against another country (*e.g.*, China) or region (*e.g.*, the Far East), or against the rest of the world (*i.e.*, all other countries).

In the post-Second World War era, there have been two premises underlying American trade policy. First, the march toward trade liberalization is in the long-term interest of the United States, and of all other countries. Second, a rule of international trade law, under the auspices of the General Agreement on Tariffs and Trade (GATT) and World Trade Organization (WTO), is the best way to preserve the free trading system. Some experienced practitioners and scholars question these two premises, and even argue they are false.

The essence of this skeptical argument — "skeptical" because it is contrary to the conventional free-trade wisdom — is that imbalances in trade flows have existed for years, indeed decades, that they are not automatically self-correcting by virtue of market forces (such as foreign exchange movements and the J-curve effect), and that there is nothing in the GATT–WTO legal or institutional regime that helps resolve them. Underlying this argument is that structural imbalances matter, at least in a political if not economic sense, and that they are not sustainable in perpetuity. Associated with this argument is the observation that the global economic recession that began in 2008 is linked to structural imbalances.

As a factual matter, the United States is a structural trade deficit country. China, Germany, Japan, and Korea are structural trade surplus countries. China is at the heart of the problem of structural imbalances, so the argument goes, but it is neither fair nor productive to single China out for blame. Germany, Japan, and Korea have long been neo-mercantilist in their approach to international trade. Moreover, it appears Brazil, India, and Taiwan actively structure their economies in favor of export-led growth. None of the structural surplus countries allow for the creative destruction of capitalism that Joseph Schumpeter famously discusses in his classic *Capitalism, Socialism, and Democracy* (1943), and to some degree in his earlier work *The Theory of Economic Development: An Inquiry into Profits, Capital, Credit, Interest and the Business Cycle* (first published in German in 1911 as *Theorie der wirtschaftlichen Entwicklung*, and translated into English in 1934). Generally, the governments of structural surplus economies allow little room for entrepreneurship through debt-leveraging, nor have bankruptcy laws favorable to debtors. Rather, they rely on export-targeting (*i.e.*, government identification of industries to lead the country in exports).

That said, the United States is in part to blame for its structural deficit position. The American capitalist economy is a consumption-driven one, with a faith in the proposition that what is good for consumers is good for producers, and *vice versa*. The argument against this proposition is that the proposition holds true in a closed domestic economy. But, when a consumption-driven economy is an open one, and the appetite for consumption is fed by imports, then imbalances are inevitable.

Among the key elements of the argument of the skeptics are the following:

- Patience of Capital —

  Capital (that is, financial capital) is far more patient in Japan than in the United States. This patience is demonstrated in the auto industry, when the question of why structural imbalances in auto trade between the United States and Japan are considered. The Italian producer Fiat, and the French producers Peugeot and Renault, withdrew from the American auto market. The German producer, Mercedes, had a disastrous experience in teaming with Chrysler. Yet, the Japanese giants, Honda and Toyota, have stayed in the American market, producing millions of vehicles in the United States. Why? One reason is the Japanese *keiretsu* system, *i.e.*, the Japanese system of corporate organization, characterized by interlocking directorates, close relationships between lenders and borrowers, and vertical integration. In this system, corporations take a long-term view of their product and its success. Rather than measuring achievement by quarterly movements in share prices, or short-term sales revenues, as the American and even European firms do, the Japanese companies emphasize long-term performance indicators, like product quality, market share, and reputation.

- Significance of Profitability —

Profitability is far less significant to Japanese than to American companies. That is one reason why they are less willing to outsource than American companies. That is, profitability is relatively insignificant in Japan compared to the United States, but long-term relationships are relatively more important than in Japan. Consequently, Japanese companies are not eager to outsource work and workers.

- Distribution —

Ricardo's principle of comparative advantage emphasizes the ability to produce a good at lower marginal cost. But, it entirely ignores the problem of selling a good in a foreign country. That is, that principle says nothing about the system of distribution. In the United States, it is relatively easy for a foreign producer-exporter to sell its product. That is not true in the structural surplus countries of Germany, Japan, and Korea.

Consider the fact that there are only three major countries in which Wal-Mart has had problems, and failed — Germany, Japan, and Korea. In all three countries, the distribution system is one that Wal-Mart has not been able to own or operate. Rather, local companies exercise that control, making it difficult for Wal-Mart to distribute its products. This control, *i.e.*, the closed distribution system, contributes to structural imbalances. Despite negotiations under the *General Agreement on Trade in Services* (*GATS*), the multilateral trade regime does not aggressively promote the opening of distribution channels.

Similarly, the *Korea–United States Free Trade Agreement* (*KORUS*) does nothing to loosen the grip of *chaebols* (in effect, the Korean version of *keiretsu*). Thus, for example, the American white-goods producer, Whirlpool, will not be able to sell easily its washers, dryers, and other consumer durables in Korea, because the distribution network — even the producer of boxes for the appliances — are owned by Korean companies like LG.

- Exchange Rates —

Exchange rates have not operated to correct structural trade imbalances, at least not between the United States and Japan.

Between 1985 and 1995, the Japanese yen appreciated relative to the U.S. dollar by 2.5 times. But, denominated in yen terms, Japan's trade surplus with the United States dropped only marginally, and in dollar terms, its surplus tripled.

- Dispute Settlement —

  The WTO *Understanding on Rules and Procedures Governing the Settlement of Disputes* (*Dispute Settlement Understanding*, or *DSU*), forces companies to think narrowly. That is, the DSU compels them to focus on litigation, not on structural imbalances. Thus, the *DSU* can resolve infractions of trade rules in relatively minor sectors, but it is not designed to deal with structural imbalances in the international aircraft industry that pit Boeing and Airbus against each other over reciprocal allegations about unfair subsidization.

  Notably, China has articulated a goal of being the world's largest producer of civil aircraft by 2020. That goal reflects the fact that China does not see itself as the "factory floor" of the world in perpetuity, *i.e.*, that it seeks to ascend the chain of value-added manufacturing. The entry of Airbus into the world civil aviation market ultimately hastened the exit of Lockheed and McDonnell–Douglas from that market. Were China to reach its goal, Boeing, Airbus, or both could be put under severe competitive pressure. Focusing on *DSU* litigation misses the mark, namely, the big picture of China's ascendancy in world commercial aviation.

- Asymmetric Distribution of Rights and Duties —

  The GATT–WTO system distributes rights and obligations unevenly. There is no mechanism, no leverage, for the United States to force the kind of wrenching change necessary to balance trade flows. The best available legal tools to correct structural imbalances are in GATT Articles XII and XVIII. Yet, despite an *Understanding* from the Uruguay Round on these GATT balance of payments (BOP) provisions, they are out-of-date.

- The Doha Round —

  The Doha Round holds little promise of correcting structural imbalances. Updating the GATT BOP provisions is not an item on the Doha Development Agenda (DDA). From the American perspective, nothing on the DDA addresses its structural trade deficit, and most other WTO Members have not made committed to significant enhancements in market access opportunities for American exporters. Even most developing and least developing countries will not prosper from the Doha Round. If most-favored nation (MFN) tariffs are cut and bound at lower levels, the major beneficiary will be China. That is because it is a huge export platform relative to developing and least developed countries. To observers of the Multi-Fiber Agreement (MFA) and Uruguay Round *Agreement on Textiles and Clothing* (*ATC*), this prospect is no surprise. The *MFA* was a development-enhancing tool, insofar as it assured many small, poor countries access for their textile and apparel (T&A) exports into the American and other developed country markets. With the abolition of global *MFA* quotas, as called for by the *ATC*, T&A manufacturers rationalized their production facilities, closing operations in small countries like Sri Lanka, and concentrating them in China and India.

*Suggestions for Further Research:*

Article:

1.　Lovett, William A., *Beyond Doha: Multipolar Challenges for a Globalized World*, 17 TULANE JOURNAL OF INTERNATIONAL & COMPARATIVE LAW 3–37 (winter 2008).

## STUFFING

*See* Point of Stuffing.

## SUBJECT MERCHANDISE

Merchandise subject to an antidumping (AD) or countervailing duty (CVD) investigation.[590]

Under pre-Uruguay Round United States law, the term for "subject merchandise" was "class or kind of merchandise subject to investigation." Since the Uruguay Round, that statute has been amended to define subject merchandise as a "class or kind of foreign merchandise that is being, or is likely to be, sold in the United States at less than its fair value." Merchandise recently subject to investigation covers a huge gamut of products, including, for instance, glass windshields and honey from China.

## SUBSIDY

*See* CVD, *SCM Agreement*, Traffic Light System.

## SUBSTANTIAL TRANSFORMATION (SUBSTANTIAL TRANSFORMATION TEST)

A rule of origin that may arise in the context of either non-preferential or preferential treatment of merchandise.

Essentially, "substantial transformation" of a product into a new and different article in a particular country confers origin on that country with respect to the product. For instance, if cocoa beans imported into the United States from Ghana are made into refined chocolate in Kansas at Russell Stover, then a substantial transformation of cocoa beans has occurred in the United States. The chocolates are the product of, or originate in, the United States.

---

[590] *See* 19 U.S.C. §1673.

The classic statement of the substantial transformation test is in the United States Supreme Court case of *Anheuser Busch*.[591] That case involved the question of whether an importer had sufficiently manufactured a product in the United States, and was thus entitled to a reimbursement of a previously-imposed tariff. The Court held that for there to be a "transformation," a new and different article must emerge from the domestic manufacturing process, "having a distinctive name, character, or use."[592] Accordingly, the *Anheuser Busch* test for substantial transformation is sometimes called the "change in name, character, or use" test.

Notably, that is not the only test for substantial transformation. Another test, which relies on Harmonized System, another test is Change in Tariff Classification (CTC), or more specifically, Change in Tariff Heading (CTH) or Change in Tariff Sub-Heading (CTSH). Essentially, if an article undergoes a CTC — at the Heading (four digit) or sub-heading (six digit level) — then a "substantial transformation" is said to have occurred.

What if more than one substantial transformation occurs in a production chain, under the applicable rule? In such a case, the merchandise in question is deemed to originate in the country in which the last substantial transformation occurred.

## SUNSET REVIEW

A review of an antidumping (AD) or countervailing duty (CVD) order at the end of five years from the date of publication of that order.

Sunset Reviews are required under Article 9 and under United States AD and CVD law. Their purpose is to ensure that AD and CVD orders do not persist beyond their useful life, and thus become unjustified protectionism. In a Sunset Review, the relevant administering agency, such as the United States Department of Commerce (DOC) must determine whether revocation of the AD or CVD order at issue would be likely to lead to a continuation or recurrence of dumping or illegal subsidization, and of material injury.

## SUNSHINE POLICY

A policy of the government of South Korea toward reunification of the Korean peninsula.

Via the Sunshine Policy, South Korea seeks peaceful reunification with North Korea. The core of the approach is to establish and expand markets and market mechanisms in the North. Thus, for instance, South Korea has supported the development of industrial complexes north of the De-Militarized Zone (DMZ), such as at Kaesong, which is about one hour drive north of the DMZ. These complexes contain factories employing mainly North Korean workers, employed by South Korean businesses.

---

[591] *See Anheuser-Busch Brewing Association v. United States* 207 U.S. 556 (1908).
[592] *Anheuser-Busch* at 562.

During negotiations for the *United States–Korea Free Trade Agreement* (*KORUS*), South Korea and the United States argues over whether products made in Kaesong would qualify as originating in Korea, and thus entitled to duty-free treatment under *KORUS*. The United States refused to accept origin on this basis, because it did not want to support the regime of Kim Jong-Il of North Korea. Shortly after the terrorist attacks of 11 September 2001, President George W. Bush had dubbed that regime part of the Axis of Evil (along with Iran and Syria), and accused it of seeking and proliferating nuclear weapons. The American strategy of isolating North Korea openly conflicted with the Sunshine Policy of South Korea.

In the end, the two sides agreed to fudge the issue in *KORUS*. *KORUS* establishes a "Committee on Outward Processing Zones." Based on yet-to-be finalized criteria, the Committee will designate which, if any, industrial complexes outside of South Korean territory might count under *KORUS*, *i.e.*, in which merchandise made could qualify as originating and thereby obtain preferential treatment. In principle, then, Kaesong products might one day receive this treatment.

## SUPER 301

A unilateral trade remedy of the United States, which calls on the United States Trade Representative to identify the most egregious trade barriers that adversely affect American exports. It is part of the *Trade Act of 1974*, as amended, and codified at 19 U.S.C. § 2420. Once the USTR identifies an act, policy, or practice of a foreign government — that is, a trade measure — as a "priority foreign country practice," then it is required to launch a Section 301 investigation.

Under the Administration of President Bill Clinton, such identification was a basis for commencing a dispute settlement proceeding in the WTO. However, Super 301 lapsed, and was not renewed. In October 2009, Senators Sherrod Brown (Democrat — Ohio) and Debbie Stabenow (Democrat — Michigan) introduced the *Trade Enforcement Priorities Act of 2009*.[593] This legislation would:

- Renew Super 301.
- Obligate the USTR to identify the most serious foreign trade measures that adversely affect American exports or jobs. Examples could include currency manipulation and unfair subsidies. The USTR would have to put the list in its annual *National Trade Estimates (NTE) Report*. This Report covers not only goods, but also services, intellectual property rights (IPRs), and foreign direct investment (FDI).
- Establish that if a dispute settlement mechanism applied to the particular measure and issue, and the measure identified by the USTR is

---

[593] *See* Rossella Brevetti, *Brown — Stabenow Trade Enforcement Bill Would Revive Super 301*, 26 International Trade Reporter (BNA) 1495 (5 November 2009).

maintained by a country with which the United States has a trade agreement, then that mechanism would be used. If no such agreement existed, then the United States would enter into bilateral consultations with the target foreign country.

- Require the USTR to make clear its enforcement priorities, and work with countries that show a pattern of unfair trade practices.

Notably, legislation introduced in 2009 to the House of Representatives would revive Super 301, such as H.R. 496, sponsored by Charles Rangel (Democrat — New York) and Sander Levin (Democrat — Michigan), the Chairmen of the House Ways and Means Committee and Trade Subcommittee, respectively.

## SUSTAINABLE DEVELOPMENT

As generally understood, and as used in a variety of contexts, notably international environmental law, "sustainable development" refers to development in a manner that enables the current generation to meet its needs without compromising the ability of future generations to meet their needs.

The term inherently contains an inter-generational ethical obligation, namely, that the present generation should preserve, even enhance, the global environment in good stewardship for subsequent generations.

However, the definition of sustainable development is not limited to environmental concerns. Rather, the United Nations Division for Sustainable Development has expanded the definition to consider poverty, technology, finance, and health, amongst others, as obstacles to sustainable development.

*Suggestions for Further Research:*

Books:

1. INTERNATIONAL COUNCIL FOR SCIENCE, SCIENTIFIC COMMITTEE ON PROBLEMS OF THE ENVIRONMENT, SUSTAINABILITY INDICATORS: A SCIENTIFIC ASSESSMENT (2007).

2. MURPHY, JOSEPH, ED., GOVERNING TECHNOLOGY FOR SUSTAINABILITY (2007).

3. PEZZEY, JOHN, SUSTAINABLE DEVELOPMENT CONCEPTS: AN ECONOMIC ANALYSIS (1992).

4. SAMPSON, GARY P., THE WTO AND SUSTAINABLE DEVELOPMENT (2005).

5. SPOOR, MAX, *ET. AL.* EDS., DRAGONS WITH CLAY FEET?: TRANSITION, SUSTAINABLE LAND USE, AND RURAL ENVIRONMENT IN CHINA AND VIETNAM (2007).

6. WHITEHEAD, MARK, SPACES OF SUSTAINABILITY: GEOGRAPHICAL PERSPECTIVES ON THE SUSTAINABLE SOCIETY (2007).

Book Chapters:

1. Chavanich, Chotiras, *Trade in Services and Sustainable Development in the Context of the WTO: The Case of Higher Education, in* THE WTO IN THE TWENTY-FIRST CENTURY — DISPUTE SETTLEMENT, NEGOTIATIONS, AND REGIONALISM IN ASIA 381–395 (Yasuhei Taniguchi, Alan Yanovich & Jan Bohanes eds. 2007).

2. Halle, Mark, *The WTO and Sustainable Development, in* THE WTO IN THE TWENTY-FIRST CENTURY — DISPUTE SETTLEMENT, NEGOTIATIONS, AND REGIONALISM IN ASIA 395–408 (Yasuhei Taniguchi, Alan Yanovich & Jan Bohanes eds. 2007).

Articles:

1. Carroll, Ellie, Comment, *Twenty-Five Years in the Making: Why Sustainable Development Has Eluded the U.N., and How Community-Driven Development Offers the Solution*, 32 HOUSTON JOURNAL OF INTERNATIONAL LAW 545-585 (2010).

2. Czarneski, Jason J., *Food, Law & the Environment: Informational and Structural Changes for a Sustainable Food System*, 31 UTAH ENVIRONMENTAL LAW REVIEW 263–290 (2011).

3. Dwyer, Lorna, *Biopiracy, Trade, and Sustainable Development*, 19 COLORADO JOURNAL OF INTERNATIONAL ENVIRONMENTAL LAW & POLICY 219–257 (2008).

4. Elizalde Carranza, Miguel A., *MEAs with Trade Measures and the WTO: Aiming Toward Sustainable Development?*, 15 BUFFALO ENVIRONMENTAL LAW JOURNAL 43–96 (2007–2008).

5. Healy, Michael P., *The Sustainable Development Principle in United States Environmental Law*, 2 GEORGE WASHINGTON JOURNAL OF ENERGY & ENVIRONMENTAL LAW 19–41 (2011).

6. Lagomarsino, Jeffrey, *WTO Dispute Settlement and Sustainable Development: Legitimacy through Holistic Treaty Interpretation*, 28 PACE ENVIRONMENTAL LAW REVIEW 545–567 (2011).

7. Kennedy, Kevin C., *The Status of the Trade-Environment-Sustainable Development Triad in the Doha Round Negotiations and in Recent U.S. Trade Policy*, 19 INDIANA INTERNATIONAL & COMPARATIVE LAW REVIEW 529–552 (2009).

8. Kershen, Drew L., *Sustainable Intensive Agriculture: High Technology and Environmental Benefits*, 16 KANSAS JOURNAL OF LAW AND PUBLIC POLICY number 3, 424–450 (spring 2007).

9. Lappé, Anna, *Food, Fuel, and the Future of Farming: Conference of Sustainable Agriculture*, 10 VERMONT JOURNAL OF ENVIRONMENTAL LAW 367–378 (2009).

10. Nightengale, Gwendolyn K., *A Sustainable Future: A Proposal for Improving the Effectiveness of Farmer Fields Schools in Indonesia and Ghana*, 3 HUMAN RIGHTS & GLOBALIZATION LAW REVIEW 9–31 (2009/2011).

11. Nowicki, Meghan, Note, *Implementing Sustainable Industrial Development in the United States and Abroad: the Need for Legislation and International Cooperation*, 62 ALABAMA LAW REVIEW 1093–1117 (2011).

12. Rene de Vera, Enrique, Development, *The WTO and Biofuels: The Possibility of Unilateral Sustainability Requirements*, 8 CHICAGO JOURNAL OF INTERNATIONAL LAW 661–679 (2008).

13. *Small, Slow, and Local: Essays on Building a More Sustainable and Local Food System*, 12 VERMONT JOURNAL OF ENVIRONMENTAL LAW 353–425 (2011).

14. Stevens, Lisa, Ballenger-Green Diversity Paper, Note, *The Illusion of Sustainable Development: How Nigeria's Environmental Laws Are Failing the Niger Delta*, 36 VERMONT LAW REVIEW 387–407 (2011).

15. Werksman, Jacob, *Book Review* (reviewing Gary Sampson, *The WTO and Sustainable Development* (2005), 25 BERKELEY JOURNAL OF INTERNATIONAL LAW 459–484 (2007).

## SVE

Small Vulnerable Economy.

As proposed by the SVE group of WTO Members during the Doha Round, an acceptable definition of an "SVE" is one with an economy that, in the period 1999 to 2004, had an average share of world merchandise trade of 0.16 percent or less, of world trade in non-agricultural products of 0.1 percent or less, and world trade in agricultural products of 0.4 percent or less. WTO Members falling under this definition include Barbados, Bolivia, Mauritius, Mongolia, and Papua New Guinea (PNG).

This definition was accepted by Chairman of the WTO agricultural negotiations, Ambassador Crawford Falconer of New Zealand, in the Second Installment of his "Challenges Paper" (at ¶ 18), dated 25 May 2007, which was posted on the WTO website.[594] During the Doha Round, a consensus emerged that the export interests of SVEs should receive enhanced improvements in market access. Similar proposals would grant SVEs more favorable treatment as regards their tariff barriers on agriculture, including a prohibition on tariff capping and exemptions from tariff reduction and tariff rate quota (TRQ) commitments.

*Suggestions for Further Research:*

Books:

1. CASTELLO, SERGIO, GLOBALIZATION OF SMALL ECONOMIES AS A STRATEGIC BEHAVIOR IN INTERNATIONAL BUSINESS (1999).

2. MCKEE, DAVID, EXTERNAL LINKAGES AND GROWTH IN SMALL ECONOMIES (1994).

Articles:

1. Gounder, Neelesh & Biman Chand Prasad, *Regional Trade Agreements and the New Theory of Trade — Implications for Trade Policy in Pacific Island Countries*, 10 JOURNAL OF INTERNATIONAL TRADE LAW AND POLICY 49–63 (2011).

2. Kelsey, Jane, *World Trade and Small Nations in the South Pacific Region*, 14 KANSAS JOURNAL OF LAW AND PUBLIC POLICY 247, 247–275 (2005).

3. von Tigerstrom, Barbara, *Small Island Developing States and International Trade: Special Challenges in the Global Partnership for Development*, 6 MELBOURNE JOURNAL OF INTERNATIONAL LAW 402 (2005).

---

[594] *See* Communication from the Chairman of the Committee on Agriculture, Special Session Second Installment (25 May 2007), *posted at,* www.wto.org (commonly known as the "Challenges Paper").

Other Sources:

1. WORLD BANK, FIVE SMALL OPEN ECONOMIES (Ronald Findlay & Stanislaw Wellisz eds., 1993).

## SOVEREIGN WEALTH FUND

A vehicle by which a government invests money, other than foreign exchange reserves, in financial assets on behalf of the country.

States establish Sovereign Wealth Funds (SWF) when they have surpluses to invest. SWFs have been around for years, but are now starting to take on a new role as surpluses and investments increase worldwide. Morgan Stanley estimated in 2007 there was close to $2,500 billion in SWFs, and that by 2010 the figure would increase to $5,000 billion, and reach $12,000 billion by 2015.[595]

The growth of SWFs and their role in the global financial market has increased overall concern about regulation, or lack thereof. Guidelines for investors and recipient countries are needed to manage successfully SWFs on a global scale. Such a "code of conduct" governing SWF behavior at the very least must cover transparency.[596]

The current regulation (or lack of regulation) leaves some SWFs "unaccountable" to their domestic legislatures.[597] According to research supported by the International Monetary Fund (IMF), 21 percent of a total of 20 funds surveyed were not accountable at all to their domestic legislature. A further 58 percent did not report directly to their domestic legislature, but reported through a board chair or minister of finance.[598] The survey further found that only some SWFs complied with the international financial reporting standards (IFRS) while the remaining respondents applied standards they considered "equivalent to" or "materially" similar to the IFRS.[599]

Regulation of SWFs entered the forefront of American politics as a reaction to concerns about national security and "interference" in the economy by foreign governments through investment. Lawmakers called for increased safeguards and stricter controls of foreign investments through regulations that would establish transparency and control the overall behavior of SWFs.[600] In 2007, the *Foreign Investment and National Security Act of 2007* became law

---

[595] Lawrence Summers, *Sovereign Funds Shake the Logic of Capitalism*, FINANCIAL TIMES, 30 July 2007, at 9.

[596] *How to Deal with Sovereign Wealth*, FINANCIAL TIMES, 28 January 2008, at 8.

[597] *See* Demetri Sevastopulo & Krishna Guha, *Fifth of SWFs 'unaccountable'*, FINANCIAL TIMES, 15 September 2008, at 4.

[598] *See* Demetri Sevastopulo & Krishna Guha, *Fifth of SWFs 'unaccountable'*, FINANCIAL TIMES, 15 September 2008, at 4.

[599] Demetri Sevastopulo & Krishna Guha, *Fifth of SWFs 'unaccountable'*, FINANCIAL TIMES, 15 September 2008, at 4.

[600] *See* Amy Tsui, *Lawmakers Calll for Rules to Govern Behavior of Sovereign Wealth Funds at China Hearing*, 25 International Trade Reporter (BNA) 229 (14 February 2008).

and reformed the Committee on Foreign Investment in the United States (CFIUS). Congress looked to regulations that would implement the law and offer a balance between control and open investment. Congress, while supporting increased control of SWF investments, recognized that regulations must be reasonable to insure that the country remain attractive to foreign investors.

On the opposite side of the American political spectrum, there exits strong arguments opposed to increased regulation of SWFs. Such opposition extends beyond the fact that many believe the regulatory framework to control SWFs already exists by means of CFIUS. Those opposed to increased regulation view excessive control of SWFs as protectionist, and recognize the role SWFs played in stabilizing the global economy, given the financial turmoil of the past few years.[601] The United States is both the world's largest recipient of inbound foreign domestic investment (FDI), and the world's largest source of outbound FDI.[602] An example of the economic benefit rather than the destabilizing effects of SWFs is, in 2007 the United States received half of the total $43 billion generated from SWFs. The United States clearly benefits as an FDI recipient.[603]

However, both those who support and oppose increased SWF regulation agree that common ground rules and transparency are essential for successful SWF investments. Furthermore, they emphasize that SWF investments must be made for commercial reasons, not as political or strategic moves.

In striking a balance between the two camps, in March of 2008 the United States reached an agreement with Abu Dhabi and Singapore on a code of conduct for investment by SWFs. The code focuses on SWF investment decisions based on commercial grounds and not on the geopolitical goals of the controlling government. The agreed principles in the code include:

- greater information disclosure,
- strong governance structure and internal controls,
- fair competition between SWFs and the private sector, and
- respect of host-country rules.[604]

At that time, the Abu Dhabi Investment Authority (ADIA) held between $500 billion and $875 billion in assets and Singapore's Government of Singapore Investment Corporation had estimated assets between $100 billion and $330 billion.[605]

---

[601] *See* Joe Kirwin, *EC to Release Proposed Code of Conduct for Sovereign Wealth Funds, Barroso Says*, 25 International Trade Reporter (BNA) 298 (28 February 2008).

[602] *See* John Herzfeld, *Veroneau Warns Against Protectionism Over Sovereign Wealth Fund Investments*, 25 International Trade Reporter (BNA) 291 (28 February 2008).

[603] *See* Ali Qassim, *Voluntary Code Will Help Build Trust for Sovereign Funds, Business Leaders Say*, 25 International Trade Reporter (BNA) 474 (3 April 2008).

[604] *See* Diana I. Gregg & Aaron Lorenzo, *Treasury Unveils Accord on Set of Principles for Wealth Funds with Singapore, Abu Dhabi*, 25 International Trade Reporter (BNA) 440 (27 March 2008).

[605] *See* Daniel Dombey, *Wealth Funds Strike Deal with Washington,* FINANCIAL TIMES, 22–23 March 2008, at 4.

The United States is not alone in creating regulation of SWFs with various individual countries. The EU executive body proposed a voluntary code of conduct for SWFs of foreign governments who wish to invest in the European Union (EU). The code would create a commitment to transparency and establish a harmonized approach among all EU states. This code of conduct includes the following standards regarding transparency: annual disclosure of investment positions; size and source of an entity's resources; and disclosure of home country regulation and oversight governing the SWF among other standards.[606]

On 16 October 2008, a group of 23 government owned SWFs presented a set of 24 generally agreed upon principles governing SWFs.[607] The International Working Group of Sovereign Wealth Funds (IWG) presented the principles to the International Monetary Fund (IMF).[608] The work of the IWG focuses on lessening concerns about sovereign investments and quelling suspicions regarding the economic power of SWFs. The 24 Principles include assurances that SWFs:

- have a transparent governance structure that provides for adequate operational controls, risk management and accountability;

- invest on the basis of economic and financial risk and return-related considerations;

- comply with regulatory and disclosure requirements in the countries in which they invest; and

- help maintain a stable global financial system and free flow of capital and investment.[609]

The principles will be reviewed and examined by the members over the course of their voluntary implementation. The third annual meeting of the International Forum of Sovereign Wealth Funds took place on 11–13 May 2011 in Beijing, China, with future meetings scheduled for 2012 in Mexico and 2013 in Norway.[610]

*Suggestions for Further Research:*

Articles:

1. Backer, Larry Catá, *Sovereign Investing in Times of Crisis: Global Regulation of Sovereign Wealth Funds, Sate-Owned Enterprises, and the*

---

[606] Joe Kirwin, *EC to Release Proposed Code of Conduct for Sovereign Wealth Funds, Barroso Says*, 25 International Trade Reporter (BNA) 298 (28 February 2008).

[607] Rita McWilliams, *Sovereign Wealth Funds Release Voluntary Principles to Add Transparency*, 25 International Trade Reporter (BNA) 1475 (10 October 2008).

[608] *See* The IWG's set of voluntary principles, *"The Santiago Principles"* posted at www.iwg-swf.org/pubs/gapplist.htm. *See generally* www.ifswf.org.

[609] Rita McWilliams, *Sovereign Wealth Funds Release Voluntary Principles to Add Transparency*, 25 International Trade Reporter (BNA) 1475 (10 October 2008).

[610] *See* International Forum of Sovereign Wealth Funds *posted at* www.ifswf.org/index. htm.

*Chinese Experience*, 19 TRANSNATIONAL LAW & CONTEMPORARY PROBLEMS 3–144 (2010).

2. Gilson, Ronald J. & Curtis Milhaupt, *Sovereign Wealth Funds and Corporate Governance: A Minimalist Response to the New Mercantilism*, 60 STANFORD LAW REVIEW 1345–1369 (2008).

3. Langland, Eric, Comment, *Misplaced Fears Put to Rest: Financial Crisis Reveals the True Motives of Sovereign Wealth Funds*, 18 TULANE JOURNAL OF INTERNATIONAL & COMPARATIVE LAW 263–286 (2009).

4. Lee, Yvonne C.L., *A Reversal of Neo-Colonialism: The Pitfalls and Prospects of Sovereign Wealth Funds*, 40 GEORGETOWN JOURNAL OF INTERNATIONAL LAW 1103–1149 (2009).

5. Lindberg, Seth Robert, Note, *Sovereign Wealth Fund Regulation in the E.U. and U.S.: A Call for Workable and Uniform Sovereign Wealth Fund Review within the E.U.*, 37 SYRACUSE JOURNAL OF INTERNATIONAL LAW & COMMERCE 95–126 (2009).

6. Keller, Amy, Note, *Sovereign Wealth Funds: Trustworthy Investors or Vehicles of Strategic Ambition? An Assessment of the Benefits, Risks, and Possible Regulation of Sovereign Wealth Funds*, 7 GEORGETOWN JOURNAL OF LAW & PUBLIC POLICY 333–372 (2009).

7. Norton, Joseph J., *The "Santiago Principles" for Sovereign Wealth Funds: A Case Study on the International Financial Standard-Setting Process*, 13 JOURNAL OF INTERNATIONAL ECONOMIC LAW 645–662 (2010).

8. O'Brien, Justin, *Barriers to Entry: Foreign Direct Investment and the Regulation of Sovereign Wealth Funds*, 42 THE INTERNATIONAL LAWYER 1231–1257 (2008).

9. Piro, John (Student Article), *Welcome to Fabulous Las Vegas: The Nevada Gaming Regulatory Response to Sovereign Wealth Fund Investment*, 2 UNLV GAMING LAW JOURNAL 167–194 (2011).

10. Reed, Brendan J., Note, *Sovereign Wealth Funds: The New Barbarians at the Gate? An Analysis of the Legal and Business Implications of Their Ascendancy*, 4 VIRGINIA LAW & BUSINESS REVIEW 97–138 (2009).

11. Slawotsky, Joel, *Sovereign Wealth Funds and Jurisdiction under the FISA*, 11 UNIVERSITY OF PENNSYLVANIA JOURNAL OF BUSINESS LAW 967–1005 (2009).

12. Wong, Anthony, Note, *Sovereign Wealth Funds and the Problem of Asymmetric Information: The Santiago Principles and International Regulations*, 34 BROOKLYN JOURNAL OF INTERNATIONAL LAW 1081–1109 (2009).

## SWING

A situation where an exporting country transfers part of the quota from one product subject to a quota regime to another product also constrained by the regime.

This phenomenon is most common in the textiles and clothing sector.

## SWISS FORMULA

A formula for reducing tariffs in a non-linear manner so that larger cuts are made to higher tariffs and smaller cuts are made to lower tariffs.

The Swiss formula combats the problem of tariff disparities both among and within countries. Countries with high overall average tariffs must impose steeper cuts, while countries with low overall average tariffs impose lesser cuts. The end goal is to bring the overall average tariffs across countries more in line with one another. Likewise, within the tariff schedule of a particular country, application of the Swiss formula should reduce tariff disparity. In brief, precisely because of its non-linearity, the Swiss formula results in harmonizing reductions.

The Swiss formula is:

$$Z = \frac{(\text{coefficient})(X)}{(\text{coefficient})+(X)}$$

That is,

$$Z = \frac{(A)(X)}{(A)+(X)}$$

where

X = initial rate of duty

Z = final rate of duty

A = coefficient

The name of the formula originates from the 1973–79 Tokyo Round, during which Switzerland proposed it. The formula was used to some degree in that Round, but not in the Uruguay Round. In the Doha Round, ironically, Switzerland opposed its use, while Uruguay — and most other WTO Members — advocated its application.

*Suggestions for Further Research:*

Book:

1. HODA, ANWARUL, TARIFF NEGOTIATIONS AND RENEGOTIATIONS UNDER THE GATT AND THE WTO (2001).

Articles:

1. Johnson, Clete D., *A Barren Harvest for the Developing World? Presidential "Trade Promotion Authority" and the Unfulfilled Promise of Agriculture Negotiations in the Doha Round*, 32 GEORGIA JOURNAL OF INTERNATIONAL & COMPARATIVE LAW 437 (2004).

2. Thacker, Cody A., *Agricultural Trade Liberalization in the Doha Round: The Search for a Modalities Draft*, 33 GEORGIA JOURNAL OF INTERNATIONAL & COMPARATIVE LAW 721 (2005).

## SWISS FORMULA COEFFICIENT

The critical arithmetic variable in the Swiss formula is known as the coefficient.

The larger the coefficient, the lower the reductions in tariffs demanded by the formula. A smaller coefficient imposes the obligation to make larger cuts. In brief, there is an inverse relationship between the value of the coefficient and the significance of the tariff reduction.

Not surprisingly, in non-agricultural market access (NAMA) negotiations in the Doha Round, industrialized countries with low bound tariff rates, such as the United States and European Union (EU) states, called for a low Swiss formula coefficient, so that developing countries with high tariffs, such as Brazil and India, would be compelled to reduce their tariffs on industrial products. That is, developed countries sought market access for their industrial exports in developing countries via a low Swiss formula coefficient. Developing countries opposed this demand, and some — such as China and India — urged a coefficient as high as 35.

The coefficient also plays an important second role. Its value determines the maximum allowable *ad valorem* tariff rate permitted for a country. For example, a coefficient of 35 means no country can have a duty rate above 35 percent. (To be sure, there may be exceptions for sensitive products.)

To illustrate the centrality of the Swiss Formula coefficient, consider the following hypothetical scenario, which the Table below summarizes. Assume developed countries start with a tariff rate of 10 percent, and developing countries with a rate of 50 percent. That is, X is 10 percent for rich countries, and 50 percent for poor countries. Consider the different final tariff rates, Z, the magnitude of tariff cuts, and the maximum bound tariff levels, under two different values for the coefficient, A. Under the first scenario, advocated by developed countries, A is 5. Under the second scenario, preferred by developing countries, A is 35.

When A = 5, developed countries are obligated to cut their tariffs from 10 percent (X) to 3.3 percent (Z), which is a 66.7 percent reduction. Developing countries must cut their tariffs from 50 percent (X) to 4.6 percent (Z), which is a 90.9 percent cut. What happens if A = 35? In that scenario, developed countries cut their tariffs from 10 percent (X) to 7.8 percent (Z), which is a 22.2 percent drop. Developing countries reduce their tariffs from 50 percent (X) down to 20.6 percent (Z), which is a 58.8 percent cut.

There are four obvious repercussions, for developed and developing countries alike, which follow from the value of A:

- With the higher Swiss formula coefficient (A = 35), the final tariff (Z) remains higher than with a lower coefficient (A = 5). For developed countries, Z is 7.8 percent at A = 35, but is 3.3 percent at A = 5. For developing countries, Z is 20.6 percent at A = 35, but 4.6 percent at A = 5. Simply put, the higher the coefficient, the higher the final tariff level.

- The higher Swiss formula coefficient (A = 35) results in a lower percentage reduction in tariffs from their initial levels (X). For developed countries, the tariff cut is 22.2 percent at A = 35, but 66.7 percent at A = 5. For developing countries, the tariff cut is 58.8 percent at A = 5, but 90.9 percent at A = 5. Simply put, the higher the Swiss formula coefficient, the smaller the percentage cut made to initial tariff levels.

TABLE:

HYPOTHETICAL EXAMPLE OF EFFECTS OF DIFFERENT SWISS FORMULA COEFFICIENTS

| Country ⟶ ⟍ Variable ↓ | Developed Countries | Developing Countries |
|---|---|---|
| Initial Tariff Level (X) | 10 percent | 50 percent |
| Coefficient (A) = 5 in Swiss Formula, $Z = \dfrac{(A)(X)}{(A)+(X)}$ | | |
| Final Tariff Level (Z) | 3.3 percent | 4.6 percent |
| Percentage Reduction from Initial Tariff Level (X) to Final Tariff Level (Z) | Drop from 10 to 3.3 percent tariff, *i.e.*, a 66.7 percent reduction. | Drop from 50 to 4.6 percent, *i.e.*, a 90.9 percent reduction. |
| Coefficient (A) = 35 in Swiss Formula, $Z = \dfrac{(A)(X)}{(A)+(X)}$ | | |
| Final Tariff Level (Z) | 7.8 percent | 20.6 percent |
| Percentage Reduction from Initial Tariff Level (X) to Final Tariff Level (Z) | Drop from 10 to 7.8 percent tariff, *i.e.*, a 22.2 percent reduction. | Drop from 50 to 20.6 percent tariff, *i.e.*, a 58.8 percent reduction. |

- The higher Swiss formula coefficient (A = 35) leaves in place greater disharmony among tariffs across countries than the lower coefficient (A = 5). Before any tariff cuts, the gap between tariffs in rich and poor countries is 40 percentage points (because X is 10 and 50 percent, in developed and developing countries, respectively). With A = 35, developed country tariffs drop to 7.8 percent, and developing country tariffs fall to 20.6 percent. The gap between tariffs in rich and poor countries is 12.8 percent. But, with A = 5, developed country tariffs are cut to 3.3 percent, and developing country tariffs slashed to 4.6 percent. The gap is down to just 1.3 percent. Simply put, the higher the Swiss formula coefficient, the greater the tariff dispersion across countries that remains in place. The cuts still are non-linear, but the extent to which harmonizing reductions occur is less than with a low coefficient value.

- The Swiss formula coefficient establishes the maximum bound rate a country can impose — meaning 5 or 35 percent, depending on which value for A is used. Thus, the higher the coefficient, the higher the ceiling rate, and concomitantly, the greater the possibility of a tariff peak to protect an industry making the merchandise in question.

In sum, the higher the coefficient, the less ambitious the tariff reduction.

Note, however, the political economy — which resonated in the Doha Round — of negotiating over the value of A. Developed countries have cut their industrial tariff levels through successive rounds of GATT negotiations since 1947. Many developing countries, which for much of the post-Second World War era either were not GATT contracting parties, or which pursued socialist policies, including import substitution, did not make significant industrial tariff concessions. Consequently, initial tariff rates — X — are asymmetric. There is little room left for rich countries to cut their tariffs on most manufactured items, whereas poor countries have considerable room to do so. Yet, many of those poor countries look askance at demands on them to agree to a low value for A, and thereby make deep cuts. First, such demands are inconsistent with the GATT Article XXXVI:8 non-reciprocity expectation. Second, those countries have infant industries they seek to protect, at least until maturity — as did many now-developed countries during similar stages of their development. Third, poor countries link any agreement on the value of the coefficient to enhanced market access, and reduced subsidies, for farm products, in which they have a keen export interest. In brief, agreeing on a value for "A" is a marvelous illustration of how the "devil" truly is "in the details," and of how complex those details are.

Note, too, the above example does not differentiate between bound and actual (*i.e.*, applied) tariff rates. If an initial tariff rate, X, is both a bound and applied rate, then a cut to X, as per the Swiss Formula, is not controversial. That is, the applied rate falls as does the bound rate. The problem arises when a bound rate exceeds the applied rate, and a Swiss Formula cuts is made to the bound rate. If that cut is small or modest, the applied rate may not fall much, or at all. That is, the cut in the initial bound rate, X, to the final bound rate, Z, is such that the applied rate still is below Z. From the perspective of exporting countries, there is no substantive improvement in market access. (There are two additional possible scenarios. First, the initial rate, X, is a bound rate, which cut as per the Swiss Formula, but which is less than the applied rate. Second, X is an applied rate, which is reduced, but which exceeds the bound rate. In either scenario, the key fact is the applied rate exceeds the bound rate, hence there is a violation of GATT Article II:1(b).)

In sum, the commercial significance of Swiss Formula reductions depends critically not only on the coefficient, A, but also on whether initial bound tariffs exceed applied rates, (and if so, then by how much), and on whether cuts are made to bound or applied rates. These issues were very much a source of controversy during Doha Round negotiations on non-agricultural market access (NAMA). The United States and other developed countries argued for a low coefficient, partly because of the considerable gap between bound and applied rates in major developing country markets like Brazil and India.

*Suggestions for Further Research:*

Book:

1.   HODA, ANWARUL, TARIFF NEGOTIATIONS AND RENEGOTIATIONS UNDER THE GATT AND THE WTO (2001).

Articles:

1.   Johnson, Clete D., *A Barren Harvest for the Developing World? Presidential "Trade Promotion Authority" and the Unfulfilled Promise of Agriculture Negotiations in the Doha Round*, 32 GEORGIA JOURNAL OF INTERNATIONAL & COMPARATIVE LAW 437 (2004).

2.   Thacker, Cody A., *Agricultural Trade Liberalization in the Doha Round: The Search for a Modalities Draft*, 33 GEORGIA JOURNAL OF INTERNATIONAL & COMPARATIVE LAW 721 (2005).

# T

## T&A

*See* Textiles and Apparel.

## TAA

Trade Adjustment Assistance.

Commencing under the *Trade Expansion Act of 1962*, TAA is a program designed to provide benefits to workers dislocated by trade liberalization.[611] The program has been renewed from time to time, including under the *Trade Act of 2002*, when it was combined with the TAA program provided under the *North American Free Trade Agreement (NAFTA)*. Under the program, eligible workers may obtain funds for re-training, re-tooling, relocation, and job search, as well as tax credits for health-care.

A number of criticisms have been made of TAA. One of them is TAA is episodically, if not chronically, under-funded. A second is that the requirements for proving entitlement to benefits are procedurally too complex and substantively too difficult. Only a modest percentage of workers dislocated by trade liberalization are able to obtain certification and become eligible. A third concern is that TAA does not apply to the roughly four of five American workers employed in service sector jobs. Only workers who manufacture products ("articles" in the statutory language) are covered, and then only those associated with a primary firm that faces difficulty or shuts down. Upstream, concomitant, or downstream service workers, *i.e.*, workers who supply services to the primary firm, are ineligible.

Senators Max Baucus (Democrat-Montana) and Norm Coleman (Republican-Minnesota) introduced bipartisan legislation in January 2007 (Senate Bill 122) to renew TAA through 2012. In response to the third point, this bipartisan bill proposed to give TAA benefits to three categories of service sector workers:

- those who lose their jobs as a result of competition from imported services, such as a lab technician who might lose an X-ray reading job to a technician at a company in India;
- those who lose their jobs when a service facility relocates overseas; for example, a call center or software designer, and — unlike the current program — even in cases where the overseas operation is not located in a country with a free trade agreement with the United States;

---

[611] *See* 19 U.S.C. §§ 2271–2321 (TAA for workers). *See also* 19 U.S.C. § 2341–52, § 2354–55 (TAA for firms).

- secondary service workers who provide input to a primary firm where workers are eligible for TAA.[612]

The proposal also would allow an entire industry to be certified as eligible, if the Secretary of Labor receives three or more petitions from the industry, or Congress passes a resolution calling for such certification. Senator Baucus believes that other agencies, such as the International Trade Commission, should play a role in the eligibility determination. The proposal also calls upon employers to assure the accuracy of information in TAA petitions, and upon the Department of Labor (DOL) to upgrade data collection and public information. Lastly, the proposal aims to send TAA to employees before they lose their jobs.

Senate Bill 122 was read to the Senate on 4 January 2007. Thereafter, it was referred to the Senate Committee on Finance. Later, in July 2007, Senator Baucus co-sponsored TAA reform with Senator Olympia Snowe (Republican-Maine). The Baucus-Snowe bill, titled the *Trade and Globalization Adjustment Assistance Act* (Senate Bill 1848), called for the following changes to TAA:[613]

- Benefits would be expanded to service workers, not restricted to workers engaged in the production of an "article."

- Benefits would cover workers who lose their jobs to countries that have not signed a free trade agreement (FTA) with the United States (*e.g.*, China or India), not just workers who lose their jobs to FTA partner countries (*e.g.*, Canada and Mexico under the *North American Free Trade Agreement* (*NAFTA*)).

- The health care tax credit under TAA would rise from paying 65 percent of a health care insurance premium to 85 percent, because at the 65 percent level, dislocated workers had to pay a larger share of their health insurance premium than when they were employed, and thus were not using the tax credit.

- Double the cap on funding for training, raising it to $440 million.

Notably, the Administration of President George W. Bush opposed the extension of TAA to service workers, when that extension was set out in a House proposal (House of Representatives Bill 3920, which the House of Representatives passed in October 2007).

---

[612] *Bipartisan Bill Would Extend TAA to 2012, Add Coverage for Displaced Service Workers*, 24 International Trade Reporter (BNA) 38 (11 January 2007); See also Michael R. Triplett, *DOL's TAA Program Faces Intense Criticism As House Panel Suggests Oversight Ahead*, 24 INTERNATIONAL TRADE REPORTER (BNA) 442–44 (29 March 2007); Rossella Brevetti, *Finance Chairman Baucus Says TPA Renewal Can Wait for New Pacts, Gives Priority to TAA*, 24 INTERNATIONAL TRADE REPORTER (BNA) 538–39 (19 April 2007); Michael R. Triplett, *Trade Court Issues Two Rulings Criticizing DOL's Handling of TAA Certification Cases*, 24 INTERNATIONAL TRADE REPORTER (BNA) 534–26 (12 April 2007).

[613] *See* Michael R. Triplett, *Baucus Says TAA Proposal Must be Approved Before Senate Will Consider Free Trade Deals*, 25 International Trade Reporter (BNA) 186–87 (7 February 2008).

In 2009, the most significant amendments to the TAA program since its inception with the *Trade Act of 1974*, as amended (*1974 Act*), were made. They were part of the *American Recovery and Reinvestment Act of 2009* (*2009 Act*), the stimulus bill sought by the Administration of President Barack H. Obama to help combat the global economic recession. The *2009 Act* extends and expands the TAA program of the *1974 Act*. The *2009 Act* was the controversial stimulus package of the Administration of President Barack H. Obama designed to boost the American economy out of the Great Recession that commenced in 2008. The relevant portion of this *Act* is known as the *Trade and Globalization Adjustment Assistance Act*. That is, the specific legislation amending Chapters 3 and 4 of the *1974 Act* was entitled the *Trade and Globalization Adjustment Assistance Act of 2009*, or "*TGAAA*."

The essence of the *TGAAA* is to reauthorize and alter significantly the TAA program. This program is supposed to deal with the adverse effects of globalization, specifically, dislocations caused by international trade competition, by offering income support, re-training, and re-allocation expenses to adversely affected parties. The *2009 Act*, including the *TGAAA*, entered into force on 17 February 2009. However, most of these statutory amendments expired on 31 December 2010, and applied only to workers covered by petitions filed between 18 May 2009 and 1 January 2011.

Accordingly, a threshold grand-level policy question is to consider how generous the *TGAAA* really was. Generosity is evident — or not — in the technicalities of the statute. Thus, to consider a response, there is no getting around the detailed rules. These rules also evince a practical point: TAA is good work for private and government international trade lawyers, not only because they can do good by helping people in need, but also because they are needed to understand and follow the rules to get that help for people.

Under the *TGAAA*, the existing coverage of the TAA program was expanded for workers, firms, communities, and farmers, where coverage was once either offered to a lesser extent, or not at all. In addition, the *TGAAA* improved healthcare coverage to TAA beneficiaries. The portion of the stimulus package that contains the amendments to the TAA program begins with Subtitle I at Section 1800 of the *2009 Act* and continues through Section 1899K. It is broken down logically into six Parts:

Part I:    Trade Adjustment Assistance for Workers.

Part II:   Trade Adjustment Assistance for Firms.

Part III:  Trade Adjustment Assistance for Communities.

Part IV:   Trade Adjustment Assistance for Farmers.

Part V:    General Provisions.

Part VI:   Health Coverage Improvement.

The Department of Labor began administering the TAA program in 1975, and its role as the lead governmental agency continues under the *2009 Act*. As is clear from the discussion below about disbursing funds, the DOL works with state governments.[614] The DOL set out the details of the administration of the entire TAA program through promulgating new regulations in the Code of Federal Regulations (C.F.R.) at 20 C.F.R. Part 618.

Among a few of the highlights of the *TGAAA* were the following:[615]

- Enhancement of the "Trade Adjustment Assistance for Firms (TAAF) Program."

  Under this Program, a national network of 11 TAA centers were established to give technical assistance to any firm that has lost domestic sales, and cut employment, because of an increase in imports. This Program is administered by the Economic Development Administration (EDA) of the Department of Commerce (DOC). Significantly, under the TAAF, service sector firms are authorized to seek technical assistance. In addition, any firm — industrial or service — may show harm (that is, damage to its business caused by an increase in imports) using the average of one, two, or three years worth of data. This change, known as a "look back" period, may help firms in proving dislocation from imports. Before the change, the period was restricted to the 12 months immediately preceding the most recent 12 month period for which data are available.

- Establishment of a "Community Trade Adjustment Assistance Program."

  The goal of this Program is to help local economies deal with the adjustment costs imposed by changes in trade patterns. This Program also is administered by the EDA. Essentially, a community must petition for assistance as a "trade-impacted community." The petition must give data about the impact on the community of actual or threatened job losses caused by import competition. The EDA determines whether the community is, in fact, a trade-impacted one. If so, then the EDA helps the community set a strategic plan to improve its economy. That plan may

---

[614] An interesting feature of the *TGAAA* regulations implemented by the DOL is that a state must employ only state government merit system personnel to perform functions funded by the TAA and implement TAA programs. A state can out-source training programs to private sector or non-governmental organization (NGO) providers, and also out-source non-inherently governmental functions, like information technology and janitorial services. But, it cannot out-source core tasks like the approval of training. Three states — Colorado, Massachusetts, and Michigan — are exempt from this limitation on the use of non-state, non-merit personnel (though they must use state merit personnel to administer trade re-adjustment allowances).

[615] *See Commerce Department Proposes Rules for TAA Programs for Firms, Communities*, 26 International Trade Reporter (BNA) 606 (7 May 2009).

include infrastructure projects, market research, public services, and training. The amount of assistance is capped at $5 million per community, with priority for granting funds to small- and medium-sized communities.

Because of the *TGAAA*, the time-frame for administrative decision-making is reduced, so as to afford as rapid a response as possible to potentially dislocated firms or communities. For example, the EDA has a maximum of 40 days to make decisions such as whether a community is "trade-impacted." Under the previous scheme, the typical period the EDA had to take decisions was 60 days.

Pursuant to the *Omnibus Trade Act of 2010*, H.R. 6517, Pub. L. No. 111-344, 124 Stat. 3611 (29 December 2010), Congress extended the entire TAA program, as amended, for just six weeks. This extension was essential to continue not only the conventional TAA benefits of compensation and training, but also and health care benefits, for workers adversely impacted because of trade. Roughly 50,000 Americans would have lost health care benefits had TAA not been renewed.

*Suggestions for Further Research:*

Book:

1.   BACCHETTA, MARC, ADJUSTING TO TRADE LIBERALIZATION: THE ROLE OF POLICY, INSTITUTIONS AND WTO DISCIPLINES (2003).

Articles:

1.   Mateikis, William J., *The Fair Track to Expanded Fair Trade: Making TAA Benefits More Accessible to American Workers*, 30 HOUSTON JOURNAL OF INTERNATIONAL LAW 1–87 (2007).

2.   McCarthy, Patricia M. & Emily S. Ullman, *Trade Adjustment Assistance Cases: 28 U.S.C. § 1581(d) — Department of Labor and Department of Agriculture Decisions Under the Trade Adjustment Assistance Statutes*, 39 GEORGETOWN JOURNAL OF INTERNATIONAL LAW 105–126 (2007).

3.   Morgan, Frank H. & Helen Wong, *Trade Adjustment Assistance Cases: 2007 Developments*, 40 GEORGETOWN JOURNAL OF INTERNATIONAL LAW 99–121 (2008).

4.   Rangel, Rep. Charles B., *Moving Forward: A New, Bipartisan Trade Policy that Reflects American Values*, 45 HARVARD JOURNAL ON LEGISLATION 377–419 (2008).

5.   Rosenblatt, Samuel M., *Trade Adjustment Assistance Programs: Crossroads or Dead End?*, 9 LAW & POLICY IN INTERNATIONAL BUSINESS 1065, 1092 (1977).

6.   Schwinn, Steven D., *Trade Adjustment Assistance at the U.S. Court of International Trade: The Year in Review*, 41 GEORGETOWN JOURNAL OF INTERNATIONAL LAW 137–160 (2009).

## TABD

The Trans-Atlantic Business Dialogue.

Formed in 1995, the TABD is a private-sector organization comprised of roughly 100–150 chief executive officers (CEOs) of major American and European corporations. TABD members are companies with strong trans-Atlantic ties, including Coca-Cola, Ernst & Young, Microsoft, PricewaterhouseCoopers, Pfizer, Unilever, Seimens, and BASF. The TABD is co-chaired by a Chief Executive Officer (CEO) from the United States and Europe for a period of two years. Thirty CEOs from a group of companies, including small and medium sized enterprises (SMEs), are selected to maintain a balance of sectoral and regional representation to serve on the TABD Executive Board (Board). The Board helps determine the direction and focus of the group. The TABD is funded exclusively by its members.

Historically, the TABD advocated not only for increased trade liberalization, but also for quick resolution of trade disputes between the United States and the European Union (EU). TABD greatly favors frequent communication between the two governments to ensure small disputes are resolved quickly and do not become barriers to trans-Atlantic commercial activity. According to the TABD, the United States and the EU should view the WTO dispute settlement system as a mechanism of last resort. Instead of running straight to the WTO when a disagreement emerges, TABD advocates trade disputes be resolved bilaterally, promptly and in good faith.

Despite a preference for holding bilateral talks, TABD still fully supports the WTO dispute system.[616] TABD urges both governments to comply quickly with all recommendations of the Dispute Settlement Body (DSB). To help stem future disputes, TABD calls upon the United States and Europe to comply fully with current WTO rules and regulations.[617]

TABD helped create an "early warning" system aimed to detect and prevent future trade disagreements.[618] Central to this idea is an early onset dialogue between the two governments as soon as a trade disagreement emerges. TABD often argues trade disputes increase protectionism on both sides of the Atlantic. These disputes, as TABD points out, affect not only economic and business relationships between the United States and EU, but also social and political interactions.[619]

---

[616] *See* Reinhard Quick, *TABD Still Supports Trade Dispute Settlement System*, FINANCIAL TIMES, 11 December 2000, at 14.

[617] *See* Gary G. Yerkey, *Business Leaders Voice Concern Over Energy, Resources Expended on EU- US Trade Spats*, 19 International Trade Reporter (BNA) 1947 (14 November 2002).

[618] *See* Gary G. Yerkey, *Business Execs From U.S., EU Will Urge Further Trade Liberalization, Other Steps*, 16 International Trade Reporter (BNA) 850 (19 May 1999).

[619] *See* Gary G. Yerkey, *Corporate Leaders Say U.S. — EU Disputes Harming Business, Urge Quick Resolution*, 17 International Trade Reporter (BNA) 1774 (23 November 2000).

In addition to the early warning system, TABD successfully directed attention to issues regarding e-commerce and helped facilitate the *U.S.-EU Mutual Recognition Agreement (MRA)*.[620] TABD also is credited with helping to reinvigorate stymied talks over the 2002 U.S.-EU *Guidelines on Regulatory Cooperation and Transparency*.[621] The *Guidelines* aim to boost trans-Atlantic trade and facilitate commercial transactions. The *Guidelines* are seen as particularly important to the Euro-American relationship, in the wake of major trade disputes such as over steel safeguards and aircraft subsidies.[622]

Although TABD saw several early successes, including those mentioned above, the organization was increasingly perceived as too "unwieldy" and began suffering from internal "fatigue."[623] In 2003, the TABD shifted its focus to the overall goal of the establishment of a trans-Atlantic free exchange of goods, services and capital.[624] That is, the TABD operates as a forum for discussions on ways for the United States and EU to reduce trade barriers and trade friction, develop a common negotiating agenda, and possibly work towards a free trade agreement (FTA).[625] It includes separate dialogues for consumers, labor, environment and business. Through increased trade liberalization, the TABD believes unified markets will create a business environment, which will stimulate innovation, investment and new jobs. Other goals of the TABD include:

- Improving regulatory cooperation to promote growth.
- Strengthening security to enhance business.
- Protecting intellectual property rights.
- Commitment to the completion of the Doha Round.

TABD also encourages the United States and Europe to adopt similar financial and economic policies that facilitate, rather than create barriers to, trans-Atlantic business.[626]

---

[620] *See* Yerkey, Gary G. Yerkey, *Trans-Atlantic Business Group Names Co-Chairs 'Relaunched' Forum Thru 2005*, 20 INTERNATIONAL TRADE REPORTER (BNA) 2028 (11 December 2003).

[621] *See* Gary G. Yerkey, *U.S., EU Agree on New Guidelines to Improve Cooperation on Regulatory Policy*, 19 International Trade Reporter (BNA) 696 (18 April 2002).

[622] *See* Michael Mann, *Move to Avert Transatlantic Trade Barriers*, FINANCIAL TIMES, 14 April 2002, at 4.

[623] *See* Gary G. Yerkey, *U.S. and EU Agree to Revamp TABD, citing "Fatigue Problem," Fading Interest*, 20 International Trade Reporter (BNA) 464 (13 March 2003); Gary G. Yerkey, *U.S., EU Agree to Re-Energize TABD by Focusing Work on Cost-Cutting Initiatives*, 20, International Trade Reporter (BNA) 753 (1 May 2003).

[624] *See* Gary G. Yerkey, *U.S., European Business Leaders to Call for Barrier-Free Trans-Atlantic Trade in 10 Years*, 21 International Trade Reporter (BNA) 643 (15 April 2004).

[625] *See* Gary G. Yerkey, *U.S., EU Business Leaders Warn of Growing Protectionist Sentiment*, 23 International Trade Reporter (BNA) 720 (11 May 2006); Arthur Rogers, *EU Trade Commissioner Dampens Hopes for "Bigger Bang" Trans-Atlantic Trade Pact*, 23 International Trade Rep. (BNA) 864–65 (8 June 2006).

[626] *See* Gary G. Yerkey, *Trans-Atlantic Business Group Names Co-Chairs for 'Relaunched' Forum Thru 2005*, 20 International Trade Reporter (BNA) 2028 (11 December 2003).

The TABD operates without government involvement, but does provide advice to governments. In this relationship, it works closely with government agencies on both sides of the Atlantic. For example, TABD participates in Transatlantic Economic Council (TEC) advisory group meetings, where it offers a business perspective to government officials from the United States and the EU.[627] For the United States, the Department of Commerce (DOC) is the TABD's liaison to other government agencies, namely, the United States Trade Representative (USTR) and Departments of Homeland Security, State, and Treasury. For the EU, the TABD partners with the European Commissions for Enterprise and Trade, and the Presidency of the European Council.

The relationship between TABD and government officials occasionally comes under fire. In 2001, a European NGO requested documents from two meetings that occurred in 1999 between EU Commission officials and the TABD in an effort to shed light on their relationship.[628] The Commission refused to release some of the documents, citing concerns about how their release may affect its relationship with the United States. The Commission emphasized that Commissioners had spoken in their personal capacities at several points during the meetings, and not as members of the Commission. It was concerned the United States would misinterpret what was said in a personal versus official capacity, leading to unnecessary disagreements. At a Euro-American summit in June 2004, the consumer group Trans-Atlantic Consumer Dialogue (TACD) criticized leaders from the United States and EU for allowing TABD "direct access to the summit leaders" while prohibiting TACD and other consumer groups from offering their own proposals.[629] However, in 2009, the TEC listened to ideas not only from TABD, but also opinions from TACD and labor union representatives.[630]

*Suggestions for Further Research:*

Articles:

1. Schammo, Pierre, *Regulating Transatlantic Stock Exchanges*, 57 INTERNATIONAL & COMPARATIVE LAW QUARTERLY 827–868 (2008).

2. Blinken, Tony, *The False Crisis Over the Atlantic*, 80 FOREIGN AFFAIRS 35 (2001).

3. Zoellick, Robert B., *Do Europeans and Americans Share an Enlightened Self-Interest?*, 6 AMERICAN COUNCIL ON GERMANY (6 June 2002).

---

[627] *See* Gary G. Yerkey, *U.S., EU to Hold High-Level Talks May 13 to Promote Greater Economic Integration*, 24 International Trade Reporter (BNA) 420 (20 March 2008).

[628] *See* Gary G. Yerkey, *EU Watchdog Rejects Argument Release of Documents would Harm U.S.-EU Relations*, 19 International Trade Reporter (BNA) 1306 (25 July 2002).

[629] *See* Gary G. Yerkey, *U.S., European Consumer Groups Skip Meeting with U.S. and EU Officials at Summit*, 21 International Trade Reporter (BNA) 1100 (1 July 2004).

[630] *See* Gary G. Yerkey, *Labor Unions Being Invited to Offer Input to Revamped U.S.-EU Economic Forum*, 26 International Trade Reporter (BNA) 643 (14 May 2009)

## *TAFTA* (FIRST MEANING)

*Trans-Atlantic Free Trade Area* or *Trans-Atlantic Free Trade Agreement*.

The idea of a trans-Atlantic free trade agreement (FTA) was raised in September 2006 by German Chancellor Angela Merkel. Her interest in the idea was motivated in part by the relative increase in China's economic prominence, though she insisted a *TAFTA* would be a tool to encourage free trade, and not a fortress against Chinese and other third country goods.

The idea of free trade between the United States and Europe is not a new one. In 1997, Klaus Kinkel — then Germany's then Foreign Minister — considered it, as did the Trade Commissioner of the European Union (EU) Sir Leon Brittan in 1998. Various studies in the United States have discussed the idea.

*Suggestions for Further Research:*

Book:

1.  STEINGART, GABOR, WORLD WAR FOR PROSPERITY (2006).

## *TAFTA* (SECOND MEANING)

*Thailand — Australia Free Trade Agreement*, which entered into force on 1 January 2005.

*Suggestions for Further Research:*

Article:

1.  Rennie, Jane, *The Evolution of Competition Law in Singapore and Thailand and its Implications for Bilateral Competition Policy in SAFTA and TAFTA*, 15 INTERNATIONAL TRADE LAW & REGULATION issue 1, 1–13 (2009).

## TARGETED DUMPING

Selling merchandise in an importing country at less than Normal Value (the price of a foreign like product in the home market of a producer-exporter) to particular customers in the importing country, in certain (but not all) regions of the country, or for a particular period of time. In other words, dumping that is aimed at specific customers or geographic regions, or at specific times.

Under Article 2:4:2 (first sentence) of the WTO *Agreement on Antidumping*, an administering authority normally must calculate a dumping margin by comparing a weighted average of Normal Value to a weighted average of Export Price (or Constructed Export Price), or by comparing individual transaction prices of Normal Value to Export Price (or Constructed Export Price). In other words, the *Agreement* mandates average-to-average or individual-to-individual comparisons of relevant price data.

However, Article 2:4:2 (second sentence) of the *Agreement* authorizes a comparison between a weighted average Normal Value and individual Export Prices (or Constructed Export Prices) if there is "a pattern of export prices that differ significantly among different purchasers, regions or time periods . . ." This exception is for average-to-individual price comparisons in instances of alleged targeted dumping. The average-to-average and individual-to-individual methodologies might not reveal targeted dumping, hence the need for this exception. The *Agreement* does not define the critical term "differ significantly" is not defined, and thus leaves it to agencies in individual WTO Members.

The United States Department of Commerce (DOC) has regulations on targeted dumping investigations. They are published at 19 C.F.R. §§ 351.301(d)(5) and 351.414(f)-(g). Such investigations are rare. Indeed, when the DOC first published these regulations — on 19 May 1997 — it had yet to perform its first targeted dumping analysis.

## TARIFFICATION (OR TARIFFY)

The process of converting quota and other non-tariff barrier (NTB) limitations on imports into tariff equivalent amounts. That is, a tariff rate providing a level of trade restriction equivalent to that provided by a quota or other NTB.

Tariffication is seen as a way to make import barriers more transparent, and comply with the general prohibition against quantitative restrictions (QRs) in GATT Article XI. It also may be a stepping stone toward the gradual reduction or elimination of tariffs. Indeed, it is commonly used as such for trade liberalization in agriculture. Article 4:2 of the WTO *Agreement Agriculture* calls on Members to "tariffy" their duties on imports of primary and processed farm products by converting NTBs to tariffs. Notably, however, tariff rate quotas (TRQs) are deemed tariffs, not QRs, hence tariffication is not required for TRQs.

*Suggestions for Further Research:*

Book Chapters:

1.   de Gorter, H. & T.G. Schmitz, *Consequences of Tariffication, in* REGULATION AND PROTECTIONISM UNDER GATT: CASE STUDIES IN NORTH AMERICAN AGRICULTURE (Andrew Schmitz *et al.*, eds., 1996).

2.   Hathaway, Dale E. & Melinda D. Ingco, *Agricultural Liberalization and the Uruguay Round, in* THE URUGUAY ROUND AND THE DEVELOPING ECONOMIES, 1, 158 (Will Martin & L. Alan Winters eds. 1995).

Articles:

1.   Cramer, Gail L., *et al.*, *Impact of Rice Tariffication on Japan and the World Rice Market*, 81 AMERICAN JOURNAL OF AGRICULTURAL ECONOMICS 1149–56 (1999).

2.   Steinle, Jeffrey J., *The Problem Child of World Trade: Reform School for Agriculture*, 4 MINNESOTA JOURNAL OF GLOBAL TRADE 333, 348–49 (1995).

## TARIFF ESCALATION

A situation in the tariff schedule of a country whereby tariff rates increase with the degree of processing, with the effect of taxing each step every other country takes in the value chain.

Tariff escalation is the opposite of an inverted tariff.

In other words, tariff escalation means there are higher duties on semi-processed products than on raw materials, and still higher tariffs on finished goods. For example, if the tariff on shoes is higher than the tariff on shoe components, like leather, then there is tariff escalation. There is tariff escalation, in a general sense, when tariffs on manufactured articles exceed tariffs on agricultural commodities. Tariff escalation protects domestic processing industries, and discourages the development of processing activity in the countries in which raw materials originate. Notably, tariff escalation in developed countries hinders processing for export of raw materials in developing and least developed countries. That hindrance, in turn, retards export diversification in poor countries — the very policy goal they are encouraged to achieve.

Generally speaking, where the tariff on an escalated processed product exceeds the tariff on an unprocessed product by a five percent or more, tariff escalation is said to occur. That also is true in respect of the tariff on a processed versus semi-processed product, or the tariff on a semi-processed versus unfinished item.

According to the United States Department of Agriculture (USDA), tariff escalation is most common in the schedules of Eastern Europe and the Middle East, followed by North America, South Asia and the European Union (EU). North African countries furnish the largest example of escalation, where the mean tariff on sweeteners increases by over 100 percentage points over similar tariffs on sugarcane and sugar beets. The most common processed goods subject to tariff escalation include meats, sweeteners, vegetable oils, vegetable juice and tobacco products.

Tariff escalation in an importing country poses a problem for an exporting country. While domestic producers of semi-processed or processed goods in the importing country receive protection from foreign competition, foreign producers and exporters are hindered. For the exporting country, its upward development on the industrialization path is hindered by tariff escalation.

## TARIFF LINE

A line in tariff schedules reflecting standard product classifications in the Harmonized System (HS).

That is, a tariff line refers to the category to which the legally established tariff applies, and may cover just one product, or it may encompass several products. The number of products a tariff line covers depends on the digit level of the tariff line at issue. A number is identified with each tariff line and generally ranges from four to 10 digits. Tariff lines specified at the four digit level are broad, *i.e.*, many products are covered. Tariff lines at the six digit level would be narrower, and at the eight digit level narrower still.

Identifying digit levels in respect of tariff lines was a source of controversy in agricultural trade talks during the Doha Round. The issue arose in the context of protection of "sensitive" farm products from the full force of any agreed-upon tariff cuts, and in the context of expanding tariff rate quotas (TRQs) as compensation to exporting countries for the designation by importing countries of a product as "sensitive." The most protectionist approach would be to designate "sensitivity" at the six digit level, rather than the eight digit level, thus covering a broader number of products, but expanding TRQs at the eight digit level, rather than the six digit level, thus pinpointing the items subject to higher quota thresholds. The most free trade approach would be the mirror image.

## TARIFF PEAK

A situation in a country's tariff schedule where there are relatively high tariffs on a few so-called "sensitive products," but otherwise generally low tariffs prevail.

In other words, a tariff that is substantially higher than the average tariff. For developed countries, a tariff of 15 percent or above is considered a tariff peak. Common examples include tariff peaks on textiles, clothing, fish, and fish products.

## TARIFF QUOTA

A synonym for tariff rate quota (TRQ).

*See* Tariff Rate Quota.

## TARIFF RATE QUOTA (TARIFF-RATE QUOTA)

A non-tariff barrier to trade (NTB), specifically, a quantitative restriction (QR) on market access.

Tariff rate quotas (TRQs) have features of both tariffs and quotas, but generally are considered tariff barriers. For example, in Article 4:2 of the WTO *Agreement on Agriculture*, TRQs are not subject to tariffication.

The application of one tariff rate for imports of an article up to a specified quota level of that article, followed by the application of a second, higher rate for imports in excess of that quota level. Shipments receiving the lower rate because they are less than the quota threshold are called "in-quota" amounts, and the corresponding rate is called the "in-quota" rate. Shipments in excess of the threshold are "out-of-quota" (or "above-quota," or "over-quota"), and bear the "out-of-quota" rate. The government of the country in which the goods are imported defines the size of the quota, usually on an annual basis. In brief, a good subject to a TRQ may be imported free of duty, or at a low duty-rate, up to the in-quota threshold. Once that threshold is reached, subsequent shipments are considered "over-quota," and face a stiff tariff.

A TRQ need not be limited to two-tiers. Sometimes, TRQs are called simply "tariff-quotas." Conceptually, there can be any number of tiers of quota thresholds and associated rates in a TRQ. Also, where the importing country imposing a TRQ allocates to exporting countries specific shares in the in-quota amount of a TRQ, such shares are referred to as "allocated tariff-rate quota access." The most notorious example of the use of TRQs and allocated access through a complex licensing scheme is found in the *EC — Bananas* case. That case sets forth important jurisprudence under GATT Article XIII, namely, that TRQs be applied in a non-discriminatory fashion.

TRQs and all other QRs are generally prohibited by Article XI of GATT. Article XIII, however, provides an exception to Article XI so long as the WTO Member applies the TRQ in a non-discriminatory manner. In addition, the WTO Member imposing the TRQ must first seek approval from the exporting countries of the goods in question. If no approval can be had, the WTO Member must set its quota regime in accordance with exporting trends, usually under the most recent three-year period where there is reliable data, and its QRs to reflect the market trend. In the *EC — Bananas* Case, the EC failed to complete either of these requirements.

TRQs are common in agricultural trade, particularly for beef, dairy products, and sugar. They are difficult to discipline, because negotiations about their reduction require agreement on a number of key variables:

* The in-quota threshold.
* The amount by which the in-quota threshold should grow.
* The base period for measuring the in-quota threshold and its growth.
* The period for phasing in growth in the in-quota threshold.
* The tariff (if any) on in-quota shipments.
* The tariff on above-quota shipments.
* The amount by which the above-quota tariff should be reduced.
* The base period for measuring the above-quota tariff and its reduction.
* The period for phasing out the above-quota tariff.
* Possible exemptions or exceptions to agreed-upon reductions in TRQs for sensitive products.

In the Doha Round, TRQs were a source of major controversy.

In that Round, TRQs were proposed as a key device for protecting "Sensitive Products." With a TRQ, which in-quota shipments of those products may be imported at low duties, and the duty rates and quota thresholds, may be negotiated. That is, a Sensitive Product can be shielded partially from the full force of any tariff reduction to which Doha Round negotiators ultimately agree, by setting an appropriate volume threshold dividing in-quota from out-of-quota shipments. A low or zero duty rate applies to in-quota shipments, but a high tariff is imposed on imports that are above the quota limit, thus providing some protection. Of course, if no TRQ exists for a particular good that a country seeks to designate as "Sensitive," then it is necessary to establish one. The key bargaining points as between exporting and importing countries of a Sensitive

Product are the threshold and duty rates. Exporting countries prefer a high threshold, zero duty for in-quota shipments, and a low duty for over-quota shipments. Importing countries have the diametrically opposite incentive. Not surprisingly, a zero-sum game approach becomes difficult to avoid, and that mentality was common in the Doha Round.

*Suggestions for Further Research:*

Other Source:

1.  SKULLY, DAVID W., UNITED STATES DEPARTMENT OF AGRICULTURE, ECONOMIC RESEARCH SERVICE, TECHNICAL BULLETIN NUMBER 1893, ECONOMICS OF TARIFF-RATE QUOTA ADMINISTRATION (April 2001), posted at http://www.ers.usda.gov/publications/tb1893/tb1893.pdf.

## *TBT AGREEMENT*

The Uruguay Round *Agreement on Technical Barriers to Trade.*

The *TBT Agreement* is one of the Multilateral Agreements on Trade in Goods contained in Annex 1A to the *WTO Agreement.*

Among the most significant potential cases that the United States or other major developed countries may consider against China are ones that involve TBTs. For example, China sets unique standards for various products, such as 3G wireless technology (used for communication devices such as the iPhone). These *sui generis* standards pose a barrier to American exports to China. Moreover, the standard-setting process may be opaque, and the testing procedures (*i.e.*, conformity assessment) discriminatory against those exports. Such cases are difficult to mount and prove. Another instance of a possible challengeable TBT is China's use of national security to regulate its domestic economy and imports into it. They often involve *de facto*, not *de jure*, TBT barriers, which means different kinds of evidence and argumentation are required from a conventional tariff barrier complaint. Complicating challenges to China's TBTs is the fact the Chinese government sometimes behaves vengefully (as do some other WTO Member governments) against American companies that encourage the United States Trade Representative (USTR) to bring a WTO action against China.

*Suggestions for Further Research:*

Book:

1.  MIDLER, PAUL, POORLY MADE IN CHINA: AN INSIDE ACCOUNT OF THE TACTICS BEHIND CHINA'S PRODUCTION GAME (New York: Wiley, 2009). *See also* the review of this book, *Shoddy Work*, THE ECONOMIST, 16 May 2009, at 89–90.

Articles:

1.  *Achieving Canada — United States Economic Competitiveness through Regulatory Convergence — A Common Cause Agenda*, 36 CANADA — UNITED STATES LAW JOURNAL 77–120 (2011) (presentations by various speakers).

2. Bernstein, Steven & Erin Hannah, *Non-State Global Standard Setting and the WTO: Legitimacy and the Need for Regulatory Space*, 11 JOURNAL OF INTERNATIONAL ECONOMIC LAW 575–608 (2008).

3. Bradley, Caroline, *Consultation and Legitimacy in Transnational Standard-Setting*, 20 MINNESOTA JOURNAL OF INTERNATIONAL LAW 480–512 (2011).

4. Carmody, Meghan Josephine, Comment, *The Price of Cheap Goods: International Trade with China and the Need for Stringent Enforcement of Manufacturing Regulations*, 34 NORTH CAROLINA JOURNAL OF INTERNATIONAL LAW & COMMERCIAL REGULATION 655–697 (2009).

5. Feeney, Adam, Note, *In Search of a Remedy: Do State Laws Exempting Sellers from Strict Product Liability Adequately Protect Consumers Harmed by Defective Chinese-Manufactured Products?*, 34 JOURNAL OF CORPORATION LAW 567–585 (2009).

6. Feld, Danielle Spiegel, *Ensuring that Imported Biofuels Abide by Domestic Environmental Standards: Will the Agreement on Technical Barriers to Trade Tolerate Asymmetrical Compliance Regimes?*, 29 PACE ENVIRONMENTAL LAW REVIEW 79–120 (2011).

7. Fontanelli, Filippo, *ISO and Codex Standards and International Trade Law: What Gets Said is Not What's Heard*, 60 INTERNATIONAL & COMPARATIVE LAW QUARTERLY 895–932 (2011).

8. Irish, Maureen, *Regulatory Convergence, Security, and Global Administrative Law in Canada–United States Trade*, 12 JOURNAL OF INTERNATIONAL ECONOMIC LAW 333–355 (2009).

9. Luan, Xinjie & Julien Chaisse, *Preliminary Comments on the WTO Seals Products Dispute: Traditional Hunting, Public Morals, and Technical Barriers to Trade*, 22 COLORADO JOURNAL OF INTERNATIONAL ENVIRONMENTAL LAW & POLICY 79–121 (2011).

10. *The Canada — United States Regulatory Regime as the Road to Recovery*, 36 CANADA — UNITED STATES LAW JOURNAL 261–284 (2011) (presentations by various speakers).

11. *The Economic Impact of Canada — United States Regulatory Convergence: From the Canada — United States Auto Pact to the North American Free Trade Agreement and Beyond*, 36 CANADA — UNITED STATES LAW JOURNAL 41–75 (2011) (presentations by various speakers).

12. Winn, Jane K., *Globalization and Standards: The Logic of Two-Level Games*, 5 I/S: A JOURNAL OF LAW AND POLICY FOR THE INFORMATION SOCIETY 185–218 (2009).

## *TCP*

*Tratado de Comercio de los Pueblos*, or sometimes called *Tratado Comercial de los Pueblos*, the Spanish acronym for "Trade Treaty of the Peoples." A synonym occasionally used is "Peoples' Trade Agreement," or "PTA."

The *TCP* concept was inspired partly by some socialist-oriented Latin American leaders during the first decade of the new millennium, such as Bolivian President Eva Morales and Venezuelan President Hugo Chávez. The *TCP* is a new kind of trade agreement, being an economic alternative and political challenge to an FTA. On 28 April 2006, Bolivia and Venezuela joined Cuba in signing a 10 point *TCP* under the auspices of the *Acuerdo Para La Aplicación de la Alternativa Bolivariana para los Pueblos de Nuestra América (ALBA) y el Tratrado de Comercio de los Pueblos (TCP)* (*Accord for the Application of the Bolivarian Alternative for the Peoples of our America and the Peoples' Trade Agreements*). In 2007, Nicaragua joined *ALBA*, and in 2008 Dominica also joined.

In other words, *ALBA* is the actual trade agreement, and the *TCP* embodies the principles on which *ALBA* is based. The first point says the trilateral accord:

> is a response to the failed neo-liberal model, based as it is on deregulation, privatization and indiscriminate opening of markets.

Accordingly, the accord aims to promote:

> a model of trade integration between people that limits and regulates the rights of foreign investors and multinationals so that they serve the purpose of national productive development.

Additionally, the agreement acknowledges the cultural similarities of the Member nations and mandates the governments of each nation consider such idiosyncrasies while developing their regional integration platform:

> [The *TCP* should] achieve a true integration among peoples that transcends the commercial and economic arenas, recognizing the differences of each country, and at the same time prioritizing the protection of internal production and national companies. A treaty which holds, above all, the well being of the people and a respect for their history and cultures.

What motivated Bolivia, Venezuela, and Cuba to sign a PTA?

One answer is they resurrected — consciously or not — socialist-style trade policies popular in Latin America in the 1950s and 1960s. These policies were advocated by leading economists like Paul Baran, Raul Prebisch, and Hans Singer.

Another triggering event was the conclusion of a free trade agreement (FTA) between Colombia and the United States on terms that Bolivia's president Morales considered harmful to his country. Bolivia was an observer to the bilateral FTA talks between the United States and Colombia, which began in May 2004. Colombia and the United States penned the FTA in early March 2006. (Panama and Peru followed suit, on 28 June 2007 and in April 2006, respectively.) As part of the FTA, Colombia agreed to buy nearly 900,000 tons of American soy. Until that point, Bolivia had shipped 500,000 tons of soybeans to Colombia, worth $166 million (in 2005). This specific element of the United States–Colombia agreement effectively closed the door on Bolivian soy exports to Colombia, which was then the largest importer of Bolivian soy.

To be sure, there is a genuine sense that a conventional market capitalist FTA will not work for Bolivia. President Morales vowed in March 2006 vowed Bolivia "never" would negotiate an FTA with the United States, and in August 2006 Bolivian Vice President Alvaro Garcia Linera explained:

> Bolivia wants trade relations with the entire world. I traveled to the United States to try to advance a trade pact. But, we can't just have free trade under the old rules, because it is too aggressive for our economy.
>
> For example, how is a small farmer in Bolivia going to compete with farmers from countries that use the latest tractors and other technologies? It's like trying to make the 2nd century compete with the 21st century. The same goes for our urban small businesses. How are we going to compete with giant factories under such conditions?[631]

A third answer is Venezuela's departure from the *Comunidad Andina de Naciones* (CAN) in April 2006. Though Venezuela had been a member since 1973, it left the group after Colombia and Peru signed FTAs with the United States. Venezuela's President Chávez stated that the FTAs caused irreparable damage to CAN and that Colombia and Peru would be swamped by super-subsidized American goods, which would ultimately hurt Venezuelan exports. Indeed, President Chávez called the Peruvian President, Alejandro Toledo, a traitor to South America for signing an FTA with the United States. Consequently, because of Venezuela's exit from CAN Colombia lost an estimated $2.1 billion in exports to Venezuela. However, few of Venezuela's non-oil export products were affected by Colombia's and Peru's FTAs with the US.

Finally, President Chávez's desire to make *MERCOSUR* an anti-American bloc similar to TCP Member countries may also have been significant. On 21 July 2006, Venezuela was inaugurated as the fifth member of *MERCOSUR* at a summit in Córdoba, Argentina. President Chávez stressed that the summit marked a new dawn for Latin American integration and development. Chávez argued that Venezuela, the world's fifth largest oil exporter, would help cover Latin America's energy needs for 100 to 200 years. Chavez cited the European Coal and Steel Community (ECSC), which paved the way for the creation of the European Union (EU), as an example of how regional integration can build around agreements on key commodities.

---

[631] *Quoted in* James Langman, *Bolivia Looks for New Kind of Trade Pace With U.S., While Seeking ATPDEA Extension*, 23 International Trade Reporter (BNA) 1198–2000 (10 August 2006).

*Suggestions for Further Research:*

Articles:

1. Backer, Larry Catá & Augusto Molina, *Cuba and the Construction of Alternative Global Trade Systems: ALBA and Free Trade in the Americas*, 31 University of Pennsylvania Journal of International Economic Law 679–752 (2010).

2. Siptroth, Stephen M., *Welcoming All to a Table of Plenty: The Free Trade Area and the Bolivarian Alternative as Competing Means of Economic Integration in the Americas*, 12 UCLA Journal of International Law & Foreign Affairs 359–391 (2007).

Other Source:

1. Sikes, Devin S., *Diverging Trade Policies and Integration Theories in Latin America* (13 February 2007) (unpublished article, University of Kansas School of Law) (manuscript on file with author).

# TDI

Trade defense instruments, a synonym for trade remedies, specifically, anti-dumping (AD), anti-subsidy (*i.e.*, countervailing duty (CVD)), and safeguard measures. The term is used commonly in the European Union (EU). Synonymous terms are "trade defense measures" and "contingency measures."

There is a vigorous debate about the efficacy of TDIs, in terms of the extent to which they reduce import competition.[632] Specifically, at issue is whether TDIs help an afflicted domestic industry (which produces a produce like the foreign merchandise targeted by at TDI) restructure and (if applicable) modernize technologically. Predictably, the WTO takes the position that there is no conclusive empirical evidence to support the proposition that TDIs help domestic industries. Yet, there is plenty of evidence to show that TDIs have a net negative welfare effect on importing countries that impose them, primarily by raising prices to consumers of the targeted foreign merchandise.

*Suggestions for Further Research:*

Book:

1. Gehring, Markus W., Jarrod Hepburn & Marie-Claire Cordonier Segger, World Trade Law in Practice (2006).

Articles:

1. Bjorklund, Andrea K., *Causation, Morality, and Quantum*, 32 Suffolk Transnational Law Review 435–450 (2009).

2. Voon, Tania, *Eliminating Trade Remedies from the WTO: Lessons from Regional Trade Agreements*, 59 International & Comparative Law Quarterly 625–667 (2010).

---

[632] *See* Daniel Pruzin, *WTO Report Calls for Restraint in Use of Trade Defense Measures*, 26 International Trade Law (BNA) 1025 (30 July 2009).

3.  Zang, Michelle Q., *The WTO Contingent Trade Instruments Against China: What Does Accession Bring?*, 58 INTERNATIONAL & COMPARATIVE LAW QUARTERLY 321–351 (2009).

## *TELECOMMUNICATIONS AGREEMENT*

The 1998 WTO *Basic Telecommunications Agreement*.

This *Agreement*, which developed under the auspices of the *General Agreement on Trade in Services (GATS)*, initially was signed by 69 WTO Members in 1998. There are 107 Members (as of March 2008) that have joined the *Agreement*. The increase is due largely to the accession of new countries to the WTO.

Trade liberalization in the cross-border supply of telecommunications services is the goal of the *Telecommunications Agreement*. Included in this goal is the establishment and expansion of the right of foreign firms to own and operate a commercial presence, *i.e.*, *GATS* Mode III service supply (foreign direct investment (FDI)). In turn, a commercial presence includes an independent telecommunications network infrastructure.

Associated with, but separate from, the *Telecommunications Agreement* is a Reference Paper. This Paper contains principles about telecommunications regulations that affect cross-border service supply. That is, the Paper lays out disciplines on the following regulatory subjects:

- Fair allocation of resources, particularly frequencies, numbers, and rights of way
- Independence of telecommunications regulators from telecommunications operators
- Interconnection guarantees
- Telecommunications competition safeguards
- Transparency in licensing

Fifty-seven WTO Members (as of March 2008) have made commitments under the Reference paper.

It would appear the *Telecommunications Agreement* and Reference Paper have been successful in facilitating cross-border telecommunications trade. Between 1998 and 2007, *i.e.*, the first decade following the signing of the *Agreement*[633] —

- The number of telephone subscribers around the world increased by 20 times, specifically from 1 billion in 1997 to roughly 4.2 billion in 2007, with most of the increase in the mobile phone sector. The majority

---

[633] The statistics are from the United Nations International Telecommunication Union (ITU) and reported (*inter alia*) in Daniel Pruzin, *Lamy Calls for "Quantum" Improvement in Doha Round Market Access Services Offers*, 25 International Trade Reporter (BNA) 292–293 (28 February 2008).

of new mobile phone subscribers were in the BRIC countries (Brazil, Russia, India, and China), with 15 million new subscribers in Brazil, 20 million in Russia, 45 million in India, and 80 million in China.

- The number of internet users rose by 1,500 percent.

- Revenues of telecommunications companies grew from U.S. $620 billion to over $1.4 trillion.

However, these statistics do not prove a causal relationship between the *Agreement* and Reference Paper, on the one hand, and telecommunications trade liberalization, on the other hand. First, many telecommunications sectors, such as mobile telephony, still are relatively new and the markets are under-saturated. Overall, the telecommunications industry overall accounts for 3.2 percent of world economic growth. Second, between 1998 and 2007, two of the BRIC countries were not parties to the *Agreement*. Russia was not a WTO Member, and Brazil signed, but has not (as of March 2008) ratified, the *Agreement*.

*Suggestions for Further Research:*

Article:

1. Lin, Chun Hung, *Selected International Rules of Foreign Direct Investment in the Telecommunications Sector and Its Influences on Taiwan's Telecommunications Legislation*, 16 ANNUAL SURVEY OF INTERNATIONAL & COMPARATIVE LAW 27–62 (2010).

# TEO

Temporary Exclusion Order.

An order to exclude temporarily from a territorial jurisdiction specified articles from overseas. The articles may be, for example, foreign merchandise that infringes on an intellectual property right (IPR) in the jurisdiction in which, but for the TEO, the merchandise would enter.

In the United States, a TEO is awarded when the International Trade Commission (ITC) determines there is reason to believe that articles in question violate Section 337 of the *Tariff Act of 1930*, as amended.[634] Generally, a petitioner must demonstrate that the imported articles pose an irreparable injury. The International Trade Commission (ITC) has 90 days (and up to 150 days in complicated cases) to render a determination on a request for preliminary relief. A TEO, however, may be undesirable for three reasons:

(1) Doing so may adversely affect the public health and welfare, competitive conditions in the American economy, the production of like or directly competitive products, or American consumers;

(2) The ITC must apply the same standards to a request for a TEO that a Federal district court would apply in a motion for a preliminary injunction; and

---

[634] *See* 19 U.S.C. § 1337.

(3) The ITC may require the complainant to post a bond as a prerequisite to issuance of a TEO. The bond must be forfeited to the government if the complainant is unsuccessful in obtaining the order.

If a TEO is issued, the ITC notifies the Secretary of the Treasury, who provides notice to the Customs and Border Protection (CBP) to exclude the infringing goods from the United States. In some instances, the CBP will seize and destroy the goods. If the ITC renders a final determination that Section 337 is violated, a permanent exclusion order (PEO) of the offending articles is a remedy that may be obtained.

## TEPAC

Trade and Environment Policy Advisory Committee.

TEPAC is a 24 member private sector body that assists the United States Trade Representative (USTR) on formulating positions on trade matters relating to the environment, such as government subsidies to fisheries, fuel, and vessel construction. Members of civil society, private sector, business, non-governmental organizations (NGOs) and academia comprise the TEPAC.

The general aim of TEPAC is to strengthen the nexus between the environment and trade through environmental reviews of each United States free trade agreement (FTA). Pursuant to Executive Order Number 13,141, the review conducted by the TEPAC is to assess and consider environmental impacts of America's trade agreements.[635]

## TERMS OF TRADE

A country's terms of trade, or TOT, is the ratio of that country's export prices to its import prices. In practice, an index of export and import prices is used to calculate the TOT.

Thus, formulaically,

$$TOT = \frac{Index \ of \ Export \ Prices}{Index \ of \ Import \ Prices}$$

A country's TOT "improve" if the TOT increases in value. When the TOT falls, it is said to "deteriorate" or "worsen." However, some care is needed when using these normative terms. Whether TOT really gets better or worse, in terms of the effect of the TOT on a country's economy, depends on the source of the change in the TOT.

Suppose a country's TOT increases because the country's goods are fetching higher prices, while import prices have declined, stayed the same, or not risen

---

[635] *See* Executive Order Number 13,141, 64 Federal Register 63169 (18 November 1999); Guidelines for Implementation of Executive Order 13141: Environmental Review of Trade Agreements, 65 Federal Register 79442–49 (19 December 2000).

as much as export prices. In effect, each exported article pays for more imports. This is a genuine blessing for the country's standard of living. However, suppose export prices remain flat, but import prices have fallen. There has been no increase in foreign demand for the country's products, which could harbinger overseas market saturation and the need to find new markets, or develop different products. Suppose TOT increase because domestic inflation exceeds inflation in the country's trading partners. The relatively higher domestic inflation rate translates into higher export prices relative to import prices. But, this development hardly can be seen as positive. It may spell worsening monetary conditions and higher interest rates in the country.

Speaking of the "terms of trade" without an adjective is somewhat imprecise. In most cases, the speaker wishes to refer to what is technically known as the "net barter terms of trade" (or, equivalently, the "commodity terms of trade"). The word "net" is used to differentiate the concept from the "gross" barter terms of trade. This measure is simply the quantity of exports divided by the quantity of imports (based on an assumption that the values of exports and imports are equal).

There is yet another measure of a country's terms of trade, known as the "factoral terms of trade" (or, equivalently, the "single factorial terms of trade"). These are the amount of imports that can be purchased per unit of factors of production (e.g., labor, land, and capital). The factoral terms of trade measure is useful when considering the effect of productivity on exports. For example, suppose there is a decline in a country's export prices that originates from an increase in productivity in that country. Spurred by competition for foreign markets, workers in the export sectors are able to generate more output per labor-hour. The country exports more of its articles, putting downward pressure on prices. The net barter TOT worsens because of the decline in export prices. But, it masks the salubrious reason for the drop, namely, the productivity gain. Indeed, assuming it is accompanied by rising wages (which it should be if wages reflect marginal productivity), then it suggests a rise in the standard of export sector workers. In contrast, the factoral TOT will show the productivity gain. After all, this measure captures the amount of imports purchasable per unit of factor input. The productivity gain will translate into more imports that can be purchased per unit of factor input.

In practice, the factoral TOT is calculated by multiplying the net barter TOT by an index of productivity change in a country's export industries. The formula is:

$$\text{Factroal TOT} = \text{Net Barter TOT} \times \frac{\text{Index of Productivity}}{\text{Changes in Export Sectors}}$$

$$= \frac{\text{Index of Export Prices}}{\text{Index of Import Prices}} \times \frac{\text{Index of Productivity}}{\text{Changes in Export Sectors}}$$

It is evident from the formula that absent any productivity change, the factoral TOT could shift because of changes in the net barter TOT. The factoral TOT is sometimes called the "single" factoral TOT, the word "single" connoting that the productivity of only the exporting country is considered. The "double" factoral TOT is calculated by taking the net barter TOT and multiplying it with an index that accounts for productivity change in the country's export sectors and in the export sectors of the country's trading partners. That index is simply the quotient of the productivity changes, hence formulaically,

$$\text{Double Factoral TOT} = \text{Net Barter TOT} \times \text{Relative Productivity Indexes}$$

$$= \frac{\text{Index of Export Prices}}{\text{Index of Import Prices}} \times \frac{\text{Index of Productivity Changes in Export Sectors}}{\text{Index of Productivity Changes in Trading Partner's Export Sectors}}$$

The double factoral TOT is the most comprehensive indicator of a country's terms of trade, because it captures not only demand and supply conditions in output markets through export and import prices, but also developments in input markets through productivity changes.

Indeed, a criticism leveled by economist Paul Krugman against the so-called East Asian economic "miracle" of the 1950s-early 1990s, and the economic recovery of East Asia in the late 1990s, is that most East Asian countries have experienced little or no growth in productivity, partly as a result of a failure to incorporate new technology into the production process. Thus, the improvement in the net barter TOT is deceptive.

Some studies attempt to demonstrate the ill effects of trade liberalization through declining TOT. The arguments claim trade liberalization is manipulated by developed countries to the detriment of developing countries. Specifically, the First World inflicts unfavorable and deteriorating TOT (*i.e.*, developed countries orchestrate the decline in the share of international trade held by developing countries). Lord Bauer rebuts these studies, contending the accusation that major powers inflict bad and worsening TOT on the Third World wrongly presumes the share of a country in total world trade is, by itself, an indicator of the prosperity or wealth of that country. Lord Bauer also argues there are several other factors within a particular country that contribute to its declining TOT. They include changes in cost of production, export diversification, trade volume and import purchasing power.

*Suggestions for Further Research:*

Books:

1.  BAUER, LORD PETER T., EQUALITY, THE THIRD WORLD AND ECONOMIC DELUSION (1981).

2.  DOSMAN, EDGAR J., THE LIFE AND TIMES OF RAÚL PREBISCH, 1901–1986 (2009).

3.  SCANDIZZO, PASQUALE L. & DIMITRIS DIAKOSAWAS, INSTABILITY IN THE TERMS OF TRADE OF PRIMARY COMMODITIES: 1900–1982 (1987).

Book Chapters:

1.  Cassetti, Mario, *Conflict, Inflation, Distribution and Terms-of-Trade in the Kaleckian Model, in* THE ECONOMICS OF DEMAND-LED GROWTH: CHALLENGING THE SUPPLY-SIDE VISION OF THE LONG RUN (Mark Setterfield ed., 2002).

2.  Zheng, Zhihai, *China's Terms of Trade in Manufactures: 1993–2000, in* UNITED NATIONS CONFERENCE ON TRADE AND DEVELOPMENT (June 2002).

Articles:

1.  Broda, Christian & Cédric Tille, *Coping with Terms-of-Trade Shocks in Developing Countries*, 9 CURRENT ISSUES IN ECONOMICS & FINANCE 11 (2003).

2.  Ocran, Matthew Kofi & Charles K.D. Adjasi, *Trade Liberalisation and Poverty: Empirical Evidence from Household Surveys in Ghana*, 8 JOURNAL OF INTERNATIONAL TRADE LAW & POLICY number 1, 40–59 (2009).

## TEU

Twenty foot equivalent unit.

The dimensions of a standard container used to ship goods by sea, rail, and land. The largest of sea vessels can carry 11,000 TEUs. By comparison, a train carrying 11,000 TEUs would stretch over 44 miles (71km) long.

## TEXTILES AND APPAREL

This sector sometimes is abbreviated "T&A."

It is important to distinguish textiles from apparel. Textiles are those goods that serve as a base or are components in the manufacturing of a finished good. Apparel, on the other hand, is that finished good comprised of any number of textile components. An example illustrates the point.

In May 2003, before the *Multi-Fiber Agreement (MFA)* was phased out on 31 December 2004, by operation of the WTO *Agreement on Textiles and Clothing (ATC)*, the world market share of Chinese apparel products was forecast to grow from 18.9 to 45.9 percent. The world market share of Taiwanese apparel was forecast to fall from 1.5 to 0.4 percent. These forecasts suggested China would be the largest exporter of apparel products in the world.[636] But,

---

[636] *See* Rossella Brevetti, *China to Monopolize Quota-Free Apparel Trade in U.S., EU, NCTO Warns*, 23 International Trade Rep. (BNA) 365 (9 March 2006).

China would be the largest importer of textiles in the world. The reasons, of course, would be China (1) needs textiles as an input to apparel, and (2) does not have a comparative advantage in textile production (only apparel production). Those countries with the greatest comparative advantage in textiles include India, Pakistan, and Vietnam, amongst others.

For some developed countries, notably the United States and several European Union (EU) states, textiles and apparel are a sensitive sector. This sector long had been protected by the *MFA*, but the *ATC* phased out global quotas.

## T-FTA

*Tripartite Free Trade Area*, a planned free trade agreement (FTA) among the three major regional economic communities in Sub-Saharan Africa, namely, the *Common Market for Eastern and Southern Africa (COMESA)*, the *East African Community (EAC)*, and the *Southern African Development Community (SADC)*.

Negotiations for the T-FTA began in June 2011. Such and FTA would be ambitious. There are 26 countries in *COMESA, EAC*, and *SADC*, and they hold 57 percent of the population of the African Union (AU).[637] Yet, only 10 percent of trade among these countries is intra-African trade.

In October 2008, in Uganda, *COMESA, EAC*, and *SADC* held their first Tripartite Summit. At that Summit, they set upon a program to harmonize trading arrangements, allow for free movement of businesspersons, implement joint programs on infrastructure, and establish institutions to promote cooperation. This Summit was followed by three years of preparatory work toward the June 2011 announcement of negotiations for the *T-FTA*.

The first phase of these negotiations focuses on free trade in goods. This phase is scheduled to last three years.

## TGAAA

*Trade and Globalization Adjustment Assistance Act of 2009*, which amended Chapters 3 and 4 (concerning Trade Adjustment Assistance (TAA)) of the *Trade Act of 1974. See* TAA.

## THERAPEUTIC JURISPRUDENCE

### Introduction

Therapeutic Jurisprudence (TJ) is a theoretical framework to acknowledge the importance of professional relationships with clients. In this framework, the subtle, unintended consequences of a legal rule or procedure are identified,

---

[637] *See* Len Bracken, *African Leaders Launch Negotiations for 26-Country Tripartite Free Trade Area,* 28 International Trade Reporter (BNA) 1002 (16 June 2011).

especially to see whether those consequences are anti-therapeutic. A concept related to TJ is Narrative Medicine (NM), whereby how physicians can experience the lives of patients to improve diagnostic and treatment options is analyzed.[638] Possibly, there may be some application of TJ, NM, or both to international trade law.

Professor Brookbanks of the University of Auckland (New Zealand) Faculty of Law attempts to link TJ and NM by incorporating NM into a legal setting to explore "the use of narrative in the lived experience of law and legal processes and to investigate how the lawyer/client relationship might be enhanced through the narrative dynamic."[639] This way, legal processes can be transformed by putting people as the central focus and using law as a tool to make social structures personal.

According to Professor Brookbanks, the main focus of TJ is to identify and minimize the "psychologically damaging effects of laws and legal processes."[640] He argues incorporating the patient-centered approach of NM into law can better express TJ principles.[641] In turn, legal events can be analyzed to understand the human dynamics that created the problem and discern how it could have been avoided.[642]

### Narrative Medicine Defined

Through her experience as a prominent American internal medicine practitioner, Dr. Rita Charon came to realize that patients expected her to understand their personal narratives to understand better their illnesses.[643] She researched communication between patients and doctors, hoping to improve the ability of doctor to understand their patients.[644] Dr. Charon created the term "narrative medicine" to describe practicing medicine with narrative competence, with an understanding of the complex narrative relationships it involves.[645] She believes doctors will improve their capacity for empathy, reflection, and professionalism by striving for ideal medical care through NM.[646]

The goal of NM is to cut across divides between doctors and patients, doctors and doctors, and doctors and themselves by describing common human experience.[647] The approach is bottom-up, and it depends on multiple sources of authorities, the reliance on which Professor Brookbanks believes is a current

---

[638] *See* Warren Brookbanks, *Narrative Medical Competence and Therapeutic Jurisprudence: Some Preliminary Thoughts*, 4 New Zealand Bioethics Journal 16, 16 (2003). [Hereinafter, Brookbanks.]

[639] Brookbanks, *supra*, at 16.

[640] Brookbanks, *supra*, at 17.

[641] Brookbanks, *supra*, at 17.

[642] Brookbanks, *supra*, at 17.

[643] *See* Brookbanks, *supra*, at 17.

[644] *See* Brookbanks, *supra*, at 17.

[645] *See* Brookbanks, *supra*, at 17.

[646] *See* Brookbanks, *supra*, at 17.

[647] *See* Brookbanks, *supra*, at 17.

trend in legal reform through TJ.[648] Though not meant to eclipse traditional practices, NM is meant to enhance them.[649] By embracing a narrative approach in law, legal relationships may be similarly affected.[650]

In the medical field, NM provides a holistic approach to the problems of a patient. Legal commentators are now investigating how the practice of law can be more holistic in relation to clients through TJ.[651] Professor Brookbanks believes that a key tie between the two theories is hope, because both work towards something good, and both should try to provide hope in the future for patients and clients.[652]

### Synthesis

Professor Brookbanks believes both TJ and NM are headed in similar directions.[653] They are both relational methods meant to improve relationships between doctors and patients, and lawyers and clients. Further research is required to learn more about their interrelationship and determine how each can aid the other in reaching goals.[654] Additionally, they can both offer a critique of the impact institutional structures have on individuals as well as offer ways to minimize it.[655]

Affective lawyering, its focus being the value of emotional engagement, is being recognized as a valid aspect of professional interactions with clients.[656] It focuses on intuition, experience, and passion, which is prevalent in narrative competence.[657]

The narrative process is empowering, and recognizes the importance of procedural justice.[658] By focusing on the narrative, a person's inner reality can be discovered allowing their pain to be discovered.[659] This focus may even avoid adversarial conflict.[660]

Professor Brookbanks gives five features of a narrative approach to law as adapted from NM:[661]

(1) Dealing with a legal problem can be seen as an enacted narrative within the story of someone's life.

---

[648] See Brookbanks, *supra*, at 18.
[649] See Brookbanks, *supra*, at 18.
[650] See Brookbanks, *supra*, at 17.
[651] See Brookbanks, *supra*, at 18.
[652] See Brookbanks, *supra*, at 19.
[653] See Brookbanks, *supra*, at 19.
[654] See Brookbanks, *supra*, at 19.
[655] See Brookbanks, *supra*, at 19.
[656] See Brookbanks, *supra*, at 19.
[657] See Brookbanks, *supra*, at 19.
[658] See Brookbanks, *supra*, at 20.
[659] See Brookbanks, *supra*, at 20.
[660] See Brookbanks, *supra*, at 20.
[661] See Brookbanks, *supra*, at 20.

(2) Using narratives provides a framework for approaching a client's problems holistically, and discovering solutions.

(3) The interpretation of history aids the analysis of narratives.

(4) Narratives provide a method for dealing with the emotions that accompany legal disputes.

(5) Narrative can revive teaching and practicing law.

Professor Brookbanks believes many areas of law could be directly impacted by these ideas, such as family law, mental health law, and employment law.

International trade law may be one such field. For example, there may be applications to trade negotiations between rich and poor nations. Yet, such applications are arguable. At their core, medicine and law pursue different ends. The ultimate goal of medicine is healing, while the ultimate goal of law is justice. Medicine is not an adversarial process in which the healing of one person necessarily produces the death of another (putting aside, of course, questions of scarce resource allocation and triage). In law, including international trade law, the "game" sometimes is zero sum, with a clear winner and loser. Attempting to be therapeutic to both parties in a legal dispute can lead to additional conflict, insofar as what might be therapeutic for one client is in direct opposition to the other. It is difficult to conceive of the WTO Appellate Body acting as a "marriage counselor" applying TJ or NM principles. Victims of violations of international trade rules might not be comforted by therapeutic approaches to offenders. Rather, they might seek punishment, in the form of authorization for trade retaliation, instead.

## THIRD COUNTRY FABRIC PROVISION
## (THIRD-COUNTRY FABRIC PROVISION)

*See AGOA.*

## TIDCA

Trade, Investment, and Development Cooperation Agreement.

A TIDCA is a bilateral accord used by the United States, often as a precursor to a Trade and Investment Framework Agreement, and ultimately — possibly — a free trade agreement (FTA). The United States offers TIDCAs for countries at early stages of development that indicate they are not prepared for a Trade and Investment Framework Agreement (TIFA) or FTA.

## TIERED FORMULA

A method of reducing tariffs or subsidies in a non-linear fashion, so that larger cuts are made to higher figures, and smaller cuts to smaller figures.

Tariffs or subsidies are classified into different categories, or tiers. Duty rates and subsidy payments in the highest (or top) tier are cut most steeply. Duty rates and subsidy payments in the lowest (or bottom) tier are cut least drastically. Duty rates and subsidy payments in the middle tier or tiers are cut by moderate degrees.

The end result of tiered reduction is greater harmonization of tariffs and subsidies across countries, including the elimination of tariff peaks. However, this result is jeopardized by exemptions, sometimes called flexibilities, from the tiered formula. The tiered reduction formula was used extensively in the Doha Round for cutting agricultural tariffs and subsidies.

## TIFA

Trade and Investment Framework Agreement.

A TIFA is a bilateral accord used by the United States, often as a precursor and pre-condition for a free trade agreement (FTA). TIFAs are negotiated mainly with countries whose economies were once closed or isolated and are now beginning to open to international trade and investment. TIFAs also establish joint working groups between the United States and its partner country to discuss how an FTA might proceed. These working groups address issues pertaining to trade and investment liberalization, including intellectual property protection, labor and the environment, small and medium sized enterprises (SMEs), and trade capacity building.

By addressing these issues in a mutually satisfactory manner, the TIFA can serve as a building block to an FTA. Moreover, the TIFA discussions may illuminate issues involving sensitive sectors, which may help shape future FTA negotiations. More bluntly, the TIFA process is to some degree a take it-or-leave-it proposition. The United States more or less insists on a country agreeing to the terms of, and implementing obligations and standards in, a TIFA, if it ever hopes to have an FTA with the United States.

Examples and counter-examples exist as to whether a TIFA is an FTA building block. Jordan signed a Bilateral Investment Treaty (BIT) with the United States in 1997, a TIFA in 1999, and an FTA on 24 October 2000. Note that the FTA effectively replaces the TIFA. Indonesia signed a TIFA with the United States in 1996. The possibility of an FTA between the United States and Indonesia is remote.

The United States has negotiated TIFAs with the countries listed below. TIFAs currently in effect (as of March 2011) are listed by region:[662]

### Africa

- United States — Angola TIFA (English)
- United States — Angola TIFA (Portuguese)
- United States — Common Market for Eastern and Southern Africa (COMESA) TIFA

---

[662] This list of TIFAs is taken and adapted from the Office of the United States Trade Representative, *posted at* www.ustr.gov/trade-agreements/trade-investment-framework-agreements.

- United States — East African Community TIFA
- United States — Ghana TIFA
- United States — Liberia TIFA
- United States — Mauritius TIFA
- United States — Mozambique TIFA
- United States — Nigeria TIFA
- United States — Rwanda TIFA
- United States — South Africa TIFA
- United States — West African Economic and Monetary Union (WAEMU) TIFA

### Americas

- United States — Caricom TIFA
- United States — Uruguay TIFA
- United States — Uruguay TIFA Protocol on Trade and Environment
- United States — Uruguay TIFA Protocol on Trade Facilitation

### Europe and the Middle East

- United States — Algeria TIFA
- United States — Bahrain TIFA
- United States — Egypt TIFA
- United States — Georgia TIFA
- United States — Iceland TICF
- United States — Iraq TIFA
- United States — Kuwait TIFA
- United States — Lebanon TIFA
- United States — Libya TIFA
- United States — Oman TIFA
- United States — Qatar TIFA
- United States — Saudi Arabia

  TIFAhttp://www.ustr.gov/sites/default/files/uploads/agreements/tifa/asset_upload_file920_7738.pdf
- United States — Switzerland TICF
- United States — Tunisia TIFA
- United States — Ukraine TICA
- United States — Ukraine TICA (Ukrainian)
- United States — United Arab Emirates TIFA
- United States — Yemen TIFA

**South and Central Asia**

- United States — Afghanistan TIFA
- United States — Central Asian TIFA (Kazakhstan, Kyrgyzstan, Tajikistan, Turkmenistan, and Uzbekistan)
- United States — Pakistan TIFA
- United States — Sri Lanka TIFA

**Southeast Asia and the Pacific**

- United States — ASEAN TIFA
- United States — Brunei TIFA
- United States — Cambodia TIFA
- United States — Indonesia TIFA
- United States — Malaysia TIFA
- United States — New Zealand TIFA
- United States — Philippines TIFA
- United States — Thailand TIFA
- United States — Vietnam TIFA

Additionally, the United States is negotiating TIFAs with several countries, including (as of March 2011), Taiwan.

As a legal matter, all TIFAs are non-binding. Yet, they yield direct benefits by helping partner countries address issues vital to trade and investment liberalization. TIFA councils normally meet once a year to review progress and encourage continued trade development between the countries. Recent talks with Uruguay recognized action in the areas of energy, environment, and climate change, while the United States and Sri Lanka have used meetings to discuss agriculture biotechnology and intellectual property rights and talks with Indonesia have included illegal logging and restrictions on pork products and pharmaceutical trade.

While progress with many countries has been successful, in May 2010, Bangladesh rejected a TIFA with the United States after six years of negotiations. It appeared to be disputes over labour, intellectual property rights and environmental issues that prevented the TIFA from being signed.

*Suggestions for Further Research:*

Article:

1. Gillman, Eric, *Note, Legal Transplants in Trade and Investment Agreements: Understanding the Exportation of U.S. Law to Latin America*, 41 GEORGETOWN JOURNAL OF INTERNATIONAL LAW 263–301 (2009).

# TNC

Transnational Corporation, a synonym for Multinational Corporation (MNC).

## TOP/BOTTOM RATIO

The second of three major methods to measure income poverty, the others being an absolute poverty threshold and a Gini coefficient.

As its name suggests, the "Top/Bottom Ratio" is the ratio of the share of income the top 20 percent of the population in a country receives to the share of income the bottom 20 percent gets:

$$\frac{\text{Top/Bottom}}{\text{Ratio}} = \frac{\text{Income received by Top 20 Percent}}{\text{Income received by Bottom 20 Percent}}$$

Clearly, a higher ratio connotes more severe inequality than a lower ratio. While 20 percent is the typical benchmark, others — such as 10 or 25 percent — can be used.

For example, the poorest 10 percent of people in China control only 1.4 percent of total income (as of May 2008).[663] In contrast, the top 10 percent own 45 percent of all assets. On the absolute poverty scale of U.S. $1 per day, between 130 and 200 million (according to different World Bank estimates) fall below the threshold. Notably, as of late 2006, 19 of China's top 100 business tycoons (gauged by a Chinese publication akin to *Forbes*) are deputies to the National People's Congress, double that number in one year. What do these data suggest?

The advantage of using a Top/Bottom Ratio over an absolute threshold is it comports with an important psychological fact about poverty. Poverty is not just about living below a minimum acceptable standard. Rather, it is a relational concept. To be "poor" has meaning in part because someone else is "rich." Consequently there is a sense of deprivation in relation to a reference group. Accordingly, the Ratio in China is helpful in gauging poverty in this sense. But, the sheer number of people still below an absolute threshold is itself staggering. And, the number of tycoons in, or with easy access to, high office, may indicate stronger efforts are needed to ensure poor people are not excluded from the political process.

The Top/Bottom Ratio, like an absolute poverty threshold and Gini coefficient, are measures of income poverty. However, as Nobel Prize winning economist Amartya Sen points out in *Development as Freedom* (1999), poverty may be conceptualized in terms broader than just income. Poverty may be thought of as capability deprivation.

*Suggestions for Further Research:*

Books:

1.  COLLIER, PAUL, THE BOTTOM BILLION — WHY THE POOREST COUNTRIES ARE FAILING AND WHAT CAN BE DONE ABOUT IT (2007).

---

[663] *See* Dorothy J. Solinger, *Inequality's Specter Haunts China*, 171 FAR EASTERN ECONOMIC REVIEW 19, 20, 22 (June 2008).

2. POMFRET, RICHARD, THE AGE OF EQUALITY: THE TWENTIETH CENTURY IN ECONOMIC PERSPECTIVE (Cambridge, Massachusetts: Belknap Press, 2011). See also the review of this book, Richard N. Cooper, *Economic, Social, and Environmental*, 90 FOREIGN AFFAIRS 179 (November/December 2011).

Articles:

1. Lee, Nancy, *More Growth with Income Equality in the Americas: Can Regional Cooperation Help?*, 14 LAW & BUSINESS REVIEW OF THE AMERICAS 665–675 (2008).

2. Ocran, Matthew Kofi & Charles K.D. Adjasi, *Trade Liberalisation and Poverty: Empirical Evidence from Household Surveys in Ghana*, 8 JOURNAL OF INTERNATIONAL TRADE LAW & POLICY number 1, 40–59 (2009).

## *TPA*

*See* Fast Track.

## *TPP (TPP FTA)*

*Trans-Pacific Strategic Economic Partnership*, a vehicle for trade liberalization through expanded market access, and increased foreign direct investment (FDI), for the United States and countries in the Asia-Pacific region.

The proposed *TPP* free trade agreement (FTA) might include the United States, Australia, Brunei, Chile, Malaysia, New Zealand, Peru, Singapore, and Vietnam. The agreement to negotiate toward a *TPP FTA* went into effect in 2006 with four original members, the so-called P-4, Brunei, Chile, New Zealand, and Singapore.

In 2008, the United States was the first country outside of the P-4 to seek membership in the existing agreement.[664] That is, in November 2009 President Obama officially announced the United Sates would join the *TPP* talks with a view to establishing the *FTA*.[665] Malaysia and Vietnam joined the negotiations in November 2010, after the third round of talks.

Is the likelihood of additional countries joining the *TPP FTA* is fading? Arguably, no. If countries are able to meet the high standards required of the *TPP* parties, then they could be considered for inclusion in the discussions. Canada, Japan, and Mexico have shown interest in joining the *TPP* talks.[666]

---

[664] *See* Stephen Joyce, *United States Agrees to Launch Negotiations On Joining Trans-Pacific Economic Agreement*, 25 International Trade Reporter (BNA) 1382 (25 September 2008).

[665] *See* Murray Griffin, *Inaugural Trans-Pacific Partnership Negotiations Launched in Australia*, 27 International Trade Reporter (BNA) 389 (18 March 2010).

[666] *See* Amy Tsui, *U.S. Discusses with Mexico Joining Talks on TPP Following Japan, Canada Meetings*, 29 International Trade Reporter (BNA) 293 (23 February 2012); Amy Tsui, *TPP Members Meet on Sidelines of APEC, Seek Broad Outline of TPP Deal by November*, 28 International Trade Reporter (BNA) 860 (26 May 2011).

Indeed, in November 2011, alongside a summit of the *Asia Pacific Economic Cooperation (APEC)* forum meeting, Japan, along with Canada, made clear its interest to enter the *TPP* negotiations. Japan's decision increased the likelihood of difficult negotiations over market access in Japan for agricultural products Japan deems sensitive (such as rice).

Even though the initial deal to negotiate a *TPP FTA* dates from 2006, the inaugural five-day round of *TPP* discussions did not occur until March 2010, in Melbourne, Australia.[667] The second round of talks began on 14 June 2010, in San Francisco, California. Negotiating sessions covered technical barriers to trade (TBT), market access, legal and institutional issues, cross-border services, competition policy, investment, and the environment.[668] Brunei hosted the third round in October of the same year, and the fourth round has held in December in Auckland, New Zealand. The fifth round of talks were held in Santiago, Chile between 14–18 February 2011. Negotiations included the areas of goods market access, investment, rules of origin and intellectual property. Discussions also included areas of labor services, government procurement and competition policy. The sixth round of talks took place in Singapore in late March 2011, and Vietnam sponsored the seventh round of talks the week of 20 June 2011. By March 2012, an 11th round of *TPP* talks had been held, that one in Melbourne, Australia.[669]

The overall goal is to conclude the *TPP* talks by the time of the Asia-Pacific Economic Cooperation (APEC) forum leaders' summit in November 2011 in Honolulu. The *TPP* is a possible foundation for a broad trade agreement between the 21 economies in APEC.[670] Almost certainly, the collapse of the Doha Round in July and December 2008, and the failure to resuscitate the Round thereafter, helped motivate interest in a *TPP FTA*.

Overall, *TPP* negotiating objectives focus on the elimination or reduction of tariff and non-tariff barriers (NTBs) for all goods (agricultural and industrial) in the Harmonized Tariff Schedule (HTS). Accordingly conventional issues of tariff and NTBs, and rules of origin (ROO) are covered. Negotiations regarding e-commerce and digital technology, and intellectual property (IP) are also covered, as are issues of foreign direct investment (FDI), government procurement, labor and the environment, sanitary and phytosanitary (SPS) measures, trade capacity building, and regulatory cooperation and coherence. With respect to

---

[667] *See* Murray Griffin, *Inaugural Trans-Pacific Partnership Negotiations Launched in Australia*, 27 International Trade Reporter (BNA) 389 (18 March 2010).

[668] *See* Amy Tsui, *Negotiators Discuss How to Start Drafting Texts for Next Round of TPP Talks in October*, 27 International Trade Reporter (BNA) 899 (17 June 2010).

[669] *See* Murray Griffin, *Trade Officials Cautious on TPP Timing, Say Expansion Contingent on "Consensus,"* 29 International Trade Reporter (BNA) 413 (15 March 2012).

[670] *See* Lucien O. Chauvin, *Peru Optimistic for Fifth Round of TPP Talks in Chile Next Week*, 28 International Trade Reporter (BNA) 230 (10 February 2011).

services, which play a key role in the *TPP* negotiations, important sectors like finance, and modes of delivery like temporary entry, are included.[671]

Additionally, provisions in a *TPP* that might emerge on state owned enterprises (SOEs) could become a template for future regional trade agreements (RTAs), and perhaps the World Trade Organization (WTO). The GATT-WTO texts speak of SOEs operating in accordance with normal commercial considerations. The *TPP* negotiations aspire to deal specifically with situations such as where an:

- SOE from one country and private business association of another country compete in a third country;
- SOE is engaged in government procurement;
- SOE is a holding company with many entities under it;
- SOE gains preferential access to export credits; and
- SOE benefits from exemptions in domestic bankruptcy law that allow it to continue in operation.

Such topics deserve coverage given the continued prominence of SOEs in many countries. For example (as of March 2012), SOEs constitute 80 percent of the value of China's stock market, 62 percent of the market capitalization of the Russian stock market, and 38 percent of that in Brazil.[672]

A critical, unanswered question is whether and how any *TPP* accord would relate to a country's existing FTAs. How would rights and duties under a TPP affect the provisions of those FTAs? The United States has FTAs with Australia, Chile, Peru, and Singapore.

But for the opposition of New Zealand under the former Labor government of Prime Minister Helen Clark to the Iraq War resolution in early 2003 in the United Nations Security Council, it might well have signed an FTA with New Zealand, too. The *United States — Australia FTA* was drafted to allow for the possibility of New Zealand docking on to it. The United States and Vietnam have a bilateral accession agreement as part of Vietnam's entry into the WTO in 2007. As for Brunei, it has no significant agricultural sector. All these points further indicate a *TPP FTA* may be reasonably easy to negotiate successfully.

Motivations for United States participation in the *TPP FTA* talks are varied, and to some degree a matter of speculation. One possibility, intimated above, is the American strategy of competitive liberalization. With multilateral trade

---

[671] *See* Murray Griffin, *TPP Should Set Benchmark for Rules on State-Owned Enterprises, Forum Told*, 29 International Trade Law Reporter (BNA) 370 (8 March 2012).

[672] *See* Murray Griffin, *TPP Should Set Benchmark for Rules on State-Owned Enterprises, Forum Told*, 29 International Trade Law Reporter (BNA) 370 (8 March 2012).

talks in the Doha Round moribund or dead, the United States seeks market access through regional and bilateral venues.

A second possibility is American efforts to vie for influence in the Asia-Pacific region with the People's Republic of China (PRC), which most definitely is excluded from the talks. The PRC has an active FTA agenda, and has expanded its ties with neighboring Taiwan under the Economic Cooperation Framework Agreement. This possibility manifestly puts American trade strategy in the broader context of its national security policy, and is redolent of Cold War efforts in the 1950s and 1960s to forge alliances in the Far East, such as through the *South East Asia Treaty Organization (SEATO)*.

A third possibility is a more cynical one. It is that the *TPP FTA* is nothing more than motion, with no *bona fide* expectation of progress, by the United States. That is, as the Administration of President Barack H. Obama lacks fast-track trade negotiating authority, at least engaging in *TPP* talks helps immunize the Administration from the criticism of free traders that it has no trade policy.

*Suggestions for Further Research:*

Book:

1.  KELSEY, JANE, ED., NO ORDINARY DEAL — UNMASKING THE TRANS-PACIFIC PARTNERSHIP FREE TRADE AGREEMENT (2010).

Articles:

1.  Lewis, Meredith Kolsky, *The Trans-Pacific Partnership: New Paradigm or Wolf in Sheep's Clothing?*, 34 BOSTON COLLEGE INTERNATIONAL & COMPARATIVE LAW REVIEW 27–52 (2011).

2.  Sell, Susan K., *TRIPs Was Never Enough: Vertical Forum Shifting, FTAs, ACTA, and TPP*, 18 JOURNAL OF INTELLECTUAL PROPERTY 447–478 (2011).

## TPRB

The Trade Policy Review Body.

The General Council of the WTO meets periodically as the TPRB to review the trade laws and policies of individual Members. This review is called for under the Trade Policy Review Mechanism (TPRM), and occurs periodically for each Member. Each year, at its initial meeting, the TPRB elects its Chairperson for the year from among the Member representatives. The Members that are subject to TPRB review are selected by the middle of the previous calendar year. The TPRB also selects two discussants before each meeting to stimulate debate.

## TPRM

The Trade Policy Review Mechanism, which is Annex 3 of the *WTO Agreement*.

The TPRM was an early accomplishment of the Uruguay Round: in December 1988, it was provisionally established at the Montreal Mid-Term Review of the

Round. Originally, the TPRM called for review of trade policies of Members only as regards goods. However, with the signing of the *WTO Agreement*, the jurisdiction of the TPRM was extended to cover services trade and intellectual property (IP).

The overall aim of the TPRM is to enhance the transparency of its Members' trade policies. The WTO, specifically, the TPRB, reviews every two years the trade laws and policies of the four largest Members — China, the European Union (EU), Japan, and the United States. It reviews every four years the next 16 largest Members. The TPRB reviews all other Members, except least developed countries, every six years. For least-developed countries, the review period is in excess of six years.

*Suggestions for Further Research:*

Book Chapters:

1.   Francois, Joseph F., *Maximizing the Benefits of the Trade Policy Review Mechanism for Developing Countries, in* DEVELOPING COUNTRIES AND THE WTO: A PRO-ACTIVE AGENDA (Bernard Hoekman & Will Martin *et al.*, eds. 2001).

Article:

1.   Gao, Henry, *China's Participation in the WTO: A Lawyer's Perspective,* 11 SINGAPORE YEAR BOOK OF INTERNATIONAL LAW 1–34 (2007).

## TOT

*See* Terms of Trade.

## TRADE ADJUSTMENT ASSISTANCE

*See* TAA.

## TRADE BALANCING REQUIREMENT

A requirement imposed by a host country government on foreign direct investors that, in exchange for permission to invest in the country, the investors must use earnings from exports of their products from the country to pay for any imports into the country that they require for their production process.

The term is synonymous with "trade-balancing measure." Along with export performance and local content requirements, trade balancing is a tactic used by host country governments to regulate foreign direct investment (FDI).

Trade balancing is a topic arising in the 2002 WTO case concerning India and the automotive sector.[673]

---

[673] WTO Appellate Body Report, *India — Measures Affecting the Automotive Sector,* WT/DS146/AB/R, WT/DS175/AB/R (adopted 5 April 2002).

## TRADE CREATION

"Trade creation" occurs when consumers within a regional trade agreement (RTA) shift purchases from relatively high-cost producers in their country to relatively low-cost producers in another country that also is a member of the same RTA.

Because low-cost suppliers are substituted for high-cost suppliers, the outcome is efficient, in the sense of an improvement of the allocation of productive resources within the RTA. The cheapest-cost producers are given business, and thus their countries in the RTA are able to maximize their comparative advantages.

Trade creation mostly occurs whenever the applicable tariff imposed by an importing country, before the RTA eliminated the tariff, exceeded the difference between the (1) price charged by the high-cost producers in the importing country and (2) price charged by the low-cost producers in the exporting country. In other words, trade creation is likely to happen when the pre-RTA tariff served to protect the high-cost producers in the importing country from external competition from another country that joins the RTA.

The converse of trade creation is trade diversion.

*Suggestions for Further Research:*

Book:

1.   DAM, KENNETH W., THE GATT 284–86 (1970).

## TRADE DEFENSE MEASURES

*See* TDI.

## TRADE DEFLECTION

A phenomenon whereby products originating in a third country that do not have preferential access to the market of one country, because it is not a member of the same free trade agreement (FTA) or customs union (CU) of that country, are re-routed through a second country that does have preferential access, either through an FTA or CU, to the market of the first country.

That is, trade deflection is the rerouting of shipment of a good through one or more third countries. The term is largely synonymous with "transshipment," and usually reflects the fraudulent behavior of an exporter and/or importer.

Trade deflection can also occur through methods other than simple transshipment. For example, a basic operation can be done to the goods, such as re-packaging, cleaning, or sorting, when they are in and being re-routed through the second country. This allows the goods to be affixed with false country of origin labels. In addition, trade deflection arises when products are shipped through a third country to avoid antidumping duties. That is, if goods from one country are subject to antidumping duties, those goods may attempt to gain duty-free access through a third country. However, rules of origin of an FTA, CU or other PTA are designed to counteract trade deflection in either instance.

A recent example of trade deflection is the shipping of Brazilian ethanol to El Salvador. In this case, ethanol is shipped first from Brazil to El Salvador and later re-exported to the United States so that it may gain duty-free treatment thanks to the *Central American Free Trade Agreement — Dominican Republic (CAFTA-DR)*.

*Suggestions for Further Research:*

Articles:

1.   Brown, Chad P. & Meredith A. Crowley, *Trade Deflection and Trade Depression*, 72 JOURNAL OF INTERNATIONAL ECONOMICS 176–201 (2007).

2.   Durling, James P. & Thomas J. Prusa, *The Trade Effects Associated with an Antidumping Epidemic: The Hot-Rolled Steel Market, 1996–2001*, 22 EUROPEAN JOURNAL OF POLITICAL ECONOMY 675–95 (2006).

## TRADE DIVERSION

"Trade diversion" is a shift in consumption patterns within a regional trade agreement (RTA) from relatively low-cost producers outside of the RTA to relatively high-cost producers in the RTA.

That is not a salubrious economic change, because the suppliers with the cheaper costs — those in countries outside the RTA — are not given business. To the contrary, they lose sales by virtue of the protection the RTA gives to producers in the countries that are parties to it. That is, the allocation of factors of production is less efficient than before. Trade diversion is likely to occur when the price of the good made outside of the RTA, inclusive of the applicable tariff, exceeds the price of the like product made within the RTA (on which the tariff was eliminated.

The converse of trade diversion is trade creation.

*Suggestions for Further Research:*

Book:

1.   DAM, KENNETH W., THE GATT 284–86 (1970).

## TRADE — ENERGY LINK

International trade and energy are linked in a theoretical and practical sense. In theory, the obligations of GATT and the WTO are applicable to energy, such as fossil fuels and natural gas, which crosses an international boundary. That is, the purpose and framework of the GATT—WTO regime are relevant to world trade in energy. In practice, much of the energy supply of many countries indeed is imported from abroad. However, major energy commodities like oil generally have not been made subject to GATT—WTO commitments. In part, that is because GATT contracting parties, and now WTO Members, have preferred not to make such commitments that might undermine their policy space to operate domestic energy policies, for example, by imposing taxes on oil imports. That also has been because some major energy producer-exporters were not GATT contracting parties. For example, the Kingdom of Saudi Arabia did not accede to the WTO until 11 December 2005, and Iran, Iraq, and Russia remains non-Members.

Energy is a peculiarity within international trade, because it is not as vulnerable to the standard free trade arguments of the Classical economists, Adam Smith and David Ricardo, and their Neo-Classical successors.[674] First, much of the energy supply in the world is concentrated geographically. That is, the location of the supply is relatively fixed in a few countries that are endowed with the relevant resource, such as oil or natural gas. Thus, on the supply side, the pattern of trade — which countries export which energy products — does not change in the short term (one - two years) or even medium term (two – five or two - 10 years). It is pre-determined based on natural resource endowments. Only over the long-term (10 years or more) are changes possible. In other words, the specialization of production that Ricardo identified as a gain from free trade cannot easily or quickly occur with respect to energy if a country does not naturally have that energy product.

Second, also on the supply side, traditional energy sources — especially fossil fuels and natural gas — are scarce and non-renewable. (That is not true, of course, of new sources like solar and wind energy.) In consequence, there is less direct competition in the market to produce conventional energy products than there is in the market for a normal good.

Third, on the demand side of the energy market, there are intense political complications. All countries need energy. Hence, the demand for it is widespread, and it is inelastic, as there are no substitutes available in the short- or medium-term to traditional energy products. Some countries obviously need more energy than others — major economies like that of the United States, EU, and Japan, and big emerging developing countries like Brazil, China, and India. China and India are said to compete with the United States, EU, and Japan, and with each other, in traditional energy markets, and in finding new sources of supply in Africa. The United States balances a generally pro-Israeli Middle East policy with efforts not to alienate Middle East oil suppliers (as occurred in the 1973 Arab oil embargo). Hoping to enhance its energy security, Japan — which imports nearly 100 percent of its energy — invests directly in various energy supply countries as a way of bolstering its relations in a not-too-overtly political manner. The list goes on, but the point is that the demand for energy among countries is not as simple as the standard economics

---

[674] *See* World Trade Organization, *WTO Culture of International Trade Cooperation is Relevant to the Energy Sector — Lamy*, 22 October 2009, *posted at* www.wto.org (speech of Pascal Lamy, WTO Director-General, at Conference on "Energy, Trade and Global Governance," Centre for Trade and Economic Integration, Graduate Institute of International and Development Studies, Geneva).

models that emphasize the price of a good as the key determinant of the quantity of that good that is demanded.

Fourth, in respect of price, it is quite volatile. That is, energy commodity markets are subject to considerable price volatility. This volatility results from a variety of factors, such as inelastic demand, speculation by financiers, political risk, and supply uncertainties. In the markets for normal goods, prices of course rise and fall over time, but are not usually subject to volatility except in periods of extreme stress (such as a natural disaster).

The "bottom line" from these four special features of global energy markets is that international trade in energy products does not result in specialization of production, nor enhance competition among suppliers, as it does for a normal good under Ricardo's Law of Comparative Advantage. Moreover, consumption is subject to political factors and price volatility not generally associated with a normal good. In turn, international trade does not lead to adjustments in the allocation of energy resources as it would for a normal good.

All this said, the WTO has endeavored to address energy issues. To be sure, GATT—WTO rules do not single out energy as a distinct sector. But, the key rules of this regime are appropriate for the sector. These rules include GATT obligations on non-discrimination (both most-favored nation and national treatment), transit rights (*i.e.*, rights for transporting energy), transparency, and WTO provisions on dispute settlement. Indeed, such rules are critical to enhancing certainty and predictability in energy markets. In addition, such rules include disciplines on export restrictions, state trading enterprises (STEs), and trade-distorting subsidies for energy products.

Importantly, the WTO also has established a framework, under the *General Agreement on Trade in Services (GATS)* for energy services. These services include distribution, drilling, engineering, pipeline construction, technical testing, plus services incidental to the extraction of oil and gas, and services incidental to energy distribution and pipeline transportation of fuels. However, the extent to which WTO Members make ambitious commitments in energy services remains to be seen.

*Suggestions for Further Research:*

Articles:

1.   Alvarez, José E., *The WTO as Linkage Machine*, 96 AMERICAN JOURNAL OF INTERNATIONAL LAW issue 1, 146–158 (2002).

2.   Bejesky, Robert, *Geopolitics, Oil Law Reform, and Commodity Market Expectations*, 63 OKLAHOMA LAW REVIEW 193–277 (2011).

3.   Blyschak, Paul M., *Yukos Universal v. Russia: Shell Companies and Treaty Shopping in International Energy Disputes*, 10 RICHMOND JOURNAL OF GLOBAL LAW & BUSINESS 179–210 (2011).

4.   Glassman, Sasha, *Proposed Amendments to Multilateral Trading Agreements to Encourage U.S. — Mexico Trade in Biofuels*, 17 UNIVERSITY OF BALTIMORE JOURNAL OF ENVIRONMENTAL LAW 107–143 (2010).

5.   Lavín, Antonio Riva Palacio, *Comments on the Reforms to the Mexican Energy Laws of 2008*, 15 ILSA JOURNAL OF INTERNATIONAL & COMPARATIVE LAW 629–650 (2009).

6.   McMahon, Joe A. & Stephanie Switzer, *EU Biofuels Policy — Raising the Question of WTO Compatibility*, 60 INTERNATIONAL & COMPARATIVE LAW QUARTERLY 713–736 (2011).

7.   Miranda, Martin, Note, *The Legal Obstacles to Foreign Direct Investment in Mexico's Oil Sector*, 33 FORDHAM INTERNATIONAL LAW JOURNAL 206–242 (2009).

8.   Sakmar, Susan L., *Bringing Energy Trade into the WTO: The Historical Context, Current Status, and Potential Implications for the Middle East Region*, 18 INDIANA INTERNATIONAL & COMPARATIVE LAW REVIEW 89–111 (2008).

9.   Shih, Wen-Chen, *Energy Security, GATT / WTO, and Regional Agreements*, 49 NATURAL RESOURCES JOURNAL 433–484 (2009).

10.  Urdaneta, Karla, *Transboundary Petroleum Reservoirs: A Recommended Approach for the United States and Mexico in the Deepwaters of the Gulf of Mexico*, 32 HOUSTON JOURNAL OF INTERNATIONAL LAW 333–391 (2010).

## TRADE — ENVIRONMENT LINK

*See* Environmental Side Agreement, MEA.

## TRADE — ETHICS LINK

A lack of regulation in the monitoring of ethical behavior of legal practitioners before various United States trade agencies and trade courts has lent itself to an increase in fraud and misrepresentations in cases before such agencies and courts.

As it stands, United States trade agencies, such as the Department of Commerce (DOC), International Trade Administration (ITA), and International Trade Commission (ITC), which lack regulatory and disciplinary authority over the professional ethical behavior of lawyers, can report complaints to the District of Columbia Court of Appeals (D.C. Court of Appeals). The D.C. Court of Appeals will investigate and sanction abuses of rules, including ethical canons.

However, not only are complaints rarely made to the Court, but also the regulatory mechanism available to the Court is little used and ineffective. Furthermore, the regulations cover only the actions of a barred attorney (*i.e.*, a lawyer who has passed a relevant bar examination and thereby is licensed to practice). So, the regulations do not govern actions of a non-lawyer representative (*e.g.*, an accountant or consultant) appearing before the agencies. If a representative of a client perpetrates fraud in a case before an agency, then the only remedy of the agency is to punish the client by applying adverse inferences (against the client) in the case. The case of the client might suffer, yet the culpable practitioner is in no way directly accountable for her actions, even if her involvement in the fraudulent activity is clear.

As a result of increased fraud and misrepresentation in international trade cases, more vigorous remedies have been considered. One such proposal is greater application of Rule 11 sanctions by the Court of International Trade (CIT) and the development of a licensing system that individuals must be a part of prior to appearing before a United States trade agency. This version of Rule 11, arising under the CITs procedures, tracks Rule 11 of the *Federal Rules of Civil Procedure* (*FRCP*), which technically are inapplicable in CIT proceedings.

CIT Rule 11 reads:

> By presenting to the court a pleading, written motion, or other paper — whether by signing, filing, submitting, or later advocating it — an attorney or unrepresented party certifies that to the best of the person's knowledge, information, and belief, formed after any inquiry reasonable under the circumstances:
>
> (1)    it is not being presented for any improper purpose, such as to harass, cause necessary delay, or needlessly increase the cost of litigation;
>
> (2)    the claims, defenses, and other legal contentions are warranted by existing law or by a non-frivolous argument for extending, modifying, or reversing existing law or for establishing new law;
>
> (3)    the factual contentions have evidentiary support or, if specifically so identified, will likely have evidentiary support after a reasonable opportunity for further investigation or discovery; and
>
> (4)    the denials of factual contentions are warranted on the evidence or, if specifically so identified, are reasonable based on belief or a lack of information.[675]

Traditionally, the CIT has not granted Rule 11 sanctions with much frequency.

However, if the trend of increasing fraud and misrepresentations continues, then the CIT most likely will be forced to impose sanctions on legal counsel who violate ethical obligations. To be sure, this regulatory mechanism always has been available to the Court, even if rarely used. Therefore, in dealing with fraud and misrepresentation before the CIT, there is no need to implement a new regulatory system, but simply to utilize the one already in place.

While the CIT has its own regulatory provisions available to it, United States trade agencies, which lack such provisions, possibly could stop violations before they occur by implementing a licensing system for any individual (*e.g.*, barred attorney, foreign lawyer, lay person consultant) appearing before the agency. Various federal agencies already regulate individuals, both lawyers and lay persons, who appear before the agency, such as the Bureau of Alcohol, Tobacco,

---

[675] Court of International Trade Rule 11(b).

Firearms, and Explosives (ATF or Bureau). Practitioners must be enrolled to represent a client before the Bureau. Enrollment consists of completing an application that includes naming their technical qualifications and paying a small fee. Once enrolled the Bureau has the authority to suspend or disbar an individual from appearing before it for reasons such as incompetency, or refusal to comply with the rules set forth by the Bureau.

Similarly, the Federal Energy Regulatory Commission (FERC) conditions appearances before it on the individual, lawyer or lay person, being in good standing with the Commission. Furthermore, the United States Patent and Trademark Office (PTO) has regulated individuals appearing before it since 1861. The PTO has this authority: "for gross misconduct he [the PTO Commissioner] may refuse to recognize any person as a patent agent, either generally or in any particular case."[676] In 1899, the PTO increased its regulation by requiring registration of all individuals practicing before it.

Specifically, the ITA and ITC, in implementing a licensing system to stem fraud and misrepresentation, would not be in the minority, but would join the numerous federal agencies that already successfully use such a system. Suggestions for the licensing system include:

- filing an application with the agency, a requirement that would apply to both lawyers and non-lawyers;

- requiring a licensed practitioner to disclose to the agencies the names of those assisting her in the matter;

- granting a license to a practicing individual, not the firm or employer of the individual;

- prohibiting an individual from appearing before the agency without a license;

- granting the agency removal authority in the case of incompetence or unethical behavior.

*Suggestions for Further Research:*

Articles:

1.  Pierce, Kenneth J. & Alexandra B. Hess, *Proposal to License All Antidumping and Countervailing Duty Agency Practitioners to Better Ensure Competency and Ethical Behavior*, 28 International Trade Reporter (BNA Insights) 410 (10 March 2011).

2.  Hadfield, Frances P., *A Question of Evidence, Ethics, and Interpretation: Possible Perils and Pitfalls of United States Court of International Trade Rules 8 and 11*, 19 TULANE JOURNAL OF INTERNATIONAL AND COMPARATIVE LAW 573 (Spring 2011).

3.  Pickard, Daniel B. & Laura El-Sabaawi, *The Future of Rule 11 Sanctions for Unethical Conduct Before the U.S. Court of International Trade*, 19 TULANE JOURNAL OF INTERNATIONAL AND COMPARATIVE LAW 587 (Spring 2011).

---

[676] Act of March 2, 1861, c. 88, s 8, (12 Stat. 247).

## TRADE FACILITATION

Simplifying, streamlining, and otherwise making more efficient the process of customs clearance and the regulations governing this process.

Trade facilitation, also called "customs facilitation," is one of the Four "Singapore Issues." In 1996, the Council for the Trade in Goods established a work program to assess the scope of rules concerning simplification of customs procedures.

WTO Members formally agreed to launch negotiations on trade facilitation in July 2004 under the auspices of modalities contained in Annex D of the "July Package." In the Doha Round negotiations, no less than 50 WTO Members had, by October 2005, submitted proposals on facilitation of trade through reform of customs procedures. Some suggestions cut across the First World—Third World divide. The United States, for example, had submitted a joint proposal with India, and another one with Uganda, while Rwanda teamed with Switzerland to make an offer. Such plans focused on three provisions in GATT, namely, Article V, concerning freedom of transit, Article VIII, concerning fees and formalities for importation and exportation, and Article X, concerning transparency through publication and administration of trade measures.

A number of studies bolster the case for emphasizing trade facilitation in multilateral trade talks. Generally, these studies, while admitting the topic is not glamorous, point out benefits from customs facilitation can rival the gains from tariff cuts. Indeed, an Asia Pacific Economic Cooperation (APEC) study, discussed in 2006 by the *Financial Times*, observed that comprehensive trade facilitation is twice as valuable, as regards increasing trade, as tariff reduction. Some countries, such as Morocco, have implemented trade facilitation programs — and the results are evident. In 1996, it took 18 to 20 days to process a container in the port of Casablanca. By April 2006, the time was cut to a few hours. Analysts also cite to red tape, not tariff barriers, as the reason for many small and medium sized enterprises (SMEs) being inactive participants in international trade.

Product and packaging standards are a key area for simplification and streamlining. These standards, even when motivated by bona fide public policy concerns, can retard shipment processing. For instance, as reported by the *Financial Times*:[677]

- Expensive Packaging Standards:

  A traditional Zambian export, copper wire, which is loaded on wooden pallets, can take a week to clear customs in South Africa. That is because South African officials may demand proof the Zambian exporter has conducted a pest risk analysis on the pallets. The exporter must show a registered inspector from the Zambian Ministry of Agriculture has certified the wood used to construct the pallets has

---

[677] Alan Beattie, *Forget Tariff Cuts, the Poor Need Trade Facilitation*, FINANCIAL TIMES, 1–2 April 2006, at 4.

been dried in a kiln, or fumigated, to kill pests. However, the certification costs the exporter U.S. $100.

- Sophisticated International Quality Tests:

  To export cotton to the United States, strict American quality tests must be met. The tests ensure compliance of foreign cotton with international standards. However, some poor countries — such as Zambia — do not have the technology to provide international standards testing. Therefore, to sell cotton in the American market, Zambian exporters must first ship their cotton to Mauritius, which has a sophisticated textile industry and can perform the necessary quality assessment.

- Independent Certifications:

  The European Union (EU) has strict quality and safety rules for imports of flowers and food. The rules are set not by an international body, but by European grocery chains. The chains demand independent certification of foreign farms from which the flowers or food originate.

Perhaps the most obvious justification for customs facilitation — and the resistance to among certain constituencies and countries — concerns corruption. Every check in the process of clearing goods through customs is an opportunity to solicit a bribe from an exporter or importer.

*Suggestions for Further Research:*

Books:

1.   LAKSHMANAN, T.R., ET AL., INTEGRATION OF TRANSPORT AND TRADE FACILITATION: SELECTED REGIONAL CASE STUDIES (2001).

2.   SENGUPTA, NIRMAL, THE ECONOMICS OF TRADE FACILITATION (2007).

Book Chapters:

1.   Messerlin, Patrick A. and Jamel Zarrouk, *Trade Facilitation: Technical Regulations and Customs Procedures, in* DEVELOPING COUNTRIES AND THE WTO: A PRO-ACTIVE AGENDA (2001).

# TRADE FINANCE

A general term referring to the means by which importers of merchandise pay, or arrange for payment to be made to, exporters of that merchandise.

Trade finance is a market worth about U.S. $10 trillion annually. This market consists of three major instruments:

- Credit, specifically, commercial letter of credit.
- Guarantees, including standby letters of credit.
- Insurance.

Over 90 percent of trade transactions in the world use some form of trade finance. Thus, trade finance sometimes is called the "grease" that facilitates the cross-border flow of goods.[678] Banks (specifically, commercial banks) are the main providers (suppliers) of trade finance, and importers and exporters are the main consumers (demanders) of it.

As a result of the global economic recession and the reluctance or inability of many banks to lend, trade finance shrank dramatically in the fall 2008 and spring 2009. In turn, that seizing up of the trade finance market had a deleterious knock-on effect on the value and volume of world trade, which shrank dramatically. Put simply, goods cannot flow if exporters cannot get paid, and exporters cannot get paid if importers cannot get their banks to extend trade finance to them for the benefit of the exporters. Thus, at the April 2009 Group of 20 (G-20) Summit in London, leaders pledged $250 billion of support for trade finance during the subsequent two years. This assistance would be through export credit and investment agencies, and multilateral development banks such as the World Bank, under the umbrella rubric of the "Global Trade Liquidity Program (GTLP)."

## TRADE — HUMAN RIGHTS LINK

Along with the relationships between trade and the environment, and trade and labor rights, the topic of trade and human rights became a major issue during and after the Uruguay Round of 1986–94. In truth, these linkage issues always existed, and are reflected not only in the Charter for an International Trade Organization (ITO or Havana Charter), but also in the writings of ancient and medieval scholars. The central questions on all such issues are two-fold: first, to what extent, if any, does trade liberalization advance, or retard, the promotion of environmental, labor, or human rights; second, what is the causal mechanism in the link between trade and environmental, labor, or human rights?

In contemporary times, there are at least six relationships between trade and human rights that scholars and policy makers consider and explore. They are as follows:

(1) Law and Economics Approach

By increasing trade with countries like China, the human rights situation in those countries will improve. The causal link is that increased trade generates wealth, citizens become less concerned with economic rights, and more concerned with political and human rights, as they gain increased wealth. This approach is a passive, long-term one, and does not call for any additional or interventionist mechanism beyond trade liberalization. Among its proponents are law and economics scholars like Professor Alan O. Sykes.

---

[678] *See, e.g.,* Daniel Pruzin, *WTO Cites "Race Against Time" for Countries to Revive Trade Finance for Exports, Imports,* 26 International Trade Reporter (BNA) 477 (9 April 2009).

(2) Property Rights Approach

By increasing trade with countries like China, property rights are enhanced in those countries. That is, the delineation and recordation of who owns what, and the free alienation of property by its owners, is a natural concomitant of freer trade. In turn, as citizens become used to enhanced and better-protected property rights, including intellectual property (IP) rights, they become more interested in human rights. This approach also is a passive, long-term one, calling for no serious intervention other than a rule-of-law framework for property rights. Among its proponents is Professor Ernst-Ulrich Petersmann.

(3) Transparency Approach

The WTO contributes to the advancement of human rights through the implementation and enforcement of transparency obligations set out in the GATT–WTO texts. That also is true of free trade agreements (FTAs), insofar as they contain transparency rules. For instance, under GATT Article X, China has to publish rules before applying them. In turn, as rules become more transparent, citizens better understand their rights and duties — and, critically, the obligations owed by government to them. The next logical step they take is to consider their political and human rights. Under this approach, no active intervention is needed, other than a stringent adherence to transparency rules.

(4) Multinational Corporation (MNC) Approach

Trade liberalization under the GATT—WTO regime or FTAs contributes to the advancement of human rights insofar as it facilitates cross-border foreign direct investment (FDI) by MNCs. Many MNCs, including ones that operate in China, have adopted voluntary corporate codes of conduct. The codes contain provisions about the environment and labor, and typically at least touch on human rights-related topics. Cynics say that such codes, because they are voluntary, are just for show, and designed to buy consumer goodwill. In fact, corporations tend to take them seriously, because their reputations are at stake. Reputation is a sanction that should not be underestimated.

(5) Human Rights Treaty Approach

The Appellate Body should use human rights law as an interpretative tool to decide WTO cases. After all, the Appellate Body has stated that under the Vienna Convention on the Law of Treaties, non-WTO agreements can be used to interpret provisions of WTO accords. Certain cases the Appellate Body has adjudicated under GATT Article XX and *General Agreement on Trade and Services (GATS)* Article XIV suggest that human rights concerns can and should be considered overtly in deciding trade cases. Thus, for instance, human rights law might be used to decide a case about an origin-neutral law that bars imports of a particular good or service on the grounds of (1) public morals (*e.g.*, under Article XIV of *GATS*), or (2) the way in which the good is produced or service is provided (which allegedly offends human rights standards).

(6) Explicit Obligations Approach

There are explicit (or nearly explicit) human rights obligations already built into international trade law, and they should be enforced vigorously. The examples include:

- The GATT Article XX(a) exception for the protection of public morals, and the Article XX(e) exception for prison labor products, are closely related to human rights.

- The Kimberly Process waiver, under which signatories to the Kimberly Process that are WTO Members obtained a waiver from GATT—WTO obligations to allow them to respect the Process. They obtained the waiver at the December 2005 Hong Kong Ministerial Conference. The process is designed to ban imports of conflict diamonds (*i.e.*, diamonds from a war zone that are sold by an army or insurgency to finance its combat operations). Absent the waiver, a WTO Member following the ban might violate an obligation, like most-favored nation (MFN) treatment under GATT Article I:1 or the rule against quantitative restrictions under Article XI:1.

- The Doha Development Agenda (DDA), which recognizes that the *Agreement on Trade-Related Aspects of Intellectual Property Rights (TRIPs Agreement)* should be interpreted in a way to promote public health, and the amendment to Article 31 of, which allows poor countries lacking manufacturing capacity to import generic pharmaceuticals produced overseas under a compulsory license. Public health, in turn, is (or is closely related to) a human right.

*Suggestions for Further Research:*

Books:

1.   ABBOTT, FREDRICK M., ET AL., EDS., INTERNATIONAL TRADE AND HUMAN RIGHTS (2006).

2.   BOUCHER, DAVID, THE LIMITS OF ETHICS IN INTERNATIONAL RELATIONS — NATURAL LAW, NATURAL RIGHTS, AND HUMAN RIGHTS IN TRANSITION (2009).

3.   HARRISON, JAMES, THE HUMAN RIGHTS IMPACT OF THE WORLD TRADE ORGANIZATION (Hart Publishing, 2007).

4.   KINLEY, DAVID, CIVILIZING GLOBALISATION: HUMAN RIGHTS AND THE GLOBAL ECONOMY (2009). *See also* Kanstansin Dzehtsiarou, *Book Review*, 13 *Journal of International Economic Law* 521–524 (2010).

Articles:

1.   Alvarez, José E., *The WTO as Linkage Machine*, 96 AMERICAN JOURNAL OF INTERNATIONAL LAW issue 1, 146–158 (2002).

2.  Ashby, Timothy, *U.S. Certified Claims Against Cuba: Legal Reality and Likely Settlement Mechanisms*, 40 UNIVERSITY OF MIAMI INTER-AMERICAN LAW REVIEW 413–431 (2009).

3.  Choudhury, Barnali, *The Façade of Neutrality: Uncovering Gender Silences in International Trade*, 15 WILLIAM & MARY JOURNAL OF WOMEN & LAW 113–159 (2008).

4.  Choudhury, Barnali, *Exception Provisions as a Gateway to Incorporating Human Rights Issues into International Investment Agreements*, 49 COLUMBIA JOURNAL OF TRANSNATIONAL LAW 670–716 (2011).

5.  Coll, Alberto R., *Wielding Human Rights and Constitutional Procedure to Temper the Harms of Globalization: Costa Rica's Battle Over the Central American Free Trade Agreement*, 33 University of Pennsylvania Journal of International Law 461–561 (2011).

6.  Cottier, Thomas, *Trade and Human Rights: A Relationship to Discover*, 5 JOURNAL OF INTERNATIONAL ECONOMIC LAW issue 1, 111–132 (2002).

7.  Gao, Pengcheng, *Rethinking the Relationship between the WTO and International Human Rights*, 8 RICHMOND JOURNAL OF GLOBAL LAW & BUSINESS 397–426 (2009).

8.  Goldenziel, Jill I., *Sanctioning Faith: Religion, State, and U.S.—Cuban Relations*, 25 JOURNAL OF LAW & POLITICS 179–210 (2009).

9.  Harrington, Alexandra R., *Faceting the Future: The Need for and Proposal of the Adoption of a Kimberly Process-Styled Legitimacy Certification System for the Global Gemstone Market*, 18 TRANSNATIONAL LAW & CONTEMPORARY PROBLEMS 353–417 (2009).

10. Hilpold, Peter, *Human Rights and WTO Law: From Conflict to Coordination*, ARCHIV DES VÖLKERRECHTS, 45 Band, 4 Heft, (2007), S. 484–516.

11. Howse, Robert L. & Jared M. Genser, *Are EU Trade Sanctions on Burma Compatible with WTO Law?*, 29 MICHIGAN JOURNAL OF INTERNATIONAL LAW 165–196 (2008).

12. Jernudd, Sigrid Ursula, Comment, *China, State Secrets, and the Case of Xue Feng: The Implication for International Trade*, 12 CHICAGO JOURNAL OF INTERNATIONAL LAW 309–339 (2011).

13. Kopel, David P., Paul Gallant & Joanne D. Eisen, *The Arms Trade Treaty: Zimbabwe, the Democratic Republic of the Congo, and the Prospects for Arms Embargoes on Human Rights Violators*, 114 PENN STATE LAW REVIEW 891–953 (2010).

14. Likosky, Michael B., *Gender Arbitrage: Law, Luxury and Labor*, 23 WISCONSIN JOURNAL OF LAW, GENDER & SOCIETY 293–311 (2008).

15. Moon, Gillian, *Fair in Form, but Discriminatory in Operation — WTO Law's Discriminatory Effects on Human Rights in Developing Countries*, 14 JOURNAL OF INTERNATIONAL ECONOMIC LAW 553–592 (2011).

16. Murphy, Shannon K., Student Article, *Clouded Diamonds: Without Binding Arbitration and More Sophisticated Dispute Resolution Mechanisms,*

*the Kimberley Process Will Ultimately Fail in Ending Conflicts Fueled by Blood Diamonds*, 11 PEPPERDINE DISPUTE RESOLUTION LAW JOURNAL 207–228 (2011).

17. Panday, Agatha, *The Role of International Human Rights Law in WTO Dispute Settlement*, 16 UNIVERSITY OF CALIFORNIA DAVIS JOURNAL OF INTERNATIONAL LAW & POLICY 245–271 (2009) (Pritkin Prize Winner).

18. Powell, Stephen Joseph & Patricia Camino Pérez, *Global Laws, Local Lives: Impact of the New Regionalism on Human Rights Compliance*, 17 BUFFALO HUMAN RIGHTS LAW REVIEW 117–153 (2011).

19. Sharp, Dustin N., *Requiem for a Pipedream: Oil, the World Bank, and the Need for Human Rights Assessments*, 25 EMORY INTERNATIONAL LAW REVIEW 379–410 (2011).

20. Sheffer, Megan Wells, 2009–2010 V.B. Sutton Award: First Place, Note, *Bilateral Investment Treaties: A Friend or Foe to Human Rights?*, 39 DENVER JOURNAL OF INTERNATIONAL LAW & POLICY 483–521 (2011).

21. Simma, Honorable Bruno, *Foreign Investment Arbitration: A Place for Human Rights?*, 60 INTERNATIONAL & COMPARATIVE LAW QUARTERLY 573–596 (2011).

22. Smith, Tyler, Note, *Much Needed Reform in the Realm of Public Morals: A Proposed Addition to the GATT Article XX(a) "Public Morals" Framework Resulting from China — Audiovisual (China — Measures Affecting Trading Rights and Distribution Services for Certain Publications and Audiovisual Entertainment Products, WT/DS363/R (2009)*, 19 CARDOZO JOURNAL OF INTERNATIONAL & COMPARATIVE LAW 733–773 (2011).

23. Symposium, *The Cuban Embargo and Human Rights*, 4 INTERCULTURAL HUMAN RIGHTS LAW REVIEW 1–173 (2009).

24. *The Human Element: The Impact of Regional Trade Agreements on Human Rights and the Rule of Law*, 42 UNIVERSITY OF MIAMI INTER-AMERICAN LAW REVIEW 197–366 (2011).

25. Wexler, Lesley, *Regulating Resource Curses: Institutional Design and Evolution of the Blood Diamond Regime*, 31 CARDOZO LAW REVIEW 1717–1780 (2010).

26. Wilets, James D., *A Unified Theory of International Law, the State, and the Individual: Transnational Legal Harmonization in the Context of Economic and Legal Globalization*, 31 UNIVERSITY OF PENNSYLVANIA JOURNAL OF INTERNATIONAL ECONOMIC LAW 753–825 (2010).

27. Wright, Claire, *Censoring the Censors in the WTO: Reconciling the Communitarian and Human Rights Theories of International Law*, 3 JOURNAL OF INTERNATIONAL MEDIA & ENTERTAINMENT LAW 17–119 (2010).

## TRADE IN VALUE ADDED

The concept and attendant measurement of the contribution to the total value of a product made in a particular country.

Because of global supply (also called global value) production chains, many products are manufactured in multiple countries. That is, production of the finished good does not occur entirely in one country. Rather, certain aspects of the production occur in one country, other aspects in another country, and still other aspects in a third country. The entire chain of production is the global supply or global value chain. Put differently, producers engage in different tasks in different countries, sourcing inputs and intermediate goods based on a variety of considerations, not the least of which is cost.

Global supply chains challenge the traditional Balance of Payments (BOP) statistical approach whereby the entire value of a finished product is attributed to the last country of origin of that product. For example, suppose a t-shirt has cotton from Egypt worth $1, yarn (that is, cotton fabric) produced in Pakistan worth $5, a design from France worth $4, cutting and sewing in Bangladesh worth $2, and assembly in China worth $3. Suppose further that the shirt is imported into the United States at a cost of $20. While the typical Rule of Origin (ROO) would be yarn-forward for purposes of determining country of origin, which is not China, but rather Pakistan, for purposes of customs valuation, the entire value of the shirt, $15, would be attributed to China.

Thus, in trade balance statistics, $15 is attributed to China as an export to the United States. Yet, in fact, $15 of the value of the shirt was not added in China. Hence, this attribution overstates the true export position of China relative to the United States. That is, assuming China has a trade surplus, this attribution overstates the trade surplus. In turn, poor or ill-informed political decisions may result because of a failure to appreciate the true domestic value added to the finished good in each country in the global production chain.

The World Trade Organization (WTO) and Organization for Economic Cooperation and Development (OECD) have a "Made in the World" Initiative as of spring 2012 in which they have established a publicly accessible date base on international trade flows estimated in value added terms.

## TRADE — LABOR LINK

*See* ILO, Labor Side Agreement.

## TRADE REMEDIES

A generic term encompassing legal action taken against imported merchandise.

Action may be taken to rectify alleged unfair trade practices, principally dumping, illegal subsidies, or intellectual property right (IPR) infringement. Alternatively, remedial action may be taken against fairly traded foreign merchandise, as in the case of safeguards, such as the Escape Clause of GATT Article XIX and Section 201 of Untied States trade law.

As tariff and non-tariff barriers have generally been reduced through successive rounds of GATT—WTO negotiations, trade remedies remain as the critical policy tool to protect domestic industries. Not surprisingly, then, efforts to weaken trade remedy laws have met with strong resistance, including in the United States Congress. Indeed, at many opportunities in several trade rounds, the ability to use remedial actions has been expanded or strengthened. Likewise, WTO Appellate Body decisions that are read (or, perhaps, misread) to restrict the use of trade remedies in a manner not grounded on a relevant GATT—WTO text, meet with harsh criticism in some quarters, again including in the United States.

*Suggestions for Further Research:*

Books:

1.   BARRINGTON, LOUISE, ED., DUMPING — A COMPARATIVE APPROACH (1995).

2.   BOWMAN, GREGORY W., NICK COVELLI, DAVID A. GANTZ & IHN HO UHM, TRADE REMEDIES IN NORTH AMERICA (2009). *See also* the review of this book, Kevin C. Kennedy, *Book Review*, 19 MICHIGAN STATE JOURNAL OF INTERNATIONAL LAW 145–161.

3.   BOVARD, JAMES, THE FAIR TRADE FRAUD — HOW CONGRESS PILLAGES THE CONSUMER AND DECIMATES AMERICAN COMPETITIVENESS (1992).

4.   CZAKO, JUDITH, JOHANN HUMAN & JORGE MIRANDA, A HANDBOOK ON ANTI-DUMPING INVESTIGATIONS (2003).

5.   GEHRING, MARKUS W., JARROD HEPBURN & MARIE-CLAIRE CORDONIER SEGGER, WORLD TRADE LAW IN PRACTICE (2006).

6.   MASTEL, GREG, ANTIDUMPING LAWS AND THE U.S. ECONOMY (1998).

7.   MASTEL, GREG & ANDREW SZAMOSSZEGI, LEVELING THE PLAYING FIELD: ANTIDUMPING AND THE U.S. STEEL INDUSTRY (February 1999).

8.   STEWART, TERRENCE P. & AMY S. DWYER, WTO ANTIDUMPING AND SUBSIDY AGREEMENTS (1998).

9.   VAKERICS, THOMAS V., DAVID I. WILSON & KENNETH G. WEIGEL, ANTIDUMPING, COUNTERVAILING DUTY, AND OTHER TRADE ACTIONS (December 1987).

Book Chapters:

1.   Davey, William J., *Antidumping Laws in the GATT and the EC*, IN ANTIDUMPING LAW AND PRACTICE: A COMPARATIVE STUDY 295–301 at 296 (John H. Jackson & Edwin A. Vermulst eds., 1989).

2.   Horlick, Gary N., *The United States Antidumping System in* ANTIDUMPING LAW AND PRACTICE 160 (John H. Jackson & Edwin A. Vermulst, eds., 1989).

Articles:

1.   Bentes, Pablo M., et al., *International Trade*, 45 THE INTERNATIONAL LAWYER 79–94 (2011).

2.   Bernstein, Mark A. & Andrea C. Casson, *How Useful is 28 U.S.C. § 1292(d)(1) in Preventing Protracted Litigation and Uncorrectable harm to*

*Litigants in Trade Remedies Cases?*, 19 TULANE JOURNAL OF INTERNATIONAL & COMPARATIVE LAW 455–467 (2011).

3.   Cammarano, Dennis A., *Impacts of the Supreme Court Decision in Regal-Beloit: Exporting Import Litigation*, 85 TULANE LAW REVIEW 1207–1220 (2011).

4.   Horlick, Gary N. & Eleanor C. Shea, *The World Trade Organization Antidumping Agreement*, 29 JOURNAL OF WORLD TRADE 5, 26 (1995).

5.   Laroski Jr., Joseph A., & Valentin A. Povarchuk eds., *International Trade*, 45 THE INTERNATIONAL LAWYER 79–94 (spring 2011).

6.   Sebastian, Thomas, *World Trade Organization Remedies and the Assessment of Proportionality: Equivalence and Appropriateness*, 48 HARVARD INTERNATIONAL LAW JOURNAL 337–382 (2007).

7.   Stewart, Terence P., Amy S. Dwyer & Elizabeth M. Hein, *Trends in the Last Decade of Trade Remedy Decisions: Problems and Opportunities for the WTO Dispute Settlement System*, 24 ARIZONA JOURNAL OF INTERNATIONAL AND COMPARATIVE LAW 251–297 (2007).

8.   Voon, Tania, *Eliminating Trade Remedies from the WTO: Lessons from Regional Trade Agreements*, 59 INTERNATIONAL & COMPARATIVE LAW QUARTERLY 625–667 (2010).

9.   White Jr., Franklin E., *The Bell Atlantic Corp. v. Twombly Pleading Standard: Has Its Application Been Outcome Determinative in Court of International Trade Cases?*, 19 TULANE JOURNAL OF INTERNATIONAL & COMPARATIVE LAW 543–564 (2011).

10.  Yu, Yanning, *Trade Remedies: The Impact on the Proposed Australia — China Free Trade Agreement*, 18 MICHIGAN STATE JOURNAL OF INTERNATIONAL LAW 267–296 (2010).

Other Source:

1.   COMMITTEE ON WAYS AND MEANS, UNITED STATES HOUSE OF REPRESENTATIVES, OVERVIEW AND COMPILATION OF U.S. TRADE STATUTES, 109TH CONGRESS, 1ST SESSION parts I and II (Committee Print June 2005).

## TRADE ROUND

*See* GATT, MTN, WTO.

## TRADEMARK

A trademark is a form of intellectual property (IP).

A trademark is any word, name, phrase, symbol or design (or combination of words, names, symbols, or designs) used in the trade of a good to identify the source or origin of that good, and to distinguish the good from all other goods.[679] The Nike check symbol is an example. Ethiopia's attempt to trademark a number of coffee varieties originating within its borders, namely, Sidamo, Harar

---

[679] *See* BLACK'S LAW DICTIONARY 1530–33 (8th ed. 2004).

and Yirgacheffe, is another example.[680] In effect, the trademark is the commercial substitute for one's signature.

A trademark arises from either (1) actual use of the mark, or (2) filing an application to register the mark with the appropriate governmental authority stating that the applicant already has used, or intends to use, the mark in commerce. In the United States, the Patent and Trademark Office (PTO) is responsible for handling applications for, and registering, trademarks. Note, therefore, that because use can establish the right to a mark, it is not necessary to register the mark to have that right. Anyone claiming rights in a trademark can use the "TM" designation to alert the public to the claim. However, under American law, federal registration creates a presumption of ownership of a mark, and only as a result of this registration can the ® symbol be used. American trademark law is set forth in the *Trademark Act of 1946*, commonly known as the *"Lanham Act."*[681]

The first party who either uses the mark in commerce or files an application has the ultimate right to register the mark. A trademark can last indefinitely if the owner continues to use the mark to identify its goods. The term of federal registration is 10 years, with 10 year renewal terms.

The key criterion in determining whether to grant a registration request is whether there is a conflict between the proposed trademark and an existing trademark. Where there is a likelihood of confusion, *i.e.*, where consumers would be likely to associate the applicant's good with the good of another party that already has a trademark, the application will be denied. To find a conflict, the proposed and extant trademarks need not be identical, and the goods do not have to be identical. A second criterion used to determine whether to grant an application request is the nature of the trademark. If it is merely descriptive of the good, or a feature of the good, then an application for registration likely will be refused. A trademark must be affixed to the product actually sold in the market place to receive protection. Moreover, applications to register a geographic term or surname also may be refused. Finally, a trademark cannot consist of (1) immoral, deceptive, or scandalous material, (2) the name, picture, or signature of a living person (without that person's consent), or (3) the official flag of a country or sub-central government.

As with a copyright, patent, or service mark, it is up to a trademark owner to enforce the property right in the event of possible infringement. A prominent recent example of trademark infringement is Anheuser-Busch's improper use of the brand name "Budweiser" in Portugal, where a Czech firm, *Budejovicky Budvar*, had established prior rights to the name.[682]

---

[680] *See* Carey Lening, *Oxfam Urges Starbucks to Support Ethiopia in its Bid for Coffee Trademark Registration*, 23 INTERNATIONAL TRADE REPORTER (BNA) 1645–46 (16 November 2006).

[681] *See* 15 U.S.C. §§ 1051 *et seq.*

[682] *See* Arthur Rogers, *Anheuser-Busch Will Appeal European Court Ruling in Favor of Budejovicky Budvar*, 23 INTERNATIONAL TRADE REPORTER (BNA) 71 (1 January 2006).

*Suggestions for Further Research:*

Articles:

1.   Calboli, Irene, *Market Integration and (the Limits of) the First Sale Rule in North American and European Trademark Law*, 51 SANTA CLARA LAW REVIEW 1241–1282 (2011).

2.   Chow, Daniel, *Exhaustion of Trademarks and Parallel Imports in China*, 51 SANTA CLARA LAW REVIEW 1283–1309 (2011).

3.   Kaunelis, Brian S., Note, *Securing Global Trademark Exceptions: Why the United States Should Negotiate Mandatory Exceptions into Future International Bilateral Agreements*, 85 CHICAGO-KENT LAW REVIEW 1147–1170 (2010).

4.   Lau, Timothy, Kyle Niemi & Lanna Wu, Note, *Protecting Trademark Rights in China Through Litigation*, 47 STANFORD JOURNAL OF INTERNATIONAL LAW 441–451 (2011).

5.   Liu, Kung-Chung, Xinliang Tao & Eric Wang, *The Use and Misuse of Well-Known Marks Listings*, 40 IIC: INTERNATIONAL REVIEW OF INTELLECTUAL PROPERTY & COMPETITION LAW 685–697 (2009).

6.   McGill, Aileen M., *How China Succeeded in Protecting Olympic Trademarks and Why This Success May Not Generate Immediate Improvements in Intellectual Property Protection in China*, 9 LOYOLA LAW TECHNOLOGY ANNUAL 1–29 (2009–2010).

7.   Pava, Mindy, Comment, *The Cuban Conundrum: Proposing An International Trademark Registry for Well-Known Foreign Marks*, 25 EMORY INTERNATIONAL LAW REVIEW 631–679 (2011).

8.   Ramsey, Lisa P., *Free Speech and International Obligations to Protect Trademarks*, 35 YALE JOURNAL OF INTERNATIONAL LAW 405–467 (2010).

9.   Senftleben, Martin, *Trade Mark Protection — A Black Hole in the Intellectual Property Galaxy?*, 42 IIC: INTERNATIONAL REVIEW OF INTELLECTUAL PROPERTY & COMPETITION LAW 383–386 (2011).

10.   Tan, Ashley, Note, *GoogleAdWorks: Trademark Infringer or Trade Liberalizer?*, 16 MICHIGAN TELECOMMUNICATIONS & TECHNOLOGY LAW REVIEW 473–509 (2010).

11.   Vadi, Valentina, *Trademark Protection, Public Health, and International Investment Law: Strains and Paradoxes*, 20 EUROPEAN JOURNAL OF INTERNATIONAL LAW 773–803 (2009).

Other Sources:

1.   AMERICAN BAR ASSOCIATION SECTION OF INTELLECTUAL PROPERTY LAW, THE INTELLECTUAL PROPERTY HANDBOOK 1–140 (William A. Finkelstein & James R. Sims III eds., 2005).

2.   AMERICAN BAR ASSOCIATION SECTION OF INTELLECTUAL PROPERTY LAW, WHAT IS A TRADEMARK? (2006).

3.   Hill, Breann M., Comment, *Achieving Protection of the Well-Known Mark in China: Is there a Lasting Solution?*, 34 UNIVERSITY OF DAYTON LAW REVIEW 281–303 (2009).

# TRADE TREATY FOR THE PEOPLES

*See TCP.*

# TRAFFIC LIGHT SYSTEM

A term associated with the WTO *Agreement on Subsidies and Countervailing Measures (SCM Agreement)* to differentiate among Prohibited, Actionable, and Non-Actionable subsidies. Specifically, subsidies are categorized according to their trade distorting impact.

The term "Traffic Light," and the related terms "Red Light," "Yellow Light" and "Dark Amber," and "Green Light" subsidies, are not used expressly in the *SCM Agreement*, nor in United States countervailing duty (CVD) law.[683] However, they are in widespread use in the literature and among practicing international trade lawyers, and they are found throughout the legislative history to the United States law.[684]

Accordingly, Prohibited Subsidies are in the "Red Light" category, such as subsidies contingent on export performance or on the use of domestic rather than imported goods. Actionable Subsidies are those in the "Yellow Light" or "Dark Amber" categories, including subsidies covering operating losses sustained by an industry or an by a particular enterprise, other than a onetime measure that is non-recurrent. "Yellow Light" and "Dark Amber" are not synonymous categories; rather, they are distinguishable in two ways.

First, Dark Amber subsidies have associated with them a rebuttable presumption of a serious adverse trade affect. Second, if a subsidy scheme can be put in no other category, it qualifies for the Yellow Light category by default. Subsidies that provide government assistance to disadvantaged regions or for research and development are non-actionable and thus in the "Green Light" category.

Provisions for "Dark Amber" and "Green Light" subsidies lapsed in 2000, following a five year period set by Article 31 of the *SCM Agreement*. There has been no renewal of either category, though in the Doha Round proposals for renewal in some manner were floated.

Note that the term "Non-Actionable" is not exactly synonymous with the term "non-countervailable." Articles 4 and 7 of the *SCM Agreement* mention remedies available in WTO dispute resolution cases in addition to the imposition of a countervailing duty. These additional remedies include a WTO panel or Appellate Body recommendation that an offending subsidy be withdrawn,

---

[683] *See, e.g.*, WTO Appellate Body Report, *Canada — Certain Measures Affecting the Automotive Industry*, WT/DS139/AB/R and WT/DS142/AB/R (adopted 19 June 2000).

[684] *See* Uruguay Round Trade Agreement, Statement of Administrative Action, Agreement on Subsidies and Countervailing Measures, House of Representatives Document Number 316, 103d Congress, 2d Session, Vol. 1, 911-23 (27 September 1994).

and a recommendation that adverse effects caused by an offending subsidy be removed.

*Suggestions for Further Research:*

Article:

1.   Diamond, Richard, *Privatization and the Definition of Subsidy: A Critical Study of Appellate Body Texturalism*, 11 JOURNAL OF INTERNATIONAL ECONOMIC LAW 649–678 (2008).

## TRANSPARENCY

World Trade Organization (WTO) law defines "transparency" as the "degree to which trade policies and practices, and the process by which they are established, are open and predictable."[685]

Transparency in the WTO context has both internal and external dimensions. "Internal" transparency focuses on the WTO Member states and includes ". . . equal access to WTO negotiations and decision by all Members, and in particular the transparency of the WTO decision-making process to its Members."[686] In contrast, "external" transparency focuses on the access of the public, that is, citizens at large, to information regarding WTO procedures and decisions.[687]

Increased transparency in trade laws and policies reduces the likelihood of illegitimate government practices and increases the confidence of foreign purchasers seeking to do business in another country. Transparency facilitates, but is distinct from, participation. The latter concept suggests a relationship with the substance of trade law and policy formulation, and trade dispute adjudication. Transparency, by contrast, concerns the clarity of observation.

There are a number of measures that have been established to increase transparency in international trade law. For example, GATT Article X:1 requires all WTO Members to publish their trade regulations ". . . promptly in such a manner as to enable governments and traders to be acquainted with them."[688] The aim of such a notification obligation is to ". . . ensure transparency of and trust in the new international trade order."[689] However, GATT

---

[685] *See* WTO Glossary, *posted at* www.wto.org/english/thewto_e/glossary_e/glossary_e.htm.

[686] Friedl Weiss, *Transparency as an Element of Good Governance in the Practice of the EU and the WTO: Overview and Comparison*, 30 FORDHAM INTERNATIONAL LAW JOURNAL 1545, 1572 (May 2007).

[687] *Id.*

[688] Raj Bhala, *International Trade Law: Interdisciplinary Theory and Practice —Documents Supplement* 130 (LexisNexis 3rd ed. 2008).

[689] Friedl Weiss, *Transparency as an Element of Good Governance in the Practice of the EU and the WTO: Overview and Comparison*, 30 FORDHAM INTERNATIONAL LAW JOURNAL 1545, 1573 (May 2007).

Article X has never been enforced, despite being cited in dispute settlement proceedings and complaints, mostly due to violations of other, more substantive GATT or WTO obligations within those same complaints.[690] For example, in the *Indonesia — Autos case*, a WTO Panel examined Indonesia's domestic automobile industry in regard to inconsistencies with GATT Article I, III, and X.[691] The Panel found violations of Article I and/or Article II GATT and, therefore, did not examine the claims brought forth under Article X.[692]

A second example of transparency obligations is found in, Article III of the General Agreement on Trade in Services (GATS). The Article requires Members to promptly publish no later than by the time of entry into force, "all relevant measures of general application which pertain to or affect the operation of this Agreement. Where publication . . . is not practicable, such information shall be made otherwise publicly available."[693] Members are also required to publish international agreements to which they are a signatory that pertains to or affects trade in services.

Finally, the Trade Policy Review Mechanism (TPRM) in another measure aimed at enhancing transparency, by reviewing periodically the trade and related policies of the WTO Members made under Multilateral Trade Agreements or Plurilateral Trade Agreements.[694]

Further steps taken by the WTO to expand transparency include the establishment of a working group at the 1996 Ministerial Conference in Singapore to study transparency in members' government procurement practices. Ten years later, on 14 December 2006, the WTO established a provisional mechanism to increase transparency in regional trade agreements (RTAs). Under this mechanism, any Member entering into an RTA would need to provide early announcement of such an accord to all other Members and the WTO.

Despite the progress in expanding transparency, the WTO has come under considerable criticism for failing to practice the transparency it preaches. The criticism is in respect to two processes — negotiations, and dispute resolution. Critics charge that interested parties that are not sovereign states are closed

---

[690] Friedl Weiss, *Transparency as an Element of Good Governance in the Practice of the EU and the WTO: Overview and Comparison*, 30 FORDHAM INTERNATIONAL LAW JOURNAL 1545, 1573 (May 2007).

[691] Friedl Weiss, *Transparency as an Element of Good Governance in the Practice of the EU and the WTO: Overview and Comparison*, 30 FORDHAM INTERNATIONAL LAW JOURNAL 1545, 1574 (May 2007) (citing WTO Panel Report, *Indonesia — Certain Measures Affecting the Automobile Industry*, WT/DS54/R, WT/DS55/R,WT/DS59/R, WT/DS64/R (adopted 23 July 1998).

[692] Friedl Weiss, *Transparency as an Element of Good Governance in the Practice of the EU and the WTO: Overview and Comparison*, 30 FORDHAM INTERNATIONAL LAW JOURNAL 1545, 1573 (May 2007).

[693] Raj Bhala, *International Trade Law: Interdisciplinary Theory and Practice — Documents Supplement* 491 (LexisNexis 3rd ed. 2008).

[694] Raj Bhala, *International Trade Law: Interdisciplinary Theory and Practice — Documents Supplement* 587 (LexisNexis 3rd ed. 2008).

out of both processes. Negotiations occur behind closed doors, sometimes through rather secretive Green Room discussions, and oral arguments before a panel or the Appellate Body are not open to the public. WTO supporters point to innovations that allow for greater access to negotiations, such as meetings held by Secretariat officials (including the Director-General) and Members with non-governmental organizations (NGOs). Supporters also highlight the increase in public observation of selected dispute settlement proceedings.

The first public observation of an appeals hearing before the Appellate Body occurred in the dispute between the United States European Union (EU), and Canada in the *Beef Hormones* case.[695] The dispute concerned the continued United States and Canadian trade sanctions on EU imports in response to the EU exclusion of American and Canadian hormone-treated beef.[696] The parties themselves requested of the Appellate Body that the public be allowed to listen in on the hearing.[697] The hearing was broadcast live on closed-circuit television network, and observers could watch the telecast from designated rooms — all of which were in Geneva.[698]

While the *Beef Hormones* dispute was the first public hearing before the Appellate Body, there have previously been several open Panel proceedings. All of the previous open Panel hearings involved the United States, EU, and Canada, three countries that advocate increased transparency in WTO dispute proceedings.[699] In 2004, the United States and EU agreed to open panel proceedings in a dispute over alleged government subsidies to aircraft manufacturers — the *Boeing—Airbus* case.[700] Those hearings were taped, and broadcast after a one-day delay, to alleviate the risk of disclosure of confidential business information. Subsequently, the United States and European Union (EU) agreed to open to the public additional hearings, including:

(1) In November 2007, a compliance panel in the *Bananas*[701] dispute concerning the American complaint on EU banana import tariffs, namely, the EU maintains a preferential tariff that unfairly discriminates in favor of African,

---

[695] WTO Appellate Body Report, *EC Measures Concerning Meat and Meat Products (Hormones)*, WT/DS48/AB/R (adopted 13 February 1998).

[696] *See* Daniel Pruzin, *WTO Appellate Body to Open Hearings to Public in Dispute Over Beef Hormones*, 25 International Trade Reporter (BNA) 1061 (17 July 2008).

[697] *See* Daniel Pruzin, *WTO Appellate Body to Open Hearings to Public in Dispute Over Beef Hormones*, 25 International Trade Reporter (BNA) 1061 (17 July 2008).

[698] *See* Daniel Pruzin, *WTO Appellate Body to Open Hearings to Public in Dispute Over Beef Hormones*, 25 International Trade Reporter (BNA) 1061 (17 July 2008).

[699] *See* Daniel Pruzin, *WTO Appellate Body to Open Hearings to Public in Dispute Over Beef Hormones*, 25 International Trade Reporter (BNA) 1061 (17 July 2008).

[700] *See* European Communities and Certain Member States — Measures Affecting Trade in Large Civil Aircraft, WT/DS316/AB/R, WT/DS317/AB/R, WT/DS347/AB/R, WT/DS353/AB/R (1 June 2011)

[701] WTO Appellate Body Report, *European Communities — Regime for the Importation, Sale and Distribution of Bananas*, WT/DS27/AB/R (adopted 25 September 1997).

Caribbean, and Pacific (ACP) Members of the WTO, and against Latin American Members;[702] and

(2) In November 2007 and February 2008, panel hearings on the EU complaint against the American methodology of zeroing in 18 antidumping (AD) cases (covering original investigations, Administrative Reviews, and Sunset Reviews concerning anti-friction bearings, ball bearings, chemicals, pasta, and steel products from Belgium, Finland, France, Germany, Italy, Latvia, Netherlands, Spain, Sweden, and the United Kingdom), where zeroing led to the imposition of AD duties above the actual dumping margin.

In the *Bananas* case, the United States and EU agreed the public could be in the same room as the panelists and parties, thereby observing the proceedings live. In the *Zeroing* case, the two sides agreed to broadcast the hearing to members of the public who were seated in a separate room.

From these instances of increased transparency in Appellate Body and Panel hearings, four points can be inferred. First, the instances of transparency arise under the WTO *Understanding on Rules and Procedures Governing the Settlement of Disputes* (*Dispute Settlement Understanding*, or *DSU*).[703] The instances of transparency are not evidence of transparency in dispute settlement proceedings under a free trade agreement (FTA) or customs union (CU).

Second, all of the public hearings involve disputes that include the United States and EU. Furthermore, the United States and EU agreed that, in principle, *all* of their dispute settlement proceedings should be open to the public in some way. The basis for such agreement could be the potentially democracy-enhancing effect of transparency especially within the *DSU*. However, the same enthusiasm for transparency has not gathered interest from, for example, developing or Islamic countries, or more generally, countries that are not democracies.

Third, the nature and extent of the transparency tends to differ from case to case. There is no general rule of live broadcasting, but rather ad hoc arrangements depending on the needs and interests of the parties and underlying businesses engaged in a dispute.

Fourth, transparency does not exist for members of the public not physically present at the hearing (other than a possible delayed videotaping). Live webcasting, or telecasting beyond a closed circuit, is currently not implemented.

*Suggestions for Further Research:*

Book:

1.   HOLZNER, LESLIE, TRANSPARENCY IN GLOBAL CHANGE: THE VANGUARD OF THE OPEN SOCIETY (2006).

---

[702] *See* Daniel Pruzin, *U.S., EU Agree to Open Up Panel Hearings at WTO on Banana, Zeroing Complaints*, 24 International Trade Reporter (BNA) 1541 (1 November 2007).

[703] RAJ BHALA, INTERNATIONAL TRADE LAW: INTERDISCIPLINARY THEORY AND PRACTICE — DOCUMENTS SUPPLEMENT 559 (LexisNexis, 3rd ed. 2008).

Articles:

1. Ala'i, Padideh, *From the Periphery to the Center? The Evolving WTO Jurisprudence on Transparency and Good Governance*, 11 JOURNAL OF INTERNATIONAL ECONOMIC LAW 779–802 (2008).

2. Alvarez-,Jiménez Alberto, *Public Hearings at the WTO Appellate Body: The Next Step*, 59 INTERNATIONAL & COMPARATIVE LAW QUARTERLY 1079–1098 (2010).

3. Biukovic, Ljiljana, *Selective Adaptation of WTO Transparency Norms and Local Practices in China and Japan*, 11 JOURNAL OF INTERNATIONAL ECONOMIC LAW 803–825 (2008).

4. Carmody, Chi, *Metrics and the Measurement of International Trade: Some Thoughts on the Early Operation of the WTO RTA Transparency Mechanism*, 28 SAINT LOUIS UNIVERSITY PUBLIC LAW REVIEW 273–294 (2008).

5. Charnovitz, Steve, *Transparency and Participation in the World Trade Organization*, 56 RUTGERS LAW REVIEW 927–959 (2004).

6. Ehring, Lothar, *Public Access to the Dispute Settlement Hearings in the World Trade Organization*, 11 JOURNAL OF INTERNATIONAL ECONOMIC LAW 1021–1034 (2008).

7. Esty, Daniel C., *Good Governance at the World Trade Organization: Building a Foundation of Administrative Law*, 10 JOURNAL OF INTERNATIONAL ECONOMIC LAW 509–527 (2007).

8. Gathii, James Thuo, *Process and Substance in WTO Reform*, 56 RUTGERS LAW REVIEW 885–925 (2004).

9. Howse, Robert, *For a Citizen's Task Force on the Future of the World Trade Organization*, 56 RUTGERS LAW REVIEW 877–884 (2004).

10. Kaufmann, Christine & Rolf H. Weber, *The Role of Transparency in Financial Regulation*, 13 JOURNAL OF INTERNATIONAL ECONOMIC LAW 779–797 (2010).

11. Markell, David, *The Role of Spotlighting Procedures in Promoting Citizen Participation, Transparency, and Accountability*, 45 WAKE FOREST LAW REVIEW 425–467 (2010).

## TRANSSHIPMENT

Routing the shipment of a good through one or more third countries.

Transshipment may reflect fraudulent behavior by an exporter and/or importer. Specifically, the purpose of transshipment may be to disguise the true country of origin of a good, in order for that good to qualify for duty-free treatment under a free trade agreement (FTA), customs union (CU), or preferential trading arrangement (PTA). Transshipment also may involve affixing false country of origin labels.

## *TRIMS (TRIMS AGREEMENT)*

The WTO *Agreement on Trade-Related Investment Measures*, reached during the Uruguay Round.

The *TRIMs Agreement* is one of the Multilateral Agreements on Trade in Goods contained in Annex 1A to the *Agreement Establishing the World trade Organization (WTO Agreement)*.

## TRIPS (TRIPS AGREEMENT)

The WTO *Agreement on Trade-Related Aspects of Intellectual Property Rights*, reached during the Uruguay Round.

The *TRIPs Agreement* is set forth in Annex 1C to the *Agreement Establishing the World trade Organization (WTO Agreement)*. The *TRIPs Agreement* sets out minimum standards for the protection of different kinds of intellectual property (IP), most notably, patents, trademarks, copyrights, and semi-conductor mask works. Generally speaking, the Agreement borrows from, or piggy-backs on, the world's leading IP conventions, rather than establish entirely new or different protections.

In respect of minimum IP protections, on patents, for example, the *TRIPs Agreement* contains the following provisions —

- Article 28 —

In accordance with the basic definition of a patent, this Article explains what kind of property right a patent must confer. A patent must prevent anyone, without the consent of the patent holder, from using, offering for sale, selling, or importing, the product that is the subject of the patent, for a prescribed, limited period.

- Article 33—

This Article prescribes the minimum term of patent protection, which is 20 years. The period starts from the date of filing (the rule in virtually every WTO Member), not (as under United States patent law) from the date of invention.

- Article 27 —

This Article sets out exceptions — or flexibilities — to patent protection. A WTO Member may prevent patents on diagnostic, therapeutic, or surgical methods that are used to treat humans or animals.

- Article 31 —

This Article sets out conditions for invoking another exception to patent protection, namely, compulsory licensing.

Comparable provisions, appropriate for trademarks and copyrights, exist elsewhere in the *TRIPs Agreement*. Critically, the *Agreement* also contains provisions on intellectual property right (IPR) enforcement, which have been the subject (in 2006–2007) of complaints against China by a number of WTO Members.

The *TRIPs Agreement* also contains special and differential treatment for developing and least developed countries. Developing countries had until the end of 2005 to implement the *Agreement*. Least developed countries initially had until the end of 2010 — a 10, instead of five year long phase-in period. However, for least developed countries that had no pre-existing IP laws, the period for establishing minimum IP standards extends to 2016. Interestingly, unlike all other Uruguay Round agreements, which entered into force on 1 January 2005 for developed countries, the *TRIPs Agreement* took effect a year later, on 1 January 2006.

*Suggestions for Further Research:*

Books:

1.   ARUP, CHRISTOPHER, THE NEW WORLD TRADE ORGANIZATION AGREEMENTS — GLOBALIZING LAW THROUGH SERVICES AND INTELLECTUAL PROPERTY (2000).

2.   EL SAID, MOHAMMED, THE DEVELOPMENT OF INTELLECTUAL PROPERTY PROTECTION IN THE ARAB WORLD (2008).

3.   EL SAID, MOHAMMED K., PUBLIC HEALTH RELATED TRIPS-PLUS PROVISIONS IN BILATERAL TRADE AGREEMENTS: A POLICY GUIDE FOR NEGOTIATORS AND IMPLEMENTERS IN THE WHO EASTERN MEDITERRANEAN REGION (World Health Organization and International Centre for Trade and Sustainable Development, 2010).

4.   GERVAIS, DANIEL, THE TRIPs AGREEMENT: DRAFTING HISTORY AND ANALYSIS (3rd ed. 2008).

5.   MASKUS, KEITH E., ED., THE WTO, INTELLECTUAL PROPERTY RIGHTS AND THE KNOWLEDGE ECONOMY (2004).

Articles:

1.   Abbott, Frederick M. & Jerome H. Reichman, *The Doha Round's Public Health Legacy: Strategies for the Production and Diffusion of Patented Medicines Under the Amended TRIPs Provisions*, 10 JOURNAL OF INTERNATIONAL ECONOMIC LAW 921–987 (2007).

2.   Abrams, David S., *Did TRIPS Spur Innovation? An Analysis of Patent Duration and Incentives to Innovate*, 157 UNIVERSITY OF PENNSYLVANIA LAW REVIEW 1613–1647 (2009).

3.   Anderson, Alan M. & Bobak Razavi, *The Globalization of Intellectual Property Rights: TRIPs, BITs, and the Search for Uniform Protection*, 38 GEORGIA JOURNAL OF INTERNATIONAL & COMPARATIVE LAW 265–292 (2010)

4.   Athanasakou, Konstantina, *China IPR Enforcement: Hard as Steel or Soft as Tofu?, Bringing the Question to the WTO Under TRIPs*, 39 GEORGETOWN JOURNAL OF INTERNATIONAL LAW 217–245 (2007).

5.   Benoliel, Daniel & Bruno Salama, *Towards an Intellectual Property Bargaining Theory: The Post-WTO Era*, 32 UNIVERSITY OF PENNSYLVANIA JOURNAL OF INTERNATIONAL LAW 265–368 (2010).

6.   Berg, Thomas C., *Intellectual Property and the Preferential Option for the Poor*, 5 JOURNAL OF CATHOLIC SOCIAL THOUGHT number 1, 193–233 (2008).

7.   Brewster, Rachel, *The Surprising Benefits to Developing Countries of Linking International Trade and Intellectual Property*, 12 CHICAGO JOURNAL OF INTERNATIONAL LAW 1–54 (2011).

8. Cekola, James, Comment, *Outsourcing Drug Investigations to India: A Comment on U.S., Indian, and International Regulation of Clinical Trials in Cross-Border Pharmaceutical Research*, 28 NORTHWESTERN JOURNAL OF INTERNATIONAL LAW AND BUSINESS 125–145 (2007).

9. Chaves, Amanda, Note, *A Growing Headache: The Prevalence of International Counterfeit Pharmaceutical Trade in Developing African Nations*, 32 SUFFOLK TRANSNATIONAL LAW REVIEW 631–654 (2009).

10. Crowne, Emir Aly & Cristina Mihalceanu (Student), Innovators and Generics: *Proposals for Balancing Pharmaceutical Patent Protection and Public Access to Cheaper Medicines in Canada (Or, Don't NOC the Players, Hate the Regulations)*, 51 IDEA 693–723 (2011).

11. Cullen, Chad M., *Can TRIPs Live in Harmony with Islamic Law? An Investigation of the Relationship between Intellectual Property and Islamic Law*, 14 SMU SCIENCE & TECHNOLOGY LAW REVIEW 45–68 (2010).

12. Dziuba, Dawn, *TRIPs Article 31bis and H1N1 Swine Flu: Any Emergency or Urgency Exception to Patent Protection?*, 20 INDIANA INTERNATIONAL & COMPARATIVE LAW REVIEW 195–212 (2010).

13. El Said, Mohammed, *The Implementation Paradox: Intellectual Property Regulation in the Arab World*, 9 JOURNAL OF INTERNATIONAL TRADE LAW & POLICY issue 3, 221–235 (2010).

14. Fukunaga, Yoshifumi, *Enforcing TRIPs: Challenges of Adjudicating Minimum Standards Agreements*, 23 BERKELEY TECHNOLOGY LAW JOURNAL 867–931 (2008).

15. Geller, Paul Edward, *A German Approach to Fair Use: Test Cases for TRIPs Criteria for Copyright Limitations?*, 57 JOURNAL OF THE COPYRIGHT SOCIETY U.S.A. 553–571 (2010).

16. Gibbons, Llewellyn Joseph, *Do As I Say (Not As I Did): Punitive Intellectual Property Lessons for Emerging Economies from the Not So Long Past of the Developed Nations*, 64 SMU LAW REVIEW 923–973 (2011).

17. Gostin, Lawrence O., *A Proposal for a Framework Convention on Global Health*, 10 JOURNAL OF INTERNATIONAL ECONOMIC LAW 989–1008 (2007).

18. Haag, Darya, Student Article, *Time to Pay the Dues or Can Intellectual Property Rights Feel Safe with the WTO?*, 8 RICHMOND JOURNAL OF GLOBAL LAW & BUSINESS 427–452 (2009).

19. Harris, Donald, *TRIPs After Fifteen Years: Success or Failure, as Measured by Compulsory Licensing*, 18 JOURNAL OF INTELLECTUAL PROPERTY LAW 367–400 (2011).

20. Herren, Jaime B., Comment, *TRIPs and Pharmaceutical Patents: The Pharmaceutical Industry vs. the World*, 14 INTELLECTUAL PROPERTY LAW BULLETIN 43–65 (2009).

21. Judd, Patricia L., *Towards a TRIPs Truce*, 32 MICHIGAN JOURNAL OF INTERNATIONAL LAW 613–662 (2011).

22. Kapczynski, Amy, *Harmonization and Its Discontents: A Case Study of TRIPs Implementation in India's Pharmaceutical Sector*, 97 CALIFORNIA LAW REVIEW 1571–1649 (2009).

23. Kennedy, Matthew, *When Will the Protocol Amending the TRIPs Agreement Enter into Force?*, 13 JOURNAL OF INTERNATIONAL ECONOMIC LAW 459–473 (2010).

24. Lee, Edward, *Measuring TRIPs Compliance and Defiance: The WTO Compliance Scorecard*, 18 JOURNAL OF INTELLECTUAL PROPERTY LAW 401–445 (2011).

25. Liang, Mark, Comment, *A Three-Pronged Approach: How the United States Can Use WTO Disclosure Requirements to Curb Intellectual Property Infringement in China*, 11 CHICAGO JOURNAL OF INTERNATIONAL LAW 285–319 (2010).

26. Manne, Caroline, Note, *Pharmaceutical Patent Protection and TRIPs: The Countries That Cried Wolf and Why Defining "National Emergency" Will Save Them From Themselves*, 42 GEORGE WASHINGTON INTERNATIONAL LAW REVIEW 349–379 (2010).

27. McCabe, Justin, *Enforcing Intellectual Property Rights: A Methodology for Understanding the Enforcement Problem in China*, 8 PIERCE LAW REVIEW 1–29 (2009).

28. McCurdy, Lindsey, Comment, *Lessons from U.S. Trade with China: How to Use the World Trade Organization to Promote Public Health in Trade Relations with India*, 14 JOURNAL OF HEALTH CARE LAW & POLICY 405–430 (2011).

29. Mellino, Marla L., Note, *The TRIPS Agreement: Helping or Hurting Least Developed Countries Access to Essential Pharmaceuticals?*, 20 FORDHAM INTELLECTUAL PROPERTY, MEDIA & ENTERTAINMENT LAW JOURNAL 1349–1388 (2010).

30. Nesheiwat, Ferris K., *The Adoption of Intellectual Property Standards Beyond TRIPs — Is It a Misguided Legal and Economic Obsession by Developing Countries?*, 32 LOYOLA OF LOS ANGELES INTERNATIONAL & COMPARATIVE LAW REVIEW 361–394 (2010).

31. Osborn, Jacob R., *A View of the Hierarchy of Patent Rights, TRIPs, and the Canadian Patent Act*, 4 AKRON INTELLECTUAL PROPERTY JOURNAL 261–280 (2010).

32. Rajkumar, Rahul, *The Central American Free Trade Agreement: An End Run Around the Doha Declaration on TRIPs and Public Health*, 15 ALBANY LAW JOURNAL OF SCIENCE & TECHNOLOGY 433–475 (2005).

33. Rao, Sasha S., Student Article, *Improving Access To Patented Humanitarian Products via TRIPs: A Study of the Plumpy'nut Problem*, 15 MICHIGAN STATE UNIVERSITY JOURNAL OF MEDICINE & LAW 111–136 (2010).

34. Reichman, Jerome H., *Intellectual Property in the Twenty-First Century: Will the Developing Countries Lead or Follow?*, 46 HOUSTON LAW REVIEW 1115–1185 (2009).

35. Rogoyski, Robert S. & Kenneth Basin, *The Bloody Case that Started from a Parody: American Intellectual Property and the Pursuit of Democratic Ideals in Modern China*, 16 UCLA ENTERTAINMENT LAW REVIEW 237–264 (2009).

36. Ruse-Khan, Henning Grosse, *A Pirate of the Caribbean? The Attractions of Suspending TRIPs Obligations*, 11 JOURNAL OF INTERNATIONAL ECONOMIC LAW 313–364 (2008).

37. Ruse-Khan, Henning Grosse, *Time for a Paradigm Shift? Exploring Maximum Standards in International Intellectual Property Protection*, 1 TRADE, LAW AND DEVELOPMENT number 1, 56–102 (spring 2009).

38. Sanders, Anselm Kamperman, *Intellectual Property, Free Trade and Economic Development*, 23 GEORGIA STATE UNIVERSITY LAW REVIEW 893–911 (2007).

39. Sell, Susan K., *TRIPs Was Never Enough: Vertical Forum Shifting, FTAs, ACTA, and TPP*, 18 JOURNAL OF INTELLECTUAL PROPERTY 447–478 (2011).

40. Sen, Rajarshi & Adarsh Ramanujan, *Pruning the Evergreen Tree or Tripping Over TRIPS? — Section 3(d) of the Indian Patents Act, 1970*, 41 IIC: INTERNATIONAL REVIEW INTELLECTUAL PROPERTY & COMPETITION LAW 170–186 (2010).

41. Slater, Gabriel L., Note, *The Suspension of Intellectual Property Obligations under TRIPs: A Proposal for Retaliating Against Technology-Exporting Countries in the World Trade Organization*, 97 GEORGETOWN LAW JOURNAL 1365–1408 (2009).

42. Strauss, Debra M., *The Application of TRIPs to GMOs: International Intellectual Property Rights and Biotechnology*, 45 STANFORD JOURNAL OF INTERNATIONAL LAW 287–320 (2009).

43. Subramanian, Sujitha, *EU Obligation to the TRIPs Agreement: EU Microsoft Decision*, 21 EUROPEAN JOURNAL OF INTERNATIONAL LAW 997–1023 (2010).

44. Taubman, Antony, *Rethinking TRIPs: "Adequate Remuneration" for Non-Voluntary Patent Licensing*, 11 JOURNAL OF INTERNATIONAL ECONOMIC LAW 927–970 (2008).

45. Winter, Lauren, Note, *Cultivating Farmers' Rights: Reconciling Food Security, Indigenous Agriculture, and TRIPs*, 43 VANDERBILT JOURNAL OF TRANSNATIONAL LAW 223–254 (2010).

46. Yu, Peter K., *The Objectives and Principles of the TRIPS Agreement*, 46 HOUSTON LAW REVIEW 979–1046 (2009).

47. Yu, Peter K., *TRIPs and its Achilles' Heel*, 18 JOURNAL OF INTELLECTUAL PROPERTY LAW 479–531 (2011).

48. Yu, Peter K., *The TRIPS Enforcement Dispute*, 89 NEBRASKA LAW REVIEW 1046–1131 (2011).

49. Zhou, Weighou, Comment, *Pirates Behind an Ajar Door, and an Ocean Away: U.S.-China WTO Disputes, Intellectual Property, and Market Access*, 25 TEMPLE INTERNATIONAL & COMPARATIVE LAW JOURNAL 139–177 (2011).

## *TRIPS-PLUS*

*See* WTO-Plus.

## TRQ

*See* Tariff Rate Quota.

## TSA

Transportation Security Administration, a part of the Department of Homeland Security (DHS).

On 19 November 2001, TSA was formed under the auspices of the *Aviation and Transportation Security Act*.[704] TSA was originally organized under the United States Department of Transportation, but was moved to the DHS on 1 March 2003.

The aim of the TSA is to protect the transportation systems within the United States by conducting various security measures, such as airport security checkpoints, rail car and port container inspections, amongst others, to ensure freedom of movement for people and commerce. In all, the TSA oversees security for the highways, railroads, buses, mass transit systems, ports and 450 United States airports.

The TSA has been subject to considerable criticism since its inception.[705] Allegations against it have included employees sleeping on the job and stealing from passenger suitcases, as well as general incompetence.

## TSUS

Tariff Schedule of the United States.

The TSUS was replaced by the Harmonized Tariff Schedule (HTS) on 1 January 1989.[706]

## TWO VERSUS THREE DIMENSIONAL VIEW

The traditional debate in trade policy, not only in the United States, but also in most countries, is between free trade and protectionism. This debate arises in four contexts — (1) multilateral trade liberalization, (2) regional (or bilateral)

---

[704] *See Aviation and Transportation Security Act of 2001*, Public Law Number 107-71, 115 Stat. 597 (2001)

[705] *See Transportation Security Administration Has Made Progress in Managing a Federal Security Workforce and Ensuring Security at U.S. Airports, but Challenges Remain: Hearing before the Subcommittee on Federal Workforce and Agency Organization of the H. Comm. on Government Reform*, 109th Cong. GAO-06-597T (2006) (statement of Cathleen A. Berrick, Director, Homeland Security and Justice Issues).

[706] *See Floating Initial Negotiating Rights, Decision of 15 June 1988*, B.I.S.D. (35th Supp.) at 336 (1988).

trade liberalization, (3) enforcement of trade agreements, and (4) the role of developing countries. Arguably, however, the trade policy debate has moved beyond this old-fashioned divide between free trade and protectionism, and toward a new dynamic. The new dynamic is characterized as a discussion between a Two Dimensional View versus a Three Dimensional View of trade.

According to the Two Dimensional View, trade policy is about (1) reaching trade agreements that expand trade, and (2) putting into place Trade Adjustment Assistance (TAA) programs that take care of the "losers" from free trade. Advocates of this view, therefore, backed the fiscal stimulus bill passed by Congress in February 2009 and signed by President Barack H. Obama. The bill contained the most dramatic improvements in TAA since 1962, when that program was founded.

The Three Dimensional View accepts the two dimensions outlined above, but says there is one more indispensable element to trade policy. That element is getting trade agreements "right," which means ensuring that the deals to expand trade have provisions in them, or operate in a way, to increase living standards and promote environmental, labor, and human rights. In other words, the third dimension is to engage in outward transactions in a more intelligent way than in recent years.

Proponents of the Three Dimensional View argue that the third dimension is essential if trade liberalization is to be sustained, and if the expansion of trade is to be sustainable in respect of being mindful of environmental, labor, and human rights issues. While the classical absolute and comparative advantage theories, developed by Adam Smith and David Ricardo, respectively, state that net societal welfare increases with free trade, these theories do not address the environmental, labor, and human rights aspects of trade. Without focusing on those issues, there will be a backlash against trade — indeed, there already has been, with the anti-globalization movement that erupted in the 1990s. The third dimension puts trade policy on sounder footing than relying on just the first two dimensions.

# U

## UEMOA

West African Economic and Monetary Union (WAEMU).

"UEMOA" stands for the French appellation *Union Économique et Monétaire Ouest-Africaine*. UEMOA was established by the Treaty of Dakar, signed on 10 January 1994 by the heads of state of seven West African nations. On 2 May 1997, Guinea Bissau joined the group. Members of the UEMOA include:

- Benin
- Burkina Faso
- Côte d'Ivoire
- Guinea Bissau
- Mali
- Niger
- Senegal
- Togo

The principal aim of the UEMOA is to facilitate economic integration among countries that share a common currency, the CFA franc, which is pegged to the euro (€). The primary objectives of the group are:

- To increase the economic and financial competitiveness of its Member States through open market principles;

- To ensure the convergence of marcroeconomic performance and policy across Member States;

- To create a common market for the Member States to allow the free flow of people, goods, services and capital, as well as maintain a common external tariff (CET) and common trade policy;

- To promote the coordination of national sectoral policy and implementation in the areas of agriculture, environment, transport, infrastructure, telecommunications, human resources, energy, industry, mining and crafts; and

- To enact legislation across Member States concerning fiscal policies to provide for the smooth operation of the common market.

By early 2000, UEMOA adopted a customs union (CU) and a CET, and harmonized indirect taxation regulations. In 2002, the group signed a *Trade and Investment Framework Agreement* (TIFA) with the United States.[707] UEMOA houses a regional central bank in Dakar, as well as a regional development bank in Lomé.

---

[707] *See Agreement between the Government of the United States of America and the West African Economic and Monetary Union Concerning the Development of Trade and Investment Relations,* 12 April 2002, posted at www.ustr.gov/assets/Trade_Agreements/ TIFA/asset_upload_file935_7730.pdf.

*Suggestions for Further Research:*

Books:

1.   PONDI, MAKON MA, THE EUROPEAN UNION, THE COUNTRIES OF WEST AFRICA AND WAEMU (1997).

2.   UNION ÉCONOMIQUE ET MONÉTAIRE OUEST AFRICAINE, UN NOUVEAU MARCHÉ POUR VOS INVESTISSEMENTS: LE DÉVELOPPEMENT DE LA ZONE FRANC CFA (1998).

Article:

1.   Udombana, Nsongurua J., *How Should We Then Live? Globalization and the New Partnership for Africa's Development*, 20 BOSTON UNIVERSITY INTERNATIONAL LAW JOURNAL 293–354 (2002).

# UIGEA

*Unlawful Internet Gambling Enforcement Act of 2006*, codified at 31 U.S.C. § 5631 *et seq.*

A United States statute passed by Congress, signed by President George W. Bush, and implemented through regulations jointly promulgated by the Department of the Treasury and Board of Governors of the Federal Reserve System. The statute is linked to the adverse WTO Appellate Body decision of April 2005 in the case brought by Antigua and Baruba, *United States — Measures Affecting the Cross-Border Supply of Gambling and Betting Services*, WT/DS285/AB/R (adopted 20 April 2005). However, the *UIGEA* does not necessarily put the United States in compliance with that decision.

In its April 2005 Report, the Appellate Body agreed with the complainant that Internet gambling was included in the America's Schedule of Services Concessions (specifically, Section 10.D under "other recreational services") under the *General Agreement on Trade in Services* (*GATS*). The Appellate Body thereby rejected the American defense that the United States did not intend to include Internet gambling in the schedule, nor did it intend to allow cross-border supply of Internet gambling services. It also rejected the defense under *GATS* Article XIV, concerning public morality, for failure to satisfy the requirements of the *chapeau* of that Article. Thus, concluded the Appellate Body, American restrictions on Internet gambling violated the market access commitments.

In March 2007, a WTO Compliance Panel held the United States still had not brought its laws into conformity with the Appellate Body Report. On 4 May 2007, the United States said it would modify its Services Schedule to exclude any market access commitments on gambling services, thereby correcting what it called a "drafting 'oversight' made at the end of the Uruguay Round negotiations in 1993."[708] The United States contended that this change allowed

---

[708] *See* Alexei Alexis, *Bush Administration Finalizes Rules to Block Online Gambling Transactions*, 25 International Trade Reporter (BNA) 1651–1652 (20 November 2008).

it to comply with the WTO Appellate Body Report, and simultaneously retain its extant rules against cross-border service provision of Internet gambling.

To make the Schedule change in conformity with *GATS*, the United States had to pay compensation to affected WTO Members. It paid compensation in late 2007 and early 2008 to four of the five complainants — Canada, Costa Rica, EU, and Japan. However, Antigua pressed the case for retaliation, on the ground the United States failed to comply with the Appellate Body Report. Antigua sought the right to retaliate against the United States in the amount of $3.443 billion. In December 2007, a WTO arbitration panel granted Antigua the right to impose $21 million annually in trade sanctions against the United States.

The *UIGEA* (*inter alia*) defines "unlawful Internet gambling" Critics of the *UIGEA* said the legislation did not clearly or adequately define "unlawful Internet gambling." The joint Treasury–Federal Reserve regulations were designed partly to rectify that problem, for example, by encompassing the placement of a bet or wager using the Internet that is unlawful under any Federal or State law that applies in the jurisdiction in which the bet or wager is made or received. Those regulations also require financial firms to establish and implement policies and procedures "reasonably" designed to block payments to a business involved in unlawful internet gambling.[709] The regulations apply to a "designated payment system" that might be used to facilitate an unlawful payment, such as a credit card system.

## UMAU

The United Maghreb Arab Union, commonly known as the Arab Maghreb Union.

The UMAU was founded on 17 February 1989 in Marrakesh, Morocco. The UMAU aims to create a common market among Algeria, Libya, Mauritania, Morocco, and Tunisia. The UMAU is led by a rotating chairmanship, which is held in turn by each nation. The primary objectives of the UMAU include:

- Consolidation of the reports/ratios of fraternity which bind the Member States and their people; the realization of the progress and the wellbeing of their communities and the defense of their rights;

- The progressive realization of freedom of movement of the people of the services, the goods and the capital between the Member States; and

- Adoption of a common policy in all the fields. Out of economic material, the common policy aims at ensuring industrial development, agricultural, commercial and social of the Member States.

---

[709] *See* Alexei Alexis, *Bush Administration Finalizes Rules to Block Online Gambling Transactions*, 25 International Trade Reporter (BNA) 1651–1652 (20 November 2008).

In addition to these objectives, long term goals were set with the aim of achieving an economic union between the five member States. With the view of such a Union in mind, the following stages were fixed:

- First, the establishment of a free trade zone (FTZ) with the dismantling of tariff and non-tariff barriers between the Member States;

- Second, a customs union (CU) that institutes a common tariff schedule along with the adoption of a common external tariff;

- Last, a common market, which must be devoted to the integration of the Maghrebi economies with the elimination of all restrictions on goods and services between the Member States.

For most of the 1990s, the efforts were sidetracked, not only because of political instability in Algeria (a civil war between the government and Islamic extremists) and the international ostracism of Libya (owing to its sponsorship of terrorism), but also because of bickering between Algeria and Morocco. Those two countries are suspicious of each other because of a long-running dispute over the Western Sahara: Morocco claims sovereignty over the territory, and Algeria backs the Polisario Front, which demands independence.

However, the United States and European Union (EU) have urged Algeria and Tunisia to set aside their differences and form a common economic area that would attract foreign investment. In 1998, the United States launched an initiative to create an economic partnership with Algeria, Tunisia, and Morocco. The EU has its own Euro-Mediterranean initiative, which seeks to promote economic integration between the Arab world and the EU through modifications in the EU's rules of origin governing exports from Arab countries to the EU. Thus, Egypt, Jordan, Morocco, and Tunisia have signed association accords with the EU to bring them into an FTA with the EU — a Mediterranean free trade zone — by 2010. Algeria is negotiating a similar deal. Interestingly, some of these agreements, such as the deal with Tunisia, obligate the would-be EU partners to respect democratic principles.

*Suggestions for Further Research:*

Articles:

1.   Fakhri, Michael, *Images of the Arab World and Middle East — Debates about Development and Regional Integration*, 28 WISCONSIN INTERNATIONAL LAW JOURNAL 391–429 (2010).

2.   McKeon Jr., Robert W., *The Arab Maghreb Union: Possibilities of Maghrebine Political and Economic Unity, and Enhanced Trade in the World Community*, 10 DICKINSON JOURNAL OF INTERNATIONAL LAW 263, 302 (1992).

3.   Mohammedi, Omar T., *International Trade and Investment in Algeria: An Overview*, 18 MICHIGAN STATE JOURNAL OF INTERNATIONAL LAW 375–409 (2010).

4.   Sakmar, Susan L., *Globalization and Trade Initiatives in the Arab World: Historical Context, Progress to Date, and Prospects for the Future*, 42 UNIVERSITY OF SOUTH FLORIDA LAW REVIEW 919–939 (2008).

## U.N. (UN)

United Nations.

The U.N. is headquartered with its Secretariat in New York, and has offices and agencies around the world.

The U.N. was established with the signing of the United Nations Charter on 26 June 1945 in San Francisco. The U.N. was preceded by the League of Nations, which was established by the *Treaty of Versailles* shortly after the First World War but whose activities ceased after failing to prevent the outbreak of the Second World War. There are 192 U.N. members (as of December 2007), encompassing almost every recognized independent state. Five members hold permanent seats on the U.N. Security Council, a body which can veto any UN resolution: People's Republic of China; French Republic; Russian Federation; United Kingdom; and United States. Reform of the permanent membership of the Council is one among many controversies plaguing the U.N.

The general aim of the U.N. is to facilitate cooperation in international law, international security, economic development, human rights and environmental protection. In the traditional sense, the U.N. provides a forum to allow disputing parties to peacefully resolve conflicts and avoid war. However, the U.N. has evolved into one body that protects human rights and the environment; combats the spread of disease, such as AIDS; works to alleviate poverty by providing know-how and technical assistance to help increase food production; assists displaced persons; and many other humanitarian efforts. In these areas, the U.N. is one among several bodies, joined by sovereign states and non-governmental organizations (NGOs), and even high-net worth private investors and entertainers. Indeed, the efficacy of non-state actors — in terms of efficiency and contribution — coupled with high-profile scandals (such as corruption in the Iraq oil-for-food program after the first Gulf War) causes many observers to question whether the U.N. is increasingly marginalized.

The U.N. is divided into five organs:

- General Assembly
- Security Council
- Economic and Social Council (ECOSOC)
- Secretariat
- International Court of Justice (ICJ).

The General Assembly is the main deliberative organ of the U.N. and comprised of one representative from each Member State. Though most decisions are made by simple majority, a special two-thirds majority is required for decisions relating to peace, security, the accession of new members and budgetary matters. Unlike Security Council resolutions, however, all General Assembly decisions are non-binding. The Security Council has the responsibility, under the U.N. Charter, to maintain international peace and security. ECOSOC serves as the principal forum for discussing international economic and social issues. In particular, by its own account, ECOSOC is responsible for:

> . . . promoting higher standards of living, full employment and economic and social progress; identifying solutions to international economic, social and health problems; facilitating international cultural and educational cooperation; and encouraging universal respect for human rights and fundamental freedoms.

The Secretariat carries out the day-to-day work of the Organization. The Secretary General heads this organ, and ensures the policies promulgated by the other principal U.N. bodies are administered and followed. Lastly, the ICJ is the principal judicial organ of the U.N. The ICJ settles legal disputes between States and gives advisory opinions on legal questions referred to it by other U.N. organs and agencies.

The U.N. is linked to international trade law in several ways. In 1947, GATT established one of the first links. In particular, Article XXI(c) states GATT is in no way to prevent contracting parties from taking "any action in pursuance of its obligations under the United Nations Charter for the maintenance of international peace and security." That is, GATT mandates that it is not an "escape clause" for contracting parties that breach its obligations of maintaining international peace and security due under the U.N. Charter.

Two U.N. bodies, namely, United Nations Commission on International Trade Law (UNCITRAL) and United Nations Commission on Trade and Development (UNCTAD), continue to preserve the Organization's close ties with international trade law under the auspices of the WTO. In addition, several groups within the WTO have granted observer status to the U.N., including: General Council; Council for Trade in Goods; Council for Trade in Services; Council for Trade-Related Aspects of Intellectual Property Rights; Committee on Trade and Environment; Committee on Trade-Related Investment Measures; Committee on Trade in Financial Services; Working Party on GATS Rules; Working Party on Domestic Regulation; Working Group on Trade, Debt and Finance; and the Council for Trade in Services, Special Session. The U.N. was granted such status to enable it to follow discussions within the WTO on matters of direct interest to them.

*Suggestions for Further Research:*

Books:

1.  ALGER, CHADWICK F., UNITED NATIONS SYSTEM: A REFERENCE HANDBOOK (2006).

2.  FOMERAND, JACQUES, HISTORICAL DICTIONARY OF THE UNITED NATIONS (2007).

3.  SMITH, COURTNEY B., POLITICS AND PROCESS AT THE UNITED NATIONS: THE GLOBAL DANCE (2006).

4.  WEISS, THOMAS G., ET AL., THE UNITED NATIONS AND CHANGING WORLD POLITICS (2007).

## UNBALANCED GROWTH

*See* Big Push.

## UNCITRAL

United Nations Commission for International Trade Law.

Established on 17 December 1966 by the United Nations General Assembly Resolution 2205(XXI), UNCITRAL is the core legal body within the United Nations (U.N.) system in the field of international trade law and works towards the progressive harmonization and unification of the law of international trade.

That is, UNCITRAL aims to identify, reduce and remove disparities in national laws governing international trade that creates obstacles to the flow of trade. UNCITRAL has produced many leading commercial conventions, rules, and model laws, including the United Nations *Convention for Contracts on the International Sale of Goods (CISG)*, the United Nations *Model Law on International Credit Transfers*, and the UNCITRAL *Model Law on International Commercial Arbitration*. There are 60 members of UNCITRAL, elected to six year terms, all of whom are selected by the General Assembly so as to represent the world's various geographic regions and its principal economic and legal systems. The term of half of the Members expire every three years.

The appellation of UNCITRAL is rather a misnomer, reflecting an old, English-style meaning of "international trade law." That meaning concerns private contractual arrangements among importers, exporters, carriers, and other commercial players. This meaning is reflected in the work product of UNCITRAL, which covers (*inter alia*) contracts (sales), insolvency, payments, project finance, and secured transactions. In modern American legal parlance, this field goes by "international commercial law," as reflected in law school courses with such or similar titles. "UNCICRAL," with the second "C" standing for "Commercial," would be a more appropriate title for the body.

UNCITRAL carries out its work at annual sessions and is comprised of six Working Groups, which meet twice annually. These six Working Groups perform the substantive preparatory work on topics discussed by UNCITRAL. These groups focus on:

- Procurement
- International Arbitration and Conciliation
- Transport Law
- Electronic Commerce
- Insolvency Law
- Security Interests

UNCITRAL has been granted observer status to only one WTO working group, namely, the Working Group on Transparency in Government

Procurement. The purpose of this grant is to allow UNCITRAL to follow discussions within the WTO concerning a matter of direct interest to it.

*Suggestions for Further Research:*

Book:

1.  CARON, DAVID D., UNCITRAL ARBITRATION RULES: A COMMENTARY (2006).

## UNCTAD

United Nations Conference on Trade and Development.

The core legal body in the United Nations system dealing with issues at the intersection of international trade and development. Established in 1964, the principal aim of UNCTAD is to promote development in, and friendly integration of, poor countries into the world economy. UNCTAD looks to shape current thinking on the concept of "development" and ensure domestic policies and multilateral rules are mutually supportive and that they promote sustainable development.

The first Secretary-General of UNCTAD was the towering Argentine economist, Raúl Prebisch, who had served since 1948 as the head of the United Nations Economic Commission for Latin America (ECLA).

> Though undermined by the cold war, UNCTAD managed to negotiate the general[ized] system of preferences under which rich countries give tariff-free access to products from the developing world.[710]

Prebisch also coined the term "New International Economic Order" (NIEO).

UNCTAD performs three key functions to help operationalize its aim:

*   Serving as a forum for intergovernmental deliberations, aimed at consensus building;
*   Undertaking research, policy analysis and data collection for government representatives and experts; and
*   Providing technical assistance to developing countries.

Some developed nations, including the United States, tend to view UNCTAD as a highly politicized, anti-western entity. That view in part reflects the prominence of developing and least developed countries in UNCTAD, many positions it has taken on trade issues, and the economic philosophies of some of its Secretary Generals, including Raul Prebisch. Prebisch, the UNCTAD chief in the 1960s, called for a re-balancing of the global trading system to help improve the terms of trade (TOT) of developing countries, which he (with colleague Hans Singer) argued had deteriorated through free trade. From the 1960s to the 1980s, UNCTAD was closely related idea of a New International Economic Order (NIEO).

---

[710] *Misunderstood Moderate*, THE ECONOMIST, 7 March 2009, at 90 (reviewing Edgar J. Dorfman, *The Life and Times of Raúl Prebisch, 1901–1986* (2009)).

In 2003, the WTO and UNCTAD established a legal framework for technical assistance cooperation. The agreement between the organizations has a number of aims, including:

- Implementing the Doha Development Agenda (DDA).
- Enhancing cooperation to ensure trade serves development goals.
- Increasing assistance to facilitate the beneficial integration of developing and least developed countries into the global economy and multilateral trading system.

The WTO and UNCTAD agreed to cooperate for the purposes of technical cooperation, capacity-building, training, research and analysis as regards both specific inter-agency programs and such other specific areas as may be agreed between the two organizations.

Further, many agencies within the WTO have granted UNCTAD Observer Status for the purpose of permitting UNCTAD to follow discussions within the WTO that are in its general sphere or direct area of interest.[711] The specific WTO entities in which UNCTAD has Observer Status are:

- General Council
- Trade Policy Review Body (TPRB)
- Council for Trade in Goods
- Council for Trade in Services
- Council for Trade-Related Aspects of Intellectual Property Rights
- Committee on Anti-dumping Practices
- Committee on Subsidies and Countervailing Measures
- Committee on Safeguards; Committee on Agriculture
- Committee on Sanitary and Phytosanitary Measures
- Committee on Balance of Payment Restrictions
- Committee on Regional Trade Agreements
- Committee on Trade and Development
- Committee on Trade and the Environment
- Committee on Market Access
- Committee on Import Licensing
- Committee on Rules of Origin
- Committee on Technical Barriers to Trade
- Committee on Trade-Related Investment Measures
- Committee on Customs Valuation

---

[711] *See* Daniel Pruzin, *Developing Countries Reach Framework for Future "South-South" Tariff-Cutting Deal*, 23 INTERNATIONAL TRADE REPORTER (BNA) 1793–94 (21 December 2006).

- Committee on Trade in Financial Services
- Working Party on GATS Rules
- Working Party on Domestic Regulation
- Committee on Specific Commitments
- Working Group on Transparency in Government Procurement
- Working Group on the Relationship between Trade and Investment
- Working Group on the Interaction between Trade and Competition Policy
- Working Group on Trade, Debt and Finance
- Working Group on Trade and Transfer of Technology
- Committee on Government Procurement
- Committee on Trade in Civil Aircraft
- Committee of Participants on the Expansion of Trade in Information Technology Products.

*Suggestions for Further Research:*

Books:

1.   ,DOSMAN EDGAR J., THE LIFE AND TIMES OF RAÚL PREBISCH, 1901–1986 (2009).

Other Sources:

1.   UNITED NATIONS CONFERENCE ON TRADE AND DEVELOPMENT, A PARTNERSHIP FOR GROWTH AND DEVELOPMENT: UNCTAD (1998).

2.   UNITED NATIONS CONFERENCE ON TRADE AND DEVELOPMENT, BEYOND CONVENTIONAL WISDOM IN DEVELOPMENT POLICY: AN INTELLECTUAL HISTORY OF UNCTAD 1964–2004 (2004).

3.   UNITED NATIONS CONFERENCE ON TRADE AND DEVELOPMENT, BILATERAL TREATIES 1995–2006: TRENDS IN INVESTMENT RULEMAKING (2007).

## UNFREEDOM

*See* Development as Freedom.

## U.N. HDI (UN HDI)

United Nations Human Development Index.

*See* HDI

## UNICE

The French acronym for the Confederation of European Business, now called "Business Europe."

*See* Business Europe.

## UNIDROIT

*Institut International Pour L'Unification du Droit Prive*, which is the French acronym for the International Institute for the Unification of Private Law.

UNIDROIT was established as an auxiliary organ to the League of Nations in 1926. After the demise of the League, UNIDROIT was reestablished in 1940 under the auspices of a multilateral agreement, the UNIDROIT Statute. Membership of UNIDROIT is limited to States that accede to the UNIDROIT statute. They are:

- Argentina
- Australia
- Austria
- Belgium
- Bolivia
- Brazil
- Bulgaria
- Canada
- Chile
- China
- Colombia
- Croatia
- Cuba
- Cyprus
- Czech Republic
- Denmark
- Egypt
- Estonia
- Finland
- France
- Germany

- Greece
- Holy See
- Hungary
- India
- Iran
- Iraq
- Ireland
- Israel
- Italy
- Japan
- Latvia
- Lithuania
- Luxemburg
- Malta
- Mexico
- The Netherlands
- Nicaragua
- Nigeria
- Norway
- Pakistan
- Paraguay

- Poland
- Portugal
- Republic of Korea
- Republic of Serbia
- Romania
- Russian Federation
- San Marino
- Slovakia
- Slovenia
- South Africa
- Spain
- Sweden
- Switzerland
- Tunisia
- Turkey
- United Kingdom
- United States
- Uruguay
- Venezuela

Headquartered in Rome, the purpose of UNIDROIT is to study the needs and methods for modernizing, harmonizing, and coordinating private law, especially in the commercial arena, between states and groups of states. That focus has led to some overlap, even tension, between UNIDROIT and UNCITRAL. One example, in the area of international contract (sales) law, is the UNIDROIT *Principles of International Commercial Contracts* and UNCITRAL-drafted United Nations *Convention on Contracts for the International Sales of Goods* (*CISG*). Where there is not been overlap, UNIDROIT publishes a number of widely recognized legal guides. Some of the Institute's most recent publications include the UNIDROIT *Model Disclosure Franchise Law* and the UNIDROIT *Convention on International Financial Leasing*.

UNIDROIT boasts a three-tiered structure, comprised of a Secretariat, a Governing Council and a General Assembly. The Secretariat, led by the Secretary General, is the executive organ of UNIDROIT and is responsible for the day-to-day activities of the Institute. The Governing Council, headed by the President, oversees all policy aspects of the means by which the Institute's objectives are attained. The General Assembly is in charge of the fundamental operations of UNIDROIT and consists of one representative for each member state. That is, the General Assembly votes on the Institute's annual budget; approves the Work Program of the Institute every three years; and elects the General Council every five years.

.The Work Program is the instrument that details the various projects and aspirations of what UNIDROIT hopes to achieve in a given term, each of which lasts three years. From 2006–2008, the UNIDROIT Work Program included the preparation of uniform law instruments and exercising of depository functions in respect of:

- Principles on International Commercial Contracts.
- Model Law on Leasing.
- International Interests in Mobile Equipment.
- Transactions on Transnational and Connected Capital Markets.

*Suggestions for Further Research:*

Book:

1.  HEIDERMANN, MAREN, METHODOLOGY OF UNIFORM CONTRACT LAW: THE UNIDROIT PRINCIPLES IN INTERNATIONAL LEGAL DOCTRINE AND PRACTICE (2006).

Other Source:

1.  THE UNIDROIT PRINCIPLES IN PRACTICE: CASE LAW AND BIBLIOGRAPHY ON THE UNIDROIT PRINCIPLES OF INTERNATIONAL COMMERCIAL CONTRACTS (Michael Joachim Bonell ed., 2006).

## UNILAW

An electronic database maintained by UNIDROIT.

Established by the UNIDROIT Governing Council, this database consists of case law on uniform law conventions and other instruments. The database contains texts in both English and French.

*Suggestions for Further Research:*

Article:

1.  Bernardeau, Ludovich & Lena Peters, *The Computerization of the UNIDROIT Library and the Proposed Uniform Law Database*, 27 INTERNATIONAL JOURNAL OF LEGAL INFORMATION 202 (1999).

## UNILEX

An electronic database maintained by UNIDROIT.

The database consists of international case law and a bibliography relating to the United Nations (UN) *Convention on the International Sales of Goods (CISG)* and the UNIDROIT *Principles of International Commercial Contracts*. In addition to the full texts of both the *CISG* and the *Principles of International Commercial Contracts*, UNILEX contains detailed abstracts and full texts of the most important cases decided under both instruments by courts and arbitral tribunals.

*Suggestions for Further Research:*

Book:

1. BONELL, MICHAEL JOACHIM, ED., UNILEX: INTERNATIONAL CASE LAW & BIBLIOGRAPHY ON THE UN CONVENTION ON CONTRACTS FOR THE SALE OF INTERNATIONAL GOODS (1999).

## UPOV

*Union internationale pour la **p**rotection des **o**btentions **v**égétales*, or the International Union for the Protection of New Varieties of Plants.

The principal aim of UPOV is to afford intellectual property right (IPR) protection to newly developed varieties of plants. It is an intergovernmental organization headquartered in Geneva, Switzerland established by the *Convention for the Protection of New Varieties of Plants* on 2 December 1961 in Paris. The *Convention* came into force on 10 August 1968 after being ratified by the United Kingdom, the Netherlands, and Germany. The *Convention* has since been amended three times: in 1972, 1978 and 1991 to reflect technological advancements in plant breeding.

There are 64 Members of UPOV, as follows:

- Albania
- Argentina
- Australia
- Austria
- Azerbaijan
- Belarus
- Belgium
- Bolivia
- Brazil
- Bulgaria
- Canada
- Chile
- China

- Colombia
- Croatia
- Czech Republic
- Denmark
- Dominican Republic
- Ecuador
- Estonia
- European Community
- Finland
- France
- Germany

- Hungary
- Iceland
- Ireland
- Israel
- Italy
- Japan
- Jordan
- Kenya
- Kyrgyzstan
- Latvia
- Lithuania
- Mexico
- Moldova

- Morocco
- Netherlands
- New Zealand
- Nicaragua
- Norway
- Panama
- Paraguay
- Poland
- Portugal
- Republic of Korea
- Romania
- Russian Federation
- Singapore
- Slovakia
- Slovenia
- South Africa
- Spain
- Sweden
- Switzerland
- Trinidad & Tobago
- Tunisia
- Ukraine
- United Kingdom
- United States
- Uruguay
- Uzbekistan
- Vietnam

The *Convention* provides for a unique type of intellectual property (IP) protection specifically designed for the process of plant breeding. The UPOV affords this protection to encourage the development of new varieties of plants, for the benefit of society. To be sure, the UPOV System of plant variety protection is *sui generis*: UPOV classifies a plant on six different levels. In the broadest category, plants are classified by the "species" to which they belong. Accordingly, the plant can be further classified then by "genus," "family," "order," "class," and, in the narrowest sense, by "division."

For a plant breeder's rights to be acknowledged, the new variety must meet four criteria established by the UPOV. First, the new plant must be novel. That is, the plant must not have been previously marketed in a country where it seeks protection. Second, new plants must be distinct from other varieties. Third, plants must display homogeneity. Last, the trait or traits endemic to the new variety must be constant so that the plant remains true to type after repeated cycles of propagation.

UPOV has come under heavy criticism over the last decade, particularly from non-governmental organizations (NGOs) and developing countries. The contention is UPOV enables corporations from developed nations to extend their hegemonic control over the food supply of developing countries by forcing them to comply with IPRs. That is, NGOs and developing countries argue UPOV enables corporations to undo customs and traditions associated with thousands of years of farming.

*Suggestions for Further Research:*

Articles:

1.   Kennedy, Rónan, *International Conflicts Over Plant Genetic Resources: Future Developments?*, 20 TULANE ENVIRONMENTAL LAW JOURNAL 1 (2006).

2.   Nelson, Amy, *Is There an International Solution to Intellectual Property Protection for Plants?*, 37 GEORGE WASHINGTON INTERNATIONAL LAW REVIEW 997 (2005).

## U.S.C.

United States Code.

The official statutes of the United States, divided into titles based on subject area. Title 19 of the U.S.C. contains virtually all statutes relating to international trade. Certain statues are found in other titles, namely, for criminal matters in Title 18, and for the jurisdiction of the Court of International Trade (CIT) in Title 28.

## USDA

United States Department of Agriculture.

Established in 1862, the USDA is the Executive agency responsible promoting American agriculture interests both here and abroad. Working with the Food and Drug Administration (FDA), the USDA promotes food safety through inspection of American and imported food products. The agency also funds research into new agricultural technology, collects and distributes data on American and world agriculture trends, and assists in marketing agricultural commodities both in the United States and overseas. The USDA has a special commitment to rural areas to help them meet the unique needs of twenty first century life, based on their isolation from urban areas which may receive better services.

The USDA is headed by the Secretary of Agriculture, who is appointed by the President. It is a Cabinet-level appointment, meaning the Secretary is part of the President's Cabinet. The USDA has several agencies. Each agency is headed by an Under Secretary. The groups are defined on functional lines. In turn, each agency has divisions and sub-divisions, which in turn, are headed by administrators. Among the most prominent agencies and divisions are the following:

- Natural Resources and Environment
  Forest Service
  Natural Resources Conservation Service
- Farm and Foreign Agricultural Services
  Farm Service Agency
  Foreign Agricultural Service
  Risk Management Agency
- Rural Development
  Rural Utilities Service
  Rural Housing Service
  Rural Business Cooperative Service
- Food, Nutrition and Consumer Services
  Food and Nutrition Service
  Center for nutrition Policy and Promotion

- Food Safety

    Food Safety Inspection Service

- Research Education and Economics

    Agricultural Research Service

    Cooperative State Research, Education, and Extension Service

    Economic Research Service

    National Agricultural Library

    National Agricultural Statistics Service

- Marking and Regulatory Programs

    Agricultural Marketing Service

    Animal and Plant Health Inspection Service

    Grain Inspection, Packers and Stockyards Administration

In addition, the USDA has an Office of General Counsel.

*Suggestions for Further Research:*

Articles:

1.  Liu, Chenglin, *Is "USDA ORGANIC" a Seal of Deceit?: The Pitfalls of USDA Certified Organics Produced in the United States, China, and Beyond*, 47 STANFORD JOURNAL OF INTERNATIONAL LAW 333–378 (2011).

2.  Pape, Eileen Starbranch, Comment, *A Flawed Inspection System: Improvements to Current USDA Inspection Practices Needed to Ensure Safer Beef Products*, 48 HOUSTON LAW REVIEW 421–455 (2011).

## U.S. — INDIA ECONOMIC AND FINANCIAL PARTNERSHIP

A bilateral body designed to improve relations on issues pertaining to the financial sector, infrastructure, and macroeconomics.

In late 2009, to coincide with a State Visit to the White House by Indian Prime Minister Manmohan Singh, the United States and India agreed to create an Economic and Financial Partnership. The first meeting of the cooperative venture was held in April 2010. Issues discussed by the key participants, American Treasury Secretary Timothy Geithner and Indian Finance Minister Pranab Mukherjee, included deepening capital markets to improve growth, financial regulatory reforms, increasing infrastructure finance, and macroeconomic policies to generate growth in incomes and jobs.

## U.S. — INDIA TRADE POLICY FORUM

A bilateral body designed to discuss trade and investment issues between the United States and India.

The two countries established the Forum on 18 July 2005, and the inaugural session occurred on 12 November of the same year. The Forum focuses primarily on bilateral trade between the two countries, which totaled nearly

U.S. $30 billion in 2005 ($7.96 billion in American exports to India whereas India's exports to the United States reached $18.8). The Forum assists in bolstering transparency in government measures affecting trade; eliminating tariff and non-tariff barriers (NTBs); harmonizing customs procedures; subsidies; intellectual property rights (IPRs); sanitary and phytosanitary (SPS) measures; government procurement; and services.[712]

To facilitate development in these areas, the Forum agreed to a number of measures in June 2006, hoping to boost trade between India and the United States to about $60 billion within three years.[713] As regards IPRs, the Forum agreed to strengthen the Indian Patent Office through sharing of experiences and technical cooperation in all fields, and to make patents systems more effective. The Forum also agreed to help the India Trademark Registry fulfill the requirements of the Madrid Protocol. India also agreed to consider measures to strengthen disclosure laws regarding certain agricultural chemicals and pharmaceuticals. Lastly, the Forum agreed to familiarize enforcement agencies in both countries about IPR laws, as well a systems that determine the best practices to enforce those rights, particularly against counterfeiting and piracy of intellectual property (IP).

In April 2007, the Forum helped liberalize trade in agriculture, resulting in American almond exports to India, and Indian mangoes entering the American market for the first time in 18 years. Generally, through the Forum the United States has offered technical assistance and training to Indian agricultural scientists through a program called "AKI."

The Forum also works to improve the climate for foreign direct investment (FDI) in India. These efforts were manifested when the Forum initiated a Bilateral Investment Program in 2006, whereby infrastructure investment opportunities were identified, including power, roads, airports and ports. India also announced in April 2007 it would allow up to 74 percent ownership in local telecommunication firms.

## USIPER

Office of the United States Intellectual Property Enforcement Representative.

The USIPER was created by the *Prioritizing Resources and Organization for Intellectual Property Act of 2008* (*PRO-IP Act*), Pub. L. No. 110-403, 122 Stat. 4256, codified in scattered sections of 15, 17, 18, 19, and 42 U.S.C. This *Act* increased anti-piracy enforcement tools in the Executive branch through the creation of the USIPER, appointment by the President (subject to Senate confirmation) of an Intellectual Property Enforcement Coordinator, and civil and

---

[712] *See* Gary G. Yerkey, *U.S., India Hold High-Level Talks on Boosting Bilateral Trade and Investment*, 23 INTERNATIONAL TRADE REPORTER (BNA) 277 (23 February 2006).

[713] *See* Rossella Brevetti, *U.S.-India Trade Meeting Could Produce Results in Agriculture, Legal Services Areas*, 23 INTERNATIONAL TRADE REPORTER (BNA) 949–50 (22 June 2006).

criminal penalties for copyright and trademark infringement. The Coordinator must draft a joint strategic plan to combat infringement and counterfeiting, including through cooperation with foreign governments. The Coordinator also must work with foreign governments.

## U.S. — JAPAN ECONOMIC HARMONIZATION INITIATIVE

A program established in 2011 between the United States and Japan to harmonize their respective regulatory measures and thereby facilitate bilateral trade.

## USP

United States Price.

The generic term used in pre-Uruguay Round American antidumping (AD) law to refer to either Purchase Price (PP) or Exporters Sales Price (ESP). Under former Section 353.41(a) of 19 C.F.R, United States Price was determined by "sales, or in the absence of sales, likely sales."[714] The use of "likely sales" to calculate United States Price occurred only when no actual sales were available. "Likely sales" included unaccepted tender bids, whether rejected or not yet accepted, to the extent the bids constituted irrevocable offers. The term "United States Price" was eliminated as of 1 January 1995 and has no analog in post-Uruguay Round law.

*Suggestions for Further Research:*

Books:

1.  BRYAN, GREYSON, TAXING UNFAIR INTERNATIONAL TRADE PRACTICES: A STUDY OF U.S. ANTIDUMPING AND COUNTERVAILING DUTY LAWS (1980).

2.  JACKSON, JOHN H. & EDWIN VERMULST EDS., ANTIDUMPING LAW AND PRACTICE: A COMPARATIVE STUDY (1989).

Article:

1.  Hendrick, James Pomeroy, *The United States Antidumping Act*, 58 AMERICAN JOURNAL OF INTERNATIONAL LAW 914–34 (1964).

## USTR

The United States Trade Representative, formerly the Special Trade Representative (STR), with its head office in Washington, D.C., and an office in Geneva, Switzerland.

The USTR is responsible for developing and coordinating United States international trade, commodity and direct investment policy and is part of the Executive Office of the President. The USTR also resolves trade-related disagreements and assists the President in making decisions on trade policy.

---

[714] *See generally* 19 C.F.R. § 353 (28 March 1989) (on AD duties).

In particular, the USTR provides trade policy and negotiating expertise in areas including (as the USTR itself describes on its website (www.ustr.gov)):

- Bilateral, regional and multilateral trade and investment issues;

- Expansion of market access for American goods and services;

- International commodity agreements;

- Negotiations affecting United States import policies;

- Oversight of the Generalized System of Preferences (GSP) and Section 301 complaints against foreign unfair trade practices, as well as Section 1377, Section 337 and import relief cases under Section 201;

- Trade, commodity, and direct investment matters managed by international institutions such as the Organization for Economic Cooperation and Development (OECD) and the United Nations Conference on Trade and Development (UNCTAD);

- Trade-related intellectual property protection issues; and

- World Trade Organization (WTO) issues.

Indeed, the *1994 Uruguay Round Agreements Act* specifies the USTR is the chief negotiator for all discussions under the auspices of the WTO. In 2000, the *Trade and Development Act* granted the additional titles of Chief Agricultural Negotiator and Assistant United States Trade Representative for African Affairs to the USTR. Other duties of the USTR include the Vice Chairmanship of the Overseas Private Investment Corporation (OPIC), a non-voting membership to the Export-Import Bank, and a membership to the National Advisory Council on International Monetary and Financial Policies.

The Figure below summarizes the organizational structure of the USTR. The Office of the USTR is led by the United States Trade Representative, who is appointed by the President, serves in his Cabinet, and holds the rank of Ambassador. The Trade Representative is the President's principal trade advisor, negotiator and spokesperson on trade-related issues.

**FIGURE:**

**ORGANIZATION OF THE USTR**

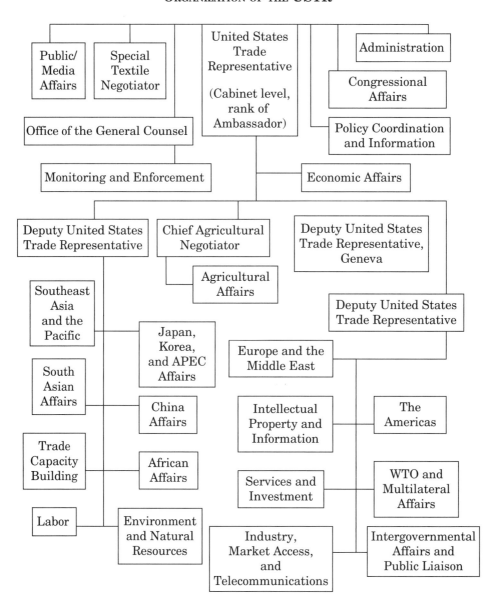

In 2006, Susan C. Schwab was appointed by President George W. Bush as the Trade Representative. Previous Trade Representatives are set out in the Table below, beginning with the first STR:

**TABLE:**
**AMERICA'S TRADE REPRESENTATIVES**[715]
*(reverse chronological order)*

| United States Trade Representative (or STR prior to 1979) | Term | Appointed By (President): |
|---|---|---|
| Ron Kirk | 2009– | Barack H. Obama |
| Susan Schwab | 2006–2009 | George W. Bush |
| Rob Portman | 2005–2006 | George W. Bush |
| Robert B. Zoellick | 2001–2005 | George W. Bush |
| Charlene Barshefsky | 1997–2000 | William J. Clinton |
| Michael Kantor | 1993–1996 | William J. Clinton |
| Carla A. Hills | 1989–1993 | George H. W. Bush |
| Clayton K. Yeutter | 1985–1989 | Ronald W. Reagan |
| William E. Brock III | 1981–1985 | Ronald W. Reagan |
| Reubin O'Donovan Askew | 1979–1981 | Jimmy Carter |
| Robert S. Strauss | 1977–1979 | Jimmy Carter |
| Frederick B. Dent | 1975–1977 | Gerald R. Ford |
| William D. Eberle | 1971–1975 | Richard M. Nixon |
| Carl J. Gilbert | 1969–1971 | Richard M. Nixon |
| William M. Roth | 1967–1969 | Lyndon B. Johnson |
| Christian A. Herter | 1962–1966 | John F. Kennedy |

The USTR coordinates trade policy under the auspices of three agencies, each of which operates as a sub-cabinet level mechanism to develop and explicate position of the United States government on international trade and trade-related matters:

- Trade Policy Review Group (TPRG).
- Trade Policy Staff Committee (TPSC)
- National Economic Council (NEC).

The TPSC runs the day-to-day activities of 90 subcommittees that focus on particular issues pertinent to international trade. If an agreement is not reached at the subcommittee level under the TPSC, then the TPRG takes up the controversy. The NEC is chaired by the President. Memoranda from the TPRG, as well as other important or controversial trade-related matters, are considered by the NEC Deputies' committee.

---

[715] Modified from United States Trade Representative, 1962-Present, *posted at* www.ustr.gov/Who_We_Are/United_States_Trade_Representatives,_1962_-_Present.html.

The USTR also maintains a close working relationship with a number of executive agencies, including the Department of Commerce (DOC), Department of Labor (DOL), Department of Agriculture (USDA), Environmental Protection Agency (EPA), and Small Business Administration (SBA). Each relationship helps foster concrete, cogent American government positions on international trade.

The USTR has come under scrutiny lately for its inability to maximize human capital tools and minimize retention challenges.[716] More generally, at least five features of the USTR are noteworthy.

First, the USTR has a wide area of responsibility. Second, despite that width, both its budget and the size of its staff are relatively small. Third, foreign governments do not always appreciate the negotiating style and tactics of the USTR. Critics charge the USTR with — put bluntly — a combination of ignorance of local conditions and problems in foreign countries coupled with arrogance. Fourth, in discharging its responsibilities, the USTR articulates clearly the theory and rhetoric of free trade and comparative advantage, but — again, critics charge — with some hypocrisy. That is because of an overwhelming focus, in some trade negotiations, on market access into foreign countries. Fifth, the USTR tends to spend at least as much time negotiating with the United States Congress as it does with foreign countries. That fact alone helps account for some of its behavior that foreign governments target for criticism. That is, the USTR literally is often in the middle position, between American legislators and foreign governments.

A sixth feature is perhaps the most significant in the post-9/11 world. The power of the USTR, as a practical matter, may have been relegated to that of national security officials. Major — and even minor — trade deals tend increasingly to be viewed through the lens of national security. It is difficult, for example, to justify free trade agreements with countries like Bahrain for their broad commercial significance. Consequently, the ability of the USTR to act autonomously, and report directly to the President, seems to have been circumscribed. The post-9/11 reality appears to be the USTR must operate through national security channels, in the White House, Department of Defense, and so forth.

*Suggestions for Further Research:*

Books:

1.   DESTLER, IRVING M., AMERICAN TRADE POLITICS (4th ed. June 2005).

2.   DEVEREAUX, CHARAN, ROBERT Z. LAWRENCE & MICHAEL D. WATKINS, CASE STUDIES IN TRADE NEGOTIATION, VOLUME 1: MAKING THE RULES, AND VOLUME 2: RESOLVING DISPUTES (Washington, D.C.: Peterson Institute for International Economics, 2008). *See also* the review of these books by Larry Crump & John S. Odell, *Analyzing Complex U.S. Trade Negotiations*, 24 NEGOTIATION JOURNAL 355–369 (2008).

---

[716] *See* Rossella Brevetti, *GAO Urges USTR to Better Use Tools for Human Capital to Manage Challenges*, 23 INTERNATIONAL TRADE REPORTER (BNA) 37 (12 January 2006).

3. DRYDEN, STEVE, TRADE WARRIORS: USTR AND THE AMERICAN CRUSADE FOR FREE TRADE 33–59 (1995).

4. LOVETT, WILLIAM A., ET AL., U.S. TRADE POLICY: HISTORY, THEORY, AND THE WTO (2004).

## UNASUR

Union of South American Nations, a group of 12 countries in South America that seeks to boost South — South trade, that is, trade with other developing and emerging countries. "UNASUR" reflects the Spanish name for the group.

## UNBOUND TARIFF

A tariff not subject to a binding commitment under GATT Article II:1(b).

An unbound tariff means there is no legal upper boundary constraint on the applied tariff. Effectively, it refers to a category of merchandise in the Harmonized Tariff Schedule of a particular country for which that country has not agreed to a maximum ceiling above which the applied duty cannot rise.

During the Doha Round, in the July 2007 draft modalities text on non-agriculture market access (NAMA) proposed by negotiating chairman Don Stephenson (Canada's WTO Ambassador), developing countries should bind at least 90 percent of their tariff lines. That is, in respect of product coverage — the percentage of tariff lines covered by a binding commitment, the modalities text said developing countries would have to ensure they bound at least 90 percent of their lines. Further, they would have to limit their average bound rate to 28.5 percent. Many Sub-Saharan African countries, along with Sri Lanka, rejected binding any more than 70 percent of their tariff lines, and ruled out a 28.5 percent average duty rate cap.

# V

## VALIDATION (OR VALIDATION SELECTION PROCEDURE)

A term arising in connection with the United States *Customs Trade Partnership Against Terrorism* (*C-TPAT*).

"Validation" refers to the process by which the United States Customs and Border Protection (CBP) meets with company representatives, and visits domestic and foreign sites to verify company statements about security. The principal aim of validation is to ensure the *C-TPAT* security profile of a selected company is reliable, accurate, and effective. In addition, validation helps a company share "best practices" with similarly situated businesses, as well as identifies potential vulnerabilities. Most validations last no more than 10 business days. A company is selected for validation based on the risk in its import supply chain. That is, a company is selected for validation based on risk management principles. In turn, risk is assessed on factors such as security-related anomalies, strategic threats posed in particular geographic regions, import volumes, or as a matter of routine oversight. All companies selected for validation are given 30 days notice.

At the conclusion of a validation, each company is briefed on the findings of the validation. If the findings are satisfactory, then the company's benefits may increase under *C-TPAT*. But, if the findings reveal weaknesses in the security policy of a company, then *C-TPAT* benefits may be suspended or removed until corrective action is implemented.

The *C-TPAT* has considered using private contractors to carry out validations.[717] Various labor unions have resisted this kind of privatization.

As of mid-2006, over 10,000 companies have joined *C-TPAT*. Of the participants, over 6,000 have been certified as having implemented *C-TPAT* security criteria through validation.

*Suggestions for Further Research:*

Article:

1. Ferrara, Jennifer M., *Regulation Consolidation: How Recent United States Customs and Securities and Exchange Commission Pronouncements Will Cause a Sea of Change*, 30 TULANE MARITIME LAW JOURNAL 335 (2006).

## VALUE ADDED

The additional value of a good created at a particular stage in production or distribution.

---

[717] See *Union Criticized Any Privitizing of C-TPAT Validations*, 23 INTERNATIONAL TRADE REPORTER (BNA) 527 (6 April 2006); Rosella Brevetti, *Ways and Means Subcommittee Criticizes CBP for Import Specialist Staffing Shortfalls*, 23 INTERNATIONAL TRADE REPORTER (BNA) 1129–30 (27 July 2006).

That is, the value added to a particular good is the sale price of a good less the value of all inputs, including rents, wages and other charges associated with the manufacture or distribution of that good. In essence, it is the measure of profit earned on each product or products. Value added is used as the basis for a value added tax (VAT), and also for many non-preferential and preferential rules of origin

*Suggestions for Further Research:*

Book:

1. AJAMI, RIAD A. & MARCA MARIE BEAR EDS., THE GLOBAL ENTERPRISE: ENTREPRENEURSHIP AND VALUE CREATION (2007).

## VARIABLE LEVY

A tax on an imported article whose amount changes with changes in the price of that article.

The purpose of a variable levy is to ensure merchandise is not admitted into the importing country at below a set price level, and thereby maintain domestic prices at a target level. Thus, the level of protection afforded generally to domestic producers always remains the same.

Prior to the 1992 MacSharry Reform of the Common Agricultural Policy (CAP), the European Community (EC) commonly used variable levy to protect agricultural producers. The variable levy was the difference between the lower world market price for a farm product and a higher internal (domestic) target price. The goal of the levy was to keep the internal price above the world market price, at or near a target price set by the EC, and thereby guarantee producers a level of income.

*Suggestions for Further Research:*

Article:

1. Meester, Gerrit, *European Union, Common Agricultural Policy, and World Trade*, 14 KANSAS JOURNAL OF LAW & PUBLIC POLICY 389–412 (Winter 2005).

## VAT

Value Added Tax.

A tariff levied on the value added that results from each exchange or step in a commercial chain.

That is, a VAT is a consumption tax assessed on the value added to a good or service at each stage of its production. A VAT is not a charge on a business (*i.e.*, on the income of a business). Rather, it is a levy calculated as a percentage of price, whereby the actual tax burden is visible at each stage. Generally, the consumer pays a VAT as part of the selling price of a good or service purchased. Hence, the VAT is an indirect tax. (An income tax would be a direct tax.) A VAT is generally not imposed on exported goods (or, if imposed at an earlier stage, is rebated upon exportation). A VAT is seen as more favorable than a traditional sales tax, which is used in most American states. That is because a VAT undermines tax-evading activity by charging a tax at each level of the production and distribution chains.

VATs are widely used. Many countries have adopted them, including Argentina, European Union (EU), India, Mexico, and New Zealand, amongst others. In the United States, only the state of Michigan has a VAT tax, though it expired on 31 December 2007. The United States considered, but rejected, implementation of a VAT in the mid 1980s.

In June 2007, newly-elected President Nicolas Sarkozy sought to increase the VAT in France as a means of financing cuts in payroll taxes.[718]

*Suggestions for Further Research:*

Book:

1.   BEBI, HOSTER, VALUE ADDED TAX (VAT) IN SADC: POTENTIAL IMPACT: CASE STUDIES OF NAMIBIA AND SOUTH AFRICA (2001).

Articles:

1.   Bird, Richard M. & Pierre-Pascal Gendron, *Sales Tax in Canada: The GST — HST — QST — RST "System,"* 63 TAX LAW REVIEW 517–582 (2010).

2.   Cnossen, Sijbren, *VAT Coordination in Common Markets and Federations: Lessons from the European Experience,* 63 TAX LAW REVIEW 583–622 (2010).

3.   Keen, Michael & Walter Hellerstein, *Interjurisdictional Issues in the Design of a VAT,* 63 TAX LAW REVIEW 359–408 (2010).

4.   Kirsch, Michael S., *Taxing Citizens in a Global Economy,* 82 NEW YORK UNIVERSITY LAW REVIEW 443 (2007).

5.   Perry, Victoria J., *International Experience in Implementing VATs in Federal Jurisdictions: A Summary,* 63 TAX LAW REVIEW 623–638 (2010).

6.   Van Brederode, Robert F., *A Normative Evaluation of Consumption Tax Design: The Treatment of the Sales of Goods Under VAT in the European Union and Sales Tax of the United States,* 62 TAX LAWYER 1055–1084 (2009).

Other Source:

1.   INTERNATIONAL MONETARY FUND, MODERN VAT (2001).

## VER

Voluntary Export Restraint.

Also known as a "Voluntary Restraint Agreement" (VRA) or "Orderly Marketing Arrangement" (OMA), a VER is an undertaking to limit quantities of a product exported to a particular market. That is, VER is an agreement

---

[718] *See The Reforming Juggernaut,* ECONOMIST, 21 June 2007, at 57–58.

whereby an industry in an exporting country, or the government of that country, voluntarily undertakes to limit exports of a particular article to another (or other) countries. Typically, a specific volume of exports is specified across a certain time.

The undertaking may be made between the governments of the exporting and importing countries, the government of the exporting country and a private association in the importing country, a private association in the exporting country and the government of the exporting country, or private associations in each country. Private associations can be any private-sector group, such as an industry association, employer federation, workers' group or union, or consumer group. Thus, for example, under a VRA between the governments of the United States and Japan during the early 1980s, Japan agreed to limit car exports to approximately 1.5 million vehicles annually. The United States government negotiated the VRA after the near collapse of Chrysler and heavy losses suffered by Ford and General Motors (GM).

While stylized as "voluntary," in fact such deals usually involve bargained-for consideration and are enforceable. Article 11:1(b) of the WTO *Agreement on Safeguards* prohibits all VRAs, except for ones negotiated between private parties in the exporting and importing countries. This strong rule reflects distaste for the proliferation of VRAs that occurred in the 1970s and 1980s, up to the Uruguay Round. VRAs were used, or abused, as a non-transparent means to create the same effect as a trade remedy (*e.g.*, a formal safeguard action), but without fulfilling all the legal obligations for such a remedy. In brief, VRAs tend to distort trade and lack transparency.

*Suggestions for Further Research:*

Articles:

1. Berry, Steven, *et al.*, *Voluntary Export Restraints on Automobiles: Evaluating a Trade Policy*, 89 AMERICAN ECONOMIC REVIEW 400–30 (1999).

2. Immenga, Ulrich, *Export Cartels and Voluntary Export Restraints Between Trade and Competition Policy*, 4 PACIFIC RIM LAW AND POLICY JOURNAL 93, 132–33 (1995).

3. Kitt, Dennis, Note, *What's Wrong with Volunteering? The Futility of the WTO's Ban on Voluntary Export Restraints*, 47 COLUMBIA JOURNAL OF TRANSNATIONAL LAW 359–386 (2009).

4. Maruyama, Warren H., *The Wonderful World of VRAs: Free Trade and the Goblet of Fire*, 24 ARIZONA JOURNAL OF INTERNATIONAL AND COMPARATIVE LAW 149–197 (2007).

5. Wolf, Martin, *Why Voluntary Export Restraints? An Historical Analysis*, 12 WORLD ECONOMICS 273–93 (1989).

Book Chapters:

1. Hindley, Brian, *Safeguards, VERs and Anti-Dumping Action*, in THE NEW WORLD TRADING SYSTEM: READINGS (Organization for Economic Co-operation and Development, ed.) 93 (1994).

2.   Okawa, Masayuki, *Quotas, Voluntary Export Restraints and Welfare, in* ECONOMIC THEORY AND INTERNATIONAL TRADE (Alan D. Woodland ed., 2002).

Other Source:

1.   *The Legacy of the Japanese Voluntary Export Restraints*, HEARING BEFORE THE SUBCOMMITTEE ON TRADE, PRODUCTIVITY AND ECONOMIC GROWTH OF THE JOINT ECONOMIC COMMITTEE, 99th Congress (1986).

## VERTICAL

Within a product category or services sector.

"Vertical" is used to connote the scope of coverage of trade negotiations or a trade agreement. That scope is deep, applying within a specific area. The opposite adjective, of course, is "horizontal," which connotes breadth across product categories or service sectors.

## VEU

A United States export control term standing for "validated end-user."

VEU status permits the export, re-export, and transfer of certain eligible items without a license to certain end-users in eligible countries that have been verified by the United States government, specifically, the Department of Commerce (DOC). Generally, a VEU has demonstrated to the United States that it is committed to obeying American export control rules.[719]

One such rule is that a VEU will employ dual-use goods or technology exclusively in non-military activities. Unlike the End-User Certification, a VEU does not require the exporter to first obtain a license from the Bureau of Industry and Security (BIS) before shipping particular goods. In reviewing the request of a party to be listed as a VEU, the DOC applies the following criteria in respect of that party:

- The record of exclusive engagement in civil end-use activities.
- Compliance with United States export controls.
- Capability to comply with the requirements of Authorization VEU.
- Agreement to permit the United States government to conduct on-site compliance reviews.
- Relationships with American and foreign companies.
- Status of export controls, and support and adherence to multilateral export control regimes in the eligible destination.

A request to be considered a VEU must be submitted to the DOC in the form of an advisory opinion request. In addition, it must be accompanied by a list of items, sorted by Export Control Classification Number (ECCN), to be exported or re-exported under the authorization and a description of how the items will

---

[719] *See* Export Administration Regulations, 15 C.F.R. §§ 740, 742, 744, 748 (2006).

be used by the VEU. All VEUs are listed in Supplement Number 4 to Part 740 of the Export Administration Regulations (EAR).

On 6 July 2006, the BIS began assigning VEU status to exporters who ship goods to China.[720] The VEU program allows the United States government to pre-approve the transfer of certain items without a license to qualified end-users in China. The United States acknowledged all end-users in China are eligible to obtain VEU status, subject to satisfactory fulfillment of certain criteria (listed above). However, exporters who export, re-export, or transfer items to China for military end-uses may not obtain VEU status. India has been mentioned as the next target for the VEU program.

*Suggestions for Further Research:*

Article:

1. Berlack, Evan R., *"End Use" Controls in the Export Administration Regulations*, 892 PLI/COMM 125 (2006).

## VIENNA CONVENTION

The *Vienna Convention on the Law of Treaties* (the *"Convention"*).

The *Convention* was signed at Vienna on 23 May 1969 by the United Nations (U.N.) Conference on the Laws of Treaties (the "Conference"), and entered into force on 27 January 1980.[721] The Conference convened pursuant to U.N. General Assembly Resolutions 2166 (XXI) and 2287 (XXII).[722] The *Convention* applies to treaties signed by States, but not treaties between states and international organizations or treaties between international organizations. The *Convention* acknowledges that each State has the capacity to conclude treaties, as well as provides substantive rules regarding the interpretation of treaties.

As of May 2007, 108 states have ratified the *Convention*. The United States is not a party to the *Vienna Convention*. However, it has stated on numerous occasions before international tribunals it regards Articles 31-32 of the *Convention* (concerning general and supplementary rules of treaty interpretation, respectively) as reflecting customary international law. These key provisions state:

*Article 31: General rule of interpretation*

1. A treaty shall be interpreted in good faith in accordance with the ordinary meaning to be given to the terms of the treaty in their context and in the light of its object and purpose.

---

[720] *See Revisions and Clarifications of Export and Reexport Controls for the People's Republic of China*, 71 Federal Register 38,313–321 (6 July 2006); *Meetings in Boston, Chicago, Houston and La Jolla with Interested Public on the Proposed Rule: Revisions and Clarifications of Export and Reexport Controls for the People's Republic of China*, 71 Federal Register 44,943 (8 August 2006).

[721] *See* 1155 U.N.T.S. 331 (1969), *reprinted in* 8 INTERNATIONAL LEGAL MATERIALS 679 (1969).

[722] *See* U.N. Doc. A/CONF. 39/27 (1969).

2. The context for the purpose of the interpretation of a treaty shall comprise, in addition to the text, including its preamble and annexes:

    (a)   any agreement relating to the treaty which was made between all the parties in connection with the conclusion of the treaty;

    (b)   any instrument which was made by one or more parties in connection with the conclusion of the treaty and accepted by the other parties as an instrument related to the treaty.

3. There shall be taken into account, together with the context:

    (a)   any subsequent agreement between the parties regarding the interpretation of the treaty or the application of its provisions;

    (b)   any subsequent practice in the application of the treaty which establishes the agreement of the parties regarding its interpretation;

    (c)   any relevant rules of international law applicable in the relations between the parties.

4. A special meaning shall be given to a term if it is established that the parties so intended.

*Article 32: Supplementary means of interpretation*

Recourse may be had to supplementary means of interpretation, including the preparatory work of the treaty and the circumstances of its conclusion, in order to confirm the meaning resulting from the application of article 31, or to determine the meaning when the interpretation according to article 31:

    (a)   leaves the meaning ambiguous or obscure; or

    (b)   leads to a result which is manifestly absurd or unreasonable.

The *Convention*, particularly Articles 31-32, frequently is cited by WTO panels and the Appellate Body when called upon to interpret a provision of the GATT or WTO agreements.

*Suggestions for Further Research:*

Books:

1. SINCLAIR, I.M., THE VIENNA CONVENTION ON THE LAWS OF TREATIES (1984).

2. SZTUCKI, JERZY, JUS COGENS AND THE VIENNA CONVENTION ON THE LAWS OF TREATIES: A CRITICAL APPRAISAL (1974).

3. VILLIGER, MARK E., CUSTOMARY INTERNATIONAL LAW AND TREATIES: A STUDY OF THEIR INTERACTIONS AND INTERRELATIONS, WITH SPECIAL CONSIDERATION OF THE 1969 VIENNA CONVENTION ON THE LAW OF TREATIES (1985).

Article:

1. Maki, Peter C., *Interpreting GATT Using the Vienna Convention on the Law of Treaties: A Method to Increase the Legitimacy of the Dispute Settlement System*, 9 MINNESOTA JOURNAL OF GLOBAL TRADE 343–60 (2000).

## VIRTUAL WATER

A term connoting the amount of water required to produce a good or service. It also is known as "embodied water."

Tony Allan first coined the term in 1993, and has applied the concept to the analysis of water as a factor of production, especially in food, and the cost of producing a good in a drought prone area, as a way to analyze food consumption choices. When this measurement is done on an aggregate country wide basis, the term "water footprint" is used to represent the total water use by a country to produce the goods and services it consumes. The term "water footprint" was first used in 2002 by Arjen Hoekstra. Along with virtual water analysis, a water footprint provides insight into a use of water by a country as a resource, and in its overall consumption and demand especially relating to food.

*Suggestions for Further Research:*

Articles:

1.   Allan, J.A., *Virtual Water: A Strategic Resource, Global Solutions to Regional Deficits*, 36 GROUND WATER number 4 (July-August 1998).

2.   Hoekstra, A. Y. & A. K. Chapagain, *Water Footprints of Nations: Water Use by People as a Function of Their Consumption Pattern* (paper posted at www.waterfootprint.org).

## VRA

Voluntary Restraint Agreement.

*See* VER.

# W

## W120 (W120 LIST, W120 GATS SECTORAL CLASSIFICATION LIST)

The system of classifying services used for purposes of the WTO *General Agreement on Trade in Services (GATS)*.

The W120 List contains 11 broad services sectors, which are divided into approximately 161 sub-sectors.

## WAIVER

A dispensation granted by an authority to one or more entities subject to the jurisdiction of that authority to derogate from obligations that arise under an agreement applicable to it or them, and which otherwise would be incumbent on it or them. In the WTO context, a waiver is a permission granted by the Members to another allowing a Member not to comply with normal commitments in the usual time frame.[723] In effect, a waiver allows one or more WTO Members to bypass an otherwise obligatory WTO rule.

The basic wavier authority in GATT is contained in Article XXV:5. Under the *Agreement Establishing the World Trade Organization (WTO Agreement)*, Article IX requires Member states to request a waiver from the Ministerial Conference. A waiver is granted by consensus; if no consensus is reached, a waiver may be granted by three-fourths vote of all Member states.

Normally, waivers have time limits, and a Member must justify any request for an extension. However, some waivers, such as preferential tariff treatment for least-developed countries, may be granted on a permanent basis. Another example is Article 31(f) of the *Agreement on the Trade-Related Aspects of Intellectual Property (TRIPS)*, whereby a Member may grant to another a compulsory license for the purposes of production of pharmaceutical products in the event of a national health care crisis.

A request for a waiver or for an extension of an existing waiver must describe the measures a WTO Member wishes to take, the objective for requesting such relief, and the reasons that prevent the Member from complying with its obligations. The Member granting the waiver may file a claim under the WTO *Understanding on Rules and Procedures Governing the Settlement of Disputes (Dispute Settlement Understanding, or DSU)* if (a) the WTO Member receiving the waiver fails to comply with the conditions of the waiver, or (b) the application of the waiver impairs a benefit accruing to the waiver-granting Member.

---

[723] *See, e.g.*, Decision on Waiver, *Preferential Tariff Treatment for Least-Developed Countries*, WT/L/304 (17 June 1999).

*Suggestions for Further Research:*

Article:

1. Parrish, Roberta, *Does Waiver of Patent Restrictions Clear Way for Generics in Poor Countries?*, 3 HEALTH LAWYER 12–19 (2004).

## WASHINGTON CONSENSUS

An ideology that emerged at the end of the Cold War, particularly in the late 1980s and through most of the 1990s, about free markets, free trade, and economic policy.

The Consensus is so-named because it captured the minds and hearts of many leading international organizations, such as the IMF and World Bank, think tanks, and non-governmental organizations (NGOs) inside the Washington, D.C. beltway. The essence of the Consensus is that post-Second World War economic history showed government planned economies — *i.e.*, socialism and communism — had failed. To develop economically, free markets and free trade should be promoted, meaning that economic reforms designed to liberalize strictures on private agents in an economy should be pursued. Concomitant with these reforms ought to be political change that permits, if not American-style democracy, greater freedom of expression to support economic liberalization.

In the early part of the new millennium, the Washington Consensus has been criticized. As an economic strategy, free markets and free trade may not work effectively in all countries at all times in the same way. More attention to nuances is needed than the Consensus admits. In particular, attention to income distribution is necessary, and pro-active government strategies for poverty alleviation that are more interventionist than the Consensus would have it are called for to offset harsh blows of globalization sometimes by vulnerable groups within a society. Notably, even WTO Director-General Pascal Lamy concedes "elements of the Washington Consensus . . . have failed, such as deregulation," though understandably he warns against increased protectionism.[724] As a matter of style, the Consensus has been challenged has being arrogant, insensitive, and even as advancing a neo-conservative American imperial agenda in some parts of the world.

*Suggestions for Further Research:*

Article:

1. Symposium, *Trade Integration in the Americas: Revisiting the Washington Consensus*, 16 LAW & BUSINESS REVIEW OF THE AMERICAS 3–269 (2009).

---

[724] *Lamy Underscores Doha Round Benefits for Japan*, Speech before the Japan Institute of International Affairs, 25 February 2009, posted at www.wto.org.

## WASHINGTON TREATY

*Treaty on Intellectual Property in Respect of Integrated Circuits*, a precursor to the WTO *Agreement on the Trade Related Aspects of Intellectual Property (TRIPs)*.

Done at Washington, D.C., on 26 May 1989, the *Washington Treaty* was established under the direction of the World Intellectual Property Organization (WIPO).[725] The principal aim of the Washington Treaty is to establish a union to facilitate the protection of integrated circuits. The *Washington Treaty* has yet to enter into force, owing to a number of deficiencies. While *TRIPs* requires WTO Members to provide protection to integrated circuits on the basis of the *Washington Treaty*, it seeks to correct the deficiencies in the *Treaty*. In particular, *TRIPs* requires

- Protection must be available for a minimum period of 10 years.

- The rights must extend to articles incorporating infringing layout designs.

- Innocent infringers must be allowed to use or sell stock in hand or ordered before learning of the infringement against a suitable royalty.

- Compulsory licensing and government use is only allowed under a number of strict conditions.

Unlike the *Washington Treaty*, *TRIPs* also expressly covers articles incorporating protected chips and assures a reasonable royalty to the right-holder after notice in connection with the disposition of stock on hand.

## WASSENAAR ARRANGEMENT

*The Wassenaar Arrangement on Export Controls for Conventional Arms and Dual-Use Goods and Technologies.*

This *Arrangement* is a 1996 agreement establishing a new international group to perform many of the same export control functions as COCOM. At the end of the Cold War, members of Coordinating Committee for Multilateral Export Controls (COCOM) determined that an East-West focus was no longer the best approach to international stability and security. On 16 November 1993, 17 members of COCOM agreed to terminate COCOM and establish a new group. On 19 December 1995, the *Agreement to Establish the "Wassenaar Arrangement"* was reached in Wassenaar, The Netherlands. The *Arrangement* began operations in September 1996, and is headquartered in Vienna, Austria.

The principal aim of the *Arrangement* is to contribute to regional and international security and stability by promoting transparency and greater responsibility in transfers of conventional arms and dual-use goods and technologies. In addition, the *Arrangement* complements and reinforces exiting control regimes for weapons of mass destruction and their delivery systems. The deci-

---

[725] *See* World Intellectual Property Organization: Treaty on Intellectual Property In Respect of Integrated Circuits, 26 May 1989, 28 International Legal Materials 1477 (1989).

sion to permit or deny transfer of any item is the sole responsibility of each participating state. Indeed, all measures with respect to the *Arrangement* are adopted and implemented on the basis of national discretion. Forty states are party to the *Arrangement*. They include:

- Argentina
- Australia
- Austria
- Belgium
- Bulgaria
- Canada
- Croatia
- Czech Republic
- Denmark
- Estonia
- Finland
- France
- Germany
- Greece
- Hungary

- Ireland
- Italy
- Japan
- Latvia
- Lithuania
- Luxembourg
- Malta
- Netherlands
- New Zealand
- Norway
- Poland
- Portugal
- Korea (Republic of)
- Romania

- Russian Federation
- Slovakia
- Slovenia
- South Africa
- Spain
- Sweden
- Switzerland
- Turkey
- Ukraine
- United Kingdom
- United States

Two principal bodies govern the *Arrangement*. The decision making body of the *Arrangement* is the *Wassenaar Arrangement* (WA) Plenary, which is comprised of representatives from each member states and meets annually. The WA Plenary also establishes several subsidiary bodies, such as the Licensing and Enforcement Officers Meeting, which prepare recommendations for Plenary decisions. The Plenary Chair rotates annually among member States. The other principal body, the Secretariat, is based in Vienna. It provides necessary support to *Arrangement* operations.

The *Arrangement* has adopted several control lists, each of which identifies military and dual-use goods and technologies. One such list, the Munitions List, contains 22 entries on items marked for military use. These goods include:

- Small arms and light weapons (and related ammunition).
- Tanks and other military armed vehicles.
- Combat vessels (surface or underwater).
- Armored and protective equipment.
- Aircraft and unmanned airborne vehicles, aero engines, and related equipment.

The Official Website of the *Wassenaar Arrangement* (www.wassenaar.org) sets out comprehensive details concerning the Munitions List.

The List of Dual-Use Goods and Technologies is divided into nine primary categories, each of which corresponds to a particular dual-use good or technology, such as material processing, electronics, computers, navigations and avionics and propulsion, amongst others.

States participating in the *Arrangement* also agree to report the transfer of particular goods to non-*Arrangement* countries. In particular, each participating state must issue reports detailing any transfers of particular arms, such as battle tanks, warships and armored combat vehicles, outside of the Arrangement. The reporting requirements equally apply to sensitive dual-use goods and technologies, as determined by the *Arrangement*.

In late 2006, the *Arrangement* increased efforts to prevent the intangible transfer of dual-use and conventional weapons technology to non-states. Examples of technical data transferred by intangible means, include blueprints, plans, diagrams, models, formulae and tables for the development, production or use of controlled products.[726]

*Suggestions for Further Research:*

Book:

1. WETTER, ANNA, ENFORCING EUROPEAN UNION LAW ON EXPORTS OF DUAL-USE GOODS (2009).

Book Chapters:

1. Lipson, Michael, *The Wassenaar Arrangement: Transparency and Restraint through Trans-Governmental Cooperation?*, *in* NON-PROLIFERATION EXPORT CONTROLS: ORIGINS, CHALLENGES, AND PROPOSALS FOR STRENGTHENING (Daniel Joyner ed., 2006).

Articles:

1. Allen, Karri, Comment, *Communications Satellites and U.S. Export Controls: Correcting the Balance*, 18 COMMUNICATIONS LAW CONSPECTUS 463–486 (2010).

2. Badaway, Antonia Alica, *Controlling the Export of Dual-Use Technology in a Post-9/11 World*, 18 TRANSNATIONAL LAWYER 431–54 (2005).

3. Baker, Lee, Note, *The Unintended Consequences of U.S. Export Restrictions on Software and Online Services for American Foreign Policy and Human Rights*, 23 HARVARD JOURNAL OF LAW & TECHNOLOGY 537–566 (2010).

4. Bartlett III, James E., *et al.*, *Export Controls and Economic Sanctions*, 43 THE INTERNATIONAL LAWYER 311–333 (2009).

5. Boscariol, John, *et al.*, *Export Controls and Economic Sanctions*, 44 THE INTERNATIONAL LAWYER 25–44 (2010).

6. Burton, Michael L., *et al.*, *Export Controls and Economic Sanctions*, 45 THE INTERNATIONAL LAWYER 19–38 (2011).

---

[726] Gary G. Yerkey, *Multilateral Regime Agrees to Tighten Controls on Exports of "Intangible" Technology"*, 23 INTERNATIONAL TRADE REPORTER (BNA) 1788 (21 December 2006).

7. Burton, Michael L., Kara M. Bombach, and Dan Fisher-Owens, *et al.*, *Export Controls and Economic Sanctions*, 45 THE INTERNATIONAL LAWYER 19–38 (spring 2011).

8. Carrier, Michael K., *An Introduction to U.S. Export Control: Regulations for Patent Practitioners*, 5 AKRON INTELLECTUAL PROPERTY JOURNAL 1–17 (2011).

9. Damast, David, Note, *Export Control Reform and the Space Industry*, 42 GEORGETOWN JOURNAL OF INTERNATIONAL LAW 211–232 (2010).

10. Diamond, Andrew F., Note, *Dueling Over Dual-Use Goods: The U.S. Department of Commerce's Misguided Attempt to Promote U.S. Security and Trade with China Through Restrictive Export Controls*, 3 BROOKLYN JOURNAL OF CORPORATE FINANCE & COMMERCIAL LAW 153–183 (2008).

11. Gold, Mike N., *Thomas Jefferson, We Have A Problem: The Unconstitutional Nature of the U.S.'s Aerospace Export Control Regime as Supported by Bernstein v. U.S. Department of Justice*, 57 CLEVELAND STATE LAW REVIEW 629–643 (2009).

12. Kurth, Alison N., Note, *Rethinking the Syria Accountability Act: Are Sanctions on Syria in the Best Interests of the United States?*, 20 TRANSNATIONAL LAW & CONTEMPORARY PROBLEMS 239–277 (2011).

13. Lipson, Michael, *The Reincarnation of COCOM: Explaining Post-Cold War Export Controls*, VI THE NONPROLIFERATION REVIEW number 2, 34 (winter 1999).

14. McKenzie, John F., *U.S. Export Controls on Internet Software Transactions*, 44 THE INTERNATIONAL LAWYER 857–870 (summer 2010).

15. Nichols, Philip M., *Using Sociological Theories of Isomorphism to Evaluate the Possibility of Regime Change Through Trade Sanctions*, 30 UNIVERSITY OF PENNSYLVANIA JOURNAL OF INTERNATIONAL ECONOMIC LAW 753–788 (spring 2009).

16. Reyes, Carla L., Comment, *International Governance of Domestic National Security Measures: The Forgotten Role of the World Trade Organization*, 14 UCLA JOURNAL OF INTERNATIONAL LAW & FOREIGN AFFAIRS 531–566 (2009).

17. Trachy, Elizabeth, *Comment, State & Local Economic Sanctions: The Constitutionality of New York's Divestment Actions and the Sudan Accountability & Divestment Act of 2007*, 74 ALBANY LAW REVIEW 1019–1065 (2010/2011).

18. Westbrook, Amy Deen, *What's In Your Portfolio? U.S. Investors Are Unknowingly Financing State Sponsors of Terrorism*, 59 DEPAUL LAW REVIEW 1151–1221 (2010).

19. Wuestehube, Linda, *U.S. Patent Applications and Export Control Regulations: Seven Habits for Highly Effective Offshore Outsourcing*, 14 INTELLECTUAL PROPERTY LAW BULLETIN 109–122 (2010) (SFIPLA Writing Competition Winner).

## WATER (THE WATER)

*See* Binding Overhang.

## WATER FOOTPRINT

*See* Virtual Water.

## WCO

The World Customs Organization, the new name of the Customs Co-Operation Council (CCC).

Though the CCC was established in 1952, operations began under the auspices of the title "WCO" in 1994. The 170 members of the WCO — a figure slightly larger than the number of WTO Members — are responsible for the movement of more than 98 percent of all international trade.

The WCO Council, comprised of one representative from each member, who is entitled to one-vote, heads the WCO. The 24 of the Council and Policy Commission (CPC) maintain the day-to-day activities of the WCO. In addition, the Finance Committee provides financial advice to the organization. Other prominent committees in the WCO include the Permanent Technical Committee; Enforcement Committee; Harmonized System Committee; Technical Committee on Customs Valuation; and Technical Committee on the Rules of Origin. Finally, the Secretariat ensures that all decisions of the Council and the CPC are executed and enforced.

Headquartered in Brussels, the principal aim of the WCO is to promote a transparent and predictable customs environment. In particular, the WCO aspires to harmonize customs systems and procedures amongst its Members by facilitating communication and cooperation on customs issues. To this aim, the WCO develops rules on customs and provides technical advice and assistance for developing customs procedures.

Significantly, the WCO also worked to establish the *Harmonized Commodity Description and Coding System* (the *"HS"*), an international standardized system that classifies certain products by name and number, namely, by a six-digit nomenclature. This system is used to classify goods for tariff purposes. The HS came into force on 1 January 1988. Some of the other notable international conventions of the WCO include:

- GATT *Customs Valuation Agreement*;
- *Nairobi* and *Johannesburg Conventions*, both dealing with the sharing of information;
- 1973 *Kyoto Convention* on customs procedures; and,
- the 1999 revised *Kyoto Convention*, formally known as the *International Convention on the Harmonization and Simplification of Customs Procedures*.

In 2002, the WCO Council unanimously approved a resolution on security and the facilitation of the international trade supply chain. This resolution contained numerous benchmarks and best practices. The United States

Customs and Border Patrol (CBP) assists the WCO in writing these standards.

In conjunction with the World Trade Organization (WTO), the WCO has been hard pressed to harmonize procedures concerning customs valuation and rules of origin. In 1999, the WCO Technical Committee on Rules of Origin transmitted 500 outstanding issues for discussion to the WTO Committee on Rules of Origin (CRO). To date, the CRO aims to complete its work by the end of 2007. The WCO Technical Committee on Customs Valuation (TCCV) was established in 1980. The TCCV and the WTO Committee on Customs Valuation provide advisory opinions, commentaries, explanatory notes and case studies adopted by the TCCV. The WCO is also an observer member to several WTO bodies, including the Council for Trade in Goods; Council for Trade-Related Aspects of Intellectual Property Rights; Committee on Trade and Environment; Committee on Market Access; Committee of Participants on the Expansion of Trade in Information Technology Products; and the Negotiating Group on Trade Facilitation.

*Suggestions for Further Research:*

Article:

1.   Friedman, Lawrence M. & Christine H. Martinez, *What is Persuasive? Pushing World Customs Organizations Materials Through the Skidmore Sieve,* 17 TULANE JOURNAL OF INTERNATIONAL & COMPARATIVE LAW 515–531 (2009).

## WFP

World Food Program. *See* Food Security.

## WHO

World Health Organization.

Under the auspices of the United Nations (U.N.) system, the WHO began operations on 7 April 1948 when its Constitution came into force. The WHO is headquartered in Geneva, Switzerland, and has six regional offices:

- Brazzaville, Congo
- Cairo, Egypt
- Copenhagen, Denmark
- Manila, Philippines
- New Delhi, India
- Washington, D.C., United States

The WHO is the directing and coordinating authority for health within the United Nations (UN) system. The primary objective of the WHO is attainment for all peoples of the highest possible level of health. "Health" is defined under the WHO Constitution encompasses physical, mental, and social well-being, and not consisting only of the absence of disease or infirmity. To achieve this object, the WHO operates on six principles, which include:

- Providing leadership on global health matters;
- Shaping the health research agenda;
- Setting norms and standards;
- Articulating evidenced-based policy options;
- Proving technical support to countries; and
- Monitoring and assessing global health trends.

In addition, the WHO promotes development and alleviates poverty by increasing access to medical facilities. That is, the WHO aims to increase access to life-saving or health-promoting interventions, regardless of one's economic status. The WHO also safeguards world health security by strengthening mechanisms to prevent the outbreak of epidemics and diseases. Strengthening health systems by expanding health coverage to lower-income peoples is an important element of WHO operations. This requires the WHO to ensure such facilities are equipped with a properly trained staff, proper funds, and appropriate technology, including essential drugs.

The WHO is led by four principal bodies, namely the:

- World Health Assembly
- Executive Board
- Director-General
- Secretariat.

The supreme governing body of the WHO is the World Health Assembly. Meeting each May in Geneva, it is attended by delegations from all 193 member states. The Health Assembly supervises the financial policies of the organization, including the budget, and appoints the Director General. It also considers reports from the Executive Board and mandates any further action to the Board that may be required.

The Executive Board is comprised of 34 members technically qualified in the field of health. The main function of the Executive Board is to execute the decisions and policies of the Health Assembly, and to facilitate its work. Members of the Executive Board are elected to three-year terms. The duties of the Executive Board include setting the agenda for the upcoming Health Assembly, as well as deciding which resolutions will be forwarded to the Assembly.

A Director-General heads the WHO. The Executive Board nominates the Director-General. The Health Assembly formally appoints the nominee to the post. The Secretariat carries out day-to-day operations of the WHO. The Secretariat is staffed with some 8,500 health experts and support staff.

In September 2000, the WHO adopted the Millennium Development Goals (MDGs). The eight goals include

(1) Eradication of extreme poverty and hunger.

(2) Achievement of universal primary education.

(3) Promoting gender equality and empowering women.

(4) Reducing child mortality.

(5) Improving maternal health.

(6) Combating HIV/AIDS, malaria and other diseases.

(7) Ensuring environmental sustainability.

(8) Establishing a global partnership for development.

The target date for achieving these goals is 2015.

The WHO collaborates with the World Trade Organization (WTO) on a number of issues related to trade and health. The WHO also has observer status with the WTO, and regularly participates in the WTO Councils for Trade in Services and Trade-Related Aspects of Intellectual Property, as well as the WTO Committees on Sanitary and Phytosanitary Measures and Technical Barriers to Trade. The WTO and the WHO hope to increase policy coherence between trade and health matters at the national and international levels.

*Suggestions for Further Research:*

Book:

1.   SIDDIQI, JAVED, WORLD HEALTH AND WORLD POLITICS: THE WORLD HEALTH ORGANIZATION AND THE U.N. SYSTEM (1995).

Article:

1.   Countryman, Philip, *International Trade and World Health Policy: Helping People Reach their Full Potential*, 21 PACE INTERNATIONAL LAW REVIEW 241–279 (2009).

# WIPO

The World Intellectual Property Organization, founded on 14 July 1967 by the *Convention Establishing the World Intellectual Property Organization* and located in Geneva, Switzerland.

WIPO membership is comprised of 184 Member states. WIPO is a specialized agency of the United Nations (UN) that is dedicated to developing a balanced and accessible intellectual property (IP) system that rewards creativity, stimulates innovation and contributes to economic development whilst protecting the public interest. For WIPO, "IP" consists of any creation of the mind, including, but not limited to, inventions, literary and artistic works, and symbols, names, images, and designs used in commerce. Indeed, WIPO divides IP into two categories, namely, industrial property (such as trademarks, patents, industrial designs and geographic indications of source) and copyright (which includes literary and artistic works, such as novels, poems, plays, films and architectural works, among others).

WIPO hopes to utilize IP to promote cultural, economic, and social development of all countries. WIPO seeks to maximize the benefits of IP by promoting IP culture; integrating IP into national development policies and programs; developing international IP laws and standards; delivering quality services in global IP protection systems; and increasing the efficiency of its management and support processes.

WIPO is led by three principal governing bodies. First, the WIPO General Assembly is comprised of one representative from each Member state. The Assembly approves the budget and financial regulations of the organization. It also appoints the Director-General, and nominates new members.

Second, the WIPO Conference, which contains one representative from each Member, discusses matters of general interest in the field of IP and adopts recommendations relating to such matters. The Conference also sets forth the legal-technical assistance programs of WIPO, as well as appoints states to become members to the organization.

Third, the WIPO Coordination Committee oversees the *Paris Convention for the Protection of Industrial Property* (originally completed in 1883 and subsequently revised on several occasions) and the *Berne Convention for the Protection of Literary and Artistic Works* (originally completed in 1886 and subsequently revised on several occasions). In particular, the Coordination Committee gives advice to the organs of WIPO and each Convention on all administrative and financial matters of common interest. The Committee also nominates a Director-General to lead the day-to-day functions of the Organization. WIPO also has several permanent committees, including:

- Program and Budget Committee,
- Committee on Intellectual Property and Development,
- Intergovernmental Committee on IP and Genetic Resources,
- Traditional Knowledge and Folklore, and
- Advisory Committee on Enforcement.

Several standing committees and working groups also toil over specific topics to further promote WIPO's principal aims.

On 22 December 1995, WIPO and the WTO signed the *Agreement between the World Intellectual Property Organization and the World Trade Organization*.[727] The *Agreement* promotes cooperation between the two organizations, particularly in the notifications of countries' laws, technical assistance, and implementing obligations under the WTO *Agreement on Trade Related Aspects of Intellectual Property Rights (TRIPs)*. As part of this initiative, the

---

[727] *See* World Trade Organization, WTO-WIPO Cooperation Agreement, *posted at* www.wto.org/english/tratop_e/trips_e/wtowip_e.htm.

two organizations have launched a number of joint-efforts on technical cooperation.

In recent years, there has been increased deadlock between Member States in regards to the Development Agenda (not to be confused with the Doha Development Agenda (DDA)).[728] The Development Agenda, proposed by Argentina and Brazil in 2004, would require development needs to be taken into account in all of the organization's activities. Accordingly, there would be provisions on transfer of technology; anticompetitive practices; the safeguarding of public-interest flexibilities; and longer implementation periods for developing countries in treaties now under negotiation.

*Suggestions for Further Research:*

Book:

1. MAY, CHRISTOPHER, WORLD INTELLECTUAL PROPERTY ORGANIZATION: RESURGENCE AND THE DEVELOPMENT AGENDA (2007).

Article:

1. Dinwoodie, Graeme B. & Rochelle C. Dreyfuss, *Designing a Global Intellectual Property System Responsive to Change: The WTO, WIPO, and Beyond*, 46 HOUSTON LAW REVIEW 1187–1234 (2009).

## WMD

Weapons of Mass Destruction.

Such weapons include biological, chemical, nuclear and radiological devices. Under a broader definition, however, the term WMD has come to include any means capable of inflicting mass casualties. American statutory law adopts the broader definition of WMD: a "weapon of mass destruction" is defined as "any weapon that is designed or intended to cause death or serious bodily injury through the release, dissemination, or impact of toxic or poisonous chemicals."[729]

Preventing the use and proliferation of such devices, particularly by terrorist groups, has become the top national security priority of a number of nations. Such task has also become a goal of many international organizations, including the North Atlantic Treaty Organization (NATO), and the United Nations (U.N.).

*Suggestions for Further Research:*

Book:

1. LANGFORD, ROLAND E., INTRODUCTION TO WEAPONS OF MASS DESTRUCTION: RADIOLOGICAL, CHEMICAL AND BIOLOGICAL (2004).

---

[728] *See* Daniel Pruzin, *U.S. Officials Warn of Deadlock in WIPO Development Negotiations*, 23 INTERNATIONAL TRADE REPORTER (BNA) 309 (2 March 2006).

[729] *See* 18 U.S.C. § 2332a(c)(2)(b).

Article:

1.  Alvarez-Verdugo, Milagros, *Comparing U.S. and E.U. Strategies against Weapons of Mass Destruction*, 11 ANNUAL SURVEY OF INTERNATIONAL & COMPARATIVE LAW 119–40 (2005).

## WORLD BANK

The World Bank, headquartered in Washington, D.C.

The World Bank is an international development bank that makes low-interest and interest-free loans to developing and least developed countries with the avowed objective of reducing poverty. Conceived in July 1944 at the Bretton Woods Conference (along with its sister institution, the International Monetary Fund (IMF)), the Bank is comprised of two separate bodies:

- International Bank for Reconstruction and Development (IBRD)

- International Development Association (IDA)

The IBRD targets its efforts primarily on middle-income developing countries, while the IDA focuses on the poorest countries of the world. The IBRD acquires funding for its operations primarily through the sale of AAA-rated bonds in world financial markets, and from lending its own capital. The IDA obtains the majority of its funds from donor countries and loan repayments.

Overall, the World Bank has 185 members, considerably more than the WTO. The President of the World Bank leads the daily operations of the Bank, and helps chart its course, and 24 Executive Directors oversee these operations and plan strategy. By common understanding, the World Bank President invariably is an American citizen, while the Managing Director of the IMF is a European. That understanding, however, has come in for considerable criticism in recent years, led by Russia and a number of developing countries. They urge that selecting a citizen from the developing world would be fairer than picking an American at every go, break the dominance of hegemonic powers over major international organizations, and possibly even contribute to human capital advancement in poor countries. Moreover, there is plenty of world-class talent emerging from poor countries to fill the senior-most positions at the World Bank.

While the Bank has achieved some notable successes in reducing poverty in parts of the world, it has also come under severe criticism from diverse groups of observers. Many critics argue the Bank's policies champion American business interests, often at the expense of the environment, public health, and cultural diversity. Some reports of the Bank-funded projects and operations suggest a success rate of no more than about 50 percent. The World Bank also has been accused of turning a blind eye toward corruption in developing countries, paying insufficient emphasis to rule of law development, and stocking its own ranks with officials not through merit, but rather on the basis of insider connections, even nepotistic ones. The 2007 resignation in disgrace of World

Bank President Paul Wolfowitz, who championed anti-corruption efforts, highlighted the latter point, because of the causal event that led to it.

As with the IMF, the practical import of criticisms of the World Bank may be less than the elevated rhetorical volume suggests. Private capital flows — by, for example, mutual funds, hedge funds, and other investment vehicles channeled by major private sector players such as Goldman Sachs, Hong Kong Shanghai Bank, Merrill Lynch, Morgan Stanley, and the like — dwarf the entire portfolio of loanable funds of both the IMF and World Bank combined. A country needing a soft (*i.e.*, long-term, low- or-no-interest loan) is in bad shape indeed, as it can attract only the most risk-loving of investors. The extent to which the country follows a World Bank-style reform package may be a signal to private portfolio investors that it is on a sound economic path, and thereby might have attractive investment opportunities. In sum, neither the magnitude nor the nature of World Bank assistance is as significant as the enormous attention devoted to it intimates.

*Suggestions for Further Research:*

Books:

1.   BIRD, GRAHAM, THE IMF AND THE FUTURE: ISSUES AND OPTIONS FACING THE FUND (2003).

2.   DAM, KENNETH W., THE RULES OF THE GAME — REFORM AND EVOLUTION IN THE INTERNATIONAL MONETARY SYSTEM (1982).

3.   GRANVILLE, BRIGITTE, ED., ESSAYS ON THE WORLD ECONOMY AND ITS FINANCIAL SYSTEM (2000).

4.   HEAD, JOHN W., LOSING THE GLOBAL DEVELOPMENT WAR: THE FUTURE OF THE GLOBAL ECONOMIC ORGANIZATIONS: A CONTEMPORARY CRITIQUE OF THE IMF, THE WORLD BANK, AND THE WTO (2005).

5.   HEAD, JOHN W., GLOBAL BUSINESS LAW: PRINCIPLES AND PRACTICE OF INTERNATIONAL COMMERCE AND INVESTMENT (2nd ed. 2007).

6.   JAMES, HAROLD, INTERNATIONAL MONETARY COOPERATION SINCE BRETTON WOODS (1996).

7.   LISSAKERS, KARIN, BANKS, BORROWERS, AND THE ESTABLISHMENT — A REVISIONIST ACCOUNT OF THE INTERNATIONAL DEBT CRISIS (1991).

8.   QURESHI, ASIF H. & ANDREAS R. ZIEGLER, INTERNATIONAL ECONOMIC LAW chs. 17–18 (2nd ed. 2007).

Articles:

1.   Feldstein, Martin, *Refocusing the IMF* 77, FOREIGN AFFAIRS number 2, 20–33 (March/April 1998).

2.   Head, John W., *Supranational Law: How the Move Towards Multilateral Solutions Is Changing the Character of "International Law"* 16 UNIVERSITY OF KANSAS LAW REVIEW 627–28 (1993).

3.   Symposium: Fifteenth Annual Herbert and Justice Rose Luttan Rubin International Law Symposium, *The Privatization of Development Assistance,*

42 New York University Journal of International Law & Politics 1079–1426 (2010).

4. Symposium: *Law-Based Nature of the New International Financial Infrastructure*, 33 The International Lawyer number 4, 847–1014 (winter 1999).

5. Symposium: *Law-Based Nature of the New International Financial Architecture*, Part II: Articles and Selected Essays, 34 The International Lawyer number 1, 85–234 (spring 2000).

6. Symposium — *International Monetary and Financial Law in the New Millennium: Dedication Conference of Sir Joseph Gold Library Collection*, 35 The International Lawyer number 4, 1335–1669 (winter 2001).

7. Symposium — *Developing the IMF, the World Bank, and the Regional Development Banks: The Future of Law and Policy in Global Financial Institutions*, 17 Kansas Journal of Law and Public Policy (fall 2007).

Other Sources:

1. Auboin, Marc, *The Trade, Debt and Finance Nexus: At the Cross-Roads of Micro- and Macroeconomics*, WTO Discussion Paper Number 6 (2004).

2. Bandow, Doug & Ian Vásquez, eds. Perpetuating Poverty — The World Bank, the IMF, and the Developing World (Cato Institute, 1994).

3. Bergsten, C. Fred, ed., International Adjustment and Financing: The Lessons of 1985–1991 (Institute for International Economics 1991).

4. Cartellieri, Ulrich & Alan Greenspan, *Global Risk Management*, Group of Thirty, The William Taylor Memorial Lectures Number 3 (1996).

5. Corrigan, E. Gerald, *The Financial Disruptions of the 1980s: A Central Banker Looks Back*, Group of Thirty, The William Taylor Memorial Lectures Number 1 (1993).

6. Eatwell, John, *International Financial Liberalization: the Impact on World Development*, United Nations Development Program (UNDP) Office of Development Studies, Discussion Paper Number 12 (September 1996).

7. Hakim, Jonathan R., ed., *Investment Banking and Development Banking*, IFC Occasional Papers, Capital Markets Series (1985).

8. Wyplosz, Charles, *Exchange Rate Regimes: Some Lessons from Postwar Europe*, Group of Thirty Occasional Paper Number 63 (2000).

## WORLD BANK GROUP

An umbrella term covering all of the institutions affiliated with the World Bank.

## WORLD ECONOMIC FORUM

*See* Davos Summit

## WORLD ORGANIZATION FOR ANIMAL HEALTH

*See* OIE.

## WORLD SOCIAL FORUM

An alternative meeting to the Davos Summit.

Typically held annually in a developing country, participants examine, and sometimes protest against, the deleterious effects of globalization. Social movements, networks, NGOs, and other civil society organizations are invited to participate in the World Social Forum (the "Forum"). Under its motto "another world is possible," the Forum promotes the sharing of ideas that facilitates economic development without capitalism. That is, the Forum is a group comprised of organizations who oppose classic models of economic growth based on capitalism. The Forum's Charter of Principles, approved by the World Social Forum International Council on 10 June 2001, captures the principle aims of the group. In particular, these principles echo the Forum's ultimate aim of economic development without the use of neoliberal reforms and greater understanding for culture considerations and the environment.

Founded 25 January 2001 in Porto Alegre, Brazil, the Forum holds annual meetings in January to counter those of the World Economic Forum (*i.e.*, the Davos Summit). Since the initial gathering, subsequent meetings have been held in Porto Alegre (2002, 2003, 2005); Mumbai, India (2004); Caracas, Venezuela (2006); Bamako, Mali (2006); Karachi, Pakistan (2006); Nairobi, Kenya (2007); and Belém, Brazil (2008).

A committee native to the location, *i.e.*, a local committee, leads each annual summit. The International Council (IC) is the highest governing body of the Forum. General political questions and discussion concerning the Forum's agenda and methodologies for each annual event is debated within the IC. The IC is comprised of 129 organizations and committees, including Greenpeace and OXFAM, amongst others, that focus on six primary themes: methodology; content and themes; expansion; strategies; resources; and communication.

*Suggestions for Further Research:*

Books:

1. FISHER, WILLIAM F. & THOMAS PONNIAH EDS., ANOTHER WORLD IS POSSIBLE: POPULAR ALTERNATIVES TO GLOBALIZATION AT THE WORLD SOCIAL FORUM (2003).

2. DE SOUSA SANTOS, BOAVENTURA, RISE OF THE GLOBAL LEFT: THE WORLD SOCIAL FORUM AND BEYOND (2006).

Article:

1. Smith, Jackie, *Economic Globalization and Labor Rights: Towards Global Solidarity?*, 20 NOTRE DAME JOURNAL OF LAW, ETHICS & PUBLIC POLICY 873, 879–81 (2006).

## WTO

World Trade Organization.

The WTO is the governing body of international trade, setting and enforcing rules of trade between nations. It was established on 1 January 1995, pursuant to the *Agreement Establishing the World Trade Organization (WTO Agreement)*, which was negotiated under the auspices of the Uruguay Round of talks under the General Agreement on Tariffs and Trade (GATT).[730]

Since the Uruguay Round, the WTO has replaced the institution of the GATT, which was established shortly after the Second World War, as the principal international body governing international trade. There are a total of 151 parties, comprised of nation-states and separate customs territories, which have acceded to the WTO (as of December 2007). They are officially known as "Members."

Perhaps the most important distinctions as to the make-up of the WTO in comparison with GATT concern size and poverty. The GATT began with 23 contracting parties, and for years if not decades was dominated by developed countries. The WTO is roughly seven times larger, and about 80 percent of the Membership consists of developing or least developed countries. Yet, like the old GATT, the WTO is a Member-driven organization. All major decisions are made by the Membership as a whole, either by ministers at the Ministerial Conference, or by their ambassadors or delegates under the General Council. This distinguishes the WTO from other international organizations, such as the International Monetary Fund (IMF) and the World Bank. The major decisions at the IMF and World Bank are taken by a Board of Directors, or by the head of the organization. Manifestly, as the Membership grows in size and economic, social, cultural, and religious diversity, consensus-based decision making and single-undertaking requirements for trade deals is increasingly different.

The principal goal of the WTO is to help producers of goods and services, exporters, and importers conduct their business and to improve the welfare of the peoples of its member countries by lowering tariff barriers and providing a platform for negotiation of trade. In other words, the primary objective of the WTO is to ensure trade flows as smoothly, predictably, and freely as possible. To achieve this aim, the primary functions of the WTO include:

- Administering trade agreements;
- Acting as the forum for trade negotiations;
- Settling trade disputes;
- Reviewing national trade policies;
- Assisting developing countries in trade policy issues, through technical assistance and training programs; and
- Cooperating with other international organizations.

The WTO abides by five principles when carrying out its primary functions. Put differently, five points define the *raison d'être* of the WTO.

---

[730] *See* 19 U.S.C. § 3501(8).

First, the WTO requires non-discrimination amongst its members. The two elements of this principle include the (a) most-favored nation (MFN) principle and (b) national treatment requirement. The MFN principle forbids discrimination in respect of like products originating in different Members. National treatment requires equal treatment of imported and locally produced goods in respect of like or directly competitive or substitutable products. Second, the WTO seeks achievement of freer trade through negotiations. Trade liberalization occurs progressively as countries mutually agree to reduce their tariff and non-tariff barriers to trade. Third, the WTO aims to facilitate trade by requiring Members to bind their tariff rates and increase transparency. Enduring commitments encourages stable, predictable terms for commercial intercourse between and among public and private parties. Lastly, the fourth and fifth principles ensure WTO operations promote fair competition, while also supporting development and economic reform.

The Figure below sets out the basic organizational framework of the WTO. The WTO is led by three governing bodies. First, the Ministerial Conference is the WTO's top decision making body. It is comprised of trade ministers from each Member. The Ministerial Conference meets once every two years. The Conference takes decisions concerning the fundamental operations of the organization, such as the accession of new members and selection of a new Director-General.

## FIGURE:
### BASIC STRUCTURE OF THE WORLD TRADE ORGANIZATION
### *(WTO Agreement Articles IV, VI-VII, XII)*

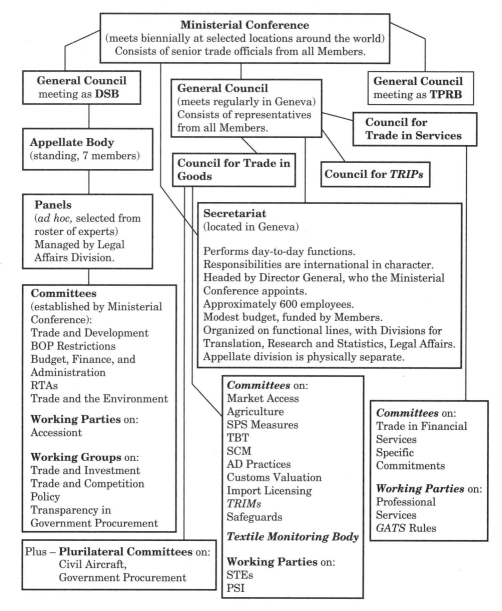

**Ministerial Conference**
(meets biennially at selected locations around the world)
Consists of senior trade officials from all Members.

**General Council**
meeting as **DSB**

**General Council**
(meets regularly in Geneva)
Consists of representatives
from all Members.

**General Council**
meeting as **TPRB**

**Council for**
**Trade in Services**

**Appellate Body**
(standing, 7 members)

**Council for Trade in**
**Goods**

**Council for *TRIPs***

**Panels**
(*ad hoc,* selected from
roster of experts)
Managed by Legal
Affairs Division.

**Secretariat**
(located in Geneva)

Performs day-to-day functions.
Responsibilities are international in character.
Headed by Director General, who the Ministerial
Conference appoints.
Approximately 600 employees.
Modest budget, funded by Members.
Organized on functional lines, with Divisions for
Translation, Research and Statistics, Legal Affairs.
Appellate division is physically separate.

**Committees**
(established by Ministerial
Conference):
Trade and Development
BOP Restrictions
Budget, Finance, and
Administration
RTAs
Trade and the Environment

**Working Parties** on:
Accessiont

**Working Groups** on:
Trade and Investment
Trade and Competition
Policy
Transparency in
Government Procurement

***Committees*** on:
Market Access
Agriculture
SPS Measures
TBT
SCM
AD Practices
Customs Valuation
Import Licensing
*TRIMs*
Safeguards

***Textile Monitoring Body***

**Working Parties** on:
STEs
PSI

***Committees*** on:
Trade in Financial
Services
Specific
Commitments

***Working Parties*** on:
Professional
Services
*GATS* Rules

Plus – **Plurilateral Committees** on:
Civil Aircraft,
Government Procurement

There have been eight Ministerial Conferences since the birth of the WTO in 1995:

- Singapore (9–13 December 1996)
- Geneva, Switzerland (18–20 May 1998)
- Seattle, Washington, United States (30 November-3 December 1999)
- Doha, Qatar (9–14 November 2001)
- Cancún, Mexico (10–14 September 2003)
- Hong Kong, SAR, China (13–18 December 2005).
- Geneva, Switzerland (30 November-2 December 2009).
- Geneva, Switzerland (15–17 December 2011).

Note that Article IV:1 of the *WTO Agreement* calls for a Ministerial Conference every two years. Hence, the WTO violated its own rules with the four-year gap between 2005 and 2009.

Note, too, the 2009 Geneva Ministerial Conference was not intended as a venue for negotiations on the Doha Development Agenda (DDA). Doha Round negotiations continued on a separate track. Of course, the tracks were not entirely separate. One reason for the four year delay was exhaustion — negotiating fatigue — over the DDA. Moreover, the theme of the 2009 Geneva Conference, which was "The WTO, the Multilateral Trading System, and the Current Global Economic Environment," certainly was wide enough to include Doha Round discussions at the margin. This Conference also sought to be a so-called "FIT" one, meaning full participation, inclusiveness, and transparency, amidst a lean, non-extravagant atmosphere.

And, note the cities that host Ministerial Conferences are in the firing line of anti-globalization and anti-WTO protestors. Not surprisingly, given its reputation for order and security, Geneva is a favorite spot for the Conferences. To be sure (and at the risk of some cynicism), some WTO diplomats from dreadfully poor, dangerous, or uneventful capital cities enjoy these attractions of Geneva, as well as the shopping opportunities there. Yet, the fact is some cities understandably prefer not to host a major international economic gathering of "establishment" figures knowing that the event will trigger "anti-establishment" protestors, and thus require an investment of time and money on logistics and security.

Second, directly below the Ministerial Conference is the General Council. This Council is composed of ambassadors and heads of delegation in Geneva, Switzerland. The General Council undertakes the day-to-day operations of the WTO. Meeting several times a year, the General Council also meets as the Trade Policy Review Body (TPRB) to review Member States national trade laws, and as the Dispute Settlement Body (DSB), to settle disputes between Member states.

Three additional entities operate under the General Council. These subsidiary entities are the Goods Council, Services Council, and Intellectual Property

(TRIPS) Council. Under these Councils, several further subsidiary bodies, such as committees, work to formulate policies on particular trade issues. Examples of these committees include the Committee on Trade and the Environment, Committee on Regional Trade Agreements, and the Working Party on Accession.

Last, the WTO Secretariat is located in Geneva and operates with a staff of about 625 and a modest budget of approximately 182 million Swiss francs (U.S. $150 million). The main function of the Secretariat, which is led by a Director-General, is to supply technical support for the various councils, committees and ministerial conferences. It also provides technical assistance to developing countries, analyzes world trade, and serves as the official medium by which the WTO relays its policies to the public and the media. Four Director-Generals have served the WTO, including:

- Renato Ruggeiro (1 May 1995 to 31 August 1999), from Italy
- Mike Moore (1 September 1999 to 31 August 2002), from New Zealand
- Supachai Panitchpakdi (1 September 2002 to 31 August 2005), from Thailand
- Pascal Lamy (1 September 2005 to 31 August 2009, and reappointed for a second term from 1 September 2009 to 31 August 2013), from France

Selection of the Director-General is a four-step process. First, WTO Members make nominations of individuals for the post. Second, the nominated candidates go to Geneva for interviews with Members. Third, a Selection Committee consisting of the Chairmen of the WTO General Council, Dispute Settlement Body, and Trade Policy Review Body, consults with the Members as to the candidates. The goal of the consultations is to allow the Committee to narrow the field of candidates to one finalist. Following each round of consultations, the Committee asks the candidate with the least support to withdraw his or her name from consideration. Iterations of this process continue until one candidate is left. Finally, the Committee puts forth the single name to the WTO Members with the recommendation that he or she be selected as Director-General by consensus. In the final step, the Members may request the single candidate to make a presentation outlining his or her vision for the future of the WTO, and engage in a question-and-answer session with them. They did so, for example, in April 2009 with respect to the re-appointment of Pascal Lamy as Director-General.

Selection of the Director-General has at times been acrimonious, revealing schisms in the Membership between rich and poor countries, and among rich countries, and among poor countries. For example, in 1998–1999, Members divided themselves into various coalitions over the selection of Mike Moore versus Supachai Panitchpakdi, and ultimately compromised by splitting one full term between the two men. A bitter aftertaste persisted among many Members. Top management of the Secretariat, beneath the Director-General level, consists of four Deputy Director-Generals. They are chosen in part to embody regional balance.

Decisions at the WTO are reached by consensus. Beginning in early GATT trade rounds, tradition has held that decisions are reached by a consensus of all contracting parties — *i.e.*, the CONTRACTING PARTIES (with large/small capitals, or all capitals, signifying joint action by consensus). The tradition carries into the WTO (without the corresponding use of "MEMBERS" or "MEMBERS"). Effectively, then, "consensus" means unanimity, in that all Members agree to take the proposed decision, with no Member or group of Members raising objections in a way to block movement forward. The process of reaching consensus can be time-consuming, as (among many examples) the Doha Round suggests. Notably, WTO Director-General Pascal Lamy once described the WTO as a "medieval" organization because of its tradition of consensus-based decision making.[731]

What happens if a consensus is not possible? Then, the *WTO Agreement* allows for voting. On the basis of one country, one vote, a vote is won with a majority of the votes cast. However, actual votes rarely, if ever, occur. That was true under the old GATT system, and remains the case in the WTO.

Observe the consensus system, with the underlying possibility of equal voting rights, is — on paper, at least — highly democratic. It is not "might is right." It is not budget weighted voting. It is not voting based on share ownership, which in turn depends on capital contributions. Again, in theory, it is not nearly so antithetical to small, poor countries, nor so skewed in favor of a few, rich, powerful countries, as many anti-WTO critics contend. That said, of course, in practice certain countries — developed and developing — do wield disproportionate influence. That, however, may well be a feature of any human institution.

There are four exceptions to this general rule. A vote of three-fourths of all WTO Members is required to (1) adopt an interpretation of a multilateral trade agreement, or (2) waive an obligation due from a WTO Member state under a multilateral trade agreement. A two-thirds majority vote of all WTO Members is needed to (3) admit a new member to the WTO, or (4) amend provisions of any multilateral trade agreement. Amendments to multilateral agreements may be enforced against only those countries that adopted them.

Note that decisions by the General Council operating as the DSB are taken by the "reverse consensus" rule, also called the "negative consensus" rule. That means the DSB agrees to a proposed course of action (typically, formation of a panel, or adoption of a panel or Appellate Body report), unless there is a consensus not to do so. The reverse consensus rule is an important innovation of the *Understanding on Rules and Procedures Governing the Settlement of Disputes* (*Dispute Settlement Understanding*, or *DSU*), to facilitate adjudication and avoid problems of delays, blockage, and enforcement, which plagued the pre-Uruguay Round dispute settlement system under GATT Article XXIII.

---

[731] *See* Daniel Pruzin, *Lamy Moves Early, Gets Support in Bid for Second Term as WTO Director-General*, 25 International Trade Reporter (BNA) 1601–1602 (13 November 2008).

Since its inception in 1995, the WTO has only attempted one trade round, namely, the Doha Development Agenda (DDA), commonly called the "Doha Round."[732] As of April 2009, it appears that Round has collapsed, or at least stalled indefinitely, despite several years of negotiations.

*Suggestions for Further Research:*

Books:

1. BARFIELD, CLAUDE E., FREE TRADE, SOVEREIGNTY, DEMOCRACY — THE FUTURE OF THE WORLD TRADE ORGANIZATION (2001).

2. BHAGWATI, JAGDISH & MATHIAS HIRSCH EDS., THE URUGUAY ROUND AND BEYOND — ESSAYS IN HONOR OF ARTHUR DUNKEL (1998).

3. BOSSCHE, PETER VAN DEN, THE LAW AND POLICY OF THE WORLD TRADE ORGANIZATION: TEXT, CASES AND MATERIALS (2005).

4. BUCKLEY, ROSS P., ED., THE WTO AND THE DOHA ROUND: THE CHANGING FACE OF WORLD TRADE (2003).

5. CASS, DEBORAH Z., CONSTITUTIONALIZATION OF THE WORLD TRADE ORGANIZATION: LEGITIMACY, DEMOCRACY, AND COMMUNITY IN THE INTERNATIONAL TRADING SYSTEM (2005).

6. CROOME, JOHN, RESHAPING THE WORLD TRADING SYSTEM — A HISTORY OF THE URUGUAY ROUND (1995).

7. CROOME, JOHN, GUIDE TO THE URUGUAY ROUND AGREEMENTS (1999).

8. FOOTER, MARY E., INSTITUTIONAL AND NORMATIVE ANALYSIS OF THE WORLD TRADE ORGANIZATION (2006).

9. GEHRING, MARKUS W., JARROD HEPBURN & MARIE-CLAIRE CORDONIER SEGGER, WORLD TRADE LAW IN PRACTICE (2006).

10. HEAD, JOHN W., THE FUTURE OF THE GLOBAL ECONOMIC ORGANIZATIONS: AN EVALUATION OF CRITICISMS LEVELED AT THE IMF, THE MULTILATERAL DEVELOPMENT BANKS, AND THE WTO (2005).

11. HOEKMAN, BERNARD M. & MICHEL M. KOSTECKI, THE POLITICAL ECONOMY OF THE WORLD TRADING SYSTEM — THE WTO AND BEYOND (3rd ed. 2009).

12. JACKSON, JOHN H., RESTRUCTURING THE GATT SYSTEM (1990).

13. JACKSON, JOHN H., THE WORLD TRADING SYSTEM — LAW AND POLICY OF INTERNATIONAL ECONOMIC ORGANIZATIONS (2nd ed. 1997).

14. JACKSON, JOHN H., THE WORLD TRADE ORGANIZATION — CONSTITUTION AND JURISPRUDENCE 81–89 (1998).

15. JACKSON, JOHN H., SOVEREIGNTY; THE WTO AND CHANGING FUNDAMENTALS OF INTERNATIONAL LAW (2006).

16. JOERGES, CHRISTIAN & ERNST-ULRICH PETERSMANN EDS., CONSTITUTIONALISM, MULTILEVEL TRADE GOVERNANCE AND SOCIAL REGULATION (2006).

---

[732] *Mangling Trade*, ECONOMIST, 28 June 2007, at 86.

17. Kotera, Akira, Ichiro Araki and Tsuyoshi Kawase, The Future of the Multilateral Trading System: East Asian Perspectives (2009).

18. Krueger, Anne O., ed., The WTO as an International Organization (1998).

19. Matsushita, Mitsuo, Thomas J. Schoenbaum & Petros C. Mavroidis, The World Trade Organization — Law, Practice, and Policy (2nd ed. 2005).

20. O'Rourke, Kevin H., ed., The International Trading System, Globalization and History vols. I and II (2005).

21. Porter, Roger B., Pierre Sauvé, Arvind Subramanian & Americo Beviglia Zampetti eds., Efficiency, Equity, Legitimacy — The Multilateral Trading System at the Millennium (2001).

22. Qureshi, Asif H. & Andreas R. Ziegler, International Economic Law chs. 11–13 (2nd ed. 2007).

23. Ruttley, Philip, Iain MacVay & Carol George, The WTO and International Trade Regulation (1998).

24. Sally, Razeen, New Frontiers in Free Trade — Globalization's Future and Asia's Rising Role (2008).

25. Schott, Jeffrey J., ed., The WTO After Seattle (July 2000).

26. Steger, Debra P., ed., Redesigning the World Trade Organization for the Twenty-First Century (2009).

27. Stewart, Terence P., ed., The World Trade Organization — Multilateral Trade Framework for the 21st Century and U.S. Implementing Legislation (1996).

28. Thomas, Jeffrey S. & Michael A. Meyer, The New Rules of Global Trade — A Guide to the World Trade Organization (1997).

29. Trebilcock, Michael J. & Robert Howse, The Regulation of International Trade (3rd ed. 2005).

30. Wallach, Lori & Michelle Sforza, The WTO — Five Years of Reasons to Resist Corporate Globalization (1999).

31. Whalley, John & Colleen Hamilton, The Trading System After the Uruguay Round (July 1996).

32. Wouters, Jan & Bart de Meester, The World Trade Organization: A Legal and Institutional Analysis (Antwerpen, The Netherlands: Intersentia, 2007). *See also* the Book Review by Peter McLaverty, 8 Journal of International Trade Law & Policy number 1, 95 (2009).

Book Chapters:

1. Weiss, Friedl, *Competition as a WTO Subject, in* Economic Law as an Economic Good — Its Rule Function and its Tool Function in the Competition of Systems 243–267 (Karl M. Meessen, ed., München, Germany: Sellier European Law Publishers, 2009).

Articles:

1. Alvarez, José E., *Contemporary International Law: An "Empire of Law" or the "Law of Empire"?*, 24 American University International Law Review 811–842 (2009).

2. Bradford, Anu, *When the WTO Works, and How It Fails*, 51 VIRGINIA JOURNAL OF INTERNATIONAL LAW 1–56 (2010).

3. Busch, Marc L., Eric Reinhardt & Gregory Shaffer, *Does Legal Capacity Matter? A Survey of WTO Members*, 8 WORLD TRADE REVIEW issue 4, 559–577 (2009).

4. Cho, Sungjoon, *Global Constitutional Lawmaking*, 31 UNIVERSITY OF PENNSYLVANIA JOURNAL OF INTERNATIONAL ECONOMIC LAW 621–678 2010).

5. Coffield, Shirley A., *Book Review*, 23 GEORGE WASHINGTON JOURNAL OF INTERNATIONAL LAW & ECONOMICS 825–830 (1990) (reviewing John H. Jackson, *Restructuring the GATT System* (1990)).

6. Cooney, Rosie & Andrew T.F. Lang, *Taking Uncertainty Seriously: Adaptive Governance and International Trade*, 18 EUROPEAN JOURNAL OF INTERNATIONAL LAW 523–551 (2007).

7. Cottier, Thomas, *Preparing for Structural Reform in the WTO*, 10 JOURNAL OF INTERNATIONAL ECONOMIC LAW 497–508 (2007).

8. Dam, Kenneth W., *Cordell Hull, The Reciprocal Trade Agreements Act, and the WTO — An Essay on the Concept of Rights in International Trade*, 1 NEW YORK UNIVERSITY JOURNAL OF LAW AND BUSINESS 709–730 (2005).

9. Diebold, Nicolas F., *The Morals and Order Exceptions in WTO Law: Balancing the Toothless Tiger and the Undermining Mole*, 11 JOURNAL OF INTERNATIONAL ECONOMIC LAW 43–74 (2008).

10. Du, Michael Ming, *The Rise of National Regulatory Autonomy in the GATT/WTO Regime*, 14 JOURNAL OF INTERNATIONAL ECONOMIC LAW 639–675 (2011).

11. EJIL: Debate!, *Taking Uncertainty Seriously: Adaptive Governance and International Trade*, reply by Mónica García-Salmones, rejoinder by Andrew Lang and Rosie Cooney, 20 EUROPEAN JOURNAL OF INTERNATIONAL LAW 167–192 (2009).

12. Emmerson, Andrew, *Conceptualizing Security Exceptions: Legal Doctrine or Political Excuse?*, 11 JOURNAL OF INTERNATIONAL ECONOMIC LAW 135–154 (2008).

13. Esty, Daniel C., *Good Governance at the World Trade Organization: Building a Foundation of Administrative Law*, 10 JOURNAL OF INTERNATIONAL ECONOMIC LAW 509–527 (2007).

14. Feichtner, Isabel, *The Waiver Power of the WTO: Opening the WTO for Political Debate on the Reconciliation of Competing Interests*, EUROPEAN JOURNAL OF INTERNATIONAL LAW 615–645 (2009).

15. Gerber, David J., *Competition Law and the WTO: Rethinking the Relationship*, 10 JOURNAL OF INTERNATIONAL ECONOMIC LAW 707–724 (2007).

16. Harrison, James, *Legal and Political Oversight of WTO Waivers*, 11 JOURNAL OF INTERNATIONAL ECONOMIC LAW 411–425 (2008).

17. Hoekman, Bernard, Proposals for WTO Reform: A Synthesis and Assessment, 20 MINNESOTA JOURNAL OF INTERNATIONAL LAW 324–364 (2011).

18. Hsieh, Pasha L., *China's Development of International Economic Law and WTO Legal Capacity Building*, 13 JOURNAL OF INTERNATIONAL ECONOMIC LAW 997–1036 (2010).

19. Kill, Theodore, *The Evidence for Constitutionalization of the WTO: Revisiting the Telmex Report*, 20 MINNESOTA JOURNAL OF INTERNATIONAL LAW 65–122 (2011).

20. Kolbein, Kevin, *The WTO Distraction*, 21 STANFORD LAW & POLICY REVIEW 461–491 (2010).

21. Lang, Andrew & Joanne Scott, *The Hidden World of WTO Governance*, EUROPEAN JOURNAL OF INTERNATIONAL LAW 575–614 (2009).

22. Leader, Sheldon, *The Collateral Protection of Rights in a Global Economy*, 53 NEW YORK LAW SCHOOL LAW REVIEW 805–814 (2008–09).

23. Lockhart, Nicholas & Elizabeth Sheargold, *In Search of Relevant Discretion: The Role of Mandatory/Discretionary Distinction in WTO Law*, 13 JOURNAL OF INTERNATIONAL ECONOMIC LAW 379–421 (2010).

24. Lodge, Aaron, *Globalization: Panacea for the World or Conquistador of International Law and Statehood?*, 7 OREGON REVIEW OF INTERNATIONAL LAW 224-303 (2005).

25. Lynch, Elizabeth M., *China's Rule of Law Mirage: The Regression of the Legal Profession Since the Adoption of the 2007 Lawyers Law*, 42 GEORGE WASHINGTON INTERNATIONAL LAW REVIEW 535–585 (2010).

26. Martin, Mervyn & Maryam Shademan Pajouh, *Rebalancing the Balance: How the WTO's HR Policy Impacts on Its Very Objectives for Welfare Enhancement and Development*, 10 JOURNAL OF INTERNATIONAL TRADE LAW AND POLICY number 3, 243–254 (2011).

27. McGrady, Benn, *Necessity Exceptions in WTO Law: Retreaded Tyres, Regulatory Purpose, and Cumulative Regulatory Measures*, 12 JOURNAL OF INTERNATIONAL ECONOMIC LAW 153–173 (2009).

28. Pavel, Carmen, *Normative Conflict in International Law*, 46 SAN DIEGO LAW REVIEW 883–907 (2009).

29. Pavoni, Riccardo, *Mutual Supportiveness as a Principle of Interpretation and Law-Making: A Watershed for the "WTO-and-Competing-Regimes" Debate?*, 21 EUROPEAN JOURNAL OF INTERNATIONAL LAW 649–679 (2010).

30. Pérez, Jorge, *The Decay of Commercial Multilateralism in South America*, 28 SAINT LOUIS UNIVERSITY PUBLIC LAW REVIEW 295–315 (2008).

31. Petersmann, Ernst-Ulrich, *Multilevel Judicial Governance of International Trade Requires a Common Conception of Rule of Law and Justice*, 10 JOURNAL OF INTERNATIONAL ECONOMIC LAW 529–551 (2007).

32. Reyes, Carla L., Comment, *International Governance of Domestic National Security Measures: The Forgotten Role of the World Trade Organization*, 14 UCLA JOURNAL OF INTERNATIONAL LAW & FOREIGN AFFAIRS 531–566 (2009).

33. Roessler, Frieder, *et al.*, *Performance of the System IV: Implementation — Comments*, 32 THE INTERNATIONAL LAWYER 789, 790, 792–93 (1998) (question

and answer summary; views of Timothy Reif; comments of Professor Roessler; question and answer summary; views of Professor Jackson; comments of Richard Elliott).

34. Rolland, Sonia E., *Redesigning the Negotiation Process at the WTO*, 13 JOURNAL OF INTERNATIONAL ECONOMIC LAW 65–110 (2010).

35. Rothchild, John A., *Exhausting Extraterritoriality*, 51 SANTA CLARA LAW REVIEW 1187–1239 (2011).

36. Ruddy, Brendan, Note, *The Critical Success of the WTO: Trade Policies of the Current Economic Crisis*, 13 JOURNAL OF INTERNATIONAL ECONOMIC LAW 475–495 (2010).

37. Shaffer, Gregory & Joel Trachtman, *Interpretation and Institutional Choice at the WTO*, 52 VIRGINIA JOURNAL OF INTERNATIONAL LAW 103–153 (2011).

38. Simmons, Beth A. & Student Andrew B. Breudenbach, *The Empirical turn in International Economic Law*, 20 MINNESOTA JOURNAL OF INTERNATIONAL LAW 198–222 (2011).

39. Sreejith, S.G., *Public International Law and the WTO: A Reckoning of Legal Positivism and Neoliberalism*, 9 SAN DIEGO INTERNATIONAL LAW JOURNAL 5–79 (2007).

40. Steger, Debra P., *The Culture of the WTO: Why it Needs to Change*, 10 JOURNAL OF INTERNATIONAL ECONOMIC LAW 483–495 (2007).

41. Steger, Debra P., *The Future of the WTO: The Case for Institutional Reform*, 12 JOURNAL OF INTERNATIONAL ECONOMIC LAW 803–833 (2009).

42. *Symposium: The Boundaries of the WTO*, 96 AMERICAN JOURNAL OF INTERNATIONAL LAW number 1–158 (January 2002).

43. *Symposium — The WTO at 10 and the Road to Hong Kong*, 24 ARIZONA JOURNAL OF INTERNATIONAL AND COMPARATIVE LAW 1–297 (2007).

44. *Symposium: Operationalizing Global Governance*, 16 INDIANA JOURNAL OF GLOBAL LEGAL STUDIES 1–361 (2009).

45. *The Future of the WTO*, 19 THE CATO JOURNAL number 3 345–461 (winter 2000).

46. Toohey, Lisa, *China and the World Trade Organization: The First Decade*, 60 INTERNATIONAL & COMPARATIVE LAW QUARTERLY 788–795 (2011).

47. Trachtman, Joel P., *Regulatory Jurisdiction and the WTO*, 10 JOURNAL OF INTERNATIONAL ECONOMIC LAW 631–651 (2007).

48. Vranes, Erich, *The WTO and Regulatory Freedom: WTO Disciplines on Market Access, Non-Discrimination and Domestic Regulation Relating to Trade in Goods and Services*, 12 JOURNAL OF INTERNATIONAL ECONOMIC LAW 953–987 (2009).

49. Zang, Dongsheng, *Divided by a Common Language: "Capture" Theories in GATT/WTO and the Communicative Impasse*, 32 HASTINGS INTERNATIONAL & COMPARATIVE LAW REVIEW 423–476 (2009).

50. Zhao, Jun & Timothy Webster, *Taking Stock: China's First Decade of Free Trade*, 33 UNIVERSITY OF PENNSYLVANIA JOURNAL OF INTERNATIONAL LAW 65–119 (2011).

Other Sources:

1.   Hoekman, Bernard M., *Trade Laws and Institutions — Good Practices and the World Trade Organization*, World Bank Discussion Paper number 282 (1995).

2.   ORGANIZATION FOR ECONOMIC COOPERATION AND DEVELOPMENT (OECD), THE NEW WORLD TRADING SYSTEM — READINGS (1994).

3.   Weiss, Wolfgang, *Shift in Paradigm: From the New International Economic Order to the World Trade Organization — Germany's Contribution to the Development of International Economic Law*, 46 GERMAN YEARBOOK OF INTERNATIONAL LAW 171–225 (2003).

## *WTO AGREEMENT*

*Agreement Establishing the World Trade Organization.*

The *WTO Agreement* was reached on 15 December 1993, at the end of the Uruguay Round, and signed on 15 April 1994 in Marrakech, Morocco.[733] It entered into force in the United States and all other Members on 1 January 1995.

The *WTO Agreement* defines the scope, structure, and functions of the WTO. In particular, the *Agreement* calls for a single institutional framework that encompasses the General Agreement on Tariffs and Trade (GATT) and all agreements and arrangements concluded under the auspices of the Uruguay Round. These agreements are included in the Annexes 1, 2, 3 and 4. Annexes 1, 2, and 3 contain the multilateral trade agreements (MTAs), and Annex 4 consists of the plurilateral trade agreements (PTAs).

The *WTO Agreement* has no expiration date. With certain important exceptions, under Article X of the *Agreement*, any amendment to the *Agreement* requires a two-thirds majority vote of the WTO Members. Under Article X:1, X:3, and X:5, an amendment is not binding on an objecting Member, unless three-fourths of the Members state otherwise.

*Suggestions for Further Research:*

Books:

1.   BOSSCHE, PETER VAN DEN, THE LAW AND POLICY OF THE WORLD TRADE ORGANIZATION: TEXT, CASES AND MATERIALS (2005).

2.   BUCKLEY, ROSS P., ED., THE WTO AND THE DOHA ROUND: THE CHANGING FACE OF WORLD TRADE (2003).

3.   CROOME, JOHN, GUIDE TO THE URUGUAY ROUND AGREEMENTS (1999).

4.   DALHUISEN, JAN, TRANSNATIONAL AND COMPARATIVE COMMERCIAL, FINANCE, AND TRADE LAW (Hart Publishing, 2007).

5.   GEHRING, MARKUS W., JARROD HEPBURN & MARIE-CLAIRE CORDONIER SEGGER, WORLD TRADE LAW IN PRACTICE (2006).

---

[733] *See* 19 U.S.C. § 3501(9).

6.  JACKSON, JOHN H., THE WORLD TRADING SYSTEM — LAW AND POLICY OF INTERNATIONAL ECONOMIC ORGANIZATIONS (2nd ed. 1997).

7.  MATSUSHITA, MITSUO, THOMAS J. SCHOENBAUM & PETROS C. MAVROIDIS, THE WORLD TRADE ORGANIZATION — LAW, PRACTICE, AND POLICY (2nd ed. 2005).

8.  STEWART, TERENCE P., ED., THE WORLD TRADE ORGANIZATION — MULTILATERAL TRADE FRAMEWORK FOR THE 21ST CENTURY AND U.S. IMPLEMENTING LEGISLATION (1996).

9.  TREBILCOCK, MICHAEL J. & ROBERT HOWSE, THE REGULATION OF INTERNATIONAL TRADE (3rd ed. 2005).

Articles:

1.  Andenas, Mads & Stefan Zleptnig, *Proportionality: WTO Law in Comparative Perspective*, 42 TEXAS INTERNATIONAL LAW JOURNAL 371–427 (2007).

2.  Carmody, Chios, *A Theory of WTO Law*, 11 JOURNAL OF INTERNATIONAL ECONOMIC LAW 527–557 (2008).

3.  Sloss, David, *The Constitutional Right to a Treaty Preemption Defense*, 40 UNIVERSITY OF TOLEDO LAW REVIEW 971–997 (2009).

Other Source:

1.  ORGANIZATION FOR ECONOMIC COOPERATION AND DEVELOPMENT (OECD), THE NEW WORLD TRADING SYSTEM — READINGS (1994).

## WTO AGREEMENTS

A generic term to embrace all agreements reached among and approved by WTO Members.

The term *"WTO Agreement"* should not be confused with "WTO agreements." The former term refers to a particular agreement, evidenced by the use of the singular. The latter term, which is in the plural, generically covers all WTO accords — the *WTO Agreement*, plus the accords in the four Annexes to that *Agreement*.

*Suggestions for Further Research:*

Article:

1.  Schaffer, Gregory C. & Mark A. Pollack, *Hard vs. Soft Law: Alternatives, Complements, and Antagonists in International Governance*, 94 MINNESOTA LAW REVIEW 706–799 (February 2010).

## WTO MEMBER

A country or separate customs territory that has acceded to the WTO.

Any state or customs territory that has full sovereignty over its trade policy is eligible for accession to the WTO.

Following the rules set out in the *Agreement Establishing the World Trade Organization* (*WTO Agreement*), GATT, plus traditional practice, the accession of a party to the WTO includes four stages.

- First, the government applying for membership must disclose all aspects of its trade and economic policies that have a bearing on WTO agreements, usually in the form of a memorandum. A working party is assigned to review the document.

- Second, while the working party reviews the memorandum, bilateral talks begin between the prospective new member and individual Member countries. These talks cover tariff rates and specific market access commitments.

- Third, after the working group has completed its review of the prospective new member's trade regime and the bilateral talks are complete, the working party finalizes the terms of accession.

- Last, the final package, consisting of a report, protocol and list of commitments is presented to the WTO Ministerial Conference or General Council.

Upon two-thirds approval of all members, the party will successfully accede to the WTO. The legislature or parliament of the newly approved Member must ratify the agreement before membership is complete.

*Suggestions for Further Research:*

Articles:

1. Mushkat, Miron & Roda Mushkat, *The Political Economy of State Accession to International Legal Regimes — A Re-Assessment of the China–World Trade Organization Nexus*, 10 JOURNAL OF INTERNATIONAL TRADE LAW AND POLICY issue 1, 5–28 (2011).

2. Santoro, Thomas H., Student Work, *In the Club: A Study of the Correlation between World Trade Organization Membership and National Wealth*, 42 WAKE FOREST LAW REVIEW 1201–1223 (2007).

## WTO MINISTERIAL CONFERENCE

*See* Ministerial Conference.

## WTO-MINUS

The opposite of WTO-Plus.

"WTO-Minus" is an adjective to characterize an obligation created by a bilateral trade agreement, or a regional trade agreement (RTA), such as a free trade agreement (FTA). A "WTO-Minus" obligation is less demanding than a corresponding commitment in a WTO agreement. That is, a WTO-minus provision is a reduction in regular WTO obligations imposed on a Member state. Depending on the circumstances, a WTO-Minus commitment could be inconsistent with WTO rules.

The term "WTO-Minus" also refers to particular rights or benefits forgone by a newly acceded Member State to the WTO that other Members enjoy. That is, WTO-Minus obligations are those requirements that weaken the rights or privileges afforded to newly acceded WTO Members. For example, a tariff quota on particular goods from a country would be a WTO-Minus provision. As another example, a condition on the accession of China's to the WTO was acceptance by China of temporary restrictions on the use of antidumping (AD) and safeguard measures, as well as permanent special subsidy rules.

*Suggestions for Further Research:*

Articles:

1.   Charnovitz, Steve, *Taiwan's WTO Membership and its International Implications*, 1 ASIAN JOURNAL OF WTO & INTERNATIONAL HEALTH LAW & POLICY 401–31 (2006).

2.   Nguyen, Nhan, Comment, *WTO Accession at Any Cost? Examining the Use of WTO-Plus and WTO-Minus Obligations for Least-Developed Country Applicants*, 22 TEMPLE INTERNATIONAL & COMPARATIVE LAW JOURNAL 243–277 (2009).

3.   Ya Qin, Julia, *WTO-Plus Obligations and their Implications for the World Trade Organization Legal System: An Appraisal of the China Accession Protocol*, 37 Journal of World Trade 483–522 (2003).

## WTO PANEL

An independent group of three experts established by the Dispute Settlement Body (DSB) to examine and issue recommendations on a particular dispute in light of WTO provisions.

If a dispute arises between WTO Members, then each Member must engage in a consultation to try resolving the issue. If, after 60 days, the consultations do not resolve the dispute, a request may be made for the establishment of a WTO Panel. The request must identify specific measures at issue and provide a brief summary of the legal basis of the problem sufficient to present the problem clearly. A Panel is then established no later than the second DSB meeting at which the request is made (and is decided by a negative consensus).

Once the Panel is established, Article 7 of the WTO *Understanding on Rules and Procedures Governing the Settlement of Disputes (Dispute Settlement Understanding, or DSU)* requires the Panel to set forth its Terms of Reference, which are either standard or special terms. Article 8 of the *DSU* states the panel is comprised of "well qualified government and/or non-governmental individuals." These individuals are usually nominated by the Director-General.

The principal function of a WTO Panel, according to *DSU* Article 11, is to

> make an *objective assessment of the matter before it*, including an *objective assessment of the facts* of the case and the *applicability* of and *conformity* with the relevant covered agreements. . . . [Emphasis added.]

When a dispute is brought before the Panel, usually two oral hearings are held. In addition, the Panel may seek factual information from any relevant source or scientific or technical advice from an expert under Article 13 and Appendix 4 of the *DSU*. After the hearings, the Panel will issue the descriptive part of a drafted report to the Parties. The Panel then reviews the draft in the interim before it issues a final report to the parties. All final reports are circulated to all Members. Upon the establishment of a Panel, a final report must be issued within nine months. If there is an appeal, however, then the Panel will have 12 months to issue a report. Panel reports are adopted within 60 days of circulation by reverse (negative) consensus.

*Suggestions for Further Research:*

Book:

1. YERXA, RUFUS & BRUCE WILSON EDS., KEY ISSUES IN WTO DISPUTE SETTLEMENT (2005).

Articles:

1. Chua, Adrian T.L., *Precedent and Principles of WTO Panel Jurisprudence*, 16 BERKLEY JOURNAL OF INTERNATIONAL LAW 171–96 (1998).

2. Kantchevski, Petko D., *The Differences Between the Panel Procedures of the GATT and the Role of GATT and WTO Panels in Trade Dispute Settlement*, 3 BRIGHAM YOUNG UNIVERSITY INTERNATIONAL LAW & MANAGEMENT REVIEW 79–139 (2006).

3. Nichols, Dan, *Use of WTO Panel Decisions in Judicial Review of Administrative Action under U.S. Antidumping Law*, 1 BRIGHAM YOUNG UNIVERSITY INTERNATIONAL LAW & MANAGEMENT REVIEW 237–81 (2005).

4. Stewart, Terence P., *The WTO Panel Process: An Evaluation of the First Three Years*, 32 THE INTERNATIONAL LAWYER 709–35 (1998).

## WTO-PLUS

The opposite of WTO-Minus.

"WTO-Plus" is an adjective to characterize an obligation created by a bilateral trade agreement, or a regional trade agreement (RTA), such as a free trade agreement (FTA). A "WTO-Plus" obligation goes beyond what is set forth in an analogous WTO agreement, or what is required by WTO rules.

For example, the *Agreement on Trade-Related Aspects of Intellectual Property Rights (TRIPs)* requires WTO Members to provide for patent protection for 20 years. A WTO-Plus commitment — specifically, a *TRIPs-Plus* obligation — would mandate 25 years. In 2005–06, the United States called for such a commitment in FTA negotiations with Thailand. It is typical for the United States to negotiate WTO-Plus provisions in its FTAs. As another example, Chapter 15 of the *North American Free Trade Agreement (NAFTA)* on competition policy, monopolies, and state enterprises, contains WTO-Plus obligations. That is because there are no provisions in the WTO texts dealing with antitrust matters.

The term "WTO-Plus" may also mean obligations exceeding the existing requirements of WTO agreements. That is, WTO-Plus obligations are requirements going beyond minimum standards stated in WTO agreements. For example, China agreed to enhanced obligations concerning the rule of law and foreign investment when it acceded to the WTO in 2001.

*Suggestions for Further Research:*

Books:

1. EL SAID, MOHAMMED, THE DEVELOPMENT OF INTELLECTUAL PROPERTY PROTECTION IN THE ARAB WORLD (2008).

2. EL SAID, MOHAMMED K., PUBLIC HEALTH RELATED TRIPS-PLUS PROVISIONS IN BILATERAL TRADE AGREEMENTS: A POLICY GUIDE FOR NEGOTIATORS AND IMPLEMENTERS IN THE WHO EASTERN MEDITERRANEAN REGION (World Health Organization and International Centre for Trade and Sustainable Development, 2010).

Book Chapters:

1. Woolcock, Stephen, *A Framework for Assessing Regional Trade Agreements: WTO-Plus*, in REGIONALISM, MULTILATERALISM, AND ECONOMIC INTEGRATION: THE RECENT EXPERIENCE (Gary P. Sampson & Stephen Woolcock eds., 2003).

Articles:

1. Charnovitz, Steve, *Taiwan's WTO Membership and its International Implications*, 1 ASIAN JOURNAL OF WTO & INTERNATIONAL HEALTH LAW & POLICY 401–31 (2006).

2. El Said, Mohammed, *Surpassing Checks, Overriding Balances and Diminishing Flexibilities — FTA-IPRs Plus Bilateral Trade Agreements: From Jordan to Oman*, 8 THE JOURNAL OF WORLD INVESTMENT & TRADE 243–268 (2007).

3. El Said, Mohammed K., Editorial: *Free Trade, Intellectual Property, and TRIPs-Plus World*, 28 LIVERPOOL LAW REVIEW 1–9 (2007).

4. El Said, Mohammed K., *The European TRIPs-Plus Model and the Arab World: From Co-operation to Association — A New Era in the Global IPRs Regime?*, 28 LIVERPOOL LAW REVIEW 143–174 (2007).

5. Frankel, Susy, *Challenging TRIPs-Plus Agreements: The Potential Utility of Non-Violation Disputes*, 12 JOURNAL OF INTERNATIONAL ECONOMIC LAW 1023–1065 (2009).

6. Grosse Ruse-Khan, Henning, *The International Law Relation between TRIPs and Subsequent TRIPs-Plus Free Trade Agreements: Towards Safeguarding TRIPs Flexibilities*, 18 JOURNAL OF INTELLECTUAL PROPERTY LAW 325–365 (2011).

7. Lin, Tsai-Yu, *Compulsory Licenses for Access to Medicines, Expropriation, and Investor-State Arbitration Under Bilateral Investment Agreements — Are There Issues Beyond the TRIPs Agreement?*, 40 IIC: INTERNATIONAL REVIEW OF INTELLECTUAL PROPERTY & COMPETITION LAW 152–173 (2009).

8. Lindstrom, Beatrice, Note, *Scaling Back TRIPs-Plus: An Analysis of Intellectual Property Provisions in Trade Agreements and Implications for Asia and the Pacific*, 42 NEW YORK UNIVERSITY JOURNAL OF INTERNATIONAL LAW & POLITICS 917–980 (2010).

9.  Nesheiwat, Ferris K., *The Adoption of Intellectual Property Standards Beyond TRIPs — Is It a Misguided Legal and Economic Obsession by Developing Countries?*, 32 LOYOLA OF LOS ANGELES INTERNATIONAL & COMPARATIVE LAW REVIEW 361–394 (2010).

10. Nguyen, Nhan, Comment, *WTO Accession at Any Cost? Examining the Use of WTO-Plus and WTO-Minus Obligations for Least-Developed Country Applicants*, 22 TEMPLE INTERNATIONAL & COMPARATIVE LAW JOURNAL 243–277 (2009).

11. Sell, Susan K., *TRIPs Was Never Enough: Vertical Forum Shifting, FTAs, ACTA, and TPP*, 18 JOURNAL OF INTELLECTUAL PROPERTY 447–478 (2011).

12. Turk, Matthew, Note, *Bargaining and Intellectual Property Treaties: the Case for a Pro-Development Interpretation of TRIPs But Not TRIPs Plus*, 42 NEW YORK UNIVERSITY JOURNAL OF INTERNATIONAL LAW & POLITICS 981–1029 (2010).

13. Ya Qin, Julia, *WTO-Plus Obligations and their Implications for the World Trade Organization Legal System: An Appraisal of the China Accession Protocol*, 37 JOURNAL OF WORLD TRADE 483–522 (2003).

## WTO OBSERVER

A country or separate customs territory that is an Observer at the WTO.

Observer status is given to a Party once a working group on their accession has been established. Generally, WTO Observer status provides the Party access to WTO capacity building assistance and the opportunity to attend and learn from WTO meetings. Indeed, observers can participate in meetings but they cannot take part in the decision-making process. Only the Holy See has permanent status as an Observer. All other Observers are supposed to commence accession negotiations within five years of gaining that status.

Observers, other than the Holy See, include:

- Afghanistan
- Algeria
- Andorra
- Azerbaijan
- Bahamas
- Belarus
- Bhutan
- Bosnia and Herzegovina
- Cape Verde
- Equitorial Guinea
- Ethiopia
- Iran
- Iraq
- Kazakhstan
- Laos (Lao People's Democratic Republic)
- Lebanese Republic
- Libya
- Montenegro
- Russian Federation
- Samoa
- Sao Tomé and Príncipe
- Serbia
- Seychelles

- Sudan
- Tajikistan
- Tonga
- Ukraine
- Uzbekistan
- Vanuatu
- Yemen

Several international intergovernmental organizations have been granted observer status to several WTO bodies. Observer status is granted to enable those organizations to follow discussions within the WTO on matters of direct interest to them. Observer organizations include:

- African Caribbean and Pacific Group of States (ACP)
- African Union (AU)
- Caribbean Community Secretariat
- Central African Economic and Monetary Community
- Common Fund for Commodities
- Commonwealth Secretariat
- Convention on Biological Diversity
- Convention on International Trade in Endangered Species of Wild Fauna and Flora
- Cooperation Council for the Arab States of the Gulf (GCC)
- Economic Community of West African States (ECOWAS)
- Economic Cooperation Organization
- European Bank for Reconstruction and Development (EBRD)
- European Free Trade Association (EFTA)
- Food and Agriculture Organization (FAO)
- FAO International Plant Protection Convention
- Inter-American Development Bank (IADB)
- Inter-American Institute for Agricultural Cooperation
- Inter-Arab Investment Guarantee Cooperation
- International Electrotechnical Commission
- International Commission for the Conservation of Atlantic Tunas
- International Grains Council
- International Monetary Fund (IMF)
- International Office of Epizootics
- International Organization of Legal Metrology
- International Organization for Standardization
- International Plant Genetic Resources Institute
- International Telecommunication Union (ITU)
- International Textiles and Clothing Bureau
- International Union for the Protection of New Varieties of Plants

- Islamic Development Bank
- Latin American Economic System
- Latin American Integration Association
- Organization of American States (OAS)
- Organization for Economic Cooperation and Development (OECD)
- Organization of the Islamic Conference (OIC)
- Pacific Islands Forum
- Permanent Secretariat of the General Treaty on Central American Economic Integration
- Regional International Organization for Plant Protection and Animal Health
- South Centre
- Southeast Asian Fisheries Development Center
- Southern African Development Community (SADC)
- United Nations (U.N.)
- United Nations Commission for Sustainable Development
- United Nations Conference on Trade and Development (UNCTAD)
- United Nations Development Program (UNDP)
- United Nations Economic Commission for Africa
- United Nations Economic Commission for Europe
- United Nations Economic Commission for Latin America and the Caribbean
- United Nations Economic and Social Commission for Asia and the Pacific
- United Nations Environment Program
- United Nations Framework Convention on Climate Change
- United Nations Industrial Development Organization (UNIDO)
- United Nations World Food Program
- United Postal Union
- West African Economic and Monetary Union
- World Bank
- World Customs Organization (WCO)
- World Health Organization (WHO)
- World Intellectual Property Organization (WIPO)
- World Tourism Organization

To date, no non-governmental organization (NGO) has been granted Observer status to the WTO. The WTO does, however, grant NGOs limited access to Ministerial Conferences and various other events.

# Y

## YARN

"Yarn" is a product of substantial length, but relatively thin cross-section, comprised of interlocking fibers, and is used to produce textiles, as well as for sewing, knitting, weaving, and rope making.

Fibers themselves come from plants and animals. Cotton is the most common plant fiber used to produce yarn. The most common animal fiber, wool, is collected from sheep. Synthetic materials, such as acrylic and nylon, also are used to produce yarn. Moreover, yarn may be a blend of any of the three classes of fiber mentioned above. Cotton-polyester is an example of a widely-used blend.

Yarn is made by either a spinning or air texturizing ("taslanizing") process. Essentially, a yarn is made from twisting plies together, with each ply being a single thread. Twisting together two or more plies produces a different type of yarn, namely, cord yarn. The final yarn is a result of twisting, or plying, the threads together. Generally, plies are twisted in opposite directions to make the yarn thicker. The more the plies are twisted, the stronger the yarn becomes. In the end, the yarn will be known as "s- or z-twist yarn," depending on the direction of the final twisting. In brief, "yarn" is simply "thin fibers spun together." A "thread," then, is a thin yarn used to make textiles, and of course in sewing.

With 34 million spinners, India produces more yarn than any other country in the world, with China spinning its way into second place.[734] In 2006, the United States produced over 7 billion pounds of yarn.

*Suggestions for Further Research:*

Books:

1. GOSWAMI, BHUVENESH CHANDRA, TEXTILE YARNS: TECHNOLOGY, STRUCTURE, AND APPLICATIONS (1977).

2. KADOLPH, SARA J., TEXTILES (2007).

3. LONG, A.C., ED., DESIGN AND MANUFACTURE OF TEXTILE COMPOSITES (2005).

4. NEEDLES, H.L., TEXTILE FIBERS, DYES, FINISHES AND PROCESSES (1986).

## YARN-FORWARD

A rule of origin for textile and apparel (T&A) merchandise that requires the production process, from the making of yarn to the completion of the finished article, be conducted in a particular country for the article to qualify as originating in that country.

---

[734] *See The Looming Revolution,* ECONOMIST, 11 November 2004, at 68.

As an example, suppose the Member countries of the *Mercado Común del Sur* (*MERCOSUR*) implement a yarn-forward rule of origin for all *sungas* (the Brazilian-Portuguese word for a male bathing suit, commonly known as a "Speedo") produced within that customs union (CU). For the *sungas* to qualify as originating within *MERCOSUR*, the production process from the making of the yarn to the completion of the finished *sunga* must occur within one or multiple *MERCOSUR* countries. Another example is Chapter 5 of the *North American Free Trade Agreement* (*NAFTA*), which requires that any yarn used to form fabric must originate in a *NAFTA* country.

The United States imposes a yarn-forward rule of origin in most of its free trade agreements (FTAs). Those FTAs with yarn-forward rules of origin include:

- Australia
- Bahrain
- *Central American Free Trade Agreement–Dominican Republic* (*CAFTA-DR*)
- Chile
- *Korea–United States Free Trade Agreement* (*KORUS*)
- Morocco
- *NAFTA*
- Oman
- Singapore

Although most rules of origin requirements in *CAFTA-DR* and *NAFTA* are yarn-forward, there are limited exceptions. These exceptions deal mainly with yarn produced from fibers that are in short supply in the region, such as silk. United States FTAs with Israel and Jordan do not, however, include a yarn-forward rule of origin. Rather, those FTAs permit unlimited third-country yarn and fabric to be used in apparel eligible for duty-free treatment.

To be sure, there are stricter and less demanding rules of origin. A "fiber-forward" rule of origin is an example of a rule that is more strict than yarn-forward. It requires that the fabric used to produce yarn and any subsequent processing must occur in a particular country. Conversely, an example of a more lenient rule of origin is a "single-transformation" rule. It requires that a good undergo a "single transformation" in a particular country to be considered originating in that country. An example of a single transformation includes the sewing on of sleeves or collars on dress shirts.

Notwithstanding distinct rules of origin, a yarn-forward requirement is protectionist. That requirement is the second most restrictive type of specified process requirement. Indeed, placement of a yarn-forward rule of origin in the *African Growth and Opportunity Act* (*AGOA*) draws heavy criticism from many members in the international trade community.

*Suggestions for Further Research:*

Article:

1.   Baker, Mark B., *No Country Left Behind: The Exporting of U.S. Legal Norms Under the Guise of Economic Integration*, 19 EMORY INTERNATIONAL LAW REVIEW 1321, 1361 (2005).

# Z

## ZERO FOR X

A rule, or proposal, typically in the context of cutting tariffs as between developed and developing countries.

In the Doha Round of multilateral trade negotiations, specifically in sectoral negotiations on non-agricultural market access (NAMA), one proposal (among many offered) was "zero for X." Under it, developed countries would eliminate their industrial tariffs on imports of products within an industrial sector. That elimination represented the "zero." In exchange — the "X" — developing countries would reduce their tariffs by more than the cut applicable generally to industrial products (under the Swiss Formula). But, X would exceed zero, meaning the cut would not reduce developing country tariffs in that same sector to zero. In that Round, the sectors under negotiation included automobiles and auto parts, bicycles and bicycle parts, chemicals, electronics and electronic products, fish and fish products, forestry products, gems and jewelry, hand tools, health care products, pharmaceuticals, raw materials, sports equipment, textiles, and toys.

## ZEROING

The artificial setting to zero a dumping margin that is negative for the purpose of determining whether dumping has occurred.

That is, zeroing refers to treating all non-dumped sales as having a dumping margin of zero, and thereby preventing non-dumped sales from offsetting dumped sales. In turn, zeroing increases the dumping margin and, thus, makes it more likely subject merchandise was dumped in an importing country. In addition, a higher positive dumping margin results in imposition of a greater antidumping (AD) duty on the alleged dumped goods, at least in the United States, which (in contrast to the EU and many WTO Members) does not employ the Lesser Duty Rule. Evidently, zeroing is a practice biased in favor of the petitioner.

To summarize by example, suppose bicycle tires imported into Argentina from Brazil have an average dumping margin of U.S. $10. Further, assume tricycle tires, which are like products, imported from Brazil have an average dumping margin of -$5. Normally, the weighted average dumping margin would be $2.50 (*i.e.*, 10 + -5 / 2 = $2.50). However, if the Argentine government engages in zeroing, the weighted average dumping margin would be $5.00. That is because Argentina would set non-dumped sales to zero, and thus 10 + 0 / 2 = $5).

This illustration is one of "Simple Zeroing." It involves a "transaction-to-transaction" methodology. That is, Simple Zeroing relies on comparisons of individual transactions of Export Price and Normal Value. It can entail an average-to-transaction methodology, which uses comparisons of a weighted average Normal Value against individual Export Price transactions. Average-to-transaction comparisons are particularly common in the context of a review of an AD order, such as an Administrative, New Shipper, Expedited AD, or Sunset Review.

Still another technique is known as "Model Zeroing," which involves a weighted average-to-weighted average methodology. With Model Zeroing, subject merchandise is divided into product categories, or groups. A weighted average dumping margin is calculated for each group. If the weighted average dumping margin for a particular group is negative (*i.e.*, Export Price or Constructed Export Price exceeds Normal Value for that group), then that margin is set to zero. An aggregate dumping margin for the entire subject merchandise then is calculated, based on the margins within each group. Critically, non-dumped sales do not offset dumped sales across groups. That is, zeroing occurs because the aggregate dumping margin is calculated by summing up the margins for each group, and any negative margin for a group has been set to zero.

Zeroing is a major subject of litigation at the WTO, and indeed as of April 2010 is the most litigated topic in the history of GATT—WTO adjudication.[735] The pertinent legal texts of the WTO, namely, GATT and the *Agreement on the Implementation of Article VI (Antidumping* or *AD Agreement)*, are silent on the legality of zeroing. However, in 2001, India successfully brought a case against the European Communities (EC) for zeroing dumping margins of bed linens from India.[736] The Appellate Body agreed with India, holding that the practice of zeroing was illegal under the *AD Agreement*. In 2002, Canada, the EC and Japan have also brought claims against the United States for its zeroing practice. Again, the Appellate Body found that zeroing was illegal under the *AD Agreement*. However, the Appellate Body stated its ruling was limited to the use of zeroing in the context of a weighted average Normal value-to-weighted average Export Price comparison. Interestingly, the Appellate Body also cited to the 2001 *EC — Bed Linen* Case as another legal justification for its holding.

The Table below summarizes Appellate Body precedents on zeroing.

---

[735] *See* Len Bracken, *WTO Dispute System at Record Level of Activity, Wilson Says, Predicts AB Surge*, 27 International Trade Reporter (BNA) 660 (6 May 2010) (reporting the remarks of Bruce Wilson, outgoing Director, Legal Affairs Division, WTO Secretariat, who noted there had been 20 zeroing cases to date).

[736] *See* Appellate Body Report, *European Communities — Anti-Dumping Duties on Imports of Cotton-Type Bed Linen from India*, WT/DS141/AB/R (adopted 12 March 2001); Panel Report, *European Communities — Antidumping Duties on Imports of Cotton-Type Bed Linen from India*, (adopted as modified by the Appellate Body Report, 12 March 2001).

**TABLE:**

SUMMARY OF WTO PRECEDENTS ON ZEROING

| *Type of Zeroing* → <br><br> *Context of Zeroing* ↓ | *Simple Zeroing* <br><br> **(Comparisons of individual Export Price transactions, or Constructed Export Price transactions, with an individual or weighted average Normal Value; no division of subject merchandise into product sub-groups)** | *Model Zeroing* <br><br> **(Comparison of weighted average Export Price, or Constructed Export Price, with weighted average Normal Value; division of subject merchandise into product sub-groups)** |
|---|---|---|
| *Original Investigation* | Illegal under WTO rules. <br><br> In the *Softwood Lumber Zeroing* Compliance Report (¶ 124), the Appellate Body (reversing the compliance Panel) ruled Simple Zeroing is illegal. The Appellate Body emphasized it is "illogical to interpret the transaction-to-transaction comparison methodology in a manner that would lead to results that are systematically different from those obtained under the weighted average-to-weighted average methodology."[737] Thus, the Appellate Body held Simple Zeroing in transaction-to-transaction comparisons of Normal Value to Export Price violates the "fair comparison" requirement of Article 2:4 of the *Antidumping Agreement*, and also is inconsistent with Article 2:4:2 of that *Agreement*, because the methodology systematic disregards comparisons in which Export Price exceeds Normal Value. <br> The *Japan Zeroing* Panel upheld use of Simple Zeroing in original investigations, saying a prophylactic prohibition was "manifestly absurd and | Illegal under WTO rules. <br><br> In *EC — Bed Linens* (¶ 66), the Appellate Body ruled Model Zeroing violates Article 2:4:2 (first sentence) of the *Antidumping Agreement*. <br><br> In *Softwood Lumber Zeroing* (¶ 117), the Appellate Body ruled Model Zeroing violates Article 2:4 and 2:4:2 of the *Antidumping Agreement*. <br><br> In *U.S. — Zeroing (EC)* (¶ 222), the Appellate Body upheld a Panel finding that Model Zeroing violates Article 2:4:2 |

---

[737] *See* Appellate Body Report, *United States — Final Dumping Determination on Softwood Lumber from Canada (Article 21:5 — Canada)*, WT/DS264/AB/RW (adopted 1 September 2006). This case, and the substantive decision underlying it, *United States — Final Dumping Determination on Softwood Lumber from Canada*, WT/DS264/AB/R (adopted 31 August 2004), sometimes are referred to as "*Softwood Lumber V.*"

**TABLE (continued)**

| Type of ──▶ Zeroing<br><br>Context of ↓<br>Zeroing | Simple Zeroing | Model Zeroing |
|---|---|---|
| **Original Investigation, continued** | unreasonable."[738] (The case involved 15 instances between 1999–2004 in which the United States imposed antidumping duties on Japanese carbon-quality steel plate products, and various kinds of bearings (antifriction, ball, cylindrical, spherical plain, tapered and cylindrical roller bearings). The Panel specifically rejected Japan's claim that Appellate Body precedents indicate zeroing is, or should be, prohibited in all contexts, because the method unfairly inflates the dumping margin, and thereby the amount of antidumping duties imposed. The Panel said the Appellate Body "has never actually made a legal finding in a specific case that the use of zeroing is inconsistent" with the *Antidumping Agreement*.<br><br>But, in *Japan Zeroing* (¶ 138), the Appellate Body reversed the Panel's decision. The Appellate Body held Simple Zeroing violates Articles 2:4 and 2:4:2, of the *Antidumping Agreement*. The Appellate Body chastised the Panel, saying it had "no reason to depart" from its finding in the *Softwood Lumber Zeroing* Compliance Report. | of the *Antidumping Agreement*.[739]<br><br>The *Japan Zeroing* Panel agreed with Japan that the use of Model Zeroing in original investigations violates the *Antidumping Agreement*. The U.S. did not appeal this ruling.<br><br>The U.S. did not contest the facts or arguments made by Ecuador in the *Ecuador Zeroing* case,[740] the first time a respondent in a WTO case essentially has pled *nolo contendere* (no contest). Ecuador protested the imposition in three cases of AD duties on frozen, warm water shrimp ranging from 2.35 to 4.48 percent, claiming that but for Model Zeroing in the original investigation, there would have been no dumping margin. |

[738] *See* Appellate Body Report, *United States — Laws, Regulations and Methodology for Calculating Dumping Margins ("Zeroing")*, WT/DS294/AB/R (adopted 9 May 2006). This case sometimes is referred to as "*EC — Zeroing.*"

[739] *See* WTO Panel Report, *United States — Measures Relating to Zeroing and Sunset Reviews*, WT/DS322/R (adopted as modified by the Appellate Body 23 January 2007) (complaint by Japan); WTO Appellate Body Report, *United States — Measures Relating to Zeroing and Sunset Reviews*, WT/DS322/AB/R (adopted 23 January 2007) (complaint by Japan).

[740] See WTO Panel Report, *United States — Anti-Dumping Measure on Shrimp from Ecuador,* WT/DS335/R (adopted 30 January 2007) (complaint by Ecuador); Daniel Pruzin, *U.S. Does Not Contest Ecuador Shrimp Case After WTO Panel Rules Against U.S. Zeroing,* 24 International Trade Reporter (BNA) 174–75 (1 February 2007).

TABLE (continued)

| Type of ——▶ Zeroing<br><br>Context of ↓ Zeroing | Simple Zeroing | Model Zeroing |
|---|---|---|
| Original Investigation, continued | | Under the *de facto nolo contendere* plea, arranged before the Panel ruling, the U.S. agreed to a six month compliance period, to recalculate dumping margins to conform to the foreseeable Panel ruling (in accordance with Section 129(b) of the *1994 Uruguay Round Agreements Act*), and to give prospective effect only to any new cash deposit rate resulting from recalculated margins.<br><br>In return, Ecuador agreed it would not ask the Panel to recommend ways the U.S. ought to implement the ruling, thereby avoiding for the U.S. the discomfort of yet another call from Geneva for the U.S. to revoke an AD order. The two sides also agreed to share drafts of their written submission, a rare instance of such cooperation.<br><br>At the same time, Ecuador did not drop the case, in order to retain its future rights, especially concerning implementation and, should it be necessary to exercise, retaliation.<br><br>(Interestingly, Ecuador suffered no real injury from Zeroing, because third country competi |

TABLE **(continued)**

| Type of → Zeroing<br><br>Context of ↓ Zeroing | *Simple Zeroing* | *Model Zeroing* |
|---|---|---|
| **Original Investigation, continued** | | tors, *i.e.*, shrimp from Brazil, China, India, Thailand, and Vietnam, were hit with relatively higher AD duties on their shipments to the U.S. But, injury was irrelevant to its claim.)<br><br>Thus, the Panel in *Ecuador — Zeroing* followed the *Softwood Lumber Zeroing* Appellate Body decision, and said Model Zeroing in original investigations violates Article 2:4:2 (first sentence) of the *Antidumping Agreement*. That was true, held the Panel, in respect of the dumping margins calculated by the Department of Commerce for the three largest Ecuadorian shrimp producer-exporters, and for the all others rate computation. |
| ***Administrative (Periodic) Reviews*** | Illegal under WTO rules.<br><br>The *Japan Zeroing* Panel upheld use of Simple Zeroing in an Administrative Review of existing AD order.<br><br>But, in *Japan Zeroing* (¶ 166), the Appellate Body reversed this decision, holding Simple Zeroing violates Articles 2:4, 9:3, and 9:5 of the *Antidumping Agreement*, and GATT Article VI:2. The violation lies in the fact Simple Zeroing leads to an artificial inflation of the dumping margin, which in turn leads to an AD duty that exceeds the margin. The dumping margin established for | Illegal under WTO rules.<br><br>In *EC — Zeroing* (¶¶ 132–135), the Appellate Body held Model Zeroing in Administrative Reviews violates Article 9:3 of the *Antidumping Agreement* and Article VI:2 of GATT. That is because systematic disregard of any individual transaction in which Export Price exceeds the contempora- |

TABLE (continued)

| Type of Zeroing → Context of Zeroing ↓ | Simple Zeroing | Model Zeroing |
|---|---|---|
| Administrative (Periodic) Reviews continued | an exporter is a ceiling on the total amount of AD duties that can be levied on subject merchandise from that exporter, and this same ceiling applies in original investigations and reviews, in both prospective and retrospective AD regimes. | neous weighted average Normal Value leads to an assessment of an AD duty that exceeds the actual margin of dumping for a particular exporter. |

In *Stainless Steel* (¶¶ 133–139, 165(a)-(b)), the Appellate Body (reversing the Panel, and re-affirming its *Japan Zeroing* precedent) held that Simple Zeroing in Administrative Reviews violates GATT Article VI:2 and Article 9:3 of the *Antidumping Agreement*.[741] That is because Simple Zeroing is inconsistent with the plain meaning of the relevant textual provisions that an AD duty imposed does not exceed the margin of dumping. Further, when the Uruguay Round negotiators meant to exclude information from an AD investigation, they stated so explicitly (as in Articles 2:2:1 and 9:4), but they did not do so in respect of disregarding instances in which Export Price exceeds Normal Value. Finally, zeroing would enter an AD case through the back door if it were permitted in the Review when it is barred from the original investigation.

Citing precedents, in *Continued Zeroing* (¶¶ 145, 242–317, 395(d)), the Appellate Body held Simple Zeroing in Administrative Reviews violates Article 9:3 of the *Antidumping Agreement* and Article VI:2 of GATT.[742]

---

[741] *United States — Final Anti-dumping Measures on Stainless Steel from Mexico* (complaint by Mexico), WT/DS344/AB/R (adopted 20 May 2008). This case sometimes is referred to as "2008 *Mexico Zeroing.*"

[742] *United States — Continued Existence and Application of Zeroing Methodology* (complaint by European Communities (EC)), WT/DS/350/AB/R (adopted 19 February 2009). This case sometimes is referred to as "2009 *Continued Zeroing.*"

TABLE (continued)

| Type of Zeroing → | Simple Zeroing | Model Zeroing |
|---|---|---|
| Context of Zeroing ↓ | | |
| Sunset Reviews | Illegal under WTO rules.<br><br>The *Japan Zeroing* Panel upheld use of Simple Zeroing in an Administrative Review of existing AD order.<br><br>But, in *Japan Zeroing*, the Appellate Body reversed this decision, holding Simple Zeroing violates Article 11:3 of the *Antidumping Agreement*. The Appellate Body said dumping margins calculated with zeroing did not, contrary to Article 11:3, provide a "rigorous examination," yield "reasoned and adequate conclusions [supported by] positive evidence," or have a "sufficient factual basis." | Illegal under WTO rules.<br><br>The *Continued Zeroing* Appellate Body (¶¶ 147, 369–383, 395(f)) agreed with the Panel: Model Zeroing in an original investigation, violates Article 2:4:2 of the *AD Agreement* (based on precedents); hence, relying on Model Zeroing in a Sunset Review also must be illegal, specifically under Article 11:3 of the *Agreement*.<br><br>In addition, reversing the Panel, the *Continued Zeroing* Appellate Body (¶¶ 143(a)-(b), 149–199, 395(a)(i)-(v)) held that the claims of the respondent (EC) concerning 18 AD duty orders and the application of zeroing in the original investigations, Administrative Reviews, and Sunset Reviews were justiciable. These claims were neither "as such" nor "as applied." Rather, they were claims about "ongoing conduct," namely, the continued use of zeroing starting in an original investigation and through subsequent Reviews. Such claims are a potentially new category of measures that may be challenged under WTO dispute settlement rules. |

**TABLE (continued)**

| Type of → Zeroing

Context of ↓ Zeroing | Simple Zeroing | Model Zeroing |
|---|---|---|
| **New Shipper Reviews** | Illegal under WTO rules.

The *Japan Zeroing* Panel held Japan failed to prove zeroing is illegal in a Changed Circumstances Review of an existing AD order.

But, in *Japan Zeroing* (¶¶ 165–166), the Appellate Body reversed this decision, holding Simple Zeroing violates Articles 2:4, 9:3, and 9:5 of the *Antidumping Agreement*, and GATT Article VI:2. Essentially, it applied the same rationale in this context as in Administrative Reviews. | No case (yet). |
| **Changed Circumstances Reviews** | Illegal under WTO rules.

The *Japan Zeroing* Panel upheld use of Simple Zeroing in New Shipper Reviews connected with an existing AD order.

But, in *Japan Zeroing*, the Appellate Body reversed this decision, holding Simple Zeroing violates Articles 2:4, 2:4:2, 9:3, 9:5, and 11:3 of the *Antidumping Agreement*. | No case (yet). |
| **Targeted Dumping**[743] | No case (yet). | No case (yet). |

Indeed, the practice of zeroing was deemed a prohibited practice again in January 2007. This time, Ecuador, along with Brazil, China, the EC, India, Japan, Korea, and Thailand, successfully brought a claim against the United States practice of zeroing. The WTO Panel found the United States had been illegally zeroing the dumping margin of shrimp and shrimp products from Ecuador. The Table below summarizes the zeroing precedents set by the Appellate Body. The Table highlights the fact that zeroing can and does occur

---

[743] That is, rare investigations, using comparisons of average Normal Value to individual Export Price, of allegations that the pattern of Export Prices differs markedly across exporters of subject merchandise, buyers of that merchandise, or time periods.

in many contexts — original investigations, and different kinds of reviews of existing AD orders.

Despite the declaration of its illegality by the Appellate Body, some American courts, namely, the United States Court of International Trade (CIT) and the Court of Appeals for the Federal Circuit have held that the practice is legal. These courts have found the practice to be legal because it is still permitted by the United States Code (U.S.C.) and the Code of Federal Regulations (C.F.R.).[744]

Notably, following the *U.S. — Zeroing (EC)* decision, in a 27 December 2006 *Federal Register* notice, the United States Department of Commerce (DOC) announced it would abandon Model Zeroing (in which the DOC relies on average-to-average comparisons, *i.e.*, weighted average Export Prices against weighted average Normal Value) in original investigations. The DOC deferred the implementation date, originally in January, until February, at the request of Congress. Section 123(b) and (g) of the *Uruguay Round Agreements Act of 1994* requires a 60 day consultation period between the appropriate Congressional committees (namely, the Senate Finance and House Ways and Means Committee) and an Executive Branch department or agency seeking to modify its regulation to implement a WTO decision. During the 60 days, the appropriate committee may vote to show its support or opposition to the proposed regulatory change. Because of the November 2006 election and transition from the 109th to 110th Congress, the appropriate committees did not have enough time to consider the issue. However, the December 2006 change did not affect the use of Model Zeroing in other contexts, nor did it affect the use of Simple Zeroing.

In June 2007, the United States submitted to a proposal to the WTO Negotiating Group on Rules, which called for the adoption of clear and precise rules permitting the use of zeroing in investigations and administrative reviews. The proposal was submitted as part of the ongoing Rules negotiations in the Doha Development Agenda (DDA). The United States suggested a successful Doha Round outcome was not possible without approval of its proposal. Nevertheless, the proposal drew fierce opposition from the vast majority of WTO Members. To be sure, certain other WTO Members continue to engage in zeroing.

Yet, on 28 December 2010, the DOC proposed to change its zeroing practices in Administrative Reviews, Sunset Reviews, expedited AD Reviews, and New

---

[744] *See* 19 U.S.C. §§ 1673, 1677; 19 C.F.R. § 351 (2006); *Corus Staal BV v. United States*, 395 F.3d 1343 (Fed. Cir. 2005); *Timken Co. v. United States*, 354 F.3d 1334 (Fed. Cir. 2004); *SKF USA Inc. v. United States*, 491 F. Supp. 2d 1354, (Ct. Int'l Trade 2007).

Shipper Reviews.[745] The DOC finalized this proposal on 8 February 2012.[746] The final rule was part of a deal between the United States, on the one hand, and the European Union (EU) and Japan on the other hand, whereby the EU and Japan agreed to withdraw their requests to the WTO to retaliate against the United States by impose hundreds of millions of dollars of duties on American imports because of the failure of the United States to implement several WTO adjudicatory rulings against zeroing.

The DOC said it would grant an offset for comparisons of monthly weighted average Export Prices with monthly weighted average Normal Values, whenever the comparisons show Export Price exceeds Normal Value. The offset would be granted in Administrative Reviews, new Shipper Reviews, Expedited AD Reviews, and Sunset Reviews. In other words, the DOC indicated it would cease Model Zeroing in these Reviews. Thus, the offset would apply to calculations of the dumping margin determination for purposes of an AD duty assessment rate, which is established in these (particularly Administrative) Reviews. Whenever the DOC finds the weighted average dumping margin is zero or *de minimis*, then it will not order assessment of AD duties.

Note that technically, the question in 5-year Sunset Reviews is not zeroing *per se*, but rather whether zeroing occurred in the underlying original investigation or Administrative Review that is being analyzed in a Sunset Review. In its February 2012 regulation, the DOC agreed not to base a Sunset Review on a prior determination that involved weighted average dumping margins calculated by zeroing. It opined that except for the most extraordinary circumstances, it would be able to rely on prior dumping margin calculations in the batch of Sunset Reviews now on its docket, and not have to recalculate margins in each and every instance.

On a case-by-case basis, the DOC reserved the right to determine if a different method of comparing Export Price and Normal Value might be appropriate, such as a transaction-to-transaction (T-T) comparison of Export Price and

---

[745] *See* 75 Federal Register 81533; Daniel Pruzin, *U.S. Says Proposed Changes to Zeroing Will Bring It In Line with WTO Rulings*, 28 International Trade Reporter (BNA) 95 (20 January 2011). The DOC regulations on Administrative Reviews are at 19 C.F.R. § 351.213, on New Shipper Reviews at 19 C.F.R. § 351.214, and on Expedited AD Reviews at 19 C.F.R. § 351.215.

Typically in these Reviews, the DOC makes comparisons between a weighted average Normal Value and transaction-specific Export Prices, *i.e.*, also called an average-to-transaction comparison. The December 2010 proposal would modify 19 C.F.R. § 351.414(a) and (c) by removing the preference for making average-to-transaction comparisons in Administrative Reviews, and permit application of average-to-average comparisons, just like original investigations, without zeroing. Additionally, modifications to 19 C.F.R. § 351.414(d)(3) and (e) would clarify that the DOC could calculating weighted averages on a monthly basis in a Review.

[746] See 77 Fed. Reg. 8,101 (14 February 2012; Daniel Pruzin, *Commerce Publishes Final Rule Amending Zeroing Practice in Administrative Reviews,* 29 International Trade Reporter (BNA) 234 (16 February 2012)

Normal Value. To be sure, the Appellate Body had ruled a T-T comparison with no offset is illegal zeroing. To avoid any conflict with this ruling, the DOC made clear in February 2012 it had abandoned its prior practice of not allowing offsets when using the T-T method, *i.e.*, Simple Zeroing. The last time the DOC used the T-T method was in 2005, involving AD duties on softwood lumber from Canada. Moreover, in its December 2010 proposal, the DOC said it would end Simple Zeroing (*i.e.*, using the T-T methodology and not allowing offsets) in original investigations.

In January 2011, the United States communicated the December 2010 DOC proposal to the WTO, thereby hinting at a possible shift in its Doha Round position. By the time of that communication, WTO panels and the Appellate Body had issued over 20 rulings against zeroing. However, many politicians in the House of Representatives and Senate strongly oppose any weakening of the zeroing methodology.[747]

Note that the DOC has yet to declare that it will eschew zeroing in respect of petitioner complaints about targeted dumping.

*Suggestions for Further Research:*

Articles:

1.   Greenwald, John D., *After Corus Staal — Is There Any Role, and Should There Be for WTO Jurisprudence in the Review of U.S. Trade Measures by U.S. Courts?*, 39 GEORGETOWN JOURNAL OF INTERNATIONAL TRADE LAW 199–216 (2007).

2.   Langland, Eric, Recent Development, *United States — Final Antidumping Measures on Stainless Steel from Mexico: Row Over Zeroing Reveals Judicial Quagmire (United States — Final Antidumping Measures on Stainless Steel from Mexico, WT/DS344/AB/R, 2008)*, 17 TULANE JOURNAL OF INTERNATIONAL & COMPARATIVE LAW 555–570 (2009).

2.   Reeder, Casey, *Zeroing in on Charming Betsy: How an Antidumping Controversy Threatens to Sink the Schooner*, 36 STETSON LAW REVIEW 255–291 (2006).

3.   Spaulding, Jeffrey W., *Do International Fences Really Make Good Neighbors? The Zeroing Conflict Between Antidumping Law and International Obligations*, 41 NEW ENGLAND LAW REVIEW 379–433 (2007).

# ANNEX A

# MAPS

## Map A-1: World (Political)

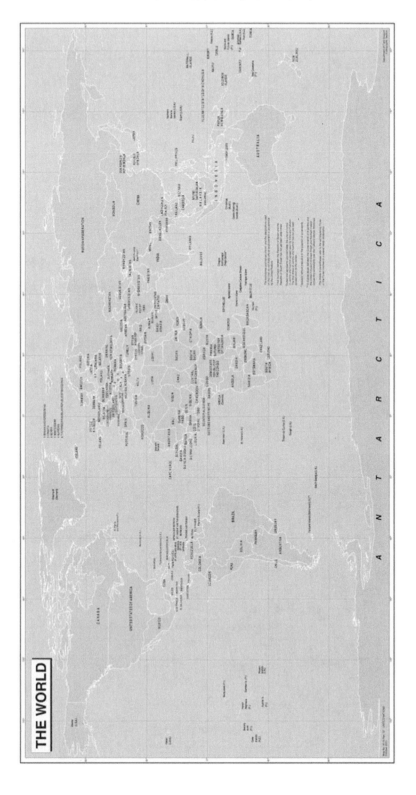

## MAP A-2:    WORLD (TIME ZONES)

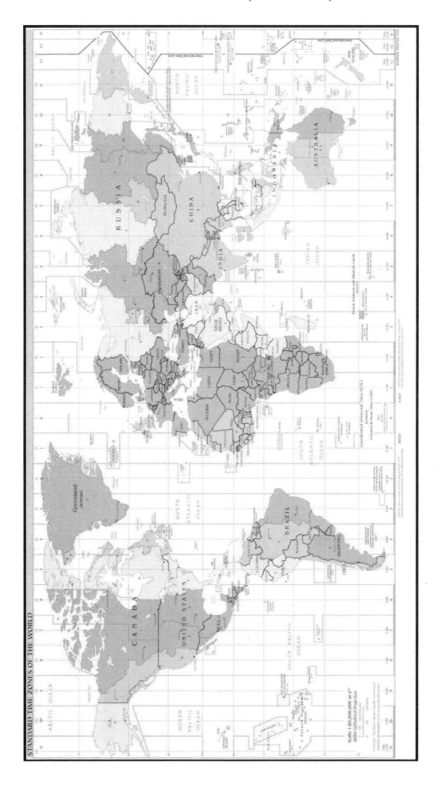

## MAP A-3: AFRICA

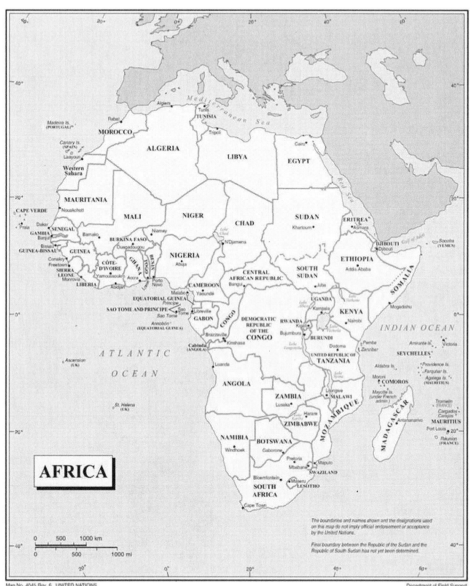

## MAP A-4:     ARCTIC REGION

## MAP A-5:    ASIA

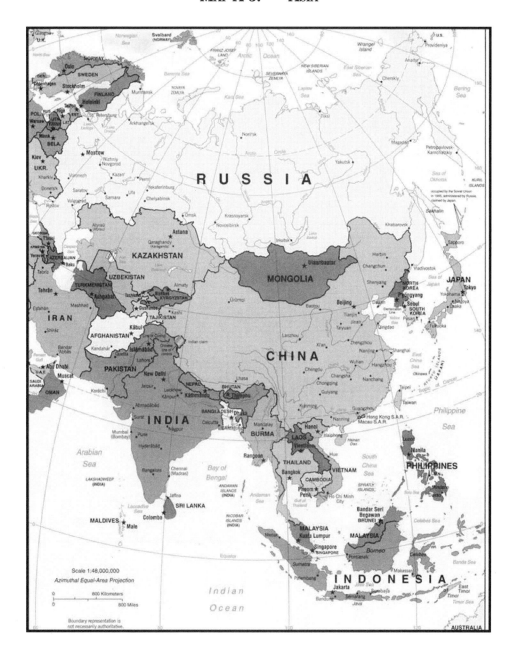

## MAP A-6:     AUSTRALIA

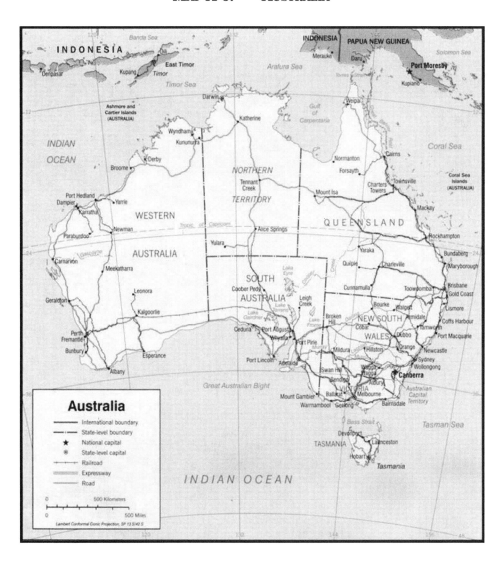

## MAP A-7:    BRAZIL

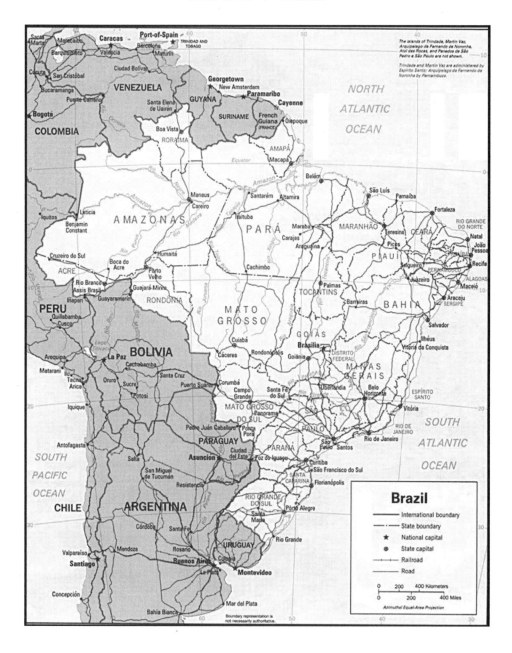

## MAP A-8:    CANADA

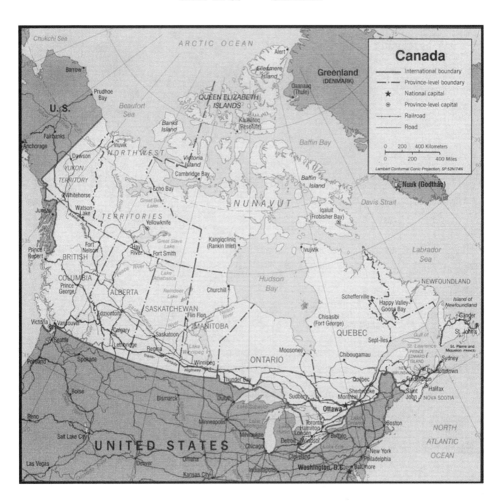

**MAP A-9:     CENTRAL AMERICA AND THE CARIBBEAN**

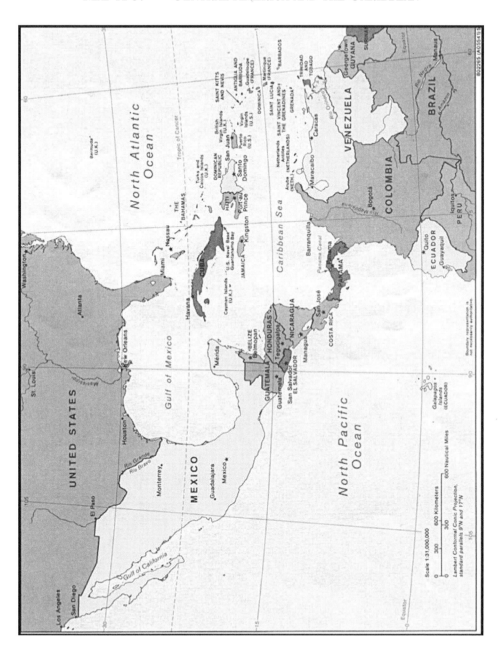

## Map A-10: China

## Map A-11:     East Asia

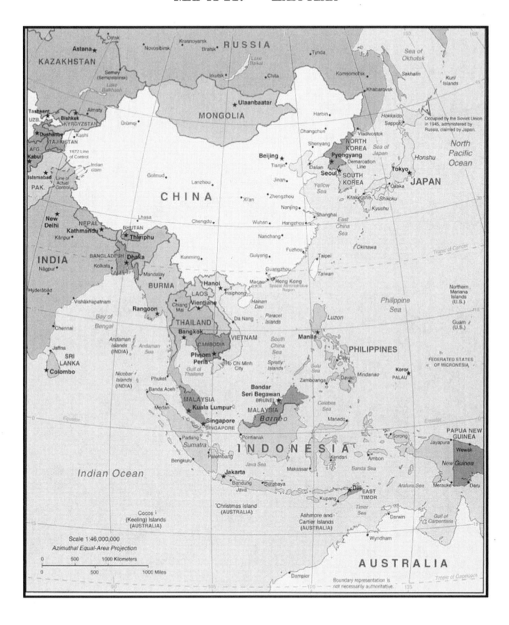

## MAP A-12: EUROPE

## MAP A-13:    INDIAN SUBCONTINENT

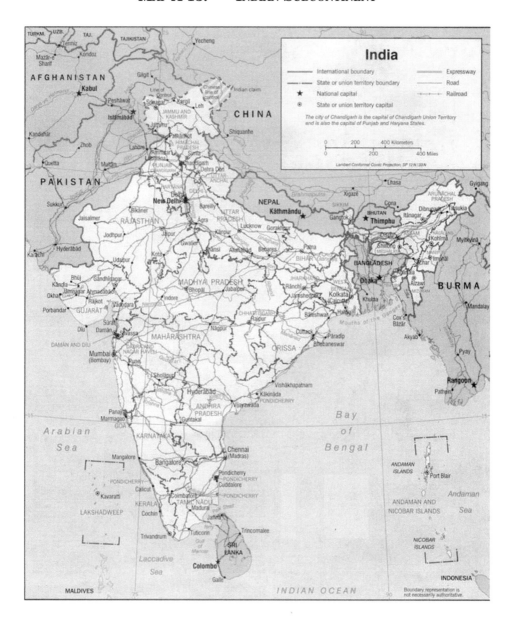

## MAP A-14: JAPAN

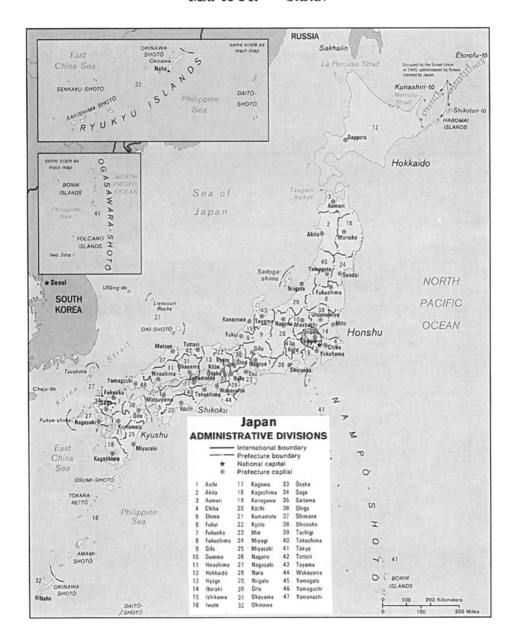

## MAP A-15: KOREA

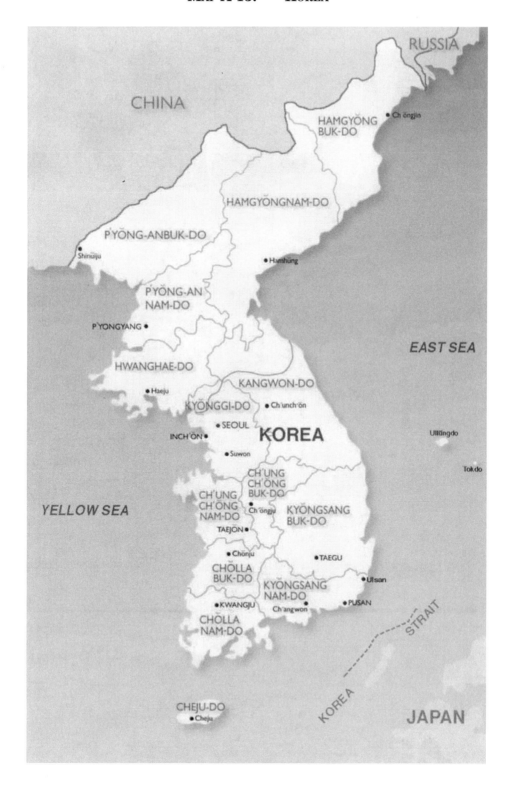

**MAP A-16:     MEXICO**

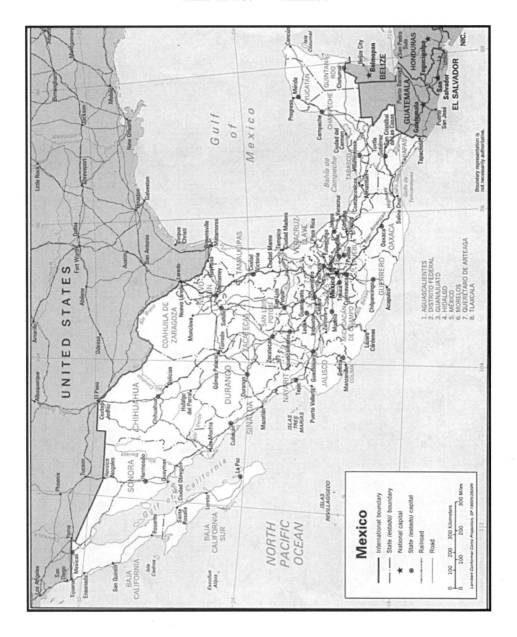

## Map A-17:　　Middle East

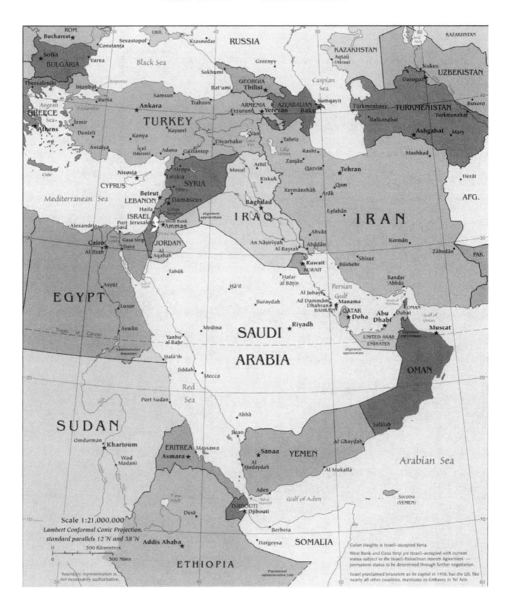

## MAP A-18:    NORTH AMERICA

## MAP A-19: OCEANIA

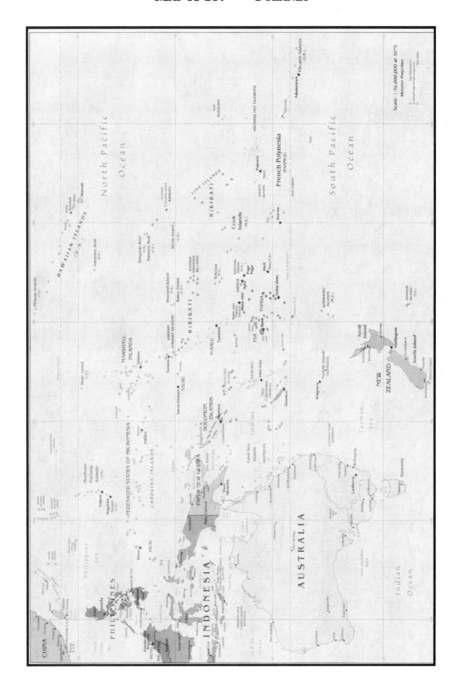

## MAP A-20:     RUSSIA

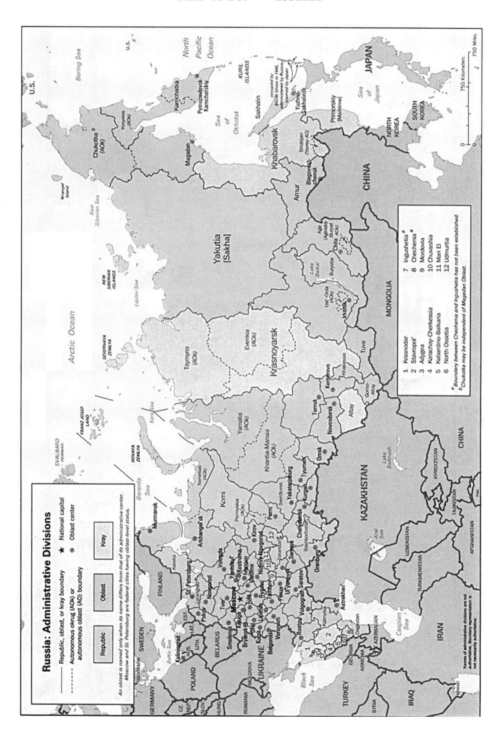

## MAP A-21:     SOUTH AFRICA

South Africa's Former Provinces

## MAP A-22:     SOUTH AMERICA

## MAP A-23: SOUTHERN ASIA

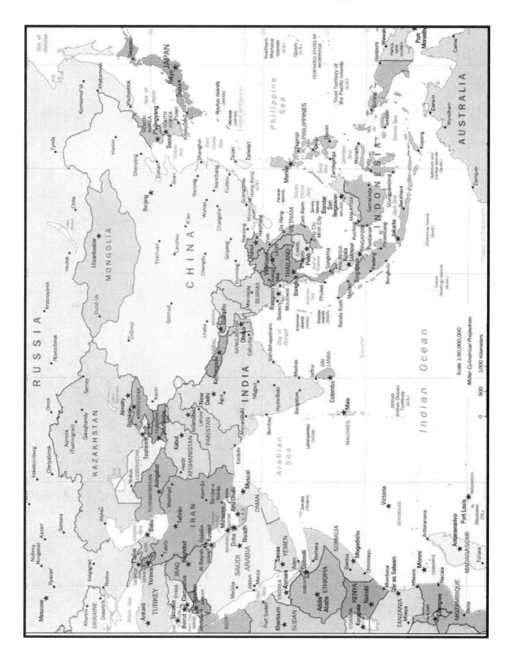

## MAP A-24: UNITED STATES

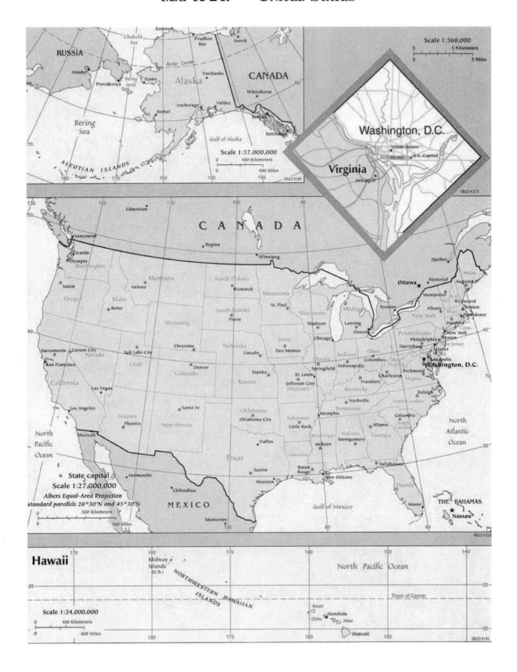

## MAP A-25:     KANSAS

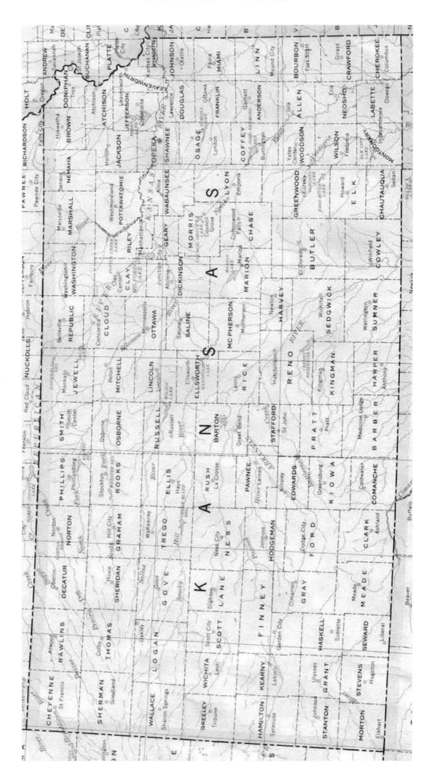

# ANNEX B

# RESEARCH TOOLS

## TABLE B-1:

## FREE INTERNATIONAL TRADE LAW WEBSITES[1]

| Organization | Website Address |
|---|---|
| **A** | |
| Advisory Center on WTO Law | www.acwl.ch |
| Afghan-American Chamber of Commerce | www.a-acc.org |
| AFL-CIO Solidarity Center | www.solidaritycenter.org |
| African, Caribbean, and Pacific (ACP) Group of States | www.acpsec.org |
| African Growth and Opportunity Act (AGOA) | www.agoa.gov |
| African Union | www.africa-union.org |
| American Bar Association (ABA) Section of International Law | www.abanet.org/intlaw/ |
| American Farm Bureau | www.fb.org |
| American Society for International Law (ASIL) — Election Information System for International Law | www.eisil.org |
| Asian Development Bank (ADB) | www.adb.org |
| Asian Pacific Economic Cooperation (APEC) forum | www.apec.org |
| Association of South East Asian Nations (ASEAN) | www.aseansec.org |
| Australian Bureau of Agriculture Resource Economics (ABARE) | www.abare.gov.au |
| Australia — Department of Foreign Affairs and Trade (DFAT) | www.dfat.gov.au |
| **B** | |
| Bank for International Settlements | www.bis.org |
| Bankers Association for Finance and Trade | www.baft.org |
| Bilaterals.Org | www.bilaterals.org |
| BioSafety Clearinghouse | http://bch.biodiv.org |

---

[1] For convenience, this Table runs continuously.

## TABLE (continued)

| Organization | Website Address |
| --- | --- |
| Brazil — Embassy of Brazil in the United States (Washington, D.C.) | www.brasilemb.org |
| Business Roundtable | www.businessroundtable.org |
| **C** | |
| Cairns Group | www.cairnsgroup.org |
| Canada — Department of Foreign Affairs and International Trade (DFAIT) | www.dfait-maeci.gc.ca |
| Canada — International Trade Canada (CITC) | www.itcan-cican.gc.ca |
| Canadian International Trade Tribunal (CITT) | www.citt.gc.ca |
| Caribbean Community (CARICOM) | www.caricom.org |
| Catholic News Service | www.catholicnews.com |
| Center for Transnational Law (CENTRAL) University of Cologne (Germany) | www.tlbd.net |
| China — Ministry of Commerce (MOFCOM) | http://english.mofcom.gov.cn/ |
| Codex Alimentarius Commission (Codex) | www.codexalimentarius.net |
| Commonwealth Secretariat | www.thecommonwealth.org |
| Confederation of British Industry (CBI) | www.cbi.org.uk |
| Consultative Group on International Agricultural Research | www.cgiar.org |
| Convention on Biological Diversity | www.cbd.int |
| Council on Foreign Relations (CFR) | www.cfr.org |
| **D** — | |
| **E** | |
| East African Community (EAC) | www.eac.int |
| Economic Commission for Latin America and the Caribbean (ECLAC) | www.eclac.org |

## TABLE (continued)

| Organization | Website Address |
| --- | --- |
| Economic Community of Central African States (ECCAS) | www.ceeac-eccas.org |
| Economic Community of West African States (ECOWAS) | www.ecowas.int |
| Environmental Working Group (lists recipients of American agricultural subsidies) | www.ewg.org |
| European Central Bank (ECB) | www.ecb.int |
| European Centre for International Political Economy (ECIPE) | www.ecipe.org |
| European Free Trade Association (EFTA) | www.efta.int |
| European Judicial Network in Civil and Commercial Matters | www.ec.europa.eu/civiljustice/ |
| European Union (EU) | http://europa.eu.int |
| European Union (EU) — Director General of Trade (DG Trade) | http://europa.eu.int/comm/trade |
| European Union (EU) — Registration, Evaluation and Authorization of Chemicals (REACH) | http://ec.curopa.eu/environment/ chemicals/reach/ |
| **F** | |
| Fairtrade Labeling Organizations International | www.fairtrade.net |
| Food and Agriculture Organization (FAO) | www.fao.org |
| Free Trade Area of the Americas (FTAA) | www.ftaa-alca.org |
| **G** | |
| Geary Kamis System — | www.stats.oecd.org/glossary/ detail.asp?ID=5528 |
| For estimated synthetic world market agricultural prices | http://unstats.un.org/unsd/ methods/icp/icpo_htm.htm |
| | www.fao.org/es/ess/top/prices_ en.htm |

TABLE **(continued)**

| Organization | Website Address |
|---|---|
| Global Environment Facility | www.gefweb.org |
| Government of Colombia, Office of the President (for June 2006 Tripartite Agreement and other labor reforms implemented pursuant to the *United States — Colombia Free Trade Agreement*) | http://wsp.presidencia.gov.co/ Especiales/2011/Documents |
| Group of Thirty | www.group30.org |
| **H** | |
| Hague Conference on Private International Law | www.hcch.net |
| Hong Kong Special Administrative Region (HKSAR) — Department of Trade and Industry | www.tid.gov.hk |
| Hong Kong Special Administrative Region (HKSAR) — Department of Trade and Industry 2011 *Free Trade Agreement between Hong Kong and the European Free Trade Association (EFTA)* | www.tid.gov.hk/english/trade_ relations/hkefta |
| Hong Kong Special Administrative Region (HKSAR) — Government of Hong Kong | www.gov.hk |
| **I** | |
| India (Directory of Official Websites of the Government of India) | http://goidirectory.nic.in |
| India — Department of Commerce, Ministry of Commerce and Industry | http://commerce.nic.in |
| Institute for International Finance (IIF) | www.iif.com |
| Institute of International Banking | www.iib.org |
| Inter-American Development Bank (IADB) | www.iadb.org |
| Inter-American Institute for Cooperation on Agriculture | www.iica.int |

## TABLE (continued)

| *Organization* | *Website Address* |
|---|---|
| Intergovernmental Forum on Chemical Safety | www.who.int/ifcs |
| International Centre for Genetic Engineering and Biotechnology | www.icgeb.trieste.it |
| International Centre for Trade and Sustainable Development (ICTSD) | www.ictsd.org |
| International Chamber of Commerce (ICC) | www.iccwbo.org |
| International Court of Justice (ICJ) | www.icj-cij.org |
| International Energy Agency | www.iea.org |
| International Food Policy Research Institute | www.ifpri.org |
| International Fund Agriculture Development | www.ifad.org |
| International Grains Council | www.igc.org.uk |
| International Labor Organization | www.ilo.org |
| International Monetary Fund (IMF) | www.imf.org |
| International Plant Protection Convention | www.ippc.int |
| International Program on Chemical Safety | www.who.int.ipcs/en/ |
| International Rice Research Institute (IRRI) | www.irri.org |
| International Seed Federation | www.worldseed.org |
| International Seed Testing Association | www.seedtest.org |
| International Telecommunications Union | www.itu.int |
| International Tropic Timber Organization | www.itto.or.jp |
| International Union of Food Science and Technology | www.iufost.org |
| International Union for the Protection of New Varieties (UPOV) | www.upov.int |
| International Water and Sanitation Centre | www.irc.nl |

## TABLE (continued)

| Organization | Website Address |
|---|---|
| Internet Corporation for Assigned Names and Numbers | www.icann.org |
| **J** ||
| Japan — Ministry of Economy, Trade, and Industry (METI) | www.meti.go.jp |
| **K** ||
| Kansas — Trade Development, State of Kansas Department of Commerce | www.kdoch.state.ks.us |
| Kansas City — International Affairs and Trade Office of Kansas City | www.kcmo.org/international |
| Kansas City — International Relations Council of Kansas City | www.irckc.org |
| Kansas City — International Trade Council of Greater Kansas City | www.itckc.org |
| Kenya — Kenyan Institute for Public Policy Research (KIPPRA) | www.kippra.org |
| Korea — Ministry of Foreign Affairs and Trade (MOFAT) | www.mofat.go.kr |
| Kyoto Protocol (official website) | http://unfccc.int/kyoto_protocol |
| **L** ||
| Lex Mercatoria (collection of international cases, conventions, model laws and treaties) | www.lexmercatoria.org and www.jus.uio.no/lm |
| Louisiana State University Agricultural Center | www.lsuagcenter.com |
| **M** ||
| Make Trade Fair | www.maketradefair.org |
| Maximum Residue Levels | www.codexalimentarius.net |

## TABLE (continued)

| Organization | Website Address |
|---|---|
|  | www.mrldatabase.com |
|  | www.clubdeparis.org |
| *MERCOSUR* | www.mercosur.org |
| Mexico — Ministry of the Economy (Secretaría de Economía) | www.economia.gob.mx |
| Millennium Challenge Corporation | www.mcc.gov |
| Millennium Development Goals (MDGs) | www.un.org/millenniumgoals |
| Militarily Critical Technologies List (MCTL) | www.dtic.mil/mctl/ |
| Moldova — Ministry of Foreign Affairs and European Integration of the Republic of Moldova | www.mfa.md |
| **N** | |
| National Association of Manufacturers (NAM) | www.nam.org |
| National Foreign Trade Council (NFTC) | www.nftc.org |
| New York — Customs and International Trade Bar Association (CITBA) | www.citba.org |
| New Zealand — Ministry of Foreign Affairs and Trade (MFAT) | www.fta.govt.nz |
| Nobel Prizes | www.nobelprize.org |
| North American Agreement on Environmental Cooperation (NAAEC) | www.naaec.gc.ca |
| North American Commission on Environment Cooperation | www.cec.org |
| North American Free Trade Agreement (NAFTA) | www.nafta-sec-alena.org |
| North Atlantic Treaty Organization (NATO) | www.nato.int |

## TABLE (continued)

| Organization | Website Address |
|---|---|
| **O** | |
| Observatory of European and Comparative Private Law (University of Girona, Catalonia, Spain) | civil.udg.es/epclp |
| Organization of American States (OAS) | www.oas.org |
| Organization of American States — Department of International Legal Affairs | www.oas.org/dil |
| Organization of American States — Trade Unit | www.sice.oas.org |
| Organization for Economic Cooperation and Development | www.oecd.org |
| Organization of Petroleum Exporting Countries (OPEC) | www.opec.org |
| Organization of the Islamic Conference (OIC) | www.oic-oci.org |
| Overseas Private Investment Corporation | www.opic.gov |
| Oxfam United States | www.oxfamamerica.org |
| Oxfam United Kingdom | www.oxfam.org.uk |
| **P** | |
| Pan American Health Organization | www.paho.org |
| Pharmaceutical Research and Manufacturers of America (PhRMA) | www.phrma.org |
| Public Citizen | www.citizen.org |
| Public Citizen Global Trade Watch | www.tradewatch.org |
| **Q** | |
| — | |
| **R** | |
| Royal Institute for International Affairs (United Kingdom) | www.chathamhouse.org.uk |
| Royal Society for Asian Affairs (United Kingdom) | www.rssa.org.uk |

## Table (continued)

| Organization | Website Address |
|---|---|
| **S** | |
| Saudi Arabia (Kingdom of) — Tariff Schedule | www.customs.gov.sa/ CustomsNew/tariff/trfmain_E. aspx |
| Secretariat for Central American Economic Integration (SIECA) | www.sieca.org.gt |
| South Africa Department of Foreign Affairs | www.dfa.gov.za |
| South African Customs Union (SACU) | www.sacu.int |
| South Asian Association for Regional Cooperation (SAARC) | www.saarc-sec.org |
| South Centre | www.southcentre.org |
| Southern African Development Community (SADC) | www.sadc.int |
| Sustainable Development Gateway | www.sdgateway.net |
| **T** | |
| Taiwan — Bureau of Foreign Trade (BOFT) | eweb.trade.gov.tw |
| Texas Tech University — Cotton Economics Research Institute | www.aaec.ttu.edu/ceri |
| Third World Network (Singapore) | www.twnside.org.sg |
| T. M. C. Asser Institute (Private International Law Database) | www.asser.nl/ipr/index.html |
| Trade Law Centre for Southern Africa (TRALAC) | www.tralac.org |
| Trans-Atlantic Business Dialogue (TABD) | www.tabd.com |
| Transparency International | www.transparency.org |
| **U** | |
| **Non-United States Government Websites** | |
| United Maghreb Arab Union (UMAU) | www.maghrebarabe.org |
| United Nations (UN) | www.un.org |
| United Nations Commission on Sustainable Development | www.un.org/esa/sustdev |

## TABLE (continued)

| Organization | Website Address |
|---|---|
| United Nations Commission for International Trade Law (UNCITRAL) | www.uncitral.org |
| United Nations Commission on International Trade Law (UNCITRAL) — Case Law on UNICTRAL Texts (CLOUT) | www.uncitral.org/uncitral/en/case_law.html |
| United Nations Conference on Trade and Development (UNCTAD) | www.unctad.org |
| United Nations Convention to Combat Desertification | www.unccd.int |
| United Nations Department of Economic and Social Affairs | www.un.org/esa/desa.html |
| United Nations Development Program (UNDP) | www.undp.org |
| United Nations Economic and Social Commission for Asia and the Pacific (UNESCAP) | www.unescap.org |
| United Nations Economic Commission for Europe | www.unece.org |
| United Nations Educational, Scientific and Cultural Organization (UNESCO) | www.unesco.org |
| United Nations Framework Convention on Climate Change | unfccc.int |
| United Nations Industrial Development Organization (UNIDO) | www.unido.org |
| United Nations International Institute for the Unification of Private Law (UNIDROIT) | www.unidroit.org |
| United Nations International Law Commission (ILC) | www.un.org/law/ilc |
| UNILAW (Database of Uniform Law Conventions, maintained by UNIDROIT) | www.unidroit.info |

**TABLE (continued)**

| *Organization* | *Website Address* |
|---|---|
| UNILEX<br>(Database of International Contract<br>  Law and Cases, maintained by<br>  UNIDROIT) | www.unilex.info |
| United Nations International<br>  Strategy for Disaster Reduction | www.unisdr.org |
| United Nations Joint Program on<br>  HIV/AIDS | www.unaids.org |
| United Nations University | www.unu.edu |
| United Nations World Food Program | www.wfp.org |
| United Nations World Tourism<br>  Organization (UNWTO) | www.world-tourism.org |
| United States Coalition of Service<br>  Industries | www.uscsi.org |
| United States Conference of Catholic<br>  Bishops (USCCB)<br>(social justice, including<br>  international, issues) | www.nccbuscc.org |
| United States Council for<br>  International Business | www.uscib.org |
| USA — Engage | www.usaengage.org |
| Universal Postal Union | www.upu.int |
| University of Arkansas —<br>National Agricultural Law Center | www.nationalaglawcenter.org |
| University of Southern Australia<br>  Adelaide | www.economics.adelaide.edu.au |
| University of Toronto —<br>Munk Centre for International<br>  Studies | http://webapp.mcis.utoronto.ca |
| **United States Government Executive Branch Websites** | |
| Agency for International Development<br>  (USAID) | www.usaid.gov |
| Central Intelligence Agency (CIA) | www.cia.gov |
| Central Intelligence Agency (CIA)<br>  World Fact Book | www.cia.gov/library/publications/<br>the-world-factbook/index.html |
| Customs and Border Protection (CBP) | www.cbp.gov |

**TABLE (continued)**

| *Organization* | *Website Address* |
| --- | --- |
| Department of Agriculture (USDA) — Animal and Plant Health Inspection Service (APHIS) | www.aphis.usda.gov |
| Department of Agriculture (USDA) — Economic Research Service (ERS) | www.ers.usda.gov |
| Department of Agriculture (USDA) — Farm Services Agency (FSA) | www.fsa.usda.gov |
| Department of Agriculture (USDA) — Foreign Agricultural Service | www.fas.usda.gov |
| Department of Commerce (DOC) | www.doc.gov |
| Department of Commerce (DOC) — Balance of Payments (BOP) Statistics, Census Bureau | www.census.gov/foreign-trade |
| Department of Commerce (DOC) — Balance of Payment (BOP) Statistics, Bureau of Economic Analysis, | www.bea.gov |
| Department of Commerce (DOC) — Bureau of Industry and Security (BIS) | www.bis.doc.gov |
| Department of Commerce (DOC) — Foreign Trade Zones (FTZs) | http://ia.ita.doc.gov/ftzpage |
| Department of Commerce (DOC) — Import Administration (IA) | www.ita.doc.gov/import_admin/records |
| Department of Commerce (DOC) — International Trade Administration (ITA) | www.ita.doc.gov |
| Department of Commerce (DOC) — National Oceanic and Atmospheric Administration (NOAA) | www.noaa.gov |
| Department of Commerce (DOC) — Office of Textiles and Apparel (OTEXA), International Trade Administration (ITA) | otexa.ita.doc.gov |
| Department of Commerce (DOC) — Trade Compliance Center (TCC) | www.tcc.export.gov |

**TABLE (continued)**

| Organization | Website Address |
|---|---|
| Department of Commerce — Trade Stats Express, Office of Trade and Economic Analysis, International Trade Administration (ITA) | tse.export.gov |
| Department of Defense (Pentagon) | www.dod.gov |
| Department of Defense — Special Operations Forces Command | www.socom.mil |
| Department of Energy (DOE) — Energy Information Administration (EIA) | www.eia.doe.gov |
| Department of Homeland Security (DHS) | www.dhs.org |
| Department of Homeland Security (DHS) — Transportation Security Administration (TSA) | www.tsa.gov |
| Department of Labor (DOL) | www.dol.gov |
| Department of Labor (DOL) — Education and Training Administration (for Trade Adjustment Assistance) | www.doleta.gov |
| Department of State | www.state.gov |
| Department of State — Office of the Legal Advisor | www.state.gov/s/l |
| Department of Transportation (DOT) — Federal Highway Administration (FHA) | www.fhwa.dot.gov |
| Environmental Protection Agency (EPA) | www.epa.gov |
| Export Import Bank | www.exim.org |
| Federal Motor Carrier Safety Administration (FMCSA) | www.fmcsa.dot.gov |
| Immigration and Customs Enforcement (ICE) | www.ice.gov |
| International Trade Commission (ITC) | www.usitc.gov |

**TABLE (continued)**

| Organization | Website Address |
|---|---|
| Patent and Trademark Office (PTO) | www.uspto.gov |
| Trade and Development Agency (TDA) | www.tda.gov |
| United States Trade Representative (USTR) | www.ustr.gov |
| **United States Government, Non-Executive Branch Websites** | |
| Congress — Congressional Budget Office (CBO) | www.cbo.gov |
| Congress — Congressional Reports of the United States Congress | www.gpoaccess.gov/serialset/ creports |
| Congress — Government Accountability Office (GAO) | www.gao.org |
| Congress — House of Representatives | www.house.gov |
| Congress — Senate | www.senate.gov |
| Courts — Court of Appeals for the Federal Circuit (CAFC) | www.cafc.uscourts.gov |
| Courts — Court of International Trade (CIT) | www.cit.uscourts.gov |
| Embassies — Embassy in China (Beijing) | www.usembassy-china.org.cn |
| Federal Reserve — Federal Reserve Bank of New York | www.newyorkfed.org |
| Law — Code of Federal Regulations (CFR) | www.gpoaccess.gov/cfr/index.html |
| Law — Government Printing Office (GPO) (includes Federal Register Notices, Public Law Texts) | www.gpoaccess.gov |
| Law — Harmonized Tariff Schedule of the United States (HTSUS) | www.usitc.gov/tata/hts/bychapter/ index.html |
| Law — Library of Congress | thomas.loc.gov |

## TABLE (continued)

| Organization | Website Address |
|---|---|
| Law — United States Code (U.S.C.) (including Title 19) | www.gpoaccess.gov/uscode/index. html |
| President of the United States — White House | www.whitehouse.gov |
| **V** | |
| Vatican (The Holy See) | www.vatican.va |
| **W** | |
| Washington International Trade Association (WITA) | www.wita.org |
| Wassenaar Arrangement | www.wassenaar.org |
| West African Economic and Monetary Union (UEMOA) | www.uemoa.int |
| World Bank | www.worldbank.org |
| World Conservation Union | www.iucn.org |
| World Council of Churches | www.wcc-coe.org |
| World Courts (Permanent Court of International Justice (PCIJ), Central American Court of Justice, International Commissions of Inquiry, International Prize Court, Economic Court of the Commonwealth of Independent States) | www.worldcourts.com |
| World Customs Organization (WCO) | www.wcoomd.org |
| World Economic Forum (Davos Summit) | www.weforum.org |
| World Health Organization (WHO) | www.who.int |
| World Health Organization (WHO) — Global Health Atlas | http://globalatlas.who.int |
| World Intellectual Property Organization (WIPO) | www.wipo.int |
| World Intellectual Property Organization (WIPO) — Collection of Laws for Electronic Access (CLEA) | www.wipo.int/clea/en |

TABLE **(continued)**

| *Organization* | *Website Address* |
|---|---|
| World Meteorological Organization | www.wmo.ch/index-en.html |
| World Organization for Animal Health (OIE) | www.oie.int |
| World Social Forum | www.forumsocialmundial.org |
| World Trade Organization (WTO) | www.wto.org |
| **X** — | |
| **Y** — | |
| **Z** — | |

## TABLE B-2:

## POLITICAL AND ECONOMIC MILESTONES IN CHINESE HISTORY[1]

| Period | |
|---|---|
| *Date* | *Event* |
| **Early Dynastic Period**<br>Unification of China (followed by periods of disunion and reunion)<br><br>Early Contact with Foreigners<br><br>Golden Age of Chinese Culture (Tang Dynasty) | |
| c. 2200 BC - c. 1700 BC | Xia Dynasty (17 kings over 14 generations) |
| c. 1700 BC - c. 1200 BC | Shang Dynasty (31 kings over 17 generations) |
| c. 1200 BC - 771 BC | Zhou Dynasty (Western Zhou) (12 kings over 11 generations) |

---

[1] This Table synthesizes information from a large number of sources, including many articles published in the *Economist* and *Financial Times*, and the following books:

1. IRIS CHANG, THE RAPE OF NANKING (Basic Books Publishers, 1997).

2. DANIEL C.K. CHOW, THE LEGAL SYSTEM OF THE PEOPLE'S REPUBLIC OF CHINA (Thomson West Nutshell, 2003).

3. CHIH H. LU, THE SINO INDIAN BORDER DISPUTE — A LEGAL STUDY (Greenwood Press, 1986).

4. COLIN MACKERRAS & ROBERT CHAN, MODERN CHINA A CHRONOLOGY FROM 1842 TO THE PRESENT (Thames and Hudson Ltd., London 1982).

5. GAVIN MENZIES, 1421 THE YEAR CHINA DISCOVERED THE WORLD (Transworld/Bantam Press 2002).

6. J.A.G. ROBERTS, A HISTORY OF CHINA (Palgrave Macmillan, 2nd ed., 2006).

7. WITOLD RODZINSKI, A HISTORY OF CHINA vols. 1 and 2 (Pergamon Press, 1979).

8. BAI SHOUYI, AN OUTLINE HISTORY OF CHINA (Foreign Languages Press, Beijing, 2002).

9. PAN WEI TUNG, THE CHINESE CONSTITUTION: A STUDY OF FORTY YEARS OF CONSTITUTION-MAKING IN CHINA (Institute of Chinese Culture, Washington D.C., 1945).

10. HAROLD M. VINACKE, MODERN CONSTITUTIONAL DEVELOPMENT IN CHINA (Dissertation, Princeton University Press, 1920).

## TABLE (continued)

| Date | Event |
|---|---|
| 771 BC - 256 BC | Eastern Zhou Dynasty (25 kings) |
| 722 BC - 404 BC | Spring and Autumn Period (end of period in dispute 481 BC and 404 BC)<br><br>Confucius (551 BC - 479 BC) |
| 403 BC - 221 BC | Warring States Period (start of period in dispute between 476 BC, 475 BC, and 403 BC) |
| 221 BC - 207 BC | Qin Dynasty (2 emperors)<br><br>First Chinese Emperor Qin Shi Huang Di rules from 221 BC to 210 BC (death). He constructs the Great Wall of China as a northern defensive border to protect against invasion. |
| c. 202 BC - 5 AD | Western Han Dynasty (12 emperors) |
| c. 9 AD - 25 AD | Supposed Xin Dynasty (2 rulers Wang Mang 9 AD - 23 AD and Liu Xuan 23AD - 25 AD) regarded as a transition period in the Han Dynasty |
| c. 25 AD - 220 | Eastern Han Dynasty (14 emperors) |
| 220 - 266 | Three Kingdoms Period (three different kingdoms ruled in China simultaneously)<br>Wei 220-265<br>Shu (Shu-Han) 221-263<br>Wu 222-280 |
| 265 - 317 | Western Jin Dynasty (4 emperors over 3 generations) |
| 317 - 420 | Eastern Jin Dynasty (11 emperors over 4 generations) |
| 420 - 589 | Southern and Northern Dynasties Period (2 separate dynastic lines concurrently ruled in China in the South and North)<br><br>Southern Dynasties<br>420 - 479 Song (8 rulers)<br>479 - 502 Southern Qi (7 rulers)<br>502 - 557 Liang (4 rulers)<br>557 - 589 Chen (5 rulers) |

## TABLE (continued)

| Date | Event |
|------|-------|
| | Northern Dynasties<br>386 - 534 Northern Wei (11 rulers)<br>534 - 550 Eastern Wei (1 ruler)<br>535 - 556 Western Wei (3 rulers)<br>550 - 557 Northern Qi (6 rulers)<br>557 - 581 Northern Zhou (5 rulers) |
| 581- 618 | Sui Dynasty<br>(2 emperors over 2 generations) |
| 618 - 907 | Tang Dynasty<br>(20 emperors, 1 empress over 14 generations)<br><br>Celebrated Golden Age of Chinese Culture<br><br>*The Book of Tea* by Lu Yu (733–804) discussed cultivation and processing of tea<br><br>Trade and Foreign Commerce between China and Japan and China Arabia established (over the silk road trade routes)<br><br>Early skirmishes between Chinese and Tibetan armies during 600s. Tibetan King Srong-brtsans-Gam-po marries Wen-Chen, a Chinese princess, in the early 600s.<br><br>China develops early "foreign currency script" to facilitate foreign exchange transactions called *fei qian* (flying money). |
| 907 - 960 | Five Dynasties Period |
| | 907 – 923<br>Later Liang (2 emperors)<br>923 – 936<br>Later Tang (4 emperors)<br>936 – 947<br>Later Jin (2 emperors)<br>947 – 950<br>Later Han (2 emperors)<br>950 – 960<br>Later Zhou (3 emperors) |

## TABLE (continued)

| Date | Event |
|---|---|
| 960 - 1279 | Song Dynasty |
| | Educational exchanges between China and Korea and China and Japan especially in Chinese medicine- but also cultural exchanges as well |
| | 960 – 1127<br>Northern Song (9 emperors over 7 generations) |
| | 1127 – 1279<br>Southern Song (7 emperors over 7 generations) |
| | During Song Dynasty, other Dynasties ruled parts of China |
| | 907 – 1125<br>Liao Dynasty (9 emperors) |
| | 1038 – 1227<br>Western Xia Dynasty (10 emperors) |
| | 1115 – 1234<br>Jin Dynasty (7 emperors) |
| **Later Dynastic Period**<br>Foreigners invade and stay to rule in China<br>China loses territory<br>Dynastic system crumbles in 20th century | |
| 1206 - 1368 | Yuan Dynasty (18 rulers, 15 emperors, 1 regent 2 temporary rulers) |
| | Mongols invade and rule China<br>Chinese Agricultural Production increased<br>Much trade between Arabs and Persians<br>Muslims installed in government roles especially in Astronomical Department |
| | Notable Yuan Emperor Reigns:<br>1206 - 1228 Genghis Khan<br>1260 - 1295 Kublai Khan (grandson to Genghis Khan) |
| | 1253<br>Kublai Khan invades and conquers Tibet, prior to becoming emperor. |

TABLE (continued)

| Date | Event |
|------|-------|
| | 1275 – 1292<br>Marco Polo visits China, meets Kublai Khan and wins his favor. Marco Polo writes a book of his travels which will continue to influence European perceptions of China for centuries. |
| 1368 - 1644 | Ming Dynasty (17 emperors over 12 generations)<br><br>1408, 1421<br>Zhong He (a Muslim military commander) leads Chinese exploration missions around Arabia and Africa- some claim he circumnavigates the globe a century prior to Magellan.<br><br>1557<br>Portuguese establish Macau as a trading port, the first of its kind in China. A Jesuit Mission is also established. |
| 1644 - 1912 | Qing Dynasty (10 emperors over 9 generations)<br><br>Manchus overthrow last Ming Dynasty emperor establish Qing Dynasty, last imperial dynasty of China<br><br>1720<br>Emperor Kang Xi marches Qing armies into Lhasa, deposing the Dalai Lama, and installing a more favorable to the Qing Dalai Lama. A regional government outpost is established in Tibet, keeping it under Qing control for nearly 200 years.<br><br>1840–1842<br>The Opium War, a trade war between Britain and China ends with the *Treaty of Nanking* (Nanjing) on 29 August 1842, ceding Hong Kong (specifically, Hong Kong island and Kowloon, but not the New Territories, which become subject later to a 99 year lease) to the British. |

## TABLE (continued)

| Date | Event |
|---|---|
| | **1849**<br>Portuguese seize Macau following the British claim of Hong Kong, later negotiating a formal accession treaty with China.<br><br>**1858**<br>In a series of treaties concluded in Tianjin, Russian (13 June 1858), American (18 June 1858), British (26 July 1858), and French (27 July 1858) governments negotiate trade pacts to open ports to foreign trade. These treaties along with other subsequent treaties carve up China into spheres of influence, weakening the power of the Qing against foreigners.<br><br>**1861–1908**<br>Empress Dowager Ci Xi (Tzu-Hsi) effectively takes power from the weakened Qing Emperor Xianfeng, and rules China *de facto* until her death (15 November), and the suspicious death of the 37-year old Emperor Guang Xu (14 November) both in 1908. |
| 1644–1912, continued | Qing Dynasty, continued<br><br>**1850s–1900**<br>Taiping Rebellion (1850–1866) and Boxer Rebellion (1898–1900), which are populist uprisings against both the Qing Dynasty and foreign influence. Neither Rebellion drives western powers from China or weakened their spheres of influence. But, they succeed in increase animosity against the weakened Qing Dynasty, which is perceived as kowtowing to those powers. Notably, during the Taiping Rebellion, the rebels succeed in capturing Nanking (Nanjing), which is 19 March 1853. During the Boxer Rebellion Empress Dowager Ci Xi expresses her favor for the Boxers on 21 June 1900, seeing an opportunity in their Rebellion to reassert power of the |

## TABLE (continued)

| Date | Event |
|---|---|
|  | Qing Dynasty. She orders General Yuan Shikai to assist the Boxers in their struggle. However, western forces prove far too strong for the Qing Army, which surrenders on 27 December 1900. |
|  | 17 March 1890 *Convention between Great Britain and China Relating to Sikkim and Tibet* regarding the Himalayan kingdoms between British controlled India and a weak and one might argue British influenced China allowing Britain expanded trade routes on the Silk Road. |
|  | 1 August 1894 - 17 April 1895 First Sino-Japanese War China and Japan fight over control of Korea. Conflict ends with the signing of the *Treaty of Shimonoseki*. China loses war and possession of Taiwan and Korea to Japan. |
|  | 27 August 1908 Nine year plan to develop a Constitution is begun. The *"Principles of Constitution"* document creates a National Assembly with the ultimate goal of constitutional monarchy. |
| 1644–1912, continued | Qing Dynasty, continued 2 December 1908 Pu Yi, the last emperor of China, ascends after the deaths of Ci Xi and Emperor Guang Xu. Pu Yi is the 2 ½ year old nephew of Ci Xi. |
|  | 1910 Development of first Chinese Civil Code, influenced by the 1898 German Civil Code and the 1896 Japanese Civil Code (developed during the Meiji Restoration period in Japan). |
|  | 10 October 1911 Wuchang Uprising, the start of the revolution ending Qing rule in China after two and half centuries. |

## TABLE (continued)

| Date | Event |
|---|---|
| | 11 November 1911<br>*"Nineteen Articles"* promulgated under the rapidly deteriorating rule of the Qing specifying a constitution be drafted.<br>12 February 1912<br>The 6-year old emperor, Pu Yi, abdicates his throne. |
| **Republic of China**<br>Development of Chinese Constitution<br>War with Japan<br>Rise of Communism<br>Civil War in China | |
| 1 January 1912 | Dr. Sun Yatsen establishes of the Republic of China, and becomes the first provisional president. |
| 13 February 1912 | Dr. Sun Yatsen resigns as provisional president, following the formal abdication of Pu Yi and collapse of Qing power. |
| 15 February 1912 | Yuan Shikai elected by Chinese senate as the new President of China. Yuan Shikai was seen by many as being supported by the foreign powers still occupying China, because he was a favored general in the Qing dynasty. |
| 11 March 1912 | Provisional constitution drafted under the new Republic of China. |
| July 1912 | Tibet claims its independence from China after the fall of the Qing. |
| 6–8 October 1913 | Simla Conference, a three day meeting between representatives of the Chinese, Tibetan, and British governments to demarcate the borders between China, Tibet, and British India. British negotiator, Henry McMahon helps facilitate a boundary between Tibet and India called the "McMahon Line" which still persists as a *de facto* boundary. |

## TABLE (continued)

| Date | Event |
|------|-------|
| | The agreement is concluded on 3 July 1914. China claims never to have assented fully to this agreement, and maintains that Tibet is a part of China, not recognizing the claim of independence from the year before. However, Britain does recognize Tibet's claim of sovereignty. |
| 1 May 1914 | Constitutional Compact drafted to assist in development of Chinese constitution. |
| 22 March 1916 | Yuan Shikai resigns as President. He later dies on 6 June 1916. |
| 4 May 1919 | May 4th rebellion, a political response to the failure of the Paris Peace Conference to adequately address Chinese concerns over lingering foreign influence in China. Riots continue over the next few years. |
| April 1921 | Dr. Sun Yatsen assumes provisional presidency of China once again. |
| 1 July 1921 | Formation of the Communist Party in China by 13 activists, which eventually becomes the largest political organization in the world. |
| 10 October 1923 | First Constitution of China completed. Never operational however, due to a lack of agreement among the KouMinTang (KMT), the Beiyang Warlords who followed Yuan Shikai, and the rise of the Communists in China following Lenin's rise to power in Russia in 1917 |
| 12 April 1924 | Fundamentals of National Reconstruction, Dr. Sun Yatsen led this effort to codify the 3 principles (San Min Chu I) as the KuoMinTang (KMT) claim more power and work with the Communists initially. The 3 Principles are: Nationalism (self emancipation of the Chinese nation), Livelihood (freedom from imperialist aggression), and Democracy (full equality for all the ethnic groups in China). |
| 12 March 1925 | Dr. Sun Yatsen dies. |

**TABLE (continued)**

| Date | Event |
|------|-------|
| 23 May 1929 | Second Civil Code promulgated. Still in use in Taiwan today. |
| 18 September 1931 | Japan invades and conquers Manchuria. Start of Japanese aggression in the Pacific and the beginnings of its second war with China. |
| 1934–36 | The Long March<br><br>Communist forces re-group via a Long March. Edgar Snow chronicles it, and the popularity of the Communists among the Chinese peasants, in his classic *Red Star Over China* (1936). |
| 7 July 1937 | Japan and China skirmish at Lugouqiao (Marco Polo Bridge) northwest of Beijing. This is generally defined as the start of the Second Sino-Japanese War (1937–1945). The United States assists China after its entry into the War following the Japanese attack on Pearl Harbor. |
| 13 December 1937 | Japan attacks Nanjing (Nanking) and proceeds to plunder, rape, and to kill 300,000 civilians. *"The Rape of Nanking"* a 1997 book by Iris Chang discusses in detail the events surrounding the taking of the city. The Japanese will later deny the atrocities committed and China will maintain cool relations with Japan following the end of the war. |
| 9 September 1945 | The Sino-Japanese war ends as a part of the end of Second World War. Taiwan (Formosa) was liberated from the Japanese at the end of the war, and returned to China 50 years of Japanese rule. |
| 25 December 1946 | Second Constitution of China adopted. Still in use in Taiwan today. |
| 1945–1949 | The Nationalists KuoMinTang (KMT) led by Chiang Kai Shek fight the Communists for control of China after the end of the Sino Japanese war. This animosity had been brewing since the late 1920s, but had been |

## TABLE (continued)

| Date | Event |
|---|---|
| | interrupted due to the war. General Chiang characterizes the Japanese as a "disease of the skin," but the Communists as a "disease of the heart." |
| | The United States supports General Chiang, but this support — led by General Joe Stilwell — proves modest. Supplies come via air, over the Himalayas, from Burma and India, and amount to feeding an elephant with an eyedropper. (The American support is chronicled dramatically by Barbara Tuchman in *Stilwell and the American Experience in China*.) |
| | Moreover, Nationalist forces, aligned with warlords and often corrupt, are deeply unpopular throughout the Chinese countryside. The Nationalists lose the battle for control of China, and flee the Mainland. They take refuge on the island of Formosa (Taiwan), establishing the Republic of China on the island. |
| | Years of debate ensue in the United States over "who lost China?," and is associated with the anti-communist McCarthy movement. |
| | To this day, both the Communists and Nationalists claim they are the rightful political rulers of both Taiwan and the Mainland as one China. |
| **People's Republic of China** China reclaims border lands and begins communist rule. China retreats from the International Stage focusing on radical domestic policies to modernize its economy. China aligns itself with other Communist countries during the "cold war." | |
| 1 October 1949 | Formation of the People's Republic of China (PRC) under the leadership of Mao Zedong and Communist Party. |
| 7 October 1950 | China marches People's Liberation Army (PLA) troops into Tibet, starting an occupation of the territory based on |

TABLE (continued)

| Date | Event |
|------|-------|
| | ancestral claim to the land as a part of China. A newly independent India begins to annex the Sikkim kingdom region in 1950 as well, revisiting the disputed boundary (McMahon Line) between China, Tibet, and India. |
| 14 February 1950 | China normalizes relations with the Union of Soviet Socialist Republics (USSR) signing a treaty of alliance, friendship, and mutual assistance. |
| 7 March 1950 | Withdrawal of Chinese membership in the GATT by telegram from Taipei effective 5 May 1950. |
| 24 October 1950–27 July 1953 | Chinese involvement in the Korean War. China fights United States directly (only a few years after the end of the Second World War, in which the countries had been allies) after the Chinese cross the Yalu River (bordering China and North Korea), in support of the North Korean communists. China fights to the end of the war and participates in the signing of the armistice agreement. |
| 21 July 1954 | Geneva Conference ends the fighting in French Indochina (Vietnam), following French military defeat by Vietnamese forces at Dienbenphu. Vietnamese nationalists and communists are led by Ho Chi Minh. As French forces leave, United States military advisers — and, in 1965, combat troops — continue their presence, and gradually expand through the 1960s and into the 1970s. The 1964 Gulf of Tonkin resolution authorizes the United States to take an active combat role. (It is later shown the Gulf of Tonkin incident never happened.) Fighting between Communist forces in the North and United States-backed South escalates and draws the United States and China into another conflict between communist and democratic forces. |

## TABLE (continued)

| Date | Event |
|------|-------|
| 20 September 1954 | Third Constitution is ratified. The first Communist Constitution and first Constitution of the People's Republic of China. |
| c. 1956–1969 | Sino-Soviet Split. Following Nikita Khrushchev's rise to power in the Soviet Union, the special bond between the two communist countries degrades due to ideological conflicts between Mao and Khrushchev. China feels the Soviets are supporting India in the unsettled border skirmishes, and the Soviets are concerned about Mao's nuclear ambitions and radical domestic policies. |
|  | February 1956 During the 20th meeting of the Communist Party of the Soviet Union, Khrushchev criticizes the recently deceased Joseph Stalin (death in 1953), and denounces personality cults in general. Mao takes offense to both actions, as he and Stalin had been compatriots. |
|  | 3 August 1958 A joint Sino-Russian communiqué expresses concern over United States military intervention in Lebanon (15 July 1958) and calls for a global nuclear test ban. China is disappointed there is no mention in the document about its claim to sovereignty over Taiwan. |
|  | 2 July 1960 The Soviets announce the withdrawal of their academic experts due to their dissatisfaction with China's economic policies and ideological differences of Communism. |
|  | 19 November 1960 Zhou Enlai addresses the conference of the Communist Party of the Soviet Union, criticizing the Soviet stance on Albania, and leaves the conference early. |

**TABLE (continued)**

| Date | Event |
|---|---|
|  | 5 July 1963<br>Bilateral talks between China and the Soviet Union fail to reach agreement. The erosion of relations continues throughout the 1960s. |
| 1958–1960 | Great Leap Forward<br>Started as the second economic 5-year plan, which is Mao's radical policy to drive industrial production at the expense of agricultural labor. This shift of human capital, a subsequent drought, and falsification of production data by local Communist Party cadres to show their districts meet central planning production targets (resulting in higher targets and further over-statements of output) leads to food shortages and mass starvation. Foreign demographers discover decades later that between 20 million and 35 million people died as a result of the Great Leap Forward. |
| 28 March 1959 | China formally annexes Tibet, reclaims it as part of China, and establishes it as the Xizang Autonomous Region. The 25-year old Dalai Lama flees Lhasa, and takes refuge in Dharamsala, India. Buddhists (and others) around the world protest peacefully Chinese aggression and the destruction of traditional Tibetan culture, and continue to do so. |
| 20 October – 21 November 1962 | Sino-Indian Border War, as Chinese and India military forces actively combat over the still-disputed border between India (Kashmir) and China (Tibet). The active fighting is preceded by small skirmishes in 1954, 1959, and 1961. On 10 December 1962, six party talks are held in Colombo, Ceylon (modern day Sri Lanka) among Burma, Ghana, Indonesia, the United Arab Republic (the ill-fated union of Egypt, Syria, and Libya), and China and India, to resolve the border issue. |

## Table (continued)

| Date | Event |
|------|-------|
| | The talks lead to no permanent solution. China unilaterally pulls troops back on 21 November. The stalemate continues to the present day, although economic opportunities may provide a way to finally bridge the border issue. |
| 16 May 1963 | China formally confirms support for Communist forces in Vietnam, and denounces the prolonged American presence in the region. |
| 27 January 1964 | France normalizes relations with China, the first Western country to do so. |
| 16 October 1964 | China detonates its first atomic bomb. |
| 1966–1976 | Cultural Revolution. Mao Zedong launches the Cultural Revolution in an effort to reclaim power (particularly from Hua Guafeng and Deng Xiaoping, following the debacle of the Great Leap Forward). The Revolution emboldens the youth of China to rise up against their parents, teachers, and the establishment to reinvigorate Communist ideals. Universities, government institutions, and the legal apparatus are defunct for a decade. Intellectuals are sent to fields and factories to labor as peasants. In 1976, the son of Deng Xiaoping, a university student, is thrown from a window in Beijing and paralyzed. The success of this effort allows Mao to maintain power in China until his death. But, the dismantling of Chinese economic infrastructure haunts the country for years afterward. The rise of industrial Japan in the 1960s helps motivate China to reconsider its policy of isolation and consider a different economic path. The psychological impact of Cultural Revolution lasts for decades, with criticism of it possible only in recent years, some of which is a proxy for criticism of the Tiananmen Square incident of 4 June 1989. |

**TABLE (continued)**

| Date | Event |
|------|-------|
| 9–11 July 1971 | Henry Kissinger, Secretary of State under President Richard Nixon, secretly visits China and meets with Mao Zedong. |
| 25 October 1971 | The People's Republic of China joins the United Nations and takes the China seat currently occupied by the Republic of China's (Taiwan's) representative. |
| 14–28 February 1972 | President Nixon visits China, meets with Mao Zedong, and begins the process to normalize relations between the United States and the People's Republic of China. On 28 February 1972, the Shanghai Communiqué, which adopts the One China Policy (one country, two systems), is signed. |
| 29 March 1973 | United States armed forces withdraw from Vietnam. The communist North Vietnamese take over the country in 1975, capturing Saigon (subsequently renamed Ho Chi Minh City) in April. Cambodia and Laos also fall to communists. The United States is plagued by perceived failure in defending pro-democratic regimes against communists. The "Vietnam Syndrome" persists for decades, coloring the modern United States view of whether and how to intervene militarily overseas, and what constitutes victory in warfare. |
| 4–5 April 1976 | Pro democracy riots erupt in Beijing. Following the death of Zhou Enlai on 8 January 1976, mourners begin to congregate in Tiananmen Square. The People's Liberation Army (PLA) is sent in to break up the demonstrations which evolved from a memorial to a claim of more freedoms. This event will eerily foreshadow another similar clash in the Square thirteen years later. |
| 9 September 1976 | Mao Zedong dies. |

**TABLE (continued)**

| Date | Event |
|------|-------|
| 21 July 1977 | Deng Xiaoping emerges as the next leader of China after Mao's death, and the capture of the Gang of Four (including Madame Jiang Qing, the wife of Chairman Mao). The subsequent trial will be a celebrated media event and the Court sentences Madame Mao to death, but later commutes the sentence to life in prison. |
| 17 February–1 March 1979 | Vietnam-China border conflict. In a rapid deterioration of foreign diplomatic relations following the Communist victory in Vietnam, skirmishes over the border erupt into 2 weeks of active combat before a truce is called. |

**Open Door Policy**
Development of modern foreign trade relations between China and the rest of the world
Rebuilding of Chinese infrastructure and the gradual development of modern legal infrastructure after the end of the Cultural Revolution
China begins participation in international organizations.

| Date | Event |
|------|-------|
| November–December 1978 | Critical meetings of the Central Committee of the Chinese Communist Party (CCP) (November), and a plenary session of the CCP (December), at which Deng Xiaopeng demonstrates political authority over Maoists, and discusses economic reforms. By 1984, communes in Anhui are formally dismantled. |
| Late 1978 | Rural economic reforms begin in the central Chinese province of Anhui. Peasants in one commune divide land into individual plots, at first secretly, but later with official support and are not punished. |
| 1 January 1979 | Diplomatic relations between the United States and China are established by President Jimmy Carter. The United States pledges to continue to provide informal support to the people of Taiwan. |

## TABLE (continued)

| Date | Event |
|------|-------|
| 29 January–4 February 1979 | President Carter hosts Deng Xiaoping on his visit to the United States from. This visit marks the first time a leader from the People's Republic of China visits the United States. |
| 10 April 1979 | *Taiwan Relations Act*, enacted by the United States Congress, authorizes the United States to provide military aid to the island. |
| 1 June 1979 | The first modern law for Chinese and Foreign Joint Venture Investment is promulgated. |
| 1 July 1979 | Deng Xiaoping launches his Open Door Policy of economic reform. Four Special Economic Zones (SEZs) are launched, in Zhuhai, Shenzhen, Xiamen, and Shantou. Other SEZs will follow in Beijing and Shanghai. |
| 2 April 1980 | China becomes a member of the International Monetary Fund (IMF). |
| 15 May 1980 | China becomes a member of the World Bank. |
| 13 December 1981 | China promulgates the Economic Contract Law (domestic), the first of three sets of laws governing contracts in China. |
| 4 December 1982 | Fourth Constitution of China adopted (currently in use in the People's Republic of China) includes provisions for freedom of the press and of religion. Former President Carter claims these freedoms are included at his urging to Deng Xiaoping. |
| 20 December 1984 | China and Great Britain conclude the Anglo Chinese agreement effectively setting the stage for Hong Kong's return to China, the Sino-British Joint Declaration. |
| 1 July 1985 | Foreign Economic Contract law promulgated. |
| 10 July 1986 | China expresses interest in joining (or re-joining) the GATT, and begins the negotiation process toward accession. |

## TABLE (continued)

| Date | Event |
|------|-------|
| 23 June 1987 | Technology Contract law promulgated. The third of the contract laws which govern Chinese transactions. |
| 1 July 1987 | Customs Law is promulgated, replacing the 1951 provisional law still on the books. |
| 13 April 1988 | Chinese Foreign Contractual Joint Ventures Law promulgated. |
| 4 June 1989 | Tiananmen Square riots erupt. After months of pro democracy demonstrations by university students and other workers in the public square, the People's Liberation Army (PLA) is dispatched to break up the demonstrations, which were gaining more and more world-wide media attention. The estimated death toll is between several hundred and up to three thousand. The event shows the Communist control exerted over the people. The rest of the world looks on in horror. |
| 10 December 1989 | The Dalai Lama of Tibet accepts the Nobel Peace Prize for his non-violent efforts to free Tibet from Chinese control. This award comes after the Tiananmen Square Riots and almost in counterpoint to Chinese aggression. |
| 1990 | Opening of the Shanghai stock exchange on 26 November 1990, and of the Shenzhen stock exchange on 1 December 1990. |
| 1 January 1994 | China establishes first exchange rate for the Renminbi (RMB) and other world currencies eliminating the previous dual system of domestic RMB and foreign exchange certificates. |
| 1 July 1994 | Company Law enters force. This legislation dictates the formation of companies and corporations in China. |

**TABLE (continued)**

| Date | Event |
|---|---|
| 31 August 1994 | Arbitration Law enters force. This legislation provided an alternate form of dispute resolution for Chinese and Foreign companies, rather than using the Chinese court system. |
| 26 April 1996 | First meeting of the Shanghai Five, which consists of China, Russia, Kazakhstan, Kyrgyzstan, and Tajikistan. The countries form this economic group to promote trade in Central Asia. |
| 19 February 1997 | Deng Xiaoping dies. |
| 1 July 1997 | Hong Kong returns to China from British rule. |
| 15 March 1999 | A single unified Contracts Law is promulgated. |
| 20 December 1999 | Macau returns to China from Portuguese rule. |

**On the World Stage**
Continued Progressive Legal Developments Through Promulgation of Laws by Subject
China participates as an emerging world leader in Global Affairs
Unprecedented economic success drives larger and larger infrastructure projects

| Date | Event |
|---|---|
| 13 July 2001 | China is selected as the host for the 2008 Olympic games. |
| 5 December 2001 | Chinese Law on Wholly Owned Foreign Enterprises is promulgated. |
| 11 December 2001 | China joins the WTO 50 years after withdrawing from the GATT contracting parties. |
| 1 January 2002 | Chinese Taipei (Taiwan) joins the World Trade Organization as an independent member. |
| 25 March 2003 | China's Ministry of Foreign Trade and Economic Cooperation (MOFTEC) becomes the Ministry of Commerce (MOFCOM). |

## TABLE (continued)

| Date | Event |
|---|---|
| 2003 | The Closer Economic Partnership Agreement (CEPA) between China and Hong Kong and Macau is signed, A testament to the One China Two Systems approach, this agreement establishes a free trade agreement (FTA) between the 3 economies of China eliminating tariffs and setting the stage for broader economic integration. 29 June 2003 Hong Kong and China sign CEPA. 17 October 2003 Macau and China sign CEPA. |
| 1 July 2004 | Foreign Trade Law of the People's Republic of China enters into force. Covering technology trade and antidumping (AD) measures. |
| 29 January 2005 | First direct airline connection between China and Taiwan since 1949, prior to the start of Spring Festival (Chinese New Year) a traditional time for families to gather. |
| 20 May 2006 | Construction of the Three Gorges Dam, the world's largest dam, is completed. This project engenders great controversy in China and around the world for environmental and human rights reasons. |
| 1 July 2006 | New technologically advanced railway opened offering direct travel between Beijing and Lhasa. |
| 11 December 2006 | Banking, securities, and insurance services opened to foreign financial service providers. The first time since the beginning of the 20th century. |
| 2007 | China enacts its first antitrust law, the Anti-Monopoly Law (AML). In 2005, the Committee on Foreign Investment in the United States (CFIUS) blocked a proposed acquisition by the China National Offshore Oil Company Ltd. |

## TABLE (continued)

| Date | Event |
|------|-------|
| | (CNOOC) of Unocal. Stung by the CFIUS decision, part of China's motivation for the AML was to develop an antitrust apparatus and regulatory procedures to block foreign acquisitions of Chinese companies, and obtain some control over global merger and acquisition (M&A) activity. Of course, antitrust measures are based on sound economic analysis of markets and competition, whereas a national security review of M&A transactions is an entirely different matter. |
| | Under the AML, the key regulatory authority is The AML resembles the United States *Sherman* and *Clayton Acts*, in that it covers anti-competitive mergers, horizontal cartels, monopolization, and unreasonable restraints on distribution. But, there are differences between the Chinese and American regimes. |
| | First, American antitrust law forbids monopolization. The AML is broader, as it forbids not only monopolization, but also abuse of dominant market positions and monopoly agreements. Market power is not a pre-requisite under the AML to prove a monopoly agreement. |
| | Second, the AML expressly allows the relevant governmental authority to incorporate non-competition factors into its analysis. Such factors can include not only national security, but also national economic development. For example, in an abuse-of-dominance case, Chinese officials could consider non-competition factors like the impact of the proposed transaction on operational efficiency, social and public interests, and economic development. Under U.S. antitrust law, only competition criteria are applied. |

## TABLE (continued)

| Date | Event |
|------|-------|
|  | Third, in he American scheme, there are two key regulatory authorities, the Department of Justice and Federal Trade Commission. Under the AML, there are three authorities: the Ministry of Commerce (MOFCOM), which has the power to block or impose conditions on transactions involving foreign firms, and two other entities. |
|  | The AML provisions on mergers have affected American firms, because they require pre-merger notification of the total sales of a party in China, not just the nexus of the proposed merger transaction with China. Still, during the first year of its |
|  | use, Chinese authorities reviewed over 52 mergers, prohibited one, and approved five others with conditions. |
|  | There is concern about the AML in respect of certain overly broad and ambiguous provisions, possible rigid prohibitions, and potential for selective enforcement (to the benefit of individual competitors rather than the competitive process and consumer welfare). Moreover, in the first 2 years of its operation, China applied the AML, by imposing merger conditions or blocking mergers, only in cases involving foreign companies. In a high-profile case, China blocked the planned acquisition of the Huiyuan Juice Group (a major Chinese name-brand company) by Coca-Cola. |
|  | Nonetheless, the AML was an important step for China in its transition to a market economy. |

## TABLE (continued)

| Date | Event |
| --- | --- |
| 1 January 2008 | New Labor Law enters into force, enforceable by monetary fines. The Law guarantees minimum pay (*e.g.*, 1,000 yuan per month in Guangdong province), health, and pension benefits, and limiting maximum weekly work hours (40 in Guangdong) and weekly overtime hours (32 in Guandong). However, enforcement has been uneven, especially with global competitive pressures (such as cheaper wages in Vietnam and other nearby countries), and severe recession, leaving some factory owners unable or unwilling to comply. Wal-Mart instructs its 20,000 Chinese suppliers to comply with the Labor Law, or face replacement. |
| 8 August 2008 | The 2008 Summer Olympic Games opens in Beijing. After years of negotiation and preparation, China emerges on the world sport stage. |
| 11–12 October 2008 | Property Law liberalization agreed to in closed door plenary session of the Central Committee of the Communist Party. Decision taken is to establish exchanges for peasants to trade freely their land use rights. Since the 1949 Communist Revolution, all land has been owned by the state or rural collectives. Buying and selling land by individuals has been illegal. Most of China's 730 million peasant farmers hold 30-year land use contracts, according to which they may use farm plots they are allocated by local Communist Party officials. The contracts make it nearly impossible for them to sell their land use rights, or pledge these rights as collateral for loans. In taking the decision, the Communist Party balances two fears. First, it fears a return to pre-Revolution feudalism in which a few wealthy landlords hoard land, and millions of rural poor flood into China's cities. |

TABLE (continued)

| Date | Event |
|------|-------|
| | Second, it fears stagnant or declining agricultural productivity, and appreciates concentrating land into large, efficient farms will boost output. The decision to allow for trading on an organized exchange, protected by law, of land rights, is a step toward privatization, but short of permitting full ownership (title holding) by individuals, *i.e.*, the decision contributes to a kind of *de facto* privatization. |
| 13 October 2008 | Property Law liberalization (above) is implemented through establishment of first exchange, in Chengdu, on which peasant farmers can trade their land use rights freely. |
| 20 May 2009 | Court in Beijing, the Daxing District Court, issues first decision in favor of a victim of internet censorship. |
| | The plaintiff, Hu Xingdou, a professor of economics, maintained a website on which he regularly discussed controversial topics such as official corruption and police brutality. Beijing Xin Net, the company hosting that web site informed him in April 2009 via e-mail that it had shut down his site because the site contained illegal content. The specific article that led Xin Net to take action was one posted by Professor Hu calling for the abolition of re-education through labor prison camps. In such camps, sometimes referred to as gulags, authorities place political prisoners without trial. |
| | Xin Net countered it was following orders from the Chinese internet surveillance officials, who apparently were with the Suzhou police. In so doing, the Chinese government was following its usual practice of not blocking a website itself, but rather having a host company (like Xin Net) do so under order, or having the host company exercise self-censorship under pressure. |

## TABLE (continued)

| Date | Event |
| --- | --- |
| | The Court ruled the defendant hosting company failed to prove its claim concerning "illegal content," and breached its contract with Professor Hu by not giving him the opportunity to remove the controversial content before closing down the site. The Court ordered Xin Net to return to Professor Hu the $201 fee he paid for two years of services. |
| | The Court did not reach broader, deeper issues of free speech. Nevertheless, both the winning plaintiff and observers praised the ruling as a step in favor of greater rule of law, judicial independence, and transparency, and was a modest warning to internet censorship authorities to eschew arbitrary and capricious behavior. |
| 26 December 2009 | The Standing Committee of the National People's Congress passes a Tort Liability Law, after 7 years of deliberation and 3 drafts. (The Standing Committee is the senior-most legislative body in China.) The Law took effect on 1 July 2010, and has equal legal status with the Property Law. |
| | The Tort Liability Law has 92 Articles, covering compensation for a broad range of unlawful acts, including work-related accidents and privacy infringement. |
| | Though the Law does not create any new environmental torts, it reinforces the liability scheme in China's environmental laws, because four of the articles in the law specify compensation for environmental torts. |
| 1 July 2010 | New Tort Law covering Products Liability and Personal Injury takes effect. Under this law, a plaintiff can file for potentially unlimited punitive damages against a company that harms it. |

**TABLE (continued)**

| Date | Event |
|---|---|
| 30 December 2010 | First victory for non-governmental organizations (NGOs) in a lawsuit in one of China's pilot Environmental Courts.

In 2008, China established pilot Environmental Courts in five provinces: Guizhou, Hebei, Jiangsu, Liaoning, and Yunnan.

Subsequently, two NGOs — the All-China Environment Federation (ACEF) and the Public Environmental Education Center (PEEC) — filed suit against the Dingpa Paper Company in the pilot court in Qingzhen, Guizhou. (Note the ACEF is not a pure NGO, as it is affiliated with the Ministry of Environmental Protection.) They alleged Dingpa was dumping wastewater into the Nanming River without treating the effluent. The court agreed with the plaintiffs, and ordered Dingpa not only to cease the discharges until it treated the water, but also to pay litigation fees and court costs. |

## TABLE B-3:

## ECONOMIC LANDSCAPE OF THE PEOPLE'S REPUBLIC OF CHINA[1]

| Political Unit (Name, Type, Capital) | Economic Information | Industries and Companies |
|---|---|---|
| **Anhui** (Province) Hefei | GDP (U.S.$ billion, 2005) 67.9% of all provinces 2.7 Real GDP growth (% 96-05) 10.1 Population (million, 2005) 65.2 GDP per capita (U.S.$) 1,042 | Iron/Steel (Maanshan Iron and Steel) Building Materials (Anhui Conch Cement) Commercial Services (Anhui Expressway) Mining (Anhui Tongdu Copper) Auto Parts and Equipment (Anhui Jianghuai Automobile) |
| **Fujian** (Province) Fuzhou | GDP (U.S. $ billion, 2005) 82.9% of all provinces 3.3 Real GDP growth (% 96-05) 10.1 Population (million, 2005) 35.4 GDP per capita (U.S.$) 2,345 | Agriculture (Chaoda Modern Agriculture) Mining (Ziijin Mining Group) Commercial Services (Fujian Expressway, Xiamen Port Development) Auto Parts and Equipment (Fuyao Glass) |

---

[1] *Notes:*

(1) Data in this Table are drawn, adapted, and condensed from China Research Team, Credit Suisse (Hong Kong) Limited, October 2006, Map and Data/Text Box Insets entitled "Economic Landscape of Mainland China."

(2) These data do not account for two regions — Hong Kong and Macao. They are Special Administrative Regions (SARs), with their own independently functioning economies. China manages trade via Hong Kong and Macao under the *Closer Economic Partnership Arrangement* (CEPA), a free trade agreement (FTA) among China, Hong Kong, and Macao which entered into force on 1 January 2004.

(3) These data do not include Taiwan.

## TABLE (continued)

| Political Unit (Name, Type, Capital) | Economic Information | Industries and Companies |
|---|---|---|
| **Gansu** (Province) Lanzhou | GDP (U.S. $ billion, 2005) 24.4 % of all provinces 1.0 Real GDP growth (% 96-05) 9.8 Population (million, 2005) 25.9 GDP per capita (U.S.$) 939 | None listed |
| **Guangdong** (Province) Guangzhou | GDP (U.S. $ billion 2005) 274.2 % of all provinces 11.1 Real GDP growth (% 96-05) 10.3 Population (million, 2005) 91.9 GDP per capita (U.S. $) 2,982 | Banks (China Merchants Bank, Shenzhen Development Bank) Insurance (Ping An Insurance) Diversified Financial Services (CITIC Securities, Foxcomm International Holdings) Telecom (ZTE Corp., Hauwei Technology), Internet (Tencent Holdings), Packaging Containers (China International Marine Containers), Real Estate (China Vanke, Guangzhou F and F Properties), Engineering/ Construction (Shenzhen Yantian Port, Guangzhou Baiyun Airport), Commercial Services Shenzhen Chiwan Wharf), Electric Components and Equipment (BYD), Forest Products and Paper (Nine Dragons Paper), Medical Devices (Mindray Medical Technologies), Media (Clear Media) |

TABLE (continued)

| Political Unit (Name, Type, Capital) | Economic Information | Industries and Companies |
|---|---|---|
| **Guizhou** (Province) Guiyang | GDP (U.S. $ billion, 2005) 24.5 % of all provinces 1.0 Real GDP growth (% 96-05) 9.4 Population (million, 2005) 39.3 GDP per capita (U.S. $) 624 | Beverages (Kweichow Moutai) |
| **Hainan** (Province) Haikou | GDP (U.S. $ billion, 2005) 11.4 % of all provinces 0.5 Real GDP growth (% 96-05) 10.7 Population (million, 2005) 8.3 GDP per capita (U.S.$) 1,379 | Chemicals (China Blue Chemical) Airlines (Hainan Airlines) |
| **Hebei** (Province) Shijiazhuang | GDP (U.S. $ billion, 2005) 127.8 % of all provinces 5.2 Real GDP growth (% 96-05) 9.9 Population (million, 2005) 68.5 GDP per capita (U.S.$) 1,866 | None Listed |
| **Heilongjiang** (Province) Harbin | GDP (U.S.$ billion, 2005) 69.6 % of all provinces 2.8 Real GDP growth (% 96-05) 10.7 Population (million, 2005) 38.2 GDP per capita (U.S.$) 1,823 | Agriculture (Heilongjiang Agriculture), Pharmaceutical (Harbin Pharmaceuticals), Electric Components and Equipment (Harbin Power Equipment), Aerospace / Defense (Hafei Aviation) |

## TABLE (continued)

| Political Unit (Name, Type, Capital) | Economic Information | Industries and Companies |
|---|---|---|
| **Henan** (Province) Zhengzhou | GDP (U.S.$ billion, 2005) 133.1 % of all provinces 5.4 Real GDP growth (% 96-05) 13.1 Population (million, 2005) 97.7 GDP per capita (U.S.$) 1,363 | Food (Henan Shuanghui) Auto Manufacturers (Zhengzhou Yutong Bus) Electric Components and Equipment (XJ Electric) Cosmetics/Personal Care (Henan Rebecca) |
| **Hubei** (Province) Wuhan | GDP (U.S.$ billion, 2005) 81.9 % of all provinces 3.3 Real GDP growth (% 96-05) 10.2 Population (million, 2005) 60.3 GDP per capita (U.S.$) 1,359 | Iron/Steel (Wuhan Iron and Steel) Electric (China Yangtze Power (headquarters in Beijing) Auto Manufacturing (Dongfeng Motor Group) |
| **Hunan** (Province) Changsha | GDP (U.S.$ billion, 2005) 81.8 % of all provinces 3.3 Real GDP growth (% 96-05) 9.8 Population (million, 2005) 67.3 GDP per capita (U.S.$) 1,215 | Iron / Steel (Hunan Valin Steel Tube and Wire) Machinery-Construction and Mining (Changsha Zoomlion Heavy Industry, Sany Heavy Industry) |
| **Jiangsu** (Province) Nanjing | GDP (U.S.$ billion, 2005) 230.9 % of all provinces 9.3 Real GDP growth (% 96-05) 10.1 Population (million, 2005) 74.7 GDP per capita (U.S.$) 3,089 | Retail (Golden Eagle, Suning Appliance), Commercial Services (Jiangsu Expressway), Food (China Yurun), Auto Parts and Equipment (Weifu High Technology), Machinery Diversified (NARI Technology) |

TABLE **(continued)**

| Political Unit (Name, Type, Capital) | Economic Information | Industries and Companies |
|---|---|---|
| **Jiangxi** (Province) Nanchang | GDP (U.S.$ billion, 2005) 51.3 % of all provinces 2.1 Real GDP growth (% 96-05) 12.6 Population (million, 2005) 43.1 GDP per capita (U.S.$) 1,189 | Metal Fabricate Hardware (Jiangxi Cooper), Commercial Services (Jiangxi Ganyue Expressway) |
| **Jilin** (Province) Changchun | GDP (U.S.$ billion, 2005) 45.7 % of all provinces 1.8 Real GDP growth (% 96-05) 12.1 Population (million, 2005) 27.2 GDP per capita (U.S.$) 1,682 | Biotechnology (Global Bio-Chem) Auto Manufacturing (FAW CAR) Pharmaceutical (Jilin Aodong Medicine) |
| **Liaoning** (Province) Shenyang | GDP (U.S.$ billion, 2005) 101.1 % of all provinces 4.1 Real GDP growth (% 96-05) 11.9 Population (million, 2005) 42.2 GDP per capita (U.S.$) 2,396 | Iron/Steel (Angang New Steel), Engineering and Construction (Dalian Port), Retail (Dashang Group), Hand/Machine Tools (Shenyang Machine Tool), Transportation (China Railway Container Logistics) |
| **Qinghai** (Province) Xining | GDP (U.S. $ billion, 2005) 6.9 % of all provinces 0.3 Real GDP growth (% 96-05) 10.5 Population (million, 2005) 5.4 GDP per capita (US$) 1,264 | Chemicals (Qinghai Salt Lake Potash) |

## TABLE (continued)

| Political Unit (Name, Type, Capital) | Economic Information | Industries and Companies |
|---|---|---|
| **Shaanxi** (Province) Xi'an | GDP (U.S.$ billion, 2005) 46.4 % of all provinces 1.9 Real GDP growth (% 96-05) 10.2 Population (million, 2005) 37.2 GDP per capita (U.S.$) 1,248 | None listed |
| **Shanxi** (Province) Taiyuan | GDP (U.S.$ billion, 2005) 46.4 % of all provinces 1.9 Real GDP growth (% 96-05) 11.5 Population (million, 2005) 33.6 GDP per capita (U.S.$) 1,384 | Transportation (Daqin Railway) Coal (Xishan Coal, Datong Coal) Iron/Steel (Taigang Stainless Steel) |
| **Shandong** (Province) Jinan | GDP (U.S.$ billion, 2005) 233.4 % of all provinces 9.4 Real GDP growth (% 96-05) 10.5 Population (million, 2005) 92.5 GDP per capita (U.S.$) 2,523 | Coal (Yanzhou Coal), Textiles (Weiqiao Textiles), Electric (Hudian Power), Food (People's Food, Xiwang Sugar), Chemicals (Yantai Wanhua), Forest Products and Paper Beverages (Yantai Changyu, Tsingtao Brewery), Apparel (Luthai Textiles), Home Furnishings (Qingdao Haier), Healthcare-Productions (Shandong Weigao), Machinery-Construction and Mining (Shantui Construction Machinery) |

## TABLE (continued)

| Political Unit (Name, Type, Capital) | Economic Information | Industries and Companies |
|---|---|---|
| **Sichuan** (Province) Chengdu | GDP (U.S.$ billion, 2005) 93.3 % of all provinces 3.8 Real GDP growth (% 96-05) 8.7 Population (million, 2005) 87.5 GDP per capita (U.S.$) 1,066 | Iron/Steel (Panzhihua New Steel and Vanadium) Beverages (Wuliangye Yibin) Machinery- Diversified (Dongfang Electric Machinery) |
| **Yunnan** (Province) Kunming | GDP (U.S.$ billion, 2005) 43.9 % of all provinces 1.8 Real GDP growth (% 96-05) 8.6 Population (million, 2005) 44.5 GDP per capita (U.S.$) 986 | Chemicals (Yunnan Yuntianhua) Mining (Yunnan Copper, Yunnan Tin) Pharmaceuticals (Yunnan Baiyao) |
| **Zhejiang** (Province) Hangzhou | GDP (U.S.$ billion, 2005) 168.9 % of all provinces 6.8 Real GDP growth (% 96-05) 11.6 Population (million, 2005) 49.0 GDP per capita (U.S.$) 3,448 | Commercial Services (Zhejiang Expressway), Energy Alternate Sources (Suntech Power), Auto Parts and Equipment (Minth Group), Pharmaceutical (Zhejiang Hisun), Electronics (Hengdian Magnetics), Housewares (Zhejiang Supor Cookware) |
| **Beijing** Municipality | GDP (U.S.$ billion, 2005) 87.0 % of all provinces 3.5 Real GDP growth (% 96-05) 11.1 Population (million, 2005) 15.4 GDP per capita (U.S.$) 5,657 | Oil and Gas (Petro China, Sinopec, CNOOC Ltd., China Oilfield Services),Telecom (China Mobile, China Telecom, China Netcom, China Unicom), |

TABLE (continued)

| Political Unit (Name, Type, Capital) | Economic Information | Industries and Companies |
|---|---|---|
| | | Banks (China Construction Bank, Bank of China Ltd., China Minsheng Bank, Industrial and Commercial Bank of China), Coal (China Shenhua Energy), Insurance (China Life, PICC P&C), Mining (Chalco), Electric (Huaneng Power, China Yangtze Power, Datang Power), Airlines (Air China), Computers (Lenovo), Internet (Netease.com, Sina Corp., Baidu), Engineering and Construction (Beijing Capital Airport), Education (New Oriental School), Healthcare Products (China Medical Technologies) |
| **Chongqing** Municipality | GDP (U.S.$ billion, 2005) 38.8 % of all provinces 1.6 Real GDP growth (% 96-05) 9.4 Population (million, 2005) 28.0 GDP per capita (U.S.$) 1,386 | Auto Manufacturers (Chongqing Changan Auto) |
| **Shanghai** Municipality | GDP (U.S. $ billion, 2005) 115.5 % of all provinces 4.7 Real GDP growth (% 96-05) 10.0 | Iron / Steel (Baosteel), Banking (Bank of Communication, Shanghai Pudong Development Bank), Transportation (China Shipping and Development), |

## TABLE (continued)

| Political Unit (Name, Type, Capital) | Economic Information | Industries and Companies |
| --- | --- | --- |
| | Population (million, 2005) 17.8<br>GDP per capita (U.S.$) 6,498 | Chemicals (Sinopec Shanghai Petrochemical), Machinery Diversified (Shanghai Electric, Zhenhua Port Machinery),<br><br>Engineering and Construction (Shanghai Airport), Commercial Services (Shanghai Port), Food (Lianhua Supermarket), Internet (Ctrip.com, Shanda), Advertising (Focus Media), Airlines (China Eastern Airlines), Semiconductors (SMIC- Semiconductor Manufacturing International Corp.) |
| **Tianjin** Municipality | GDP (U.S. $ billion, 2005) 46.3<br>% of all provinces 1.9<br>Real GDP growth (% 96-05) 11.1<br>Population (million, 2005) 10.4<br>GDP per capita (U.S. $) 4,439 | Food (Tingyi Holding), Commercial Services (Tianjin Port), Oil and Gas Services (Offshore Oil Engineering), Auto Manufacturing (Tianjin Faw Xiali Auto), Pharmaceutical (Tianjin Tasly Pharmaceuticals), Beverages (Dynasty Fine Wines Group Ltd.), Environmental Controls (Tianjin Capital Environmental Protection) |

## TABLE (continued)

| Political Unit (Name, Type, Capital) | Economic Information | Industries and Companies |
|---|---|---|
| **Guangxi** (Autonomous Region) Nanning | GDP (U.S. $ billion, 2005) 51.3 % of all provinces 2.1 Real GDP growth (% 96-05) 11.5 Population (million, 2005) 49.3 GDP per capita (U.S.$) 1,042 | Electric (Guangxi Guiguan Electric Power) Machinery-Construction and Mining (Guangxi Liugong Machinery Food (Nanning Sugar Manufacturing) |
| **Inner Mongolia** (Autonomous Region) Hohhot | GDP (U.S. $ billion, 2005) 48.3 % of all provinces 1.9 Real GDP growth (% 96-05) 12.1 Population (million, 2005) 23.9 GDP per capita (U.S. $) 2,024 | Coal (China Shenhua Energy (headquartered in Beijing)) Food (China Mengniu Dairy, Inner Mongolia Yili) Apparel (Inner Mongolia Eerduosi Cashmere) |
| **Ningxia** (Autonomous Region) Yinchuan | GDP (U.S.$ billion, 2005) 7.6 % of all provinces 0.3 Real GDP growth (% 96-05) 10.7 Population (million, 2005) 6.0 GDP per capita (U.S. $) 1,270 | None listed |
| **Xinjiang** (Autonomous Region) Ürümqi | GDP (U.S. $ billion, 2005) 33.0 % of all provinces 1.3 Real GDP growth (% 96-05) 8.9 Population (million, 2005) 20.1 GDP per capita (U.S. $) 1,640 | Electric Components and Equipment (Xinjiang Tebian Electric Apparatus) Environmental Control (Tianye Water) |

## TABLE (continued)

| Political Unit (Name, Type, Capital) | Economic Information | Industries and Companies |
|---|---|---|
| **Xizang** (Tibet) (Autonomous Region) Lhasa | GDP (U.S. $ billion, 2005) 3.2 % of all provinces 0.1 Real GDP growth (% 96-05) 11.6 Population (million, 2005) 2.8 GDP per capita (U.S.$) 1,143 | None listed |
| **CHINA** <br><br> TOTAL | GDP (U.S.$ billion, 2005) 2,313 % of all provinces 100 Real GDP growth (% 96-05) 9.0 Population (million, 2005) 1,308 GDP per capita (U.S. $) 1,769 | Oil and Gas (Petro China, Sinopec, CNOOC Ltd.), Telecom (China Mobile, China Telecom, China Netcom, China Unicom) Banks (China Construction Bank, Bank of China Ltd., China Merchants Bank, Bank of Communication), Coal (China Shenhua Energy), Iron/Steel (Baosteel), Insurance (China Life, Ping An Insurance), Mining (Chalco), Electric (Huaneng Power, China Yangtze Power), Diversified (CITIC Pacific), Transportation (Daqin Railway), Commercial Services (Foxconn International Holdings) |

TABLE B-4:

POLITICAL AND ECONOMIC MILESTONES IN EU HISTORY[1]

| Date | Document | Who | More Information |
|------|----------|-----|------------------|
| 19 September 1946 | Zurich University Speech | Winston Churchill | Creation of the United States of Europe |
| Signed 18 April 1951, entered into Force 23 July 1952, expired 23 July 2002 | Treaty of Paris | European Coal and Steel Community (ECSC) | Formation of the first multilateral European organization — which united France and Germany |
| Signed on 25 March 1957, entered into force 1 January 1958 | Treaties of Rome —<br><br>Established the European Economic Community | European Economic Community (EEC). Same countries as ECSC, namely, France Germany Italy Belgium, the Netherlands, and Luxembourg | Formed the European Economic Community, the basis (or forerunner) for the European Union. Treaties of Rome still a foundational document in the EU currently. Lead by Jean Monnet, the agricultural interests of the French (leading to the development of the Common Agricultural Policy (CAP) were balanced by German industrial concerns for market access for industrial goods. |

---

[1] Adapted from Ralph Folsom, *European Union Law in a Nutshell* (5th ed. 2005), "The History of the EU" available at http://www.europa.eu/abc/history/index_en.htm, and the European Treaties website available at http://www.uiuc.edu/edx/EU/treaties.htm.

TABLE **(continued)**

| Date | Document | Who | More Information |
|------|----------|-----|-----------------|
| Also signed 25 March 1957, entered into force 1 January 1958 | Treaties of Rome —<br><br>Established EURATOM Treaty | (Same as above) | Formation of the European Atomic Energy Community, for research and development of peaceful atomic energy. Established many of the same institutions the Treaty of Rome set up. (Institutions later merged into the TEU under Merger Treaty provisions) |
| 3 May 1960 | European Free Trade Area (EFTA) comes into force | Austria, Denmark, Great Britain, Iceland, Norway, Portugal, Sweden and Switzerland | EFTA formed. Limited to free trade in industrial goods- this trade bloc acted in counter balance to the European Economic Community. |
| 1 July 1967 | Merger Treaty | EEC | Consolidated the institutions formed by the two Treaties of Rome. |
| 1 January 1973 | First Enlargement | Great Britain, Denmark, and Ireland | EFTA reduced in importance as Great Britain pulled out of EFTA and led charge to join the European Economic Community. |

### TABLE (continued)

| Date | Document | Who | More Information |
|------|----------|-----|------------------|
| 1 January 1981 | Second Enlargement | Greece | 10 member states |
| 1 January 1986 | Third Enlargement | Spain and Portugal | 12 member states |
| Signed 17 and 28 February 1986, entered into force 1 July 1987 | Single European Act | Within the EEC | Major amendments to the Treaty of Rome. Broadened economic integration. |
| 19 June 1990 | Schengen Accord | Belgium, France, Germany, the Netherlands, and Luxembourg (Italy signs 27 November 1990) | Removes internal controls limiting border crossing, allowing for free movement of people across the signatory states of the European Community |
| Signed 7 February 1992, entered into force 1 November 1993 | Maastricht Treaty on the European Union (TEU) | All EU (some states opted out of the Schengen Accord provisions | Creation of Economic and Monetary Union. EEC renamed the EU. |
| 1 January 1995 | Fourth Enlargement | Austria, Finland, and Sweden added | Expansion brought about in part by Maastricht Treaty. 15 countries now members (these were former EFTA members) |

TABLE **(continued)**

| Date | Document | Who | More Information |
|---|---|---|---|
| Signed 2 October 1997 Entered into Force 1 May 1999 | Amsterdam Treaty | European Union | More amendments to the Treaty of Rome/ TEU, including renumbering of the provisions, full incorporation of the Schengen Accords, increasing the powers of the European Parliament powers, and allowing members to establish "closer cooperation" within the EU. |
| 1 January 2002 | Full Debut of the Euro | Austria, Belgium, Finland, France, Germany Greece, Ireland, Italy, Luxembourg, the Netherlands, Portugal, and Spain | Euro coins and banknotes enter circulation, replacing the individual currencies of each country with a single, uniform currency. |
| Signed 26 February 2001, entered into force 1 February 2003 | Treaty of Nice | European Union | Amends the Treaty of Rome. Establishes an enlargement protocol for incoming member countries |
| 1 May 2004 | Fifth Enlargement | Cyprus, the Czech Republic, Estonia, Hungary, Latvia, Lithuania, Malta, Poland, the Slovak Republic, and Slovenia | Largest single increase in European Union membership, now 25 member countries. |

## TABLE (continued)

| Date | Document | Who | More Information |
|---|---|---|---|
| Signed 18 June 2004, no entry into force as of December 2007 | Constitution for European Union drafted | European Union | 29 May 2005 French voters declined to ratify the EU constitution in a referendum vote (55% to 45%). 1 June 2005 Dutch votes also declined to ratify the EU constitution in a referendum vote (62% to 38%). These two votes effectively terminate the possibility of the EU constitution becoming effective in the foreseeable future. |
| 1 January 2007 | Sixth Enlargement | Bulgaria and Romania | Accession to the European Union based on preliminary work done during the Fifth Enlargement. 27 member countries |
| Fall 2008 through at least Summer 2012 | Various proposals and plans, both from Brussels and individual countries, to reduce debt and deficits, and restructure existing sovereign debt | Entire EU, but particularly the Eurozone countries, threatening the long-term viability of the Euro as a currency | Eurozone crisis associated with unsustainably high debt and deficit levels, credit rating agency downgrades of sovereign debt, particularly in the "PIIGS" countries Portugal, Italy, Ireland, Greece, and Spain |

TABLE B-5:

MAJOR UNITED STATES TRADE STATUTES SINCE 1916

*(reverse chronological order)*

| YEAR ENACTED | FULL NAME (note "as amended" to indicate one or more subsequent significant changes) | SHORT-HAND NAME | BRIEF HIGHLIGHTS | LOCATION OF SECTIONS WHERE CODIFIED |
|---|---|---|---|---|
| 2011 | | United States — Korea Free Trade Agreement (KORUS) | Implementing legislation for KORUS. | 19 U.S.C. |
| 2011 | | United States — Colombia Trade Promotion Agreement (CTPA) | Implementing legislation for CTPA, and also includes extension of Andean Trade Preference Act (ATPA), which covers Ecuador, and which had lapsed on 12 February 2011, through 31 July 2013. | 19 U.S.C. |
| 2011 | | United States — Panama Free Trade Agreement (Panama FTA) | Implementing legislation for Panama FTA. | 19 U.S.C. |

| 2011 | Renewal of *Trade Adjustment Assistance* (*TAA*) and *Generalized System of Preferences* (*GSP*), or *TAA – GSP* bill | *TAA* provides help to workers, farmers, and firms dislocated by foreign competition. The 2011 renewal extends the *TAA* expansion legislation enacted in 2009, which had lapsed on 31 December 2010, to the *TAA* program so as to (1) cover service workers and workers adversely affected by trade with countries that are not partners to a FTA with the United States, and (2) offer a Health Coverage Tax Credit for health care premiums of 72.5 percent. The HCTC (*i.e.*, the 72.5 percent subsidy for health insurance premiums) under the 2011 renewal was less than the 80 percent in the 2009 expansion bill, but higher than the 2002 level of 65 percent. The 2011 HCTC amended the definition of "qualifying insurance and credit." But, along with the other provisions of the renewal, the 2011 HCTC sunset on 31 December 2013 for all qualifying individuals.<br><br>*GSP* provides preferences on up to 4,800 eligible products from 129 Beneficiary Developing Countries (BDCs). These preferences expired on 31 December 2010, but the 2011 legislation renewed them retroactively to 1 January 2011 through 31 July 2013. | 19 U.S.C. |

**TABLE (continued)**

| YEAR ENACTED | FULL NAME (note "as amended" to indicate one or more subsequent significant changes) | SHORT-HAND NAME | BRIEF HIGHLIGHTS | LOCATION OF SECTIONS WHERE CODIFIED |
|---|---|---|---|---|
| 2010 | Omnibus Trade Act of 2010 H.R. 6517, Pub. L. No. 111-344, 124 Stat. 3611 (29 December 2010) | 2010 Act | Temporarily (for 6 weeks) extends the Andean Trade Preference Act (ATPA), which grants duty-free treatment to selected merchandise from Colombia and Ecuador (but not Peru, which gets such treatment under its Free Trade Agreement with the U.S.), and Trade Adjustment Assistance (TAA), which offers compensation, training, and health care benefits to workers adversely impacted because of trade. (Roughly 50,000 Americans would have lost health care benefits had TAA not been renewed.) But, excludes (i.e., fails to extend) the Generalized System of Preferences (GSP) and tariff suspensions for hundreds of products not made in the U.S. | Codified in scattered sections of 19 U.S.C. |

| 2010 | *Comprehensive Iran Sanctions, Accountability, and Divestment Act of 2010* H.R. 2194, Public Law No. 111-195 | CISADA | Amends the *Iran Sanctions Act of 1996*, Public Law No. 111-195, 50 U.S.C. 1701 note. Significantly strengthens financial sanctions against Iran, generally prohibiting United States financial institutions from doing business with Iran. *CISADA* is designed (*inter alia*) to make it difficult for Iran to obtain trade finance, and either pay for imports or receive payment for exports. In turn, *CISADA* may help prevent the Central Bank of Iran from reversing the erosion in the value of the Iranian currency, and thereby bring about a collapse in that value. *CISADA* also authorizes the Financial Crimes Enforcement Network (FinCEN) of the Department of the Treasury to request information from United States financial institutions about correspondent banking accounts and funds transfers that may violate *CISADA*. However, *CISADA* does not bar Iran from selling crude oil to Europe, nor does it bar the United States from buying Iranian oil that is refined in and sold from Europe. | Codified in scattered sections of titles 5, 7, 8, 21, 41, and 50. |

**TABLE** (continued)

| YEAR ENACTED | FULL NAME (note "as amended" to indicate one or more subsequent significant changes) | SHORT-HAND NAME | BRIEF HIGHLIGHTS | LOCATION OF SECTIONS WHERE CODIFIED |
|---|---|---|---|---|
| | | | *CISADA* contains a so-called "Special Rule" whereby the U.S. government tries to persuade companies to cease doing business with Iran, and energy traders to stop sales of refined petroleum products to Iran. Those outcomes have occurred. Further, foreign direct investment (FDI) in the upstream oil and gas sector of Iran has plummeted, forcing Iran to give up on many projects. Under *CISADA*, the Treasury Department conducts financial investigations, and its Office of Foreign Assets Control (OFAC) makes designations concerning prohibited entities and license exceptions. The Bureau of Economic, Energy, and Business Affairs of the Department of State investigates possible violations about *CISADA* sanctions on refined oil products. | |

| 2008 | *Prioritizing Resources and Organization for Intellectual Property Act of 2008* Pub. L. No. 110-403, 122 Stat. 4256 (13 Oct. 2008) | *PRO-IP Act* | Increases anti-piracy enforcement tools in the Executive branch through the creation of the Office of the United States Intellectual Property Enforcement Representative (USIPER), appointment by the President (subject to Senate confirmation) of an Intellectual Property Enforcement Coordinator, and civil and criminal penalties for copyright and trademark infringement. The Coordinator must draft a joint strategic plan to combat infringement and counterfeiting, including through cooperation with foreign governments. The Coordinator also must work with foreign governments. | Codified in scattered sections of 15, 17, 18, 19, and 42 U.S.C. |
| 2007 | *Implementing Recommendations of the 9/11 Commission Act of 2007* Pub. L. 110-53, 121 Stat. 266 (3 August 2007) | *2007 Act* | Mandates 100 percent container security screening. | Scattered sections. |

**TABLE (continued)**

| Year Enacted | Full Name (note "as amended" to indicate one or more subsequent significant changes) | Short-Hand Name | Brief Highlights | Location of Sections where Codified |
|---|---|---|---|---|
| 2006 | The Tax Relief and Health Care Act of 2006 Pub. L. No. 109-432, 120 Stat. 2922 (20 December 2006) | Comprehensive Trade Legislation | Grants Permanent Normal Trade Relations (PNTR) to Vietnam, thereby eschewing the necessity of invoking non-application upon Vietnam's accession to the WTO (effective 11 January 2007). Renews GSP program for 133 beneficiary countries for 2 years (otherwise scheduled to expire on 31 December 2006). Renews *ATPA* for Bolivia, Colombia, Ecuador, and Peru for 2 years (otherwise scheduled to expire on 31 December 2006), for six-month renewable periods. Extends third country fabric provision in *AGOA* (to allow for benefits for certain apparel made in Sub-Saharan Africa using third country fabric). Amends *CBI* to allow duty-free treatment for certain articles from Haiti. | Scattered sections. |

| | | | | |
|---|---|---|---|---|
| **2006** | *Security and Accountability For Every Port Act of 2006* Pub. L. No. 109-347, 120 Stat. 1884 (13 October 2006) | *SAFE Port Act* | Codifies the *Container Security Initiative* (*CSI*) and *Customs-Trade Partnership Against Terrorism* (*C-TPAT*) programs into law. | 6 U.S.C. §§ 115, 220, 314a, 470, 592a, 901, 968; 31 U.S.C. § 5361; 42 U.S.C. § 300hh14; 46 U.S.C. §§ 70105, 70107, 70107A, 70111 |
| **2004** | *African Growth and Opportunity Acceleration Act of 2004* Pub. L. No. 108-274, 118 Stat. 820 (13 July 2004) | *AGOA III* | Renews AGOA, including the third country fabric provisions. | Scattered sections |
| **2002** | *Trade Act of 2002* Pub. L. No. 107-210, 116 Stat. 933 (6 August 2002) | *Trade Act* | Renews Presidential trade negotiating authority (*Trade Promotion Authority*, or *TPA*), which had expired in 1994. Significantly revises *Trade Adjustment Assistance Programs* (through the *Trade Adjustment Assistance Reform Act of 2002*, a portion of the overall legislation). Amends AGOA, known as *AGOA II*. Contains the *Andean Trade Promotion and Drug Eradication Act* (*ATPDEA*). | Scattered sections |

**TABLE (continued)**

| YEAR ENACTED | FULL NAME (note "as amended" to indicate one or more subsequent significant changes) | SHORT-HAND NAME | BRIEF HIGHLIGHTS | LOCATION OF SECTIONS WHERE CODIFIED |
|---|---|---|---|---|
| 2002 | Homeland Security Act<br><br>Pub. L. No. 107-296, 116 Stat. 2135 (25 November 2002) | Homeland Security Act | Creates the Customs and Border Protection (CBP) from the Customs Service and other agencies (including bodies involved in information gathering and security), dramatically alters the organizational structure of customs functions, and effects a shift in paradigm from customs-as-a-trade-agency to customs-as-a-security agency. | 5 U.S.C. §§ 1401-1402, 3319, 3521-3525, 9701, and App. 3 § 8J; 6 U.S.C. §§ 101-103, 111-113, 121-122, 131-134, 141-145, 161-165, 181-193, 195, 195a, 201-203, 211-218, 231-239, 251-256, 271-279, |

| 2002 | Public Health Security and Bioterrorism Preparedness and Response Act of 2002 | Bioterrorism Act (BTA) | Establishes a nation-wide plan to combat bio-terrorism, addressing (inter alia) public health emergencies, biological agents and toxins, and drinking water safety. | 291-298, 311-321, 321a-321j, 331, 341-346, 361, 381, 391-395, 411-415, 421-428, 441-444, 451-468, 481-484, 491-496, 511-512, 521-522, 531-533, 541-543, 551-557, 571-578, 591-596; 18 U.S.C. § 3051; 44 U.S.C. § 3537, 3538; 49 U.S.C. § 44921 | 42 U.S.C §§ 201 et seq |

**TABLE (continued)**

| YEAR ENACTED | FULL NAME (note "as amended" to indicate one or more subsequent significant changes) | SHORT-HAND NAME | BRIEF HIGHLIGHTS | LOCATION OF SECTIONS WHERE CODIFIED |
|---|---|---|---|---|
| | Pub. L. 107-188, 116 Stat. 594 (12 June 2002) | | | |
| 2000 | Trade and Development Act Pub. L. 106-200, 114 Stat. 251 (18 May 2000) | TDA | Contains the African Growth and Opportunity Act (AGOA), at 114 Stat. 252, which provides limited duty-free treatment for certain products from certain sub-Saharan African – known as AGOA I. Re-authorizes GSP, CBI, and Trade Adjustment Assistance. | Scattered sections |
| 1996 | Iran and Libya Sanctions Act | ILSA | Imposes controversial secondary boycott against foreign investment in the Iranian and Libyan petroleum sectors. | 50 U.S.C. Section 1701 note |

| 1996 | *Cuban Liberty and Democracy Solidarity (Libertad) Act* | *Helms-Burton Act* | Imposes another controversial secondary boycott. (However, key sanctions are waived regularly by the President in light of a major row with European Union (EU)). | 22 U.S.C. Sections 6021 *et seq.* |
|---|---|---|---|---|
| 1994 | *Uruguay Round Agreements Act* Pub. L. 103-465, 108 Stat. 4809 (8 December 1994) | *1994 Act* | Implements the results of the Uruguay Round. | 19 U.S.C. §§ 3501 *et seq.*, plus scattered sections |
| 1993 | *North American Free Trade Implementation Act* Pub. L. 103-182, 107 Stat. 2057 (14 December 1993) | *1993 Act, or NAFTA Act* | Implements the *North American Free Trade Agreement (NAFTA)*. Also contains the Customs Modernization Act, which sets forth the most extensive changes to the customs laws since the *1978 Act.* | Scattered sections |

**TABLE (continued)**

| YEAR ENACTED | FULL NAME (note "as amended" to indicate one or more subsequent significant changes) | SHORT-HAND NAME | BRIEF HIGHLIGHTS | LOCATION OF SECTIONS WHERE CODIFIED |
|---|---|---|---|---|
| 1991 | Andean Trade Preference Act Pub. L. 102-182, 105 Stat. 1236 (4 December 1991) | ATPA, Andean Initiative, or Andean Trade Pact | Creates preferential trade benefits for Bolivia, Colombia, Ecuador, and Peru. | 19 U.S.C. §§ 3201-3206 |
| 1990 | Customs and Trade Act | 1990 Act | Renames the Customs Court the "CIT." Clarifies the exclusive jurisdiction of the CIT and expands it to include civil actions involving import and a statute, Constitutional provision, or international trade agreement. Calls for the development and implementation of accounting systems and surveys to determine the allocation of responsibilities among Customs Service personnel, and sets forth enforcement priorities of the Customs Service. | 16 U.S.C. § 620a-j, 1 9 U.S.C. §§ 2082-2083, 20 U.S.C. § 226, plus scattered sections |

| 1988 | United States — Canada Free Trade Implementation Act | 1988 Act | Implements the Canada — United States Free Trade Agreement (CUSFTA). | 19 U.S.C. § 2112 note |
| 1988 | Omnibus Trade and Competitiveness Act, as amended | 1988 Act or OTCA | Contains the Uruguay Round negotiating authority and objectives.

Replaces the Tariff Schedule of the United States (TSUS) with the Harmonized Tariff Schedule (HTS).
Adds Special 301 and Super 301.
Makes significant changes to Trade Adjustment Assistance (TAA) program. | Scattered sections |
| 1985 | United States — Israel Free Trade Implementation Act | 1985 Act | Implements the Israel — United States Free Trade Agreement, which is America's first comprehensive free trade agreement (FTA) with another country. | 19 U.S.C. § 2112 note |
| 1984 | International Trade and Investment Act of 1984 | Trade and Tariff Act of 1984, or 1984 Act | Provides negotiating authority for a bilateral free trade agreement (FTA) with Israel. | Scattered sections |

**TABLE (continued)**

| YEAR ENACTED | FULL NAME (note "as amended" to indicate one or more subsequent significant changes) | SHORT-HAND NAME | BRIEF HIGHLIGHTS | LOCATION OF SECTIONS WHERE CODIFIED |
|---|---|---|---|---|
| | Pub. L. No. 98-573, 98 Stat. 2948 (30 October 1984) | | | |
| 1983 | Trade and Development Enhancement Act of 1983 Pub. L. No. 98-181, 97 Stat. 1263 (30 November 1983) | TDEA | Related to the Caribbean Basin Economic Recovery Act, Pub. L. 98-67, 97 Stat. 384, which creates the Caribbean Basin Initiative (CBI). | 19 U.S.C. § 2701 et seq |
| 1979 | Trade Agreements Act | 1979 Act | Implements the results of Tokyo Round. | Scattered sections |
| 1978 | Customs Procedural Reform and Implementation Act | 1978 Act | Makes major reforms in customs laws and procedures. | 19 U.S.C. § 2075 |

| 1977 | *International Emergency Economic Powers Act* | IEEPA | Authorizes the President to regulate a broad range of financial and commercial transactions involving foreign parties in order to deal with unusual and extraordinary threats arising from outside the United States. | 50 U.S.C. §§ 1701-1706 |
| --- | --- | --- | --- | --- |
| 1977 | *Foreign Corrupt Practices Act, as amended* | FCPA | Makes illegal certain types of payments to foreign government officials. | 15 U.S.C. §§ 78dd-1, dd-2, and 78ff |
| 1975 | *Trade Act of 1974, as amended* Pub. L. 93-618, 88 Stat. 1978 (3 January 1975) | 1974 Act | Contains the Tokyo Round negotiating authority and objectives. Expands the duties of the Special Trade Representative (STR). Introduces Section 301 (concerning unilateral retaliation) and the *Generalized System of Preference* (*GSP*). Includes major changes to the Escape Clause (Section 201). Expands Trade Adjustment Assistance (TAA) program. Contains the *Jackson-Vanik Amendment*. | Scattered sections. |

**TABLE (continued)**

| YEAR ENACTED | FULL NAME (note "as amended" to indicate one or more subsequent significant changes) | SHORT-HAND NAME | BRIEF HIGHLIGHTS | LOCATION OF SECTIONS WHERE CODIFIED |
|---|---|---|---|---|
| 1972 | Marine Mammal Protection Act, as amended | MMPA | Bans importation of marine mammals and marine mammal products. (In 1991 and 1994, GATT panels found the tuna embargo procedures were inconsistent with GATT, but their reports are not adopted.) | 16 U.S.C. §§ 1361 et seq. |
| 1962 | Trade Expansion Act, as amended | 1962 Act | Establishes the Office of the Special Trade Representative (STR). Establishes the first Trade Adjustment Assistance (TAA) program. Contains the predecessor to Section 301 (concerning unilateral retaliation). Section 232 authorizes the President to impose national security import restrictions. | Scattered sections |
| 1956 | Agricultural Act of 1956, as amended | 1956 Act | Authorizes the President to negotiate agreements with other countries to limit agricultural and textile exports. | 7 U.S.C. § 1854 |

| | | | Provides the legal basis for the Multi-Fiber Agreement (MFA), and is the legal basis for implementation of the Uruguay Round Agreement on Textiles and Clothing (ATC). | |
|---|---|---|---|---|
| 1934 | *Foreign Trade Zones Act,* as amended | *FTZ Act* | Authorizes the establishment of foreign trade zones (FTZs). | 19 U.S.C. §§ 81a-81u. |
| 1934 | *Reciprocal Trade Agreements Act* | *1934 Act* | Empowers President Franklin D. Roosevelt to undo the *Smoot-Hawley Act* tariffs through a series of bilateral deals. | Scattered sections |
| **1933** | *Buy American Act* | *Buy American Act* | Requires the United States government to purchase domestic goods and services, unless the head of the department involved determines the prices of domestic supplies are unreasonable or their purchase would not be in the public interest. | 41 U.S.C. §§ 10a-10d |
| **1930** | *Tariff Act of 1930,* as amended Pub. L. No. 71-361, 46 Stat. 590 (17 June 1930) | *1930 Act,* or *Smoot-Hawley Act* | Implemented shortly after the Great Crash of 1929. Establishes the notoriously high tariff rates, thereby stifling trade and exacerbating the Great Depression. Contains the core provisions of many features of American trade law, including antidumping (AD), countervailing (CVD), and Section 337 remedies. | Scattered sections |

**TABLE** (continued)

| YEAR ENACTED | FULL NAME (note "as amended" to indicate one or more subsequent significant changes) | SHORT-HAND NAME | BRIEF HIGHLIGHTS | LOCATION OF SECTIONS WHERE CODIFIED |
|---|---|---|---|---|
| 1917 | Trading With the Enemy Act, as amended | TWEA | Prohibits trade with any enemy or ally of an enemy during war time. | 50 App. U.S.C. §§ 1-44 |
| 1916 | Antidumping Act of 1916 | 1916 Act | Creates criminal liability for dumping.<br><br>However, no successful prosecutions ever occur, because of the difficulty of proving intent.<br><br>Following an adverse ruling in the WTO nearly a century later, the 1916 Act was repealed. | 15 U.S.C. § 72 |

*Note:*

There are two provisions of the United States Constitution directly concerning international trade. First, Article 1, Section 8, Clause 3 — the Commerce Clause — states that "The Congress shall have Power . . . To regulate Commerce with foreign Nations." Second, Article I, Section 9, Clause 5 of the Constitution bars state taxation of exports. A third provision of the Constitution, Article I, Section Clause 1, relates to trade, in that it mandates any revenue bill (including one that affects tariffs) originate in the House of Representatives.

## TABLE B-6:

### SERVICE SECTOR CLASSIFICATIONS
### (W120 LIST)[1]

| Sector | Sub-Sector | Sub-Sub-Sector |
|---|---|---|
| Business Services | Professional | Legal Services. Accounting, auditing and bookkeeping services. Taxation Services. Architectural services. Engineering services. Integrated engineering services. Urban planning and landscape architectural services. Medical and dental services Veterinary services. Services provided by midwives, nurses, physiotherapists and para-medical personnel. Other. |
| | Computer and Related Services | Consultancy services related to the installation of computer hardware. Software implementation services. Data processing services d. Data base services. Other. |
| | Research and Development Services | R&D services on natural sciences. R&D services on social sciences and humanities Interdisciplinary R&D services. |
| | Real Estate Services | Involving own or leased property. On a fee or contract basis. |

---

[1] Drawn from www.ita.doc.gov/td/sif/GATS/W120.htm. For convenience, this Table flows continuously from start to finish.

## TABLE (continued)

| Sector | Sub-Sector | Sub-Sub-Sector |
|---|---|---|
| | Rental/Leasing Services without Operators | Relating to ships. Relating to aircraft. Relating to other transport equipment. Relating to other machinery and equipment. Other. |
| | Other Business Services | Advertising services. Market research and public opinion polling services. Management consulting service. Services related to man. Consulting. Technical testing and analysis services. Services incidental to agriculture, hunting and forestry. Services incidental to fishing. Services incidental to mining. Services incidental to manufacturing. Services incidental to energy distribution. Placement and supply services of personnel. Investigation and security. Related scientific and technical consulting services. Maintenance and repair of equipment (not including maritime vessels, aircraft or other transport equipment). Building-cleaning services. Photographic services. Packaging services. Printing, publishing. Convention services. Other. |

TABLE **(continued)**

| *Sector* | *Sub-Sector* | *Sub-Sub-Sector* |
|---|---|---|
| Communication Services | Postal services | |
| | Courier services | |
| | Telecommunication services | Voice telephone services. Packet-switched data transmission services. Circuit-switched data transmission services. Telex services. Telegraph services. Facsimile services. Private leased circuit services. Electronic mail. Voice mail. On-line information and data base retrieval. Electronic data interchange (EDI). Enhanced/value-added facsimile services, including store and forward, store and retrieve. Code and protocol conversion. On-line information and/or data processing (including transaction processing. Other. |
| | Audiovisual services | Motion picture and video tape production and distribution services. Motion picture projection service. Radio and television services. Radio and television transmission services. Sound recording. Other. |
| | Other | |

**TABLE (continued)**

| Sector | Sub-Sector | Sub-Sub-Sector |
|---|---|---|
| Construction and Related Engineering Services | General construction work for buildings | |
| | General construction work for civil engineering | |
| | Installation and assembly work | |
| | Building completion and finishing work | |
| | Other | |
| Distribution Services | Commission agents' services | |
| | Wholesale trade services | |
| | Retailing services | |
| | Franchising | |
| | Other | |
| Educational Services | Primary education services | |
| | Secondary education services | |
| | Higher education services | |
| | Adult education | |
| | Other education services | |
| Environmental Services | Sewage services | |
| | Refuse disposal services | |
| | Sanitation and similar services | |
| | Other | |
| Engineering Services | | |

## TABLE (continued)

| Sector | Sub-Sector | Sub-Sub-Sector |
|---|---|---|
| Financial Services | All insurance and insurance-related services | Life, accident and health insurance services.<br>Non-life insurance services.<br>Reinsurance and retrocession.<br>Services auxiliary to insurance (including broking and agency services). |
|  | Banking and other financial service (excluding insurance) | Acceptance of deposits and other repayable funds from the public.<br>Lending of all types, including (*inter alia*) consumer credit, mortgage credit, factoring and financing of commercial transaction.<br>Financial leasing.<br>All payment and money transmission services.<br>Guarantees and commitments.<br>Trading for own account or for account of customers, whether on an exchange, in an over-the-counter market or otherwise, the following:<br>- money market instruments (cheques, bills, certificate of deposits, etc.)<br>- foreign exchange<br>- derivative products incl., but not limited to, futures and options<br>- exchange rate and interest rate instruments, including products such as swaps, forward rate agreements, etc.<br>- transferable securities<br>- other negotiable instruments and financial assets, including bullion.<br>Participation in issues of all kinds of securities, including under-writing and placement as agent (whether publicly or privately) and provision of service related to such issues.<br>Money broking. |

**TABLE (continued)**

| Sector | Sub-Sector | Sub-Sub-Sector |
|---|---|---|
| | | Asset management, such as cash or portfolio management, all forms of collective investment management, pension fund management, custodial depository and trust services. Settlement and clearing services for financial assets, including securities, derivative products, or and other negotiable instruments. Advisory and other auxiliary financial services on all the activities listed or in Article 1B of MTN.TNC/W/50, including credit reference and analysis, investment and portfolio research and advice, advice on acquisitions and on corporate restructuring and strategy. Provision and transfer of financial information, and financial data processing and related software by providers of other financial services. |
| | Other | |
| Health Related and Social Services (other than those listed under Business/ Professional) | Hospital Services Other Human Health Services Social Services Other | |
| Tourism and Travel Related Services | Hotels and restaurants (including catering) Travel agencies and tour operators' services Tourist guides services | Cleaning. Hotel. Transportation (land, air, sea). Sports and recreation. |
| | Other | |

## TABLE (continued)

| Sector | Sub-Sector | Sub-Sub-Sector |
|---|---|---|
| Recreational, Cultural and Sporting Services (other than Audiovisual Services) | Entertainment services (including theatre, live bands and circus services) | *Note:* Some WTO Members specify WT120 Schedules with Tourism and Travel Related Services, and Recreational, Cultural, and Sporting Services, as one large category. |
| | News agency services | |
| | Libraries, archives, museums and other cultural services | |
| | Sporting and other recreational services | |
| | Other | |
| Transport Services | Maritime Transport Services | Passenger transportation. Freight transportation. Rental of vessels with crew. Maintenance and repair of vessels. Pushing and towing services. Supporting services for maritime transport. |
| | Internal Waterways Transport | Passenger transportation. Freight transportation. Rental of vessels with crew. Maintenance and repair of vessels. Pushing and towing services. Supporting services for internal waterway transport. |
| | Air Transport Services | Passenger transportation. Freight transportation. Rental of aircraft with crew. Maintenance and repair of aircraft. Supporting services for air transport. |
| | Space Transport | |

## TABLE (continued)

| Sector | Sub-Sector | Sub-Sub-Sector |
|---|---|---|
| | Rail Transport Services | Passenger transportation. Freight transportation. Pushing and towing services. Maintenance and repair of rail transport equipment. Supporting services for rail transport services. |
| | Road Transport Services | Passenger transportation. Freight transportation. Rental of commercial vehicles with operator. Maintenance and repair of road transport equipment. Supporting services for road transport services. |
| | Pipeline Transport | Transportation of fuels. Transportation of other goods. |
| | Services auxiliary to all modes of transport | Cargo-handling services Storage and warehouse services Freight transport agency services Other |
| | Other Transport Services | |
| Other Services Not Included Elsewhere | | |

# ANNEX C

# FREE TRADE AGREEMENTS DATA

## Introductory Note

The Tables below summarize free trade agreements (FTAs) in which the United States is involved. The FTAs are arranged chronologically by date of signature. Table I provides legal facts about each FTA — its name, when it was negotiated and signed, the date of entry into force, and the implementing legislation. Table II offers political facts about America's FTAs. It shows the votes in the United States Congress on each FTA, overall and the "no" vote by political party, and indicates political control in Congress at the time of the vote. From these Tables, a number of legal and political patterns or trends may be inferred. Legally, inferences may be drawn about the time between commencing negotiations and entry into force. Politically, query whether there is anything left of the famed post-Second World War bipartisan consensus in favor of free trade. Subsequent Tables provide data on the market access — and limitations thereon — in specific sectors arising out of FTAs.

Obviously, there are an enormous number of FTAs — planned, in negotiations, and implemented — not involving the United States. For instance, Australia, Japan, Mexico, New Zealand, and Singapore have FTA "dockets," as it were, differing in activity, history, and purpose. So, too, does the European Union (EU). Indeed, the EU has entered into, and continues to pursue, "association agreements." These free trade deals are more than an economic link. They are designed as the first step toward accession into the EU, at least for some of the former Soviet bloc countries. However, it is dubious as to whether the EU ever would admit all of the countries in the Mediterranean region with which it has such agreements.

TABLE C-1:
UNITED STATES FTAS — LEGAL FACTS

| FTA | When Negotiations Commenced | Date FTA Signed and Post-Signature Accords (if any) | U.S. Implementing Legislation | Date of Presidential Signature on Implementing Legislation | Implementation Date (i.e., entry into force) |
|---|---|---|---|---|---|
| *Israel* | Mid-January 1984 | 22 April 1985 | *United States— Israel Free Trade Area Implementation Act of 1985,* Public Law Number 99-47, 99 Stat. 82. Amendment *to Trade and Tariff Act of 1984.* Noted at 19 U.S.C. § 2112 | 11 June 1985 | 30 August 1985, by Executive Order No. 5365, 50 Fed. Reg. 36220 (30 August 1985). Original FTA extended to encourage greater regional integration by Israel with its neighbors. H.R. 3074, *West Bank and Gaza Strip Free Trade Benefits,* Pub. L. No. 104-234, approved 2 October 1996, amends *1985 Act* gives duty-free treatment to articles from designated industrial parks between West Bank— Israel, Gaza Strip—Israel, and Qualified Industrial Zones (QIZs) between Israel— Jordan and Egypt— Jordan. *See also* Presidential Proclamation 6955, 13 November 1996, 61 Fed. Reg. 58761 (18 November 1996). Original FTA also supplemented by a 1996 *Agreement on Trade in Agricultural Products (ATAP).* |

| | | | | | |
|---|---|---|---|---|---|
| *Canada* | Dates back to 1965 *U.S.—Canada Auto Pact*. Discussions between President Ronald Reagan and Prime Minister Brian Mulroney in mid-1980s. | 2 January 1988 | *United States—Canada Free Trade Agreement Implementation Act of 1988*, Public Law Number 100–449, 102 Stat. 1851 (1988) Noted at 19 U.S.C. § 2112 | 28 September 1988 | 1 January 1989, by Executive Order Number 5923, 53 Fed Reg. 50638 (14 December 1988) *NAFTA* suspends provisions in the earlier *FTA* that overlap with *NAFTA* until such time as Canada may terminate its participation in *NAFTA*. |
| *NAFTA* | June 1991. Preliminary ideas floated in late 1980s. | 17 December 1992 | *North American Free Trade Agreement Implementation Act of 1993*, Public Law Number 103–182, 107 Stat. 2057 19 U.S.C. §§ 3301 note, 3311 | 8 December 1993 | 1 January 1994, by Executive Order Number 12889, 58 Fed. Reg. 69681 (27 December 1993) |

**TABLE (continued)**

| FTA | When Negotiations Commenced | Date FTA Signed and Post-Signature Accords (if any) | U.S. Implementing Legislation | Date of Presidential Signature on Implementing Legislation | Implementation Date (i.e., entry into force) |
|---|---|---|---|---|---|
| *Jordan* | June 2000 | 24 October 2000 | *United States—Jordan Free Trade Area Implementation Act*, Public Law Number 107—43, 115 Stat. 243 (2001) Noted at 19 U.S.C. § 2112 | 28 September 2001 | 17 December 2001, by Executive Proclamation Number 7512, 66 Fed. Reg. 64497, 7 December 2001 Ratification of *FTA* by Jordanian Parliament occurred in May 2001. |
| *Singapore* | December 2000 | 6 May 2003 | *United States—Singapore Free Trade Agreement Implementation Act*, Public Law Number 108—78, 117 Stat. 948 Noted at 19 U.S.C. § 2805 | 3 August 2003 | 1 January 2004, by Executive Proclamation Number 7747, 30 December 2003, 68 Fed. Reg. 75793 |

| | | | | |
|---|---|---|---|---|
| *Chile* | December 2000 | 6 June 2003 | *United States—Chile Free Trade Agreement Implementation Act*, Public Law Number 108–77, 117 Stat. 909<br><br>Noted at 19 U.S.C. § 2805 | 3 August 2003 | 1 January 2004, by Executive Proclamation Number 7746, 30 December 2003, 68 Fed. Reg. 75789 |
| *Australia* | March 2003 | 18 May 2004 | *United States—Australia Free Trade Agreement Implementation Act*, Public Law Number 108–286, 118 Stat. 919<br><br>Noted at 19 U.S.C. § 3805 | 3 August 2004 | 1 January 2005, by Executive Proclamation Number 7857, 20 December 2004, 69 Fed. Reg. 77135 |
| *Morocco* | January 2003 | 15 June 2004 | *United States—Morocco Free Trade Implementation Act*, Public Law Number 108–302, 118 Stat. 1103 | 17 August 2004 | 1 January 2006, by Executive Proclamation Number 7971, 22 December 2005, 70 Fed. Reg. 76651 |

**TABLE (continued)**

| FTA | When Negotiations Commenced | Date FTA Signed and Post-Signature Accords (if any) | U.S. Implementing Legislation | Date of Presidential Signature on Implementing Legislation | Implementation Date (i.e., entry into force) |
|---|---|---|---|---|---|
| | | | Noted at 19 U.S.C. § 3805 | | |
| CAFTA—DR | January 2003 (November 2003 for negotiations with Dominican Republic.) | 5 August 2004 | Dominican Republic—Central America—United States Free Trade Implementation Act, Public Law Number 109–53, 119 Stat. 462 Noted at 19 U.S.C. § 3805 | 2 August 2005 | Initial implementation date supposed to be 1 January 2006, but delayed over need for change in agriculture and IP regimes in CAFTA—DR countries. Rolling (staggered) implementation. Implemented in U.S. effective 1 March 2006 by Executive Proclamation Number 7987, 28 February 2006, 71 Fed. Reg. 10827, and in El Salvador. Implemented 1 April 2006 in Honduras and Nicaragua, and 1 July 2006 in Guatemala. Not implemented in Costa Rica or Dominican Republic as of December 2007. But, narrowly approved in Costa Rica in an October 2007 referendum (the country's first one) by a 51.6 to 48.3 percent margin. |

| **Bahrain** | January 2004 | 14 September 2004 | *United States—Bahrain Free Trade Agreement Implementation Act*, Public Law Number 109–169, 119 Stat. 3581 Noted at 19 U.S.C. § 3805 | 11 January 2006 | 1 August 2006, by Executive Proclamation Number 8039, 27 July 2006, 71 Federal Register 43,633. |
|---|---|---|---|---|---|
| **Oman** | March 2005 | 19 January 2006 | *United States—Oman Free Trade Implementation Act*, Public Law Number 109–283 | 26 September 2006 | Under the *Implementation Act*, Congress authorized the President to implement, by Presidential Proclamation, the *Oman FTA* no earlier than 1 January 2007. As of December 2008, no Proclamation had been issued. Entry into force finally occurred on 1 January 2009. |

**TABLE (continued)**

| FTA | When Negotiations Commenced | Date FTA Signed and Post-Signature Accords (if any) | U.S. Implementing Legislation | Date of Presidential Signature on Implementing Legislation | Implementation Date (i.e., entry into force) |
|-----|------------------------------|------------------------------------------------------|-------------------------------|------------------------------------------------------------|-----------------------------------------------|
| *Peru* | May 2004 | 12 April 2006 | *U.S.—Peru Trade Promotion Agreement (PTPA)*, H.R. 3688, Public Law Number 110–138, 121 Stat. 1455 Noted at 19 U.S.C. § 3805, with certain sections codified at 19 U.S.C. §§ 58c, 1508, 1514, 1520, 1592, 2518, 2252, and 26 U.S.C. § 6655 note. | 14 December 2007. House Ways and Means Committee approved draft implementing bill in July 2006. Passed by that Committee, and by Senate Finance Committee, in September 2007. | 1 February 2009. |

| Colombia | May 2004 | 22 November 2006<br><br>Subsequent negotiations on labor issues, leading to April 2011 agreement by Colombia on an *Action Plan Related to Labor Rights* established by the USTR. | *U.S.—Colombia Trade Promotion Agreement (CTPA)*<br><br>H.R. 3078, S. 1641, Public Law Number 112–42 | Enacted by Congress 12 October 2011, signed by President Barack H. Obama 21 October 2011. | 15 May 2012 |
|---|---|---|---|---|---|
| Panama | 2004 | Initial signing in December 2006<br><br>Subsequent negotiations on labor issues following guidance from Congress.<br><br>Final accord signed 28 June 2007. | H.R. 3079, S. 1643, Public Law Number 112–43 | Enacted by Congress 12 October 2011, signed by President Barack H. Obama 21 October 2011. | |

**Table (continued)**

| FTA | When Negotiations Commenced | Date FTA Signed and Post-Signature Accords (if any) | U.S. Implementing Legislation | Date of Presidential Signature on Implementing Legislation | Implementation Date (i.e., entry into force) |
|---|---|---|---|---|---|
| *Korea* | June 2006 (FTA idea launched in February 2006, and first formal negotiation round occurred in June 2006) | 31 March 2007 Signed in Seoul, on 30 June 2007, about 25 minutes before *Trade Promotion Authority (TPA)* deadline, Eastern Standard Time (EST). Signed with amended labor and environmental provisions. In April 2008, *Beef Import Protocol* signed by U.S. and Korea. | H.R. 3080, S. 1642, Public Law Number 112–41 | Enacted by Congress 12 October 2011, signed by President Barack H. Obama 21 October 2011. | 15 March 2012 Presidential Proclamation 8783, 6 March 2012 (77 Federal Register 14,265), implements the provisions of KORUS that modify the Harmonized Tariff Schedule of the United States (HTSUS). |

*See* Table C–4 on Deferred Market Access.

In December 2010, a *Supplemental Agreement* revising the initial *KORUS* terms was reached, and was officially signed in February 2011. This *Agreement* consisted of a

*Supplemental Auto Agreement* (an exchange of letters), *Agreed Minutes* on fuel economy and $CO_2$ gas emissions standards, and *Agreed minutes* on L-1 (intercompany transferee) visas.

**Table (continued)**

| FTA | When Negotiations Commenced | Date FTA Signed and Post-Signature Accords (if any) | U.S. Implementing Legislation | Date of Presidential Signature on Implementing Legislation | Implementation Date (i.e., entry into force) |
|---|---|---|---|---|---|
| Korea continued | | The Supplemental Agreement did not cover beef trade. See Table C-4 on Deferred Market Access. | | | |
| Malaysia | March 2005 | Negotiations slowed as of March 2007, and failed to meet Trade Promotion Authority notification deadline of 31 March 2007. | | | |

| | | |
|---|---|---|
| | | |
| Negotiations subsumed under Trans Pacific Partnership (TPP) initiative, launched by the Administration of President George W. Bush, and continued by President Barack H. Obama.<br><br>Prospective TPP partners are Australia, Brunei, Chile, Malaysia, New Zealand, Peru, Singapore, and Vietnam. | March 2005 | Episodic negotiations ongoing as of June 2010. |
| | | *Qatar, Thailand, United Arab Emirates (UAE)* |

TABLE C-2:

UNITED STATES FTAs — POLITICAL FACTS

*(FTAs listed chronologically by Implementation Date)*

| FTA (Implementation Date) | Bills | U.S. Senate Vote (Overall Political Control) | Vote Breakdown | U.S. House of Representatives Vote (Overall Political Control) | Vote Breakdown |
|---|---|---|---|---|---|
| **Israel** (30 August 1985) | H.R. 2268 and S. 1114 House Bill enacted. | Unanimous by voice vote. (The Senate resolved to let the House Bill pass.) 23 May 1985, Senate Journal 263 (Senate divided between 47 Democrats, 53 Republicans.) | Not Applicable. | 422 to 0, with 3 voting "Present," and 9 not voting. 7 May 1985, House Journal 319–320 (House divided between 253 Democrats, 182 Republicans.) | The 3 Representatives voting as "present" were Democrats. Of the 9 Representatives not voting, 8 were Democrats, 1 was Republican. |
| **Canada** (1 January 1989) | H.R. 5090 and S. 2651 House Bill enacted. | 83 to 9 19 September 1988, Senate Journal H-234 (Senate divided between 55 Democrats, 45 Republicans.) | 9 No votes, split between 7 Democrats, 2 Republicans. | 366 to 40, with 24 not voting 9 August 1988, House Journal 1399–1400 (House divided between 258 Democrats, 177 Republicans.) | 40 No votes, split between 23 Democrats, 10 Republicans. Of the 24 Representatives not voting, 8 were Democrats, 16 were Republican. |

| | | | | | |
|---|---|---|---|---|---|
| **NAFTA** (1 January 1994) | H.R. 3450 and S. 1627 House Bill enacted. | 61 to 38, with 1 not voting. 20 November 1993, Senate Journal 718. (Senate divided between 57 Democrats, 43 Republicans.) | 38 No votes, split between 28 Democrats, 10 Republicans. The Senator not voting was Democrat. | 234 to 200 17 November 1993, 139 Congressional Record H10048 (House divided between 258 Democrats, 178 Republicans, 1 Independent.) | 200 No votes, split between 156 Democrats, 43 Republicans, 1 Independent. |
| **Jordan** (December 17, 2001) | H.R. 2603 and S. 643 House Bill enacted. | Voice vote. September 24, 2001, Senate Journal 768. (Senate divided between 50 Democrats, 49 Republicans, 1 Independent.) | Voice vote, thus not available. | Voice vote. 31 July 2001, House Journal 932. (House divided between 212 Democrats, 221 Republicans, 2 Independents.) | Voice vote, thus not available. |
| **Singapore** (1 January 2004) | H.R. 2739 and S. 1417 | 66 to 32, with 2 not voting. | 32 No votes, split between 24 Democrats, 7 Republicans, 1 Independent. | 272 to 155, with 7 not voting. | 155 No votes, split between 127 Democrats, 27 Republicans, and 1 Independent. |

**TABLE (continued)**

| FTA (Implementation Date) | Bills | U.S. Senate Vote (Overall Political Control) | Vote Breakdown | U.S. House of Representatives Vote (Overall Political Control) | Vote Breakdown |
|---|---|---|---|---|---|
| | House Bill enacted. | 31 July 2003 Senate Journal 764. (Senate divided between 48 Democrats, 51 Republicans, 1 Independent.) | Both Senators not voting were Democrats. | 24 July 2003, 149 Congressional Record H7489-03 (House divided between 204 Democrats, 229 Republicans, 1 Independent.) | Of the 7 Representatives not voting, 3 were Democrats, 4 were Republicans. |
| *Chile* (1 January 2004) | H.R. 2738 and S. 1416 House Bill enacted. | 65 to 32, with 3 not voting. 31 July 2003 Senate Journal 764. (Senate divided between 48 Democrats, 51 Republicans, 1 Independent.) | 31 No votes, split between 22 Democrats, 8 Republicans, 1 Independent. Of the 3 Senators not voting, 2 were Democrats, 1 was Republican. | 270 to 156, with 8 not voting. 24 July 2003, 149 Congressional Record H7514-01 (House divided between 204 Democrats, 229 Republicans, 1 Independent.) | 156 No votes, split between 128 Democrats, 27 Republicans, and 1 Independent. Of the 8 Representatives not voting, 2 were Democrats, 6 were Republicans. |

| | | | | | |
|---|---|---|---|---|---|
| *Australia* (1 January 2005) | H.R. 4759 and S. 2610 House Bill enacted. | 80 to 16, with 4 not voting. 15 July 2004, Senate Journal 549 (Senate divided between 48 Democrats, 51 Republicans, 1 Independent.) | 16 No votes, split between 14 Democrats, 2 Republicans. Of the 4 not voting, 3 were Democrats (including 2004 Presidential and Vice Presidential Candidates Kerry and Edwards), 1 was Republican. | 314 to 109, with 9 not voting and 1 voting "Pre-sent." 14 July 2004, 150 Congressional Record H5690-01 (House divided between 204 Democrats, 229 Republicans, 1 Independent.) | 109 No votes, split between 85 Democrats, 23 Republicans, 1 Independent. Of the 9 Representatives not voting, 5 were Democrats, 4 were Republican. |
| *Morocco* (1 January 2006) | H.R. 4842 | 85 to 13, with 2 not voting. July 22, 2004 Senate Journal 596 (Senate divided between 48 Democrats, 51 Republicans, 1 Independent.) | 13 No votes, split between 8 Democrats, 5 Republicans. The 2 Senators not voting were Democrats (2004 Presidential and Vice Presidential Candidates Kerry and Edwards.) | 323 to 99, with 12 not voting. 22 July 2004, 150 Congressional Record H6569-01 (House divided between 206 Democrats, 227 Republicans, 1 Independent.) | 99 No votes, split between 80 Democrats, 18 Republicans, 1 Independent. Of the 12 Representatives not voting, 6 were Democrats, 6 were Republicans. |

**TABLE (continued)**

| FTA (Implementation Date) | Bills | U.S. Senate Vote (Overall Political Control) | Vote Breakdown | U.S. House of Representatives Vote (Overall Political Control) | Vote Breakdown |
|---|---|---|---|---|---|
| **CAFTA—DR** (1 March 2006 in U.S., but later dates in other CAFTA—DR countries) | H.R. 3045 | 55 to 45. 28 July 2005, 151 Congressional Record S9253-01 (Senate divided between 48 Democrats, 51 Republicans, 1 Independent.) | 45 No votes, split between 33 Democrats, 12 Republicans. | 217 to 215, with 2 not voting. 27 July 2005, 151 Congressional Record H6884-03 (House divided between 202 Democrats, 232 Republicans, 1 Independent.) | 215 No votes, split between 188 Democrats and 27 Republicans. Both Representatives not voting were Republican. |
| **Bahrain** (1 August 2006) | H.R. 4340, S.2027 | Voice vote. 13 December 2005, 151 Congressional Record S13507-03. (Senate divided between 48 Democrats, 51 Republicans, 1 Independent.) | Voice vote, thus not available. | 327 to 95, with 10 not voting. 7 December 2005, 151 Congressional Record H11181 (House divided between 202 Democrats, 229 Republicans, 1 Independent.) | 95 No votes, split between 81 Democrats, 13 Republicans, 1 Independent. Of the 10 Representatives not voting, 6 were Democrats, 4 were Republicans. |

| | | | | | |
|---|---|---|---|---|---|
| *Oman*<br>(1 January 2009) | H.R. 5684,<br>S. 3569 | 60 to 34, with 6 not voting.<br>29 June 2006,<br>152 Congressional Record S6763.<br>Later approval of House bill by 63–31.<br>(Senate divided between 48 Democrats, 51 Republicans, 1 Independent.) | 34 No votes, split between 29 Democrats, 5 Republicans.<br>Of the 6 Senators not voting, 4 were Democrats, 2 were Republicans. | 221 to 205, with 7 non-voting.<br>20 July 2006.<br>(House divided between 202 Democrats, 229 Republicans, 1 Independent.) | 205 No votes, split between 176 Democrats, 28 Republicans, and 1 Independent.<br>Of the 7 Representatives not voting, 3 were Democrats, 4 were Republicans. |
| *Peru*<br>(1 February 2009) | H.R. 3688 | 77 to 18.<br>4 December 2007. | 18 No votes, split between 16 Democrats, 1 Republican, and 1 Independent. | 285 to 132.<br>8 November 2007.<br>(November 2006 elections shift House control to Democrats, 234 to 201.) | 132 No votes, split between 116 Democrats, 16 Republicans.<br>Of the 16 Representatives not voting, 6 were Democrat, 6 Republican. |

**TABLE (continued)**

| FTA (Implementation Date) | Bills | U.S. Senate Vote (Overall Political Control) | Vote Breakdown | U.S. House of Representatives Vote (Overall Political Control) | Vote Breakdown |
|---|---|---|---|---|---|
| **Peru, continued** | | (November 2006 elections shift Senate control to Democrats 51–49.) | Of the 5 Senators not voting, 4 were Democrats (including 2008 Presidential and Vice-Presidential candidates Obama and Biden), 1 was Republican (2008 Presidential candidate McCain). | | The *Peru FTA* is the first and only FTA approved during the Administration of George W. Bush that contains the 10 May 2007 understanding between that Administration and Congress on enhanced labor and environmental provisions. The FTA contains these provisions.<br><br>Accordingly, in 2007 Peru changed its labor laws to end the use of sub-contracting as a way to undermine the ability of workers to unionize. (However, |

| | | | | | |
|---|---|---|---|---|---|
| | | | | | to the chagrin of some in Congress, Peru subsequently adopted a vague exception allowing for sub-contracting if its Ministry of Labor finds that reasonable.) |
| *Colombia* (15 May 2012) | H.R. 3078, S. 1641 | 66 to 33. 12 October 2011. (Senate divided among 51 Democrats, 47 Republicans, 2 Independents.) | 33 No votes, split between 30 Democrats, 2 Republicans, 1 Independent. | 262 to 167 12 October 2011. (November 2010 elections shift control of House to Republicans. House divided between 242 Republicans, 192 Democrats.) | 167 No votes, split between 158 Democrats, 9 Republicans. The *Colombia TPA* contains the 10 May 2007 understanding between the Administration and Congress on enhanced labor and environmental provisions. The *TPA* contains enhanced commitments on these topics. In April 2011, the USTR established an *Action Plan Related to Labor Rights*, to which Colombia agreed. |

**TABLE (continued)**

| FTA (Implementation Date) | Bills | U.S. Senate Vote (Overall Political Control) | Vote Breakdown | U.S. House of Representatives Vote (Overall Political Control) | Vote Breakdown |
|---|---|---|---|---|---|
| *Panama* (2012–2013) | H.R. 3079, S. 1643 | 77 to 22. 12 October 2011. (Senate divided among 51 Democrats, 47 Republicans, 2 Independents.) | 22 No votes, split between 21 Democrats and 1 Independent. | 300 to 129. 12 October 2011. (November 2010 elections shift control of House to Republicans. House divided between 242 Republicans, 192 Democrats.) | 129 No votes, split between 123 Democrats, 6 Republicans. The *Panama FTA* contains the 10 May 2007 understanding between the Administration and Congress on enhanced labor and environmental provisions. The FTA contains enhanced commitments on these topics. |

| Country (date) | Bill | Senate vote | House vote | Notes |
|---|---|---|---|---|
| | | | | Under American pressure, in spring 2011, Panama made several changes to strengthen its labor laws, in April 2011 it agreed to a *Tax Information Exchange Agreement (TIEA)* with the U.S., and it amended its law on "Bearer Shares." |
| *Korea* (15 March 2012) | H.R. 3080, S. 1642 | 83 to 15. 12 October 2011. (Senate divided among 51 Democrats, 47 Republicans, 2 Independents.) 15 No votes, split between 14 Democrats, 1 Republican. | 278 to 151. 12 October 2011. (November 2010 elections shift control of House to Republicans. House divided between 242 Republicans, 192 Democrats.) 151 No votes, split between 130 Democrats, 21 Republicans. | The *Korea FTA* contains the 10 May 2007 understanding between the Administration and Congress on |

TABLE (continued)

| FTA (Implementation Date) | Bills | U.S. Senate Vote (Overall Political Control) | Vote Breakdown | U.S. House of Representatives Vote (Overall Political Control) | Vote Breakdown |
|---|---|---|---|---|---|
| Korea Continued | | | | | enhanced labor and environmental provisions. The FTA contains enhanced commitments on these topics.<br><br>It also contains the February 2011 *Supplemental Agreement*, which consists of a *Supplemental Auto Agreement* (on auto market access), plus two sets of *Agreed Minutes* (covering fuel economy and emission standards, and business visas, respectively). |

TABLE C-3:

MARKET ACCESS RULES FOR GOODS IN UNITED STATES FTAs — IMMEDIATE DUTY FREE TREATMENT

*(FTAs listed chronologically by Implementation Date)*

| *FTA and Relevant Provisions* | *Date of Immediate Duty-Free Treatment (typically Implementation Date)* | *Percentage of Articles Eligible for Immediate Duty-Free Treatment* | *Other Notable Market Access Commitments* |
|---|---|---|---|
| *Israel* Annexes I (imports from Israel to the U.S.) and II (imports from the U.S. to Israel) | 1 September 1985 | Not available. Agricultural goods not covered under original FTA until 1996, when *Agreement on Trade in Agricultural Products (ATAP)* added as adjunct to FTA. Original FTA does not cover electronic commerce, intellectual property (IP), or technical barriers to trade (TBT). Thus: concerning electronic commerce, there is no rule against tariffs or discriminatory taxes on electronic transmission, and no consumer guarantees or privacy protections. On TBT, there is formal standard setting arrangement, beyond the | Israel reduced or eliminated export subsidies, limited its GATT rights as a developing country to use tariffs to protect infant industries. Israel and the U.S. agreed not to impose import licensing requirements for FDI, except in certain instances of export or purchase performance requirements. Israel and U.S. reviewed veterinary and plant health rules to ensure they are non-discriminatory and not undue trade obstructions. Israel and U.S. agreed to limit the duration of any restrictions imposed in a balance of payments (BOP) crisis. |

**TABLE (continued)**

| FTA and Relevant Provisions | Date of Immediate Duty-Free Treatment (typically Implementation Date) | Percentage of Articles Eligible for Immediate Duty-Free Treatment | Other Notable Market Access Commitments |
|---|---|---|---|
| Israel Continued | | existing "Notice and Consultation" obligation in the FTA, to ensure harmonization, transparency, or use of international standards. On IP, there is no conformity with digital copyright treaties of the World Intellectual Property Organization (WIPO), nor provisions on Israeli patent law reaching a specified level of protection. | |
| Canada | 1 January 1989 | Substantial. | Preferential rules of origin rely primarily on Change in Tariff Classification (CTH). Customs user fees and duty drawback were phased out by 1994. Import and export quotas not specifically permitted by FTA or GATT were prohibited. Technical standards were liberalized or harmonized. |

| | | | |
|---|---|---|---|
| **NAFTA**<br>Chapters 3 (goods) and 7 (agriculture) | 1 January 1994 | Substantial.<br>All products have duty free entry into Canada, and all products except for C+ goods have duty free entry into Mexico.<br>Mexico eliminated tariffs on 50% of industrial goods, and many non-tariff barriers, immediately upon entry into force. | Some reservations for sensitive goods, *i.e.*, the C+ category.<br>Non-tariff barriers to trade are reduced or eliminated. |
| *Jordan*<br>Annex 2.1 (general goods schedule) and Article 7 (e-commerce) | 17 December 2001 | Tariffs on 95% of goods eliminated (as of 1 January 2005). | E-commerce is covered through an obligation to seek to avoid (1) imposing tariffs on electronic transmissions, (2) placing unnecessary barriers to trade in digitized products, and (3) impeding the ability to deliver services through electronic means. |
| *Singapore*<br>Chapter 2 | 1 January 2004 | Singapore guaranteed zero tariff treatment immediately on all U.S. products.<br>The U.S. guaranteed zero tariff treatment immediately on most Singaporean goods, and phased out remaining tariffs over 3–10 years. | Chewing gum may be imported into Singapore, but only for its therapeutic value as a health product under Article 2:11 (possibly requiring a prescription). |

**TABLE (continued)**

| FTA and Relevant Provisions | Date of Immediate Duty-Free Treatment (typically Implementation Date) | Percentage of Articles Eligible for Immediate Duty-Free Treatment | Other Notable Market Access Commitments |
|---|---|---|---|
| **Chile** Chapter 3 | 1 January 2004 | Over 85 % of bilateral trade in consumer and industrial products received immediate duty-free treatment. | Chile's status as a beneficiary of the Generalized System of Preferences (GSP) terminated. Preferential rules of origin are designed to be easier to administer than NAFTA rules of origin. The origin rules must be transparent and efficient. Chile agreed to phase out its price band system, under which the import duties it levied on the same product depended on price level. The U.S. and Chile agreed to resolve SPS issues that inhibit market access. While agreeing that controls on the flow of financial capital are illegal, Chile won an exception to the obligation not to restrict capital transfers. |

| | | | |
|---|---|---|---|
| **Australia**<br>Chapter 2 | 1 January 2005 | Duties on more than 99% of tariff lines for industrial and consumer goods (equaling 93% of U.S. goods exports to Australia) eliminated immediately.<br>Duties on all U.S. agricultural exports to Australia eliminated immediately.<br>Duties on most Australian agricultural imports not eliminated immediately. | Non-tariff barriers that restrict or distort trade flows must be eliminated.<br>A new forum is created for cooperation to resolve animal and plant health matters, focusing on the application of scientific standards with a view to facilitating trade. |
| **Morocco**<br>Chapter 2 | 1 January 2006 | 95% of goods receive immediate duty free treatment.<br>Duties on virtually all trade between U.S. and Morocco eliminated over 10–18 years.<br>Immediate bilateral tariff elimination on many agricultural products. | Morocco's status as a beneficiary of the Generalized System of Preferences (GSP) terminated. |
| **CAFTA—DR**<br>Chapter 2 | 1 March 2006 | 80% of U.S. exports receive duty-free treatment. | Separate tariff schedules for country. |
| **Bahrain**<br>Chapter 2 | 1 August 2006 | 98% of agricultural products and virtually industrial and commercial goods. | Remaining tariffs phased out over 10 years. |
| **Oman**<br>Chapter 2 | 1 January 2009 | 100% of two-way trade in consumer and industrial products, including major U.S. exports to Oman like automobiles, electrical and other machinery, and medical and optical instruments.<br>87% of agricultural products, including beverage bases, sugars, sweeteners, and vegetable oils. | Oman agreed to Side Letter on SPS barriers in which it accepts U.S. food safety inspection, including on meat products such as beef, pork, and poultry.<br>Oman also agreed to enhanced IP protection. |

TABLE (continued)

| FTA and Relevant Provisions | Date of Immediate Duty-Free Treatment (typically Implementation Date) | Percentage of Articles Eligible for Immediate Duty-Free Treatment | Other Notable Market Access Commitments |
|---|---|---|---|
| *Peru* Chapter 2 | 1 February 2009 | Overall, 90% of tariff lines are duty free. 92% of industrial tariff lines are duty-free, and 78% of agricultural tariff lines are duty free. 80% of U.S. exports of consumer and industrial products, and over two-thirds of U.S. exports of agricultural products, receive duty free treatment. Examples include (1) agricultural goods such as high-quality beef, fruits and vegetables, and other processed foods, (2) agricultural, construction, and mining equipment, and (3) technology products. | Peru agreed to eliminate its price band system, which imposes variable tariffs on imports of keen export interest to the U.S., such as corn, pork, and wheat. The tariff variations are linked to external market conditions, but the variation creates uncertainty and diminishes transparency for exporters. Peru also agreed to *Side Letter* on SPS barriers in which it accepts U.S. food safety inspection, including on meat products such as beef, pork, and poultry. In a so-called "Timber Annex," formally called the "Annex on Forest Sector Governance," Peru agreed to strictures against illegal timber logging (*e.g.*, of mahogany from natural reserves, or from Indian land, |

in the Peruvian Amazon), and illegal trade in wildlife. Peru had 18 months from the date of implementation to hire additional forestry inspectors, strengthen its forestry regulator, and increase penalties for illegal logging. U.S. inspectors may bar suspicious shipments at the border, and may conduct on-site investigations in Peru.

In June 2011, Peru's Congress passed the forestry legislation necessary to comply with the Timber Annex. The bill (04141-2009-PE) contained 161 articles. It created a National Wildlife and Forestry Service (SERFOR), which is responsible for forestry formulating and critiquing policy, and the National Forestry and Wildlife Management System (SINAFOR), which manages forests and wildlife and

**TABLE (continued)**

| FTA and Relevant Provisions | Date of Immediate Duty-Free Treatment (typically Implementation Date) | Percentage of Articles Eligible for Immediate Duty-Free Treatment | Other Notable Market Access Commitments |
|---|---|---|---|
| *Peru Continued* | | | operationalizes policy. The bill establishes four categories of forests, namely, areas for: (1) permanent production; (2) protection and conservation; (3) recuperation (reforestation); and (4) special treatment. The bill limits logging concessions to 5,000-40,000 hectares, for up to 40 years, with no restriction on the number of concessions a single entity can hold. The bill also amends Peru's Criminal Code, to increase penalties for forestry and wildlife crimes, and boosts the number of ecological police officers and prosecutors. This legislation replaced a June 2008 Legislative Decree (1090), which was intended to comply with the *FTA*, but which triggered violent, deadly protests over land tenure |

| | | | | |
|---|---|---|---|---|
| *Colombia*<br>Chapter 2 | 15 May 2012 | 80% of U.S. consumer and industrial products to Colombia receive immediate duty free treatment. (The pre-*FTA* average tariff Colombia imposed on manufactured products was 14%.)<br>Colombia agreed to phase out remaining tariffs on such goods over 10 years. | Colombia agreed to a Side Letter on SPS barriers in which it accepts U.S. food safety inspection, including on meat products such as beef, pork, and poultry.<br><br>In April 2011, the USTR established an *Action Plan Related to Labor Rights* by which Colombia would | in the Amazon. The bill remains controversial, as it does not recognize the right of indigenous peoples to ancestral territories unless they hold a land title granted by the government.<br><br>Annex 10-E of the FTA sets limits on the amount of damages a foreign direct investor can receive as compensation arising from certain capital controls implemented by a host government, and imposes a cooling off period before filing such claims. |

**TABLE (continued)**

| FTA and Relevant Provisions | Date of Immediate Duty-Free Treatment (typically Implementation Date) | Percentage of Articles Eligible for Immediate Duty-Free Treatment | Other Notable Market Access Commitments |
|---|---|---|---|
| Colombia Continued | | Colombia grants immediate duty-free treatment to many U.S. agricultural products, including beef, cotton, frozen French fries, soybeans, soybean meal, and wheat, plus certain horticultural products.<br><br>U.S. grants textile and apparel (T&A) exports from Colombia immediate duty-free, quota-free treatment, subject to rules of origin. | enhance its enforcement of internationally recognized workers' rights, protect labor leaders from violence, and prosecute perpetrators of such violence.<br><br>Under the *Action Plan*, Colombia agreed to its labor laws, expand its protection program for labor leaders and union activists, prosecute and punish persons for violence against union activists, and revise its program for relocating and protecting teachers.<br><br>Under the *Action Plan*, Colombia also agreed to increase the number and capacity of prosecutors and judicial police, and make necessary reforms to its criminal code to criminalize acts or threats against worker rights. |

However, the *Action Plan* does not cover the use of cooperatives, which replace direct hiring in Colombia, and deny basic labor rights to the workers hired through them.

In June 2011, the USTR announced Colombia met the requirements of the *Action Plan related to Labor Rights*, namely:

(1) Update a June 2006 Tripartite Agreement among the Colombian government, unions, and businesses to strengthen workers' rights.

(2) Create a new Ministry of Law and Justice, and reorganize existing Ministries (including of Labor, Health, and Social Protection) to strengthen the judiciary, protect workers' rights, and safeguard unions.

**TABLE (continued)**

| FTA and Relevant Provisions | Date of Immediate Duty-Free Treatment (typically Implementation Date) | Percentage of Articles Eligible for Immediate Duty-Free Treatment | Other Notable Market Access Commitments |
|---|---|---|---|
| Colombia Continued | | | (3) Enact or reform penal code provisions to strengthen penalties for violations of workers' or union rights or threats to union leaders, and enhance protection of workers in cooperatives, and increase protection, including criminal penalties (imprisonment) for an employer that undermines the right of workers to organize and bargain collectively or threatens a worker who exercises that right. (4) Issue a memorandum on the right of public service workers to strike, except for workers providing essential services (who must seek governmental permission to strike). (5) Reduce by 75% the backlog of risk assessments for union activists and leaders seeking protection. |

| | | | |
|---|---|---|---|
| | | | (6) Establish a process for posting on the Internet information about completed criminal cases on labor violence. (7) Increase financial and manpower (*e.g.*, labor inspector) resources for governmental agencies responsible for protecting workers and unionists. (8) Analyze prior cases involving homicide of unionists. Colombia posted its reforms on an official governmental website. The *Action Plan* sets benchmarks for Colombia to meet in subsequent years (*e.g.*, hiring 380 additional labor inspectors by 2014). | Special provisions exist on the protection and promotion of labor and environmental rights. |
| *Panama* | 2012–2013 | Immediate duty-free treatment for over 50% of U.S. agricultural exports to Panama, including beef (high-quality), | |

**TABLE (continued)**

| FTA and Relevant Provisions | Date of Immediate Duty-Free Treatment (typically Implementation Date) | Percentage of Articles Eligible for Immediate Duty-Free Treatment | Other Notable Market Access Commitments |
|---|---|---|---|
| *Panama Continued* | | cotton, fresh fruits, nuts, pork and poultry products soybeans, soybean meal, and wheat, as well as certain processed products, distilled spirits, and wine.<br><br>Immediate duty-free treatment for 88% of U.S. exports of consumer and industrial goods to Panama, with remaining Panamanian tariffs phased out over 10 years.<br><br>Panama consolidates its market access benefits to the U.S. through the Caribbean Basin Initiative (CBI), under which 96% of exports already enter duty free. | In spring 2011, to meet American concerns about labor rights, Panama issued executive decrees<br><br>(1) against the misuse of sub-contract and temporary contract labor,<br><br>(2) strengthening collective bargaining and the right to strike, and<br><br>(3) preventing employers from interfering with union activities.<br><br>Additionally, the Panamanian Ministry of Labor issued a resolution to increase the number of inspections in the maritime sector.<br><br>Finally, Panama agreed to amend its labor laws to eliminate restrictions on labor rights in free trade and export processing zones to give the right to strike and collective bargaining rights to all workers in those zones (including the special economic zone |

of Barú), and eliminate an exemption from these rights for temporary workers hired for up to 3 years.

In April 2011, Panama's legislature approved a U.S. — Panama *Tax Information Exchange Agreement* (*TIEA*), which the two countries had signed in November 2010. (*See* Law 33, *Official Gazette of Panama*, 20 June 2010.)

The *TIEA*, which entered into force on 18 April 2011, makes it more difficult for Panama to be a tax haven. It allows each country to seek evidence from the other on civil and criminal tax matters in accordance with international conventions on information exchange (including the 1985 *Hague Convention on the Law Applicable to Trusts and Their Recognition*, which entered into force in 1992, and which Panama joined in connection with the *TIEA*), beginning on or after 30 November 2007, even if the evidence sought is not of interest to the domestic authority from which it is sought.

**TABLE (continued)**

| FTA and Relevant Provisions | Date of Immediate Duty-Free Treatment (typically Implementation Date) | Percentage of Articles Eligible for Immediate Duty-Free Treatment | Other Notable Market Access Commitments |
|---|---|---|---|
| Panama Continued | | | Relatedly, Panama also changed its law on anonymous accounts, called "Bearer Shares," obligating law firms that incorporate a business to engage in due diligence to verify the true owners of the business and provide this information to the Panamanian government, *i.e.*, to "Know Your Client." (*See* Law 2, *Official Gazette of Panama*, 1 February 2011.)

In the auto sector, under the initially agreed provisions as revised by the February 2011 *Supplemental Auto Agreement*, Korea agreed to eliminate immediately its 10% tariff on trucks, |

| *Korea* <br> Chapters One (Initial Provisions and Definitions), Two (National Treatment and Market Access for Goods), Three (Agriculture), Four (Textiles and Apparel), plus February 2011*Supplemental Agreement* | 15 March 2012 | Immediate duty-free treatment of nearly two-thirds (over $1 billion) of American farm exports to Korea. Examples include cherries, corn, cotton, hides and skins, soybeans for crushing, wheat, whey for feed use, and high-value added agricultural goods such as almonds, bourbon, fresh cherries, frozen French fries, frozen orange juice concentrate, grape juice, orange juice, pet food, pistachios, raisins, whisky, and wine. <br><br> 80.5% of American exports of agricultural and industrial goods (over 9,000 products) to Korea were duty free immediately. Specifically, over two-thirds of American exports of agricultural goods to Korea, and 80% of American exports of industrial goods to Korea, received immediate | and to eliminating its 8% tariff on cars (including non-American brands, *e.g.*, German and Japanese cars, made in the U.S.) in two stages: from 8% to 4% immediately (staying at 4% until the end of the 4th year of implementation of *KORUS*), and to zero on 1 January 2016. <br><br> Also in the auto sector, Korea agreed to eliminate engine displacement-based taxes. (These levies include the Annual Vehicle Tax, Special Consumption Tax, and Subway/Regional Development Bond.) The U.S. contended these taxes discriminated against foreign-produced cars because the amount of the tax depended on engine size, and foreign cars have larger-sized engines than Korean cars. |

**TABLE (continued)**

| FTA and Relevant Provisions | Date of Immediate Duty-Free Treatment (typically Implementation Date) | Percentage of Articles Eligible for Immediate Duty-Free Treatment | Other Notable Market Access Commitments |
|---|---|---|---|
| *Korea Continued* | | duty-free treatment. The agricultural goods included almonds, certain meats, cherries, cotton, orange juice, and wheat. The industrial goods included aerospace equipment, agricultural equipment, autos, auto parts, building products, chemicals, consumer goods, electrical equipment, environmental goods, all footwear and travel goods, paper and paper products, scientific equipment, and shipping and transportation equipment. | As for Korean auto exports to America, the United States maintains its 2.5% car tariff until the end of the 4th year of implementation of *KORUS*, and then drops this tariff to zero. *KORUS* also establishes an Automotive Working Group to review auto-related regulations, promote good regulatory practices in Korea, and ensure Korea shares the same information on technical standards with U.S. automakers as it does with Korean companies. Also in the auto sector, *KORUS* has an enhanced dispute settlement mechanism for controversies over auto-related measures, requiring a decision by a panel within 6 months of commencing a case, and allowing the winning country to snap back the tariff at issue to the pre-*KORUS* MFN level. |

| | |
| --- | --- |
| 95% of bilateral trade in consumer and industrial products is duty-free within 5 years of entry into force. Examples include auto parts, most chemicals, cosmetics, electronic machinery and parts, medical and scientific equipment, motorcycles, perfume, toothpaste, and certain wood products. Products also include re-manufactured goods (which is significant in respect of auto parts, machinery, and medical equipment). | At the same time, Korea agreed to the U.S. demands Korea ensure that (1) the preferential rule of origin for T&A products is yarn forward, (2) T&A products using Chinese yarn are not eligible for duty free status, (3) there are strict rules against trans-shipment and mislabeling origins of T&A products, and (4) a special textile safeguard remedy exists (in Article 4:1) for temporary relief from Korean T&A merchandise proven to cause damage to U.S. domestic producers.<br><br>National treatment guaranteed to U.S. direct investors, including the right to establish, acquire, and operate investments. Transparent, binding international arbitration mechanism will be used to resolve any FDI disputes. |

**TABLE (continued)**

| FTA and Relevant Provisions | Date of Immediate Duty-Free Treatment (typically Implementation Date) | Percentage of Articles Eligible for Immediate Duty-Free Treatment | Other Notable Market Access Commitments |
|---|---|---|---|
| *Korea Continued* | | But, the initial deal on priority passenger vehicles and trucks was revised in a *Supplemental Auto Agreement* reached in December 2010 and officially initialed in February 2011. Under the *Supplemental Agreement*, Korea agreed to cut its electric car tariffs from 8 to 4% immediately, and phase out the remaining 4% by the end of the 5th year of implementation of *KORUS*. E-commerce also covered by immediate, non-discriminatory, duty-free treatment. Merchandise includes all digital products (*e.g.*, audio-visual and software), whether imported physically or through the internet. Most remaining tariffs are phased out over 10 years. | Korea will strengthen its competition laws and enforcement regime to ensure practices by private parties, government monopolies, and state owned enterprises (SOEs) do not undermine *KORUS* benefits. Korea will provide due process protections apply in competition law proceedings in Korean administrative hearings (*e.g.*, opportunity to present evidence, be heard, review and rebut information, cross examine witnesses), and ensure antitrust authorities have the authority to enter into settlement agreements with respondents in enforcement actions. |

## TABLE C-4:
## MARKET ACCESS RULES FOR GOODS IN *U.S.—ISRAEL FTA* — DEFERRED DUTY FREE (OR QUOTA FREE) TREATMENT

| | |
|---|---|
| ***Implementation Date*** | 30 August 1985 |
| ***Relevant Provisions*** | Annexes I (imports from Israel to the U.S.) and II (imports from the U.S. to Israel), and Agreement on Trade in Agricultural Products (ATAP) Annexes A-D |
| ***Number of Staging Categories*** | 4 |
| ***Tariff Elimination Methodology*** | Israel imposes fees on U.S. exports to Israel based on CIF value of merchandise: <br><br> 1% port fee, and 0.5 % stevedoring (unloading) fee. <br><br> Also, Israel imposes a compulsory levy on food and agriculture. <br><br> Israel imposes a purchase tax on luxury goods (Israeli or foreign), and a 17% Value Added Tax (VAT), which importer may recover on resale. |
| ***Maximum Tariff (or Quota) Phase Out Period*** | 10 years, *i.e.*, by 1995. |
| ***Examples of Deferred Tariff (or Quota) Elimination*** | Products that are import sensitive for domestic producers. <br><br> Agriculture not covered under original FTA. In 1996, *Agreement on Trade in Agricultural Products (ATAP)* added as adjunct to FTA. *ATAP* expired on December 31, 2002, renewed in 2004. The 2004 renewal continued through 2008, and was extended through 2009. On 31 August 2009, President Barack H. Obama issued a Proclamation to modify the Harmonized Tariff Schedule (HTS) to provide the tariff treatment intended under the FTA, *ATAP*, and 2004 renewal. |
| ***Final Date for Elimination of all Tariffs (or Quotas)*** | 1 January 1995 <br><br> Also, ban on any new import limitations after 1990. |

TABLE C-4, (continued)
MARKET ACCESS RULES FOR GOODS IN *U.S.—CANADA FTA* —
DEFERRED DUTY FREE (OR QUOTA FREE) TREATMENT

| | |
|---|---|
| *Implementation Date* | 1 January 1989 |
| *Relevant Provisions* | Not available |
| *Number of Staging Categories* | 3 — A, B, and C |
| *Tariff Elimination Methodology* | Category A goods received immediate duty free treatment (as of 1 January 1989). |
| | Tariffs on Category B goods were eliminated in 5 equal stages (duty free as of 1 January 1993). |
| | Tariffs on Category C goods were eliminated in 10 equal stages (duty free as of 1 January 1998) |
| *Maximum Tariff (or Quota) Phase Out Period* | 10 years |
| *Examples of Deferred Tariff (or Quota) Elimination* | Certain agricultural products (e.g., softwood lumber and wheat for Canada), automotive products (covered by the 1965 *Auto Pact*), distilled spirits and wine (for the U.S. and Canada), and fish (for Canada). |
| | Certain cultural industries are exempt from trade liberalization obligations. |
| *Final Date for Elimination of all Tariffs (or Quotas)* | 1 January 1998, subsumed under *NAFTA*. |

TABLE **C-4, (continued)**
MARKET ACCESS RULES FOR GOODS IN *NAFTA* —
DEFERRED DUTY FREE (OR QUOTA FREE) TREATMENT

| | |
|---|---|
| *Implementation Date* | 1 January 1994 |
| *Relevant Provisions* | Chapters 3 (goods) and 7 (agriculture) |
| *Number of Staging Categories* | 4 — A, B, C, and C+ |
| *Tariff Elimination Methodology* | Category A goods received immediate duty free treatment (as of 1 January 1994). Tariffs on Category B goods were eliminated in 5 equal stages (duty free as of 1 January 1999). Tariffs on Category C goods were eliminated in 10 equal stages (duty free as of 1 January 2004). Tariffs on Category C+ goods were eliminated in 15 equal stages (duty free as of 1 January 2008). |
| *Maximum Tariff (or Quota) Phase Out Period* | 15 years |
| *Examples of Deferred Tariff (or Quota) Elimination* | For Mexico: Beans, corn, non-fat dry (powdered) milk, and sugar For U.S.: Sugar |
| *Final Date for Elimination of all Tariffs (or Quotas)* | 1 January 2008 |

TABLE C-4, (continued)
MARKET ACCESS RULES FOR GOODS IN *U.S.—JORDAN FTA* —
DEFERRED DUTY FREE (OR QUOTA FREE) TREATMENT

| | |
|---|---|
| ***Implementation Date*** | 17 December 2001 |
| ***Relevant Provisions*** | Annex 2:1 and Article 7 (e-commerce) |
| ***Number of Staging Categories*** | 10 total staging categories. |
| | 5 general categories for U.S. and Jordan — A, B. C, D, and E |
| | 5 additional country-specific categories for U.S. or Jordan |
| | Jordan FTA is the only U.S. accord where staging categories (A, B, C, and D) depend on the pre-FTA tariff level. |
| ***Tariff Elimination Methodology*** | Tariffs on Category A goods (less than 5%) were eliminated in 2 years (duty free on 18 December 2003). |
| | Tariffs on Category B goods (between 5-10 %) were eliminated in 4 years (duty free on 18 December 2005). |
| | Tariffs on Category C goods (between 10-20%) were eliminated in 5 years (duty free on 18 December 2006). |
| | Tariffs on Category D goods (over 20%) are eliminated in 10 years (duty free on 18 December 2011). |
| | For Category E goods, tariffs are maintained at existing WTO commitment levels (as of *Jordan FTA* signing). |
| ***Maximum Tariff (or Quota) Phase Out Period*** | 10 years |
| ***Examples of Deferred Tariff (or Quota) Elimination*** | Category D goods for Jordan includes handwoven rugs most vegetables, shellfish, spices, refined petroleum (*e.g.*, butane, petroleum jelly). |
| | Also for Jordan, Category D includes most textiles (HTS Chapters 61, 62, and 63), most machinery (HTS Chapter 85), some metals and alloy combinations, and most rubber products. |
| ***Final Date for Elimination of All Tariffs (or Quotas)*** | 17 December 2011 |

TABLE C-4, (continued)
MARKET ACCESS RULES FOR GOODS IN *U.S.—SINGAPORE FTA* —
DEFERRED DUTY FREE (OR QUOTA FREE) TREATMENT

| | |
|---|---|
| *Implementation Date* | 1 January 2004 |
| *Relevant Provisions* | Chapter 2 |
| *Number of Staging Categories* | 7 Categories for the U.S. — A, B. C, D, E, F, and G. 2 Categories for Singapore — A and E |
| *Tariff Elimination Methodology* | The U.S. phased out tariffs, in equal annual installments, on Singaporean goods through 7 Categories: Category A (immediate duty free treatment); Category B (duty free treatment in year 4 following entry into force, *i.e.*, as of 1 January 2008); Category C (duty free in year 8, *i.e.*, as of 1 January 2012); Category D (duty free in year 10, *i.e.*, as of 1 January 2014); Category E (goods that received duty-free treatment before the *FTA* continue to receive this treatment); Category F (goods that receive duty-free treatment and may enter the U.S. without bond); Category G (HTS Chapter 98 goods, duty free in year 10). Annex 2A to Chapter 2 covers reservations (*e.g.*, for U.S., export controls on logs and shipping). Annex 2B to Chapter 2 is the U.S. tariff schedule. This Annex sets out 4 staging categories for quota elimination, according to commodity: (1) Immediate quota-free treatment (as of 1 January 2004); |

**TABLE C-4:  *U.S.—SINGAPORE FTA* DEFERRALS, (continued)**

|  | |
|---|---|
|  | (2) quota-free treatment in 4 years (as of 1 January 2008); |
|  | (3) quota-free treatment in 8 years (as of 1 January 2012); and |
|  | (4) quota-free treatment in 10 years (as of 1 January 2014). |
|  | Singapore gave immediate duty free treatment for all U.S. goods under Categories A and E. |
|  | Annex 2C to Chapter 2 is the Singapore tariff schedule. This schedule says every good gets immediate duty-free, quota-free treatment, including beer, stout, *samsu*, and medicated *samsu* (*ban siew tong*). |
|  | Note Singapore imposes a 5% sales tax on all imports and domestic goods. |
| ***Maximum Tariff (or Quota) Phase Out Period*** | 10 years (for tariff and quota elimination by the U.S.) |
| ***Examples of Deferred Tariff (or Quota) Elimination*** | U.S. imposes quota limits for 10 years on beef, butter, cheese, cotton, liquid dairy products, sugar, and tobacco. |
|  | Note that Singapore has neither an export agriculture industry nor a Ministry of Agriculture. |
|  | The quota limits appear to be a precedent for the U.S. to cite, or template to impose, in subsequent FTA negotiations. |
| ***Final Date for Elimination of All Tariffs (or Quotas)*** | 1 January 2014 |

TABLE C-4: (continued)
MARKET ACCESS RULES FOR GOODS IN *U.S.—CHILE FTA* —
DEFERRED DUTY FREE (OR QUOTA FREE) TREATMENT

| | |
|---|---|
| *Implementation Date* | 1 January 2004 |
| *Relevant Provisions* | Chapter 3 |
| *Number of Staging Categories* | 16 total staging categories. |
| | 8 general staging categories for U.S. and Chile — |
| | A, B. C, D, E, F, G, and H. |
| | 8 additional country-specific categories for U.S. or Chile (*e.g.*, for non-linear phase outs of tariffs, and for certain products such as agricultural goods). |
| *Tariff Elimination Methodology* | Goods in Category A got immediate duty free treatment (as of 1 January 2004). |
| | Tariffs on goods in Categories B through E phase out over 4, 8, 10, or 12 years (from the date of entry into force), respectively, and in equal annual installments. |
| | Tariffs on Category F goods continue to receive duty free treatment. Tariffs on Category G goods remain at base rates in years 1-4, and are reduced by 8.3% of the base rate in year 5, and by an annual 8.3% of the base rate in each year thereafter through year 8. In Year 9, duties on Category G goods are reduced by an additional 16.7% through year 12, and become duty free on 1 January of year 12. |
| | Tariffs on Category H goods are at base rates in years 1 and 2, and duties are removed beginning in year 3 in 8 equal annual installments, with duty-free treatment on 1 January of year 10. |
| *Maximum Tariff (or Quota) Phase Out Period* | 4 year phase out period for consumer and industrial products. |
| | 12 year phase out period for agricultural products. |

TABLE C-4:    *U.S.—CHILE FTA* DEFERRALS, (continued)

| | |
|---|---|
| ***Examples of Deferred Tariff (or Quota) Elimination*** | Certain agricultural products.<br><br>More than 75% of U.S. farm goods enter Chile duty-free within 4 years. Tariffs on remaining U.S. farm goods phased out over 12 years.<br><br>Annex 3:3 to Chapter 3 contains 8 staging categories for quota elimination by the U.S., as follows:<br><br>2 years for copper;<br><br>4 years for beef;<br><br>8 years for tires;<br><br>10 years for hotel china ware and poultry;<br><br>12 years for butter, cheese, condensed milk, milk powder, other dairy, sugar, and tobacco.<br><br>For avocados, 12 year quota phase out is applicable year around, but threshold changes seasonally, with higher threshold for shipments between 1 October and 31 December, and lower thresholds for shipments between 1 January and 30 September.<br><br>Chile imposes its MFN tariff rate for 4 product categories in HTS Chapter 2 (0207.13.00, 0207.14.00, 0207.26.00, and 0207.27.00). These categories are poultry. The MFN rate is 25%. The phase out period is Category H (10 years), and quotas apply.<br><br>Chile imposes its MFN tariff rate for 27 product categories in HTS Chapter 15. These products are vegetable oils. The MFN rate is 31.5%. There is no phase out period.<br><br>Chile imposes its MFN tariff rate for 4 categories of goods in HTS Chapter 1701 (1701.11, 1701.12, 1701.91, and 1701.99). These categories are cane or beet sugar products). The MFN rate is 98 %. The phase out period is Category G (12 years). |
| ***Final Date for Elimination of All Tariffs (or Quotas)*** | 1 January 2008 for consumer and industrial products.<br><br>1 January 2016 for agricultural goods. |

TABLE C-4: (continued)

MARKET ACCESS RULES FOR GOODS IN *U.S.—AUSTRALIA FTA* —
DEFERRED DUTY FREE (OR QUOTA FREE) TREATMENT

| | |
|---|---|
| *Implementation Date* | 1 January 2005 |
| *Relevant Provisions* | Chapter 2 |
| *Number of Staging Categories* | 5 staging categories |
| *Tariff Elimination Methodology* | Goods in Category A got immediate duty free treatment (as of 1 January 2005). |
| | Tariffs on goods in Categories B through D phase out over 4, 8, or 10 years (from the date of entry into force), respectively, and in equal annual installments. |
| | Tariffs on goods in Category E received duty free treatment before the *FTA* and continue to receive it. |
| | For specific goods, the U.S. has are 5 country-specific staging categories, and Australia has 3 country-specific staging categories. |
| | For example, U.S. staging categories F, G, and H phase out tariffs across 18 years. Category I covers sugar, and exempts it from the *FTA*. |
| *Maximum Tariff (or Quota) Phase Out Period* | 10 year phase out period for a small number of industrial goods. |
| | 4-18 year phase out period of U.S. tariffs on Australian agricultural goods. |
| *Examples of Deferred Tariff (or Quota) Elimination* | Small number of industrial goods from U.S. or Australia. |
| | Most Australian agricultural imports into the U.S. |
| | Special mechanisms, including preferential TRQs and safeguards, apply to certain agricultural products (e.g., beef, cotton, dairy, peanuts, and some horticultural products). |
| *Final Date for Elimination of All Tariffs (or Quotas)* | 1 January 2015 for industrial and consumer goods. |
| | 1 January 2023 for agricultural goods. |
| | However, sugar excluded from FTA coverage. |

## TABLE C-4: (continued)
### MARKET ACCESS RULES FOR GOODS IN *U.S.—MOROCCO FTA* — DEFERRED DUTY FREE (OR QUOTA FREE) TREATMENT

| | |
|---|---|
| ***Implementation Date*** | 1 January 2006 |
| ***Relevant Provisions*** | Chapter 2, Annex 4 (Goods Schedule) |
| ***Number of Staging Categories*** | 12 staging categories, plus 9 country-specific categories. |
| ***Tariff Elimination Methodology*** | Category A goods receive immediate duty free treatment (*i.e.*, as of 1 January 2006). |
| | Category B goods receive duty free treatment in year 2 (as of 1 January 2008). Tariffs are eliminated in 2 equal annual installments. |
| | Category C goods receive duty free treatment in year 5 (as of 1 January 2011). Tariffs are eliminated in 5 equal annual installments. |
| | Category D goods received an immediate 50% duty reduction (as of 1 January 2006), and beginning in year 2 duties on them were eliminated in 5 equal annual installments, with duty-free treatment in year 6 (*i.e.*, as of 1 January 2012). |
| | Category E goods receive duty free treatment in year 8 (as of 1 January 2014). Tariffs are eliminated in 8 equal annual installments. |
| | Category F goods receive duty free treatment in year 9 (as of 1 January 2015). Tariffs are eliminated in 9 equal annual installments. |
| | Category G goods receive duty free treatment in year 10 (as of 1 January 2016). Tariffs are eliminated in 10 equal annual installments. |
| | Tariffs on Category H goods are eliminated in 10 non-linear stages. In year 1, duties were cut by 3%, and by an additional 3% in years 2-3. Beginning in year 5, duties were eliminated in 6 equal annual installments, with duty free treatment in year 10 (*i.e.*, 1 January 2016). |

**TABLE C-4:   *U.S.—MOROCCO FTA* DEFERRALS, (continued)**

| *Tariff Elimination Methodology, continued* | Category I goods receive duty free treatment in year 12 (as of 1 January 2018). Tariffs are eliminated in 12 equal annual installments. |
|---|---|
| | Category J goods receive duty free treatment in year 15 (as of 1 January 2021). Tariffs are eliminated in 15 equal annual installments. |
| | Tariffs on Category K goods remain at the base rate during years 1-6. During year 7, duties are cut by 5.6% of the base rate. During years 8-12, duties are cut by an additional 5.6% of the base rate. In year 13, duties are cut by an additional 11.1%, in years 14-18 by an additional 11.1%. Category K goods are duty free in year 18 (*i.e.*, 1 January 2024). |
| | Category L goods received duty free treatment before the *FTA*, and continue to receive it. |
| | For certain goods, Morocco has 9 additional country-specific staging categories (Categories M-U), including a 19 year phase out period (Category R), and a 25 year phase out (Category S). |
| *Maximum Tariff (or Quota) Phase Out Period* | 10 year phase out period for non-agricultural products, 10 year phase out period for textiles and apparel, and 15 year phase out period for agricultural products. |
| | 18 year phase out period for certain goods imported by U.S. from Morocco. |
| | 25 year phase out period for U.S. turkey meat cuts imported by Morocco (HTS 0207.26.00.29). |
| *Examples of Deferred Tariff (or Quota) Elimination* | Certain textile and apparel articles, and certain horticultural products. |
| *Final Date for Elimination of All Tariffs (or Quotas)* | 1 January 2016 for certain non-agricultural products and textile and apparel. |
| | 1 January 2021 for certain agricultural products. |
| | 1 January 2031 for final elimination of all duties. |

**TABLE C-4: (continued)**
**MARKET ACCESS RULES FOR GOODS IN *CAFTA—DR* —**
**DEFERRED DUTY FREE (OR QUOTA FREE) TREATMENT**

| | |
|---|---|
| ***Implementation Date*** | 1 March 2006 (later date for Costa Rica and Dominican Republic) |
| ***Relevant Provisions*** | Article 3:3 and Annex 3:3 |
| ***Number of Staging Categories*** | 8 general staging categories — A, B, C, D, E, F, G, and H. |
| ***Tariff Elimination Methodology*** | Category A goods receive immediate duty-free treatment. |
| | Category B goods receive duty-free treatment in year 5 |
| | (*i.e.*, 5 years after the implementation date). |
| | Category C goods receive duty-free treatment in year 10 |
| | (*i.e.*, 10 years after the implementation date). |
| | Category D goods receive duty-free treatment in year 15 |
| | (*i.e.*, 15 years after the implementation date). |
| | Category F goods receive duty-free treatment in year 20 |
| | (*i.e.*, 20 years after the implementation date). |
| | Categories E, G, and H receive alternative treatment. |
| ***Maximum Tariff (or Quota) Phase Out Period*** | 20 years |
| ***Examples of Deferred Tariff (or Quota) Elimination*** | Appendix 3:3:6:4 covers General Exceptions from Tariff Treatment. |
| | This Appendix includes chicken (certain items under HS 0207), milk powder (HS 0402.10, 0402.21, and 0402.29), onions (HS 0703.10), garlic (HS 0703.20), beans (HS 0713.31, 0713.32, and 0713.33), coffee (certain items under HS 0901), rice (certain items under HS 1006), wheat flour (HS 1100.00), sugar (HS 1701.00, 1701.91, and 1701.99), beer (HS 2203), alcohol (HS 2207 and 2209), and tobacco (HS 2401.20, 2402.20, and 2403.10). |

**TABLE C-4: _U.S.—CAFTA—DR_ DEFERRALS, (continued)**

| | |
|---|---|
| | Note several of these product categories are staple items in the diets of people in the U.S. or Central America. |
| _Final Date for Elimination of All Tariffs (or Quotas)_ | 1 January 2027 |

TABLE C-4: (continued)
MARKET ACCESS RULES FOR GOODS IN *U.S.—BAHRAIN FTA —*
DEFERRED DUTY FREE (OR QUOTA FREE) TREATMENT

| | |
|---|---|
| ***Implementation Date*** | 1 August 2006 |
| ***Relevant Provisions*** | Chapter 2 |
| ***Number of Staging Categories*** | 3 general staging categories, plus 6 country-specific staging categories (4 for U.S. and 2 for Bahrain). |
| ***Tariff Elimination Methodology*** | Category A goods received immediate duty-free treatment (as of 1 August 2006). |
| | Category A embraces all meat goods, including pork and pork products (*e.g.*, meat and carcasses of swine, HS 0203, pig fat, HS 1501.00.30, and pork sausages, HS 1601), and cocoa and chocolates that include alcohol (HS 1806.31.10 and HS 1806.32.10). |
| | Category B goods received duty-free treatment in 10 years (effective 1 January 2017), with tariff elimination in 10 equal annual installments. |
| | Category C goods received duty-free treatment before the *FTA*, and continue to receive it. |
| | For certain goods, the U.S. has 4 additional country-specific staging categories. |
| | Bahrain has 2 additional country-specific staging categories. |
| | Bahrain reserves the right to regulate goods in Category H. Category H includes beer (HS 2203), wine (HS 2204), vermouth (HS 2205), spirits (HS 2207, except medical alcohol, which is in Category A), re-treaded automobile tires (HS 4012). |
| | Under Category I, duties remain at the base rates for years 1-9 (*i.e.*, the rates as of 1 January 2003), and are eliminated in year 10 (effective 1 January 2017). But, Bahrain may continue to prohibit importation of Category I goods. Category I goods include live swine (HS 0103), ivory (HS 0507.10.00), illicit drugs (cocoa leaf, HS 1211.30.00, cannibis, HS 1211.90.60, and opium extract, HS 1302.11.00, and hashish, HS 1302.19.10). |

**TABLE C-4:   *U.S.—BAHRAIN FTA* DEFERRALS, (continued)**

| | |
|---|---|
| ***Tariff Elimination Methodology, continued*** | Note:<br><br>(1) In their *FTAs* with the U.S., different Muslim countries treat some goods, the consumption of which Islamic Law (*Shari'a*) forbids (*i.e.*, *haram* goods) differently. For example, Oman, but not Bahrain, bans certain meat goods, including pork and pork products, chocolate containing cocoa and alcohol.<br><br>(2) Categories H and I cover other goods the consumption of which is forbidden under Islamic Law (*Shari'a*).<br><br>(3) Bahrain bans ivory and re-treated automobile tires under Category I, which Oman in its *FTA* with the U.S. grants immediate duty-free access. |
| ***Maximum Tariff (or Quota) Phase Out Period*** | 10 years |
| ***Examples of Deferred Tariff (or Quota) Elimination*** | For the U.S., quotas apply for 10 years to imports from Bahrain of beef, butter, cheese, cotton, liquid dairy, and milk powder, peanuts, sugar, and tobacco.<br><br>Note:<br><br>Bahrain does not export most of these products to the U.S. |
| ***Final Date for Elimination of All Tariffs (or Quotas)*** | 1 January 2017 |

TABLE C-4: (continued)

MARKET ACCESS RULES FOR GOODS IN *U.S.—OMAN FTA* —
DEFERRED DUTY FREE (OR QUOTA FREE) TREATMENT

| | |
|---|---|
| *Implementation Date* | 1 January 2009 |
| *Relevant Provisions* | Chapter 2 |
| *Number of Staging Categories* | 5 staging categories, plus country-specific staging categories (2 for Oman). |
| *Tariff Elimination Methodology* | Category A goods receive immediate duty-free treatment (as of 1 January 2007). |
| | Category B goods received duty-free treatment in 5 years (effective 1 January 2012), with tariff elimination in 5 equal annual installments. |
| | Category C goods received duty-free treatment in 10 years (effective 1 January 2017), with tariff elimination in 10 equal annual installments. |
| | Category D goods received deferred duty-free treatment, with tariff elimination in equal annual installments. |
| | Category E goods received duty-free treatment before the *FTA*, and continue to receive it. |
| | Oman has 2 additional country-specific staging categories. |
| | Oman reserves the right to regulate goods in Category H. Category H includes meat goods, including pork and pork products (*e.g.*, meat and carcasses of swine, HS 0203, pig fat, HS 1501.00.30, and pork sausages, HS 1601), chocolate containing cocoa and alcohol (HS 1806.31.10 and 1806.32.10), beer (HS 2203), wine (HS 2204), vermouth (HS 2205), and spirits (HS 2207, except medical alcohol, which is in Category A. |

**TABLE C-4:** *U.S.—OMAN FTA* **DEFERRALS, (continued)**

| | |
|---|---|
| *Tariff Elimination Methodology, continued* | Under Category I, duties remain at the base rates for years 1-9 (*i.e.*, the rates as of 1 January 2003), and are eliminated in year 10 (effective 1 January 2017). But, Oman may continue to prohibit importation of Category I goods. Category I goods include live swine (HS 0103), illicit drugs (cocoa leaf, HS 1211.30.00, cannibis, HS 1211.90.60, and opium extract, HS 1302.11.00, and hashish, HS 1302.19.10). |
| | Note: |
| | (1) In their *FTAs* with the U.S., different Muslim countries treat some goods, the consumption of which Islamic Law (*Shari'a*) forbids (*i.e.*, *haram* goods) differently. For example, Oman, but not Bahrain, bans certain meat goods, including pork and pork products, chocolate containing cocoa and alcohol. |
| | (2) Category A, as above, grants immediate duty free treatment to some products, whereas Bahrain places them in Categories H or I. Examples of such goods are ivory (HS 0507.10.00), re-treaded automobile tires (HS 4012). |
| | (3) Oman treats hops (HS 1302.13.00), an ingredient in beer, the consumption of which is forbidden in Islamic Law (*Shari'a*), as a Category A good. |
| | (4) Categories H and I cover other goods the consumption of which is forbidden under Islamic Law (*Shari'a*). |
| *Maximum Tariff (or Quota) Phase Out Period* | 10 year phase out period for remaining Omani tariffs on agricultural products. |

**TABLE C-4:** *U.S.—OMAN FTA* DEFERRALS, (continued)

| | |
|---|---|
| ***Examples of Deferred Tariff (or Quota) Elimination*** | 13% of agricultural products. <br><br> As with the *Bahrain FTA*, for the U.S., quotas apply for 10 years to imports from Oman of beef, butter, cheese, cotton, liquid dairy, and milk powder, peanuts, sugar, and tobacco. <br><br> Note Oman does not export most of these products to the U.S. |
| ***Final Date for Elimination of All Tariffs (or Quotas)*** | 10 years (1 January 2017) |

TABLE C-4:　(continued)
MARKET ACCESS RULES FOR GOODS IN *U.S.—PERU TPA* —
DEFERRED DUTY FREE (OR QUOTA FREE) TREATMENT

| *Implementation Date* | 1 February 2009 |
|---|---|
| *Relevant Provisions* | Chapter 2 and Annexes 2:18 and 2:3 |
| *Number of Staging Categories* | 6 staging categories — A, B, C, D, E, and F. |
| *Tariff Elimination Methodology* | Category A goods receive immediate duty-free treatment. |
| | Category B goods receive duty-free treatment in year 5 |
| | (*i.e.*, 5 years after the implementation date). |
| | Category C goods receive duty-free treatment in year 10 |
| | (*i.e.*, 10 years after the implementation date). |
| | Category D goods receive duty-free treatment in year 15 |
| | (*i.e.*, 15 years after the implementation date). |
| | Category E goods receive duty-free treatment in year 17 |
| | (*i.e.*, 17 years after the implementation date). |
| | Tariffs on goods in Category F received duty free treatment before the *TPA* and continue to receive it. |
| *Maximum Tariff (or Quota) Phase Out Period* | 17 years, but no phase out of TRQs on certain products, such as the U.S. TRQ on sugar imports. |

TABLE C-4:   *U.S.—PERU TPA* DEFERRALS, (continued)

| | |
|---|---|
| ***Examples of Deferred Tariff (or Quota) Elimination*** | 20% of U.S. exports of consumer and industrial products, and roughly one-third of U.S. exports of agricultural products. |
| | The U.S. maintains TRQs for certain types of condensed and evaporated milk (classified under HS 0402), certain kinds of cheese (classified under HS 0406 and 1901), and sugar and sugar-containing products. For example, for sugar and sugar containing products (*i.e.*, as with the *Colombia TPA*, certain items classified in HS 1701, 1702, 1704, 1806, 1901, 2101, 2103, and 2106), the U.S. TRQ accords duty-free treatment in year 1 to 9,000 metric tons of Peruvian sugar. The in quota threshold rises by 180 metric tons per year in perpetuity. In other words, the U.S. never phases out its sugar TRQ. |
| | The U.S. retains the right to impose an agricultural safeguard, triggered by volume (140% of the beef TRQ), on condensed and evaporated milk, and on cheese. |
| | Peru maintains TRQs, and retains the right to impose agricultural safeguards, based on a trigger volume (between 130% and 150% of the relevant TRQ) for certain beef products (classified under HS 0201 and 0202), chicken leg quarters (HS 0207.13.00, 0207.14.00, and 1602.32.00), rice (classified under HS 1006),certain milk powder products (classified under HS 0402), certain butter and dairy spreads (classified under HS 0405), and certain kinds of cheese (classified under HS 0406). |
| ***Final Date for Elimination of All Tariffs (or Quotas)*** | 1 January of year 17, but no free trade in sugar. |

## TABLE C-4:
## MARKET ACCESS RULES FOR GOODS IN *U.S.—COLOMBIA TPA* — DEFERRED DUTY FREE (OR QUOTA FREE) TREATMENT

| | |
|---|---|
| *Implementation Date* | 15 May 2012 |
| *Relevant Provisions* | Chapter 2 and Annexes 2:18 and 2:3 |
| *Number of Staging Categories* | 7 staging categories — A, B, C, D, E, F, G. |
| *Tariff Elimination Methodology* | Category A goods receive immediate duty-free treatment. |
| | Category B goods receive duty-free treatment in year 5 |
| | (*i.e.*, 5 years after the implementation date). |
| | Category C goods receive duty-free treatment in year 10 |
| | (*i.e.*, 10 years after the implementation date). |
| | Category D goods receive duty-free treatment in year 11 |
| | (*i.e.*, 11 years after the implementation date). |
| | Category E goods receive duty-free treatment in year 15 |
| | (*i.e.*, 15 years after the implementation date). |
| | Category F goods receive duty-free treatment in year 17 |
| | (*i.e.*, 17 years after the implementation date). |
| | Tariffs on goods in Category G received duty free treatment before the *TPA* and continue to receive it. |
| *Maximum Tariff (or Quota) Phase Out Period* | 19 year phase out period for Colombia's TRQ on American rice, 18 years for its TRQ on American chicken leg quarters, and 12 years for its TRQ on American corn. |
| | But, no phase out date for U.S. TRQ on sugar. |

TABLE **C-4:**   *U.S.—COLOMBIA TPA* DEFERRALS, **(continued)**

| *Examples of Deferred Tariff (or Quota) Elimination* | The U.S. maintains TRQs for condensed and evaporated milk, cheese, and sugar and sugar-containing products. For example, for sugar and sugar containing products (*i.e.*, as with the *Peru FTA*, certain items classified in HS 1701, 1702, 1704, 1806, 1901, 2101, 2103, and 2106), the U.S. TRQ accords duty-free treatment in year 1 to 50,000 metric tons of Colombian sugar. The in quota threshold rises by 750 metric tons per year in perpetuity. In other words, the U.S. never phases out its sugar TRQ. |
|---|---|
| | The U.S. retains the right to impose an agricultural safeguard, triggered by volume (140% of the beef TRQ), on certain beef products (classified under HS 0201 and 0202). |
| | Colombia maintains TRQs, and retains the right to impose agricultural safeguards, based on a trigger volume (between 120% and 140% of the relevant TRQ) for certain beef products (classified under HS 0201 and 0202), spent fowl, *i.e.*, chickens (HS 0207.11.00 and 0207.12.00), chicken leg quarters (HS 0207.13.00, 0207.14.00, and 1602.32.00), dried beans (classified under 0713.33), and rice (classified under HS 1006). |
| *Final Date for Elimination of All Tariffs (or Quotas)* | For consumer and industrial products, 10 years from implementation date. |
| | For agricultural products, 19 years for last Colombian TRQ to be eliminated (on rice). |
| | No free trade in sugar. |

TABLE C-4:<br>
MARKET ACCESS RULES FOR GOODS IN <i>U.S.—PANAMA FTA</i> —<br>
DEFERRED DUTY FREE (OR QUOTA FREE) TREATMENT

| | |
|---|---|
| *Implementation Date* | 2012-2013 |
| *Relevant Provisions* | |
| *Number of Staging Categories* | |
| *Tariff Elimination Methodology* | On consumer and industrial exported by U.S. to Panama, nearly 90% receive immediate duty-free treatment, with remaining Panamanian tariffs eliminated over 10 years. |
| *Maximum Tariff (or Quota) Phase Out Period* | 10 years |
| *Examples of Deferred Tariff (or Quota) Elimination* | |
| *Final Date for Elimination of All Tariffs (or Quotas)* | |

## TABLE C-4:
## MARKET ACCESS RULES FOR GOODS IN *KOREA.—U.S. FTA (KORUS)* — DEFERRED DUTY FREE (OR QUOTA FREE) TREATMENT

| | |
|---|---|
| ***Implementation Date*** | 15 March 2012 |
| ***Relevant Provisions*** | February 2011 *Supplemental Agreement* |
| ***Number of Staging Categories*** | |
| ***Tariff Elimination Methodology*** | On agricultural exports, over $1 billion worth of American farm products receive immediate duty-free treatment. |
| | 2-year tariff phase out period applies to avocados, dried prunes, lemons, and sunflower seeds. |
| | 5-year tariff phase out period applies to alfalfa (and other fodder and forage), breads and pastry, chocolate, chocolate confectionary, dried mushrooms, food preparations, grapefruit, sauces and preparations, sweet corn. |
| | Korea expands tariff rate quotas (TRQs) over time on apples, barley, beef, cheese, dextrins and modified starches, grapes, oranges, pears, popcorn, pork, skim and whole milk powder, soybeans for food use, whey for food use |
| | Most remaining tariffs and quotas are phased out over the first 10 years of *KORUS* implementation. |
| | Korea phases out its 40% tariff on beef over 15 years. |
| | However, rice excluded entirely from *KORUS*, and Korea made no commitment on sanitary and phytosanitary (SPS) measures in respect of U.S. beef. |

**TABLE C-4:  *KORUS* DEFERRALS, (continued)**

| Tariff Elimination Methodology, continued | In April 2008, a *Beef Import Protocol* signed by U.S. Trade Representative (USTR) and Korea, followed by an exchange of side letters, called for immediate access of U.S. beef from cattle of 30 months of age or less to the Korean market, allowed Korea to exclude certain additional cattle parts, and clarified the right of Korea to protect the health of its citizens. The U.S. Department of Agriculture (USDA) agreed to monitor a voluntary agreement by American beef exporters that they would ship to Korea only beef from cattle of less than 30 months age. |
| --- | --- |
| | Massive public protests erupted in Korea over the *Protocol*, thus delaying its implementation. As of February 2011, this *Protocol* was not satisfactory to certain Congressional officials, including Senate Finance Committee Chairman Max Baucus (Democrat—Montana), who demanded Korea re-open fully its market to all American beef. |
| | On consumer and industrial products, 95% of bilateral trade is duty-free within 3 years of the entry into force of *KORUS*. Most remaining tariffs are eliminated within 10 years. |
| | Initially, Korea agreed to drop its tariff of 8% on 2 of the 3 major categories of auto imports drops to zero immediately (covering priority U.S. passenger vehicles and trucks), but on the third category is phased out. |
| | As of April 2009, these auto provisions remained unsatisfactory to certain Congressional officials, including Representative Carl Levin (Democrat—Michigan), Chairman of the Trade Subcommittee of the House Ways and Means Committee. Political pressure from him, other Congressmen and Senators, and the U.S. auto industry forced the U.S. to re-open *KORUS* negotiations. |

TABLE C-4:   *KORUS* DEFERRALS, (continued)

| | |
|---|---|
| | In December 2010, the U.S. and Korea negotiated a *Supplemental Auto Agreement*, along with an agreement on fuel economy and $CO_2$ emission standards for motor vehicles, which they signed in February 2011. The *Supplemental Auto Agreement* took the form of an exchange of letters between the U.S. Trade Representative and Korean Trade Minister, and the accord on fuel economy and emission standards took the form of *Agreed Minutes*. |
| | Under the original *KORUS* terms, the U.S. agreed to phase out over 10 years its 2.5% tariff on cars with small engines, and 25% truck tariff, on Korean vehicles (beginning with small-engine capacity cars). Under the January-February 2011 *Supplemental Auto Agreement*, the U.S. agreed to end its 2.5% car tariff after 5 years (*i.e.*, to eliminate the 2.5% duty at the end of the fifth implementation year), and to begin phasing out its 25% truck tariff after 7 years (*i.e.*, to begin the phase out in the 8th implementation year). This agreement took the form of a modification to *KORUS* Article 2:3(2) and Annex 2-B. |
| | In exchange, Korea agreed to the following points: |
| | (1) Allowing in annually up to 75,000 American cars that meet U.S., rather than Korean, safety standards, and to ensure new environmental standards for cars proposed by Korea in the prior 3 years would not become *de facto* tariff barriers. |

TABLE C-4: *KORUS* DEFERRALS, (continued)

| *Tariff Elimination Methodology, continued* | (2) Cutting its 8% car tariff not to zero immediately, but rather to 4% immediately, and then to zero after 5 years (*i.e.*, as of 1 January 2016). In contrast, under the *Korea—EU FTA*, which took effect in July 2011, Korea phased out its 2-6% duties on European cars gradually over 4 years. Therefore, the *Supplemental Agreement* removed what would have been a margin of preference for American vis-à-vis European cars of zero versus 2-6% in years 1 through 4. And, near the end of year 5, Korean tariffs on American cars will be higher than those on European ones (because American cars will face a 4% duty until after year 5). This agreement took the form of a modification to *KORUS* Article 2:3(2) and Annex 2-B. |
|---|---|
| | (3) Certain rules on transparency. |
| | (4) Special procedures for a motor vehicle safeguard under the *KORUS* Chapter 10 bilateral safeguard. |
| | (5) Accelerated implementation of certain pharmaceutical product provisions in *KORUS* Chapter 18, Article 18:5(b). |
| | (6) A 2-year delay, to 1 January 2016 (instead of 1 January 2014), to eliminate tariffs on pork. Yet, under the *Korea—Chile FTA*, Chilean pork enters the Korean market with lower duties than American pork has under the revised *KORUS* deal. |
| | Under the original *KORUS* terms and the *Supplemental Agreement*, the rule of origin for autos is the same: 35% value added, *i.e.*, 35% American or Korean content. Further, Korea may continue to grant duty drawback to Korean producers on auto parts (*e.g.*, steel, tires) they import from China (or any other countries) and use in the production of cars they export duty-free under *KORUS* to the U.S. |

**TABLE C-4:** *KORUS* DEFERRALS, (continued)

| | |
|---|---|
| ***Maximum Tariff (or Quota) Phase Out Period*** | 15 years |
| ***Examples of Deferred Tariff (or Quota) Elimination*** | Beef (15 years) |
| ***Final Date for Elimination of All Tariffs (or Quotas)*** | Approximately 2027 |

## TABLE C-5:
## MARKET ACCESS RULES FOR SERVICES IN UNITED STATES FTAS

### *(FTAs listed chronologically by Implementation Date)*

| FTA, Implementation Date, and Relevant Services Provisions | Service Sectors and Sub-Sectors with Liberalized versus Deferred Access, and Reservations |
|---|---|
| **Israel** <br><br> 30 August 1985 <br><br> Article 16 | None. FTA does not cover services. <br><br> Article 16 covers services, albeit in a skeletal way. It calls for the Parties to agree "to develop a means for cooperation on trade in services pursuant to the provisions of a *Declaration* to be made by the Parties." But, there is no Negative List Annex that lays out the services sectors to which trade liberalization obligations would not apply. |
| **Canada** <br><br> 1 January 1989 <br><br> Chapters 14-15 | Temporary entry for business persons (Mode IV delivery) facilitated. <br><br> Deferred access for financial, legal services. |
| **NAFTA** <br><br> 1 January 1994 <br><br> Chapter 12-14 | Substantial liberalization. <br><br> Deferred access for energy distribution, financial, and legal services. <br><br> The U.S. strictly limits or forbids foreign service provision of atomic energy, aviation (*e.g.*, running a domestic airline), fisheries, maritime matters (including salvage), and telecommunications. |
| **Jordan** <br><br> 17 December 2001 <br><br> Article 3, Annex 3:1 (services side letter and *GATS* Article V) | U.S. service markets generally were open to Jordan before *FTA*. <br><br> Under the *FTA*, the U.S. liberalized Mode IV services access (temporary movement of persons) by permitting Jordanian national (plus souse and children) to enter U.S. as non-immigrant, if entry is solely to carry on substantial trade or develop a business in which the national invests substantial capital. <br><br> Under the *FTA*, Jordan opened service markets such as business, communications, construction and engineering, distribution, education, energy distribution, environment, finance, health, printing and publishing, recreation, tourism, transportation. |

## TABLE (continued)

| FTA, Implementation Date, and Relevant Services Provisions | Service Sectors and Sub-Sectors with Liberalized versus Deferred Access, and Reservations |
|---|---|
| | Both U.S. and Jordan defer access for financial and legal services. |
| **Singapore** 1 January 2004 Chapters 8-10 | The U.S. grants substantial market access in most services markets to Singaporean providers. The U.S. strictly limits or forbids foreign service provision of atomic energy, aviation (*e.g.*, running a domestic airline), fisheries, maritime matters (including salvage), and telecommunications. Singapore grants substantial market access in all service markets, with few exceptions, to U.S. providers. The exceptions include certain air services (*e.g.*, participation in domestic air services) and banking services (*e.g.*, board of director composition, number of customer service locations, and the number and locations of ATMs). On Mode IV, Singapore created separate categories of entry for businesspersons to engage temporarily in a wide range of activities. They may enter Singapore without a labor market test. There are Side Letters on Financial Services, Legal Services, Temporary Entry, and Telecommunications. The Singapore Side Letter on Temporary Entry, concerning Mode IV, specifies a minimum salary threshold for businesspersons to be exempt from the labor market test. |
| **Chile** 1 January 2004 Chapters 11-13, and associated Annexes | Chile committed to a Negative List approach, providing substantial market access in virtually all service sectors, with very few exceptions. Liberalization through Modes I (cross-border supply), III (FDI), and IV (temporary migration of persons). On Mode IV, entry facilitated for business visitors, traders, investors, intra-company transferees, and professionals. For example, U.S. established a special *FTA* visa for a limited number of persons, capped annually, holding a 4-year degree. |

TABLE **(continued)**

| FTA, Implementation Date, and Relevant Services Provisions | Service Sectors and Sub-Sectors with Liberalized versus Deferred Access, and Reservations |
|---|---|
| | However, in Annex III, Chile imposes a kind of financial capital control. Essentially, capital of a foreign capital investment fund may not be remitted overseas until 5 years after the date on which that capital was contributed. |
| **Australia** <br><br> 1 January 2005 <br><br> Chapters 10, 12-13 | Generally open access, with a small number of explicitly excluded service sectors. <br><br> National and MFN treatment for all service sectors not explicitly excluded. <br><br> Local presence requirements prohibited. |
| **Morocco** <br><br> 1 January 2006 <br><br> Chapters 11-13 | Following a Negative List approach, Morocco opened its service markets to U.S. providers, with very few exceptions. Morocco's commitments go beyond the WTO *General Agreement on Trade in Services* (*GATS*), *i.e.*, they are "*GATS* Plus." The principal exceptions are financial services, where Morocco maintains certain restrictions on U.S. service providers. |
| **CAFTA—DR** <br><br> 1 March 2006 (later date for Costa Rica and Dominican Republic) <br><br> Annex I plus country-specific Side Letters | The U.S. strictly limits or forbids foreign service provision of atomic energy, aviation (*e.g.*, running a domestic airline), fisheries, maritime matters (including salvage), and telecommunications. <br><br> Some Central American countries, and the Dominican Republic, impose limitations on real estate ownership by foreigners within a specified number of kilometers of a national border. <br><br> Costa Rica includes the following reservations: <br><br> (1) State control is required of lottery and liquor licenses. <br><br> (2) Limits on ownership of local newspapers, radio, and TV. <br><br> (3) Government ownership is required of airports, docks, and railroads. <br><br> (4) Limits on activities in free zone activity. <br><br> (5) Tour guides must be Costa Rican nationals. <br><br> (6) Limits on hydrocarbon exploration. |

**TABLE (continued)**

| FTA, Implementation Date, and Relevant Services Provisions | Service Sectors and Sub-Sectors with Liberalized versus Deferred Access, and Reservations |
|---|---|
| *CAFTA—DR, continued* | (7) Limits on foreign professionals in accounting, architecture, dentistry, education, law, medicine, and scientific research. |
| | Dominican Republic includes the following reservations: |
| | (1) Limits on public utilities (especially electricity). |
| | (2) Limits on ownership of local newspapers, radio, and TV, and local cultural content requirements. |
| | (3) Limits on air transport services. |
| | (4) Geographic restrictions on pharmaceutical establishments (drug stores, pharmacies, and labs must be 500 meters from one another). |
| | (5) Limits on mining. |
| | (6) Limits on foreign professionals in accounting, architecture, dentistry, education, law, medicine, and scientific research. |
| | Guatemala includes the following reservations: |
| | (1) Limits on air transport services. |
| | (2) Limits on foreign ownership of land. |
| | (3) Only Guatemalan citizens can access forestry resources. |
| | (4) Geographic restrictions on gas stations (must be 600 meters from one another in urban areas, and 10 kilometers from one another in rural areas). |
| | (5) Tour guides must be Guatemalan nationals. |
| | (6) Limits on foreign professionals in accounting, architecture, dentistry, education, law, medicine, notarization, performing arts and scientific research. |
| | Honduras includes the following reservations: |
| | (1) State control is required of lottery and utilities (especially electricity and water). |
| | (2) Only Honduran citizens (by birth) may own casinos. |

TABLE (continued)

| FTA, Implementation Date, and Relevant Services Provisions | Service Sectors and Sub-Sectors with Liberalized versus Deferred Access, and Reservations |
|---|---|
| CAFTA—DR, continued | (3) Limits on ownership and management of local newspapers, radio, and TV. |
| | (4) Foreign governments are barred from telecommunications services. |
| | (5) Limits on air transport. |
| | (6) Limits on construction and petroleum services. |
| | (7) Limits on foreign professionals in accounting, architecture, dentistry, education, law, medicine, musicians, notarization, and scientific research, and on the number of foreigners on a Honduran soccer team. |
| | Nicaragua includes the following reservations: |
| | (1) State control is required of lottery and liquor licenses. |
| | (2) Limits on licenses for radio and TV stations. |
| | (3) Limits on air services, and domestic land transport services. |
| | (4) Limits on activities in free zone activity. |
| | (5) Tour guides must be Nicaraguan nationals. |
| | (6) Limits on hydrocarbon research and mineral exploration. |
| | (7) Limits on foreign professionals in accounting, architecture, cartography, dentistry, education, law, medicine, musicians, notarization, and scientific research. |
| | El Salvador includes the following reservations: |
| | (1) Limits on ownership of local newspapers, radio, and TV, and local content requirements for advertising and programming. |
| | (2) Limits on air transport services. |
| | (3) Limits on foreign ownership of rural land. |
| | (4) Geographic restrictions on gas stations (must be 600 meters from one another in urban areas, and 10 kilometers in rural areas). |

TABLE (continued)

| FTA, Implementation Date, and Relevant Services Provisions | Service Sectors and Sub-Sectors with Liberalized versus Deferred Access, and Reservations |
|---|---|
| | (5) Taxation of foreign circuses. |
| | (6) Limits on foreign professionals in accounting, architecture, dentistry, education, law, medicine, and notarization, scientific research. |
| **Bahrain** <br> 1 August 2006 | The U.S. grants substantial market access in most services markets to Bahraini providers. |
| | The U.S. strictly limits or forbids foreign service provision of atomic energy, aviation (*e.g.*, running a domestic airline), fisheries, maritime matters (including salvage), and telecommunications. |
| Chapters 11-12, 14 | Bahrain grants substantial market access in virtually all services markets to U.S. providers, with several exceptions. |
| | The exceptions include: |
| | (1) Finance. |
| | (2) Port and customs services. |
| | (3) Legal services (*e.g.*, foreigners are limited to 70% ownership of a Bahraini law firm). |
| | (4) Utilities (especially electricity, petrol, and water). |
| | (5) Real estate (*e.g.*, ownership restrictions). |
| | (6) Telecommunications. |
| | The exceptions also include matters related to Islamic Law (*Sharī'a*). namely, *Hajj* and *'Umrah* services, and gambling, which Bahrain prohibits in a Side Letter. |
| **Oman** <br> 1 January 2009 <br> Chapters 11-13 | The U.S. grants substantial market access in most services markets to Omani providers. |
| | The U.S. strictly limits or forbids foreign service provision of atomic energy, aviation (*e.g.*, running a domestic airline), customs brokerage services (which are restricted to U.S. citizens), fisheries, maritime matters (including salvage), patent attorney or agency services, radio licenses, telecommunications, technology exportation, trading on U.S. securities exchanges. |

TABLE (continued)

| FTA, Implementation Date, and Relevant Services Provisions | Service Sectors and Sub-Sectors with Liberalized versus Deferred Access, and Reservations |
|---|---|
| | Oman grants substantial market access in virtually all services markets to U.S. providers, with several exceptions. |
| | The exceptions include: |
| | (1) Employment placement. |
| | (2) Legal services (*e.g.*, foreigners are limited to 70% ownership of an Omani law firm). |
| | (3) Newspaper and book publishing. |
| | (4) Photographic services. |
| | (5) Real estate ownership (which is restricted) and real estate brokerage. |
| | (6) Radio and TV. |
| | Note in contrast to the *Bahrain FTA*, the *Oman FTA* contains no restrictions concerning services raising Islamic Law (*Shari'a*) issues. |
| *Peru*<br><br>1 February 2009<br><br>Chapters 11-12, 14, plus Side Letters | The *FTA* covers many sectors, including "landside" port functions whereby Peruvian companies can operate and maintain docks in the U.S., load and unload vessels, and clean ships. |
| | In a Side Letter, the U.S. government promises Peru it will review state laws (specifically, California, D.C., Florida, New Jersey, New York, and Texas) that restrict foreign participation in certain professional services (accounting, architecture, dentistry, engineering, law, medicine, nursing, and paramedical). |
| | The U.S. strictly limits or forbids foreign service provision of atomic energy, aviation (*e.g.*, running a domestic airline), fisheries, maritime matters (including salvage), and telecommunications. |
| | Peru includes the following reservations: |
| | (1) At least one bull fighter in a bullfighting event must be Peruvian. |
| | (2) Limits on ownership of local newspapers, radio, TV, and local cultural content requirements. |

## TABLE (continued)

| FTA, Implementation Date, and Relevant Services Provisions | Service Sectors and Sub-Sectors with Liberalized versus Deferred Access, and Reservations |
|---|---|
| | (3) Cinematographic prizes are restricted to Peruvian filmmakers. |
| | (4) Tax credits are available only to Peruvian publishers. |
| | (5) Limits on aviation and customs services. |
| | (6) Foreign ownership of land within 50 kilometers of the Peruvian border is forbidden. |
| | (7) Limits on archaeological research. |
| | (9) Limits on foreign professionals in accounting, architecture, dentistry, education, law, medicine, notaries, and scientific research. |
| *Colombia* <br> 15 May 2012 | The same Side Letter on state law review that associated with the *Peru TPA* accompanies the *Colombia TPA*. <br><br> The U.S. strictly limits or forbids foreign service provision of atomic energy, aviation (*e.g.*, running a domestic airline), fisheries, maritime matters (including salvage), and telecommunications. |
| Chapters 11-12, 14, plus Side Letters | Colombia includes the following reservations: <br><br> (1) Limits on utilities (*e.g.*, electricity) and telecommunications. <br><br> (2) Limits on FDI, which must be conducted through a foreign capital investment fund (*Fondo de Inversion de Capital Extranjero*). <br><br> (3) Limits on ownership of local movie theaters, political periodicals, radio, TV, and local cultural content requirements. <br><br> (4) Limits on air transport and port services, and foreign involvement in certain port cities is restricted. <br><br> (5) Tourism services must be provided by persons domiciled in Colombia. <br><br> (6) Limits on foreign professionals in accounting, architecture, dentistry, education, law, medicine, notaries, and scientific research. |

## TABLE (continued)

| FTA, Implementation Date, and Relevant Services Provisions | Service Sectors and Sub-Sectors with Liberalized versus Deferred Access, and Reservations |
|---|---|
| **Panama**<br><br>2012-2013 | Substantial market access, including by Panama in banking and financial services. |
| **Korea**<br><br>15 March 2012 | Overall, a Negative List approach to services trade liberalization.<br><br>Korea provides enhanced market access for audio-visual, e-commerce, and telecommunications services, including 100 percent ownership by U.S. firms of telecom operations in Korea.<br><br>Significant market access for express delivery services (with Korea agreeing to commitments on international delivery services and reform of domestic services), and for financial services (including national treatment for cooperatives selling insurance and Korea Post, and private insurers), as well as accounting, audio-visual (AV) and broadcasting (including 100 percent foreign ownership within 3 years of program providers by U.S. firms, reducing quotas on animation and film, increasing allowable content from a single country, and locking in current quotas applicable in other areas), education, environmental, health, maintenance and repair of equipment, research and development, services incidental to mining, telecommunications (including 100 percent U.S. ownership of telecom operations in Korea within 2 years of the effective date of *KORUS*, an increase from the 49 percent cap, a requirement that dominant phone companies provide cost-based interconnection and access to essential facilities, including submarine cable landing stations, and protections for technology choices by operators, particularly in respect of wireless technologies).<br><br>Korea also provides greatly enhanced market access for legal services, with market opening (for the first time) for American lawyers and law firms in 5 years from the date of entry into force of *KORUS*, through 3 stages. |

TABLE **(continued)**

| *FTA, Implementation Date, and Relevant Services Provisions* | *Service Sectors and Sub-Sectors with Liberalized versus Deferred Access, and Reservations* |
| --- | --- |
| *Korea, continued* | (Before *KORUS*, foreign law firms could not set up an office in Korea. The *Korean Attorney-At-Law Act* prevents a foreign attorney from provide counsel in Korea, even on the laws of the jurisdiction in which the attorney is licensed, unless that attorney passes the Korean Bar Examination (which is administered only in the Korean language) and registers with the Korean Bar Association. Consequently, foreign attorneys work in Korea as "Foreign legal Consultants," practice the law of their home jurisdictions, but ensure any final transaction is completed and approved by a Korean lawyer. *KORUS* does away with these strictures.)<br><br>Specifically, under *KORUS*, in Phase I (years 1 and 2), American law firms may open a branch office in Korea and offer legal advisory services on American or international, but not Korean, law. In Phase II (years 3 and 4), American law firms can work directly with Korean law firms on specific cases, and share profits and fees. In Phase III (year 5), American firms may establish a partnership or joint venture (JV) with Korean firms, and directly hire local Korean attorneys who have passed the Korean Bar Examination. In all likelihood, the ownership stake of an American firm in a partnership or JV will be limited to 49 percent, thereby ensuring Korean management control. |

## TABLE C-6:

## MARKET ACCESS RULES FOR GOVERNMENT PROCUREMENT IN UNITED STATES FTAS

*(FTAs listed chronologically by Implementation Date)*

| FTA, Implementation Date, and Relevant Government Procurement Provisions | Contract Value Thresholds for Eligibility for Government Procurement, and Scope of Coverage for Access to Government Procurement |
|---|---|
| **Israel**<br>30 August 1985<br>Article 15 | U.S. and Israel waived "Buy National" (*e.g.*, "Buy American) restrictions on contracts valued $50,000 or more for goods or services covered by 1979 GATT *Agreement on Government Procurement*. For defense purchases, both countries deferred by at least 1 year the waiver.<br><br>Following an amendment by the 1994 *Uruguay Round Agreements Act*, the $50,000 threshold applies to central government goods and services procurement contracts under the 1994 WTO *Agreement on Government Procurement*, if Israel reciprocally agrees. |
| **Canada**<br>1 January 1989<br>Chapter 13 | Exempts from *Buy American Act* restrictions goods from Canada covered by the 1979 GATT *Government Procurement Agreement* for contracts valued at U.S. $25,000 or more. |
| **NAFTA**<br>1 January 1994<br>Chapter 10 | Substantial liberalization, use of Negative List approach.<br><br>Government procurement rules apply to contracts for goods or services valued at U.S. $50,000 or more (U.S. $6.5 million for construction services) with federal government entities.<br><br>Government procurement rules apply to contracts for goods or services valued at U.S. $250,000 or more (U.S. $8 million for construction services) with federal government enterprises.<br><br>Government procurement rules apply to contracts for goods or services with state and provincial government entities, with values negotiated after entry into force. |

**TABLE (continued)**

| FTA, Implementation Date, and Relevant Government Procurement Provisions | Contract Value Thresholds for Eligibility for Government Procurement, and Scope of Coverage for Access to Government Procurement |
|---|---|
| **Jordan** <br> 17 December 2001 <br> Article 9 | The scope of government procurement rules under the *FTA* was deferred pending Jordan's accession to the WTO *Agreement on Government Procurement*. (Jordan applied to join this *Agreement* on 12 July 2000.) The *FTA* rules were to be negotiated separately, but with a view to Jordan's WTO commitments. |
| **Singapore** <br> 1 January 2004 <br> Chapter 13, Annex 13A | Singapore committed to a Negative List approach, thereby giving U.S. contractors non-discriminatory access unless specifically excluded. It also agreed to "WTO *Agreement on Government Procurement* Plus" monetary thresholds for U.S. contractors, *i.e.*, lower thresholds than in the *Agreement*, thereby expanding contracts with U.S. firms subject to *FTA* disciplines. <br><br> Annex 13A covers U.S. entities, and says: <br><br> (1) Government procurement rules apply to contracts for goods or services valued at U.S. $56,190 or more (U.S. $6.481 million for construction services) with federal government entities. <br><br> (2) Government procurement rules apply to contracts for goods or services with state government entities valued at U.S. $460,000 (U.S. $6.481 million for construction services). <br><br> (3) Government procurement rules apply to contracts for goods or services valued at U.S. $250,000 or more (U.S. $6.481 million for construction services) with quasi-federal government bodies (*e.g.*, enterprises and authorities). <br><br> (4) The U.S. adjusts these thresholds periodically in accordance with a formula articulated in the *FTA*. |

**TABLE (continued)**

| FTA, Implementation Date, and Relevant Government Procurement Provisions | Contract Value Thresholds for Eligibility for Government Procurement, and Scope of Coverage for Access to Government Procurement |
|---|---|
| | Annex 13 A also covers Singaporean entities, and says: <br><br> (1) Government procurement rules apply to contracts for goods or services valued at S$102,710 or more (S$11.376 million for construction services) with central government entities. <br><br> (2) Government procurement rules apply to contracts for goods or services valued at S$910,000 or more (S$ 11.376 million for construction services) with quasi-central government bodies (*e.g.*, enterprises and authorities). <br><br> (3) Singapore adjusts these thresholds periodically in accordance with a formula articulated in the *FTA*. |
| *Chile* <br> 1 January 2004 <br> Chapter 9 | Government procurement rules cover 20 Chilean central government and 13 regional government entities, 341 Chilean municipalities, 79 U.S. government entities, and 37 U.S. states. <br><br> Applies to national government procurement contracts for goods and services over $56,190, and construction services over $6,481,000. <br><br> Applies to contracts with state-owned enterprises (SOEs) for procurement of goods and services over $280,951 or $518,000, and construction services over $6,481,000. <br><br> Applies to contracts with Chilean sub-central governments, and U.S. states, for goods and services over $460,000, and construction services over $6,481,000. <br><br> Chilean ministries, and regional and municipal governments, must not discriminate against U.S. contractors, or in favor of Chilean firms. Chilean government procurement procedures must be transparent, and bribery is a criminal offense under Chilean (and U.S.) law. |

TABLE (continued)

| FTA, Implementation Date, and Relevant Government Procurement Provisions | Contract Value Thresholds for Eligibility for Government Procurement, and Scope of Coverage for Access to Government Procurement |
|---|---|
| **Australia**<br><br>1 January 2005<br><br>Chapter 15 | U.S. contractors have non-discriminatory rights to bid on Australian government procurement contracts for all major procuring entities. These entities include the Prime Minister and Cabinet, Departments of Communications, Defense, Information Technology and the Arts, Transport and Regional Services, and 31 administrative and public bodies such as the Australian Broadcasting Authority, Australian Nuclear Science and Technology Organization, and Reserve Bank of Australia.<br><br>Tendering procedures must be transparent, predictable, and fair, and bribery of procurement officials is a criminal or administrative offense. |
| **Morocco**<br><br>1 January 2006<br><br>Chapter 9 | U.S. contractors have access to procurements by 30 Moroccan central government entities, including the Prime Minister's Office, and the Ministries of Defense, Foreign Affairs, and Interior, plus 136 Moroccan administrative and public bodies, such as the National Office of Airports, National Office of Electricity, National Office of Potable Water, the National Railroad Office, and the Office of Ports Utilization. They also have access to procurements by Moroccan provinces and prefectures.<br><br>Government procurement thresholds apply to contracts for goods and services worth more than U.S. $175,000, or construction services worth more than $ 6,725,000.<br><br>Moroccan government purchasers must afford national treatment to U.S. contractors, and thus cannot discriminate against American in favor of Moroccan contractors, and they must adhere to transparent procurement procedures (*e.g.*, advance notice of purchases, timely and effective bid review procedures). |

## TABLE (continued)

| FTA, Implementation Date, and Relevant Government Procurement Provisions | Contract Value Thresholds for Eligibility for Government Procurement, and Scope of Coverage for Access to Government Procurement |
|---|---|
| **CAFTA–DR**<br><br>1 March 2006 (later date for Costa Rica and Dominican Republic)<br><br>Chapter 9 and Annex 9:1:2(b) (i), (ii), and (iii) | Three regimes exist (Article 9:1:2(b)) —<br><br>1st: Government procurement between the U.S. and each other *CAFTA* Party.<br><br>2nd: Government procurement among the Central American *CAFTA* Parties.<br><br>3rd: Government procurement between any Central American *CAFTA* Party, on the one hand, and the Dominican Republic, on the other hand.<br><br>For the 1st regime, for access into the U.S. market —<br><br>(1) Government procurement rules apply to contracts for goods or services valued at U.S. $58,550 or more (U.S. $6.725 million for construction services) with central government entities.<br><br>(2) Government procurement rules apply to contracts for goods or services with sub-central government entities valued at U.S. $ 477,000 (U.S. $6.725 million for construction services).<br><br>(3) Government procurement rules apply to contracts for goods or services valued at U.S. $250,000 or more (U.S. $6.725 million for construction services) with other covered entities (*e.g.*, quasi- governmental bodies).<br><br>(4) The thresholds are adjusted periodically in accordance with a formula articulated in *CAFTA*.<br><br>Also for the 1st regime, for access into the Central American *CAFTA* Parties and the Dominican Republic, but only for the first 3 years of the life of *CAFTA* for the purpose of giving protection to local government procurement providers, the following transitional thresholds apply —<br><br>(1) Government procurement rules apply to contracts for goods or services valued at U.S. $ 117,100 or more (U.S. $8 million for construction services) with central government entities. |

TABLE **(continued)**

| *FTA, Implementation Date, and Relevant Government Procurement Provisions* | *Contract Value Thresholds for Eligibility for Government Procurement, and Scope of Coverage for Access to Government Procurement* |
|---|---|
| | (2) Government procurement rules apply to contracts for goods or services valued at U.S. $650,000 or more (U.S. $8 million for construction services) with sub-central government bodies (*e.g.*, enterprises and authorities). |
| | (3) Government procurement rules apply to contracts for goods or services valued at U.S. $250,000 or more (U.S. $8 million for construction services) with other covered entities (*e.g.*, quasi-governmental bodies). |
| | (4) These thresholds are adjusted periodically in accordance with a formula articulated in the *FTA*. |
| | (5) After the first 3 years of *CAFTA*, the U.S. thresholds (as adjusted) apply. |
| | For the 2ⁿᵈ regime, for access into the market of another Central American *CAFTA* Party — |
| | (1) The same thresholds (as adjusted) that exist under the 1ˢᵗ regime between the U.S. and Central American *CAFTA* Parties apply. |
| | (2) For government procurement contracts below those thresholds, the national law of the Central American *CAFTA* Party applies. |
| | For the 3ʳᵈ regime, for access between the Central American *CAFTA* Parties and the Dominican Republic, the same rules as for the 2ⁿᵈ regime apply. |
| *Bahrain*<br>1 August 2006<br>Chapter 9 | Bahrain committed to a Negative List approach, thereby giving U.S. contractors non-discriminatory access unless specifically excluded. It also agreed to "WTO *Agreement on Government Procurement* Plus" monetary thresholds for U.S. contractors, *i.e.*, lower thresholds than in the *Agreement*, thereby expanding contracts with U.S. firms subject to *FTA* disciplines.<br><br>Annex 9-A-1 covers U.S. entities, and says:<br><br>(1) Government procurement rules apply to contracts for goods or services valued at U.S. $175,000 or more (U.S. $7,611,532 for construction services) with federal government entities. |

TABLE (continued)

| FTA, Implementation Date, and Relevant Government Procurement Provisions | Contract Value Thresholds for Eligibility for Government Procurement, and Scope of Coverage for Access to Government Procurement |
| --- | --- |
| | (2) Government procurement rules apply to contracts with quasi-federal government bodies (*e.g.*, enterprises and authorities) for goods or services valued at, depending on the body, U.S. $250,000 and $538,000 or more (U.S. $9,368,478 for construction services). |
| | (3) The U.S. adjusts (starting two years after the *FTA* entered into force) these thresholds periodically in accordance with a formula articulated in the *FTA*. |
| | No commitments are made for state government entities. |
| | Annex 9-A-1 also covers Bahraini entities, and says: |
| | (1) Government procurement rules apply to contracts for goods or services valued at U.S. $200,000 or more (U.S. $8 million for construction services) with central government entities. |
| | (2) Bahrain adjusts (starting two years after the *FTA* entered into force) these thresholds periodically in accordance with a formula articulated in the *FTA*. |
| ***Oman*** <br><br> 1 January 2009 <br><br> Chapter 9 and Annex 9 | Oman committed to a Negative List approach, thereby giving U.S. contractors non-discriminatory access unless specifically excluded. It also agreed to "WTO *Agreement on Government Procurement* Plus" monetary thresholds for U.S. contractors, *i.e.*, lower thresholds than in the *Agreement*, thereby expanding contracts with U.S. firms subject to *FTA* disciplines. |
| | Annex 9 covers U.S. entities, and says: |
| | (1) Government procurement rules apply to contracts for goods or services valued at U.S. $193,000 or more (U.S. $8,422,165 for construction services) with federal government entities. |

**TABLE (continued)**

| FTA, Implementation Date, and Relevant Government Procurement Provisions | Contract Value Thresholds for Eligibility for Government Procurement, and Scope of Coverage for Access to Government Procurement |
|---|---|
| | (2) Government procurement rules apply to contracts with quasi-federal government bodies (*e.g.*, enterprises and authorities) for goods or services valued at, depending on the body, U.S. $250,000 and $593,000 or more (U.S. $10,366,227 for construction services). |
| | (3) The U.S. adjusts (starting two years after the *FTA* entered into force) these thresholds periodically in accordance with a formula articulated in the *FTA*. |
| | No commitments are made for state government entities. |
| | Annex 9 also covers Omani entities, and says: |
| | (1) Government procurement rules apply to contracts for goods or services valued at U.S. $260,000 or more (U.S. $8,422,165 for construction services) with central government entities. |
| | (2) Oman adjusts (starting two years after the *FTA* entered into force) these thresholds periodically in accordance with a formula articulated in the *FTA*. |
| *Peru* <br> 1 February 2009 <br> Chapter 9 and Annex 9:1 | Annex 9:1 covers both U.S. and Peruvian entities, and says: |
| | (1) Government procurement rules apply to contracts for goods or services valued at U.S. $193,000 or more (U.S. $7.407 million for construction services) with central government entities. |
| | (2) Government procurement rules apply to contracts for goods or services valued at U.S. $526,000 or more (U.S. $7.407 million for construction services) with sub-central government entities. |
| | (3) Government procurement rules apply to contracts with other covered entities (*e.g.*, quasi-governmental bodies) for goods or services valued at, depending on the body, U.S. $250,000 and $593,000 or more (U.S. $7.407 million for construction services). |

**TABLE (continued)**

| FTA, Implementation Date, and Relevant Government Procurement Provisions | Contract Value Thresholds for Eligibility for Government Procurement, and Scope of Coverage for Access to Government Procurement |
|---|---|
| | (4) These thresholds are adjusted periodically in accordance with a formula articulated in the Peru *TPA*. |
| *Colombia* <br><br> 15 May 2012 <br><br> Chapter 9 and Annex 9:1 | Annex 9:1 covers U.S. entities, and creates nearly identical thresholds as the Peru *TPA*: <br><br> (1) Government procurement rules apply to contracts for goods or services valued at U.S. $64,786 or more (U.S. $7.407 million for construction services) with central government entities. <br><br> (2) Government procurement rules apply to contracts for goods or services valued at U.S. $526,000 or more (U.S. $7.407 million for construction services) with sub-central government entities. <br><br> (3) Government procurement rules apply to contracts with other covered entities (*e.g.*, quasi-governmental bodies) for goods or services valued at, depending on the body, U.S. $250,000 and $593,000 or more (U.S. $7.407 million for construction services). <br><br> (4) These thresholds are adjusted periodically in accordance with a formula articulated in the *FTA*. <br><br> Annex 9:1 also covers Colombian entities, setting out a transitional rule for the first 3 years of the life of the *FTA*, as follows: <br><br> The threshold for construction services is U.S. $8 million. The same U.S. levels apply for all other procurement contracts. |
| *Panama* <br><br> 2012–2013 | Substantial market access within defined thresholds. <br><br> U.S. firms seeking contracts associated with the $5.25 billion Panama Canal expansion project potentially benefit from government procurement mechanisms. |

Tᴀʙʟᴇ **(continued)**

| *FTA, Implementation Date, and Relevant Government Procurement Provisions* | *Contract Value Thresholds for Eligibility for Government Procurement, and Scope of Coverage for Access to Government Procurement* |
|---|---|
| *Korea* <br><br> 15 March 2012 <br><br> Annex 13-B, Section H, Chapter 17, Annex 17-A | Substantial market access within defined thresholds. <br><br> The U.S. waived the obligation of Korea to adhere to the plurilateral WTO *Government Procurement Agreement* (*GPA*), because Chapter 17 and Annex 17-A, which cover government procurement, provide for greater market access than does the *GPA*. In particular, *KORUS* prohibits a procuring entity from imposing as a condition for award of a contract that a bidder for the contract have been awarded a contract previously, or have work experience in the territory of that entity. In contrast, the *GPA* mandates only reciprocal opportunities in Korea, hence Korea could impose such a condition. |

## TABLE C-7:

## ECONOMIC PARTNERSHIP AGREEMENTS (EPAs) OF JAPAN

### (FTAs listed chronologically by Implementation Date)

| Issue Foreign Country (EPAs in Chronological Order, formal title) | Date EPA Entered into Force | Trade Coverage and Duty Reduction Phase In Rules | Important Issues Not Covered by EPA | Other Important Issues Covered by EPA |
|---|---|---|---|---|
| Japan — Singapore Economic Partnership Agreement<br><br>(Japan — Singapore EPA) | 30 November 2002 | **Goods:**<br>*Schedule of Singapore:*<br>Singapore eliminated customs duties on all originating goods of Japan as of the date of entry into force.[1]<br><br>*Schedule of Japan:*<br>Category A Goods:<br>Customs duties were eliminated as of the date of entry into force.<br><br>Category B Goods:<br>Customs duties were eliminated as of 1 April 2006.<br><br>Category C1 Goods: | Environment, Labor, Human Rights | |

---

[1] Japan — Singapore Economic Partnership Agreement, Annex 1, posted at, www.mofa.go.jp/region/asia-paci/singapore/jsepa-2.pdf.

**TABLE (continued)**

| Issue Foreign Country (EPAs in Chronological Order, formal title) | Date EPA Entered into Force | Trade Coverage and Duty Reduction Phase In Rules | Important Issues Not Covered by EPA | Other Important Issues Covered by EPA |
|---|---|---|---|---|
| | | The rate of customs duties was 2.8 percent as of the date of entry into force, and reduced annually in 8 equal installments from 2.8 percent to zero percent. Category C2 Goods: The rate of customs duties was 3.1 percent as of the date of entry into force, and reduced annually in 8 equal installments from 3.1 percent to zero percent. Category C3 Goods: The rate of customs duties was 3.9 percent as of the date of entry into force, and reduced annually in 8 equal installments from 3.9 percent to zero percent. Category D Goods: The rate of customs duties was 6.5 percent as of 1 January 2004, and reduced annually in 6 equal installments from 6.5 percent to zero percent. | | |

Japan may accord more favorable tariff treatment to the products provided for in its Schedule than that provided for in Column 3 of its Schedule.[2]

*Agriculture*:

Includes items whose tariff rates were previously conceded to zero in the Uruguay Round negotiations.

*Services:*

Positive List approach with sectoral exemptions.

Japan conceded 32 items (102 already covered in *GATS* Uruguay Round). Those items include distribution, education, and transportation.

Singapore conceded 77 items (62 already covered in *GATS* Uruguay Round negotiations) for a total of 139.

Chapter 7 of the *Japan — Singapore EPA* covers trade in services.

Chapter 7 and related Annexes set out specific exemptions from coverage.

For example, in respect of air transport services, the *Japan — Singapore EPA* does not apply to:

[2] *Japan—Singapore Economic Partnership Agreement*, Annex 1, *posted at*, www.mofa.go.jp/region/asia-paci/singapore/jsepa-2.pdf.

**TABLE (continued)**

| Issue Foreign Country (EPAs in Chronological Order, formal title) | Date EPA Entered into Force | Trade Coverage and Duty Reduction Phase In Rules | Important Issues Not Covered by EPA | Other Important Issues Covered by EPA |
|---|---|---|---|---|
| | | measures affecting traffic rights, or services directly related to the exercise of traffic rights, other than measures affecting: (a) aircraft repair and maintenance services; (b) selling and marketing of air transport services; and (c) computer reservation system services. Likewise, the *Japan — Singapore EPA* does not apply to cabotage in maritime transport services.[3] Japan's Schedule of Specific Commitments on Services is set out in Annex IVC.[4] Singapore's Schedule of Specific Commitment on Services also is in Annex IVC. Further details on commitments in specific sectors are set out in Annexes, particularly: | | |

| | | | | |
|---|---|---|---|---|
| | | Annex IVA: Financial Services<br>Annex IVB: Telecommunications Services<br>**Additional:**<br>**Technical Barriers to Trade — Inspection:**<br>A Mutual Recognition Agreement (MRA) requires only a domestic inspection prior to export on products such as electronics.[5] | Labor, Human Rights | **Environment:**<br>*Article 74:*<br>It is inappropriate to relax or derogate from domestic environmental measures to encourage investment. |
| *Japan - Mexico Economic Partnership Agreement* | 1 April 2005<br>*Amended:*<br>22 September 2011 | **Overall:**<br>Japan eliminated tariffs on 95 percent of goods.<br>Mexico eliminated tariffs on 44 percent of goods.[6] | | |

[3] *See Japan — Singapore Economic Partnership Agreement*, Chapter 7, *posted at*, www.mofa.go.jp/region/asia-paci/singapore/jsepa-1.pdf.
[4] *See Overview of Japan (JESPA)*, *posted at*, www.fta.gov.sg/fta_jsepa.asp?hl=7.
[5] *See* Hatakeyama Noboru, *A Short History of Japan's Movement to FTAs (Part 2)*, JOURNAL OF JAPANESE TRADE & INDUSTRY (January/February 2003), at 40.
[6] *See* John Nagel & Toshio Aritake, *Mexico, Japan Agree on Substantive Terms for Free Trade Pact, Economy Ministry Says*, 21 International Trade Reporter (BNA) 493 (18 March 2004).

**TABLE (continued)**

| Issue Foreign Country (EPAs in Chronological Order, formal title) | Date EPA Entered into Force | Trade Coverage and Duty Reduction Phase In Rules | Important Issues Not Covered by EPA | Other Important Issues Covered by EPA |
|---|---|---|---|---|
| (Japan — Mexico EPA) | | **Agriculture:** Japan eliminated tariffs on 43.9 percent of agriculture and fishery imports from Mexico, and lowered tariffs on 49.1 percent of agriculture and fishery imports. **Goods:** *Schedules in relation to Article 5:* *Section 1, General Notes* *Section 2, Schedule of Japan and Notes* *Section3, Schedule of Mexico and Notes* *Section 2 and Section 3 were amended by the Protocol Amending the Agreement between Japan and the United Mexican States for the Strengthening of the Economic Partnership.*[7] Below are the Categories of goods in *Section 1, General Notes.* Category A goods: Tariffs on originating goods were eliminated as of the date of entry into force. | | *Article 147:* Cooperation among Parties to promote environmental preservation, improvement, and sustainable development. |

Category B1 goods:

The most-favored nation (MFN) tariff as of 1 April 2003 was applied to originating goods as of the date of entry into force, and duty-free treatment was given as of 1 April 2006.

Category B2 goods:

Japan applied to originating goods a specific duty of 0.5 *yen* per kilogram, and Mexico applied an ad valorem duty of 2.6 percent, on the date of entry into force, and both countries granted duty free treatment as of 1 April 2010.

Category B4 goods:

Tariffs on originating goods were eliminated in 4 equal annual installments from the Base Rate to zero, beginning on the date of entry into force.

Category B5 goods:

Tariffs on originating goods were eliminated in 5 equal annual installments from the Base Rate to zero, beginning on the date of entry into force.

Category B6 goods:

Tariffs on originating goods were eliminated in 6 equal annual installments from the Base Rate to zero, beginning on the date of entry into force.

---

[7] *Protocol Amending the Agreement between Japan and the United Mexican States for the Strengthening of the Economic Partnership, posted at* www.mofa.go.jp/region/latin/mexico/agreement/pdfs/protocol1109e.pdf.

**TABLE (continued)**

| Issue Foreign Country (EPAs in Chronological Order, formal title) | Date EPA Entered into Force | Trade Coverage and Duty Reduction Phase In Rules | Important Issues Not Covered by EPA | Other Important Issues Covered by EPA |
|---|---|---|---|---|
| | | Category B7 goods: | | |
| | | Tariffs on originating goods were eliminated in 7 equal annual installments from the Base Rate to zero, beginning on the date of entry into force. | | |
| | | Category B8 goods: | | |
| | | Tariffs on originating goods were eliminated in 8 equal annual installments from the Base Rate to zero, beginning on the date of entry into force. | | |
| | | Category C goods: | | |
| | | Tariffs on originating goods were eliminated in 10 equal annual installments from the Base Rate to zero, beginning on the date of entry into force. | | |
| | | Category Ca goods: | | |
| | | Tariffs on originating goods were eliminated in 11 equal annual installments from the Base Rate to zero, beginning on the date of entry into force. | | |
| | | Category D goods: | | |

Beginning on the date of entry into force, tariffs on originating goods were the applied MFN rates as of 1 January 2004, and were eliminated tariffs in 6 equal annual installments from the Base Rate to zero, as of the first day of the 6$^{th}$ year of entry into force.

Category E goods:

Tariffs on originating goods were eliminated from the first day of the 11$^{th}$ year of entry into force.

Category P goods:

Tariffs on originating goods were reduced to the rate specified in the Note in the Schedule of each Party beginning on the date of entry into force.

Category Q goods:

Tariffs on originating goods are laid out in the terms and conditions in the Note in the Schedule of each Party.

Category X goods:

These goods are excluded from any reduction or elimination of tariffs.[8]

---

[8] *Japan — Mexico Economic Partnership Agreement*, Annex 1, *posted at* www.mofa.go.jp/region/latin/mexico/agreement/annex1.pdf.

**TABLE (continued)**

| Issue Foreign Country (EPAs in Chronological Order, formal title) | Date EPA Entered into Force | Trade Coverage and Duty Reduction Phase In Rules | Important Issues Not Covered by EPA | Other Important Issues Covered by EPA |
|---|---|---|---|---|
| | | **Services:** Positive List approach with sectoral exemptions. Chapter 8 of the *Japan — Mexico EPA* covers trade in services, and applied to: the supply of a service; the purchase or use of, or payment for, a service; the access to services offered to the public generally and the use of them, in connection with the supply of a service; and the presence in its Area of a service supplier of the other Party. Chapter 8 and related Annexes set out specific exemptions from coverage. For example, the *Japan — Mexico EPA* does not apply to: "financial services," as defined in Chapter 9; cabotage in maritime transport services, including navigation in inland waters; | | |

measures affecting traffic rights, or services directly related to the exercise of traffic rights, other than measures affecting:

(i) aircraft repair and maintenance services;

(ii) selling and marketing of air transport services; and

(iii) computer reservation system (CRS) services;

government procurement;

subsidies provided by a Party or state enterprise, including grants, government supported loans, guarantees and insurance;

measures pursuant to immigration laws and regulations;

services supplied in the exercise of governmental authority; and

measures of a Party with respect to a national of the other Party seeking access to its employment market, or employed on a permanent basis in that Party.[9]

Annex 13 sets out the Services covered by Japan.[10]

[9] *Japan — Mexico Economic Partnership Agreement*, Chapter 8, *posted at* www.mofa.go.jp/region/latin/mexico/agreement/agreement.pdf.

[10] Japan — Mexico Economic Partnership Agreement, Annex 13, *posted at* www.mofa.go.jp/region/latin/mexico/agreement/annex13.pdf.

**TABLE (continued)**

| Issue Foreign Country (EPAs in Chronological Order, formal title) | Date EPA Entered into Force | Trade Coverage and Duty Reduction Phase In Rules | Important Issues Not Covered by EPA | Other Important Issues Covered by EPA |
|---|---|---|---|---|
| | | **Additional — Auto and Steel Sectors:** Mexico fully liberalized tariffs on Japanese auto imports after 7 years, and abolished steel tariffs after 10 years. | | |
| **Japan — Malaysia Economic Partnership Agreement (Japan — Malaysia EPA)** | 13 July 2006 | **Goods:** *Schedules in relation to Article 19:* *Part 1, General Notes* *Part 2, Schedule of Japan and Notes* *Part 3, Schedule of Malaysia and Notes* Below are the Categories of goods in *Part 1, General Notes.* Category A goods: Tariffs on originating goods were eliminated as of the date of entry into force. Category B3 goods: Tariffs on originating goods were eliminated in 4 equal annual installments from the Base Rate to zero, beginning on the date of entry into force. | Labor, Human Rights | **Environment:** *Article 90:* A country shall not relax its domestic environmental measures to encourage investment. |

Category B4 goods:

Tariffs on originating goods were eliminated in 5 equal annual installments from the Base Rate to zero, beginning on the date of entry into force.

Category B5 goods:

Tariffs on originating goods were eliminated in 6 equal annual installments from the Base Rate to zero, beginning on the date of entry into force.

Category B6 goods:

Tariffs on originating goods were eliminated in 7 equal annual installments from the Base Rate to zero, beginning on the date of entry into force.

Category B7 goods:

Tariffs on originating goods were eliminated in 8 equal annual installments from the Base Rate to zero, beginning on the date of entry into force.

Category B9 goods:

Tariffs on originating goods were eliminated in 10 equal annual installments from the Base Rate to zero, beginning on the date of entry into force.

Category B10 goods:

Tariffs on originating goods were eliminated in 11 equal annual installments from the Base Rate to zero, beginning on the date of entry into force.

**TABLE (continued)**

| Issue Foreign Country (EPAs in Chronological Order, formal title) | Date EPA Entered into Force | Trade Coverage and Duty Reduction Phase In Rules | Important Issues Not Covered by EPA | Other Important Issues Covered by EPA |
|---|---|---|---|---|
| | | originating goods classified<br><br>Category B15 goods:<br><br>Tariffs on originating goods were eliminated in 16 equal annual installments from the Base Rate to zero, beginning on the date of entry into force.<br><br>Category P goods:<br><br>Tariffs on originating goods are provided in the terms and conditions in the note in each Country's Schedule.<br><br>Category Q goods:<br><br>Tariffs on originating goods are provided in the terms and conditions in the note in each Country's Schedule.<br><br>Category R goods:<br><br>Tariffs on originating goods are subject to negotiation under the terms and conditions in the note in the Schedule of Japan.<br><br>Category X goods: | | |

These goods are excluded from any commitment to reduce or eliminate tariffs, and from having to negotiate tariff cuts on them in the future.[11]

**Services:**

Positive List approach with sectoral exemptions.

Chapter 8 of the *Japan — Malaysia EPA* covers trade in services.

Chapter 8 and related Annexes set out specific exemptions from coverage.

For example, in respect of air transport services, the *Japan — Malaysia EPA* does not apply to:

measures affecting traffic rights, or directly related to the exercise of traffic rights, other than measures affecting:

(i) aircraft repair and maintenance services;

(ii) selling and marketing of air transport services; and

(iii) computer reservation system services;

Likewise, the *Japan — Malaysia EPA* does not apply to cabotage in maritime transport services;

subsidies provided by a Country or state enterprise, including grants, government supported loans, guarantees and insurance; and

[11] *Japan — Malaysia Economic Partnership Agreement*, Annex 1, *posted at*, www.mofa.go.jp/region/asia-paci/malaysia/epa/annex1.pdf.

**TABLE (continued)**

| Issue Foreign Country (EPAs in Chronological Order, formal title) | Date EPA Entered into Force | Trade Coverage and Duty Reduction Phase In Rules | Important Issues Not Covered by EPA | Other Important Issues Covered by EPA |
|---|---|---|---|---|
| | | measures affecting natural persons seeking access to the employment market of a Country, or regarding nationality, citizenship, or residence or employment on a permanent basis.<br><br>Annex 6 sets out the Schedule of Specific Commitments.[12] | | |
| *Japan - Brunei Darussalam Economic Partnership Agreement*<br><br>*(Japan — Brunei EPA)* | 31 July 2008 | ***Overall:***<br><br>The *Japan — Brunei EPA* consists of 11 Chapters that cover: Trade in Goods; Rules of Origin; Trade in Services; Investment, Energy, Cooperation; Improvement of Business Environment, Custom Procedures; General Provisions; Final Provisions; and Dispute Settlement.[13] | Labor, Human Rights | ***Environment:***<br><br>*Preamble*<br><br>*Article 71:*<br><br>It is inappropriate to relax or derogate from domestic environmental measures to encourage investment. |

| | |
|---|---|
| | *Article 93:*<br><br>The Parties shall minimize the harmful environmental impacts of their activities related to energy in its Area in pursuit of sustainable development. |
| | ***Goods***<br><br>*Schedules in relation to Article 16:*<br><br>*Part 1, General Notes*<br>*Part 2, Schedule of Japan and Schedule of Brunei*<br><br>Below are the Categories of goods in *Part 1, General Notes.*<br><br>Category A goods:<br><br>Tariffs on originating goods were eliminated as of the date of entry into force.<br><br>Category B3 goods:<br><br>Tariffs on originating goods were eliminated in 4 equal annual installments from the Base Rate to zero, beginning on the date of entry into force.<br><br>Category B5 goods:<br><br>Tariffs on originating goods were eliminated in 6 equal annual installments from the Base Rate to zero, beginning on the date of entry into force.<br><br>Category B7 goods:<br><br>Tariffs on originating goods were eliminated in 8 equal annual installments from the Base Rate to zero, beginning on the date of entry into force. |

---

[12] *Japan — Malaysia Economic Partnership Agreement*, Annex 6, *posted at* www.mofa.go.jp/region/asia-paci/malaysia/epa/annex6.pdf.

[13] Ministry of Foreign Affairs and Trade, Brunei Darussalam, *The Brunei — Japan Economic Partnership Agreement (BJEPA) posted at* www.mofat.gov.bn/index.php?option=com_k2&view=item&layout=item&id=339&Itemid=346.

**TABLE (continued)**

| Issue Foreign Country (EPAs in Chronological Order, formal title) | Date EPA Entered into Force | Trade Coverage and Duty Reduction Phase In Rules | Important Issues Not Covered by EPA | Other Important Issues Covered by EPA |
|---|---|---|---|---|
| | | Category B10 goods: Tariffs on originating goods were eliminated in 11 equal annual installments from the Base Rate to zero, beginning on the date of entry into force. Category B15 goods: Tariffs on originating goods were eliminated in 16 equal annual installments from the Base Rate to zero, beginning on the date of entry into force. Category R goods: Tariffs on originating goods were subject to negotiation between the Parties in the 5th year, unless otherwise agreed by the Parties. Category X goods: These goods are excluded from any commitment to reduce or eliminate tariffs, and from having to negotiate tariff cuts on them in the future.[14] | | |

***Services:***

Positive List approach with sectoral exemptions.

Chapter 6 of the *Japan — Brunei EPA* covers trade in services.

Chapter 6 and related Annexes set out specific exemptions from coverage.

For example, in respect of air transport services, the *Japan — Brunei EPA* does not apply to:

measures affecting traffic rights, or services directly related to the exercise of traffic rights, except measures affecting:

(i) aircraft repair and maintenance services;

(ii) selling and marketing of air transport services; and

(iii) computer reservation system (CRS) services;

The *Japan — Brunei EPA* also does not cover:

government procurement,

cabotage in maritime transport services;

measures affecting natural persons of a Party seeking access to the employment market of the other Party, or measures regarding nationality, or residence or employment on a permanent basis; and

[14] *Japan — Brunei Darussalam Economic Partnership Agreement*, Annex 1, *posted at* www.mofa.go.jp/region/asia-paci/brunei/epa0706/annex1.pdf.

**TABLE (continued)**

| Issue Foreign Country (EPAs in Chronological Order, formal title) | Date EPA Entered into Force | Trade Coverage and Duty Reduction Phase In Rules | Important Issues Not Covered by EPA | Other Important Issues Covered by EPA |
|---|---|---|---|---|
| | | subsidies provided by a Party or state enterprise, including grants, government-supported loans, guarantees and insurance.[15] Annex 7 sets out the Schedule of Specific Commitments.[16] | | |
| Japan — Chile Economic Partnership Agreement | 3 September 2007 | *Overall:* The *Japan — Chile* EPA covers: Trade and investment liberalization and facilitation; improvement of the business environment; entry and temporary stay of nationals for business purposes; intellectual property; competition; government procurement; technical barriers to trade (TBT); and sanitary and phytosanitary measures (SPS). | Labor, Human Rights | *Environment:* Preamble Article 87: It is inappropriate to relax or derogate from domestic environmental measures to encourage investment. |
| (Japan — Chile EPA) | | *Goods:* Schedules in relation to Article 14: Part 1, General Notes | | |

*Part 2, Schedule of Japan and Notes*

*Part 3, Schedule of Chile and Notes*

Below are the Categories of good for *Part 1, General Notes.*

Category A goods:

Tariffs on originating goods were eliminated as of the date of entry into force.

Category B5 goods:

Tariffs on originating goods were eliminated in 6 equal annual installments from the Base Rate to zero, beginning on the date of entry into force.

Category B7 goods:

Tariffs on originating goods were eliminated in 8 equal annual installments from the Base Rate to zero, beginning on the date of entry into force.

Category B10 goods:

Tariffs on originating goods were eliminated in 11 equal annual installments from the Base Rate to zero, beginning on the date of entry into force.

[15] Japan — Brunei Darussalam Economic Partnership Agreement, Chapter 6, *posted at* www.mofa.go.jp/region/asia-paci/brunei/epa0706/agreement.pdf.

[16] Japan — Brunei Darussalam Economic Partnership Agreement, Annex 7, *posted at* www.mofa.go.jp/region/asia-paci/brunei/epa0706/annex7.pdf.

**TABLE (continued)**

| Issue Foreign Country (EPAs in Chronological Order, formal title) | Date EPA Entered into Force | Trade Coverage and Duty Reduction Phase In Rules | Important Issues Not Covered by EPA | Other Important Issues Covered by EPA |
|---|---|---|---|---|
| | | Category B12 goods:<br><br>Tariffs on originating goods were eliminated in 13 equal annual installments from the Base Rate to zero, beginning on the date of entry into force.<br><br>Category B12* goods:<br><br>Tariffs on originating goods were eliminated according to the terms and conditions in the Note in the Schedule of Japan.<br><br>Category B15 goods:<br><br>Tariffs on originating goods were eliminated in 16 equal annual installments from the Base Rate to zero, beginning on the date of entry into force.<br><br>Category P goods:<br><br>Tariffs on originating goods were reduced according to the terms and conditions in the Note in the Schedule of each Party. | | |

Category Q goods:

Tariffs on originating goods were provided in the terms and conditions in the Note in the Schedule of each Party.

Category R goods:

Tariffs on originating goods are subject to negotiation according to the terms and conditions in the Note in the Schedule of each Party.

Category X goods:

These goods are excluded from any commitment to reduce or eliminate tariffs on them.[17]

**Services**

Positive List approach with sectoral exemptions.

Chapter 9 of the *Japan — Chile EPA* covers trade in services and includes measures affecting the:

(a) supply of a service;
(b) purchase or use of, or payment for, a service;

[17] *Japan — Chile Economic Partnership Agreement*, Annex 1, *posted at* www.mofa.go.jp/region/latin/chile/joint0703/annex.pdf.

**TABLE (continued)**

| Issue Foreign Country (EPAs in Chronological Order, formal title) | Date EPA Entered into Force | Trade Coverage and Duty Reduction Phase In Rules | Important Issues Not Covered by EPA | Other Important Issues Covered by EPA |
|---|---|---|---|---|
| | | (c) access to and the use of services offered to the public generally, including distribution, transport or telecommunications networks, in connection with the supply of a service; and <br><br> (d) presence in its Area of a service supplier of the other Party. <br><br> Chapter 9 and related Annexes set out specific exemptions from coverage. <br><br> For example, in respect of air transport services, the Agreement does not apply to: <br><br> measures affecting traffic rights, or directly related to the exercise of traffic rights, other than measures affecting: <br><br> (i) aircraft repair and maintenance services; <br><br> (ii) selling and marketing of air transport services; and <br><br> (iii) computer reservation system services;" <br><br> Furthermore, the *Japan — Chile EPA* does not apply to: | | |

| | | | | Environment: |
|---|---|---|---|---|
| | | | Labor, Human Rights | Article 111: It is inappropriate to relax or derogate from domestic environmental measures to encourage investment. |
| | "financial services," as defined in Article 128; cabotage in maritime transport services; government procurement; subsidies provided by a Party or state enterprise, including grants, government supported loans, guarantees and insurance; measures affecting natural persons of a Party seeking access to the employment market of the other Party, or measures regarding nationality or citizenship, or residence or employment on a permanent basis; and services supplied in the exercise of governmental authority.[18] | Overall: The Japan — Thailand EPA eliminates over 90 percent of tariffs over 10 years. | | |
| *Japan — Thailand Economic Partnership Agreement* | | 3 April 2007 | | |

[18] *Japan — Chile Economic Partnership Agreement*, Chapter 9, *posted at*, www.mofa.go.jp/region/latin/chile/joint0703/agreement.pdf.

**TABLE (continued)**

| Issue Foreign Country (EPAs in Chronological Order, formal title) | Date EPA Entered into Force | Trade Coverage and Duty Reduction Phase In Rules | Important Issues Not Covered by EPA | Other Important Issues Covered by EPA |
|---|---|---|---|---|
| (Japan — Thailand EPA) | | **Goods:** Schedules in relation to Article 18: Part 1, General Notes Part 2, Schedule of Japan and Notes Part 3, Schedule of Thailand and Notes Below are the Categories of goods in Part 1, General Notes. Category A goods: Tariffs on originating goods were eliminated as of the date of entry into force. Category B goods: Tariffs on originating goods were eliminated in annual installments according to the Schedule of each Party. Category P goods: Tariffs on originating goods are covered, where applicable, in the Note in the Schedule of each Party. | | Article 153: To enhance partnership the Governments of the Parties and the Parties shall promote cooperation in numerous fields, including the environment. |

Category Q goods:

Tariffs on originating goods are covered in the Note relating to tariff rate quotas (TRQs) in the Schedule of each Party.

Category R goods:

Tariffs on originating goods are subject to negotiation according to the Note in the Schedule of each Party.

Category X goods:

These goods are excluded from any commitment to reduce or eliminate tariffs, and from having to negotiate tariff cuts on them in the future.[19]

*Agriculture:*

Excludes rice and other sensitive products.

*Services:*

Positive List approach with sectoral exemptions.

Chapter 7 of the *Japan — Thailand EPA* covers trade in services.

Chapter 7 and related Annexes set out specific exemptions from coverage.

For example, in respect of air transport services, the *Japan — Thailand EPA* does not apply to:

[19] Agreement between Japan and the Kingdom of Thailand for an Economic Partnership, Annex 1, *posted at* www.mofa.go.jp/region/asia-paci/thailand/epa0704/annex1.pdf.

**TABLE (continued)**

| Issue Foreign Country (EPAs in Chronological Order, formal title) | Date EPA Entered into Force | Trade Coverage and Duty Reduction Phase In Rules | Important Issues Not Covered by EPA | Other Important Issues Covered by EPA |
|---|---|---|---|---|
| | | measures affecting traffic rights, or the exercise of traffic rights, other than measures affecting: (i) aircraft repair and maintenance services; (ii) selling and marketing of air transport services; and (iii) computer reservation system services. Furthermore, the *Japan — Thailand EPA* does not cover: cabotage in maritime transport services; subsidies or grants provided by a Party or a state enterprise, including government-supported loans, guarantees, insurance and any conditions attached to the receipt or continued receipt of such subsidies or grants; measures pursuant to immigration laws and regulations; | | |

measures affecting natural persons seeking access to the employment market of a Party, or measures regarding citizenship, residence or employment on a permanent basis; and government procurement.[20]

Annex 5 sets out the Schedule of Specific Commitments.[21]

Also, under the *Japan — Thailand EPA*, special visas are issued to Thai cooks to enable them to work in Japan.[22]

*Additional:*

The *Japan — Thailand EPA* includes coverage of protection of foreign direct investment (FDI) and intellectual property (IP).[23]

*Industrial:*

The *Japan — Thailand EPA* eliminated immediately tariffs on many Japanese steel products. It also abolished, during its first 5 years, tariffs on Japanese auto parts.

[20] *Agreement between Japan and the Kingdom of Thailand for an Economic Partnership*, Chapter 7, *posted at*, www.mofa.go.jp/region/asia-paci/thailand/epa0704/agreement.pdf.

[21] *Agreement between Japan and the Kingdom of Thailand for an Economic Partnership*, Annex 5, *posted at* www.mofa.go.jp/region/asia-paci/thailand/epa0704/annex5.pdf.

[22] Toshio Aritake, *Japan, Thailand Sign Economic Partnership Agreement Covering Cars, Steel, Farm Goods*, 24 International Trade Reporter (BNA) 519 (12 April 2007).

[23] Toshio Aritake, *Japan, Thailand Exchange Documents to Start Economic Partnership Pact Nov. 1*, 24 International Trade Reporter (BNA) 1433 (11 October 2007).

**TABLE (continued)**

| Issue Foreign Country (EPAs in Chronological Order, formal title) | Date EPA Entered into Force | Trade Coverage and Duty Reduction Phase In Rules | Important Issues Not Covered by EPA | Other Important Issues Covered by EPA |
|---|---|---|---|---|
| *Japan — Indonesia Economic Partnership Agreement* (*Japan — Indonesia EPA*) | 1 July 2008 | ***Overall:*** The *Japan — Indonesia EPA* calls for immediate duty-free treatment on approximately 92 percent of goods traded between Japan and Indonesia.[24] Specifically, 90 percent of Indonesia's exports to Japan are free of import duties and 93 percent of Japan's exports to Indonesia are free of import duties. ***Goods*** *Schedules in relation to Article 20:* *Part 1, General Notes* *Part 2, Schedule of Japan and Notes* *Part 3, Schedule of Indonesia and Notes* Below are the Categories of goods in *Part 1, General Notes.* Category A goods: Tariffs on originating goods were eliminated as of the date of entry into force. | Labor, Human Rights | ***Historic:*** Indonesia's first bilateral trade deal. ***Standards:*** Disagreement between the two countries was often about the quality standards of products, rather than tariffs.[25] ***Foreign Direct Investment:*** |

| | |
|---|---|
| Category B3 goods:<br><br>Tariffs on originating goods were eliminated in 4 equal annual installments from the Base Rate to zero, beginning on the date of entry into force.<br><br>Category B5 goods:<br><br>Tariffs on originating goods were eliminated in 6 equal annual installments from the Base Rate to zero, beginning on the date of entry into force.<br><br>Category B7 goods:<br><br>Tariffs on originating goods were eliminated in 8 equal annual installments from the Base Rate to zero, beginning on the date of entry into force. | Japan needs to invest more in Indonesia's manufacturing industry within the framework of the *EPA*.<br><br>*Environment:*<br><br>*Article 74:* |

[24] *See* Toshio Aritake, *Japanese Cabinet Decides to Put Japan-Indonesia EPA into Effect July 1*, 25 International Trade Reporter (BNA) 842 (5 June 2008);

[25] *Agreement between Japan and the Republic of Indonesia for an Economic Partnership*, Annex 1, *posted at* www.mofa.go.jp/region/asia-paci/indonesia/epa0708/annex1.pdf.

**TABLE (continued)**

| Issue Foreign Country (EPAs in Chronological Order, formal title) | Date EPA Entered into Force | Trade Coverage and Duty Reduction Phase In Rules | Important Issues Not Covered by EPA | Other Important Issues Covered by EPA |
|---|---|---|---|---|
| | | | | It is inappropriate to relax or derogate from domestic environmental measures to encourage investment. |
| | | Category B10 goods:<br><br>Tariffs on originating goods were eliminated in 11 equal annual installments from the Base Rate to zero, beginning on the date of entry into force.<br><br>Category B15 goods:<br><br>Tariffs on originating goods were eliminated in 16 equal annual installments from the Base Rate to zero, beginning on the date of entry into force.<br><br>Category P goods:<br><br>Tariffs on originating goods are provided in the terms and conditions in the note in the Schedule of each Party. | | *Article 102:* |

| | | The Parties shall minimize the harmful environmental impacts of their activities related to energy and mineral resources in its Area in pursuit of sustainable development. |
|---|---|---|
| | Category Q goods:<br><br>Tariffs on originating goods are provided in the terms and conditions in the Note in the Schedule of Japan.<br><br>Category R goods:<br><br>Tariffs on originating goods are subject to negotiations according to the terms and conditions in the Schedule of each Party.<br><br>Category X goods:<br><br>These goods are excluded from any commitment to reduce or eliminate tariffs, and from having to negotiate tariff cuts on them in the future.[26] | |

[26] *Agreement between Japan and the Republic of Indonesia for an Economic Partnership*, Chapter 6, *posted at* www.mofa.go.jp/region/asia-paci/indonesia/epa0708/agreement.pdf.

TABLE (continued)

| Issue Foreign Country (EPAs in Chronological Order, formal title) | Date EPA Entered into Force | Trade Coverage and Duty Reduction Phase In Rules | Important Issues Not Covered by EPA | Other Important Issues Covered by EPA |
|---|---|---|---|---|
| | | **Agriculture:** Indonesia's main agricultural and timber products face non-tariff and market-access barriers in Japan due to strict quality standards. **Services:** Positive List approach with sectoral exemptions. Chapter 6 of the *Japan — Indonesia EPA* covers trade in services. Chapter 6 and related Annexes set out specific exemptions from coverage. For example, in respect of air transport services, the *Japan — Indonesia EPA* does not apply to: measures affecting traffic rights, or directly related to the exercise of traffic rights, other than measures affecting: (i) aircraft repair and maintenance services; (ii) selling and marketing of air transport services; and | | |

(iii) computer reservation system services."

Furthermore, the *Japan — Indonesia EPA* does not cover:

cabotage in maritime transport services;

subsidies provided by a Party or state enterprise, including grants, government supported loans, guarantees and insurance;

measures affecting the movement of natural persons of a Party, unless otherwise provided in a Schedule of Specific Commitments in Annex 8;

measures affecting natural persons of a Party seeking access to employment market of the other Party, or measures regarding nationality, residence, or employment on a permanent basis; and

government procurement.[27]

Annex 8 sets out the Schedule of Specific Commitments.[28]

---

[27] *Agreement between Japan and the Republic of Indonesia for an Economic Partnership*, Annex 8, *posted at* www.mofa.go.jp/region/asia-paci/indonesia/epa0708/annex8.pdf.

[28] Eliswan Azly, Antara News, Indonesia, *Indonesia-Japan economic partnership agreement goes into effect tomorrow*, (1 July 2008), *posted at* www.bilaterals.org/spip.php?article12551.

**TABLE (continued)**

| Issue Foreign Country (EPAs in Chronological Order, formal title) | Date EPA Entered into Force | Trade Coverage and Duty Reduction Phase In Rules | Important Issues Not Covered by EPA | Other Important Issues Covered by EPA |
|---|---|---|---|---|
| **ASEAN 2008 Agreement on Comprehensive Economic Partnership among Member States of the Association of Southeast Asian Nations and Japan**<br><br>**(Japan — ASEAN EPA)** | Entered into force on 1 December 2008 for: *Japan, Singapore, Laos, Vietnam, and Myanmar*<br><br>Entered into force on 1 January 2009 for: *Brunei* | **Overall:**<br><br>The *Japan — ASEAN EPA* eliminates more than 90 percent of tariffs over 10 years.<br><br>**Goods:**<br><br>The *Japan — ASEAN EPA* contains 12 different Schedules, one for each country. The Categories of the goods differ from one country to the other, meaning the exact nature and timing of tariff phase-outs depends on the country.<br><br>Below are the Categories of goods in *Part 12, Schedule of Japan.*<br><br>Category A goods: | Labor, Human Rights | **Environment:**<br><br>*Article 53:* Parties shall explore and undertake economic cooperation activities in numerous fields, including the environment. |

| | |
|---|---|
| 1 February 2009: *Malaysia* | Tariffs on originating goods were eliminated as of the date of entry into force. Category B5 goods: |
| 1 June 2009: *Thailand* | Tariffs on originating goods were eliminated in 6 equal annual installments from the Base Rate to zero. Category B7 goods: |
| 1 December 2009: *Cambodia* | Tariffs on originating goods were eliminated in 8 equal annual installments from the Base Rate to zero. Category B10 goods: |
| No entry into force as of 1 October 2011: *Indonesia, Philippines* | Tariffs on originating goods were eliminated in 11 equal annual installments from the Base Rate to zero. Category B15 goods: |
| | Tariffs on originating goods were eliminated in 16 equal annual installments from the Base Rate to zero. |

**TABLE (continued)**

| Issue Foreign Country (EPAs in Chronological Order, formal title) | Date EPA Entered into Force | Trade Coverage and Duty Reduction Phase In Rules | Important Issues Not Covered by EPA | Other Important Issues Covered by EPA |
|---|---|---|---|---|
| | | Category C goods: Tariffs on originating goods applied the Base Rate from the date of entry into force. Category R goods: Tariffs on originating goods were reduced according to the terms and conditions in the Note in the Schedule of Japan. Category X goods: These goods are excluded from any tariff commitment.[29] **Agriculture:** Excludes rice and other sensitive products. **Services:** Chapter 6 of the *Japan — ASEAN EPA* covers trade in services. The Parties to the *EPA* agree to negotiate liberalizing trade in services among them. Ultimately, Chapter 6 will incorporate the results of any services trade liberalization.[30] | | |

| Japan — Philippines Economic Partnership Agreement (Japan — Philippines EPA) | 11 December 2008 | Overall: | Human Rights | Environment: |
|---|---|---|---|---|
| | | The Japan — Philippines EPA eliminates 90 percent of tariffs over 10 years; including agriculture and mineral exports, industrial goods, and labor mobility.[31] Japan excluded over 200 products, mostly agricultural and fisheries. The Philippines excluded rice and salt.[32] Goods: Schedules in relation to Article 18: Part 1, General Notes Part 2, Schedule of Japan and Notes Part 3, Schedule of the Philippines and Notes | | Article 102: It is inappropriate to relax or derogate from domestic environmental measures to encourage investment. Labor: |

[29] *Japan — ASEAN Economic Partnership Agreement*, Part 12, *posted at* www.mofa.go.jp/policy/economy/fta/asean/part12.pdf.

[30] *Japan — ASEAN Economic Partnership Agreement*, Chapter 6, *posted at* www.mofa.go.jp/policy/economy/fta/asean/agreement.pdf.

[31] Toshio Aritake, *Japan-Philippines Free Trade Agreement Goes Into Effect, Ends 90 Percent of Tariffs*, 25 International Trade Reporter (BNA) 1783 (18 December 2008).

[32] Emir M. Castro, *Landmark Japan-Philippines trade deal: a recap*, (9 January 2009) *posted at* www.bilaterals.org/article.php3?id_article=14181.

**TABLE (continued)**

| Issue Foreign Country (EPAs in Chronological Order; formal title) | Date EPA Entered into Force | Trade Coverage and Duty Reduction Phase In Rules | Important Issues Not Covered by EPA | Other Important Issues Covered by EPA |
|---|---|---|---|---|
| | | Below are the Categories of goods in *Part 1*, *General Notes*. | | *Article 103:* It is inappropriate to relax or derogate from domestic labor laws to encourage investment. Likewise, Parties will not waive or derogate from such labor laws in a way that would reduce adherence to the internationally recognized labor rights, to encourage investment. |

Category A goods:

Tariffs on originating goods were eliminated as of the date of entry into force.

Category B3 goods:

Tariffs on originating goods were eliminated in 4 equal annual installments from the Base Rate to zero, beginning on the date of entry into force.

Category B4 goods:

Tariffs on originating goods were eliminated in equal installments from the Base Rate to zero, beginning on the date of entry into force according to:

(i) The first and subsequent reductions occurred according to subparagraphs 6 (a) and (b); and

(ii) The final reduction occurred 1 January 2010.

Category B4* goods:

Beginning on the date of entry into force, tariffs on originating goods were the applied MFN rates as of 1 January 2004, and were eliminated on 1 January 2010.

Category B4**

Beginning on the date of entry into force, tariffs on originating goods were the applied MFN rates on 31 December 2003, and were eliminated the first day of the 5th year of entry into force.

**TABLE (continued)**

| Issue Foreign Country (EPAs in Chronological Order, formal title) | Date EPA Entered into Force | Trade Coverage and Duty Reduction Phase In Rules | Important Issues Not Covered by EPA | Other Important Issues Covered by EPA |
|---|---|---|---|---|
| | | Category B5 goods: Tariffs on originating goods were eliminated in 6 equal annual installments from the Base Rate to zero, beginning on the date of entry into force. Category B5* goods: Beginning on the date of entry into force, tariffs on originating goods were the applied MFN rates on 31 December 2003, and were eliminated in 5 equal annual installments from the Base Rate to zero. Category B5** goods: Beginning on the date of entry into force, tariffs on originating goods were the applied MFN rates on 31 December 2003, and were eliminated on the first day of the 6th year of entry into force. Category B7 goods: Tariffs on originating goods were eliminated in 8 equal annual installments from the Base Rate to zero, beginning on the date of entry into force. | | |

Category B10 goods;

Tariffs on originating goods were eliminated in 11 equal annual installments from the Base Rate to zero, beginning on the date of entry into force.

Category B10* goods:

Beginning on the date of entry into force, tariffs on originating goods were the applied MFN rates on 31 December 2003, and were eliminated in 10 equal annual installments from the Base Rate to zero.

Category B10** goods:

Beginning on the date of entry into force, tariffs on originating goods were the applied MFN rates on 31 December 2003, and were eliminated in 6 equal annual installments from the Base Rate to zero.

Category B15 goods:

Tariffs on originating goods were eliminated in 16 equal annual installments from the Base Rate to zero, beginning on the date of entry into force.

Category P goods:

Tariffs on originating goods are provided in the terms and conditions in the Note in the Schedule of each Party.

Category Q goods:

**TABLE (continued)**

| Issue Foreign Country (EPAs in Chronological Order, formal title) | Date EPA Entered into Force | Trade Coverage and Duty Reduction Phase In Rules | Important Issues Not Covered by EPA | Other Important Issues Covered by EPA |
|---|---|---|---|---|
| | | Tariffs on originating goods are provided in the terms and conditions in the Note in the Schedule of Japan.<br><br>Category S goods:<br><br>Tariffs on originating goods are provided in the terms and conditions in the Note in the Schedule of the Philippines.<br><br>Category R goods:<br><br>Tariffs on originating goods are subject to negotiations according to terms and conditions in the Note in the Schedule of each Party.<br><br>Category X goods:<br><br>These goods are excluded from any commitment to reduce or eliminate tariffs, and from having to negotiate tariff cuts on them in the future.[33]<br><br>*Services:*<br><br>Positive List approach with sectoral exemptions. | | |

Chapter 7 of the *Japan — Philippines EPA* covers trade in services.

Chapter 7 and related Annexes set out specific exemptions from coverage.

For example, in respect of air transport services, the *Japan — Philippines EPA* does not apply to:

measures affecting traffic rights, or directly related to the exercise of traffic rights, other than measures affecting:

(i) aircraft repair and maintenance services;

(ii) selling and marketing of air transport services; and

(iii) computer reservation system services."

Furthermore, the *Japan — Philippines EPA* does not cover:

cabotage in maritime transport services;

subsidies provided by a Party or state enterprise thereof, including grants, government supported loans, guarantees and insurance;

measures pursuant to immigration laws and regulations; and

33 *Agreement between Japan and the Republic of the Philippines for an Economic Partnership*, Annex 1, *posted at*, www.mofa.go.jp/region/asia-paci/philippine/epa0609/annex1.pdf.

**TABLE (continued)**

| Issue Foreign Country (EPAs in Chronological Order, formal title) | Date EPA Entered into Force | Trade Coverage and Duty Reduction Phase In Rules | Important Issues Not Covered by EPA | Other Important Issues Covered by EPA |
|---|---|---|---|---|
| | | measures affecting natural persons seeking access to the employment market of a Party, or measures regarding nationality, citizenship, residence, or employment on a permanent basis.[34] Annex 6 sets out Schedules of Specific Commitments.[35] | | |
| Agreement on Free Trade and Economic Partnership between Japan and the Swiss Confederation | 19 February 2009 | *Overall:* The *Japan — Switzerland EPA* eliminates tariffs on 99 percent of trade in goods over 10 years[36] This *EPA* includes, among other areas of coverage: a Place of Origin Certification System by independent certifiers (first time in a Japanese *EPA*), Services, Intellectual Property (IP), Relaxation of visas, and E-commerce[37] | Labor | *Environment:* *Preamble* *Article 9:* The Parties will promote trade in environmental products and environment — related services to support environmental protection and development goals. |

| (Japan — Switzerland EPA) | | **Goods:**<br>Schedules in relation to Article 15:<br>Appendix 1, Schedule of Japan and Notes<br>Appendix 2, Schedule of Switzerland and Notes |
| --- | --- | --- |

---

[34] *Agreement between Japan and the Republic of the Philippines for an Economic Partnership*, Chapter 7, *posted at* www.mofa.go.jp/region/asia-paci/philippine/epa0609/main.pdf.

[35] *Agreement between Japan and the Republic of the Philippines for an Economic Partnership*, Annex 6, *posted at* www.mofa.go.jp/region/asia-paci/philippine/epa0609/annex6.pdf.

[36] *Japanese-Swiss FTA takes effect*, (2 September 2009) *posted at* www.bilaterals.org/article.php3?id_article=15837.

[37] Toshio Aritake, *Japan-Swiss FTA to Enter into Force Sept. 1 Japanese Government Announces*, 26 International Trade Reporter (BNA) 1132 (20 August 2009).

**TABLE (continued)**

| Issue Foreign Country (EPAs in Chronological Order, formal title) | Date EPA Entered into Force | Trade Coverage and Duty Reduction Phase In Rules | Important Issues Not Covered by EPA | Other Important Issues Covered by EPA |
|---|---|---|---|---|
| | | Below are the Categories of goods indicated in Column 4 in *Appendix 1, Schedule of Japan.* | | *Article 101:* |
| | | Category A goods: | | It is inappropriate to relax or derogate from domestic environmental measures to encourage investment. |
| | | Tariffs on originating goods were eliminated as of the date of entry into force. | | |
| | | Category B3 goods: | | |
| | | Tariffs on originating goods were eliminated in 4 equal annual installments from the Base Rate to zero. | | |
| | | Category B5 goods: | | |

***Labour:***

*Article 101:*

It is inappropriate to lower or derogate from domestic labour standards to encourage investment.

Tariffs on originating goods were eliminated in 6 equal annual installments from the Base Rate to zero.

Category B7 goods:

Tariffs on originating goods were eliminated in 8 equal annual installments from the Base Rate to zero.

Category B9 goods:

Tariffs on originating goods were eliminated in 10 equal annual installments from the Base Rate to zero.

Category B10 goods:

Tariffs on originating goods were eliminated in 11 equal annual installments from the Base Rate to zero.

**TABLE (continued)**

| Issue Foreign Country (EPAs in Chronological Order, formal title) | Date EPA Entered into Force | Trade Coverage and Duty Reduction Phase In Rules | Important Issues Not Covered by EPA | Other Important Issues Covered by EPA |
|---|---|---|---|---|
| | | Category B12 goods: Tariffs on originating goods were eliminated in 13 equal annual installments from the Base Rate to zero. Category B15 goods: Tariffs on originating goods were eliminated in 6 equal annual installments from the Base Rate to zero. Category Pa goods: Beginning on the date of entry into force, a tariff of 6.3 percent was applied to originating goods. Category Pb goods: Beginning on the date of entry into force, a tariff of 8.1 percent was applied to originating goods. Category Pc goods: | | *Human Rights:* *Preamble* |

Beginning on the date of entry into force, a tariff of 8.5 percent was applied to originating goods.

Category Pd goods:

Beginning on the date of entry into force, a tariff of 9.6 percent was applied to originating goods.

Category Pe goods:

Beginning on the date of entry into force, a tariff of 12 percent was applied to originating goods.

Category Pf goods:

Beginning on the date of entry into force, a tariff of 12.6 percent was applied to originating goods.

Category Pg goods:

Beginning on the date of entry into force, a tariff of 13.4 percent was applied to originating goods.

Category Ph goods:

Beginning on the date of entry into force, a tariff of 17 percent was applied to originating goods.

Category Pi goods:

Beginning on the date of entry into force, a tariff of 19 percent was applied to originating goods.

Category Pj goods:

Beginning on the date of entry into force, a tariff of 20 percent was applied to originating goods.

TABLE (continued)

| Issue Foreign Country (EPAs in Chronological Order, formal title) | Date EPA Entered into Force | Trade Coverage and Duty Reduction Phase In Rules | Important Issues Not Covered by EPA | Other Important Issues Covered by EPA |
|---|---|---|---|---|
| | | Category Pk goods: Beginning on the date of entry into force, a tariff of 23.8 percent was applied to originating goods. Category Pl goods: Beginning on the date of entry into force, a tariff of 27.2 percent was applied to originating goods. Category Pm goods: Beginning on the date of entry into force, a tariff of 32 percent was applied to originating goods. Category Pn goods: Tariffs on originating goods were reduced in 11 equal annual installments from the Base Rate to 5 percent. Category Q goods: Tariffs on originating goods are provided in the terms and conditions in the Note in the Schedule of Japan. | | |

| | |
|---|---|
| | Category X goods:<br><br>These goods are excluded from any tariff commitment.[38]<br><br>**Services:**<br><br>Positive List approach with sectoral exemptions.<br><br>Chapter 6 of the *Japan — Switzerland EPA* covers trade in services and applies to all services sectors.<br><br>But, Chapter 6 and related Annexes set out one specific exemption from coverage, namely, air transport services.<br><br>The *Japan — Switzerland EPA* does not apply to:<br><br>measures affecting traffic rights, or services directly related to the exercise of traffic rights, other than those affecting:<br><br>(a) aircraft repair and maintenance services;<br><br>(b) selling and marketing of air transport services; or<br><br>(c) computer reservation system (CRS) services."[39] |

[38] *Agreement on Free Trade and Economic Partnership between Japan and the Swiss Confederation*, Annex 1, *posted at* www.mofa.go.jp/region/**europe**/switzerland/epa0902/annex1.pdf.

[39] *Agreement on Free Trade and Economic Partnership between Japan and the Swiss Confederation*, Chapter 6, *posted at* www.mofa.go.jp/region/europe/switzerland/epa0902/agreement.pdf.

TABLE (continued)

| Issue Foreign Country (EPAs in Chronological Order, formal title) | Date EPA Entered into Force | Trade Coverage and Duty Reduction Phase In Rules | Important Issues Not Covered by EPA | Other Important Issues Covered by EPA |
|---|---|---|---|---|
| Agreement between Japan and the Socialist Republic of Viet Nam for an Economic Partnership | 1 October 2009 | Overall:<br><br>Japan eliminated tariffs on 95 percent of imports from Vietnam over a 10 year period.[40]<br><br>Vietnam eliminated tariffs on 88 percent of imports from Japan over 10 years, but retained tariffs on a number of industrial products.[41] | Labor, Human Rights | Environment:<br><br>Article 111:<br><br>Parties shall explore and undertake economic cooperation activities in numerous fields, including the environment. |

| (Japan - Vietnam EPA) | **Goods:** |
| --- | --- |
| | *Schedules in relation to Article 16:* |
| | *Part 1, General Notes* |
| | *Part 2, Schedule of Japan and Notes* |
| | *Part 3, Schedule of Viet Nam and Notes* |
| | *Below are the Categories of goods in Part 2, Schedule of Japan.* |
| | Category A goods: |
| | Tariffs on originating goods were eliminated as of the date of entry into force. |
| | Category B3 goods: |
| | Tariffs on originating goods were eliminated in 4 equal annual installments from the Base Rate to zero. |
| | Category B5 goods: |
| | Tariffs on originating goods were eliminated in 6 equal annual installments from the Base Rate to zero. |

[40] See *Japan-Vietnam FTA in Effect as of Oct. 1*, 26 International Trade Reporter (BNA) 1363 (8 October 2009).
[41] See *Japan Signs EPA with Vietnam*, 26 International Trade Reporter (BNA) 49 (8 January 2009).

**TABLE (continued)**

| Issue Foreign Country (EPAs in Chronological Order, formal title) | Date EPA Entered into Force | Trade Coverage and Duty Reduction Phase In Rules | Important Issues Not Covered by EPA | Other Important Issues Covered by EPA |
|---|---|---|---|---|
| | | Category B7 goods:<br><br>Tariffs on originating goods were eliminated in 8 equal annual installments from the Base Rate to zero.<br><br>Category B10 goods:<br><br>Tariffs on originating goods were eliminated in 11 equal annual installments from the Base Rate to zero.<br><br>Category B15 goods:<br><br>Tariffs on originating goods were eliminated in 16 equal annual installments from the Base Rate to zero.<br><br>Category C goods:<br><br>Tariffs on originating goods were applied at the Base Rate existing on the date of entry into force.<br><br>Category P goods:<br><br>Tariffs on originating goods were reduced according to the terms and conditions in the Notes of the Schedule of Japan. | | |

Category Q goods:

There are two kinds of Category Q goods, ones that are subject to a tariff rate quota (TRQ), and ones that are not subject to a TRQ.

For Category Q goods subject to a TRQ —

A tariff of 12.8 percent applies to quantities up to the in-quota threshold. This threshold is called the "aggregate quota quantity." Shipments above this quantity are prohibited. But, the quantity increases annually for 11 years, according to the following terms:

(aa) 100 metric tons for the 1st year;

(bb) 105 metric tons for the 2nd year;

(cc) 110 metric tons for the 3rd year;

(dd) 115 metric tons for the 4th year;

(ee) 120 metric tons for the 5th year;

(ff) 125 metric tons for the 6th year;

(gg) 130 metric tons for the 7th year;

(hh) 135 metric tons for the 8th year;

(ii) 140 metric tons for the 9th year;

(jj) 145 metric tons for the 10th year, and;

(kk) 150 metric tons for the 11th year, and each subsequent year.

**TABLE (continued)**

| Issue Foreign Country (EPAs in Chronological Order, formal title) | Date EPA Entered into Force | Trade Coverage and Duty Reduction Phase In Rules | Important Issues Not Covered by EPA | Other Important Issues Covered by EPA |
|---|---|---|---|---|
| | | For Category Q goods not subject to a TRQ — These goods are excluded from any commitment to reduce or eliminate the tariff on them. Category R goods: These goods are excluded from any tariff commitment, but are subject to negotiation in the 5th year from the date of entry into force. Category X goods: These goods are excluded from any tariff commitment.[42] **Agriculture:** Excludes rice and sensitive products. **Services:** Positive List approach with sectoral exemptions. Chapter 7 of the *Japan — Vietnam EPA* covers trade in services. Chapter 7 and related Annexes set out specific exemptions from coverage. | | |

For example, in respect to air transport services, the *Japan — Vietnam EPA* does not apply to:

Measures affecting traffic rights, or services directly related to the exercise of traffic rights, other than measures affecting:

(i) aircraft repair and maintenance services;

(ii) selling and marketing of air transport services; and

(iii) computer reservation system services."

Furthermore, the *Japan — Vietnam EPA* does not cover:

cabotage in maritime transport services;

measures pursuant to immigration laws and regulations;

measures affecting natural persons of a Party seeking access to employment market of the other Party, nor measures regarding nationality, or residence or employment on a permanent basis; and government procurement.[43]

[42] *Agreement between Japan and the Socialist Republic of Viet Nam*, Annex 1, *posted at* www.mofa.go.jp/region/asia-paci/vietnam/epa0812/annex1.pdf.

[43] *Agreement between Japan and the Socialist Republic of Viet Nam*, Chapter 7, *posted at* www.mofa.go.jp/region/asia-paci/vietnam/epa0812/agreement.pdf.

**TABLE (continued)**

| Issue Foreign Country (EPAs in Chronological Order, formal title) | Date EPA Entered into Force | Trade Coverage and Duty Reduction Phase In Rules | Important Issues Not Covered by EPA | Other Important Issues Covered by EPA |
|---|---|---|---|---|
| | | Annex 5 sets of the Schedule of Specific Commitments.[44] | | |
| **Agreement between Japan and the Republic of Peru for an Economic Partnership** | Signed 31 May 2011 | **Overall:** | Labor, Human Rights | **Environment:** |
| | | | | *Preamble* |
| | Not entered into force as of November 2011 | The *Japan — Peru EPA* eliminates tariffs on 99 percent of imported products over 10 years. | | *Article 200:* Parties shall explore and undertake economic cooperation |
| | | **Goods:** | | |

activities in numerous fields, including science, technology, and environment.

**(Japan — Peru EPA)**

*Schedules in relation to Article 21:*

*Part 1, General Notes*

*Part 2, Schedule of Japan and Notes*

*Part 3, Schedule of Peru and Notes*

Below are the Categories of goods indicated in Column 4 of *Part 2, Schedule of Japan*.

Category A goods:

Tariffs on originating goods were eliminated as of the date of entry into force.

Category B3 goods:

---

[44] *Agreement between Japan and the Socialist Republic of Viet Nam*, Annex 5, *posted at* www.mofa.go.jp/region/asia-paci/vietnam/epa0812/annex5.pdf.

**TABLE (continued)**

| Issue Foreign Country (EPAs in Chronological Order, formal title) | Date EPA Entered into Force | Trade Coverage and Duty Reduction Phase In Rules | Important Issues Not Covered by EPA | Other Important Issues Covered by EPA |
|---|---|---|---|---|
| | | Tariffs on originating goods were eliminated in 4 equal annual installments from Base Rate to free beginning on the date of entry into force, and duty free effective 1 April of the 4th year.<br><br>Category B5 goods:<br><br>Tariffs on originating goods were eliminated in 6 equal annual installments from the Base Rate to zero beginning on the date of entry into force, and duty free effective 1 April of the 6th year.<br><br>Category B7 goods:<br><br>Tariffs on originating goods were eliminated in 8 equal annual installments from the Base Rate to zero beginning on the date of entry into force, and duty free effective 1 April of the 8th year.<br><br>Category B10 goods:<br><br>Tariffs on originating goods were eliminated in 11 equal annual installments from the Base Rate to zero beginning on the date of entry into force and duty free effective 1 April of the 11th year. | | |

Category B15 goods:

Tariffs on originating goods were eliminated in 16 equal annual installments from the Base Rate to zero beginning on the date of entry into force, and duty free effective 1 April of the 16th year.

Category B16 goods:

Tariffs on originating goods were eliminated in 17 equal annual installments from the Base Rate to zero beginning on the date of entry into force, and duty free effective 1 April of the 17th year.

Category P goods:

Tariffs on originating goods were reduced according to the terms and conditions in the Notes in the Schedule of Japan.

Category Q goods:

Tariffs on originating goods are provided in the terms and conditions in the Notes in the Schedule of Japan.

Category R goods:

These goods are excluded from any tariff commitment and subject to negotiation in the 5th year from the date of entry into force.

**TABLE (continued)**

| Issue Foreign Country (EPAs in Chronological Order, formal title) | Date EPA Entered into Force | Trade Coverage and Duty Reduction Phase In Rules | Important Issues Not Covered by EPA | Other Important Issues Covered by EPA |
|---|---|---|---|---|
| | | Category X goods:<br><br>These goods are excluded from any tariff commitment.[45]<br><br>**Agriculture:**<br><br>Excludes sensitive products such as rice and frozen fish.<br><br>**Services:**<br><br>Positive List approach with sectoral exemptions.<br><br>Chapter 7 of the Agreement covers trade in services, including measures affecting the:<br><br>(a) supply of a service;<br><br>(b) purchase or use of, or payment for, a service;<br><br>(c) access to and the use of services offered to the public generally, including distribution, transport or telecommunications networks and services, in connection with the supply of a service;<br><br>(d) presence in its Area of a service supplier of the other Party; and | | |

(e) provision of a bond or other form of financial security as a condition for the supply of a service.

Chapter 7 and related Annexes set out specific exemptions from coverage.

For example, in respect of air transport services, the *Japan — Peru EPA* does not apply to: measures affecting traffic rights, or services directly related to the exercise of traffic rights, other than measures affecting:

(i) aircraft repair and maintenance services;

(ii) selling and marketing of air transport services; and

(iii) computer reservation system (CRS) services. Furthermore, the *Japan — Peru EPA* does not cover:

"government procurement" as defined in Article 144;

any obligation on a Party with respect to a national of the other Party seeking access to its employment market, or employed on a permanent basis in that Party; and

services supplied in the exercise of governmental authority.[46]

[45] *Agreement between Japan and the Republic of Peru for an Economic Partnership*, Annex1, *posted at* www.mofa.go.jp/region/latin/peru/epa201105/pdfs/jpepa_x01_e.pdf.

[46] *See Agreement between Japan and the Republic of Peru for an Economic Partnership*, Chapter 7, *posted at* www.mofa.go.jp/region/latin/peru/epa201105/pdfs/jpepa_ba_e.pdf.

**TABLE (continued)**

| Issue Foreign Country (EPAs in Chronological Order, formal title) | Date EPA Entered into Force | Trade Coverage and Duty Reduction Phase In Rules | Important Issues Not Covered by EPA | Other Important Issues Covered by EPA |
|---|---|---|---|---|
| | | *Additional:* *Industrial:* The *Japan — Peru EPA* eliminates Peru's 9 percent tariff on industrial products over 10 years.[47] | | *Environment:* |
| *Comprehensive Economic Partnership Agreement between Japan and the Republic of India* | 1 August 2011 | *Overall:* | Labor, Human Rights | |
| | | The *Japan — India EPA* eliminates 94 percent of import duties over 10 years, mostly in the non-agriculture sector.[48] | | *Preamble* |
| | | *Goods:* | | *Article 8:* Each Party shall ensure its domestic laws and regulations |

provide for adequate levels of environmental protection and work to improve such laws and regulations. Furthermore, the Parties affirm their commitment to any international agreements regarding the environment to which they are both parties.

*Schedules in relation to Article 19:*

---

[47] *See* Toshio Aritake, *Japan, Peru Sign Free Trade Agreement; Covers 99% of Goods Except Agriculture,* 28 International Trade Reporter (BNA) 937 (9 June 2011).

[48] *See* Toshio Aritake, *Japan, India Reach Agreement on Bilateral FTA, to Take Effect in 2011,* 27 International Trade Reporter (BNA) 1389 (16 September 2010).

**TABLE (continued)**

| Issue Foreign Country (EPAs in Chronological Order, formal title) | Date EPA Entered into Force | Trade Coverage and Duty Reduction Phase In Rules | Important Issues Not Covered by EPA | Other Important Issues Covered by EPA |
|---|---|---|---|---|
| *(Japan - India EPA)* | | *Part 1, General Notes*<br><br>*Part 2, Schedule of India*<br><br>*Part 3, Schedule of Japan*<br><br>Below are the Categories of goods of *Part 1, General Notes.*<br><br>Category A goods:<br><br>Tariffs on originating goods were eliminated as of the date of entry into force.<br><br>Category B5 goods:<br><br>Tariffs on originating goods were eliminated in 6 equal annual installments from the Base Rate to zero.<br><br>Category B7 goods:<br><br>Tariffs on originating goods were eliminated in 8 equal annual installments from the Base Rate to zero. | | |

| | | |
|---|---|---|
| | Category B10 goods:<br><br>Tariffs on originating goods were eliminated in 11 equal annual installments from the Base Rate to zero.<br><br>Category B15 goods:<br><br>Tariffs on originating goods were eliminated in 16 equal annual installments from the Base Rate to zero.<br><br>Category Pa and Pb goods:<br><br>Tariffs on originating goods were reduced according to the terms and conditions in the Notes in the Schedule of India.<br><br>Category X goods:<br><br>These goods are excluded from any reduction or elimination of tariffs.[49]<br><br>*Services:*<br><br>Positive List approach with sectoral exemptions.<br><br>Chapter 6 of the *Japan — India EPA* covers trade in services.<br><br>Chapter 6 and related Annexes set out specific exemptions from coverage. | *Article 99:*<br><br>It is inappropriate to relax or derogate from domestic environmental measures to encourage investment. |

[49] *Comprehensive Economic Partnership Agreement between Japan and the Republic of India*, Annex 1, *posted at* www.mofa.go.jp/region/asia-paci/india/epa201102/pdfs/ijcepa_x01_e.pdf.

**TABLE (continued)**

| Issue Foreign Country (EPAs in Chronological Order, formal title) | Date EPA Entered into Force | Trade Coverage and Duty Reduction Phase In Rules | Important Issues Not Covered by EPA | Other Important Issues Covered by EPA |
|---|---|---|---|---|
| | | For example, in respect of air transport services, the *Japan — India EPA* does not apply to: measures affecting traffic rights, or services directly related to the exercise of traffic rights, other than measures affecting: (i) aircraft repair and maintenance services; (ii) selling and marketing of air transport services; and (iii) computer reservation system services." Furthermore, the *Japan — India EPA* does not cover: cabotage in maritime transport services; and measures affecting natural persons seeking access to the employment market of a Party, or regarding nationality, citizenship, or residence or employment on a permanent basis.[50] Annex 6 sets out the Schedule of Specific Commitments.[51] | | |

| | |
|---|---|
| ***Japan — Republic of Korea Economic Partnership Agreement*** ***(Japan — Korea EPA)*** | April 2008, discussions to consider resuming *EPA* negotiations<br><br>Signed a bilateral Investment Agreement in 2002 as a first step towards a future *EPA* |
| ***Japan — Mongolia Economic Partnership Agreement*** ***(Japan — Mongolia EPA)*** | 24-25 June 2010, first meeting to discuss possible *EPA*<br><br>Parties agreed in November 2011 to start negotiations in 2012. |

[50] *Comprehensive Economic Partnership Agreement between Japan and the Republic of India, posted at* www.mofa.go.jp/region/asia-paci/india/epa201102/pdfs/ijcepa_ba_e.pdf.

[51] *Comprehensive Economic Partnership Agreement between Japan and the Republic of India,* Annex 6, *posted at* www.mofa.go.jp/region/asia-paci/india/epa201102/pdfs/ijcepa_x06_e.pdf.

Table (continued)

| Issue Foreign Country (EPAs in Chronological Order, formal title) | Date EPA Entered into Force | Trade Coverage and Duty Reduction Phase In Rules | Important Issues Not Covered by EPA | Other Important Issues Covered by EPA |
|---|---|---|---|---|
| *Japan — Australia Economic Partnership Agreement*<br><br>*(Japan — Australia EPA)* | 12th Round of Negotiations:<br><br>January 2011 | | | |